GERMAN

MILITARY DICTIONARY

Lancer Militaria

Originally published by the War Department, 1944

Printed in the United States of America

ISBN 0-935856-06-4

Lancer Militaria
P.O. Box 886
Mt. Ida, Arkansas 71957
USA

PART I
GERMAN—ENGLISH

Abbau *m*   dismantling *(a structure, etc.)*; mining *(ore)*.

abbauen   to dismantle *(a structure, etc.)*; to mine *(ore)*.

abbefördern evacuate *(PW, wounded, etc.)*.

Abbildung *f*   illustration, figure, diagram.

abbinden   to tie, lash *(Tp wire)*.

abblasen   to release gas *(CWS)*.

abblenden   dim *(a light)*.

"Abblenden!"   "Out of action!" *(AA SL)*.

Abblendlicht *n*   dim light *(on auto headlight)*.

abbrechen   break off; cease; withdraw.

das Lager abbrechen   to break camp.

das Gefecht abbrechen   to withdraw from action.

Abbrechen des Gefechts   withdrawal from action.

abbremsen   to brake.

Abbremsvorrichtung *f*   arresting gear *(aircraft carrier)*.

abbrücken   dismantle *(a bridge)*.

Abdachung *f*   slope *(Top)*.

Abdeckplatte *f*   cover plate *(G)*.

abdichten   to seal, calk, pack.

Abdichtung gegen Kampfgas   gasproofing *(CWS)*.

Abdichtungsring *m*   sealing ring, washer.

abdienen   complete a period of service.

Abdrift *f*   drift *(Avn, Nav)*.

Abdriftmesser *m*   driftmeter *(Ap)*.

Abdriftplatz *m*   landing area, jump area *(Prcht troops)*.

Abdriftvisier *n*   driftmeter *(Ap)*.

abdrosseln   to throttle *(an engine)*.

abdrücken   to fire, *i.e.* pull *(a trigger)*; press *(a button)*.

Abdrückvorrichtung *f*   release mechanism *(G)*.

Abendgesellschaftsanzug *m*   special evening dress uniform.

Abfahrt *f*   departure, start; downhill run *(skiing)*.

Abfahrtzeit *f*   time of departure, time of starting; time of descent *(skiing)*.

Abfall *m*   waste; drop *(Elec)*.

abfallen   to slope *(Top)*.

abfallendes Gelände   sloping terrain.

abfangen   pull out, level off, flatten out *(Avn)*; intercept *(Tac)*.

Abfangradius *m*   pull-out radius *(in dive bombing)*.

Abfangwalze *f*   front roller, roller bumper *(MT, Tk)*.

Abfederung *f*   spring system, suspension *(MT)*.

abfertigen   to dispatch *(messages, vehicles, trains, etc.)*; to process further disposition.

Abfertigungsgebäude *n*   control tower *(Adrm)*.

abfeuern   to fire.

Abfeuerungseinrichtung *f*   release mechanism *(Mort)*.

Abfeuerungshebel *m*   firing lever *(G)*.

Abfeuerungsverbindung *f*   firing circuit for machine gun or gun *(Tk)*.

Abfeuerungsvorrichtung *f*   firing mechanism.

Abfindung *f*   pay and/or reimbursement, financial settlement.

Abflug *m*   take-off *(Avn)*; going flight, departing flight, receding flight *(AAA)*.

Abfluggeschwindigkeit *f*   take-off speed.

Abflugleistung *f*   take-off rating.

Abfrageapparat *m*   operator's telephone.

Abfrageklinke *f*   operator's answering jack.

abfragen inquire as to party or line desired *(Tp)*.

abfüttern to feed *(an animal)*.

Abgangsfehler *m* jump, vertical jump *(Arty)*.

Abgangsfehlerwinkel *m* angle of jump, jump, vertical jump *(Arty)*.

Abgangsrichtung *f* line of departure *(Ballistics)*.

Abgangswinkel *m* quadrant angle of departure *(Ballistics)*.

Abgase *npl* exhaust gases, waste gases.

Abgasturbine *f* exhaust turbine *(Ap)*.

abgeflacht flattened, flat.

abgeflachter Teil der Patrone méplat *(SA Am)*.

abgekämpft battle-weary.

abgejagt winded, worn out.

abgenutzt worn, worn out, worn away; eroded *(G barrel)*.

Abgeschobener *m* evacuee.

abgesessen dismounted *(Pers)*.

abgesondert detached *(unit, etc.)*.

abgestellt parked.

abgetragen worn *(Clo)*.

abgießen to spray chemical warfare agents *(Avn)*.

Abgleitschienen *fpl* bullet-deflection rails *(Tk)*.

abgreifen to transfer map distances with compass or dividers, to plot *(in this sense)*.

Abgreifen der Entfernung measuring map range with dividers or compass.

Abgrenzung *f* demarcation, delimitation.

abhängen take off *(a pack)*; unhook *(a trailer)*; hang up *(Tp)*; overtake and leave behind *(slang)*.

abhauen to cut down; to "beat it" *(slang)*.

abheben lift up; pull up, take off *(Avn)*.

Abholkommando *n* party detailed to fetch anything; aircraft ferrying detachment.

abhören intercept, listen in, monitor *(Rad, Tp)*.

Abhörgefahr *f* danger of interception *(Tp, Rad)*.

Abhörstelle *f* intercept station *(Sig C)*; monitoring station *(Rad)*.

abkippen wing over *(Avn)*; withdraw from action *(slang)*.

abklemmen disconnect from binding post *(Elec)*.

abkommandieren to detach, to detail.

Abkommen *n* deviation; agreement, convention; point of aim *(at instant of firing)*.

das Abkommen melden to call the shot.

abkommen deviate.

Abkommpunkt *m* point of called shot, point of aim.

Abkommrohr *n* subcaliber tube *(G)*.

Abkommschießen *n* subcaliber firing, subcaliber practice.

Abkrümmen *n* trigger squeeze.

abkrümmen to squeeze *(a trigger)*.

Abladekommando *n* unloading detail.

abladen unload, detruck, detrain.

Ablage *f* dump.

Ablagerungszaun *m* drift fence *(a type of snow fence for winter operations)*.

Ablaßschraube *f* drain plug.

Ablauf *m* completion, termination; launching, starting.

Ablaufbahn *f* runway *(Adrm)*; landing ramp *(for seaplanes)*.

Ablaufberg *m* hump, incline *(RR)*.

Ablaufposten *m* bridge-traffic control post.

Ablaufventil *n* relief valve *(Hydraulics)*.

ablauschen listen in, intercept *(Rad)*.

abläuten to ring off *(Tp)*.

ableiten divert *(a stream, etc.)*.

Ableitung *f* derivation; derivative *(Math)*; leakage *(Elec)*.

Ablenkung *f* diversion *(Tac)*; deflection, refraction.

Ablenkungsangriff *m* diversion, feint attack *(Tac)*.

Ablesemarke *f* index line, index mark.

ablesen to read *(instruments, etc.)*.

Ablesefehler *m* index error.

Ablesung *f* setting, reading.

abliefern deliver.

Ablösung *f* relief *(Tac)*.

ablösen relieve, take over.

Abmarsch *m* , half-squad *(Cav)*; departure, start.

abmarschbereit ready to start.

Abmarschführer *m* half-squad leader *(Cav)*.

abmarschieren depart, start the march.

abnehmen remove, take off; decrease; accept, take.

Abnutzung *f* erosion, wear; wear and tear; attrition.

Abnutzung des Rohres erosion of the bore.

Abnutzungskampf *m* battle of attrition.

Abort *m* toilet, latrine.

abprallen to ricochet.

Abpraller *m* ricochet.

Abprallerschießen *n* ricochet fire.

Abprallwinkel *m* angle of ricochet.

abprotzen uncouple, unlimber *(Arty)*.

Abregnen *n* aerial spraying *(CWS)*.

abreißen to rip, tear off.

Abreißknopf *m* fuze-cord button *(hand grenade)*.

Abreißschnur *f* rip cord *(Prcht)*; fuze cord *(hand grenade)*.

Abreißzünder *m* friction igniter, ripcord igniter.

abriebbeständig wear-resistant.

abriegeln to block, interdict, box in, seal off *(Tac)*; to bolt *(a door, etc.)*.

Abriegelungsfeuer *n* box barrage *(Arty)*.

Abrücken *n* departure.

abrufen to ring off *(Tp)*.

abrüsten disarm.

Abrüstung *f* disarmament.

abrutschen to slip *(Avn)*.

sich seitlich abrutschen lassen to fall off *(Avn)*.

absacken to drop, pancake *(Avn)*; to founder, sink *(slang)*.

Absatteltrupp *m* unsaddling detail *(Cav)*.

Absatz *m* berm *(Ft)*; heel *(of shoe)*; paragraph.

abschätzen to estimate *(distance, etc.)*.

Abscheren *n* shear *(Mech)*.

abschieben evacuate; expel, deport.

Abschied *m* departure; discharge; resignation.

ehrenvoller Abschied honorable discharge.

abschießen to down, to shoot down *(an Ap)*; to disable, put out of action *(a Tk or vehicle)*; to shoot *(a person)*.

abschirmen to blanket, screen, cover, protect, shield.

Abschirmung *f* shielding, screening *(Rad)*.

abschlachten to massacre, slaughter.

abschlagen repel; reject.

Abschleppdienst *m* recovery service, towing service *(MT)*.

Abschleppen *n* towing.

Abschleppgerät *n* towing equipment.

Abschleppkommando *n* recovery party, wrecking section.

Abschleppkraftwagen *m* wrecking truck.

Abschleppzug *m* wrecker platoon, maintenance platoon *(MT)*.

Abschlußplättchen *n* base cover *(Am)*.

abschmieren lubricate.

abschneiden to cut off, isolate *(Tac)*; to cut *(wire, etc.)*.

Abschnitt *m* sector, phase *(Tac)*; area, section.

Abschnittsgrenze *f* sector boundary.

Abschnittsreserve *f* sector reserve.

abschnittsweise by sectors; in phases.

abschraubbar unscrewable, detachable.

abschreiten pace off *(a distance)*.

Abschrift *f* copy.

Abschub *m* evacuation *(of PW, wounded, etc.)*; transportation to the rear *(of salvage, supplies, etc.)*.

Abschubstelle *f* evacuation station.

Abschuß *m* discharge *(of a gun)*; downed enemy airplane; disabled tank or vehicle.

Abschußentfernung *f* slant range to present position *(at instant of firing)* *(AAA)*.

abschüssig steep *(Top)*.

Abschußpunkt *m* present position *(at instant of firing)* *(AAA)*.

Abschußrohr *n* projector *(CWS, Sig)*.

abschwächen reduce *(Photo)*; weaken.

Absetzbewegung *f* withdrawal, disengagement.

absetzen, sich disengage, withdraw *(Tac)*; increase distance between aircraft in flight.

Absetzer *m* jumpmaster *(Prcht troops)*.

Absetzgelände *n* landing area *(Prcht troops)*.

Absicht *f* intent, intention.

absitzen dismount *(from H or vehicle)*; do time, serve a sentence.

absondern isolate *(Med)*; divide, separate; segregate *(PW)*.

Absonderung *f* isolation *(Mcd)*; division, separation; segregation *(PW)*.

Absonderungsabteilung *f* isolation quarters *(Med)*.

abspannen relieve strain on wire by tying *(Tp)*; relieve tension, unharness, uncock, relax.

absperren close or block *(a road, etc.)*; lock *(a door, etc.)*; cut off, isolate *(Tac)*.

abspreizen to brace.

abspringen bail out, jump *(Avn)*.

Absprung *m* jump *(Prcht)*.

Absprunghafen *m* jump-off base *(Avn)*.

Absprung mit verzögerter Öffnung delayed jump *(Prcht)*.

abspulen unreel, unwind.

abspülen rinse out, wash out.

Abspuler *m* paying-out reel, axle of hand reel *(Tp)*.

Abspüren *n* gas detection *(CWS)*.

Abstand *m* distance *(from front to rear)*. See also **Zeitabstand**.

Abstandslicht *n* marker light *(MT)*.

Abstandwerfen *n* pattern bombing.

abstecken stake off *(Engr, Surv)*; plot *(a course, etc.)*; trace, tape off *(a mine field, etc.)*.

Absteckpfahl *m* stake *(Surv)*.

absteifen to brace, stiffen.

absteigender Ast descending branch *(of trajectory)*.

Abstellbahnhof *m* railroad yard.

abstellen to park, stop; to turn off *(an engine or motor)*.

Abstellgleis *n* classification track, siding *(RR)*.

Abstellplatz *m* parking place, parking area, dispersal area *(Adrm)*.

abstimmen to tune *(Rad)*.

Abstimmkondensator *m* tuning condenser *(Rad)*.

Abstimmschärfe *f* selectivity, sharpness of resonance *(Rad)*.

Abstimmskala *f* tuning dial *(Rad)*.

Abstimmspule *f* tuning coil *(Rad)*.

abstreifen to patrol *(a road, area, etc.)*.

abstufen graduate *(into degrees)*.

Absturz *m* crash, plunge *(Avn)*.

zum Absturz bringen to down *(an Ap)*.

absuchen to search, sweep.

Abszisse *f* abscissa, X-coordinate.

Abtastdose *f* pick-up unit *(record player)*.

Abteilung *f* battalion *(Cav, Arty, Armd Comd)*; detachment, unit *(Tac)*; department, section *(Adm)*.

"Abteilung, Halt!" "Squad *(company, detail, etc.)*, halt!"

Abteilungsadjutant *m* battalion adjutant.

Abteilungskommandeur *m* battalion commander.

Abteilungsnachrichtenstaffel *f* battalion communication section.

Abteilungsstab *m* battalion headquarters.

Abtransport *m* evacuation.

abtransportieren evacuate.

abtrennen cut off, separate, isolate, disconnect.

"Abtreten!" "Dismissed!" *(formal style, to an individual)*. Compare **"Weggetreten!"**

abtreten lassen dismiss *(an individual)*.

Abtrift *f* drift *(Avn)*.

Abtriftmesser *m* driftmeter *(Avn)*.

Abtriftvisier *n* See **Abdriftvisier**.

Abtriftwinkel *m* drift angle *(Avn)*.

abtrudeln go into a spin *(Avn)*.

Abwälzstößel *m* tappet rod *(eccentric-cam type)*.

abwärts downward, downhill.

abwässern to drain *(water)*.

Abwehr *f* defense, active defense; military security.

Abwehrangelegenheiten *fpl* security matters.

Abwehrdienst *m* counterintelligence.

Abwehrerfolg *m* defensive success.

Abwehrgeschütz *n* antiaircraft gun.

Abwehrkampf *m* defensive combat.

Abwehrmaßnahme *f* defensive measure; security measure.

Abwehroffizier *m* security officer.

Abwehrvorbereitung *f* defensive preparation, preparation of defensive measures.

Abwehrwaffe *f* defensive arm; defensive weapon.

abwehrweise defensively.

Abwehrzone *f* defensive zone.

abweichen deviate.

abweichende Anfangsgeschwindigkeit velocity error.

Abweichung *f* deviation, deflection, error.

abweisen repel.

Abweiser *m* fender; recoil guard *(G mount)*.

abwerfen to drop, jettison *(Avn)*.

abwesend absent.

Abwind *m* descending air current *(Met)*.

Abwurf *m* release *(bombing)*. See also **Wurf**.

Abwurfbehälter *m* slip tank, belly

tank *(Ap)*; aerial delivery unit *(airborne operations)*.

Abwurfgerät *n* bomb-release mechanism *(Ap)*.

Abwurfgondel *f* See **Abwurfkiste**.

Abwurfhöhe *f* bombing altitude, bomb-release altitude *(Avn)*.

Abwurfkiste *f* aerial delivery container *(airborne operations)*.

Abwurfmeldung *f* drop message.

Abwurfpatrone *f* message container *(for drop message) (Avn)*.

Abwurfschacht *m* bomb rack *(Ap)*.

Abwurfstelle *f* message-dropping ground; drop point *(airborne supply)*.

Abwurfvorrichtung *f* bomb-release mechanism *(Ap)*.

Abwurfzielgerät *n* bomb sight *(Ap)*.

abwürgen to stall *(an engine)*.

"**Abzählen!**" "Count off!"

Abzeichen *n* badge, device, emblem, insignia; marking *(Ap, Tk)*.

abziehen pull *(a trigger)*; withdraw *(Tac)*; hone, whet, sharpen; make a print *(Photo)*; subtract, deduct, draw off.

Abzug *m* trigger *(SA)*; withdrawal *(Tac)*; contact print *(Photo)*; deduction *(of pay, etc.)*.

Abzugsbügel *m* trigger guard *(R)*.

Abzugsfeder *f* sear spring *(R)*.

Abzugsgabel *f* trigger-sear fork *(R)*.

Abzugsgewicht *n* trigger pull *(SA)*.

Abzugsgriff *m* lanyard handle *(G)*.

Abzugshebel *m* trigger lever *(MG)*; firing lever *(G)*.

Abzugsschiene *f* trigger bar *(AA gun)*.

Abzugsschnur *f* lanyard *(Ord)*.

Abzugsstange *f* sear *(pistol)*.

Abzugsstift *m* trigger pin *(R)*.

Abzugsstollen *m* sear, sear nose *(R)*.

Abzugsstück *n* trigger piece, firing lever *(G)*.

Abzugsvorrichtung *f* trigger mechanism *(SA)*; firing mechanism *(Ord)*.

Abzugswelle *f* firing rod *(AA gun)*.

Abzweigung *f* branch; junction line *(RR)*.

Achsantrieb *m* axle drive *(MT)*.

Achsdruck *m* axle load *(MT)*.

Achse *f* axis; ordinate; axle; shaft.

Achsel *f* shoulder. See *also* **Schulter**.

Achsenverschränkbarkeit *f* angle of axle swing *(MT)*.

Achsfeder *f* axle spring.

Achsfederung *f* axle suspension.

Achslager *n* axle bearing.

Achsmutter *f* axle nut.

Achsschenkel *m* wheel spindle *(MT)*.

Achsschenkellenkung *f* steering-knuckle type of steering, Ackerman steering *(MT)*.

Achsschwingschenkel *m* wheel spindle *(G)*.

Achssitze *mpl* axle seats *(for gunners)*.

Achssturz *m* pivot inclination, kingpin inclination *(MT)*.

Achszapfen *m* kingpin, steering knuckle pivot *(MT)*.

Achszapfensturz *m* pivot inclination, kingpin inclination *(MT)*.

Achterzelt *n* eight-man tent.

Achtganggetriebe *n* eight-speed transmission *(MT)*.

"**Achtung!**" "Attention!", "Caution!", "Danger!", "Look out!"

"**Achtung! Präsentiert das, Gewehr!**" "Present, Arms!"

Adamsit *m* adamsite *(CWS)*.

Aderpresse *f* tourniquet.

Adjutant *m* adjutant, aide, aide-de-camp, executive officer.

Adjutantur *f* Adjutant's Office *(department of the* Oberkommando des Heeres *serving as central clearing office for routine matters; in no sense equivalent to US Adjutant General's Department); personnel group of general staff sections (in army, corps, and Div)*.

Adler *m* eagle.

Admiral *m* admiral.

Afrikakämpfer *m* veteran of the African Campaign.

Aggregat *n* unit, set; charging unit *(Elec)*.

Ago name of an aircraft manufacturing company.

Akja *m* boat-type runner *(placed under gun wheels for operations in deep snow; also used as a swamp conveyance for wounded, etc.)*.

Akten *fpl* documents, records, papers, file.

Aktenmaterial *n* official documents.

Aktenschrank *m* filing cabinet.

Aktionsbereich *m* See **Fahrbereich, Flugbereich,** *etc.*

Aktionsradius *m* See **Wirkungsbereich.**

aktiv active; regular.
aktive Truppe line troops, combat troops.
akustische Ortung sound location, acoustic orientation *(AAA)*.
Alarm *m* alarm; air-raid warning.
"Alarm aus!" "All clear!"
alarmbereit on the alert.
Alarmbereitschaft *f* alert, stand-by.
Alarmplatz *m* alarm station.
Alarmschußgerät *n* trip-wire alarm.
Alkalipatrone *f* alkali cartridge *(oxygen breathing apparatus)*.
Alleinflug *m* solo flight.
allgemeines Aufgebot levée en masse.
Allgemeines Heeresamt General Army Office *(central section in rear echelon of* Oberkommando des Heeres) *(abbr. AHA)*.
Allgemeines Luftamt General Air Office *(section of Ger Air Ministry)*.
Allgemeines Wehrmachtamt General Office of the Armed Forces *(central section in rear echelon of* Oberkommando der Wehrmacht).
allgemeingültige Anordnungen general orders.
Allradantrieb *m* all-wheel drive *(MT)*.
Alp *f* mountain pasturage.
Alter *n* age.
Altersgrenze *f* age limit.
Alterungsbeständigkeit *f* resistance to aging.
alte Wache old guard.
Altgummi *n-m* scrap rubber.
Altmaterial *n* junk, scrap, waste.
Altmetall *n* scrap metal.
Alulegierung *f* See Aluminiumlegierung.
Aluminiumlegierung *f* aluminum alloy.
Amatol *n* amatol *(Am)*.
Amboß *m* anvil *(Am)*.
amboßförmiger Kumulo-Nimbus incus *(Met)*.
Amboßschraube *f* threaded anvil *(Am)*.
Ammoniumpikrat *n* ammonium picrate *(Am)*.
Ammonpulver *n* ammonal *(Am)*.
Ammonsalpeter-Sprengmittel *n* ammonium nitrate explosive.
Amperemeter *n* ammeter.
Amperezahl *f* amperage.
Amphibienflugzeug *n* amphibian airplane.

Amphibienkampfwagen *m* amphibian tank.
Amt *n* office, bureau; administrative function; telephone central.
amtlich official.
Amtsanschließer *m* telephone-exchange connecting device *(connects field Tp with country-wide network)*.
Amtswalter *m* administrator *(Reich Labor Service)*.
Amtszusatz *m* telephone-exchange auxiliary set *(connects field central with country-wide network)*.
Anaglypt *n* anaglyph *(Surv)*.
Analphabet *m* illiterate.
Anblasrichtung *f* direction of air flow *(Avn)*.
Anderthalbdecker *m* sesquiplane.
Änderungsgeschwindigkeit *f* remaining velocity *(Ballistics)*.
andrehen to crank, to turn over *(an engine)*.
Andrehkurbel *f* crank *(MT)*.
Anerkennung *f* recognition, acknowledgment.
Anerkennungsschreiben *n* commendation.
Anfahrtsgang *m* low gear *(MT, Tk)*.
Anfall *m* surprise attack, raid.
Anfangsbuchstabe *m* initial, first letter.
Anfangsdrall *m* initial twist *(Ord)*.
Anfangsgeschwindigkeit *f* initial velocity, muzzle velocity *(Ballistics)*.
Anfangsladung *f* initial charge.
Anfangsstellung *f* initial position.
Anfeuerung *f* combustible composition *(in a flare cartridge)*.
Anfeuerungssatz *m* booster charge *(Am)*.
anfliegen to approach *(a target)* *(Avn)*.
Anflug *m* coming flight *(AAA)*; approach run *(bombing)*; approach flight *(Avn)*.
Anfluggrundlinie *f* principal course of approach *(Inst landing)*.
Anflugkurs *m* approaching course *(Avn)*.
Anflugrichtung *f* direction of approach *(Avn)*.
Anflugsektor *m* on-course zone *(Inst landing)*; approach zone *(Adrm)*.
Anflugwinkel *m* approach angle, angle of approach *(Avn)*.
anfordern to requisition *(Adm)*.

Anforderung *f* requisition.

Anforderungszeichen *n* requisition number.

Anführer *m* file leader.

Angaben *fpl* data, statements.

Angehöriger *m* member; relative. **die nächsten Angehörigen** next of kin.

angelehnt supported by, in contact with, covered by *(Tac)*.

angelehnter Flügel supported flank.

"Angetreten!" "Fall in!" *(at attention)*.

angliedern to attach.

angreifen to attack.

Angreifer *m* attacker, aggressor.

angrenzend adjacent.

Angriff *m* attack *(Tac)*; charge *(Cav)*.

Angriff auf Stellungen attack of organized positions.

Angriff aus der Bewegung attack from march column.

Angriff mit begrenztem Ziel limited attack, attack with limited objective.

Angriffsabschnitt *m* attack sector, zone of action in attack.

Angriffsart *f* form of attack, form of offensive action.

Angriffsbefehl *m* attack order.

Angriffsbeginn *m* time of attack.

Angriffsbereitstellung *f* assembly (area) for attack.

Angriffsbreite *f* frontage in attack, attack frontage *(Tac)*.

Angriffsflug *m* air-attack flight, raid *(Avn)*.

Angriffsflügel *m* attacking wing.

Angriffsform *f* form of attack; attack formation.

angriffsfreudig aggressive.

Angriffsgefecht *n* offensive combat.

Angriffsgelände *n* terrain of attack, attack zone.

Angriffsgraben *m* assault trench.

Angriffsgruppe *f* attack group, attack echelon.

Angriffshandlung *f* offensive action.

Angriffshöhe *f* air-attack altitude, bombing altitude *(Avn)*.

angriffslustig aggressive.

Angriffsplan *m* plan of attack.

Angriffsrichtung *f* direction of attack.

Angriffsstreifen *m* attack sector.

Angriffstruppen *fpl* attack units, attack troops.

Angriffsverlauf *m* progress of an attack.

Angriffsversuch *m* attempted attack.

Angriffswelle *f* attack wave, attacking echelon.

Angriffsziel *n* objective *(of attack)*. **erstes Angriffsziel** immediate objective.

Angriffszwischenziel *n* intermediate objective.

Anhalt *m* guide, general principle.

Anhaltspunkt *m* check point *(Gunnery, Air Navigation, Surv)*; item in a check list *(combat orders)*.

Anhang *m* appendix *(to a manual, etc.)*.

Anhängelast *f* trailer load *(MT)*.

Anhängen *n* See **Vermessung durch Anhängen.**

Anhänger *m* trailer *(MT)*; tender *(RR)*; tie-on tag.

Anhängezettel *m* tie-on tag.

Anhäufung *f* accumulation, concentration, piling up.

Anhöhe *f* height, hill, rise.

Anker *m* armature, rotor *(Elec)*; anchor *(Nav)*.

Ankerachse *f* armature shaft *(field Tp)*.

Ankerbalken *m* anchor stock.

Ankerflunken *m* anchor fluke.

Ankergrund *m* anchorage *(Nav)*.

Ankerlicht *n* anchor light.

Ankerlichten *n* weighing anchor.

Ankerlinie *f* line of anchors *(Bdg)*.

Ankermine *f* anchored mine, moored mine.

Ankermast *m* mooring mast.

Ankerpfahl *m* anchor stake *(for a guy line)*.

Ankerplatte *f* anchor plate *(part of a clockwork fuze)*.

Ankerplatz *m* anchorage *(Nav)*.

Ankerrödel *m* anchor rack stick *(Bdg)*.

Ankerrute *f* anchor shank.

Ankerseil *n* guy line.

Ankerstelle *f* anchorage *(Nav)*.

Ankerstich *m* anchor hitch.

Ankersucher *m* grapnel.

Ankertau *n* anchor cable.

Ankerturm *m* mooring tower.

Ankerwelle *f* armature shaft *(Elec)*.

Ankerwicklung *f* armature winding.

Ankerwinde *f* capstan.

Anklage *f*   charge, complaint.
anklammern   to cling tenaciously, to hold fast.
ankleben   to paste, adhere, stick, fasten with adhesive.
Ankündigung *f*   announcement, bulletin, notice.
Ankündigungskommando *n*   preparatory command.
Ankündigungssignal *n*   warning signal.
Ankunft *f*   arrival.
ankurbeln   to crank.
Anlage *f*   installation; annex, inclosure *(in a manual)*.
anlassen   to start *(an engine)*; to temper *(steel)*.
Anlasser *m*   starter *(Mtr)*.
Anlaßknopf *m*   starter button *(Mtr)*.
Anlaßmotor *m*   starter motor *(Mtr)*.
Anlaßpatrone *f*   cartridge for cartridge starter *(Mtr)*.
Anlaßpistole *f*   cartridge starter *(Mtr)*.
Anlaßschalter *m*   starter switch *(Mtr)*.
Anlauf *m*   take-off run *(Avn)*.
Anlaufstrecke *f*   take-off distance *(Avn)*.
anläuten   to ring *(Tp)*.
anlegen   to aim *(R)*; to dock; to put ashore; to construct.
Anlegepunkt *m*   aiming point.
Anlegestelle *f*   pier, wharf.
anleuchten   illuminate.
Anmarsch *m*   approach, approach march, advance *(Tac)*.
Anmarschweg *m*   approach, approach route.
annähernd   approximate.
Annäherung *f*   approach.
Annäherungsformation *f*   approach march formation.
Annäherungsmarsch *m*   approach march *(Tac)*.
Annahme *f*   assumption; acceptance, reception.
Annahmestelle *f*   recruiting office; receiving office *(letters, etc.)*.
Anode *f*   plate, anode *(Elec)*.
Anodenbatterie *f*   plate battery, "B" battery *(Rad)*.
Anodengleichspannung *f*   direct plate voltage *(Rad)*.
Anodenkreis *m*   plate circuit *(Rad)*.
Anodenrückkopplung *f*   plate feedback coupling *(Rad)*.

Anodenverlustleistung *f*   plate dissipation *(Rad)*.
Anorak *m*   parka *(Clo)*.
Anordnung *f*   order.
anpassen   adapt, blend *(Cam)*.
Anpeilen *n*   taking of bearings, radio direction finding *(Avn)*.
anpirschen   to creep up, to stalk.
Anrecht *n*   claim.
Anregungsmittel *n*   stimulant.
anrichten   to sight, sight in, align; to cause *(damage, etc.)*.
anrollen   to roll along runway *(on take-off run)*.
Anruf *m*   call, call-up *(Rad, Tp)*; challenge.
Anrufantwort *f*   answer to call-up *(Rad)*.
Anrufklappe *f*   switchboard drop *(Tp)*.
Anrufsschauzeichen *n*   incoming-call signal light *(Tp)*.
Anrufzeichen *n*   call signal *(Tp)*.
Ansammlung *f*   concentration *(Tac)*.
Ansatzflügel *m*   stub wing *(Ap)*.
Ansaugetakt *m*   intake stroke, suction stroke *(Mtr)*.
Ansaughub *m*   intake stroke *(Mtr)*.
Ansaugkrümmer *m*   air-intake horn *(carburetor)*.
Ansaugleitung *f*   intake duct *(Mtr, Ft)*.
Ansaugrohr *n*   intake pipe *(Mtr)*.
Ansaugung *f*   suction.
anschaffen   procure.
anschalten   connect, switch on; tap *(a wire)*.
Anreicherung *f*   concentration *(CWS)*.
Anschauungsmittel *npl*   illustrative material, demonstration material *(Tng aids)*.
Anschießen *n*   harmonization *(Ord)*.
anschießen   to sight in.
Anschlag *m*   aiming or firing position with rifle or machine gun; stop *(Ord)*.
anschlagen   to post *(a notice, etc.)*.
Anschlagsart *f*   firing position *(of the soldier)*.
Anschlagtafel *f*   bulletin board.
Anschlagwinkel *m*   try square.
anschließen   join, close up, connect.
Anschluß *m*   liaison, support, contact *(Tac)*; connection, junction, coupling.
Anschlußbahnhof *m*   junction *(RR)*.
Anschlußklemme *f*   binding post *(Elec)*.

Anschlußklinke *f* line jack, stationline jack *(Tp)*.

Anschlußmann *m* connecting file.

Anschlußpunkt *m* connecting point *(in axes of Sig Com)*.

Anschlußschnur *f* connecting cord *(Elec)*.

Anschlußstecker *m* plug, connecting plug *(Elec, Tp)*.

Anschlußstück *n* connecting piece, joint, coupling, union.

Anschlußteil der Garbe margin of the sheaf of fire.

Anschnallgurt *m* safety belt *(Avn)*.

Anschneidelinie *f* line of intersection.

Anschneiden *n* intersection *(Surv)*.

anschneiden to intersect; determine a fix *(air navigation)*; obtain a bearing *(Rad, FR)*.

Anschnitte *mpl* cross bearings.

Anschuß *m* sighting shot.

ansetzen launch, commit *(Tac)*; ram *(G)*.

Ansetzer *m* rammer *(G)*.

Ansichtsskizze *f* panoramic sketch *(Top)*.

Ansprache *f* designation *(of a target)*.

Anspruch *m* claim.

Anstalt *f* institution, establishment, station.

anstauen to dam up, flood.

Anstauung *f* damming, flooding; flooded area.

anstechen to tie, fasten, hitch.

Ansteckblech *n* float plate *(on a trail spade)*.

anstecken to attach, fasten, hitch; to infect.

ansteckende Krankheit communicable disease, contagious disease.

Ansteckung *f* infection.

Anstellwinkel *m* angle of pitch, blade angle *(propeller)*; angle of attack *(Avn)*.

Ansteuerungsfeuer *n* directional beacon *(Avn)*.

anstreichen run weapon up and down side of tree, etc., *(to find firing support)*; to paint.

Anstrich *m* paint.

Anströmrichtung *f* direction of air flow *(Avn)*.

anstürmen to assault, attack, charge.

ansuchen to request.

Ansumpfung *f* inundation, inundated area.

Antenne *f* antenna, aerial.

Antenne mit Rundwirkung omnidirectional antenna.

Antennenanschluß *m* antenna binding post.

Antennen-Anschlußbuchse *f* See Antennenbuchse.

Antennenbuchse *f* antenna jack.

Antennengebilde *n* antenna array, antenna structure, antenna system.

Antennengerät *n* antenna outfit, antenna equipment.

Antennenhaspel *f* antenna reel *(Ap)*.

Antennenkapazität *f* antenna capacitance.

Antennenkondensator *m* antenna condenser.

Antennenkopplung *f* antenna coupling.

Antennenkreis *m* antenna circuit.

Antennenleistung *f* antenna power.

Antennenmast *m* antenna mast.

Antennenspule *f* antenna tuning coil.

Antennenstab *m* antenna rod.

Antennenstellung *f* directional position of the antenna.

Antennenstromanzeiger *m* antenna ammeter.

Antennenwiderstand *m* antenna resistance.

Antiflatterbock *m* antishimmy shackle *(MT)*.

Antrag *m* request; recommendation, suggestion, proposal.

antreiben to drive, impel, propel.

antreten to fall in; begin *(an assignment)*; assume *(duties, etc.)*.

"Antreten!" "Fall in!" *(not at attention)*.

Antrieb *m* drive *(Mech)*.

Antriebsachse *f* driving axle *(MT)*.

Antriebsart *f* type of drive *(MT)*.

Antriebskegelrad *n* bevel drive pinion *(differential gear)*.

Antriebsrad *n* drive wheel *(MT)*.

Antriebsritzel *m* starter pinion *(on armature shaft of starter)*.

Antriebswelle *f* drive shaft.

Antriebszahnrad *n* drive gear *(MT)*.

A.N.-Verfahren *n* A.N. method *(of instrument landing)*.

anvisieren to sight at.

Anwärmeschuß *m* warming-up shot.

Anwärter *m* candidate; cadet.

anweisen to direct, instruct, allot.

Anweisung *f* directive; instructions; allotment.

anwerfen to crank *(an engine)*.
Anzapfleitung *f* power lead-in *(Rad)*.
Anzeiger *m* indicator, marker.
Anzeigerschiene *f* indicator slide *(MG)*.
Anziehungskraft *f* force of attraction.
anzielen to sight, to aim.
Anzug *m* uniform; suit of clothes.
anzünden to ignite, light.
Aphongetriebe *n* constant-mesh transmission *(MT)*.
Apotheker *m* pharmacist.
Apparattornister *m* instrument case *(portable Rad)*.
Apparatur *f* chassis *(Rad)*; fixtures *(Tech)*.
Appell *m* roll call; muster; inspection.
Aquadag *m* aquadag *(lubricant)*.
Arado name of an aircraft manufacturing company.
Aräometer *m* hydrometer.
Arbeiten *fpl* works *(Ft)*.
Arbeitsanzug *m* fatigue uniform, work uniform.
Arbeitsdienst *m* See **Reichsarbeitsdienst**.
Arbeitsdienstpflicht *f* liability to labor service.
Arbeitsführer *m* captain *(Reich Labor Service)*.
Arbeitsgeschütz *n* roving gun *(Arty)*.
Arbeitshub *m* power stroke *(Mtr)*.
Arbeitskommando *n* fatigue detail.
Arbeitslager *n* labor camp.
Arbeitsmann *m* workman *(Reich Labor Service)*.
Arbeitsspiel *n* functioning, action *(Mech)*.
Arbeitstakt *m* power stroke *(Mtr)*.
Arbeitsurlaub *m* leave for purposes of war work.
arbeitsverwendungsfähig fit for labor duty only *(abbr. a.v.)*.
a.v. Heimat fit for labor duty in zone of interior only.
Arktik *f* smoke acid for use in extremely cold weather *(CWS)*.
arktische Kaltluft polar air *(Met)*.
Armaturenbrett *n* instrument board, instrument panel.
Armauflage *f* elbow rest *(trench or firing pit)*.
Armband *n* See **Armbinde**.
Armbanduhr *f* wrist watch.
Armbinde *f* arm band, brassard.

Armee *f* army *(a tactical unit, distinguished from* Heer, the Army*)*.
Armeebefehl *m* army field order.
Armeebekleidungsamt *n* army clothing depot.
Armeebriefstelle *f* army postal station.
Armeefeldlazarett *n* army surgical hospital.
Armeegebiet *n* army area.
Armeegruppe *f* task force usually comprising one army and miscellaneous units.
Armeeintendant *m* army intendant *(Adm official at army Hq in charge of rations, clothing, equipment, pay, etc.)*.
Armeekartenlager *n* army map depot.
Armeekorps *n* army corps.
Armeekraftfahrpark *m* army motor transport park.
Armeemunitionslager *n* army ammunition depot.
Armeenachrichtenabteilung *f* army signal battalion.
Armeenachrichtenregiment *n* army signal regiment.
Armeenachschubführer *m* commander of army services of supply *(also known as* Kommandeur der Armeenachschubtruppen*)*.
Armeeoberkommando *n* high command of an army, army headquarters *(abbr.* OAK*)*.
Armeesanitätsabteilung *f* army medical battalion.
Armeeverpflegungsamt *n* office of army ration supply.
Armeeverpflegungslager *n* army ration-supply depot.
Ärmel *m* sleeve *(Clo)*.
Ärmelaufschlag *m* cuff *(Clo)*.
Ärmelabzeichen *n* sleeve badge.
Ärmelpatte *f* cuff patch.
Armschiene *f* splint *(for arm fracture)*.
Armzeichen *n* arm and hand signal, arm signal.
Arrestant *m* person under arrest.
Arrestanstalt *f* military prison.
Arrestlokal *n* detention room, guardhouse cell, guardhouse.
Arreststrafe *f* confinement, sentence of confinement.
Arrestraum im Lazarett detention ward.
Arsin *n* arsine *(CWS)*.

Art *f* kind, manner, method, type.
Art. B.-Stelle *f* See **Artilleriebeobachtungsstelle.**
Artillerie *f* artillery.
leichte **Artillerie** light artillery.
schwere **Artillerie** medium artillery.
schwerste **Artillerie** heavy artillery.
Artillerieabteilung *f* artillery battalion.
Artillerieaufmarsch *m* moving up to positions *(Arty)*.
Artilleriebekämpfung *f* counterbattery fire.
Artilleriebeobachter *m* artillery observer, spotter.
Artilleriebeobachtungsabteilung *f* observation battalion *(Arty)*.
Artilleriebeobachtungsstelle *f* artillery observation post.
Artilleriebeschuß *m* artillery fire.
Artillerieeinschlag *m* shell hit, shell burst, point of impact *(Arty)*.
Artillerieflieger *mpl* artillery reconnaissance aviation.
Artillerieflug *m* artillery mission *(Avn)*.
Artillerieflugzeug *n* artillery observation airplane.
Artillerieführer *m* division artillery commander *(special staff Arty officer and Arty commander at Div Hq)*.
Artilleriegliederung *f* organization of artillery.
Artilleriegruppe *f* artillery group, artillery groupment.
Artilleriekolonne *f* ammunition supply column *(Arty)*.
Artilleriekommandeur *m* corps artillery commander *(in GHQ pool)*; division artillery commander *(when GHQ artillery is attached)*.
Höherer Artilleriekommandeur special staff artillery officer *(at army Hq)*.
Artillerienachrichtenstelle *f* artillery intelligence center.
Artillerienachrichtentrupp *m* artillery intelligence section.
Artilleriepark *m* artillery equipment park.
Artilleriepunkttafel *f* point-designation grid.
Artillerierechenschieber *m* graphical firing table.
Artilleriespähtrupp *m* artillery reconnaissance detail.

Artilleriesperrfeuer *n* artillery barrage.
Artilleriestaffel *f* artillery train.
Artillerieunterstützung *f* artillery support.
Artillerieverbindungskommando *n* artillery liaison command post, artillery liaison detachment.
Artillerieverbindungsoffizier *m* artillery liaison officer.
Artillerievermessung *f* artillery survey.
Artillerievermessungstrupp *m* artillery survey section.
Artillerievorbereitung *f* artillery preparation.
Artilleriezugmaschine *f* artillery prime mover.
Artillerist *m* artilleryman.
artilleristische Aufklärung artillery reconnaissance.
artilleristische Punkte *mpl* artillery reference points.
Arznei *f* drug, medicine, medicament.
Arzneikasten *m* medicine chest.
Arzneikiste *f* See **Arzneikasten.**
Arzneimittel *n* medicine, medicament.
Arzt *m* doctor, medical officer.
Ärztliche Akademie der Luftwaffe school of aviation medicine.
ärztliche Behandlung medical treatment, medical attendance.
ärztliche Untersuchung *f* medical examination, physical examination.
Asbest *m* asbestos.
Äskulapstab *m* caduceus.
Assistenzarzt *m* second lieutenant *(Med)*.
Ast *m* branch; knot *(in wood)*.
Astro *m* celestial navigator *(Avn slang)*.
astronomische Navigation celestial navigation *(Avn)*.
astronomischer Meßzug *m* astronomical survey platoon.
Astverhau *m* dead abatis made of tree branches.
Atemeinsatz *m* filter element *(gas mask)*.
Atemgerät *n* oxygen apparatus *(Avn)*.
Atemmaske *f* oxygen mask *(Avn)*.
Atemmundstück *n* mouthpiece *(oxygen breathing apparatus)*.
Atemsack *m* respirator bag *(oxygen breathing apparatus)*.

Atemschlauch *m* hose *(gas mask, oxygen breathing apparatus).*

Äthylarsindichlorid *n* ethyldichlorarsine, ED *(CWS).*

Äthyldichlorarsin *n* ethyldichlorarsine, ED *(CWS). (Ger abbr.* Dick*).*

Attacke *f* charge *(Cav).*

Attrappe *f* dummy *(target, vehicle, etc.).*

ätzender Kampfstoff vesicant, vesicant agent, blister agent, blister gas.

Ätzmittel *n* caustic.

Ätznatron *n* lye, caustic soda, sodium hydroxide.

Aubo-Fähre *f* outboard-motor ferry *(Aubo = Außenbord).*

Aubomotor *m* outboard motor *(Aubo = Außenbord).*

Audion *n* grid-leak detector, detector, 2nd detector *(Rad).*

Aufbau *m* body *(MT);* superstructure, *i.e.* sponson and turret *(Tk).*

Aufbaulüfter *m* ventilator *(in Tk sponson or turret).*

Aufbewahrung *f* storage.

aufbieten mobilize.

aufblasen inflate, blow up.

Aufblitzen *n* flash *(Arty fire).*

aufbrauchen to exhaust, use up.

aufbrechen to depart, start.

Aufbruchsort *m* departure point, starting point.

Aufbruchszeit *f* departure time, starting time.

aufbumsen collide, strike *(slang).*

Aufenthaltspunkt *m* stop *(RR, MT).*

auffangen to detect *(Rad);* intercept, catch; to absorb *(recoil, etc.).*

Auffangstellung *f* prepared position in rear, rear position *(in defense).*

Auffangvorrichtung *f* buffer *(G).*

auffinden to locate *(a target).*

Aufführender *m* corporal of the guard.

Aufgabe *f* mission, task, problem.

aufgeben abandon, give up; register *(baggage, etc.);* send *(a telegram, etc.).*

Aufgebot *m* *See* **allgemeines Aufgebot.**

aufgesessen mounted *(Pers).*

Aufgleitfront *f* warm front *(Met).*

Aufhaken *n* message pick-up *(Avn).*

Aufhängeöse *f* suspension lug *(bomb).*

Aufhängung *f* suspension *(of bombs, etc.).*

aufhetzen incite.

aufklären reconnoiter, scout, observe, patrol.

Aufklärer *m* scout, observer; reconnaissance airplane.

Aufklärertätigkeit *f* reconnaissance activity, patrol activity.

Aufklärung *f* reconnaissance *(Tac).*

Aufklärungsabteilung *f* reconnaissance battalion.

Aufklärungsbreite *f* width of reconnaissance sector *(in which Obsn Bn locates targets).*

Aufklärungsergebnis *n* results of reconnaissance.

Aufklärungsflieger *m* aircraft observer; reconnaissance aircraft.

Aufklärungsflug *m* reconnaissance mission, reconnaissance flight *(Avn).*

Aufklärungsflugzeug *m* reconnaissance airplane.

Aufklärungsgebiet *n* reconnaissance area.

Aufklärungskörper *mpl* reconnaissance elements.

Aufklärungsmaterial *n* reconnaissance information.

Aufklärungsraum *m* reconnaissance area.

Aufklärungsschwadron *f* reconnaissance troop *(Cav).*

Aufklärungsspähtrupp *m* reconnaissance patrol.

Aufklärungsstaffel *f* reconnaissance squadron *(Avn).*

Aufklärungsstreifen *m* reconnaissance sector.

Aufklärungstiefe *f* reconnaissance depth *(in which Obsn Bn locates targets).*

Aufklärungstrupp *m* reconnaissance patrol.

Aufklärungszug *m* scout car platoon; reconnaissance platoon.

Aufladekommando *n* loading detail.

Auflademotor *m* supercharged engine *(Avn).*

aufladen to boost, supercharge; to load.

Aufladung *f* detonating charge *(blasting cap).*

Auflagefläche *f* bearing surface, contact surface.

Auflagepunkt *m* center of tire impact *(MT);* point of support *(Tech).*

Auflager *n* pedestal, support *(Bdg);* hanger bar *(harness).*

Auflaufstück *n* knuckle lug *(G).*

auflösen disintegrate, disband, dissolve, scatter, demobilize.

Aufmarsch *m* concentration or assembly of troops for action; strategic concentration; moving up to positions *(Arty)*.

Aufmarschgebiet *n* concentration area *(Tac)*.

Aufmarschplan *m* plan for strategic concentration.

Aufnahme *f* covering force *(reserve force covering withdrawal from action)*; reception; photograph; taking up, establishment *(of contact, etc.)*.

Aufnahmefähigkeit *f* capacity *(of roads, structures, etc.)*.

Aufnahmehaken *m* pick-up hook *(for message pick-up)* *(Ap)*.

Aufnahmering *m* receiving ring *(AA gun)*.

Aufnahmestellung *f* covering position *(covering withdrawal from action)*.

Aufnahmestreifen *m* tape *(Tg printer.)*

aufnehmen to record *(sound, etc.)*; to receive, take up; to photograph; to survey; to establish *(contact, etc.)*.

aufpflanzen to fix bayonets.

aufprotzen to couple, limber, place a gun in traveling position *(Arty)*.

Aufrauhbürste *f* rotary sweeper *(road construction)*.

aufräumen to clear away, mop up.

aufrecht erect, upright.

aufreißen to rip, tear up.

Aufriß *m* design, sketch, vertical section.

aufrollen to roll up *(Tac)*; to coil *(wire)*.

aufrücken to move up, advance.

Aufruhr *m* riot.

Aufrüstung *f* plank scaffolding *(on a Pon)*.

Aufsatz *m* sight mount, telescope mount *(in a loose sense, either the optical sight alone or the entire sight assembly)*; essay, composition.

Aufsatzeinteilung *f* elevation graduations *(sight mount)*.

Aufsatzentfernung *f* corrected range *(Arty)*.

Aufsatzerhöhung *f* corrected elevation *(Arty)*.

Aufsatzgehäuse *n* sight-mount housing *(G)*.

Aufsatzstange *f* sight adjustment rod *(G)*.

Aufsatzträger *m* sight bracket, sight support *(G)*.

Aufsatztrieb *m* elevation mechanism *(G)*.

Aufsatztrommel *f* angle-of-elevation dial *(G)*.

Aufsatzwinkel *m* angle of elevation *(Gunnery)*; superelevation *(AAA)*.

Aufsatzwinkeltrieb *m* angle-of-elevation mechanism *(G)*.

Aufsatzzeiger *m* telescope mount reference pointer *(matches with Rohrzeiger when gun is laid for elevation)*.

aufschablonieren to stencil on.

aufschirren to harness.

Aufschlag *m* impact, percussion; cuff *(Clo)*.

Aufschlaggelände *n* impact area.

Aufschlaggeschwindigkeit *f* striking velocity.

Aufschlagpunkt *m* point of impact, objective point.

Aufschlagweite *f* burst interval.

Aufschlagwinkel *m* angle of impact.

Aufschlagzünder *m* impact fuze, percussion fuze.

Aufschlagzünder mit Verzögerung delay fuze.

Aufschlagzünder ohne Verzögerung nondelay fuze.

Aufschreiber *m* recorder *(Arty)*.

Aufschrumpfen *n* heat shrinking *(Ord)*.

Aufschub *m* delay.

Aufschüttung *f* fill *(Engr, Top)*.

Aufsichtsturm *m* control tower *(Adrm)*.

aufsitzen to mount *(a horse or vehicle)*.

das Ziel aufsitzen lassen to hold below the target in aiming.

Aufspuler *m* reel *(Tp)*.

Aufsteckschlüssel *m* socket wrench.

aufsteigen to ascend, mount, rise.

aufsteigender Ast ascending branch *(of trajectory)*.

Aufstellbahnhof *m* make-up yard *(RR)*.

aufstellen to post *(a sentry)*; to activate or constitute *(a unit)*; to emplace *(a gun)*; to install *(an engine, etc.)*; to mount *(a gun)*; to place, to distribute *(troops, etc.)*; to establish *(an agency)*; to park *(vehicles)*.

Aufstellgleis *n* make-up track *(RR)*.

Aufstellung *f* formation *(of troops)*; initial organization *(of a unit)*; establishment *(of an agency)*; disposition *(Tac)*.

Aufstellungsbefehl *m* initial organization order *(to activate a unit)*.

Aufstromvergaser *m* updraft carburetor.

Auftakt *m* initial phase *(of an operation)*.

auftanken refuel.

Auftrag *m* mission, task *(Tac)*.

"**Auftrag erledigt!**" "Mission accomplished!"

Auftragserteilung *f* assignment of missions, assignment of tasks.

Auftragskarte *f* flight diagram *(aerial Photo)*.

Auftreffen *n* impact.

Auftreffgeschwindigkeit *f* striking velocity *(of projectile)*.

Auftreffpunkt *m* point of impact.

Auftreffwinkel *m* angle of impact.

Auftrieb *m* buoyancy, lift *(Avn)*.

Auftriebsmittelpunkt *m* center of lift *(Avn)*.

Auftritt *m* fire step.

Aufwind *m* anabatic wind, up-slope wind.

Aufzeichnung *f* record, notation, sketch.

Aufziehachse *f* winding stem *(on blasting machine, watch, etc.)*.

aufziehen to mount *(Photo)*; pull up, lift, hoist; to mount *(guard)*; to wind *(a watch, etc.)*.

Aufziehen der Wache guard mount.

Aufziehleine *f* static line *(Prcht)*.

Aufzug *m* elevator, hoist.

Augenabstand *m* interpupillary distance *(Optics)*.

Augenaufklärung *f* visual reconnaissance.

Augenblicksziel *n* fleeting target, transient target, fleeting objective.

Augenblickszünder *m* instantaneous fuze, nondelay fuze, quick fuze.

Augenfenster *n* eyepiece *(gas mask)*.

"**Augen gerade, aus!**" "Ready, front!"

"**Augen, links!**" "Eyes, left!" *(strictly,* "Die Augen, links!" *to distinguish preparatory command from that in* "Augen, rechts!"*)*.

Augenmuschel *f* eyeguard *(Optics)*.

"**Augen, rechts!**" "Eyes, right!"

Augenreizstoff *m* lacrimator *(CWS)*.

Augenring *m* eyepiece frame of goggles *(gas mask)*.

Augenschlitz *m* viewing slit *(telescopic sight)*.

Augenverbindung *f* visual communication.

Ausatemventil *n* outlet valve *(gas mask)*.

Ausbau *m* construction; improvement *(of a position)*; dismantling, removing, dismounting *(of a gun, etc.)*.

ausbauen dismount *(Ord)*; improve *(Ft)*; remove, dismantle.

Ausbilder *m* instructor.

Ausbildung *f* training, drill.

Ausbildungsanweisungen *fpl* training order.

Ausbildungsgerät *n* training equipment, training instrument.

Ausbildungslager *n* training camp.

Ausbildungsplan *m* training schedule.

Ausbildungsrichtlinien *fpl* training outlines, training regulations.

Ausbildungsstab *m* training staff.

Ausbildungsstufe *f* training phase.

Ausbildungsvorschrift *f* training manual, drill regulations.

Ausblick *m* objective lens *(Optics)*; prospect, view.

Ausblickprismengehäuse *n* objective-prism housing *(BC telescope)*.

Ausblickstutzen *m* objective-lens socket *(Optics)*.

Ausbootung *f* debarkation.

Ausbrennung *f* barrel erosion, erosion of the bore *(Ord)*.

Ausbruch der Feindseligkeiten outbreak of hostilities.

Ausbuchtung *f* salient.

Ausdauer *f* endurance.

Ausdehnung *f* frontage *(Tac)*; expansion, extension, spreading.

auseinandergehen diverge, separate.

auseinandernehmen to strip, disassemble, dismantle, take apart.

auseinanderziehen deploy, extend, spread out *(Tac)*.

ausfahren to extend, to lower *(Ap landing gear, etc.)*; to ride out, drive out.

Ausfahrgleis *n* outgoing track *(RR)*.

Ausfall *m* sortie *(Tac)*; long lunge, long thrust *(bayonet thrust)*; casualty; failure, breakdown *(of an engine, etc.)*; gun out of battery *(Arty)*.

Ausfertigung *f* drawing up, writing out *(a report, etc.)*.

in dreifacher Ausfertigung in triplicate.

ausfragen interrogate, question.

ausführen accomplish, carry out, execute.

Ausführung *f* execution, carrying out; design, model *(Tech)*.

in zweifacher Ausführung in duplicate.

Ausführungskommando *n* command of execution *(drill)*.

Ausgabe *f* issue; edition.

Ausgabestelle *f* point of issue, distributing point.

Ausgang *m* departure, outcome, exit, outlet, start.

Ausgangslage *f* assault position *(Tac)*; starting position, original position.

Ausgangslinie *f* line of departure, jump-off line.

Ausgangsort *m* point of departure *(air navigation)*.

Ausgangspunkt *m* initial point, origin, point of departure.

Ausgangsspannung *f* output voltage.

Ausgangsstellung *f* line of departure, jump-off position *(Tac)*.

Ausgangstransformator *m* output transformer *(Rad)*.

ausgeben to issue, distribute.

ausgeglichen balanced, equalized, equilibrated.

Ausgehanzug *m* dress uniform.

ausgehoben drafted; silenced *(slang)*.

Ausgehobener *m* draftee.

Ausgehverbot *n* curfew *(Mil Govt)*.

ausgemustert rejected as unfit. See Musterung, Ausmusterungsschein.

Ausgießgerät *n* See Aus- und Abgießgerät.

Ausgleich *m* equalization, compensation, equilibration, balancing.

Ausgleichdüse *f* compensating jet *(Mtr)*.

ausgleichen to balance, compensate, equalize.

Ausgleicher *m* compensator *(Ord, Mech)*; equilibrator *(G)*.

Ausgleicherarm *m* equilibrator anchor *(G)*.

Ausgleichfläche *f* balance tab, trim tab *(Ap)*.

Ausgleichgetriebe *n* differential gear.

Ausgleichsperre *f* differential lock *(MT)*.

ausglühen anneal.

ausheben to conscript, draft.

Aushebung *f* draft, conscription.

Aushilfe *f* expedient, substitute, auxiliary.

ausholen to lunge.

ausklinken to release *(bombs, etc.)*.

Auskolkung *f* scour *(in a river bed)*.

Auskreuzung *f* bracing, cross bracing *(Ap)*.

auskundschaften to spy, to scout.

Auskunft *f* information.

Auskunftsstelle *f* information center, information office; control point.

auskuppeln disengage the clutch.

Ausladebahnhof *m* detraining point, railhead.

Ausladeeinheit *f* unloading unit.

Ausladegebiet *n* detrucking area.

Ausladekommando *n* unloading detail.

ausladen to unload, detruck, detrain, etc.

Ausladeplatz *m* detrucking point.

Auslader *m* stevedore.

Ausladespitze *f* railhead, truckhead.

Ausladestelle *f* detrucking point.

Ausladeübersicht *f* detraining or unloading table.

Ausland *n* foreign country.

im Ausland abroad.

Ausländer *m* alien, foreigner.

feindlicher Ausländer enemy alien.

Auslaßrohr *n* eduction tube *(Cml cylinder)*.

Auslaßventil *n* exhaust valve *(Mtr)*.

Auslaßventilkammer *f* exhaust port.

Auslauf *m* outlet *(for liquids, etc.)*.

auslaufen to run out; to complete a run after landing; to put to sea.

auslegen to pay out *(rope, wire, etc.)*; to explain, interpret; to expose, extend; to lay out *(money)*.

Ausleger *m* pack rest *(harness)*; outrigger *(boats and floats)* *(AA gun)*; boom *(of a crane or derrick)*.

Auslegerbrücke *f* cantilever bridge.

Auslegezeichen *n* ground panel *(Sig C)*.

Ausleseknopf *m* selector switch *(Ap armament control)*.

Auslieferung *f* delivery; exposure *(to danger, the elements, etc.)*.

auslöschen extinguish, put out *(a fire)*.

Auslöseeinrichtung *f* release mechanism *(bombing)*.

Auslöseknopf *m* release button.

Auslösepunkt *m* bomb release point, release point.

Auslösung *f* release *(of bombs, etc.)*.

Ausmaß *n* dimension.
ausmerzen eliminate, eradicate.
Ausmusterungsschein *m* certificate of rejection *(for those unfit for Mil service)*.
Ausnahmegespräch *n* urgent call *(Tp)*.
Ausnahmezustand *m* state of emergency.
ausnutzen to exploit, to utilize fully.
Auspuff *m* exhaust, exhaust system *(Mtr)*.
Auspuffgeräusch *n* exhaust noise.
Auspuffhub *m* exhaust stroke *(Mtr)*.
Auspuffkanal *m* exhaust duct *(Mtr)*.
Auspuffklappe *f* cutout *(Mtr)*.
Auspuffkrümmer *m* exhaust manifold *(Mtr)*.
Auspuffleitung *f* exhaust duct *(Mtr)*.
Auspufftakt *m* exhaust stroke *(Mtr)*.
Auspufftopf *m* muffler *(Mtr)*.
Auspuffwolke *f* exhaust smoke *(Mtr)*.
ausräuchern to smoke out; to fumigate.
ausrichten to dress *(drill)*; to perform; to level, straighten.
sich nach links ausrichten to dress left.
Ausrichtung *f* orientation; straightening, leveling.
Ausrollen *n* landing run *(Avn)*.
ausrotten wipe out, crush, annihilate.
ausrücken disengage *(gears, etc.)*; depart, move up.
Ausrüstung *f* equipment, outfit, accessories, accouterments.
Ausrüstungsgegenstand *m* item of equipment.
Ausrüstungsnachweisung *f* table of equipment.
Ausrüstungsstück *n* accessory, piece of equipment.
Aussage *f* statement.
Ausschalen *n* stripping the forms *(concrete construction)*.
Ausschaltehebel *m* throwout lever *(aiming circle)*.
ausschalten disconnect, detach, cut out, eliminate, switch off, throw out; compensate for, correct *(an error, etc.) (Gunnery)*.
Ausschalten der besonderen und Witterungseinflüsse ballistic correction, *i.e.* correction for interior and exterior ballistic factors.
Ausschalten der Grundstufe calibration correction, correction for velocity

error *(Gunnery)*. See *also* **Grundstufe**.
Ausschalten der Schnittbildversetzung halving adjustment *(coincidence range finder)*.
Ausschalten der Temperatureinflüsse elasticity correction *(Gunnery)*.
Ausschalten des Schallverzuges acoustic correction *(sound locator)*.
Ausschalten des Windes wind correction *(Gunnery)*.
Ausschalter *m* switch; throwout *(lever)*.
ausscheiden to detach, to detail; to eliminate *(impurities, etc.)*; to drop out, leave, separate.
ausscheren to fall out of formation *(Avn)*; to fall out of line *(Nav)*.
ausschiffen debark, disembark.
Ausschiffung *f* debarkation, disembarkation.
ausschirren unharness.
Ausschlag *m* decisive factor; rash *(Med)*.
ausschlaggebend decisive.
ausschließen interdict; exclude.
Ausschließungsschein *m* certificate of exclusion from military service *(for criminals, subversive elements, etc.)*.
Ausschuß *m* board, committee, commission.
ausschwärmen deploy *(Tac)*.
ausschweben hold off *(in landing) (Avn)*.
ausschwingen die out, die down *(oscillations)*.
Außenantenne *f* outside antenna.
Außenaufhängung *f* external suspension *(of bombs)*.
Außenbackenbremse *f* external contracting brake *(MT)*.
Außenbefestigungen *fpl* outworks *(Ft)*.
Außenbordmotor *m* outboard motor.
Außengrenzlehre *f* snap gage.
Außenhafen *m* outer harbor.
Außenhaut *f* skin, skin cover, covering *(Ap)*.
Außenlandung *f* off-field landing *(Avn)*.
Außenluftdruck *m* barometric pressure *(Avn)*.
Außenluft-Thermometer *n* free-air thermometer *(Ap)*.
Außenschieber *m* outer sleeve *(sleeve-type engine)*.

Außenstelle *f* outlying station or post.

Außenverspannung *f* external bracing *(Ap)*.

Außenwache *f* exterior guard.

Außenwerke *npl* outworks *(Ft)*.

außerballistisch pertaining to exterior ballistics.

außer Betrieb out of order, not working.

außer Dienst retired *(abbr. a.D.)*.

außer Gefecht gesetzt put out of action.

äußere Ballistik exterior ballistics.

außerplanmäßig exceeding authorized basic allowance or strength; not in accordance with plans; extraordinary.

aussenden to dispatch, send out, transmit.

Aussetzen *n* posting *(of guards)*; cessation *(of rain, fire, etc.)*.

Aussichtsturm *m* observation tower.

aussondern to sort.

ausspähen to spy, reconnoiter.

Ausspähung *f* espionage, reconnaissance, spying.

aussparen to leave untouched, to bypass.

ausspringender Winkel salient.

ausstatten equip.

aussteigen bail out *(Avn slang)*.

Ausstoßbüchse *f* smoke canister ejected from projectile on burst.

Ausstoßen *n* exhaust stroke *(Mtr)*; expulsion.

ausstoßen to expel, eliminate, cashier.

Ausstrahlung *f* radiation.

Austausch *m* exchange *(PW, etc.)*.

austauschbar interchangeable.

Austauschschiff *n* exchange ship, cartel ship *(Nav)*.

Austauschstoff *m* substitute material.

austreten relieve oneself, attend to one's needs.

Aus- und Abgießgerät *n* gas-spraying apparatus *(Ap, CWS)*.

Auswanderungsmesser *m* lead computer *(AA)*.

Auswanderungsstrecke *f* linear travel of target, leg between present and future positions *(AAA)*.

auswärtig foreign.

auswechselbar interchangeable, removable.

auswechselbares Seelenrohr removable liner *(G)*.

Ausweichbewegung *f* evading movement, withdrawing movement to new position *(Tac)*.

ausweichen evade, give way, withdraw, fall back *(Tac)*.

Ausweichflugplatz *m* dispersal landing field.

Ausweichgleis *n* siding *(RR)*.

Ausweichhafen *m* alternate airport.

Ausweichstelle *f* bypass *(Road)*; siding *(RR)*.

Ausweichstellung *f* alternate position.

Ausweichvermittlung *f* alternate routing *(emergency Tp Com)*.

Ausweichziel *n* alternate target, secondary target *(bombing)*.

Ausweis *m* identification *(card, document, etc.)*; pass, permit.

Ausweiskarte *f* identification card, pass, permit.

Ausweispapier *n* identification papers.

Auswerfer *m* ejector *(Ord)*.

Auswerfervorrichtung *f* ejector mechanism *(Ord)*.

Auswertelineal *n* computing slide rule *(FR)*.

auswerten evaluate, interpret, compute, plot *(maps)*.

Auswertestelle *f* computing station *(SR)*.

Auswertung *f* evaluation, interpretation.

Auszeichnung *f* decoration, medal.

ausziehen extract, draw out, pull out.

Auszieher *m* extractor *(Ord)*.

Ausziehgleis *n* lead track *(RR)*.

Auszug *m* extract, summary, departure; extension *(Tech)*.

Autobahn *f* automobile express highway.

Autofrettage *f* cold-drawing, autofrettage *(Ord)*.

Autokartograph *m* stereoscopic plotting machine.

Autokolonne *f* motor vehicle column, motor march column.

automatische Kurssteuerung automatic pilot, mechanical pilot *(Ap)*.

Autoschleppstart *m* auto-tow take-off *(glider)*.

Axt *f* ax.

Azetylen *n* acetylene.
Azetylensauerstoffbrenner *m* oxyacet-
ylene torch.
Azimut *n* azimuth.

Azimutalprojektion *f* azimuthal projection.
Azimutentfernungsmesser *m* depression position finder.

B

Bach *m* stream, brook, rivulet.
Bachübergang *m* stream crossing.
Backbord *n* port side.
Backbordmotor *m* port engine.
Backe *f* cheek.
Backenbremse *f* shoe brake *(MT)*.
Backenschiene *f* stock rail *(RR)*.
Backenstück *n* cheek strap *(harness)*.
Bäckerei *f* bakery.
Bäckereikompanie *f* bakery company.
Badewagen *m* shower-bath truck.
Bagger *m* excavator, dredge, power
shovel.
Bahn *f* path, road; runway; rail-
road; orbit; course; trajectory.
Bahnanlage *f* railroad installation.
Bahndamm *m* railroad embankment.
Bahnhof *m* railroad station; trolley
or bus station.
Bahnhofsleistung *f* station capacity
*(number of trains loaded or unloaded
per day)*.
Bahnhofsoffizier *m* railroad station
traffic officer.
Bahnhofswachabteilung *f* railroad
station guard detachment.
Bahnkörper *m* roadbed *(RR)*.
Bahnkrone *f* crown of roadbed
(RR).
Bahnplanum *n* subgrade *(RR)*.
Bahnsteig *m* platform *(RR)*.
Bahnsteigunterführung *f* platform
underpass *(RR)*.
Bahntransport *m* railroad transpor-
tation.
Bahnüberführung *f* overpass *(RR)*.
Bahnübergang *m* railroad crossing.
Bahnunterführung *f* underpass *(RR)*.
Bahnverbindung *f* railroad line, rail-
road communication.
Bajonett *n* bayonet. *See also* Seiten-
gewehr.
Bajonettangriff *m* bayonet charge.
Bajonettfechten *n* bayonet fighting.
Bajonettgriff *m* bayonet grip.
Bajonettkupplung *f* bayonet joint.

Bajonettstoß *m* bayonet thrust.
Bajonettverschluß *m* bayonet lock,
bayonet joint.
Bake *f* beacon; navigation guide,
channel marker, landmark *(Nav)*.
Bakenempfang *m* radio-beacon recep-
tion.
Bakterienkrieg *m* bacteriological
warfare.
Baldachin *m* canopy *(center section
of upper wing of biplane)*.
Balken *m* balk, beam; girder; log.
Balkenbahn *f* timber road.
Balkenfloß *n* timber raft.
Balkensperre *f* timber road block.
schwimmende Balkensperre floating
boom.
Balkenstapel *m* log crib, timber crib
(Bdg).
Balkenverhau *m* timber obstacle.
Ballen *m* bulb *(horse)*; heel *(har-
ness)*; bale.
Ballistik *f* ballistics.
ballistische Tageseinflüsse ballistic
density and wind factors.
Ballistit *n* ballistite *(Am)*.
Ballon *m* balloon.
Ballonabweiser *m* anti-balloon device
(Ap).
Ballonamme *f* supply balloon, nurse
balloon.
Ballonaufstiegplatz *m* balloon site.
Ballonbatterie *f* observation balloon
section *(Arty)*.
Ballonbeobachter *m* balloon observer.
Ballonbeobachtung *f* balloon observa-
tion.
Ballonführer *m* balloon pilot.
Ballongurt *m* rigging band *(captive
Bln)*.
Ballonhülle *f* envelope, gas bag, outer
cover, balloon cover.
Ballonkorb *m* balloon basket.
Ballonmannschaft *f* balloon crew.
Ballonnetz *n* balloon net.
Ballonreifen *m* balloon tire.

Ballonsperre *f* balloon barrage.
Ballonstoff *m* balloon fabric.
Ballonvariometer *n* balloon stato-
scope.
Ballonventil *n* gas valve *(Bln)*.
Ballonwinde *f* balloon winch.
Balta *See* **ballistische Tageseinflüsse.**
Baltasekunden *fpl* ballistic density
and wind factors in time-of-flight
seconds.
Baltasekunden-Verfahren *n* procedure
in correcting for ballistic density and
wind.
Bananenstecker *m* banana plug.
Band *n* band, cord, tape, strip, rib-
bon.
Bandbreite *f* band width *(Rad)*.
Bandbremse *f* band brake *(MT)*.
Bändchenmikrophon *n* *See* **Bandmi-
krophon.**
Bandfeder *f* flat coil spring *(fuze)*.
Bandgestell *n* harness *(gas mask)*.
Bandmikrophon *n* ribbon microphone.
Bandsäge *f* band saw.
Bandspreizung *f* bandspread *(Rad)*.
Bank *f* bench; lathe; bank; parapet,
barbette.
Bannware *f* contraband of war.
Baracke *f* temporary barracks, semi-
permanent cantonment building.
Barackenlager *n* cantonment, camp
having semipermanent buildings.
Barbarabehelfsmeldung *f* hasty mete-
orological message *(Arty)*.
Barbarameldung *f* meteorological
message *(Arty)* *(from* Barbara,
patron saint of Arty).
Barbarist *m* artilleryman *(slang)*.
See also **Barbarameldung.**
Barbarasondermeldung *f* special
meteorological message *(Arty)*.
Barbette *f* barbette.
Barbettelafette *f* barbette carriage,
barbette mount *(G)*.
Bargeld *n* cash.
barometrische Reglerdose control
aneroid *(Ap engine)*.
barometrisches Gefälle pressure
gradient *(Met)*.
Basis *f* base; horizontal base *(Btry
Surv)*.
Basislineal *n* base-line arm *(plotting
protractor)*.
Bataillon *n* battalion.
Bataillonsabschnitt *m* battalion sector.
Bataillons-Adjutant *m* battalion ex-

ecutive officer, aide to battalion com-
mander.
Bataillonsführer *m* battalion com-
mander; acting battalion commander.
Bataillonsgefechtsstand *m* battalion
command post.
Bataillonshornist *m* drum major
(formerly called Tambourmajor*)*.
Bataillonskolonne *f* battalion train.
Bataillons-Kommandeur *m* battalion
commander.
Bataillonsnachrichtenstaffel *f* bat-
talion communication section.
Bataillonsstab *m* battalion staff, bat-
talion headquarters.
Bataillonstambourstock *m* baton.
Bataillonstroß *m* battalion train.
Bataillonsverbandplatz *m* battalion
aid station.
Batterie *f* battery *(Arty, Elec)*.
Batteriebild *n* battery-location plot
(SR).
Batteriechef *m* battery commander.
Batteriefront *f* battery front.
Batterieführer *m* battery commander;
acting battery commander.
Batteriekasten *m* battery box *(Elec)*.
Batteriekran *m* gun hoist, loading
crane *(Arty)*.
Batterieoffizier *m* executive *(firing
Btry)*.
Batterieplan *m* firing chart *(Arty)*.
Batteriestand *m* *See* **Batteriestellung.**
Batteriestellung *f* battery position
(Arty).
Batterietafel *f* battery manning table
(Arty).
Batterietrupp *m* battery detail, bat-
tery headquarters detail, battery
commander's detail *(Arty)*.
Batteriezündung *f* battery ignition
(Mtr).
Bau *m* construction, structure, type
of construction.
Bauart *f* type of construction.
Bauausführung *f* construction, struc-
tural design.
Baubataillon *n* construction bat-
talion.
Bauch *m* abdomen, belly.
Bauchfreiheit *f* chassis clearance
(MT).
Bauchgurt *m* front cinch *(pack
saddle)*.
Bauchlandung *f* belly landing *(Avn)*.
Bauchtreffer *m* sidewise-striking
projectile.

Bauglied n structural unit, section of a structure, structure element.
Bauholz n lumber.
Baukompanie f construction company *(Mil)*.
Baumaß n structural dimensions.
Baumbeobachtungsstand m observation post in a tree.
Baumschütze m sniper in a tree.
Baumsperre f abatis, dead abatis.
Baumstamm m tree trunk.
Baumstammkufe f log runner *(log sled)*.
Baumstumpf m tree stump.
Baumuster n model, type *(Ap, MT)*.
Baumverhau m live abatis.
Baumwollabfall m cotton waste, cotton linters.
Baumwolle f cotton.
Bausoldat m engineer soldier in construction unit.
Baustab m construction staff.
Baustange f lance pole *(Tp)*.
Bautrupp m construction detail, construction squad.
Bautruppen fpl construction troops.
Bauunternehmer m contractor, builder.
Bauweise f type of construction or structure, method of construction.
Beamter m official, civil servant. *See also* **Wehrmachtbeamter.**
Beanspruchung f load, stress, strain.
beaufsichtigen supervise.
Beauftragter m representative.
bebaute Felder cultivated fields.
bebautes Gelände built-up area.
Bedarf m requirements.
bedeckt covered, overgrown; overcast *(Met)*.
fast bedeckt broken *(Met)*.
Bedeckung f coverage *(Met)*; escort, convoy, cover *(Tac)*.
Bedeckungsabteilung f covering party, escort detachment.
Bedeckungsmannschaft f escort personnel.
Bediener m controller *(AA SL)*.
Bedienung f gun squad; service of the piece.
Bedienungsanweisung f operating directions.
Bedienungseinrichtung f control device, operating device.
Bedienungsentlastung f relief of strain on pilot *(Avn)*.
Bedienungsmannschaft f gun crew, gun squad.

Bedienungsplatte f operating panel *(Rad)*.
Bedienungsschalter m operating switch *(Elec)*.
Bedienungsvorschrift f operating instructions.
bedingungslose Übergabe unconditional surrender.
Bedrohung f threat.
Beendigung der Luftgefahr "all clear."
Beerdigung f burial.
Befehl m order, command.
"Zu Befehl!" "Yes, sir!" *(in acknowledgment of an order)*.
Befehlsausgabe f briefing, issuance of orders.
Befehlsbefugnis f authority *(Mil)*.
Befehlsbereich m extent of command.
Befehlsbestätigung f confirmatory order.
Befehlserteilung f issuance of orders.
Befehlsgebäude n control tower *(Adrm)*.
Befehlsgebung f giving of commands.
befehlsgemäß according to instructions, as ordered.
Befehlsgewalt f command, authority of command.
Befehlsgruppe f command group.
Befehlshaber m commander.
Befehlshaber des Ersatzheeres *See* **Chef der Heeresrüstung und Befehlshaber des Ersatzheeres.**
Befehlsnetz n command net.
Befehlspanzer m command tank.
Befehlssprache f terminology of orders.
Befehlsstand m command post, headquarters.
Befehlsstelle f control tower *(Adrm)*; command post, headquarters.
Befehlsübermittlung f transmission of orders.
Befehlsverhältnisse npl chain of command.
Befehlswagen m command car, command truck, commander's car, staff car.
Befehlsweg m chain of command, command channel.
befestigt fortified; secured, tied, fastened.
Befestigung f fortification.
Befestigungsanlage f fortified defense system.

Befestigungsarbeiten *fpl* fortifications, works.

Befestigungswerk *n* permanent fortification, work.

befeuern to mark or light with beacon lights *(an airway or Adrm)*.

befördern to forward *(supplies, etc.)*; promote; transmit.

Beförderung *f* advancement, promotion; transmission, forwarding, transportation.

Beförderungsliste *f* promotion list.

Beförderungsmittel *n* carrier, vehicle; means of transportation; means of transmission.

Befragung *f* questioning *(of PW, etc.)*.

Befugnis *f* authority, powers.

begasen to gas *(CWS)*.

Begasung *f* laying of gas obstacles, gassing *(CWS)*.

Begegnungsgefecht *n* meeting engagement.

beglaubigen certify, authenticate, verify, confirm.

beglaubigt authenticated, certified, notarized, verified, confirmed.

Beglaubigung *f* authentication, certification, confirmation, verification.

Begleitartillerie *f* accompanying artillery.

Begleitbatterie *f* accompanying battery.

Begleiter *m* escort; assistant driver.

Begleitfeuer *n* accompanying fire.

Begleitgeschütz *n* accompanying gun.

Begleitkommando *n* escort party, escort detachment, covering party.

Begleitpanzer *m* accompanying tank.

Begleitschiff *n* escort vessel.

Begleitschutz *m* escort, fighter escort *(Avn)*.

Begleitzettel *m* emergency medical tag.

Begleitzug *m* convoy.

Begräbnis *n* burial.

begrenztes Ziel limited objective.

Begrenzungshebel *m* clamping lever *(MG)*.

Begrenzungsstift *m* traversing stop *(MG)*.

Behälter *m* gasoline tank; container.

Behandlung *f* treatment.

Beharrungsvermögen *n* inertia.

Behelf *m* expedient, makeshift.

Behelfsantenne *f* emergency antenna.

Behelfsbrücke *f* emergency bridge, hasty bridge.

Behelfsfloßsack *m* emergency pneumatic boat.

Behelfsgasschutz *m* emergency gas protection.

Behelfslandebrücke *f* hasty landing stage.

behelfsmäßig improvised, hasty, emergency, temporary, auxiliary, makeshift.

Behelfsmaterial *n* emergency construction material.

beherrschend commanding, dominating.

Behinderungsschießen *n* interdiction fire.

Behmlot *n* fathometer, echo depth sounder *(Nav)*; Behm sound-ranging altimeter, sonic altimeter *(Ap)*.

Behörde *f* authority *(Adm, Law)*.

behördlich zugelassen authorized, officially sanctioned.

beibringen inflict *(losses, etc.)*.

Beiende *n* warp *(of a rope)*.

Beifahrer *m* rear rider, sidecar rider *(Mtcl)*; assistant driver *(MT)*.

beifügen add; attach, enclose.

beiklappbar folding.

Beil *n* ax.

Beiladung *f* igniting charge, igniter, booster charge *(Am)*.

Beilage *f* enclosure, supplement *(in a manual, etc.)*.

Beilpicke *f* pickax.

Beinleder *npl* leather puttees, leather leggins.

Beisitzer *m* law member.

Beißzange *f* nippers.

beitragen contribute to, cooperate.

beitreiben to requisition *(from civilians)*; to commandeer.

Beitreibung *f* requisitioning *(from civilians)*.

Beitreibungsschein *m* requisition receipt *(for civilian property)*.

Beiwagen *m* sidecar *(Mtcl)*.

Beiwagenkrad *n* sidecar motorcycle.

Beiwert *m* coefficient.

Bekanntgabe *f* announcement.

bekleiden to revet *(Ft)*; to clothe; to hold *(office)*.

Bekleidung *f* revetment *(Ft)*; clothing.

Bekleidungsentgiftung *f* clothing decontamination.

Bekleidungsnachweis *m* clothing account.

Bekleidungssack *m* duffle bag, barrack(s) bag.

Bekleidungsstück *n* article of clothing.

Beköstigungsgeld *n* garrison ration.

Beköstigungsmittel *npl* ration supplies, subsistence supplies.

Beladeplan *m* stowage chart *(for vehicle)*.

Belag *m* planking *(Bdg)*; reinforcing strap *(harness)*.

belagern besiege.

Belagerung *f* siege.

Belagerungszustand *m* state of siege.

belästigen to annoy, harass *(Tac)*.

Belastung *f* load, maximum load *(Engr)*; inductance *(Rad)*.

bleibende Belastung basic load *(Ap)*.

Belastungsfaktor *m* load coefficient.

Belastungsprobe *f* load test.

Beleg *m* voucher, proof, evidence, document.

belegen to cover *(with fire)*, to fire on, to shell; to billet.

Belegung *f* coverage; shelling; billeting, quartering; condenser plate *(Rad)*.

Belegungsstärke *f* density of gas coverage *(CWS)*.

Belehrungsschießen *n* instruction firing.

Belehrungs- und Versuchsschießen *n* special service practice *(Arty)*.

beleuchten illuminate, light.

Beleuchtung *f* illumination.

Beleuchtungsfenster *n* illuminating window *(panoramic sight)*.

Belichtung *f* exposure *(Photo)*.

beliefern to deliver, to supply.

Belüftung *f* ventilation.

Belüftungsanlage *f* ventilation system.

Bemannung *f* complement, crew.

benachrichtigen inform.

Benennung *f* nomenclature.

Benzin *n* gasoline.

Benzinbehälter *m* gasoline tank.

Benzinkanister *m* gasoline container.

Benzinmanometer *m* gasoline pressure gage.

Benzinstandmesser *m* fuel gage.

Benzol *n* benzol.

Beobachter *m* observer; air observer, navigator-observer.

Beobachterabzeichen *n* observer badge *(decoration)*.

Beobachterfernrohr *n* observer telescope.

Beobachtersitz *m* observer's seat *(Ap)*.

beobachtetes Schießen observed fire.

Beobachtung *f* observation; spotting *(Arty)*.

Beobachtung der Längenabweichung vertical spotting *(Arty)*.

Beobachtungsabteilung *f* observation battalion *(Arty)*.

Beobachtungsbereich *m* observation area *(Arty)*.

Beobachtungsfehler *m* personnel error.

Beobachtungsfernrohr *n* observation telescope *(BC telescope)*.

Beobachtungskorb *m* observer's basket *(captive Bln)*.

Beobachtungskuppel *f* cupola *(Tk)*.

Beobachtungsmine *f* controlled mine, observation mine *(Nav)*.

Beobachtungsnetz *n* observation post system *(Arty)*.

Beobachtungsoffizier *m* observation post officer *(Arty)*.

Beobachtungspatrone *f* explosive smoke-producing observation cartridge.

Beobachtungsraum *m* searching sector *(AAA)*; observation area.

Beobachtungsrohr *n* trench periscope.

Beobachtungsstand *m* See **Beobachtungsstelle**.

Beobachtungsstelle *f* observation post.

Beobachtungsturm *m* cupola *(Tk)*.

Beobachtungs- und Wirkungsstreifen *m* sector of fire *(SA firing)*.

Beobachtungswagen *m* observer's car.

Beobachtungswinkel *m* aiming point offset *(Arty)*.

Beobachtung von seitlicher Beobachtungsstelle flank spotting *(Arty)*.

Berater *m* adviser.

berechnen calculate.

Berechtigung *f* authorization; justification.

Bereich *m* area, district, zone; range, scope.

Bereifung *f* tires, set of tires.

bereit ready.

Bereitschaft *f* alert, preparedness, readiness.

Bereitschaften *fpl* alerted reserve troops or police.

Bereitschaftsbaracke *f* cantonment building for troops on the alert, alert hut.

Bereitschaftsbataillon *n* reserve battalion.

Bereitschaftslazarett *n* mobile surgical unit.

Bereitschaftsmunition *f* ammunition at the gun, ammunition kept in readiness *(Arty)*.

Bereitstellung *f* moving into assembly area or position; assembly position, position of readiness *(Tac)*; making ready, preparation.

Bereitstellungsbefehl *m* assembly order.

Bereitstellungsplatz *m* assembly position, assembly point *(Tac)*.

Bereitstellungsraum *m* assembly area *(Tac)*.

Berg *m* hill, mountain *(collective: Gebirge n)*.

bergab downhill.

bergauf uphill.

Bergedienst *m* recovery service, salvage collecting service.

Bergegerät *n* recovery equipment, salvage collecting equipment.

Bergekolonne *f* recovery column, salvage column.

Bergekommando *n* collecting unit, salvage party, recovery party.

Bergen *n* recovery, salvage.

Bergenge *f* defile.

Berger-Mischung *f* Berger-type smoke agent *(mixture composed of two parts of zinc dust to three parts of hexachlorethane)*.

Berghang *m* mountain slope, hillside.

Bergjoch *n* saddle *(Top)*.

Bergkamm *m* crest *(Top)*.

Bergmütze *f* mountain cap, alpine cap.

Bergrücken *m* ridge *(Top)*.

Bergschuhe *mpl* mountain boots, ski boots.

Bergstriche *mpl* hachures.

Bergung *f* rescue, salvage, recovery.

Bergungskolonne *f* See Bergekolonne.

Bergungsschiff *n* rescue vessel, salvage vessel.

Bericht *m* report; communiqué, news dispatch.

Berichter *m* correspondent, reporter.

berichtigen collimate *(Surv)*; correct, rectify, adjust.

Berichtigung *f* collimation *(Surv)*; adjustment, correction, rectification.

Berichtigungswalze *f* adjustment drum *(range finder)*.

beritten mounted *(on horse)*.

berittene Artillerie horse artillery.

Berme *f* berm *(Ft)*.

bersten to burst, explode.

berücksichtigen to consider, to allow for, take into consideration.

Berücksichtigung *f* consideration, allowance for, correction for.

Berührung *f* touch, contact.

Berührungslinie *f* tangent.

Berührungspunkt *m* point of contact.

Berührungswarngerät *n* high-voltage warning device.

Berührungszeichen *n* touch signal *(Tk)*.

Berührungszündung *f* contact fire *(Nav)*.

Besatzung *f* garrison, crew.

Besatzungsheer *n* army of occupation.

Beschädigung *f* damage, injury.

beschaffen procure.

Beschaffung *f* procurement.

bescheinigen certify, authenticate, receipt for.

Bescheinigung *f* authentication, certificate, receipt, voucher.

beschießen to shell, to fire at.

der Länge nach beschießen to enfilade.

Beschlag *m* ferrule.

beschlagen to shoe.

Beschlagmeister *m* horseshoer *(with rank of Tech Sgt)*.

Beschlagnahme *f* confiscation, seizure.

Beschlagschmied *m* horseshoer.

Beschlagschmiedobergefreiter *m* horseshoer *(with rank of Cpl)*.

beschleunigen accelerate.

Beschleuniger *m* accelerator.

Beschleunigung *f* acceleration.

Beschleunigungsmesser *m* accelerometer *(Ap)*.

Beschuß *m* fire, shooting.

Beschußfestigkeit *f* resistance to fire, resistance to penetration *(armor)*.

beschußsicher bulletproof.

beschützen protect.

Beschwerde *f* complaint.

Beschwerungsrohr *n* counterpoise, counterweight *(G)*.

Beschwerungsstück n   *See* **Beschwerungsrohr.**
beseitigen   reduce *(a stoppage)* *(Ord)*; remove *(an obstacle).*
Beselersteg m   hasty trestle footbridge *(named after General H. H. von Beseler: 1850-1921).*
besetzt busy *(Tp)*; occupied, invaded.
Besetztschauzeichen n   "busy" signal light *(Tp).*
Besetztzeichen n busy signal *(Tp).*
Besetzung f   occupation.
Besetzungsarmee f   army of occupation.
besichtigen inspect, review.
Besichtigung f inspection, review.
besiegen to defeat.
Besitz m   property.
Besoldung f   payment, pay, wages.
Besoldungsdienstalter n   seniority for computation of pay.
Besoldungseinbehaltung f   detention of pay.
Besoldungswesen n   pay and allowance administration.
Besoldungszulage f   additional pay.
Besoldungszulage nach dem Dienstalter longevity pay.
besonder special.
besondere Anordnungen   administrative details in combat orders.
besondere Dienstzweige   special services.
besondere Einflüsse   interior ballistic factors.
besondere und Witterungseinflüsse interior and exterior ballistic factors.
besorgen procure.
Besorgung f procurement.
bespannt animal-drawn; covered with stressed skin *(Ap).*
Bespannung f covering *(Ap skin or fabric)*; team of horses.
Besprechung f consultation, critique, discussion, conference.
Bestallungsurkunde f   certificate of appointment.
Bestand m stock *(supplies, equipment, etc.)*; inventory, supply, strength, balance, cash on hand.
Bestandsbuch n   stock book.
Bestandsliste f inventory of supplies, equipment, etc.; property book.
Bestandsnachweisung f   stock inventory, stock report.
Bestandteil m   component.
bestätigen confirm.

Bestattung f   burial.
Bestattungskommando n   burial detail.
bestechen to bribe.
Bestechung f   bribery.
Besteck n   ship's position; set of instruments or utensils; knife, fork and spoon *(considered as unit of mess kit).*
Bestellnummer f   requisition number.
Bestellschein m   requisition ticket *(Adm).*
Bestellung f   requisition *(Adm).*
Bestimmung f   regulation; decision; destination; determination.
Bestrafung f   punishment.
bestreichen   to graze, sweep *(with fire)*; to spread, cover, coat.
bestreichendes Feuer   grazing fire *(Arty).*
bestrichener Raum   beaten zone *(firing).*
bestrichener Raum der Kerngarbe effective beaten zone, 85% zone *(MG fire).*
Bestückung f   armament *(Ap, Tk).*
betätigen   actuate, bring into play, set going, put into operation.
Betäubungsmittel n   anesthetic.
Beton m   concrete.
Betonbau m   concrete construction.
Betonbombe f   concrete bomb.
Betonbrücke f   concrete bridge.
Betonbunker m   concrete bunker, concrete pillbox.
betoniert   concrete, built of or reinforced with concrete.
Betonmischmaschine f   concrete mixer.
Betonschicht f   layer of concrete, concrete burster course.
Betonsperre f   concrete obstacle.
Betonstärke f   thickness of concrete.
Betonturm m   concrete turret *(Ft).*
Betonunterstand m   concrete shelter, concrete dugout.
Betrag m   amount, sum.
Betrauung f   charge, trust.
Betrieb m   operation *(Tp, Rad)*; traffic; action; factory.
außer Betrieb   not in use, out of order, not running.
Betriebsbuch n   station log *(Rad).*
Betriebsfunkspruch m   routine radio message.
Betriebskompanie f   operating company *(Adrm, RR, Tp).*

Betriebsschalter *m* operating switch *(Tp)*.

Betriebssicherheit *f* reliability of operation, safety of operation.

Betriebsstoff *m* fuel, gasoline, Diesel fuel.

Betriebsstoffausgabestelle *f* gasoline and lubricants distributing point.

Betriebsstoffkesselkraftwagen *m* gasoline tank truck.

Betriebsstoffkolonne *f* gasoline and lubricants supply column.

Betriebsstoffversorgung *f* gasoline and lubricants supply.

Betriebsstoffverwaltungskompanie *f* gasoline and lubricants administration company.

Betriebsstoffzusatzmittel *n* dope *(for Avn gasoline)*.

Betriebsstrom *m* operating current.

Betriebsstunde *f* hour of operation.

Betriebsunterlagen *fpl* consolidated plan of telephone communication.

Bettung *f* roadbed *(RR)*; ground platform *(RR gun)*; base *(fixed G)*; foundation *(G emplacement)*.

Bettungsloch *n* gun platform excavation *(RR gun)*.

Beugung *f* diffraction.

beunruhigen to disturb, harass, cause uneasiness.

Beunruhigung *f* harassment, uneasiness, disturbance, alarm.

Beunruhigungsfeuer *n* harassing fire.

beurlaubt on leave.

Beurlaubtenstand *m* reserve status. Offizier des Beurlaubtenstandes officer commissioned for the duration *(abbr. d.B.)*.

beurteilen estimate, judge, evaluate, interpret.

Beurteilung *f* estimate, appreciation, judgment.

Beute *f* booty, captured matériel, prize, pillage, loot.

Beutebergungsabteilung *f* salvage detachment for captured matériel.

Beutegeschütz *n* captured gun.

Beute-Kraftfahrzeug *n* captured motor vehicle.

Beutel *m* bag, pouch.

Beutesammelstelle *f* See Beutestelle.

Beutestab *m* salvage staff for captured enemy matériel.

Beutestelle *f* salvage depot, salvage dump *(for enemy matériel)*.

Bevölkerung *f* population.

bevollmächtigen to authorize, empower.

bevollmächtigter Transportoffizier chief transportation officer *(on an army staff)*.

bewachen to guard.

Bewachungsfahrzeug *n* patrol vessel, escort vessel *(Nav)*.

bewaffnet armed.

Bewaffnung *f* armament.

Bewährung *f* proving of fitness, competence or durability.

beweglich mobile, movable, moving, flexible, portable.

bewegliches Geschütz flexible gun.

bewegliches Hindernis portable obstacle.

bewegliches Maschinengewehr flexible machine gun.

bewegliches Ziel moving target.

Beweglichkeit *f* mobility, maneuverability.

Bewegung *f* movement.

Bewegungsbuch *n* record of transactions.

Bewegungskontrolle *f* flight control *(Avn)*.

Bewegungskrieg *m* war of movement, mobile warfare.

Bewegungsgröße *f* momentum.

bewegungsunfähig incapable of moving, immobilized; stuck, stalled *(MT)*.

Bewehrung *f* cable armor *(Tp)*; iron reinforcement *(concrete construction)*.

Beweismaterial *n* written evidence.

Bewetterung *f* mine ventilation.

bewirken to cause, bring about, effect.

bezeugen to certify, witness.

beziehen to mount *(guard)*; occupy *(a position)*; collect *(pay)*.

Bezirk *m* district.

Bezug *m* datum, reference, relation.

Bezugsebene *f* datum level, datum plane *(Surv)*.

Bezugsfläche *f* See Bezugsebene.

Bezugslinie *f* datum line, reference line *(Surv)*.

Bezugspunkt *m* check point, datum point.

Bezugsschein *m* ration card; requisition ticket.

bezwingen to reduce, overcome *(Tac)*.

Biberwehr *n* beaver dam.

Biegemaschine *f* bending machine.

Biegung *f* bend, turn, flexure.
Bild *n* picture, photograph.
Bildaufklärung *f* photographic reconnaissance.
Bildauswertung *f* interpretation of photographs.
Bildberichter *m* war photographer (in Ger propaganda company).
Bilderkundung *f* photographic reconnaissance.
Bildflieger *m* aerial photographer.
Bildfunk *m* radiophotography, radiophoto transmission.
Bildmeßwesen *n* photogrammetry.
Bildoffizier *m* photographer (officer).
Bildplan *m* controlled mosaic (aerial Photo).
Bildplanskizze *f* partially controlled mosaic (aerial Photo).
Bildpunkt *m* picture point (aerial Photo).
Bildreihe *f* strip mosaic (aerial Photo).
Bildskizze *f* uncontrolled mosaic (aerial Photo).
Bildwerfer *m* still projector (Photo).
Binauralverfahren *n* binaural method (sound locator).
Binde *f* bandage.
binden contain (Tac); bind, tie.
Binder *m* necktie (Clo).
Bindereifen *m* rim (G-carriage wheel).
Binnenwasserstraße *f* inland waterway.
Bittschrift *f* petition.
Biwak *n* bivouac.
Biwakskommandant *m* bivouac commander (ranking officer at bivouac).
Biwaksplatz *m* bivouac (site).
blanker Draht bare wire (Tp).
blanke Waffe "cold steel."
blanke Waffen armes blanches, hand weapons.
Blasangriff *m* cloud attack, cloud gas attack, gas-cylinder attack.
Blase *f* blister.
blasenziehend blistering, vesicant.
blasenziehender Kampfstoff vesicant agent (CWS).
Blasflasche *f* gas cylinder (CWS).
Blaspistole *f* air gun, compressed-air cleaner (MT).
Blasverfahren *n* gas-cylinder method (of gas release) (CWS).
Blatt *n* leaf; blade; sheet; propeller blade.

Blättchenpulver *n* flake powder (Am).
Blattern *fpl* smallpox.
Blattfeder *f* leaf spring (MT).
Blaukreuz *n* sternutators (Ger. marking "Blue Cross") (CWS).
Blaupause *f* blueprint.
Blausäure *f* hydrocyanic acid, prussic acid (CWS).
Blech *n* sheet metal; nonsense (slang).
Blechbehälter *m* metal container.
Blechbeplankung *f* metal skin (Ap).
Blechbüchse *f* can; sheet-metal box or container.
Blechgehäuse *n* sheet-metal case, sheet-metal housing.
Blechkanister *m* metal container (for water, gasoline, etc.).
Blechschmied *m* tinsmith.
Blechtrommel *f* metal drum.
Blei *n* lead (metal).
Bleichmittel *n* bleach.
Bleimantel *m* lead jacket (Am); lead sheath (armored cable).
Bleiplombe *f* lead seal.
Bleisammler *m* lead-plate storage battery.
Bleispritzer *m* lead spatter, bullet spatter.
Bleitetraäthyl *n* tetraethyl lead.
Blendabdeckung *f* shutter cover (Tk).
Blende *f* gun mantlet, gun shield, shielded port (Tk); diaphragm (Photo); occulter (SL); shutter.
blenden to blind, to dazzle; to cover or shield; to lay a smoke screen.
Blendenhebel *m* shutter lever (SL).
Blendkörper *m* frangible glass smoke grenade.
Blendschutz-Scheibe *f* anti-glare windshield.
Blendungsschießen *n* smoke-screening fire (Arty).
Blickfeld *n* field of view (Optics).
Blindabwurf *m* emergency release (bombing).
Blindflug *m* blind flying, instrument flying.
Blindgänger *m* dud.
blindgeladen blank, with inert filling.
blindgeladene Granate blank shell.
Blindkurbeln *n* blindfold operation of crankwheels (gun-laying exercise).
Blindlandung *f* instrument landing.
Blindwiderstand *m* reactance (Elec).
Blinken *n* signal-lamp transmission.

Blinkfeuer *n* flashing light, blinker light *(Avn)*.
Blinkgerät *n* signal lamp, signal-lamp apparatus.
Blinklampe *f* signal lamp.
Blinkspruch *m* signal-lamp message.
Blinkstelle *f* signal-lamp station.
Blinksuchtrupp *m* signal-lamp spotting squad.
Blinktornister *m* portable signal-lamp case.
Blinktrupp *m* signal-lamp team.
Blinkverbindung *f* signal-lamp communication.
Blinkverfahren *n* lamp-signaling method.
Blinkzeichen *n* flash signal *(Sig lamp)*.
Blitz *m* lightning, lightning flash.
Blitzableiter *m* lightning arrester.
Blitzbündel *n* lightning-flash cluster *(badge worn by Sig Pers)*.
Blitzkrieg *m* lightning war, blitzkrieg.
Blitzlichtbombe *f* photo flashbomb.
Blitzschutzsicherung *f* lightning arrester.
Blitzstrahl *m* lightning flash.
Block *m* block; writing pad.
Blockwart *m* block warden.
Blumenkohl *m* cauliflower; Oak Leaf Cluster *(slang)*.
Bluse *f* service coat, blouse.
Blut *n* blood.
Blutgruppe *f* blood group, blood type.
Blutopfer *n* heavy losses, heavy casualties.
Blutorden *m* medal awarded to participants in Munich riots of 1923.
Blutspender *m* blood donor.
blutstillend styptic.
Blutvergiftung *f* blood-poisoning.
Bö *f* squall, gust.
Bock *m* trestle, bent *(Bdg)*; wagon-driver's seat.
Bockbein *n* trestle leg *(Bdg)*.
Bockbrücke *f* trestle bridge.
Bockschnellsteg *m* hasty trestle bridge.
Bockschnürbund *m* square lashing *(Bdg)*.
Bocksprengwerk *n* lock-spar support *(Bdg)*.
Bockwagen *m* trestle carrier *(MT)*.
Boden *m* ground *(Top)*; base *(Am)*; floor; earth; bottom.
Bodenabstandszünder *m* base delay-action fuze *(Am)*.

Bodenabwehr *f* antiaircraft defense, antiaircraft artillery, ground defense.
Bodenanlage *f* ground installation.
Bodenanlage der Luftwaffe air-base service area.
Bodenantenne *f* surface antenna.
Bodenaushub *m* spoil *(Engr, Ft)*.
Bodenbedienung *f* ground crew *(Avn)*.
Bodenbewachsung *f* vegetation *(Top)*.
Boden-Bord air-ground *(Sig Com)*.
Bodenbrett *n* floor board *(MT)*.
Bodendienst *m* base services *(Avn)*.
Bodendruck *m* ground pressure. **spezifischer Bodendruck** ground pressure per unit area *(MT, Tk)*.
Bodenerhebung *f* elevation, rise *(Top)*.
Bodenfalte *f* furrow, gully *(Top)*.
Bodenfreiheit *f* road clearance *(MT)*.
Bodenfunkdienst *m* ground radio service *(Avn)*.
Bodenfunkstelle *f* ground radio station.
Bodengestaltung *f* configuration of ground, terrain features.
Bodenhaftung *f* road traction *(MT)*.
Bodenkammerladung *f* base charge *(Am)*.
Bodenkanzel *f* ball turret, belly turret, ventral turret *(Ap)*.
Bodenkrepierer *m* dud.
Bodenlader *m* supercharger with low blower ratio *(Ap)*.
Bodenlafette *f* ventral gun mount *(Ap)*.
Bodenleitung *f* surface line *(Tp)*.
Bodenluke *f* escape hatch in belly or floor *(Ap, Tk)*.
Bodennavigation *f* pilotage *(Avn)*.
Bodennebel *m* ground fog.
Bodenorganisation *f* ground personnel *(Avn)*.
Bodenpeilfunkstelle *f* radio direction-finder station *(Avn)*.
Bodenpeilstelle *f* See **Bodenpeilfunkstelle**.
Bodenpersonal *n* air base troops; ground crew, ground personnel, maintenance personnel, service personnel *(Avn)*.
Bodenplatte *f* base plate *(Mort)*.
Bodenpunkt *m* place mark *(Surv)*.
Bodenschwanz *m* tail *(of a bomb)*.
Bodensicht *f* ground visibility *(Avn)*. **auf Bodensicht** in sight of the ground.

Bodenstelle *f* ground station *(Rad)*.
Bodenstrahlung *f* ground radiation *(Rad)*.
Bodenstück *n* floor plate, butt assembly *(MG)*; breech, breech ring *(G)*.
Bodenstücksperre *f* floor-plate lock *(MG)*.
Bodentreffbild *n* dispersion pattern, horizontal shot group.
Bodentreffer *m* overended shot.
Bodenverdichter *m* road grader and tamper.
Bodenwanne *f* bottom gondola *(Ap)*.
Bodenwelle *f* ground wave *(Rad)*.
Bodenwellenempfangszone *f* ground-wave reception zone *(Rad)*.
Bodenwind *m* surface wind.
Bodenziel *n* ground target.
Bodenzünder *m* base detonating fuze.
Böenkragen *m* arcus, scud roll *(Met)*.
Bogen *m* arc, arch; bend, curve; sheet *(of paper)*.
Bogenbrücke *f* arched bridge.
Bogenlampe *f* arc lamp.
Bogenspitze *f* ogive *(Am)*.
Bohle *f* plank.
Bohlenbahn *f* plank road.
bohren to drill, bore.
Bohrer *m* bit, drill, auger.
Bohrladung *f* borehole blasting charge.
Bohrloch *n* borehole.
Bohrpatrone *f* blasting cartridge.
Bohrung *f* bore *(Mech)*.
Bohrwinde *f* brace *(a tool)*.
Böigkeit *f* turbulence *(Met)*.
Boje *f* buoy.
Bola *f* *See* **Bodenlafette**.
Bölinie *f* squall line.
Bolzen *m* bolt, pin.
Bombardierung *f* bombing, bombardment.
Bombe *f* bomb.
Bombe mit Verzugszeit time bomb.
Bombenabwurf *m* bomb release.
Bombenabwurf auf Flächenziel area bombing.
Bombenabwurfgerät *n* bomb release controls.
Bombenabwurfkurve *f* bomb trajectory.
Bombenabwurfvorrichtung *f* bomb control mechanism, bomb release mechanism *(Ap)*.
Bombenabwurfwinkel *m* dropping angle *(bombing)*.

Bombenabwurfzielgerät *n* *See* **Bombenzielgerät**.
Bombenabzughebel *m* bomb control, bomb rack control *(Ap)*.
Bombenangriff *m* bombing attack, bombing raid *(Avn)*.
Bombenauslösung *f* bomb release.
Bombenauslösungsvorrichtung *f* bomb control mechanism, bomb release mechanism *(Ap)*.
Bombeneinschlag *m* bomb hit.
Bombenfallkurve *f* bomb trajectory.
Bombenfallzeit *f* time of fall *(bombing)*.
Bombenfernrohr *n* telescopic bomb sight *(Ap)*.
bombenfest bomb-resistant, bomb-proof.
Bombenflieger *mpl* bombardment aviation.
Bombenflugbahn *f* bomb trajectory.
Bombenflugzeug *n* bombardment airplane, bomber.
Bombengeschwader *n* bomber wing. *See also* **Geschwader**.
Bombenhebel *m* bomb release handle.
Bombenhülle *f* bomb case.
Bombenjäger *m* "bomber destroyer" *(airplane employed to combat bombers by dropping bombs on them)*.
Bombenkammer *f* bomb bay *(Ap)*.
Bombenklappe *f* bomb-bay doors, bomb doors *(Ap)*.
Bombenkopf *m* bomb nose.
Bombenlast *f* bomb load.
Bombenloch *n* bomb crater.
Bombenmagazin *n* bomb bay *(Ap)*.
Bombenreihe *f* train of bombs, bomb train.
Bombenrichtgerät *n* bomb sight.
Bombenschacht *m* bomb rack *(Ap)*.
Bombenschütze *m* bombardier.
Bombenschützenstand *m* bombardier's position, bombardier's compartment.
bombensicher bomb-resistant, bomb-proof, heavy shellproof.
bombensichere Deckung bombproof shelter.
Bombenteppich *m* practice-bombing panel.
Bombentiefangriff *m* low-level bombing attack *(Avn)*.
Bombentreffer *m* bomb hit.
Bombenvisier *n* bomb sight *(Ap)*.
Bombenvolltreffer *m* direct bomb hit.
Bombenwurf *m* bomb release, bombing.

gezielter Bombenwurf precision bombing.

Bombenwurfplatz *m* target area *(bombing)*.

Bombenzielapparat *m* *See* **Bombenzielgerät.**

Bombenzielgerät *n* bomb sight.

Bomben-Zubringewagen *m* bomb trailer.

Bombenzünder *m* bomb fuze.

Boot *n* boat; hull *(of flying boat)*.

Bootshaken *m* boathook.

Bootsmann *m* boatswain *(Nav)*.

Bordaufklärer *m* shipboard reconnaissance airplane.

Bordbatterie *f* aircraft radio battery.

Bordbesatzung *f* air crew.

Bordbuch *n* log book *(Ap)*.

Borderkunder *m* shipboard reconnaissance airplane.

Bordflak *f* shipboard antiaircraft artillery.

Bordfliegerstaffel *f* squadron of carrier-based airplanes.

Bordflugzeug *n* shipboard airplane.

Bordfunker *m* radio operator *(Avn)*.

Bordgerät *n* intercommunication telephone *(Ap, Tk)*.

Bordgeräte *npl* aircraft equipment; aircraft instruments.

Bordlafette *f* gun mount on ship or airplane.

Bordlandefackel *f* landing flare *(Avn)*.

Bordmannschaft *f* air crew.

Bord-Maschinengewehr *n* aircraft machine gun.

Bordmechaniker *m* flight engineer.

Bordmonteur *m* aircraft mechanic; flight engineer *(Avn)*.

Bordmunition *f* aircraft ammunition.

Bordnetz *n* aircraft wiring system *(Elec)*.

Bordpeiler *m* radio compass, direction finder, direction-finder operator *(Ap)*.

Bordschütze *m* aerial gunner, gunner *(Avn)*.

Bordsprechanlage *f* intercommunication system, interphone system *(Ap, Tk)*.

Bordsprechgerät *n* intercommunication telephone, interphone *(Ap, Tk)*.

Bordtelephon *n* interphone *(Ap, Tk)*.

Bordverpflegung *f* flight ration *(Avn)*.

Bordverständigung *f* interphone communication.

Bordverständigungsanlage *f* intercommunication system *(Ap, Tk)*.

Bordwaffen *fpl* aircraft armament; tank armament.

Bordwaffenbeschuß *m* fire from aircraft weapons.

Bordwandwagen *m* gondola car *(RR)*.

Bordwart *m* flight mechanic, flight engineer *(Avn)*.

Bord zu Boden air-ground *(Sig Com)*.

Borsalbe *f* boric acid ointment.

Borsäure *f* boric acid.

Borte *f* braid *(Clo)*.

Böschung *f* escarpment, scarp, slope.

Böschung im Abtrag downward slope.

Böschung in Auftrag upward slope.

Böschungsanlage *f* batter *(Ft)*.

Böschungskante *f* military crest *(Top)*.

Böschungsfuß *m* foot of slope *(Top)*.

Böschungskrone *f* *See* **Böschungskante.**

Böschungswinkel *m* angle of slope, gradient angle, gradient *(Top)*.

Botschaft *f* embassy; message.

Bowdenzug *m* bowden control cable *(control cable in flexible steel conduit)*.

Boxe *f* submarine pen; aircraft revetment *(colloquial)*.

Boxermotor *m* opposed-piston engine.

B.-Patrone *f* *See* **Beobachtungspatrone.**

Brakenstange *f* side rail (limber).

Bramo *f* name of a type of aircraft engine *(abbr. of* **Brandenburgische Motorenwerke)**.

Brand *m* fire; gangrene.

Brandbinde *f* absorbent gauze treated with bismuth for burns.

Brandbombe *f* incendiary bomb.

Brandbombenbündel *n* cluster of incendiary bombs.

Brander *m* fire raft.

Brandflasche *f* frangible grenade, incendiary bottle, "Molotov cocktail."

Brandgeschoß *n* incendiary bullet, incendiary projectile.

Brandgranate *f* incendiary shell.

Brandhahn *m* distributor cock *(of Ap fire extinguisher)*.

Brandmasse *f* incendiary composition.

Brandmeister *m* fire marshal.

Brandmittel *n* incendiary agent.

Brandmunition *f* incendiary ammunition.

Brandsatz m incendiary composition, incendiary filling (Am).
Brandschott n fire wall (Ap).
Brandschutz m fire prevention, fire protection.
Brandspant m See **Brandschott**.
Brandstoff m incendiary agent.
Brand- und Asche-Taktik f scorched earth tactics.
Brandwirkung f incendiary effect.
Brandwunde f burn.
Bratling m soya-bean meat substitute.
Bratlingspulver n soya-bean flour.
brauchbar serviceable, usable; practicable.
Braunkohle f lignite.
Braunsche Röhre cathode-ray tube.
Braunstein m manganese dioxide.
Braunsteinbeutel m manganese dioxide compartment (of Elec cell).
Brecheisen n See **Brechstange**.
Brechreiz m nausea.
Brechstange f crowbar, pinch-bar.
Breite f width.
Breitenausdehnung f extension in width (Tac).
Breitenfeuer n distributed fire (R, MG); sweeping fire, traversing fire (MG).
Breitenfeuer mit Tiefenfeuer traversing and searching fire (MG).
Breitengliederung f distribution, formation, or organization in width (Tac).
Breitengrad m degree of latitude.
Breitenhöhe f meridian altitude (celestial navigation).
Breitenkreis m parallel of latitude.
Breitenstreuung f direction dispersion, deflection dispersion (Ballistics).
Breiten- und Tiefenfeuer n traversing and searching fire (MG).
Breitenziel n linear target.
Breitkeil m inverted wedge formation (Tac).
Breitseite f flank (Tac); broadside (Nav).
Breitspur f wide gage (RR).
Bremsarm m brake arm (G-carriage wheel brake).
Bremsausgleich m brake equalization; brake equalizer.
Bremsbacke f brake shoe.
Bremsband n brake band.
Bremsbelag m brake lining.

Bremsbock m brake carrier (G carriage).
Bremsbuchse f brake bushing (recoil mechanism).
Bremse f brake, buffer.
Bremsfeder f brake release spring (MT).
Bremsflüssigkeit f recoil oil (G); brake fluid (MT).
Bremsfußhebel m brake pedal (MT).
Bremsgestänge n brake rod (MT).
Bremsgitter n suppressor grid (Rad tube).
Bremshebel m brake level (G, MT); locking lever (panoramic telescope).
Bremsklappe f landing flap, wing flap (Ap).
Bremsklaue f brake shoe (G-carriage wheel).
Bremsklotz m brake shoe; chock, wheel block.
Bremskolben m recoil piston (G).
Bremsleistung f brake horsepower.
Bremslicht n stop light (MT).
Bremsscheibe f brake drum.
Bremsspur f skid mark (MT).
Bremsstrecke f stopping distance (MT); braking section (Ap catapult).
Bremsträger m anchor pin (of brake shoes).
Bremstritt m brake pedal.
Bremstrommel f brake drum.
Bremsvorrichtung f recoil mechanism (G); brake mechanism (MT).
Bremsweg m stopping distance (MT).
Bremswirkung f braking effect.
Bremszylinder m recoil cylinder (G); brake cylinder (MT).
Brenndauer f burning rate, burning time (fuze).
Brennebene f focal plane (Optics).
Brennermotor m internal combustion engine.
Brenngemisch n gasoline mixture.
Brenngeschwindigkeit f burning rate, rate of burning (fuze).
Brennlängenschieber m corrector (fuze).
Brennpunkt m focus (Optics).
Brennstoff m gasoline, fuel, Diesel fuel.
Brennstofflager n gasoline dump, fuel dump.
Brennstofftankwagen m gasoline tank truck.
Brennstoffverbrauch m gasoline consumption, fuel consumption.

Brennstoffvorrat *m* gasoline supply, fuel supply.
Brennweite *f* focal distance *(Optics)*.
Brennzünder *m* powder-train fuze *(shell)*; igniting fuze, time fuze *(hand grenade)*.
Brennzünderschuß *m* time fire *(Arty)*.
Bresche *f* breach.
Brett *n* board, panel.
Bretterbahn *f* boardwalk, duckboard *(trench)*.
Bretterbock *m* plank trestle.
Bretterstapel *m* plank crib *(Bdg)*.
Brettertafel *f* plank floor *(Bdg)*.
Bretterteppich *m* plank flooring *(rope Bdg)*.
Brettstückmine *f* duckboard mine, pressure-board mine.
Briefmarke *f* postage stamp.
Brieftaube *f* carrier pigeon, homing pigeon, messenger pigeon.
Brieftaubenmeister *m* pigeoneer *(Tech Sgt)*.
Brieftaubenpfleger *m* pigeoneer.
Brieftaubenschlag *m* pigeon loft.
Brieftaubenstelle *f* *See* **Brieftaubenschlag.**
Brigade *f* brigade.
Brigadeführer *m* brigade commander. *See also* **SS-Brigadeführer.**
Brigadekommando *n* brigade headquarters.
Brillenglassalbe *f* antidim compound *(for gas mask)*.
brisant high-explosive.
Brisanz *f* brisance, explosive effect.
Brisanzgranate *f* high-explosive shell.
Brisanzschrapnell *n* high-explosive shrapnel.
Brisanzsprengstoff *m* detonating explosive.
Brombenzylzyanid *n* brombenzylcyanide *(CWS)*.
Bromzyan *n* cyanogen bromide *(CWS)*.
Brotbeutel *m* field bag, musette bag.
Brotsatz *m* bread ration.
Bruch *m* crack-up, crash *(Avn)*; fraction *(Math)*; fracture, rupture.
Bruchfestigkeit *f* breaking strength.
Bruchgrenze *f* point of rupture *(Mech)*.
Bruchlandung *f* crash landing *(Avn)*.
bruchsicher breakproof, shatterproof.
Bruchstück *n* fragment.
Brücke *f* bridge.

Brücke mit festen Stützen fixed bridge.
Brücke mit schwimmenden Stützen floating bridge.
Brückenachse *f* bridge center line.
Brückenbahn *f* bridge roadway.
Brückenbau *m* bridge construction; bridge structure; bridging.
Brückenbaubataillon *n* bridge construction battalion.
Brückenbaugerät *n* bridge-building equipment.
Brückenbelag *m* chess, planking *(Bdg)*.
Brückenbock *m* bridge trestle.
Brückenbogen *m* arch, span *(Bdg)*.
Brückendamm *m* approach embankment *(Bdg)*.
Brückenendwiderlager *n* abutment *(Bdg)*.
Brückenfahrbahn *f* *See* **Brückenbahn.**
Brückenfahrzeug *n* bridge-carrying vehicle.
Brückengeländer *n* bridge railing.
Brückengerät *n* bridge equipage, bridge equipment.
Brückenglied *n* bay, section *(Bdg)*.
Brückenkolonne *f* bridge column, ponton train, bridge train.
Brückenkommandant *m* bridge commander.
Brückenkopf *m* bridgehead.
Brückenkopflinie *f* bridgehead line.
Brückenkopfstellung *f* bridgehead position.
Brückenlinie *f* bridge center line.
Brückenoberbau *m* superstructure *(Bdg)*.
Brückenpanzerkampfwagen *m* bridge-carrying tank.
Brückenpfeiler *m* pile *(Bdg)*.
Brückenschlag *m* bridge construction, bridging.
Brückenskizze *f* bridge diagram.
Brückenspitze *f* open end of bridge under construction.
Brückenstelle *f* bridge site.
Brückenstrecke *f* bay *(Bdg)*.
Brückenstützweite *f* span of bridge.
Brückentrupp *m* bridge-construction party.
Brückenüberbau *m* *See* **Brückenoberbau.**
Brückenunterbau *m* foundation, substructure *(Bdg)*.
Brückenwiderlager *n* abutment *(Bdg)*.
Brünierung *f* browning *(anti-rust*

treatment or coating on R or G barrel).

Brunnen *m* well.

Brustblatt *n* breast-collar body *(pack saddle).*

Brustbohrer *m* hand drill.

Brustfallschirm *m* chest pack parachute.

Brustfernsprecher *m* head and chest set *(Tp).*

Brustschild *m* shield *(G).*

Brustwehr *f* breastwork, parapet.

Brustwehrkrone *f* fire crest *(trench).*

Bruttotonnengehalt *m* gross tonnage *(Nav).*

B.-Stelle *f* See **Beobachtungsstelle.**

B-Stoff *m* bromaceton *(CWS).*

Buchse *f* jack, socket *(Rad);* bushing.

Büchse *f* box, can, canister; case; gas-mask carrier; filter canister.

Büchsenfilter *m* canister filter *(gas mask).*

Büchsenfleisch *n* canned meat.

Büchsenkonserven *fpl* canned food, canned ration.

Buchsring *m* bushing *(G).*

Buchstabengruppe *f* code group *(Sig C).*

Buchstabiertafel *f* phonetic alphabet *(Sig C).*

Bucht *f* inlet, creek, bay.

Buchung *f* accounting.

Bug *m* bow, front, nose *(Ap, Nav, Tk).*

Bügel *m* trigger guard; stirrup.

Buggeschütz *n* bow gun, front gun *(Tk).*

Bugkanzel *f* forward gunner's compartment, nose turret, nose compartment *(Ap).*

Bugpanzer *m* front armor *(Tk).*

Bugradfahrgestell *n* tricycle landing gear *(Ap).*

Bugschütze *m* nose gunner, bow gunner, front gunner *(Ap, Tk).*

Bugstand *m* nose-gun station *(Ap).*

Buhne *f* diversion dam *(Engr).*

Bullauge *n* porthole.

Bumslandung *f* pancake landing, rough landing *(slang).*

Buna *n* buna *(rubber).*

Bunareifen *m* buna tire *(MT).*

Bund *m* tie, lashing *(Engr, Tp);* league, alliance; bunch *(of keys, etc.).*

Bündel *n* bundle; cluster; package.

Bundesgenosse *m* ally.

Bunde und Knoten knots and ties.

Bunker *m* concrete emplacement, concrete shelter, pillbox, bunker, submarine pen.

Bunkeranlagen *fpl* group of bunkers *(Ft).*

Bunkerlinie *f* line of concrete emplacements and pillboxes.

Bunkerstand *m* concrete emplacement.

Bunkerstellung *f* position fortified with concrete emplacements and shelters.

bunt varicolored, bright, dazzling; mixed, confused.

bunt bemalt dazzle-painted *(Cam).*

bunte Lappen colored cloth garnish, garlands *(Cam).*

Buntfarbenanstrich *m* camouflage painting, dazzle painting.

Buntkreuze *npl* colored cross markings *(to identify CWS munitions).*

Buntschießen *n* simultaneous or alternate shelling with HE and Cml shells of different type.

Bürger *m* citizen.

Bürgerkrieg *m* civil war.

Bursche *m* orderly.

Bürste *f* brush.

Bussole *f* compass; declinator *(aiming circle).*

Bussolengehäuse *n* compass case.

Bussolenring *m* compass azimuth circle.

Bussolenzug *m* compass traverse *(Arty, Surv).*

Bz.-Schuß *m* See **Brennzünderschuß.**

C

Calypsol *n* a cold-resistant grease.

Ce-Stoff *m* cyanogen bromide *(CWS)*

Celsius centigrade.

Cetenzahl *f* cetane rating *(Diesel fuel).*

Charakter *m* honorary rank carrying specific seniority but not the pay; character, quality, peculiarity; qualification *(Law).*

Charakterisierung *f* conferment of

honorary rank as defined under *Charakter.*
Chausseewalze *f* road roller.
Chef *m* chief.
Chef der Heeresrüstung und Befehlshaber des Ersatzheeres Chief of Army Equipment and Commander of Replacement Training Army *(Commander of rear echelon of* Oberkommando des Heeres, *in charge of all non-operational branches and whole basic Army structure) (abbr. Ch Rü u B d E).*
Chef der Luftwehr chief of administrative and supply services of German Air Ministry.
Chef der Schnellen Truppen Chief of Mobile Troops *(branch of* Oberkommando des Heeres). *See also* **Schnelle Truppen.**
Chef der Zivilverwaltung chief of civil affairs section at an army headquarters.
Chef des Generalstab(e)s Chief of Staff.
Chef des Heeres-Waffenamtes Chief of Ordnance.
Chef des Transportwesens Chief of Transportation *(Tac, RR).*
Chefveterinär *m* Chief of Veterinary Service.
chemische Kampfstoffe chemical warfare agents.
chemischer Krieg chemical warfare.
Chiffre *f* cipher.
chiffrieren encipher.
Chiffriermaschine *f* cipher device, converter *(Sig C).*
Chiffrierung *f* encipherment.
Chinin *n* quinine.
Chirurg *m* surgeon.
Chlor *n* chlorine *(CWS).*

Chloramin *n* chloramine-T *(CWS).*
Chlorarsinkampfstoff *m* diphenylchlorarsine *(CWS, abbr.* Clark).
Chlorat-Sprengmittel *n* chlorate explosive.
Chlorazetophenon *n* CN, chloracetophenone *(CWS).*
Chlorazetophenon-Chlorpikrin-Lösung *f* chloracetophenone solution, CNS *(CWS).*
Chlorcyan *n* cyanogen chloride *(CWS).*
Chlorgas *n* chlorine *(CWS).*
Chlorkalk *m* calcium chloride, chloride of lime, chlorinated lime, calcium bleach *(CWS).*
Chlorkohlenoxyd *n* carbonylchloride, phosgene *(CWS).*
Chlornatron *n* sodium hypochlorite.
Chlorpikrin *n* chlorpicrin *(CWS).*
Chlorsulfonsäure *f* chlorsulfonic acid *(CWS).*
Chlorvinyldichlorarsin *n* lewisite *(CWS).*
Cholmschild *m* shield-shaped insignia awarded to troops besieged at *Kholm-on-Lovat.*
Christie-Panzerkraftwagen *m* Christie tank.
Chrom *n* chrome, chromium.
Chronograph *m* chronograph.
Chronometer *n* chronometer.
Cirruswolke *f* cirrus cloud.
Clark I diphenylchlorarsine *(CWS).*
Clark II diphenylcyanarsine *(CWS).*
Cletrac-Lenkgetriebe *n* Cleveland-tractor type of steering mechanism.
Cyan-Chlorarsinkampfstoff *m* diphenylcyanarsine *(CWS).*
Cyan Clark *See* **Cyan-Chlorarsinkampfstoff.**

D

Dach *n* roof.
Dachluke *f* turret hatch *(Tk).*
Dachpappe *f* roofing paper.
daktyloskopieren to fingerprint.
Dammkörper *m* dam embankment.
Dämpfer *m* stabilizer (Ap); silencer, flash hider *(Ord);* damper *(Tech).*

Dampfmaschine *f* steam engine.
Dampfrohr *n* steam tube *(MG).*
Dämpfung *f* damping *(Elec, Rad).*
Dämpfungsfläche *f* stabilizing surface *(Ap).*
Dämpfungsflosse *f* tail turface *(Ap).*
Dampfwalze *f* steam roller.
Daten *npl* data.

Daube *f* stave.
Dauer *f* duration.
Dauerabzug *m* trigger for full-automatic fire *(MG)*.
Dauerbefehl *m* standing order.
Dauerfährbetrieb *m* permanent ferrying operations.
Dauerfestigkeit *f* fatigue strength, endurance limit *(Mech)*.
Dauerfeuer *n* full-automatic fire, automatic fire *(MG, R)*; continuous fire, sustained fire.
Dauerfleisch *n* preserved meat.
Dauerleistung *f* normal rating, continuous output *(Mtr)*; feat of endurance.
Dauerleitung *f* permanent line *(Tp)*.
Dauermarsch *m* forced march.
Dauerstörung *f* continuous interference *(Rad)*.
Dauerstrich *m* long dash *(Tg)*.
Dauerton *m* continuous note *(Rad)*.
Dauerunterkünfte *fpl* permanent billets.
Dauerwirkung *f* lasting effect, permanent effect.
Daumen *m* cam; thumb.
Daumenbreite *f* thumb width *(range estimation)*.
Daumensprung *m* thumb jump *(method of range estimation)*.
Daumenwelle *f* camshaft.
Dazwischensprechen *n* break-in procedure *(Rad)*.
dechiffrieren decipher.
Deckanruf *m* code call *(Tp)*.
Deckblatt *n* change sheet *(to be inserted in a manual)*.
Decke *f* casing, shoe *(of a tire)*; ceiling *(of a room)*; blanket, cover, tarpaulin.
Deckel *m* cover.
Deckelriegel *m* cover-plate latch *(MG)*.
Deckelsperre *f* cover-plate lock *(MG)*.
decken to cover, support *(Tac)*.
Deckengurt *m* surcingle *(harness)*.
Deckenlicht *n* dome light, tonneau light *(MT)*.
Deckenventilator *m* ceiling ventilator *(MT)*.
Decklandeflugzeug *n* deck-landing airplane.
Deckname *m* code name.
Deckplatte *f* casing, cover plate.

Deckung *f* cover, shelter *(Ft)*; mask *(Gunnery)*; concealment *(Tac)*.
Deckungsfeuer *n* covering fire.
Deckungsgraben *m* cover trench, slit trench, shelter trench.
Deckungshöhe *f* height of mask *(Arty)*.
Deckungsloch *n* foxhole.
Deckungsspiegel *m* trench periscope.
Deckungsstärke *f* strength of cover *(Ft)*.
Deckungstrupp *m* support party, covering party, covering detachment.
Deckungstruppe *f* covering force.
Deckungswinkel *m* angle of site to mask *(Ballistics)*.
Deckungswinkelmesser *m* site-to-mask clinometer.
Deckvermögen *n* effective coverage *(of smoke screen)*.
Deckwort *n* code word.
Deckzeichen *n* code sign, code signal.
defilieren to pass in review.
Degen *m* sword.
Degradation *f* demotion.
degradieren to break, reduce in rank.
Dehnung *f* lengthening, elongation; strain *(Mech)*.
Deich *m* dike.
Deichsel *f* limber pole, wagon shaft.
Deichselbolzen *m* pole pin *(limber)*.
Deichselstütze *f* pole prop *(limber)*.
dejustiert out of alinement.
Dekade *f* 10-day pay period.
demobilmachen demobilize.
Demobilmachung *f* demobilization.
Demolierung *f* demolition.
Denkmal *n* monument.
Desinfektionskammer *f* disinfecting chamber *(Med)*.
Desinfektionsmittel *n* disinfectant.
Detektor *m* detector *(Rad and Radar)*.
Detonationsdruck *m* blast pressure.
deuten interpret, explain, indicate.
Deutpatrone *f* indicator cartridge *(for Ger grenade pistol)*.
Deutsche Industrie-Norm German Industrial Standard *(abbr. DIN)*.
Deutscher Gruß Nazi salute.
Deutsches Kreuz German Cross *(decoration)*.
Dezimetergerät *n* microwave radio set.
Diatomitschicht *f* diatomite layer *(gas filter) (CWS)*.
dicht compact, dense, leakproof, thick.

Dichte *f* density; concentration *(CWS)*.

Dichtemesser *m* densimeter, aerometer.

dichten to calk, pack, seal.

Dichtigkeit *f* density; impermeability.

Dichtigkeitsmesser *m* densimeter, aerometer; viscometer.

Dichtlinie *f* sealing band *(gas mask)*.

Dichtrahmen *m* sealing frame *(gas mask)*.

Dichtring *m* binder ring *(gas mask)*.

Dichtung *f* gasket; washer; insulation; packing.

Dichtungsring *m* sealing ring, washer.

Dick *See* **Äthyldichlorarsin.**

Dienst *m* duty, service, detail.

außer Dienst retired *(abbr.* a.D.).

Dienstalter *n* seniority.

Dienstaltersgrenze *f* age limit.

Dienstältester *m* senior officer.

Dienstanweisung *f* service regulations, list of instructions.

Dienstanzug *m* service uniform.

Dienstausrüstung *f* service equipment.

Dienstbefehl *m* routine order.

Dienst bei der Truppe service with troops, field duty.

Dienstbeschädigung *f* damage or injury occurring while in service.

Dienstbescheinigung *f* certificate of service.

Diensteid *m* oath of enlistment; oath of office.

Diensteinteilung *f* duty roster.

Dienstentlassung *f* discharge without honor, dismissal.

dienstfähig fit for duty, fit for active service.

dienstfrei off duty.

Dienstgebrauch *m* service use, service tradition.

nur für den Dienstgebrauch restricted *(manuals, etc.)*.

Dienstgipfelhöhe *f* service ceiling *(Avn)*.

Dienstgrad *m* grade; rating *(Nav)*.

Dienstgradabzeichen *n* grade chevron.

Dienstgradherabsetzung *f* demotion.

Dienstgrad mit Patent permanent rank.

dienstlich authorized, official.

Dienstpflicht *f* liability for service, obligation to serve.

Dienstpflichtiger *m* one who is subject to military service.

Dienstplan *m* duty roster.

Dienststelle *f* duty station, command headquarters, administrative center or office.

Dienststellung *f* appointment.

Dienststempel *m* official stamp.

Dienstumschlag *m* official envelope.

Dienstunfähiger *m* noneffective, one who is unfit for service.

Dienstvorschrift *f* service regulation; service manual.

Dienstweg *m* military channel *(Adm)*.

auf dem Dienstweg through channels.

Dienstzweig *m* branch of the service.

Dieselkraftstoff *m* Diesel fuel.

Diesel-Lastwagen *m* Diesel truck.

Dieselmotor *m* Diesel engine.

Dieselschlepper *m* Diesel tractor.

diesig hazy *(Met)*.

Diglykolnitrat-Blättchenpulver *n* diglycolnitrate flake powder *(abbr.* Digl. Bl. P.).

DIN *See* **Deutsche Industrie-Norm.**

Dina *f See* **Divisionsnachrichtenabteilung.**

Dinafü *m See* **Divisionsnachrichtenführer.**

Diopter *m* diopter, alidade.

Diopterfaden *m* diopter hair *(Optics)*.

Diopterlineal *n* alidade ruler *(aiming circle)*.

Diopterschlitz *m* diopter slit *(Optics)*.

Diphenylaminchlorarsin *n* adamsite.

Diphenylchlorarsin *n* diphenylchlorarsine *(CWS)*.

Dipolantenne *f* dipole antenna.

Disziplin *f* discipline.

Disziplinarstrafe *f* punishment for breach of discipline.

Disziplinarverfahren *n* disciplinary action.

Division *f* division.

Divisionsarzt *m* division surgeon *(generally with rank of Oberstarzt, colonel)*.

Divisionsbataillon *n* divisional battalion *(provisional unit whose primary mission is counterattack)*.

Divisionsbefehl *m* division order, division combat order.

Divisionsbegleitkompanie *f* division escort company *(for protection of Div Hq)*.

Divisionsfeldlazarett n division surgical hospital.

Divisionsgefechtsstand m division command post.

Divisionsintendant m See **Intendant.**

Divisionskommando z.b.V. special administrative division (consists of Landesschützen Bns and GHQ troops in a Wehrkreis).

Divisionsnachrichtenabteilung f division signal battalion.

Divisionsnachschubführer m chief of division supply services.

Divisionsnachschubkolonne f division supply column.

Divisionspanzerabwehrabteilung f division antitank battalion.

Divisionspferdelazarett n division veterinary clearing station.

Divisionspferdepark m division remount depot.

Divisionsstab m division headquarters or headquarters personnel.

Divisionsstammleitung f division trunk line (axis of Sig Com).

Dixol n an antifreeze solution.

Docht m wick.

Dockanlagen fpl dock installations.

Dolch m dagger.

Dollbord n gunwale (rowboat).

Dolmetscher m interpreter, translator.

Doppelanschnitt m two-station pilot-balloon spotting (Met).

Doppelbereifung f double tires, dual tires (MT).

Doppelbetriebsschaltung f composite connection (Tp).

Doppeldecker m biplane.

Doppelfernglas n field glass, binocular.

Doppelfernrohr n See **Doppelfernglas.**

Doppelflügel m "double wing" (wing with double ailerons and flaps).

Doppelglas n See **Doppelfernglas.**

Doppellafette f two-barreled mount.

doppelläufig double-barreled.

Doppelleitung f metallic circuit (Tp).

Doppelposten m double sentry.

Doppelpropeller m coaxial contra-rotating propellers (Ap).

Doppelreihe f column of twos, double file.

"In Doppelreihe, angetreten!" "In column of twos, fall in!"

Doppelringtrensengebiß n double-ring snaffle bit.

Doppelringvisier n double ring sight.

Doppelschieber m · double slide (plotting protractor).

Doppelschraubenrichtmaschine f twin-screw elevating mechanism (G).

Doppelschritt m stride (2 paces).

Doppelseitensteuer n twin rudders (Ap).

Doppelsprechen n phantoming (Tp).

Doppelsprechschaltung f phantom circuit (Tp).

Doppelsprengkabel n two-conductor firing wire (demolitions).

Doppelstecker m two-way plug (Tp, Rad).

Doppelsternmotor m double-row radial engine.

Doppelsteuerung f dual controls (Ap).

Doppelumfassung f double envelopment (Tac).

Doppelverkehr m two-way communication, two-way traffic.

Doppelzünder m combination fuze.

Dörrfleisch n dehydrated meat.

Dörrgemüse n dehydrated vegetables.

Dose f box, can.

Dosenbarometer n aneroid barometer.

Dosenlibelle f box level.

Drache(n) m kite.

Drachenballon m kite balloon.

Dragge f grapnel.

Draht m wire.

Drahtbund n wire-cable lashing.

Drahteinzäunung f wire inclosure.

Drahtgabel f wire pike (Tp construction).

Drahtgeflecht n wire netting.

Drahthindernis n protective wire, wire entanglement.

Drahtigel m gooseberry (obstacle).

Drahtleitung f wire line (Tp).

Drahtmatte f wire mesh mat.

Drahtnachrichtenmittel n means of wire communication.

Drahtnachrichtennetz n wire net, wire system (Sig C).

Drahtnetz n wire net, wire mesh.

Drahtnetz zum Tarnen chicken wire (Cam).

Drahtrohr n wire-wound gun barrel.

Drahtrolle *f* wire roll, concertina, wire-roll entanglement.

Drahtschere *f* wire cutters.

Drahtschleife *f* wire winding, wire turn, wire loop *(Elec)*.

Drahtschlinge *f* wire snare, trip wire.

Drantseil *n* wire cable.

Drahtseilhindernis *n* cable block, wire-cable obstacle.

Drahtspirale *f* spiral wire, helical wire.

Drahtstraße *f* metal mesh road, wire mesh road.

Drahttelegraphie *f* wire telegraphy.

Drahttelephonie *f* wire telephony.

Drahtverbindung *f* wire circuit, wire communication, connecting wire, wire connection *(Tg, Tp)*.

Drahtverhau *m* wire entanglement.

Drahtwalze *f* reinforced concertina roll.

Drahtzange *f* pliers *(for handling wire)*.

Drahtzaun *m* double-apron entanglement, double-apron fence, wire fence.

Drahtzug *m* flexible steel cable *(Ap)*.

Drall *m* rifling, twist *(Ord)*; spin *(of a projectile)*.

Drallabweichung *f* drift *(due to spin of projectile)*.

Drallänge *f* length of rifling *(Ord)*.

Drallwinkel *m* angle of twist *(rifling)*.

Drallwirkung *f* twist effect of slipstream *(Avn)*.

Drallzüge *mpl* grooves *(rifling)*.

Draufgängertum *n* audacity, daring.

Drauflosfahrt *f* headlong movement *(MT, Tk)*.

Drehbank *f* lathe.

Drehbewegung *f* rotation *(of projectile)*.

Drehbolzen *m* pivot pin.

Dreher *m* lathe operator.

Drehflügelflugzeug *n* rotor airplane.

Drehgestell *n* truck *(RR car)*; turntable.

Drehgriff *m* control grip *(Mtcl)*.

Drehkolbenpumpe *f* port-control fuel-injection pump *(Diesel engine)*.

Drehkondensator *m* variable capacitor, variable condenser.

Drehkranz *m* circular track *(MG mount)*.

Drehkuppel *f* revolving turret.

Drehlichtscheinwerfer *m* revolving searchlight, revolving beacon light.

Drehlichtsignal *n* revolving beacon.

Drehmoment *n* torque.

Drehpunkt *m* pivot, fulcrum.

Drehrahmenantenne *f* rotating loop antenna.

Drehring *m* racer *(AA gun)*.

Drehscheibenlafette *f* turntable gun carriage.

Drehschemellenkung *f* fifth-wheel steering.

Drehschieber *m* rotor-type valve *(Mtr)*.

Drehschwingung *f* torsional vibration.

Drehsinn *m* direction of rotation.

Drehspule *f* moving coil *(Elec)*.

Drehspulinstrument *n* moving coil instrument *(Elec)*.

Drehstabfeder *f* torsion-rod spring *(MT)*.

Drehstrom *m* three-phase alternating current.

Drehturm *m* revolving turret.

Drehzahl *f* number of revolutions, rpm.

Drehzahlmesser *m* tachometer.

Drehzahlregler *m* governor *(Mtr)*.

Drehzahlschwankung *f* rpm fluctuations *(Mtr)*.

Drehzapfen *m* pivot.

Dreiachser *m* six-wheel vehicle.

Dreibein *n* tripod.

Dreibeinlafette *f* tripod mount.

Dreibeinmast *m* tripod mast.

Dreiblattverstellschraube *f* three-blade controllable propeller *(Ap)*.

Dreibock *m* tripod cable support.

Dreieck *n* triangle.

Dreieckbalkensperre *f* triangular timber obstacle.

Dreieckrechner *m* computer *(circular slide rule for air navigation)*.

Dreiecksaufnahme *f* triangulation *(Surv)*.

Dreieckschaltung *f* delta connection *(Elec)*.

Dreieckzielen *n* sighting-triangle aiming exercise *(Gunnery)*; triangle exercise *(R practice)*.

Dreielektrodenröhre *f* triode tube.

Dreiergemisch *n* triple mixture *(gasoline 50%, benzol 40%, alcohol 10%)*.

Dreifachzünder *m* combination fuze *(superquick, delay and time)*.

Dreiflügelschraube *f* three-bladed propeller *(Ap)*.
Dreifuß *m* tripod.
Dreifußaufsatzstück *n* tripod extension piece *(MG)*.
Dreiganggetriebe *n* three-speed transmission *(MT)*.
dreigliedrige Division triangular division.
Dreipolröhre *f* triode tube *(Rad)*.
Dreipunktlandung *f* normal landing, three-point landing *(Avn)*.
Dreipunktschaltung *f* Hartley oscillator *(Rad)*.
Dreiradfahrgestell *n* tricycle landing gear *(Ap)*.
Dreireihenstandmotor *m* three-bank upright engine.
Dreiwegehahn *m* three-way selector cock.
Drillich *m* denim *(also spelled Drilch)*.
Drillichanzug *m* fatigue uniform, work uniform.
Drillstab *m* torsion rod *(MT)*.
dringend urgent.
Dringlichkeitsliste *f* priority list.
Dringlichkeitszeichen *n* urgent signal *(Sig Com)*.
DRK-Helfer *m* German Red Cross attendant.
DRK-Helferin *f* German Red Cross nurse apprentice.
DRK-Schwester *f* German Red Cross nurse.
DRK-Schwesternhelferin *f* German Red Cross junior nurse, nurse's aid.
Drohung *f* threat.
Drossel *f* throttle *(Mtr)*.
Drosselgriff *m* throttle grip.
Drosselhebel *m* throttle lever.
Drosselklappe *f* throttle valve.
Drosselklappenwelle *f* throttle shaft.
Drosselrinne *f* jugular groove *(horse)*.
Drosselspule *f* choke coil *(Elec)*.
Drosselung *f* choking, throttling.
Druck *m* pressure.
Druckänderung *f* pressure change *(Met)*.
Druckausgleicher *m* pressure equalizer.
Druckbohlenmine *f* pressure-plank mine.
Druckbrettmine *f* pressure-board mine.
drucken to print.

drücken to press, push; to push control stick or wheel forward *(Ap)*.
Drücker *n* thumb nut *(sight)*; trigger.
Druckgurt *m* compression chord *(truss)*.
Druckkabine *f* pressure cabin *(Ap)*.
Druckknopf *m* pushbutton; snap, snap fastener.
Druckleitung *f* pressure line.
Druckluft *f* compressed air.
Druckluftbremse *f* air brake.
Drucklufterzeuger *m* air compressor.
Drucklufthammer *m* pneumatic hammer.
Druckluft-Niethammer *m* pneumatic riveter.
Druckluftramme *f* pneumatic pile driver.
Druckmesser *m* pressure gage.
Drucknase *f* trigger cam *(R)*.
Druckplatte *f* pressure plate *(clutch)*.
Druckpunkt *m* pressure point.
Druckpunkt nehmen to take up the slack *(of the trigger)*.
Druckraum *m* surge chamber.
Druckregler *m* pressure regulator.
Druckschmierung *f* pressure lubrication.
Druckschraube *f* pusher propeller *(Ap)*.
Druckschrauber *m* pusher airplane.
Druckseite *f* pressure side, pressure surface *(Ap wing)*.
Druckstelle *f* pressure point.
Druckstempel *m* pressure plug *(Arty)*.
Druckstück *n* contact piece on trigger *(R)*.
Drucktaster *m* sending key.
Druckumlaufschmierung *f* See Druckschmierung.
Druckvorschrift *f* Field Regulations, Field Manual *(abbr. Dv.)*.
Druckzerstäuber *m* pressure spray gun *(CWS)*.
Druckzünder *m* pressure firing device, pressure igniter, push igniter *(LM)*.
Druckzylinder *m* master cylinder *(hydraulic brake)*.
Dschungel *f* jungle.
D-Stoff *m* dimethylsulfate *(CWS)*.
Dübel *m* lug *(G)*.
Ducht *f* crosspiece, thwart *(boat or Pon)*.

Dücker *m* sluice pipe.

Dulag *See* Durchgangslager.

Dulagluft *See* Durchgangslager Luftwaffe.

Dumdum-Geschoß *n* dumdum bullet.

Dunkelheit *f* darkness.

Dunkelkammer *f* darkroom.

Dunnit *n* dunnite *(Am)*.

Dunst *m* haze, vapor.

Durchbiegung *f* deflection *(of a beam or girder)*.

durchbrechen to break through, pierce.

durchbrennen to burn out *(Elec fuse)*.

Durchbruch *m* break-through *(Tac)*.

"Durchdecken!" "Dress and Cover!"

durchdrehen to pull *(a propeller)* through.

Durchführung *f* gland *(Bln)*; carrying out, execution.

Durchgabe *f* transmission *(of Rad messages, etc.)*.

Durchgangsbahnhof *m* through station *(RR)*.

Durchgangsfernspruch *m* long-distance telephone call.

Durchgangslager *n* PW transit camp *(abbr. Dulag)*.

Durchgangslager Luftwaffe PW transit camp for Air Forces personnel *(abbr. Dulagluft)*.

durchgeben to transmit *(Sig C)*.

Durchgriff *m* reciprocal of amplification factor in percent *(Rad)*.

Durchhang *m* sag.

Durchhängen *n* droop *(Mech)*.

durchkrümmen to squeeze *(the trigger)*.

Durchlaß *m* culvert, passage, conduit, opening.

durchladen to load *(a magazine or belt)*.

Durchlaufgleis *n* through track *(RR)*.

durchlöchern pierce.

Durchmesser *m* diameter.

durchpausen to trace *(a map, etc.)*.

Durchpunkt *m* point at which trajectory intersects plane of aerial target perpendicular to line of sighting.

durchsacken to drop, to do a power stall, to sink, to pancake *(Avn)*.

Durchsackgeschwindigkeit *f* critical speed, stalling speed *(Avn)*.

durchsagen to pass the word along.

Durchschlag *m* carbon copy *(typed)*; drift pin.

Durchschläger *m* punch, drift *(tool)*.

Durchschlagskraft *f* penetration, force of penetration *(Am)*.

durchschmelzen to burn out *(Elec fuse)*.

Durchschnitt *m* average, mean; cross section.

Durchschnittsleistung *f* average performance.

Durchschnittspanzerstärke *f* average thickness of armor *(Tk)*.

Durchschreibeblock *m* carbon-copy pad.

Durchschrift *f* carbon copy *(written)*.

durchsichtig transparent.

Durchstich *n* cut *(Engr, RR)*.

Durchstoß *m* penetration by assault.

durchstoßen pierce, penetrate; fly through *(a layer of clouds)*.

durchsuchen to search.

Durchtrittsöffnung *f* cutaway *(for ejected cartridge cases)*.

durchwaten to ford.

durchziehen to pull out *(dive bombing)*.

Dusche *f* shower bath.

Düse *f* injector, jet, nozzle; vent *(rocket)*.

Düsenkorrektor *m* mixture control.

Dynamomaschine *f* dynamo, generator.

Dynastart *m* starter-generator.

E

Echolot *n* sonic altimeter, sound-ranging altimeter *(Avn)*; fathometer, echo depth sounder *(Nav)*.

Eckplatte *f* gusset.

Edelgas *n* rare gas.

Edisonsammler *m* Edison storage battery.

Edler *m* knight, noble.

Ehre *f* honor.

Ehrenbezeigungen bei Beerdigung graveside service *(Mil funeral)*.

Ehrenbezeugung *f* salute.

Ehrengeleit *n* escort of honor.

Ehrenparade *f* dress parade.

Ehrenposten *m* guard of honor.
Ehrenrang *m* honorary rank.
Ehrenrat *m* court of honor.
Ehrensalve *f* volley *(at burials)*.
Ehrensold *m* award.
Ehrenwache *f* guard of honor, honor guard.
Ehrenwort *n* parole, word of honor.
Ehrenzeichen *n* decoration.
eichen calibrate.
Eichenlaub *n* oak leaf cluster.
Eichstrich *m* measuring line, graduation.
Eichung *f* calibration, adjustment.
Eierhandgranate *f* egg-shaped hand grenade, "pineapple" hand grenade.
Eigenfrequenz *f* natural frequency *(Rad)*.
Eigengeschwindigkeit *f* indicated air speed *(Avn)*.
Eigengewicht *n* empty weight.
eigenmächtig on one's own authority, unauthorized.
eigenmächtige Entfernung absence without leave.
Eigenpeilung *f* direction finding by taking bearings from an aircraft on two or more radio stations.
Eigenschaft *f* quality, characteristic, property.
Eigenschatten *m* shadow on object *(as distinguished from shadow cast by the object) (Cam)*.
Eigenschwingung *f* natural oscillation *(Rad)*.
Eigentum *n* property.
Eigenverständigung *f* interphone *(Ap)*; intravehicular communication *(Tk)*.
Eignungsprüfung *f* aptitude test.
Eihandgranate *f* See Eierhandgranate.
Eimer *m* bucket.
"Ein!" "Contact!" *(Avn)*.
Einankerumformer *m* dynamotor.
Einatemventil *n* inlet valve *(gas mask, oxygen breathing apparatus)*.
Einbahnstraße *f* one-way road or street.
Einbahnverkehr *m* one-way traffic *(MT)*.
Einbaufähre *f* construction float *(Bdg)*.
Einbehaltung *f* detention *(of pay, etc.)*.
Einbeinfahrgestell *n* landing gear with individual cantilever legs *(Ap)*.

einberufen to induct into the armed forces, to call to the colors, to order to report for active duty. See Einberufung.-
Einberufung *f* call to the colors *(corresponds roughly to US induction, and is followed by Einstellung, assignment to a unit)*.
Einberufungsbefehl *m* order to report for active duty.
Einberufungskarte *f* notice of induction.
Einberufungsort *m* induction station.
Einblick *m* view into *(enemy positions, etc.)*; insight; eyepiece *(Optics)*.
Einblicklinse *f* eyepiece lens *(Optics)*.
Einblickrohr *n* eyepiece tube.
Einblickstutzen *m* eyepiece mount.
Einbruch *m* penetration *(Tac)*.
Einbruchsfeuer *n* assault fire.
Einbruchsfront *f* frontage of penetration *(Tac)*; cold front *(Met)*.
Einbruchstelle *f* breach, point of penetration, point chosen for penetration *(Tac)*.
Einbuchtung *f* dent in the enemy's line, salient *(Tac)*.
Eindecker *m* monoplane.
Eindeckung *f* cover *(Ft)*.
eindringen infiltrate, penetrate.
Eindringungstiefe *f* depth of penetration or infiltration *(Tac)*.
Eineinhalbdecker *m* sesquiplane.
Einerzelt *n* one-man shelter tent, pup tent.
Einfachanschnitt *m* single-station pilot-balloon spotting *(Met)*.
Einfachleitung *f* ground-return circuit *(Tp)*.
einfädeln to thread *(a needle)*; to join a march column, to get into line.
einfahren to float bridge-sections into place; to break in *(a horse, etc.)*; to harness; to drive in.
Einfahrgleis *n* incoming track *(RR)*.
Einfallwinkel *m* angle of incidence.
einfetten to grease, lubricate.
einfliegen to penetrate *(air attack tactics)*; make a test flight.
Einflieger *m* test pilot.
Einfliegerei *f* aircraft-testing department.
Einfluchten *n* marking out *(in fixing the azimuth) (Surv)*.
Einflug *m* penetration *(air attack

tactics); approach flight *(Avn);* approach of a target *(AWS).*

Einfluggenehmigung *f* traffic-control clearance *(Avn).*

Einflugsmeldung *f* report of approaching target *(AWS).*

Einflugzeichen *n* "come in" signal *(Inst landing).*

Einflüsse *mpl* See **besondere und Witterungseinflüsse.**

einführen introduce, initiate, lead in.

Einfuhrhafen *m* port of entry.

Einführungsdraht *m* lead-in *(Rad).*

Einfüllstutzen *m* oil-filling plug *(recoil mechanism);* filler neck *(of gasoline or oil tank).*

eingabeln to bracket *(Arty).*

Eingabelung *f* bracket, bracketing.

Eingang *m* entrance.

Eingangswerte *mpl* initial data *(AAA).*

Eingangszündung *f* priming charge.

eingesehen exposed to observation *(emplacement, trench, etc.).*

Eingitterröhre *f* single-grid tube, triode *(Rad).*

eingleisig single-track.

eingliedern assign; incorporate, make an organic part of; classify.

Eingliederung *f* assignment; incorporation, o r g a n i c arrangement; classification.

eingraben dig in, entrench; bury.

Eingreifdivision *f* reserve division.

eingreifen intervene, come to the aid of, take a hand in; to catch, mesh, engage.

einhängen suspend *(a bomb).*

Einheit *f* unit, element *(Tac).*

kleinste taktische Einheit basic tactical unit.

Einheitsführer *m* commander of a unit.

Einheitsgeschütz *m* dual-purpose gun.

Einheitsgewicht *n* specific gravity.

Einheitsgranate *f* combination high-explosive and shrapnel shell.

Einheitskanister *m* standard gasoline container, unit container.

Einheitsmaß *n* unit of measurement.

Einheitsmunition *f* fixed ammunition.

Einheitsmunitionszug *m* ammunition train carrying only one type and caliber of ammunition *(RR).*

Einheitsmütze *f* regulation field cap *(replaces the* Feldmütze*).*

Einheitsprinzip *n* unit principle *(Ger Mil doctrine providing maximum independence and self-sufficiency for each unit).*

Einheitswaffe *f* dual-purpose weapon.

Einheitszeit *f* standard time.

Einheitszünder *m* combination fuze, standard fuze *(Am).*

einholen overtake, collect, bring in; haul down.

einigeln take up a position of all-around defense.

einkesseln to encircle, trap, pocket.

Einkesselung *f* encirclement.

Einkipptrieb *m* leveling mechanism *(Mort).*

Einkleidungsbeihilfe *f* clothing money allowance.

Einkreisempfänger *m* receiver with one resonant circuit *(Rad).*

Einkreisung *f* encirclement.

Einkreisungsmanöver *n* encircling maneuver.

Einkreisungsschlacht *f* battle of encirclement *(Tac).*

Einkreisungsversuch *m* attempted encirclement.

einkuppeln engage, thrown in *(the clutch).*

einladen to load, entrain, entruck, etc.

Einladeübersicht *f* entraining table, entrucking table.

Einlaß *m* inlet, intake.

Einlaßkanal *m* intake line *(Mtr).*

Einlaßventil *n* intake valve *(Mtr).*

Einlaßventilkammer *f* intake-valve chamber *(Mtr).*

einläufig single-barreled.

Einlegerohr *n* liner, subcaliber tube *(Ord).*

einleiten begin, introduce, initiate, commence.

einleitendes Gefecht preliminary action or engagement.

einmessen to survey *(Arty).*

Einnahme *f* capture, occupation, seizure *(of a locality);* reception, acceptance *(of equipment, Ord, etc.);* receipts *(money, etc.).*

Einnahmeschein *m* receipt.

einnebeln to blanket, to lay a smoke screen.

einölen to oil, lubricate.

einpeilen take a radio bearing.

Einpolluftleiter *m* Marconi antenna, quarter-wave v e r t i c a l antenna.

einrasten engage; lock; ram home; snap shut; catch.

einrichten adjust *(fire, etc.)*; orient *(a map)*; prepare, improve *(a position)*; install; furnish, equip.

Einrichten einer Karte orientation of a map.

Einrichten einer Stellung preparation or improvement of a position.

Einrichtung *f* installation; organization, establishment; adjustment; arrangement; device; orientation.

Einrumpfflugzeug *n* single-fuselage airplane.

Einsatz *m* commitment, employment; mission; operation, action; effort; insertion; duty; sortie *(Avn)*.

bei besonderem Einsatz on active duty; during special commitment *(in time of war or national emergency)*.

Einsatzbereitschaft *f* aggressiveness, initiative, readiness for action.

Einsatzbesprechung *f* orders conference, "briefing" *(Avn)*.

einsatzfähig available for assignment, commitment or employment.

Einsatz fliegen to fly a sortie *(Avn)*.

Einsatzhafen *m* home field *(Avn)*.

Einsatzhafenkommandantur *f* operational airdrome command *(sub-division of Lufthafenbereichkommandantur)*.

Einsatzort *m* locality to be occupied, area where units are to be sent into action.

Einsatzraum *m* operational area.

Einsatztopf *m* filter-element container *(gas mask)*.

Einschaltung *f* switching on, throwing into gear.

einschanzen dig in, entrench.

Einscheibenkupplung *f* single-plate clutch *(MT)*.

Einschießen *n* adjustment fire, trial fire *(Arty)*.

Einschießen mit hohen Sprengpunkten high-burst ranging.

Einschießen nach der Länge range adjustment.

Einschießpunkt *m* adjusting point *(adjustment fire)*.

Einschießziel *n* adjustment target *(Arty)*.

Einschiffung *f* embarkation.

Einschlag *m* impact, strike *(Arty)*; toe-in *(MT)*.

Einschlagsgarbe *f* sheaf of fire at point of impact, shot group, shot pattern *(Arty)*.

Einschlagsgruppe *f* shot group, shot pattern *(of a volley)*.

Einschleifen einer Leitung connecting a line into a telephone circuit.

einschneiden to intersect, to take cross bearings.

Einschneiden auf Richtungslinie point determination along an orienting line *(Surv)*.

Einschneiden nach drei Punkten three-point resection *(Surv)*.

Einschnitt *m* cut *(Engr, RR)*.

Einschuß *m* hit.

einschwenken to pivot *(Tac, drill)*.

seitlich einschwenken to pivot to the left or right, to fan out *(Tac)*.

einsetzen to commit, employ, insert.

einsickern infiltrate *(Tac)*.

Einsitzer *m* single-seater airplane.

einspielen bring into play, throw in, engage, actuate.

Einspielen der Libellen leveling, cross-leveling *(Arty)*.

Einsprache *f* mouthpiece *(Tp)*.

einspringender Winkel reentrant.

Einspritzdüse *f* fuel injector, injection nozzle *(Mtr)*.

Einspritzpumpe *f* injection pump.

Einspruch *m* challenge.

Einstecklauf *m* subcaliber tube.

Einsteigluke *f* entrance hatch *(Tk)*.

Einsteigöffnung *f* manhole.

einstellbare Luftschraube adjustable propeller *(Ap)*.

einstellen tune in *(Rad)*; to dial *(Tp)*; adjust, set *(a fuze, etc.)*; cease *(fire, etc.)*.

Einstellhülse *f* adjustable holder *(panoramic telescope)*.

Einstellmarke *f* index; adjustable marker.

Einstellmutter *f* adjustment nut, regulating nut.

Einstellring *m* adjusting ring *(fuze)*.

Einstellung *f* adjustment, setting; cessation. *See also* Einberufung.

Einstellvorrichtung *f* adjustment device, setting device.

Einstellwinkel *m* angle of wing setting, angle of incidence.

Einstiegklappe *f* hatch cover *(Ap)*.

Einstiegluke *f* hatch *(Ap)*.
einstöpseln plug in *(Rad, Tp)*.
einstürzen to cave in.
einteilen graduate *(into degrees, etc.)*; to divide, classify, separate into groups.
Einteilung *f* classification; scale; graduation, division *(into degrees or units)*.
eintreffen arrive.
Eintreffzeit *f* arrival time.
Einweiser *m* guide.
Einweisungskommando *m* party of guides.
Einwohnerschaft *f* population, inhabitants.
Einzäunung *f* enclosure, stockade, compound *(PW)*.
Einzelabfederung *f* independent suspension *(of wheels)*.
Einzelabwurf *m* individual release, single release *(Bombing)*.
Einzelaufhängung *f* independent suspension *(of wheels)*.
Einzelausbildung *f* individual training.
Einzelbefehl *m* fragmentary order, extract order *(Tac)*.
Einzelfeuer *n* single-shot fire, semiautomatic fire *(MG)*.
Einzelhaft *f* solitary confinement.
Einzelkrad *n* solo motorcycle.
Einzellader *m* single loader, singleshot weapon.
Einzelschnittverfahren *n* single-intersection method *(target location in FR)*.
Einzelschuß *m* single shot, single round.
Einzelschutz *m* individual protection.
Einzelsprünge *mpl* bounds *(method of advancing)*.
Einzelwurf *m* individual release, single release *(Bombing)*.
Einzelziel *n* point target *(Bombing)*.
einziehbar retractable *(landing gear, etc.)*.
einziehen draw in, retract; withdraw *(a sentry)*; conscript, draft *(recruits)*; confiscate.
Einziehfahrgestell *n* retractable landing gear *(Ap)*.
Eisansatz *m* accumulation of ice.
Eisbrecher *m* ice apron *(Bdg)*.
Eisenbahn *f* railroad, railway.
Eisenbahnanlage *f* railroad installation.

Eisenbahnaufmarsch *m* strategic concentration by rail.
Eisenbahnbatterie *f* railway artillery battery.
Eisenbahnbaubataillon *n* railway construction battalion.
Eisenbahnbeförderung *f* transportation by rail.
Eisenbahnbetrieb *m* railway traffic; railway operation.
Eisenbahnbetriebskompanie *f* railway operating company.
Eisenbahnendpunkt *m* railway terminal, railhead.
Eisenbahnflak *f* railway antiaircraft gun; railway antiaircraft artillery.
Eisenbahngeleise *n* railroad track.
Eisenbahngeschütz *n* railway gun.
Eisenbahnhaubitze *f* railway howitzer.
Eisenbahnkesselwagen *m* tank car *(RR)*.
Eisenbahnklaue *f* spur track.
Eisenbahnknotenpunkt *m* railway center, railway junction.
Eisenbahnküchenwagen *m* kitchen car *(RR)*.
Eisenbahnnachschublinie *f* railway supply line.
Eisenbahnpanzerzug *m* armored train *(RR)*.
Eisenbahn-Pfeilerbaukompanie *f* railway pile-driving or pier-building company *(Mil)*.
Eisenbahnpioniere *mpl* railway engineer troops.
Eisenbahnstellwerk *n* railway signal tower, switch control room.
Eisenbahntankstelle *f* gasoline and lubricant railhead, bulk reduction point.
Eisenbahntransportfolge *f* railway transportation timetable.
Eisenbahntruppen *fpl* railway operating troops.
Eisenbahnwagen *m* railway car.
Eisenbeton *m* reinforced concrete, ferro-concrete.
Eisenblech *n* sheet iron.
Eiseneinlage *f* iron reinforcement *(in ferro-concrete)*.
Eisenkern *m* iron core *(Elec)*.
Eisenwalze *f* iron roller *(mine clearance)*.
eiserne Portion emergency ration *(for Pers)*.

eiserne Ration emergency ration *(for animals)*.

Eisernes Kreuz Iron Cross *(decoration)*.

Eisregen *m* sleet.

Eissporn *m* ice spade *(trail spade)*.

Ekrasit *n* ecrasite *(explosive)*.

E-Latte *f* aiming stake, aiming post (E=Entfernung, *range)*.

Elektrizitätszähler *m* electric meter.

Elektrode *f* electrode; grounded electrode *(spark plug)*.

Elektrodenröhre *f* radio tube.

Elektromechaniker *m* electrician.

Elektron *n* electron; trade name of a magnesium-aluminum alloy.

Elektronbrandbombe *f* electron incendiary bomb.

Elektrotechniker *m* electrical engineer.

Element *n* cell, element *(Elec)*.

Elementbecher *m* cell container *(Elec)*.

Elementekühler *m* cellular-type radiator *(MT)*.

Elementprüfer *m* battery tester *(Elec)*.

Ellbogen *m* elbow.

E.Meßgerät *n* See Entfernungsmeßgerät.

E.Meßmann *m* See Entfernungsmeßmann.

E.Messer *m* See Entfernungsmesser.

Emfang *m* receipt, reception.

Empfänger *m* indicator *(follow-the-pointer mechanism of AA gun)*; indicator *(fuze setter)*; receiver, receiving set *(Rad)*; data receiver, indicator-regulator *(data transmission system of AA gun)*.

Empfangsapparatur *f* receiver chassis, receiving equipment *(Rad)*.

Empfangsberechtigter *m* beneficiary.

Empfangsbescheinigung *f* See Empfangsschein.

Empfangsbestätigung *f* acknowledgment of receipt *(Sig C)*.

Empfangslautstärke *f* volume of reception *(Rad)*.

Empfangsschaltung *f* receiver circuit *(Rad)*.

Empfangsschein *m* receipt form.

Empfangswelle *f* receiving frequency *(Rad)*.

Empfangszone *f* reception zone *(Rad)*.

empfindlich sensitive.

empfindlicher Aufschlagzünder superquick impact fuze.

empfindlicher Kopfzünder allways fuze.

empfindlicher Zünder superquick fuze.

Endauflager *n* abutment *(Bdg)*.

Endbahnhof *m* railhead, terminal.

Enddrall *m* terminal twist *(Ord)*.

Endgeschwindigkeit *f* terminal velocity.

Endmontage *f* final assembly.

Endverstärker *m* terminal repeater *(Tp)*; final amplifier, power amplifier *(Rad)*.

Endziel *n* final objective.

Energieleitung *f* feeder cable *(Elec)*.

Energienachfuhr *f* additional supply of power *(Elec)*.

Energieverlust *m* power loss *(Elec, Rad)*.

Energievorrat *m* power supply.

Enge *f* defile *(Tac)*.

Engländer *m* Englishman; monkey wrench.

Engpaß *m* bottleneck, defile.

entblößen uncover *(Tac)*.

Ente *f* duck; canard airplane.

Enteiser *m* de-icer *(Ap)*.

Enteisungsanlage *f* de-icer system, ice-eliminating system *(Ap)*.

Enteisungsgerät *n* de-icer *(Ap)*.

Enteisungmittel *n* anti-icer solution.

Entenflugzeug *n* canard airplane.

entfalten develop *(a route column, etc.)*; unfold.

entfalteter Anmarsch advance in developed formation *(Tac)*.

Entfaltung *f* development *(followed by* Entwicklung, *deployment)*.

Entfaltung aus dem Marsch development from march column.

Entfaltungszeit *f* parachute opening time.

Entfernung *f* range, distance; removal; departure.

mittlere Entfernung medium range *(up to 800 m)*.

nächste Entfernung close range *(up to 100 m)*.

nahe Entfernung close range *(up to 400 m)*.

weite Entfernung long range *(beyond 800 m)*.

Entfernungsermittlung *f* range determination.

Entfernungsgerät *n* range finder.

Entfernungslineal *n* range ruler *(Arty)*.

Entfernungsmarke *f* range indicator *(practice firing)*.

Entfernungsmeßgerät *n* range-finder, altimeter, height-finder *(AAA)*.

Entfernungsmeßmann *m* range-finder operator; height-finder sergeant *(AAA)*.

Entfernungsmeßmann zur Seitenbeobachtung lateral tracker *(AAA)*.

Entfernungsmesser *m* range-finder; range-finder operator; height-finder sergeant *(AAA)*.

Entfernungsschätzen *n* range estimation.

Entfernungsteilung *f* range scale.

Entfernungstrommel *f* range knob *(G)*.

Entfernungsunterschied *m* range difference.

Entfernungsvorhalt *m* linear difference between present slant range *(at instant of range determination)* and future slant range *(AAA)*.

Entfettung *f* degreasing.

Entgasung *f* degassing.

entgegenwirken counteract, act against, work against.

Entgiftung *f* decontamination.

Entgiftungsabteilung *f* decontamination battalion.

Entgiftungsdienst *m* decontamination service.

Entgiftungsgerät *n* decontamination apparatus.

Entgiftungskompanie *f* decontamination company.

Entgiftungskraftwagen *m* decontamination truck.

Entgiftungsmittel *n* decontamination agent.

Entgiftungspflug *m* decontamination plow.

Entgiftungsplatz *m* decontamination point.

Entgiftungsstoff *m* decontamination agent.

Entgiftungstrommel *f* perforated decontamination drum.

  fahrbare Entgiftungstrommel decontamination cart.

Entgiftungstrupp *m* decontamination squad.

entheben relieve *(of a command, etc.)*.

entkeimen sterilize.

entkohlen decarbonize.

entkupfern decopper.

entladen unload, empty; discharge.

Entladestab *m* unloading staff *(harbor)*.

Entladung *f* to discharge *(Am, Elec, etc.)*.

Entladungsstoß *m* discharge surge *(Elec)*.

entlassen to dismiss, discharge; release; disband, demobilize.

Entlassung *f* discharge; dismissal; release.

Entlassung auf Ehrenwort release on parole, home parole.

Entlassungsjahrgang *m* age class due for discharge.

Entlassungsschein *m* certificate of discharge.

Entlassungsstelle *f* demobilization center, discharge center.

entlasten relieve *(of pressure)*.

Entlastung *f* relief *(of pressure)*.

Entlastungsangriff *m* relief attack *(made to relieve enemy pressure elsewhere)*.

entlaufen to escape.

entlausen delouse.

Entlausungsanstalt *f* delousing station.

entlüften ventilate; bleed *(recoil mechanism)*.

Entlüfter *m* ventilator.

Entlüftungsstutzen *m* breather *(Mtr)*.

Entmagnetisierung *f* de-gaussing.

entrollen to unfurl or uncase *(a flag)*.

Entsatz *m* relief *(of a fortress, etc.)*.

Entschädigung *f* compensation, reimbursement, allowance, recoupment.

entschärfen disarm *(Am)*.

Entscheidung *f* decision.

Entscheidungsgefecht *n* decisive action, decisive battle *(Tac)*.

Entschluß *m* decision *(Tac)*.

Entschlußfassung *f* formulation of decision(s).

Entschlußkraft *f* power of decision.

entschlüsseln decode, decryptograph.

entsenden to dispatch, send off.

entsetzen relieve *(a fortress, etc.)*; be terrified; relieve *(of a command)*.

Entsetzung *f* relief *(of a fortress, etc.)*.

entseuchen disinfect.

Entseuchungsgerät *n* disinfestor.

Entseuchungsmittel *n* disinfecting agent.

Entseuchungsschrank *m* disinfecting chamber.

entsichern to disengage or release the safety *(SA, R, etc.)*; to arm or activate *(a mine, bomb, etc.)*.

Entsicherungsflügel *m* arming vane *(bomb)*.

entspannen to uncock; to relieve tension.

Entstaubung *f* dust filtering *(MT)*.

Entstörkappe *f* ignition shield *(over spark plug)*.

Entstörung *f* interference elimination *(Rad)*.

enttarnen remove camouflage.

entwaffnen disarm.

Entwarnung *f* "all clear" signal.

Entwässerungsgraben *m* drainage ditch.

Entweichen *n* escape, evasion.

Entwesung *f* sterilization.

entwickeln deploy *(Tac)*; develop *(Photo)*; generate *(smoke, etc.)*.

Entwicklung *f* deployment *(follows Entfaltung, development)*; development *(Photo)*; generation *(of smoke, etc.)*.

Entwurf *m* sketch, outline; plan, scheme.

Entzerrer *m* balancing network *(Rad, Tp)*.

Entzerrung *f* rectification, restitution *(aerial Photo)*; correction, compensation *(of frequency response, Rad, Tp)*.

Entzerrungsgerät *n* rectifying camera *(aerial Photo)*.

entziehen remove, withdraw, deprive.

sich entziehen avoid, evade, disengage *(Tac)*.

entziffern decipher, decryptograph.

Entzifferung *f* deciphering.

entzurren unlock, unclamp.

Episkop *n* reflecting projector, episcope.

erbeuten to capture *(matériel)*.

Erdanschluß *m* ground connection *(Elec)*.

Erdarbeit *f* excavation work; earthwork *(Ft)*.

Erdartillerie *f* artillery used against ground targets *(as distinguished from AAA)*.

Erdaufklärung *f* ground reconnaissance *(Tac)*.

Erdbeobachtung *f* ground observation.

Erdbeschuß *m* anti-aircraft fire *(as seen from target)*.

Erdbildmessung *f* phototopography.

Erde *f* earth, soil; ground *(Elec)*.

Erdei *See* **Erdeinschießziel.**

Erdeinschießziel *n* ground adjustment target *(Gunnery)*.

erden to ground *(Elec)*.

Erder *m* ground *(Elec)*.

Erdfernsprechverbindung *f* ground-return telephone circuit.

Erdgegner *m* hostile ground force.

Erdgleiche *f* ground level *(Ft)*.

Erdgrube *f* borrow pit.

Erdhörer *m* geophone.

Erdkabel *n* underground cable or wire *(Tp)*.

Erdkrümmungslineal *n* altitude-correction ruler.

Erdleitung *f* ground, ground lead *(Elec)*.

Erdleitungsdraht *m* ground wire *(Elec)*.

Erdleitungsrohr *n* ground pipe, underground pipe.

Erdmine *f* land mine.

Erdöl *n* petroleum.

Erdortung *f* pilotage *(Air Navigation)*.

erdrosseln to throttle, strangle.

Erdrückleitung *f* ground-return circuit *(Tp)*.

Erdschluß *m* ground leak, ground short *(Elec)*.

Erdschwere *f* gravitation, gravity.

Erdsporn *m* trail spade *(G)*.

Erdstecker *m* grounding rod *(Elec)*.

Erdtelegraphieverbindung *f* ground-return telegraph circuit.

Erdtruppen *fpl* ground forces.

Erdung *f* ground, grounding *(Elec)*.

Erdvergleichsziel *n* auxiliary ground target *(Arty)*.

Erdvermessung *f* topographic survey.

Erdwinde *f* winch *(for Bln)*.

Erdzielbeschuß *m* firing against ground targets *(AAA)*.

Erdzuleitung *f* ground lead *(Elec)*.

Ergänzung *f* supplement, replacement(s), reserve(s); completion, rounding out, bringing to full strength.

Ergänzungsbedarf *m* deficiency, shortage, replacement requirements.

Ergänzungsgruppe *f* replacement training group *(Air Force group composed of 2 or more* Ergänzungsstaffeln).

Ergänzungsstaffel *f* See Ergänzungsgruppe.

Ergänzungsstelle *f* replacement center.

ergeben, sich to surrender, capitulate.

Ergebnis *n* result; score.

Erhebungswinkel *m* quadrant angle *(Surv)*.

Erhöhung *f* quadrant elevation *(Gunnery)*.

Erhöhungsskala *f* elevation scale *(G, MG)*.

Erhöhungswinkel *m* quadrant angle of elevation *(Gunnery)*.

Erholungsurlaub *m* leave; arrest, imprisonment *(slang)*.

Erinnerungsmedaille *f* campaign medal.

erkämpfen to force *(a crossing, etc.)*.

Erkennungsmarke *f* identification tag, "dog tag."

Erkennungsmunition *f* signal ammunition.

Erkennungstuch *n* identification panel, ground panel.

Erkennungswort *n* countersign, password.

Erkennungszeichen *n* marking, insignia, identification mark; recognition signal.

Erker *m* "bay window" type gun mount in front right sponson *(Tk)*.

Erkunder *m* scout; reconnaissance airplane.

Erkundung *f* reconnaissance *(Tac)*.

Erkundungsfahrzeug *n* reconnaissance vehicle, scout vehicle.

Erkundungsorgan *n* reconnaissance element.

Erkundungsvorstoß *m* scouting raid.

Erlaubnis *f* permission.

Erlaubnisschein *m* leave pass.

Erledigung *f* accomplishment, completion.

Ermäßigung der Strafe remission of sentence.

ermächtigen empower.

Ermattungsstrategie *f* strategy of attrition.

Ermessen *n* discretion.

Ermüdung *f* fatigue, exhaustion.

Ermüdungskampfstoff *m* harassing agent *(CWS)*.

Ermüdungsschießen *n* harassing fire, gas-shell fire *(Arty)*.

ernannt See Ernennung.

Ernennung *f* appointment to brevet rank.

Ernstfall *m* emergency.

erobern conquer *(territory or locality)*.

Eroberung *f* conquest.

Erreger *m* exciter *(Rad)*.

Erregerstrom *m* excitation current *(Elec)*.

Erregerwicklung *f* excitation winding *(Elec)*.

Ersatz *m* replacement; substitute, synthetic material; spare part; compensation, damages.

Ersatzbataillon *n* replacement training battalion.

Ersatzbatterie *f* spare battery *(Elec)*.

Ersatzbedienung *f* gun crew replacements, reserve gun crew.

Ersatzdienststelle *f* recruiting center.

Ersatzeinheit *f* replacement unit, replacement training unit.

Ersatzfunkstelle *f* secondary radio station.

Ersatzheer *n* replacement training Army.

Ersatzkarte *f* provisional map, substitute map.

Ersatzmann *m* replacement.

Ersatzmannschaften *fpl* replacements.

Ersatzpferd *n* remount.

Ersatzregiment *n* replacement training regiment.

Ersatzreifen *m* spare tire.

Ersatzreserve *f* replacement reserves.

Ersatzreserve I reserves comprising untrained men under 35.

Ersatzreserve II reserves comprising physically unfit, untrained men under 35.

Ersatzreserveausbildung *f* training of replacement reserves.

Ersatzschaltschema *n* equivalent circuit *(Elec)*.

Ersatzteil *n* reserve unit *(Tac)*; spare part.

Ersatztruppen *fpl* replacements.

Ersatzverpflegungsmagazin *n*   ration depot *(Z of I)*.

Ersatzwesen *n*   recruiting and replacement administration.

Erschießen der Tageseinflüsse   obtaining metro data by registration *(FA)*.

erschöpfen   to exhaust, wear out, use up.

Erschütterung *f*   concussion, shock.

erstarren   become rigid or stiff; "freeze" in position.

Erstausstattung *f*   initial issue.

erste Hilfe   first aid.

Erster Offizier   first officer *(Nav)*.

ersticken   asphyxiate, choke, stifle, suffocate.

erstickender Kampfstoff   lung irritant.

Erststrom *m*   primary current.

erstürmen   to rush, take by assault *(Tac)*.

Erträglichkeitsgrenze *f*   harassing concentration *(CWS)*.

Erwa-Meldung *f*   stand-by message *(preliminary to metro message) (Arty)*.

Erwiderungsfeuer *n*   retaliation fire, counterfire.

erzwingen   force *(a crossing, etc.)*.

Etappe *f*   communications zone *(superseded by rückwärtiges Armeegebiet, but still frequently used)*.

Etappenmarsch *m*   administrative march.

Etat *m*   budget.

Etatposten *m*   budget item.

Exerzierbombe *f*   drill bomb, practice bomb.

Exerzieren *n*   drill, practice.

Exerzierform *f*   drill formation.

Exerziergeschoß *n*   dummy projectile.

Exerzierhalle *f*   drill hall.

Exerzierhaus *n*   armory.

Exerziermarsch *m*   goose step.

Exerziermunition *f*   drill ammunition, dummy ammunition.

Exerzierordnung *f*   drill formation; drill regulations.

Exerzierpatrone *f*   dummy cartridge.

Exerzierplatz *m*   drill ground, parade ground.

Exerzierschritt *m*   *See* **Exerziermarsch.**

Exerziervorschrift *f*   drill regulations.

Exzenterhülse *f*   eccentric sleeve *(aiming circle)*.

F

Fabrik *f*   factory.

Fach *n*   field of competency, trade, profession; branch of knowledge; specialty; compartment, pigeonhole.

Fachabteilungen *fpl*   professional service units *(Med)*.

Facharbeiter *m*   technician, skilled workman, specialist.

Fachausdruck *m*   technical term.

Fachbearbeiter *m*   staff officer or official in charge of some technical branch or administrative department.

Fachberater *m*   technical adviser.

Fächermotor *m*   fan-type engine, double-V engine.

Fächerturn *m*   half-loop wing-over *(Avn)*.

Fachmann *m*   specialist, expert.

Fachsprache *f*   technical terminology.

Fachverständiger *m*   specialist, expert.

Fachwerk *n*   latticework, grillage; truss.

Fachwerkbrücke *f*   truss bridge.

Fachwerkträger *m*   truss *(Bdg)*.

Fackel *f*   flare, torch.

Faden *m*   thread, filament; string; fathom *(Nav)*; front-sight slit *(aiming circle)*; hair *(Optics)*.

Fadenkreuz *n*   cross hairs, cross wires *(Optics)*.

Fadenstück *n*   front-sight piece *(aiming circle)*.

Fahne *f*   colors, flag, guidon.

Fahnenband *n*   battle honors.

Fahneneid *m*   oath of allegiance, oath of enlistment.

Fahnenflucht *f*   desertion.

Fahnenflüchtiger *m*   deserter.

Fahnenjunker *m*   officer candidate *(from enlistment until promotion to Fähnrich)*.

Fahnenjunker-Gefreiter *m* officer candidate *(with grade of* Gefreiter).

Fahnenjunker-Unteroffizier *m* NCO officer candidate *(with grade of* Sgt).

Fahnenkompanie *f* color guard company.

Fahnenmast *m* fixed flagpole.

Fahnenposten *m* color sentinel.

Fahnenschaft *m* flagpole.

Fahnenstange *f* flagpole, pike.

Fahnenträger *m* color bearer, guidon.

Fahnentrupp *m* color guard.

Fahnentuch *n* bunting.

Fahnenwache *f* color guard, color sentinel.

Fähnrich *m* officer candidate *(grade above* Fahnenjunker-Unteroffizier).

Fahrabteilung *f* supply-train battalion *(H-Dr)*.

Fahrausweis *m* travel order, traveling permit.

Fahrbahn *f* roadway.

Fahrbahnträger *m* floor beam, roadway girder *(Bdg)*.

fahrbar passable *(for vehicles)*; mobile; practicable; navigable.

Fahrbefehl *m* transportation order *(MT)*.

Fahrbenzin *n* standard gasoline.

Fahrbereich *m* operating range, traveling distance, cruising radius *(MT, Tk)*.

Fährbetrieb *m* ferrying operations.

Fahrbremse *f* wheel brake *(G carriage)*.

Fähre *f* ferry.

fahren to drive, travel, ride.

fahrendes Ziel moving target *(Tk, vehicle)*.

Fahrer *m* driver *(MT, Tk, etc.)*; private *(H-Dr Transport)*.

Fahrerhaus *n* cab *(Trk)*.

Fahreroptik *f* driver's periscope *(Tk)*.

Fahrgast *m* passenger.

Fahrgerät *n* propelling equipment *(Engr)*.

Fahrgestell *n* chassis *(MT)*; landing gear, landing-gear frame *(Ap)*.

Fahrkarte *f* transportation ticket *(RR, bus, etc.)*.

Fahrkolonne *f* horse-drawn column.

Fahrkostenentschädigung *f* travel allowance *(reimbursement)*.

Fahrküche *f* rolling kitchen.

Fahrlässigkeit *f* negligence.

Fahrleistung *f* traveling capacity *(MT, Tk)*.

Fahrplan *m* timetable, train schedule.

Fährprahm *m* tank landing craft.

Fahrrad *n* bicycle.

Fahrrinne *f* rut.

Fährseil *n* ferry cable.

Fährstelle *f* ferrying site, ferry embarkation point.

Fahrstellung *f* traveling position *(Ord)*.

Fahrt *f* ride, run; trip, journey; speed.

Fahrtenschwimmer *m* qualified swimmer *(on basis of time-endurance test)*.

Fahrtliste *f* entraining table.

Fahrtmesser *m* airspeed indicator.

Fahrtrupp *m* boat crew *(Engr)*.

Fahrtruppen *fpl* transportation units *(H-Dr)*.

Fahrweg *m* dirt road.

Fahrwerk *n* landing gear *(Ap)*; running gear, chassis *(MT)*; suspensions and tracks *(Tk)*.

Fahrwerkachse *f* landing-gear axle *(Ap)*.

Fahrwerkrahmen *m* chassis frame *(MT)*.

Fahrwerkstrebe *f* landing-gear strut *(Ap)*.

Fahrwiderstand *m* tractional resistance *(MT)*.

Fahrwind *m* air stream, airflow.

Fahrzeug *n* vehicle; craft.

Fahrzeugüberhang *m* overhang, angle of approach *(MT)*.

Fall *m* drop, fall; case, instance.

Fallbahn *f* bomb trajectory.

Fallbenzintank *m* gravity tank *(MT)*.

Fallbeschleunigung *f* downward acceleration *(Ballistics)*.

Fallbö *f* downdraft *(Met)*.

Fallblockverschluß *m* drop-block type breechblock *(G)*.

Falle *f* trap, decoy; catch *(MG)*.

Fallenachse *f* catch pivot *(MG)*.

Fallgeschwindigkeit *f* velocity of fall *(Ballistics)*.

Fallgesetz *n* law of falling bodies.

Fallhöhe *f* drop, height of drop.

Fallklappe *f* drop *(Tp switchboard)*.

Fallpunkt *m* level point, point of fall *(Ballistics)*.

Fallschirm *m* parachute.
Fallschirmabsprung *m* parachute jump.
Fallschirmabsprungturm *m* parachute tower, controlled tower.
Fallschirmbombe *f* parachute bomb.
Fallschirmgerät *n* parachute equipment.
Fallschirmgewehr *n* parachutist's automatic rifle.
Fallschirmgurt *m* parachute harness.
Fallschirmjäger *m* parachutist.
Fallschirmjäger-Abteilung *f* parachute detachment.
Fallschirmjägerbataillon *n* parachute battalion.
Fallschirmlast *f* delivery unit *(airborne operations)*.
Fallschirmleuchtbombe *f* aircraft parachute flare.
Fallschirmleuchtkugel *f* parachute flare.
Fallschirmleuchtpatrone *f* parachute-flare cartridge *(for Sig pistol)*.
Fallschirmrakete *f* parachute rocket signal.
Fallschirmsack *m* pack assembly, pack *(Prcht)*.
Fallschirmschütze *m* parachutist rifleman.
Fallschirmschützen-Abzeichen *n* parachute badge *(decoration)*.
Fallschirmspringer *m* parachutist.
Fallschirmtruppen *fpl* parachute troops.
Fallschirmturm *m* parachute tower.
Fallstromvergaser *m* downdraft carburetor.
Falltafel *f* bomb trajectory table.
Falltür *f* trapdoor; escape hatch *(Ap)*.
Fallwind *m* katabatic wind *(Met)*.
Fallwinkel *m* angle of fall *(Ballistics)*.
Fallzeit *f* time of fall *(Bombing)*.
Faltboot *n* faltboat, collapsible boat with rubberized-cloth skin.
Familienunterhalt *m* dependency benefits.
Fangleine *f* shroud line *(Prcht)*.
Fangnetz *n* anti-submarine net.
Fangschnur *f* aiguillette, fourragere.
Fangstoß *m* parry.
farbenblind color blind.
Farbentüchtigkeit *f* color vision.
farblos colorless.

Farb-Spritzanlage *f* spray painting unit.
farbtonrichtig orthochromatic.
Faschine *f* fascine.
Faschinenbahn *f* fascine road.
Faschinendamm *m* raised fascine road.
Faser *f* fiber.
Fassung *f* receptacle, socket *(Elec)*; text or wording, version; composure.
Fassungsvermögen *n* volumetric capacity.
fäulnisbekämpfend antiseptic.
Faust *f* fist.
Faustachse *f* Mercedes-type front axle *(MT)*.
Fäustel *n* mallet.
Fausthandschuh *m* mitten.
Faustriemen *m* sword knot.
Faustskizze *f* rough sketch.
F-Boot *n* tank landing craft.
Feder *f* pen; spring; feather.
Federantrieb *m* spring action *(clockwork fuze)*.
Federaufhängung *f* spring suspension *(MT)*.
Federausgleicher *m* spring equilibrator *(G)*.
Federbarometer *n* aneroid barometer.
Federbein *n* shock-absorbing strut *(Ap)*.
Federbock *m* spring hanger *(MT)*.
Federbolzen *m* spring bolt *(MT)*.
Federbund *n* spring clip *(MT)*.
Federeinrichtung *f* spring mechanism *(MG)*.
Federgehänge *n* spring suspension.
Federhand *f* spring bracket *(MT)*.
Federkolben *m* breechblock endpiece *(self-loading pistol)*.
Federkopf *m* follower-spring stud *(self-loading pistol)*.
Federkraft *f* elasticity.
Federlasche *f* shackle, spring shackle *(MT)*.
Federluftdruckmesser *m* aneroid barometer.
Federring *m* lockwasher.
Federteller *m* valve-spring retainer *(Mtr)*.
Federung *f* suspension *(MT)*.
Federvorholer *m* spring counterrecoil mechanism, spring recuperator *(G)*.
Federwolke *f* cirrus cloud.

Fehlbestand *m* shortage, discrepancy *(supplies, etc.)*.

Fehler *m* error; defect; miss.

Fehlerdreieck *n* triangle of error *(Surv)*.

fehlerhaft defective.

Fehlgänger *m* miss.

Fehlgriff *m* blunder.

Fehlleistung *f* malfunction.

fehlschlagen fail.

Fehlschuß *m* miss.

Fehlstart *m* unsuccessful take-off *(Avn)*.

Fehlstelle *f* vacancy *(Adm)*.

Fehltreffer *m* near miss.

Fehlweisung *f* deviation *(Rad)*.

Fehlzerspringer *m* low-order burst, low-order shell *(Am)*.

Fehlzündung *f* backfire *(Mtr)*.

Feigheit *f* cowardice.

Feile *f* file *(tool)*.

Feind *m* enemy.

Feindbeobachtung *f* observation of or by the enemy.

Feindberührung *f* contact with the enemy.

Feindbeschuß *m* enemy fire.

Feindbesetzung *f* occupation by the enemy.

Feinddruck *m* enemy pressure.

Feindeinsicht *f* enemy observation.

Feindeinwirkung *f* enemy action.

Feindesland *n* enemy territory, hostile territory.

Feindflug *m* raid, sortie, combat mission *(Avn)*.

Feindflugausweis *m* special identification card carried on missions during which capture by enemy is likely *(Avn)*.

feindfrei clear of the enemy.

Feindgelände *n* enemy terrain.

Feindnachrichten *fpl* information about the enemy.

Feindnähe *f* closeness to the enemy, nearness to the enemy.

Feindraum *m* enemy zone.

Feindseligkeiten *fpl* hostilities.

Feindsicht *f* enemy observation.

Feindtätigkeit *f* enemy activity.

Feindzusammenstoß *m* collision with the enemy.

Feineinstellung *f* fine tuning *(Rad)*; fine setting, precision adjustment.

Feinhöhenmesser *m* sensitive altimeter *(Ap)*.

Feinkorn *n* fine sight *(R aiming)*; fine grain *(Photo)*.

Feld *n* field *(Top, Elec)*; land *(rifling)*; bay *(Ap)*.

langes Feld chase of gun barrel.

Feldanzug *m* field uniform.

Feldarmee *f* field army.

Feldausbildungsdivision *f* field training division.

Feldausrüstung *f* field equipment.

Feldausstattung *f* field equipment; ammunition reserve.

Feldbäckerei *f* field bakery.

Feldbahn *f* narrow-gage field railway.

Feldbauamt *n* airdrome maintenance office.

Feldbefestigung *f* field fortification.

Feldbischof *m* Chief of Chaplains.

Feldbluse *f* service coat.

feldbrauchbar serviceable for use in the field.

Feldbrunnen *m* field well.

Feldbücherei *f* military field library.

Felddauerlinie *f* permanent field-telephone line.

Felddienst *m* field duty.

felddienstfähig fit for active duty.

Felddienstordnung *f* field service regulations.

Felddienstübung *f* field exercise.

Feldeisenbahn *f* field railway.

Feldeisenbahnbetriebsamt *n* field railway operations office.

Feldeisenbahndirektion *f* field railway command station.

Feldeisenbahner *m* field railway engineer.

Feldeisenbahnmaschinenamt *n* field railway machinery office.

Feldeisenbahnwerkstättenamt *n* field railway workshop office.

Feldelement *n* field cell *(Tp)*.

Felder *npl* lands *(Ord)*; fields *(Top)*.

Feldersatzbataillon *n* replacement training battalion *(assigned to the field forces)*.

Felderscheibe *f* target divided into squares.

Felder und Züge lands and grooves.

Feldfernkabel *n* field trunk wire *(Tp)*.

Feldfernkabeltrupp *m* wire-laying team *(Tp)*.

Feldfernsprecher *m* field telephone; field telephone operator.

Feldflasche *f* canteen *(for water)*.

Feldflughafen *m* field airdrome.

Feldflugplatz *m* advanced airfield.

Feldfunksprecher *m* See **Feldfunksprechgerät.**

Feldfunksprechgerät *n* field radio set.

Feldgeistlicher *m* chaplain.

Feldgendarm *m* military policeman.

Feldgendarmerie *f* military police.

Feldgendarmerievorschrift *f* military police regulations.

Feldgerät *n* field equipment.

Feldgericht *n* provost court, court-martial.

Feldgeschütz *n* field gun.

Feldhandapparat *m* field handset *(Tp).*

Feldhaubitze *f* field howitzer.

Feldheer *n* field forces.

Feldherrnkunst *f* strategy, generalship.

Feldinstandsetzung *f* line maintenance.

Feldjustizamt *n* legal branch of army, corps and division general staffs *(consists of civilian officials).*

Feldkabel *n* field wire *(Tp).*

Feldkabelader *f* field-wire strand *(Tp).*

Feldkabelbau *m* field-wire laying *(Tp).*

Feldkabelleitung *f* field-wire line *(Tp).*

Feldkanone *f* field gun.

Feldkaplan *m* chaplain.

Feldklappenschrank *m* portable switchboard.

Feldkochherd *m* field range *(cooker).*

Feldkochunteroffizier *m* cook *(NCO).*

Feldkommandantur *f* military administration headquarters *(in Com Z and occupied countries).* Compare **Ortskommandantur, Stadtkommandantur.**

Feldküche *f* field kitchen, rolling kitchen.

Feldlaboratorium *n* field laboratory *(Med).*

Feldlager *n* bivouac, encampment.

Feldlazarett *n* surgical hospital.

Feldmarschall *m* Field Marshal *(Ger).*

Feldmeister *m* first sergeant *(Reich Labor Service).*

Feldmeßkästchen *n* field testing set *(Tp).*

Feldmütze *f* garrison cap.

Feldnachrichtenkommandantur *f* field signal command *(signal Hq for an area of occupied territory or in rear area of T of Opns).*

Feldpolizei *f* See **Geheime Feldpolizei.**

Feldportion *f* field ration *(for Pers).*

Feldpost *f* army postal service.

Feldpostamt *n* army post office.

Feldpostbeamter *m* army mail clerk *(Civ official).*

Feldposteinheit *f* army postal unit.

Feldposten *m* outguard sentinel.

Feldpostwesen *n* army postal service.

Feldprediger *m* chaplain.

Feldprüfschrank *m* field testing box *(Tp).*

Feldrain *m* uncultivated strip at edge of field.

Feldration *f* field ration *(for animals).*

Feldschanze *f* field fortification, earthwork.

Feldsicherungskästchen *n* field fuse box *(Tp).*

Feldsonderbataillon *n* field disciplinary battalion.

Feldstraflager *n* field disciplinary camp.

Feldtrage *f* field litter *(Med).*

Feldunterarzt *m* acting medical officer.

Feldverpflegung *f* field messing.

Feldwache *f* outguard.

Feldwagen *m* field wagon.

Feldwebel *m* technical sergeant.

Feldweg *m* cross-country dirt road.

Feldwerkstatt *f* field workshop.

Feldwerkstattzug *m* field workshop platoon.

Feldwetterstelle *f* field weather station.

Feldwetterwarte *f* See **Feldwetterstelle.**

Feldzeugbataillon *n* ordnance battalion.

Feldzeugkommando *n* ordnance command *(one in each Wehrkreis and some in occupied countries).*

Feldzeuglager *n* ordnance depot.

Feldzeugstab *m* ordnance staff.

Feldzug *m* campaign.

Felge *f* felloe, rim.

Felgenband *n* tire flap *(MT).*

Fels *m* rock, cliff.

Felsblock *m* boulder, rock.

Felsenklippe *f* bluff *(Top).*

Fenster *n* sight peephole *(AA sight);* window.

Fepo *f* *See* **Geheime Feldpolizei.**

Ferdinand name of a heavily-armored German self-propelled gun.

Fernantrieb *m* remote drive, remote control.

Fernaufklärer *m* long-range reconnaissance airplane.

Fernaufklärung *f* distant reconnaissance; long-range reconnaissance *(Avn).*

Fernaufklärungsflugboot *n* patrol bomber, long-range reconnaissance flying boat.

Fernaufklärungsflugzeug *n* *See* **Fernaufklärer.**

Fernaufklärungsgruppe *f* air force long-range reconnaissance group *(attached to ground forces and composed of two or more* F-Staffeln).

Fernaufklärungsstaffel *f* long-range reconnaissance squadron attached to army ground units *(abbr.* F-Staffel).

Fernbesprechgerät *n* remote control unit *(Rad).*

Fernbesprechung *f* remote control operation *(Rad).*

Fernbild *n* telephoto.

Fernbomber *m* long-range bomber.

Ferndrucker *m* teletype, teletypewriter, telegraph printer.

Fernempfang *m* long-distance reception *(Rad).*

Fernempfangszone *f* reception zone beyond the skip distance *(Rad).*

Fernerkunder *m* *See* **Fernaufklärer.**

Fernfahrtmesser *m* remote-reading airspeed indicator *(Ap).*

ferngelenkt remote-controlled.

Ferngeschütz *n* *See* **Fernkampfgeschütz.**

Ferngespräch *n* telephone call, telephone conversation.

ferngesteuert remote-controlled.

Fernglas *n* binoculars, field glass.

Fernhörer *m* receiver *(Tp, Rad Tp).*

Fernkabel *n* trunk wire *(Tp).*

Fernkampfartillerie *f* long-range artillery.

Fernkampfflugzeug *n* long-range bombardment airplane.

Fernkampfgeschütz *n* long-range gun.

Fernkompaß *m* remote-reading compass *(Ap).*

Fernkurs *m* correspondence course.

Fernleitung *f* long-distance circuit, interurban line *(Tp).*

Fernlenkung *f* remote control.

Fernlicht *n* bright light *(on auto headlight).*

Fernmeßgerät *n* range finder.

Fernmeldeanlage *f* communication station *(Sig C).*

Fernmesser *m* range finder; rangefinder operator.

fernmündlich by telephone.

Fernrichten des Geschützes remote gun control *(CA, Nav).*

Fernrohr *n* telescope; binoculars *(in this sense, generally* Doppelfernrohr).

Fernrohrarme *mpl* telescope tubes *(BC telescope).*

Fernrohraufnahme *f* telephoto.

Fernrohraufsatz *m* telescopic sight.

fernrohrbesetzt equipped with telescopic sight *(R).*

Fernrohrhals *m* telescope center section.

Fernrohrhülse *f* telescope housing.

Fernrohrkopf *m* telescope head.

Fernrohrkörper *m* telescope tube; body *(of binoculars).*

Fernrohrlager *n* telescope seat.

Fernrohrsteg *m* telescope support.

Fernschreiber *m* teletype, teletypewriter, telegraph printer; teletype operator.

Fernschreibkompanie *f* teletype company, telegraph-printer company.

Fernschreibleitung *f* teletype circuit.

Fernschreibnetz *n* teletype net *(Luftwaffe).*

Fernschreibwagen *m* teletype truck.

Fernsehen *n* television.

Fernsicht *f* visibility.

Fernsprechanschluß *m* telephone connection.

Fernsprechbaukompanie *f* telephone-construction company.

Fernsprechbautrupp *m* telephone-construction crew.

Fernsprechbauwagen *m* telephone-construction truck.

Fernsprechbetriebstrupp *m* telephone-operations team.

Fernsprechbetriebswagen *m* telephone-operations truck.

Fernsprechbetriebszug *m* telephone operating platoon.

Fernsprechdoppelleitung *f* metallic telephone circuit.

Fernsprecher *m* telephone; telephone operator.

Fernsprechfahrzeug *n* telephone-operations vehicle.

Fernsprechgerät *n* telephone equipment.

Fernsprechkompanie *f* telephone-communications company.

Fernsprechkraftwagen *m* telephone motor truck.

Fernsprechleitung *f* telephone line.

Fernsprechnetz *n* wire net *(Tp)*.

Fernsprechrelais *n* telephone relay.

Fernsprechstelle *f* telephone station.

Fernsprechtrupp *m* telephone section.

Fernsprechverkehr *m* telephone traffic.

Fernsprechvermittlung *f* telephone central, switching central.

Fernsprechwagen *m* telephone wagon, telephone truck.

Fernspruch *m* telephone transcription, telephone message.

Fernsteuerung *f* remote control.

Fernthermometer *n* water temperature gage *(MT)*.

Ferntrauung *f* marriage by proxy *(while on active duty)*.

Ferntroß *m* third echelon supply train *(behind the* Mitteltroß).

Fernunterricht *m* instruction by correspondence.

Ferse *f* heel *(Anatomy)*.

"Fertig!" "Ready!" *(Arty)*.

Fertigaufschlagzünder *m* ready-fixed percussion fuze *(Am)*.

Fertigerzeugnis *n* finished product.

Fertigmontage *f* final assembly *(Tech)*.

Fertigung *f* production, manufacture, construction.

Fertigungshalle *f* factory shop.

Fertigungsjahr *n* year of manufacture.

Fertigzünder *m* ready-fixed fuze *(Am)*.

Fessel *f* pastern *(horse)*.

Fesselballon *m* captive balloon.

Fesselgelenk *n* pastern joint *(horse)*.

Fesselkabel *n* ground cable, mooring cable *(Bln)*.

fesseln to contain, to fix, pin down *(Tac)*; to chain, tie up.

Fesselseil *n* ground cable, mooring cable *(Bln)*.

Fesseltau *n* *See* Fesselseil.

Fesselung *f* pinning down, containing *(Tac)*.

Fesselungsvorstoß *m* containing attack, holding attack.

fest firm, solid, steady; locked; fixed, stationary; fastened.

Festantenne *f* fixed antenna.

festfressen, sich to seize, freeze *(piston, etc.)*.

festhalten to contain, hold, immobilize *(Tac)*; to track *(a target)*.

Festhaltevorrichtung *f* locking device *(MG)*.

Festigkeitslehre *f* strength of materials.

Festigkeitsnachweis *m* stress analysis.

Festklemmvorrichtung *f* clamping mechanism *(MG tripod)*.

Festland *n* mainland, continent.

festlegen to refer *(Gunnery)*; to fix; pinpoint, plot, determine; to sense, spot.

Festlegepunkt *m* reference point.

Festlegezahl *f* deflection reading, new reading *(in referring the piece) (Gunnery)*.

festmachen to make fast, secure, tie, moor.

Festnahme *f* arrest, seizure.

Festpunkt *m* control point, reference point.

Festpunktnetz *n* control-point net *(Surv)*.

festschießen seat the base plate by firing *(Mort)*.

Festung *f* fortress, fort.

Festungsartillerie *f* fortress artillery.

Festungsartilleriekommandeur *m* fortress artillery commander.

Festungsbaubataillon *n* fortress construction battalion.

Festungsgraben *m* moat.

Festungsgürtel *m* cordon of forts.

Festungshaft *f* confinement in a fortress.

Festungsingenieur *m* civilian engineer in charge of fortifications.

Festungsinspekteur *m* superintendent of fortress engineering service *(superior of* Festungspionierkommandeur).

Festungskrieg *m* siege warfare.

Festungsnachrichtenkommandantur *f* fortress signal command *(attached to staff of Ft Engr units)*.

Festungspionier *m* fortress engineer.

Festungspionierfeldwebel *m* technical sergeant *(Ft Engr)*.

Festungspionierkommandeur *m* fortress engineer brigade commander.

Fett *n* grease.

Fettpresse *f* grease gun.

Fettüberzug *m* grease coating.

Feuchtigkeit *f* humidity, moisture, dampness.

Feuchtigkeitsgehalt *m* moisture content, humidity *(Met)*.

Feuchtigkeitsmesser *m* hygrometer.

Feuchtigkeitsschreiber *m* hygrograph *(Met)*.

Feuer *n* fire.

unter Feuer nehmen to shell, to strafe.

Feuerabriegelung *f* box barrage.

Feuerabriegelung schießen to box in, to lay down a box barrage.

Feuerart *f* method of fire.

Feuerauftrag *m* fire mission *(Arty)*.

Feuerbefehl *m* fire order, fire command.

Feuerbegriffe *mpl* fire classification *(Arty)*.

Feuerbeobachtung *f* observation of fire *(Gunnery)*.

Feuerbereich *m* zone of fire.

feuerbereit in firing position; uncoupled, unlimbered, ready for action *(Arty)*.

Feuerdämpfer *m* flash hider.

Feuerdichte *f* density of fire.

Feuereinheit *f* fire unit *(Arty)*.

Feuereinheit der Artillerie basic tactical unit of the artillery.

Feuer einstellen to cease fire.

Feuer eröffnen to open fire.

Feuereröffnung *f* commencement of fire, opening of fire.

feuerfest fireproof.

Feuerformen *fpl* types of fire, forms of fire *(Arty, MG)*.

"Feuer frei!" "Fire!"

Feuergarbe *f* sheaf of fire, cone of dispersion, cone of fire.

feuergefährlich inflammable.

Feuergefecht *n* fire fight, fire duel.

Feuergeschwindigkeit *f* rate of fire *(MG)*.

Feuerhöhe *f* height of muzzle.

Feuer in der oberen Winkelgruppe high-angle fire.

Feuer in der unteren Winkelgruppe low-angle fire.

Feuerkampf *m* fire fight, fire duel, weapons duel.

Feuerkette *f* line of skirmishers.

Feuerkommando *n* firing command *(Arty)*.

Feuerkraft *f* fire power.

Feuer kreuzen to cross fire.

Feuerleitgerät *n* fire-control equipment, ballistic director *(Arty)*.

Feuerleitung *f* fire direction, fire control.

Feuerleitungsnetz *n* fire control net, fire direction net *(Arty)*.

Feuerleitungsplan *m* fire-control map *(Arty)*.

Feuerleitungsstand *m* fire-direction center.

Feuerleitungsstelle *f* See **Feuerleitungsstand**.

Feuerlinie *f* firing line.

Feuerlöscher *m* fire extinguisher.

Feuerlöschordnung *f* fire plan *(fire prevention measure)*.

Feueröffnung *f* commencement of firing.

Feuerpatsche *f* fire swatter *(used in fire fighting)*.

Feuerpause *f* cessation of fire *(Arty)*.

"Feuerpause!" "Cease firing!"

Feuerplan *m* plan of fire *(Tac)*.

Feuerplattform *f* gun platform.

Feuerregelung *f* fire control, conduct of fire.

Feuerriegel *m* box barrage.

Feuersäule *f* column of flames.

Feuerschiff *n* lightship.

Feuerschlag *m* sudden concentration *(Arty)*.

Feuerschutz *m* covering fire, protective fire; fire support, coverage by supporting fire; artillery protection.

Feuerschütze *m* aerial gunner.

Feuerschutzpolizei *f* fire protection police.

feuersicher fireproof.

Feuersignal *n* fire call.

Feuersperre *f* barrage.

Feuerspritze *f* fire engine.

Feuerspucker *m* Spitfire *(slang)*.

Feuerstärke *f* density of fire.

Feuersteigerung *f* increased rate of fire, intensification of fire.

Feuerstellung *f* firing position, field emplacement, gun position.

in Feuerstellung in abatage, in firing position.

verdeckte Feuerstellung position defilade.

Feuerstoß *m* burst *(MG)*.

Feuerstrahl *m* jet of liquid fire; gun flash.

Feuertaufe *f* baptism of fire.

Feuerüberfall *m* sudden concentration *(Arty)*; surprise fire *(Arty, MG)*.

Feuerüberlegenheit *f* fire superiority.

Feuer und Bewegung fire and movement, fire and maneuver.

Feuerunterstützung *f* fire support.

Feuervereinigung *f* concentration of fire *(Arty)*.

Feuervereinigungswinkel *m* deflection difference *(Btry firing)*.

Feuerverlegen *n* shift of fire *(Arty)*.

Feuer verlegen to shift fire.

Feuerverteilung *f* fire distribution *(Arty, MG)*.

Feuerverteilungswinkel *m* divergence difference *(Btry firing)*.

Feuervorbereitung *f* fire preparation *(Tac)*.

Feuervorhang *m* fire curtain, curtain of fire.

Feuer vorverlegen to lift fire, to advance fire *(Arty)*.

Feuerwaffe *f* firearm.

Feuerwalze *f* rolling barrage.

Feuerwand *f* fire curtain, curtain of fire.

Feuerwehr *f* fire department.

Feuerwerker *m* technical sergeant *(Ord)*.

Feuerwerkskörper *m* pyrotechnic composition *(Am)*.

Feuerwirkung *f* effect of fire *(Gunnery)*.

Feuerzeug *n* cigarette lighter.

Feuerzone *f* zone of fire.

Feuerzucht *f* fire discipline.

F-Haube *f* cowling *(Ap)*.

Fieber *n* fever.

Fieseler-Storch *m* a German liaison airplane.

Filmkammer *f* roll-film camera.

Filmkassette *f* film cartridge, film-pack adapter *(Photo)*.

Filmstreifen *m* film strip.

Filmvorführapparat *m* motion-picture projector.

Filterbüchse *f* gas mask canister.

Filtereinsatz *m* filter element *(gas mask)*.

Filtergehäuse *n* filter container *(gas mask)*.

Filterkolonne *f* water purification column.

Filterwechsel *m* filter replacement *(gas mask)*.

Filz *m* felt.

Filzstiefel *m* felt boot.

Fingerabdruck *m* fingerprint.

Finnenzelt *n* plywood shelter *(winter operations)*.

Finsternis *f* darkness.

Firnis *m* varnish.

Fischgrätenhindernis *n* fishbone obstacle pattern.

Fla *f* antiaircraft defense *(originally abbr. of Flugabwehr; now used as independent word)*. Compare **Flak.**

Flabataillon *n* antiaircraft battalion.

flach flat.

Flachbahngeschütz *n* flat-trajectory gun.

Flachbettfelge *f* flat-base rim *(MT)*.

Fläche *f* wing *(Ap)*; surface, area.

flache Böschung gentle slope.

Flächenausgleich *m* aerodynamic balance *(Ap)*.

Flächenbelastung *f* wing loading.

Flächenbrand *m* area conflagration *(Bombing)*.

Flächendrahthindernis *n* multiple-belt entanglement.

Flächenfeuer *n* area fire, zone fire.

Flächeninhalt *m* area.

Flächenmeßplan *m* plotting board *(FR)*.

Flächenschießen *n* area fire, zone fire.

flächentreue Projektion equal area projection *(mapping)*.

Flächenziel *n* area target.

Flachfeuer *n* flat fire, flat trajectory fire.

Flachfeuergeschütz *n* flat-trajectory gun.

Flachkeilverschluß *m* sliding square-wedge breechblock *(G)*.

Flachlasche *f* butt strap.

Flachmeißel *m* flat chisel.

Flachtrudeln *n* flat spin *(Avn)*.

Flachzange f flat-jawed pliers.

Flackertaste f flicker-signal calling key *(Tp)*.

Fladdermine f land mine.

Fla-Einheit f antiaircraft machinegun unit.

Flagge f flag.

Flaggentruppen fpl units represented by flags *(in maneuvers)*.

Flaggentuch n bunting.

Flaggoffizier m flag officer *(Nav)*.

Flaggschiff n flagship.

Flak f antiaircraft gun, antiaircraft artillery *(originally abbr. of Flugabwehrkanone; now used as independent word). Compare* **Fla.**

Flakabteilung f antiaircraft artillery battalion.

Flakabwehr f antiaircraft defense.

Flakalarm m air warning for antiaircraft artillery units.

Flakartillerie f antiaircraft artillery.

Flakbatterie f antiaircraft battery.

Flakbedienung f antiaircraft gun crew.

Flakbrigade f antiaircraft brigade *(sometimes known as* Flakdivision).

Flakdivision f antiaircraft artillery "division" *(contains two to five* Flakregimenter). *See also* **Flakbrigade.**

Flakfeuer n antiaircraft fire.

Flakgeschütz n antiaircraft gun.

Flakgranate f antiaircraft shell.

Flakgruppe f antiaircraft artillery group *(for the defense of an air district)*.

Flakgürtel m cordon of antiaircraft fire.

Flakhelferin f antiaircraft artillery woman auxiliary.

Flak-Kampfgruppe f antiaircraft combat group.

Flakkommandeur m antiaircraft artillery commander.

Höherer Flakkommandeur antiaircraft artillery commander of a *Luftgau*.

Flakkommandogerät n antiaircraft director.

Flakkorps n antiaircraft artillery corps *(contains from two to four* Flakdivisionen *or two to three* Flakbrigaden).

Flakkreuzer m antiaircraft cruiser.

Flakmaschinengewehr n antiaircraft machine gun.

Flakmeßgerät n plane spotter and range finder *(AAA)*.

Flakmunition f ammunition for antiaircraft weapons.

Fla-Kompanie f antiaircraft company.

Flakregiment n antiaircraft regiment.

Flakscheinwerfer m antiaircraft searchlight.

Flakschießen n antiaircraft fire.

Flakschießlehre f theory of antiaircraft fire.

Flakschutz m antiaircraft-artillery protection.

Flaksperre f antiaircraft barrage, curtain of antiaircraft fire.

Flakstellung f antiaircraft gun emplacement.

Flaksturmabzeichen n antiaircraft-artillery assault badge *(decoration)*.

Flaktreffer m hit by antiaircraft fire, antiaircraft hit.

Flaktruppe f antiaircraft artillery *(as a branch of the Army)*.

Flakuntergruppe f subdivision of a *Flakgruppe*.

Flakvierling m four-barreled antiaircraft gun.

Flakvisier n antiaircraft gun sight.

Fla-Maschinengewehr n antiaircraft machine gun.

Fla-Maschinenkanone f automatic antiaircraft gun.

Flammendämpfer m flash hider *(Ord)*.

Flammenverzehrer m flame dampener exhaust stack *(Ap)*.

Flamm(en)öl n flame thrower fuel.

Flammenstrahl m jet of liquid fire.

Flammenwerfer m flame thrower.

Flammenwerfer-Füllwagen m recharging trailer for flame throwers.

Flammenwerferpanzerwagen m flame-throwing tank.

Flammenwerferschutzanzug m flame-thrower operator's protective clothing.

Flandernzaun m double-apron entanglement, double-apron fence.

Flanke f flank.

Flankenangriff m flank attack.

Flankenbewegung f flanking movement.

Flankeneinbruch *m*   flanking penetration.

Flankenfeuer *n*   flanking fire, enfilade fire.

Flankenmarsch *m*   flanking march.

Flankenschutz *m*   flank protection.

Flankensicherung *f*   flank security.

Flankenstellung *f*   flanking position.

flankieren   to flank, outflank.

Flankierungsdurchbruch *m*   flanking break-through.

Flansch *m*   flange.

Flaschenhals *m*   bottleneck.

Flaschenzug *m*   block and tackle.

Flata *m*   flame-thrower tank *(probably abbr. of* Flammenwerfertank).

Flattermine *f*   *See* **Fladdermine.**

Flattern *n*   shimmying *(MT)*.

Fla-Waffe *f*   antiaircraft weapon.

Flechtwerk *n*   brushwork, brushwood revetment.

Fleckfieber *n*   typhus.

Fleischbeschau *m*   meat inspection.

Fleischer *m*   butcher.

Fleischhackmaschine *f*   meat grinder.

Fleischkonserve *f*   canned meat.

Flettner-Seitenruder *n*   servo rudder *(Ap)*.

fliegen   to fly.

fliegendes Personal   flying personnel.

Flieger *m*   private *(Luftwaffe)*; pilot, flier; airplane *(as seen from ground)*.

Fliegeralarm *m*   air alert warning, air raid warning.

Fliegerabwehr *f*   antiaircraft defense.

Fliegerabzeichen *n*   aviation badge.

Fliegerangriff *m*   air attack, air raid.

Fliegerarzt *m*   flight surgeon.

Fliegerausbildungsregiment *n*   air force preflight training regiment.

Fliegerbenzin *n*   aviation gasoline.

Fliegerbluse *f*   flight blouse, pilot's blouse.

Fliegerbombe *f*   aircraft bomb.

Fliegerdeckung *f*   cover from air observation or attack.

Fliegerdivision *f*   airborne division, parachute division.

Fliegerei *f*   aviation.

Fliegerfilz *m*   grenades ejected from airplanes into the path of attacking fighters *(slang)*.

Fliegerformation *f*   formation of airplanes.

Fliegerführer *m*   air force commander *(commander of a* Luftflotte *or of an area of air operations)*.

Fliegergasbombe *f*   chemical bomb *(Avn)*.

Fliegergruppe *f*   group *(Avn)*.

Fliegerhandkammer *f*   aerial hand camera.

Fliegerhaube *f*   helmet *(Avn)*.

Fliegerheld *m*   ace.

Fliegerhilfe *f*   aviation support.

Fliegerhorizont *m*   artificial horizon.

Fliegerhorst *m*   airdrome, air base airdrome.

Fliegerhorstkommandant *m*   air base commander.

Fliegerhorstkompanie *f*   airdrome protection company.

Fliegerkammer *f*   aircraft camera, aerial camera.

Fliegerkarte *f*   air map, flight map, pilot chart.

Fliegerkorps *n*   air force corps *(subordinate operational command of a* Luftflotte).

Fliegerkräfte *fpl*   air forces.

Fliegerkraftstoff *m*   aviation fuel.

Fliegerkrankheit *f*   fliers' sickness *(complex of disorders affecting flying* Pers; *not to be confused with* Höhenkrankheit).

Fliegerleuchtpistole *f*   aircraft signal pistol.

Fliegermarschbreite *f*   dispersed formation in width *(AA security)*.

Fliegermarschtiefe *f*   dispersed formation in depth *(AA security)*.

Fliegermaske *f*   camouflage net *(AA defense)*.

Fliegermütze *f*   pilot's garrison cap.

Fliegeroffizier *m*   flying officer.

Fliegerschule *f*   flying school.

Fliegerschule für technische Ausbildung   ground school *(Avn)*.

Fliegerschulung *f*   pilot training *(Avn)*.

Fliegerschutz *m*   antiaircraft defense.

Fliegerschutzanzug *m*   flying suit.

Fliegerschütze *m*   aerial gunner.

Fliegerschutzgraben *m*   slit trench *(AA security)*.

Fliegersirene *f*   air raid siren.

Fliegersoldat *m*   enlisted man *(Luftwaffe)*.

Fliegertätigkeit *f*   air activity.

Fliegertauglichkeit *f*   fitness for flying.

fliegertechnisches Personal ground crew *(Avn)*.

Fliegertruppe *f* flying and maintenance personnel of the *Luftwaffe*.

Fliegertuch *n* ground panel, marking panel.

Fliegerunterstützung *f* aviation support, air support.

Fliegerverband *m* formation of airplanes, air task force.

Fliegerverbindungsoffizier *m* air support officer *(air force liaison officer between* Luftwaffe *and* Army; *abbr.* Flivo).

Fliegervisier *n* antiaircraft sight.

Fliegervisiereinrichtung *f* antiaircraft sight assembly, aircraft gun sights.

Fliegerwaffenpersonal *n* aircraft armament personnel.

Fliegerwarnung *f* aircraft warning, air raid alarm.

Fliegerwetter *n* good flying weather; bad flying weather *(ironic)*.

Fliegerzeugnis *n* pilot's rating, pilot's certificate.

Fliegerzulage *f* aviation pay, flight pay, flying pay.

Fliehbacke *f* centrifugal arming device *(fuze)*.

Fliehbackenfeder *f* spring of centrifugal arming device *(fuze)*.

Fliehbolzen *m* centrifugal bolt *(fuze)*.

fliehen flee, escape.

Fliehgewicht *n* flyweight *(engine governor)*.

Fliehkraftantrieb *m* centrifugal action *(fuze)*.

Fliehkraftregler *m* centrifugal governor *(Mtr)*.

Fliehkraftzünder *m* centrifugal fuze.

Fließrichtung *f* direction of flow.

Flinte *f* shotgun.

Flivo *m* *See* **Fliegerverbindungsoffizier.**

Floß *n* float, raft.

Floßbrücke *f* floating bridge.

Flosse *f* fin *(Ap)*.

Flossenstummel *m* inboard stabilizing float *(seaplane)*.

Floßsack *m* pneumatic float, pneumatic ponton, pneumatic boat.

Floßsacksteg *m* pneumatic-boat footbridge.

Flotille *f* flotilla.

Flotte *f* fleet *(Nav)*. *See also* **Luftflotte.**

Flottenchef *m* Commander-in-Chief of a fleet *(Nav)*. *See also* **Luftflottenchef.**

Flotteneinheit *f* naval unit.

Flottenstützpunkt *m* naval base.

flottmachen to free *(stuck or stalled vehicle)*; to float *(a grounded vessel)*.

Flucht *f* flight, escape.

flüchten flee, escape.

flüchtig hasty *(Ft)*; nonpersistent *(CWS)*; fleeting; volatile.

flüchtige Feldbefestigung hasty field fortification.

flüchtiger Kampfstoff nonpersistent chemical agent.

Flüchtigkeit *f* volatility *(CWS)*.

Fluchtlinie *f* directional traverse.

Flüchtling *m* refugee.

Fluchtstab *m* range pole *(Surv)*.

Fluchtversuch *m* attempt to escape.

Flug *m* flight, flying. *See also terms under* **Flieger** *and* **Luft.**

Flugabwehr *f* antiaircraft defense.

Flugabwehrbezirk *m* air defense region.

Flugabwehrführer *m* antiaircraft commander.

Flugabwehrgeschütz *n* antiaircraft gun.

Flugabwehrkanone *f* antiaircraft gun *(abbr.* Flak).

Flugabwehrmaschinengewehr *n* antiaircraft machine gun.

Flugabwehrmaschinenkanone *f* automatic antiaircraft gun.

Flugabwehrmaschinenwaffen *fpl* automatic antiaircraft weapons.

Fluganwärterkompanie *f* pool company for pilot candidates *(waiting for assignment to a pilot school)*.

Flugbahn *f* trajectory.

Flugbahnaufriß *m* *See* **Flugbahnbild.**

Flugbahnbild *n* trajectory diagram.

Flugbahngrundriß *m* *See* **Flugbahnbild.**

Flugbereich *m* range, maximum range *(Ap)*.

flugbereit "on the hangar line" *(after servicing)*.

Flugbereitschaft *f* ground readiness *(Avn)*.

Flugbesprechung *f* orders conference, "briefing" *(Avn)*.

Flugbetrieb *m* airdrome traffic, airdrome activities, routine flying operations.

Flugbetriebsstoffkolonne *f* aviation gasoline, oil and lubricants column.

Flugblatt *n* propaganda leaflet.

Flugboot *n* flying boat.

Flugbuch *n* flight log.

Flugdauer *f* endurance, duration of flight *(Avn)*.

Flugdeck *n* landing deck, flight deck *(aircraft carrier)*.

Flugebene *f* slant plane determined by lines of present and future position *(AA gunnery)*.

Flügel *m* wing *(Ap, Tac)*; fin *(Mort shell, R grenade, bomb)*; vane *(Cml shell, bomb)*; propeller blade.

Flügelangriff *m* frontal attack directed obliquely against one wing.

Flügelanordnung *f* wing setting *(Ap)*.

Flügelblech *n* stabilizing fin (Mort Am).

Flügeleinstellwinkel *m* angle of wing setting *(Ap)*.

Flügeleinteilung *f* classification of wing parts *(Ap)*.

Flügeleintrittskante *f* leading edge *(Ap)*.

Flügelende *n* wing tip.

Flügelgeschütz *n* outside or end gun of a battery.

Flügelhaut *f* wing skin.

Flügelholm *m* wing spar.

Flügelinhalt *m* wing area.

Flügelkanone *f* wing-mounted cannon.

Flügelkolben *m* pump vane.

flügellastig wingheavy.

Flügelleuchtpatrone *f* wing-tip flare.

Flügelmann *m* flank man *(drill)*.

Flügelmann am Drehpunkt fixed pivot, pivot man *(drill)*.

Flügel-Mittelstück *n* wing center section *(Ap)*.

Flügelmutter *f* wing nut.

Flügelnase *f* leading edge *(Ap)*.

Flügelprofil *n* wing profile.

Flügelrippe *f* wing rib.

Flügelschaft *m* fin shaft *(Mort shell)*.

Flügelschiene *f* wing rail *(RR)*.

Flügelschnitt *m* wing section *(Ap)*.

Flügelschraube *f* thumbscrew.

Flügelsehne *f* wing chord.

Flügelsignal *n* wing signal.

Flügelspannweite *f* wing span.

Flügelspitzenkurve *f* ninety-degree turn *(Avn)*.

Flügelstiel *m* interplane strut.

Flügelstrebe *f* wing strut.

Flügelstreckung *f* aspect ratio.

Flügeltiefe *f* depth of wing profile.

Flügelverspannung *f* wing bracing.

Flügelverstrebung *f* wing strut system.

Flügelvorderkante *f* leading edge.

flügelweise in width, in line.

flügelweise Aufstellung disposition in width *(Tac)*.

Flügelwurzel *f* wing root *(Ap)*

Flügelzelle *f* cell, cellule *(Ap)*.

Flugfigur *f* flight maneuver.

Flugform *f* flight formation.

Fluggast *m* airplane passenger.

Fluggerät *n* aircraft instruments.

Fluggeschwindigkeit *f* flying speed.

Fluggewicht *n* gross weight *(Ap)*.

Flughafen *m* airport, airdrome.

Flughafenbautrupp *m* airdrome construction detachment.

Flughafengrenze *f* airdrome boundary.

Flughöhe *f* altitude *(Avn)*; ordinate of trajectory, vertical height *(Ballistics)*.

höchste Flughöhe absolute ceiling *(Avn)*.

Flughöhe über dem Erdboden absolute altitude *(Avn)*.

flugklar airworthy, capable of flying; cleared for take-off.

Fluglage *f* attitude, attitude of flight *(Avn)*.

Fluglehre *f* theory of flight.

Fluglehrer *m* flight instructor.

Flugleistung *f* flight performance *(Ap)*.

Fluglinie *f* flight line.

Flugmeldedienst *m* aircraft warning service.

Flugmeldekommando *n* information center *(AWS, Z of I)*.

Flugmeldenetz *n* aircraft warning net.

Flugmeldeposten *m* antiaircraft lookout, air guard observer *(AWS)*.

Flugmelderose *f* orientation card *(AWS)*; orientation clock *(to indicate target's direction of approach)* *(AAA)*.

Flugmeldezentrale *f* information center *(AWS, T of Opns)*.

Flugmeldung *f* flight report *(Avn)*; report of approaching aircraft *(AWS)*.

Flugmotor *m* aircraft engine.

Flugneigungswinkel *m* angle of dive *(AA gunnery)*.

Flugordnung *f* flight formation.

Flugpeildienst *m* airways navigation service.

Flugplatz *m* airfield, airdrome.

Flugplatzanlagen *fpl* airdrome installations.

Flugplatzbefeuerung *f* airdrome lighting.

Flugplatzfeld *n* landing field.

Flugplatzzone *f* control zone *(Adrm)*.

Flugrichtung *f* direction of flight, course *(Avn)*.

Flugrichtungspfeil *m* path-of-flight pointer *(reflector sight)*.

Flugschüler *m* pilot trainee.

Flugsicherheit *f* flying safety *(Avn)*.

Flugsicherung *f* air-traffic safety control.

Flugsicherungsbereich *m* air-traffic control area.

Flugsicherungsdienst *m* air-traffic control service.

Flugsicherungshauptstelle *f* air-traffic control station.

Flugsicherungsschiff *n* air-traffic safety ship *(vessel employed as radio aid for air navigation and in aircraft rescue service)*.

Flugstrecke *f* airway, flight route, flight line, leg of a flight.

Flugstreckenfeuer *n* airway beacon, course light.

Flugstreckenkarte *f* strip map, air navigation map.

Flugstützpunkt *m* air base.

Flugtagebuch *n* flight log.

flugtechnisch pertaining to aeronautical technology or technique of flying.

Flugtorpedoboot *n* torpedo-carrying flying boat.

flugtüchtig airworthy, capable of flying.

Flugwache *f* observation post *(AWS, Z of I)*.

Flugwachkommando *n* filter center *(AWS, Z of I)*.

Flugweg *m* airway, course, path of flight.

Flugwegbestimmung *f* course determination *(Air Navigation)*.

Flugweite *f* range of flight, flying distance.

Flugwesen *n* aviation.

Flugwetter *n* (good) flying weather.

Flugwetterdienst *m* aviation weather reporting service.

Flugwetterwarte *f* aviation weather station.

Flugwinkel *m* angle of approach *(AAA)*.

Flugwinkel im Abschußpunkt angle of approach at instant of firing. *(AAA)*.

Flugwinkel im Meßpunkt angle of approach at instant of range determination. *(AAA)*.

Flugwinkel im Treffpunkt angle of approach at future position. *(AAA)*.

Flugwissenschaft *f* aeronautics.

Flugzeit *f* flying time, endurance *(Ap)*; time of flight *(of projectile)*.

Flugzeitkurve *f* time-of-flight curve *(imaginary curve indicating different points of burst at constant time setting with varying elevation)*.

Flugzeitsekunden *fpl* time of flight in seconds *(Ballistics)*.

Flugzeug *n* airplane, aircraft.

Flugzeugabwehrscheinwerfer *m* antiaircraft searchlight.

Flugzeugachse *f* axis of an aircraft.

Flugzeugbaumuster *n* airplane model.

Flugzeugbein *n* shock strut *(Ap)*.

Flugzeugbesatzung *f* air crew.

Flugzeugbewaffnung *f* airplane armament.

Flugzeug-Flügelkanone *f* wing-mounted cannon *(Ap)*.

Flugzeugführer *m* pilot.

zweiter Flugzeugführer co-pilot.

Flugzeugführerschein *m* pilot's certificate.

Flugzeugführerschule *f* pilot school.

Flugzeuggerippe *n* airframe.

Flugzeuggeschwindigkeitslineal *n* airplane speed slide rule *(AAA)*.

Flugzeughalle *f* hangar.

Flugzeugkanone *f* aircraft cannon, aircraft automatic gun.

Flugzeugmechaniker *m* air mechanic.

Flugzeugmetaller *m* metalsmith *(Avn)*.

Flugzeug-M.G.-Steuerung *f* impulse generator mechanism *(Ap MG)*.

Flugzeugmotor *m* aircraft engine.

Flugzeugmutterschiff *n* seaplane tender.

Flugzeugortung *f* air navigation.

Flugzeugrumpf *m* fuselage.

Flugzeugrüstpersonal *n* aircraft armorer-artificers.

Flugzeugschlepp *m* airplane towing.

Flugzeugschleuder *f* catapult *(Avn)*.

Flugzeugschleuderschiff *n* seaplane tender with catapult facilities.

Flugzeug-Schwerölmotor *m* Diesel-type aircraft engine.

Flugzeugsteuerung *f* airplane controls, flight control.

Flugzeugtender *m* seaplane tender.

Flugzeugtorpedo *n* aerial torpedo.

Flugzeugträger *m* aircraft carrier.

Flugzeugwart *m* airplane mechanic.

Flugzeug zu Flugzeug air-air *(Sig Com)*.

Flugziel *n* air target, air objective.

Flugzielbeschuß *m* firing at air target.

Flugzustand *m* attitude, attitude of flight *(Avn)*.

Fluoreszenzfarbe *f* luminous paint.

Fluß *m* river.

Flußbreitenmesser *m* river-width measuring instrument.

Flußerkundung *f* river reconnaissance.

Flüssigkeit *f* liquid.

Flüssigkeitsausgleicher *m* fluid equalizer *(recoil mechanism)*.

flüssigkeitsgekühlt liquid-cooled.

Flüssigkeitsgetriebe *n* fluid drive *(MT)*.

Flüssigkeitskühlung *f* liquid cooling *(Mtr)*.

Flüssigkeitsrücklaufbremse *f* hydraulic recoil brake *(G)*.

Flüssigkeitsstoßdämpfer *m* hydraulic shock absorber *(MT)*.

Flüssigkeitszerstäuber *m* decontamination sprayer.

Flußkabel *n* marine cable, underwater cable *(Tp)*.

Flußpolizei *f* river police.

Flußübergang *m* river crossing, ford.

Flutlicht *n* floodlight.

Folgeladung *f* induced-detonation charge.

Folgezeiger *m* pointer, indicator *(follow-the-pointer mechanism in data transmission system)*.

Folgezeigerantrieb *m* follow-the-pointer drive *(AAA)*.

Folgezeigereinrichtung *f* follow-the-pointer mechanism *(AAA)*.

Folgezeigerempfänger *m* fuze indi-

cator *(follow-the-pointer-type fuze setter)*.

Förderbahn *f* miners' tramway.

Formel *f* formula.

Formgebung *f* lofting *(Ap)*.

Formular *n* form, blank.

Formveränderung *f* evolution *(Tac)*.

Formwert *m* coefficient of form *(Ballistics)*.

Forstamt *n* forest service office.

Försterei *f* forest service station.

Fortbewegung *f* propulsion, movement.

Fortbildung *f* advanced training.

Fortschritt *m* effective pitch *(propeller)*; progress.

Fracht *f* freight.

Frachtbrief *m* bill of lading.

Frachtdampfer *m* freighter.

Frachtenbeförderung *f* transportation of freight.

Frachter *m* freighter.

Frachtflugzeug *n* cargo-transport plane.

Fragebogen *m* questionnaire.

"fraglich" "doubtful" *(uncertain regarding effect of a projectile)*.

Fräsmaschine *f* milling machine.

Fregattenkapitän *m* commander *(Nav)*.

Freibord *m* freeboard.

Freigabe *f* clearance.

Freihandnivellierinstrument *n* hand level *(Surv)*.

Freiheitsstrafe *f* sentence of confinement.

Freiherr *m* baron.

Freilassung *f* release *(of prisoner)*.

Freilassung auf Ehrenwort release on parole.

Freilauf *m* freewheeling *(MT)*.

Freileitung *f* overhead line *(Tp)*.

Freischärler *m* guerrilla.

Freischwimmer *m* qualified swimmer. *See also* **Fahrtenschwimmer**.

Freischwimmertrupp *m* swimmer detail *(for swimming horses across a stream)*.

freitragend cantilever.

Freiübung *f* setting-up exercise.

freiwillig voluntary, volunteer.

sich freiwillig melden to volunteer, enlist, enroll.

Freiwilliger *m* volunteer.

Freiwilligenlegion *f* legion composed of non-German volunteers.

Freizeichen *n* dial hum *(Tp)*.

Fremdpeilung *f* direction finding by means of bearings radioed to the aircraft by surface direction-finder stations.

Frequenz *f* frequency.

Frequenzangabe *f* frequency designation *(Rad)*.

Frequenzband *n* frequency band *(Rad)*.

Frequenzbereich *m* frequency range *(Rad)*.

Frequenzeinstellung *f* tuning control *(Rad)*.

Frequenzkorrektur *f* calibration adjustment *(Rad)*.

Frequenzmesser *m* frequency meter *(Rad)*.

Frequenzmodulation *f* frequency modulation *(Rad)*.

Freßbeutel *m* feed bag.

Friede *m* peace.

Friedensstärke *f* peace strength.

Friedensstärkenachweisung *f* table of organization *(peacetime)*.

Friedensverhandlungen *fpl* peace negotiations.

Friedhof *m* cemetery.

Front *f* front *(Mil, Met)*.

innere Front home front.

Frontabschnitt *m* front sector.

Frontalangriff *m* frontal attack.

Frontalfeuer *n* frontal fire.

Frontantrieb *m* front-wheel drive *(MT)*.

Frontbogen *m* front arc, curved front line.

Frontdienst *m* service at the front.

Fronteinsatz *m* commitment to the front, employment at the front.

Frontensegeln *n* frontal soaring *(glider)*.

Frontflugspange *f* combat aviation clasp *(decoration)*.

Frontflugzeug *n* combat airplane.

Frontkämpfer *m* fighter at the front; combatant; veteran.

Frontkämpferkreuz *n* veterans cross *(decoration awarded to all veterans of World War 1)*.

Frontingenieur *m* engineer of the Todt Organization *(Ft)*.

Frontleitstelle *f* forward directing center for personnel in transit.

Front-MG. *n* bow machine gun *(Tk)*.

Frontmitte *f* center of the front *(Tac)*.

Frontoffizier *m* line officer.

Frontpanzer *m* front armor *(Tk)*.

Frontsammelstelle *f* front collecting point *(for reception of trained replacements and distribution to units)*.

Frontsoldat *m* soldier at the front, combatant.

Frontstalag *n* forward prisoner of war camp. See also **Stalag**.

Fronturlaub *m* furlough from the combat zone.

Frontverband *m* combat element *(Tac)*; support force, formation of support aircraft *(Avn)*.

Frontvorsprung *m* salient *(Tac)*.

Frontzeitung *f* army newspaper in combat zone.

Frontzulage *f* combat pay *(additional pay for personnel in the combat zone)*.

Frostgraupeln *pl* sleet.

Frostschutzmittel *n* antifreeze solution.

Frostschutzsalbe *f* antifrostbite ointment.

frostsicher nonfreezable, frost-resistant.

Frühzerspringer *m* premature burst *(Arty)*.

Frühzündung *f* preignition *(Mtr)*.

F-Staffel *f* See **Fernaufklärungsstaffel**.

F-Stoff *m* titanium tetrachloride *(a smoke agent) (CWS)*.

F.T.-Anlage *f* radio installation, radio equipment, radio set *(Ap)*.

F.T.-Gerät *n* radiotelegraph set, radio equipment, radio set *(Ap)*.

F.T.-Haube *f* helmet with built-in headset and throat-type microphone.

F.T.-Verbindung *f* radiotelegraph communication.

Fuchsloch *n* niche *(Ft)* *(Note:* fox hole = *Schützenloch)*.

Fugasse *f* fougasse.

Fühlerlehre *f* thickness gage.

Fühlung *f* contact *(Tac)*.

Fühlung aufnehmen to make contact *(with friendly or enemy troops)*.

Fühlunghalten *n* contact mission *(Avn)*.

Fühlunghalter *m* airplane maintaining contact with enemy force *(Avn, Nav)*.

Fühlungnahme *f* establishment of contact *(Tac)*.

führen to lead, direct, manage; to drive; to guide; to pilot.

Führer *m* leader; commander, commanding officer; chief; guide; driver; pilot.

Führeranwärter *m* SS officer candidate.

Führerbesprechung *f* conference.

Führer der Luft air liaison officer with the Navy.

Führereigenschaft *f* quality(-ies) of leadership.

Führerflugzeug *n* commander's airplane, leading airplane, command airplane.

Führergehilfe *m* assistant chief of staff.

Führergondel *f* control car *(Ash)*.

Führerhauptquartier *n* Hitler's headquarters in the field.

Führerkanzel *f* pilot's cockpit, control cabin *(Ap)*.

Führerkompaß *m* pilot's compass *(Ap)*.

Führerkurs *m* officer training course.

Führerraum *m* control cabin, pilot's compartment, pilot's cockpit *(Ap)*.

Führerschaft *f* leadership; group of leaders.

Führerschein *m* operator's permit, driver's permit *(MT)*.

Führersitz *m* cockpit; pilot's seat; driver's seat.

Führerstab *m* command group.

Führerstand *m* control cabin, pilot's cockpit, pilot's compartment *(Ap)*; tank commander's position.

Führerzügel *m* lead rein *(harness)*.

Führung *f* command, conduct, leadership; command post, headquarters; guide *(Mech)*.

obere Führung higher command *(Div and up)*.

untere Führung lower command *(Regt and down)*.

Führungsabteilung *f* tactical group of general staff sections.

Führungsband *n* rotating band *(Am)*.

Führungsfläche *f* flank *(G barrel)*.

Führungshülse *f* traversing slide *(MG)*.

Führungskante *f* edge of land *(G barrel)*.

Führungskette *f* squadron commander's flight, leading flight *(Avn)*.

Führungsklaue *f* assembly guide claw *(G)*.

Führungskunst *f* art of leadership, art of command *(Tac)*.

Führungsleiste *f* ribbed guide *(breechblock)*.

Führungs-Nachrichtenregiment *n* signal regiment which provides communication down to Army Hq.

Führungsring *m* rotating band *(Am)*.

Führungsrolle *f* guide roller *(Tk)*.

Führungsschiene *f* guide rail *(G cradle)*.

Führungsstab *m* operations staff *(Luftwaffe)*.

Führungsstück *n* traversing arc *(MG)*.

Führungsvermittlung *f* command telephone central.

Führungswulst *m* rear bourrelet *(Am)*.

Führungszeichen *n* driving signal.

Füllansatz *m* appendix *(Bln)*.

Füllelement *n* desiccated cell, "add-water" cell *(Elec)*.

Füllfunkspruch *m* dummy radio message.

Füllpulver 02 *n* TNT.

Füllschraube *f* filler cap *(MG)*.

Fülltrichter *m* filling funnel.

Füllung *f* filler *(Am)*; filling *(CWS)*.

Füllzapfen *m* filling plug.

Fundamentring *m* base ring *(Ord)*.

Fünfer-Schwarmwinkel *m* wedge formation of 5 airplanes.

Fünfte Kolonne fifth column.

Funk *m* radio.

Funkabkürzung *f* procedure sign, code group, prosine, prosig.

Funkanlage *f* radio installation.

Funkaufklärung *f* radio intelligence.

Funkauswertekraftwagen *m* radio-intelligence truck.

Funkbake *f* radio beacon.

Funkbefehl *m* radio command, radio order.

Funkbereitschaft *f* radio alert.

Funkbeschickung *f* radio compass calibration *(Air Navigation)*.

Funkbeschickungskurve *f* deviation curve *(Rad)*.

Funkbeschränkung *f* limited radio silence.

Funkbetrieb *m* radio operations.

Funkbetriebskraftwagen *m* radio operations truck.
Funkbetriebsstelle *f* radio operations station.
Funkdauerbereitschaft *f* continuous radio alert.
Funkdienst *m* radio communication service.
Funkdoppelverkehr *m* simultaneous two-way radio traffic.
Funke *m* spark.
Funkeinsatz *m* employment of radio.
Funkempfang *m* radio reception.
Funkempfänger *m* radio receiver.
funken to radio, send by radio.
Funkenbildung *f* production of sparks *(Elec)*.
Funkenstrecke *f* spark gap.
Funkentelegraphie *f* radiotelegraphy.
Funkentelephonie *f* radiotelephony.
Funkentladung *f* spark discharge *(Elec)*.
Funkentstörer *m* static eliminator *(Rad)*.
Funker *m* radio operator *(with grade of private)*.
Funkfeuer *n* radio beacon.
Funkgefreiter *m* radio operator *(with grade of* Gefreiter*)*.
Funkgerät *n* radio set, radio equipment.
Funkgerätkraftwagen *m* radio truck, radio-equipment truck.
Funkgerätmechaniker *m* radio repairman.
Funkhorchdienst *m* radio intercept service.
Funkhorchkraftwagen *m* radio intercept truck.
Funkhorchstelle *f* radio intercept station.
Funkkiste *f* radio chest, radio case.
Funkkompanie *f* radio company.
Funkkraftwagen *m* radio car, radio truck, radio command truck.
Funklinie *f* radio line, two-station net.
Funkmast *m* antenna mast, mast-type antenna.
Funkmastkraftwagen *m* radio antenna truck.
Funkmeister *m* technical sergeant *(Rad)*.
Funkmeisterei *f* signal supply and radio maintenance shop.
Funkmeldung *f* radio message.

Funkmeßgerät *n* radar.
Funkmeßturm *m* radar tower, radar station.
Funknachrichten *fpl* radio messages, radio communications.
Funknavigation *f* radio navigation *(Avn)*.
Funknetz *n* radio net.
Funknetz für den Verkehr Boden-Bord air-ground net *(Rad)*.
Funkpanzerkampfwagen *m* radio command tank.
Funkpeiler *m* radio direction finder.
Funkpeilgerät *n* radio direction-finding apparatus.
Funkpeilung *f* radio direction finding.
Funkquerverbindung *f* intercommunication channel *(Rad)*.
Funkrufzeichen *n* radio call signal.
Funksender *m* radio transmitter.
Funksendung *f* radio transmission.
Funksignal *n* radio signal.
Funkskizze *f* radio net diagram.
Funksprechen *n* radio voice transmission, radiotelephone communication, voice-radio communication.
Funksprechgerät *n* radiotelephone.
Funksprechübermittlung *f* voice-radio communication.
Funkspruch *m* radio message.
Funkspruchkopf *m* heading on radio message.
Funkspruchübersicht *f* radio signal unit journal, number sheet.
Funkspruchvermittlung *f* radio-message transmission, radio message relay (station).
Funkspruchweg *m* radio channel.
auf dem Funkspruchweg by radio, via radio.
Funkstaffel *f* echelon of radio units; radio detachment.
Funkstelle *f* radio station.
Funkstille *f* radio silence.
Funkstörung *f* radio interference, radio jamming.
Funktafel *f* radio code table.
Funktasten *n* keying *(Rad)*.
Funktäuschung *f* radio deception.
Funktechnik *f* radio engineering.
Funktechniker *m* radio engineer.
Funktrupp *m* radio section.
Funkturm *m* radio tower.
Funküberwachung *f* radio monitoring.

Funkübung *f* radio-communication exercise.

Funkunteroffizier *m* radio operator *(Sgt)*.

Funkverbindung *f* radio communication.

Funkverbot *n* radio silence.

Funkverkehr *m* radio traffic.

Funkverkehrsabkürzungen *fpl* brevity code, prosigs *(Rad)*.

Funkverkehrsart *f* type of radio-net traffic.

Funkverkehrsform *f* method of radio communication.

Funkwagen *m* radio car, truck, or wagon.

Funkwart *m* radio technician.

Funkwechselsprechen *n* alternate two-way radiophone communication.

Funkwechselverkehr *m* alternate two-way radio traffic.

Funkweg *m* radio channel.

auf dem Funkweg by radio, via radio.

Funkwelle *f* radio wave.

Funkwerkstatt *f* radio maintenance shop.

Funkwetterwarte *f* radio weather station.

Funkzucht *f* radio discipline.

furagieren to forage.

Furagierleine *f* picket line *(for horse)*.

Furche *f* furrow; scour *(river bed)*; groove; white line *(hoof)*.

Furier *m* quartermaster sergeant.

Furnier *n* veneer.

Fürsorge *f* welfare.

Furt *f* ford.

Füsilier *m* private, infantry rifleman.

Fußbremshebel *m* brake pedal.

Fußhebel *m* pedal *(Ord, MT)*.

fußkrank footsore.

Fußlappen *m* foot rag, foot cloth; cabbage *(slang)*.

Fußlatscher *m* "foot-slogger," infantryman *(slang)*.

Fußlatte *f* sill *(Bdg)*.

Fußmelder *m* runner.

Fußplatte *f* foot plate, float *(AA gun outrigger)*.

Fußpunkt *m* nadir point.

Fußschalter *m* foot switch *(Elec)*; foot starter *(MT)*.

Fußschaltung *f* foot shifter *(MT)*.

Fußschlingenmine *f* foot snare mine.

Fußstütze *f* footrest.

Fußteller *m* float, float plate, jack float *(AA gun)*.

Fußweg *m* footpath.

Futter *n* forage, fodder; lining *(Clo)*; bushing, liner *(Tech)*; chuck *(of lathe, etc.)*.

Futteral *n* case; scabbard; sheath.

Futterholz *n* frame, shim *(Engr)*.

Futterration *f* forage ration.

Futterrohr *n* removable liner *(G)*.

Futterstück *n* bushing *(breechblock)*.

G

Gabel *f* fork *(utensil)*; bracket *(Arty)*.

eine Gabel bilden to bracket *(Arty)*.

Gabelachse *f* Elliot-type front axle *(MT)*.

Gabelbildung *f* bracketing method, bracket adjustment *(Arty)*.

Gabeldeichsel *f* pair of wagon shafts.

Gabellafette *f* gun carriage with shafts.

Gabelmotor *m* V-engine.

gabeln to bracket *(Arty)*.

Gabelschießen *n* bracket fire.

Gabelschwanz *m* twin tail *(Ap)*.

Gabelstütze *f* bipod *(MG)*.

Gabelumschalter *m* hook switch *(Tp)*.

Gabelung *f* bracket *(Arty)*.

Gamaschen *fpl* leggins, puttees.

Ganasche *f* jaw *(horse)*.

Gang *m* gear, speed, action, play, motion, travel *(Mech)*; passage, gangway.

Gangart *f* gait *(horse)*.

gangbar passable.

Gangrolle *f* pivoted dial *(speedometer)*.

Gangschaltung *f* gearshift *(MT)*.

Gangspill *m* capstan.

Gänsemarsch *m* Indian file, single file.

"Ganze Abteilung, Kehrt!" "About Face!" *(to a detail, squad, company, etc.).*

Ganzmetallflugzeug *n* all-metal airplane.

Garbe *f* sheaf of fire, cone of dispersion, cone of fire.

Garnison *f* garrison *(now Standort).*

garnisonverwendungsfähig fit for limited service *(i.e., in a garrison post, station or in Com Z) (abbr. g.v.).*

Gasabblaseverfahren *n* gas-release method *(CWS).*

Gasabdichtung *f* gas check *(breechblock).*

Gasabwehr *f* gas defense.

Gasabwehrdienst *m* chemical defense service.

Gasabwehrmaßnahmen *fpl* tactical protection *(CWS).*

Gasabwehrmittel *n* gas-defense equipment.

Gasabwehrwaffe *f* gas-defense weapon.

Gasalarm *m* gas alarm.

Gasalarmsirene *f* gas-alarm siren.

Gasalarmzeichen *n* gas-alarm signal.

Gasangriff *m* gas attack.

Gasanzeiger *m* gas detector kit.

Gasanzug *m* gas-protection suit.

Gasaufklärung *f* gas reconnaissance.

Gasausbildung *f* gas-defense instruction.

Gasbehälter *m* gas container.

Gasbekleidung *f* protective clothing *(CWS).*

Gasbereitschaft *f* gas alert.

Gasbeschuß *m* gas-shell fire *(Arty).*

Gasbrand *m* gas gangrene.

Gasbrille *f* gas goggles *(CWS).*

Gasbrisanzgranate *f* high-explosive chemical shell.

gasdicht gasproof, gastight.

Gasdichte *f* gas concentration.

Gasdichtigkeit *f* impermeability to gas.

Gasdisziplin *f* gas discipline.

Gasdruck *m* blowback, gas pressure *(Ord).*

Gasdrucklader *m* blowback-operated weapon.

Gasdruckmeßgerät *n* pressure gage *(Arty).*

Gasdruckprüfung *f* pressure test *(Ord).*

Gasdüse *f* gas-cylinder nozzle.

Gasentladungsröhre *f* gas tube *(Rad).*

Gas-Erdmine *f* chemical mine, chemical land mine.

Gaserkennungsdienst *m* gas-detecting service.

Gasflasche *f* chemical cylinder, gas cylinder.

Gasfußhebel *m* accelerator pedal *(Mtr).*

Gasfußtritt *m* See Gasfußhebel.

Gasgenerator *m* wood-gas generator *(MT).*

Gasgeschoß *n* chemical projectile.

gasgeschützt gasproofed.

Gasgewehrgranate *f* gas rifle grenade.

Gasgranate *f* chemical shell, gas shell.

Gashandgranate *f* gas hand grenade, chemical hand grenade.

Gashandschuh *m* gas-protection glove.

Gashandwerfer *m* chemical mortar.

Gashebel *m* throttle lever *(Ap);* accelerator *(Mtr).*

Gaskampf *m* chemical warfare.

Gaskampfgerät *n* chemical warfare equipment.

Gaskampfmittel *npl* chemical warfare material.

Gaskrieg *m* chemical warfare.

Gasläufer *m* antigas runner *(roll of impregnated paper on which to cross contaminated ground).*

Gasleitung *f* gas line, gas pipe.

Gasmaske *f* gas mask.

Gasmaskenkörper *m* body of gas mask.

Gasmaskenprüfgerät *n* gas-mask testing apparatus.

Gasmaskentragbüchse *f* gas-mask carrier *(canister type).*

Gasmaskenzubehör *n* gas-mask accessories.

Gasmörser *m* chemical mortar.

Gasmunition *f* chemical munitions.

Gasoffizier *m* gas officer, chemical officer.

Gasöl *n* gas oil, Diesel fuel.

Gasplane *f* antigas paulin, protective awning *(CWS).*

Gasraum *m* gas chamber *(Bln, CWS).*

Gasraumprobe *f* gas-chamber test *(CWS)*.

Gasraumprüfung *f* *See* **Gasraumprobe**.

Gasschießen *n* gas-shell fire *(Arty)*.

Gasschleuse *f* gas trap, air lock *(CWS)*.

Gasschutz *m* chemical defense.

Gasschutzdecke *f* protective mat *(CWS)*.

Gasschutzfilm *m* chemical-defense training film.

Gasschutzgerät *n* gas protective equipment.

Gasschutzgerätepark *m* chemical defense equipment park.

Gasschutzgerätwerkstatt *f* repair shop for gas protective equipment.

Gasschutzsalbe *f* protective ointment *(CWS)*.

Gassschutzübungsmittel *n* chemical defense training agent.

Gasschutzunteroffizier *m* gas noncommissioned officer.

Gasschutzvorhang *m* gas curtain, blanket door.

Gasschutzvorrat *m* stock of chemical defense equipment.

Gasschutzvorschrift *f* gas-defense regulations.

Gasschwaden *mpl* gas fumes *(CWS)*.

Gasse *f* gap *(in obstacle or mine field)*; alley, street.

gassicher gasproof.

Gassperre *f* gas barrier, contaminated area.

Gasspüren *n* gas detection.

Gasspürer *m* gas sentry.

Gasspürfähnchen *n* gassed-area marker.

Gasspürgerät *n* gas-detection apparatus.

Gasspürkraftwagen *m* gas-detection car.

Gasspürmittel *npl* gas-detection equipment.

Gasspürstoff *m* gas-detection agent.

Gasspürtrupp *m* gas-detection squad.

Gasstiefel *mpl* gas-protection boots.

Gastruppen *fpl* chemical troops.

Gasüberfall *m* surprise gas attack, surprise gas-shell fire.

Gasumhang *m* gas-protection cloak.

Gasvergifteter *m* gas casualty.

Gasvergiftung *f* gas poisoning, contamination.

Gasverluste *mpl* gas casualties.

Gasvorhang *m* gas curtain.

Gaswarnung *f* gas warning.

Gaswerfen *n* chemical-projector fire.

Gaswerfer *m* chemical projector.

Gaswolke *f* gas cloud.

Gaszelle *f* cell, cellule *(Ash)*.

Gaszucht *f* gas discipline.

Gaze *f* gauze.

geballt concentrated.

geballte Ladung concentrated charge *(consisting of several explosive blocks tied together)*.

geben to give; transmit *(Rad, Tg)*.

Geber *m* sender, transmitter; data transmitter *(data transmission system)*; azimuth and elevation indicator *(AA director)*.

Gebiet *n* region; territory; zone.

Gebirgsartillerie *f* mountain artillery, pack artillery.

Gebirgsfahrkolonne *f* mountain supply column *(H-Dr)*.

Gebirgsgeschütz *n* mountain gun, pack gun.

Gebirgshang *m* mountainside.

Gebirgskanone *f* mountain gun.

Gebirgsinfanteriegeschütz *n* mountain infantry howitzer.

Gebirgsjäger *m* mountain infantryman.

Gebirgsjäger-Bataillon *n* mountain infantry battalion.

Gebirgsjäger-Regiment *n* mountain infantry regiment.

Gebirgskampf *m* mountain combat.

Gebirgskorps *n* mountain corps.

Gebirgskorpskommando *n* mountain corps headquarters.

Gebirgskrieg *m* mountain warfare.

Gebirgsmütze *f* mountain cap.

Gebirgspaß *m* mountain pass.

Gebirgs-Pionier-Regiment *n* mountain engineer regiment.

Gebirgsträgerkompanie *f* mountain carrier company *(on foot)*.

Gebirgstruppen *fpl* mountain troops.

Gebiß *n* bit *(harness)*.

Gebläse *n* blower, supercharger; ventilator.

Gebläsemotor *m* supercharged engine.

Gebläsewind *m* airflow.

Gebrauch *m* use, custom.

Gebrauchsanweisung *f* instructions for use, operating instructions.

Gebrauchsflugzeug *n* general-purpose airplane.

Gebrauchsladung *f* normal charge.

Gebrauchsstufe *f* the sum of all interior ballistic factors. *See also* Grundstufe.

Gebühr *f* charge, rate, allowance, fee.

Gebührnisse *fpl* allowances, rates.

Geburtsjahrgang *m* age class.

Geburtsurkunde *f* birth certificate.

gedämpft damped *(Elec, Mech)*.

gedeckt covered, concealed, defiladed, masked, sheltered.

gedeckte Bahn shooting gallery.

gedeckte Batterie masked battery.

gedeckter Raum dead space, safety zone.

gedeckte Stellung cover position.

geeicht calibrated.

geerdet grounded *(Elec)*.

Gefahr *f* danger.

gefährden endanger.

gefährlich dangerous.

Gefahrpunkt *m* critical point *(Tac)*.

Gefälle *n* gradient *(Met, Top)*.

Gefällemesser *m* clinometer *(Engr)*.

gefallen fallen, dead, killed.

im Felde gefallen killed in action.

Gefangenenabschub *m* evacuation of prisoners.

Gefangenenaussage *f* prisoner's statement.

Gefangenenaustausch *m* exchange of prisoners.

Gefangenenbewachungskommando *n* prisoner guard detachment.

Gefangenenlager *n* prisoner-of-war camp.

Gefangenensammelkommando *n* prisoner-collecting detachment.

Gefangenensammelstelle *f* prisoner collecting point.

Gefangenenverhör *n* *See* Gefangenenvernehmung.

Gefangenenvernehmung *f* interrogation of prisoners.

Gefangener *m* prisoner.

Gefangennahme *f* capture.

Gefängnis *n* prison.

Gefängnisstrafe *f* sentence of confinement to a prison.

Gefecht *n* action, battle, combat, engagement, fight. *See also terms under* Kampf, Krieg.

Gefechte unter besonderen Verhältnissen special operations.

Gefecht im Gebirge mountain combat.

Gefechtsabschnitt *m* combat sector, zone of action.

Gefechtsaufgabe *f* combat task.

Gefechtsaufklärung *f* battle reconnaissance, combat reconnaissance.

Gefechtsauftrag *m* combat mission.

Gefechtsausbildung *f* combat practice, tactical training.

Gefechtsbatterie *f* firing battery.

Gefechtsbefehl *m* combat order.

Gefechtsbefehlsstelle *f* command post.

Gefechtsbereich *m* zone of action.

Gefechtsbereitschaft *f* readiness for action.

Gefechtsbericht *m* combat report.

Gefechtsberührung *f* contact with the enemy.

Gefechtsbreite *f* combat frontage.

Gefechtseinheit *f* combat unit.

Gefechtseinsatz *m* employment in action, commitment to action.

Gefechtsentwicklung *f* deployment for action *(Tac)*.

Gefechtsfahrzeug *n* combat vehicle.

Gefechtsform *f* combat formation.

Gefechtsgebiet *n* combat zone.

Gefechtsgliederung *f* tactical grouping.

Gefechtsgruppe *f* combat unit; armored support unit.

Gefechtshandlung *f* operation, action, engagement, battle.

Gefechtskarren *m* ammunition and weapons cart *(H-Dr)*.

Gefechtskarte *f* battle map.

Gefechtskasten *m* medical supplies and equipment chest.

gefechtsklar cleared for action *(Nav)*.

Gefechtskompanie *f* assault company *(Prcht troops)*.

Gefechtskopf *m* warhead *(torpedo)*.

Gefechtskraftwagen *m* combat car.

Gefechtslage *f* combat situation.

Gefechtslandeplatz *m* advance(d) landing field.

Gefechtslärm *m* noise of battle.

Gefechtslehre *f* tactics.

Gefechtslinie *f* line of battle.

Gefechtsluftaufklärung *f* combat air reconnaissance.

gefechtsmäßig similar to actual combat or conditions in the field.

gefechtsmäßiges Schießen combat practice firing.

Gefechtsmeldung *f* combat message, combat report.

Gefechtspause *f* lull in combat.

Gefechtsraum *m* zone of action, combat area *(Tac)*; fighting compartment, turret basket *(Tk)*.

Gefechtsscheibe *f* field target, aiming silhouette.

Gefechtsschießen *n* advanced combat practice firing.

Gefechtsschießstand *m* field firing range *(R)*.

Gefechtsschlitten *m* combat sled.

Gefechtsschreiber *m* clerk at a command post.

Gefechtsspähtrupp *m* combat patrol.

Gefechtsstab *m* command group; tactical operations staff.

Gefechtsstaffel *f* combat-train echelon.

Gefechtsstand *m* command post *(in combat)*; headquarters *(Avn)*; gun position, gunner's station *(Ap)*.

Gefechtsstellung *f* action station.

Gefechtsstreifen *m* combat sector, zone of action.

Gefechtstätigkeit *f* combat activity.

Gefechtstroß *m* combat train; maintenance section *(Btry)*.

Gefechtsübung *f* combat practice.

Gefechtsverlauf *m* progress of action *(Tac)*.

Gefechtsverwendung *f* employment in combat.

Gefechtsvorposten *m* combat outpost.

Gefechtswagen *m* ammunition and weapons wagon.

Gefechtszeitangabe *f* chronology of battle.

Gefechtszweck *m* objective of combat, purpose of an action.

Gefecht um Engen combat at defiles.

Gefolgschaft *f* collective term for subordinate officers and/or enlisted personnel.

Gefreitenarmwinkel *m* acting corporal's chevron.

Gefreitenwinkel *m* See **Gefreitenarmwinkel.**

Gefreiter *m* acting corporal *(grade between Pvt 1cl and Cpl, strictly not NCO in Ger definition of term; translated as acting Cpl, lance Cpl, etc.).*

Gefrierschutz *m* antifreeze *(MT)*.

Gefrierschutzmittel *n* antifreeze solution *(MT)*.

Gegenangriff *m* counterattack *(Tac)*.

Gegenaufklärung *f* counterreconnaissance.

Gegenbefehl *m* counterorder.

einen Gegenbefehl geben to countermand.

Gegenböschung *f* counterslope.

Gegend *f* region, vicinity, neighborhood.

Gegenfeuer *n* counterfire, retaliation fire.

Gegenfunkstelle *f* called station *(Rad)*.

Gegengewicht *n* counterpoise *(Rad)*; counterweight, counterbalance.

Gegenhang *m* counterslope.

Gegenkolbenmotor *m* opposed-piston engine.

Gegenlaufgraben *m* counterapproach trench.

gegenläufige Luftschrauben contrarotating propellers.

Gegenlicht *n* "counter-light" *(sunlight against the attacker, defender or observer)*.

Gegenlosung *f* countersign.

Gegenmarsch *m* countermarch.

Gegenmaßnahme *f* countermeasure.

Gegenmine *f* countermine.

Gegenmutter *f* lock nut.

Gegenoffensive *f* counteroffensive.

Gegenpropaganda *f* counterpropaganda.

Gegenseil *n* stagger wire *(biplane)*.

gegenseitig two-way, mutual, reciprocal.

gegenseitige Sprechverbindung two-way telephone circuit.

Gegensignal *n* answer signal.

Gegensinn *m* counterclockwise direction, opposite direction.

im Gegensinn zum Uhrzeiger counterclockwise.

Gegenspionage *f* counterespionage.

Gegensprechen *n* duplex operation, two-way break-in communication *(Rad)*; duplexing *(Tp)*.

Gegenstand *m* item, object, article.

Gegenstelle *f* called station *(Rad)*.

Gegensteuern *n* trimming *(with one or more engines inoperative) (Avn)*.

Gegenstollen *m* countermine.

Gegenstoß *m* counterthrust, counterattack *(Tac)*.

Gegentakt-Verstärker *m* push-pull amplifier *(Rad)*.
Gegenvorbereitungsfeuer *n* counter preparation, counterpreparation fire.
Gegenwehr *f* resistance *(Tac)*.
Gegenwind *m* head wind.
Gegenzeiger *m* pointer, indicator *(follow-the-pointer mechanism)*.
Gegenzeigersinn *m* counterclockwise direction.
Gegner *m* opponent.
Gegnerpfeil *m* path-of-flight pointer *(reflector sight)*.
Gegnerpunkt *m* future position at moment of burst *(AAA)*.
gegossen cast *(metals, armor, etc.)*.
gegurtet belted *(Am, etc.)*.
Gehalt *m* concentration *(CWS)*; content, volume.
Gehäuse *n* case, casing, housing.
geheim secret, confidential.
Geheime Feldpolizei secret field police *(special MP units attached to armies and Mil Adm of occupied countries; abbr. G.F.P.)*.
geheimer Gegenstand classified military item, secret item.
Geheime Staatspolizei secret state police *(political police; abbr. Gestapo)*.
Geheimhaltung *f* secrecy.
Geheimnis *n* secret.
Geheimschrift *f* cryptography.
Geheimschriftanalyse *f* cryptanalysis.
Geheimtext *m* cipher text.
Geheimwort *n* cipher key.
Gehilfe *m* aid, assistant.
Gehilfe des Richtschützen assistant gunner *(MG squad)*.
Gehirnerschütterung *f* concussion of the brain.
gehoben raised, lifted, elevated; higher grade *(of Wehrmachtbeamter)*.
Gehorsam *m* obedience.
Gehorsamsverweigerung *f* insubordination.
Geisel *f* hostage.
geladen loaded, armed, charged, activated.
geladener Draht live wire.
Gelände *n* terrain, ground, country.
Geländeabschnitt *m* terrain sector, terrain compartment.
Geländeanpassung *f* adaptation to

the terrain, blending with the ground *(Cam)*.
Geländeaufnahme *f* terrain photo-survey.
Geländeausbildung *f* field training.
Geländeausnutzung *f* utilization of terrain.
Geländeausschnitt *m* coverage *(aerial Photo)*.
Geländebedeckung *f* mask *(Gunnery)*.
Geländebesprechung *f* tactical ride, tactical walk.
Geländebeurteilung *f* terrain appreciation, estimate of terrain.
Geländedarstellung *f* terrain representation *(Surv)*.
Geländeentgiftung *f* ground decontamination.
Geländeerkundung *f* terrain reconnaissance.
geländefähig capable of cross-country travel *(MT)*.
Geländefahren *n* cross-country driving.
Geländefahrzeug *n* cross-country vehicle *(MT)*.
Geländegang *m* auxiliary gear, underdrive *(MT)*.
geländegängig capable of cross-country travel, having cross-country mobility *(MT)*.
Geländegängigkeit *f* cross-country traveling ability, cross-country mobility *(MT)*.
Geländegegenstand *m* terrain feature, landmark.
Geländegestaltung *f* configuration of terrain, terrain features.
Geländehindernis *n* natural obstacle, terrain obstacle.
Geländekampfstoff *m* ground-contaminating agent, persistent agent *(CWS)*.
Geländekette *f* traction band *(MT)*.
Geländekraftfahrzeug *n* cross-country motor vehicle.
Geländenachbildung *f* simulation of terrain.
Geländeneigung *f* slope.
Geländeorientierung *f* orientation by map.
Geländepunkt *m* terrain point, landmark.
Geländer *n* railing; handrail *(Bdg)*.
Geländeraum *m* terrain area.

Geländerstütze *f* railing post; handrail post *(Bdg)*.

Geländescheibe *f* landscape target *(Tng)*.

Geländeschutz *m* defilade, natural protection.

Geländeskizze *f* military sketch.

Geländestreifen *m* terrain sector.

Geländeübung *f* field exercise.

Geländevergiftung *f* terrain contamination *(CWS)*.

Geländeverhältnisse *npl* terrain conditions.

Geländevermessung *f* terrain survey.

Geländeverstärkung *f* organization of the ground *(Tac)*.

Geländewinkel *m* angle of site *(Gunnery)*; angle of slope *(Top)*.

negativer Geländewinkel angle of depression, negative angle of site.

Geländewinkellibelle *f* angle-of-site level.

Geländewinkelmesser *m* angle-of-site instrument, clinometer.

Geländewinkelmeßvorrichtung *f* angle-of-site mechanism *(telescopic sight)*.

Gelatit *n* a rock-blasting explosive.

gelb yellow.

Gelbkreuz *n* Yellow Cross *(Ger marking for vesicants) (CWS)*.

Gelbkreuzbeschuß *m* chemical-shell fire *(vesicant filler)*.

Geldabfindung *f* money allowance, reimbursement, cash settlement.

Geldstrafe *f* fine *(Law)*.

Geldwert der Verpflegungsersparnisse ration savings.

Gelegenheitsziel *n* target of opportunity.

Geleise *n* track *(RR)*.

Geleit *n* escort, convoy.

Geleitmannschaft *f* escort personnel.

Geleitschiff *n* convoy vessel, escort vessel.

Geleitschutz *m* convoy guard *(Nav)*.

Geleitzug *m* convoy *(Nav)*.

Gelenk *n* knuckle, joint, flexible coupling.

Gelenkbinden *fpl* ankle wrap puttees.

Gelenkbogenbrücke *f* hinged-arch bridge.

Gelenkgehäuse *n* universal-joint housing *(MT)*.

Gelenkstück *n* joint piece *(MG tripod)*.

Gelenkwelle *f* flexible drive shaft,

drive shaft and universal joint, propeller shaft.

gelöste Flugordnung route formation *(Avn)*.

Gemeiner *m* private, common soldier or sailor *(in disuse)*.

Gemischbildung *f* mixing, mixture formation *(carburetor)*.

gemischt mixed, combined.

Gemischtbauweise *f* composite construction.

gemischter Verband combined-arms unit.

gemodelte Welle modulated wave.

genau accurate, exact, precise; tight; close; strict.

genaues Einschießen precision adjustment fire.

Gendarm *m* rural policeman.

Gendarmerie *f* rural police.

genehmigen authorize, approve.

General *m* lieutenant general; general; general officer *(specifically, Lt Gen)*. *Compare* Generaloberst.

Generaladmiral *m* admiral *(commander of a fleet)*.

Generalarzt *m* brigadier general *(Med)*.

Generalarbeitsführer *m* brigadier general *(Reich Labor Service)*.

Generalfeldmarschall *m* Field Marshal.

Generalgouvernement *n* Government General *(administrative region established in occupied territory; specifically, in Central Poland in 1939)*.

Generalinspekteur für die Panzerwaffe Inspector General of Armored Forces.

Generalintendant *m* civilian official in administrative services ranking as brigadier general.

Generalkommando *n* corps headquarters.

Generalleutnant *m* major general.

Generalluftzeugmeister *m* chief of air forces special supply and procurement service.

Generalmajor *m* brigadier general.

Generaloberst *m* general *(full general)*.

Generaloberstabsarzt *m* surgeon general *(lieutenant general)*.

Generaloberstabsveterinär *m* lieutenant general *(Vet)*.

Generalquartiermeister *m* general staff officer Ib in charge of supply and administration at headquarters of field forces.

Generalstab *m* general staff.

Generalstab des Heeres General Staff of the Army.

Generalstabsarzt *m* major general *(Med)*.

Generalstabschef *m* Chief of Staff.

Generalstabskarte *f* strategic map *(1:100,000)*.

Generalstabskorps *n* General Staff Corps.

Generalstabsoffizier *m* general staff officer.

Generalstabsveterinär *m* major general *(Vet)*.

Generalveterinär *m* brigadier general *(Vet)*.

Generatoranhänger *m* wood-gas generator trailer *(MT)*; generator trailer *(Elec)*.

Genesung *f* convalescence.

Genesungskompanie *f* convalescent company, rehabilitation company.

Genesungsurlaub *m* sick leave.

Genfer Abkommen Geneva Convention.

Genfer Rotes Kreuz Geneva Cross.

genormt standardized.

geöffnet open, extended.

geöffnete Ordnung extended order.

geographische Breite latitude.

geographische Karte geographic map.

geographische Koordinaten geographic coordinates.

geographische Länge longitude.

Geographisch-Nord *m* true north.

Gepäck *n* baggage, impedimenta.

Gepäcktroß *m* baggage train.

Gepäckwagen *m* baggage car *(RR)*.

gepanzert armored.

gepflastert paved.

gerade straight.

geradeaus straight ahead.

Geradeausflug *m* horizontal flight, level flight *(Avn)*.

Geradseitfelge *f* straight-side rim *(MT)*.

Gerät *n* nonexpendable supplies, matériel, ordnance, equipment; instrument; apparatus.

Gerätart *f* type of equipment.

Gerätausstattung *f* allotment of equipment.

Gerätbrett *n* instrument panel.

Gerätedurchsicht *f* inspection of equipment or ordnance.

Geräteeinheit *f* unit assemblage *(of equipment, etc.)*.

Geräteentgiftung *f* decontamination of equipment.

Gerätelicht *n* instrument light.

Geräteoffizier *m* ordnance staff officer, ordnance officer, property officer.

Geräteunteroffizier *m* ordnance sergeant.

Geräteverwalter *m* quartermaster sergeant.

Gerätewagen *m* *See* **Gerätwagen.**

Gerätinspizient *m* equipment inspector.

Gerätklasse *f* class of equipment.

Gerätsammelstelle *f* ordnance collecting point.

Gerätsatz *m* unit of equipment.

Gerätstück *n* piece of equipment, item of equipment.

Gerätwagen *m* equipment truck, equipment wagon.

Geräusch *n* noise, sound.

Geräuschtarnung *f* "noise camouflage" *(any noise-producing means intended to deceive enemy as to position of guns, advance of tanks, etc.)*.

Gerbersche Anordnung Gerber design *(a type of cantilever bridge)*.

Gerberträger *m* cantilever span *(two cantilever arms with suspended span)*.

Gericht *n* court.

gerichteter Empfang directional reception *(Rad)*.

Gerichtsherr *m* appointing authority *(Law)*.

Gerippe *n* skeleton, framework, outline.

Gerippeabteil *n* bay *(Ap)*.

Germanisches SS-Panzerkorps SS armored corps composed of non-German volunteers from "Germanic" countries.

Geruch *m* odor.

geruchlos odorless.

Gerücht *n* rumor.

Gerüst *n* scaffold, frame.

Gesamtausfall *m* total loss(es).

Gesamtauswanderungsstrecke *f* linear travel of target from position at instant of range determination to future position *(AA gunnery)*.

Gesamtauswanderungszeit *f* dead time plus time of flight *(AA gunnery)*.

Gesamtbefehl *m* complete order *(Tac)*.

Gesamtdruck *m* total pressure.

Gesamterhöhung *f* quadrant elevation *(Gunnery)*.

Gesamtkilometerzähler *m* total mileage odometer *(on speedometer)*.

Gesamtkriegführung *f* grand strategy, general conduct of the war.

Gesamtlage *f* total situation, over-all situation *(Tac)*.

Gesamtrohrerhöhung *f* total elevation *(G)*.

Gesamtseitenrichtung *f* total traverse, total deflection *(G)*.

Gesamtvorhaltewinkel *m* principal lateral deflection angle *(AA gunnery)*.

Gesandtschaft *f* legation.

Geschirr *n* harness; utensils.

Geschirrtau *n* trace *(harness)*.

Geschlechtskrankheit *f* venereal disease.

geschlossen closed, close; combined; compact.

geschlossene Ordnung close order.

geschlossener Bau close-order construction *(method of Tp line construction by a single crew)*.

geschlossenes Exerzieren close-order drill.

geschlüsselt encoded, secret.

geschlüsselter Funkspruch radio code message.

Geschoß *n* projectile, bullet, shell.

Geschoßabweichung *f* deviation, absolute deviation *(Gunnery)*.

Geschoßanlage *f* clearance space *(R)*.

Geschoßaufschlag *m* impact of projectile, point of impact.

Geschoßbahn *f* trajectory, ballistic curve.

Geschoßbö *f* blast effect of antiaircraft shell.

Geschoßboden *m* base of projectile.

Geschoßdrall *m* spin of projectile.

Geschoßdrehung *f* See **Geschoßdrall**.

Geschoßdurchmesser *m* diameter of projectile.

Geschoßeinschlag *m* impact of projectile, point of impact.

Geschoßflugzeit *f* time of flight of projectile.

Geschoßform *f* shape of projectile.

Geschoßführung *f* seating of projectile.

Geschoßgarbe *f* cone or sheaf of fire, cone of dispersion.

Geschoßgewicht *n* weight of projectile.

Geschoßheber *m* gun hoist.

Geschoßhöhlung *f* shell cavity *(Am)*.

Geschoßhülle *f* body of projectile *(Am)*.

Geschoßhülse *f* cartridge case *(Am)*.

Geschoßkanal *m* bullet tube *(grenade launcher)*.

Geschoßkappe *f* cap of projectile.

Geschoßkern *m* core of bullet.

Geschoßknall *m* report produced by shell wave *(SR)*.

Geschoßkopf *m* head of projectile.

Geschoßkran *m* gun hoist.

Geschoßmantel *m* jacket of bullet.

Geschoßmine *f* improvised antitank mine made of a high-explosive shell.

Geschoßspitze *f* ogive of shell.

Geschoßwagen *m* ammunition truck.

Geschoßwirkung *f* effect of projectile.

Geschoß-Zubringewagen *m* ammunition truck *(for carrying heavy projectile to the piece)*.

Geschütz *n* gun *(Arty piece)*. See **Artillerie** *for classification as light, medium and heavy.*

Geschützart *f* type of gun *(Arty)*.

Geschützbank *f* barbette.

Geschützbedienung *f* gun crew; service of the piece.

Geschützbettung *f* ground platform *(RR gun)*.

Geschützexerzieren *n* service of the piece drill.

Geschützführer *m* chief of section *(FA)*.

Geschützkompanie *f* howitzer company *(Inf)*.

Geschützladung *f* propelling charge *(Am)*.

Geschützmannschaft *f* gun crew.

Geschütznullpunkt *m* position of gun *(on firing charts and diagrams)*.

Geschützort *m* See **Geschütznullpunkt**.

Geschützpark *m* ordnance park.

Geschützplane *f* gun cover.

Geschützrohr *n* gun barrel.

Geschützschlepper *m* prime mover *(Arty)*.

Geschützstaffel *f* gun section.

Geschützstand *m* gun position, gun emplacement, position of the piece *(Arty)*.

Geschützstellung *f* gun position, gun emplacement.

geschützt protected.

geschützter Behälter self-sealing tank *(Ap)*.

Geschützverschluß *m* breech mechanism, breechblock *(Ord)*.

Geschützwagen *m* gun car *(RR)*.

geschützweises Feuer fire by piece at command *(Arty)*.

Geschützwinde *f* firing jack *(G)*.

Geschützzielfeuer *n* simulated fire representing an enemy gun target *(Tng)*.

Geschützzug *m* howitzer platoon *(Inf)*.

Geschwader *n* wing *(air force operational unit consisting of about 100 aircraft organized into from 3 to 5 Gruppen)*; squadron *(Nav)*.

Geschwaderflugform *f* wing flight formation.

Geschwaderkeil *m* wing wedge formation *(Avn)*.

Geschwaderkolonne *f* wing column formation *(Avn)*.

Geschwaderkommodore *m* wing commander *(Avn)*.

geschweißt welded.

Geschwindigkeit *f* speed, velocity; rate *(of fire)*.

Geschwindigkeitsdreieck *n* triangle of velocities *(Avn)*.

Geschwindigkeitsmesser *m* speedometer *(MT)*.

Geschwindigkeitssteigerung *f* speed increase.

Geschwindigkeitsverlust *m* loss of velocity *(Ballistics)*.

Geschwindigkeit zur Luft indicated airspeed.

Gesellschaftsanzug *m* dress uniform for social occasions.

Gesenk *n* die *(for stamping or punching)*.

Gesetz *n* law, statute.

Gesetze und Gebräuche des Landkrieges Laws and Customs of War on Land *(Hague Convention, 1907)*.

gesichert safe; secured.

Gesichtsfeld *n* field of view *(Optics)*.

Gespann *n* team of horses.

Gespräch *n* conversation; telephone call.

Gesprächsschluß *m* completion of call *(Tp)*.

Gesprächsverbindung *f* call, connection *(Tp)*.

gestaffelt echeloned, staggered.

Gestalt *f* form, shape, figure, configuration.

Gestalt der Flugbahn curve of the trajectory.

Gestänge *n* bars, poles, rods, linkage.

Gestapo *f* See **Geheime Staatspolizei**.

gestattet allowed, allowable, granted, permitted.

gestattete Abweichung tolerance *(Tech)*.

Gesteinssprengmittel *n* rock-blasting explosive.

Gestell *n* stand; mount; frame; block; trestle; carriage; gear.

Gestellungsbefehl *m* induction order.

Gestellungspflicht *f* obligation to appear before draft board.

gesteuert controlled, steered; synchronized.

gesteuertes Maschinengewehr synchronized machine gun *(Ap)*.

Gesträuch *n* underbrush, shrubbery.

gestreckt elongated, extended; stretched; flat.

gestreckte Flugbahn flat trajectory.

gestreckte Ladung elongated charge. See also **Reihenladung**.

gestrichenes Korn medium sight *(R aiming)*.

Gestrüpp *n* underbrush, brush.

Gesuch *n* petition, request, application.

Gesundheit *f* health.

Gesundheitsappell *m* physical inspection.

Gesundheitsdienst *m* Sanitary Corps.

Gesundheitsoffizier *m* health officer.

Gesundheitszustand *m* physical condition.

Getränk *n* beverage.

getrennt separate(d); cut off *(Tp)*.

getrennte Munition separate-loading ammunition.

getrennter Bau extended-order construction *(method of Tp line construction by two separate crews)*.

Getriebe *n* gear, transmission *(MT)*.

Getriebebremse *f* transmission brake *(MT)*.

Getriebefett *n* transmission grease *(MT)*.

Getriebehauptwelle *f* transmission main shaft *(MT)*.

Getriebegehäuse *n* transmission case *(MT)*.
Getriebewelle *f* transmission shaft *(MT)*.
Gewahrsam *m* custody.
Gewaltmarsch *m* forced march.
gewaltsam forceful, in force.
gewaltsame Erkundung reconnaissance in force.
Gewehr *n* rifle.
"Gewehr, ab!" "Order, arms!"
"Gewehr abnehmen!" "Unsling, arms!"
Gewehrappell *m* rifle inspection.
Gewehrauflage *f* fire crest *(Ft)*.
Gewehrfeuer *n* rifle fire.
Gewehrführer *m* machine-gun squad leader, gun leader *(heavy MG)*.
Gewehrgeschoß *n* rifle bullet.
Gewehrgranate *f* rifle grenade.
Gewehrgranatenschütze *m* rifle grenadier.
"Gewehr in die, Hand!" "Take, arms!"
Gewehrkartusche *f* propelling cartridge for rifle grenade.
Gewehrkolben *m* rifle butt.
Gewehrkupplungsstück *n* barrel-locking stud *(MG)*.
Gewehrmieke *f* arms rack.
Gewehrmücke *f* See Gewehrmieke.
Gewehrmunition *f* rifle ammunition.
Gewehr-Panzergranate *f* armor-piercing rifle grenade.
Gewehr-Propagandagranate *f* rifle propaganda grenade *(scatters leaflets)*.
Gewehrriemen *m* rifle sling.
Gewehrschaft *m* rifle stock.
Gewehrschießstand *m* rifle range.
Gewehrschuß *m* rifle shot.
Gewehrschütze *m* rifleman.
Gewehrsprenggranate *f* high-explosive rifle grenade.
Gewehrstock *m* cleaning rod *(R)*.
Gewehrstütze *f* arms rack.
Gewehrträger *m* rifleman; machine-gun carrier *(gunner No. 1)*; cradle *(on MG sleigh mount or tripod)*.
Gewehrtragevorrichtung *f* rifle scabbard *(Cav)*.
"Gewehr, über!" "Left shoulder, arms!" *(with tightened sling)*; "Sling arms!" *(with loosened sling)*.
Gewehrübung *f* rifle exercise *(calisthenics)*.

"Gewehr umhängen!" "Sling arms!"
Gewehrzielfeuer *n* simulated fire representing enemy rifle or MG target *(Tng)*.
Gewehrzubehör *n* rifle accessories.
gewerblich industrial.
Gewicht *n* weight; gravity.
Gewichtsverteilung *f* weight distribution, balance.
Gewinde *n* thread *(Tech)*.
Gewindebacken *fpl* die *(for cutting threads)*.
Gewindegang *m* pitch *(of screw thread)*.
Gewindeschablone *f* screw pitch gage.
Gewitter *n* thunderstorm.
gewitterdrohend ugly, threatening sky *(Met)*.
Gewitterflug *m* frontal soaring *(glider)*.
Gewitterstörung *f* atmospherics, static *(Rad)*.
gewöhnliches Ferngespräch routine call *(Tp)*.
gewölbt convex, arched, vaulted.
gewölbte Böschung convex slope.
Gezeiten *pl* tide(s).
Gezeitentafel *f* tide table.
gezogen rifled *(barrel)*; drawn, towed.
gezogene Kurve climbing turn *(Avn)*.
gezogenes Geschütz rifled gun *(Arty)*.
gezogenes Ziel towed target.
Gieren *n* yawing; trail-ferrying.
Gierfähre *f* trail ferry.
Gierungsmesser *m* yawmeter *(Ap)*.
Gierwinkel *m* angle of yaw *(Avn)*.
Gießerei *f* foundry.
Gift *n* poison.
giftig poisonous, toxic.
Giftnebel *m* toxic smoke *(CWS)*.
Giftnebelkerze *f* gas candle, irritant gas candle *(CWS)*.
Giftnebelwolke *f* gas cloud.
Giftrauch *m* irritant smoke *(CWS)*.
Giftrauchkerze *f* toxic-smoke candle, gas candle *(CWS)*.
Giftregen *m* aerial gas spray *(CWS)*.
Giftregenangriff *m* spray attack *(CWS)*.
Giftstoff *m* toxic agent *(CWS)*.
Gipfel *m* peak, summit.
Gipfelentfernung *f* abscissa for maximum ordinate *(of trajectory)*.

Gipfelhöhe *f* maximum ordinate *(of trajectory)*; absolute ceiling *(Avn)*.

Gipfelhöhe mit einem stehenden Motor emergency ceiling *(Avn)*.

Gipfelpunkt *m* summit *(of trajectory, etc.)*.

Gitter *n* grid *(maps, Rad)*; trellis, lattice, grillage.

Gitterantenne *f* parasol-type antenna.

Gitterdrossel *f* grid resistor *(Rad)*.

Gittergleichrichter *m* grid rectifier *(Rad)*.

Gitterkondensator *m* grid condenser, grid capacitor *(Rad)*.

Gitterkreis *m* grid circuit, grid resonant circuit *(Rad)*.

Gitterlinie *f* grid line.

Gittermast *m* trellis mast.

Gitternetz *n* coordinate map grid, grid system, military grid.

Gitternetzkarte *f* gridded map.

Gitternetzlinie *f* *See* Gitterlinie.

Gitter-Nord *m* grid north.

Gitterrichtung *f* grid base-line direction *(Gunnery)*.

Gitterschießplan *m* fire-control grid *(Gunnery)*.

Gitterschwanz *m* open tail *(Ap)*.

Gitterspannung *f* grid voltage *(Rad)*.

Gittervorspannung *f* bias *(Rad)*.

Gitterwerte *mpl* grid coordinates, grid numbers *(maps)*.

Gitterwiderstand *m* grid resistance *(Rad)*.

Glas *n* glass; binoculars, field glass.

glasartig glasslike.

glasartige Vereisung clear ice, glaze *(Avn)*.

Glasbeobachtung *f* observation with field glass or telescope.

Glasgefäß *n* envelope *(of Rad tube)*.

Glasmaßstab *m* glass scale *(Optics)*.

glatt smooth, smooth-bore.

glattes Geschütz smooth-bore gun.

gleichachsig coaxial.

gleichbleibend uniform, constant.

gleichbleibender Drall uniform twist *(Ord)*.

gleichförmiger Drall *See* gleichbleibender Drall.

Gleichgewicht *n* balance, equilibrium.

Gleichlauf *m* synchronism.

Gleichlaufende *f* parallel line.

Gleichlaufstellung *f* laying pieces reciprocally *(Btry)*.

Gleichlaufverfahren *n* reciprocal laying *(Btry)*.

Gleichrichter *m* rectifier *(Elec)*.

Gleichrichterröhre *f* rectifier tube.

Gleichrichtung *f* rectification *(Rad)*.

Gleichschritt *m* cadence; quick time. "Im Gleichschritt, marsch!" "Forward, march!" *(being at a halt)*. "Im Gleichschritt!" "Quick time, march!" *(being in march in double time)*.

gleichstellen synchronize *(watches)*; equalize.

Gleichstrom *m* direct current.

Gleichung *f* equation.

gleichzeitig simultaneous.

Gleis *n* rail, track *(RR)*.

Gleisanlage *f* railroad yard.

Gleisbalken *m* stringer *(Bdg)*.

Gleiskette *f* caterpillar track.

Gleiskettenantrieb *m* caterpillar drive.

Gleiskettenfahrzeug *n* track-laying vehicle.

Gleiskettenschlepper *m* caterpillar tractor.

Gleiskettenzugmaschine *f* caterpillar prime mover.

Gleiskurve *f* epi, curved spur track *(RR gun)*.

Gleitbahn *f* slide *(G cradle)*.

Gleitbombe *f* glider bomb *(Avn)*.

gleiten to glide.

Gleiter *m* glider.

Gleitfähigkeit *f* gliding ability; sliding ability.

Gleitflug *m* glide, gliding *(Avn)*.

Gleitflugwinkel *m* gliding angle *(Avn)*.

Gleitflugzeug *n* glider.

Gleithebel *m* sliding lever *(breechblock)*.

Gleithebelverschluß *m* sliding-lever breechblock.

Gleitkufe *f* landing ski *(Ap)*.

Gleitlager *n* plain bearing.

Gleitmittel *n* lubricant.

Gleitriegel *m* sliding bolt *(breechblock)*.

Gleitschiene *f* guide slide, guide rail *(G cradle)*; track *(of a catapult)*.

Gleitschuh *m* gun slide.

Gleitschutz *m* nonskid tread *(MT)*.

Gleitschutzkette *f* skid chain *(MT)*.

Gleitschutzmittel *n* nonskid device, traction aid *(MT)*.

Gleitstein *m* cam plate *(G)*.

Gleitstößel *m* tappet rod *(sliding-cam type)*.

Gleitvorrichtung f slide mechanism *(MG)*.

Gleitwand f slide plate *(MG)*.

Gleitwinkel m gliding angle *(Avn)*.

Glied n rank *(in formation)*; limb; link; member; unit; penis.

Gliederung f formation, organization; distribution; classification, arrangement; composition.

Gliedersäge f chain saw.

Glimmer m mica.

Glimmlampe f neon lamp.

Glühdraht m *See* **Glühfaden.**

Glühfaden m filament.

Glühkathode f hot cathode *(Rad)*.

Glühkathodenröhre f vacuum tube, incandescent cathode tube *(Rad)*.

Glühkerze f glow plug *(Diesel engine)*.

Glühköpfchen n hot-wire-bridge head *(Elec igniting device)*.

Glühlampe f incandescent lamp.

Glührohrzündapparat m hot-tube igniter.

Glühzündapparat m blasting machine, exploder *(Engr)*.

Glühzünder m electric igniter *(blasting cap)*.

Glühzündstück n electric detonator, electric igniter *(Engr)*.

Glysantin n an antifreeze solution *(MT)*.

Gnade f quarter, mercy; grace; pardon.

Goerz-Visier n bomb sight manufactured by Goerz Company.

Gondel f gondola, nacelle *(Ap)*.

Goniometer n goniometer *(Surv)*.

Goniometrie f goniometry *(Surv)*.

Graben m trench; ditch.

Grabenbagger m trench excavator.

Grabenbekleidung f trench revetment.

Grabendurchfahrt f crossing of trenches or ditches *(MT)*.

Grabenkopf f saphead *(Ft)*.

Grabenkrieg m trench warfare.

Grabenprofil n trench profile *(Ft)*; ditch profile *(Engr)*.

Grabenrost m trench boards, boardwalk.

Grabensohle f trench bottom.

Grabenspiegel m trench periscope.

Grabenstellung f trench position.

Grabenstufe f firing step.

Grabenwehr f parapet.

Gräberoffizier m graves registration officer.

Grabkreuz n grave marker.

Grabtafel f grave marker.

Gradabteilung f map square.

Gradabzeichen n *See* **Dienstgradabzeichen.**

Gradbogen m quadrant scale *(G)*.

Gradeinteilung f graduation, scale.

Gradfeld n map square.

Gradnetz n map grid.

Gradzahl f number of degrees, number of graduations.

Granatbüchse f antitank grenade rifle.

Granate f shell *(Am)*.

Granatfüllung f shell filler *(Am)*.

Granathülse f shell case.

Granatloch n shell hole.

Granatsignal n projector signal, star shell.

Granatsplitter m shell splinter.

Granattreffer m hit *(shell fire)*.

Granattrichter m shell crater.

Granatwerfer m mortar *(Ord)*; gunner *(Mort squad)*.

Granatwerfergeschoß n mortar shell.

Granatwerfer-Gruppe f mortar section.

Granatwerfernest n mortar pit.

Granatwerferstand m mortar emplacement.

Granatwerfertrupp m mortar team.

Granatwerferzug m mortar platoon.

graphisch graphic; mapped, surveyed or plotted.

graphischer Punkt topographical point *(on map)*.

graphische Schußtafel trajectory chart *(not to be confused with US graphical firing table)*.

Graphitschmiermittel n graphite lubricant.

Grat m ridge *(especially a sharp, rocky ridge)*; scoring *(in bore of gun)*.

Gräte f fishbone.

Graupelschauer m snow-pellet shower, graupel shower *(Met)*.

Greifer m cleat, grouser *(MT, Tk)*.

Greifervorrichtung f traction device *(MT)*.

Greifzirkel m calipers, dividers.

Grenadier m private, infantry rifleman *(historical term reintroduced)*. *See also* **Panzergrenadier.**

Grenadierbataillon *n* rifle battalion.
Grenadierkompanie *f* rifle company.
Grenadier-Panzerwagen *m* armored personnel carrier *(MT)*.
Grenadierregiment *n* rifle regiment, infantry regiment.
Grenzbahnhof *m* frontier station *(RR)*.
Grenzbezirk *m* frontier district.
Grenze *f* frontier, border; boundary; limit.
Grenzfrequenz *f* cut-off frequency *(Rad)*.
Grenzgebiet *n* border area, frontier area.
Grenzlehre *f* fixed gage, plug or snap gage.
Grenzschicht *f* boundary layer *(fluid mechanics)*.
Grenzschraube *f* setscrew.
Grenzschutz *m* frontier guard; frontier protection.
Grenzschutzabschnittskommando *n* frontier guard sector command *(Regtl Hq)*.
Grenzschutzunterabschnitt *m* frontier guard sub-sector *(Bn Hq)*.
Grenzüberschreitung *f* crossing a frontier.
Grenzwache *f* frontier sentry, frontier guard.
Grenzwacht *f* frontier guard.
Grenzwachtdivision *f* frontier guard division.
Grenzzwischenfall *m* border incident, frontier incident.
Griff *m* grip; hold; handle; doorknob.
Griffigkeit *f* grip, traction *(tires)*; traction, ground-gripping ability *(Mt, Tk)*.
Griffplatte *f* holding plate *(G sight)*.
Griffrohr *n* tubular handle *(trail spade)*.
Griffschale *f* stock *(pistol)*.
Griffstück *n* grip *(MG)*; receiver *(pistol)*.
grob approximate, rough, gross, coarse; bad, serious *(mistake)*.
Grobeinstellung *f* frequency selection *(Rad)*; coarse setting *(Optics)*.
grobes Einschießen approximate adjustment fire.
Grobfeile *f* coarse file.
Grobsicherung *f* fuse *(Elec)*.
Grobstufenschalter *m* band switch *(Rad)*.

Grof *m* heavy flame thrower *(on two-wheel carrier)* *(abbr. of* grosser Flammenwerfer).
Gros *n* main body *(Tac)*.
Großadmiral *m* Admiral of the Fleet; Commander-in-Chief *(operational and/or administrative)* *(Nav)*.
Großangriff *m* large-scale attack, major attack, major offensive operation.
Größe *f* quantity *(Math)*; greatness, magnitude, size.
Großeinsatz *m* major commitment, commitment of large forces, employment of great numbers *(Tac)*.
Großer Bär Big Dipper.
Großfertigung *f* mass production.
Großfunkstelle *f* high-power long-distance radio station.
großkalibrig large-caliber.
Großkampfschiff *n* capital ship.
Großkreis *m* great circle.
Großreihenfertigung *f* large-scale series production.
Größtgeschwindigkeit *f* maximum speed.
Großvernebelung *f* extensive smoke screen, large-area screening.
Grube *f* pit.
Grundausbildung *f* basic training.
Grundbegriffe *mpl* fundamentals, basic concepts.
Grundbuchse *f* base bushing *(counterrecoil mechanism)*.
Grundgehalt *n* base pay.
Grundgeschütz *n* base piece, directing gun.
Grundgeschwindigkeit *f* ground speed *(Avn)*.
Grundlagen *fpl* data.
Grundlinie *f* base line.
Grundmaschinengewehr *n* base machine gun.
Grundmine *f* ground mine, controlled mine, observation mine *(Nav)*.
Grundplatte *f* base plate.
Grundrichtung *f* base-line direction *(Gunnery)*.
Grundrichtungslinie *f* base line *(Gunnery)*.
Grundrichtungspunkt *m* base point *(Gunnery)*.
Grundrichtungswinkel *m* base angle *(Gunnery)*.
Grundrißskizze *f* area sketch.
Grundschwelle *f* ground sill *(Bdg)*.

Grundstellung *f* position of attention, position of the soldier *(drill)*.

Grundstufe *f* a factor used for correction of velocity error *(expressed in units — Stufeneinheiten — each equal to ⅓ of 1% of standard muzzle velocity)*.

Grundwasser *n* subsoil water, underground water.

Grundzahl *f* reference-point reading *(Gunnery)*.

Grünkreuz *n* green cross *(Ger marking for lung irritants) (CWS)*.

Gruppe *f* group, groupment *(Tac)*; rifle squad *(Inf)*; section *(Cav)*; volley *(Arty)*; group *(air force operational unit of 3* Staffeln, *about 27 aircraft)*.

Gruppenfeuer *n* volley fire *(Arty)*.

Gruppenflugform *f* group formation *(Avn)*.

Gruppenführer *m* squad leader *(Inf)*; section leader *(Cav)*. See also SS-Gruppenführer.

Gruppenführerabmarsch *m* section-leader half-squad *(Cav)*.

Gruppengefechtsstand *m* group command post *(Avn)*.

Gruppengetriebe *n* auxiliary transmission *(MT)*.

Gruppenkeil *m* group wedge *(Avn)*.

Gruppenkolonne *f* group of squadron javelins *(Avn)*.

Gruppenkolonne aus geschlossenen Winkeln group column of squadron wedges.

Gruppenkolonne links group of squadron javelins echeloned left.

Gruppenkommandeur *m* commander of a *Gruppe (Luftwaffe)*.

Gruppenkommando *n* army group headquarters; air force headquarters of a *Gruppe*.

Gruppenschaltung *f* series-parallel connection *(Elec)*.

Gruppenschießen *n* volley fire *(Arty)*.

gruppenweise by squads; by sections; by groups.

Gruppenwinkel *m* group cclumn of squadron V's *(Avn)*.

Gruppe zu Pferde mounted section *(Cav)*.

Gruß *m* hand salute.

Grußpflicht *f* obligation to salute.

Grußweite *f* saluting distance.

Guerillakämpfer *m* guerrilla.

Guerillakrieg *m* guerrilla warfare.

Gulasch *n* beef stew.

Gulaschkanone *f* field kitchen *(slang)*.

Gummi *m-n* rubber; gum.

Gummierung *f* rubberizing, rubber coating; gumming.

Gummifederung *f* rubber shock absorber.

Gummigleiskette *f* rubber track *(Tk)*.

Gummikabel *n* rubber-insulated wire *(Tp)*.

Gummiknüppel *m* rubber truncheon, rubber club.

Gummipolster *n* rubber block *(caterpillar track)*.

Gummirad *n* rubber-tired wheel.

Gummistoff *m* rubberized material.

günstig favorable.

Gurt *m* belt, strap, web *(Clo)*; ammunition belt, feed belt *(MG)*; chord *(of a truss)*.

Gürtel *m* belt, strap; cordon; zone.

Gürtelfestung *f* fortress with an outer cordon of smaller forts.

gurten to load an ammunition belt.

Gurtförderer *m* belt conveyor.

Gurtfüller *m* belt-filling machine, belt-loading machine, link-loading machine.

Gurthebel *m* belt-feed guide *(MG)*.

Gurtladung *f* belt feed.

Gurtschieber *m* belt-feed pawl *(MG)*.

Gurtstrippe *f* rear cinch (pack-saddle).

Gurttrommel *f* belt drum *(MG)*.

Gurtwerk *n* parachute harness.

Gurtzuführer *m* belt feed *(MG)*.

Gußeisen *n* cast iron.

Gußgehäuse *n* cast-metal case or housing.

Gußstahl *m* cast steel.

Güterbahnhof *m* freight station *(RR)*.

Güterwagen *m* freight car *(RR)*.

Güterzug *m* freight train *(RR)*.

Guttaperchapapier *n* gutta-percha paper, waterproof paper.

G.W.-Stand *m* See Granatwerferstand.

Gyrorektor *m* gyro flight indicator *(Ap)*.

H

Haager Abkommen Hague Convention.

Haarrohr *n* capillary tube.

Hacke *f* hatchet, ax, pickax; point of hock *(horse)*.

Hackmesser *n* machete; meat cleaver.

Hafen *m* harbor, port.

Hafenanlage *f* port installation.

Hafenarbeiter *m* longshoreman.

Hafenbecken *n* harbor basin.

Hafendamm *m* mole, jetty.

Hafengebiet *n* harbor area.

Hafenoffizier *m* port officer, port control officer.

Hafenschlepper *m* harbor tugboat.

Hafenschutz *m* harbor defense.

Hafenschutzboot *n* harbor defense boat.

Hafenüberwachung *f* port control.

Haft *f* custody, arrest, detention, confinement.

Haft-Hohlladung *f* magnetic anti-tank hollow charge.

Haftlokal *n* guardhouse, detention room.

Haftpflock *m* steel picket or stake *(Bdg)*.

Haftung *f* adhesion.

Haftung am Erdboden stability, low center of gravity *(of a vehicle)*.

Hagel *m* hail *(Met)*.

Hahn *m* hammer *(SA)*; cock; stopcock, faucet.

Hahnbolzen *m* trigger pin *(MG)*.

Hahngewehr *n* hammer gun *(as distinguished from* hahnloses Gewehr, hammerless gun*)*.

hahnlos hammerless *(Ord)*.

Haken *m* hook; clasp; clamp; catch.

Hakenkreuz *n* swastika.

Hakenumschalter *m* hook switch *(Tp)*.

halbautomatisch semiautomatic.

Halbbildentfernungsmesser *m* split-field coincidence range finder.

Halbflachbettfelge *f* semiflat-base rim *(MT)*.

Halbflachfelge *f* See **Halbflachbettfelge**.

halbfreitragend semicantilever.

Halbholz *n* split post, split log.

Halbinsel *f* peninsula.

Halbkettenantrieb *m* half-track drive *(MT)*.

Halbkettenfahrzeug *n* half-track vehicle.

Halbkettenkraftfahrzeug *n* half-track motor vehicle.

Halbketten-Lastkraftwagen *m* half-track motor truck.

"Halblinks schwenkt, Marsch!" "Column half left, march!"

Halbmesser *m* radius.

"Halbrechts schwenkt, Marsch!" "Column half right, march!"

halbstarr semirigid.

halbstarres Luftschiff semirigid airship.

halbstocks half-mast, half-staff.

Halbzelt *n* lean-to tent.

Halbzug *m* section *(of MG platoon)*.

Halbzugführer *m* section leader *(MG section)*.

Halfter *f* halter *(harness)*.

Halfterkinnkette *f* halter chain *(harness)*.

Halfterriemen *m* halter strap, halter tie *(harness)*.

Halfterstrick *m* picket line.

Halftertasche *f* holster.

Halle *f* hangar; garage; shed; hall.

Hallenvorplatz *m* apron *(Adrm)*.

Halsbinde *f* neckband *(Clo)*.

Halshalfter *f* neck halter *(harness)*.

Halshalfterriemen *m* neck-halter tie *(harness)*.

Halskerbe *f* neck groove *(horse)*.

Halskoppel *f* breast strap *(harness)*.

Halsriemen *m* neck strap *(harness)*.

Halt *m* halt.

Halteleinenbund *m* maneuvering spider *(Bln)*.

halten to hold; to carry *(AA SL)*; to aim.

Halteplatz *m* halt area; stopping place; parking place; loading place.

Haltepunkt *m* point of aim; stop *(halting place)*.

Halterung *f* arms rack, ammunition rack.

Haltestelle *f* halting place, stop.

Haltetau *n* handling line *(Bln)*; guy line.

Haltezeichen *n* stop signal *(MT)*; block signal *(RR)*.

"Halt, wer da!" "Halt! Who is there?"

Handanlasser *m* crank starter, hand starter *(Mtr).*

Handapparat *m* handset *(Rad, Tp).*

Handbeil *n* hatchet.

Handbohrmaschine *f* hand drill.

Handbremse *f* hand brake, emergency brake.

Handdrehmaschine *f* hand-crank generator *(Tp).*

Handelsmarine *f* merchant marine.

Handelsschiff *n* merchantman *(Nav).*

Handelsschiffsraum *m* merchant tonnage *(Nav).*

Handelssperre *f* embargo on commerce.

handelsüblich commercial.

Handfäustel *n* mallet.

Handfesseln *fpl* handcuffs, manacles.

Handfeuerlöscher *m* hand fire extinguisher.

Handfeuerwaffen *fpl* small arms.

Handgeld *n* See **Kapitulantenhandgeld.**

Handgemenge *n* hand-to-hand fighting.

Handgranate *f* hand grenade.

Handgranatenwurfstand *m* grenade court.

Handgriff *m* grip, handle; single manual operation.

Handhabungstau *n* prolonge, drag rope *(Arty).*

Handkammer *f* hand camera.

Handkurbel *f* hand crank.

Handleuchtzeichen *n* ground signal flare.

Handloch *n* hand hole *(G carriage wheel).*

Handlüfter *m* hand-operated ventilator.

Handpferd off horse, led horse.

Handrad *n* handwheel.

Handrädchen *n* micrometer-scale knob *(angle-of-site Instr)*; small handwheel.

Handrad zur Höhenrichtung elevating handwheel *(G).*

Handrad zur Seitenrichtung traversing handwheel *(G).*

Handramme *f* hand piledriver; maul.

Handrauchzeichen *n* hand smoke signal.

Handschellen *fpl* handcuffs, manacles.

Handschuh *m* glove.

Handschutz *m* hand guard.

Handstreich *m* surprise raid; coup de main.

Handstreutrommel *f* hand sprinkler *(CWS).*

Handstütze *f* pistol grip.

handtätig hand-operated, manually operated, manual *adj.*

Handwaffe *f* hand weapon, hand arm.

Handwagen *m* handcart.

Handwerfer *m* mortar.

Hang *m* slope.

Hängeantenne *f* trailing wire antenna *(Ap).*

Hängebrücke *f* suspension bridge.

Hängeleine *f* suspension line *(Prcht).*

Hängematte *f* hammock.

Hängemine *f* hanging mine.

Hängesäule *f* king post.

Hängeventil *n* inverted valve *(Mtr).*

Hängewerk *n* erect truss *(Bdg).*

Hangfaktor *m* slope factor *(influence of slope of target surface on longitudinal dispersion) (Ballistics).*

Hangsegeln *n* ridge soaring *(glider).*

Hangstellung *f* slope position *(Tac).*

Hangwind *m* anabatic wind.

Hangwinkel *m* gradient *(Top).*

Hardyscheibe *f* flexible disk *(MT).*

Harke *f* rake.

Hartfutter *n* oats and grain.

Hartgummi *n* ebonite.

Haschee *n* hash.

Haube *f* cap *(Am)*; hood *(Mtr)*; spinner *(Ap propeller).*

Haubenverkleidung *f* engine cowling *(Ap).*

Haubitze *f* howitzer *(light and medium).*

Haue *f* pickax.

Haufenwolke *f* cumulus cloud.

Hauptangriff *m* main attack, main effort.

Hauptanschluß *m* trunk station *(Tp).*

Hauptauswanderungsstrecke *f* linear travel of target during time of flight *(AA gunnery).*

Hauptbeobachtungsstelle *f* fire direction center *(Arty).*

Haupteinbruchsstelle *f* main point of penetration *(Tac).*

Hauptfeldwebel *m* first sergeant.

Hauptfunkstelle *f* net control station *(Rad).*

Hauptgefreiter *m* a grade in the *Luftwaffe* between *Obergefreiter (Cpl)* and *Unteroffizier (Sgt)*; seaman, 1st class *(highest rated 1st* *class seaman, with 4½ years' seniority).*

Hauptgestell *n* headstall *(harness).*

Hauptgetriebe *n* main transmission gear *(MT).*

Hauptkampffeld *n* main defensive area, battle position.

Hauptkampflinie *f* main line of resistance.

Hauptladung *f* main charge *(blasting cap).*

Hauptleute *pl* captains.

Hauptmacht *f* main striking force.

Hauptmann *m* captain.

Hauptmasse *f* main body.

Hauptquartier *n* headquarters.

Hauptreinigung *f* complete cleaning *(R).*

Hauptschlußmotor *m* series motor *(Elec).*

Hauptschlußschaltung *f* series connection *(Elec).*

Hauptschnittverfahren *n* mainstation intersection method *(FR).*

Hauptsender *m* final amplifier, power amplifier *(Rad).*

Hauptstelle *f* trunk station *(Tp).*

Hauptsturmführer *m* *See* SS-Hauptsturmführer.

Hauptträger *m* longeron *(Ap);* main beam or girder *(Bdg).*

Haupttrupp *m* advance guard reserve *(in Adv Gd of large unit);* rear guard reserve *(in rear Gd of large unit);* advance guard support *(in Adv Gd of smaller unit);* rear guard support *(in rear Gd of smaller unit).*

Hauptuhr *f* master watch.

Hauptverbandplatz *m* clearing station *(Med).*

Hauptvorgelege *n* main reduction gear *(Tk).*

Hauptwache *f* main guard.

Hauptwachtmeister *m* first sergeant *(Arty, Cav).*

Hauptwelle *f* mainshaft.

Hauptzündung *f* main ignition lead *(blasting).*

Haushaltsjahr *n* fiscal year.

Hauswart *m* house warden; janitor.

Hauszelt *n* "house tent" *(a 16-man tent constructed from shelter halves).*

Haut *f* skin.

hautätzend vesicant *(CWS).*

Hautentgiftungsmittel *n* skin decontamination agent.

Hautentgiftungssalbe *f* decontamination ointment.

Hautgift *n* blister agent, vesicant agent *(CWS).*

Hautwirkung *f* skin effect *(Rad).*

Heavisideschicht *f* Heaviside layer.

Hebebaum *m* crowbar, handspike, lever.

Hebel *m* lever.

heben elevate *(a gun);* raise, lift.

Hebezeug *n* hoisting gear, hoist.

Heck *n* stern *(Nav, Ash);* tail *(Ap);* rear *(Tk).*

Heckantrieb *m* rear drive *(MT).*

Hecke *f* hedge.

Heckenschütze *m* sniper.

Heckenspringen *n* hedge-hopping *(Avn).*

Heckkanzel *f* tail turret *(Ap).*

Heckmaschinengewehr *n* tail gun *(Ap).*

Heckmotorwagen *m* rear-engine motor car.

Heckpanzer *m* rear armor *(Tk).*

Heckschütze *m* tail gunner *(Ap).*

Heckstand *f* tail-gun position *(Ap).*

Heckwaffe *f* tail gun *(Ap).*

Heer *n* Army *(the Army, as distinguished from* Armee, *a tactical unit).*

Heeresakja *f* *See* Akja.

Heeresamt *n* *See* Allgemeines Heeresamt.

Heeresanstalt *f* Army establishment, organization, or institution.

Heeresartillerie *f* GHQ artillery.

Heeresarzt *m* chief representative of Army Medical Department at *Oberkommando des Heeres (subordinate to* Heeressanitätsinspekteur).

Heeresatmer *m* service oxygen breathing apparatus *(automatically operated).*

Heeresbaudienst *m* Army construction service.

Heeresbeamter *m* civilian official of the Army.

Heeresbedürfnisse *npl* military necessities.

Heeresbergführer *m* Army mountain guide *(mountaineer specialist).*

Heeresbericht *m* official Army communiqué.

Heeresbestände *mpl* military stores.

Heeresbetreuungsabteilung *f* Army welfare unit, Army morale unit.

Heeresbetriebsstofflager *n* Army

gasoline and lubricant bulk storage plant.

Heeresbildungsanstalt *f* military school.

Heeresbücherei *f* Army library.

Heeresdruckvorschrift *f* Army Manual *(abbr. H. Dv.)*.

Heereseinrichtung *f* Army establishment, organization, or institution.

Heeresflak *f* Army antiaircraft artillery *(as distinguished from AAA of the* Luftwaffe*)*.

Heeresgerät *n* Army equipment *(in its broadest sense; to be distinguished from* Heergerät*)*.

Heeresgruppe *f* group of armies.

Heeresgruppenkommando *n* headquarters of a group of armies.

Heereshochgebirgsschule *f* Army training school for mountain warfare.

Heeresintendant *m* *See* Intendant.

Heeresjustizbeamter *m* military law official.

Heereskavallerie *f* GHQ cavalry.

Heereskraftfahrpark *m* GHQ motor transport park.

Heereskrankenschwester *f* Army nurse.

Heeresküstenartillerie *f* Army coast artillery *(as distinguished from the* Marineartillerie*)*.

Heereslazarett *n* general hospital, Army hospital.

Heeresleitung *f* GHQ, Army Command.

Heeresmunitionslager *n* Army ammunition-supply depot.

Heeresnachrichtenregiment *n* GHQ signal regiment.

Heeresnachschubführer *m* GHQ chief of rear services.

Heeresnachschubkolonne *f* GHQ supply column.

Heerespersonalamt *n* Army Personnel Office *(branch of the* Oberkommando des Heeres*)* *(abbr.* HPA, PA*)*.

Heerespferdelazarett *n* GHQ veterinary hospital.

Heerespsychologe *m* personnel consultant.

Heeresreserve *f* GHQ reserve.

Heeressanitätsabteilung *f* GHQ medical battalion.

Heeres-Sanitätsinspekteur *m* surgeon

general *(with rank of* Generaloberstabsarzt*)*.

Heeres-Sauerstoffschutzgerät *n* service oxygen breathing apparatus *(manually operated)*.

Heeresstandort *m* army post.

Heeresstandortkasse *f* army post finance office.

Heeresstandortverwaltung *f* army post administration.

Heerestruppen *fpl* GHQ troops.

Heeresversorgung *f* Army supply.

Heeresverwaltung *f* Army administration, administrative services.

Heeresverwaltungsamt *n* Army Administration Office *(branch of the* Oberkommando des Heeres*)* *(abbr.* HVA, VA*)*.

Heereswaffenamt *n* Army Ordnance Office *(branch of the* Oberkommando des Heeres*)* *(abbr.* HWaA*)*.

Heeres-Zeugamt *n* Army ordnance supply office or depot.

Heergerät *n* Army transport equipment *(includes transport accessories; to be distinguished from* Heeresgerät*)*.

Heimatgebiet *n* zone of the interior.

Heimatflughafen *m* home base *(Avn)*.

Heimat-Pferdelazarett *n* veterinary general hospital *(Z of I)*.

Heimathorst *m* home base *(Avn)*.

Heimatstaat *m* country of origin *(PW)*.

Heimatwachbataillon *n* guard battalion *(Z of I)*.

Heimsendung *f* repatriation.

heißen to hoist *(a flag)*.

heiter bright, cheerful; scattered *(Met)*.

Heizbatterie *f* "A" battery, filament battery *(Rad)*.

Heizfaden *m* filament *(Rad)*.

Heizkanal *m* hot-air duct *(thermo anti-icer)*.

Heizkreis *m* filament circuit *(Rad)*.

Heizöl *n* fuel oil *(for heating)*.

Heizregler *m* variable filament resistor *(Rad)*.

Heizsammler *m* filament battery *(Rad)*.

Heizstrom *m* filament current *(Rad)*.

Heldenfriedhof *m* military cemetery.

Heldentat *f* heroic deed, exploit.

Helm *m* helmet.

Helmband n   identification helmet band *(Tng)*.

Helmbezug m   helmet cover.

Helmüberzug m   *See* **Helmbezug**.

hemmen   to check *(recoil, etc.)*; to jam *(a gun, etc.)*; to obstruct, hinder, slow down; inhibit.

Hemmung f   stoppage *(Ord)*; obstruction; inhibition.

Beseitigen von Hemmungen   immediate action *(Ord)*.

herabsetzen   reduce *(in rank)*.

heranlocken   to decoy, to lure.

heranpirschen, sich   to creep or stalk up to.

herausmanövrieren   to maneuver the enemy out of position.

"Heraustreten!"   "Fall out!" *(to men in barracks)*.

Herbertgerät n   Herbert bridge unit *(similar to US Bailey-type bridge)*.

Hereinlotsen n   "piloting-in" by ground-air radio communication.

Hering m   tent pin.

Hersteller m   maker, manufacturer.

Hertz n   cycles per second *(Ger unit of frequency)*.

Herzstück n   switch point *(RR)*.

Heulsignal n   siren.

Hexachloräthan n   hexachlorethane *(CWS)*.

Hieb m   slash *(bayonet)*; cut *(saber, etc.)*.

Hiebwaffe f   slashing weapon.

Hilfe f   help, aid, assistance.

Hilfsantenne f   sensing antenna *(Rad direction finder)*.

Hilfsbeobachter m   assistant observer *(Avn)*.

Hilfsflügel m   slat, auxiliary airfoil.

Hilfskette f   auxiliary track *(MT)*.

Hilfskettenfahrzeug n   combination wheel-track vehicle.

Hilfskreuzer m   auxiliary cruiser.

Hilfslafette f   improvised mount *(MG)*.

Hilfslandeplatz m   auxiliary landing field.

Hilfsmaßstab m   auxiliary scale *(Inst)*.

Hilfsmotor m   auxiliary engine.

Hilfsschirm m   pilot parachute.

Hilfstruppen fpl   auxiliary troops. *See also* **Hilfswilliger**.

Hilfswaffe f   auxiliary arm.

Hilfswilliger m   auxiliary volunteer *(East-European or PW volunteer for non-combat service with the German Army)*.

Hilfsziel n   auxiliary target; reference point.

Himmelskugel f   celestial sphere.

Himmelsrichtung f   point of the compass, cardinal point.

Hindernis n   obstacle, hurdle, obstruction; accessory defense *(Tac)*.

Hindernisbahn f   obstacle course.

Hindernisfeuer n   obstacle light, obstruction light *(Avn)*.

Hindernisschlagpfahl m   driving-type obstacle picket *(i.e., set up by driving into ground)*.

Hindernisschraubpfahl m   screw-type obstacle picket *(i.e., set up by screwing into ground)*.

Hindernissprengtrupp m   obstacle demolition squad.

Hindernisstrecke f   obstacle course.

Hindernistrupp m   obstacle construction squad.

hinhaltend   delaying.

hinhaltender Widerstand   delaying action *(in successive positions)*.

hinhaltendes Gefecht   delaying action.

Hinterachsantrieb m   rear-axle drive *(MT)*.

Hinterachsgehäuse n   differential housing, differential case *(MT)*.

Hintereinanderschaltung f   series connection *(Elec)*.

Hintergelenk n   rear toggle joint *(pistol)*.

Hinterhalt m   ambush, concealment; trap.

Hinterhand f   hindquarters *(horse)*.

Hinterhang m   reverse slope.

Hinterhangstellung f   reverse-slope position.

Hinterholm m   rear outrigger *(AA gun)*.

Hinterkaffe f   stern compartment *(Pon)*.

Hinterkante f   trailing edge *(Ap wing)*.

Hinterradantrieb m   rear-wheel drive *(MT)*.

Hintersielengeschirr n   wheel harness.

Hintersteven m   sternpost.

Hinterstütze f   trail *(MG tripod)*.

Hinterwagen m   caisson.

Hinterzeug n   breeching *(harness)*.

Hinterzwiesel m   cantle of saddle; rear of packsaddle arch.

Hirnsäge f   crosscut saw.

hissen to hoist *(a flag)*.

Hitler-Jugend *f* Nazi party youth organization.

hitzebeständig heat-resistant.

Hitzschlag *m* heatstroke.

Hochachse *f* vertical axis *(Ap)*.

Hochangriff *m* high-altitude bombing attack *(Avn)*.

Hochbau *m* overhead construction *(Tp line)*.

hochbrisant high-explosive.

Hochdecker *m* high-wing monoplane.

Hochdruckgebiet *n* high-pressure area *(Met)*.

Hochdruckreifen *m* high-pressure tire *(MT)*.

Hochdruckschmierung *f* high-pressure lubrication.

Hochebene *f* plateau.

Hochelastikreifen *m* cushion tire *(MT)*.

hochempfindlich supersensitive.

hochempfindlicher Aufschlagzünder supersensitive fuze *(AA Am)*.

Hochfrequenz *f* radio frequency, high frequency.

Hochfrequenzdrossel *f* radio-frequency choke.

Hochfrequenzstörungen *fpl* high-frequency interference *(Rad)*.

Hochfrequenzstufe *f* radio-frequency stage.

Hochfrequenztransformator *m* radio frequency transformer.

Hochfrequenzverstärker *m* radio frequency amplifier.

Hochgebirgsbataillon *n* high-mountain rifle battalion *(consists entirely of mountaineer specialists)*.

hochgezogene Kehrkurve Immelmann turn.

Hochleitung *f* overhead line.

Hochofen *m* blast furnace.

Hochseeschlepper *m* ocean-going tugboat.

Hochspannungsleitung *f* high-tension line, power transmission line *(Elec)*.

Hochstand *m* high lookout post.

Höchstgasdruck *m* maximum gas pressure *(Ord)*.

Höchstgeschwindigkeit *f* maximum speed.

Höchstlast *f* maximum load.

Höchstleistung *f* maximum power, maximum performance.

Höchstschußweite *f* extreme range, maximum range *(Ord)*.

Höchstwertverfahren *n* maximum intensity method *(sound locator)*.

Höchstzahl *f* maximum number.

Hochwert *m* Y-coordinate number *(map grid or coordinate scale)*.

Hochziehen *n* steep climb, zoom *(Ap)*.

Höckerhindernisse *npl* "dragon's teeth" *(AT obstacle)*.

Hockloch *n* crouching foxhole.

Hof *m* yard, courtyard; farm.

Höhe *f* altitude, elevation, height; hill; rate, amount.

Hoheitsabzeichen *n* nationality marking *(Ap, Tk)*; national insignia, national emblem *(Clo)*.

Hoheitsgewässer *npl* territorial waters.

Hoheitszeichen *n* See **Hoheitsabzeichen**.

Höhenabstand *m* vertical interval.

Höhenabweichung *f* range deviation, vertical deviation *(Gunnery)*.

Höhenangabe *f* altitude indication, altitude reading.

Höhenänderung *f* change of height *(AA predictor)*.

Höhenatmer *m* oxygen apparatus *(Avn)*.

Höhenbegrenzer *m* elevating stop *(Ord)*.

Höhenbestimmung *f* determination of altitude.

Höhenbombenwurf *m* high-altitude bombing.

Höhenebene *f* horizontal plane through path of target in horizontal flight *(AA gunnery)*.

Höhenempfänger *m* elevation indicator, elevation indicator-regulator *(AA gun)*.

Höhenentfernungsmesser *m* height finder, altimeter *(AAA)*.

Höhenflosse *f* stabilizer *(Ap)*.

Höhenflug *m* high-altitude flight *(Avn)*.

Höhenflugzeug *n* sub-stratoplane.

Höhengradbogen *m* elevating sector *(G)*.

Höhenhebel *m* elevating gear lever *(MG)*.

Höhenkabine *f* pressure cabin *(Ap)*.

Höhenkrankheit *f* aeroembolism, bends *(Avn)*.

Höhenlader *m* supercharger with high blower ratio *(Ap)*.

Höhenleitwerk *n* elevator assembly *(Ap)*.

Höhenlibelle *f* elevation level *(MG sight)*.

Höhenlinie *f* contour line.

Höhenmesser *m* altimeter *(Ap)*; height finder, altimeter *(AAA)*.

Höhenmeßplan *m* elevation plotting board *(Gunnery)*.

Höhenmessung *f* hypsometry *(Surv)*.

Höhenmischregelung *f* high-altitude mixture control *(Ap)*.

Höhenmotor *m* supercharged engine *(Ap)*.

Höhenrichtfeld *n* elevation, total movement in elevation *(Ord)*.

Höhenrichtfernrohr *n* elevation tracking telescope *(height finder)*.

Höhenrichtkanonier *m* elevation setter.

Höhenrichtmaschine *f* elevating mechanism *(Ord)*.

Höhenrichtrad *n* elevating handwheel *(G)*.

Höhenrichtschraube *f* elevation screw *(prismatic sight)*.

Höhenrichttrieb *m* elevating drive, elevating mechanism *(Ord)*.

Höhenrichtung *f* adjusted range; laying for elevation *(Gunnery)*.

Höhenrichtwelle *f* elevating shaft *(G)*.

Höhenrichtwerk *n* elevating mechanism *(Ord)*.

Höhenrichtzeiger *m* elevation indicator *(Ord)*.

Höhenrippe *f* ridge *(Top)*.

Höhenrücken *m* ridge, crest of ridge.

Höhenruder *n* elevator *(Ap)*.

Höhenruderhebel *m* elevator control lever *(Ap)*.

Höhenschicht *f* altitude bracket *(Avn, Met)*.

Höhenschichtlinie *f* contour line.

Höhenschreiber *m* barograph *(Avn)*.

Höhenstaffelung *f* stepped-up formation *(Avn)*.

Höhenstellung *f* position on dominant height.

Höhensteuer *n* elevator *(Ap)*.

Höhensteuerung *f* elevator control *(Ap)*.

Höhenstreuung *f* range dispersion on vertical target *(Ballistics)*.

Höhenteilung *f* elevation scale *(G, MG)*.

Höhentemperatur *f* temperature at various altitudes *(Met)*.

Höhentrieb *m* elevating worm *(sight mechanism)*.

Höhenunterschied *m* difference in altitude between target and piece *(Gunnery)*; elevation difference *(Surv, Top)*; vertical interval, vertical offset.

Höhenvorhalt *m* See **Höhenwinkelvorhalt.**

Höhenwinkel *m* angular height, vertical visual angle *(AA gunnery)*.

Höhenwinkelverbesserungsknopf *m* vertical correction knob *(AA gun)*.

Höhenwinkelvorhalt *m* vertical lead, vertical deflection *(AA gunnery)*.

Höherer...Offizier Senior...Officer *(with mention of arm or service)* *(at Army Hq, e.g. Höh. Kav. Offz., Senior Cav Officer at Army Hq)*.

hohl hollow, concave, sunken.

Höhle *f* cave.

Hohlkopfgeschoß *n* hollow-charge projectile.

Hohlladung *f* hollow charge.

Hohlraumpanzerung *f* spaced armor *(Tk)*.

Hohlringladung *f* hollow ring charge.

Hohlweg *m* sunken road.

Holm *m* spar *(Ap)*; stringer, spar *(Bdg)*; outrigger *(AA gun)*; trail *(right or left trail of a split trail)*.

die Holme spreizen to spread the trails.

Holmzurrung *f* outrigger lock *(G)*.

Holzbunker *m* log bunker, timber shelter *(Ft)*.

Holzgasanlage *f* wood-gas generator.

Holzgas-Lastkraftwagen *m* wood-gas motor truck.

Holzgehäuse *n* wooden baffle, cabinet *(Rad)*.

Holzgeist *m* wood alcohol.

Holzkohle *f* charcoal.

Holzkohlen-Gasgenerator *m* wood-gas generator *(MT)*.

Holzmine *f* wooden box mine.

Holzrost *m* wooden grating; trench flooring, catwalk, boardwalk *(trench)*.

Holz-Tankstelle *f* filling station for wood-gas motor vehicles.

Holzverkleidung *f* wood revetment.

Holzweg *m* dead-end loggers' road.

Holzzwischenlage *f* wood separator *(storage battery)*.

Horchauswertestelle *f* radio intelligence post.

Horchdienst *m* intercept service *(Rad, Tp)*.

Horchempfang *m* stand-by operation *(Rad)*.

Horchempfänger *m* intercept set *(Rad)*.

Horcherprüf- und Übungsgerät *n* binaural trainer, binaural training instrument.

Horchgerät *n* sound locator, sound detector; intercept receiver.

Horchkompanie *f* intercept company *(Sig C)*.

Horchortung *f* sound location, sound ranging *(AAA)*.

Horchposten *m* listening sentry, listening post.

Horchstelle *f* listening post, intercept post.

Hörfrequenz *f* audio frequency.

Hörer *m* telephone receiver, headphone.

Horizont *m* horizon; artificial horizon *(Ap)*.

Horizontalebene *f* horizontal plane.

Horizontalflug *m* horizontal flight, level flight *(Avn)*.

Horizontalgeschwindigkeit *f* ground speed *(of target) (AA gunnery)*.

Horizontiergriff *m* leveling jack handle *(AA gun outrigger)*.

Horizontierung *f* leveling jack *(AA gun outrigger)*.

Horizontierungsvorrichtung *f* leveling device *(AA gun mount)*.

Hörmuschel *f* earpiece *(Tp)*.

Horn *n* bugle, horn.

Hornisse *f* hornet *(name of Ger self-propelled AT gun)*.

Hornist *m* bugler.

Hornsignal *n* bugle call; horn signal *(MT)*.

Hörsaalflugzeug *n* "flying classroom."

Hörsaalsummer *m* oscillator-amplifier *(code practice)*.

Horst *m* *See* Fliegerhorst.

H-Staffel *f* tactical reconnaissance squadron attached to army ground units *(Luftwaffe)*.

Hub *m* stroke *(Mtr)*.

Hubhöhe *f* angle of axle displacement *(MT)*.

Hubraum *m* piston displacement *(Mtr)*.

Hubschrauber *m* helicopter.

Hubvolumen *n* *See* Hubraum.

Hufbeschlag *m* horseshoeing.

Hufkrone *f* hoof coronet *(horse)*.

Hügel *m* hill.

Hülle *f* case, envelope, skin, cover, shell.

Hüllenbahn *f* panel *(Bln)*.

Hülse *f* hoop *(Mort)*; gas-cylinder plug *(MG)*; receiver *(pistol, R)*; socket *(G carriage)*; cartridge or shell case.

Hülsenauswurf *m* ejection of cartridge case.

Hülsenauszieher *m* extractor *(Ord)*.

Hülsenboden *m* base of cartridge case.

Hülsenbrücke *f* receiver cover *(R)*.

Hülsenfänger *m* deflector bag *(AA gun, MG)*.

Hülsenhals *m* neck of cartridge.

Hülsenkartusche *f* semifixed cartridge.

Hülsenkasten *m* deflector box *(AA gun, MG)*.

Hülsenkopf *m* front end of receiver *(R)*.

Hülsenmantel *m* cartridge-case jacket.

Hülsenrand *m* cartridge-case rim.

Hülsenreißer *m* stoppage caused by broken cartridge case.

Hülsenzapfen *m* recoil lug *(R)*.

Hummel *f* bumblebee *(nickname for Ger self-propelled medium field howitzer)*.

Hundeführer *m* dog handler, dog guard.

Hundeführerrotte *f* dog-handler party.

Hüpflinie *f* short hop, short leg of flight *(Avn)*.

Hurde *f* brush hurdle.

Hütchen *n* blasting cap; cup *(cartridge)*.

Hütte *f* hut, cottage; iron works; rolling mill.

Hüttenlager *n* cantonment.

Hydrozyansäure *f* hydrocyanic acid, prussic acid *(CWS)*.

Hyperbelplan *m* asymptote correction chart *(SR)*.

I

Igel *m* hedgehog *(AT obstacle);* all-around defense *(Tac).*

Igelit *n* a type of electric wire insulation.

Igelstellung *f* "hedgehog" defense position, position of all-around defense.

Ilag *n* See **Interniertenlager.**

impfen inoculate, vaccinate.

Impfschein *m* vaccination certificate.

Impfung *f* inoculation, vaccination.

Imprägniermittel *n* impregnite.

Inaktive Offiziere inactive reserve.

Inaugenscheinnahme *f* inspection.

Inausgabegenehmigung *f* authorized permission to delete from stock record items issued.

Inbesitznahme *f* occupation *(Tac);* act of taking possession.

Indienststellung *f* commissioning *(of a vessel).*

Indizienbeweis *m* circumstantial evidence.

indizierte Leistung indicated horsepower.

Industrieanlagen *fpl* industrial installations.

Induktor *m* generator *(Tp).*

Ineinklangbringen *n* harmonization.

Infanterie *f* infantry.

Infanteriebegleitgeschütz *n* infantry accompanying gun.

Infanteriefliegerstaffel *f* air support squadron. *See also* **Staffel.**

Infanterieflug *m* contact patrol *(Avn).*

Infanteriegeschütz *n* infantry gun, infantry howitzer.

Infanteriegranate *f* shell fired by infantry gun or howitzer.

Infanteriekolonne *f* infantry supply column *(generally prefixed by* leichte).

Infanteriekommandeur *m* infantry commander *(supervises training of Inf units under Div Commander).*

Infanterienachspitze *f* infantry rear point *(march column).*

Infanteriepark *m* infantry equipment park.

Infanteriepionier *m* infantry pioneer.

Infanteriepionierzug *m* pioneer platoon *(Inf Regt).*

Infanterie-Reiterzug *m* mounted rifle platoon *(Inf Regt).*

Infanteriespitze *f* infantry point *(march column).*

Infanteriesturmabzeichen *n* infantry assault badge *(decoration).*

Infanterist *m* infantryman.

Infinitesimalrechnung *f* calculus *(Math).*

Influenz *f* electrostatic induction.

Ingangsetzen *n* starting.

Ingenieur *m* engineer *(a Civ official with nominal Mil rank serving in technical capacity generally in MT, Ft Engr, or Avn).*

Initialzünder *m* initiator *(Am).*

Inklination *f* dip *(compass).*

Innenauskreuzung *f* interior bracing *(Ap).*

Innenbackenbremse *f* internal expanding brake.

Innendienst *m* interior duty, duty in barracks.

Innengrenzlehre *f* plug gage.

Innenhafen *m* inner harbor.

Innenhütchen *n* plug, inner cap *(blasting cap).*

Innenraum *m* interior.

Innenschieber *m* inner sleeve *(sleeve-valve engine).*

Innenverspannung *f* interior bracing *(Ap).*

Innenwache *f* interior guard.

innerballistisch pertaining to interior ballistics.

Insel *f* island.

Inspektion *f* inspectorate *(any of the sections devoted to various arms and services in the* Allgemeines Heeresamt).

Inspekteur *m* inspector *(chief of an inspectorate in the* Allgemeines Heeresamt, *as* Waffeninspekteur [Ord]).

Inspizient *m* inspector.

Inspizierung *f* inspection.

Installateur *m* plumber; electrician.

Installationsplan *m* wiring diagram; pipe layout.

Instandhaltung *f* maintenance.

Instandsetzung *f* repair.

nach Bedarf durchgeführte Instandsetzung march maintenance, operating maintenance.

regelmäßig durchgeführte Instandsetzung scheduled maintenance.
Instandsetzungsabteilung *f* maintenance unit.
Instandsetzungsdienst *m* damage-clearance and repair service *(Civ defense)*.
Instandsetzungskraftwagen *m* maintenance truck, repair truck.
Instandsetzungsstaffel *f* maintenance echelon.
Instandsetzungswerkstätte *f* repair shop.
Instandsetzung und Unterhaltung repair and maintenance.
Instanz *f* authority, court *(Law)*.
Instellungbringen *n* emplacing *(Arty)*.
Instellunggehen *n* moving into position *(Tac)*.
Instrumentenbrett *n* instrument panel.
Instrumentfehler *m* instrumental error.
Intendant *m* civilian official in administrative services *(ranking as colonel)*.
Intendantur *f* general staff administrative section *(section IV of an army, corps, or Div general staff, dealing mostly with supply)*.
Intendanturassessor *m* civilian official in administrative services *(ranking as captain)*.

Intendanturinspektor *m* civilian official in administrative services *(ranking as 1st Lt)*.
Intendanturrat *m* civilian official in administrative services *(ranking as major)*.
internieren to intern.
Internierter *m* internee.
Interniertenlager *n* internment camp.
Invarol *n* a cold-resistant grease.
Invertentfernungsmesser *m* inverted-image range finder.
Irrung *f* correction *(Rad procedure)*.
Isolator *m* insulator *(Elec)*.
Isolierband *n* friction tape *(Elec)*.
Isolierbecher *m* insulating case *(circuit tester)*.
isolieren to insulate *(Elec)*; isolate *(Med)*.
Isoliergerät *n* oxygen breathing apparatus.
Isolierschutz *m* insulation *(Elec)*.
Isolierstoff *m* insulating material, insulator *(Elec)*.
Isolierstreifen *m* friction tape, insulating tape.
Isolierung *f* isolation, absolute quarantine.
Istbestand *m* equipment on hand.
Iststand *m* See **Iststärke**.
Iststärke *f* actual strength, morning-report strength.
Iststärkenachweisung *f* daily strength report.

J

Jabo *m* See **Jagdbomber**.
Jackenwiege *f* jacket cradle, ring cradle *(G)*.
Jafü *m* See **Jagdführer**.
Jagdabwehr *f* fighter defense *(Avn)*.
Jagdbomber *m* fighter bomber.
Jagdeinsitzer *m* single-seater fighter *(Avn)*.
Jagdflieger *m* fighter pilot *(Avn)* *(same word used in plural to denote fighter aviation)*.
Jagdflieger-Ergänzungsstaffel *f* fighter replacement squadron *(Avn)*.
Jagdflug *m* fighter patrol, fighter sweep *(Avn)*.
Jagdflugzeug *n* single-engine fighter airplane.

Jagdführer *m* commander of all fighter units of a *Luftflotte*.
Jagdgeschwader *n* fighter wing *(Avn)*. See also **Geschwader**.
Jagdgruppe *f* fighter group *(Avn)*. See also **Gruppe**.
Jagdmehrsitzer *m* multi-seater fighter airplane.
Jagdraum *m* patrol area for fighter aircraft.
Jagdschutz *m* fighter escort *(Avn)*.
Jagdsperre *f* fighter screen *(Avn)*.
Jagdstaffel *f* fighter squadron *(Avn)*. See also **Staffel**.
Jagdverband *m* fighter formation *(Avn)*.

Jagen *n* subarea of forest *(for mapping purposes)*.

Jäger *m* rifleman *(in a light Mtz Inf Div,* Jägerdivision); private *(in mountain Inf,* Gebirgsjäger); fighter airplane, pursuit airplane.

Jägerbataillon *n* rifle battalion. See **Jägerdivision.**

Jägerdivision *f* light infantry division *(so-called "light division" somewhat similar to Ger Mtz Inf Div).*

Jägerplatz *m* fighter airdrome.

Jäger-Regiment *n* rifle regiment. See **Jägerdivision.**

Jägerschutz *m* fighter escort *(Avn).*

Jahrgang *m* age class; year *(of a publication, etc.).*

Joch *n* bent, trestle *(Bdg);* yoke.

Jochleiste *f* cheekbone *(horse).*

Jochpfahl *m* pile of pile bent *(Bdg).*

Jod *n* iodine.

Jodessigester *m* ethyliodoacetate *(CWS).*

Jodtinktur *f* tincture of iodine.

Jolle *f* yawl *(Nav).*

Jugendherberge *f* youth hostel.

justieren to adjust, to collimate *(bore-sight alinement, etc.).*

Justiergerät *n* bore sight.

K

Kabel *n* cable, wire *(Tp).*

Kabelader *f* strand, conductor *(of Tp wire).*

Kabelaufführungspunkt *m* wire lead-in point *(Tp).*

Kabelgraben *m* wire trench *(Tp).*

Kabelleitung *f* wire line *(Tp).*

Kabelmantel *m* cable sheath *(Elec, Tp).*

Kabelmeßgerät *n* wire-testing instrument *(Tp).*

Kabelmesser *n* electrician's knife.

Kabelschuh *m* loop-tip terminal *(Elec).*

Kabelseele *f* core conductor *(Tp wire).*

Kabelstecker *m* wire plug *(Elec).*

Kabeltau *n* hawser.

Kabeltrommel *f* reel *(Tp).*

Kabelverbinder *n* connecting sleeve *(Tp wire).*

Kabelverbindung *f* wire splice *(Tp).*

Kabelwachs *n* cable wax, adhesive pitch *(Tp).*

Kabine *f* compartment, cockpit *(Ap).*

Kader *m* cadre.

Kadett *m* cadet.

Kaffe *f* compartment, sponson *(Pon).*

Kahn *m* boat.

Kahnfähre *f* punt ferry, boat ferry.

Kai *m* quay.

Kajüte *f* cabin *(Nav).*

Kaliber *n* caliber.

Kalibereinheit *f* unit load of single-caliber ammunition *(approximately 18-ton unit for one RR car).*

Kaliberlänge *f* barrel length expressed in calibers.

Kaliberring *m* bore gage, breech bore gage.

Kaliberzylinder *m* See **Kaliberring.**

Kalipatrone *f* potassium cartridge *(oxygen breathing apparatus).*

Kaliumpermanganat *n* potassium permanganate.

Kalk *m* lime.

Kalkmilch *f* lime solution *(CWS).*

kältebeständig cold-resistant.

kaltgereckt cold-worked.

Kaltklebekitt *m* cold adhesive putty *(for attaching demolition charges) (abbr.* Kat).

Kaltluftfront *f* cold front *(Met).*

Kaltmeißel *m* cold chisel.

Kaltrecken *n* cold-working process, autofrettage *(Ord).*

Kameradschaftsheim *n* service club, canteen.

Kamm *m* crest, ridge; comb.

Kammer *f* bolt *(R, pistol);* camera; chamber; stockroom.

Kammerbahn *f* bolt slide *(R).*

Kammerfang *m* bolt catch *(MG).*

Kammerfangstück *n* bolt-catch piece *(pistol).*

Kammergriff *m* bolt handle *(MG).*

Kammerhülse *f* central tube, flash tube *(shrapnel).*

Kammerhülsenladung f   flash-tube charge (shrapnel).
Kammerhülsenrohr n   burster tube (Am).
Kammerknopf m   bolt knob (R).
Kammerstengel m   bolt handle (R).
Kammerunteroffizier m   supply sergeant.
Kammerwarze f   bolt lug (R).
Kammkissen n   back pad (harness).
Kammkissengurt m   back-pad strap (harness).
Kammlinie f   ridge line (Top).
Kampf m   battle, combat, fight. See also terms under **Gefecht**, **Krieg**.
Kampfabschnitt m   combat sector.
Kampfabteil m   fighting compartment, turret basket (Tk).
Kampfaufgabe f   combat task (Tac).
Kampfauftrag m   combat mission.
Kampfeinheit f   combat unit, tactical unit.
kämpfen to fight.
kämpfende Truppe combat element.
Kämpfer m   fighter; abutment (of an arch).
kampferprobt seasoned, battle-tried, having combat experience.
Kampffahrzeug n   combat vehicle.
Kampffeld n   field of combat.
Kampfflieger m   bomber pilot; any member of a combat crew (same word used in plural to denote bombardment aviation).
Kampffliegerei f   bombardment aviation.
Kampffliegergruppe f   bombardment group (Avn). See also **Gruppe**.
Kampffliegerstaffel f   bombardment squadron (Avn). See also **Staffel**.
Kampffliegerverband m   bombardment formation (Avn).
Kampfflugzeug n   bombardment airplane.
Kampfführung f   battle command, conduct of battle.
Kampfgas n   war gas (CWS).
Kampfgebiet n   combat zone, forward area, combat area.
Kampfgelände n   battle terrain.
Kampfgemeinschaft f   combat team.
Kampfgeschwader n   bombardment wing (Avn). See also **Geschwader**.
Kampfgeschwader z.b.V. special purpose transport wing (airborne operations).

Kampfgruppe f   bombardment group (Avn); combat command (Armd Comd); combat team, task force.
Kampfhandlung f   engagement, action.
Kampfkraft f   fighting power.
Kampflage f   tactical situation.
Kampfleistung f   battle performance, combat performance.
Kampflinie f   line of battle.
Kampfmehrsitzer m   multiseater bomber.
Kampfmittel npl   means of combat, arms and ammunition.
Kampfnachricht f   combat message (Rad).
Kampfpistole f   rifled Very pistol (for Sig and/or incendiary cartridges).
Kampfraum m   combat zone, forward area, combat area.
Kampfruf m   password, slogan, battle cry.
Kampfschule f   bombardment school (Avn).
Kampfstaffel f   combat echelon (Tac); bombardment squadron (Avn). See also **Staffel**.
Kampfstellung f   battle position.
Kampfstoff m   chemical warfare agent.
Kampfstoffbelegung f   gas coverage.
Kampstoffbeschuß m   chemical-shell fire.
Kampfstoffbombe f   chemical bomb.
Kampfstoffgehalt m   gas concentration (CWS).
Kampfstoffgruppen fpl   classification of chemical warfare agents.
Kampfstoffriegel m   chemical obstacle; chemical-shell box barrage.
Kampfstoffschwaden mpl   chemical fumes (CWS).
Kampfstoffsperre f   chemical obstacle, contaminated area (CWS).
Kampfstoffverwendung f   employment of chemical warfare agents.
Kampfstoffzerstäuber m   chemical-spray apparatus.
Kampftätigkeit f   combat activity, active combat, action.
Kampftruppe f   combat element.
Kampfverband m   bomber formation (Avn); combined arms unit, combat team.
Kampfwagen m   tank, combat car.
Kampfwagenfalle f   tank trap.

Kampfwagengeschütz n See Kampfwagenkanone.
Kampfwagenkanone f tank gun.
Kampfwagennachbildung f tank silhouette, dummy tank.
Kampfwagenscheibe f tank-silhouette target.
Kampfwagenwerk n tank factory.
Kampfwert m fighting qualities (of a unit).
Kampfwunde f battle injury, wound.
Kampfziel n objective (Tac).
Kampfzone f battle zone.
Kampfzweck m tactical purpose, intention.
Kandare f curb bit (harness).
Kandarenzügel m curb rein (harness).
Kanone f gun, cannon.
Kanonenboot n gunboat.
Kanonenflugzeug n cannon-armed airplane.
Kanonenjagdflieger m cannon-armed fighter airplane.
Kanonenrohr n gun barrel.
Kanonensalut m gun salute.
Kanonenschlag m firecracker (simulated fire).
Kanonenschlag mit Knallerscheinung firecracker.
Kanonenschlag mit Raucherscheinung smoke-puff charge.
Kanonenschuß m gun shot.
Kanonenwagen m assault gun car.
Kanonier m private (Arty); cannoneer.
Kante f edge; ridge.
Kantholz n squared timber.
Kantine f canteen.
Kanzel f cockpit, turret (Ap); pillbox (Ft).
vordere Kanzel nose turret (Ap).
Kap n cape (point of land).
Kapelle f band (music); chapel.
Kaperfahrt f naval raid against enemy merchant shipping.
kapern to capture (a ship).
Kapitänleutnant m lieutenant (Nav).
Kapitän zur See captain (Nav).
Kapitulant m reenlisted man.
Kapitulantenhandgeld n reenlistment bonus.
Kapitulation f capitulation, surrender; reenlistment.
kapitulieren capitulate, surrender; reenlist.
Kappagerät n predictor (AA).

Kappe f cap (of a projectile).
Kapsel f detonator, blasting cap; capsule.
Kapuze f hood.
Karabiner m carbine.
Karabinertragevorrichtung f carbine scabbard carrier.
Karbolsäure f carbolic acid, phenol.
Kardangelenk n universal joint.
kardanische Aufhängung compass gimbal.
Kardanwelle f flexible drive shaft, propeller shaft.
Karosserie f body (MT).
Kartätsche f canister (separate-loading Am).
Karte f map, chart; card, ticket.
Kartei f card file.
Karteikarte f filing card.
Kartenausschnitt m map section.
Kartenbatterie f topographic section, mapping section.
Kartenblatt n map sheet, zone map.
Kartenblatt mit Gitter grid sheet.
Kartenblattnummer f geographic index number.
Kartenbrett n map-mounting board, military sketching board.
Kartendruckerei f map-printing office or plant.
Kartenebene f horizontal plane through base of trajectory.
Kartenentfernung f horizontal range, map range.
Kartenentfernung zum Abschußpunkt horizontal range to present position (instant of firing) (AAA).
Kartenentfernung zum Meßpunkt horizontal range to present position (instant of range determination) (AAA).
Kartenentfernung zum Treffpunkt horizontal range to future position (AAA).
Kartenentfernung zum Wechselpunkt horizontal range to midpoint, minimum horizontal range (AAA).
Kartenentwurf m map projection.
Kartengitternetz n map grid.
Kartenkurs m map course (Navigation).
Kartenlesen n map reading.
Kartenmaßstab m map scale.
Kartenprojektion f map projection.
Kartenraum m chartroom (Nav).
Kartensignatur f conventional sign (on maps).

Karten- und Vermessungstruppen *fpl* topographic troops.

Kartenunterlage *f* plane table.

Kartenvervollständigung *f* map compilation.

Kartenwinkelmesser *m* map protractor.

Kartenzeichen *n* conventional sign *(on maps)*.

Kartenzeichner *m* cartographer.

kartieren to map.

Karton *m* cardboard.

Kartothek *f* card file.

Kartuschbeutel *m* cartridge bag, powder bag *(Am)*.

Kartusche *f* cartridge; cartridge case; powder bag; any container of the propelling charge *(generally for separate-loading Am)*; cartridge pouch *(Cav)*.

Kartuschenwagen *m* ammunition vehicle for cartridge cases.

Kartuschhülse *f* cartridge case.

Kartuschmunition *f* separate-loading ammunition.

Kartuschraum *m* chamber *(G)*.

Kartuschvorlage *f* flash-reducing wad *(Am)*.

Kaseinleim *m* casein glue.

Kasematte *f* casemate.

Kasemattenlafette *f* casemate gun mount.

Kaserne *f* permanent barracks.

Kasernenarrest *m* restriction to barracks.

Kasernenhof *m* barracks yard.

kaserniert quartered in barracks.

kasernierungspflichtig obliged to live in barracks.

Kasino *n* officers' mess, officers' club.

Kasino-Ordonnanz *f* dining room orderly.

Kasinovorstand *m* mess council.

Kassenabteilung *f* finance department.

Kassenordnung *f* finance regulations.

Kassenverwaltung *f* finance administration.

Kassenwesen *n* finance.

Kasten *m* receiver *(MG)*; magazine *(R)*; tank, airplane *(slang)*; box, case.

Kastenboden *m* receiver floor plate *(MG)*; magazine floor plate *(R)*.

Kastendeckel *m* receiver top *(MG)*.

Kastenlafette *f* box-trail gun carriage.

Kastenleitwerk *n* box tail unit *(Ap)*.

Kastenmagazin *n* box magazine.

Kastenschlüssel *m* transposition cipher *(Sig C)*.

Kastenträger *m* box girder.

Kastenwand *f* side of receiver *(MG)*.

Kat *m* See Kaltklebekitt.

Katapultflugzeug *n* catapult airplane.

Kathodenstrahlröhre *f* cathode-ray tube.

Kausche *f* grommet; thimble *(rigging, etc.)*.

kaustisches Natron lye, caustic soda, sodium hydroxide.

Kautschuk *m* rubber.

Kavalierstart *m* climbing take-off *(Avn)*.

Kavallerie *f* cavalry.

Kavallerist *m* cavalryman.

K.-Blink *n* portable signal lamp.

K-Brückengerät *n* portable bridge unit.

Kegel *m* cone; conical peak *(Top)*.

Kegelfeder *f* volute spring.

Kegelkupplung *f* cone clutch *(MT)*.

Kegelprojektion *f* conic projection.

Kegelrad *n* bevel gear.

Kegelrollenlager *n* conical roller bearing.

Kegelzahnrad *n* bevel gear.

Kehlriemen *m* throatlatch *(harness)*.

Kehlkopfmikrophon *n* throat-type microphone *(Avn)*.

Kehrbildentfernungsmesser *m* inverted-image range finder.

Kehrichtofen *m* incinerator.

Kehrkurve *f* turn *(Avn)*.

kehrtmachen to face about.

Kehrtwendung *f* turn *(Avn)*; about face *(drill)*.

Kehrtwendung links left-about *(drill)*.

Kehrwert *m* inverse value, reciprocal value.

Keil *m* breech wedge *(G)*; wedge formation *(Tac)*; wedge; key; cotter pin.

Keilloch *n* breech recess *(G)*.

Keillochfläche *f* breech-recess surface *(G)*.

Keilnut *f* keyway.

Keilriemen *m* V-type belt *(Tech)*.

Keil und Kessel breakthrough and encirclement.

Keilverschluß *m* wedge-type breechblock.

Keilwelle *f* spline shaft *(MT)*.

Keim *m* germ.

Keks *m-n* biscuit.

Kelle *f* signaling disk; marking disk; trowel.

Kellerwart *m* shelter warden *(Civ defense)*.

Kennbuchstabe *m* identification letter.

Kennfaden *m* tracer thread *(Tp wire)*.

Kennkarte *f* civilian identity card.

Kennlicht *n* identification light, navigation light *(Ap)*.

Kennscheinwerfer *m* identification light *(Ap)*.

Kenntlichmachen *n* marking, identification.

Kennummer *f* identification number.

Kennung *f* identification signal, marker beacon signal *(Avn)*.

Kennwort *n* password.

Kennzeichen *n* identification mark.

Kern *m* core.

Kerngarbe *f* effective part of cone *(Ballistics)*.

Kerngeschoß *n* armor-piercing bullet.

Kernladung *f* base section *(separate-loading Am)*.

Kernrohr *n* liner *(G)*.

Kernschußweite *f* point-blank range.

Kerntruppen *fpl* crack troops, picked troops, elite troops.

Kerze *f* candle; spark plug.

Kessel *m* pocket, encircled area *(Tac)*; deep hollow *(Top)*; meat can *(mess kit)*; boiler; kettle.

Kesselhaus *n* boiler house.

Kesselschlacht *f* battle of encirclement.

Kesselwagen *m* tank truck *(MT)*.

Kette *f* chain; track *(Tk)*; flight *(3 airplanes)*.

Kettenabdeckung *f* track shield *(Tk)*.

Kettenbolzen *m* track pin *(Tk track)*.

Kettenfahrzeug *n* track-laying vehicle *(MT)*.

Kettenführer *m* flight commander *(Avn)*.

Kettenglied *n* track shoe, track block *(Tk)*; chain link.

Kettenhund *m* rear outside airplane in a formation, "tail-end Charlie," "wing man."

Kettenkeil *m* flight wedge *(Avn)*. *See* **Kette.**

Kettenkrad *n* half-track motorcycle.

Kettenkraftrad *n* *See* **Kettenkrad.**

Kettenkurbel *f* connector *(MG)*.

Kettenlaufräder *npl* bogie wheels *(Tk)*.

Kettenreihe *f* flight of airplanes echeloned left or right. *See also* **Kette.**

Kettenspanner *m* track-connecting fixture, track-connecting tool *(for Tk track)*.

Kettentriebrad *n* driving sprocket *(Tk)*.

Kettenwinde *f* chain winch.

K.-Gerät *n* *See* **Kraftfahrgerät.**

Kiel *m* keel.

Kielflosse *f* keel fin *(of flying-boat hull or seaplane float)*.

Kielwasser *n* wake *(of a ship)*.

Kiesgrube *f* gravel pit.

Kiesstraße *f* gravel road.

Kilohertz *n* kilocycles per second *(Ger unit of frequency)*.

Kilometerzähler *m* mileage indicator, odometer *(MT)*.

Kimme *f* sight notch *(MG, R, etc.)*.

Kimmtiefe *f* dip *(Avn)*.

Kinderzulage *f* dependency allowance for children.

Kinnkette *f* curb chain *(harness)*.

Kinnkettengrube *f* chin groove.

Kinnriemen *m* chin strap *(helmet)*.

Kinnstößel *m* chin strap *(harness)*.

Kinnstütze *f* chin support *(gas mask)*.

Kinotheodolit *m* recording theodolite *(practice firing)*.

kippen to tip, tilt.

Kippfrequenz *f* sweep frequency *(Rad)*.

Kippgerät *n* sweep generator *(Rad)*.

Kipphebel *m* rocker arm *(Mtr)*.

Kipplore *f* dump car *(field RR)*.

Kippneigung *f* tipping gradient *(MT)*.

Kippregel *f* alidade *(Surv)*.

Kippschalter *m* toggle switch *(Elec)*.

Kippschnecke *f* elevating worm *(aiming circle, BC telescope)*.

Kippschwingung *f* sawtooth oscillation, relaxation oscillation *(Rad)*.

Kippvorrichtung *f* dumping mechanism *(dump truck)*.

Kippwagen *m* dump truck.

Kirche *f* church.

Kissen *n* cushion; pad *(Clo, harness, etc.)*; gas-check pad *(G)*; pillow.

Kiste *f* case, crate, chest, box; airplane *(slang)*.

Kitt *m* putty.
Klage *f* complaint.
Klammer *f* butt swivel *(R)*; clip, paper clip; clamp, clasp; parenthesis.
Klammerfuß *m* butt-swivel plate *(R)*.
Klapparm *m* extension arm *(AA sight)*.
Klappblende *f* drop cover *(Ft)*.
Klappbrücke *f* drawbridge, bascule bridge.
Klappe *f* drop *(Tp switchboard)*; tailboard *(Trk)*; flap *(Ap)*; landing ramp *(on landing craft)*.
Klappenschrank *m* portable switchboard.
Klappflügel *m* folding wing *(Ap)*.
Klapphacke *f* pick mattock.
Klapplafette *f* extendable mount *(Ap MG)*.
Klappmesser *n* jackknife.
Klappscheibe *f* bobbing target *(practice firing)*.
Klappsporn *m* folding trail spade.
Klappvisier *n* leaf sight.
Klarinol *n* a cleaning fluid for optical glass.
Klarscheibe *f* antidim eyeglass.
Klarsichtsalbe *f* antidim compound.
Klartext *m* text in clear *(Sig C)*.
Klartextfunken *n* transmitting in clear *(Rad)*.
Klaue *f* dog *(clutch)*; epi, curved spur track *(RR gun)*; claw.
Klauenbeil *n* claw hatchet.
Klauenfutter *n* guide lining *(G)*.
Klauenkupplung *f* dog clutch *(MT)*.
Klauenring *m* guide ring *(G)*.
Klebeflugzeug *n* intruding airplane, intruder *(one which trails an enemy plane back to its home base)*.
Klebelack *m* dope *(Ap)*.
kleben to adhere, to stick to; to follow closely, to trail.
Klebestreifen *m* adhesive tape.
Klebezettel *m* paster, sticker *(sticker-type baggage tag, etc.)*.
Kleiderkarte *f* ration card for clothing.
Kleif *m* portable flame thrower *(abbr. of* kleiner Flammenwerfer*)*.
Kleinbahn *f* substandard-gage railway.
Kleiner Bär Little Dipper.
Kleiner Krieg guerrilla warfare, partisan warfare.

Kleinfunkkraftwagen *m* small radio truck.
Kleinfunktrupp *m* portable-radio section.
Kleinfunkwagen *m* *See* Kleinfunkkraftwagen.
Kleinkaliberlauf *m* subcaliber tube *(G)*; small-bore barrel *(R)*.
Kleinkalibermunition *f* subcaliber ammunition.
Kleinkaliberschießen *n* subcaliber target practice *(Arty)*; small-bore target practice *(R)*.
Kleinkraftrad *n* light motorcycle.
Kleinkrieg *m* guerrilla warfare.
Kleinluftschiff *n* blimp.
Kleinmaschinensatz *m* portable generating unit *(Elec)*.
Klein-Panzerkampfwagen *m* light tank.
Kleinschießplatz *m* miniature range; subcaliber target range *(Arty)*; small-bore target range *(R)*.
Kleinsendegerät *n* portable radio transmitter.
Kleinvernebelung *f* limited-area smoke screen, local smoke screening.
Kleister *m* adhesive paste.
Klemme *f* clip; clamp; terminal; binding post.
klemmen to hold right or left *(R aiming)*; to clamp, to jam, to become wedged.
Klemmenspannung *f* voltage across terminals.
Klemmhebel *m* clamping lever *(MG)*.
Klemmplatte *f* clamping plate *(G barrel guide)*.
Klemmring *m* clamping ring *(grenade launcher)*.
Klemmschraube *f* setscrew; clamping screw *(aiming circle)*.
Klemmzange *f* clamp *(blasting-cap fuze)*.
Klempner *m* plumber.
Klettereisen *npl* climbers, climbing irons.
Kletterfähigkeit *f* vertical axle displacement *(MT)*.
Kletterschuhe *mpl* rock-climbing shoes *(mountain operations)*.
Klettersporn *m* gaff *(of climbers)*.
Kletterwalze *f* front roller *(MT)*.
Klima *n* climate.
Klimaanlage *f* air conditioning plant.
Klinke *f* pawl, catch; jack *(Tp)*.
Klippe *f* bluff, cliff *(Top)*.

Klop *n* *See* **Chlorpikrin.**

Klopfen *n* detonation, knock, pinking *(of an engine).*

Klopfer *m* telegraph sounder.

klopffest antiknock.

Klopffestigkeit *f* antiknock quality *(engine fuel).*

Klotz *m* block, log.

Kluppe *f* stock *(die holder).*

Knagge *f* prop, wedge.

Knall *m* report *(G);* bang, crack, detonation.

Knallbild *n* sound track *(on SR film).*

Knalldämpfer *m* silencer *(R, pistol, etc.).*

Knallerscheinung *f* sound effect *(SR).*

Knallkörper *m* firecracker *(simulated fire).*

Knallmeß- *See* **Schallmeß-.**

Knallnetz *n* mine-exploding net, primacord net.

Knallquecksilber *n* mercury fulminate.

Knallzündschnur *f* detonating cord, primacord *(Engr).*

Knebel *m* gag.

Kneifzange *f* pincers.

Knemeyer *m* computer *(circular slide rule used in air navigation).*

Knetlegierung *f* malleable alloy.

Knick *m* break; crack; kink; knee *(Rad).*

knicken to buckle.

Knickfestigkeit *f* resistance to buckling.

Knickflügel *m* gull wing *(Ap).*

Knie *n* knee; salient *(Tac);* stifle joint *(horse);* elbow, bend *(of pipe, etc.).*

Kniegelenk *n* toggle joint *(pistol).*

kniender Anschlag kneeling position *(in firing).*

Kniepausche *f* knee pad *(harness).*

Knieschützer *mpl* knee pads *(Prcht troops).*

Kniestellung *f* salient *(Tac).*

Kniff *m* knack; helpful hint, handy device; "shortcut," trick.

Knochen *m* bone.

Knochenbruch *m* fracture *(Med).*

Knopf *m* button.

Knorrbremse *f* Knorr air brake.

Knoten *m* knot.

Bunde und Knoten knots and ties.

Knotenpunkt *m* intersection, junction.

Knüppel *m* control stick *(Ap);* club, bludgeon; log, round timber.

Knüppeldamm *m* corduroy road.

Knüppelgriff *m* grip of control stick *(Ap).*

Knüppelsteuerung *f* stick control *(Ap).*

Knüppelweg *m* corduroy road.

Kobona chocolate with caffeine *(Prcht ration).*

Kochgeschirr *n* mess kit, mess gear.

Kochgeschirrhülle *f* mess-kit cover.

Kochloch *n* cooking pit.

Kohle *f* carbon, coal; carbon brush, carbon rod *(Elec).*

Kohlebürste *f* carbon brush *(Elec).*

Kohleklotz *m* carbon block *(microphone).*

Kohlenelektrode *f* carbon electrode.

Kohlenkörner *npl* carbon granules *(microphone).*

Kohlenmikrophon *n* carbon microphone.

Kohlenoxyd *n* carbon monoxide.

Kohlensäure *f* carbon dioxide.

Kohlenstoff *m* carbon.

Kohlenstoffträger *m* carbon filler *(in liquid-oxygen blasting charges).*

Kohlepapier *n* carbon paper.

Kohleschicht *f* charcoal layer *(gas mask).*

Kohlestab *m* carbon rod *(Elec).*

Kohle-Zink-Element *n* carbon-zinc cell *(Elec).*

Kohle-Zinksammler *m* carbon-zinc battery.

Koinzidenzentfernungsmesser *m* coincidence range finder.

Koje *f* cabin *(Nav).*

Kokillenguß *m* chilled casting.

Kolben *m* piston *(Mech);* butt *(MG, R).*

Kolbenbolzen *m* piston pin *(Mtr).*

Kolbenbolzenlager *n* piston-pin bushing *(Mtr).*

Kolbenhals *m* small of the stock *(R).*

Kolbenhieb *m* butt stroke.

Kolbenhub *m* piston stroke *(Mtr).*

Kolbenkappe *f* butt plate *(R).*

Kolbenpistole *f* submachine gun consisting of automatic pistol with telescope or skeleton stock.

Kolbenring *m* piston ring *(Mtr).*

Kolbenstange *f* piston rod *(Mtr).*

Kolk *m* scour *(in river bottom).*

Kollektor *m* commutator, collector ring *(Elec).*

Kollimationslinie *f* collimating mark *(Optics)*.

Kollodiumwolle *f* pyroxylin *(Am)*.

Kolonne *f* column; train *(supply)*; javelin *(Avn)*.

Kolonnenbrücke *f* portable bridge.

Kolonnenchef *m* column commander *(MT)*.

Kolonnengebiet *n* communications zone.

Kolonnenspitze *f* head of column.

Kolonnenstaffel *f* rear echelon train.

Kolonnenverkehr *m* column traffic.

Kolonne zu Einem column of files.

Kolonne zu Zweien column of twos.

Koluft *m* See **Kommandeur der Luftwaffe.**

Kombination *f* flying suit, coverall.

Kombüse *f* galley *(Nav)*.

Kommandant *m* commander *(of an Ap, Tk, ship, etc.)*; commanding officer *(of a post, garrison, or station)*.

Kommandantur *f* commander's office, garrison headquarters. *See also* **Feldkommandantur, Ortskommandantur.**

Kommandeur *m* commander, commanding officer *(Bn and higher units, including entire arm or service)*; commandant *(of a service school)*.

Kommandeur der Luftwaffe air support commander.

Kommandeurpanzer *m* commander's tank.

kommandieren to command; to detach, to detail.

kommandierender General commanding general *(of a corps or service command)*.

Kommandierrolle *f* duty roster.

Kommando *n* order, command; headquarters *(Div and larger units)*; detached duty or service; detached unit; party or detail.

Kommandobehörde *f* command, command agency, headquarters *(Div and larger units)*.

Kommandoflagge *f* command post flag *(Bn or higher unit)*.

Kommandoführer *m* commander of a detachment, leader of a party.

Kommandogerät *n* data computer, ballistic director *(AAA)*; command set *(Rad)*.

Kommandohilfsgerät *n* auxiliary fire director *(AAA)*.

Kommandopanzer *m* command tank.

Kommandosache *f* confidential military document.

Kommandospruch *m* radio message from commander's tank.

Kommandostelle *f* command post, headquarters.

Kommandotafel *f* range conversion table *(Gunnery)*.

Kommando- und Ladeverzugszeit dead time *(Gunnery)*.

Kommando- und Stabsschwadron headquarters troop *(Cav)*.

Kommandowagen *m* command car, command truck.

Kommandowerte *mpl* fire-director data *(AAA)*.

"Kommando zurück!" "As you were!"

Kommiß *m* military service, "the service" *(corresponds in many cases to the term "G.I." as used colloquially)*.

Kommißbrot *n* G.I. bread.

Kommißstiefel *m* G.I. boot.

Kommodore *m* wing commander *(Avn)*.

Kommodor und Lufttransportführer chief of air transport *(at Ger Air Ministry)*.

Kompanie *f* company.

Kompanieabschnitt *m* company sector.

Kompaniebezirk *m* company area.

Kompaniebreitkeil *m* company inverted wedge formation.

Kompaniechef *m* company commander.

Kompanieführer *m* officer in charge of company, temporary company commander.

Kompaniegefechtsstand *m* company command post *(in combat)*.

Kompaniegelder *npl* company fund.

Kompaniegrenze *f* company boundary.

Kompaniekeil *m* company wedge formation.

Kompanierevier *n* company area.

Kompanieschreiber *m* company clerk.

Kompanietrupp *m* company headquarters (personnel).

Kompanietruppführer *m* leader of company headquarters personnel.

Kompaß *m* compass.

Kompaßablenkung *f* compass error.

Kompaßausgleichung *f* compass compensation.

Kompaßkessel *m* compass bowl *(Ap)*.

Kompaßkurs *m* compass heading, compass course *(Avn)*.

Kompaßkurswinkel *m* compass azimuth.

Kompaßlenkung *f* compass deviation.

Kompaßmißweisung *f* compass declination.

Kompaßpeilung *f* compass bearing.

Kompaßrose *f* compass rose, compass card.

Kompaßstrich *m* point of the compass.

Kompaßzahl *f* azimuth, compass reading, bearing.

Komplize *m* accomplice *(Law)*.

Kompressionsraum *m* compression chamber *(Mtr)*.

Kompressor *m* compressor, supercharger.

Kompressormotor *m* supercharged engine.

Kondensationswärme *f* heat of condensation *(Met)*.

Kondensator *m* condenser, capacitor *(Rad)*.

Kondensatormikrophon *n* condenser microphone.

Kondensstreifen *m* vapor trail *(Avn)*.

konisch conical, tapered.

konisches Rohr tapered-bore barrel *(G)*.

Konstrukteur *m* technical designer.

Konstruktion *f* design; construction; structure.

Konstruktionsfehler *m* faulty design, structural defect.

Konstruktionszeichner *m* designer, draftsman.

Kontaktmesser *n* knife-switch prong *(Elec)*.

Kontaktmine *f* contact mine *(Nav)*.

Kontaktstift *m* prong of jack *(Elec)*.

Kontaktstück *n* contact, contact piece *(Elec)*.

Konteradmiral *m* rear admiral.

Konterbande *f* contraband.

Kontrollkarte *f* intercept board *(AWS)*.

Kontrollampe *f* pilot light *(Ap, MT)*.

Kontrolliste *f* check list.

Konuskupplung *f* cone clutch *(MT)*.

konvergieren to converge.

Konzentrationslager *n* concentration camp.

konzentrisch concentric, converging.

Koordinate *f* coordinate.

Koordinatennetz *n* map grid, coordinate grid system.

Koordinatenschieber *mpl* coordinate cards.

Koordinatenverzeichnis *n* table of coordinates *(Surv)*.

Koordinationsausgangspunkt *m* point of origin of coordinates.

Kopf *m* head; heading *(on a message)*; nose or point *(of a shell)*.

Kopfbahnhof *m* terminal; railhead.

Kopfbänder *npl* head straps *(gas mask)*.

Kopfbänderung *f* head harness *(Gas mask)*.

Kopfbedeckung *f* headgear, hat or helmet.

Kopffernhörer *m* headphone, headset.

Kopfgestell *n* headstall *(harness)*.

Kopfhaube *f* helmet *(Avn)*.

Kopfhörer *m* headphone, headset.

kopflastig noseheavy *(Ap)*.

Kopfplatte *f* head-strap cushion *(Gas mask)*.

Kopframpe *f* end ramp *(RR)*.

Kopfschützer *m* woolen cap, winter cap.

Kopfstand *m* nose-over *(Avn)*.

Kopfstärke *f* strength *(of a unit)*.

Kopfstück *n* crownpiece *(harness)*; head *(MG)*.

Kopfsturz *m* vertical dive, nose dive *(Avn)*.

Kopfteil *n* nose section of shell *(Am)*.

Kopfteilung *f* graduation on head of panoramic telescope.

Kopfwelle *f* shell wave, ballistic wave, bow wave *(Ballistics)*.

Kopfzünder *m* point-detonating fuze *(Am)*; nose fuze *(bomb)*.

Koppel *n* belt.

koppeln to determine a course or establish a fix by dead reckoning *(Avn)*; to couple *(Arty)*.

Koppelnavigation *f* navigation by dead reckoning *(Avn)*.

Koppelort *m* fix, dead reckoning position *(Air Navigation)*.

Koppelschloß *n* belt buckle.

Koppelzeit *f* time at which exact position is ascertained by means of dead reckoning *(Air Navigation)*.

Kopplung *f* coupling *(Arty, Rad)*.

Korb *m* basket *(Bln, etc.)*; cluster of bombs *(slang)*.

Korbring *m* concentration ring *(Bln)*.

Kordelmutter *f* knurled nut.

Kordelung *f* knurl, knurling.

kordieren to knurl.

Kordit *n* cordite.

Korkenzieher *m* spiral dive, "corkscrew dive" *(Ap)*.

Korn *n* front sight *(R, pistol, etc.)*; muzzle sight *(G)*; grain; bead; acorn.

das Korn klemmen to hold right or left.

geklemmtes Korn incorrectly centered front sight.

Körnchen *n* granule.

Körner *m* center punch.

Körnerform *f* granular form *(powder)*.

Kornfuß *m* front-sight base *(R)*.

Kornhalter *m* front-sight holder *(R)*.

Kornwarze *f* front-sight stud *(R)*.

Körperschutzmittel *n* protective clothing *(CWS)*.

Korps *n* corps.

Korpsbezirk *m* corps area.

Korpsführer *m* assistant band leader.

Korpsgeist *m* esprit de corps, group spirit, group morale.

Korpskommando *n* corps headquarters.

Korpsnachschubführer *m* chief of corps supply services.

Korpsstab *m* corps headquarters staff.

Korrekturluftdüse *f* air-adjustment jet *(Mtr)*.

Korrosionsbeständigkeit *f* resistance to corrosion.

Korvettenkapitän *m* lieutenant commander *(Nav)*.

Kost *f* meal, food; diet.

Kot *m* mud, excrement, filth.

Köte *f* fetlock.

Kotflügel *m* mudguard, fender.

Krad *n* motorcycle *(abbr. of* Kraftrad*)*.

Kradfahrer *m* motorcyclist.

Kradmantel *m* motorcyclist's overcoat.

Kradmelder *m* motorcycle messenger.

Kradmeldetrupp *m* motorcycle messenger detachment.

Kradschütze *m* motorcycle rifleman.

Kradschützen-Bataillon *n* motorcycle battalion.

Kradschützenschwadron *f* motorcycle troop.

Kradschützensteg *m* floating wooden treadway bridge.

Kradschützenzug *m* motorcycle platoon.

Kradspäher *m* motorcycle scout.

Kradspitze *f* motorcycle point of advance guard.

Kraft durch Freude Strength Through Joy *(Ger Civ morale and travel organization)*.

Kräfte *fpl* forces; power; strength.

Kräfteersparnis *f* economy of manpower, sparing of personnel.

Kräfteverteilung *f* distribution of forces, tactical grouping *(Tac)*.

Kräftezersplitterung *f* splitting up of forces, dissipation of forces *(Tac)*.

Kraftfahrabteilung *f* motor transport battalion.

Kraftfahrausbildung *f* driver training *(MT)*.

Kraftfahrer *m* driver; private *(MT)*.

Kraftfahr-Ersatzteil-Staffel *f* spare parts section *(MT)*.

Kraftfahrgerät *n* motor-transport equipment.

Kraftfahrkampftruppen *fpl* armored troops.

Kraftfahrkorps *n* See National-sozialistisches Kraftfahrkorps.

Kraftfahrlehrstab *m* motor transport training staff.

Kraftfahrpark *m* motor transport park *(GHQ or Army)*; motor pool, vehicle park.

Kraftfahrparkkompanie *f* motor transport company *(component unit of a* Kraftfahrpark*)*.

kraftfahrtechnisch pertaining to automotive mechanics.

Kraftfahrtransport *m* motor transport.

Kraftfahrtruppen *fpl* motor transport troops.

Kraftfahrversorgung *f* motor transport supply.

Kraftfahrwesen *n* motor transport service.

Kraftfahrzeug *n* motor vehicle.

Kraftfahrzeugkolonne *f* motor convoy, motor column.

Kraftfahrzeugpark *m* motor vehicle park.

Kraftfahrzeug-Verwertung *f* sorting and classification of motor vehicle salvage.

Kraftfahrzeugzubehör *n* motor-vehicle accessories.

Kraftlinien *fpl* lines of force *(Elec)*.

Kraftmoment *n* moment of force.

Kraftomnibus *m* bus.

Kraftquelle *f* power source.

Kraftquellenwagen *m* horse-drawn generating unit.

Kraftrad *n* motorcycle. *For compounds see under* **Krad.**

Kraftsäge *f* power saw.

Kraftschlepper *m* tractor, prime mover.

Kraftspeicher *m* closing spring cylinder *(AA gun)*; storage battery.

Kraftstoff *m* fuel, gasoline.

Kraftstoffabstellhahn *m* fuel shut-off valve *(Mtr)*.

Kraftstoffanlage *f* fuel system *(Mtr)*.

Kraftstoffausgabestelle *f* gasoline distributing point.

Kraftstoffbehälter *m* fuel tank, gasoline tank.

Kraftstoffdruckmesser *m* fuel pressure gage *(Ap)*.

Kraftstoffdüse *f* fuel jet *(Mtr)*.

Kraftstoffgemisch *n* fuel mixture *(Mtr)*.

Kraftstofflager *n* fuel dump.

Kraftstoffleitung *f* fuel line *(MT)*.

Kraftstoff-Luftgemisch *n* fuel-air mixture *(Mtr)*.

Kraftstoffmeßuhr *f* fuel gage *(Mtr)*.

Kraftstoffnachschub *m* fuel supply, gasoline supply.

Kraftstoffnormverbrauch *m* normal fuel consumption *(MT)*.

Kraftstoffölmischung *f* gasoline-oil mixture.

Kraftstofförderpumpe *f* fuel pump *(Mtr)*.

Kraftstofförderung *f* fuel feed *(Mtr)*.

Kraftstoffreiniger *m* fuel filter *(Mtr)*.

Kraftstoffsieb *n* *See* **Kraftstoffreiniger.**

Kraftstoffstaffel *f* gasoline supply section *(Tk Bn)*.

Kraftstoffverbrauch *m* fuel consumption *(MT)*.

Kraftstoffverbrauchssatz *m* rate of fuel consumption *(MT)*.

Kraftstoffversorgung *f* gasoline supply.

Kraftstoffvorratsmesser *m* fuel level gage *(Ap)*.

Kraftstoffzufluß *m* fuel feed *(Mtr)*.

Kraftstoffzug *m* gasoline-supply train *(RR)*.

Kraftübertragung *f* power transmission, power train *(MT)*.

Kraftübertragungsteile *mpl* power train *(MT)*.

Kraftverstärker *m* power amplifier *(Rad)*.

Kraftverstärker-Anlage *f* public-address system *(Elec)*.

Kraftwagen *m* automobile, motor vehicle *(occasionally used in sense of* Lastkraftwagen, *truck)*.

Kraftwagenanhänger *m* trailer.

Kraftwagenbegleiter *m* assistant driver *(MT)*.

Kraftwagenflak *f* mobile antiaircraft artillery.

Kraftwagengeschütz *n* *See* **Kraftwagenkanone.**

Kraftwagenkanone *f* gun mounted on motor carriage.

Kraftwagenkanonenwagen *m* assault gun car, motor carriage for gun.

Kraftwagenkolonne *f* motor transport column.

große **Kraftwagenkolonne** heavy motor transport column *(capacity 60 tons)*.

kleine **Kraftwagenkolonne** light motor transport column *(capacity 30 tons)*.

Kraftwagenkolonne für Betriebsstoffe gasoline and lubricant supply column.

Kraftwagenküchenkompanie *f* mobile kitchen company.

Kraftwagenmarsch *m* motorized march.

Kraftwagenpark *m* motor park.

Kraftwagentransport *m* motor transport.

Kraftwagentransportabteilung *f* motor transport battalion.

Kraftwagentransportkolonne *f* motor transport column.

Kraftwagenwerkstatt *f* motor vehicle repair shop.

Kraftwagenwerkstattzug *m* motor maintenance repair shop platoon.

Kraftwerk *n* power house, power station.

Kraftzug *m* power traction *(as of a prime mover)*.

mit **Kraftzug** tractor-drawn, truck-drawn.

Kraftzugartillerie *f* motorized artillery.

Kraftzuggeschütz *n* motorized gun.

Kraftzugmaschine *f* prime mover.

Kragen *m* collar *(Clo)*.

Kragenlitze *f* collar badge *(facing sewn on the* Kragenpatte*)*.

Kragenpatte *f* collar patch *(cloth backing for the* Kragenlitze).
Kragenspiegel *m* collar patch *(Luftwaffe)*.
Kragträger *m* cantilever beam.
Kragträgerbrücke *f* cantilever bridge.
Krähennest *m* "crow's nest," gunner's compartment *(Ap upper turret)*.
Krampe *f* staple *(Tech)*.
Kran *m* crane, hoist; crane tractor *(used as a power shovel)*.
krängen to heel *(Avn)*.
Krängungsfehler *m* heeling error *(Avn)*.
krank sick, ill.
sich krank melden to go on sick call, to report sick.
Krankenabschub *m* evacuation of the sick.
Kranken-Absonderung *f* medical isolation.
Krankenabteilung *f* ward *(Med)*.
Krankenabtransport *m* evacuation of the sick.
Krankenbehandlung *f* treatment of sick.
Krankenblatt *n* clinical record.
Krankenbuch *n* See **Krankenmeldebuch**.
Kranken-Isolierung *f* medical isolation.
Krankenkraftwagen *m* motor ambulance.
Krankenkraftwagenzug *m* motor ambulance platoon.
Krankenmeldebuch *n* sick report book or folder.
Krankenmeldung *f* daily sick report.
Krankenrevier *n* infirmary, dispensary.
Krankensammelpunkt *m* See **Krankensammelstelle**.
Krankensammelstelle *f* collecting station *(Med)*.
Krankenschwester *f* nurse.
Krankenstall *m* veterinary hospital.
Krankenstube *f* infirmary, ward.
Krankentrage *m* litter, stretcher.
Krankentragenfahrgerät *n* wheeled litter carrier *(Med)*.
Krankenträger *m* litter bearer *(Med)*.
Krankentransportabteilung *f* ambulance battalion.
Krankenunterkunft *f* field hospital.
feste Krankenunterkunft fixed hospital.

Krankenurlaub *m* sick leave.
Krankenwärter *m* ward attendant *(Med)*.
Kranz *m* circular track *(MG mount)*.
Kratze *f* scraper, hoe.
Kraxe *f* wood frame pack carrier.
Kreis *m* circle; area; circuit.
Kreisbogen *m* arc of a circle.
Kreisbogenabsteckung *f* measuring or transferring an arc with dividers.
Kreisel *m* gyroscope.
Kreiselabfeuergerät *n* gyro control, gyro-stabilizer *(Tk)*.
Kreiselkompaß *m* gyro compass.
Kreiselkompressor *m* centrifugal compressor.
Kreiselneigungsmesser *m* bank-and-turn indicator *(Ap)*.
Kreiselpumpe *f* centrifugal pump.
Kreiselsteuerzeiger *m* gyro indicator, gyroscopic turn indicator *(Ap)*.
Kreiselwendezeiger *m* gyro turn indicator, gyroscopic turn indicator *(Ap)*.
kreisen to circle, to maneuver in circles.
Kreisflug *m* circular course *(Avn)*.
Kreisfunkfeuer *n* fan-marker beacon, omnidirectional beacon *(Rad)*.
Kreisfunktion *f* trigonometric function.
Kreiskimme *f* rear ring sight *(MG)*.
Kreiskommandantur *f* area headquarters *(Mil Govt)*.
Kreiskorn *n* front ring sight *(MG)*.
Kreiskornfuß *m* front ring sight base *(MG)*.
Kreiskornhalter *m* front ring sight support *(MG)*.
Kreiskornrahmen *m* front ring sight frame *(MG)*.
Kreislauf *m* cycle.
Kreisleitung *f* series circuit *(demolitions)*.
Kreisprozeß *m* cycle.
Kreisverkehr *m* "circular" radio traffic *(radio-net traffic in which stations communicate directly with each other on a common frequency with different call signs and without a net control station)*.
Kreisvisier *n* ring sight *(Ord)*.
krepieren to explode, burst; to die.
Kresolseifenlösung *f* cresol soap solution.
Kresolwasser *n* cresol solution.

Kreuz *n* cross; crosspiece *(of universal joint).*
Kreuzbund *n* shear lashing *(for diagonal timbers).*
Kreuzen *n* traffic crossing.
kreuzen to cross; to cruise *(Nav).*
Kreuzer *m* cruiser.
Kreuzfeuer *n* cross fire.
Kreuzgelenk *n* universal joint.
Kreuzhacke *f* double-bitted pickax.
Kreuzlafette *f* outrigger-type gun mount.
Kreuzleinen *fpl* cross line *(reins).*
Kreuzlochschraube *f* cross-hole screw.
Kreuzmuffe *f* cross pipe fitting, four-way pipe joint.
Kreuzpeilung *f* determining a fix, taking cross bearings *(Air Navigation).*
Kreuzschraube *f* trigger-guard screw *(R).*
Kreuzteil *n* rear of receiver well *(R).*
Kreuzung *f* intersection.
Kreuzungsbahnhof *m* crossing station *(RR).*
Kreuzverhör *n* cross-examination.
kriechen to creep or crawl.
Kriechgraben *m* crawl trench, shallow communication trench.
Krieg *m* war. *See also terms under* Gefecht, Kampf.
kriegführend belligerent.
kriegführende Macht belligerent power.
Kriegführung *f* warfare.
Kriegsakademie *f* war college.
Kriegsartikel *mpl* Articles of War *(now replaced by brief summary of military ideals and obligations called* Pflichten des deutschen Soldaten).
Kriegsausgang *m* outcome of war.
Kriegsausrüstungsnachweisung *f* table of basic allowances *(wartime).*
Kriegsband *n* battle honors.
Kriegsbeorderung *f See* Kriegsbeordnung.
Kriegsbeordnung *f* mobilization order for reservists.
Kriegsbericht *m* war communiqué, war news report.
Kriegsberichter *m* accredited correspondent *(in a Ger propaganda Co).*
kriegsbeschädigt disabled on active duty.
Kriegsbeteiligung *f* participation in war.
Kriegsbrauch *m* customs of war.
Kriegsbrücke *f* military bridge.

Kriegsbrückengerät *n* military bridge equipment.
Kriegsdauer *f* duration of war.
auf Kriegsdauer for the duration *(abbr.* a.K.).
Kriegsdenkmünze *f* campaign medal.
Kriegsdienstverweigerer *m* conscientious objector.
Kriegserfordernisse *fpl* military requirements in wartime.
Kriegserklärung *f* declaration of war.
Kriegsflagge *f* ensign.
Kriegsfuß *m* war footing.
Kriegsgebiet *n* theater of operations.
Kriegsgebrauch *m* customs of war.
Kriegsgefangenenbau- und Arbeitsbataillon PW construction and labor battalion *(for guarding PWs working in Germany or rear areas).*
Kriegsgefangeneneinsatz *m* employment of prisoners of war.
Kriegsgefangenensammelstelle *f* prisoner-of-war collecting point.
Kriegsgefangener *m* prisoner of war.
Kriegsgerät *n* war matériel.
Kriegsgericht *n* court-martial.
Kriegsgerichtsrat *m* judge advocate.
Kriegsgerichtsrechtsprechung *f* military justice.
Kriegsgerichtsverfahren *n* court-martial proceedings.
Kriegsgliederung *f* order of battle.
Kriegskasse *f* field safe; war chest.
Kriegskonterbande *f* contraband of war.
Kriegskunst *f* art of war.
Kriegslazarett *n* base hospital.
Kriegslist *f* stratagem, ruse *(Tac).*
Kriegsmarine *f* navy.
Kriegsmarsch *m* tactical march.
kriegsmäßig warlike, similar to actual conditions in the field.
Kriegsneurose *f* war neurosis.
Kriegsoffizier-Bewerber *m* applicant for wartime commission.
Kriegsrangliste *f* army directory.
Kriegsräson *f* military necessity.
Kriegsrecht *n* military law.
Kriegssanitätsordnung *f* medical field regulations or manual.
Kriegsschauplatz *m* theater of war.
Kriegsschiff *n* warship.
Kriegsschule *f* officer candidate school.
Kriegsspiel *n* war game, map maneuver.
Kriegsstammrolle *f* personnel roster *(wartime).*

Kriegsstand m See Kriegsstärke.
Kriegsstärke f war strength (of a unit, etc.).
Kriegsstärkenachweisung f table of organization (wartime).
Kriegstagebuch n war diary; journal, daybook.
Kriegsverdienstkreuz n War Service Cross (decoration).
Kriegsverrat m war treason.
Kriegsverräter m war traitor.
kriegsverwendungsfähig fit for active service (abbr. k.v.).
Kriegswerft f navy yard.
kriegswichtig of military importance.
Kriegswissenschaft f military science.
Kriegszahnarzt m dental surgeon.
Kriegszustand m state of war.
Kriminalpolizei f criminal investigation police.
Krimschild m Crimea Shield (decoration on upper left sleeve, worn by all veterans of the battle in the Crimea).
Kripo f See Kriminalpolizei.
K.-Rolle f plain-wire concertina (abbr. of Klaviersaitendraht-Rolle).
Kronenmutter f castellated nut.
Kröpfung f right-angle bend; throw (of a crankshaft).
Krümmer m elbow pipe; manifold.
Krümmung f bend; turn; camber; curvature.
Kruppe f croup (horse).
K-Stoff m diphosgene (CWS).
Kübel m bucket; jeep.
Kübelsitzer m See Kübelwagen.
Kübelsitzwagen m See Kübelwagen.
Kübelwagen m command car, jeep.
Kubikzahl f cube (Math).
Küche f kitchen.
Küchendienst m kitchen police, KP; mess orderly, mess attendant.
Küchenunteroffizier m mess sergeant.
Kufe f sled runner; skid.
Kugel f bullet; ball; sphere.
Kugelblende f mantlet of flexible ball mount, ball mount (Tk).
Kugelfang m target butt, range butt.
kugelfest bulletproof.
Kugelfüllung f ball filler (shrapnel).
Kugelgelenk n ball-and-socket joint.
Kugellafette f ball mount (MG).
Kugellager m ball bearing.
Kugelpfanne f ball socket (Mort).
kugelsicher bulletproof.
Kühlanlage f cooling system (Mtr).

Kühler m radiator (Mtr).
Kühler-Einfüllverschluß m radiator cap (MT).
Kühlerklappe f louver (Mt, Tk).
Kühlerschutzhaube f radiator guard (MT).
Kühlerverschluß m radiator cap (MT).
Kühlflüssigkeit f cooling liquid (Mtr).
Kühlmantel m water jacket (Mtr, MG).
Kühlmittel n coolant (Mtr).
Kühlrippe f cooling fin (Mtr).
Kühlstoff m coolant.
Kühlung f cooling system (Mtr).
Kühlwagen m refrigerator truck, refrigerator car.
Kühlwassermantel m water jacket.
Kulissenschaltung f gate-type gear shift.
Kumpel m buddy.
Kumuluswolke f cumulus cloud.
Kundschafter m spy.
Kunstflug m stunt flying.
Kunstflugfigur f stunt-flying maneuver.
Kunstleder n artificial leather.
künstliche Antenne artificial antenna (Rad).
künstliche Atmung artificial respiration.
künstliche Lüftung artificial ventilation.
künstlicher Gummi synthetic rubber.
künstlicher Horizont absolute inclinometer, gyro horizon indicator, artificial horizon (Ap Inst).
künstlicher Nebel screening smoke (CWS).
künstliches Hindernis artificial obstacle.
künstliche Spur artificial scent (for army dogs).
Kunstschaltung f superposed connection (Tp).
Kunstseide f rayon.
Kunststoff m synthetic plastic.
Kupfer n copper.
Kupferdraht m copper wire.
Kupferkapsel f copper shell (detonator cap).
Kuppe f knoll, knob, rounded hilltop.
Kuppel f cupola.
Kuppellafette f cupola mount (Ap).
Kuppelstange f tie rod (split-trail carriage).

Kupplung f clutch *(MT)*; coupling *(Mech)*; recoil connection *(pistol)*.
Kupplungsfeder f clutch spring *(MT)*.
Kupplungsfußhebel m clutch pedal *(MT)*.
Kupplungsgehäuse n clutch housing *(MT)*.
Kupplungshebel m clutch lever *(MT)*; recoil-spring lever *(pistol)*.
Kupplungskasten m junction box, gun junction box, control box *(AA director)*.
Kupplungskegel m clutch cone *(MT)*.
Kupplungskopf m coupling head *(trailer)*.
Kupplungspedal n clutch pedal *(MT)*.
Kupplungsscheibe f clutch plate *(MT)*.
Kupplungsstange f recoil-spring lever bar *(pistol)*.
Kupplungstritt m clutch pedal *(MT)*.
Kupplungswelle f clutch shaft *(MT)*.
Kurbel f crank.
Kurbelarm m crank arm *(of crankshaft)*.
Kurbeldynamo f hand-crank generator.
Kurbelgehäuse n crankcase *(Mtr)*.
Kurbelgriff m crank handle.
Kurbelinduktor m hand-crank generator *(Tp)*.
Kurbelkröpfung f crankshaft throw.
Kurbellager n crankshaft bearing, pillow block.
Kurbelrad n crankwheel *(G)*.
Kurbelstange f connecting rod *(Mtr)*.
Kurbeltrieb m crank mechanism.
Kurbeltriebwerk n crankshaft assembly *(Mtr)*.
Kurbelübung f crankwheel operation exercise *(gun laying)*.
Kurbelwelle f crankshaft *(Mtr)*.
Kurbelzapfen m crank pin *(Mtr)*.
Kurier m courier, special messenger.
Kurierflugzeug n liaison airplane.
Kurierpost f courier mail.
Kurier-Staffel f special communication squadon *(Luftwaffe)*. See also **Staffel.**
Kurs m course, heading.
Kursgleiche f rhumb line *(Air Navigation)*.
Kurskreisel m directional gyro.
Kursscheibe f bearing plate *(Avn)*.
Kursstabilität f directional stability *(Ap)*.

Kurssteuerung f piloting, navigating, pilot control.
automatische Kurssteuerung automatic pilot, mechanical pilot *(Ap)*.
Kursverbesserung f off-course correction *(Air Navigation)*.
Kursvisier n bomb sight *(Ap)*.
Kurswechsel m change of course, change of direction *(Avn)*.
Kurswinkel m azimuth of target *(AAA)*.
Kurszeiger m navigator's compass *(Ap)*.
Kurve f curve, turn.
Kurvenblatt n graph.
Kurvenflug m curvilinear flight *(Avn)*.
Kurvengleitflug m spiral *(Avn)*.
Kurvenkampf m turning combat, dogfight *(Avn)*.
Kurvenmesser m map measurer *(Inst)*.
Kurvenscheibe f cam plate *(Ord)*; curvilinear target *(Tng)*.
Kurvenvisier n tangent sight *(SA)*.
Kurzleistung f military rating *(of an Ap engine)*.
Kurzschluß m short circuit, short *(Elec)*.
Kurzschlußankermotor m squirrel-cage motor.
Kurzschuß m short *(Gunnery)*.
Kurzsignal n code group.
Kurzwelle f short wave *(Rad)*.
Kurzwellensender m short-wave transmitter.
Küste f coast, shore.
Küstenartillerie f coast artillery.
Küstenaufklärer m coast reconnaissance airplane.
Küstenaufklärung f coast reconnaissance.
Küstenbatterie f coast battery, shore battery.
Küstenflak f coast antiaircraft gun, coast antiaircraft artillery.
Küstenfliegergruppe f coast reconnaissance and naval support group *(Avn)*. See also **Gruppe.**
Küstengebiet n coastal area.
Küstengeschütz n coast artillery gun.
Küstengewässer npl coastal zone, coastal waters.
Küstenlafette f coast artillery gun mount.

Küstenstaffel *f*   coastal squadron *(Avn)*. *See also* **Staffel.**
Küstenstation *f*   coast guard station.
Küstenverteidigung *f*   coast defense.
Küstenvorfeld *n*   coastal zone.
Küstenwache *f*   coast guard, coast guard station.
Küstenwacht *f*   coast patrol.

Küstenwehr *f*   coast defense, coast defense troops.
Kutonnase *f*   cable cutter on leading edge of wing *(an anti-barrage-balloon device)*.
Kuvi *n*   *See* **Kursvisier.**
KWK.-Stand *m*   fixed emplacement made of tank gun turret.

L

Lack *m*   lacquer, varnish.
Ladebaum *m*   boom, derrick, crane.
Ladebrücke *f*   loading ramp *(on trailer)*.
Ladedruck *m*   manifold pressure *(Mtr)*.
Ladedruckmesser *m*   manifold pressure gage *(Ap engine)*.
Ladedruckregler *m*   manifold pressure control *(Ap engine)*.
Ladeeinheit *f*   load unit, unit load.
Ladefähigkeit *f*   load capacity; serviceable condition of ammunition.
Ladegewicht *n*   load capacity, weight of load.
Ladegleis *n*   loading siding *(RR)*.
Ladegurt *m*   cartridge belt.
Ladehemmung *f*   stoppage in loading mechanism *(Ord)*.
Ladekanonier *m*   gun loader, loader, assistant gunner, cannoneer No. 1.
Ladeklappe *f*   breechblock.
Ladekran *m*   gun hoist.
Ladelaufrad *n*   impeller *(supercharger)*.
Ladeleitrad *n*   diffuser *(supercharger)*.
Ladeloch *n*   loading recess *(G)*.
Ladeluftkühler *m*   intercooler *(Ap supercharger)*.
Ladeluke *f*   loading hatch *(Ap)*.
Lademaschine *f*   battery charger *(Elec)*.
Lademaschinensatz *m*   battery charging unit *(Elec)*.
Lademulde *f*   loading tray *(G)*.
laden   to load *(R, G, etc.)*.
"Laden und sichern!"   "Load and lock!"
Ladeplatz *m*   pier, wharf, quay.

Lader *m*   stevedore, loader, supercharger *(Mtr)*.
Laderampe *f*   loading ramp.
Laderaum *m*   chamber, powder chamber *(G)*; hold *(Nav)*.
Laderaumverlängerung *f*   advance of forcing cone *(G)*.
Ladergetriebe *n*   supercharger drive.
Ladeschale *f*   loading tray *(G)*.
Ladeschütze *m*   assistant gunner, loader *(Tk)*.
Ladesitz *m*   loader's seat *(G)*.
Ladespannung *f*   charging voltage *(battery charger)*.
Ladestelle *f*   loading point, entraining or entrucking point; battery-charging station.
Ladestock *m*   rammer.
Ladestörung *f*   stoppage in loading mechanism *(Ord)*.
Ladestraße *f*   delivery roadway *(RR freight station)*.
Ladestreifen *m*   cartridge clip, ammunition clip.
Ladetätigkeit *f*   loading operations *(service of the piece)*.
Ladetisch *m*   loading tray *(G)*.
Ladetrommel *f*   cartridge drum.
Ladetrupp *m*   loading detail.
Ladeverzug *m*   loading lag *(Gunnery)*.
Ladeverzugszeit *f*   loading lag, loading time *(Gunnery)*.
Ladevorgang *m*   loading action *(semi- or full-automatic weapons)*.
Ladevorrichtung *f*   breech mechanism, loading device *(Ord)*; feeding device *(SA)*.
Ladezeit *f*   loading time, entrucking time, entraining time; charging time *(Elec battery)*.

Ladung *f* cargo, load; charge.

Ladungsbüchse *f* blasting-charge container *(generally of galvanized metal)*.

Ladungsgefäß *n* blasting-charge container.

Ladungskasten *m* blasting-charge box.

Ladungsraum *m* *See* **Laderaum.**

Ladungsverhältnis *n* loading ratio *(ratio between weight of charge and weight of projectile)*.

Ladungswerfer *m* spigot mortar.

Lafette *f* gun carriage, gun mount.

Lafettenachse *f* gun-carriage axle.

Lafettenart *f* type of gun carriage or mount.

Lafettenaufsatzstück *n* adapter, tripod extension piece *(MG)*.

Lafettendreieck *n* triangular base *(AA gun)*.

Lafettenfahrzeug *n* trailer mount *(Arty)*.

Lafettenholm *m* gun-mount outrigger; gun-trail crosspiece.

Lafettenkasten *m* trail box *(G)*.

Lafettenkranz *m* circular track mount *(Ap, Tk)*.

Lafettenkreuz *n* outriggers *(AA gun)*.

Lafettenschwanz *m* trail *(G)*.

Lafettensporn *m* trail spade *(G)*.

Lafettenstütze *f* firing base *(G)*.

Lafettentisch *m* gun-carriage bed.

Lafettenwand *f* gun-carriage side plate.

Lage *f* situation *(Tac)*; position, site; salvo *(pieces fire in succession)*; layer, stratum *(Met)*.

Lagebericht *m* situation report.

Lagebeurteilung *f* estimate of the situation *(Tac)*.

Lagenfeuer *n* salvo fire *(pieces fire in succession)*.

Lagenkarte *f* situation map *(Tac)*.

Lagenmeldung *f* situation report.

Lager *n* camp; depot, dump; bearing, support.

das Lager abbrechen to strike camp.

das Lager aufschlagen to pitch camp.

Lagerbestand *m* stock, stockage.

Lagerbock *m* support *(for piston rod of counterrecoil mechanism)*; pillow block.

Lagergehäuse *n* housing or case enclosing a bearing or bushing.

Lagergeld *n* pay *(PW)*.

Lagergerüst *n* storage-closet rack.

Lagerhaus *n* warehouse.

Lagerkommandant *m* prison camp or internment camp commander.

Lagerleitung *f* camp authorities *(PW)*.

Lagermetall *n* bearing metal.

Lagern *n* storage.

Lagerort *m* camp site.

Lagerplatz *m* storage place; camp site.

Lagerraum *m* storeroom.

Lagerschale *f* bushing.

Lagerschuppen *m* storage shed.

Lagerstelle *f* camp site.

Lagerung *f* storage, stowage.

Lagerzapfen *m* journal *(crankshaft)*; pivot pin *(trail spade)*; trunnion *(aiming circle)*.

lähmen paralyze, immobilize, neutralize *(Tac)*.

lahmlegen neutralize *(an attack)*.

Lahmlegung *f* neutralization *(Tac)*.

Lähmungsschießen *n* harassing fire *(with Cml shell)*.

Lamelle *f* disk; leaf; plate; shim; cooling fin.

Lamellenkupplung *f* multiple-disk clutch *(MT)*.

Lamellenschluß *m* armature short *(Elec)*.

Lampenfassung *f* lamp socket *(Elec)*.

Lampengehäuse *n* lamp case *(Sig lamp)*.

Landankertau *n* shore anchor line *(Pon Bdg)*.

Landbatterie *f* land-based antiaircraft battery *(as distinguished from ship-based battery)*.

Landbord *m* shoreward side.

Landbrücke *f* landing stage *(Engr)*.

Landebahn *f* landing strip, runway.

Landebahnfeuer *n* contact light *(Adrm)*.

Landedeck *n* landing deck, flight deck *(aircraft carrier)*.

Landefackel *f* wing-tip flare *(Ap)*.

Landefeuer *n* landing light *(Ap)*.

Landefunkfeuer *n* runway localizing beacon *(Rad)*.

Landegeschwindigkeit *f* landing speed *(Ap)*.

Landeklappe *f* landing flap *(Ap).*
Landekopf *m* beachhead.
Landekreuz *n* landing T *(Avn).*
Landelicht *n* landing light *(Ap).*
Landemannschaft *f* ground crew *(Bln).*
Landeplatz *m* landing area, landing field *(Avn).*
Landesaufnahme *f* topographic survey, geodetic survey.
landeseigener Verband "native" unit *(composed of inhabitants of German-occupied country who fight, on their own soil, as auxiliaries of German Army).*
Landesschützeneinheit *f* regional defense unit *(such as Landesschützen-division, -regiment, -bataillon, and -kompanie; mainly for guard duty in Com Z and Z of I).*
Landesteg *m* landing ramp *(Nav).*
Landesverrat *m* treason.
Landesverteidigung *f* home defense.
Landetrupp *m* landing and saddling detail *(at stream crossing) (Cav).*
Landezeichen *n* landing signal.
Landezone *f* landing zone *(Adrm).*
Landfahrwerk *n* wheel-type landing gear *(Ap).*
Landfahrzeug *n* land vehicle; shore-ward ponton *(Bdg).*
Landkrieg *m* war on land, land warfare.
Landkriegsordnung *f* Rules of Land Warfare.
Landmeile *f* statute mile (1.609 *km*).
Landmine *f* land mine.
Landser *m* doughboy.
Landstraße *f* road, highway.
Landsturm *m* territorial reserve, replacement reserves *(age over 45).*
Landsturm I trained reserves *(age over 45).*
Landsturm II untrained reserves *(age over 45).*
Landtruppen *fpl* ground troops.
Landung *f* landing.
Landung mit Seitenwind cross-wind landing.
Landungsabteilung *f* beach party or detachment.
Landungsboot *n* landing barge, landing boat.
Landungsfahrzeug *n* landing craft.
Landungsklappe *f* landing ramp *(of a landing craft or ship).*

Landungsplatz *m* landing area.
Landungsrauchzeichen *n* landing smoke signal *(Avn).*
Landungstrupp *m* landing party.
Landungsunternehmung *f* landing operation.
Landverankerung *f* guy-line anchorage *(Pon).*
Landwehr *f* reserves *(age group 35-45).*
Landwehr I trained reserves (35-45).
Landwehr II untrained reserves (35-45).
Landwehroffizier *m* reserve officer. *See* **Landwehr.**
Langbasis *f* horizontal base *(Arty, Surv).*
Langbasisanlage *f* base end station.
Langbasisverfahren *n* horizontal base method, long base method *(Gunnery).*
Länge *f* length.
der Länge nach beschießen to enfilade.
Längenabweichung *f* longitudinal deviation, range deviation *(Gunnery).*
Festlegen der Längenabweichung range sensing, range spotting *(Arty Obsn).*
Längengrad *m* degree of longitude.
Längenkreis *m* circle of longitude.
Längenmessung *f* linear measurement.
Längenstreuung *f* range dispersion on horizontal target *(Ballistics).*
Längenverbesserung *f* range correction *(Gunnery).*
Längenverhältnis *n* aspect ratio *(Ap).*
Länge über alles over-all length.
Längsachse *f* longitudinal axis.
Langsamflug *m* stalling flight *(Ap).*
Längsbestreichung *f* enfilade fire.
Längsfeld *n* chase of gun barrel.
Längsfeuer *n* enfilade fire.
Längslibelle *f* longitudinal level *(sighting mechanism).*
Längsneigungsmesser *m* pitch indicator, fore-and-aft inclinometer *(Ap).*
Längsschnitt *m* longitudinal section.
Längsseitgehen *n* pulling alongside.
Längsstabilität *f* longitudinal stability *(Ap).*

Längsträger *m* stringer, balk *(Bdg)*; longitudinal outrigger *(AA gun)*; longeron *(Ap)*; long channel bar of chassis frame *(MT)*.
Langstreckenbomber *m* long-range bomber.
Langstreckenjäger *m* long-range fighter airplane.
Langstrecken-Seeflugzeug *n* long-range seaplane.
Längszapfen *m* axle pivot pin *(split trail carriage)*.
Langwellen *fpl* long waves *(Rad)*.
Langwellenpeiler *m* long-wave direction finder *(Rad)*.
Lasche *f* butt strap *(Engr)*.
Last *f* load.
Lastanhänger *m* truck trailer *(MT)*.
Lastensegelflugzeug *n* *See* **Lastensegler.**
Lastensegler *m* troop-carrying glider, cargo-carrying glider.
Lastfallschirm *m* cargo parachute.
Lastflugzeug *n* cargo transport airplane.
Lastigkeitsregelung *f* trimming *(Ap)*.
Lastigkeitswaage *f* balance indicator *(Ap)*.
Lastkraftwagen *m* truck, cargo truck.
Lastwagenschlepper *m* truck-tractor.
Latte *f* batten, lath, board; propeller *(Ap)*; stadia rod *(Surv)*.
Lattenführung *f* pitch control *(propeller)*.
Lattenpunkt *m* place mark *(Surv)*.
Lattenrost *m* boardwalk, duckboard *(trench)*.
Laubwald *m* deciduous forest, deciduous wood.
Lauerstellung *f* ambush gun emplacement, ambush.
Lauf *m* barrel *(MG, R)*; run, course.
Laufbahn *f* career *(as an officer, specialist, etc.)*; runway *(Adrm)*.
Laufbahnabzeichen *n* specialist's insignia or badge.
Laufbrücke *f* gangplank.
Laufdecke *f* tire casing *(MT)*.
laufend running; current; continuous; serial.
laufende Nummer serial number.
Läufer *m* runner, messenger.
Lauffläche *f* tread *(of a tire)*; sliding surface *(of a sled runner)*;

bearing surface, friction surface.
Laufgraben *m* approach trench, communication trench.
Laufinneres *n* bore *(SA)*.
Laufmantel *m* jacket *(MG)*.
Laufmundstück *n* breech piece *(R)*.
Laufrad *n* landing wheel *(Ap)*; bogie wheel *(Tk)*; impeller *(of pump, etc.)*.
Laufring *m* race *(ball bearing)*.
Laufrolle *f* bogie wheel *(Tk)*.
Laufschritt *m* double time.
"Im Laufschritt, Marsch! Marsch!" "Double time, march!"
Laufseele *f* bore *(SA)*.
Laufseelenprüfer *m* barrel reflector *(SA)*.
Laufsitzring *m* barrel-locking ring *(MG)*
Laufweite *f* caliber.
Laufwerk *n* tracks and suspensions *(Tk)*; running gear *(of a vehicle)*.
Laufwerkpanzerung *f* track shield, armored skirting *(Tk)*.
Lauschdienst *m* intercept service *(Sig C)*.
Lauschempfänger *m* intercept receiver *(Sig C)*.
Lauschgerät *n* intercept set *(Rad)*.
Lauschstelle *f* intercept station *(Sig C)*.
Lauschzange *f* wire-tapping clamp.
Lauthörknopf *m* handset switch, amplifier knob *(Tp)*.
Lautsprecher *m* loudspeaker *(Rad)*.
Lautsprechertrichter *m* horn, cone, trumpet *(of loud speaker)*.
Lautsprechertruhe *f* baffle, speaker cabinet *(Rad)*.
Lautstärke *f* signal strength, volume, readability *(Rad)*; sound intensity *(sound locator)*.
Lautstärkenregler *m* volume control *(Rad)*.
Lautverstärker *m* volume amplifier *(Rad)*.
Lazarett *n* hospital.
Lazarettaufnahme *f* hospitalization.
Lazarettbehandlung *f* hospital treatment, hospitalization.
Lazarettflagge *f* flag of protection.
Lazarettschiff *n* hospital ship.
Lazarettzug *m* hospital train.
Lebensdauer *f* accuracy life *(G)*.
Lebensmittel *npl* subsistence supplies.

Lebensmittelkarte *f* food ration card.

Lederfett *n* dubbin.

Lederring *m* *See* **Lederscheibe.**

Lederscheibe *f* leather washer.

Ledertasche *f* leather case, leather bag.

Leere *f* vacuum.

Leergang *m* backlash, lost motion; neutral gear *(Mtr)*.

Leergewicht *n* empty weight.

Leergut *n* empties *(Am)*.

Leerlauf *m* idling, neutral, idling speed *(Mtr)*.

Leerlaufdüse *f* idler jet *(Mtr)*.

Leermaterial *n* train of empties *(RR)*.

Leerschraube *f* drain plug.

Legierung *f* alloy.

Legionsschütze *m* non-German rifleman in the *Wehrmacht.*

Lehmgrube *f* clay pit.

Lehrbataillon *n* instruction battalion *(used for demonstrations, etc.)*.

Lehre *f* doctrine, theory; gage.

Lehrfilm *m* training film.

Lehrflugwesen *n* training aviation.

Lehrgang *m* course of instruction.

Lehrgangsleiter *m* instructor.

Lehrgruppe *f* instruction group *(Avn)*.

Lehrregiment *n* instruction regiment *(used for demonstrations, etc.)*.

Lehrtruppe *f* instruction unit.

Leibgarde *f* bodyguard.

Leibgurt *m* belt *(Clo)*.

Leibgurt mit Schulterriemen Sam Browne belt.

Leibriemen *m* garrison belt *(Clo)*.

Leibstandarte *f* *See* **SS-Leibstandarte.**

Leibwache *f* bodyguard.

Leiche *f* corpse; carcass.

leichte Division motorized division, "light division."

Leichtkrankenkriegslazarett *n* base hospital for minor cases *(Com Z)*.

Leichtkrankenschiff *n* hospital ship for minor cases.

Leichtkrankenzug *m* hospital train for minor cases.

Leichtkranker *m* ambulatory case, minor case *(sick, not wounded)*.

Leichtöl *n* light fuel *(as distinguished from Diesel fuel)*.

Leichtverwundetensammelplatz *m*

collecting station for walking wounded.

Leichtverwundeter *m* minor casualty.

Leinenbund *n* rope lashing.

Leinöl *n* linseed oil.

Leinwand *f* linen; cloth; projection screen.

Leiste *f* strip; edge; fillet; batten.

Leistenbruch *m* hernia.

Leistengegend *f* groin.

Leistung *f* output, performance, capacity; power *(Rad)*.

Leistungsbelastung *f* power loading *(Ap)*.

Leistungsfähigkeit *f* efficiency, capacity.

Leistungsgewicht *n* weight per horsepower.

Leistungsregler *m* power control *(Rad)*.

Leistungsröhre *f* power amplifier tube.

Leistungssegelflugzeug *n* performance-type glider *(Avn)*.

Leistungssteigerung *f* increase of efficiency *(Mtr)*.

Leistungsstufe *f* power amplifier, final amplifier *(of a Rad transmitter)*.

Leistungswählhebel *m* output selector lever *(Ap engine)*.

leiten conduct, lead, direct, manage.

Leitender *m* director *(maneuvers)*.

Leitender Arzt ward officer *(Med)*.

Leitender Ingenieur chief engineer *(a Civ official in the Armed Forces)*.

Leitender Offizier executive officer.

Leiter *m* leader, director; conductor *(Elec)*.

Leiter *f* ladder.

Leiterschleife *f* armature turn *(Elec)*.

Leitfähigkeit *f* ~ conductivity *(Elec)*.

Leitfeuer *n* cord fuze, safety fuze.

Leitfeuerzündmittel *n* cord fuze detonator.

Leitfeuerzündung *f* cord fuze detonation.

Leitfunkstelle *f* net control station *(Rad)*.

Leitkante *f* leading edge *(Ap wing)*.

Leitrad *n* idler, idler wheel *(Tk)*; diffuser *(supercharger)*.

Leitradachse *f* idler wheel shaft *(Tk)*.

Leitstand *m* fire-direction center *(Arty)*; command post.

Leitstelle *f* net control station *(Rad)*.

Leitstrahl *m* localizer beam *(Inst landing)*.

Leitstrahlverfahren *n* localizer-beam method *(Inst landing)*.

Leitung *f* line *(Tp)*; command; direction; control; management.

Leitungsbau *m* line construction *(Tp)*.

Leitungsgehilfe *m* director's aide *(maneuvers)*.

Leitungskapazität *f* capacity of a line, traffic capacity of a line *(Elec, Tp, Tg)*.

Leitungsmast *m* telephone pole.

Leitungsmaterial *n* conducting material, electric wire.

Leitungsmittel *n* line wire *(Tp)*.

Leitungsnetz *n* wire net, circuit, wiring system, wire-communication net.

Leitungsoffizier *m* assistant director *(maneuvers)*.

Leitungsplan *m* wiring diagram.

Leitungsprüfer *m* galvanometer *(Engr)*; circuit tester *(Elec)*.

Leitungsskizze *f* circuit diagram *(Tp)*.

Leitungssondertruppen *fpl* special troops of director headquarters *(maneuvers)*.

Leitungsstab *m* directing staff *(maneuvers)*.

Leitungssystem *n* wiring system *(Elec)*.

Leitungstruppen *fpl* troops assigned to director headquarters *(maneuvers)*.

Leitungs- und Schiedsrichterdienst *m* directing and umpiring service *(maneuvers)*.

Leitungswiderstand *m* line resistance *(Elec)*.

Leitverkehr *m* control-station traffic *(Rad)*.

Leitwand *f* baffle.

Leitwellverschluß *m* sliding-wedge-type breechblock *(G)*.

Leitwerk *n* empennage, tail assembly, tail unit *(Ap)*.

Leitwert *m* conductance *(Elec)*.

Leitzaun *m* guide fence *(a type of snow fence)*.

Lenden *fpl* loins *(horse)*.

Lenkballon *m* dirigible

Lenkbremse *f* steering brake *(Tk)*.

Lenkeinrichtung *f* steering mechanism.

Lenkeinschlag *m* maximum angle of turn *(steering wheels)*.

Lenker *m* steering arm *(of a gun wheel)*.

Lenkgehäuse *n* steering-gear housing *(MT)*.

Lenkgestänge *n* tie rods *(MT)*.

Lenkgetriebe *n* steering mechanism *(track-laying vehicles)*.

Lenkhebel *m* steering-knuckle gearrod arm *(MT)*; steering lever *(track-laying vehicle)*.

Lenkknüppel *m* steering lever *(track-laying vehicle)*.

Lenkluftschiff *n* dirigible.

Lenkrad *n* steering wheel *(MT)*.

Lenksäule *f* steering column *(MT)*.

Lenkschnecke *f* steering worm *(MT)*.

Lenkschraube *f* cylindrical cam on steering column *(MT)*.

Lenkschubstange *f* steering gear connecting rod *(MT)*.

Lenksegment *n* steering-worm sector *(MT)*.

Lenkstange *f* tie rod *(MT)*; handle bar *(Mtcl)*.

Lenkstock *m* See **Lenkstockhebel.**

Lenkstockhebel *m* steering arm *(MT)*.

Lenkstoßfang *m* steering shock suspension *(MT)*.

Lenkung *f* steering, steering system *(MT)*.

Lettenhaue *f* mattock hoe *(Engr)*.

leuchtbereit ready for action *(SL)*.

Leuchtblatt *n* luminous dial.

Leuchtboje *f* light buoy.

Leuchtbombe *f* aircraft parachute flare.

Leuchtdauer *f* burning time *(of a ground Sig, etc.)*.

Leuchtfallschirm *m* parachute flare *(Avn)*.

Leuchtfarbe *f* luminous paint.

Leuchtfeuer *n* beacon light *(Avn)*.

Leuchtgeschoß *n* See **Leuchtgranate.**

Leuchtgranate *f* star shell *(Am)*.

Leuchtgranatwerfer *m* pyrotechnic projector.

Leuchtkompaß *m* luminous compass.

Leuchtkreuze *npl* reticle image *(reflector sight).*

Leuchtkugel *f* ground signal, Very signal light.

Leuchtmittel *n* pyrotechnic device.

Leuchtmunition *f* pyrotechnics; tracer ammunition.

Leuchtpatrone *f* signal case; signal cartridge; cartridge-type ground signal.

Leuchtpfad *m* flare path *(Avn).*

Leuchtpistole *f* pyrotechnic pistol, signal pistol, Very pistol.

Leuchtrakete *f* signal rocket.

Leuchtraketengestell *n* pyrotechnic projector *(for Sig rockets).*

Leuchtröhre *f* fluorescent tube.

Leuchtsatz *m* pyrotechnic composition, flare composition, illuminant charge; tracer composition.

Leuchtschiff *n* lightship.

Leuchtspur *f* tracer trajectory.

Leuchtspurgeschoß *n* tracer bullet, tracer.

Leuchtspurgranate *f* tracer shell *(Am).*

Leuchtspurmunition *f* tracer ammunition.

Leuchtspursatz *m* tracer composition *(Am).*

Leuchtstern *m* star *(signal).*

Leuchttonne *f* light buoy.

Leuchtturm *m* lighthouse.

Leuchtvisier *n* luminous sight.

Leuchtzeichen *n* ground signal, light signal.

Leuchtzifferblatt *n* luminous dial *(Inst).*

Leukoplast *n* court plaster.

Leute *fpl* personnel.

Leutnant *m* second lieutenant; lieutenant *(specifically, 2nd Lt).*

Leutnant der Flieger second lieutenant *(Luftwaffe).*

Leutnant zur See ensign *(Nav).*

Lewisit *n* Lewisite *(CWS).*

Libelle *f* level *(Inst);* clinometer *(Arty, Surv).*

die Libelle einspielen to center the bubble in a level.

Libelleneinstellung *f* level setting, level adjustment.

Libellengehäuse *n* level housing *(panoramic telescope).*

Libellenquadrant *m* gunner's quadrant *(with spirit level).*

Libellentafel *f* angle-of-site table *(Gunnery).*

Lichtanlasser *m* generator-starter *(MT).*

"Licht auf!" **"In action!"** *(AA SL).*

Lichtbild *n* photograph.

Lichtbildaufnahme *f* See **Lichtbild.**

Lichtbildauswertung *f* interpretation of photographs.

lichtbilden to photograph.

Lichtbildentzerrung *f* rectification of aerial photographs.

Lichtbilderkundung *f* photographic reconnaissance.

Lichtbildmaschinengewehr *n* machine-gun camera.

Lichtbildmessung *f* phototopography.

Lichtbild-MG *n* camera gun *(Avn).*

Lichtbildner *m* photographer.

Lichtbildpause *f* photographic overlay.

Lichtbildwesen *n* photography.

Lichtbogenschweißung *f* arc welding.

Lichtkegel *m* beam of light, cone of light.

Lichtmaschine *f* generator *(MT).*

Lichtmeßbatterie *f* flash ranging section *(Obsn Bn).*

Lichtmeßdienst *m* flash ranging service.

Lichtmessen *n* flash ranging.

Lichtmeßstelle *f* flash ranging station.

Lichtmeßtrupp *m* flash ranging team.

Lichtnetz *n* lighting system.

Lichtpause *f* photostatic reproduction; photocopy; blueprint.

Lichtrufanlage *f* light-signal call system *(in hospitals, etc.).*

Lichtschallmessen *n* sound and flash ranging.

Lichtschalter *m* light switch.

Lichtsprechgerät *n* modulated light-ray communication set.

Lichtspruch *m* signal-lamp message.

Lichtspur- See **Leuchtspur-.**

Lichtstärke *f* luminous intensity, intensity of light.

Lichtung *f* forest clearing.

lidern to pack, seal, obturate.

Liderung *f* gas check, obturator (G).

Liderungskopf *m* mushroom head *(of obturator).*

Liderungspolster *n* gas-check pad.

Lieferant *m* supplier, contractor.

Lieferdienst *m* ferrying service *(Avn)*.
Lieferschein *m* shipping ticket.
Lieferung *f* lot, shipment.
liegend prone, lying; berthed.
Liegeplatz *m* berth *(in port)*.
Linealvisier *n* linear sight *(Ger AA gun)*.
lineares System linear speed method *(AA Gunnery)*.
Linie *f* line, rank.
"In Linie zu einem Gliede, angetreten!" "In single rank, fall in!"
Linie B-Stelle-Ziel OP-target line.
Linie Geschütz-Ziel gun-target line.
Linienaufstellung *f* line formation.
Linienbö *f* line squall.
Linienkarte *f* line route map *(Tp)*.
Linienverkehr *m* "line" traffic *(two-station Rad Com on one or two frequencies)*.
Linie zu einem Glied single rank *(Inf)*; line *(Cav)*.
links left, to the left, on the left.
Linkskurve *f* left turn *(MT)*; left bank *(Avn)*.
linkslaufend counterclockwise.
Linksdrall *m* left-hand twist *(rifling)*.
linksgängig counterclockwise; left-hand *(threads, etc.)*.
Linksgewinde *n* left-hand thread *(MT)*.
linkslaufend counterclockwise.
"Links schwenkt, Marsch!" "Column left, march!"
"Links, um!" "Left, face!" *(being at a halt)*; "By the left flank, march!" *(given in marching)*.
Linkswendung *f* left face.
Linse *f* lens.
List *f* cunning, ruse, trick; stratagem *(Tac)*.
Litze *f* stranded wire *(Elec)*; colored facing on collar *(Clo)*.
Litzenspiegel *m* two narrow colored strips on collar *(Clo)*.
Livens-Handwerfer *m* Livens projector *(CWS)*.
l.M.G.-Abmarsch *m* light MG half squad *(Cav)*.
l.M.G.-Trupp *m* light machine-gun team *(of Ger R squad)*.
Ln.-Helferin *f* See **Luftnachrichten-Helferin**.
Ln.-Zugführer *m* See **Luftnachrichten-Zugführer**.

Locken *n* call to quarters.
Löffelbagger *m* power shovel.
Löhnung *f* base pay.
Lokomotivbahnhof *m* engine yard *(RR)*.
Lokomotivschuppen *m* engine house, roundhouse *(RR)*.
Looping *m* loop *(Avn)*.
Losantin *n* ,a German decontaminating agent *(calcium hypochlorite preparation in powder or in tablet form)*.
Losantinbrei *m* calcium hypochlorite slurry *(CWS)*.
löschen to unload *(a ship)*; to extinguish *(a fire)*; to slake *(lime)*.
Löschflüssigkeit *f* extinguisher fluid.
Löschgerät *n* fire extinguisher.
Löschmeister *m* sergeant fireman (Luftwaffe *official ranking as Master Sgt)*.
Löschplatz *m* pier, wharf.
Löschtrupp *m* fire-fighting crew.
lose loose, unlocked.
loslösen, sich disengage *(Tac)*.
Loslösung *f* disengagement *(Tac)*.
Lost *n* mustard gas.
Losung *f* password.
Lösung *f* solution; mixture.
Lösungsmittel *n* solvent.
Losungswort *n* password, countersign.
Lot *n* plumb bob, sounding lead; solder.
löten to solder.
Lotfe *n* See **Lofternrohr**.
Lotfernrohr *n* bomb sight.
Lötkolben *m* soldering iron.
Lötlampe *f* blowtorch.
Lötmetall *m* solder.
lotrecht perpendicular.
Lotrechte *f* perpendicular *(line)*.
Lotschnur *f* plumb line.
Lotse *m* pilot *(Nav)*.
Lotsenflagge *f* Union Jack *(Nav)*.
Lötzinn *n* solder.
Loxodrome *f* rhumb line *(Navigation)*.
L'Spur *f* See **Leuchtspur**.
Lücke *f* gap.
Luft *f* air *(in compounds: Air Forces, airborne, aircraft, aviation, etc.)*. See also terms under **Flieger**, **Flug**.
Luftabflußklappen *fpl* cowling flaps.
Luftabwehr *f* active air defense.

Luftabwehrdienst *m* air defense service.

Luftabwehrstelle *f* air defense post.

Luftabwehrwaffe *f* antiaircraft weapon.

Luftalarm *m* air-raid alarm.

Luftamt *n* See **Allgemeines Luftamt**.

Luftangriff *m* air attack, air raid.

Luftangriffsziel *n* air objective.

Luftanreicherung *f* concentration of gas in the air *(CWS)*.

Luftaufklärung *f* air reconnaissance.

Luftaufklärungsraum *m* air reconnaissance area.

Luftaufsichtsdienst *m* flight control service *(a branch of the Ger Air Ministry)*.

Luftausgleicher *m* pneumatic equilibrator *(G)*.

Luftbauamt *n* Air Ministry construction office.

Luftbehälter *m* compressed-air tank *(Engr, MT)*; air chamber *(counterrecoil mechanism, vehicle brake)*.

Luftbehälter des Vorholers recuperator cylinder *(G)*.

Luftbeobachtung *f* air observation.

Luftbild *n* aerial photograph.

Luftbildauswertung *f* interpretation of aerial photographs.

Luftbildentzerrung *f* rectification of aerial photographs.

Luftbildgerät *n* aircraft camera.

Luftbildkammer *f* aerial camera, aircraft camera.

Luftbildkarte *f* aerial mosaic; photographic map.

Luftbildplan *m* photomap.

Luftbildreihe *f* photographic strip.

Luftbildwesen *n* aerial photography.

luftdicht airtight.

Luftdichte *f* air density.

Luftdienstzulage *f* aviation pay, flying pay.

Luftdraht *m* antenna wire, overhead antenna.

Luftdruck *m* air pressure *(Mech)*; atmospheric pressure *(Met)*; blast *(effect of explosion)*.

Luftdruckbremse *f* air brake.

Luftdruck-Fettpresse *f* grease gun.

Luftdruckgradient *m* pressure gradient *(Met)*.

Luftdruckmesser *m* barometer.

Luftdrucktür *f* blast baffle *(Ft)*.

Luftdruckwirkung *f* blast effect.

Luftdüse *f* air jet *(Mtr)*.

Lufteinschießziel *n* high-burst adjustment target *(Arty)*.

lüften to air, to ventilate.

Lüfter *m* ventilator, fan, blower.

Lufterkundung *f* air reconnaissance.

Luftfahrt *f* aeronautics, aviation.

Luftfahrthindernis *n* airway obstruction.

Luftfahrtmedizin *f* aviation medicine.

Luftfahrtministerium *n* See **Reichsluftahrtministerium**.

Luftfahrwesen *n* aeronautics.

Luftfahrzeug *n* aircraft.

Luftfelddivision *f* air forces field division *(fighting as ground force with Army)*.

Luftfilter *m* air filter.

Luftflasche *f* compressed-air cylinder, oxygen flask.

Luftflotte *f* air force *(a territorial and tactical command of the Luftwaffe)*.

Luftflottenchef *m* air force commander. See also **Luftflotte**.

Luftgau *m* air force administrative command *(administrative area of a Luftflotte)*.

Luftgaukommado *n* air force administrative command headquarters. See also **Luftgau**, **Luftflotte**.

Luftgegner *m* hostile aircraft.

luftgekühlt air-cooled.

Luftgeschwader *n* See **Geschwader**.

Luftgewicht *n* density of the air.

ballistisches Luftgewicht ballistic density.

Lufthafenbereichkommandantur *f* airdrome regional command *(subdivision of a Luftgau)*.

Luftherrschaft *f* air supremacy, mastery of the air, control of the air.

Lufthoheit *f* air sovereignty.

Luftinfanterie *f* airborne infantry.

Luftkabel *n* overhead wire *(Tp)*.

Luftkampf *m* air fighting, air attack.

Luftkampfgeschwader *n* bombardment wing. See also **Geschwader**.

Luftkampfstoff *m* volatile chemical agent *(as distinguished from Geländekampfstoff, ground contaminating agent)*.

Luftkampfübung *f* air fighting or air attack exercise.

Luftkarte *f* air map.

Luftklappenventil *n* choke valve *(carburetor)*.

Luftkraft *f* aerodynamic force.

Luftkreis *m* air force service area.

Luftkreiskommando *n* air force service area headquarters.

Luftkrieg *m* air war, air warfare.

Luftkriegführung *f* air warfare.

Luftkriegsschule *f* officer candidate school *(Luftwaffe)*.

Luftkühlung *f* air cooling.

Luftlager *n* PW camp for air forces personnel.

Luftlandegeschwader *n* glider wing *(strictly, a wing of transport airplanes for towing gliders)*.

Luftlandekette *f* glider flight *(airborne operations)*. See also **Luftlandegeschwader**.

Luftlandestaffel *f* glider squadron *(airborne operations)*. See also **Luftlandegeschwader**.

Luftlandetruppen *fpl* air landing troops.

Luftleere *f* vacuum.

Luftleiter *m* antenna.

Luftloch *n* air pocket *(Avn)*.

Luftmacht *f* air power.

Luftmarsch *m* "air march" *(flight of airborne troops from departure Adrm to destination)*.

Luftmeer *n* atmosphere.

Luftmeldequadrat *n* grid square *(for reporting locations in air reconnaissance)*.

Luftmine *f* aerial mine.

Luftnachrichten *fpl* signal communication *(Luftwaffe)*.

Luftnachrichtenabteilung *f* signal battalion *(Luftwaffe)*.

Luftnachrichtenhelferin *f* woman signal auxiliary *(Luftwaffe)*.

Luftnachrichtenkompanie *f* signal company *(Luftwaffe)*.

Luftnachrichtenstelle *f* signal center of an airdrome.

Luftnachrichtentruppe *f* signal communication troops *(Luftwaffe)*.

Luftnavigation *f* air navigation.

Luftoffensive *f* air offensive.

Luftparade *f* aerial review, aerial pass in review.

Luftpersonalamt *n* See **Luftwaffenpersonalamt**.

Luftpresser *m* air compressor.

Luftraum *m* air area; air space; sky.

Luftreibung *f* air friction.

Luftreifen *m* pneumatic tire.

Luftreiniger *m* air filter.

Luftsack *m* wind sock, wind sleeve, wind cone *(Avn)*; towed-sleeve target *(AAA practice)*; ballonet *(Bln)*.

Luftsackmaul *n* air scoop *(Bln)*.

Luftsackventil *n* ballonet valve *(Bln)*.

Luftsäule *f* column of air *(Met)*.

Luftscheibe *f* antiaircraft practice target.

Luftschicht *f* atmospheric layer *(Met)*.

Luftschiff *n* airship.

Luftschlacht *f* air battle.

Luftschlauch *m* inner tube *(MT)*.

Luftschlitz *m* louver *(Tk)*.

Luftschraube *f* propeller *(Ap)*. See also **Propeller**.

Luftschraubenblatt *n* propeller blade *(Ap)*.

Luftschraubendrehzahl *f* propeller rpm.

Luftschraubenebene *f* plane of propeller rotation *(Ap)*.

Luftschraubenflügel *m* propeller blade *(Ap)*.

Luftschraubenhaube *f* propeller spinner *(Ap)*.

Luftschraubenkreis *m* propeller-disk area *(Ap)*.

Luftschraubensteigungsmesser *m* propeller pitch indicator.

Luftschraubenstrahl *m* slipstream.

Luftschraubennabenstück *n* propeller boss *(Ap)*.

Luftschraubenverstellgerät *n* pitch-control mechanism *(propeller)*.

Luftschutz *m* air raid protection, passive air defense *(Civ defense)*.

Luftschutzabschnitt *m* civilian defense sector *(air raid protection)*.

Luftschutzbezirk *m* civilian defense district *(air raid protection)*.

Luftschutzbrandspritze *f* stirrup pump.

Luftschutzbund *m* See **Reichsluftschutzbund**.

Luftschutzkeller *m* air raid shelter.

Luftschutzleiter *m* chief of air defense *(in a local defense council)*.

Luftschutzmaßnahmen *fpl* air raid precautionary measures.

Luftschutzordnungsdienst *m* civilian

defense police service (air raid protection).

Luftschutzpolizei f civilian defense police (air raid protection).

Luftschutzraum m air raid shelter.

Luftschutzrevier n civilian defense zone (air raid protection).

Luftschutzsanitätsdienst m civilian defense medical service (air raid protection).

Luftschutzsirene f air raid siren.

Luftschutztruppen fpl civilian defense troops (air raid protection).

Luftschutzturm m air raid tower.

Luftschutzübung f air raid drill, practice alert.

Luftschutzveterinärdienst m civilian defense veterinary service (air raid protection).

Luftschutzwarndienst m aircraft warning service (Civ defense).

Luftschutzwarnstelle f district warning center (AWS).

Luftschutzwarnzentrale f control center (AWS).

Luftschutzwart m air raid warden.

Luftschutzzentrale f See **Luftschutzwarnzentrale**.

Luftsog m vacuum (resulting from explosion).

Luftspäher m ground observer (AWS); antiaircraft scout or lookout, air sentinel, air guard.

Luftspäh- und Warndienst m aircraft scout and warning service.

Luftsperre f antiaircraft defenses (balloon barrage, fighter patrol, etc.).

Luftsperrgebiet n prohibited zone, airspace reservation (Avn).

Luftsperrtruppen fpl barrage balloon troops.

Luftsprengpunkt m point of air burst (Arty).

Luftstörungen fpl atmospheric disturbances.

Luftstoß m blast, concussion of air (resulting from an explosion).

Luftstreitkräfte fpl air forces.

Luftstrom m air current.

Luftstromgerät n airplane chemical spray apparatus.

Luftstützpunkt m air base.

lufttanken to refuel in flight.

Lufttorpedo n aerial torpedo.

Lufttransport m air transport.

Lufttreffbild n air-burst pattern.

Lufttüchtigkeit f airworthiness.

Lufttüchtigkeitsschein m airworthiness certificate.

Luftüberlegenheit f air superiority.

Lüftung f ventilation.

Lüftungsrohr n ventilation shaft (Tk).

Luftverankerung f overhead cable anchorage (Pon Bdg).

Luftverdichter m air compressor.

Luftvergleichsziel n high-burst auxiliary target (Arty).

Luftverkehrslinie f civil airway.

Luftversorgung f supply by air.

Luftverteidigung f air defense, antiaircraft defense; air defense system.

Luftverteidigungsgebiet n special air defense command in vital areas.

Luftvorholer m pneumatic recuperator (G).

Luftwache f ground observer (AWS); air sentinel, air guard.

Luftwaffe f German Air Forces.

Luftwaffenbautruppe f aviation construction engineers.

Luftwaffenbetriebskompanie f airdrome maintenance and service unit.

Luftwaffen-Druckvorschrift f air forces manual (abbr. L.Dv.).

Luftwaffen-Felddivision f air forces field division (fighting as ground force with the Army).

Luftwaffenflak f air forces antiaircraft artillery (as distinguished from Army antiaircraft artillery).

Luftwaffengruppenkommando n air force headquarters of a Gruppe.

Luftwaffenhelfer m air forces orderly (messenger or clerk of premilitary age).

Luftwaffenhelferin f air forces woman auxiliary.

Luftwaffen-Jäger-Regiment n air forces rifle regiment.

Luftwaffenkommando n air forces headquarters.

Luftwaffenpersonalamt n Air Forces Personnel Office (a branch of the Ger Air Ministry).

Luftwaffenschützenregiment n air forces rifle regiment.

Luftwaffen-Sturm-Bataillon n Air Forces assault battalion (air-landing troops).

Luftwaffenverordnungsblatt n Air Forces Regulations (a publication).

Luftwaffenverwaltungsamt n Air

Forces Administration Office (a branch of the Ger Air Ministry).

Luftwichte f specific gravity of air.

Luftwiderstand m air resistance (Ballistics, MT, etc.); drag (Avn).

Luftzielapparat m azimuth instrument.

Luger 08 f German standard military pistol.

Luke f door, hatch (Ap, Tk).

Lukendeckel m hatch cover (Tk).

Lungengift n See **Lungenreizstoff.**

Lungenreizstoff m lung irritant (CWS).

Lunte f slow match (fuze lighter).

Luv f weather side.

Luvwinkel m crab, angle of crab, drift angle (Air Navigation).

M

Maat m petty officer, third class (Nav).

Macht f power; country.

Maderfelge f quick-detachable rim (with side ring) (MT).

Magazin n storage depot; magazine.

Magazinfeuer n automatic fire.

Magazingehäuse n magazine housing (pistol).

Magazinhaltehebel m magazine catch lever (MG).

Magazinhalter m magazine holder (MG); magazine catch (pistol).

Magazinlager n magazine rack (Ord).

Magnesiumthermit n thermit filler (incendiary bomb).

Magnetapparat m magneto (Mtr).

Magnetisch-Nord m compass north, magnetic north.

Magnetkompaß m magnetic compass.

Magnetmine f magnetic mine.

Magnetspule f solenoid (Elec).

Magnetzündapparat m magneto.

Magnetzündung f magneto ignition.

Magnus-Effekt m Magnus effect (of air rotation caused by projectile spin).

Major m major.

Mangan n manganese.

Männchen n whipstall (Avn).

Manneszucht f military discipline.

Mannschaft f crew, team, party, squad, "outfit." See also **Mannschaften.**

Mannschaften fpl enlisted personnel (up to and including Obergefreiter, Cpl).

Mannschaftsentgiftungskraftwagen m decontamination truck for personnel.

Mannschaftsstube f squad room.

Mannschaftswagen m personnel carrier (MT).

Manöver n maneuver.

Manöverkartusche f blank cartridge.

Manövrierfähigkeit f maneuverability.

Manövrierventil n maneuvering valve (Bln).

Mantel m overcoat (Clo); jacket (MG, Am); casing (of a tire).

Mantelboden m jacket base (MG).

Mantelkopf m jacket end cap (MG).

Mantelringrohr n built-up barrel (G); jacketed barrel (MG).

Marine f navy.

Marineakademie f naval academy.

Marineartillerie f naval coast artillery.

Marineartillerieabteilung f naval coast artillery battalion.

Marineartilleriemaat m petty officer, third class, in naval coast artillery.

Marineattaché m naval attaché.

Marinebaubataillon n naval construction battalion.

Marine-Flak f naval antiaircraft artillery.

Marineflieger m naval aviator, naval pilot.

Marineflugwesen n naval aviation.

Marinelager n See **Marlag.**

Marineministerium n Admiralty of the German Navy.

Marke f mark, index mark, reading on range drum (Arty); label; brand; stamp.

Markenplatte f index plate (on aiming circle or telescopic sight).

Markenring m index ring (MG telescopic sight).

Marinestation f naval base.

Marinestoßtrupp *m* naval landing party.

Marinewaffenamt *n* Bureau of Ordnance *(Nav)*.

Marinewerft *f* navy yard.

Markenstück *n* line-up stud *(on top gun carriage)*.

Marketenderei *f* post exchange.

Marketenderware *f* sales article *(sold at PX)*.

Markscheidegerät *n* mine-surveying set *(Engr)*.

Marlag *n* prisoner-of-war camp for sailors *(abbr. of* Marinelager).

Marschabstand *m* distance between march units.

Marschallstab *m* baton.

Marschbataillon *n* personnel replacement transfer battalion *(conducting replacements from* Wehrkreis *to* T *of Opns)*.

Marschbefehl *m* march order; official travel order.

Marschbereitschaft *f* march readiness.

Marschbreite *f* width of march column.

Marschdecke *f* blanket.

marschfähig capable of walking, fit for marching.

marschfähige Verwundete walking wounded, ambulant cases.

Marschfähigkeit *f* marching ability.

Marschfolge *f* order of march.

Marschfühlung *f* maintenance of contact on the march.

Marschführer *m* control officer *(march column)*.

Marschgepäck *n* full pack.

Marschgeschwindigkeit *f* cruising speed *(Ap)*; rate of march.

Marschgliederung *f* march formation, organization of march.

Marschgruppe *f* march group, march section, march unit.

Marschhalt *m* march halt.

Marschieren ohne Tritt route march, route step.

Marschkolonne *f* march column, route column.

Marschkompanie *f* trained replacement company.

Marschkompaß *m* prismatic compass.

Marschkontrollstelle *f* control point.

Marschlänge *f* road space *(march column)*.

Marschleistung *f* march capacity, march performance.

Marschlinie *f* line of march.

"Marsch! Marsch!" "Double time, march!"; "On the double!"

Marschordnung *f* column of threes *(Inf drill)*; close order march formation; line of march.

"In Marschordnung, angetreten!" "In column of threes, fall in!"

"Marschordnung!" "March order!" *(Arty)*.

Marschpause *f* march halt.

Marschrast *f* march rest.

Marschsicherung *f* security on the march.

Marschskizze *f* strip map *(MT)*.

Marschstockung *f* road jam.

Marschstraße *f* march route.

Marschstrecke *f* march route, stretch or leg of a march.

Marschtafel *f* march table.

Marschtiefe *f* road space *(march column)*.

Marschübersicht *f* march schedule.

Marschvorposten *m* march outpost.

Marschweg *m* route of march.

Marschzeit *f* time of march, time distance.

Marschziel *n* march objective, march destination.

Marschzucht *f* march discipline.

Maschendraht *m* woven wire, wire netting, wire mesh.

Maschendrahtzaun *m* woven-wire fence, woven-wire obstacle.

Maschine *f* motor, engine; machine; airplane *(colloquial)*.

Maschinenflak *f* antiaircraft automatic weapons.

Maschinengewehr *n* machine gun. See also terms under **MG**.

Maschinengewehrangriff *m* strafing assault, strafing attack *(Avn)*.

Maschinengewehr-Bedienung *f* machine-gun crew.

Maschinengewehrgarbe *f* sheaf of fire *(MG)*.

Maschinengewehrgruppe *f* machine-gun section.

Maschinengewehr-Halbzug *m* machine-gun squad.

Maschinengewehrschlitten *m* machine-gun sleigh mount.

Maschinengewehrschütze *m* machine gunner.

Maschinengewehrstand *m* machine-gun emplacement; machine gunner's station *(Ap)*.

Maschinengewehrsteuerung *f* synchronization *(Ap MG's)*.

Maschinengewehrtrupp *m* light MG team *(of Inf squad)*.

Maschinengewehrzug *m* MG platoon.

Maschinenkanone *f* automatic cannon *(Ap)*; automatic gun.

Maschinenkarabiner *m* automatic rifle.

Maschinenpistole *f* submachine gun.

Maschinensatz *m* generating unit, power unit.

Maschinenschlosser *m* mechanic.

Maschinenschreiber *m* typist.

Maschinenwaffe *f* automatic weapon.

Maschinist *m* machinist *(Nav)*.

Maske *f* mask, screen, camouflage net, flat-top, overhead screen *(Cam)*; gas mask; oxygen mask.

Maskenbrille *f* special type of eyeglasses for wear under gas mask.

Maskenkörper *m* facepiece *(gas mask)*.

Maskenspanner *m* face form *(to prevent gas-mask distortion)*.

Maß *n* measure *(of quantity, etc.)*.

Masse *f* mass.

Massenabwurf *m* salvo release *(Bombing)*.

Massenausgleich *m* counterbalance, counterweight *(Ap)*.

Massenbeschuß *m* concentrated fire.

Masseneinsatz *m* commitment of major forces, employment of major forces *(Tac)*.

Massenfertigung *f* mass production.

Massentaktik *f* grand tactics.

Massenwirkung *f* mass effect *(Tac)*.

massieren to mass, concentrate; to massage.

Massierung *f* mass, massing, line of masses *(Tac)*.

Maßnahme *f* measure; step; enactment.

Maßstab *m* scale; proportion.

maßstabgerecht according to scale.

Mast *m* mast.

Mastwurf *m* clove hitch.

Materialfehler *m* defect of material.

Materialsammelstelle *f* salvage dump.

Materialschlacht *f* battle of matériel.

Materialwirkung *f* effect of fire against material objects *(Gunnery)*.

Matrose *m* apprentice seaman; sailor.

Matrosengefreiter *m* seaman, second class.

Matrosenhaupgefreiter *m* seaman, first class *(highest rated, with 4½ years seniority)*.

Matrosenobergefreiter *m* seaman, first class.

Mattanstrich *m* lusterless paint.

Mattscheibe *f* ground-glass plate.

Mauer *f* stone, brick or concrete wall.

Maultier *n* mule.

Maultierkolonne *f* mule train.

Maximaleffekt *m* maximum intensity *(sound locator)*.

M.-Blink *n* portable signal lamp *(abbr. of mittleres Blinkgerät)*.

Mechaniker *m* mechanic.

mechanischer Zünder mechanical fuze.

mechanisierter Verband mechanized unit.

mechanisiertes Fahrzeug armored combat vehicle.

Mechanisierung *f* mechanization.

Medaille *f* medal.

Meer *n* ocean, sea.

Meeresküste *f* seacoast.

Meeresspiegel *m* sea level.

Mehrachsantrieb *m* multi-axle drive.

Mehrachser *m* multi-axle vehicle.

Mehrbestand *m* surplus stock *(i.e. above authorized basic allowance)*.

Mehrdecker *m* multiplane *(Ap)*.

mehrfach multiple; multiplex; combination.

Mehrfachbetrieb *m* multiplex operation *(Tp)*.

Mehrfach-Reihenbildkammer *f* multiple lens camera *(aerial Photo)*.

Mehrfachsprechen *n* multiplex telephony.

Mehrfachzünder *m* combination fuze *(Am)*.

Mehrgitterröhre *f* multiple-grid tube, multielement tube *(Rad)*.

mehrgleisig multiple-tracked *(RR)*.

Mehrlader *m* magazine-fed rifle or carbine, clip-fed rifle or carbine.

Mehrladevorrichtung *f* magazine feeding device *(R)*.

mehrläufige Fla-Waffe multiple-barrel antiaircraft weapon.

Mehrlauflafette *f* multiple-gun mount.

Mehrlochdüse *f* multiple-hole nozzle *(Mtr)*.

mehrmotorig multiple-engine.

Mehrscheibenkupplung *f* multiple-disk clutch.

Mehrsitzer *m* multiseater airplane.

Mehrzweckfahrzeug *n* general-purpose vehicle.

Mehrzweckflugzeug *n* general-purpose airplane.

Mehrzweckgeschütz *n* multipurpose gun.

Meilenstein *m* milestone.

Meißel *m* chisel.

Meldeabwurf *m* message dropping.

Meldeabwurfhülle *f* drop-message bag.

Meldeabwurfstelle *f* message-dropping ground.

Meldeblatt *n* message blank.

Meldeblock *m* message pad.

Meldebuch *n* field message book.

Meldebüchse *f* message container *(for dropping messages).*

Meldedienst *m* message communication service.

Meldefahrer *m* mounted messenger *(MT);* dispatch rider, dispatch driver.

Meldefahrzeug *n* messenger vehicle.

Meldeformular *n* message blank.

Meldegänger *m* runner, messenger.

Meldehund *m* messenger dog.

Meldehundführer *m* messenger-dog handler, messenger-dog guard.

Meldehundtrupp *m* dog-handler team *(for messenger dogs).*

Meldekapsel *f* message-dropping container.

Meldekarte *f* message blank.

Meldekopf *m* wire head *(line construction);* advance message center.

Meldelauf *m* message run *(messenger dog).*

Meldeläufer *m* runner, messenger.

melden to report.

sich **melden** to report *(to present oneself);* to register with the police; to volunteer.

sich **krank melden** to report sick, to go on sick call.

sich **freiwillig melden** to volunteer, enlist, enroll.

Meldepatrone *f* ground signal cartridge.

Meldepflicht *f* obligation to report to, or register with, the police.

Meldequadrat *n* grid square *(for reporting locations).*

Melder *m* messenger.

Melderakete *f* message-carrying rocket.

Meldereiter *m* mounted messenger.

Melderose *f* orientation card *(AWS);* orientation clock *(to indicate target's direction of approach) (AAA).*

Meldesammelstelle *f* message center.

Meldestelle *f* control point *(march column);* local reporting office.

Meldetasche *f* dispatch case.

Meldeweg *m* message channel.

Meldung *f* message, report, dispatch.

Membran *f* diaphragm.

Membranmaske *f* diaphragm gas mask.

Membranpumpe *f* diaphragm pump.

mengenmäßig quantitative; volumetric.

Meridiankonvergenz *f* gisement, grid declination *(Surv).*

Merkblatt *n* supplement *(to a manual);* instructional pamphlet or booklet.

Merkzettel *m* data card, memo.

Meßband *n* surveyor's tape.

Meßbatterie *f* survey battery *(Arty).*

Meßbecher *m* dispenser, graduate.

Meßbildpaare *npl* stereoscopic complements *(Photo Surv).*

Meßbildverfahren *n* phototopography.

Meßbrücke *f* measuring bridge circuit, Wheatstone bridge *(Elec).*

Meßdreieck *n* plotting protractor *(Arty).*

Meßdreieckverfahren *n* plotting-protractor method *(protractor compensates for position offset and determines firing range on basis of range-finder and aiming-circle data).*

Meßei *n* pressure gage *(Arty).*

Meßeinheit *f* unit of measurement.

Meßentfernung *f* slant range to present position *(at instant of range determination) (AA gunnery).*

Messerflug *m* steep-bank flight.

Messerschalter *m* knife switch *(Elec).*

Meßflug *m* test flight *(Avn).*

Meßgerät *n* range-finder; survey equipment or instrument.

Meßhöhe *f* altitude of target at instant of range determination *(AA gunnery).*

Messing *n* brass.

Meßkammer *f* topographic-survey camera.

Meßkartusche *f* test cartridge; charge temperature cartridge *(Arty)*.

Meßkette *f* surveyor's chain.

Meßknopf *m* measuring knob *(range finder)*.

Meßkreis *m* protractor arc *(plotting protractor)*; azimuth circle *(BC telescope)*.

Meßlatte *f* stadia rod *(Surv)*.

Meßleitung *f* measuring circuit *(SR, FR)*.

Meßmann *m* range-finder operator.

Meßmarke *f* measuring mark *(range finder)*.

Meßpatrone *f* bore gage *(SA)*.

Meßpunkt *m* present position of target *(at instant of range determination) (AA gunnery)*.

Meßspiegel *m* reference mirror *(river-width measuring Inst)*.

Meßstab *m* stadia rod *(Surv)*.

Meßstand *m* base end station *(AAA)*.

Meßstelle *f* ranging station *(SR, FR)*.

Meßtisch *m* plane table *(Surv)*.

Meßtischblatt *n* plane table sheet.

Meßtrupp *m* survey team, flash or sound ranging team *(Arty)*.

Meßwalze *f* measuring knob *(height finder)*.

Meßzentrale *f* flash central station, sound central station *(FR, SR)*.

Metallgefäß *n* metal container.

Metallgliedergurt *m* metallic-link ammunition belt *(MG)*.

Metallgliederkette *f* metallic-link belt *(MG)*.

Metallsäge *f* hacksaw.

Meteorograph *m* aerometeorograph, aerograph, meteorograph *(Avn, Met)*.

Meteorologe *m* meteorologist.

Meterspur *f* one-meter track gage *(RR)*.

Methyldichlorarsin *n* methyldichlorarsine *(CWS)*.

Meuterei *f* mutiny.

M.-Flak *f* automatic antiaircraft gun *(abbr. of* Flugabwehrmaschinenkanone).

MG.-Dreifuß *m* tripod *(MG)*.

MG.-Gerät *n* machine-gun matériel.

MG.-Gurt *m* machine-gun ammunition belt.

MG.-Mann *m* machine gunner.

MG.-Richtaufsatz *m* machine-gun sight.

MG.-Richtkreis *m* machine-gun aiming circle.

MG.-Staffel *f* heavy machine-gun section *(Cav)*.

MG.-Träger *m* machine-gun carrier.

MG.-Wagen *m* machine-gun cart *(H-Dr)*.

MG.-Warze *f* blister *(Ap)*.

MG.-Zieleinrichtung *f* machine-gun sighting mechanism.

MG.-Zielfernrohr *n* machine-gun telescopic sight.

MG.-Zwilling *m* twin machine gun.

Mikrometerschraube *f* micrometer, micrometer calipers.

Milag *n* See **Militärlager.**

Milchglas *n* frosted glass.

Militär *n* military, military forces, soldiery. See *also terms under* **Heer, Wehrmacht.**

Militärärztliche Akademie army medical school.

Militärattaché *m* military attaché.

Militärausschuß *m* military commission.

Militärbefehlshaber *m* military commander in occupied territory.

Militärbehörde *f* military authorities.

Militärbevollmächtigter *m* military plenipotentiary.

Militärbezirk *m* military district.

Militärfriedhof *m* military cemetery.

Militärgefängnis *n* military prison.

Militärgericht *n* military court, military tribunal.

Militärgerichtsbarkeit *f* military jurisdiction.

militärische Besetzung military occupation.

militärische Formen military courtesy.

militärischer Auftrag military mission.

militärischer Schriftverkehr military correspondence.

militärisch räumen demilitarize.

Militärkommission *f* military commission.

Militärlager *n* prisoner of war camp *(abbr.* Milag).

Militärluftfahrt *f* military aviation.

Militärpfarrer *m* chaplain.

Militärstrafgesetzbuch *n* military penal code.

Militärverwaltung *f* military administration; military government.
Militärverwaltungsbezirk *m* military subdistrict.
Miliz *f* militia.
Mindestnutzbreite *f* minimum useful width of roadway.
Mine *f* mine.
Minenabweiser *m* parävane *(Nav)*.
Minenanker mit Tiefensteller automatic anchor *(Nav)*.
Minenanlage *f* demolition installation *(in a Bdg, etc.)*; mine system *(mine warfare)*.
Minenboje *f* mine buoy.
Minenbombe *f* aerial mine.
Minenfahrzeug *n* mine layer, mine planter *(Nav)*.
Minenfeld *n* mine field.
Minenflugzeug *n* mine-laying airplane.
Minengang *m* mine gallery.
Minengefäß *n* mine case *(container)*.
Minenhund *m* miner's tramcar *(Engr)*; remote-controlled explosive-laden tank, "robot tank."
Minenkammer *f* demolition chamber *(Bdg, mine)*.
Minenkampf *m* military mining, mine warfare.
Minenkratze *f* grub hoe.
Minenkrieg *m* military mining, mine warfare.
Minenlegen *n* mine laying.
Minenleger *m* mine layer, mine planter *(Nav)*.
Minenlegermotorboot *n* mine yawl *(Nav)*.
Minenlegerpanzerkampfwagen *m* mine-laying tank.
Minenräumboot *m* mine sweeper *(Nav)*.
Minenräumer *m* mine sweeper *(Nav)*.
Minenräumpanzer *m* mine-clearance tank.
Minenräumung *f* mine sweeping; mine clearance.
Minenrohr *n* borehole.
Minenschacht *m* mine shaft.
Minenschleppen *n* mine dragging *(Nav)*.
Minensperre *f* mine field, mine obstacle; submarine mine field *(Nav)*; mine defense *(Tac)*.
Minenstollen *m* gallery, tunnel.

Minensuchboot *n* mine sweeper *(Nav)*.
Minensucher *m* mine sweeper *(Nav)*.
Minensuchgerät *n* mine detector.
Minensuchstab *m* mine-probing rod.
Minensuchtrupp *m* mine-locating detail.
Minentonne *f* mine buoy.
Minentrichter *m* mine crater.
minenverseuchtes Gebiet mined area, mine-infested area.
Minenwirkung *f* mining effect *(Am)*.
Minierdienst *m* mining service *(tunneling)*.
Miniergerät *n* mining tools.
Miniergut *n* spoil *(mining)*.
Mißbilligung *f* disapproval.
mißlingen fail.
mißweisender Kurs magnetic heading, magnetic course *(Air Navigation)*.
mißweisender Kurswinkel magnetic azimuth *(Air Navigation)*.
Mißweisung *f* magnetic declination, magnetic variation, declination constant, compass declination.
Mithöreinrichtung *f* sidetone circuit *(Rad, Tp)*.
mithören to listen in, to monitor *(Rad, Tp)*.
Mithörstelle *f* intercept station.
Mitklingen *n* resonance *(Rad)*.
Mitkoppeln *n* determining of course or fix by dead reckoning *(Avn)*.
Mitlesen *n* interception *(of visual signals)*.
Mitnehmer *m* translating lever *(sight mechanism)*; lathe dog; catch; lifter; cam; lug.
Mitschuldiger *m* accomplice.
mitteilen inform.
Mitteilung *f* communication, message, information.
Mittelbalken *m* center balk *(Bdg)*.
Mitteldecker *m* midwing monoplane.
Mittelhand *f* barrel *(horse)*.
Mittelpferde *npl* swing team.
Mittelpfropfen *m* tompion *(G)*.
Mittelrohrrahmen *m* tubular-center chassis *(MT)*.
Mittelspiegel *m* a colored center strip between the halves of the Kragenlitze *(Clo)*.
Mitteltroß *m* second echelon supply train *(behind the Gefechtstroß)*.
Mitteneindruck *m* binaural balance *(sound locating)*.

mittlere Flugbahn mean trajectory.
mittlerer Fehler average error, mean error.
mittlerer Panzerkampfwagen medium tank.
mittlerer Sprengpunkt center of burst.
mittlerer Treffpunkt center of impact, center of dispersion.
mittlere Sonnenzeit mean solar time.
Mitwirkung f cooperation.
mobil mobilized.
mobil machen to mobilize.
Mobilmachung f mobilization.
Mobilmachungsbestimmungen fpl mobilization regulations.
Mobilmachungsplan m mobilization plan.
Modell n model, type, pattern.
Modelung f modulation (Rad, Tp).
modulierte Welle modulated wave.
Moment m moment, instant.
Moment n factor, element.
Momentstrom m instantaneous current (Elec).
Montage f assembly, erection, mounting, installation.
Montagehalle f assembly shop.
Montageluke f inspection hatch (Tk).
Montageplatte f chassis panel (Rad).
Montagewerk n assembly plant.
Monteur m mechanic, assembler.
montieren to assemble, make up, erect, mount.
Montierhebel m tire tool.
Moor n bog, marsh, moor.
Morast m bog.
Morgenkost f breakfast, morning meal.
Morsealphabet n Morse code.
Morsen n transmitting by Morse code.
Mörser m howitzer (caliber 210 mm and larger).
Morsespruch m telegraph message.
Morsetaste f telegraph key.
Morsezeichen n Morse code character.
Motor m engine, motor.
Motorblock m cylinder block (Mtr).
Motorbremse f engine brake (MT).
Motordrehmoment n engine torque.
Motordrehzahl f engine rpm.
Motoren-Instandsetzung f engine repair.

Motorenkühlung f engine cooling.
Motorenlüftung f engine ventilation, engine louvers (Tk).
Motorenraum m engine compartment (Tk).
Motorgleiter m powered glider.
Motorgondel f engine nacelle (Ap).
Motorhaube f engine cowling (Ap); hood (MT).
motorisiert motorized; mechanized; mobile.
motorisierte Kavallerie mechanized cavalry.
Motorpanne f engine failure.
Motorponton m ponton with outboard motor.
Motorrad n See Kraftrad.
Motorregler m engine governor.
Motorsäge f power saw.
Motorschaden m engine damage, engine trouble.
Motorschlitten m motor sled, aerosled.
Motorschnellboot n motor torpedo boat, PT boat.
Motorsegler m powered glider.
Motorstörung f engine trouble.
Motortorpedoboot n motor torpedo boat, PT boat.
Motorverkleidung f engine cowling (Ap).
Motorverschalung f See Motorverkleidung.
Motorwelle f engine crankshaft.
m.Pak f medium antitank gun.
M.Patrone f ground signal cartridge (abbr. of Meldepatrone).
Mucken n flinching (SA firing).
Müdigkeit f fatigue.
Mudrasteg m a type of portable hasty footbridge.
Muffe f threaded sleeve (for pipe connections).
Mühle f mill.
Mulde f pit, hole, depression, hollow.
Muldenlinie f centerline of depression (Top).
mündlich oral.
Mundloch n adapter opening (Am).
Mundlochfries m muzzle bell, muzzle swell (G).
Mundlochgewinde n adapter thread (Am).
Mundlochschraube f adapter plug (Am).
Mundpfropfen m tompion (G).

Mundschicht *f* chemical layer *(gas mask)*.

Mundstück *n* mouthpiece *(harness)*.

Mündung *f* muzzle *(Ord)*; mouth, outlet *(of a river)*.

Mündungsarbeit *f* kinetic energy at the muzzle.

Mündungsbremse *f* muzzle brake *(G)*.

Mündungsdeckel *m* muzzle cover.

Mündungsenergie *f* kinetic energy at the muzzle.

Mündungsfeuer *n* muzzle flash.

Mündungsfeuerdämpfer *m* flash hider.

Mündungsgasdruck *m* muzzle gas pressure.

Mündungsgeschwindigkeit *f* muzzle velocity.

Mündungskappe *f* tompion, muzzle cover *(G)*.

Mündungsknall *m* report produced by gun or muzzle wave *(SR)*.

Mündungspfropfen *m* tompion *(G)*.

Mündungsrauch *m* muzzle-blast smoke.

Mündungsschoner *m* muzzle cover *(R)*.

Mündungswaagerechte *f* base of the trajectory.

Mündungswucht *f* kinetic energy at the muzzle.

Munition *f* ammunition.

Munitionieren *n* loading *(Ap weapons)*.

Munitionsart *f* grade of ammunition.

Munitionsaufzug *m* shell hoist.

Munitionsausgabestelle *f* ammunition distributing point.

Munitionsausstattung *f* issue of ammunition.

Munitionsbestand *m* stock of ammunition.

Munitionseinsatz *m* commitment or employment of ammunition.

Munitionsersatz *m* resupply of ammunition.

Munitionsfahrzeug *n* ammunition carrier *(vehicle)*.

Munitionskammer *f* ammunition sponson *(Tk)*; ammunition storage chamber, magazine.

Munitionskarren *m* loading barrow; ammunition carrier *(H-Dr)*.

Munitionskasten *m* ammunition box.

Munitionskolonne *f* ammunition train, ammunition column.

Munitionslager *n* ammunition dump, ammunition depot.

Munitionslager in Geschütznähe ready magazine *(Arty)*.

Munitionsloch *n* ammunition pit.

Munitionsmangel *m* ammunition shortage.

Munitionsnachschub *m* ammunition supply.

Munitionsnische *f* ammunition niche, hasty ammunition shelter *(Ft)*.

Munitionsschlepper *m* ammunition prime mover *(MT)*.

Munitionsschuppen *m* ammunition storage shed.

Munitionsschütze *m* ammunition bearer, ammunition carrier.

Munitionsstaffel *f* ammunition section *(of firing Btry, Tk Bn, etc.)*.

Munitions-Staffelführer *m* ammunition supply officer.

Munitionsstapelplatz *m* ammunition dump.

Munitionsträger *m* ammunition bearer, ammunition carrier.

Munitionstrommel *f* ammunition drum.

Munitionstrupp *m* ammunition detail.

Munitionsumschlagstelle *f* ammunition supply point.

Munitionsunteroffizier *m* chief of ammunition *(NCO, Arty)*.

Munitionsverbrauch *m* expenditure of ammunition.

Munitionsvergeudung *f* waste of ammunition.

Munitionsverteilungsstelle *f* ammunition distributing point.

Munitionsverwaltung *f* ammunition administrative office *(Div and up)*.

Munitionsverwaltungskompanie *f* ammunition administration company.

Munitionswagen *m* caisson, ammunition wagon, ammunition trailer, ammunition carrier *(H-Dr)*.

Munitionswesen *n* ammunition supply service.

Munitionszug *m* ammunition train *(RR)*.

Munitionszugmaschine *f* ammunition prime mover *(MT)*.

mürbe softened up, worn out, demoralized.

M- u. R.-Patronen *fpl* signal and smoke cartridges *(abbr. of* Melde- und Rauchpatronen*)*.

Musikkorps *n* military band.

Musikmeister *m* bandmaster *(2nd Lt)*.
Muster *n* model, type, pattern.
Musterung *f* registration for the draft *(includes physical examination and tentative classification)*.
Musterungsbezirk *m* draft subdistrict *(subdivision of* Wehrmeldebezirk*)*.
Musterungsstab *m* registration staff *(for the draft)*.

Mutter *f* nut *(Tech)*.
Mutterkompaß *m* master compass *(Avn)*.
Muttermal *n* birthmark.
Mutterrohr *n* gun tube designed to receive a liner.
Mutterschiff *n* tender *(Nav)*.
Mutterschlüssel *m* wrench.
Mutteruhr *f* master watch.
Mütze *f* cap, hat.
Mützenkordel *f* hat cord.

N

Nabe *f* hub.
Nachbar *m* adjacent unit *(Tac)*; neighbor.
Nachbartruppen *fpl* adjacent troops.
Nachbildung *f* mock-up, model, dummy.
nachbrennen to hang fire *(Am)*.
Nachbrenner *m* hangfire *(Am)*.
Nachdrängen *n* direct pressure in pursuit *(Tac)*.
Nachhinken *n* hysteresis *(Mech)*.
Nachhut *f* rear guard.
Nachlässigkeit *f* negligence.
Nachlauf *m* positive caster *(MT)*.
"Nach links, richt Euch!" "Dress left, dress!"
Nachprüfung *f* verification.
Nachricht *f* information, intelligence, news, message.
Nachrichten *fpl* information, intelligence, signal communication.
Nachrichtenabteilung *f* signal battalion.
Nachrichtenachse *f* axis of signal communication.
Nachrichtenaufklärung *f* signal intelligence.
Nachrichtenbeschaffung *f* procurement of information, intelligence.
Nachrichtenbeurteilung *f* evaluation of information.
Nachrichtenblatt *n* bulletin *(publication)*.
Nachrichtendienst *m* military intelligence service, intelligence service; news service *(Rad)*.
Nachrichteneinsatz *m* commitment or employment of signal units.

Nachrichtenfahrzeug *n* signal vehicle.
Nachrichtenführer *m* signal officer of a *Fliegerkorps (in Comd of a* Luftnachrichtenregiment*)*.
Höherer Nachrichtenführer signal officer at a *Luftflotte* headquarters.
Nachrichtengerät *n* signal equipment, signal supplies.
Nachrichtengerätkarren *m* signal-equipment cart.
Nachrichtengerätpark *m* signal-supply dump.
Nachrichtenhelferin *f* signal-communication woman auxiliary.
Nachrichtenkolonne *f* signal-supply column.
Nachrichtenkompanie *f* signal company.
Nachrichtenkopf *m* wire head, advance message center.
Nachrichtenkraftfahrzeug *n* signal motor vehicle.
Nachrichtenmaid *f* woman signal auxiliary of the *SS*.
Nachrichtenmann *m* signal communication man.
Nachrichtenmittel *n* means of signal communication.
Nachrichtennetz *n* communication net.
Nachrichtenoffizier *m* signal officer, communication officer, intelligence officer.
Nachrichtenpark *m* signal-supply depot.
Nachrichtenquerverbindung *f* liaison communication.

Nachrichtensammelstelle *f* signal intelligence center.

Nachrichtenstaffel *f* communication section *(Bn, Btry, etc.)*.

Nachrichtenstelle *f* message center, signal center.

Nachrichtentrupp *m* communication detail.

Nachrichtentruppe *f* Signal Corps.

Nachrichtentruppen *fpl* signal troops.

Nachrichtenübermittlung *f* transmission of communications.

Nachrichtenverband *m* signal unit.

Nachrichtenverbindung *f* signal communication.

Nachrichtenverkehr *m* signal communication traffic.

Nachrichtenwagen *m* signal wagon, signal truck.

Nachrichtenwege *mpl* signal communication channels.

Nachrichtenwerkstattkraftwagen *m* signal repair truck.

Nachrichtenwesen *n* signal communications.

Nachrichtenzentrale *f* signal center, message center.

Nachrichtenzug *m* signal communication platoon.

Nachsatteln *n* readjustment of saddle.

Nachschub *m* supply.

Nachschubabwurf *m* dropping of supplies from aircraft.

Nachschubausgabestelle *f* supply point.

Nachschubbataillon *n* supply battalion.

Nachschubboot *n* supply boat.

Nachschubdienst *m* supply service.

Nachschubdienststelle *f* supply service headquarters, office of supply services.

Nachschubfahrzeug *n* supply vehicle.

Nachschubführer *m* chief of supply services *(Div, corps, army)*.

Nachschubgeleit *n* supply convoy *(Nav)*.

Nachschubgut *n* supply, supplies.

Nachschubkolonne *f* supply column, supply train.

Nachschubkolonnenabteilung *f* supply column battalion.

Nachschubkompanie *f* supply company.

Nachschublage *f* supply situation.

Nachschublager *n* supply depot, supply dump.

Nachschublinie *f* supply line.

Nachschubmittel *n* means of supply movement.

Nachschuboffizier *m* supply officer.

Nachschub-Panzerkampfwagen *m* armored supply and maintenance vehicle.

Nachschubpark *m* supply dump, supply depot.

Nachschubsammelgebiet *n* railhead service area.

Nachschubstab z.b.V. special supply staff.

Nachschubstraße *f* supply route, line of supply, line of communication.

Nachschubstützpunkt *m* supply base.

Nachschubtrupp *m* supply party, supply detail.

Nachschubtruppen *fpl* supply troops, supply units.

Nachschubübung *f* supply service exercise.

Nachschubumschlagstelle *f* supply point.

Nachschubverkehr *m* supply traffic, movement of supplies.

Nachschubverteilungsstelle *f* supply distributing point.

Nachschubweg *m* supply road, supply route.

Nachschubwesen *n* supply services.

Nachschubzug *m* supply train *(RR)*.

Nachsicherung *f* additional security *(Tac)*.

Nachspitze *f* rear point *(march column)*.

Nachspitzenkompanie *f* rear party *(in rear guard of large unit)*.

nachstellen to readjust; to pursue.

Nachstrom *m* slipstream *(Avn)*.

Nachtangriff *m* night attack, night raid.

nachtanken refuel.

Nachtaufklärung *f* night reconnaissance.

Nachtbefeuerung *f* night beacon lighting *(along a flight route or airway)*; lighting facilities for landing at night *(Adrm)*.

Nachtgefecht *n* night combat.

Nachtglas *n* night glasses.

Nachtjagd *f* night fighting, pursuit operations at night *(Avn)*.

Nachtjagdgeschwader *n* wing of night fighters *(Avn)*.

Nachtjagdgruppe *f* night fighter group *(Avn)*.

Nachtjagdschule *f* night fighter school *(Avn)*.

Nachtjäger *m* night fighter *(Avn)*.

Nachtjägergeschwader *n* wing of night fighters *(Avn)*.

Nachtkampfflugzeug *n* night bomber.

Nachtluftkampf *m* night fighting *(Avn)*.

Nachtmarsch *m* night march.

nachträglich supplementary.

Nachtrupp *m* rear guard support *(in rear guard of large unit)*; rear party *(in rear guard of smaller unit)*.

Nachtschießen *n* night firing.

Nachtunternehmung *f* night operation.

Nachurlaub *m* extension of leave.

Nachweis *m* proof, evidence; inventory; list; record.

Nachweisung *f* list, account, record; strength report, stock report.

Nachzügler *m* straggler.

Nachzündung *f* retarded ignition.

Nackenband *n* neck strap *(gas mask)*.

Nackenriemen *m* neck strap *(harness)*.

Nadel *f* needle; firing pin *(fuze)*.

Nadelabweichung *f* magnetic declination.

Nadellager *n* needle bearing *(MT)*.

Nadelschwankungen *fpl* oscillations of compass needle.

Nadelstück *n* firing pin support *(fuze)*.

Nadelverfahren *n* compass method *(of laying guns)*.

Nadelwald *m* coniferous forest, coniferous wood.

Nadelwehr *n* needle dam *(Engr)*.

Nadelzahl *f* magnetic azimuth, azimuth reading.

Nafü *m* *See* **Nachrichtenführer.**

Nahabwehr *f* close defense.

Nahaufklärer *m* close reconnaissance airplane.

Nahaufklärerstaffel *f* close reconnaissance squadron *(Avn)*.

Nahaufklärung *f* local reconnaissance, close reconnaissance.

Nahaufklärungsflugzeug *n* close-reconnaissance airplane, observation airplane.

Nahaufklärungsgruppe *f* close reconnaissance airplane group *(attached to ground forces)*.

Nahbeobachtung *f* local observation.

Naherkunder *m* close reconnaissance airplane, observation airplane.

nähern to approach, close in.

Nahkampf *m* close combat.

Nahkampfartillerie *f* close support artillery.

Nahkämpfer *m* close-combat fighter.

Nahkampffliegerverband *m* formation of close support airplanes.

Nahkampfführer *m* commander of a *Nahkampfgruppe (Luftwaffe)*.

Nahkampfgruppe *f* close support airplane group *(attached to ground forces)*.

Nahkampfmittel *n* close-combat munitions or weapons.

Nahkampfspange *f* close combat clasp *(decoration)*.

Nahkampfwaffe *f* close combat weapon.

Nahkampfweite *f* close range, close-combat range.

Nahkompaß *m* direct-reading compass.

Nah-Packgefäß *n* unit container *(as distinguished from a bulk container)*.

nähren to feed; to reinforce.

Nahrung *f* nourishment, food.

Nahsicherung *f* close-in security, close-in protection.

Naht *f* seam; boundary between units *(Tac)*.

Nahtkompanie *f* contact company *(occupying a boundary position between two units)*.

Nahtreffer *m* near miss.

Nahtstelle *f* boundary position *(between units)*.

Nahunterstützung *f* close support.

Nahverkehr *m* local traffic, short-range traffic.

Nahverteidigung *f* close defense.

Nahwerfer *m* short-range flame thrower.

Nähzeug *n* sewing kit.

Nalfagtafel *f* chart showing chemical warfare agents and their properties *(Tng)*.

Narbe *f* scar.

Narvikschild *m* Narvik Shield *(emblem on upper left sleeve, worn by* *all participants in reconquest of Narvik, 1940).*

Nase *f*   nose; stud; cap; lug.

Nasenklammer *f*   nose clamp *(gas mask).*

Nasenleiste *f*   leading edge *(Ap wing).*

Nasenrachenreizstoff *m*   nose and throat irritant, sternutator *(CWS).*

Nasenriemen *m* noseband *(harness).*

Nasen- und Rachenreizstoff *m*   See **Nasenrachenreizstoff.**

Naßbrandpulver *n*   black powder.

Nationale *n*   personal data *(birth, occupation, etc.).*

Nationalsozialistisches Fliegerkorps Nazi party aviation corps *(abbr.* N.S.F.K.).

Nationalsozialistisches Kraftfahrkorps Nazi party motor corps *(abbr.* N.S.K.K.).

Natrium *n*   sodium.

Natriumhypochlorit *n*   sodium hypochlorite.

Natriumkarbonat *n*   washing soda.

Natriumsulfid *n*   sodium sulfide.

Natriumsulfit *n*   sodium sulfite.

Natur *f*   nature.

in Natur   in kind *(rations, Clo, etc.).*

Naturalleistungsgesetz *n*   requisition law.

Naturalverpflegung *f*   rations in kind.

Naturgummi *m*   See **Naturkautschuk.**

Naturkautschuk *m*   natural rubber.

natürliche Deckung   accidental cover.

Naturschutzgebiet *n*   national park.

Nautiker *m*   navigator.

Navigationsfunkfeuer *n*   radio marker beacon *(Air Navigation).*

Navigationskarte *f*   navigation chart or map.

Nebel *m*   smoke *(CWS);* fog, mist, haze, vapor.

Nebelabblasen *n*   release of smoke *(CWS).*

Nebelabblasgerät *n*   smoke-filled chemical cylinder *(CWS).*

Nebelabteilung *f*   smoke-producing unit *(CWS).*

Nebelausdehnung *f*   smoke coverage.

Nebelbombe *f*   smoke bomb.

Nebeldecke *f*   smoke blanket, smoke screen.

Nebeleinsatz *m*   employment of smoke.

Nebelentwicklung *f*   generation of smoke.

Nebelgebiet *n*   fog area *(Met).*

Nebelgerät *n*   chemical tank, smoke tank *(for Cml spraying).*

Nebelgeschoß *n*   smoke projectile.

Nebelgewehrgranate *f*   smoke rifle grenade.

Nebelgranate *f*   smoke shell *(Am).*

Nebelhandgranate *f*   smoke hand grenade.

Nebelkasten *m*   box-type smoke container *(CWS).*

Nebelkerze *f*   smoke candle.

Nebelkraftwagen *m*   smoke equipment truck.

Nebelmittel *n*   smoke agent, smoke equipment.

Nebelmunition *f*   smoke munitions.

Nebelpanzerkampfwagen *m*   smoke-screen tank.

Nebelpatrone *f*   smoke cartridge.

Nebelsäure *f*   FS solution, sulfur trioxide-chlorsulfonic acid solution *(CWS).*

Nebelschießen *n*   smoke-shell firing *(Arty).*

Nebelschleier *m*   smoke screen.

Nebelstoff *m*   smoke agent, screening agent *(CWS).*

Nebeltopf *m*   smoke pot *(CWS).*

Nebeltornister *m*   pack smoke apparatus *(CWS).*

Nebeltrommel *f*   drum-type smoke container *(CWS).*

Nebeltrupp *m*   smoke party.

Nebeltruppen *fpl*   chemical troops, smoke-generator units.

Nebelübung *f*   smoke-screening exercise.

Nebelwalze *f*   creeping barrage of smoke-shell fire *(Arty);* progressive smoke screening.

Nebelwand *f*   smoke curtain, smoke screen.

Nebelwerfer *m*   chemical projector *(smoke shell);* smoke-shell mortar; rocket launcher, rocket mortar. *(Note:* Nebelwerfer 41 *is a six-tube rocket launcher for HE rockets).*

Nebelwerferabteilung *f*   smoke battalion, chemical battalion.

Nebelwerferregiment *n*   smoke regiment, chemical regiment.

Nebelwolke *f*   smoke cloud *(CWS).*

Nebelwurfgranate *f*   mortar smoke shell.

Nebelzerstäuber *m* smoke spray *(smoke-filled Cml cylinder with spray nozzle)*.

Nebelzone *f* smoke-screened area.

Nebelzündmittel *n* smoke-container firing device.

Nebenabschnitt *m* adjacent sector.

Nebenabsicht *f* secondary objective.

Nebenangriff *m* holding attack, secondary attack, secondary effort *(Tac)*.

Nebenanschluß *m* local station, extension *(Tp)*.

Nebenanschlußleitung *f* local-circuit line, extension line *(Tp)*.

Nebeneinanderschaltung *f* parallel connection *(Elec)*.

Nebenfarbe *f* secondary service color *(as distinguished from the basic service color, Waffenfarbe)*.

Nebengeräusche *npl* ambient noise *(sound locating)*.

Nebengleis *n* side track, siding *(RR)*.

Nebenkolonne *f* adjacent column, secondary column.

Nebenlager *n* branch camp *(PW)*.

Nebenluft *f* secondary air *(Mtr)*.

Nebenmann *m* man on the left or right *(Drill)*.

Nebenoperationen *fpl* secondary operations *(Tac)*.

Nebenschluß *m* shunt *(Elec)*.

Nebenschlußmotor *m* shunt motor *(Elec)*.

Nebenstachel *m* front sight *(AT gun)*.

Nebenstelle *f* local station *(Tp)*.

Nebenstraße *f* side street, side road; secondary road, auxiliary road.

Nebenstromkreis *m* shunt circuit *(Elec)*.

Nebsttreffer *m* near miss.

nehmen to take.

aus der Flanke nehmen to attack on the flank.

unter Feuer nehmen to shell, to fire on.

Nehmestaat *m* detaining power *(PW)*.

nehmestaatliche Behörde detaining authority *(PW)*.

Neigung *f* inclination, slope.

Neigungsmesser *m* clinometer *(Surv, Gunnery)*; flight indicator, inclinometer *(Ap)*.

Neigungswinkel *m* angle of slope.

Nennhöhe *f* rated altitude.

Nennleistung *f* rated horsepower.

Nest *n* nest; emplacement; position consisting of a group of foxholes with shallow connecting trenches.

Netz *n* net, network; grid; wiring system; power system.

Netzanschlußgerät *n* power-line operated radio set *(as distinguished from battery-operated or local power-supply set)*; power-supply unit, power pack *(Rad)*.

Netzleger *m* net-laying vessel.

Netzsperre *f* net obstacle, net-defense obstacle *(coastal defense)*.

Netztransformator *m* power transformer *(Rad)*.

Netzverkehr *m* "net" traffic *(includes several radio stations communicating at will on the frequency of their called stations)*.

Neuaufstellung *f* reorganization, new organization; reorganized or newly activated unit.

Neubearbeitung *f* revision.

neu einrichten re-lay *(Gunnery)*; readjust.

Neugrad *m* 1/400th of a circle *(equals 16 artillery mils, as distinguished from Grad, degree, 1/360th of a circle)*.

Neugradteilung *f* centesimal graduation. See Neugrad.

neutrale Nachrichtenverbände neutral communication units *(maneuvers)*.

neutrale Truppen neutral troops *(maneuvers)*.

neutrale Zone taxiway *(Adrm)*.

neutralisieren to neutralize.

Neutralität *f* neutrality.

nichtbrisanter Sprengstoff low explosive.

Nichtkämpfer *m* noncombatant.

Nickelsammler *m* nickel-alkaline cell *(Elec)*.

Niederdruckreifen *m* low-pressure tire *(MT)*.

Niederfrequenz *f* low frequency, audio-frequency *(Rad)*.

Niederfrequenzverstärker *m* audio-frequency amplifier *(Rad)*.

niederhalten to neutralize, immobilize, hold down.

Niederhaltungsschießen *n* neutralization fire *(Arty)*.

niederkämpfen reduce, overpower,

put out of action *(Tac);* to silence *(enemy fire).*

Niederkämpfung *f* reduction, destruction, putting out of action *(Tac);* covering with destruction fire *(Arty).*

Niederlage *f* defeat, reverse.

niedermachen kill, slaughter.

niedermetzeln to massacre, slaughter.

Niederschläge *mpl* precipitation *(Met).*

Niederspannung *f* low voltage *(Elec).*

Niederung *f* low country, depression, low ground.

Niedrigantenne *f* low antenna.

Niemandsland *n* no man's land.

Nieseln *n* drizzle *(Met).*

Niesgas *n* sneeze gas *(CWS).*

Niet *m* riveted joint, riveted assembly, riveted seam.

Niete *f* rivet.

nieten to rivet.

Niethammer *m* riveter *(tool).*

Nietung *f* riveting.

Nippel *f* nipple *(Tech).*

Nitrierung *f* nitration *(Am).*

Nitroglyzerin *n* nitroglycerin.

Nitroglyzerin-Blättchenpulver *n* nitroglycerin flake powder.

nitroglyzerinhaltiges Nitrozellulosepulver double base powder *(Am).*

Nitroglyzerinpulver *n* nitroglycerin powder.

Nitrozellulose *f* nitrocellulose, pyrocellulose.

Nitrozellulose-Blättchenpulver *n* nitrocellulose flake powder.

Nitrozellulosepulver *n* blank fire powder, E.C. powder, E.C. smokeless powder, E.C. blank fire *(SA Am).*

Nivellementspunkt *m* bench mark.

Nivellierinstrument *n* surveyor's level.

Nivellierlibelle *f* sighting level *(plane table).*

Nocken *m* cam *(also spelled die Nocke).*

Nockenwelle *f* camshaft.

Nonius *m* vernier.

Norden *m* north.

Norm *f* standard *(Tech).*

Normalbelastung *f* normal load, standard load.

Normalfluglage *f* level flight *(Avn).*

Normalkette *f* standard caterpillar track.

Normalnull *f* mean sea level *(abbr.* NN).

Normalraupe *f* standard caterpillar track.

Normalspur *f* standard gage *(RR).*

Normalstellung *f* zero position *(Arty).*

Normalvisier stellen to zero a gun sight.

normen standardize.

Normteil *m* standard part.

Normung *f* standardization.

Not *f* emergency.

Notabwurf *m* emergency salvo release *(Bombing).*

Notbeleuchtung *f* emergency illumination.

Notbremse *f* emergency brake.

Notfall *m* emergency.

Notfeuer *n* barrage, normal barrage *(now called* Sperrfeuer).

Nothilfe *f See* **Technische Nothilfe.**

nötigen compel.

Notlandehafen *m* emergency landing field.

notlanden make an emergency landing, make a forced landing *(Avn).*

Notlandeplatz *m* emergency landing field.

Notlandung *f* emergency landing, forced landing *(Avn).*

Notleitung *f* emergency line *(Tp).*

Notpiste *f* emergency trail or path.

Notruf *m* emergency call *(Tp).*

Notsender *m* emergency radio transmitter *(floatable rescue set).*

Notsignal *n* distress signal, SOS.

Notverbandpäckchen *n* first-aid packet, first-aid dressing.

Notverbandtasche, *f* first-aid pouch.

Notvisier *n* direct-fire sight *(Ord).*

notwassern to make an emergency landing on water, to "ditch" *(an Ap).*

Notwasserung *f* emergency landing on water, "ditching" *(Avn).*

Notwehr *f* self-defense.

Notwurf *m* emergency salvo release *(Bombing).*

Notzeichen *n* distress signal, SOS.

Notzug *m* emergency release handle *(Ap).*

NSKK.-Mann *m* private in the Nazi party motor corps.

NSKK.-Transportregiment *n* transportation regiment of the Nazi party motor corps.

Null *f* zero.

auf Null stellen to zero *(an Inst, scale, etc.).*

Nullpunkt *m* zero, freezing point; zero point, aiming point, directing point, point of origin *(Arty, Surv).*

Nullstellung *f* zero position *(of an Inst, scale, etc.);* neutral position, zeroing.

Nullzeit *f* zero hour.

Nummer *f* number.

Nummerscheibe *f* dial *(Tp).*

Nummerscheibenkästchen *n* dial box *(field Tp).*

Nurflügelflugzeug *n* all-wing airplane, "flying wing."

Nüstern *fpl* nostrils.

Nute *f* groove, slot, keyway *(also spelled der Nut).*

Nutzarbeit *f* useful work, brake horsepower.

Nutzfahrzeug *n* commercial vehicle *(MT).*

Nutzfrequenz *f* desired frequency *(Rad).*

Nutzlast *f* useful load, pay load.

Nutzleistung *f* net horsepower.

Nutzwiderstand *m* useful resistance *(Elec).*

O

OB-Betrieb *m* local-battery operation *(Tp) (abbr of* Ortsbatteriebetrieb).

Oberarbeitsführer *m* major *(Reich Labor Service).*

Oberarzt *m* first lieutenant *(Med).*

Oberbau *m* permanent way, top of roadbed *(RR).*

Oberbaustab *m* superior construction staff *(equivalent in status to a brigade staff).*

Oberbefehl *m* high command *(function).*

Oberbefehlshaber *m* commander in chief, commander. *See also* **Oberster Befehlshaber.**

Oberbefehlshaber des Heeres Commander-in-Chief of the Army.

Oberbefehlshaber einer Gruppe army group commander.

Oberbeschlagmeister *m* horseshoer *(master Sgt).*

Oberbrieftaubenmeister *m* pigeoneer *(master Sgt).*

obere Führung higher command *(Div and up);* higher command echelon.

Oberfähnrich *m* master sergeant *(officer candidate).*

Oberfähnrich der Flieger aviation cadet *(with rank of master Sgt).*

Oberfahrer *m* private first class *(H-Dr T).*

Oberfeldarzt *m* lieutenant colonel *(Med).*

Oberfeldkommandantur *f* military government area headquarters *(under commander of army group, in a T of Opns; under general commanding officer in charge of Mil Adm, in occupied territories).*

Oberfeldmeister *m* master sergeant *(Reich Labor Service).*

Oberfeldveterinär *m* lieutenant colonel *(Vet).*

Oberfeldwebel *m* master sergeant.

Oberfeldzeugstab *m* higher ordnance staff.

Oberfeuerwerker *m* master sergeant *(Ord).*

Oberfläche *f* surface *(outside or top).*

Oberfunker *m* radioman *(Pvt 1st class).*

Oberfunkmeister *m* radioman *(master Sgt).*

Obergefreiter *m* corporal.

Obergeneralarbeitsführer *m* major general *(Reich Labor Service).*

Obergrenadier *m* private first class *(Inf).*

Obergurt *m* top chord *(truss);* surcingle *(harness).*

Oberjäger *m* private first class *(mountain Inf).*

Oberkanonier *m* private first class *(Arty).*

Oberkommandierender *m* commander-in-chief. *See* **Oberster Befehlshaber.**
Oberkommando *n*   high command *(agency and function).*
Oberkommando der Kriegsmarine High Command of the Navy *(abbr.* OKM).
Oberkommando der Luftwaffe High Command of the Air Forces *(abbr.* OKL).
Oberkommando der Wehrmacht High Command of the Armed Forces *(abbr.* OKW).
Oberkommando des Heeres Army High Command *(abbr.* OKH).
Oberkraftfahrer *m* private first class *(MT).*
Oberlafette *f* top carriage *(G).*
Oberleutnant *m* first lieutenant.
Oberleutnant zur See lieutenant junior grade *(Nav).*
Oberpanzergrenadier *m* armored infantry rifleman *(Pvt 1st class).*
Oberpionier *m* private first class *(Engr).*
Oberquartiermeister *m* D e p u t y Chief of the General Staff *(at* Oberkommando des Heeres; *known as* Oberquartiermeister I, *Operations;* Oberquartiermeister II, *Training;* Oberquartiermeister III, *Organization;* Oberquartiermeister IV, *Intelligence;* Oberquartiermeister V, *Historical);* general staff officer at Hq of an army *(in charge of supply* and *Adm).*
Oberreiter *m* private first class *(Cav).*
Oberring *m* upper band *(R).*
Oberringfeder *f* upper-band spring *(R).*
Oberschenkel *m* thigh.
Oberschiedsrichter *m* a s s i s t a n t director *(maneuvers).*
Oberschild *m* upper shield *(G).*
Oberschirrmeister *m* master sergeant *(maintenance).*
Oberschütze *m* private first class *(Inf rifleman).*
Oberschwester *f* chief nurse.
Oberschwingungsfrequenz *f* harmonic frequency *(Rad).*
Oberst *m* colonel.
Oberstabsarzt *m* major *(Med).*
Oberstabsveterinär *m* major *(Vet).*
Oberstarbeitsführer *m* colonel *(Reich Labor Service).*

Oberstarzt *m* colonel *(Med).*
Oberster Befehlshaber der Wehrmacht Commander-in-Chief of the Armed Forces.
oberster Schiedsrichter director *(maneuvers).*
Oberstfeldmeister *m* lieutenant *(Reich Labor Service).*
Oberstintendant *m* civilian official in administrative services ranking as colonel.
Oberstleutnant *m* lieutenant colonel.
oberstrom upstream.
Oberstveterinär *m* colonel *(Vet).*
Obertruppführer *m* sergeant *(Reich Labor Service).*
Oberveterinär *m* first lieutenant *(Vet).*
Obervormann *m* chief foreman *(Reich Labor Service)*
Oberwachtmeister *m* master sergeant *(Arty, Cav).*
Oberzahlmeister *m* paymaster official *(Wehrmachtbeamter ranking as 1st Lt).* *See also* **Zahlmeister.**
Objektschutz *m* air defense of fixed installations.
OB-System *n* local-battery system *(Tp) (abbr. for* Ortsbatteriesystem).
Ofen *m* heater, oven, stove.
Ofenrohr *n* stovepipe; "bazooka" *(slang term for* Raketenpanzerbüchse, *rocket launcher).*
offen exposed *(Tac);* in clear *(Sig Com);* open, frank.
offene Flanke open flank *(Tac).*
offener Flügel exposed wing *(Tac).*
offener Funkspruch radio message in clear.
offene Stellung exposed position *(Tac).*
Offensive *f* offensive *(Tac).*
offensive Verteidigung offensive defense.
Offizier *m* officer.
Offizierbewerber *m* officer aspirant.
Offizier des Beurlaubtenstandes reserve officer.
Offizierheim *n* officers' mess, officers' club.
Offizierlaufbahn *f* officer's career.
Offizierledigenheim *n* bachelor officers' quarters.
Offiziersanwärter *m* officer candidate.
Offiziersbursche *m* officer's orderly.
Offizierskasino *n* officers' mess.

Offizierslager *n* permanent camp for officer prisoners of war *(abbr. Oflag).*

Offiziersnachwuchs *m* new crop of officers.

Offizierspähtrupp *m* officer reconnaissance patrol.

Offizierspatent *n* commission.

Offizier vom Biwakdienst bivouac security officer.

Offizier vom Dienst duty officer, officer on duty.

Offizier vom Ortsdienst officer of the guard.

Offizier vom Tagesdienst officer of the day.

Öffnerhebel *m* operating level, operating handle *(G).*

Öffnung *f* aperture, port, opening.

Oflag *n See* Offizierslager.

Ohnehaltflug *m* nonstop flight *(Avn).*

"Ohne Tritt, Marsch!" "Route step, march!"

Ohrverschlußwatte *f* cotton for ear plugs.

Oktanwert *m* octane rating.

Oktanzahl *f* octane number.

Okular *n* eyepiece.

OKW.-Bericht *m* official communiqué of the *Oberkommando der Wehrmacht.*

Öl *n* oil.

Ölablaß *m* oil drain.

Ölbehälter *m* oil tank.

ölbeständig oil-resistant.

Ölbohrloch *n* oil well.

Ölbombe *f* oil bomb.

Ölbüchse *f* oilcan.

öldicht oiltight.

Öldruckbremse *f* hydraulic brake.

Öleinfüll-Verschraubung *f* oil filler plug *(Mtr).*

Ölfederstrebe *f* oleo strut *(Ap).*

olivgrün olive drab.

Ölkanister *m* oil container *(Ap, MT).*

Ölkohle *f* carbon *(Mtr).*

Öllager *n* oil-storage depot.

Ölmanometer *n* oil pressure gage.

Ölmeßbecher *m* graduated oil dispenser *(MT).*

Ölschlitzring *m* grooved piston ring *(Mtr).*

Ölstand *m* oil level.

Ölstandanzeiger *m* oil level gage *(MT).*

Ölstandschraube *f* oil level plug *(Mtr).*

Ölstandskontrolle *f* oil level check, oil level indicator *(Mtr).*

Ölthermometer *n* oil temperature gage.

Öltropfer *m* oiler.

Ölüberlauf *m* oil overflow *(Mtr).*

Ölwanne *f* oil pan *(Mtr).*

Operation *f* operation *(Tac, Med).*

Operationsbasis *f* base of operations *(Tac).*

Operationsbefehl *m* operations order.

Operationsgebiet *n* zone of operations, theater of operations.

Operationskarte *f* operations map.

Operationslinie *f* line of operations.

Operationsplan *m* operations plan.

Operationsraum *m* zone of operations, theater of operations.

operativ operational, strategic.

operative Aufklärung strategic reconnaissance.

operative Luftaufklärung strategic air reconnaissance.

operatives Ziel strategic objective.

operative Unterstützung indirect support *(Avn, Tac).*

Opfer *n* victim.

Oppanol *n* a synthetic substance resistant to mustard gas and Lewisite *(CWS).*

Optik *f* optics; lens system, optical system or instruments; telescopic sight *(G);* periscope *(Tk).*

optische Peilung pilotage *(Avn).*

optisches Zielgerät optical sight *(Ord).*

O-Punkt *m* aiming point *(Gunnery). See also* Nullpunkt.

Orden *m* medal, decoration, order.

Ordensband *n* ribbon *(of a decoration).*

Ordensschnalle *f* bar *(decoration).* kleine Ordensschnalle miniature *(decoration).*

Ordensspange *f* bar *(decoration).*

Ordinate *f* ordinate, Y-coordinate.

Ordnung *f* order, rule.

Ordnungsdienst *m* provost service, military police service.

Ordnungsgleis *n* make-up track *(RR).*

Ordnungspolizei *f* uniformed regular police.

Ordonnanz *f* orderly.

Ordonnanzoffizier *m* special-missions staff officer.

Organisationsstab *m* organizational staff.

Organisation Todt Todt Organization *(Engr and Ft construction)*.

Orientierung *f* orientation.

Orientierungslinie *f* orienting line *(Surv)*.

Orientierungspunkt *m* control point *(Surv)*.

Orkan *m* hurricane, tropical cyclone.

Orpo *f* See **Ordnungspolizei.**

Orsatapparat *m* Orsat gas-analysis apparatus *(CWS)*.

Ort *m* locality, place; locus *(Math)*. See also **Standort.**

Ortbalken *m* exterior stringer *(on a fixed bridge)*; exterior balk *(on a floating bridge)*.

orten locate; orient; take bearings.

Orter *m* navigator *(Avn)*.

Orterkompaß *m* navigator's compass *(Avn)*.

örtlich local.

Ortsbatterie *f* local battery *(Tp)*.

Ortsbatterie-Betrieb *m* local-battery operation *(Tp)*.

Ortsbesprechung *f* local operation *(Rad)*.

Ortsbestimmung *f* orientation, position determination.

Ortsbiwak *n* billets, close billets.

Ortschaft *f* village, town, inhabited locality.

Ortscheit *n* doubletree *(limber)*.

Ortseindruck *m* sensation of direction *(sound locator)*.

Ortsempfang *m* local reception *(Rad)*.

ortsfest fixed, permanent *(Arty, Ft)*.

ortsfeste Flak fixed antiaircraft guns or artillery.

ortsfeste Küstenartillerie fixed sea-coast artillery.

ortsfeste Lafette stationary gun mount *(G)*.

Ortsgefecht *n* See **Ortskampf.**

Ortskampf *m* combat in towns.

Ortskommandant *m* commander of a garrison, post, or station; town commander *(Mil Govt)*.

Ortskommandantur *f* garrison, post, or station headquarters; town headquarters *(Mil Govt)* (Ortskommandantur I, *in large and medium-sized cities;* Ortskommandantur II, *in small cities, towns, and villages)*.

Ortskrankenlazarett *n* billet hospital. *(Med)*.

Ortskrankenstube *f* billet dispensary.

ortskundig familiar with a locality or area.

Ortsmißweisung *f* magnetic declination.

Ortsnetz *n* local net *(Tp)*.

Ortsquartier *n* See **Ortsunterkunft.**

Ortssender *m* local station *(Rad)*.

Ortsunterkunft *f* billets.

Ortsvorstand *m* local authorities, town authorities.

Ortung *f* position finding, orientation, taking of bearings.

Ortungsanforderung *f* request for a bearing *(Avn, Rad)*.

Ortungsleuchtzeichen *n* ground position signal *(ground-air Com)*.

öse *f* lug; ring; lunette; eye *(Tech)*.

Ost *m* east *(also spelled* Osten).

Ostlegion *f* legion composed of non-German volunteers and prisoners of war from East-European countries.

Ostmedaille *f* Eastern Campaign Medal *(decoration)*.

Ostsee *f* Baltic Sea.

Otter *f* paravane.

P

Packgefäß *n* bulk container.
Packriemen *m* pack strap *(harness)*.
Packsattel *m* pack saddle *(harness)*.
Packstrick *m* pack rope *(harness)*
Packtasche *f* saddlebag.

Packung *f* packing *(Mech)*.
Paddelboot *n* collapsible paddling boat.
Pak *f* antitank gun, antitank artillery *(abbr. of* Panzerabwehrkanone).

Pakethülle f wrapping.

Pak-Flak f antitank-antiaircraft gun, dual-purpose gun.

Pakgeschütz n antitank gun.

Pakgeschütz auf Selbstfahrlafette self-propelled antitank gun, tank destroyer.

Pakstellung f antitank gun position, antitank gun emplacement.

Pak-Zug m antitank platoon.

Panne f breakdown; engine failure; blowout.

Panoramakammer f panoramic camera (Avn).

Pantograph m pantograph (Surv).

Panzer m armor; tank.

Panzerabteilung f armored battalion.

Panzerabwehr f antitank defense, antimechanized defense (in compounds, now superseded by Panzerjäger-).

Panzerabwehrgewehr n antitank rifle (now called Panzerbüchse).

Panzerabwehrgeschütz n antitank gun.

Panzerabwehrgraben m antitank ditch.

Panzerabwehrkanone f antitank gun (now called Panzerjägerkanone).

Panzerabwehrmine f antitank mine.

Panzerabwehrmittel npl means of antitank defense.

Panzerabwehrrakete f a n t i t a n k rocket.

Panzerangriff m armored attack, tank attack.

Panzerartillerie f armored division artillery, armored artillery.

Panzeraufbau m tank hull and turret; armored body of a vehicle.

Panzeraufklärungsabteilung f armored reconnaissance battalion.

Panzerbataillon n armored battalion.

Panzerbefehlswagen m a r m o r e d command car.

Panzerbekämpfung f antitank combat.

Panzerbeobachtungsturm m armored observation turret.

Panzerbesatzung f tank crew, armored vehicle crew.

Panzerbeschuß m firing at tanks; test firing at armor plate.

Panzerbeschußtafel f firing table for antitank gun.

Panzerblech n armor plate.

Panzerblende f tank shutter; tank gun shield, mantlet.

Panzerbombe f antitank bomb, armor-piercing bomb, heavy-case bomb.

panzerbrechend armor-piercing.

Panzerbrigade f armored brigade, tank brigade.

Panzerbüchse f antitank rifle.

Panzerdeckungsloch n foxhole (for AT protection).

Panzerdivision f armored division.

Panzerdrehturm m revolving armored turret (Ft); revolving tank turret (Tk).

panzerdurchschlagend armor-piercing (Am).

Panzerdurchschlagsleistung f armor-piercing capacity, penetration (Am).

Panzereinsatz m commitment of armored units.

Panzererkennungsdienst m tank identification service.

Panzerfahrer m tank driver.

Panzerfahrschule f armored vehicle operators' school.

Panzerfahrzeug n armored vehicle.

Panzerfahrzeugfalle f tank trap.

Panzerfahrzeuggraben m antitank ditch.

Panzerfalle f tank trap.

Panzerführer m tank commander (NCO); armored-vehicle commander; armored-unit commander.

Panzerfunker m tank radio operator.

Panzerfunktrupp m armored radio section.

Panzerfunkwagen m armored radio car or truck.

Panzergeschoß n armor-piercing projectile.

panzergeschützt armor-protected.

Panzerglas n bulletproof glass.

Panzergraben m antitank ditch.

Panzergranate f armor-piercing shell, armor-piercing rifle grenade.

Panzergranate-Patrone f armor-piercing shell (fixed Am).

Panzergrenadier m armored infantry rifleman, private in armored infantry regiment.

Panzergrenadier-Bataillon n armored infantry battalion.

Panzergrenadier-Brigade f armored infantry brigade.

Panzergrenadier-Division f motorized division. See also SS-Panzergrenadier-Division.

Panzergrenadier-Ersatzregiment *n* armored infantry replacement regiment.

Panzergrenadier-Personenkraftwagen armored personnel carrier.

Panzergrenadier-Regiment *n* motorized infantry regiment (*of a* Panzerdivision).

Panzergruppe *f* armored group.

Panzergürtel *m* armor belt.

Panzerhindernis *n* antitank obstacle.

Panzerinstandsetzungsabteilung *f* tank repair battalion.

Panzerjäger *m* member of antitank unit.

Panzerjägerabteilung *f* antitank battalion.

Panzerjägergeschütz *n* antitank gun.

Panzerjägerkanone *f* *See* **Panzerjägergeschütz.**

Panzerjägerkompanie *f* antitank company.

Panzerjägerregiment *n* antitank regiment.

Panzerjägerzug *m* antitank platoon.

Panzerkabel *n* armored cable (*Elec*).

Panzerkampfabzeichen *n* *See* **Panzerkampfwagenabzeichen.**

Panzerkampfwagen *m* tank.

Panzerkampfwagenabzeichen *n* Tank Badge (*decoration awarded to members of armored units after participation in three separate combat actions*).

Panzerkampfwagenhindernis *n* tank obstacle.

Panzerkanone *f* tank gun.

Panzerkasten *m* tank hull.

Panzerkastenoberteil *n* sponson, upper hull (*Tk*).

Panzerkette *f* tank track.

Panzer-Kommandant *m* tank commander.

Panzerkompanie *f* tank company.

Panzerkopf *m* armor-piercing cap (*Am*).

Panzerkörper *m* hull (*Tk*).

Panzerkorps *n* armored corps.

Panzerkorpskommando *n* armored corps headquarters.

Panzerkräfte *fpl* armored forces, armored units.

Panzerkraftfahrzeug *n* armored vehicle.

Panzerkraftwagen *m* armored car.

Panzerkrieg *m* armored warfare.

Panzerkuppel *f* tank cupola, armored cupola (*Ft*).

Panzer-Lehr-Regiment *n* armored demonstration regiment.

Panzermine *f* antitank mine.

Panzermunition *f* armor-piercing ammunition; tank ammunition.

Panzernachrichtenabteilung *f* armored signal battalion.

Panzer-Obergrenadier *m* private first class (*Armd Inf Regt*).

Panzeroberschütze *m* private first class (*in Armd unit*).

Panzeroffizier *m* armored officer.

Panzerpionier *m* armored engineer.

Panzer-Pionier-Bataillon *n* armored engineer battalion.

Panzerplatte *f* armor plate.

Panzerregiment *n* armored regiment.

Panzerrichttafel *f* tank-silhouette aiming target.

Panzerscharte *f* peephole, direct vision slit (*Tk*).

Panzerschild *m* armor-plate shield (*G*).

Panzerschott *n* armor bulkhead (*Tk*).

Panzerschutz *m* armor protection (*Ft, Tk*); antitank defense.

Panzerschütze *m* private in an armored unit; tank gunner.

panzersicher secure against mechanized attack.

Panzersonderfahrzeug *n* special-purpose armored vehicle.

Panzerspähfahrzeug *n* armored reconnaissance vehicle.

Panzerspähkompanie *f* armored reconnaissance company.

Panzerspäh-Schwadron *f* mechanized cavalry reconnaissance troop.

Panzerspähtrupp *m* armored reconnaissance car section.

Panzerspähwagen *m* armored reconnaissance car, armored scout car.

Panzersperre *f* antitank obstacle.

Panzersperrgraben *m* antitank ditch.

Panzersperrmauer *f* antitank wall obstacle.

Panzerspitze *f* armored point (*Adv Gd*).

Panzersprenggeschoß *n* armor-piercing projectile.

Panzersprenggranate *f* armor-piercing shell.

Panzerstärke *f* thickness of armor (*Tk*).

Panzerstoß *m* armored thrust (*Tac*).

Panzersturmabzeichen *n* Armored Assault Badge *(decoration)*.

Panzertransportwagen *m* armored personnel carrier.

Panzertruppe *f* Armored Command.

Panzertruppen *fpl* armored troops, armored forces.

Panzerturm *m* tank turret; armored turret *(Ft)*.

Panzerung *f* armor, armor plating.

Panzerunterstützung *f* armored support *(Tac)*.

Panzerverband *m* armored formation, armored force unit, combined-arms armored force.

Panzerverbände der Heerestruppen GHQ reserve tank groups.

Panzervernichtungsabzeichen *n* decoration awarded for close-combat destruction of at least one enemy tank.

Panzer-Verschwindeturm *m* disappearing armored turret *(Ft)*.

Panzerwaffe *f* Armored Command.

Panzerwagen *m* armored car, combat car, tank.

Panzerwagenfalle *f* tank trap.

Panzerwagengraben *m* tank ditch.

Panzerwanne *f* tank hull.

Panzerwarndienst *m* antimechanized warning system.

Panzerwarnung *f* tank warning, antimechanized warning.

Panzerwart, *m* armored maintenance man.

Panzerwerk *n* steel and concrete fortification.

Panzerwerkstattkompanie *f* armored force repair shop company.

Panzerweste *f* body armor *(Avn)*.

Panzerzug *m* armored train *(RR)*; tank platoon.

Papierstreifenverfahren *n* paperstrip method *(aerial Photo)*.

Pappe *f* cardboard *(also called* **Pappdeckel** *m)*.

Parabel-Fachwerkträger *m* curved chord truss.

Parabellum *n* a type of self-loading pistol.

Parade *f* parade, review.

Paradeanzug *m* full-dress uniform.

Parademarsch *m* march in review, pass in review.

Paradeplatz *m* parade ground.

Parallaxe *f* parallax, azimuth difference.

Parallaxwinkel *m* angle of parallax, azimuth difference.

Parallel-Fachwerkträger *m* parallel-chord truss.

Parallelogrammgestänge *n* parallelogram linkage system *(AA sight)*.

Parallelschaltung *f* parallel connection *(Elec)*.

Pardon *m* quarter, mercy, clemency.

parieren to parry.

Parierstange *f* bayonet guard.

Park *m* park, depot.

parken to park.

Parklicht *n* parking light *(auto headlight)*.

Parlamentär *m* parlementaire, bearer of a flag of truce.

Parlamentärflagge *f* flag of truce.

Parole *f* password.

Parteien *fpl* opposing sides *(maneuvers)*.

Parteiführer *m* commander of one of the opposing forces in maneuvers.

Paspel *f* piping or edging on uniform.

Paß *m* pass *(Top)*; passport.

Paßgenauigkeit *f* accuracy of fit *(Tech)*.

Passierschein *m* permit, pass, safeconduct, military passport.

Paßstück *n* adapter *(Ord)*.

Passung *f* fit *(Tech)*

Patent *n* officer's commission; patent *(Tech)*

patentierter Offizier commissioned officer.

Patrone *f* cartridge *(Am)*; round of fixed ammunition *(Arty)*

Patronenauswerfer *m* ejector.

Patronenauszieher *m* extractor.

Patroneneinlage *f* breech recess *(R)*.

Patronenführungsleisten *fpl* cartridge guides *(MG)*.

Patronengurt *m* cartridge belt *(MG)*; bandoleer.

Patronenhalter *m* cartridge holder *(MG)*.

Patronenhebel *m* cartridge lever *(MG)*.

Patronenhülse *f* cartridge case.

Patronenkasten *m* cartridge box, ammunition box.

Patronenkorb *m* shell basket *(for fixed Am)*.

Patronenlager *n* cartridge chamber *(G, R)*.

Patronenmunition *f* fixed ammunition.

Patronenrahmen *m* clip *(R, AA gun)*.

Patronenraum *m* propelling-charge chamber *(Mort shell)*.

Patronenschacht *m* feed funnel *(fixed aircraft MG)*.

Patronenstreifen *m* cartridge clip.

Patronenstützfeder *f* cartridge-support spring *(MG)*.

Patronentasche *f* ammunition pocket, ammunition pouch.

Patronenträger *m* cartridge carrier *(MG)*.

Patronenträgerhebel *m* belt-feed lever *(MG)*.

Patronenzuführung *f* cartridge feed *(SA)*.

Patrouillenflug *m* patrol, patrolling *(Avn)*.

Patte *f* collar patch, cuff patch.

Pause *f* pause; tracing.

Pauspapier *n* tracing paper.

Pech *n* pitch.

Pegel *m* water-level gage *(for rivers, lakes, etc.)*.

Peilanlage *f* direction-finder station *(Air Navigation)*.

Peilantenne *f* direction-finding antenna.

Peilapparat *m* azimuth instrument.

Peilaufsatz *m* pelorus *(Avn)*.

Peilberichtigungskurve *f* deviation curve *(Rad)*.

Peilempfänger *m* radio compass, direction finder *(Air Navigation)*.

Peilen *n* direction finding *(Rad)*.

peilen to take a bearing *(Nav, Rad, Avn)*.

Peilflugleiter *m* chief of direction-finder station *(Avn)*.

Peilfunkempfänger *m* radio compass, direction finder *(Air Navigation)*.

Peilfunkgerät *n* radio direction finder.

Peilfunkstelle *f* radio direction finder station *(Avn)*.

Peilgerät *n* azimuth instrument *(Surv)*; direction-finder equipment or set *(Rad, Avn)*.

Peilkompaß *m* navigator's compass *(Avn)*.

Peilkraftwagen *m* radio direction-finding truck.

Peilleitstelle *f* radio direction-finder control station.

Peillinie *f* line of bearing, bearing line *(Air Navigation)*.

Peillot *n* sounding lead *(Nav)*.

Peilnebenstelle *f* auxiliary direction-finder station *(Air Navigation)*.

Peilrahmen *m* directional loop antenna *(Rad)*.

Peilscheibe *f* azimuth instrument.

Peilsender *m* directional transmitter.

Peilstelle *f* radio direction-finder station.

Peilstrahl *m* beam *(Rad)*.

Peilung *f* bearing, direction finding.

optische Peilung pilotage *(Avn)*.

Peilzeichen *n* direction-finder signal *(Avn)*.

pelzgefüttert fur-lined.

Pelzkombination *f* fur-lined flying suit.

Pendel *n* pendulum.

Pendelfrequenz *f* quenching frequency *(Rad)*.

Pendelfrequenzempfänger *m* super-regenerative receiver.

pendeln oscillate; swerve.

Pendelverkehr *m* shuttle traffic.

Perchlorameisensäuremethylester *m* diphosgene *(CWS)*.

Perlkorn *n* bead sight *(R)*.

Personal *n* personnel.

Personalabteilung *f* personnel section.

Personalamt *n* See **Heerespersonalamt**.

Personalausweis *m* identification papers, certificate of identification.

Personaldaten *npl* personal data *(birth, occupation, etc.)*.

Personalveränderung *f* change of personnel.

Personenbahnhof *m* passenger station *(RR)*.

Personenfähre *f* passenger ferry.

Personenkraftfahrzeug *n* personnel carrier, passenger vehicle *(MT)*.

Personenkraftwagen *m* personnel carrier, passenger car *(MT)*.

perspektivische Projection geometric projection, perspective projection.

Perstoff *m* diphosgene *(CWS)*.

Petroleum *n* kerosene.

Pfad *m* path, trail.

Pfahl *m* picket, stake; pile; post.

Pfahlhindernis *n* See **Pfahlsperre**.

Pfahljoch *n* pile bent *(Bdg)*.

Pfahljochbrücke *f* pile-bent bridge.

Pfahlsperre *f* post obstacle *(AT)*.

Pfeife f whistle, pipe.
Pfeifpatrone f whistling pyrotechnic signal cartridge *(used as gas alarm)*.
Pfeifsignal n whistle signal.
Pfeiler m pier *(Bdg)*; column, pillar *(Engr)*.
Pfeilform f sweepback *(Ap wing)*; arrow or wedge formation.
Pferd n horse.
pferdebespannt horse-drawn.
Pferdeersatz m remounts.
Pferdefahrzeug n horse-drawn vehicle.
Pferdehalter m horseholder *(Cav, Arty)*.
Pferdekrankenkraftwagen m veterinary motor ambulance.
Pferdekrankensammelplatz m veterinary collecting station.
Pferdelazarett n veterinary hospital.
Pferdepark m remount depot.
Pferdestärke f metric horsepower *(abbr.* PS) *(1* PS = *0.986* HP; *1* HP = *1.014* PS).
Pferdetransportkolonne f horse-drawn transport column.
Pferdeverbandplatz m veterinary aid station.
Pferdezug m draft *(horse traction)*.
Pferdezweigpark m branch remount depot.
Pfiff m whistle *(sound)*.
Pfiffikus n phenyldichlorarsine *(CWS)*.
Pflegeschwester f nurse.
Pflicht f duty, obligation.
Pflichten des deutschen Soldaten *See* **Kriegsartikel**.
Pflock m stake, peg, pin, picket.
Pflugbagger m tractor plow; bulldozer.
Pfropfen m plug, stopper, wad.
Phasenverschiebung f phase shift, phase displacement, phase difference *(Elec, Rad)*.
Phenyldichlorarsin n phenyldichlorarsine.
Phon n decibel.
Phosgen n carbonylchloride, phosgene *(CWS)*.
Phosphor m phosphorus.
Phosphorfliegerbombe f phosphorus bomb.
Phosphorgeschoß n phosphorus bullet, incendiary bullet.

Phosphorhandgranate f phosphorus grenade.
Photogrammetrie f photogrammetry.
Photograph m photographer.
Photographie f photography.
photographische Kartenaufnahme photographic mapping.
Photokopie f photostat.
photokopieren to photostat.
Phototopographie f phototopography.
Photozelle f photo-electric cell.
Pickettpfahl m picket, stake.
Pier m pier.
Pi-Kampfmittel npl engineer combat equipment.
Pikrinsäure f trinitrophenol, picric acid.
Pille f pill, pellet, primer.
Pilotballon m pilot balloon, trial balloon.
Pilotballonaufstieggerät n pibal equipment *(Met)*.
Pilz m mushroom head of obturator.
Pinsel m paint brush.
Pionier m engineer soldier, private in engineer unit.
Pionieraufklärung f engineer reconnaissance.
Pionier-Ausbau-Bataillon n engineer construction-improvement battalion.
Pionierbataillon n engineer battalion.
Pionierdienst m engineer service.
Pionier-Erkundungstrupp m engineer reconnaissance squad.
Pionierfahrzeug n engineer vehicle.
Pionierführer m special staff engineer officer and engineer commander *(at Div Hq)*.
Pioniergerät n engineer equipment.
Pioniergerätepark m engineer equipment depot.
Pionier-Kampfmittel npl engineer combat equipment.
Pionierkolonne f engineer equipment column.
Pionierlandungskompanie f engineer landing company.
Pioniermaschinenzug m engineer machine platoon.
Pionieroffizier m engineer officer.
Pionierpanzerkampfwagen m engineer tank.
Pionierpark m engineer park, engineer depot.
Pionierschule f engineer school.
Pioniersprengmittel npl engineer explosives.

Pionier-Sturmabzeichen n Engineer Assault Badge *(decoration)*.

Pioniersturmzug m engineer assault platoon.

Pioniertruppe f Corps of Engineers.

Pioniertruppen fpl engineer troops.

Pionierverband m engineer unit.

Pioniervermessungsgerät n engineer surveying instrument or equipment.

Pionierwerkzeug n engineer tool.

Pionierwerkzeugtasche f engineer tool bag.

Pionierzug m engineer platoon.

Pionierzwischenpark m engineer dump.

Piste f trail, path, beaten track.

Pistole f pistol.

Pistolengriff m pistol grip.

Pistolenöffnung f pistol port *(Tk)*.

Pistolentasche f pistol holster.

Pi.-Sturmabzeichen n *See* **Pionier-Sturmabzeichen.**

Pitotrohr n pitot tube.

Pivotgeschütz n swivel gun, pedestal-mounted gun.

Pivotlafette f pivot-type mount *(MG)*; turntable carriage *(G)*.

Pivotlager n trunnion bearing *(G)*.

Pi.-Zug m *See* **Pionierzug.**

PK.-Filmberichter m propaganda-company moving-picture cameraman.

P.K.-Kriegsberichter m propaganda-company war correspondent.

Plan m plan, chart, diagram, scheme.

Plane f tarpaulin.

Planfeuer n concentrated antiaircraft fire within the critical zone.

Planfeuertafel f lead chart *(AA firing)*.

Planfeuerwürfel m critical zone *(AA firing)*.

Planier-Raupenschlepper m bulldozer, angledozer, tractor with angledozer.

Planimeter n planimeter *(Surv)*.

Plänkelei f skirmish.

Planladung f computed charge *(demolitions)*.

planmäßig in accordance with table of organization or basic allowance; according to plan; systematic, deliberate, thorough.

planmäßige Feldbefestigung deliberate field fortification.

planmäßiger Nachschub automatic supply.

Planpause f overlay, traced map or firing chart.

Planquadrat n grid square.

Planrichten n laying by survey *(Arty)*.

Planschießen n map fire, unobserved fire *(Gunnery)*.

Plansektor m map-protractor set *(Arty, Surv)*.

Planspiel n map exercise *(Tng)*.

Planstärke f authorized strength, table of organization strength.

Planstelle f place authorized by table of organization.

freie Planstelle vacancy.

Planübergang m level crossing *(RR)*.

Planübung f map maneuver, map exercise *(Tng)*.

Planunterlage f plane table *(Arty, Surv)*.

Planzeichnen n plotting *(Surv)*.

Planzeiger m coordinate scale *(Arty, Surv)*.

plastische Liderung plastic-pad obturator *(G)*.

Platte f plate *(Tech)*; phonograph record.

Platteneinsatz m storage-battery cell *(Elec)*.

Plattenkondensator m parallel plate condenser *(Rad)*.

Plattenpulver n flake powder *(Am)*.

Plattensatz m storage-battery cell *(Elec)*.

Plattenventil n poppet valve *(Mtr)*.

Plattform f platform *(Arty, etc.)*.

Plattformwagen m flatcar *(RR)*.

Plattfüße mpl flat feet.

Platz m airdrome, airfield, landing field *(Avn)*; aid station *(Med, Vet)*; place, square *(in a city or town)*; site; locality; station; space; room.

platzen to burst; to blow out *(tire)*.

Platzfeuer n airdrome light.

Platzfeuerwehr f airdrome fire-fighting unit.

Platzgrenze f airdrome boundary.

Platzmembrane f bursting diaphragm *(message container)*.

Platzpatrone f blank cartridge.

Platzrunde f circle flown over airdrome.

Platzwechsel m change of station.

Pleuelstange f connecting rod, piston rod *(Mtr)*.

Plombe f lead seal.

Plünderer *m* marauder, plunderer.
plündern to plunder.
Plünderung *f* plundering, pillage, looting.
Pneumassivreifen *m* cushion tire.
Polarstern *m* North Star.
polieren to polish, to buff *(Tech)*.
Polizei *f* police.
Polizist *m* policeman.
Polklemme *f* battery-terminal binding post *(Elec)*.
Polschuh *m* pole piece *(magnet)*.
Polster *n* pad *(Clo, harness, etc.)*; track block *(Tk)*; pillow, cushion.
Polwechsler *m* pole changer *(Tp)*.
Polygonzug *m* closed traverse *(Surv)*.
Ponton *m* ponton.
Pontonbrücke *f* ponton bridge.
Pontonfähre *f* ponton ferry.
Pontonier *m* pontoneer.
Pontonoberkante *f* gunwale *(Pon)*.
Pontonstrecke *f* ponton bay.
Pontonwagen *m* ponton carrier *(MT)*.
Porontoofen *m* a small liquid-fuel stove.
Portepee *n* sword knot *(worn by Ger officers and higher-bracket NCO's)*.
Portepeeunteroffizier *m* noncommissioned officer *(from* Feldwebel *up)*.
Portion *f* ration; dose *(Med)*.
eiserne Portion emergency ration.
Portionenausgabe *f* distribution of rations.
Portionssatz *m* scale of rations, ration quantity.
Positionslicht *n* position light, running light *(Ap)*.
Post *f* mail.
Postaufnahmegerät *n* mail pick-up device *(Ap)*.
Posten *m* sentry; post; duty station; item *(in a list)*; lot *(of goods)*.
Postenanweisungen *fpl* guard orders.
allgemeine Postenanweisungen general orders *(guard duty)*.
besondere Postenanweisungen special orders *(guard duty)*.
Postenkette *f* line of sentries.
Postleitungen *fpl* civil communication lines.
Postprüfungsstelle *f* postal censor's office.
Postüberwachungsstelle *f* *See* Postprüfungsstelle.
Potenz *f* power *(Math)*.

potenzieren raise *(to a power)* *(Math)*.
Prahm *m* barge, lighter *(Engr, Nav)*.
Prallhaltevorrichtung *f* ballonet balloon *(airship)*.
Prallschuß *m* ricochet.
Prallwand *f* baffle.
Präzisionsschießen *n* precision fire.
Preis *m* price; rate; prize.
Preisübung *f* qualification course.
Prellschuß *m* ricochet.
Presseoffizier *m* public relations officer.
Preßfutter *n* compressed forage.
Preßluft *f* compressed air.
Preßluftanlasser *m* air starter, compressed-air starter *(Mtr)*.
Preßluftflasche *f* compressed-air flask.
Preßlufthammer *m* pneumatic hammer.
Preßluft-Niethammer *m* pneumatic riveter.
Preßluftzylinder *m* compressed-air cylinder.
Preßstoff *m* plastic.
Pr.Geschoß *n* *See* Phosphorgeschoß.
Primärkreis *m* primary circuit *(Rad)*.
Primärwicklung *f* primary winding *(Elec)*.
Prise *f* prize.
Prisenrecht *n* angary.
Prismenkreuz *n* an engineer surveying instrument.
Pritsche *f* wooden-board bed.
Probe *f* test, trial.
Probeflug *m* test flight.
Probelauf *m* test run *(Mtr)*.
Probeschießen *n* test firing.
Profil *n* profile, cross section; tread *(of a tire)*.
Profildicke *f* profile thickness *(Ap wing)*.
Profilhinterkante *f* trailing edge *(Ap wing profile)*.
profiliert streamlined, faired.
Profilierung *f* fairing *(Ap)*; recapping *(tires)*; streamlining.
Profilsehne *f* wing chord *(Ap)*.
Profiltiefe *f* depth of profile *(Ap wing)*.
Profilvorderkante *f* leading edge *(Ap wing profile)*.
Projektion auf die Horizontalebene horizontal projection.

Projektion auf die Senkrechtebene vertical projection.
Propaganda *f* propaganda, publicity.
Propagandakompanie *f* propaganda company *(for front-line reporting; composed of writers and cameramen)*.
Propeller *m* propeller. *See also* **Luftschraube.**
Propellerblatt *n* propeller blade *(Ap)*.
Propellerhaube *f* propeller spinner.
Propellerkreis *m* plane of propeller rotation, propeller-disk area *(Ap)*.
Propellernabe *f* propeller hub *(Ap)*.
Propellersteigung *f* propeller pitch.
Propellerwind *m* slipstream *(Avn)*.
Protzarm *m* limber drawbar *(Arty)*.
Protze *f* limber *(Arty)*.
Protzgestell *n* limber frame *(Arty)*.
Protzhaken *m* limber pintle.
Protzkasten *m* limber ammunition chest *(Arty)*.
Protzöse *f* lunette *(G)*.
Prozentsatz *m* percentage.
prüfen to check, inspect, test, verify.
Prüfgerät *n* testing apparatus.
Prüfgestell *n* testing stand.
Prüfknopf *m* testing button *(field Tp)*.
Prüfröhrchen *n* detector tube *(in CWS detector kit)*.
Prüfstand *m* testing block *(Avn, MT)*.
Prüftaste *f* testing key *(field Tp)*.
Prüfung *f* test, testing, verification.
Prüfungsschießen *n* verification fire.
Puffer *m* buffer *(Ord)*.
Puffergehäuse *n* buffer housing *(MG)*.
Pufferlager *n* buffer support *(G cradle)*.
Pulk *m* boat-type runner *(placed under gun wheels for operations in deep snow)*; formation *(Avn slang)*.

Pulver *n* powder.
Pulverbrennzündung *f* powder-train ignition *(fuze)*.
Pulverbündel *n* powder bag *(Am)*.
Pulverhaus *n* powder magazine.
Pulverkammer *f* powder chamber.
Pulverkorn *n* powder grain *(Am)*.
Pulverladung *f* powder charge *(Am)*.
Pulverraum *m* powder chamber.
Pulverrückstände *mpl* powder fouling *(G)*.
Pulversatz *m* powder train, powder pellet *(fuze)*.
Pulversprengstoff *m* low explosive.
Pulvertemperaturmessung *f* measurement of powder temperature.
Pulverthermometer *n* powder thermometer *(Am)*.
Pulvertreibladung *f* propellent charge.
Pulverzerstäuber *m* decontaminating-powder sprayer *(CWS)*.
Pumpenkühlung *f* forced-circulation cooling *(Mtr)*.
Punkt *m* point, place; dot *(Tg)*.
Punktbestimmung *f* point designation, point location.
Punktfeuer *n* point fire, fixed fire *(MG)*.
Punktplan *m* range card *(Gunnery)*.
Punktschießen *n* See **Punktfeuer.**
Punktschweißung *f* spot welding.
Punkttafel *f* point-designation grid *(Arty)*.
Punktziel *n* point target *(Gunnery)*.
Pupinspule *f* loading coil *(Tp)*.
Puppe *f* dummy *(for bayonet Tng, etc.)*.
putzen to clean, polish, shine.
Putzlappen *m* cleaning rag.
Putzwolle *f* cotton waste.
Pz.Kw.-Nachbildung *f* tank silhouette *(practice firing)*.

Q

Q-Gruppe *f* Q signal *(Rad)*.
Quadrant *m* quadrant.
Quadrantenfläche *f* quadrant plate *(G)*.
Quadrantenvisier *n* leaf-type quadrant sight *(R, MG)*.

Quadrat *n* square, grid square.
Quadratwurzel *f* square root.
Qualifikationsbericht *m* qualification card.
Qualm *m* dense smoke.
Quarantäne *f* quarantine *(Med)*.

Quartier *n* quarters, billets.
Quartierarrest *m* restriction to quarters.
Quartiermacher *m* quartering officer, billeting officer.
Quartiermacherkommando *n* quartering party, billeting party.
Quartiermachertrupp *m* quartering detail, billeting detail.
Quartiermeister *m* corps or division quartermaster *(general staff officer "Ib" in charge of supply and Adm at corps or Div Hq)*.
Quartiermeisterabteilung *f* supply group of staff sections *(comprises* Quartiermeister *and* Intendantur*)*.
Quartier und Verpflegung quarters and subsistence.
Quartier- und Verpflegungsvergütung *f* quarters and subsistence allowance *(reimbursement)*.
Quartier- und Verpflegungszuschuß *m* quarters and subsistence allowance.
Quartiervergütung *f* quarters allowance.
quarzgesteuerter Sender crystal-controlled transmitter *(Rad)*.
Quarzkristall *n* quartz crystal *(Rad)*.
Quarzsteuerung *f* crystal control *(Rad)*.
Quast *m* tassel.
Qu-Blende *f* *See* **Querschnittblende.**
Quecksilber *n* mercury.
Quelle *f* source, spring, well.
quer across, obliquely.
Querachse *f* lateral axis *(Ap)*.
Queraxt *f* adze.
Querbeil *n* *See* **Queraxt.**

Querdeckung *f* traverse *(Ft)*.
querfahrendes Ziel target moving parallel to front *(ground target)*.
Querfahrt *f* movement parallel to front *(ground target)*.
querfeldein cross-country.
Querlibelle *f* cross level *(Surv, Arty)*.
Querrinne *f* open culvert *(road)*.
Querruder *n* aileron *(Ap)*.
Querruderhebel *m* aileron horn *(Ap)*.
Quersäge *f* crosscut saw.
Querschläger *m* ricochet.
Querschnitt *m* cross section.
Querschnittbelastung *f* ballistic coefficient.
Querschnittblende *f* transverse shutter *(signal lamp)*.
Querstabilität *f* lateral stability *(Ap)*.
Querstreuung *f* *See* **Breitenstreuung.**
Querträger *m* transverse beam, transom, transverse support *(Bdg)*.
Querverbindung *f* intervehicular communication; local circuit; cross bar, transverse bracing.
Querverkehr *m* internet traffic *(Rad)*.
Querverstrebung *f* cross bracing *(Bdg)*.
Querwall *m* traverse *(Ft)*.
quetschen to crush, bruise, squeeze, pinch.
Quetschkondensator *m* trimmer condenser *(Rad)*.
Quetschladung *f* camouflet.
Quetschmine *f* *See* **Quetschladung.**
Quetschung *f* contusion *(Med)*.
quietschen to screech *(brakes)*; to squeal *(Rad)*.

R

Rache *f* revenge.
Rachen *m* throat.
Rachenreizstoff *m* *See* **Nasen- und Rachenreizstoff.**
Rad *n* wheel; bicycle.
Radachse *f* axle.
Radauflagepunkt *m* center of tire contact *(MT)*.
Raddruck *m* wheel load *(MT)*.
Räderantrieb *m* wheel drive *(MT)*.

Räderbahre *f* wheeled litter carrier.
Räderfahrzeug *n* wheeled vehicle.
Räder-Gleiskettenantrieb *m* combination wheel-track drive, convertible wheel-track drive.
Räderkettenfahrzeug *n* combination wheel-track vehicle, convertible wheel-track vehicle.
Räderraupenfahrzeug *n* *See* **Räderkettenfahrzeug.**

Räderwerk *n* tracks and suspensions *(Tk)*.
Radfahrabteilung *f* bicycle battalion.
Radfahrkompanie *f* bicycle company.
Radfahrschwadron *f* bicycle troop.
Radfahrwerk *n* wheel-type landing gear *(Ap)*.
Radfahrzug *m* bicycle platoon.
Radflügelflugzeug *n* cyclogiro *(Avn)*.
Radgürtel *m* caterpillar band *(G)*.
Radiergummi *m* rubber eraser.
Radiosonde *f* radiosonde, radio meteorograph *(Met)*.
Radizierung *f* extraction of roots.
Radkappe *f* hub cap.
Radkörper *m* disk spider *(wheel)*.
Radlafette *f* wheeled gun carriage.
Radlandung *f* two-point landing *(Avn)*.
Radlenker *m* guard rail *(RR switch)*.
Radnabe *f* hub.
Radreifen *m* tire *(of a wheel)*.
Radschlepper *m* wheeled tractor.
Radsporn *m* tail wheel *(Ap)*.
Radstand *m* wheelbase; alinement of wheels.
Radstandlibelle *f* cross level *(G)*.
Radstandtrieb *m* cross-leveling mechanism *(G sight)*.
Radsteuerung *f* wheel control *(as distinguished from stick control) (Ap)*.
Radsturz *m* camber *(MT)*.
Radzugmaschine *f* wheeled tractor.
Rahmen *m* frame.
Rahmenantenne *f* loop antenna *(Rad)*.
Rahmenheer *n* enlisted cadre.
Rahmenlafette *f* frame-type gun carriage.
Rahmenspannturm *m* frame cabane *(Ap)*.
Rahmenübung *f* command-post exercise *(staff Tng)*.
Rakete *f* rocket.
Raketenantrieb *m* rocket propulsion.
Raketenbombe *f* rocket bomb *(Avn)*.
Raketen-Panzerbüchse *f* antitank rocket launcher.
Raketenstart *m* rocket-assisted take-off *(Avn)*.
Raketenwurfmaschine *f* rocket launcher, rocket projector.
Rammbär *m* drop hammer of a pile driver.
Rammbühne *f* pile-driver staging.
Ramme *f* pile driver.

rammen to ram *(Nav)*; to drive *(a pile)*.
Rammfähre *f* pile-driver raft.
Rammgerüst *n* pile-driver frame.
Rampe *f* ramp.
Rampengerät *n* ramp equipment.
Rampenmine *f* ramp mine *(improvised mine under an inclined board)*.
Rampensperre *f* sawhorse ramp obstacle.
Rampenwagen *m* ramp carrier *(MT)*.
Rand *m* edge, border, margin, rim; perimeter *(Tac)*.
Randbemerkungen *fpl* marginal data.
Randdüsenzünder *m* rimvent fuze *(Am)*.
Rändel *m* knurled nut or knob, micrometer knob.
rändeln to knurl.
Randfeuer *n* boundary light *(Adrm)*.
Randstellungen *fpl* perimeter positions *(Tac)*.
Rang *m* rank, status.
Rangabzeichen *n* insignia of rank.
Rangältester *m* senior officer.
Rangdienstalter *n* age-in-grade, seniority.
Rangierbahnhof *m* railroad yard.
Rangliste des Heeres army register.
Rasanz der Flugbahn flatness of trajectory.
rasch quick.
Raspel *f* rasp.
Rast *f* rest *(march column)*; click, detent *(Tech)*.
Rastgruppe *f* rest group *(march rest)*.
Rasthebel *m* bolt lock *(MG)*.
Rastplatz *m* resting place *(march rest)*.
Rate *f* rate.
Ration *f* forage ration.
eiserne Ration emergency forage ration.
Rationssatz *m* scale of forage rations.
Rauch *m* smoke.
Rauchentwickler *m* smoke generator.
Rauchentwicklung *f* generation of smoke.
Raucherscheinung *f* smoke effect *(flash ranging)*.
Rauchgerät *n* smoke equipment *(Ap)*.
Rauchgranate *f* smoke shell *(Am)*.
Rauchkerze *f* smoke candle *(CWS)*.
Rauchkörper *m* smoke filler *(Am)*; smoke-puff charge *(simulated fire)*.
Rauchladung *f* smoke charge *(Am)*.

Rauchmeldepatrone *f* smoke-cartridge message container *(for dropped messages) (Avn)*.

Rauchofen *m* smoke generator *(Adrm)*.

Rauchpatrone *f* smoke signal cartridge.

Rauchsatz *m* pyrotechnic composition *(smoke signal)*; smoke composition; smoke pellet *(Am)*.

rauchschwach smokeless, semismokeless.

rauchschwaches Pulver smokeless powder.

Rauchschwimmer *m* floating smoke pot.

Rauchsignalpatrone *f* smoke signal cartridge.

rauchstark generating much smoke.

Rauchvorhang *m* smoke curtain, smoke screen.

Rauchwolke *f* smoke cloud.

Rauhreif *m* frost *(Met)*.

Raum *m* space; room, chamber; sector; area, zone, region.

Raumbild *n* stereoscopic picture.

Raumbildentfernungsmesser *m* stereoscopic range finder.

Räumboot *n* mine sweeper.

räumen to clear mines; to clear out; to evacuate *(a position)*.

Raumgehalt *m See* **Rauminhalt**.

Rauminhalt *m* volume, cubic capacity.

Raumladung *f* space charge *(radio tube)*.

Raumlöffel *m* miner's spoon *(Engr tool)*.

Raummeßbild *n* stereogram *(Photo survey)*.

Räumotter *f* paravane.

Raumstrahlung *f* free-space radiation *(Rad)*.

Raumwelle *f* sky wave *(Rad)*.

Raupe *f* caterpillar; caterpillar track; plaited shoulder strap.

Raupenantrieb *m* caterpillar drive *(MT)*.

Raupenfahrzeug *n* track-laying vehicle.

Raupenkette *f* caterpillar track.

Raupenkrad *n See* **Kettenkrad**.

Raupenschlepper *m* caterpillar tractor.

R-Boot *n See* **Räumboot**.

Rechen *m* rake.

Rechengerät *n* computer.

Rechenschieber *m* slide rule.

Rechenschieber zur Entfernungsermittlung logarithmic range scale *(Arty)*.

Rechenstelle *f* post of computing section *(firing battery)*.

Rechenzettel *m* firing-data form *(Arty)*.

rechnen to count, compute.

Rechner *m* computer, plotter *(person)*.

Rechnung *f* account, bill; computation.

Rechnungsführer *m* accountant and pay noncommissioned officer.

Rechnungslegung *f* accountability.

Rechnungswesen *n* accounting.

Recht *n* law, jurisprudence.

Rechteck *n* rectangle.

Rechtsabteilung *f* legal branch, legal section.

Rechtsdrall *m* right-hand twist *(rifling)*.

rechtsgängig clockwise; right-hand *(threads, etc.)*.

Rechtsgewinde *n* right-hand thread.

Rechtskurve *f* right bank *(Avn)*.

rechtslaufend clockwise.

"Rechts schwenkt, marsch!" "Column right, march!" *(followed by* "Gerade, aus!"*)*.

Rechtsstellung *f* legal status.

"Rechts, um!" "Right, face!"; "By the right flank, march!" *(given in marching)*.

Rechtswert *m* X-coordinate *(on co-ordinate scale in map reading)*.

rechtweisender Kurs true course *(Air Navigation)*.

rechtweisender Windkurs true heading *(Air Navigation)*.

rechtwinklig rectangular.

Reduktionsmaßstab *m* engineer's scale.

Reduziergetriebe *n* reduction gear.

Reede *f* roadstead.

Reflexglas *n* transparent reflector *(reflector sight)*.

Reflexvisier *n* reflector sight *(Ap, AA gun)*.

Regel *f* rule.

Regellast *f* standard maximum load *(Bdg)*.

regellose Flucht rout.

regelmäßig regular.

regelmäßiger Fehler systematic error, determinate error.

regeln to direct, control, regulate.

regelrecht standard, according to regulations.

Regelröhre *f* variable *μ* tube, supercontrol tube *(Rad)*.

Regelspur *f* standard gage *(RR)*.

Regelstange *f* regulator *(G recoil brake)*.

Regelvorrichtung *f* governing device *(Mtr)*.

Regen *m* rain.

Regendecke *f* tarpaulin.

regenerierter Altgummi reclaimed rubber.

Regengebiet *n* precipitation area *(Met)*.

Regenguß *m* shower *(Met)*.

Regenklappe *f* rain flap *(on haversack)*.

Regenmantel *m* raincoat.

Regenmesser *m* rain gage *(Met)*.

Regenschauer *m* shower *(Met)*.

Regenwolke *f* rain cloud *(Met)*.

Regierung *f* government.

Regiment *n* regiment.

Regimentsabschnitt *n* regimental sector.

Regimentsadjutant *m* aide to regimental commander, regimental executive.

Regimentsarzt *m* regimental surgeon.

Regimentsbefehl *m* regimental order.

Regimentsgefechtsstand *m* regimental command post.

Regimentskommandeur *m* regimental commander.

Regimentsnachrichtenzug *m* regimental communication platoon.

Regimentsstab *m* regimental headquarters, regimental staff.

Regimentstroß *m* regimental train.

Registrier-Chronograph *m* chronograph.

Regler *m* governor; automatic control; automatic corrector.

Reglerdose *f* control aneroid *(Ap engine)*.

Reglergabel *f* governor arms *(Mtr)*.

Reglergestänge *n* plunger *(engine governor)*.

Reglerschalter *m* combination voltage regulator, current regulator and cut-out relay *(Mtr)*.

Reglerteilung *f* correction scale on gun sight.

Reglerventil *n* regulating valve, check valve.

Reglerwinkel *m* principal vertical deflection angle *(AA gunnery)*.

Regulierhebel *m* throttle lever *(carburetor)*.

regungslos erstarren freeze in position.

Reibahle *f* reamer.

Reibfläche *f* head *(of SA cartridge)*.

Reibung *f* friction, galling, rubbing.

Reibungswiderstand *m* frictional resistance.

Reibzündschraube *f* friction primer.

Reichsarbeitsdienst *m* Reich Labor Service.

Reichsarbeitsführer *m* lieutenant general *(Reich Labor Service)*.

Reichsautobahn *f* Reich automobile express highway.

Reichsflagge *f* German national flag.

Reichsführer SS Reich Leader of SS troops.

Reichskokarde *f* national rosette *(worn on field and mountain cap)*.

Reichskriegerbund *m* Veterans Association of the Reich.

Reichskriegsflagge *f* German national ensign *(Nav)*.

Reichsluftfahrtministerium *n* German Air Ministry.

Reichsluftfahrtverwaltung *f* German Civil Aeronautics Administration.

Reichsluftschutzbund *f* German national air defense organization.

Reichsmeldedienst *m* German aircraft warning service.

Reichsstraße *f* national highway of the Reich.

Reichweite *f* range, maximum range.

Reif *m* rime ice, frost.

Reifen *m* tire.

Reifenerneuerung *f* recapping, retreading.

Reifenheber *m* tire tool.

Reifen-Luftdruckprüfer *m* tire pressure gage.

Reifenpanne *f* puncture, blowout.

Reihe *f* file, single file *(Inf)*; column of troopers *(H Cav)*; ladder *(six observed rounds) (Arty)*; train of bombs.

"In Reihe, angetreten!" "In single file, fall in!"

Reihenabwurf *m* train release, train bombing.

Reihenbild *n* aerial mosaic, strip mosaic.

Reihenbildkammer *f*   aerial mapping camera.
Reihenbildner *m*   *See* **Reihenbildkammer.**
Reihenfeuer *n*   ladder fire *(Gunnery).*
Reihenkammer *f*   *See* **Reihenbildkammer.**
Reihenladung *f*   elongated charge. in Rohr gefüllte Reihenladung bangalore torpedo.
Reihenmotor *m*   in-line engine.
Reihenschaltung *f*   series connection *(Elec).*
Reihenschießen *n*   ladder fire *(Gunnery).*
Reihenstandmotor *m*   in-line upright engine.
Reihenwurf *m*   train release, train bombing.
Reinigungsbürste *f*   bore brush, cleaning brush *(Ord).*
Reinigungsdocht *m*   cleaning patch *(R).*
Reinigungslappen *m*   cleaning rag.
Reisegeld *n*   travel allowance.
Reisegeschwindigkeit *f*   cruising speed *(Ap).*
Reisekostenvergütung *f*   *See* **Reisevergütung.**
Reisemarsch *m*   administrative march.
Reisevergütung *f*   travel allowance, mileage allowance *(reimbursement).*
Reiseverordnung *f*   mileage table.
Reiseverpflegung *f*   travel ration.
Reisigbündel *n*   fascine.
Reißbahn *f*   rip panel *(Bln).*
Reißbrett *n*   drawing board.
reißen   to rip.
Reißleine *f*   rip cord *(Prcht, Bln);* static line *(Prcht).*
Reißnadel *f*   scriber.
Reißnagel *m*   thumbtack.
Reißschnur *f*   quick release cord *(Prcht).*
Reißverschluß *m*   zipper, slide fastener.
Reißzeug *n*   drawing instruments, drawing set.
reitende Artillerie   horse artillery.
Reiter *m*   private *(Cav);* cavalryman, trooper.
spanischer Reiter   cheval-de-frise, knife rest *(Ft).*
Reiteraufklärungsabteilung *f*   cavalry reconnaissance detachment *(H Cav).*
Reiterbrigade *f*   cavalry brigade *(H Cav).*

Reiterei *f*   cavalry.
Reitergruppe *f*   cavalry section *(H Cav).*
Reiternachspitze *f*   cavalry rear point, rear guard cavalry detachment.
Reiterregiment *n*   cavalry regiment *(H Cav).*
Reiterreihe *f*   column of troopers *(H Cav).*
Reiterrudel *n*   flock *(H Cav).*
Reiterschwadron *f*   cavalry troop *(H Cav).*
Reiterspähtrupp *m*   cavalry reconnaissance squad, cavalry patrol *(H Cav).*
Reiterspitze *f*   cavalry point, advance guard cavalry detachment.
Reiterzug *m*   rifle platoon *(H Cav Regt);* mounted platoon *(Inf Regt).*
Reithalfter *f*   cavesson *(harness).*
Reithosen *fpl*   breeches.
Reitpferd *n*   mount, riding horse.
Reitstiefel *mpl*   riding boots.
reizender Kampfstoff   irritant agent *(lacrimator or nose and throat irritant).*
Reizgeschoß *n*   irritant gas projectile.
Reizkerze *f*   irritant candle *(CWS).*
Reizkörper *m*   CN capsule, lacrimator *(CWS).*
Reizpatrone *f*   tear-gas cartridge *(for gas chamber test).*
Reizstoff *m*   irritant, harassing agent *(CWS).*
Reiztopf *m*   irritant gas candle.
Reizwürfel *m*   irritant capsule, CN capsule *(CWS).*
Rekrut *m*   recruit.
Rekrutendepot *n*   recruit depot.
rekrutieren   to recruit.
Relais *n*   relay *(Elec).*
Relativgeschwindigkeit *f*   indicated air speed *(Avn).*
Relativhöhenmesser *m*   sonic altimeter *(Ap).*
Reliefkarte *f*   relief map.
Remonteamt *n*   remount depot.
Remonteaufkaufskommission *f*   remount purchasing board.
Remonteinspektion *f*   Remount Division.
Remontekommission *f*   *See* **Remonteaufkaufskommission.**
Remontewesen *n*   remount service.
Repatriierung *f*   repatriation.

Repetitions-Theodolit *m*   repeating theodolite *(Surv)*.

Repressalien *fpl* reprisals.

requirieren commandeer.

Reserve *f* reserve (Reserve I, *inactive reserve of fully trained men under 35;* Reserve II, *inactive reserve of partly trained men under 35).*

Reservedivision *f* reserve division *(Tng unit in occupied countries).*

Reserveeingreiftrupp *m* reserve detachment *(held in readiness for tactical commitment).*

Reservelazarett *n* general hospital.

Reserveoffizier *m* reserve officer.

Reserveoffizieranwärter *m* reserve officer candidate.

Reserveoffizier-Bewerber *m* reserve officer applicant.

Reservezündung *f* auxiliary ignition lead *(blasting).*

Resonanzkreis *m* resonant circuit *(Rad).*

Restflugweite *f* straight-line distance between point of burst and theoretical point of impact *(Ballistics).*

Rettungsboje *f* life buoy.

Rettungsdienst *m* life-saving service, rescue service.

Rettungsfahrzeug *n* lifeboat.

Rettungsgerät *n* life-saving equipment.

Rettungsgürtel *m* life belt.

Rettungsleine *f* life line.

Rettungsmannschaft *f* rescue party.

Rettungsring *m* life preserver.

Rettungsschwimmer *m* qualified swimmer *(holder of life-saver's certificate).*

Rettungsstange *f* boat hook *(for rescue work).*

Rettungstrupp *m* rescue squad *(CWS).*

Revier *n* infirmary; forest range; precinct, district.

Revierkranker *m* infirmary case, dispensary case.

Revierstunde *f* sick call.

Revolver *m* revolver.

Revolvergurt *m* revolver belt.

Revolver mit Wiederspannabzug double-action revolver.

Reynoldszahl *f* Reynolds number *(Aerodynamics).*

Richtantenne *f* directional antenna *(Rad).*

Richtaufsatz *m* sight mount, telescope mount.

Richtaufsatzträger *m* sight mount bracket.

Richtausbildung *f* training in sighting and aiming.

Richtbaum *m* trail handspike *(G).*

Richtbefehl *m* aiming order.

Richtbogen *m* clinometer *(Surv, Gunnery).*

Richtempfänger *m* radio compass, direction finder *(Air Navigation).*

Richtempfangsanlage *f* direction-finder station *(Air Navigation).*

Richtempfangsantenne *f* directional receiving antenna *(Rad).*

richten to lay, to aim, to point *(a gun).*

Richter *m* judge.

"Richt Euch!" "Dress right, dress!"

Richtfeld *n* field of fire; extent of traverse and elevation.

Richtfernrohr *n* telescopic sight.

Richtfunkfeuer *f* radio range beacon.

Richtgehäuse *n* elevating-gear housing *(MG).*

Richtgelenk *n* elevating link *(MG).*

Richtgerät *n* laying mechanism, sight equipment *(G);* direction-finding equipment *(Rad).*

Richtglas *n* collimating sight.

Richthebel *m* elevating arm *(MG).*

Richthebelwelle *f* elevating-arm shaft *(MG).*

Richthöhe *f* elevation *(Gunnery).*

Richtkanonier *m* gunner *(Arty);* gun pointer.

Richtkommando *n* aiming order.

Richtkreis *m* aiming circle *(Arty);* azimuth circle *(Surv).*

Richtkreis-Bussole *f* declinator *(aiming circle).*

Richtkreiseinteilung *f* mil graduation *(aiming circle).*

Richtkreisunteroffizier *m* instrument NCO in charge of aiming circle *(Arty).*

Richtlampe *f* aiming light, aiming post light.

Richtlatte *f* aiming stake, aiming post *(Arty);* base stake *(Surv).*

Richtlehre *f* theory of gun pointing.

Richtlehrer *m* instructor in gunnery.

Richtlinien *fpl* guiding principles, directions.

Richtmaschine *f* elevating and traversing mechanism *(G).*

Richtmittel *n* sighting device; laying device.

Richtposten *m* road sign post.

Richtpunkt *m* aiming point *(Gunnery)*.

Richtpunktverfahren *n* aiming-point and deflection method *(Gunnery)*.

Richtpunktzahl *f* aiming-point azimuth reading.

Richtsäule *f* control column *(for synchronizing sound locator and searchlight)*.

Richtscheibe *f* aiming target.

Richtschütze *m* gunner *(MG, Mort, Tk, AT)*; gun pointer.

Richtsitz *m* gunner's seat, layer's seat *(G)*.

Richtstange *f* alinement stake *(Bdg, Engr)*.

Richtstelle *f* aiming-circle station *(MG platoon)*.

Richtstock *m* aiming post.

Richtstrahl *m* radio beam.

Richtstrich *m* center line *(on inside of march-compass cover)*.

Richtübung *f* aiming practice, aiming exercise *(Gunnery)*.

Richtübungsgerät *n* practice sight.

Richtung *f* direction; pointing or laying *(of a gun)*.

Richtungsangabe *f* indication of direction.

Richtungsbestimmung *f* determining of direction, orientation.

Richtungsgleis *n* classification track *(RR)*.

Richtungshörer *m* sound locator *(AAA)*.

Richtungslinie *f* orienting line *(Gunnery, Surv)*.

Richtungspunkt *m* orienting point *(Surv)*.

Richtungsschießen *n* adjustment fire for direction *(Gunnery)*.

Richtungsschild *n* road sign.

Richtungsschüsse *mpl* adjustment shots for direction *(Gunnery)*.

Richtungsstabilität *f* directional stability *(Ap)*.

Richtungswinkel *m* firing angle.

Richtverfahren *n* method of laying *(Gunnery)*.

Richtvorrichtung *f* elevating and traversing mechanism.

Richtwirkung *f* directional effect *(Rad)*.

Richtzahnbogen *m* elevating rack, elevating arc *(G)*.

Riechprobe *f* sniffing test *(CWS)*.

Riechprobenkasten *m* gas-identification set, sniff set *(CWS)*.

Riechspur *f* artificial scent.

Riechtopf *m* irritant-gas generator, CN generator *(CWS)*.

Riechwürfel *m* chemical capsule *(to simulate gas-shell fire)*.

Riegel *m* bolt; bar; crossbar; sliding bolt; switch line, oblique defense line *(Tac, Ft)*.

Riegelbolzen *m* retaining bolt *(Ord)*.

Riegelhebel *m* locking lever *(G)*.

Riegelstellung *f* switch position *(Ft, Tac)*.

Riemen *m* strap; sling; belt.

Riemenantrieb *m* belt drive.

Riemenbügel *m* sling swivel *(R)*.

Riemenscheibe *f* pulley.

Riemenschieber *m* gun-sling keeper *(R)*.

Riesenluftreifen *m* giant tire, oversize tire *(MT)*.

Rille *f* cannelure *(Am)*; groove.

Ringen *n* combat, struggle, wrestling.

Ringfallschirm *m* parachute skirt.

Ringpulver *n* annular powder *(Am)*.

Ringrohr *n* built-up barrel *(G)*.

Ringtrichterrichtungshörer *m* trumpet-type sound locator *(AAA)*.

Ringübertrager *m* repeating coil *(Tg, Tp)*.

Ringverkleidung *f* engine ring cowling *(Ap)*.

Ringvisier *n* ring sight.

rinnen to leak.

Rippe *f* rib; cooling fin *(air-cooled engine)*.

Rippenfläche *f* fin surface *(air-cooled engine)*.

Riß *m* rip, tear; split; rupture; laceration; sectional drawing.

Rißwunde *f* lacerated wound.

Ritter *m* knight, noble.

Ritterkreuz *n* Knight's Cross *(decoration)*.

Rittmeister *m* captain *(Cav, H-Dr T)*.

Ritzel *m* pinion.

robben to crawl.

Rödelbalken *m* siderail, curb rail, guard rail *(Bdg)*.

Rödelbund *m* siderail lashing *(Bdg)*.

Rödelkeil *m* siderail wedge *(Bdg)*.

Rödeln *n*   siderail lashing *(Bdg)*.
Rödelung *f*   siderails, guard rails, siderail lashing *(Bdg)*.
Rödelzange *f*   siderail clamp *(Bdg)*.
Rodung *f*   logged-off area, cleared woodland.
Rohöl *n*   crude oil.
Rohr *n*   tube, gun barrel; pipe.
Rohrabnutzung *f*   erosion of the bore.
Rohransatz *m*   barrel extension.
Rohrbremse *f*   recoil brake *(G)*.
Rohrbuch *n*   gun book.
Röhre *f*   tube *(Rad)*.
Röhrenheizung *f*   filament heating *(Rad)*.
Röhrenkennlinie *f*   characteristic curve, tube characteristic *(Rad)*.
Röhrenlafette *f*   tubular mount.
Röhrenlibelle *f*   tubular spirit level.
Röhrenmast *m*   tubular mast.
Röhrenprüfgerät *n*   tube tester, tube checker *(Inst, Rad)*.
Röhrenpulver *n*   perforated powder *(Am)*.
Röhrensockel *m*   tube base, tube socket *(Rad)*.
Röhrenspannungsmesser *m*   vacuum-tube voltmeter.
Röhrensummer *m*   electronic audio oscillator *(Rad)*.
Rohrerhöhung *f*   quadrant elevation.
Rohrfestigkeit *f*   strength of barrel *(Ord)*.
Rohrhalter *m*   barrel bracket *(G)*.
Rohrinneres *n*   bore *(G)*.
Rohrklaue *f*   barrel guide *(G)*.
Rohrkrepierer *m*   barrel burst.
Rohrlänge *f*   length of barrel *(G)*.
Rohrleitung *f*   pipe line.
Rohrmantel *m*   jacket *(G)*.
Rohrmündung *f*   muzzle *(G)*.
Rohrrahmen *m*   tubular chassis frame *(MT)*.
Rohrrücklauf *m*   barrel recoil *(G)*.
Rohrschlitten *m*   sleigh *(G)*; gun-barrel sled *(for carrying barrel of dismantled mountain gun in deep snow)*.
Rohrschreiber *m*   practice aiming device consisting of pencil mounted on gun barrel and chart on which pencil tracks movement of target.
Rohrseele *f*   bore *(G)*.
rohrsicherer Zünder   bore-safe fuze.
Rohrsicherheit des Zünders   bore safety of fuze.

Rohrstütze *f*   tubular support *(AA gun outrigger)*.
Rohrwagen *m*   cannon transport wagon, gun-barrel trailer.
Rohrwandbeobachtungsgerät *n*   barrel reflector *(G)*.
Rohrwechsel *m*   change of barrel *(Ord)*.
Rohrweite *f*   caliber *(G)*.
Rohrwiege *f*   cradle *(G)*.
Rohrzange *f*   Stillson wrench, pipe wrench.
Rohrzeiger *m*   gun barrel reference pointer *(matches with Aufsatzzeiger when gun is laid for elevation)*.
Rohrzerspringer *m*   barrel burst.
Rollbahn *f*   taxiway *(Adrm)*; track *(of road)*.
Rollbock *m*   bogie trailer *(Arty)*.
Rolle *f*   roll *(Avn, Tech)*; roller, pulley; wire roll.
   gesteuerte Rolle   slow roll *(Avn)*.
rollen   to taxi *(Avn)*; to roll along, to roll forward *(Tks, vehicles, etc.)*.
   in rollendem Einsatz   in waves *(Tac)*.
rollendes Material   rolling stock *(RR)*.
Rollenlager *n*   roller bearing *(Mech)*.
Rollenstößel *m*   roller-type valve lifter *(Mtr)*.
Rollenwagen *m*   bogie suspensions *(Tk)*.
Rollfeld *n*   landing field, cleared zone *(Adrm)*.
Rollstraße *f*   taxiway *(Adrm)*.
Rollwerk *n*   landing gear *(Ap)*.
Rollwiderstand *m*   vehicle resistance *(MT)*; rolling friction *(Mech)*.
Röntgenbild *n*   X-ray photograph.
Röntgenstrahlen *mpl*   X-rays.
Rost *m*   rust; grate; grill; trench board.
rostig   rusty.
Rotes Kreuz   Red Cross.
Rotfilterempfangsgerät *n*   red-filter receiving attachment *(signal lamp)*.
Rotfiltergerät *n*   red-filter set *(BC telescope)*.
Rotte *f*   two-ship element *(formation of two airplanes)*; a number of men in file.
R-Patrone *f*   See **Rauchpatrone**.
Rückbau *m*   reconstruction; dismantling.
Rückbeförderung *f*   evacuation *(of wounded, etc.)*.

Rückblick *m*   backsight *(Surv);* rear glance, rear view, retrospect.

Rückblickspiegel *m* rear-view mirror.

Rückdruck *m*   reaction pressure *(rocket).*

Rücken *m*   rear *(Tac);* ridge *(Top);* back.

Rückenangriff *m*   attack against the rear; attack from the rear.

Rückendeckung *f* rear covering force, rear cover *(Tac);* parados *(Ft).*

Rückenfallschirm *m*   back-pack parachute.

Rückenfeuer *n*   enemy fire from the rear.

Rückenflug *m*   inverted flight, upsidedown flight.

Rückengepäck *n*   pack.

Rückenkissen *n*   crupper pad *(harness).*

Rückenlehne *f*   back rest *(Ap, MT).*

Rückenlinie *f*   ridge line *(Top).*

Rückenriemen *m*   leadup strap *(harness).*

Rückenring *m*   back rest *(AA MG).*

Rückentrage *f*   pack reel *(for Tp wire).*

Rückenwehr *f*   parados *(Ft).*

Rückenwind *m*   tail wind.

Rückfahrlaterne *f*   backing light *(MT).*

Rückflug *m*   return flight, homing flight *(Avn).*

Rückfrage *f*   check-back, tracer.

Rückgrat *n*   backbone.

Rückhalt *m*   support *(Tac).*

Rückholer *m*   connecting arm between firing lever and sear *(light Inf howitzer).*

Rückkehr *f*   return.

Rückkopplung *f*   feedback, regeneration *(Rad).*

Rücklauf *m*   recoil.

Rücklaufbremse *f*   recoil brake *(G).*

Rücklaufeinrichtung *f*   recoil mechanism *(G).*

rückläufig retrograde, reverse.

Rücklauffeder *f*   recoil spring, buffer spring.

Rücklaufmesser *m*   recoil marker *(G).*

Rücklaufschieber *m*   recoil marker slide *(G).*

Rücklaufwelle *f*   reverse idler gear shaft *(MT).*

Rückleitung *f*   return *(Elec, Tp);* return line *(hydraulics).*

Rücklicht *n*   taillight *(MT).*

Rückmarsch *m*   retrograde march, retirement *(Tac).*

Rückmarschbewegung *f*   retrograde movement.

Rückmarschstraße *f*   line of retirement *(Tac).*

Rückmeldung *f*   reply.

Rucksack *m*   knapsack, rucksack.

Rückschlag *m*   blowback *(Ord);* back pressure *(Mtr);* reverse *(Tac).*

Rückschlagventil *n*   check valve, oneway valve.

Rückstände *mpl*   fouling *(Ord);* carbon *(Mtr);* residue.

Rückstoß *m*   recoil, kick *(Ord);* reaction *(Mech).*

Rückstoßhülse *f*   recoil booster sleeve *(MG).*

Rückstoßlader *m*   recoil-operated weapon.

Rückstoßmotor *m*   jet-propulsion engine *(Ap).*

Rückstoßverstärker *m*   recoil booster *(MG).*

Rückstoßwirkung *f*   recoil effect.

Rückstrahler *m*   reflector.

Rücktrift *f*   trail *(bomb trajectory).*

Rücktriftwinkel *m*   trail angle *(bomb trajectory).*

rückwärtig   rear, rearward, behind the lines.

rückwärtige Dienste   rear services, supply services.

rückwärtige Einrichtungen rear installations.

rückwärtiges Armeegebiet communications zone.

rückwärtiges Gebiet   rear area, rear zone, communications zone.

rückwärtiges Heeresgebiet communications zone of a group of armies.

rückwärtiges Lazarett   base hospital.

rückwärtiges Nachschublager   base depot.

rückwärtige Stellung   rear position, reserve battle position, rear battle position.

Rückwärtseinschneiden *n*   resection *(Surv).*

Rückwärtsfahrer *m*   rear driver *(of a vehicle with double-end control).*

Rückwärtsfahrt *f*   reverse movement *(MT).*

Rückwärtsgang *m*   reverse, reverse gear, reverse speed *(MT).*

Rückwärtslenkung f rear steering system (*of a vehicle with double-end control*).

Rückwärtsstaffelung f negative stagger (*Ap wings*); echelon formation in depth.

Rückweg m withdrawal route (*Tac*); return, way back.

rückwirkend retroactive.

Rückzug m retreat, retirement, withdrawal (*Tac*).

Rückzugslinie f line of retirement, line of retreat (*Tac*).

Rückzugsstraße f withdrawal route, route of retreat.

Rudel n See **Schützenrudel, Reiterrudel.**

Ruder n oar; elevator or rudder (*Ap*).

Ruderboot n rowboat.

Ruderfahrzeug n oar-propelled craft.

Rudersteven m stern post (*assault boat, ferry, or barge*).

Ruf m call; ring (*Tp*); reputation.

Rufbatterie f a battery whose observation post is within calling distance of the battalion observation post.

rufen to call; to ring (*Tp*).

Rufname m first name.

Rufstrom m signaling current, ringing current (*Tp*).

Rufzeichen n call sign, call signal (*Rad*); calling signal (*Tp*).

Ruhe f rest, silence, quiet.

Ruhegehalt n pension.

Ruhelager n rest camp.

Ruhestand m retirement.

im **Ruhestand** retired (*abbr.* i.R.).

Ruhestellung f "at ease" position.

Ruhr f dysentery.

Ruhrast f half cock (*SA*).

"Rührt, euch!" "At ease!"

Rumpf m trunk, torso; fuselage (*Ap*); hull (*of flying boat*).

Rumpfbug m nose (*Ap*).

Rumpfende n tail (*Ap*).

Rumpfgerüst n fuselage framework (*Ap*).

Rumpfhaut f fuselage skin (*Ap*).

Rumpfholm m longeron (*Ap*).

Rumpfkanzel f cockpit (*Ap*).

Rumpfklappe f bomb doors (*Ap*).

Rumpflängsachse f longitudinal axis of fuselage.

Rumpflängsleiste f longeron (*Ap*).

Rumpfmontage f fuselage assembly (*Ap*).

Rumpfspant m bulkhead (*Ap*).

Rumpfnase f nose (*Ap*).

Rumpfspitze f nose (*Ap*).

Rumpfverband m cadre.

Rundbild n panoramic photograph (*Surv*).

Rundblickfernrohr n panoramic telescope, panoramic sight.

Runde f tour, round, circle, curve.

Runderneuerung f retreading (*MT*).

Rundflug m local flight (*Avn*).

Rundfunk m radio broadcast; broadcasting.

Rundfunkempfang m radio broadcast reception.

Rundfunksender m radio broadcasting station.

Rundholz n round timber, spar.

Rundkeilverschluß m cylindrical wedge-type breechblock (*G*).

Rundschreiben n circular.

Rundzelt n circular tent.

Rungenwagen m flatcar with side racks (*RR*).

Rüstgewicht n structural weight (*plus equipment*) (*Ap*).

Rüstung f armament.

rutschen to slip, slide, skid; to sideslip (*Avn*).

Rüttelerscheinungen fpl flutter (*Ap*).

R-Wagen m See **Rungenwagen.**

S

SA f See **Sturmabteilungen.**

Säbel m saber, sword.

Sachbearbeiter m technical staff officer; individual in charge of a special administrative department or field of subject matter.

Sachnummer f item number.

Sachschaden m material damage, damage to property.

Sack m bag, sack.

sacken to sag, settle, sink.

Sackgasse f dead-end street or road.

Sackleinen *n* burlap, osnaburg.
Saft *m* juice; electric current *(slang)*.
Säge *f* saw.
Sägewerk *n* sawmill.
Salpeter *m* saltpeter.
Salpetersäure *f* nitric acid.
Salut *m* gun salute.
Salve *f* salvo *(pieces fire simultaneously) (Arty);* volley *(fired by riflemen).*
Salvengeschütz *n* automatic gun.
Salz *n* salt.
Salzkartusche *f* flash-reducing wad *(Am).*
Salzsäure *f* hydrochloric acid.
Salzvorladung *f* flash-reducing wad.
Salzvorlage *f* See **Salzvorladung.**
SA-Mann *m* storm trooper.
Sammelgespräch *n* conference call *(Tp).*
Sammelkommando *n* recovery party, salvage collecting party.
Sammelkompanie *f* salvage collecting company.
Sammelmeldung *f* general message *(Rad).*
sammeln to salvage, to collect, to gather.
Sammelort *m* assembly place, rendezvous.
Sammelplatz *m* collecting point; assembly point, rallying point, rendezvous *(Tac);* collecting station *(Med).*
Sammelpunkt *m* See **Sammelplatz.**
Sammelrufzeichen *n* collective call sign, general call sign *(Rad).*
Sammelschutz *m* collective protection *(CWS).*
Sammelstelle *f* assembly point.
Sammeltätigkeit *f* collecting; salvage collecting.
Sammelwesen *n* salvage service.
Sammelzug *m* salvage platoon.
Sammler *m* See **Sammlerbatterie.**
Sammlerbatterie *f* storage battery.
Sammlerhaube *f* battery cover *(Elec).*
Sammlerkasten *m* battery box *(Elec).*
Sandeis *n* "ice concrete" *(a frozen mixture of sand, gravel and water).*
Sandgrube *f* sand pit.
Sandkasten *m* sand table *(Tng).*
Sandkastenspiel *n* sand table exercise.
Sandsack *m* sandbag.

Sandschutzbrille *f* sand goggles.
Sanierung *f* sanitation, introduction of sanitary measures.
Sanierungsmittel *n* prophylactic.
Sanitätsabteilung *f* medical battalion.
Sanitätsausrüstung *f* medical equipment.
Sanitätsdienst *m* medical service.
Sanitätseinrichtung *f* medical installation.
Sanitätsfahrzeug *n* ambulance.
Sanitätsfeldwebel *m* technical sergeant *(Med).*
Sanitätsflugbereitschaft *f* airplane ambulance unit.
Sanitätsflugzeug *n* airplane ambulance.
Sanitätsgefreiter *m* acting corporal *(Med).* See also **Gefreiter.**
Sanitätsgerät *n* medical equipment.
Sanitätshelferin *f* medical woman auxiliary.
Sanitätshund *m* first-aid dog.
Sanitätskasten *m* medicine chest, surgical chest.
Sanitätskolonne *f* ambulance column.
Sanitätskompanie *f* medical company.
Sanitätskorps *n* Medical Corps.
Sanitätsmaterialpark *m* medical supply depot.
Sanitätsoberfeldwebel *m* master sergeant *(Med).*
Sanitätsobergefreiter *m* corporal *(Med).*
Sanitätsobersoldat *m* private first class *(Med).*
Sanitätsoffizier *m* medical officer.
Sanitätsoffizier (Z) *m* dental officer *(Z is abbr. of* **Zahnarzt).**
Sanitätsordnung *f* regulations governing organization and operation of Medical Corps.
Sanitätspark *m* medical depot.
Sanitätspersonal *n* medical corps personnel.
Sanitätssoldat *m* private *(Med).*
Sanitätsstaffel *f* medical unit *(of Div Med Bn).*
Sanitätstroß *m* medical train.
Sanitätstruppe *f* medical corps.
Sanitätstasche *f* pouch kit.
Sanitätstruppen *fpl* medical troops.
Sanitätsunteroffizier *m* sergeant *(Med).*
Sanitätswesen *n* medical service.
Sappe *f* sap *(Ft).*
Sappenkopf *m* saphead *(Ft).*

Sarg *m* coffin.
Sattel *m* saddle *(harness, Top)*.
Sattelbaum *m* saddletree *(harness)*.
Sattelbefehl *m* field order.
Sattelbekleidung *f* saddle covering.
Sattelgurt *m* girth *(of a saddle)*.
Sattelholz *n* short wooden plate or sill placed on top of a column so as to increase its bearing surface.
Sattelkissen *n* saddle pad.
Sattelpferd *n* near horse.
Sattelschlepper *m* semitrailer *(MT)*.
Sattelsitz *m* seat *(of a saddle)*.
Satteltasche *f* skirt *(saddle)*.
Satteltracht *f* saddle cover *(pack saddle)*.
Sättigung *f* saturation.
Satz *m* sentence, axiom; rate, scale; set, unit; composition, pellet *(Am, CWS)*; jump, bound.
Satzring *m* time train ring *(time fuze)*.
Satzstück *n* powder pellet *(time fuze)*.
säubern to clean; clear up; clean out; mop up *(Tac)*.
Säuberungstrupp *m* mopping-up detachment.
Säuberungsunternehmen *n* mopping-up operation.
Sauerstoff *m* oxygen.
Sauerstoffazetylenschweißung *f* oxy-acetylene welding.
Sauerstofflasche *f* oxygen cylinder.
Sauerstoffgerät *n* oxygen apparatus.
Sauerstoff-Wiederbeleber *m* pulmotor.
Saughub *m* intake stroke, suction stroke *(Mtr)*.
Saugleitung *f* intake duct *(Mtr)*.
Saugluft *f* inflow *(Avn)*.
Saugrohr *n* intake manifold *(Mtr)*.
Saugseite *f* suction surface *(Ap wing)*.
Saugsteinbehälter *m* silicic acid gel container *(gas-detection apparatus)*.
Säule *f* column, pile.
Saumpfad *m* path *(for pack animals)*; mountain trail.
Sauna Finnish steam bath.
Säure *f* acid.
Säuremesser *m* hydrometer.
S-Beköstigungsmittel *npl* army post subsistence supplies *(abbr. for Standort-Beköstigungsmittel)*.
S-Boot *n* See Schnellboot.
Schaber *m* scraper.
Schablone *f* stencil, templet.

schablonieren to stencil.
Schacht *m* shaft *(mining)*; bomb rack; conduit *(Elec)*.
Schachtel *f* box.
Schädel *m* skull.
Schaden *m* damage.
Schadenbekämpfung *f* damage control.
Schadenersatz *m* indemnity.
schädlich injurious, harmful, destructive, pernicious, dangerous; prejudicial, disadvantageous.
schädlicher Widerstand parasite drag *(Avn)*.
Schädlichkeitsgrenze *f* point of intolerable concentration *(CWS)*.
Schaft *m* stock *(R)*; forearm *(automatic R)*; leg *(of a jackboot)*; rod, stem, handle, shank, shaft, stick.
Schaftpflegemittel *n* stock preservative *(R)*.
Schäkel *m* clevis, shackle.
Schalenbauweise *f* monocoque construction *(Ap)*.
Schalenkreuzwindmesser *m* cup anemometer *(Met)*.
Schall *m* sound.
Schallaufnahmegerät *n* oscillograph *(sound ranging)*.
Schallblech *n* diaphragm *(Tp)*.
Schalldämpfer *m* muffler *(MT)*; silencer *(Ord)*.
schalldicht soundproof.
Schalldose *f* pick-up unit *(phonograph)*.
Schallgeschwindigkeit *f* velocity of sound.
Schallmeßaufnahmegerät *n* oscillograph *(sound ranging)*.
Schallmeßbatterie *f* sound-ranging battery *(Arty)*.
Schallmeßfilm *m* oscillogram *(film)* *(sound ranging)*.
Schallmeßstelle *f* sound-ranging station *(Arty)*.
Schallmeßstellentrupp *m* sound unit *(sound ranging)*.
Schallmeßsystem *n* sound-ranging net *(Arty)*.
Schallmessung *f* sound ranging.
Schallmikrophon *n* sound-ranging microphone.
Schallmittel *n* sound-communication device.
Schallortung *f* sound location *(AAA)*.
Schallplatte *f* phonograph record.

Schallplatten-Abtastdose *f* phonograph pick-up unit, pick-up.

Schallverzug *m* sound lag *(AAA)*.

Schallwelle *f* sound wave.

Schalmesser *n* drawknife.

Schaltbrett *n* control panel, dashboard, instrument panel.

Schaltbrettlaterne *f* instrument light.

Schaltdom *m* gearshift-lever housing.

schalten to shift *(MT)*; to switch *(Elec)*.

Schalter *m* switch *(Elec)*.

Schaltgabel *f* shifter fork *(MT)*.

Schaltgetriebe *n* gearshift transmission *(MT)*.

Schalthebel *m* gearshift lever *(MT)*; throwout lever *(panoramic telescope)*.

Schaltkästchen *n* portable switchboard *(Tp)*; switchbox *(Elec)*.

Schaltkasten *m* switchbox *(Elec)*; combination switch box *(MT)*.

Schaltklaue *f* dog clutch member *(constant-mesh transmission) (MT)*.

Schaltmuffe *f* gearshift collar *(MT)*.

Schaltplan *m* circuit diagram.

Schaltschema *n* See **Schaltplan**.

Schaltskizze *f* See **Schaltplan**.

Schaltstange *f* shift rail *(MT)*.

Schaltstück *n* throwout *(sight-mount housing)*.

Schalttafel *f* control board, control panel, instrument panel.

Schalttisch *m* switchboard *(Tp)*.

Schaltung *f* connection *(Elec)*; circuit *(Rad, Tp, Tg)*; gearshift *(MT)*.

Schaltvorrichtung *f* switching device *(Elec)*.

Schalung *f* casing; form *(concrete construction)*; revetment.

Schandeck *n* gunwale *(Pon)*.

Schanzarbeiten *fpl* entrenchments, spadework *(field Ft)*.

Schanze *f* earthwork *(Ft)*.

schanzen dig, dig in, entrench.

Schanzkorb *m* gabion *(Ft)*.

Schanzzeug *n* entrenching tool(s).

scharf armed, live, primed *(Am)*; activated *(LM)*; sharp.

Schärfe *f* sharpness.

scharfe Munition live ammunition.

scharfe Panzermine activated anti-tank mine.

scharfe Patrone live cartridge, ball cartridge *(Am)*.

scharfgeladene Granate live shell *(Am)*.

scharf machen to arm *(Am)*; to activate *(a mine)*.

Scharfschütze *m* sharpshooter, sniper, marksman.

Scharfschützengewehr *n* sharpshooter's rifle.

Scharfschützennest *n* sniper's post.

scharf stellen to arm *(Am)*; to activate *(LM)*.

Scharmützel *n* skirmish.

Scharnier *n* hinge.

Scharte *f* port *(Tk)*; loophole, embrasure *(Ft)*.

Schartenblende *f* firing-port shutter *(Tk)*; gun shelter *(Ft)*.

Schartenschild *m* shield with sighting ports *(G)*; gun shelter *(Ft)*.

Schartensprengtrupp *m* pillbox demolition party.

Schatten *m* shadow.

Schattenriß *m* silhouette.

Schattenwirkung *f* shadow effect *(Cam)*.

schätzen to estimate.

Schätzung *f* estimation, estimate.

Schaufel *f* shovel.

Schauflug *m* demonstration flight *(Avn)*.

Schauloch *n* inspection hole.

Schauzeichen *n* visual signal.

Scheibe *f* disk, plate *(Tech)*; practice target; pane *(of glass)*; compass card.

Scheibenkupplung *f* plate clutch *(MT)*.

Scheibenrahmen *m* target frame.

Scheibenrose *f* compass card.

Scheibenstand *m* target butt.

Scheibentreffbild *n* vertical shot group *(Ballistics)*.

Scheibenwischer *m* windshield wiper.

Scheibenzuganlage *f* range unit with moving targets *(Tng)*.

Scheide *f* scabbard, sheath.

Scheider *m* separator *(storage battery)*.

Schein *m* card, ticket, certificate; illusion, deceptive appearance; light, blaze, flash, halo.

Scheinangriff *m* feint attack, feint, demonstration *(Tac)*.

Scheinanlage *f* dummy installation, dummy works.

Scheinflughafen *m* dummy airport.

Scheingas *n* fake gas.

Scheingefecht *n* mock combat, sham battle; feint, demonstration *(Tac)*.

Scheingraben *m* dummy trench *(Ft)*.

Scheinleitwert *m* admittance *(Elec)*.

Scheinmine *f* dummy mine.

Scheinplatz *m* dummy airfield.

Scheinsperre *f* dummy obstacle *(Ft)*.

Scheinstellung *f* dummy site, dummy position.

Scheinvergiftung *f* fake contamination *(CWS)*.

Scheinverneblung *f* deceptive smoke screen.

Scheinwerfer *m* headlight; searchlight, spotlight, projector.

führender Scheinwerfer carry light *(AAA)*.

Scheinwerferabteilung *f* searchlight battalion *(AAA)*.

Scheinwerferrichtungsweiser *m* control station *(AA SL)*.

Scheinwerferstellung *f* searchlight station *(AAA)*.

Scheinwiderstand *m* impedance *(Elec)*.

Scheitel *m* apex, summit, vertex, zenith.

Scheitelbogen *m* azimuth *(Surv)*.

Scheitelkreis *m* See **Scheitelbogen**.

Scheitelpunkt *m* apex, vertex, zenith.

Scheitelwert *m* peak value *(Elec)*.

Scheitelwinkel *m* vertical angle, opposite angle.

scheitern to be shipwrecked, run aground; fail, miscarry, be frustrated.

Schellband *n* hoop *(G)*.

Schelle *f* clamping collar *(Mort)*.

Schenkel *m* leg, thigh; side *(of an angle)*; leg *(of a tripod, etc.)*.

Scherbalken *m* ponton balk.

Scherdraht *m* shear wire *(fuze)*.

Schere *f* scissors, shears.

Scherenfernrohr *n* battery commander's telescope.

Scherfestigkeit *f* shearing strength.

Scherspannung *f* shear stress.

Scherwinkel *m* angle of yaw *(Avn)*.

Scheune *f* barn.

Schi *m* ski.

Schibataillon *n* ski battalion.

Schicht *f* course, layer, stratum; sheet, coating, film; working shift.

Schichtlinie *f* contour line.

Schichtwolke *f* stratocumulus cloud.

Schiebedach *n* sliding roof *(Ap)*.

schieben to push, slide, shove; to drift *(Avn slang)*.

Schieber *m* rear sight slide *(R)*; keeper *(R sling)*; slide; sleeve *(sleeve-type engine)*; slide rule.

Schiebermotor *m* sleeve-type engine.

Schieberwiderstand *m* rheostat.

Schiebeschnalle *f* slide buckle.

Schiebewind *m* cross wind *(Avn)*.

Schieblehre *f* vernier calipers.

Schiedsrichter *n* umpire *(maneuvers)*.

oberster Schiedsrichter director.

Schiedsrichteranweisung *f* instructions to umpires *(maneuvers)*.

Schiedsrichtergehilfe *m* umpire's aide.

Schiedsrichterstab *m* umpire staff.

schief oblique; biased; crooked; sloping, inclined.

schiefer Radstand cant *(Arty)*; misalignment of wheels *(MT)*.

Schieflaufende *f* rhumb line *(Navigation)*.

Schienbein *n* shin.

Schiene *f* rail; surgical splint.

Schienensperre *f* steel rail antimechanized obstacle.

Schießaufgabe *f* fire problem *(Arty Tng)*.

Schießauftrag *m* fire mission *(Arty)*.

Schießausbildung *f* training in firing.

Schießausbildungshilfe *f* marksmanship training aid.

Schießbahn *f* practice range.

Schießbaumwolle *f* guncotton.

Schießbecher *m* grenade launcher *(R)*.

Schießbedarf *m* ammunition requirements.

Schießbehelf *m* fire-control aid *(Gunnery)*.

Schießbremse *f* gun-wheel brake.

Schießbuch *n* score book.

Schießen mit Entfernungskommandos fire by command for range.

Schießen mit hohen Sprengpunkten air-burst registration fire.

Schießen mit Karte map fire *(Gunnery)*.

Schießen ohne Beobachtung unobserved fire *(Gunnery)*.

Schießen während der Bewegung assault fire *(automatic weapons)*.

Schießfertigkeit *f* marksmanship.

Schießgerät *n* firing equipment, practice-firing device *(Gunnery)*.

Schießgestell *n* firing stand *(MG)*.

Schießgrundlagen *fpl*   firing data *(Gunnery)*.

Schießhilfsmittel *npl*   means of fire control *(Gunnery)*.

Schießkladde *f*   battery emplacement book.

Schießklotz *m*   wheel chock *(Arty)*.

Schießlehre *f*   ballistics.

Schießlehrer *m*   gunnery instructor.

Schießlineal *n*   straightedge *(SR correction chart)*.

Schießliste *f*   battery chart.

Schießplan *m*   fire-control map *(Gunnery)*.

Schießplatz *m*   artillery range.

Schießpulver *n*   gunpowder.

Schießscharte *f*   loophole, embrasure.

Schießstand *m*   range, target range.

Schießstock *m*   projector rod *(Sig projector)*.

Schießtechnik *f*   firing technique.

Schießübung *f*   firing practice, range practice.

Schießunterlagen *fpl*   basic data *(firing)*.

Schießverfahren *n*   method of fire *(Arty)*.

Schießvorschrift *f*   firing regulations; gunnery field manual.

Schießvorschule *f*   basic training course *(Arty)*; elementary marksmanship training.

Schießwagen *m*   range car *(on target range)*.

Schießwesen *n*   gunnery.

Schießwolle *f*   *See* Schießbaumwolle.

Schiffahrt *f*   shipping *(Nav)*.

Schiffbau *m*   shipbuilding.

Schiffbauwerft *f*   shipbuilding yard.

Schiffbruch *m*   shipwreck.

Schiffsflak *f*   ship-based antiaircraft artillery.

Schiffslazarett *n*   sick bay.

Schiffsraum *m*   tonnage *(Nav)*.

Schiffsrumpf *m*   hull *(Nav)*.

Schiffstaucher *m*   diver *(Nav)* *See also* Torpedotaucher.

Schiffswerft *f*   shipyard.

Schiffswesen *n*   shipping *(Nav)*.

Schild *n*   signboard.

Schild *m*   shield *(G)*.

Schilderhaus *n*   sentry box.

Schildlager *n*   bracket seat *(G)*.

Schildstütze *f*   shield support *(G)*.

Schildzapfen *m*   trunnion *(G)*.

Schildzapfenlager *n*   trunnion bearing *(G)*.

Schildzapfenlagerdeckel *m*   trunnion cap *(G)*.

Schildzapfenpfanne *f*   trunnion socket.

Schippe *f*   shovel.

Schirm *m*   screen; visor *(of cap)*; parachute canopy, parachute; umbrella.

Schirmantenne *f*   umbrella antenna *(Rad)*.

Schirmeindecker *m*   parasol monoplane.

Schirmgitter *n*   screen grid *(Rad)*.

Schirmgitterröhre *f*   screen-grid tube *(Rad)*.

Schirmmütze *f*   service cap.

Schirrmeister *m*   maintenance technical sergeant.

Schirrunteroffizier *m*   maintenance sergeant.

Schlacht *f*   battle.

Schlächtereiabteilung *f*   butchery battalion.

Schlächtereizug *m*   butchery platoon.

Schlachtfeld *n*   battlefield.

Schlachtflieger *m*   close support airplane; ground attack airplane; pilot of close support airplane *(pl: support Avn)*.

Schlachtfliegerbombe *f*   fragmentation bomb.

Schlachtfliegerunterstützung *f*   close aviation support, support by ground attack airplanes.

Schlachtflotte *f*   battle fleet.

Schlachtflugzeug *n*   close support airplane, ground attack airplane.

Schlachtgeschwader *n*   ground attack and antitank wing, support aviation wing. *See also* Geschwader.

Schlachtkreuzer *m*   battle cruiser.

Schlachtlinie *f*   battle line.

Schlachtschiff *n*   battleship.

Schläfenband *n*   temple strap *(gas mask)*.

schlaff   slack.

Schlafsack *m*   sleeping bag.

Schlag *m*   shock, stroke, blow; pigeon loft; bay *(of a trench)*.

Schlagbolzen *m*   firing pin *(Ord)*; inertia pellet, inertia striker pellet *(fuze)*.

Schlagbolzenfeder *f*   main spring *(R)*; firing-pin spring *(pistol, fuze)*.

Schlagbolzenmutter *f*   cocking piece *(R)*.

Schlagbolzenspitze *f*   striker *(G. R.)*.

Schlagbolzen-Versager *m* hung striker *(fuze)*.

Schlägel *m* mallet; drumstick.

Schlägelstampfer *m* maul *(Tech)*.

schlagen to hit, knock, strike; to defeat; to build *(a Bdg)*.

Schlagfeder *f* firing-pin spring *(fuze)*.

schlagfertig ready for immediate action.

Schlagfertigkeit *f* readiness for action, state of tactical preparedness.

Schlagkraft *f* striking power *(Tac)*.

Schlagladung *f* booster, magazine charge *(fuze)*.

Schlagloch *n* pothole, road hole.

Schlaglot *n* hard solder.

Schlagring *m* brass knuckles.

Schlagschatten *m* shadow cast by an object *(as distinguished from shadow on the object itself) (Cam)*.

Schlagseite *f* list *(of a ship)*.

Schlagstift *m* striker *(fuze)*.

Schlagstück *n* hammer *(SA)*.

Schlagwort *n* slogan.

Schlagzünder *m* impact fuze, percussion fuze.

Schlagzündschraube *f* threaded percussion primer *(fuze)*.

Schlamm *m* mud.

Schlange *f* snake; spiral, coil, helix, worm.

Schlappe *f* reverse, defeat, setback.

Schlauch *m* hose, pipe, tube; inner tube *(MT)*.

Schlauchbinder *m* hose coupling *(MT)*.

Schlauchboot *n* pneumatic raft, pneumatic boat.

Schlauchbootfähre *f* pneumatic boat ferry.

Schlauchbrücke *f* pneumatic boat bridge.

Schlauchschoner *m* tire flap *(MT)*.

Schlaufe *f* keeper *(R sling)*; band, loop.

Schlechtwetter-Landedienst *m* station marker beacon service *(for Inst landing in bad weather) (Avn)*.

Schlechtwetterzone *f* bad-weather zone *(Met)*.

Schleichweg *m* hidden trail.

Schleier *m* screen *(Tac)*.

Schleife *f* loop *(Avn, Elec, etc.)*.

schleifen to grind, sharpen, abrade.

Schleifenflug *m* loop *(Avn)*.

Schleifmaschine *f* grinding machine *(Tech)*.

Schleifmittel *n* abrasive.

Schleifring *m* collector ring *(magneto)*; release ring *(clutch)*.

Schlenke *f* ravine, gully.

Schleppantenne *f* trailing wire antenna *(Ap)*.

schleppen to tow, drag.

Schlepper *m* tractor; tug *(Nav)*.

Schlepphaken *m* pintle *(Trac)*.

Schleppkahn *m* towed boat.

Schleppkante *f* trailing edge *(Ap)*.

Schleppkommando *n* glider-towing detachment, unit of tug airplanes.

Schleppschacht *m* inclined gallery *(Mining)*.

Schleppseil *n* See **Schlepptau**.

Schleppscheibe *f* tow target, towed-sleeve target *(AAA)*.

Schlepptau *n* trail rope *(Bln)*; tow rope, tow line.

Schleppwagen *m* beaching gear *(seaplane)*.

Schleppziel *n* flag target, towed-sleeve target *(AAA)*.

Schleppzug *m* column of tractors; train of barges.

Schleuder *f* catapult *(Avn)*.

Schleuderbund *m* sling lashing *(Engr)*.

Schleuderguß *m* centrifugal casting *(foundry)*.

Schleudermine *f* sling mine, sliding mine.

schleudern to skid, to slip, to catapult.

Schleuderstart *m* catapult take-off *(Avn)*.

Schleuderpsychrometer *n* sling psychrometer *(Met)*.

Schleuderthermometer *n* sling thermometer *(Met)*.

Schleuse *f* lock *(of a canal)*; sluice.

schließen to close, lock *(a door, etc.)*.

Schließender *m* file closer; trail officer *(MT column)*.

Schließfeder *f* main spring *(pistol)*; closing spring.

Schließkontakt *m* contact maker *(Elec)*.

Schließstelle *f* contact point *(Elec)*.

schlingern to roll.

Schlingerwand *f* baffle *(Ap tank)*.

Schlips *m* necktie.

Schlitten *m* sled; sleigh, sleigh mount *(MG)*.
Schlittenaufsatzstück *n* sleigh-mount extension piece *(MG)*.
Schlittenführer *m* sled driver.
Schlittenkufe *f* sled runner; sleigh-mount runner *(MG)*.
Schlittenstoßtrupp *m* assault detachment with sled-borne weapons and supplies.
Schlittenstütze *f* sleigh-mount leg *(MG)*.
Schlitz *m* slit; slot *(Ap wing)*.
Schlitzflügel *m* slotted wing *(Ap)*.
Schlitzquerruder *n* slotted aileron.
Schloß *n* lock; bolt mechanism, bolt assembly *(MG, R)*; castle.
Schlößchen *n* bolt sleeve *(R)*.
Schlosser *m* mechanic, locksmith, fitter.
Schloßfuß *m* bolt base *(MG)*.
Schloßgehäuse *n* bolt housing *(MG)*.
Schloßhalter *m* bolt support *(MG)*.
Schloßhebel *m* bolt handle *(MG)*.
Schloßkurbel *f* bolt shaft *(MG)*.
Schloßplatte *f* back plate *(G)*.
Schlot *m* smoke stack.
Schlucht *f* gorge *(Top)*.
Schlund *m* throat.
Schlupf *m* slip *(propeller)*.
Schlupfe *f* keeper *(R sling)*.
Schlupfjacke *f* sweater *(Clo)*.
schlüpfrig slippery.
Schluppe *f* See Schlupfe.
Schlußbesprechung *f* critique.
Schlüssel *m* key; cipher, code; wrench.
Schlüsselbolzen *m* locking pin *(limber)*; retaining pin or bolt.
Schlüsselgraben *m* main trench.
Schlüsselheft *n* code book.
Schlüsselkraftwagen *m* coding truck *(Sig C)*.
Schlüsselmaschine *f* converter, cipher device.
Schlüsselmine *f* key mine *(antivehicle mine laid as road block)*.
schlüsseln encode, encipher.
Schlüsselpunkt *m* key point *(Tac)*.
Schlüsselschieber *m* corrector pointer *(hand fuze setter)*.
Schlüsselstellung *f* key position *(Tac)*.
Schlüsseltext *m* cipher text.
Schlüsseltrupp *m* code section.
Schlüsselungsoffizier *m* cryptographer officer.

Schlüsselunterlage *f* encoding and decoding chart.
Schlüsselwort *n* cipher key.
Schlußklappe *f* disconnect drop *(Tp switchboard)*.
Schlußlicht *n* taillight *(MT)*.
Schlußzeichen *n* clearing signal *(indicating party has rung off)* *(Tp)*.
Schmalspur *f* narrow gage *(RR)*.
Schmalspurbahn *f* narrow-gage railroad.
Schmelzsicherung *f* fuse *(Elec)*.
schmiedbar malleable.
Schmiede *f* forge.
Schmiedeeisen *n* wrought iron, forged iron.
Schmierbüchse *f* grease cup; axle box.
schmieren to grease, lubricate.
Schmiermittel *n* lubricant.
Schmieröl *n* lubricating oil.
Schmierölpumpe *f* lubrication pump.
Schmierölschicht *f* oil film *(Mech)*.
Schmierplan *m* lubrication diagram.
Schmierpresse *f* grease gun.
Schmierstelle *f* lubrication point.
Schmierstoff *m* lubricant.
Schmierstoffanlage *f* lubricating system *(Mtr)*.
Schmierstoffbehälter *m* oil tank *(Ap)*.
Schmierstoffdruckmesser *m* oil pressure gage *(Ap)*.
Schmierstoffkühler *m* oil cooler.
Schmierstoffvorratsmesser *m* oil level gage.
Schmierung *f* lubrication.
Schmirgelleinwand *f* emery cloth.
Schmirgelrad *n* See Schmirgelscheibe.
Schmirgelscheibe *f* emery wheel.
Schnabel *m* beak, nose; launching nose *(Bdg)*.
Schnalle *f* buckle; gun sling hook *(R)*.
Schnecke *f* worm *(Mech)*.
Schneckenantrieb *m* worm drive.
Schneckengehäuse *n* worm-gear housing *(panoramic telescope)*.
Schneckenlenkung *f* worm and sector steering system *(MT)*.
Schneckenrad *n* worm gear *(MG, Mech)*.
Schneckenscheibe *f* spiral target *(Tng)*.
Schneckentrieb *m* See Schneckenantrieb.

Schneckenwelle *f* worm shaft.
Schnee *m* snow.
Schneefräsmaschine *f* rotary snow-plow.
Schneehemd *n* parka.
Schneehütte *f* igloo.
Schneekette *f* snow chain, skid chain *(MT)*.
Schneekufe *f* landing ski *(Ap)*.
Schneekufengestell *n* landing ski assembly *(Ap)*.
Schneeloch *n* snow pit.
Schneemann *m* "snow man" *(an improvised road marker constructed of blocks of snow)*.
Schneepflug *m* snowplow.
Schneereifen *m* snowshoe.
Schneeschuh *m* ski; snow boot, over-shoe.
Schneestauung *f* impacted snow.
Schneetreiben *n* snow flurries *(Met)*.
Schneewanne *f* boat-type runner *(placed under gun wheels for operations in deep snow)*.
Schneewolke *f* snow cloud *(Met)*.
Schneidbrennen *n* oxyacetylene cutting.
Schneide *f* edge *(of a bayonet, etc.)*.
Schneise *f* straight narrow clearing, forest aisle, firebreak; sector *(Air Navigation)*.
schneidig smart *(in appearance, deportment, etc.)*.
Schneidkluppe *f* stock *(die holder)*.
Schneidkluppe mit Schneidbacken stock and die.
schnell fast, quick, rapid, mobile.
Schnellablaß *m* quick release, jettisoning *(of fuel)*.
Schnelladeverschluß *m* rapid-fire breechblock *(G)*.
Schnelladung *f* emergency demolition charge.
Schnellboot *n* E-boat *(Ger)*, motor torpedo boat, speedboat.
Schnellbrücke *f* hasty bridge.
Schnelle Truppen Mobile Troops *(includes Tk Rgts, AT Bns, Panzergrenadier units, MG Bns, H-Cav Rgts, Div Rcn units, Mecz Rcn units and cyclist units)*.
Schnellfeuer *n* rapid fire, magazine fire.
Schnellfeuergeschütz *n* rapid-fire gun.
Schnellfeuerkanone *f* rapid-fire cannon.

Schnellfeuerwaffe *f* rapid-fire weapon.
Schnellgang *m* overdrive *(MT)*.
Schnellganggetriebe *n* overdrive transmission *(MT)*.
Schnellkampfgeschwader *m* ground attack and antitank wing *(Luftwaffe)*.
Schnellschuß *m* hasty shot *(firing)*.
Schnellsperre *f* hasty obstacle.
Schnellsteg *m* hasty footbridge.
Schnelltelegraph *m* teletype, teletypewriter, telegraph printer.
Schnellzünder *m* instantaneous fuze, nondelay fuze.
Schnitt *m* cut *(injury or wound)*; section, intersection; slice; bearing *(Navigation)*.
Schnittbildentfernungsmesser *m* split-field range finder.
Schnittlinie *f* secant; halving line *(coincidence range finder)*.
Schnittpunkt *m* point of intersection.
Schnittzeichnung *f* cut-away view *(sketching)*.
Schnur *f* rope, cord, twine, string.
Schnürbund *m* cord lashing, rope lashing.
Schnürleiste *f* rack stick *(for cord lashing)*.
Schnurrensattelgurt *m* web girth *(saddle)*.
Schnürschuh *m* laced shoe.
Schnürsenkel *m* bootlace, shoelace.
Schnürstiefel *m* lace boot.
Schokokola chocolate with kola *(Prcht ration)*.
schonen to spare, protect.
Schonganggetriebe *n* overdrive transmission *(MT)*.
Schöpfeimer *m* scoop *(excavator)*.
Schornstein *m* chimney, smoke stack.
Schott *n* bulkhead *(also spelled die Schotte)*.
Schotter *m* road metal, broken stone, gravel.
Schotterstraße *f* metalled road, gravel road.
Schottpanzerung *f* spaced armor.
Schraffen *fpl* hachures *(Surv, Top)*.
Schraffierung *f* See **Schraffen**.
schräg diagonal, oblique, inclined.
Schrägaufnahme *f* oblique aerial photograph.
Schräge *f* inclination; diagonal line; bevel *(Tech)*.

Schrägentfernung f slant range *(AA gunnery)*.

schräges Kreuz St. Andrew's cross *(used as road marker to indicate by-pass)*.

Schrägfahrt f movement at an angle *(ground target)*.

Schrägfeuer n oblique fire, flanking fire, enfilade.

Schräglage f bank *(Ap)*.

Schräglinie f diagonal.

Schrägnocke f inclined beveled cam *(Diesel engine)*.

Schrägstellung f tilt, lateral tilt.

Schranke f railroad gate; barrier.

Schränkung f dihedral *(Ap)*.

Schrapnell n shrapnel.

Schrapnellkugel f shrapnel ball.

Schrapnellmine f antipersonnel mine.

Schraube f screw *(Mech)*; propeller.

Schraubendruck m propeller thrust.

Schraubenantrieb m propeller drive.

Schraubenfeder f coil spring, helical spring, spiral spring.

Schraubenflugzeug n helicopter.

Schraubenganglenkung f cam and lever steering system *(MT)*.

Schraubenmutter f nut *(Tech)*.

Schraubenschlüssel m wrench.

Schraubenspindelrichtmaschine f elevating-screw-type elevating mechanism *(G)*.

Schraubensteigung f screw pitch; propeller pitch.

Schraubensteven m propeller post *(Nav)*.

Schraubenstrahl m slipstream *(Ap)*.

Schraubenverschluß m interrupted-screw-type breechblock *(G)*.

Schraubenzieher m screwdriver.

Schraubenzug m propeller thrust.

Schraubpfahl m screw-type post *(for obstacle construction)*.

Schraubstock m vise *(Tech)*.

Schreckladung f booby trap.

Schreckmine f booby mine.

Schreibeblock m writing pad.

Schreiber m clerk; yeoman *(Nav)*.

Schreibmaschine f typewriter.

Schreibstube f orderly room, office.

schriftlich in writing, written.

Schriftverkehr m correspondence.

Schritt m pace, step.

den **Schritt wechseln** to change step.

Schrittmesser m pedometer.

schroff steep *(Top)*.

Schrot m shot *(for shotgun)*.

Schrotgewehr n shotgun.

Schrotpatrone f shotgun shell.

Schrotsäge f ripsaw.

Schubkarren m wheelbarrow.

Schubkurbelverschluß m pusher-handle sliding-wedge-type breech-block *(G)*.

Schubstange f torque arm, torque rod; piston rod; connecting rod.

Schuh m shoe; boot *(SA scabbard or holster)*.

Schuhzeug n footgear.

Schulflugwesen n training aviation.

Schulflugzeug n training airplane, trainer.

Schulgefechtsschießen n battle service practice *(Arty)*.

Schulgefechtsschießstand m target range *(Arty Tng)*.

Schulschießen n record service practice *(Arty)*.

Schulschießstand m target range.

Schulter f shoulder.

Schulterdecker m semi-high-wing monoplane.

Schultergurt m shoulder strap *(gas mask carrier)*.

Schulterklappe f shoulder strap *(enlisted men's uniforms)*.

Schulterriemen m crossbelt *(Clo)*.

Schulterstütze f shoulder stock *(MG)*.

Schulterstück n shoulder strap *(officers' uniforms)*; shoulder piece *(MG)*.

Schulterwehr f traverse *(Ft)*.

Schulungskursus m training course, orientation course.

Schummerung f shading *(on maps)*.

Schuppen m shed, hangar.

Schupo f *See* Schutzpolizei.

Schürmanneisen n butt strap.

Schurzholz n trench timber, wooden revetment.

Schurzholzrahmen m gallery case *(Engr)*.

Schuß m shot *(discharge of fire-arm)*; round *(Am)*.

Schußbahn f line of fire; trajectory.

Schußbeobachtung f sensing, spotting, observation of fire *(Arty)*.

Schußbereich m range of gun; danger area *(on target range)*.

schußbereit ready to fire.

Schußbremse f recoil brake.

Schußebene f plane of departure, plane of fire *(Gunnery)*; plane of position at instant of firing *(AAA)*.

Schußelemente *npl* basic data, firing data *(Gunnery)*.

Schußentfernung *f* range.

schußfertig ready to fire; prepared for firing *(Am)*.

Schußfeld *n* field of fire.

Schußfeldlücke *f* gap in field of fire.

schußfest bulletproof; light shell proof.

Schußfolge *f* cyclic rate *(automatic fire)*.

Schußgarbe *f* sheaf of fire, cone of fire.

Schußleistung *f* shooting strength *(Ord)*.

Schußlinie *f* line of site, line of position *(Gunnery)*; line of future position *(AAA)*.

Schußrichtung *f* direction of fire.

Schußschneise *f* fire lane.

Schußseitenwinkel *m* firing azimuth.

schußsicher bulletproof; light shell proof.

schußsichere Deckung shellproof cover *(Ft)*.

schußsicherer Schlauch self-sealing inner tube, bullet-resisting inner tube *(tire)*.

schußsicheres Glas bulletproof glass.

Schußtafel *f* firing table, ballistic table.

graphische Schußtafel trajectory chart *(not to be confused with US graphical firing table)*.

schußtafelmäßig according to firing-table data, firing-table *(adj)*.

schußtafelmäßige Anfangsgeschwindigkeit standard muzzle velocity.

schußtafelmäßige Erhöhung firing-table elevation *(Gunnery)*.

schußtafelmäßige Flugzeit theoretical time of flight *(as indicated in firing table)*.

schußtafelmäßige Schußweite firing-table range *(Gunnery)*.

Schußverbesserung *f* firing correction *(Gunnery)*.

Schußwaffe *f* firearm.

Schußweite *f* range *(Gunnery)*.

Schußwerte *mpl* basic data, firing data *(Gunnery)*.

Schußwirkung *f* effect of fire *(Arty)*.

Schußzahl *f* number of rounds.

Schüttkasten *m* bomb magazine, "Molotov breadbasket" *(container with a number of small bombs)*.

Schüttwurf *m* salvo release *(bombing)*.

Schutz *m* cover, protection.

Schütz *m* relay *(Elec)*.

Schutzanlagen *fpl* protective works.

Schutzanstrich *m* camouflage paint (ing); protective paint(ing).

Schutzanzug *m* protective clothing *(CWS)*.

Schutzblech *n* fender, mudguard.

Schutzbrille *f* goggles.

Schütze *m* private *(Inf)*; rifleman; machine gunner *(Ap, etc.)*; marksman.

schützen to cover, protect; to support *(by fire)*.

Schützenabmarsch *m* rifle half squad *(Cav)*.

Schützenabzeichen *n* marksmanship badge.

Schützenauftritt *m* fire step *(Ft)*.

Schützenbank *f* *See* Schützenauftritt.

Schützenfeuer *n* rifle fire.

Schützengraben *m* fire trench, trench.

Schützengrabenspiegel *m* trench periscope.

Schützenhöhle *f* dugout.

Schützenkette *f* *See* Schützenlinie.

Schützenkompanie *f* rifle company *(Inf)*.

Schützenlinie *f* line of skirmishers.

Schützenloch *n* foxhole, rifle pit.

Schützenmine *f* antipersonnel mine *(abbr.* S-Mine).

Schützenmulde *f* skirmisher's trench, prone shelter, shallow rifle pit.

Schützennest *n* rifle-squad entrenchment, nest of riflemen *(Ft)*.

Schützenpanzer *m* *See* Schützenpanzerwagen.

Schützenpanzerwagen *m* armored personnel carrier.

Schützenreihe *f* squad column, file of riflemen.

Schützenrudel *n* rifle squad in grouped combat formation *(squad leader and light MG team forward, assistant squad leader and rifle team back, echeloned right or left)*.

Schützenschnur *f* marksmanship fourragère.

Schützenstand *m* gun position *(Ap)*.

Schützentrupp *m* rifle team *(riflemen of a rifle squad as distinguished from the light MG team)*.

Schützenzug *m* rifle platoon *(Inf)*.

Schutzgebiet *n* protectorate.

Schutzgitter *n* suppressor grid (*Rad tube*).

Schutzglas *n* bulletproof glass; protectoscope (*Tk*).

Schutzhülle *f* hood (*Am*).

Schutzimpfung *f* inoculation, vaccination.

Schutzmacht *f* protecting power (*PW*).

Schutzmann *m* policeman.

Schutzmittel *n* prophylactic.

Schutzmütze *f* crash helmet (*for Tk crew*).

Schutzpolizei *f* municipal police.

Schutzpolsterung *f* crash padding (*Tk*).

Schutzraum *m* shelter (*Ft*); air raid shelter.

Schutzsalbe *f* protective ointment (*CWS*).

Schutzscheibe *f* protectoscope (*Tk*).

Schutzschicht *f* burster course (*Ft*).

Schutzschild *m* shield, gun shield.

Schutzsieb *n* mechanical filter (*gas mask*).

Schutzstaffeln *fpl* elite guard of the Nazi party (*abbr.* SS). *See also* Waffen-SS.

Schutzwall *m* protective wall (*system of land defenses, as the* Westwall *on the western frontier of Germany*).

Schutzwallehrenzeichen *n* bronze medal awarded to workers excelling in the construction of German fortifications.

Schutzzaun *m* guard fence.

Schwachstrom *m* low voltage (*current*).

Schwaden *m* gas cloud, smoke cloud.

Schwadenschießen *n* gas or smoke shell fire (*Arty*).

Schwadron *f* troop (*Cav*).

Schwadronschef *m* troop commander (*Cav*).

Schwadronsführer *m* temporary troop commander, troop commander (*Cav*).

Schwadronstrupp *m* troop headquarters detail (*Cav*).

Schwalbennest *n* shoulder patch (*worn by bandsmen*).

Schwamm *m* sponge; mushroom.

Schwankung *f* fluctuation; variation; sway; oscillation.

Schwanz *m* tail; trail (*G*).

Schwanzblech *n* trail float (*G*).

Schwanzlandung *f* tail landing (*Avn*).

schwanzlastig tailheavy (*Avn*).

Schwanzsporn *m* tail skid (*Ap*); trail spade (*G*).

Schwarm *m* tactical formation of about five airplanes (*consists of two Ketten*).

schwärmen to deploy into line of skirmishers.

Schwarmkolonne *f* javelin formation of from 3 to 5 airplanes.

Schwarmwinkel *m* wedge formation of from 3 to 5 airplanes.

Schwarzpulver *n* black powder.

Schwebekreisvisier *n* pivoted ring sight (*AA*).

Schweberiemen *m* hip strap (*harness*).

Schwebstoff *m* nonpersistent chemical agent (*CWS*).

Schwebstoffilter *m* mechanical filter (*gas mask*).

Schwebstoffteilchen *n* nonpersistent chemical particle (*CWS*).

Schwebungsempfang *m* beat-frequency reception (*Rad*).

Schwebungsfrequenz *f* beat frequency (*Rad*).

Schwebungsfrequenzmesser *m* heterodyne frequency meter.

Schwebungslücke *f* *See* Schwebungsnull.

Schwebungsnull *f* zero beat (*Rad*).

Schwefel *m* sulphur.

Schwefelantimon *n* antimony sulfide (*Am*).

Schwefelnatrium *n* sodium sulfide.

Schwefelsäure *f* sulfuric acid.

Schwefeltrioxyd *n* sulfur trioxide (*CWS*).

Schwefelwasserstoff *m* hydrogen sulfide.

schwefligsaures Natrium sodium sulfite.

Schweige-MG. *n* ambush machine gun, concealed machine gun.

Schweigewaffen *fpl* concealed weapons which hold their fire until enemy has reached certain points.

Schweiß *m* sweat.

Schweißbrenner *m* welding torch.

Schweißelektrode *f* welding electrode, welding rod.

schweißen to weld.

Schweißer *m* welder.

Schweißnaht *f* welded seam.

Schweißtechnik *f* theory and practice of welding.

Schwelkerze *f* smoke candle *(CWS)*.

Schwelle *f* tie *(RR)*; sill *(Bdg)*; threshold.

Schwellenbahn *f* corduroy road.

Schwelljoch *n* trestle bent with sill *(Bdg)*.

schwenkbar traversable; rotatable; flexible *(MG)*.

Schwenkbereich *m* extent of traverse, total movement in traverse *(Ord)*.

schwenken to wheel, turn *(Tac)*; to traverse, to slew *(a gun)*.

Schwenkflügel *m* folding wing *(Ap)*.

Schwenkwinkel *m* angle of traverse *(Gunnery)*.

Schwenkung *f* pivoting or wheeling maneuver *(Tac)*; slewing, traversing motion *(of a gun)*.

Schwenkungspunkt *m* pivot *(Tac)*.

Schwenkungswinkel *m* angle of traverse *(Gunnery)*.

schwer medium *(Ord)*; heavy; grave, serious. *See also* schwerst-.

schwere Artillerie medium artillery.

schwere Kompanie heavy weapons company *(Mtz R Regt)*.

schwere Schwadron *f* weapons troop *(Cav)*.

Schwerkraft *f* force of gravity.

Schwerkraftstoff *m* Diesel fuel.

Schweröl *n* Diesel fuel.

Schweröl-Flugmotor *m* Diesel-type aircraft engine.

Schwerölmotor *m* Diesel engine.

Schwerpunkt *m* main effort, point of main effort *(Tac)*; center of gravity.

schwerst- heavy *(Ord)*; heaviest.

schwerste Artillerie heavy artillery.

Schwerverwundeter *m* serious casualty.

Schwesterwaffe *f* related arm, related branch of the service.

Schwimmdock *n* floating dock.

Schwimmer *m* float, pontoon *(Ap)*; float *(carburetor, gage, etc.)*.

Schwimmerflugzeug *n* floatplane.

Schwimmergehäuse *n* float chamber *(carburetor)*.

Schwimmergestell *n* float gear *(seaplane)*.

Schwimmernadel *f* float needle *(carburetor)*.

Schwimmerwagen *m* beaching gear *(seaplane)*.

Schwimmerwerk *n* float gear *(seaplane)*.

schwimmfähig capable of floating or swimming, amphibian.

Schwimmlastkraftwagen *m* amphibian truck.

Schwimmpanzerkampfwagen *m* amphibian tank.

Schwimmstabilität *f* flotation stability *(seaplane)*.

Schwimmwerk *n* float gear, floats.

Schwimmwerk für Landflugzeuge emergency flotation gear *(Avn)*.

Schwimmweste *f* life vest, "Mae West."

Schwindelgas *n* fake gas *(CWS)*.

schwinden fade *(Rad)*.

Schwingachse *f* flexible axle *(MT)*.

Schwinge *f* flexible shaft *(follow-the-pointer mechanism)*.

Schwingkreis *m* *See* Schwingungskreis.

Schwingschenkel *m* wheel spindle *(G)*.

Schwingung *f* oscillation *(Elec, Rad)*; vibration *(Mech)*.

Schwingungsdämpfer *m* vibration damper.

Schwingungserzeuger *m* oscillator *(Rad)*.

Schwingungskreis *m* oscillating circuit *(Rad)*.

Schwingungsweite *f* amplitude of oscillations *(Rad)*.

Schwingungszahl *f* number of oscillations, frequency *(Elec, Rad)*.

schwitzen to sweat.

Schwund *m* fading *(Rad)*.

Schwundausgleich *m* automatic volume control *(Rad)*.

Schwundwirkung *f* fading effect *(Rad)*.

Schwungkraft *f* centrifugal force.

Schwungkraftanlasser *m* inertia starter *(Mtr)*.

Schwungrad *n* flywheel.

Schwungscheibe *f* *See* Schwungrad.

Sechskantschraube *f* hexagonal-head screw.

Sechsradkraftfahrzeug *n* six-wheel motor vehicle.

See *m* lake **(die** See = *ocean or sea)*.

See *f* sea, ocean **(der** See = *lake)*.

Seeaufklärer *m* naval patrol airplane, patrol bomber, scout bomber.

Seeflieger *m* naval aircraft pilot; naval airplane, seaplane.

Seefliegerei *f* naval aviation.

Seefliegerhorst *m* seaplane base.

Seeflugwesen *n* naval aviation.

Seeflugzeug *n* naval airplane, seaplane.

Seehöhe *f* height above mean sea level.

Seekabel *n* marine cable.

Seekadett *m* midshipman.

Seekarte *f* hydrographic map.

Seele *f* bore *(Ord)*.

Seelenachse *f* axis of the bore.

Seelendurchmesser *m* caliber.

Seelenlänge *f* tube length, barrel length *(Ord)*.

Seelenmesser *m* star gage *(G)*.

Seelenrohr *n* tube, liner *(G)*.

Seelenwand *f* bore surface *(G)*.

Seelenweite *f* caliber.

seelische Wirkung moral effect *(Tac)*.

Seeluftstreitkräfte *fpl* naval aviation.

Seemeile *f* nautical mile *(1.853 km)*.

Seemine *f* submarine mine.

Seeminensperre *f* submarine mine field.

Seeenge *f* defile between lakes.

Seenotdienst *m* air forces sea rescue service.

Seenotflugkommando *n* air forces sea rescue command.

Seenotflugzeug *n* sea rescue airplane.

Seestreitkräfte *fpl* naval forces.

Seetransportübung *f* exercise in transportation by water.

seewasserbeständig salt-water resistant.

Seezünder *m* hydrostatic bomb fuze *(antisubmarine bombs and depth charges.)*

Segelflieger *m* glider, sailplane; glider pilot.

Segelflug *m* glide, gliding.

Segelflugzeug *n* glider, sailplane.

segeln to glide, soar; to sail.

Segelstellung *f* feathered position *(propeller)*.

Segeltuch *n* canvas.

Segler *m* glider; sail boat.

Segmentlenkung *f* worm and sector steering system *(MT)*.

Segmentstück *n* segment *(angle-of-site Inst)*.

Sehfehler *m* defect of vision.

Sehfeld *n* field of view *(Optics)*.

Sehklappe *f* peephole protector, lookout hole cover *(Tk)*.

Sehkraft *f* eyesight, vision.

Sehlinie *f* line of observation; line of sight *(Surv)*.

Sehne *f* tendon; chord.

Sehöffnung *f* peephole, lookout hole *(Ft, Tk)*.

Sehrohr *n* periscope.

Sehschärfe *f* eyesight, vision; focus.

Sehschärfeneinteilung *f* focusing scale *(Optics)*.

Sehschlitz *m* direct vision slot *(Tk)*; observation slit, lookout slit *(Ft)*.

Sehstreifen *m* sector of view *(from observation point to right and left ends of target)*.

Sehverbindung *f* visual communication.

Sehwinkel *m* angle of view.

Sehzeichen *n* visual signal.

seicht shallow *(water)*.

Seide *f* silk.

Seife *f* soap.

Seil *n* cord, rope, cable, line.

Seilbahn *f* overhead cable railway.

Seilbahnkommandotruppen *fpl* overhead cable railway troops.

Seilbremse *f* cable brake.

Seilfähre *f* cable ferry, rope ferry.

Seilrolle *f* cable drum.

Seiltrommel *f* cable drum.

Seilwinde *f* cable winch.

Seite *f* azimuth, direction *(Gunnery)*; side.

Seitenabgangsfehler *m* lateral jump *(Gunnery)*.

Seitenabstand *m* interval *(from left to right)*; displacement *(Gunnery)*.

Seitenabstand vom Richtpunkt angle of shift *(indirect firing)*.

Seitenabweichung *f* drift *(of a projectile)*; deflection *(Gunnery)*.

Seitenänderung *f* deflection change, deflection correction *(Gunnery)*.

Seitenansicht *f* side view.

Seitenbegrenzer *m* traverse stop *(G, MG)*.

Seitenbestimmung *f* sensing *(Rad direction finding)*.

Seitenbewegung *f* lateral movement.

Seitenblatt *n* skirt *(saddle)*.

Seitendeckung *f* flank guard, flank security *(Tac)*.

Seitenempfänger *m* azimuth indicator *(AA gun)*.

Seitenfehler *m* lateral error *(Gunnery)*.

Seitenfeuer *n* enfilade fire.

Seitenflosse *f* tail fin *(Ap)*.

Seitengewehr *n* bayonet.
"Seitengewehr, an Ort!" "Unfix, bayonets!"
Seitengewehrgriff *m* bayonet grip.
Seitengewehrhalter *m* bayonet stud *(R)*.
"Seitengewehr, pflanzt auf!" "Fix, bayonets!"
Seitengewehrtasche *f* bayonet scabbard.
Seitenhebel *m* traversing lever *(MG sleigh mount)*.
Seitenholm *m* side outrigger *(AA gun)*.
Seitenklappe *f* side door *(Tk)*.
Seitenleitwerk *n* rudder assembly *(Ap)*.
Seitenlicht *n* running light *(Ap)*.
Seiten-MG. *n* waist gun, side gun.
Seitenrampe *f* side-loading ramp.
Seitenrichtbereich *m* total movement in traverse *(G)*.
Seitenrichtfeld *n* extent of traverse, total movement in traverse *(G)*.
Seitenrichtfeld von 360° all-round traverse.
Seitenrichtfernrohr *n* azimuth tracking telescope *(height finder)*.
Seitenrichtkanonier *m* azimuth setter.
Seitenrichtmaschine *f* traversing mechanism *(G)*.
Seitenrichtrad *n* traversing handwheel *(G)*.
Seitenrichtschieber *m* deflection board *(Arty)*.
Seitenrichtschraube *f* traversing screw *(G)*.
Seitenrichtteilung *f* deflection scale.
Seitenrichttrieb *m* traversing drive *(G, Mort)*.
Seitenrichtung *f* azimuth, direction *(Gunnery)*.
Nehmen der Seitenrichtung laying for direction.
Seitenrichtwerk *n* traversing mechanism *(G)*.
Seitenrichtwinkel *m* angle of traverse, azimuth *(Gunnery)*.
Seitenruder *n* rudder *(Ap)*.
Seitenrutsch *m* side slip *(Avn)*.
Seitenschwankung *f* lateral sway *(Bdg)*.
Seitensicherung *f* flank security.
Seitensteuerung *f* rudder controls; lateral control.
Seitenstreuung *f* lateral dispersion, width of dispersion *(Arty)*.

Seitenteilring *m* azimuth scale *(AA gun)*.
Seitentrieb *m* traversing drive *(G)*.
Seitenverankerung *f* apron *(of double-apron fence)*.
Seitenverbesserung *f* deflection correction *(Gunnery)*.
Seitenverbindung *f* lateral communication *(Sig C)*.
Seitenverhältnis *n* aspect ratio *(Ap)*.
Seitenverschiebung *f* drift correction *(Gunnery)*.
Seitenvorhalt *m* lateral lead *(firing)*.
Seitenvorhaltebene *f* slant plane of lateral lead *(AA gunnery)*.
Seitenwagen *m* sidecar *(Mtcl)*.
Seitenwelle *f* jack shaft *(MT)*.
Seitenwind *m* cross wind.
Seitenwinkel *m* deflection angle *(Gunnery)*; horizontal angle *(Surv)*.
Seitenwinkelverbesserungsknopf *m* lateral correction knob *(AA gun)*.
Seitenwinkelvorhalt *m* lateral angular lead, lateral deflection angle *(AA gunnery)*.
seitlich abrutschen to fall off *(Avn)*.
seitlich einschwenken pivot to the left or right, fan out *(Tac)*.
Seitwärtsbewegung *f* yawing *(Ap)*.
Seitwärtseinschneiden *n* lateral resection *(Surv)*.
Sektor *m* sector; protractor.
Sekundärkreis *m* secondary circuit *(Rad)*.
Sekundärstrom *m* secondary current *(Rad)*.
selbständig independent.
Selbstantrieb *m* self-propulsion, automatic drive.
selbstdichtend self-sealing *(Ap tank)*.
selbsterregend self-exciting *(Rad)*.
Selbstfahrlafette *f* self-propelled mount, gun motor carriage.
Selbstinduktion *f* self-induction *(Elec)*.
Selbstinduktionsspule *f* self-induction coil *(Elec)*.
Selbstladeeinstecklauf *m* subcaliber barrel *(for semiautomatic weapon)*.
Selbstladegewehr *n* self-loading rifle, semiautomatic rifle.
Selbstladepistole *f* self-loading pistol, automatic pistol.
Selbstlader *m* self-loading rifle.
Selbstladewaffe *f* self-loading weapon, semiautomatic weapon.

Selbstretter *m* oxygen breathing apparatus.

Selbstschutz *m* self-defense; individual air raid precautions.

Selbstschutzmittel *n* prophylactic.

selbstsperrend self-locking.

Selbststeuergerät *n* automatic pilot *(Ap)*.

Selbststeuerung *f* automatic control.

selbsttätig automatic *(adj)*, automatically operated.

Selbstunterbrecher *m* automatic circuit breaker *(Elec)*.

Selbstvernebelung *f* smoke screening *(one's own troops and/or installations)*.

Selbstverstümmelung *f* self-mutilation.

Selbstverwaltung *f* self government *(PW)*.

Sendeantenne *f* transmitting antenna.

Sendebereitschaft *f* stand-by, readiness to transmit *(Rad)*.

Sendegerät *n* radio transmitter.

Sender *m* transmitter *(Rad)*.

Senderempfänger *m* transceiver *(Rad)*.

Senderöhre *f* transmitting tube *(Rad)*.

Sendestelle *f* transmitting station.

Sendung *f* shipment; transmission *(Rad)*.

Senfgas *n* mustard gas *(CWS)*.

Senkblei *n* plumb bob, sounding lead.

Senke *f* depression *(Top)*.

senken to depress *(a gun)*; to sink *(a shaft)*; to let down, to lower.

Senkfaschine *f* sunken fascine revetment.

Senkfaschinendamm *m* fascine-reveted dam.

Senkfeuer *n* plunging fire *(Arty)*.

Senkkasten *m* caisson *(Engr)*.

Senklot *n* See **Senkblei**.

senkrecht vertical, perpendicular.

Senkrechtaufnahme *f* vertical aerial photograph.

Senkrechtbild *n* See **Senkrechtaufnahme**.

Senkrechte *f* perpendicular *(line)*.

Senkrechtebene zum Zielweg vertical plane containing course of target *(AA gunnery)*.

senkrechte Gitterlinie Y-line *(of map grid)*.

senkrechter Abstand vertical interval.

senkrechtes Auftreffen normal impact *(Ballistics)*.

Senkrechtgeschwindigkeit *f* vertical speed *(Avn)*.

Senkrechtluftaufnahme *f* vertical aerial photograph.

Senkstück *n* sunken fascine mat or cribwork.

Senkungswinkel *m* depression angle *(G)*.

Serienschaltung *f* series connection *(Elec)*.

Servowirkung *f* servo action *(servo brake)*.

seßhafter Kampfstoff persistent chemical warfare agent.

Seßhaftigkeit *f* persistency *(CWS)*.

"Setzt die, Gewehre! Zusammen!" "Stack, arms!"

Setzwaage *f* builders' level *(Engr)*.

Seuche *f* epidemic, contagious disease.

S-Gerät *n* See **Suchgerät**.

S.-Geschoß *n* See **Spitzgeschoß**.

sicher safe.

Sicherer *mpl* security patrol(s).

Sicherheitsbestimmungen *fpl* safety regulations.

Sicherheitsdienst *m* security measures *(Tac)*; SS security service *(abbr.* SD).

Sicherheitsdraht *m* safety wire *(Ord)*.

Sicherheitsfunkenstrecke *f* safety spark gap *(magneto ignition)*.

Sicherheitsglas *n* safety glass, shatterproof glass.

Sicherheitshöhe *f* safe altitude *(Avn)*.

Sicherheitskoeffizient *m* factor of safety.

Sicherheitsmaß *n* clearance, safety angle *(Gunnery)*.

Sicherheitsmaßnahme *f* safety measure, security measure.

Sicherheitsoffizier *m* safety officer *(at target range)*.

Sicherheitspolizei *f* security police *(comprising* Kriminalpolizei *and* Geheime Staatspolizei).

Sicherheits- und Hilfsdienste *mpl* air raid protection services. *(Also called* Luftschutzpolizei).

Sicherheitsventil *n* safety valve.

Sicherheitszone *f* safety area *(Arty)*.

sichern to cover, protect, make secure *(Tac)*; to lock, to put at "safe" *(Ord, Am)*.

Sicherung *f* security, security detachment, covering party *(Tac)*; safety *(SA)*; safety lock *(fuze)*; safety device; fuse *(Elec)*.

Sicherungsabstand *m* security distance *(between march units)*.

Sicherungsauftrag *m* security mission *(Tac)*.

Sicherungsdienst *m* guard service *(Tac)*.

Sicherungs-Division *f* security division *(mobile* Landesschützen *units employed at rear area duties)*.

Sicherungsflügel *m* protective wing or flank *(Tac)*; interrupter *(Am)*.

Sicherungsflugzeug *n* escort airplane.

Sicherungshaken *m* release hook *(glider)*.

Sicherungshebel *m* grip safety *(pistol)*.

Sicherungskappe *f* safety device *(fuze)*; safety cap *(hand grenade)*.

Sicherungsklappe *f* interrupter *(Am)*.

Sicherungslinie *f* line of security.

vorderste **Sicherungslinie** outpost line.

Sicherungsmaßnahme *f* security measure.

Sicherungsmutter *f* lock nut.

Sicherungsschleier *m* screen *(Tac)*.

Sicherungsstift *m* safety pin *(fuze)*.

Sicherungsstück *n* safety lug *(on gun cradle)*.

Sicherungsvorrichtung *f* interrupter *(Am)*; safety device.

Sicherungsvorstecker *m* arming pin *(fuze)*; safety pin *(bomb)*.

Sicherungszuschlag *m* margin of safety *(firing)*.

Sicht *f* visibility.

Sichtabstand *m* interval permitting visual contact.

Sichtanzeigegerät *n* visual indicator *(Ap Inst)*.

sichtbar visible.

Sichtbarkeit *f* visibility.

Sichtbereich *m* radius of visibility.

Sichtberührung *f* visual contact.

Sichtdeckung *f* sight defilade; smoke and flash defilade *(Arty)*.

Sichtigkeit *f* visibility.

Sichtnavigation *f* contact flight, pilotage *(Air Navigation)*.

Sichtverhältnisse *npl* visibility conditions.

Sichtweite *f* radius of visibility.

Sichtzeichen *n* visual signal, panel signal.

Sickerschacht *m* drainage ditch, sump *(trench)*.

Sieb *n* screen, sifter, filter.

Siebkreis *m* series resonant circuit *(Rad)*.

Siebtrichter *m* filter funnel *(MT)*.

Siegel *n* seal.

Sieger *m* victor.

siegreich victorious.

Sielengeschirr *n* breast harness.

Signal *n* signal; bugle call.

Signalbombe *f* signal flare.

Signalbuch *n* signal book *(Nav)*.

internationales **Signalbuch** international code *(Nav)*.

Signalmittel *n* signal device.

Signalpatrone *f* signal cartridge.

Signalrakete *f* signal rocket.

Signalscheibe *f* signaling disk.

Signalstreifen *m* code panel *(Avn)*.

Signaltafel *f* code chart *(Sig C)*.

Signaltuch *n* code panel *(Avn)*.

Signalwerfer *m* ground signal projector, pyrotechnic projector.

Signatur *f* conventional sign *(on maps)*.

Simmerring *m* oil seal *(MT)*.

Simulant *m* malingerer.

simulieren malinger.

Simultanschaltung *f* simplexed connection *(Tg, Tp)*.

Sinkgeschwindigkeit *f* rate of drop *(Avn)*.

Sinn *m* sense, meaning; direction.

Sipo *f* See **Sicherheitspolizei**.

Sirene *f* siren.

sitzender Anschlag sitting position *(MG or R firing)*.

Sitzfallschirm *m* seat pack parachute.

Sitzriemen *m* seat strap *(saddle)*.

Skala *f* scale, dial.

Skalenring *m* micrometer *(angle-of-site Inst)*.

Skalenscheibe *f* angle-of-site scale *(Arty)*; dial plate, scale disk *(Rad)*.

Skizze *f* sketch.

S-Maske *f* See **Staubmaske**.

s.M.G.-Bedienung *m* heavy machine-gun squad.

s.M.G.-Zug *m* heavy machine-gun platoon.

S-Mine *f* antipersonnel mine *(abbr. of* Schützenmine*)*.

S-Mittel *npl* *See* **Standort-Beköstigungsmittel.**

S.m.K.Geschoß *n* pointed steel-core armor-piercing bullet.

S.m.K.L'spurgeschoß *n* pointed steel-core tracer bullet.

Sockel *m* pedestal, swivel *(G).*

Sockelgeschütz *n* swivel gun, pedestal-mounted gun.

Sockellafette *f* pedestal mount, swivel mount *(G).*

Sockelschaltung *f* socket connection *(Rad tube).*

Sog *m* suction.

Sohle *f* sole; bottom of trench.

Sold *m* pay.

Soldat *m* soldier, enlisted man.

soldatische Haltung military bearing.

Soldbuch *n* pay book *(soldier's individual pay record).*

Sollbestand *m* authorized basic allowance.

Sollstand *m* *See* **Sollstärke.**

Sollstärke *f* authorized strength.

Sollstelle *f* *See* **Planstelle.**

Solokrad *n* solo motorcycle.

Sommerweg *m* road shoulder.

Sonderanhänger *m* special trailer.

Sonderaufbau *m* special body *(MT).*

Sonderauftrag *m* special mission.

Sonderbataillon *n* special battalion, disciplinary battalion.

Sonderberichterstatter *m* visiting correspondent.

Sonderfahrzeug *n* special-purpose vehicle.

Sonderflugzeug *n* special-purpose airplane.

Sonderfrequenz *f* specially assigned frequency *(Rad).*

Sonderfrieden *m* separate peace.

Sonderführer *m* specialist *(includes interpreters, laboratory technicians, radio specialists, cameramen, etc., serving in the Ger armed forces, with nominal rank up to Bn commander but no actual Mil rank).*

Sonderfunkspruch *m* special radio message *(for Arty metro message and weather reports).*

Sondergasmaske *f* special gas mask.

Sondergespräch *n* special telephone call.

Sonderkriegsgericht *n* special court-martial.

Sonderlafette *f* special gun mount.

Sonderlastkraftwagen *m* special-purpose motor truck.

Sonderlaufbahn *f* specialist's career.

Sondermeldung *f* special message, special announcement *(Rad).*

Sondermunition *f* separate-loading ammunition; special-purpose ammunition.

Sonderstahl *m* special steel.

Sondertruppen *fpl* special units, special troops.

Sonderverband *m* special unit.

Sonderverfügungen *fpl* special orders.

Sonderverpflegung *f* special rations.

Sonderwaffe *f* special weapon.

Sonderzweck *m* special purpose.

Sondiernadel *f* probing rod *(for land mines).*

Sonnenblende *f* sun shield, sun shade.

Sonnengeflecht *n* solar plexus.

Sonnenstich *m* sunstroke.

Sonnenzeit *f* solar time.

spähen to scout.

Späher *m* scout, lookout.

Spähtrupp *m* patrol, reconnaissance patrol.

Spähtruppführer *m* patrol leader.

Spähtrupptätigkeit *f* patrol activity.

Spähtruppvorstoß *m* scouting raid.

Spähwagen *m* scout car.

s.Pak *f* heavy antitank gun.

Spalt *m* crack, split.

Spalte *f* slit; split; crevice, fissure; leak; column *(in tables).*

Spaltflügel *m* slotted wing *(Ap).*

Spaltring *m* split ring *(breechblock).*

Spaltrohr *n* collimator.

Spange *f* clasp *(decoration).*

Spanienkämpfer *m* veteran of Spanish Civil War.

spanischer Reiter knife rest, cheval-de-frise.

Spanndraht *m* tension wire, wire brace.

spannen to cock *(SA);* to stretch, strain, apply tension, tighten.

Spannfalle *f* firing pin trip *(breechblock).*

Spannfeder *f* cocking spring *(MG).*

Spannhebel *m* cocking lever *(G, MG).*

Spannlack *m* dope *(Ap).*

Spannrast *f* full cock *(SA).*

Spannriegel *m* cocking bolt *(breechblock).*

Spannschieber *m* cocking slide *(MG).*

Spannschloß *n* idler adjuster rod *(Tk)*; turnbuckle.

Spannschraube *f* threaded breech hoop *(G)*.

Spannstollen *m* cocking cam *(breechblock)*.

Spannstück *n* sear *(G)*; accelerator *(MG)*.

Spannturm *m* cabane *(Ap)*.

Spannung *f* voltage, tension *(Elec)*.

Spannungsabfall *m* voltage drop, potential drop.

Spannungs-Dehnungs-Diagramm *n* stress-strain diagram.

Spannungsmesser *m* voltmeter.

Spannungsregler *m* voltage regulator.

Spannungsschwankung *f* voltage variation.

Spannungssicherung *f* circuit breaker.

Spannungsteiler *m* voltage divider *(Rad)*.

Spannweite *f* span *(Bdg)*; wing span *(Ap)*.

Spannwelle *f* recocking shaft *(breechblock)*.

Spant *m* vertical frame, vertical ring, bulkhead frame *(Ap)*.

Spargelbeete *npl* asparagus-bed obstacle pattern.

Sparschaltung *f* autotransformer circuit *(Elec)*.

Sparstoff *m* scarce material, high-priority material.

Spartransformator *m* autotransformer *(Rad, Elec)*.

Spaten *m* spade, shovel.

Spätzerspringer *m* retarded burst.

Spätzündung *f* retarded ignition, retarded spark *(Mtr)*.

Speiche *f* spoke.

Speicher *m* storeroom.

Speiseleitung *f* feeder line *(Rad)*.

Speiseraum *m* mess.

Speisestrom *m* feeder current *(Elec)*.

Speisung *f* feed, feeding.

Sperrabschnitt *m* prohibited area; defense sector.

Sperrad *n* locking wheel *(gun cradle)*; ratchet wheel.

Sperramt *n* harbor-defense ordnance depot.

Sperrballon *m* barrage balloon.

Sperrballontruppen *fpl* barrage balloon troops.

Sperrdienst *m* obstacle-construction service.

Sperrdrache *m* barrage kite.

Sperre *f* block, obstacle, barrier, accessory defense; blockade, embargo; air alert, fighter patrol *(Avn)*.

Sperre aus Schienen steel-rail obstacle.

Sperre aus Stahlträgern steel-beam obstacle, structural-steel obstacle.

Sperre fliegen to fly on an air alert.

sperren to lock, to bar; interdict *(Tac)*; tune out *(Rad)*.

Sperrfeder *f* retard spring *(fuze)*; locking spring *(MG)*.

Sperrfeld *n* obstacle field.

Sperrfeuer *n* barrage, barrage fire.

Sperrfeuerskizze *f* barrage chart.

Sperrfeuerwand *f* curtain of antiaircraft fire.

Sperrfeuerzone *f* zone covered by barrage fire *(AAA)*.

Sperrgebiet *n* prohibited area, restricted area; blockade zone *(Nav)*.

Sperrhebel *m* locking lever *(G carriage)*.

Sperrholz *n* plywood.

Sperrholzzelt *n* plywood shelter.

Sperriegel *m* switch position, switch trench; locking bolt *(MG stock)*.

Sperrklinke *f* retaining catch *(breechblock)*; safety catch, pawl *(Mech)*.

Sperrkreis *m* tank circuit *(Rad)*.

Sperrlicht *n* barrier light.

Sperrlinie *f* obstacle line.

Sperrnase *f* catch *(fuze)*.

Sperrohr *n* outer steam tube *(MG)*.

Sperrstück *n* locking bolt *(pistol)*.

Sperrtrupp *m* obstacle-construction detachment; blocking party.

Sperrung *f* obstruction, blocking.

Sperrverband *m* obstacle-construction unit; blocking unit.

Sperrwachboot *n* boom defense vessel.

Sperrzone *f* obstacle zone.

spezifischer Bodendruck ground pressure per unit area *(MT)*.

spezifisches Gewicht specific gravity.

Spiegel *m* mirror; level mirror *(panoramic telescope)*; periscope; bull's-eye *(target)*; collar patch.

Spiegeldurchmesser *m* mirror diameter *(SL)*.

Spiegelentfernungsmesser *m* macrometer.

Spiegelfrequenz *f* image frequency *(Rad)*.

Spiegelhalter *m* mirror support *(MG prismatic sight)*.

Spiegelkreuzlibelle *f* reflector-type cross level *(panoramic telescope)*.
Spiegelneigungsmesser *m* Abney level.
Spiegelrahmen *m* mirror frame *(MG prismatic sight)*.
Spiegeltelegraph *m* heliograph, heliotrope *(Sig C)*.
Spiegelvisier *n* mirror sight.
Spiel *n* backlash, clearance, play *(Mech)*; game.
Spielmann *m* bandsman *(pl* Spielleute).
Spielraum *m* clearance, backlash.
Spieß *m* "top sergeant," "top kick."
Spill *n* winch.
Spindel *f* gear shaft *(elevating mechanism)*; spindle, pinion, mandril.
Spindellenkung *f* cam and lever steering system *(MT)*.
Spinne *f* multiple road junction; spider.
Spion *m* spy.
Spionage *f* espionage.
Spionageabwehr *f* counterespionage.
Spiralbohrer *m* twist drill.
Spiralfeder *f* spiral spring, helical spring.
Spiralfederausgleicher *m* spiral-spring equilibrator *(AA gun)*.
spitz pointed.
Spitze *f* point, advance guard point *(Tac)*; tip, peak, head.
Spitzengruppe *f* point squad; advance element *(Tac)*.
Spitzenkompanie *f* advance party *(in Adv Gd of large unit)*.
Spitzenpanzer *m* leading tank.
Spitzenwagen *m* leading car, "point" car *(MT)*.
Spitzenzug *m* advance platoon *(Armd Comd)*.
spitzer Winkel acute angle.
Spitzgeschoß *n* pointed bullet.
Spitzgeschoß mit Stahlkern pointed steel-core armor-piercing bullet.
Spitzhacke *f* pickax.
Spleißung *f* splice.
Splint *m* cotter pin, pin.
Splissung *f* splice.
Splitter *m* splinter, fragment.
Splitterbombe *f* fragmentation bomb, antipersonnel bomb.
Splitterdichte *f* density of fragments *(number of shell fragments per unit area)*.

Splittergraben *m* slit. trench, trench shelter.
Splittergranate *f* fragmentation shell.
Splitterring *m* fragmentation ring *(fits over casing of the* Stielhandgranate).
Splitterschutz *m* splinterproof protection *(Ft)*.
Splitterschutzbrille *f* protective goggles.
splittersicher splinterproof.
splittersichere Deckung splinterproof cover.
splittersicherer Unterstand splinterproof shelter.
Splitterwirkung *f* fragmentation, spray effect *(Am)*.
Sporn *m* tail skid *(Ap)*; trail spade *(G)*; spike *(MG tripod)*; spur *(Cav)*; gaff.
Spornarm *m* spade arm *(G)*.
Spornblech *n* spade plate *(G)*.
Spornkufe *f* trail-spade runner *(Arty operations in deep snow)*.
Spornrad *n* tail wheel *(Ap)*.
Spornschuh *m* tail skid *(Ap)*.
Spornteller *m* spike plate *(MG tripod)*.
Sportlehrer *m* athletic instructor.
Sprachfrequenzband *n* voice frequency band *(Rad, Tp)*.
Sprachrohr *n* megaphone.
Sprachübertragung *f* voice transmission *(Rad, Tp)*.
Sprechen *n* voice transmission *(Rad, Tp)*.
Sprechfunk *m* voice radio.
Sprechmaschine *f* phonograph.
Sprechschleife *f* loop circuit *(Tp)*.
Sprechspule *f* induction coil *(Tp)*.
Sprechstelle *f* telephone station.
Sprechtaste *f* push-to-talk switch *(Rad, Tp)*.
Sprechverbindung *f* telephone communication, telephone connection, telephone circuit.
Sprechverkehr *m* telephone traffic.
Sprechverständigung *f* talking range *(Tp)*.
Spreizklappe *f* split flap *(Ap)*.
Spreizlafette *f* split-trail gun carriage.
Spreizlafettenholme *mpl* trails *(of split-trail carriage)*.
Spreizlafettenschwanz *m* split trail.
Sprengbombe *f* demolition bomb, high-explosive bomb.

Sprengbrandbombe f combination incendiary-demolition bomb.

Sprengbüchse f explosive block (in container); demolition block.

Sprengdienst m demolition service.

sprengen to blast, blow up, detonate.

Sprengfalle f booby trap.

Sprengfüllung f filler charge (Am).

Sprenggegenstand m object to be blasted or demolished.

Sprenggerät n demolition equipment.

Sprenggeschoß n explosive projectile, explosive bullet.

Sprenggranate f high-explosive shell.

Sprenggranate-Patrone f high-explosive shell (fixed Am).

Sprenggrube f blasting pit (Engr).

Sprenghöhe f height of burst (Gunnery).

Sprengkabel n firing wire (blasting).

Sprengkammer f mine chamber (blasting).

Sprengkapsel f detonator (Am); blasting cap.

Sprengkapselröhrchen n detonator tube (hand grenade).

Sprengkapselsicherung f detonator safety (fuze).

Sprengkapselzünder m detonating-cord unit with blasting cap and fuze lighter.

Sprengkegel m spray (air burst).

Sprengkommando n bomb disposal unit; demolition party.

Sprengkörper m demolition block.

Sprengkraft f explosive force (Am).

Sprengladung f demolition charge, blasting charge (Engr); bursting charge (Am); burster (Cml shell).

Sprengladungsröhre f burster tube.

Sprengluft f liquid oxygen.

Sprengmittel n explosive (in prepared form, as distinguished from generic term Sprengstoff).

Sprengmunition O2 f TNT.

Sprengniete f explosive rivet.

Sprengöl n nitroglycerin, blasting oil.

Sprengölpulver n nitroglycerin powder.

Sprengpatrone f blasting cartridge (demolitions); explosive bullet.

Sprengplan m demolition plan.

Sprengpulver n blasting powder (black powder).

Sprengpunkt m point of burst (Gunnery).

hoher Sprengpunkt air burst.

mittlerer Sprengpunkt center of burst.

Sprengpunktentfernung f straight line from muzzle to point of burst (Gunnery).

Sprengring m retaining ring (gas mask).

Sprengsalpeter m nitrate explosive.

Sprengsatz m bursting charge (Am).

Sprengstange f charge-placing pole.

Sprengstelle f point of rupture, breaching point; demolition chamber (Bdg).

Sprengstoff m explosive.

Sprengstoffgehalt m amount of bursting charge (Am).

Sprengstoffüllung f explosive filler (Am).

Sprengstück n shell fragment, shell splinter.

sprengtechnisch pertaining to technical aspect of demolitions.

Sprengtrichter m crater, mine crater.

Sprengtrupp m demolition squad.

Sprengung f demolition, blasting.

Sprengweite f horizontal distance between point of air burst and theoretical point of impact (Gunnery).

Sprengwerk n inverted truss; strutbraced construction (Engr).

Sprengwirkung f burst effect (Am).

Sprengzünder m detonating fuze (Am).

Spreutlage f brushwork revetment.

Springschreiber m a type of telegraph printer.

Spritzdüse f spray nozzle (carburetor).

Spritzer m splash.

Spritzschlauch m spray nozzle.

Spritzumlaufschmierung f splash lubrication (Mtr).

Spritzweite f range (of a flame thrower).

Spruch m message (Tp, Rad); call (Tp); sentence, verdict.

Sprühbüchse f chemical tank for spray contamination.

Sprühpistole f spray gun (lubrication).

Sprühregen m drizzle (Met).

Sprung m bound, rush (Tac); jump (Prcht); crack, split.

Sprunggelenk n hock (horse).

Sprungkombination *f* parachute jump suit.

Sprungturm *m* controlled tower *(Prcht jump Tng).*

sprungweise by bounds, by rushes.

sprungweises Vorgehen advance by bounds.

Spulensatz *m* set of coils, coil unit *(Rad).*

Spur *f* trail, path; scent *(for messenger dogs);* track *(of road);* gage *(RR);* trace *(of a tracer bullet).*

Spürbüchse *f* gas-detector set container.

Spürfähnchen *n* gas-detection flag, gas-warning flag.

Spurgeschoß *n* tracer projectile.

Spürhund *m* tracking dog, bloodhound.

Spürmittel *npl* gas-detection equipment.

Spürpapier *n* gas-detection paper.

Spürpulver *n* gas-detection powder.

Spurpunkt *m* caster-angle vertex *(point at which line through inclined kingpin touches road) (MT).*

Spurstange *f* tie rod *(MT).*

Spurstangenhebel *m* steering-knuckle arm *(MT).*

Spurtafel *f* treadway, duckboard *(Bdg).*

Spurtafelbrücke *f* duckboard treadway bridge.

Spurweite *f* track, tread *(MT);* gage *(RR).*

S.-Rolle *f* barbed-wire concertina *(abbr. of* Stacheldraht-Rolle).

SS *f* elite guard of the Nazi party *(originally abbr. of* Schutzstaffeln *but now used as independent term; combat units of* SS *are known as* Die Waffen-SS, *The* SS *Armed Forces).*

SS-Abschnitt *m* SS area. *See also* **SS-Oberabschnitt.**

SS-Anwärter *m* candidate for rank of SS private.

SS-Brigade *f* SS brigade.

SS-Brigadeführer *m* SS brigadier general.

SS-Führer *m* SS officer.

SS-Gebirgs-Division *f* SS mountain division.

SS-Grenadier *m* SS private *(Inf).*

SS-Gruppenführer *m* SS major general.

SS-Hauptscharführer *m* SS master sergeant.

SS-Hauptsturmführer *m* SS captain.

SS-Heeres-Flakdivision *f* SS anti-aircraft artillery division.

SS-Junker *m* SS cadet *(officer candidate).*

SS-Junkerschule *f* SS officer training school.

SS-Kanonier *m* SS private *(Arty).*

SS-Kavallerie *f* SS cavalry.

SS-Kradschützen-Bataillon *n* SS motorcycle battalion.

SS-Kriegsberichter *m* SS war correspondent.

SS-Legionär *m* non-German SS man.

SS-Leibstandarte *f* SS Bodyguard Regiment *(formerly Hitler's bodyguard; increased to approximately division strength in 1943).*

SS-Mann *m* SS private.

SS-Nachrichtensturm *m* SS communication company.

SS-Oberabschnitt *m* SS region *(corresponds in most cases to a* Wehrkreis *and is composed of 2 or 3* SS-Abschnitte, SS *areas).*

SS-Oberführer *m* SS brigadier general *(below* SS-Brigadeführer).

SS-Obergruppenführer *m* SS lieutenant general.

SS-Oberscharführer *m* SS first sergeant.

SS-Oberschütze *m* SS private first class.

SS-Oberstgruppenführer *m* SS general.

SS-Obersturmbannführer *m* SS lieutenant colonel.

SS-Obersturmführer *m* SS first lieutenant.

SS-Panzergrenadier *m* SS private *(Armd Inf).*

SS-Panzergrenadier-Division *f* SS armored infantry division.

SS-Panzergrenadier-Regiment *n* SS armored infantry regiment.

SS-Panzerkorps *n* SS armored corps. *See also* **Germanisches SS-Panzerkorps.**

SS-Panzerjäger-Abteilung *f* SS anti-tank battalion.

SS-Panzerschütze *m* SS private in armored unit.

SS-Pionier *m* SS engineer.

SS-Pionierbataillon *n* SS engineer battalion.

SS-Pionier-Stoßtrupp *m* SS engineer assault detachment.

SS-PK.-Kriegsberichter *m* SS propaganda-company war correspondent.
SS-Polizei-Bataillon *n* SS police battalion.
SS-Polizei-Division *f* SS police division.
SS-Reiterei *f* SS horse cavalry.
SS-Rottenführer *m* SS corporal.
SS-Scharführer *m* SS staff sergeant.
SS-Schütze *m* SS private, SS rifleman.
SS-Sicherheitsdienst *m* SS security service.
SS-Standarte *f* SS regiment.
SS-Standartenführer *m* SS colonel.
SS-Standartenjunker *m* a graduate from *SS-Junkerschule*.
SS-Sturmbannführer *m* SS major.
SS-Sturmmann *m* SS private first class.
S-Stellung *f* dummy position *(abbr. of* Scheinstellung).
SS-Totenkopf-Verbände *mpl* SS "Death's Head" units *(primarily used as concentration camp guards and for terrorizing missions)*.
SS-Unterscharführer *m* SS sergeant.
SS-Untersturmführer *m* SS second lieutenant.
Staat *m* state, country, power.
Staatsangehörigkeit *f* nationality, citizenship.
Staatsbesitz *m* government property.
Staatsbürger *m* citizen.
Staatspolizei *f* *See* **Geheime Staatspolizei.**
Stab *m* staff; headquarters; headquarters personnel; bar, rod.
Stabantenne *f* rod antenna, "buggywhip" antenna *(Rad)*.
Stabbrandbombe *f* stick-type incendiary bomb.
Stäbchenpulver *n* cord powder, strip powder *(Am)*.
Stabilisierungsfläche *f* stabilizing surface *(Ap)*.
Stabilisierungsflügel *m* fin *(bomb)*.
Stabilisierungswulst *m* stabilizer lobe *(Bln)*.
Stabilität *f* stability.
Stabo *f* *See* **Stachelbombe.**
Stabsapotheker *m* pharmacist official *(ranking as captain)*.
Stabsarzt *m* captain *(Med)*.
Stabsbatterie *f* headquarters battery *(Arty)*.
Stabsbefehl *m* staff order.

Stabschef *m* chief of staff.
Stabsfeldwebel *m* master sergeant, regimental sergeant major.
Stabsgefreiter *m* staff lance corporal *(no US equivalent)*.
Stabshelferin *f* woman clerk auxiliary.
Stabs-Kette *f* headquarters flight *(three planes)*.
Stabskompanie *f* headquarters company.
Stabskraftwagen *m* staff car.
Stabsoffizier *m* field officer *(officer of field grade)*; staff officer *(Nav)*.
Stabsordonnanz *f* headquarters orderly.
Stabsquartier *n* headquarters; officers' quarters.
Stabsschiedsrichter *m* umpire at headquarters of a unit *(maneuvers)*.
Stabsschreiber *m* headquarters clerk.
Stabsveterinär *m* captain *(Vet)*.
Stabswache *f* headquarters guard.
Stabswachtmeister *m* master sergeant, regimental sergeant major *(Arty, Cav)*.
Stabszahlmeister *m* paymaster official *(ranking as captain)*.
Stachelbombe *f* bomb with nose spike.
Stacheldraht *m* barbed wire.
Stacheldrahthindernis *n* barbed-wire obstacle.
Stacheldrahtverhau *m* barbed-wire entanglement.
Stacheldrahtzaun *m* double-apron entanglement *(Ft)*.
Stadtkommandantur *m* garrison, post, or station headquarters in a city or large town; military government headquarters in a city or large town.
Stafetten *fpl* relay messengers.
Staffel *f* echelon *(Tac, Adm)*; squadron *(9 to 12 planes)*; section *(Arty, Cav, supply)*.
Staffelform *f* squadron formation *(Avn)*.
Staffelfront *f* squadron line of flight wedges *(Avn)*.
Staffelführer *m* echelon commander; squadron commander *(Avn)*; section leader or commander *(Arty, Cav, supply)*.
Staffelkapitän *m* squadron commander *(Avn)*.
Staffelkeil *m* squadron wedge formation of flight wedges *(Avn)*.

Staffelkolonne *f* squadron javelin formation *(Avn)*.

Staffellinie *f* squadron line formation *(Avn)*.

Staffeltrupp *m* section personnel *(Cav heavy MG section)*.

Staffelung *f* echelonment; stagger *(Ap wings)*; gun displacement *(Arty)*.

Staffelverband *m* squadron formation *(Avn)*.

staffelweise in echelon, by echelon.

Staffelwinkel *m* squadron V-formation *(Avn)*.

Stahl *m* steel.

Stahlblech *n* sheet steel.

Stahlbrücke *f* steel bridge.

Stahldrahtbeklöppelung *f* steel wire armor *(armored cable)*.

Stahlfederring *m* lockwasher.

Stahlflasche *f* steel flask, steel cylinder, steel tank.

Stahlfutter *n* steel bushing *(breechblock wedge)*.

Stahlgurt *m* metallic link belt *(MG)*.

Stahlhelm *m* steel helmet.

Stahligel *m* steel hedgehog antitank obstacle.

Stahlkerngeschoß *n* steel-core bullet, armor-piercing bullet.

Stahllegierung *f* steel alloy.

Stahlmeßband *n* steel measuring tape.

Stahlplatte *f* steel plate.

Stahlröhre *f* metal tube *(Rad)*.

Stahlschwelle *f* steel plank *(Engr)*; steel tie *(RR)*.

Stahlspurbahn *f* steel treadway *(Engr)*.

Stahlstraße *f* steel landing strip.

Staken *n* punting *(with punt pole)*.

Stalag *n* See **Stammlager.**

Stall *m* stable.

Stallhalfter *f* halter headstall *(harness)*.

Stammannschaft *f* cadre personnel.

Stammeinheit *f* parent unit.

Stammkompanie *f* cadre company *(for replacements)*.

Stammlager *n* permanent prisoner-of-war camp for NCO's and privates, base camp for prisoner-of-war labor detachments *(abbr. Stalag)*.

Stammleitung *f* trunk line, trunk circuit *(Tp)*.

Stammrolle *f* personnel roster.

Stammtafel *f* record sheet showing the formations to which a unit has belonged.

Stammtruppe *f* cadre.

Stammtruppenteil *m* parent unit.

Stampfwinkel *m* angle of pitch *(Ap)*.

Stand *m* status, state, occupation; position, station *(of crew members)* *(Ap, Tk, Nav)*; gun position.

Standarte *f* standard; guidon *(Arty, Cav, Armd Comd)*. See also SS-Standarte.

Standartenführer *m* See SS-Standartenführer.

Standartenträger *m* guidon *(Pers)*.

Stander *m* pennant.

Ständer *m* bracket, mount, support, stand, pedestal.

Standgericht *n* summary court-martial.

ständig constant, fixed.

ständige Befestigung permanent fortification.

ständige Belastung basic load *(Avn)*.

Standlinie *f* base line *(Surv)*; line of position *(Navigation)*.

Standmotor *m* upright engine.

Standort *m* post, garrison, station; position *(Surv, Navigation)*.

gekoppelter Standort dead-reckoning position *(Air Navigation)*.

Standortältester *m* garrison, post, or station commander.

Standortarzt *m* station surgeon.

Standortkommandantur *f* garrison, post, or station headquarters.

Standortlazarett *n* post hospital, station hospital.

Standortlohnstelle *f* army post pay office.

Standortmeldung *f* position report *(Air Navigation)*.

Standort-Pferdelazarett *n* veterinary station hospital.

Standortwachdienst *m* interior guard duty.

Standrecht *n* martial law.

Standsack *m* hand-grenade bag.

Standsicherheit *f* stability; steadiness *(of mobile gun mount, vehicle, etc.)*.

Standvisier *n* battle sight *(R)*.

Stange *f* pole, post, pillar, bar, rod, spar.

Stangenbau *m* line construction on poles *(Tp)*.

Stangenbild *n* pole-location diagram *(Tp)*.

Stangenbock *m* spar trestle *(Bdg)*.

Stangenhandpferd *n* off horse of wheel team.

Stangenpferde *npl* wheel team.

Stangenvisier *n* pillar-type rear sight *(MG)*.

Stangenvisiereinrichtung *f* MG sights *(blade front sight and pillar-type rear sight)*.

Stanze *f* die *(for stamping or punching)*.

Stapel *m* pile *(regular heap)*; dump; crib *(Bdg)*; launching cradle.

Stapellauf *m* launching *(Nav)*.

Stärke *f* strength.

Stärkebestand *m* actual strength.

Stärkenachweisung *f* table of organization; strength return, strength report.

Starkstrom *m* high voltage *(current)*.

Starkstromleitung *f* power line *(Elec)*.

Starkstromsperre *f* electrified obstacle, high-tension obstacle.

starr stiff, fixed, rigid.

starre Kanone fixed gun *(Ap)*.

starres Luftschiff rigid airship.

starres Maschinengewehr fixed machine gun.

Start *m* take-off *(Avn)*; take-off point *(Adrm)*.

Startbahn *f* runway.

Startbereitschaft *f* ground alert *(Avn)*.

Startdruck *m* propeller thrust at take-off *(Avn)*.

starten to start, to take off.

Starterbatterie *f* starter battery *(MT)*.

Starterklappe *f* choke *(Mtr)*.

Startflagge *f* starter flag *(Avn)*.

Startkatapult *m* catapult *(Avn)*.

startklar ready for take-off *(Avn)*.

Startlänge *f* take-off distance *(Avn)*.

Startleistung *f* power output of engine at take-off *(Avn)*.

Startschiene *f* track *(catapult)*.

Startseil *n* towline *(glider)*.

Startstelle *f* take-off point *(Adrm)*.

Startvorrichtung *f* launching device *(Avn)*; starting device *(Mtr)*.

Startzone *f* take-off zone *(Adrm)*.

statische Berechnung stress analysis.

Stativ *n* tripod, stand.

Statoskop *n* rate-of-climb indicator, climb-and-dive indicator *(Ap)*.

Stau *m* indicated air speed *(Avn)*.

Stauanlage *f* dam.

Staub *m* dust.

Staubdeckel *m* dust cover *(Ord)*.

Stäubchen *n* cloud particle, dust particle *(CWS)*.

Staubmaske *f* respirator, dust-filtering mask.

Staubschutzdeckel *m* dust cover *(Ord)*.

Staubschutzgerät *n* respirator.

Staubschutzmaske *f* See **Staubmaske**.

Stauchlafette *f* telescopic carriage, retractable gun mount.

Staudamm *m* storage dam.

Staudruck *m* dynamic pressure, velocity pressure.

Staudruckfahrtmesser *m* pitot tube.

stauen to stow; to dam up.

Stauer *m* stevedore.

Staufläche *f* area of dammed water.

Stauhöhe *f* height of upstream water.

Stausee *m* reservoir.

Stauwehr *n* weir.

Stecher *m* hair trigger *(SA)*.

Stechruder *n* paddle.

Stechschritt *m* goose step.

Stechzirkel *m* dividers.

Steckdose *f* jack, receptacle, socket.

Stecker *m* plug *(Elec)*.

Steckerstift *m* plug prong *(Elec)*.

Steckmast *m* sectional antenna mast.

Stecknadel *f* pin, plain pin.

Steckschlüssel *m* socket wrench; ignition key.

Steg *m* footbridge, footpath; web *(of girder, etc.)*.

Stegblech *n* web *(of girder, etc.)*.

stehender Spähtrupp stationary patrol.

stehendes Heer standing army.

stehendes Ziel stationary target.

steifer Wind high wind.

Steigbö *f* ascending gust *(Met)*.

Steigbügel *m* stirrup.

Steigeisen *npl* ice creepers; climbers *(Sig C)*.

steigen to climb.

Steigerung *f* intensification, increase.

Steigfähigkeit *f* grade-ascending ability *(vehicles)*; climbing ability *(Ap)*.

Steigflug *m* climb *(Avn)*.

Steighöhe *f* height of rise *(ground signal)*; altitude, ceiling *(Ap)*.

Steigleistung *f* rate of climb *(Avn)*.

Steigriemen *m* stirrup strap.

Steigung *f* gradient, grade, slope; pitch *(Mech.)*

Steigungswinkel *m* blade angle *(propeller)*; gradient angle.

Steigvermögen *n* climbing ability *(Ap)*.

Steigzeit *f* rate of climb *(Ap)*.

steil steep.

Steilfeuer *n* high-angle fire.

Steilfeuergeschütz *n* high-angle gun.

Steilfeuerwaffe *f* high-angle weapon.

Steilhang *m* steep slope, steep grade.

Steilheit *f* steepness; transconductance, mutual conductance *(Rad)*.

Steilkurve *f* steep banked turn *(Avn)*.

Steinbruch *m* quarry.

Steinflachs *m* asbestos.

Steinkohle *f* anthracite coal.

Steinschlag *m* broken stone, rubble; rock slide.

Steinschotter *m* road metal, broken stone.

Stellbecher *m* mouth of fuze setter.

Stelle *f* point, post, site, station.

Stellmarke *f* index, micrometer index *(Optics)*.

Stellmutter *f* lock nut, regulating nut, adjusting nut.

Stellring *m* adjusting ring *(fuze)*.

Stellschlüssel *m* fuze wrench; adjusting wrench.

Stellschraube *f* set screw, regulating screw, adjusting screw.

Stellung *f* position, emplacement.

Stellungnahme *f* commentary *(Tac)*; expression of opinion.

Stellungsabschnitt *m* sector of occupied position.

Stellungsbau *m* construction of field fortifications.

Stellungskampf *m* position warfare, combat from fortified positions.

Stellungskrieg *m* war of position, position warfare.

Stellungsmeßblatt *n* battery survey chart.

Stellungsunterschied *m* perpendicular distance between two parallel lines of sight *(such as that between the line: base point—aiming circle and the line parallel to it running through the base piece)*.

Stellungswechsel *m* change of position *(Tac)*; gun displacement *(Arty)*.

stellvertretend acting, deputy *(adj)*.

Stellvertretender Chef des Generalstabes Deputy Chief of Staff.

stellvertretender Führer second-in-command.

Stellvertreter *m* deputy; substitute.

Stellwerk *n* switch tower, switch control room *(RR)*.

Stempel *m* stamp, seal; punch *(Tech)*.

Stempelkissen *n* stamp pad.

Stempelplatte *f* inspection-mark plate *(R)*.

Sterbegeld *n* gratuity upon death.

Sternbild *n* constellation.

Sternbündel *n* star cluster *(signal)*.

Sternmotor *m* radial engine.

Sternplatte *f* multiple-connection plate *(stadia rod)*.

Sternschaltung *f* Y-connection *(Elec)*.

Sternsignal *n* signal flare.

Sternverkehr *m* "star" traffic *(radio net traffic in which several stations communicate only one at a time with the net control station, the other stations listening in)*.

Sternwarte *f* observatory.

stetig constant, steady, uniform, continuous.

Steuer *n* control, steering wheel.

Steuer *f* tax.

Steuerbord *m* starboard.

Steuerfläche *f* control surface *(Ap)*; stabilizing fin *(Mort shell)*.

Steuerflügel *m* stabilizing fin *(bomb)*.

Steuergitter *n* control grid *(Rad tube)*.

Steuerhebel *m* elevator control lever *(Ap)*.

Steuerknüppel *m* control stick *(Ap)*.

Steuerkompaß *m* steering compass.

Steuerkurs *m* heading *(Air Navigation)*.

steuern steer, control.

Steuerorgane *npl* controls *(Ap)*.

Steuerrad *n* control wheel *(Ap)*; steering wheel *(MT)*; timing gear *(Mtr)*.

Steuerröhre *f* master oscillator tube *(Rad)*.

Steuerruder *n* rudder *(ship)*.

Steuersack *m* rudder lobe *(Bln)*.

Steuersäule *f* control column *(Ap)*; steering column *(MT)*.

Steuersender *m* master oscillator *(Rad)*.

Steuerstrich *m* lubber line *(Ap compass)*.

Steuerstufe *f* master oscillator stage *(Rad)*.

Steuerung *f* controls *(Ap)*; timing, synchronization *(Mtr)*; steering system *(MT)*.

Steuerwelle *f* control shaft *(Ap)*; camshaft *(Mtr)*.

Steven *m* stem or stern *(Nav)*.

Stich *m* thrust, stab; stitch; bite, sting; hitch, knot.

Sticheisen *n* cutting spade *(Engr)*.

Stichgleis *n* firing spur *(RR Arty)*.

Stichprobe *f* sample taken at random.

Stichwaffe *f* thrusting weapon.

Stichwort *n* cue; catchword; code word.

Stichzähler *m* tachometer *(Ap)*.

Stickstoff *m* nitrogen.

Stickstofflost *n* nitrogen mustard gas.

Stiefel *m* boot.

Stiefelschaft *m* leg of boot.

Stiel *m* strut *(Ap)*; spar, compression member *(Bdg)*; handle, holder; stick.

Stielgranate *f* See **Stielhandgranate.**

Stielhandgranate *f* stick hand grenade, "potato-masher" hand grenade.

Stift *m* brad, holder, pin, prong, peg, tack.

"Stillgesessen!" "Attention!" *(mounted drill)*.

"Stillgestanden!" "Attention!" *(dismounted drill)*.

Stimmung *f* morale, mood, atmosphere.

Stirn *f* forehead.

Stirnangriff *m* frontal attack.

Stirnansicht *f* bow-on view *(Tk)*; front view.

Stirnband *n* forehead strap *(gas mask)*.

Stirnfläche *f* frontal area.

Stirnpanzer *m* front armor.

Stirnrad *n* spur gear.

Stirnriemen *m* brow band *(harness)*.

Stirnschattenriß *m* bow-on silhouette *(practice target)*.

Stirnseite *f* front *(Tk)*.

Stirnwiderstand *m* head resistance.

Stirnwind *m* headwind.

Stock *m* cleaning rod *(R)*; stick, baton, picket, pole; floor, story.

Stockmine *f* antipersonnel picket-type mine; stake mine *(concrete antipersonnel mine)*.

Stockung *f* block, jam, stoppage.

Stoff *m* fabric, material, substance.

Stoffbahn *f* panel, canopy *(Prcht)*.

Stoffbespannung *f* fabric covering *(Ap)*.

Stoffgliederung *f* classification of equipment.

Stoffgurt *m* web belt.

Stollen *m* tunnel *(Engr)*.

Stolperdraht *m* trip wire.

Stolperdrahtfeld *n* field of trip-wire obstacles.

Stolperdrahthindernis *n* trip-wire entanglement.

Stolperdrahtmine *f* trip-wire mine.

stolpern to trip.

Stopfbüchse *f* gland; stuffing box *(Mech)*.

"Stopfen!" "Suspend firing!" *See also* **"Feuerpause!"**

stoppen to stop; to time with a stop watch.

Stoppuhr *f* time interval recorder, stop watch.

Stopp- und Schlußlicht *n* stop and taillight *(MT)*.

Stoppzeit *f* time interval, time difference, time lag *(FR)*; sound travel time *(SR)*.

Stöpsel *m* plug *(Tp)*; stopper.

stöpseln to plug in *(Rad, Tp)*.

Störangriff *m* nuisance raid.

Storch *m* a German liaison airplane.

Storchschnabel *m* pantograph.

Störeinsatz *m* nuisance raid *(Avn)*.

stören harass *(Tac)*; jam, interfere *(Rad)*.

Störflieger *m* nuisance raider, sneak raider *(Avn)*.

Störflug *m* nuisance raid *(Avn)*.

Störflugzeug *n* nuisance raider *(Ap)*.

Störfrequenz *f* interfering frequency, undesired frequency *(Rad)*.

Störfunkstelle *f* jamming station *(Rad)*.

Störgeräusch *n* static, interference *(Rad)*.

Störschutz *m* radio noise suppressor.

Störstelle *f* See **Störfunkstelle.**

Störung *f* disturbance, annoyance; interference, static, jamming *(Rad)*; stoppage *(MG)*; breakdown.

Störungsdienst *m* trouble-shooting service, maintenance service.

Störungsfeuer *n* harassing fire *(Arty)*.

Störungsflug *m* nuisance raid.

Störungssucher *m* trouble shooter, maintenance man *(Tp)*.

Störungssuchtrupp *m* wire patrol *(field Tp)*.
Stoß *m* thrust, lunge, shock, kick, blow, push; burst *(MG fire)*.
Stoßarmee *f* main-attack army.
Stoßbalken *m* abutment beam *(Bdg)*.
Stoßboden *m* breechblock *(Ord)*; diaphragm *(shrapnel)*.
Stoßbohle *f* end dam *(Bdg)*.
Stoßdämpfer *m* shock absorber *(MT)*.
Stößel *m* valve lifter *(Mtr)*; rammer *(fuze)*.
Stößelführung *f* valve-lifter guide *(Mtr)*.
Stößelschraube *f* valve-lifter adjusting nut *(Mtr)*.
stoßempfindlich sensitive to shock *(explosives)*.
stoßen to push, thrust, lunge, strike.
Stoßfänger *m* bumper *(MT)*.
Stoßkappenmine *f* contact mine *(Nav)*.
Stoßkeil *m* spearhead *(Tac)*.
Stoßkraft *f* shock power, striking power.
Stoßlinie *f* thrust line, line of attack *(Tac)*.
Stoßmine *f* contact mine *(Nav)*.
Stoßrad *n* shock-absorber wheel *(Tk)*.
Stoßreserve *f* local supports in assault *(Tac)*.
Stoßscheibe *f* diaphragm *(shrapnel)*; lock washer *(for wheel bearing)*.
stoßsicher insensitive to shock *(explosives)*.
Stoßstange *f* push rod; bumper.
Stoßtrupp *m* combat patrol, assault detachment.
Stoßtruppen *fpl* shock troops, assault troops.
Stoßtruppspioniere *mpl* assault engineers.
Stoßtruppunternehmung *f* raid *(Tac)*.
Stoßwaffe *f* thrusting weapon.
stoßweises Feuer intermittent fire, interrupted fire, fire by bursts or volleys.
Stoßzündung *f* contact fire *(Nav)*.
Strafbuch *n* punishment book.
Strafdienst *m* extra duty.
Strafe *f* punishment.
Straffeuer *n* retaliation fire.

Strahl *m* ray, beam *(of light, etc.)*; jet, squirt *(of a liquid, etc.)*; frog *(of hoof)*.
Strahldrehung *f* rotation of the slipstream *(propeller)*.
Strahlenzieher *m* protractor.
Strahlung *f* radiation.
Strahlungsablenkung *f* radio wave deflection.
Strand *m* beach, shore.
Strang *m* strand, rope, strap.
Stranglaufe *f* lazy strap *(harness)*.
Strangträger *m* *See* **Stranglaufe**.
Straße *f* street, road, highway, route.
Straßenbaubataillon *n* road-construction battalion.
Straßenbaudienst *m* road-construction and maintenance service.
Straßenbiegung *f* road curve, road bend.
Straßendamm *m* causeway, embanked road.
Straßendecke *f* road surface.
Straßendisziplin *f* road discipline.
Straßendreieck *n* triangular road junction.
Straßeneinmündung *f* side road joining main highway.
Straßen-Entgiftungsabteilung *f* road decontamination battalion.
Straßengabel *f* road fork.
straßengängig roadbound.
Straßengraben *m* road ditch.
Straßenkampf *m* street fighting.
Straßenknie *n* V-turn *(road)*.
Straßenknotenpunkt *m* road intersection, road junction, road center.
Straßenkommandant *m* traffic control officer.
Straßenkommandantur *f* area road traffic control headquarters.
Straßenkreuzung *f* crossroads, intersection.
Straßennetz *n* road net.
Straßensperre *f* road block.
Straßenspinne *f* multiple road junction.
Straßensprengung *f* road demolition.
Straßenstreife *f* street patrol.
Straßenüberführung *f* overpass.
Straßenunterführung *f* underpass.
Straßenverhältnisse *npl* road conditions.
Straßenwalze *f* road roller.
Straßenzucht *f* road discipline.
Stratege *m* strategist.

Strategie *f* strategy.
strategisch strategic.
strategische Einheit large unit *(USA: Div and up; Ger: corps and up).*
strategischer Rückzug strategic withdrawal.
Strauch *m* bush, shrub.
Strauchbündel *n* fascine.
Strauchdamm *m* fascine road, brush road.
Strauchmaske *f* shrubbery screen, brushwood screen *(Cam).*
Strauchpackung *f* See Strauchwerk.
Strauchwerk *n* brushwork.
Strauchwerkbekleidung *f* fascine revetment.
Strebe *f* diagonal strut *(Ap);* brace, tension member *(Bdg).*
Streckbalken *m* stringer *(Bdg).*
Strecke *f* span, bay, section *(Bdg);* stretch, length, distance; leg *(of a route).*
Streckenfeuer *n* course light, airway beacon.
Streckenzug *m* traverse *(Surv).*
Streich *m* cut, slash; coup; blow; trick.
streichen cross out, strike out, eliminate; strike *(a flag);* to back water.
Streichholz *n* match.
Streifabteilung *f* raiding party.
Streife *f* patrol, raiding party; guard sentinel *(guard duty).*
Streifen *m* band, strip, belt, sector.
streifen to patrol, reconnoiter; to graze.
Streifenplan *m* diagram of patrol posts.
Streifenweg *m* patrol post.
Streifkommando *n* raiding party.
streitig machen to contest.
Streubrandbombe *f* scatter bomb.
streuen to cover with zone fire *(Arty);* to cover with searching and traversing fire *(MG);* to strew, scatter; to be erratic, to have dispersion *(G).*
Streufeuer *n* zone fire *(Arty);* searching and traversing fire *(MG).*
Streukegel *m* sheaf of fire, cone of dispersion, cone of fire.
Streumine *f* uncontrolled mine; stray mine *(not laid according to regular pattern).*
Streuschießen *n* zone fire *(Gunnery).*

Streutrommel *f* sprinkler drum or cart *(for ground decontamination).*
Streuung *f* dispersion *(Ballistics).*
Streuungsbereich *m* zone of dispersion *(Ballistics).*
Streuungsbild *n* dispersion diagram *(Ballistics).*
Streuungsfeuer *n* See Streufeuer.
Streuungsfläche *f* dispersion area *(Ballistics).*
Streuungsgarbe *f* See Streukegel.
Strich *m* artillery mil; stroke, line; dash *(Tg);* point *(of compass);* graduation, index line.
Stricheinteilung *f* graduation *(specifically, mil graduation).*
Strichfeuer *n* grazing fire *(MG).*
Strichmaß *n* marking gage.
Strichplatte *f* graduated range plate *(MG mount);* reticle *(Optics).*
Strick *m* rope, cord.
Strickjacke *f* knitted sweater *(Clo).*
Strickleiter *f* rope ladder.
Striegel *m* currycomb.
Stroboskop *n* stroboscope; protectoscope *(based on stroboscope principle) (Tk).*
Stroh *n* straw.
Strohpuppe *f* dummy *(Tng).*
Strom *m* current *(Elec);* stream, river.
Stromaggregat *n* generating unit.
Stromanker *m* upstream anchor *(Bdg).*
Stromaufnahme *f* current draw *(Elec).*
Strombord *m* offshore side.
Stromerzeuger *m* generator *(Elec).*
Stromfahrzeug *n* river craft *(Pon, assault boat, etc.).*
Stromfluß *m* current flow *(Elec).*
Stromform *f* See Stromlinienform.
Stromgeschwindigkeit *f* speed of current.
Stromkreis *m* circuit *(Elec).*
Stromleine *f* upstream tension line *(Bdg).*
Stromlinienform *f* streamline shape.
Strommesser *m* ammeter.
Strommeßgerät *n* current measuring instrument *(Elec).*
Stromquelle *f* source of current *(Elec);* power source *(Rad).*
Stromschiene *f* live rail, third rail *(RR);* bus bar *(Elec).*
Stromsicherungsbataillon *n* electric cable maintenance battalion.

Stromstärke *f* amperage.

Stromstoß *m* current impulse, current surge *(Elec)*.

Stromstrich *m* course of current *(line joining points of greatest surface speed of a river current)*.

Strömung *f* current, flow.

Strömungslehre *f* fluid mechanics.

Stromunterbrecher *m* circuit breaker *(Elec)*.

Stromverbraucher *m* outlet, current consumer *(Elec)*.

Stromzufuhr *f* current supply, power supply *(Elec)*.

Strumpf *m* stocking.

Stubenältester *m* barracks leader, squad-room leader.

Stubenarrest *m* arrest in quarters.

Stufe *f* stage, step; muzzle-velocity correction value *(Ballistics)*.

Stufeneinheit *f* See Grundstufe.

Stufenfallschirm *m* lobe parachute.

Stufenformation *f* stepped-up (or stepped-down) formation *(Avn)*.

Stufenlader *m* multistage supercharger.

Stufensender *m* multistage transmitter.

Stufung *f* step-up (-down) distance, staggering, stagger distance *(formation flying)*.

Stuhl *m* chair; excrement, feces.

Stuka *n* dive bomber *(abbr. of Sturzkampfflugzeug)*.

Stukaangriff *m* dive-bombing attack.

Stukabremse *f* diving brake *(Ap)*.

Stukaflieger *m* dive-bomber pilot.

Stumpf *m* stump.

stumpf *adj* blunt, dull; worn out; obtuse.

stumpfer Winkel obtuse angle.

Stundenwinkel *m* hour angle.

Sturm *m* assault, onrush, onslaught; storm; an SS company.

Sturmabteilung *f* storm trooper detachment of Nazi party *(abbr. SA)*.

Sturmabteilungsmann *m* storm trooper.

Sturmabzeichen *n* assault badge *(decoration)*.

Sturmangriff *m* assault, onrush, onslaught.

Sturmartillerie *f* assault artillery.

Sturmausgangsstellung *f* assault position, jump-off position.

Sturmbann *m* SS or SA battalion.

Sturmbannführer *m* See SS-Sturmbannführer.

Sturmbataillon *n* assault battalion, shock battalion.

Sturmboot *n* assault boat.

Sturmbootkommando *n* assault boat detachment.

Sturmdivision *f* assault division *(honorary title for division with reduced Inf Pers and heavy firepower)*.

stürmen to assault, storm, rush.

Sturmgasse *f* assault gap *(through obstacles)*.

Sturmgepäck *n* light equipment carried in assault *(as distinguished from field pack)*.

Sturmgeschütz *n* assault gun *(self-propelled)*.

Sturmgeschützabteilung *f* assault-gun battalion.

Sturmgeschützbatterie *f* assault-gun battery.

Sturmgeschützführer *m* assault-gun commander.

Sturmhaubitze *f* assault howitzer *(self-propelled)*.

Sturmkanone *f* assault gun *(self-propelled)*.

Sturmleiter *f* scaling ladder.

Sturmlücke *f* assault gap.

Sturmpanzer *m* assault tank.

Sturmpionier *m* combat engineer.

Sturmregiment *n* airborne assault regiment.

Sturmreifmachung *f* "softening up" *(by bombing or Arty fire)*.

Sturmreifschießen *n* artillery preparation, "softening up."

Sturmriemen *m* chin strap *(headgear)*.

Sturmschritt *m* fast run.

Sturmtrupp *m* assault detachment.

Sturmwelle *f* assault wave *(Tac)*.

Sturmwind *m* gale.

Sturz *m* plunge, dive, fall; camber, caster *(MT)*.

Sturzangriff *m* diving attack *(Avn)*.

Sturzbett *n* streambed at downstream base of dam.

Sturzbomben *n* dive bombing.

stürzen to dive, crash, plunge; to rush, assault; to fall.

Sturzflug *m* dive.

Sturzflug-Automatik *f* automatic dive control *(Ap)*.

Sturzflugbremse *f* diving brake *(Ap)*.

Sturzflug mit Endgeschwindigkeit terminal velocity dive *(Avn)*.
Sturzgeschwindigkeit *f* diving speed *(Ap)*.
Sturzhelm *m* crash helmet.
Sturzkampfflieger *m* dive-bomber pilot.
Sturzkampfflugzeug *n* dive bomber *(abbr. Stuka)*.
Sturzkampfgeschwader *n* wing of dive bombers *(Avn)*.
Sturzsirene *f* dive siren *(dive bomber)*.
Sturzspirale *f* spiral dive *(Avn)*.
Sturzvisier *n* dive-bombing sight *(Avn)*.
Sturzwehr *n* spillway weir.
Sturzwinkel *m* angle of dive, diving angle *(Avn)*.
Stütze *f* support, prop.
Stützflosse *f* inboard stabilizing float *(seaplane)*.
Stützpunkt *m* organized tactical locality, strong point; base; point of support *(structures)*.
Stützpunktschiff *n* aircraft tender.
Stützrolle *f* track-supporting roller *(Tk)*.

Stützschwimmer *m* fixed wing float *(flying boat)*.
Stützweite *f* span between supports *(Bdg)*.
Stuvi *n* dive-bombing sight *(abbr. for Sturzvisier)*.
Suchanker *m* grapnel.
suchen to search.
Sucher *m* spotlight *(MT)*; view finder *(Optics)*.
Sucherde *f* ground detector for telephone interception.
Sucherfernrohr *n* finder telescope *(height finder)*.
Suchgerätsempfänger *m* search receiver *(Ap, Rad)*.
Süden *m* south.
Summer *m* buzzer.
Summeranruf *m* buzzer signal *(Tp)*.
Summerknopf *m* buzzer button *(Tp)*.
Summerzusatz *m* buzzer set *(Tp)*.
Sumpf *m* marsh, swamp, bog.
Sumpffieber *n* malaria.
Synchrongetriebe *n* synchro-mesh transmission *(MT)*.
Synchronisator *m* impulse generator mechanism *(Ap)*.

T

Tabelle *f* chart.
Tabellenzeichner *m* cartographer.
Tachodynamo *m* generator voltmeter tachometer *(AA gun)*.
Tachograph *m* speedometer combined with odometer *(MT)*.
Tafel *f* table; list; chart, diagram; blackboard.
Tagebuch *n* log book, diary, journal.
Tagegeld *n* per diem allowance.
Tagesanbruch *m* daybreak.
Tagesangriff *m* daylight attack; daylight raid *(Avn)*.
Tagesbefehl *m* order of the day; special orders.
Tageseinflüsse *mpl* ballistic density and wind factors.
Tageskilometerzähler *m* trip mileage odometer *(speedometer)*.
Tageskost *f* day's rations, food for one day.
Tagesmarsch *m* day's march.

Tagesrate *f* basic load *(Am)*.
Tagessatz *m* daily scale or quantity; daily ration quantity.
Tagestiefangriff *m* daylight low-level attack *(Avn)*.
Tagesverpflegung *f* daily ration.
Tagesversorgung *f* daily automatic supply.
Tagesvorstoß *m* daylight raid, daylight thrust or advance.
Tagesziel *n* day's objective, day's destination; target of the day.
Tagjagd *f* daylight pursuit, daylight fighting, daylight interception *(Avn)*.
Tagmarsch *m* day march.
Takt *m* stroke *(Mtr)*.
Taktfeuer *n* blinker light.
Taktik *f* tactics.
Taktiker *m* tactician.
taktisch tactical.
taktische Feuerbegriffe tactical fire classification *(Arty)*.

taktische Unterstützung direct support *(Avn, Tac)*.

taktischer Einsatz tactical employment.

taktischer Verband tactical unit.

taktisches Hindernis tactical obstacle.

taktisches Zeichen tactical symbol.

Tal *n* valley.

Talnebel *m* ground fog *(Met)*.

Talsperre *f* dam *(large storage dam)*; reservoir.

Tambourstock *m* baton.

Tangens *m* tangent *(trigonometrical function)*.

Tangente *f* tangent *(geometry)*.

Tank *m* tank.

Tankanlagen *fpl* fuel tank installations.

Tankbüchse *f* antitank rifle.

Tankdampfer *m* tanker *(Nav)*.

tanken to fuel, refuel, to fill *(a gasoline tank)*.

Tankfalle *f* tank trap.

Tankgraben *m* antitank ditch.

Tankprahm *m* fuel tender *(Nav)*.

Tankschiff *n* tanker *(Nav)*.

Tankstelle *f* filling station *(MT)*.

Tankwagen *m* tank truck *(MT)*; tank car *(RR)*.

Tapferkeitsmedaille *f* medal awarded for bravery.

Tarnanstrich *m* camouflage painting.

Tarnausweis *m* special deceptive identification card *(carried on missions where capture by the enemy is likely)*.

Tarndecke *f* covering, flat-top *(Cam)*.

Tarndisziplin *f* camouflage discipline.

tarnen to camouflage.

Tarnjacke *f* camouflage jacket.

Tarnkappe *f* helmet cover *(Cam)*.

Tarnmittel *n* camouflage material.

Tarnnetz *n* camouflage net, drape; apron *(G emplacement, Cam)*.

Tarnscheinwerfer *m* blackout driving light *(MT)*.

Tarnüberwachung *f* camouflage inspection.

Tarnung *f* camouflage.

Tarnungsfarbe *f* camouflage paint.

Tarnungsgeflecht *n* netting *(Cam)*.

Tarnungstruppe *f* camouflage troops.

Tarnzeltbahn *f* camouflage cape.

Tasche *f* bag, pocket, pouch; link *(of cartridge belt)*; boot *(SA)*; carrier, case.

Taschenbehälter *m* pocket flask.

Taschenlampe *f* flashlight.

Taschenmesser *n* pocket knife.

Taschenmunition *f* small arms ammunition in pouches.

Taste *f* key *(Rad, Tg)*.

tasten to key, send by key *(Tg, Rad)*.

Tastfunk *m* cw transmission *(Rad)*.

Tastgerät *n* keyer *(Rad)*.

Tastverkehr *m* cw communication *(Rad)*.

Tatbericht *m* detailed report, bill of particulars.

Tätigkeit *f* activity.

tatsächliche Schußweite actual range *(Gunnery)*.

Tau *n* rope, tow rope; trace *(harness)*.

Tau *m* dew.

Taube *f* pigeon.

Taubenschießen *n* skeet shooting.

Taucher *m* diver *(Nav)*. See also **Torpedotaucher**.

Tauchgerät *n* diving apparatus *(Nav)*.

Tauchrohr *n* spray-nozzle tube *(carburetor)*.

tauglich physically fit, able-bodied.

Taukranz *m* grommet.

Taupunkt *m* dew point.

Tausch *m* exchange.

täuschen deceive.

Täuschung *f* deception.

Täuschungsangriff *m* feint attack, diversion.

Täuschungsmanöver *n* demonstration, feint *(Tac)*.

Tauträger *m* lazy strap *(harness)*.

Techniker *m* technician.

technische Dienstzweige technical services.

technische Eignungsprüfung mechanical aptitude test.

technische Kompanie BT mining company *(Mil)*.

technische Kompanie E electricity company *(Mil)*.

technische Kompanie GW gas and water company *(Mil)*.

Technische Nothilfe Technical Emergency Corps *(used for Civ defense in Z of I and for maintenance, bomb disposal, restoration of public utilities, etc., in T of Opns and occupied territory)*.

Technisches Amt Technical Office *(department of Ger Air Ministry,* *dealing with research, procurement and testing).*

Teer *m* tar.

Teich *m* pond.

Teileinheit *f* basic, self-sufficient element of a unit. *See also* **Einheitsprinzip.**

teilen to divide.

Teilgebiet *n* subarea.

Teilkreis des Höhenrichttriebs elevation circle *(G).*

Teilladung *f* increment, increment section *(separate-loading Am).*

teilmotorisiert semi-motorized.

Teilplatte *f* graduated scale.

Teilring *m* azimuth micrometer *(telescopic sight).*

Teilringänderung *f* azimuth change *(telescopic sight).*

Teilringeinstellung *f* azimuth adjustment, azimuth setting.

Teilringzahl *f* azimuth reading.

Teilscheibe *f* graduated scale; interpupillary-distance scale *(binocular);* elevation micrometer *(panoramic telescope);* graduated disk *(plotting protractor).*

Teilstrich *m* mil *(Arty);* dial division *(Rad);* scale division *(Inst).*

Teilstrichteilung *f* mil graduation.

Teiltrommel *f* micrometer knob *(on (panoramic or BC telescope);* range drum.

Teilung *f* graduation, scale; division, separation.

Telefunken trade name of German company manufacturing electronic equipment.

Telegraphenleitung *f* telegraph line.

Telegraphennetz *n* wire net *(Tg).*

Telegraphenstange *f* telegraph pole.

Tellermine *f* antitank mine.

Tellersäule *f* float column *(AA gun outrigger).*

Tellertrudeln *n* flat spin *(Avn).*

Tellerventil *n* poppet valve *(Mtr).*

Temperatureinflüsse *mpl* elasticity effect; temperature factors *(Ballistics).*

Temperaturgradient *m* temperature gradient *(Met).*

vertikaler Temperaturgradient lapse rate.

Temperaturmesser *m* temperature gage *(Mtr).*

Temperaturschwankung *f* temperature variation.

Teno *f* *See* **Technische Nothilfe.**

Termin *m* dead line.

Terrorangriff *m* terror raid *(Avn).*

Tetrachlorkohlenstoff *m* carbon tetrachloride.

Thermiksegeln *n* thermal soaring *(glider).*

Thermitbombe *f* thermite bomb.

Thermitladung *f* thermite charge *(incendiary bomb).*

Thermokreuzinstrument *n* thermocouple meter.

Thermosyphonkühlung *f* gravity-system water cooling *(Mtr).*

Tief *n* cyclone, depression *(Met).*

Tiefanflug *m* low-level approach *(Avn).*

Tiefangriff *m* low-level attack *(Avn).*

Tiefbau *m* surface construction *(Tp line);* subsurface construction *(Engr).*

Tiefbettfelge *f* drop-base rim *(MT).*

Tiefdecker *m* low-wing monoplane.

Tiefe *f* depth.

Tiefenabstand *m* distance *(from front to rear).*

Tiefenausdehnung *f* extension in depth *(Tac).*

Tiefenfeuer *n* searching fire *(MG).*

Tiefenfeuereinrichtung *f* searching-fire device *(MG).*

Tiefenfeuertafel *f* searching-fire table *(MG).*

Tiefengliederung *f* distribution in depth, disposition in depth *(Tac).*

Tiefenkreuzverspannung *f* longitudinal cross bracing *(Ap).*

Tiefenlehre *f* depth micrometer, depth gage.

Tiefenstaffelung *f* echelonment in depth *(Tac).*

Tiefenstreuung *f* range dispersion on horizontal target *(Ballistics).*

Tiefenverspannung *f* longitudinal cross bracing *(Ap).*

Tiefenwinkel *m* angle of depression *(Surv).*

Tiefenzone *f* zone of resistance *(organized in depth).*

Tiefflieger *m* low-flying airplane.

Tiefflug *m* low-level flight, hedgehopping *(Avn).*

Tiefflugangriff *m* low-level attack.

Tiefgang *m* draught *(Nav).*

tiefgegliedert distributed in depth.

tiefgestaffelt echeloned in depth.

Tiefladeanhänger *m* flatbed trailer, tank transporter trailer.

Tiefladelinie *f* load line *(Nav)*.

Tiefseekabel *n* marine cable.

Tiegelgußstahl *m* crucible steel.

Tierarzt *m* veterinarian.

Titantetrachlorid *n* titanium tetra-chloride *(CWS)*.

T-Mine *f* See Tellermine.

Tochterkompaß *m* repeater compass *(Ap)*.

tödliche Menge killing concentration *(CWS)*.

Toleranz *f* tolerance *(Tech)*.

Tolit *n* trinitrotoluol.

Tolita *n* See Tolit.

Ton *m* sound; tone *(Photo)*; clay.

Tonarm *m* pick-up arm *(phonograph)*.

tönend icw *(marking on Rad set)*.

Tonfrequenz *f* audio frequency *(Rad)*.

Tonfrequenzbereich *m* audio-frequency range *(Rad)*.

Tonhacke *f* mattock.

Tonhöhe *f* pitch *(sound)*.

tonlos cw *(marking on Rad set)*.

Tonne *f* metric ton *(=1.102 short tons)*; buoy *(Nav)*; barrel, cask, drum.

Tonnenbrücke *f* improvised floating bridge of barrels or drums.

Tonnenfähre *f* barrel raft.

Tonnenfloß *n* barrel float.

Tonnenlager *n* spherical roller bearing.

Tontaubenschießen *n* skeet shooting.

Tontaubenschießstand *m* skeet range.

Tönung *f* tone *(Photo)*.

Tonwagen *m* sound truck *(film unit)*.

Tonwiedergabe *f* sound reproduction.

Topf *m* pot; container *(hand grenade)*.

Tor *n* large gate.

Tornister *m* pack, field pack, knapsack, haversack.

Tornisterempfänger *m* portable receiver, pack receiver *(Rad)*.

Tornisterfiltergerät *n* pack-type water purification unit.

Tornisterfunkgerät *n* pack radio set, portable radio set.

Tornisterfunktrupp *m* portable-radio section.

Tornisterklappe *f* pack flap.

torpedieren to torpedo.

Torpedo *n* torpedo.

Torpedoabwurf *m* torpedo release *(Avn)*.

Torpedoausstoßrohr *n* torpedo tube.

Torpedobootzerstörer *m* destroyer *(Nav)*.

Torpedoflieger *m* torpedo bomber; torpedo-bomber pilot.

Torpedoflugzeug *n* torpedo bomber.

Torpedojäger *m* fighter-type torpedo bomber *(Ap)*.

Torpedorohr *n* torpedo tube.

Torpedoschnellboot *n* motor torpedo boat.

Torpedoschutznetz *n* torpedo defense net.

Torpedotaucher *m* deep-sea diver *(Nav)*.

Torpedotreffer *m* torpedo hit.

Torpedo-Waffenleitvormann *m* torpedoman *(Nav)*.

Torpedowulst *m* blister *(Nav)*.

Torpedowurf *m* torpedo release *(Avn)*.

Torsionsstab *m* torsion rod *(MT)*.

tot dead.

Totalausfall *m* total loss.

totaler Krieg total war.

töten to kill.

Totenkopfverbände *mpl See* SS-Totenkopfverbände.

toter Gang steering play *(MT)*; backlash, play, lost motion *(Mech)*; free travel *(of clutch pedal)*.

toter Schußraum dead area, dead space.

toter Trichter dead space *(AA gun)*.

toter Winkel dead space.

tote Zone skip zone *(Rad)*.

Totpunkt *m* dead center *(Mtr)*.

Totschläger *m* blackjack.

Tracht *f* saddle cover *(pack saddle)*.

Trachte *f* wall, periople *(hoof)*.

Trachtenkissen *n* saddle pad.

Tragbalken *m* balk, stringer *(Bdg)*.

Tragband *n* carrying strap *(gas mask)*.

tragbar portable.

Tragbeutel *m* gas-mask carrier.

Tragbüchse *f* gas-mask carrier *(metal type)*.

Tragdeck *n* wing *(Ap)*.

Trage *f* litter, stretcher *(Med)*.

Tragegestell *n* pack frame *(pack saddle)*.

Tragegurt *m* carrying strap, supporting strap.

Tragepolster *n* carrying pad *(MG)*.

Träger *m* carrier, mount, support, beam.

Tragerand *m* bearing surface *(hoof)*.

Trageriemen *m* carrying strap, carrying sling.
Trägerstrom *m* carrier current *(Tp)*.
Trägerwelle *f* carrier wave *(Rad)*.
Tragesattel *m* pack saddle.
Trageschiene *f* frame rib *(pack saddle)*.
Tragevorrichtung *f* scabbard *(R)*.
Tragfähigkeit *f* load capacity *(Bdg)*; ton capacity, passenger capacity *(MT, Ap)*; gallon capacity *(tank Trk)*.
Tragfeder *f* suspension spring *(split-trail carriage)*.
Tragfläche *f* airfoil *(Ap)*.
Tragflächenumriß *m* airfoil profile.
Tragflügel *m* wing *(Ap)*.
Tragflügelende *n* wing tip *(Ap)*.
Tragflügelhinterkante *f* trailing edge of wing *(Ap)*.
Tragflügelprofil *n* wing profile.
Trägheit *f* inertia *(Mech)*.
Trägheitsmoment *n* moment of inertia.
Traglast *f* load *(Ap, MT)*; pack *(pack animals)*.
Tragpferd *n* pack horse.
Tragriemen *m* neck strap *(pack saddle)*.
Tragrolle *f* See **Laufrolle**.
Tragschrauber *m* autogiro, gyroplane.
Tragtier *n* pack animal.
Tragtierbeförderung *f* pack transportation.
Tragtierkolonne *f* pack train.
Tragvorrichtung *f* bomb shackle *(Ap)*.
Tragwerk *n* wing assembly *(Ap)*.
Tragzapfen *m* trunnion.
Trampelpfad *m* beaten path, beaten track.
Trampelweg *m* See **Trampelpfad**.
Tränengas *n* lacrimator gas, tear gas.
Tränengaskerze *f* tear-gas candle *(CWS)*.
Tränengasstoff *m* CN solution.
Tränenstoffkerze *f* tear gas pot *(CWS)*.
Tränken *n* watering *(of animals)*.
Transportbefehl *m* movement order.
Transporter *m* transport *(Avn, Nav)*.
Transportflugwesen *n* transport aviation.
Transportflugzeug *n* transport airplane.

Transportführer *m* transportation officer, train commander *(RR)*.
Transportgeschwader *n* transport wing, transport command *(Avn)*.
Transportglied *n* ferry element *(one of a train of towed ferries)*.
Transportkolonne *f* motor transport column.
Transportkommandantur *f* transport control headquarters *(RR)*.
Transportluftfahrt *f* transport aviation.
Transportmittel *n* means of transportation.
Transportoffizier *m* transportation officer *(RR)*.
transportsicherer Zünder shipment-safe fuze *(Am)*.
Transportsperre *f* embargo *(on truck, RR, and ship movements)*.
Transportstaffel *f* transport squadron *(Avn)*.
Transporttau *n* handling line *(Bln)*.
Transportübersicht *f* transportation table, table of movements.
Transportverbot *n* embargo *(on truck, RR, and ship movements)*.
Transportwesen *n* transportation system.
Transversalmaßstab *m* interpolating scale *(Surv)*.
Trapez *n* trapezoid *(Math)*; suspension frame *(Bln)*.
Trapez-Fachwerkträger *m* Warren truss, trapezoidal truss.
Trassierband *n* tracing tape *(CWS, Engr)*.
Trauerfeier *f* funeral; commemoration services.
Trauergefolge *n* funeral escort.
Traverse *f* crossbar *(split-trail carriage)*; traverse *(Ft)*.
Trecker *m* tractor *(MT)*.
Treffaussicht *f* probability of hit.
Treffbild *n* shot group, dispersion pattern; recording target *(Tng)*.
Treffen *n* encounter, shock of assault; wave of tanks; phase of attack.
treffen to hit, meet, strike; guess; take *(measures)*.
Treffentfernung *f* slant range to future position *(AAA)*.
treffenweise in depth, in echelon.
treffenweise Aufstellung disposition in depth *(Tac)*.
Treffer *m* hit.
Treffer erzielen to score hits.

Treffergebnis *n* score *(firing or bombing).*
Trefferraum *m* zone of dispersion *(Ballistics).*
Treffer verzeichnen to register hits.
Treffgenauigkeit *f* accuracy of fire; accuracy of practice.
Treffhöhe *f* altitude of target at future position *(AA gunnery).*
Trefffläche *f* target area.
Treffpunkt *m* point of impact, objective point *(Arty);* future position *(AAA);* meeting point, rendezvous.
Treffpunktentfernung *f* slant range to future position of target *(AA gunnery).*
Treffsicherheit *f* accuracy of fire.
Treffwahrscheinlichkeit *f* expectancy or probability of hitting *(Arty).*
Treffwahrscheinlichkeit der Waffe developed armament probable error.
treiben impel, drive, propel; drift.
Treibachse *f* driving axle *(MT).*
Treibgas *n* wood gas *(MT);* propellent gas *(Bln).*
Treibgasmotor *m* wood-gas engine *(MT).*
Treibholz *n* driftwood.
Treibladung *f* propellent charge *(Am).*
Treibmine *f* floating mine, unanchored automatic contact mine.
Treibmittel *n* propellant *(Am).*
Treibscheibe *f* diaphragm *(case shot).*
Treibstoff *m* engine fuel.
Treibstoffbehälter *m* fuel tank *(MT, Ap).*
Treibstofflager *n* fuel dump.
treideln to tow boats from land.
trennen disconnect, cut off, divide, separate.
Trennklinke *f* disconnect jack *(Tp).*
Trennschärfe *f* selectivity *(Rad).*
Trennschnitt *m* line of breach *(demolitions).*
Trennung *f* break *(Rad procedure);* disconnection, separation.
Trennungsbahnhof *m* junction *(RR).*
Trennungslinie *f* boundary *(Tac).*
Trense *f* bit, snaffle *(harness).*
Trensengebiß *n* snaffle bit *(harness).*
Trensenzügel *m* snaffle rein *(harness).*
Tresse *f* braid *(Clo).*
"Treten Sie ab!" "Dismissed!" *(formal style, to an individual).*
Tretmine *f* tread mine *(pressure-ignited antipersonnel mine).*

Tretmotor *m* pedal-operated generator.
Tretsatz *m* pedal-operated generating unit.
Trichter *m* crater; funnel; cone; horn collector *(AA sound locator).*
Trichterlautsprecher *m* horn-type speaker, cone speaker *(Rad).*
Trichterfeld *n* shelled area, area pitted with shell craters.
Trichtergelände *n* shelled terrain, terrain pitted with shell craters.
Trichterladung *f* crater charge *(Engr).*
Trieb *m* drive; drift; impulse; instinct.
Triebrad *n* driving sprocket *(Tk).*
Triebsand *m* drift sand, loose sand, silt.
Triebscheibe *f* knob, micrometer head *(Optics, Ord).*
Triebscheibe zur Höhenrichtung elevating knob *(Optics, Ord).*
Triebscheibe zur Seitenrichtung azimuth knob *(Optics, Ord).*
Triebschraube *f* upper prism micrometer head *(panoramic sight).*
Triebwerk *n* power plant *(Ap, MT).*
Triebzahn *m* connector *(caterpillar track).*
trigonometrischer Punkt triangulation point, primary traverse station.
Trilit *n* trinitrotoluol.
Trimmklappe *f* trim tab *(Ap).*
Trimmruder *n* trim tab, balance tab, servo tab *(Ap).*
Trimmvorrichtung *f* flight control surfaces used for trimming *(Ap).*
trinkbar potable.
Trinkbecher *m* drinking cup.
Trinkwasser *n* drinking water.
Trinkwasserbereiter *m* water purification unit.
Tripelstreifen *m* special prism used to direct the beam of a signal lamp.
Tripper *m* gonorrhea.
Tritt *m* step, pace, tread.
Trittbrett *n* running board *(MT).*
Trockendock *n* dry dock.
Trockenelement *n* dry cell *(Elec).*
Trockengelenk *n* flexible-disk joint *(MT).*
Trockengleichrichter *m* dry cell rectifier *(Rad).*
Trockensumpfschmierung *f* dry-sump lubrication *(Mtr).*
Troddel *f* bayonet tassel.
Trog *m* trough.

Trombe *f* cyclone, tornado.
Trommel *f* drum; dial; range drum *(sight mount)*; micrometer drum *(panoramic sight)*; metal drum *(for belt Am)*.
Trommelfell *n* eardrum.
Trommelfellverletzter *m* person with punctured eardrums.
Trommelfeuer *n* drum fire, heavy barrage *(Arty)*.
Trommelmagazin *n* drum magazine *(MG)*.
Trommelmagazinzuführung *f* drum feed *(MG)*.
Trommelwirbel *m* drum roll.
Trommelzeiger *m* drum index *(sight mount, panoramic sight)*.
Trommler *m* drummer.
Trompete *f* bugle.
Trompetensignal *n* bugle call.
Trompeter *m* bugler.
tropenbeständig suitable for use in tropical climates.
Tropenhelm *m* pith helmet, sun helmet.
Tropenkraftstoff *m* tropical gasoline.
Tröpfchen *n* droplet, vapor particle *(CWS)*.
Tropfen *m* drop *(of water, etc.)*.
tropische Warmluft tropical air *(Met)*.
Troß *m* train *(combat, supply, or baggage)*.
Trosse *f* hawser.
Troßfahrzeug *n* train vehicle *(supply, baggage, etc.)*.
Trotyl *n* trinitrotoluol.
trudeln to spin *(Ap)*.
Trümmer *pl* debris.
Trupp *m* detachment, section, squad, team, detail, party *(pl Trupps)* *(to be distinguished from Truppe)*.
Truppe *f* collective term for field elements of armed forces; unit; arm or branch of service *(to be distinguished from Trupp)*.
Truppen *fpl* troops.
Truppenansammlung *f* concentration of troops.
Truppenarzt *m* medical officer.
Truppenausladung *f* detraining of troops.
Truppenausweis *f* soldier's identification card.
Truppenbefehlshaber *m* commander of troops.

Truppenbeförderung *f* transportation of troops.
Truppenbereitstellung *f* assembly of troops.
Truppenbewegung *f* troop movement.
Truppendienst *m* service with troops, duty with troops.
Truppeneinheit *f* troop unit *(usually has uniform type of weapons, as distinguished from* Truppenverband, *combined-arms unit)*.
Truppeneinladung *f* entraining of troops.
Truppeneinteilung *f* order of battle; disposition of troops; allotment or allocation of troops; conventional sequence by arms and services *(in orders)*.
Truppenentgiftung *f* decontamination of personnel *(CWS)*.
Truppenentgiftungskompanie *f* personnel decontamination company.
Truppenführer *m* commander, commanding officer *(generally of a combined-arms force)*; task force commander.
Truppenführung *f* leading of troops, conduct of field operations *(title of Ger manual corresponding to Field Service Regulations: Operations)*.
Truppengattung *f* branch of service.
Truppengebrauch *m* military usage, military custom.
Tuppengeländebesprechung *f* junior-command field critique *(maneuvers)*.
Truppengeneralstab *m* general staff with troops.
Truppenlager *n* camp.
Truppenmarketenderei *f* post exchange.
Truppenmasse *f* troop concentration.
Truppennachrichtenoffizier *m* unit communication officer.
Truppennachrichtenverband *m* communication unit.
Truppennachrichtenzug *m* unit communication platoon.
Truppenoffizier *m* line officer, officer of the line.
Truppenschiedsrichter *m* unit umpire *(maneuvers)*.
Truppenteil *m* unit.
Truppentransport *m* troop transport.
Truppentransporter *m* troop carrier *(Ap)*; troop transport *(Ap, Nav)*; troopship.

Truppentransport-Flugzeug *n* troop carrier airplane.

Truppentransportschiff *n* troop transport, troopship.

Truppentransportzug *m* troop train.

Truppenübungen *fpl* field maneuvers.

Truppenübungsplatz *m* troop training camp, troop training grounds.

Truppenunterkunft *f* barracks, quarters, billet.

Truppenverband *m* mixed force, combined-arms unit.

Truppenverbandplatz *m* aid station *(Med)*.

Truppenvermessungsdienst *m* field survey service.

Truppenwetterdienst *m* field meteorological service.

Truppführer *m* leader of a *Trupp;* corporal *(Reich Labor Service)*.

l.MG-Truppführer light MG team leader *(R squad)*.

T-Stoff *m* lacrimator *(abbr. of Tränenstoff)*.

Tucheinsatz *m* cloth filter.

Tuchzeichen *n* ground panel, code panel.

Turbokompressor *m* centrifugal compressor, turbosupercharger.

Turm *m* tower; turret.

Turmanschluß *m* turret connection *(Ap, Tk)*.

Turmaufsatz *m* cupola *(Tk)*.

Turmgeschütz *n* turret gun.

Turmklappe *f* turret hatch *(Tk)*.

Turmlafette *f* turret mount.

Turmluke *f* turret hatch *(Tk)*.

Turmlukendeckel *m* turret hatch cover *(Tk)*.

Turmschwenkwerk *n* turret traversing mechanism *(Ap, Tk)*.

Turmzurrung *f* turret locking clamp *(Ap, Tk)*.

Tutol *n* trinitrotoluol.

Typenbezeichnung *f* model designation.

Typennummer *f* model number.

Typenschild *n* name plate.

U

üben to practice, exercise, train.

Überbau *m* superstructure.

Überbeanspruchung *f* overload *(Mech)*.

Überbelichtung *f* overexposure *(Photo)*.

Überbestand *m* surplus stock *(i.e., above authorized basic allowance)*.

Überdeckung *f* overlap *(aerial Photo)*.

seitliche Überdeckung sidelap *(aerial Photo)*.

Überdruck *m* pressure above atmospheric pressure; pressure difference, excess pressure.

Überfall *m* raid, surprise attack *(Tac);* spillway *(dam)*.

Überfallkommando *n* raiding party.

Überfallkrone *f* spillway crest *(dam)*.

Überfallwehr *n* spillway weir, overfall dam.

überflügeln outflank.

Überflügelung *f* outflanking.

überfluten to flood, inundate.

Überflutung *f* flood, flooding, inundation.

überführen to ferry *(Avn);* to transport.

Überführung *f* overpass *(RR)*.

Überführungsdienst *m* ferry service *(Avn)*.

Überführungsflug *m* ferrying flight.

Übergabe *f* surrender, capitulation; handing over; giving up.

Übergabeverhandlungen *fpl* negotiations for surrender.

Übergang *m* transition; shifting; crossing.

Übergangsbahnhof *m* crossing station *(RR)*.

Übergangsgebührnisse *npl* temporary monthly allowance paid on discharge *(to ease transition to civilian life)*.

Übergangsgerät *n* stream-crossing equipment.

Übergangskegel *m* forcing cone *(G tube)*.

Übergangsmittel *npl* stream-crossing means.

Übergangsstellung *f* intermediate position.

Übergangstruppe *f* stream-crossing troops.

übergeben hand over, surrender. **sich übergeben** to vomit.

Überhang *m* overhang *(Top, etc.);* angle of approach *(MT).*

überhitzen overheat *(an engine);* superheat *(steam).*

Überhitzer *m* superheater.

überholen overtake; overhaul.

überholende Verfolgung encircling maneuver in pursuit.

Überholung *f* passing, overtaking *(MT);* encirclement *(in pursuit)* *(Tac);* overhauling *(maintenance).*

Überholungsabteilung *f* encircling detachment *(in pursuit).*

Überholungsgleis *n* passing siding *(RR).*

Überlagerungsempfänger *m* superheterodyne receiver *(Rad).*

Überlagerungsfrequenz *f* heterodyne frequency.

Überlandflug *m* cross-country flight.

überlasten to overload.

Überläufer *m* deserter *(to the enemy).*

Überlaufrohr *n* overflow pipe.

Überlegenheit *f* superiority.

Übermacht *f* superior strength, superiority.

übermannen overcome, overpower.

Übermantel *m* overcoat.

Übernahme *f* taking over, assuming *(a command, etc.);* acceptance *(of matériel, etc.).*

überplanmäßig in excess of authorized strength or allowance.

überqueren to cross *(a river, etc.).*

Überraschung *f* surprise.

Übersättigung *f* supersaturation *(Met).*

überschießen to fire over the heads of friendly troops; to fire beyond the target.

überschießen eigener Truppen overhead firing *(Gunnery).*

überschießen von Deckungen clearance of masks *(Gunnery).*

Überschießgrenze *f* corresponding range *(Gunnery).*

Überschießtafel *f* overhead firing table.

Überschlag *m* loop *(Avn).*

Überschlag auf dem Boden ground loop *(Avn).*

überschlagen, sich to tumble *(projectile);* to roll over *(Avn);* to turn over *(vehicles).*

Überschlag über den Flügel barrel roll *(Avn).*

überschreiten to cross *(a Bdg, road, etc.).*

Überschreitfähigkeit *f* trench-crossing ability *(Tk).*

Überschrift *f* heading.

Überschußwasser *n* overflow water *(dam).*

überschwemmen to flood.

Überschwemmung *f* flood.

überschwer heavy *(.50 caliber MG as distinguished from German "heavy" MG, which is .30 caliber and on tripod mount).*

übersetzen to translate; to cross, to ferry.

übersetzen über Wasserläufe stream crossing.

Übersetzer *m* translator.

Übersetzfähre *f* ferry.

Übersetzgruppe *f* crossing detail.

Übersetzmittel *n* stream-crossing equipment.

Übersetzstelle *f* stream-crossing point, ferrying point, crossing site.

Übersetzung *f* translation; gear ratio, gear transmission *(to increase speed).*

Übersetzungsgetriebe *n* gear transmission *(to increase speed).*

Übersetzungsverhältnis *n* gear ratio.

Übersicht *f* survey; chart, plan, table; summary; synoptic view.

Übersichtsbild *n* index map *(aerial Photo).*

Übersteuerung *f* over bias *(Rad);* overloading *(Elec, Rad).*

Überstromkanal *m* bypass *(Mtr).*

Übertrager *m* transformer *(Elec);* repeating coil *(Tp).*

Übertragerkästchen *n* repeating coil unit *(Tp).*

Übertragungsgerät *n* data transmission system *(AAA).*

Übertragungskörper *m* induced-detonation charge.

Übertragungsladung *f* primer charge.

Übertrommel *f* range drum *(sight mount).*

überwachen to supervise, monitor, guard, police.

Überwachung *f* surveillance, observation; monitoring; guarding, policing.

überwältigen overcome, overpower.

Überwasserstreitkräfte *fpl* surface forces *(Nav)*.

überweisen to allot; send, convey; to refer.

Überweisungsamt *n* toll station *(Tp)*.

überwinden to overcome; surmount *(obstacles)*; to force *(a crossing, etc.)*; to conquer *(the enemy, etc.)*.

überziehen to stall *(Ap)*.

Überzug *m* cover, hood.

U-Boot *n* submarine, U-boat *(abbr. of* Unterseeboot).

U-Boot-Bunker *m* submarine pen.

U-Bootjäger *m* submarine chaser.

U-Bootkrieg *m* submarine warfare.

U-Boot-Mutterschiff *n* submarine tender.

U-Bootnetz *n* submarine net.

U-Boot-Werft *f* submarine construction yard.

Übung *f* practice, exercise, training, drill, training maneuver.

Übungsflug *m* practice flight.

Übungsflugzeug *n* training airplane, trainer.

Übungsgerät *n* practice device, practice equipment.

Übungsgeschoß *n* training projectile, target-practice projectile.

Übungsgranate *f* practice shell *(Am)*.

Übungshandgranate *f* practice grenade, training grenade.

Übungsladung *f* practice charge *(Am)*.

Übungsleitung *f* director headquarters *(maneuvers)*.

Übungsmaske *f* training mask *(CWS)*.

Übungsmine *f* practice mine.

Übungsmunition *f* practice ammunition, training munitions.

Übungsreizstoff *m* irritant training agent *(CWS)*.

Übungsriechstoff *m* odor-detection training agent *(CWS)*.

Übungsschießen *n* practice firing.

Übungsverband *m* training unit.

Ufer *n* shore, bank.

Uferbalken *m* shore sill *(Bdg)*.

Uferbrücke *f* single-span stringer bridge.

Uferschnellsteg *m* hasty single-span footbridge.

Uhr *f* watch, clock, timepiece; instrument dial.

Uhrenscheibe *f* target consisting of circle of silhouettes.

Uhrvergleich *m* synchronization of watches.

Uhrwerkantrieb *m* clockwork action *(fuze)*.

Uhrwerkzünder *m* clockwork fuze *(Am)*.

Uhrzeiger *m* clock hand; indicator *(Inst)*.

im Gegensinn zum Uhrzeiger counterclockwise.

im Sinne des Uhrzeigers clockwise.

Uhrzeit *f* clock time *(such as 1345; as distinguished from* Zeit, time, in sense of "time length")*.

Uhrzeitangabe *f* time announcement, time signal.

Ultrakurzwelle *f* ultrashort wave, ultrahigh frequency *(in strict sense, very high frequency, 30 mc. to 300 mc.)*.

Ultrakurzwellenempfänger *m* ultrahigh frequency receiver. *See also* Ultrakurzwelle.

Ultrakurzwellensender *m* ultrahigh frequency transmitter. *See also* Ultrakurzwelle.

umbilden reorganize.

Umbildung *f* reorganization.

Umdrehung *f* revolution *(Mech)*.

Umdrehungszahl *f* number of revolutions, rpm.

Umdrehungszähler *m* tachometer.

Umdruck *m* mimeograph or offset reproduction.

Umfang *m* perimeter, scope, circumference.

umfassen to envelop *(Tac)*.

Umfassung *f* envelopment *(Tac)*.

Umformer *m* converter *(Elec)*.

Umformersatz *m* converter unit *(Elec)*.

Umgang *m* breeching *(harness)*.

umgehen to turn, outflank *(Tac)*; to detour, go around, bypass.

Umgehung *f* turning, outflanking *(Tac)*; bypass(ing), detour(ing).

Umgehungsbewegung *f* turning movement, outflanking movement.

umgliedern to reorganize.

Umgruppierung *f* regrouping.

Umhang *m* cape, cloak.

umhängen to sling *(arms)*; take up *(packs)*.

umkehren to reverse, turn over.
Umkehrgetriebe *n* reversing gear *(in rear-axle differential of half-track vehicle).*
umkippen to tip over, to dump.
Umklammerung *f* envelopment, encirclement *(Tac).*
Umkreis *m* perimeter, circumference, periphery; radius.
Umladung *f* transshipment.
Umlauf *m* rotation; cycle; circulation; circular; side spillway *(dam).*
in **Umlauf** to be circulated *(documents).*
Umlaufgetriebe *n* planetary gear.
Umlaufmotor *m* rotary engine *(Ap).*
umleiten to reroute *(traffic, etc.);* to divert *(a stream).*
Umlenkrolle *f* deflecting pulley.
Umpolung *f* pole reversal *(Elec).*
Umrandung *f* edge, edging, border, border strip.
Umrandungsfeuer *n* boundary light *(Adrm).*
Umrechnung *f* conversion *(Math).*
Umrechnungstafel *f* conversion table.
Umschalteklinke *f* throwout *(MG tripod).*
umschalten to switch over; to change gear.
Umschaltepause *f* switch interval, answer lag *(interphone).*
Umschalter *m* change-over switch, selector switch *(Elec).*
Umschalthebel *m* change lever *(automatic R).*
Umschlag *m* application *(Med).*
umschlagen to transload; to fell *(a tree);* to break down from bulk to unit containers; to capsize *(a boat);* to change suddenly *(wind, etc.).*
Umschlagshafen *m* transshipment port.
Umschlagstelle *f* bulk reduction point, transloading point, relay point.
umschulen to retrain.
umschwingen to veer.
Umweg *m* detour.
Umzäunung *f* enclosure.
unabhängig independent.
unabkömmlich irreplaceable, indispensable.
unangelehnte Flanke exposed flank.
unbefestigte Straße dirt road.
unbenutzbar unserviceable.

unbewaffnet unarmed.
unbrauchbar unserviceable.
Unbrauchbarmachung *f* destruction, rendering useless.
undicht leaky, permeable, not gas-proof or waterproof.
Undichtigkeit *f* permeability, leakage.
undurchdringlich impermeable, impenetrable.
Undurchdringlichkeit *f* impermeability, impenetrability.
unentzündbar inert *(Am).*
unerlaubte Entfernung absence without leave.
Unfallbearbeitung *f* accident investigation.
ungedämpft undamped *(Tech).*
ungeeignet unqualified, unsuited, unsuitable.
ungefähr approximate.
Ungehorsam *m* disobedience.
ungeklärte Lage obscure situation *(Tac).*
ungepflastert unpaved.
ungeschützt exposed *(Tac).*
ungünstig unfavorable.
Uniform *f* uniform *(Clo).*
Uniformbezugschein *m* individual clothing slip.
Universalinstrument *n* transit *(Surv).*
unmittelbare Unterstützung direct support *(Arty, Tac).*
unregelmäßig irregular.
unscharf unarmed *(fuze, etc.);* blurred, out of focus *(Optics).*
unscharf machen disarm *(Am).*
unstarres Luftschiff nonrigid airship.
untauglich physically unfit for active service.
Unterabschnitt *m* subsector.
Unterarzt *m* medical noncommissioned officer *(with rank of Master Sgt).*
Unterbau *m* subgrade, foundation, substructure.
Unterbindung *f* choking off, forestalling, preventing *(Tac).*
unterbrechen interrupt.
Unterbrecher *m* contact breaker, interrupter *(Elec).*
Unterbrechung *f* interruption; cessation; suspension *(of traffic).*
unterbringen to billet, quarter; to store, stow.
Unterbringung *f* sheltering, quarter-

ing, billeting; quarters, billets; stowage position *(of equipment in vehicle)*.

Unterbringungsgebiet *n* quartering area.

Unterdruck *m* vacuum, low pressure *(below atmospheric pressure)*.

Unterdruckförderer *m* vacuum tank *(MT)*.

Unterdruckkammer *f* low-pressure chamber.

Unterfeldmeister *m* staff sergeant *(Reich Labor Service)*.

Unterfeldwebel *m* staff sergeant.

Unterführer *m* enlisted man tentatively selected for subsequent officer's training; subordinate commander.

untere Führung lower command *(Regt and down)*.

Unterführung *f* underpass *(RR)*.

untergebene Stellen lower commands.

untergeordnet inferior in rank, subordinate.

Untergurt *m* cincha *(saddle)*; bottom chord *(truss)*.

unterhaltener Fahrweg improved road.

Unterhaltsberechtigter *m* dependent *(entitled to dependency benefits)*.

Unterhaltung *f* maintenance; conversation; recreation, entertainment.

Unterhändler *m* negotiator, bearer of a flag of truce, parlementaire.

Unterhandlung *f* parley.

Unterholz *n* underbrush, undergrowth.

Unterkalibergeschoß *n* subcaliber projectile *(Am)*.

Unterkunft *f* shelter, quarters, billets.

freie Unterkunft quarters in kind.

Unterkunftsbezirk *m* shelter area, quartering area, billeting area.

Unterkunftsgruppe *f* billeting group.

Unterkunftsraum *m* shelter area, cantonment area.

Unterlafette *f* bottom gun carriage.

Unterlage *f* plane table *(Arty, Surv)*; datum; basis; document, record.

Unterlagerungstelegraphie *f* simplexed telegraphy.

Unterlegbohlen *fpl* dunnage.

unterlegen inferior *(in numbers)*.

Unterlegenheit *f* inferiority *(Tac)*.

Unterlegeplane *f* ground cloth *(Bln)*.

Unterlegscheibe *f* washer.

Unternehmen *n* operation *(Tac)*.

Unternehmung *f* operation *(Tac)*.

Unteroffizier *m* noncommissioned officer; sergeant.

Unteroffizieranwärter *m* candidate for noncommissioned rank.

Unteroffiziere mit Portepee noncommissioned officers from *Feldwebel* up.

Unteroffiziere ohne Portepee noncommissioned officers from *Unteroffizier* down.

Unteroffiziere und Mannschaften enlisted men.

unterpolstert padded.

Unterredung *f* parley.

Unterricht *m* instruction.

unterrichten instruct, teach.

Unterrichtstafel *f* demonstration chart *(Tng)*.

Unterring *m* lower band *(R)*.

Unterringfeder *f* lower band spring.

Unterschenkel *m* gaskin *(horse)*.

Unterschied *m* difference.

Unter-Schiedsrichter *m* umpire assigned to a subordinate unit *(generally an NCO)*.

Unterschild *m* apron shield, lower shield *(G)*.

Unterschildträger *m* lower shield bracket *(G)*.

Unterschlupf *m* cut-and-cover shelter, dugout.

Unterseeboot *n* U-boat, submarine.

Unterseite *f* underside, lower side; belly *(Tk)*.

Untersetzung *f* reduction *(Mech)*.

Untersetzungsgetriebe *n* reduction gear *(MT)*.

Unterstand *m* shelter, protected shelter, dugout *(Ft)*.

unterstellt inferior in rank, subordinate.

unterstrom downstream.

Untersturmführer *m* See **SS-Untersturmführer.**

unterstützen to support.

Unterstützung *f* support *(Tac)*.

Unterstützungsartillerie *f* supporting artillery.

Unterstützungsfeuer *n* supporting fire.

untersuchen inspect, examine; test; investigate.

Untersuchung *f* investigation, examination; surveillance *(of Am and CWS supplies, etc.)*; inspection.

Untersuchungsstelle *f* test station *(Tp)*.

Unterveterinär *m* veterinary noncommissioned officer *(with rank of Master Sgt)*.

Unterwachtmeister *m* staff sergeant *(Arty, Cav)*.

Unterwasserbombe *f* depth bomb, depth charge.

Unterwasserhorchgerät *n* hydrophone *(Nav)*.

Unterwasserschneidetrupp *m* underwater cutting and welding detachment.

Unterweisung *f* indoctrination, instruction.

Unterwerfung *f* subjection, subjugation, submission, surrender.

Unterzug *m* transom *(Bdg)*.

Untiefen *fpl* shoals.

unverzüglich immediate.

unvorschriftsmäßig contrary to regulations, not prescribed, irregular.

Unwetter *n* bad weather, storm.

U-Rahmen *m* U-frame *(tubular chassis)*.

Urbaumuster *n* original model, prototype *(Ap, Tk, etc.)*.

Urkunde *f* document, permanent record.

Urkundenbeweis *m* documentary evidence.

Urlaub *m* leave, furlough, leave of absence.

Urlauber *m* man on leave, furlough, or pass.

Urlaubsschein *m* furlough certificate; leave; pass.

Ursprung *m* origin.

Urteilsmilderung *f* mitigation of sentence.

Urwald *m* jungle.

Urwaldkrieg *m* jungle warfare.

V

Vakuumröhre *f* vacuum tube.

V-Boot *n* launch *(abbr. of Verkehrsboot)*.

Velozitätsmeßzug *m* velocity measurement platoon *(Arty)*.

Ventil *n* valve.

Ventilanordnung *f* valve arrangement *(Mtr)*.

Ventilfeder *f* valve spring *(Mtr)*.

Ventilkammer *f* valve chamber *(Mtr)*.

Ventilkegel *m* valve ball *(MT)*; valve head *(pneumatic counterrecoil mechanism)*.

Ventilleine *f* valve cord, gas-valve operating line *(Bln)*.

ventilloser Motor sleeve-type engine.

Ventilschaft *m* valve stem *(Mtr)*.

Ventilschaftführung *f* valve guide *(Mtr)*.

Ventilsitz *m* valve seat *(Mtr)*.

Ventilsteuerung *f* valve-timing system *(Mtr)*.

Ventilstößel *m* valve lifter *(Mtr)*.

Ventilteller *m* valve head *(Mtr)*.

Verachtung *f* contempt, disregard.

veraltet obsolete.

verankern to moor.

Verankerung *f* anchorage, holdfast.

Verankerungsgurt *m* mooring band *(Bln)*.

Verankerungskabel *n* guy; mooring cable.

Verankerungsmast *m* mooring mast *(Bln)*.

Verankerungstau *n* ground cable, mooring cable *(Bln)*.

Verankerungsturm *m* mooring tower *(Bln)*.

veranlassen to cause, bring about, call forth.

veranschaulichen illustrate.

verantwortlich responsible.

Verantwortlichkeit *f* responsibility.

verausgaben to issue.

Verausgabung *f* issue.

Verband *m* combined-arms unit, force, task force; air force unit, force, formation *(Avn)*; bandage, dressing.

Verband aller Waffen combined-arms unit.

Verbandflug *m* formation flying.

Verbandkasten *m* first-aid box.

Verbandmittel *npl* dressing equipment *(Med)*.

Verbandpäckchen *n* first-aid packet.

Verbandplatz *m* aid station, dressing station.

Verbandsabwurf *m* formation release *(bombing)*.

Verbandsflug *m* flying in formation, formation flying.

Verbandswurf *m* *See* **Verbandsabwurf.**

Verbandtasche *f* first-aid bag.

Verbandzeug *n* first-aid kit, first-aid supplies.

verbergen to mask, conceal, hide.

Verbesserung *f* correction *(Gunnery)*.

Verbesserung für Länge range correction *(Gunnery)*.

Verbesserung für Seite lateral correction *(Gunnery)*.

Verbesserung für Witterungseinflüsse metro correction *(Arty)*.

Verbesserungsgerät *n* parallax offset mechanism *(sound locator)*.

Verbesserungswert *m* correction factor *(Gunnery)*.

Verbesserungswinkel *m* correction angle *(Gunnery)*.

verbeulte Patrone battered round.

Verbiegen *n* droop *(Mech)*.

verbieten to prohibit, forbid.

Verbindung *f* liaison, communication, contact *(Tac)*; connection *(Tp)*; compound *(Cml)*.

Verbindung aufnehmen make contact, establish communication *(with friendly troops)*.

Verbindungsachse *f* axis of communication.

Verbindungsaufnahme *f* establishment of communication, liaison, or contact *(with friendly troops)*.

Verbindungsdienst *m* liaison service, liaison duty.

Verbindungsflugzeug *n* liaison airplane.

Verbindungsgraben *m* communication trench, connecting trench.

Verbindungshülse *f* connecting sleeve, casing, collar.

Verbindungsleute *mpl* connecting file, communicating file; liaison agents.

Verbindungslinie *f* line of communication.

Verbindungsmann *m* liaison agent.

Verbindungsmittel *n* means of communication.

Verbindungsnetz *n* liaison net *(Rad)*.

Verbindungsoffizier *m* liaison officer.

Verbindungsorgane *npl* connecting elements *(march column)*.

Verbindungspatrouille *f* contact patrol *(Tac)*.

Verbindungsriemen *m* turnback *(harness)*.

Verbindungsschnur *f* connecting cord *(Tp)*.

Verbindungsschraube *f* floor plate screw *(R)*.

Verbindungsstaffel *f* liaison squadron *(Avn)*.

Verbindungsstraße *f* communication road, communication route.

Verbindungstrupp *m* liaison party, liaison detachment; connecting group; contact patrol.

Verbindungsweg *m* channel of communication *(Tp, Rad)*.

verblenden to dim or black out *(lights)*.

verbogen bent, twisted, warped.

Verbot *n* prohibition, off-limits declaration; exclusion; restriction.

Verbotstafel *f* "prohibited" sign.

Verbrauch *m* consumption, expenditure.

verbrauchbar expendable.

Verbraucherstelle *f* outlet *(Elec)*.

Verbrauchsgüter *npl* expendable supplies.

Verbrauchssatz *m* consumption per 100 kilometers *(of gasoline, oil, and lubricants)*.

Verbrauchsstoffe *mpl* *See* **Verbrauchsgüter.**

Verbrennung *f* combustion; deflagration *(of powder)*.

Verbrennungskraftmaschine *f* internal-combustion engine.

Verbrennungsraum *m* combustion chamber; powder chamber *(G)*.

Verbrennungsrückstand *m* carbon *(Mtr)*.

verbundene Waffen combined arms *(Tac)*.

Verbündete(r) *m* ally.

Verbundmaschine *f* compound-wound motor.

Verbundröhre *f* multi-unit tube *(Rad)*.

verchromt chromium-plated.

Verdämmen *n* tamping, mud capping *(demolitions)*; damming up *(a stream)*.

verdampfen to vaporize, evaporate.

Verdampfungswärme *f* heat of vaporization *(Met)*.

Verdeck *n* cover; hood; deck.

verdecken to cover, mask, conceal, defilade.

Verdeckung *f* concealment, defilade.

Verdichtung *f* compression *(Mtr)*.

Verdichtungshub *m* compression stroke *(Mtr)*.

Verdichtungsverhältnis *n* compression ratio *(Mtr)*.

Verdichtungswelle *f* burst wave, detonation wave *(SR)*; compression wave *(Physics)*.

Verdienstkreuz *n* Meritorious Service Cross *(decoration)*.

verdolmetschen interpret, translate.

verdrahten to wire, to block with wire obstacles.

Verdrängung *f* displacement.

Verdrängungszylinder *m* compression cylinder *(counterrecoil mechanism)*.

Verdunkelung *f* blackout.

Verdunkelungslampe *f* blackout lamp, blackout light.

vereinigtes Feuer collective fire *(SA)*.

Vereinheitlichung *f* standardization.

Vereisung *f* icing, formation of ice *(Avn)*.

Vereisungsschutzgerät *n* de-icer *(Ap)*.

vereiteln nullify, foil, render useless, fail.

Verfahren *n* method, procedure, process.

verfehlen to miss.

verfertigen to make, manufacture.

Verfolgung *f* pursuit *(Tac)*.

Verfolgungsabteilung *f* direct pressure detachment *(in pursuit)*.

verfügbar available.

Verfügung *f* disposal, disposition; availability; instruction, order.

zur Verfügung available for duty *(abbr. z.V.)*.

Verfügungsfrequenzen *fpl* assigned frequencies *(Rad)*.

vergasen to gas *(CWS)*.

Vergaser *m* carburetor.

Vergaseranordnung *f* carburetion *(Mtr)*.

Vergasermotor *m* carburetor engine.

Vergatterung *f* guard mount *(bugle call)*.

Vergehen *n* offense, breach *(of discipline)*, infraction *(of regulations)*.

Vergeltung *f* retaliation, reprisal.

Vergeltungsangriff *m* retaliation attack; reprisal raid *(Avn)*.

Vergeltungsmaßnahme *f* reprisal.

vergiften to poison; to contaminate, to gas *(CWS)*.

Vergiftung *f* contamination *(CWS)*.

Vergiftungsschießen *n* gas-shell fire *(Arty)*.

Vergleichsschießen *n* calibration firing *(Arty)*.

Vergleichsziel *n* auxiliary target *(Gunnery)*.

Vergrößerung *f* enlargement, magnification.

Vergrößerungsapparat *m* enlarger, enlarging projector *(Photo)*.

Vergütung *f* reimbursement, recoupment; compensation, award, allowance; heat treatment *(of metals)*.

Vergütungsanlage *f* soaking pit *(Ord)*.

Vergütungsstahl *m* heat-treated steel.

Verhaftung *f* arrest.

Verhältnis *n* relation; proportion, ratio; condition, situation.

verhandeln negotiate.

Verhandlung *f* parley, negotiation.

Verhängung von Strafen imposition of punishment *(Law, PW)*.

Verhau *m* abatis, hurdle, entanglement.

Verheerung *f* devastation.

verhindern prevent.

Verhör *n* interrogation.

verhören to interrogate.

verjüngt tapered; reduced.

Verjüngung *f* taper; reduction *(of scale)*.

verkanten to cant *(G, R)*; to tilt, incline; to become misalined.

Verkantung *f* cant *(Arty)*; misalinement of wheels *(MT)*.

Verkantungslibelle *f* cross level.

Verkantungstrieb *m* cross-level drive.

Verkehr *m* traffic; communication.

Verkehrsbestimmung *f* traffic regulation.

Verkehrsboot *n* launch *(Nav)*.

Verkehrsfliegerei *f* commercial aviation.

Verkehrsflugzeug *n* commercial airplane.

Verkehrskreis *m* traffic area.

Verkehrslast *f* bridge capacity.

Verkehrsleitung *f*   traffic control.
Verkehrslinien *fpl*   lines of communication *(Tac)*.
Verkehrsposten *m*   traffic control point.
Verkehrspunkt *m*   traffic center.
Verkehrsregel *f*   traffic rule, traffic regulation, rule for road procedure, rule of the road.
Verkehrsregelung *f*   traffic control.
Verkehrsregelungsbataillon *n*   traffic control battalion.
Verkehrsschild *n*   traffic sign.
Verkehrsstockung *f*   traffic congestion, jam, tie-up.
Verkehrsstreife *f*   traffic patrol.
Verkehrsteilnehmer *m*   traffic element.
Verkehrsüberwachung *f*   traffic supervision.
Verkehrszeichen *n*   traffic sign, traffic symbol.
verkehrt   reverse, inverse; wrong.
verkitten   fasten or seal with putty or other adhesive.
verkleiden   to revet; to mask, camouflage, disguise.
Verkleidung *f*   cowling, fairing *(Ap)*; revetment; camouflage, disguise.
verklemmen   to jam, to wedge.
Verladebahnhof *m*   loading station, entraining station *(RR)*.
Verladehafen *m*   loading port, port of embarkation.
verladen   to load, entrain, entruck, embark.
Verladeoffizier *m*   entraining officer, entrucking officer, loading officer.
Verladeplan *m*   loading table; entraining or entrucking table.
Verladeplatz *m*   loading point; entraining or entrucking point.
Verladerampe *f*   loading platform, loading ramp.
Verladestab *m*   loading staff *(sea port)*.
Verladestelle *f*   *See* **Verladeplatz**.
Verladezeit *f*   loading time, entrucking time, entraining time.
Verladung *f*   loading, entrucking, entraining.
Verladungsoffizier *m*   *See* **Verladeoffizier**.
Verladungsschein *m*   bill of lading.
Verlängerungsstück *n*   extension; sight extension *(G sight)*.
verlasten   to pack or load on vehicles

or horses *(specifically, to load on pack animals)*.
verlastete Artillerie   portée artillery.
verlastete Truppen   motorized troops.
Verlauf *m*   sequence of events, course, progress *(of an attack, etc.)*.
verlegen   to transfer; shift *(fire, etc.)*.
Verlegenheit *f*   confusion, embarrassment, perplexity.
Verlegswagen *m*   reel cart *(for Tp wire)*.
Verlegung *f*   transfer, shift.
Verlegungsbefehl *m*   movement order; order to shift fire *(Arty)*.
Verlust *m*   casualty, loss; forfeiture *(of pay, etc.)*.
Verlustliste *f*   casualty list.
Verlustmeldung *f*   casualty report.
Verlustrate *f*   casualty rate.
tägliche Verlustrate   casualty day.
vermessen   to survey, to locate.
Vermessung *f*   survey, surveying, locating *(Arty, Engr)*.
Vermessung durch Anhängen   survey by controlled traverse *(Surv)*.
Vermessungsbatterie *f*   survey battery *(Arty)*.
Vermessungs- und Kartenabteilung *f*   survey and mapping unit.
Vermessung von Feuerstellungen   field artillery survey *(Arty)*.
verminderte Ladung   reduced charge.
verminen   to mine, to lay mines.
vermißt   missing, missing in action.
vermitteln   to connect, to communicate *(Tp)*; to convey or impart *(information)*.
Vermittlung *f*   connection; switching central, telephone central.
Vermittlungskästchen *n*   portable switchboard *(Tp)*.
Vermittlungsklinke *f*   connecting jack *(Tp)*.
Vermittlungsschnur *f*   patching cord *(Tp)*.
Vermittlungsstelle *f*   switching central, telephone central.
Vernachlässigung *f*   neglect, negligence.
Vernebelung *f*   smoke screening.
vernehmen   to question, interrogate *(PW, etc.)*.
Vernehmung *f*   questioning, interrogation.
Vernehmungsoffizier *m*   interrogation officer *(PW)*.

Vernichtung *f* destruction, annihilation.

Vernichtungsfeuer *n* fire for destruction *(Arty)*.

Vernichtungskampf *m* battle of extermination.

vernieten to rivet.

verordnen to order; prescribe *(Med)*.

Verordnung *f* regulation, order.

Verpackungsgeschosse *npl* dummy ammunition *(for vehicle-loading practice)*.

Verpassung *f* fitting *(of uniforms, gas masks, etc.)*.

Verpflegung *f* feeding, messing, rationing; rations, food; food supply.

Verpflegung in Natur rations in kind.

Verpflegungsabrechnung *f* ration and savings account.

Verpflegungsabteilung *f* ration supply section.

Verpflegungsamt *n* ration supply office.

Verpflegungsausgabestelle *f* ration distribution point.

Verpflegungsbedarf *m* ration requirements.

Verpflegungsbestände *mpl* ration stores, ration stockage.

Verpflegungsbezugsschein *m* ration return.

Verpflegungsbombe *f* rations delivery unit *(airborne operations)*.

Verpflegungsdienst *m* ration supply service.

Verpflegungsersparnisse *fpl* ration savings.

Verpflegungsgebührnisse *fpl* ration allowances.

Verpflegungsgegenstände *mpl* ration articles.

Verpflegungsgeld *n* ration allowance.

Verpflegungslager *n* ration supply depot.

Verpflegungslagerausgabestelle *f* ration distributing point *(Div)*.

Verpflegungsmittel *npl* rations, subsistence supplies.

Verpflegungsnachschub *m* ration supply.

Verpflegungsoffizier *m* mess officer.

Verpflegungsportion *f* ration.

Verpflegungssatz *m* ration quantity, ration scale.

Verpflegungsstärke *f* ration strength.

Verpflegungstroß *m* ration supply train *(H-Dr or Mtz)*.

Verpflegungsunteroffizier *m* mess sergeant.

Verpflegungszug *m* ration supply train *(RR)*.

Verpflegungszuschuß *m* commutation of rations.

Verpflegung und Unterkunft rations and quarters.

verraten betray.

Verräter *m* traitor.

verriegeln to lock, cut off, block, box in.

verrostet rusty.

versacken bog down.

versagen fail.

Versager *m* misfire; dud.

Versammlung *f* assembly, concentration *(Tac)*; meeting, gathering.

Versand *m* shipment, transportation, forwarding.

verschaffen procure.

Verschalung *f* covering, skin, fairing *(Ap)*; revetment.

Verschanzung *f* entrenchment.

Verschickung *f* shipment, transportation.

Verschiebebahnhof *m* switching yard.

verschieben shift, move, displace, switch; postpone.

Verschiebung *f* displacement *(of troops, etc.)*; postponement.

verschießen , to expend *(Am)*.

verschleiern to mask, screen, blanket, conceal, camouflage.

Verschleierung *f* screening, concealment *(Tac)*.

Verschleierungsfähigkeit *f* screening capacity, density of coverage *(screening smoke)*.

Verschleierungsfeuer *n* deception fire, diversion fire; smoke-shell fire.

Verschleierungsverkehr *m* deception signal traffic.

Verschleißteil *m* part subject to wear *(Mech)*.

Verschluß *m* breechblock, breech mechanism *(Ord)*; bolt mechanism *(R, pistol)*; locking action *(Tech)*; lock; shutter.

Verschlußabstand *m* head space *(Ord)*.

Verschlußblock *m* breechblock *(screw-type breech)*.

Verschlußkeil *m* wedge-type breechblock.

verschlüsseln encode, encipher.
verschlüsselter Text secret text.
Verschlüsselung *f* coding, enciphering.
Verschlüsselungsscheibe *f* cipher disk.
Verschlußkammer *f* bolt *(R)*.
Verschlußkappe *f* filler cover *(MG)*.
Verschlußleiste *f* back plate *(MG)*.
Verschlußleistenachse *f* back plate hinge pin *(MG)*.
Verschlußplatte *f* front plate *(breechblock)*.
Verschlußring *m* breech ring *(G)*.
Verschlußschlitten *m* lock frame *(Ord)*.
Verschlußschraube *f* threaded closing cap *(fuze)*.
Verschlußstück *n* breechblock *(G, MG)*.
Verschlußträger *m* breechblock carrier *(G)*.
Verschlußüberzug *m* breech cover *(G)*.
Verschlußzylinder *m* bolt *(SA)*.
Verschränkbarkeit der Achsen compression-and-rebound range of spring suspension *(MT)*.
Verschraubung *f* threaded plug, screw.
Verschraubungsstück *n* breech ring.
Verschubbahn *f* launching track *(Bdg)*.
Verschuß *m* expenditure *(of Am)*.
Verschwertung *f* lateral truss, sway brace *(Bdg)*.
Verschwindeturm *m* disappearing turret *(Ft)*.
Verschwindlafette *f* disappearing carriage *(G)*.
Verschwindscheibe *f* bobbing target, disappearing target *(Tng)*.
Verschwörung *f* conspiracy.
Versehrtengeld *n* disability allowance or pension.
versenken to sink; to countersink.
Versenknietung *f* flush riveting.
versetzen to transfer *(Pers)*; to shift, move; to stagger *(obstacles, etc.)*.
versetzt staggered; displaced, transferred.
Versetzung *f* transfer *(Pers)*; deviation, drift *(Avn)*; stagger(ing).
Versorgung *f* supply; care *(for ex-service men)*.
Versorgungsbehälter *m* aerial delivery unit.

Versorgungsbombe *f* aerial delivery unit.
Versorgungsdienst *m* supply service.
Versorgungsfahrzeug *n* supply vehicle, train vehicle.
Versorgungsgebiet *n* supply area.
Versorgungsgüter *npl* supplies.
verspannen to brace, tighten, stretch.
Verspannung *f* bracing, fastening, tightening, stretching.
Versprengter *m* straggler; man separated from his unit in action.
versprühen to spray *(CWS)*.
verständigen inform, make known.
Verständigung *f* communication; readability, audibility *(Sig Com)*.
Verständigungsgerät *n* interphone equipment *(Ap)*.
Verständigungsmittel *n* password.
Verständigung von Bord zu Bord interaircraft communication.
Verständlichkeit *f* readability *(Sig Com)*.
verstärken reinforce, strengthen; amplify, boost, increase.
Verstärker *m* amplifier *(Rad)*.
Verstärkung *f* amplification *(Rad)*; reinforcement.
Verstärkungsfaktor *m* amplification factor *(Rad)*.
Verstärkungsring *m* hoop *(gun barrel)*.
Verstauchung *f* sprain *(Med)*.
verstauen to stow.
verstecken to hide, conceal, mask.
verstellbar controllable *(Ap propeller)*; adjustable *(tools, etc.)*.
Verstell-Luftschraube *f* controllable-pitch propeller *(Ap)*.
Verstellschlüssel *m* adjustable wrench.
Verstellschraube *f* adjusting screw *(Tech)*; controllable-pitch propeller.
Verstellung *f* adjustment, regulation, control.
Verstellwelle *f* control rod *(Ap)*.
Verstoß *m* infraction, irregularity.
Verstrebung *f* spar bracing *(Bdg)*; bracing.
verstümmeln mutilate.
Versuch *m* experiment, attempt, test, trial.
Versuchsflugzeug *n* test airplane, experimental airplane.
Versuchsladung *f* test charge *(Arty)*.
Versuchslauf *m* test run, trial run.
Versuchsschießen *n* test firing *(Ord)*.

Versuchstruppen *fpl* experimental troops.

vertäuen to moor.

Vertäumast *m* mooring mast.

Verteidigung *f* defense, defensive.

Verteidigungsabschnitt *m* defense area, defensive area, defensive sector.

Verteidigungsanlagen *fpl* defensive installations.

Verteidigungslinie *f* line of defense.

Verteidigungsnest *n* nest of resistance.

Verteidigungsplan *m* defense plan.

Verteidigungsstellung *f* defensive position.

Verteidigungszone *f* defensive zone.

verteilen to distribute, to issue.

Verteiler *m* distributor *(Mtr)*; distribution box *(data transmission system)*.

Verteilerbahnhof *m* regulating station *(RR)*.

Verteilerfinger *m* distributor arm *(Mtr)*.

Verteilerkasten *m* distribution box *(Elec, Nav)*; junction box *(data transmission system)*.

Verteilerlaufstück *n* distributor rotor, distributor arm *(Mtr)*.

Verteilerscheibe *f* distributor plate.

Verteilung *f* distribution.

Verteilungsstelle *f* distributing point.

Vertrag *m* treaty, contract, compact.

Vertragsarzt *m* contract surgeon.

vertraulich confidential.

Vertretung *f* deputy; proxy; representation.

verursachen to cause.

vervielfältigen multiply; multigraph; mimeograph; duplicate.

verwalten administer, administrate, manage.

Verwaltung *f* administration.

Verwaltungsamt *n* See **Heeresverwaltungsamt.**

Verwaltungsdienste *mpl* administrative and supply services.

Verwaltungsgebäude *n* administration building.

Verwaltungsordnung *f* administrative plan.

Verwaltungstruppenteil *m* administrative unit.

Verwaltungsübersichtskarte *f* administrative map.

Verwaltungswesen *n* administration.

Verwendung *f* employment *(Tac)*; use, utilization.

zu besonderer Verwendung on special assignment *(abbr. z.b.V.)*.

verwickeln involve, complicate; engage *(Tac)*.

verwinden to warp, to twist.

Verwirrung *f* confusion.

verwundbar vulnerable.

verwunden to wound.

Verwundetenabschub *m* evacuation of wounded.

Verwundetenabschublinie *f* chain of evacuation.

Verwundetenabtransport *m* evacuation of wounded.

Verwundetenabzeichen *n* Wound Badge *(decoration)*.

Verwundetenbetreuung *f* care of casualties.

Verwundetennest *n* aid station.

Verwüstung *f* devastation.

Verzerrung *f* distortion *(Rad)*.

verzinkt galvanized.

verzinnt tin-plated.

Verzögerung *f* delay.

verzögerungsfrei immediate, nondelay.

Verzögerungsmine *f* delayed-action mine.

Verzögerungssatz *m* delay pellet *(electric igniter)*; delay powder train *(fuze)*.

Verzögerungsschütz *m* time-delay relay *(Elec, Rad)*.

Verzögerungszünder *m* delayed-action fuze, delay fuze.

Verzug *m* delay, lag.

Verzugsrechner *m* acoustic corrector *(sound locator)*.

Veterinär *m* veterinary officer *(2nd Lt)*.

Veterinärdienst *m* veterinary service.

Veterinärgehilfe *m* veterinary aid man.

Veterinärgerät *n* veterinary equipment.

Veterinärkompanie *f* veterinary company.

Veterinärpark *m* veterinary depot.

V-Form der Tragflügel wing dihedral *(Ap)*.

V-Formwinkel *m* dihedral angle *(Ap)*.

Vieh *n* cattle, livestock.

Vielfache *n* multiple *(Math)*.

Vielfachschaltung *f* multiple connection *(Tp)*.

Viereck *n* square.
Viererleitung *f* phantom circuit *(Tp)*.
Viererschaltung *f* phantom connection *(Tp)*.
Viererzelt *n* four-man tent.
viergliedrige Division square division.
Vierlings-MG. *n* four-barreled machine gun.
Vierradantrieb *m* four-wheel drive.
Vierradlenkung *f* four-wheel steering.
Vierspitz *m* crowsfoot, four-pointed knife rest *(obstacle)*.
Viertaktmotor *m* four-cycle engine.
Viertelkreis *m* quadrant *(of a circle)*.
Visier *n* sight, rear sight *(Ord)*.
Visierbereich *m* danger space *(MG firing)*.
Visierebene *f* plane of present position *(AA gunnery)*.
Visiereinrichtung *f* sighting mechanism, sighting device, sight assembly; quadrant sight *(G)*.
visieren to sight.
Visierfeder *f* rear-sight spring *(MG, R)*.
Visierfernrohr *n* telescopic sight.
Visierfuß *m* rear-sight base *(MG, R)*.
Visiergestänge *n* parallelogram linkage system *(AA sight)*.
Visierhaltestift *m* rear-sight pin *(MG, R)*.
Visierkimme *f* rear sight; rear sight notch.
Visierklappe *f* rear-sight leaf *(MG, R)*; sight-port cover *(gun shield)*.
Visierkorn *n* front sight; bead.
Visierlinie *f* line of sight *(Ord)*; line of present position *(AA gunnery)*.
Visierlupe *f* magnifying sight lens *(site-to-mask clinometer)*.
Visierschieber *m* sight slide *(MG, R)*.
Visierschild *m* sight shield *(G)*.
Visierschuß *m* direct-fire shot.
Visierschußweite *f* direct-fire range.
Visierstange *f* rear sight pillar *(MG)*.
Visierstift *m* rear-sight pin *(MG, R)*.
Visierträger *m* sight bracket *(Ord)*.
Visiervorrichtung *f* sight mechanism *(Ord)*.
Visierwinkel *m* angle of elevation *(Gunnery)*; angular difference between present and future position *(AAA)*.
Visierzeiger *m* telescope mount reference pointer *(matches with Rohrzeiger when gun is laid for elevation)*.

Vizeadmiral *m* vice admiral.
V-Motor *m* V-engine.
V-Null *f* muzzle velocity *(abbr. Vo)*.
Völkerrecht *n* international law.
Volksdeutscher *m* German who is a citizen of another country.
Volkswagen *m* "people's car" *(general purpose car, somewhat lighter than the jeep)*.
Vollbahn *f* See Vollspurbahn.
Vollgas *n* wide-open throttle.
vollgeländegängig having complete cross-country ability *(vehicles)*.
Vollgeschoß *n* shot *(solid projectile)*; ball projectile; solid nonexplosive projectile.
Vollgummireifen *m* solid tire.
Vollkettenfahrzeug *n* full-track vehicle.
Vollkorn *n* full sight *(R aiming)*.
vollmotorisiert fully mechanized.
Vollreifen *m* solid tire.
Vollrohr *n* monobloc gun barrel.
Vollsichtkanzel *f* turret with full field of view *(Ap)*.
Vollsichtkuppel *f* See Vollsichtkanzel.
Vollspurbahn *f* standard-gage railroad *(1.435 meters)*.
vollständiger Schuß complete round *(Am)*.
Volltraghöhe *f* service ceiling *(Ap)*.
Volltreffer *m* direct hit.
vorarbeiten, sich work one's way forward *(by rushes, or crawling)*.
Vorausabteilung *f* advance detachment.
Vorausaufgabe *f* preliminary mission *(Tac)*.
Voraussage *f* prediction, forecast.
Vorauswanderungsstrecke *f* linear travel of target during dead time, linear travel of target from position at instant of range determination to present position *(AA gunnery)*.
Vorbauschnabel *m* launching nose *(Bdg)*.
Vorbefehl *m* warning order *(Tac)*.
vorbeifahren roll by, ride by.
Vorbeiflug *m* side-view flight, passing flight *(AAA)*.
Vorbeimarsch *m* pass in review, march in review.
vorbeirollen roll by, pass by.
Vorbeischlagen der Pulvergase flareback *(G)*.
vorbereiten to prearrange, prepare in

advance, to schedule in advance (*Arty fire, etc.*).

Vorbereitung *f* preparation.

Vorbereitungsfeuer *n* preparation (*Arty*).

vorbeugen prevent, anticipate.

Vorbeugung *f* prophylaxis.

Vorbeugungsmittel *n* prophylactic.

Vorderachsantrieb *m* front-axle drive (*MT*).

Vorderachse *f* front axle (*MT*).

Vordergelenk *n* front piece of toggle joint (*pistol*).

Vorderhang *m* forward slope (*Top*).

Vorderhangstellung *f* forward slope position (*Tac*).

Vorderholm *m* front outrigger (*AA gun mount*).

Vorderkaffe *f* bow compartment (*Pon*).

Vorderkante *f* leading edge (*Ap*).

Vorderlader *m* muzzle loader.

vorderlastig noseheavy (*Ap*).

Vordermann *m* the man in front (*drill*).

auf Vordermann stehen to be covered in file.

"**Vordermann!**" "Cover off!"

Vordermann nehmen to cover off, to cover in file (*drill*).

Vorderpferd *n* lead horse.

Vorderradantrieb *m* front-wheel drive.

Vordersteven *m* stem (*Nav*).

Vorderstützen *fpl* front legs (*MG tripod*).

Vorderzeug *n* martingale, breastplate harness, body of breast collar (*harness*).

Vorderzwiesel *m* pommel (*saddle*); front arch (*pack-saddle frame*).

vordringen to push forward, press forward.

Vordruck *m* printed form, blank.

Vorfahrt *f* right-of-way, priority.

Vorfahrtberechtigter *m* one who has right-of-way.

Vorfahrterlaubnis *f* permission to pass (*vehicles in column*).

Vorfahrtregelung *f* priority regulations, traffic regulations regarding right-of-way or priority.

Vorfahrtsrecht *n* priority, right-of-way.

Vorfahrtszeichen *n* priority sign (*on a vehicle*).

Vorfeld *n* foreground; outpost area (*Tac*); apron (*Adrm*).

Vorflügel *m* slat (*Ap wing*).

vorfühlen, sich to feel one's way forward, to try to establish contact.

Vorführung *f* demonstration.

Vorgang *m* occurrence, incident, event; process.

vorgehen to advance.

Vorgelegewelle *f* countershaft (*MT*).

vorgeschoben advance(d); forward.

vorgeschobene Beobachtungsstelle forward observation post.

vorgeschobener Gefechtsstand advance command post.

vorgeschobene Stellungen position of advanced covering forces (*Tac*).

vorgeschrieben prescribed.

Vorgesetzter *m* superior, superior officer or NCO.

Vorhaben *n* intent, intention, plan.

Vorhalt *m* lead (*firing*).

Vorhalteeinrichtung *f* lead computer (*AA and AT guns*).

Vorhalteeinstellung *f* positioning device for leads (*sight mechanism*).

Vorhaltemaß *n* See **Vorhaltsmaß**.

vorhalten to take a lead, apply a lead (*Gunnery*).

Vorhaltepunkt *m* future position of target (*AA gunnery*); predicted position of target, set-forward point.

Vorhaltestrecke *f* predicting interval (*AA gunnery*).

Vorhaltewinkel *m* lead angle, angle between line of present position and line of future position (*AA gunnery*); angle of lateral lead (*Gunnery*); range angle (*bombing*); drift angle (*Air Navigation*).

Vorhaltsmaß *n* amount of lead, lead factor (*in firing at moving targets*).

Vorhaltswert *m* See **Vorhaltsmaß**.

Vorhand *f* forequarters (*horse*).

Vorhersage *f* prediction, forecast.

Vorholeinrichtung *f* counterrecoil mechanism, recuperator mechanism.

Vorholer *m* recuperator, counterrecoil mechanism.

Vorholerkolben *m* recuperator piston, counterrecoil piston.

Vorholerlager *n* counterrecoil-mechanism bushing.

Vorholerstütze *f* counterrecoil-mechanism support.

Vorhut *f* advance guard.

Vorhutführer *m* advance guard commander.

Vorhutgefecht *n* advance guard action or engagement.

Vorkammer *f* precombustion chamber *(Diesel engine).*

Vorlage *f* flash-reducing wad *(Arty);* text, copy, pattern.

Vorlauf *m* counterrecoil *(G);* negative caster *(MT).*

Vorlaufbewegung *f* counterrecoil motion.

Vorlaufhemmstange *f* counterrecoil piston rod *(G).*

Vormann *m* foreman *(Reich Labor Service).*

Vormarsch *m* advance.

Vormarschlinie *f* line of advance, axis of advance.

Vormarschstraße *f* road of advance, route of advance.

Vormarschweg *m* line of advance, route of advance.

Vorposten *m* outpost.

Vorpostenabschnitt *m* outpost sector.

Vorpostenabschnittsgrenze *f* outpost-sector boundary.

Vorpostenaufstellung *f* setting up of outposts, disposition of outposts.

Vorpostenboot *n* outpost patrol boat *(Nav).*

Vorpostendienst *m* outpost duty.

Vorpostenführer *m* outpost commander.

Vorpostengefecht *n* outpost engagement.

Vorpostenkette *f* line of outguards *(Tac).*

Vorpostenkompanie *f* outpost company.

Vorpostenreserve *f* outpost reserve.

Vorpostensicherungslinie *f* outpost line of security *(Tac).*

Vorpostenstellung *f* outpost position *(Tac).*

Vorposten-Widerstandslinie *f* outpost line of resistance *(Tac).*

vorprellen to rush forward.

Vorrang *m* precedence, priority.

Vorrat *m* stock, stores, supply.

Vorratshaltung *f* maintenance of stocks or supplies.

Vorratslauf *m* spare barrel *(MG).*

Vorratsteil *n* spare part *(MT).*

Vorratszug *m* supply platoon *(Tk Bn).*

Vorrichtung *f* device, mechanism, fixture.

vorrobben, sich to crawl forward.

vorrücken to advance.

Vorschlaghammer *m* sledge hammer.

vorschreiben prescribe.

Vorschrift *f* regulation, instruction, rule; manual.

vorschiftsmäßig according to regulations.

Vorsicht *f* caution, care; foresight *(Surv).*

Vorsignal *n* preliminary signal, warning signal.

vorspringend projecting, salient.

Vorsprung *m* salient *(Tac);* start, head start, lead.

Vorspur *f* toe-in *(MT).*

Vorstecker *m* safety pin *(bombs, mines, etc.);* lug *(fuze).*

Vorsteckriemen *m* pommel-pad strap *(saddle).*

Vorstoß *m* assault, thrust, lunge; piping, edging *(along seams of uniform).*

Vorstrom *m* inflow *(Avn).*

vortäuschen to deceive, simulate, feign.

Vortäuschung von Krankheiten malingering.

Vortrag *m* lecture; verbal report and consultation *(with commanding officer).*

vortreten to step forward, to step out of the ranks.

Vortriebskraft *f* propelling power.

Vortrupp *m* advance guard support *(in Adv Gd of large unit);* advance party *(in Adv Gd of smaller unit).*

Vorverdichter *m* supercharger.

vorverlegen to lift *(Arty fire).*

Vorwähler *m* preselector *(Tp).*

Vorwärmer *m* preheater.

Vorwarner *m* outpost observer *(SR).*

Vorwarnerstelle *f* outpost station *(SR).*

Vorwärtseinschneiden *n* intersection *(Surv).*

Vorwärtsfahrer *m* front driver *(of a vehicle with double-ended drive).*

Vorwärtsgang *m* forward speed *(MT).*

Vorwärtsgeschwindigkeit *f* forward velocity *(bombing).*

Vorwärtsstaffelung *f* positive stagger *(Ap wings).*

Vorzündung *f* preignition *(Mtr).*

V-Stellung *f* dihedral setting *(Ap wings).*

W

Waage f scales, balance.

waagerecht horizontal.

Waagerechtbombenwurf m level-flight bombardment.

waagerechte Gitterlinie X-line (of map grid).

waagerechte Schußweite level-point range (Gunnery).

Waagerechtflug m level flight, horizontal flight.

Wabo f See **Wasserbombe.**

Wachanzug m guard uniform (prescribed for guard duty).

Wachbataillon n guard battalion (in rear areas and Z of I).

Wachboot n patrol vessel.

Wachbuch n guard book (guard duty).

Wachdienst m guard duty.

Wache f guard; watch (Nav).

die **Wache aufziehen** to mount the guard.

die **Wache ablösen** to relieve the guard.

Wachgebäude n guardhouse.

Wachhabender m commander of the guard.

Wachkompanie f guard company (one providing the detail for guard duty).

Wachlokal n guardroom.

Wachmannschaft f guard detail.

Wachposten m sentry.

Wachradfahrerkompanie f bicycle company of a Wachbataillon.

Wachregiment n guard regiment (in rear areas and Z of I).

Wachsamkeit f vigilance.

Wachschiff n patrol vessel.

wachsender Drall increasing twist (Ord).

Wachstaffet m oilskin.

Wachstube f guardroom.

Wachstuch n oilcloth.

Wacht f radar station (Luftwaffe).

Wachtleitstelle f radar control station (Luftwaffe).

Wachtmeister m technical sergeant (Arty, Cav, AAA of the Luftwaffe).

Wachtruppen fpl guard troops (in rear areas and Z of I).

Wachtturm m watchtower.

Wachvorgesetzter m commander of the guard.

Wachwelle f stand-by frequency (Rad).

Wackelkontakt m loose contact (Elec).

wackeln to rock (Ap wings); to shake, to be loose.

Wade f calf (of leg).

Waffe f weapon; arm.

Waffenamt n ordnance office (a branch of the Oberkommando des Heeres).

Waffenaufnahme f gun holder (multiple AA gun mount).

Waffenblende f gun shield, gun mantlet (Tk).

Waffenentgiftung f decontamination of weapons.

Waffenentgiftungsmittel n weapons decontaminating agent.

Waffenfarbe f service color.

Waffenfeldwebel m technical sergeant (armorer-artificer).

Waffenfett n gun grease, rifle grease.

Waffenführung f tactics and technique.

Waffengattung f arm or branch of the service.

Waffengruppe f group (Ord, SA).

die **Waffengruppen auseinandernehmen** to field strip (a R, etc.).

Waffeninspektion f ordnance inspectorate (a branch of the Allgemeines Heeresamt).

Waffenkasten m arms container (aerial delivery unit).

Waffenlager n ordnance depot.

waffenlos unarmed.

Waffenmeister m armorer-artificer official (Civ official ranking as 2nd Lt).

Waffenmeistergehilfe m assistant armorer-artificer.

Waffenmeisterei f armory, ordnance shop; armorer-artificer's staff or function.

Waffenmeisterschule f armorer-artificer school, ordnance school.

Waffenoffizier m ordnance staff officer, ordnance officer.

Waffenprüfung f ordnance proving or testing.

Waffenrock *m* blouse.
Waffenruhe *f* truce.
Waffenschule *f* service school.
Waffen-SS *f* SS Armed Forces.
Waffenstillstand *m* armistice.
örtlicher Waffenstillstand truce.
Waffenstillstandsbedingungen *fpl* armistice terms.
Waffenstreckung *f* surrender.
Waffenstreuung *f* armament error.
Waffentechnik *f* tactics and technique.
waffentechnisch pertaining to ordnance engineering or mechanics.
Waffenüberlegenheit *f* superiority of arms and equipment.
Waffen und Gerät ordnance matériel.
Waffen- und Gerätenachweis *m* property book.
Waffen- und Gerätuntersuchung *f* technical inspection.
Waffen-Unteroffizier *m* ordnance sergeant.
Waffenwagen *m* armament car (*armored RR train*).
Waffenwart *m* armorer-artificer.
Wagen *m* wagon; car (*MT, RR*).
Wagenfähre *f* ferry for vehicles.
Wagenführer *m* car commander (*MT*).
Wagenhalteplatz *m* ambulance loading post.
Wagenheber *m* jack.
Wagenplane *f* tarpaulin for vehicle.
Wagenzugführer *m* caisson section leader (*Arty*).
wählen to dial (*Tp*); to select, choose; to vote.
Wähler *m* dial (*Tp*); selector (*switchboard mechanism*).
Wählerbetrieb *m* dial system (*Tp*).
Wählscheibe *f* dial (*Tp*); selector disk (*switchboard mechanism*).
wahrscheinlicher Fehler probable error.
Wahrscheinlichkeitsfaktor *m* probability factor (*Ballistics*).
Waldblöße *f* forest clearing.
Waldgefecht *n* combat in woods.
Waldgelände *n* wooded area, woodland.
Waldlichtung *f* forest clearing.
Waldrand *m* edge of woods or forest.
Waldschneise *f* fire break, straight narrow forest clearing.
Waldweg *m* forest road.
Wall *m* rampart, wall (*Ft*); embankment.
Wallfeldwebel *m* technical sergeant (*Ft troops*).

Wallgraben *m* moat, ditch.
Wallmeister *m* technical official of fortifications (*Civ official ranking as 2nd Lt*).
Walloberfeldwebel *m* master sergeant (*Ft troops*).
Wallstabsfeldwebel *m* regimental sergeant major (*Ft troops*).
Walze *f* roller; body (*of a shell*); cylinder.
Walzenblende *f* cylindrical mount, mantlet for cylindrical mount (*Tk gun*).
walzenförmig cylindrical.
Wälzlager *n* antifriction bearing, ball or roller bearing.
Walzwerk *n* rolling mill.
Wand *f* interior wall; baffle; bulkhead; interior side.
Wanderbatterie *f* roving battery (*Arty*).
Wandergeschütz *n* roving gun.
Wanderungsgeschwindigkeit *f* rate of travel.
Wange *f* cheek.
Wanne *f* trough, tub; hull (*Tk*); ventral turret (*Ap*).
Wanze *f* bedbug.
Warenlager *n* warehouse.
Wärme *f* heat.
Wärmebeständigkeit *f* resistance to heat.
Wärmegleichwert *m* mechanical equivalent of heat.
Wärmeunterschied *m* temperature difference (*Met*).
Warmluftenteisung *f* thermo ice elimination (*Ap*).
Warmluftfront *f* warm front (*Met*).
Warnflagge *f* danger flag.
Warnsignal *n* danger signal.
Warnstelle *f* lookout post; district warning center (*AWS*).
Warnung *f* warning.
Warnzentrale *f* control center (*AWS*).
Wart *m* ground mechanic, maintenance man (*Avn*); mechanic, rigger; man in charge; warden, lookout.
Warte *f* watchtower; observatory.
warten to wait; to service (*Ap, Mtr, etc.*).
Wartestellung *f* stand-by position, waiting position.
Wartung *f* servicing, maintenance.
Warze *f* lug, stud.
Waschbenzin *n* gasoline used for cleaning purposes.

Wäschesack *m* laundry bag, barrack(s) bag.
Wäschetasche *f* laundry pocket *(pack)*.
Wäschewechsel *m* change of underclothing.
wasserabstoßend water-repellent.
Wasserbehälter *m* water chest; water tank.
Wasserbombe *f* depth bomb, depth charge.
Wasserdestillationskompanie *f* water distillation company.
wasserdicht waterproof, watertight.
Wasserdichtigkeit *f* impermeability to water.
Wasserfahrzeug *n* craft, vessel *(stream crossing)*.
Wasserflugzeug *n* seaplane.
wassergekühlt water-cooled.
wassergierig hygroscopic *(powder)*.
Wasserlandflugzeug *n* amphibian airplane.
Wasserlandung *f* landing on water *(Avn)*.
Wasserlauf *m* stream, watercourse.
Wasserleitung *f* water pipes, water main.
Wasserlinie *f* waterline.
Wassermantel *m* water jacket *(MG, Mtr)*.
wassern to land on water *(Avn)*.
Wasserpumpe *f* water pump.
Wasserpumpenkühlung *f* force-circulation cooling system *(Mtr)*.
Wasserreinigungssack *m* water-sterilizing bag.
Wassersäulen-Druckmesser *m* water-column pressure gage.
Wassersperre *f* water obstacle.
Wasserspiegel *m* water level, water surface.
Wasserstand *m* water level.
Wasserstandsmesser *m* water-level gage.
Wasserstoff *m* hydrogen.
Wasserstraße *f* waterway.
Wassertransport *m* transportation by water.
Wassertrense *f* watering bridle *(harness)*.
Wasserturm *m* water tower.
Wasserumlauf *m* water circulation *(Mtr)*.
Wasserung *f* landing on water *(Avn)*.
Wasserverankerung *f* anchorage in water *(Pon Bdg)*.

Wasserversorgungskompanie *f* water supply company *(Mil)*.
Wasserversorgungsstelle *f* water supply point.
Wasserverteilungsstelle *f* water distributing point.
Wasserwaage *f* builder's level, water level *(Inst)*.
wasserwärts streamward.
Wasserwerk *n* waterworks.
waten to wade.
Watfähigkeit *f* fording ability, stream-crossing ability *(MT)*.
Watte *f* absorbent cotton.
Weberknoten *m* weaver's knot.
Wechsel *m* change; displacement *(Arty)*; alternation, one-half cycle *(Elec)*; exchange, currency.
Wechselbeziehung *f* correlation.
Wechselfälle des Gefechts fortunes of war.
Wechselfestigkeit *f* fatigue strength *(Mech)*.
Wechselfeuer *n* intermittent light.
Wechselgetriebe *n* gear transmission.
Wechselpunkt *m* midpoint *(AA gunnery)*; critical point *(Top)*.
Wechselpunktentfernung *f* slant range to midpoint *(AA gunnery)*.
Wechselrichter *m* vibrator *(Rad)*.
Wechselstellung *f* alternate emplacement, alternate firing position.
Wechselstrom *m* alternating current.
Wechselstromerzeuger *m* alternating-current generator, alternator *(Elec)*.
Wechselstromwecker *m* alternating-current buzzer or ringer *(Tp)*.
Wechselverkehr *m* alternate two-way traffic *(Rad)*.
Wecken *n* reveille.
Wecker *m* buzzer, ringer *(Tp)*.
Weckerfallklappe *f* drop, shutter *(Tp)*.
Weg *m* road, route, passage, way, channel.
Wegebau *m* road construction.
Wegebiegung *f* road curve, road bend.
Wegedreieck *n* triangular road junction.
Wegeeinmündung *f* junction of side road with main road.
Wegeerkundung *f* road reconnaissance, reconnaissance of route.
Wegegabel *f* road fork.
Wegekarte *f* circulation map, road map.
Wegeknie *n* V-turn *(road)*.

Wegekreuzung *f* crossroads, intersection.

Wegenetz *n* road net, network of roads.

Wegeposten *m* marker *(traffic control)*.

Wegesperre *f* road block.

Wegespinne *f* multiple road junction.

Wegestrecke *f* stretch of road.

Wegeverhältnisse *npl* road conditions.

Wegflugpeilung *f* back bearing *(Air Navigation)*.

"Weggetreten!" "Dismissed!"

Wegskizze *f* strip map, sketched road map.

Wegsperre *f* road block.

wegtreten to break ranks.

wegtreten lassen to dismiss.

Wegweiser *m* road sign.

Wehr *n* weir *(Engr)*.

Wehr *f* defense; parapet *(G emplacement)*.

Wehrausbildung *f* military training.

Wehrbarmachung *f* activation.

Wehrbezirk *m* recruiting district *(subdivision of a* Wehrersatzbezirk).

Wehrbezirkskommandeur *m* recruiting district commander.

Wehrbezirkskommando *n* recruiting district headquarters.

Wehrdienst *m* military service; service with the armed forces.

Wehrdienstbeschädigung *f* nonbattle injury.

Wehrdienst im Beurlaubtenstande military service with reserve status.

Wehrdienstverhältnis *n* service status.

Wehrersatz *m* recruiting and replacement for the armed forces.

Wehrersatzbezirk *m* recruiting area *(subdivision of a* Wehrkreis).

Wehrersatzdienststelle *f* recruiting office.

Wehrersatzinspekteur *m* recruiting area commander.

Wehrersatzinspektion *f* recruiting area headquarters.

Wehrersatzwesen *n* armed forces recruiting and replacement administration.

Wehrertüchtigung *f* military training.

Wehrerziehung *f* military education.

wehrfähig fit for military service, eligible for military service; able-bodied.

Wehrform *f* national defense system.

Wehrgeographie *f* military geography.

Wehrgeologie *f* military geology.

Wehrgeopolitik *f* military geopolitics.

Wehrgesetz *n* compulsory service law, national defense act.

Wehrhoheit *f* military sovereignty *(right of a country to have armed forces of any strength and type)*.

Wehrkreis *m* military area *(corresponds roughly to corps area or service command; territorial Germany is divided into about 15* Wehrkreise *which form the basis for recruitment and replacements)*.

Wehrkreisbefehlshaber *m* military area commander.

Wehrkreis-Ersatzdepot *n* recruit reception center of a *Wehrkreis*.

Wehrkreiskommando *n* military area headquarters.

Wehrmacht *f* Armed Forces.

Wehrmachtakademie *f* armed forces war college.

Wehrmachtauskunftstelle *f* armed forces information office *(supplies information regarding casualties, missing, etc., upon inquiry by next of kin)*.

Wehrmachtbeamter *m* civilian official of the armed forces (Wehrmachtbeamte *have nominal rank and wear uniforms; they are classified as combatants)*.

Wehrmachtbefehlshaber *m* military district commander in occupied territory *(directly responsible to the* Oberkommando der Wehrmacht).

Wehrmachtbericht *m* communiqué of the High Command.

Wehrmachtbevollmächtigter *m* Armed Forces Plenipotentiary *(commander of a protectorate or other occupied territory)*.

Wehrmachtfahrkarte *f* soldier's reduced-rate railroad ticket.

Wehrmachtführerschein *m* military motor vehicle operator's permit.

Wehrmachtführungsstab *m* armed forces operations staff *(a joint operations staff under the* Oberkommando der Wehrmacht).

Wehrmachtgefängnis *n* disciplinary barracks.

Wehrmachtgeistlicher *m* chaplain.

Wehrmachtgelände *n* military reservation.

Wehrmachtgericht *n* military court.

Wehrmachtgesundheitsdienst *m* military hygiene service.

Wehrmachtrundfunkempfänger *m* standard broadcast receiver issued to armed forces personnel.

Wehrmachtseelsorgedienst *m* chaplains' service of the armed forces.

Wehrmachtsfahrlehrerschein *m* military motor vehicle instructor's license.

Wehrmacht-Standort *m* military post, garrison or station.

Wehrmacht-Strafgesetzbuch *n* military penal code.

Wehrmachtteil *m* branch of the armed forces (*such as Army or Navy*).

Wehrmeldeamt *n* draft board.

Wehrmeldebezirk *m* draft district (*subdivision of a* Wehrbezirk).

Wehrnummer *f* personal number (*appears on identification tag and in pay book; does not correspond to US Army Serial Number*).

Wehrordnung *f* compulsory service law regulations.

Wehrorganisation *f* armed-defense system.

Wehrpapiere *npl* military service documents.

Wehrpaß *m* service record book.

Wehrpflicht *f* obligation to serve in the armed forces.

Wehrpflichtiger *m* one who is subject to the draft.

Wehrrecht *n* military law.

Wehrsold *m* army pay.

Höhe des Wehrsoldes rate of pay.

Wehrsoldgruppe *f* pay grade.

Wehrstammblatt *n* document giving personal details (*made out at local induction center*).

Wehrstammbuch *n* service record book.

Wehrstammkarte *f* locator card.

Wehrstammrolle *f* roster of draftees (*arranged according to age groups*).

Wehrstrafrecht *n* military penal law.

Wehrsystem *n* national defense system.

wehrtauglich fit for military service.

wehrunwürdig unworthy to bear arms (*classification given to criminals, etc.*).

Wehrvergehen *n* military offense.

Wehrversammlung *f* annual assembly of reservists.

wehrwichtige Güter essential items.

wehrwichtige Nachrichten military information.

Wehrwirtschaft *f* war economy, military economics.

Wehrwissenschaft *f* military science.

wehrwürdig worthy to bear arms. *See also* **wehrunwürdig.**

Weiche *f* switch (*RR*); filter (*Rad*); flank (*horse*).

Weicheisen *n* soft iron, mild steel.

weichen give ground, give way, fall back.

Weichenbock *m* switch stand (*RR*).

Weichenhebel *m* switch lever (*RR*).

Weichenlaterne *f* switch lamp (*RR*).

Weingarten *m* vineyard.

Weingeist *m* alcohol.

Weise *f* manner, method, way.

Weißkreuz *n* lacrimator (*Ger marking "White Cross"*).

Weisung *f* directive, instruction, letter of instruction.

Weite *f* width; distance.

Weiterbildung *f* advanced training.

weitergeben to forward, pass along, relay.

Weiterleitungsstelle *f* forwarding point, forwarding station.

"Weitermachen!" "As you were!" (*In the sense of "Carry on!"*).

Weitermarsch *m* resumed march.

Weitschuß *m* over (*Gunnery*).

Weitwerfer *m* long-range flame thrower.

Weitwinkelaufnahme *f* wide-angle photograph.

Wellblech *n* corrugated sheet metal.

Welle *f* wave; frequency (*Rad*); shaft, axle, spindle.

in rollenden Wellen in waves (*Tac*).

Wellenausbreitung *f* wave propagation (*Rad*).

Wellenband *n* wave band, frequency band (*Rad*).

Wellenbereich *m* wave range (*Rad*).

Wellenbrecher *m* breakwater.

Wellenlänge *f* wave length (*Rad*).

Wellenleistung *f* brake horsepower.

Wellenmesser *m* wavemeter, frequency meter (*Rad*).

Wellenspektrum *n* frequency spectrum (*Rad*).

Wellenwechsel *m* change of frequency (*Rad*).

Wellenwiderstand *m* characteristic impedance, surge impedance (*Elec, Rad*).

Wellenzapfen m journal *(Mech)*.
wellig wavy, undulating; pulsating *(Elec)*.
Wellpappe f corrugated paper.
Weltkrieg m World War I.
Weltkriegsteilnehmer m veteran of World War I.
Wendegetriebe n reversing gear.
Wendekreis m turning radius *(MT)*.
wenden to turn, veer.
Wendepunkt m turning point, critical point.
Wendeturm m pylon *(Adrm)*.
Wendewinkel m angle of yaw *(Avn)*.
Wendezeiger m bank and turn indicator *(Ap)*.
Wendigkeit f maneuverability *(Ap)*; ease in steering or turning, mobility *(vehicles)*.
Wendung f turn *(Avn)*; facing *(drill)*; reversal; change.
werfen to throw.
Werfer m smoke-shell mortar; signal projector; rocket projector. *See also* **Nebelwerfer.**
Werferabteilung f chemical battalion, smoke battalion; rocket projector battalion.
Werferrahmen m projector frame; frame-type rocket projector.
Werferregiment n chemical regiment, smoke regiment; rocket projector regiment.
Werferschütze m mortar gunner.
Werft f shipyard, dockyard; workshop *(Adrm)*.
Werfthalle f repair hangar *(Adrm)*.
Werg n oakum.
Werk n work *(Ft, etc.)*; plant, factory.
Werkbank f workbench.
Werkflugplatz m factory airfield.
Werkluftschutz m factory air-defense system.
Werkmeister m shop foreman *(Civ official ranking as Master Sgt)*.
Werkstatt f workshop, machine shop.
Werkstattauftrag m work order.
Werkstattgerätkraftwagen m spare parts truck *(MT)*.
Werkstattkompanie f repair-shop company, workshop company.
Werkstattkraftwagen m repair-shop truck, mobile machine shop *(MT)*.
Werkstattrupp m repair-shop detachment, maintenance party.

Werkstattzug m maintenance platoon *(Tk Bn)*.
Werkstoff m material.
Werkzeug n tool.
Werkzeugkasten m tool box.
Werkzeugmaschine f machine tool.
Werkzeugstahl m tool steel.
Werkzeugtasche f tool bag, tool kit.
Wert m value, factor.
Wespe f wasp *(also nickname for Ger self-propelled light field howitzer)*.
Westa f *See* **Wettererkundungsstaffel.**
Westwall m West Wall *(a system of fortifications along Germany's western frontier)*.
Westwallabzeichen n West Wall Badge *(decoration)*.
Wetter n weather.
Wetterbeobachtung f weather observation.
Wetterberatung f *See* **Wetterbericht.**
Wetterberatungszentrale f air forces weather reporting center.
Wetterbericht m weather report.
Wetterbericht vom Pilotballon pibal *(Met)*.
Wetterbezirk m weather region, control region.
Wetterdienst m weather service.
Wetterdienstgeräte npl weather instruments *(Met)*.
Wetterdiensthelferin f air forces weather service woman auxiliary.
Wetterelement n weather factor *(Ballistics, Met)*.
Wettererkundung f weather reconnaissance *(Avn)*.
Wettererkundungsstaffel f weather reconnaissance squadron *(Avn)*.
Wetterfahne f weather vane.
Wetterführung f ventilating system *(mine)*.
Wetterfunkmeldung f weather message, meteorological message *(Rad)*.
Wetterfunkspruch m *See* **Wetterfunkmeldung.**
Wetterkarte f weather map *(Met)*.
Wetterkunde f meteorology.
Wetterlage f weather conditions.
Wetterleuchten n lightning *(Met)*.
Wettermeldung f weather report *(Avn)*; metro message *(Arty)*.
Wettermessung f meteorological measurement.
Wetterpeilzug m meteorological and direction-finding platoon.

Wetterschlüssel *m* weather code.

Wetterspinne *f* wind-component indicator *(Gunnery)*.

Wettersprengmittel *n* safety mining explosive.

Wetterstelle *f* weather station.

Wetterstörung *f* meteorological disturbance.

Wettervoraussage *f* weather forecast.

Wettervorhersage *f See* **Wettervoraussage.**

Wetterwarte *f* weather station.

Wetterzug *m* metro platoon *(Arty)*.

wetzen to sharpen, hone.

Wezu-Gerät *n* wind corrector and time scale *(SR) (Wezu = Wetterzug)*.

wichsen to polish *(leather, etc.)*.

Wickelgamaschen *fpl* wrapped leggins, wrap puttees.

Wicklung *f* winding, wrapping.

Widerlager *n* abutment *(Bdg)*.

Widerrist *m* withers *(horse)*.

Widerstand *m* resistance *(Elec, Tac)*; drag *(Avn)*.

Widerstandsgruppe *f* unit assigned to one sector of main line of resistance *(Tac)*.

Widerstandskessel *m* pocket of resistance.

Widerstandslinie *f* line of resistance.

Widerstandslinie der Vorposten outpost line of resistance *(Tac)*.

Widerstandsmesser *m* ohmmeter.

Widerstandsmoment *n* section modulus *(Engr)*.

Widerstandsnest *n* island of resistance, pocket of resistance.

Widerstandsstellung *f* delaying position.

Widerstandstruppe *f* delaying unit *(Tac)*.

Widerstandszentrum *n* center of resistance *(Tac)*.

widerstehen to withstand, resist.

wiederherstellen to repair, restore, reconstruct.

Wiederherstellung *f* reconstruction, repair, restoration.

wiederholen to repeat.

Wiederholungsunterricht *m* refresher instruction.

wieder richten to re-lay *(Gunnery)*.

Wiederspannabzug *m* double action *(SA)*.

Wiege *f* cradle *(G)*.

wiegen to weigh.

Wiegengleitbahn *f* cradle guide rails *(G)*.

Wiegenträger *m* cradle frame *(G)*.

Wiegentrog *m* cradle trough *(G)*.

Wiegenzurrung *f* cradle lock *(G)*.

Wiese und Weide grassland.

Wimpel *m* pennant.

Windabtrift *f* wind drift.

windabwärts downwind, leeward.

Windanker *m* downstream anchor cable *(Pon Bdg)*.

Windankerleine *f* downstream anchor cable *(Pon Bdg)*.

Windankerlinie *f* downstream line of anchors *(Pon Bdg)*.

Windankertau *n* downstream anchor cable *(Pon Bdg)*.

Windanzeiger *m* wind indicator.

Winddruck *m* wind pressure.

Winde *f* winch.

Windenkasten *m* winch box.

Windewagen *m* winch truck.

Windfahne *f* wind vane.

Windfahnenkorn *n* wind vane front sight *(Ap MG)*.

Windflügel *m* fan *(MT)*; arming vane *(bomb)*.

Windjacke *f* double-breasted field jacket.

Windkanal *m* wind tunnel *(Avn)*.

Windkegel *m* wind cone.

Windmesser *m See* **Windmeßgerät.**

Windmeßgerät *n* anemometer.

Windmessung *f* wind test *(Met)*.

Windmühle *f* windmill.

Windpfeil *m* wind arrow *(Met)*.

Windrichtungsanzeiger *m* wind-direction indicator *(Avn)*.

Windsack *m* wind cone, windsock.

windschief twisted, warped.

windschiefer Flug crabbing *(Avn)*.

Windschlüssel *m* key to weather code numbers and symbols *(Met)*.

Windschutz *m* windbreak.

Windschutzscheibe *f* windshield.

windseitig windward.

Windstärke *f* wind velocity *(Met)*.

Windstoß *m* squall, gust, bump.

Windung *f* twist *(Ord)*.

Windverband *m* lateral bracing *(Bdg)*.

Windverhältnisse *npl* wind factors *(Ballistics)*.

windwärts upwind, windward.

Windziffer *f* wind reference number *(Gunnery)*.

Winkel *m* angle; V-formation, wedge formation *(Avn)*; chevron.

Winkelauswanderung *f* angular movement, angular travel.
Winkelbeschleunigung *f* angular acceleration.
Winkel der Schräglage angle of bank, angle of roll *(Avn)*.
Winkelfernrohr *n* elbow telescope.
Winkelgeschwindigkeit *f* angular speed, angular velocity, angular travel.
Winkelgruppe *f* firing angles.
untere **Winkelgruppe** low firing angles (0° to 45°).
obere **Winkelgruppe** high firing angles (45° to 90°).
Winkelhebel *m* angle cam *(MG lock)*.
Winkelkopf *m* head of static rod *(river-width measuring Inst)*.
Winkellasche *f* butt strap *(made of angle iron)*.
Winkelmaß *n* angular measurement; phase constant *(Rad)*.
Winkelmesser *m* gunner's quadrant; clinometer *(Surv, Arty)*; goniometer *(Surv)*; protractor.
Winkelmesserebene *f* quadrant plate *(G)*.
Winkelmeßgerät *n* protractor.
Winkelmessung *f* goniometry *(Surv)*.
Winkelspiegel *m* periscope, protectoscope *(Tk)*.
Winkeltrommel *f* cross staff *(Surv Inst for laying out right angles)*.
Winker *m* flagman; signaler using a signal disk; signal arm or light indicating direction of turn *(MT)*.
Winkerflagge *f* See **Winkflagge**.
Winkerkelle *f* See **Winkerstab**.
Winkerstab *m* signaling disk.
Winkflagge *f* semaphore flag, control flag, signal flag.
Winkspruch *m* semaphore message, message transmitted by signaling disk or hand signals.
Winkverbindung *f* visual communication by flag or hand signals.
Winkzeichen *n* hand signal, flag signal.
Winterausrüstung *f* winter equipment.
Winterbeweglichkeit *f* mobility in winter.
Winterkettenglied *n* oversize track shoe for operations in deep snow *(MT, Tk)*.
Winterkrieg *m* winter warfare.
Winterlost *n* 50-50 mixture of lewisite and mustard *(CWS)*.
Wintermedaille des Ostkrieges Eastern

Campaign Winter Medal *(decoration)*.
Wirbel *m* vortex, eddy, whirl; whirlpool; drum roll; spine.
Wirbelbildung *f* formation of eddies *(Ballistics)*.
Wirbelkammer *f* turbulence chamber *(Diesel engine)*.
Wirbelsäule *f* spinal column.
Wirbelstrom *m* eddy current *(Elec)*.
Wirbelsturm *m* cyclone, tornado.
wirksam effective.
wirksame Schußweite effective range.
wirksame Steigung effective pitch *(propeller)*.
Wirkungsbereich *m* effective range *(Ord)*; field of fire *(Ord)*; radius of action *(Ap)*.
Wirkungsdauer *f* persistence *(of a Cml agent)*.
Wirkungsfeuer *n* fire for effect *(Arty)*.
Wirkungshalbmesser *m* radius of rupture *(demolitions)*.
Wirkungskreis *m* circle of rupture *(demolitions)*.
Wirkungsschießen *n* fire for effect *(Gunnery)*.
Wirtschaft *f* economy; tavern.
wirtschaftlich economical.
Wirtschaftskrieg *m* economic warfare.
Wirtshaus *n* tavern, inn.
Wischer *m* wiper; sponge; cleaning patch; windshield wiper.
Wischstock *m* cleaning rod *(G)*.
Wischstrick *m* pull-through rope *(for pulling brush or sponge through G barrel)*.
Witterung *f* atmospheric conditions, weather.
Witterungseinflüsse *mpl* exterior ballistic factors, weather factors.
W-Motor *m* three-bank upright engine.
Wohnungsgeldzuschuß *m* commutation of quarters, rental allowance.
Wohnviertel *n* residential quarter.
Woilach *m* saddle blanket.
Wölbung *f* droop; camber.
Wolfram *n* tungsten.
Wolfsgrube *f* obstacle pit *(Ft)*.
Wolke *f* cloud.
Wolkendecke *f* cloud cover.
Wolkenfeld *n* cloud bank.
Wolkenhöhe *f* ceiling *(Met)*.
wolkenlos clear *(Met)*.
Wolkenscheinwerfer *m* ceiling light *(Met)*.

Wolkensegeln *n* cloud soaring *(glider)*.
Wolkenspiegel *m* nephoscope *(Met)*.
Wolkenuntergrenze *f* base of cloud.
wolkig broken *(Met)*.
Wolldecke *f* wool blanket.
Wolle *f* wool.
Wolokusche *f* boat-type runner *(placed under gun wheels for operations in deep snow)*.
Wortlaut *m* text, wording.
Wriggeln *n* sculling.
Wucht *f* kinetic energy; striking power, force of impact.
Wulstband *n* rim band *(MT)*.
Wulstfelge *f* clincher rim *(MT)*.
Wundbrand *m* gangrene.
Wunde *f* wound.
Wundstarrkrampf *m* lockjaw, tetanus.
Wundverband *m* dressing, bandage.
Wurf *m* cast, throw; bomb release.
"Wurf!" "Bombs away!"
Wurfarten *fpl* types of release *(bombing)*.
Wurfbahn *f* bomb trajectory.

Würfel *m* cube; capsule, pellet.
Wurfgerät *n* projector.
schweres Wurfgerät chemical rocket projector.
Wurfgranate *f* mortar shell.
Wurfgranatzünder *m* mortar-shell fuze.
Wurfkörper *m* special projectile for signal pistols.
Wurfparabel *f* bomb trajectory.
Wurfrahmen *m* framework-type projector for high-explosive or incendiary rockets.
Wurftaubenschießstand *m* skeet range.
Wurfweite *f* mortar range; throwing range *(hand grenades)*; bombing range.
Würgebohrung *f* tapered bore, choke *(barrel) (Ord)*.
Würgezange *f* cap crimper *(Engr)*.
Würgung *f* crimp *(Am)*.
Wurzel *f* root.
Wüste *f* desert.

X

X-Tag *m* M-day, mobilization day. | **X-Uhr** *f* H-hour, zero hour.

Y

Yperit *n* mustard gas.

Z

zäh tough, tenacious; viscous; stubborn.
Zahl *f* number.
Zahlenwert *m* numerical value.
Zahlmeister *m* paymaster official (*Wehrmachtbeamter, generally ranking as 2nd Lt, responsible for pay and allowances, ration, messing, clothing accounts and company finances*).
Zahlmeisterei *f* office and function of the *Zahlmeister*.
Zahn *m* tooth.

Zahnarzt *m* dentist. *See also* Sanitätsoffizier(Z).
Zahnbehandlung *f* dental treatment.
Zahnbogen *m* elevating arc, elevating rack *(G)*.
Zahnbogenrichtmaschine *f* arc-type elevating mechanism *(G)*.
Zahnkette *f* driving chain *(MT)*.
Zahnkranz *m* traversing rack *(Tk turret, AA gun)*.
Zahnkranzlenkung *f* worm and sector steering system *(MT)*.

Zahnrad n gear, gear wheel; pinion.
Zahnradgetriebe n gear transmission *(MT)*.
Zahnradpumpe f gear pump *(Mtr)*.
Zahnstange f rack *(Tech)*.
Zahnstangenlenkung f pinion and sector steering system *(MT)*.
Zahntechniker m dental technician.
Zange f pliers, tongs.
Zangenangriff m pincer attack, double envelopment *(Tac)*.
Zangenbewegung f pincer movement.
Zapfen m pin; journal; trunnion; pivot; plug; tap; spigot; tenon.
Zapfendüse f pintle nozzle, pin nozzle *(Mtr)*.
Zapfenkreuz n cross *(of a universal joint)*.
Zapfenlager n pillow block, bushing.
Zapfenstreich m taps.
Zapfstelle f standpipe.
Zaum m bridle.
Zaun m fence.
Zehe f toe.
Zeichen n sign; signal; call; military symbol.
Zeichenbrett n drawing board.
Zeichenerklärung f legend, key to map signs.
Zeichengerät n plotting instrument, drawing instrument.
Zeichenpapier n drawing paper.
Zeichenverbindung f visual communication.
zeichnen to draw, sketch.
Zeichnung f drawing, blueprint, plan.
Zeigefinger m forefinger.
Zeiger m indicator, pointer; hand, needle *(on Inst dial)*.
Zeigerzieleinrichtung f follow-the-pointer sight mechanism *(G)*.
Zeitabstand m headway, time interval.
Zeitbombe f time bomb.
Zeiteinteilung f timetable *(Tac)*.
Zeitgruppe f time heading *(on Rad messages)*.
Zeitmaß n cadence *(marching)*.
Zeitschnur f safety fuze, blasting fuze.
Zeittafel f timetable, schedule.
Zeitunterschied m time difference *(SR)*; time interval *(AAA)*.
Zeitunterschiedverfahren n time-difference method *(SR)*.
Zeitzeichen n time signal.
Zeitzünder m time fuze *(Am)*.
Zeitzünderschuß m time fire *(Gunnery)*.

Zeitzündschnur f safety fuze, blasting fuze.
Zelle f cell, cellule.
Zellon n cellulose acetate.
Zellophan n cellophane.
Zellophanüberzug m cellophane cover.
Zellstoff m cellulose.
Zelluloidtafel f celluloid disk; protractor; templet.
Zellwolle f cellulose fiber.
Zelt n tent.
Zeltausrüstung f tent equipment.
Zeltbahn f shelter half.
Zeltbau m tent pitching.
Zeltlager n tent camp.
Zeltleine f guy rope *(tent)*.
Zeltpflock m tent pin, guy pin, guyline stake.
Zeltstock m tent pole.
Zementfliese f concrete paving block.
Zensor m censor.
Zensur f censorship.
Zentralbatterie f common battery *(Tp)*.
Zentrale f central *(Tp)*; central station *(Arty)*.
zentrale Projektion gnomonic projection.
Zentralrichtgerät n director *(AAA)*.
Zentralschmierung f central lubrication *(MT)*.
Zentrierwulst m bourrelet *(Am)*.
Zentrum n center; bull's eye.
zerbrechen to crack, break into pieces.
zerdrücken crush, crumple, squash, squeeze.
zerfallen disintegrate.
Zerfallgurt m disintegrating belt *(MG)*.
Zerknallstoß m blast, concussion.
zerlegen disassemble, dismantle, strip; decentralize, disperse; disintegrate.
Zerlegerzünder m self-destroying fuze *(AA Am)*.
zerlegte Formen broken outlines *(Cam)*.
Zerlegung f dispersal, decentralization; disintegration; dismantling, stripping.
zermalmen crush, crunch, smash, dash to pieces.
zermürben wear down.
Zermürbung f attrition.
Zermürbungskrieg m war of attrition.
Zermürbungsstrategie f strategy of attrition.

Zerschellerschicht *f* burster course, bursting layer, detonating slab *(Ft)*.

Zerschneidezünder *m* See **Zug- und Zerschneidezünder**.

zerspalten to split up.

zersplittern to shatter; to split up, dissipate *(forces, etc.)*.

zersprengen to crack, burst into pieces, shatter; to blow up; to rout.

zerspringen to explode, burst.

Zerstäuber *m* atomizer, spray.

Zerstäuberdüse *f* spray nozzle; Diesel fuel injector.

Zerstäubergerät *n* chemical spray apparatus; sprayer-type decontaminating apparatus.

Zerstörangriff *m* hit-and-run raid *(Avn)*.

zerstören destroy, demolish.

Zerstörer *m* destroyer *(Nav)*; twin-engine fighter, long-range fighter *(Ap)*.

Zerstörerflugzeug *n* twin-engine fighter airplane.

Zerstörergeschwader *n* twin-engine fighter wing.

Zerstörerschule *f* twin-engine fighter pilot school.

Zerstörung *f* destruction, demolition.

Zerstörungsarbeiten *fpl* demolitions.

Zerstörungsfeuer *n* destruction fire *(Arty)*.

Zettel *m* card, tag, ticket, slip.

Zeug *n* ordnance supplies; gear, equipment.

Zeugamt *n* ordnance office.

Zeughaus *n* arsenal.

Zeugnis *n* certificate.

Zickzackscheibe *f* zigzag target *(Tng)*.

Ziegelei *f* brickyard.

ziehen to draw, pull, drag, tow; to pull up *(Ap)*; to be drafty.

Ziehzünder *m* pull firing device *(land mine)*.

Ziel *n* target, objective, goal.

ins Ziel gehen to hold into the target.

das Ziel aufsitzen lassen to hold at bottom edge of target.

das Ziel verschwinden lassen to hold at upper edge of target.

Zielabschnitt *m* sector of fire, target sector.

Zielachse *f* sighting axis *(plane table alidade)*.

Zielanflug *m* approach flight, approach run *(Avn)*.

Zielansprache *f* target designation.

Zielaufklärung *f* artillery target reconnaissance.

Zielaufnahme mit Langbasisanlage horizontal base method.

Zielausbildung *f* training in aiming, training in laying.

Zielbild *n* target image *(telescopic sight)*.

Zielbreite *f* target length *(moving targets)*.

"Ziel dreht!" "Target changing course!" *(AA predictor)*.

Zieldreieck *n* shot group, aiming group *(sighting and aiming exercise)*.

Zieleinrichtung *f* sighting mechanism *(Ord)*.

zielen to aim, sight.

Zielentfernung *f* range to target *(Gunnery)*.

Zielerkundung *f* target reconnaissance.

Zielfehler *m* aiming error.

Zielfernrohr *n* telescopic sight, direct sighting telescope.

Zielfernrohrträger *m* telescopic sight mount.

Zielfeststellung *f* locating of target *(Gunnery)*.

Zielfläche *f* objective plane *(Gunnery)*; target area *(bombing)*.

Zielflug *m* homing *(Air Navigation)*.

Zielgelände *n* target area.

zielgenau accurate, precise.

Zielgerät *n* sight, sighting mechanism *(Ord)*; bomb sight.

Zielgeschwindigkeit *f* speed of target.

Zielgevierttafel *f* target-designation grid *(Arty Surv)*.

Zielhöhe *f* height of target, altitude of target.

Zielhöhenwinkel *m* angle of site *(Gunnery)*; angular height of target *(AAA)*.

Zielhöhenwinkel zum Abschußpunkt angular height of target at present position *(AAA)*.

Zielhöhenwinkel zum Meßpunkt angular height of target at instant of range determination *(AAA)*.

Zielhöhenwinkel zum Treffpunkt angular height of target at future position *(AAA)*.

Zielhöhenwinkel zum Wechselpunkt angular height of target at midpoint *(AAA)*.

Zielkelle *f* See **Ziellöffel**.

Zielkontrollspiegel *m* aim-checking device.

Zielkreis *m* target area *(bombing)*.

Ziellandung *f* spot landing *(Avn)*.

Ziellineal *n* orienting straightedge *(MG aiming circle)*.

Ziellinie *f* line of sight.

Ziellinienprüfer *m* bore sight *(Ord)*.

Ziellöffel *m* aiming disk, sighting disk, marking disk.

Zielmarke *f* lead mark *(telescopic sight)*.

Zielmunition *f* subcaliber ammunition.

Zielpunkt *m* target point, objective point.

Zielpunktkarte *f* battle map or firing chart showing location of probable targets.

Zielpuppe *f* dummy.

Zielraum *m* target area, sector of fire.

Zielrechenmaschine *f* predictor, prediction mechanism *(AA)*; ballistic director *(Arty)*.

Zielrichtung *f* direction of the target.

Zielscheibe *f* practice target.

Zielschiene *f* sighting bar.

Zielschiff *n* target ship.

Zielschwarze *n* bull's-eye.

Zielseitenwinkel *m* azimuth of target.

Zielseitenwinkel zum Abschußpunkt azimuth of target at present position *(AAA)*.

Zielseitenwinkel zum Treffpunkt azimuth of target at future position *(AAA)*.

Zielsetzung *f* designation of objective.

Zielsicherheit *f* accuracy of fire, marksmanship.

Zielspinne *f* range-deflection fan *(Gunnery)*.

Zielstachel *m* pointed-post reticle *(telescopic sight)*.

Zieltafel *f* data sheet *(Gunnery)*.

Zielteil *m* target sector.

Ziel- und Anschlagsübungen *fpl* aiming drill.

Zielunterlagen *fpl* information of objectives, target data.

Zielvorrichtung *f* aiming mechanism.

Zielwaagerechte *f* horizontal through base of target *(Arty)*.

Zielwechsel *m* change of target, engaging of successive targets.

Zielweg *m* course of target *(AAA)*.

Zielwurf *m* precision bombing.

Zielzuweisung *f* allocation of targets.

Ziffer *f* cipher, figure, numeral.

Zifferblatt *n* dial *(on Inst)*.

ziffern to cipher, encipher, encrypt.

Zimmerantenne *f* indoor antenna.

Zimmermann *m* carpenter.

Zimmerschießgerät *n* field artillery trainer.

Zinkbecher *m* zinc container *(dry cell)*.

Zinknebel *m* HC mixture, HC smoke mixture *(CWS)*.

Zinn *n* tin.

Zirkel *m* compasses, dividers.

Zirruswolke *f* cirrus cloud *(Met)*.

Zisternenfahrzeug *n* vehicle fitted with chemical spray apparatus.

Zisternenflugzeug *n* airplane fitted with chemical-spray apparatus.

Zivil *n* civilian clothing.

Zivilbevölkerung *f* civilian population.

Zivilgericht *n* civil court.

Zivilinternierter *m* civilian internee.

Zivilist *m* civilian.

Zivilkleidung *f* civilian clothing.

Zivilluftfahrt *f* civil aviation, commercial aviation.

Zivilperson *f* civilian.

Zivilvergehen *n* civil offense.

Zoll *m* inch *(2.54 cm)*; duty, tariff, toll.

Zollhaus *n* custom house.

Zollschranke *f* tollgate.

Zonenzeit *f* standard time.

Zubehör *n* accessories.

Zubehörteil *m* part, accessory.

Zubehörtornister *m* accessories case *(portable Rad)*.

Zubringer *m* follower *(SA)*.

Zubringerfeder *f* follower spring *(SA)*.

Zubringerhebel *m* belt-feed lever *(MG)*.

Zucht *f* discipline.

Zuchthaus *n* penitentiary.

Zuchthausstrafe *f* sentence of confinement to a penitentiary.

Zufahrtstraße *f* access road, approach road.

zufälliger Fehler nonsystematic error *(Arty)*; accidental error *(Mech, Optics)*.

Zufallstreffer *m* accidental hit.

Zufuhr *f* supply, bringing up of supplies.

Zuführer *m* belt feed *(MG)*; feed mechanism *(automatic weapon)*.

Zufuhrstraße *f* line or road of communication, line or road of supply.

Zuführung *f*   feed *(MG)*; lead-in *(Rad)*.

Zuführungsdraht *m*   lead-in *(Rad)*.

Zuführungsgehäuse *n*   feed box *(AA gun)*.

Zuführungsweg *m*   route for bringing up supplies, etc.

Zug *m*   platoon; groove *(rifling)*; train *(RR)*; pull; tension; draft.

Zugang *m*   access, approach; increase, addition.

Zugangsweg *m*   access road, approach road.

Zugbewachung *f*   train guard.

Zugbreitkeil *m*   platoon in inverted-wedge formation.

Zugbrücke *f*   drawbridge.

Zugdämpfer *m*   baffle *(engine muffler)*.

Zugdruckzünder *m*   pull-pressure igniter *(mine)*.

Zügel *m*   bridle; rein.

zugelassen   authorized, permitted; admitted.

Zügelring *m*   bit ring *(harness)*.

zugeteilt   attached; allotted.

Zugfähre *f*   rope ferry *(Engr)*.

Zugfeder *f*   safety spring *(MG)*.

Zugfederhaken *m*   safety-spring catch *(MG)*.

Zugfederschraube *f*   *See* **Zugfederspannschraube**.

Zugfederspannschraube *f*   safety-spring tension screw *(MG)*.

Zugfestigkeit *f*   tensile strength.

Zugführer *m*   platoon leader.

Zuggrenze *f*   platoon boundary.

Zuggurt *m*   tension chord *(truss)*.

Zughaken *m*   pintle *(Trac)*; singletree attachment hook *(limber)*.

Zugkeil *m*   platoon in wedge formation.

Zugkolonne *f*   column of platoons.

Zugkraft *f*   tractive power; tension force; drawbar pull *(prime mover)*.

Zugkraftwagen *m*   prime mover, half-track carrier and prime mover.

Zugleistung *f*   tractive power; drawbar pull *(Trac)*; draft efficiency *(of animals)*.

Zugmaschine *f*   prime mover *(MT)*.

Zugöse *f*   drag washer *(wheel)*; lunette *(limber, trailer)*.

Zugramme *f*   drop-hammer-type pile driver.

Zugriemen *m*   brake cable; trace *(harness)*.

Zugschraube *f*   tractor propeller *(Ap)*.

Zugschrauber *m*   tractor airplane.

Zugspannung *f*   tensile stress.

Zugstange *f*   brake rod *(vehicle brake)*; pintle drawbar *(MT, Trac)*; drawbar *(trailer)*.

Zugstreife *f*   train patrol.

Zugtau *n*   tow rope.

Zugtrupp *m*   platoon headquarters personnel, platoon command group personnel.

Zug- und Zerschneidezünder *m*   pull and cut igniter, tension release igniter *(LM)*.

Zugverkehr *m*   railroad traffic.

Zugwache *f*   train guard.

Zugzünder *m*   pull igniter *(LM)*.

Zuladung *f*   useful load *(Ap)*.

Zulage *f*   additional pay or allowance; addition; appendix.

zulässig   permissible; admissible.

Zulassung *f*   registration certificate *(MT)*; registration and airworthiness certificate *(Avn)*; admission; permission.

Zulegeplatte *f*   attachable base plate *(mine-surveying set)*.

zulegen   to add to.

Zuleitung *f*   lead-in *(Rad)*.

Zuleitungskabel *n*   lead-in cord *(signal lamp)*.

Zunahme *f*   increase, gain, addition.

Zündachse *f*   operating-piston sleeve *(blasting machine)*.

Zündapparat *m*   magneto; igniter; exploder, blasting machine.

Zündbolzen *m*   concussion plunger, percussion plunger, plunger *(powder-train time fuze)*.

Zündeinstellung *f*   timing *(ignition)*.

zünden   ignite, detonate; fire *(a demolition charge)*.

Zünder *m*   fuze *(Am)*; igniter *(land mine)*.

den Zünder einstellen   set the fuze.

Zünderdeckel *m*   false ogive *(Am)*.

Zünderdraht *m*   firing wire, lead wire *(demolitions)*.

Zündereinstellung *f*   fuze setting.

Zündereinteilung *f*   fuze scale.

Zündergehäuse *n*   fuze body *(Am)*; fuze cover *(bomb)*.

Zünderhalter *m*   shell *(of blasting cap)*.

Zünderhülse *f*   hood *(of fuze)*.

Zünderkappe *f*   closing cap *(time fuze)*; head *(point-detonating fuze)*; upper cap *(clockwork fuze)*.

Zünderkörper m body *(fuze)*.
Zünderlaufzeit f time of functioning *(fuze)*, fuze range.
Zünderstellmaschine f automatic fuze setter *(AA gun)*.
Zünderstellschlüssel m manual fuze setter.
Zünderstellsitz m fuze-setter support *(AA gun)*.
Zünderstellung f fuze setting *(Gunnery)*.
Zünderteller m body *(powder-train time fuze)*.
zündfertig armed, fuzed, ready for firing.
Zündfolge f firing order *(of engine cylinders)*.
Zündfunke m ignition spark *(Mtr)*.
Zündgerät n demolition equipment.
Zündglocke f inside bottom of cartridge case *(SA Am)*.
Zündhebel m spark control *(Ap)*.
Zündholz n match.
Zündhütchen n primer *(SA Am)*; percussion primer *(fuze)*; percussion cap, propellent primer *(Am)*.
Zündhütchenausfall m blown primer.
Zündhütchenhülse f primer cup *(Am)*.
Zündkabel n spark plug cable *(Mtr)*.
Zündkanal m vent hole *(obturator)*; primer vent *(cartridge)*; flash hole *(fuze)*; cap hole *(blasting cartridge)*.
Zündkapsel f detonator.
Zündkerze f spark plug.
Zündladung f primer, primer charge, igniting charge.
Zündladungskapsel f detonator casing *(fuze)*.
Zündladungskörper m detonator charge *(fuze)*.
Zündlage f ignition system *(Mtr)*.
Zündlichtmaschine f generator *(MT)*.
Zündloch n vent, flash vent.
Zündmagnet m magneto.
Zündmittel n detonation agent, primer, igniter, igniting mixture.
Zündnadel f firing pin *(fuze)*.
Zündpatrone f ignition cartridge *(Am)*.
Zündpunkt m flash point.
Zündpunktverstellung f timing *(engine ignition)*.
Zündsatz m powder train, primer *(Am, demolitions)*; igniter train *(pyrotechnic Sig)*; detonating composition.

Zündschalter m ignition switch *(Ap, MT)*.
Zündschlüssel m ignition key *(MT)*.
Zündschnur f safety fuze.
Zündschnuranzünder m fuze lighter.
Zündschraube f threaded primer *(Am)*.
Zündschraubengehäuse n case *(threaded percussion primer)*.
Zündspule f ignition coil *(Mtr)*.
Zündstift m insulated electrode *(spark plug)*.
Zündstrahl m igniting flash, priming flash *(Am)*.
Zündstrom m ignition current *(Mtr)*.
Zündübertragung f induced detonation *(demolitions)*.
Zündung f firing, detonation *(Am, demolitions)*; ignition *(Mtr)*.
"Zündung eingestellt!" "Contact!" *(Avn)*.
Zündverstellung f spark control, spark adjustment *(Mtr)*.
Zündverteiler m distributor *(Mtr)*.
Zündvorrichtung f firing device *(LM)*; ignition system *(Mtr)*.
Zündwilligkeit f ignition quality *(Diesel fuel)*.
Zündzeitpunkt m instant of firing *(engine ignition)*.
zunehmender Drall increasing twist *(Ord)*.
Zungenschiene f point of switch rail *(RR)*.
Zungenstuhl m knee *(RR switch)*.
Zurrbolzen m locking pin *(G)*.
Zurrbrücke f cradle lock frame *(G)*.
Zurrgriff m cradle lock handle *(G)*.
Zurrhaken m locking hook *(G carriage)*.
Zurrhebel m lock lever.
Zurrlager n lock support *(cradle lock)*.
Zurrstange f lock rod.
Zurrstellung f locked position *(Ord)*.
Zurrstück n back plate latch lock *(MG)*.
Zurrung f locking mechanism *(G, Tk, MG)*; anchorage; lashing; holdfast.
Zurückstellung f deferment.
Zurückstellungsantrag m request for deferment.
zurückweichen give ground, give way.
zurückziehen, sich fall back, retire, withdraw.
Zusammenarbeit f cooperation, mutual support.

Zusammenballung *f* concentration *(Tac)*.

Zusammenfassung *f* concentration *(Arty)*; abridgment, summary.

zusammengefaßtes Feuer concentrated fire *(Arty)*; collective fire *(SA)*.

zusammenlaufen converge.

zusammensetzen assemble; compile; compound; collect, bring together; fit together.

Zusammensetzung *f* composition.

Zusammenstoß *m* collision; clash.

Zusammenwirken *n* synchronization; coordination; liaison; cooperation.

zusammenziehen tighten, draw together, contract.

Zusatz *m* addition; supplement; appendix.

Zusatzfallschirm *m* parachute lobe.

Zusatzflügel *m* auxiliary airfoil, slat *(Ap)*.

Zusatzgetriebe *n* auxiliary transmission *(MT)*.

Zustand *m* state, condition, situation.

zuständig competent; authorized.

Zustellung *f* delivery.

zuteilen allot, attach.

Zutritt *m* entrance; admittance.

zuverlässig reliable.

zuwiderhandeln act in opposition, act against, counteract; break, violate *(a regulation, etc.)*.

zuziehen tighten, draw together.

Zwangsauslösung *f* static line device *(Prcht)*.

Zweiachser *m* two-axle vehicle, four-wheel vehicle.

zweiadrig two-stranded *(Elec)*.

zweiäugig binocular *adj.*

Zweibein *n* bipod *(MG)*.

Zweidecker *m* biplane.

Zweielektrodenröhre *f* diode tube *(Rad)*.

Zweierzelt *n* two-man shelter tent.

Zweiflügel-Luftschraube *f* two-blade propeller *(Ap)*.

Zweiglager *n* branch depot; branch camp *(PW)*.

zweigleisig double-tracked *(RR)*.

Zweiglinie *f* junction line *(RR)*.

Zweigpark *m* branch depot.

Zweigstelle *f* branch, branch office, substation.

zweimotorig twin-engine.

Zwei-Ohr-Verfahren *n* binaural method *(sound locating)*.

Zweipolröhre *f* diode tube *(Rad)*.

Zweipunktverfahren *n* two-point resection *(Surv)*.

Zweischwimmer-Seeflugzeug *n* twin-float seaplane.

Zweisitzer *m* two-place airplane; two-seater *(vehicle)*.

Zweitaktmotor *m* two-cycle engine.

Zweisternmotor *m* double-row radial engine.

Zweistieler *m* double-bay biplane.

zweistufig two-stage *(Elec, Rad)*.

Zweitaktsystem *n* two-cycle principle.

Zweiwegeatmung *f* two-way respiration *(gas mask)*.

Zwickzange *f* cutter, cutting pliers.

Zwillingslafette *f* twin mount *(Ord)*.

Zwillingsläufe *mpl* twin barrels *(MG)*.

Zwillingsmaschinengewehr *n* twin-barreled machine gun.

Zwillings-MG.-Drehturm *m* revolving turret with twin-barreled machine gun *(Ap)*.

Zwillingswaffe *f* twin-barreled weapon.

zwingen compel, force.

Zwischenbahnhof *m* intermediate station *(RR)*.

Zwischenentfernung *f* intermediate range *(Gunnery)*.

Zwischenfeld *n* ground between delaying positions, area between successive positions, intermediate area.

Zwischenfrequenz *f* intermediate frequency *(Rad)*.

Zwischenfrequenzempfänger *m* superheterodyne receiver.

Zwischengebläse *n* auxiliary stage supercharger, turbosupercharger.

Zwischengetriebe *n* auxiliary transmission *(MT)*.

Zwischenlandung *f* intermediate landing.

Zwischenlandungsplatz *m* intermediate landing field.

Zwischenraum *m* interval *(from left to right)*.

Zwischenstecker *m* adapter plug *(Elec)*.

Zwischenstelle *f* linking station; relay station *(Sig Com)*.

Zwischenstellung *f* intermediate position.

Zwischenstück *n* adapter.

Zwischenwelle *f* intermediate shaft, propeller shaft.

Zwischenziel *n* intermediate objective; reference point *(Arty, R fire)*.
Zwitterfahrzeug *n* half-track vehicle.
zwo two *(used in voice transmission to avoid confusion with* drei, *three)*.
Zyanwasserstoffsäure *f* hydrocyanic acid, prussic acid *(CWS)*.
Zylinderblock *m* cylinder block *(Mtr)*.
Zylinderinhalt *m* total volume of cylinder *(Mtr)*.
Zylinderkopf *m* cylinder head *(Mtr)*.

Zylinderlaufbüchse *f* cylinder liner *(Mtr)*.
Zylinderschleifen *n* cylinder grinding *(Mtr)*.
Zylinderverschluß *m* bolt mechanism *(R)*.
Zylinderwand *f* cylinder wall *(Mtr)*.
ZZ-Verfahren *n* method of radio approach landing *(the main let-down signal is ZZ with last letter of airport station signal in between)*.

abandon *v* räumen *(a locality)*; verlassen *(a position, etc.)*; zurücklassen *(equipment, wounded, etc.)*.

abatage   Stellung auf Fußtellern *(G)*.

abatis Baumsperre *f.*

"A" battery   Heizbatterie *f (Rad).*

abbreviation Abkürzung *f.*

authorized abbreviation   amtlich festgelegte Abkürzung.

able-bodied   wehrfähig, tauglich, wehrtauglich *(fit for Mil service).*

Abney level   Spiegelneigungsmesser *m (Surv).*

about face Kehrtwendung *f.*

"About, face!"   "Ganze Abteilung, Kehrt!"

abrasive Schleifmittel *n.*

abreast   nebeneinander, Seite an Seite, in Linie.

abscissa Abszisse *f.*

abscissa for maximum ordinate Gipfelentfernung *f (Ballistics).*

absence without leave   unerlaubte Entfernung, eigenmächtige Entfernung.

absent abwesend.

absent without leave abwesend ohne Urlaub.

absolute altitude Flughöhe *f,* Flughöhe über dem Erdboden *(Avn).*

absolute ceiling Gipfelhöhe *f (Avn).*

absolute deviation   Geschoßabweichung *f (Arty).*

absolute quarantine   Isolierung *f (Med).*

absorbent cotton Watte *f.*

abutment   Widerlager *n,* Brückenwiderlager *n,* Endauflager *n (Bdg);* Kämpfer *m (of an arch).*

abutment beam Stoßbalken *m (Bdg).*

abutment section   Pioniertrupp beauftragt mit Errichtung der Brückenendwiderlager *(Engr).*

accelerate beschleunigen.

accelerating pump Beschleunigungspumpe *f.*

acceleration Beschleunigung *f.*

acceleration downward   Fallbeschleunigung *f (of projectile).*

accelerator   Spannstück *n (MG);* Gashebel *m,* Beschleuniger *m (Mtr).*

accelerometer Beschleunigungsmesser *m (Ap).*

acceptance test Abnahmeprüfung *f.*

accessories   Ausrüstung *f,* Zubehör *n,* Zubehörteile *mpl.*

accessories case   Zubehörtornister *m (portable Rad).*

accessory   Ausrüstungsstück *n,* Zubehör *n (part);* Komplize *m,* Mitschuldiger *m (Law).*

accessory defense   Hindernis *n,* Sperre *f.*

accelerator pedal   Gasfußtritt *m,* Gasfußhebel *m.*

access road Zufahrtstraße *f.*

accident Unfall *m.*

accidental cover natürliche Deckung.

accidental error zufälliger Fehler.

accidental hit Zufallstreffer *m.*

accompanying artillery Begleitartillerie *f.*

accompanying battery   Begleitbatterie *f.*

accompanying fire Begleitfeuer *n.*

accompanying gun Begleitgeschütz *n.*

accompanying tank Begleitpanzer *m,* Begleitpanzerkampfwagen *m.*

accomplice   Mitschuldiger *m,* Komplize *m (Law).*

accomplish erledigen, erfüllen, vollenden.

accomplishment Erledigung *f (completion);* Leistung *f (feat).*

accordion action   wechselnder Fahrzeugabstand, Aufschließen und Abhängen *(MT).*

accordion effect *See* accordion action.

accountability Buchungspflicht *f*, Verantwortlichkeit *f*.

accountable zur Buchung verpflichtet.

accountable officer Verwaltungsoffizier *m*.

accouterments Ausrüstungsstücke *npl*.

accredited aviation school behördlich anerkannte Fliegerschule.

accredited correspondent Kriegsberichter *m*.

accrued leave zustehender Gesamturlaub.

accumulated leave akkumulierter Urlaub.

accuracy Genauigkeit *f*.

accuracy life Lebensdauer *f* *(G)*.

accuracy of fire Zielsicherheit *f*, Treffähigkeit *f*, Treffgenauigkeit *f*, Treffsicherheit *f*.

accuracy of fit Paßgenauigkeit *f*.

accuracy of practice Treffgenauigkeit *f*.

accurate genau, zielgenau.

ace Fliegerheld *m*, erfolgreicher Jagdflieger.

acetone Azeton *m*.

acetylene Azetylen *n*.

acetylene torch *See* oxyacetylene torch.

a-c generator Wechselstromerzeuger *m*.

acid Säure *f*.

acknowledge Bitte Quittung, Bitte Bestätigung *(Rad procedure)*.

acknowledgment of receipt Empfangsbestätigung *f* *(Rad, Tg, Tp)*.

acoustic correction Ausschalten des Schallverzuges *(sound locator)*.

acoustic corrector Verzugsrechner *m* *(sound locator)*.

acoustic orientation akustische Ortung *(sound locator)*.

act *v* wirken, handeln.

acting stellvertretend.

action Gefecht *n*, Gefechtshandlung *f*, Kampftätigkeit *f* *(Tac)*; Arbeitsspiel *n* *(Mech)*.

"In action!" "Licht auf!" *(AA SL)*.

"Action front!" "Zum Feuern nach vorwärts, protzt ab!"

"Action left!" "Zum Feuern nach links, protzt ab!"

"Action rear!" "Zum Feuern nach rückwärts, protzt ab!"

"Action right!" "Zum Feuern nach rechts, protzt ab!"

action station Gefechtsstation *f* *(Nav)*; Gefechtsstellung *f*.

activate wehrbar machen, aufstellen *(a unit)*; scharf machen *(a mine)*.

activated mine scharfe Panzermine.

activation Wehrbarmachung *f*; Aufstellung *f* *(of a unit)*.

active air defense Luftabwehr *f*, aktive Luftabwehr.

active defense Abwehr *f*.

active duty aktiver Dienst.

active list Liste der aktiven Offiziere und Mannschaften.

active service aktiver Wehrdienst.

act of sabotage Sabotageakt *m*.

actual range tatsächliche Schußweite *(Arty)*.

acute angle spitzer Winkel.

adamsite Adamsit *m*, Diphenylaminchlorarsin *n*.

adaptable anwendbar, paßlich.

adapter Lafettenaufsatzstück *n* *(MG)*; Mundlocheinschraubvorrichtung *f*, Paßstück *n* *(Ord)*; Zwischenstück *n* *(Mech)*.

adapter opening Mundloch *n* *(Am)*.

adapter plug Mundlochschraube *f* *(AM)*; Zwischenstecker *m* *(Elec)*.

adapter thread Mundlochgewinde *n* *(Am)*.

add zusammenzählen, addieren *(Math)*; hinzufügen, beifügen.

adding machine Rechengerät *n*.

adhesive paste Kleister *m*.

adhesive pitch Kabelwachs *n* *(Engr, Tp)*.

adhesive tape Klebestreifen *m* *(Tech)*; Leukoplast *n* *(court plaster)*; Isolierband *n* *(friction tape)*.

adjacent angrenzend, Nachbar—, Neben—.

adjacent unit Nachbar *m* *(Tac)*.

adjust einschießen *(G fire)*; justieren *(bore-sight alinement)*; einstellen, verstellen *(Tech)*.

adjustable verstellbar, regulierbar, verschiebbar, einstellbar.

adjustable holder Einstellhülse *f* *(panoramic telescope)*.

adjustable marker Einstellmarke *f*.

adjustable-pitch propeller einstellbare Luftschraube.

adjustable wrench verstellbarer Schraubenschlüssel.

adjusted elevation Erhöhungseinstellung *f.*

adjusted range Höhenrichtung *f (Arty).*

adjusting nut Stößelschraube *f (on valve-lifter).*

adjusting point Einschießpunkt *m (Arty).*

adjusting ring Stellring *m,* Einstellring *m (fuze).*

adjusting screw Verstellschraube *f.*

adjustment Einstellung *f,* Eichung *f,* Verstellung *f;* Berichtigung *f (correction).*

adjustment drum Berichtigungswalze *f (range finder).*

adjustment fire Richtungsschießen *n,* Einschießen *n.*

adjustment nut Einstellmutter *f.*

adjustment of fire Einschießen *n.*

adjustment shots Richtungsschüsse *mpl (for direction).*

adjustment target Einschießziel *n,* Lufteinschießziel *n (high burst).*

adjutant Adjutant *m.*

adjutant general Generaladjutant *m.* The **Adjutant General** Der Chef des Heeresverwaltungsamts *(USA).*

Adjutant General Board Die Abteilungsleiter des Heeresverwaltungsamts *(USA).*

Adjutant General's Department Heeresverwaltungsamt *n (USA).*

adjutant's office Schreibstube *f.*

administration Verwaltung *f,* Verwaltungswesen *n.*

administration building Verwaltungsgebäude *n.*

administrative inspector Verwaltungsinspektor *m.*

administrative map Verwaltungsübersichtskarte *f.*

administrative march Reisemarsch *m,* Etappenmarsch *m.*

administrative order besondere Anordnung.

administrative plan Verwaltungsordnung *f.*

administrative services Verwaltungsdienste *mpl.*

administrative unit Verwaltungstruppenteil *m.*

administrative vehicle Heeresfahrzeug *n.*

admiral Generaladmiral *m (Nav).*

advance *n* Vormarsch *m,* Vorgehen *n.*

advance *v* vorrücken, vorgehen, vordringen, vormarschieren, sich vorwärtsbewegen.

advance base Ausgabestelle im Operationsgebiet.

advance by bounds sprungweises Vorgehen.

advance by echelon staffelweises Vorgehen.

advance by rushes *See* **advance by bounds.**

advance command post vorgeschobener Gefechtsstand, vorderer Gefechtsstand.

advanced airfield Feldflugplatz *m.*

advanced detachment Vorausabteilung *f.*

advance depot Umschlagstelle *f.*

advanced specialized training militärische Sonderausbildung.

advanced training Weiterbildung *f,* Fortbildung *f.*

advance element Spitzengruppe *f (Tac).*

advance guard Vorhut *f.*

advance guard action Vorhutgefecht *n.*

advance guard cavalry detachment Reiterspitze *f.*

advance guard commander Vorhutführer *m.*

advance guard company Vorauskompanie *f.*

advance guard engagement Vorhutgefecht *n.*

advance guard point Spitze *f.*

advance guard reserve Haupttrupp *m (in Adv Gd of large unit).*

advance guard support Vortrupp *m (in Adv Gd of large unit);* Haupttrupp *m (in Adv Gd of smaller unit).*

advance in phases abschnittweises Vorgehen.

advance landing field Feldflugplatz *m,* Gefechtslandeplatz *m.*

advance message center Meldekopf, *m.*

advance of forcing cone Laderaumverlängerung *f (G).*

advance party Spitzenkompanie *f (in Adv Gd of large unit);* Vortrupp *m (in Adv Gd of smaller unit).*

advance position vorgeschobene Stellung.

advance post vorgeschobener Posten.

advance the attack sich an den Feind heranarbeiten.

"Advance to be recognized!" "Kommen Sie näher! Wer sind Sie?"
adviser Berater *m.*
adze Querbeil *n*, Queraxt *f.*
aerial *See* antenna.
aerial acrobatics Kunstflug *m.*
aerial barrage Luftsperre *f.*
aerial barrage equipment Luftsperrmittel *n.*
aerial camera Luftbildkammer *f.*
aerial combat exercise Luftkampfübung *f.*
aerial delivery container Abwurfkiste *f.*
aerial gas spray Giftregen *m.*
aerial gunner Fliegerschütze *m,* Bordschütze *m,* Feuerschütze *m.*
aerial gunnery Schießen aus der Luft.
aerial hand camera Fliegerhandkammer *f.*
aerial mapping camera Reihenkammer *f,* Reihenbildner *m,* Reihenbildkammer *f.*
aerial mine Minenbombe *f,* Luftmine *f.*
aerial mosaic Reihenbild *n,* Luftbildkarte *f.*
aerial objective Flugziel *n.*
aerial observation Luftbeobachtung *f.*
aerial observer Beobachter *m,* Beobachtungsflieger *m.*
aerial photograph Luftbild *n.*
aerial photographer Bildflieger *m.*
aerial photographic crew Flugzeugbildpersonal *n.*
aerial p h o t o g r a p h interpretation Luftbildauswertung *f.*
aerial photography Luftbildwesen *n,* Luftphotographie *f.*
aerial photomapping camera Reihenmeßkammer *f.*
aerial review Luftparade *f.*
aerial sound ranging Horchortung von Flugzielen *(AAA).*
aerial spraying Abregnen *n (CWS).*
aerial target Flugziel *n.*
aerial torpedo Lufttorpedo *n,* Flugzeugtorpedo *n.*
aerial warfare Luftkrieg *m.*
aerobatics *See* aerial acrobatics.
aerocartograph Aerokartograph *m.*
aerodynamic force Luftkraft *f.*
aerodynamics Aerodynamik *f.*
aeroembolism Höhenkrankheit *f.*
aerograph *See* aerometeorograph.

aerographer Meteorologe im Unteroffiziersrang *(Nav).*
aerologist Meteorologe im Offiziersrang *(Nav).*
aerometeorograph Meteorograph *m (Met).*
aerometer Dichtemesser *m,* Dichtigkeitsmesser *m.*
aeronautical chart Fliegerkarte *f.*
aeronautical mile Flugmeile *f (1853.25 meters).*
aeronautics Luftfahrt *f,* Luftfahrwesen *n,* Flugwissenschaft *f.*
aerosled Motorschlitten *m.*
aerostat Aerostat *m.*
affidavit beglaubigte Bescheinigung, eidliche Erklärung.
age Alter *n.*
age-in-grade Rangdienstalter *m.*
age limit Dienstaltersgrenze *f.*
agent Verbindungsmann *m,* Vertrauensmann *m.*
agent officer Verbindungsoffizier *m.*
aggressive angriffsfreudig, angriffslustig.
aggressiveness Einsatzbereitschaft *f.*
aggressor Angreifer *m.*
agonic line Agone *f.*
aide *See* aide-de-camp.
aide-de-camp Adjutant *m.*
aid man Sanitäter *m.*
aid station Truppenverbandplatz *m (Med).*
aiguillette Fangschnur *f.*
aileron Querruder *n.*
aileron horn Querruderhebel *m.*
aim *v* zielen, richten, anlegen.
aim-checking device Zielkontrollspiegel *m.*
aiming circle Richtkreis *m.*
aiming-circle station Richtstelle *f.*
aiming device Zielspiegel *m.*
aiming disk Ziellöffel *m.*
aiming drill Ziel- und Anschlagsübungen *fpl.*
aiming error Zielfehler *m.*
aiming exercise Zielübung *f.*
aiming group Zieldreieck *n (aiming triangle).*
aiming light Richtlampe *f.*
aiming mechanism Richtgerät *n,* Zieleinrichtung *f,* Zielvorrichtung *f.*
aiming order Richtkommando *n,* Richtbefehl *m.*
aiming point Richtpunkt *m,* Haltepunkt *m,* Anlegepunkt *m,* Zielpunkt *m.*

aiming-point azimuth reading Richtpunktzahl *f*.

aiming-point and deflection method Richtpunktverfahren *n*.

aiming point offset Beobachtungswinkel *m*.

aiming post Richtlatte *f*, E-Latte *f*.

aiming post light Richtlampe *f*.

aiming practice Richtübung *f*.

aiming silhouette Gefechtsscheibe *f* *(target)*.

aiming stake Richtlatte *f*, E-Latte *f*.

aiming target Richtscheibe *f*.

air *n* Luft *f*.

air *v* lüften.

"Air!" **"Hoch!"** *(firing)*.

air-adjustment jet Korrekturluftdüse *f* *(Mtr)*.

air adviser Fliegerverbindungsoffizier *m*.

air-air Flugzeug zu Flugzeug *(Sig Com)*.

air alert Jagdpatrouille in Kampfbereitschaft *(Avn)*; Fliegeralarm *m* *(AWS)*.

air ambulance Sanitätsflugzeug *n*.

air area Luftraum *m*.

air attack Luftangriff *m*.

air base Luftstützpunkt *m*, Flugstützpunkt *m* *(Tac)*; Fliegerhorst *m*, Horst *m* *(Adrm in Z of I)*.

air base airdrome Fliegerhorst *m*, Horst *m* *(Z of I)*.

air base commander Fliegerhorstkommandant *m*, Horstkommandant *m*.

air base service area Bodenanlage der Luftwaffe.

air base troops Bodenpersonal *n*.

air battle Luftschlacht *f*.

airborne auf dem Luftwege befördert.

airborne infantry Luftinfanterie *f*.

airborne troops Luftlande- und Fallschirmtruppen *fpl*.

air brake Luftdruckbremse *f* *(Mech)*; Landeklappe *f* *(Ap)*.

air burst Luftsprengpunkt *m*, hoher Sprengpunkt, S p r e n g p u n k t *m* *(Arty)*.

air-burst pattern Lufttreffbild *n* *(Arty)*.

air-burst registration fire Schießen mit hohen Sprengpunkten.

air chamber Luftbehälter *m* *(counterrecoil mechanism, vehicle brake)*.

air combat Luftgefecht *n*, Luftkampf *m*.

air command communication Funkverbindung von Flugzeug zu Flugzeug.

air command headquarters Luftwaffengruppenkommando *n*.

air compressor Drucklufterzeuger *m*, Luftverdichter *m*, Luftpresser *m*.

air conditioning plant Klimaanlage *f*.

air-cooled luftgekühlt, mit Luftkühlung.

air-cooled engine luftgekühlter Motor, Motor mit Luftkühlung.

air-cooled weapon luftgekühlte Waffe.

Air Corps *See* **Army Air Forces.**

aircraft Luftfahrzeug *n*.

aircraft ammunition Flugzeugmunition *f*, Bordmunition *f*.

aircraft armament Bordwaffen *fpl*.

aircraft automatic gun *See* **aircraft cannon.**

aircraft camera Luftbildkammer *f*, Luftbildgerät *n*, Fliegerkammer *f*.

aircraft cannon Flugzeugkanone *f*.

aircraft carrier Flugzeugträger *m*.

aircraft engine Flugmotor *m*.

aircraft equipment Bordgeräte *npl*.

aircraft factory Flugzeugwerk *n*, Flugzeugfabrik *f*.

aircraft gun sights Fliegervisiereinrichtung *f*.

aircraft industry Luftfahrzeugindustrie *f*.

aircraft instruments Bordgeräte *npl*.

aircraft landing flare Bordlandefackel *f*.

aircraft log Flugbuch *n*, Flugtagebuch *n*.

aircraft machine gun Bord-Maschinengewehr *n*.

aircraft observer Aufklärungsflieger *m*, Beobachter *m*.

aircraft parachute flare Fallschirmleuchtbombe *f*, Leuchtbombe *f*.

aircraft signal Leuchtpatrone *f*, Signalpatrone *f* *(ground-air Com)*.

aircraft signal pistol Fliegerleuchtpistole *f*.

aircraft tender Flugzeugmutterschiff *n*, Stützpunktschiff *n*.

aircraft warning Fliegerwarnung *f*.

aircraft warning company Flugmeldekompanie *f*.

aircraft warning officer Flugmeldeoffizier *m*.

aircraft warning service Flugmeldedienst *m.*

air crew Bordbesatzung *f*, Bordmannschaft *f*, fliegende Besatzung, Flugzeugbesatzung *f.*

air current Luftstrom *m.*

air defense Luftverteidigung *f;* Luftabwehr *f (active);* Luftschutz *m (passive).*

air defense area Flugabwehrgebiet *n.*

air defense region Flugabwehrbezirk *m.*

air density Luftdichte *f.*

air depot Nachschubstelle der Luftwaffe.

airdrome Flugplatz *m.*

airdrome boundary Flughafengrenze *f*, Platzgrenze *f.*

airdrome construction detachment Flughafenbautrupp *m.*

airdrome light Platzfeuer *n.*

airdrome lighting Flugplatzbefeuerung *f.*

airdrome traffic Flugbetrieb *m.*

airfield *See* **airdrome.**

air fight *See* **air combat.**

air filter Luftfilter *m*, Luftreiniger *m (Mtr).*

airflow Fahr(t)wind *m*, Gebläsewind *m (Avn).*

airfoil Tragfläche *f (Ap).*

airfoil section Flügelprofil *n*, Tragflügelprofil *n.*

air force Luftflotte *f (tactical and territorial unit).*

air force commander Flottenchef *m*, Luftflottenchef *m*, Fliegerführer *m.*

air forces Fliegerkräfte *fpl*, Luftstreitkräfte *fpl.*

Air Forces *See* **Army Air Forces.**

Air Forces Headquarters Luftwaffenkommando *n.*

airframe Flugzeuggerippe *n.*

air friction Luftreibung *f (Ballistics).*

air-ground Bord zu Boden *(Sig Com).*

air-ground communication Nachrichtenverbindung Boden-Bord.

air-ground liaison code Funkverkehrsabkürzungen *fpl.*

air-ground net Funknetz für den Verkehr Boden-Bord.

air guard Luftspäher *m.*

air-intake duct Ansaugleitung *f (Ft).*

air-intake horn Ansaugkrümmer *m (carburetor).*

air jet Luftdüse *f (Mtr).*

air landing troops Luftlandetruppen *fpl.*

airline Fluglinie *f*, Flugstrecke *f.*

air lock Gasschleuse *f (CWS).*

air mechanic Flugzeugmechaniker *m*, Bordmonteur *m.*

air mile Luftmeile *f (1,853.25 meters or 6,080 feet).*

air navigation Flugzeugortung *f*, Luftnavigation *f.*

air navigation map Flugstreckenkarte *f.*

air objective Luftangriffsziel *n.*

air observation Luftbeobachtung *f.*

air observer Beobachter *m (Avn);* Luftspäher *m (AWS).*

air obstacle Luftsperre *f (Avn).*

air offensive Luftoffensive *f.*

air officer Fliegerverbindungsoffizier *m.*

airplane Flugzeug *n;* Flieger *m (as seen from ground).*

airplane ambulance Sanitätsflugzeug *n.*

airplane armament Flugzeugbewaffnung *f*, Bordwaffen *fpl.*

airplane chemical spray apparatus Luftstromgerät *n*, Zerstäubungsgerät *n.*

airplane construction Flugzeugbau *m.*

airplane controls Flugzeugsteuerung *f.*

airplane direction finding Flugzeugortung *f.*

airplane engine Flugzeugmotor *m.*

airplane flare Fallschirmleuchtbombe *f.*

airplane mechanic Flugzeugwart *m*, Bordwart *m*, Bordmonteur *m*, Flugzeugmechaniker *m.*

airplane model Flugzeugbaumuster *n.*

airplane passenger Fluggast *m.*

airplane production Flugzeugbau *m*, Flugzeugproduktion *f.*

airplane signal Fliegerverständigungszeichen *n.*

airplane-speed slide rule Flugzeuggeschwindigkeitslineal *n (AAA).*

airplane spotter Luftspäher *m*, Flugmeldeposten *m.*

airplane towing Flugzeugschlepp *m.*

air pocket Luftloch *n.*

airport Flughafen *m.*

air power Luftmacht *f*, Luftgeltung *f*.

air pressure Luftdruck *m*.

air raid Luftangriff *m*.

air raid alarm Fliegeralarm *m*, Luftalarm *m*.

air raid drill Luftschutzübung *f* (*civilian defense*).

air raid shelter Luftschutzkeller *m*, Luftschutzraum *m*.

air raid siren Fliegersirene *f*, Luftschutzsirene *f*.

air raid warden Luftschutzwart *m*.

air raid warning district Luftwarnbezirk *m*.

air reconnaissance Luftaufklärung *f*.

air reconnaissance area Luftaufklärungsraum *m*.

air resistance Luftwiderstand *m* (*Ballistics, Avn*).

air scoop Luftsackmaul *n* (*captive Bln*).

air scout Luftspäher *m*.

air sentinel *See* **air scout.**

Air Service Command Luftgau *m*.

airship Luftschiff *n*.

airspace Luftraum *m* (*Avn, etc.*); leerer Raum (*Am*).

airspace reservation Luftsperrgebiet *n* (*Avn*).

air speed Eigengeschwindigkeit *f*, Geschwindigkeit zur Luft (*Ap*).

air speed indicator Fahrtmesser *m* (*Ap*).

Air Staff Führungsstab der Luftwaffe (*USA*).

air starter Preßluftanlasser *m* (*Mtr*).

airstream Fahrwind *m* (*Avn*).

air superiority Luftüberlegenheit *f*.

air support Fliegerunterstützung *f*.

Air Support Command Schlachtfliegerverband *m*.

air support party Luftnachrichtenverbindungsoffiziere *mpl*.

air target Flugziel *n*.

air task force fliegerischer Verband, Fliegerverband *m*.

airtight luftdicht.

air-traffic safety control Flugsicherung *f*.

air transport Transportflugzeug *n*.

air transportation Lufttransport *m*.

Air Transport Command Lufttransportkommando *n* (*USA*). *See also* **Ferry Command.**

air umpire Schiedsrichter *m* (*Avn*).

air warfare Luftkriegführung *f*.

air warning net Flugmeldenetz *n*.

airway Flugweg *m*, Flugstrecke *f*.

airway beacon Flugstreckenfeuer *n*, Streckenfeuer *n*.

airway obstruction Luftfahrthindernis *n*.

airway traffic control area Flugsicherungsbereich *m*.

airworthiness Lufttüchtigkeit *f* (*Ap*).

airworthy flugklar, flugtüchtig.

alarm Alarm *m*.

alarm station Alarmplatz *m*.

alcohol Alkohol *m*, Weingeist *m*.

alert *n* Startbereitschaft *f* (*Avn*); Bereitschaft *f*, Alarmbereitschaft *f*.

alert *v* alarmieren, in Bereitschaft stellen.

alert hut Bereitschaftsbaracke *f* (*Avn*).

alert station Jagdpatrouille *f*, Bereitschaftsstellung *f* (*Avn*).

alidade Kippregel *f* (*Surv*).

alidade ruler Diopterlineal *n* (*aiming circle*).

alignment *See* **alinement.**

alinement Nachstellung des Radstands (*of vehicle wheels*); Ausrichten *n*, Richtung *f* (*of sights*).

alinement stake Richtstange *f* (*Bdg, Engr*).

aliquot part charge aus zwei gleichen Teilladungen bestehende Treibladung (*Am*).

aliquot propelling charge *See* **aliquot part charge.**

alkali cartridge Alkalipatrone *f* (*in oxygen breathing apparatus*).

all-around defense Igelverteidigung *f*.

all-around traverse Seitenrichtfeld von 360°; mit Sockellafette.

all clear Beendigung der Luftgefahr. "All clear!" "Alarm aus!"

all clear signal Entwarnung *f*.

all-metal airplane Ganzmetallflugzeug *n*.

allocation Zuteilung *f* (*of men, supplies, etc.*); Zuweisung *f*, Anweisung *f* (*of funds*).

allocation of targets Zielzuweisung *f*.

allot anweisen.

allotment Anweisung *f*.

allotment of equipment Gerätausstattung *f*.

allowance *See* **authorized basic allowance.**

allow for berücksichtigen.

alloy Legierung *f*.

allways fuze empfindlicher Kopfzünder *(Am)*.

all-wheel drive Räderantrieb *m*, Allradantrieb *m (MT)*.

all-wing airplane Nurflügelflugzeug *n*.

ally Bundesgenosse *m*, Verbündete(r) *m*.

alphabet code flag Signalflagge *f*, internationale Signalflagge *(Nav)*.

alpine cap Bergmütze *f (Clo)*.

alternate *v* wechseln, abwechseln.

alternate airport Ausweichhaten *m*.

alternate emplacement Wechselstellung *f (G, MG)*.

alternate firing position *See* **alternate emplacement.**

alternate routing Ausweichvermittlung *f (emergency Tp Com)*.

alternate target Ausweichziel *n (bombing)*.

alternate traversing fire Breitenfeuer *n (Arty)*.

alternate two-way radiophone communication Funkwechselsprechen *n*.

alternate two-way radio traffic Funkwechselverkehr *m*.

alternating current Wechselstrom *m*; Drehstrom *m (three-phase)*.

alternating-current generator Wechselstromerzeuger *m*.

alternation Wechsel *m (Elec)*.

alternator *See* **alternating-current generator.**

altimeter Höhenmesser *m*; Höhenentfernungsmesser *m*, Höhenmesser *m*, Entfernungsmeßgerät *n (AA height finder)*.

altitude Höhe *f*.

altitude bracket Höhenschicht *f (Avn, Met)*.

altitude-correction ruler Erdkrümmungslineal *n*.

altitude indication Höhenangabe *f*.

altitude lead Höhenvorhalt *m (AAA)*.

altitude of flight Flughöhe *f*.

altitude of target Meßhöhe *f (instant of range determination)*; Zielhöhe *f (present position)*; Treffhöhe *f (future position)*.

altitude reading Höhenangabe *f*.

aluminum Aluminium *n*.

aluminum alloy Aluminiumlegierung *f*.

amatol Amatol *n (Am)*.

ambient noise störende Nebengeräusche.

ambulance Krankenkraftwagen *m*; Sanitätsfahrzeug *n (any Med vehicle)*.

ambulance battalion Krankentransportabteilung *f*.

ambulance loading post Wagenhalteplatz *m*.

ambulance station Krankentransportstelle *f*.

ambulant marschfähiger Verwundeter.

ambush *n* Hinterhalt *m*, Lauerstellung *f*.

ambush *v* aus dem Hinterhalt überfallen.

American Red Cross Amerikanisches Rotes Kreuz.

ammeter Amperemeter *n*, Strommesser *m*.

ammonal Ammonpulver *n*, Ammonal *n (Am)*.

ammonia Ammoniak *n*; Salmiakgeist *m (spirits of ammonia)*.

ammonium nitrate explosive Ammonsalpeter-Sprengmittel *n*.

ammonium picrate Ammoniumpikrat *n (Am)*.

ammunition Munition *f*. *See also* **munitions.**

ammunition bearer Munitionsschütze *m*.

ammunition belt Gurt *m*, Patronengurt *m*.

ammunition box Munitionskasten *m*.

ammunition branch depot Munitionszweiglager *n*.

ammunition carrier Munitionsfahrzeug *n*; Munitionswagen *m*, Munitionskarren *m (H·Dr)*; Gefechtskarren *m (includes weapons)*; Munitionsschütze *m*, Munitionsträger *m (bearer)*.

ammunition chest Protzkasten *m (on limber)*.

ammunition clip Ladestreifen *m*.

ammunition company Munitionsnachschub-Kompanie *f*.

ammunition depot Munitionslager *n*.

ammunition detail Munitionstrupp *m*.

ammunition distributing point Munitionsausgabestelle *f*, Munitionsverteilungsstelle *f*.

ammunition drum Munitionstrommel *f*.

ammunition dump Munitionslager *n*.

ammunition lot number laufende Nummer der Munitionslieferung.

ammunition niche Munitionsnische *f (Ft)*.

ammunition pit Munitionsloch *n*.

ammunition pocket Patronentasche *f (Clo)*.

ammunition point Munitionsausgabestelle *f*.

ammunition requirements Schießbedarf *m*.

ammunition section Munitionsstaffel *f (firing Btry)*.

ammunition shelter Munitionsnische *f (Ft)*.

ammunition shortage Munitionsmangel *m*.

ammunition sponson Munitionskammer *f (Tk)*.

ammunition stock Munitionsbestand *m*.

ammunition supply Munitionsnachschub *m*, Munitionsausstattung *f*, Munitionsbestand *m*.

ammunition supply point Munitionsumschlagstelle *f*.

ammunition supply service Munitionswesen *n*.

ammunition trailer Munitionswagen *m*.

ammunition train Munitionszug *m (RR)*; Munitionskolonne *f*.

ammunition transloading point Munitionsumschlagstelle *f*.

ammunition truck Geschoß-Zubringewagen *m*, Geschoßwagen *m*.

ammunition wagon Munitionswagen *m*.

amnesty allgemeine Begnadigung, Amnestie *f*.

amount Betrag *m*, Bestand *m*; Menge *f (quantity)*; Summe *f (sum)*.

amperage Amperezahl *f*.

ampere Ampere *n*.

amphibian airplane Wasserlandflugzeug *n*, Amphibienflugzeug *n*.

amphibian tank Schwimmpanzerkampfwagen *m*, Amphibienkampfwagen *m*.

amphibian tractor *See* tracked landing vehicle.

amphibian truck Schwimm-Lastkraftwagen *m*; Schwimmwagen *m*.

amplification Verstärkung *f (Rad)*.

amplifier Lautverstärker *m (volume)*; Kraftverstärker *m (power)*.

amplifier tube Verstärkerröhre *f (Rad)*.

amplitude of oscillations Schwingungsweite *f (Rad)*.

amputate amputieren, abnehmen.

anabatic wind Aufwind *m*, Hangwind *m (Met)*.

anaglyph Anaglyphe *f*, Anaglypt *n (Photo Surv)*.

anchor Anker *m*.

anchorage Verankerung *f*, Ankergrund *m*, Ankerplatz *m*, Ankerstelle *f (Nav)*; Verankerung *f*, Zurrung *f*.

anchor cable Ankertau *n*.

anchored mine Ankermine *f*.

anchor hitch Ankerstich *m (Engr)*.

anchoring Verankerung *f (Bdg, Nav)*.

anchor light Ankerlicht *n*.

anchor pin Bremsträger *m (of brakeshoes)*.

anchor plate Ankerplatte *f (of clockwork fuze)*.

anchor rack stick Ankerrödel *m (Bdg, Engr)*.

anchor stake Ankerpfahl *m*.

anemometer Windmesser *m*, Anemometer *n*, Windmeßgerät *n*.

aneroid barometer Dosenbarometer *n*, Federbarometer *n*, Federluftdruckmesser *m*, Aneroid-Barometer *n*.

anesthetic Betäubungsmittel *n*.

angary Prisenrecht *n*.

angle Winkel *m*.

angledozer Planier-Raupenschlepper *m*.

angle of approach Flugwinkel *m (AAA)*; Flugwinkel im Abschußpunkt *(present position)*; Flugwinkel im Treffpunkt *(future position)*; Anflugwinkel *m (Avn)*; Fahrzeugüberhang *m*, Überhang *m (MT)*.

angle of attack Anstellwinkel *m (Avn)*.

angle of axle displacement Hubhöhe *f (MT)*.

angle of axle swing Achsenverschränkbarkeit *f (MT)*.

angle of bank Winkel der Schräglage *(Avn)*.

angle of clearance Differenz zwischen Abgangswinkel und Deckungswinkel *(Ballistics)*.

angle of convergence Parallaxwinkel *m (Optics)*; Winkel zur Ausschaltung des Stellungsunterschiedes *(Arty, Surv)*.

angle of crab Luvwinkel *m (Avn)*.

angle of departure Abgangswinkel *m (Ballistics)*.

angle of depression negativer Geländewinkel *(Gunnery)*; Tiefenwinkel *m (Surv)*.

angle of dive Flugneigungswinkel *m (AA gunnery)*; Sturzwinkel *m (Avn)*.

angle of elevation Visierwinkel *m*, Aufsatzwinkel *m*, Erhöhungswinkel *m*.

angle-of-elevation dial Aufsatztrommel *f (G)*.

angle-of-elevation mechanism Aufsatzwinkeltrieb *m (G)*.

angle of fall Fallwinkel *m (Ballistics)*.

angle-offset method Kreisbogenabsteckung von einer Tangente aus *(Btry Surv)*.

angle of glide Gleitwinkel *m (Avn)*.

angle of impact Aufschlagwinkel *m*, Auftreffwinkel *m (Ballistics)*.

angle of incidence Einstellwinkel *m (Ap wing)*; Ergänzungswinkel des Auftreffwinkels *(Ballistics)*; Einfallwinkel *m*.

angle of jump Abgangsfehlerwinkel *m (Gunnery)*.

angle of parallax Parallaxe *f*, Parallaxwinkel *m (Optics)*.

angle of pitch Steigungswinkel *m*, Anstellwinkel *m (p r o p e l l e r)*; Stampfwinkel *m (Ap)*.

angle of ricochet Abprallwinkel *m*.

angle of roll Winkel der Schräglage *(Avn)*.

angle of safety Erhöhung einschließlich der Sicherheitsteilstriche *(overhead firing)*.

angle of shift Seitenabstand vom Richtpunkt *(indirect firing)*

angle of site Geländewinkel *m*, Zielhöhenwinkel *m (Gunnery)*.

angle-of-site instrument Geländewinkelmesser *m*.

angle-of-site level Geländewinkellibelle *f*.

angel-of-site mechanism Geländewinkelmeßvorrichtung *f (on telescopic sight)*.

angle-of-site micrometer Geländewinkelmesser *m (G)*.

angle-of-site scale Skalenscheibe *f*.

angle-of-site table Libellentafel *f (Gunnery)*.

angle of site to mask Deckungswinkel *m (Gunnery)*.

angle of slope Böschungswinkel *m (Top)*.

angle of traverse Schwenkwinkel *m*, Schwenkungswinkel *m*, Seitenrichtwinkel *m (Gunnery)*.

angle of twist Drallwinkel *m (rifling)*.

angle of view Sehwinkel *m*.

angle of wing setting Flügeleinstellwinkel *m (Ap)*.

angle of yaw Wendewinkel *m*, Gierwinkel *m*, Scherwinkel *m (Avn)*.

angular acceleration Winkelbeschleunigung *f*.

angular height Höhenwinkel *m (AAA)*.

angular height of target Zielhöhenwinkel *m (AAA)*; Zielhöhenwinkel zum Abschußpunkt *(present position)*; Zielhöhenwinkel zum Wechselpunkt *(midpoint)*; Zielhöhenwinkel zum Treffpunkt *(future position)*.

angular measurement Winkelmaß *n*.

angular movement Winkelauswanderung *f*; Winkelgeschwindigkeit *f (rate)*.

angular travel *See* angular movement.

angular velocity Winkelgeschwindigkeit *f*.

animal-drawn bespannt.

ankle Fußknöchel *m*, Knöchel *m*.

A.N. method of instrument landing A.N.-Verfahren *n (beam bracketing) (Avn)*.

anneal ausglühen.

annex Anlage *f*.

annihilation fire Vernichtungsfeuer *n*.

announcement Ankündigung *f*, Bekanntgabe *f*.

anode Anode *f*.

answering jack Abfrageklinke *f (Tp)*.

answer signal Gegensignal *n*.

answer to call-up Anrufantwort *f (Rad)*.

antarctic *adj* antarktisch, den Südpol betreffend.

antenna Luftleiter *m*, Antenne *f*.

antenna ammeter Antennenstromanzeiger *m.*

antenna array Antennengebilde *n.*

antenna binding post Antennenanschluß *m.*

antenna capacitance Antennenkapazität *f.*

antenna circuit Antennenkreis *m.*

antenna coupling Antennenkopplung *f.*

antenna jack Antennenbuchse *f,* Antennen-Anschlußbuchse *f.*

antenna mast Antennenstab *m (portable Rad set);* Antennenmast *m,* Funkmast *m.*

antenna outfit Antennengerät *n.*

antenna reel Antennenhaspel *f (Ap).*

antenna resistance Antennenwiderstand *m.*

antenna truck Funkmastkraftwagen *m.*

antenna tuning coil Antennenspule *f.*

antenna wire Luftdraht *m.*

anthracite coal Steinkohle *f.*

antiaircraft artillery Flakartillerie *f,* Flak *f.*

antiaircraft artillery battalion Flakabteilung *f.*

antiaircraft artillery regiment Flakregiment *n.*

antiaircraft automatic weapons Maschinenflak *f.*

antiaircraft barrage Flaksperre *f.*

antiaircraft battery Flakbatterie *f.*

antiaircraft company Fla-Kompanie *f.*

antiaircraft cruiser Flakkreuzer *m (Nav).*

antiaircraft defense Flugabwehr *f,* Flakabwehr *f,* Fliegerabwehr *f,* Luftverteidigung *f.*

antiaircraft director Kommandogerät *n,* Flakkommandogerät *n.*

antiaircraft emplacement Flakstellung *f.*

antiaircraft fire Flakfeuer *n,* Flakschießen *n.*

antiaircraft fire director Flakkommandogerät *n.*

antiaircraft gun Flugabwehrgeschütz *n,* Flakgeschütz *n,* Flugabwehrkanone *f,* Abwehrgeschütz *n.*

antiaircraft gun crew Flakbedienung *f.*

antiaircraft lookout Luftspäher *m.*

antiaircraft machine gun Flugabwehrmaschinengewehr *n,* Flakmaschinengewehr *n,* Flamaschinengewehr *n,* Fla-MG. *n.*

antiaircraft MG unit Fla-Einheit *f.*

antiaircraft protection Flakschutz *m.*

antiaircraft scout Luftspäher *m.*

antiaircraft searchlight Flugzeugabwehrscheinwerfer *m,* Flakscheinwerfer *m.*

antiaircraft security Sicherung gegen den Luftgegner *(Tac).*

antiaircraft sight Fliegervisier *n,* Flakvisier *n.*

antiaircraft weapon Luftabwehrwaffe *f,* Fla-Waffe *f.*

anticyclone Antizyklon *m,* Hoch *n (Met).*

antidim compound Klarsichtsalbe *f,* Brillenglassalbe *f.*

antidim eyeglass Klarscheibe *f (gas mask).*

antifreeze Gefrierschutz *m,* Gefrierschutzmittel *n (MT).*

antifreeze solution Frostschutzmittel *n.*

antifriction bearing Wälzlager *n.*

anti-glare windshield Blendschutzscheibe *f.*

anti-icer solution Enteisungsmittel *n.*

antiknock klopffest *(MT).*

antiknock quality Klopffestigkeit *f (of engine fuel).*

antimechanized defense Panzerabwehr *f.*

antimechanized security Sicherung gegen Panzer.

antimechanized warning Panzerwarnung *f.*

antimechanized warning system Panzerwarndienst *m.*

antimechanized weapon Panzerabwehrwaffe *f.*

antimony sulfide Schwefelantimon *n (Am).*

antipersonnel bomb Splitterbombe *f.*

antipersonnel mine S-Mine *f,* Schrapnellmine *f,* Schützenmine *f.*

antipersonnel rifle grenade Gewehrsprenggranate *f.*

antiseptic fäulnisbekämpfendes Mittel, Antiseptikum *n.*

antisubmarine net Fangnetz *n.*

antitank Pak-, Panzerabwehr-, Panzerjäger-. *See also* **tank destroyer.**

antitank artillery Pak *f.*
antitank battalion Panzerjägerabteilung *f*, Panzerabwehrabteilung *f.*
antitank bomb Panzerbombe *f.*
antitank company Panzerabwehrkompanie *f*, Panzerjägerkompanie *f.*
antitank defense Panzerabwehr *f.*
antitank ditch Panzerfahrzeuggraben *m*, Panzergraben *m*, Panzersperrgraben *m*, Tankgraben *m.*
antitank gun Pak *f*, Pak-Geschütz *n*, Panzerabwehrgeschütz *n*, Panzerabwehrkanone *f*, Panzerjägerkanone *f*, Panzerjägergeschütz *n.*
antitank gun emplacement Pakstellung *f.*
antitank hedgehog Igel *m.*
antitank lookout Panzerwarnposten *m.*
antitank mine Panzerabwehrmine *f*, Panzermine *f.*
antitank obstacle Panzersperre *f*, Panzerhindernis *n.*
antitank platoon Panzerabwehrzug *m*, Pak-Zug *m*, Panzerjägerzug *m.*
antitank regiment Panzerabwehrregiment *n*, Panzerjägerregiment *n.*
antitank rifle Panzerabwehrgewehr *n*, Tankbüchse *f*, Panzerbüchse *f.*
antitank rifle grenade panzerbrechende Gewehrgranate.
antitank rifle grenadier GewehrPanzergranatenschütze *m (USA).*
antitank rocket Panzerabwehrrakete *f.*
antitank rocket launcher RaketenPanzerbüchse *f.*
antitank squad Pak-Halbzug *m.*
antitank tetrahedron Igel *m.*
antitank wall Panzersperrmauer *f.*
antitank weapon Panzerabwehrwaffe *f.*
anvil Amboß *m (Am, blacksmith's).*
aparejo mexikanischer Packsattel.
aperiodic compass aperiodischer Kompaß.
aperture Öffnung *f (opening);* Loch *n (hole);* Spalt *m*, Schlitz *m (slit);* Scharte *f (port or peephole, Ft, Tk, etc.).*
apparatus Gerät *n*, Apparat *m.*
appeal Berufung *f (Law);* dringende Bitte *(earnest request);* Aufruf *m (public appeal).*
appendix Füllansatz *m (Bln);* Blinddarm *m (anatomy);* Anhang *m (in a manual, etc.).*

application Bewerbung *f*, Gesuch *n (request);* Umschlag *m (Med).*
appoint bestallen, ernennen.
appointing authority Gerichtsherr *m (Law).*
appointment Dienststellung *f;* Ernennung *f (to brevet rank).*
approach *n* Annäherung *f*, Herangehen an den Feind *(Tac);* Anmarschweg *m (road);* Anflug *m (bombing);* Einflug *m (of a target) (AWS).*
approach *v* anfliegen *(Avn);* sich nähern.
approach angle Anflugwinkel *m (Avn);* Fahrzeugüberhang *m*, Überhang *m (MT).*
approach embankment Brückendamm *m (Bdg).*
approaching course Anflugkurs *m (Avn).*
approaching target kommendes Ziel.
approach march Anmarsch *m*, Annäherungsmarsch *m (Tac).*
approach route Anmarschweg *m.*
approach trench Laufgraben *m.*
approach zone Anflugsektor *m (Adrm).*
appropriation Bewilligung *f (of funds, etc.).*
approximate *v* sich nähern, nahebringen, schätzen.
approximate *adj* ungefähr, annähernd, grob.
approximate adjustment fire grobes Einschießen *(Arty).*
apron Hallenvorplatz *m*, Vorfeld *n (Adrm);* Tarnnetz *n (of G emplacement);* Seitenverankerung *f (of double-apron fence).*
apron shield Unterschild *m (G).*
aptitude test Eignungsprüfung *f.*
aquadag Aquadag *m (lubricant).*
arc Kreisbogen *m (of a circle);* Bogen *m.*
arch Brückenbogen *m (Bdg).*
arched bridge Bogenbrücke *f.*
arc lamp Bogenlanrpe *f (SL).*
arctic *adj* arktisch; den Nordpol betreffend.
arctic circle nördlicher Polarkreis.
arctic zone Nordpolgebiet *n.*
arc-type elevating mechanism Zahnbogenrichtmaschine *f (G).*
arc welding Lichtbogenschweißung *f.*
area Raum *m*, Gebiet *n*, Fläche *f*, Flächeninhalt *m.*

area bombing Bombenabwurf auf Flächenziel.

area contamination Geländevergiftung f (CWS).

area fire Flächenschießen n, Flächenfeuer n (Arty).

area sketch Grundrißskizze f.

area target Flächenziel n (Gunnery).

arm n Arm m (Anatomy); Waffe f (weapon); Waffengattung f (branch of the Army).

arm v bewaffnen, bestücken (provide armament); scharf machen, entsichern (Am, mine); scharf stellen (bomb).

armament Rüstung f; Bewaffnung f, Bestückung f.

armament error Waffenstreuung f.

armament officer Waffenoffizier m.

armament plant Rüstungswerk n.

arm and hand signal Armzeichen n.

armature Anker m.

armature shaft Ankerwelle f (Elec); Ankerachse f (field Tp).

armature short Lamellenschluß m.

armature turn Leiterschleife f.

armature winding Ankerwicklung f.

armband Armbinde f.

armed bewaffnet; scharf gemacht, scharf gestellt (Am).

armed-defense system Wehrorganisation f.

Armed Forces Wehrmacht f.

armed merchantman bewaffnetes Handelsschiff.

armed reconnaissance bewaffnete Aufklärung.

armes blanches blanke Waffen, Handwaffen fpl.

arming device Fliehbacke f (centrifugal type device in fuze).

arming pin Sicherungsvorstecker m (fuze).

arming vane Entsicherungsflügel m, Windflügel m (bomb).

arming wire Entsicherungsdraht m (bomb).

armistice Waffenstillstand m.

armistice terms Waffenstillstandsbedingungen fpl.

armor Panzer m, Panzerung f (Tk, etc.); Bewehrung f (Tp cable).

armor belt Panzergürtel m.

armored gepanzert, Panzer—.

armored artillery Panzerartillerie f.

armored attack Panzerangriff m.

armored battalion Panzerbataillon n, Panzerabteilung f.

armored cable armiertes Kabel, Panzerkabel n.

armored car Panzerwagen m, Panzerkraftwagen m.

armored cargo carrier Panzertransportwagen m (MT).

armored combat Panzerkampf m, Panzergefecht n.

armored combat vehicle gepanzertes Gefechtsfahrzeug, mechanisiertes Fahrzeug.

Armored Command Panzertruppe f, Panzerwaffe f.

armored corps Panzerkorps n.

armored division Panzerdivision f.

armored engagement Panzergefecht n.

armored engineer Panzerpionier m.

armored engineer battalion Panzer-Pionier-Bataillon n.

Armored Force Panzerwaffe f, Panzertruppe f.

armored force officer Panzeroffizier m.

armored forces Panzertruppen fpl, Panzerkräfte fpl.

armored formation Panzerverband m, Panzerformation f.

armored infantry battalion Panzergrenadier-Bataillon n.

armored infantry regiment Panzergrenadier-Regiment n, Panzer-Infanterieregiment n.

armored personnel carrier Panzertransportwagen m, Schützenpanzer m, Schützenpanzerwagen m, Grenadier-Panzerwagen m (MT).

armored platoon Panzerkraftwagenzug m.

armored point Panzerspitze f (Adv Gd).

armored radio car Panzerfunkwagen m.

armored radio truck Panzerfunkwagen m.

armored reconnaissance battalion Panzeraufklärungsabteilung f.

armored reconnaissance car Panzerspähwagen m.

armored reconnaissance company Panzerspähkompanie f.

armored reconnaissance vehicle Panzerspähfahrzeug n.

armored regiment Panzerregiment n.

armored rifleman Panzergrenadier *m*.

Armored School Panzertruppenschule *f*.

armored scout car Panzerspähwagen *m*.

armored signal battalion Panzernachrichtenabteilung *f*.

armored skirting Laufwerkpanzerung *f (Tk)*.

armored support Panzerunterstützung *f (Tac)*.

armored train Eisenbahnpanzerzug *m*, Panzerzug *m (RR)*.

armored troops Panzertruppen *fpl*, Kraftfahrkampftruppen *fpl*.

armored turret Panzerturm *m;* Panzerdrehturm *m (revolving);* Panzer-Verschwindeturm *m (disappearing)*.

armored-unit commander Panzerführer *m*.

armored vehicle Panzerfahrzeug *n*, Panzerkraftfahrzeug *n*.

armored warfare Panzerkriegführung *f*, Panzerkrieg *m*.

armorer Waffenwart *m*.

armorer-artificer Waffenmeisterunteroffizier *m (NCO)*.

armor-piercing panzerbrechend, panzerdurchschlagend *(Am)*.

armor-piercing ammunition Panzermunition *f*.

armor-piercing bomb Panzerbombe *f*.

armor-piercing bullet Stahlkerngeschoß *n*, Spitzgeschoß mit Stahlkern, Panzersprenggeschoß *n*.

armor-piercing cap Panzerkopf *m*.

armor-piercing grenade Panzergranate *f (R)*.

armor-piercing projectile Stahlkerngeschoß *n*, Spitzgeschoß mit Stahlkern, Panzersprenggeschoß *n*, Panzergeschoß *n*.

armor-piercing rifle grenade Gewehr-Panzergranate *f*.

armor-piercing shell Panzersprenggranate *f*, Panzergranate *f (Am)*.

armor-piercing shot Stahlkerngeschoß *n*, Spitzgeschoß mit Stahlkern, Panzersprenggeschoß *n*.

armor plate Panzerplatte *f*, Panzerblech *n*.

armor-plate shield Panzerschild *m (G)*.

armor-protected panzergeschützt.

armor protection Panzerschutz *m (Ft, Tk)*.

armor thickness Panzerstärke *f (Tk)*.

armory Exerzierhaus *n*, Waffenmeisterei *f*.

arms Waffen *fpl (weapons);* Waffengattungen *fpl (branches of the Army)*.

arms depot Arsenal *n*, Waffenlager *n*.

arm signal Armzeichen *n*.

arms rack Gewehrstütze *f*.

army Armee *f (a tactical unit);* Heer *n (the Army)*.

army air defense Heeresluftabwehr *f*.

Army Air Forces Heeresfliegertruppe *f*, Heeresluftwaffe *f (USA.)*.

Army Air Forces Weather Service Wetterdienst der Luftwaffe.

army ammunition depot Armeemunitionslager *n*, Heeresmunitionslager *n*.

army area Armeegebiet *n*.

Army Command Heeresleitung *f*.

army corps Armeekorps *n*.

army depot Heergerätepark *m*.

Army Directory Kriegsrangliste *f*.

army dog Heereshund *m*.

army engineer Pionier *m*.

army field order Armeebefehl *m*.

Army Ground Forces Heer *n*.

army headquarters Armeeoberkommando *n*.

Army High Command Oberkommando des Heeres *(Ger)*.

army hospital Heereslazarett *n*.

army mail clerk Feldpostbeamter *m (USA: enlisted man; Ger: civilian official)*.

army medical battalion Armeesanitätsabteilung *f*.

Army Medical School Militärärztliche Akademie.

army newspaper Frontzeitung *f (T of Opns)*.

army nurse Pflegeschwester *f*, Heereskrankenschwester *f*.

Army Nurse Corps Heeres-Krankenschwesternkorps *n (USA)*.

army of occupation Besatzungsheer *n*, Besatzungsarmee *f*.

Army of the United States Das Heer der Vereinigten Staaten. *Compare* United States Army.

Army Ordnance Department Heereswaffenamt *n.*

army post Standort *m,* Heeresstandort *m.*

army post administration Heeresstandortverwaltung *f.*

army postal service Feldpostwesen *n,* Feldpost *f.*

army post office Feldpostamt *n.*

army quartermaster Höherer Kommandeur der Armeenachschubtruppen *(USA).*

army ration depot Heeresverpflegungslager *n,* Armeeverpflegungslager *n.*

Army Register Rangliste des Heeres.

army remount depot Armeepferdepark *m.*

army saddle Armeesattel *m.*

army serial number Wehrnummer *f.*

army service area Versorgungsraum *m.*

Army Service Forces Heeresversorgungs- und Nachschubdienste *mpl (USA).*

army signal unit Armeenachrichtenabteilung *f.*

army supply Heeresversorgung *f.*

army supply train Armeenachschubkolonne *f.*

army surgeon Armeearzt *m.*

army surgical hospital Armeefeldlazarett *n.*

army troops Armeetruppen *fpl.*

army veterinary hospital Armeepferdelazarett *n.*

Army War College Kriegsakademie *f.*

arrest *n* Festnahme *f,* Arrest *m,* Verhaftung *f.*

arrest *v* festnehmen, verhaften, in Haft nehmen; anhalten, aufhalten, abbremsen, hemmen *(stop).*

arresting gear Abbremsvorrichtung *f (Ap).*

arrest in quarters Stubenarrest *m.*

arrival Ankunft *f.*

arrival time Eintreffzeit *f,* Ankunftzeit *f.*

arrive ankommen, eintreffen.

arsenal Zeughaus *n,* Zeugamt *n.*

arsine Arsin *n (CWS).*

artery Arterie *f.*

article of clothing Bekleidungsstück *n.*

Articles of War Kriegsartikel *mpl.*

artificer Feuerwerker *m (NCO).*

artificial antenna künstliche Antenne *(Rad).*

artificial horizon Horizont *m,* künstlicher Horizont, Fliegerhorizont *m (Ap).*

artificial leather Kunstleder *n.*

artificial respiration künstliche Atmung.

artificial scent Riechspur *f,* künstliche Spur.

artificial ventilation künstliche Lüftung.

artillery Artillerie *f.*

heavy artillery schwerste Artillerie.

medium artillery schwere Artillerie.

light artillery leichte Artillerie.

artillery ammunition Artilleriemunition *f.*

artillery barrage Artilleriesperrfeuer *n.*

artillery battalion Artillerieabteilung *f.*

artillery commander Artillerieführer *m (corps and Div).*

artillery duel Artillerieduell *n.*

artillery fire Artilleriebeschuß *m,* Artilleriefeuer *n.*

artillery fire-control instruments Artillerie-Beobachtungs- und Vermessungsgerät *n.*

artillery group Artilleriegruppe *f.*

artillery intelligence center Artillerienachrichtenstelle *f.*

artillery intelligence section Artillerienachrichtentrupp *m.*

artillery liaison command post Artillerieverbindungskommando *n.*

artillery liaison officer Artillerieverbindungsoffizier *m.*

artilleryman Artillerist *m.*

artillery mechanic Artilleriemechaniker *m.*

artillery mil Strich *m.*

artillery mission Artillerieflug *m (Avn).*

artillery observation airplane Artilleriebeobachtungsflugzeug *n.*

artillery observation post Artilleriebeobachtungsstelle *f.*

artillery observer Artilleriebeobachter *m.*

artillery officer Höherer Artilleriekommandeur *(army and higher Hq).*

artillery order Artilleriebefehl *m.*

artillery park Artilleriepark *m.*

artillery preparation Artillerievorbereitung f.
artillery prime mover Artilleriezugmaschine f.
artillery protection Feuerschutz m.
artillery reconnaissance artilleristische Aufklärung.
artillery reconnaissance aviation Artillerieflieger mpl.
artillery reconnaissance detail Artilleriespähtrupp m.
artillery reference points artilleristische Punkte mpl.
artillery regiment Artillerieregi-
ment n.
artillery support Artillerieunterstützung f.
artillery survey section Artillerievermessungstrupp m.
artillery target reconnaissance Zielaufklärung f.
artillery train Artilleriestaffel f.
art of leadership Führungskunst f.
art of war Kriegskunst f.
asbestos Asbest m, Steinflachs m.
ascending air current Aufwind m
(Met).
ascending branch aufsteigender Ast
(of trajectory).
ascending gust Steigbö f (Met).
ashore am Ufer, an der Küste
(being ashore); ans Land, ans Ufer
(going ashore).
aspect ratio Längenverhältnis n,
Seitenverhältnis n, Flügelstreckung
f (Ap).
asphalt Asphalt m.
asphyxiate ersticken.
aspirin Aspirin n.
assault n Sturmangriff m, Sturm m,
Vorstoß m, Vorstoßen n, Erstürmung
f (Tac).
assault v erstürmen, stürmen (Tac).
to take by assault im Sturm nehmen.
assault battalion Sturmbataillon n.
assault boat Sturmboot n.
assault detachment Stoßtrupp m.
assault fire Schießen während der
Bewegung (automatic weapons);
Einbruchsfeuer n (Tac).
assault fire position Anschlag zum
Schießen während der Bewegung.
assault gap Sturmgasse f (through
obstacles).
assault gun Sturmgeschütz n (self-
propelled).

assault-gun car Kraftwagenkanonenwagen m, Kanonenwagen m.
assault howitzer Sturmhaubitze f
(self-propelled).
assault position Ausgangslage f,
Sturmausgangsstellung f.
assault trench Angriffsgraben m.
assemble (sich) versammeln (to
gather); montieren (an Ap, Tk,
etc.); zusammensetzen (a weapon).
assembly Bereitstellung f, Versammlung f (Tac); Montage f
(Tech).
assembly area Bereitstellungsraum
m (Tac).
assembly formation Versammlungs-
form f.
assembly of troops Truppenbereitstellung f.
assembly order Bereitstellungsbefehl m.
assembly plant Montagewerk n.
assembly point Sammelpunkt m,
Sammelplatz m, Sammelstelle f,
Sammelort m, Bereitstellungsplatz
m.
assembly shop Montagehalle f.
assign eingliedern (to a unit); zu-
weisen (a task, etc.). See also attach.
assigned frequencies Verfügungsfrequenzen fpl (Rad).
assignment Eingliederung f, Auftrag m, Aufgabe f.
assignment of missions Auftragserteilung f.
assistant Gehilfe m, Helfer m,
Assistent m.
Assistant Chief of Staff Abteilungs-
chef im Generalstab.
assistant chief of staff Führergehilfe m.
assistant director Oberschiedsrichter
m, Leitungsoffizier m (maneuvers).
assistant driver Begleiter m, Kraftwagenbegleiter m, Beifahrer m
(MT).
assistant gunner Ladeschütze m
(Tk); Ladekanonier m (Arty); Gehilfe des Richtschützen (MG squad).
Assistant Secretary of War Abteilungsleiter im Kriegsministerium
(USA).
asymptote correction chart Hyperbelplan m (sound ranging).
"As you were!" "Kommando
zurück!" (to revoke a command);
"Weitermachen!" (carry on).

"At ease!" "Rührt Euch!" *(silence not required).*

athletics Athletik *f.*

Atlantic Charter Atlantik-Charta *f.*

Atlantic Wall Atlantikwall *m (Ger Ft).*

atlas grid Kartengitternetz *n (aerial Photo).*

atmosphere Luftmeer *n (air);* Atmosphäre *f (unit of pressure).*

atmospheric layer Luftschicht *f (Met).*

atmospheric pressure Luftdruck *m (Met).*

atmospherics Gewitterstörung *f (Rad).*

attach zuteilen *(to a unit);* befestigen *(fasten).* See also **assign.**

attaché Attaché *m.*

attached zugeteilt *(to a unit);* befestigt *(fastened).*

attack *n* Angriff *m.*

attack *v* angreifen.

attack airplane Kampfflugzeug *n.*

attacker Angreifer *m.*

attack formation Angriffsform *f.*

attack from march formation Angriff aus der Bewegung.

attack from the rear Rückenangriff *m.*

attack frontage Angriffsbreite *f.*

attack group Angriffsgruppe *f.*

attacking flank Angriffsflügel *m.*

attack of organized positions Angriff auf Stellungen.

attack on the flank *v* aus der Flanke nehmen.

attack order Angriffsbefehl *m,* Befehl zum Angriff.

attack sector Angriffsstreifen *m.*

attack troops Stoßtruppen *fpl,* Angriffstruppen *fpl,* Sturmtruppen *fpl.*

attack wave Angriffswelle *f,* Sturmwelle *f (Tac).*

attempt *n* Versuch *m.*

attention Grundstellung *f.*

"Attention!" "Achtung!" *(on approach of an officer);* "Abteilung, Stillgestanden!" *(for formations);* "Stillgesessen!" *(mounted drill).*

attitude Fluglage *f,* Flugzustand *m (Avn).*

attrition Abnutzung *f,* Ermattung *f,* Zermürbung *f.*

audible hörbar.

audio frequency Tonfrequenz *f.*

audio-frequency amplifier Niederfrequenzverstärker *m.*

audio-frequency range Tonfrequenzbereich *m.*

audit *n* Rechnungsprüfung *f,* Buchprüfung *f.*

audit *v* Rechnungen prüfen, buchprüfen.

auger Lochbohrer *m,* Holzbohrer *m.*

authentication Beglaubigung *f,* Bescheinigung *f.*

authority Befehlsbefugnis *f (Mil);* Behörde *f,* Instanz *f (Law).*

authorization Berechtigung *f,* Genehmigung *f.*

authorize genehmigen *(approve);* bevollmächtigen *(empower).*

authorized behördlich zugelassen *(officially permitted);* dienstlich *(regulation);* genehmigt *(approved);* bevollmächtigt *(empowered);* Soll-, Plan- *(in tables of basic allowances or organization).*

authorized abbreviation amtlich festgelegte Abkürzung.

authorized basic allowance Sollbestand *m.*

authorized strength Sollstärke *f.* Compare **Iststärke.**

autofrettage Kaltrecken *n,* Autofrettage *f (Ord).*

autogiro Tragschrauber *m,* Autogiro *m.*

autoloader Selbstlader *m (Small Arms).*

automatic *n* Selbstladepistole *f.*

automatically operated selbsttätig.

automatic anchor Minenanker mit Tiefensteller *(Nav).*

automatic antiaircraft gun Flugabwehrmaschinenkanone *f,* Fla-Maschinenkanone *f.*

automatic antiaircraft weapons Flugabwehrmaschinenwaffen *fpl.*

automatic breech mechanism selbsttätiger Verschluß.

automatic cannon Maschinenkanone *f (Ap).*

automatic circuit breaker Selbstunterbrecher *m (Elec).*

automatic control Selbststeuerung *f,* Regler *m.*

automatic direction finder selbstweisendes Peilgerät *(Ap).*

automatic feed mechanism Zuführer *m (automatic weapon).*

automatic fire Dauerfeuer *n (MG, R)*.

automatic fuze setter Zünderstellmaschine *f (AA gun)*.

automatic gun Maschinenkanone *f*, Salvengeschütz *n*.

automatic pilot automatische Kurssteuerung, automatischer Pilot, Selbststeuergerät *n (Ap)*.

automatic pistol Selbstladepistole *f*.

automatic-pitch propeller vollautomatische Verstell-Luftschraube.

automatic rifle Maschinenkarabiner *m*, automatisches Gewehr.

automatic supply planmäßiger Nachschub.

automatic volume control Schwundausgleich *m*.

automatic weapon Maschinenwaffe *f*, Schnellfeuerwaffe *f (Small Arms)*.

automobile Kraftwagen *m*.

automobile engine Wagenmotor *m*.

automobile express highway Autobahn *f*.

automobile flag Kraftwagenflagge *f*.

automobile jack Wagenheber *m*.

auto-tow take-off Autoschleppstart *m (glider)*.

autotransformer Spartransformator *m (Rad, Elec)*.

autotransformer circuit Sparschaltung *f (Elec)*.

autumn Herbst *m*.

auxiliary Hilfs-, Behelfs-. *See also* woman auxiliary.

auxiliary air Nebenluft *f (Mtr)*.

auxiliary airfoil Zusatzflügel *m*, Hilfsflügel *m (Ap)*.

auxiliary arm Hilfswaffe *f*.

auxiliary cruiser Hilfskreuzer *m*.

auxiliary engine Hilfsmotor *m*.

auxiliary equipment Hilfsgerät *n*.

auxiliary gear Geländegang *m (MT)*.

auxiliary ground target Erdvergleichsziel *n (Gunnery)*.

auxiliary ignition lead Reservezündung *f (Blasting)*.

auxiliary landing field Hilfslandeplatz *m*.

auxiliary scale Hilfsmaßstab *m (Inst)*.

auxiliary stage supercharger Zwischengebläse *n (Ap engine)*.

auxiliary target Vergleichsziel *n*, Hilfsziel *n;* Luftvergleichsziel *n (high burst)*.

auxiliary track Hilfskette *f (MT)*.

auxiliary transmission Gruppengetriebe *n*, Zwischengetriebe *n*, Zusatzgetriebe *n (MT)*.

auxiliary troops Hilfstruppen *fpl*.

auxiliary vessel Hilfsschiff *n*.

auxiliary wing Hilfsflügel *m (Ap)*.

available verfügbar, zur Verwendung.

available for commitment einsatzfähig.

AVC *See* **automatic volume control.**

average *n* Durchschnitt *m*.

average *v* den Durchschnitt berechnen *(Math);* im Durchschnitt machen *(in marching, etc)*.

average *adj* durchschnittlich, Durchschnitts-.

average error mittlerer Fehler, durchschnittlicher Fehler.

average performance Durchschnittsleistung *f*.

aviation Flugwesen *n*, Luftfahrt *f*, Fliegerei *f;* Flieger *mpl (collective term for any number of airplanes)*.

aviation badge Fliegerabzeichen *n*.

aviation cadet Fähnrich der Flieger *(USA)*.

aviation engineers Luftwaffenbautruppe *f*.

aviation fuel Fliegerkraftstoff *m*.

aviation gasoline Fliegerbenzin *n*.

aviation medicine Luftfahrtmedizin *f*.

aviation pay Luftdienstzulage *f*, Fliegerzulage *f*.

aviation support Fliegerhilfe *f*, Fliegerunterstützung *f*, Schlachtfliegerunterstützung *f (Tac)*.

aviation weather service Flugwetterdienst *m*.

aviation weather station Flugwetterwarte *f*.

aviator Flieger *m*.

aviator's helmet Fliegerhaube *f*.

award Auszeichnung *f (citation);* Orden *m*, Ehrenzeichen *n (decoration);* Ehrensold *m (payment)*.

ax Axt *f*, Beil *n*.

axial observation Beobachtung aus der Schußlinie *(Arty)*.

axial road direkte Zufuhrstraße, direkte Anmarschstraße.

axial spotting Beobachtung in der Schußrichtung *(Arty)*.

axis Achse *f*, Hauptlinie *f*.

Axis forces Achsenstreitkräfte *fpl*.

axis of advance Vormarschlinie *f*.

axis of an aircraft Flugzeugachse *f.*
axis of communication Verbindungs-achse *f.*
axis of signal communication Nach-richtenachse *f.*
axis of supply Nachschublinie *f.*
axis of supply and evacuation Haupt-nachschublinie *f.*
axis of the bore Seelenachse *f.*
axis of trunnions Schildzapfenachse *f (G).*
axle Radachse *f,* Achse *f.*
axle bearing Achslager *n.*
axle displacement Kletterfähigkeit *f (MT).*
axle drive Achsantrieb *m (MT).*
axle load Achsdruck *m (MT).*
axle nut Achsmutter *f.*
axle pivot pin Längszapfen *m (split-trail carriage).*
axle seats Achssitze *mpl (for gun-ners, G).*
axle spring Achsfeder *f (G).*
azimuth Seite *f,* Seitenrichtung *f,* Richtung *f (Gunnery);* Azimut *m,* Scheitelkreis *m,* Scheitelbogen *m (Surv);* Kompaßzahl *f,* Nadelzahl *f (compass);* Kurs *m (Nav).*
azimuthal projection Azimutalpro-jektion *f.*
azimuth and elevation indicator Sei-ten- und Höhenempfänger *m (AA).*

azimuth change Teilringänderung *f (telescopic sight).*
azimuth circle Meßkreis *m (BC tel-escope),* Richtkreis *m (Surv).*
azimuth controller Seitenrichtmann *m (AAA).*
azimuth difference Parallaxe *f,* Pa-rallaxenwinkel *m (Optics).*
azimuth indicator Seitenempfänger *m (AA gun).*
azimuth instrument Peilapparat *m,* Peilgerät *n,* Peilscheibe *f,* Luftziel-apparat *m;* Theodolit *m (Surv).*
azimuth knob Triebscheibe zur Sei-tenrichtung *(Ord).*
azimuth micrometer Teilring *m (tel-escopic sight).*
azimuth of target Kurswinkel *m,* Zielseitenwinkel in der Horizontal-ebene *(AAA);* Zielseitenwinkel zum Abschußpunkt *(present position);* Zielseitenwinkel zum Treffpunkt *(fu-ture position).*
azimuth reading Teilringzahl *f,* Na-delzahl *f (magnetic);* Richtpunkt-zahl *f (aiming point).*
azimuth scale Teilring *m (panoramic sight);* Seitenteilring *m (AA gun).*
azimuth setter Seitenrichtkanonier *m.*
azimuth tracking telescope Seiten-richtfernrohr *n (height finder).*

B

bachelor officers' quarters Offizier-ledigenheim *n.*
back Rücken *m.*
back azimuth der um 180° vermehrte (oder verminderte) Richtungswinkel *(Surv).*
back azimuth method Messen der rückwärtigen Verlängerung *(Surv);* "Durchschlagen" *n (of a surveyor's transit).*
back bearing Wegflugpeilung *f (Air Navigation).*
backbone Rückgrat *n.*
backfire Fehlzündung *f (Mtr).*
backing light Rückfahrlaterne *f (MT).*
backlash Spiel *n,* Spielraum *m,* toter Gang.

back-pack parachute Rückenfall-schirm *m.*
back pad Kammkissen *n (harness).*
back-pad strap Kammkissengurt *m (harness).*
back plate Verschlußleiste *f (MG);* Schloßplatte *f (G).*
back plate hinge pin Verschlußlei-stenachse *f (MG).*
back plate latch lock Zurrstück *n (MG).*
back rest Rückenlehne *f (Ap, MT);* Rückenring *m (AA MG).*
backsight Rückblick *m (Surv).*
back step Schritt zurück.
bacteriological examination bakteri-ologische Untersuchung.

bacteriological warfare Bakterienkrieg *m*.

bacteriologist Bakteriologe *m*.

badge Abzeichen *n*.

bad weather Unwetter *n*.

baffle Truhe *f*, Lautsprechertruhe *f* *(Rad)*; Schlingerwand *f (Ap tank)*; Zugdämpfer *m (engine muffler)*; Prallwand *f*, Leitwand *f*.

bag Sack *m*, Beutel *m*, Tasche *f*.

baggage Gepäck *n*.

baggage car Gepäckwagen *m (RR)*.

baggage train Gepäcktroß *m*.

bail out abspringen, aussteigen *(Avn)*; ausschöpfen *(a boat)*.

bakery Bäckerei *f*.

bakery company Bäckereikompanie *f*.

balance *n* Gewichtsverteilung *f*, Gleichgewicht *n (equilibrium)*; Waage *f (Inst)*.

balance *v* ausgleichen.

balanced profile ausgeglichenes Profil.

balanced rudder ausgeglichenes Seitenruder, entlastetes Seitenruder *(Ap)*.

balanced stock vorschriftsmäßige Bestände.

balanced surface ausgeglichene Tragfläche *(Ap)*.

balance tab Ausgleichfläche *f*, Trimmruder *n (Ap)*.

bale *n* Ballen *m*.

bale *v* in Ballen verpacken.

baling machine Ballenpresse *f*.

balk Längsträger *m*, Tragbalken *m (Bdg)*; Scherbalken *m (Pon)*.

ball ammunition scharfe Munition.

ball-and-socket joint Kugelgelenk *n*.

ballast Ballast *m*.

ball bearing Kugellager *n*.

ball cartridge scharfe Patrone.

ball filler Kugelfüllung *f (shrapnel)*.

ballistic ballistisch.

ballistic coefficient ballistischer Beiwert, Querschnittbelastung *f*.

ballistic correction Ausschalten der besonderen und Witterungseinflüsse.

ballistic curve Flugbahn *f*, Geschoßbahn *f*, ballistische Kurve.

ballistic density ballistisches Luftgewicht.

ballistic director Feuerleitgerät *n*, Kommandogerät *n*, Zielrechenmaschine *f (Gunnery)*.

ballistic efficiency ballistische Leistungsfähigkeit *(Am)*.

ballistics Schießlehre *f*, Ballistik *f*.

ballistic table Schußtafel *f*.

ballistic wave Kopfwelle *f*.

ballistic wind ballistischer Wind.

ballistite Ballistit *n (Am)*.

ball mount Kugellafette *f*, Kugelblende *f (Tk)*.

ballonet Luftsack *m (Bln)*.

ballonet balloon Prallhaltevorrichtung *f*.

ballonet valve Luftsackventil *n*.

balloon Ballon *m*.

balloon barrage Ballonsperre *f*.

balloon basket Ballonkorb *m*.

balloon chief Ballontruppführer *m*.

balloon cover Ballonhülle *f*.

balloon crew Ballonmannschaft *f*.

balloon envelope Ballonhülle *f*.

balloon fabric Ballonstoff *m*.

balloon interval Ballonabstand *m*.

balloon net Ballonnetz *n*.

balloon observation Ballonbeobachtung *f*.

balloon observer Ballonbeobachter *m*.

balloon pilot Ballonführer *m*.

balloon position Verankerungsstelle *f (captive Bln)*.

balloon site Ballonaufstiegplatz *m*.

balloon squad Ballontrupp *m*.

balloon tire Ballonreifen *m*.

ball projectile Vollgeschoß *n*.

ball socket Kugelpfanne *f (Mort)*.

ball turret Bodenkanzel *f*.

ball turret gunner Bodenschütze *m*.

band Musikkorps *n;* Frequenzband *n (Rad)*; Band *n*, Binde *f (Clo, etc.)*.

bandage *n* Verband *m*, Binde *f*, Bandage *f*.

bandage *v* verbinden.

band brake Bandbremse *f (MT)*.

bandmaster Musikmeister *m (Ger: 2nd Lt)*.

band of fire Feuerstrahl *m (MG)*.

bandoleer Patronengurt *m*.

band saw Bandsäge *f*.

bandsman Spielmann *m (pl: Spielleute)*.

bandspread Bandspreizung *f (Rad)*.

band switch Grobstufenschalter *m (Rad)*.

band width Bandbreite *f (Rad)*.

bangalore torpedo in Rohr gefüllte Reihenladung.

bank *n* Schräglage *f (Ap)*; Ufer *n (river)*.

bank *v* sich in die Kurve legen *(Avn)*.

bank-and-turn indicator Kreiselneigungsmesser *m*, Wendezeiger *m* *(Ap)*.

banner Banner *n*.

baptism of fire Feuertaufe *f*.

bar Rangabzeichen *n*, Ordensschnalle *f*, Ordensspange *f* *(insigne or decoration)*; Stab *m*, Stange *f* *(Tech)*; Sandbank *f*, Barre *f* *(rivers, etc.)*.

barbed wire Stacheldraht *m*.

barbed-wire concertina S.-Rolle *f*, Stacheldrahtrolle *f*.

barbed-wire entanglement Stacheldrahtverhau *m*, Stacheldrahthindernis *n*.

barbette Geschützbank *f*, Barbette *f*.

barbette carriage Barbettelafette *f* *(G)*.

bare wire blanker Draht *(Tp)*.

barge Prahm *m*.

barn Scheune *f*.

barogram Barogramm *n*.

barograph Barograph *m*.

barometer Barometer *n*, Luftdruckmesser *m;* Federbarometer *n*, Federluftdruckmesser *m* *(aneroid)*.

barometric pressure Außenluftdruck *m* *(Avn)*; Luftdruck *m* *(Met)*.

barracks Kaserne *f*.

barrack(s) bag Bekleidungssack *m*, Wäschesack *m*.

barrage Sperre *f;* Feuersperre *f*, Sperrfeuer *n* *(Arty)*.

barrage balloon Sperrballon *m*.

barrage chart Sperrfeuerskizze *f*.

barrage fire Sperrfeuer *n*.

barrage kite Sperrdrache *m*.

barrel Rohr *n* *(G)*; Lauf *m* *(SA)*; Mittelhand *f* *(horse)*; Faß *n*, Tonne *f* *(container)*. See also **tube**.

barrel bracket Rohrhalter *m* *(G)*.

barrel burst Rohrzerspringer *m*.

barrel erosion Ausbrennung *f*, Rohrabnutzung *f*.

barrel extension Rohransatz *m*, Rohransatzstück *n*.

barrel float Tonnenfloß *n*.

barrel guide Rohrklaue *f* *(G)*.

barrel length Rohrlänge *f*, Seelenlänge *f* *(Ord)*.

barrel-locking ring Laufsitzring *m* *(MG)*.

barrel-locking stud Gewehrkupplungsstück *n* *(MG)*.

barrel raft Tonnenfähre *f*.

barrel recoil Rohrrücklauf *m* *(G)*.

barrel reflector Rohrwandbeobachtungsgerät *n* *(G)*; Laufseelenprüfer *m* *(R)*.

barrel roll Rolle *f*, Überschlag über den Flügel *(Avn)*.

barricade Barrikade *f*.

barrier Hindernis *n*, Sperre *f* *(Ft)*; Sperriegel *m* *(Tac)*.

barrier detachment Sperrtrupp *m*, Sperrverband *m*.

barrier light Sperrlicht *n*.

barrier line Straßensperrung *f* *(MP)*.

barrier zone Sperrzone *f*.

bascule bridge Klappbrücke *f*.

base Bettung *f* *(fixed gun)*; Boden *m*, Geschoßboden *m* ·*(Am)*; Stützpunkt *m* *(Tac)*; Visierfuß *m* *(of rear sight)*; Hülsenboden *m* *(of cartridge case)*; Wolkenuntergrenze *f* *(of cloud)*.

base angle Grundrichtungswinkel *m* *(Gunnery)*; Winkel zwischen Grundrichtungslinie und Orientierungslinie *(Surv)*.

base bushing Grundbuchse *f* *(of counterrecoil mechanism)*.

base charge Bodenkammerladung *f* *(Am)*.

base cover Abschlußplättchen *n* *(Am)*.

base deflection die vom Grundgeschütz aus gemessene Seitenänderung *(Gunnery)*.

base delay-action fuze Bodenabstandszünder *m* *(Am)*.

base depot rückwärtiges Nachschublager.

base detonating fuze Bodenzünder *m*.

base end station Stand einer Langbasisanlage *(CA)*; Meßstand *m* *(AAA)*.

base fuze Bodenzünder *m* *(Am)*.

base hospital Kriegslazarett *n*.

base line Grundrichtungslinie *f* *(Gunnery)*; Standlinie *f* *(Surv)*.

base-line arm Basislineal *n* *(plotting protractor)*.

base-line direction Grundrichtung *f* *(Gunnery)*.

base machine gun Grundmaschinengewehr *n*, Leit-Maschinengewehr *n*.

base of operations   Operationsbasis
f (Tac).
base of the trajectory   Mündungswaagerechte *f.*
base pay   Grundgehalt *n,* Löhnung *f.*
base piece   Grundgeschütz *n (Arty).*
base plate   Bodenplatte *f (Mort);*
Grundplatte *f (Tech).*
base point   Grundrichtungspunkt *m*
(Gunnery).
base ring   Fundamentring *m (Ord).*
base section   hinterer Abschnitt des
rückwärtigen Gebiets.
base services   Bodendienst *m (Avn).*
base stake   Richtlatte *f (Surv).*
basic allowance   Sollbestand *m.*
basic data   Schußwerte *mpl,* Schußelemente *npl,* Schießunterlagen *fpl,*
Schießgrundlagen *fpl.*
basic load   Tagesrate *f (Am);* ständige Belastung, bleibende Belastung
(Avn).
basic tactical unit   taktische Einheit;
Feuereinheit der Artillerie *(Arty).*
basic training   Grundausbildung *f.*
basic training course   Schießvorschule *f (Arty).*
basic unit   *See* basic tactical unit.
basket   Korb *m.*
bastion   Bastion *f.*
baton   Marschallstab *m;* Tambourstock *m,* Bataillonstambourstock *m.*
battalion   Bataillon *n,* Abteilung *f.*
battalion aid station   Bataillonsverbandplatz *m.*
battalion combat train   Gefechtstroß
eines Bataillons.
battalion commander   Abteilungskommandeur   *m,* Bataillonsführer   *m,*
Bataillonskommandeur *m.*
battalion command post   Abteilungs-
gefechtsstand *m,* Bataillonsgefechtsstand *m.*
b a t t a l i o n communication section
Bataillonsnachrichtenstaffel   *f,* Abteilungsnachrichtenstaffel *f.*
battalion headquarters   Bataillonsstab *m,* Abteilungsstab *m.*
battalion sector   Bataillonsabschnitt
m.
battalion train   Bataillonstroß *m,*
Bataillonskolonne *f.*
batter   Böschungsanlage *f (Ft).*
battered round   verbeulte Patrone
(Am).
battery   Batterie *f (Arty, Elec);*

Element *n (cell);* Sammlerbatterie *f,*
Sammler *m (storage).*
battery box   Batteriekasten *m,* Sammlerkasten *m (Elec).*
battery charger   Lademaschine *f.*
battery-charging unit   Lademaschinensatz *m.*
battery chart   Schießliste *f.*
battery commander   Batteriechef *m,*
Batterieführer *m.*
battery commander's telescope
Scherenfernrohr *n.*
battery cover   Sammlerhaube *f,*
Zellendeckel *m (Elec).*
battery detail   *See* battery headquarters detail.
battery emplacement book   Schießkladde *f.*
battery executive   Batterieoffizier *m.*
battery front   Batteriefront *f.*
battery headquarters detail   Batterietrupp *m.*
battery ignition   Batteriezündung *f*
(Mtr).
battery-location plot   Batteriebild *n*
(sound ranging).
battery manning table   Batterietafel
f.
battery position   Geschützstellung *f,*
Batteriestand *m,* Batteriestellung *f*
(Arty).
battery survey chart   Stellungsmeßblatt *n.*
battery-target line   Linie Grundge-
schütz-Ziel.
battery tester   Elementprüfer *m*
(Elec).
battle   Schlacht *f,* Kampf *m,* Gefecht *n.*
battle casualty   Ausfall *m,* Gefechts-
ausfall *m.*
battle casualty report   Verlustmeldung *f.*
battle chart   Einschießplan *m (Arty).*
battle clasp   Erinnerungsspange *f.*
battle command   Kampfführung *f.*
battle cruiser   Schlachtkreuzer *m.*
battle fatigue   Kriegsneurose *f.*
battlefield   Schlachtfeld *n,* Kampffeld *n.*
battle flag   Sturmfahne *f.*
battle fleet   Schlachtflotte *f.*
battle honor   Kriegsband *n,* Fahnenband *n.*
battle injury   Kampfwunde *f.*
battle line   Schlachtlinie *f,* Kampflinie *f.*

battle map Gefechtskarte *f.*
battle of attrition Abnutzungskampf *m.*
battle of encirclement Einkreisungsschlacht *f.*
battle of extermination Vernichtungskampf *m.*
battle performance Kampfleistung *f.*
battle position Hauptkampffeld *n,* Kampfstellung *f.*
battle reconnaissance Gefechtsaufklärung *f.*
battle reserves Reserve *f.*
battle service practice Schulgefechtsschießen *n (Arty).*
battleship Schlachtschiff *n.*
battle sight Standvisier *n (R);* Fliegervisier *n (MG).*
battle star Erinnerungsstern *m.*
battle terrain Kampfgelände *n.*
battle zone Kampfzone *f.*
bay Feld *n,* Gerippeabteil *n,* Zelle *f (Ap);* Strecke *f,* Brückenstrecke *f,* Brückenglied *n (Bdg);* Bucht *f (sea inlet).*
bayonet Seitengewehr *n,* Bajonett *n.*
bayonet charge Bajonettangriff *m.*
bayonet fighting Bajonettfechten *n.*
bayonet grip Seitengewehrgriff *m,* Bayonettgriff *m.*
bayonet guard Parierstange *f.*
bayonet joint Bajonettkupplung *f (Mech).*
bayonet lock Seitengewehrverschluß *m (R).*
bayonet practice Übung im Bajonettfechten.
bayonet scabbard Seitengewehrtasche *f.*
bayonet stud Seitengewehrhalter *m (R).*
bayonet thrust Bajonettstoß *m.*
"bazooka" "Ofenrohr" *n. See also* **antitank rocket launcher.**
"B" battery Anodenbatterie *f (Rad).*
BC telescope Scherenfernrohr *n.*
beach Strand *m.*
beach defense Strandsperre *f,* Strandverteidigung *f.*
beachhead Landekopf *m.*
beaching gear Schwimmerwagen *m,* Schleppwagen *m (seaplane).*
beaching party Landungsabteilung *f.*
beacon Bake *f,* Feuer *n;* Funkbake *f,* Funkfeuer *n (Rad).*
beacon light Leuchtfeuer *n (Avn).*

beacon lighting Nachtbefeuerung *f (Avn).*
bead sight Perlkorn *n (R).*
beam Balken *m,* Träger *m (Engr);* Strahl *m (ray);* Peilstrahl *m (Rad);* Lichtkegel *m,* Lichtstrahl *m (SL).*
bearing Peilung *f,* Peilrichtung *f,* Peillinie *f (Navigation);* Lager *n (Mech).*
bearing line Peillinie *f (Air Navigation).*
bearing metal Lagermetall *n.*
bearing plate Peilscheibe *f,* Peilaufsatz *m,* Kursscheibe *f (Air Navigation).*
bearing station Peilort *m,* Peilstelle *f (Air Navigation).*
bearing surface Lauffläche *f (Mech);* Auflagefläche *f (Engr);* Tragerand *m (hoof).*
beaten track Trampelweg *m.*
beaten zone bestrichener Raum *(firing).*
beat frequency Schwebungsfrequenz *f (Rad).*
Beaufort scale Beaufortskala *f (Met).*
beaver dam Biberwehr *n (Engr).*
bed Bett *n.*
bedbug Wanze *f.*
bedding Bettzeug *n (for Pers);* Streu *f (for animals).*
bedding roll Bettzeugrolle *f.*
bed sheets Bettbezug *m.*
beef Rindfleisch *n,* Ochsenfleisch *n.*
beef stew Gulasch *n.*
beer Bier *n.*
Behm sound-ranging altimeter Behmlot *n (Avn).*
belligerent *n* kriegführende Macht.
belligerent *adj.* kriegführend.
belly Bauch *m;* Unterseite *f (Tk).*
belly landing Bauchlandung *f (Avn)..*
belly tank Abwurfbehälter *m (Ap).*
belly turret Bodenkanzel *f (Ap).*
belt Gurt *m (MG);* Streifen *m (Top);* Gürtel *m,* Koppel *n (Clo).*
belt buckel Koppelschloß *n.*
belt conveyor Gurtförderer *m.*
belt drive Riemenantrieb *m.*
belted ammunition gegurtete Munition *(MG).*
belt-fed mit Gurtzuführung *(MG).*
belt feed Gurtladung *f,* Zuführer *m,* Gurtzuführer *m (MG).*
belt-feed guide Gurthebel *m (MG).*

belt-feed lever   Zubringerhebel *m*, Patronenträgerhebel *m (MG)*.

belt-feed pawl   Gurtschieber *m (MG)*.

belt-filling machine   *See* **belt-loading machine.**

belt-loaded   mit Gurtzuführung *(MG)*.

belt-loading machine   Gurtfüller *m*.

belt road   Querverbindungsstraße *f*.

bench   Bank *f;* Werkbank *f (Tech)*.

bench mark   Nivellementspunkt *m*.

bend   Straßenbiegung *f (road)*.

bending machine   Biegemaschine *f*.

bends   Höhenkrankheit *f (aeroembolism)*; Caisson-Krankheit *f (caisson disease)*.

beneficiary   Nutznießer *m*, Empfangsberechtigter *m*.

bent   Joch *n*, Bock *m (Bdg)*.

benzol   Benzol *n*.

benzyl bromide   Benzylbromid *n*, T-Stoff *m (CWS)*.

berm   Berme *f (Ft)*.

berth   Bett *n (Nav, RR);* Liegeplatz *m (of a ship)*.

besiege   belagern.

Bessel method   Rückwärtseinschneiden *n (Surv)*.

betray   verraten.

bevel   Schräge *f*.

bevel drive pinion   Antriebskegelrad *n (differential gear) (MT)*.

bevel gear   Kegelrad *n*, Kegelzahnrad *n*.

bevel-gear rear-axle drive   Kegelrad-Hinterachsantrieb *m*.

beverage   Getränk *n*.

bias   Gittervorspannung *f (Rad);* schräger Schnitt *(slant cut);* Voreingenommenheit *f (prejudice)*.

bible   Bibel *f*.

bicarbonate of soda   doppelkohlensaures Natrium.

Bickford fuze   Bickford-Leitfeuer *n (Engr)*.

bicycle   Fahrrad *n*, Rad *n*.

Big Dipper   Großer Bär.

bilateral observation   Beobachten mit zwei Beobachtungsstellen *(Arty)*.

bill   Rechnung *f*.

billet dispensary   Ortskrankenstube *f (Med)*.

billet hospital   Ortskrankenlazarett *n (Med)*.

billeting   Unterbringung *f*.

billeting area   Unterkunftsbezirk *m*.

billeting detail   *See* **billeting party.**

billeting equipment   Unterkunftsgerät *n*.

billeting officer   Quartiermacher *m*.

billeting party   Quartiermachertrupp *m*.

billets   Unterbringung *f*, Ortsunterkunft *f*, Ortsbiwak *n*.

bill of lading   Frachtbrief *m*, Verladungsschein *m*.

bill of particulars   Tatbericht *m*.

binaural balance   Mitteneindruck *m (Sound Locating)*.

binaural method   Zwei-Ohr-Verfahren *n*, Binauralverfahren *n (Sound Locating)*.

binaural trainer   Horcherprüf- und Übungsgerät *n*.

binder   Einbanddeckel für lose Blätter *(loose-leaf cover)*.

binder ring   Dichtring *m (gas mask)*.

binding post   Anschlußklemme *f*, Polklemme *f (Elec)*.

binocular *adj*   binokular, zweiäugig *(Optics)*.

binocular *n*   Glas *n*, Fernglas *n*, Doppelglas *n*.

biplane   Doppeldecker *m*.

bipod   Zweibein *n*, Gabelstütze *f (MG)*.

birth certificate   Geburtsurkunde *f*.

birthmark   Muttermal *n*.

biscuit   Keks *m-n*, Biskuit *m-n*.

bit   Gebiß *n*, Trense *f*, Kandare *f (curb bit, harness);* Bohrer *m*, Schneide *f (carpenter's drill)*.

bite   Stich *m (of insect);* Biß *m (of animal)*.

biting angle   kleinster Panzerdurchschlagswinkel *(Am)*.

bit ring   Zügelring *m (harness)*.

bitumen   Bitumen *n*.

bivouac   Biwak *n*, Feldlager *n*.

bivouac commander   Biwakskommandant *m (ranking officer at a bivouac)*.

bivouac security officer   Offizier vom Biwakdienst.

bivouac site   Biwakplatz *m*.

black   schwarz.

blackboard   schwarze Tafel, schwarzes Brett.

blackjack   Totschläger *m*.

blackout *n*   Verdunkelung *f*.

black-out *v*   schwarz vor den Augen werden *(Avn);* verdunkeln *(lights)*.

blackout light   Tarnscheinwerfer *m (MT)*.

blackout measures Verdunkelungs-
maßnahmen *fpl (AA defense)*.
black powder Schwarzpulver *n*,
Naßbrandpulver *n*.
blacksmith Schmied *m*. *See also*
horseshoer.
blade Blatt *n*, Flügel *m (propeller)*;
Klinge *f (of knife, etc.)*.
blade angle Steigungswinkel *m*,
Anstellwinkel *m (propeller)*.
blank Platzpatrone *(Am)*; Vordruck *m*, Formular *n (printed
form)*.
blank ammunition Platzpatronen
fpl.
blank cartridge Platzpatrone *f*,
Manöverkartusche *f*.
blanket *n* Decke *f*, Marschdecke *f*;
Wolldecke *f (woolen)*; Woilach *m
(saddle)*; künstlicher Nebel, Nebeldecke *f (CWS)*.
blanket *v* verschleiern, vernebeln,
einnebeln, abschirmen.
blanket door Gasschutzvorhang *m*.
blanketing smoke Nebelwand *f*,
Nebelschleier *m (CWS)*.
blanket roll Bettzeugrolle *f*.
blank fire powder Nitrozellulosepulver *n (Small Arms)*.
blank form Formular *n*.
blank shell blindgeladene Granate
(Am).
blast *n* Luftdruck *m*, Detonationsdruck *m*, Luftstoß *m*, Zerknallstoß *m
(pressure)*; Sprengung *f*, Explosion
f (explosion).
blast *v* sprengen.
blast effect Luftdruckwirkung *f*,
Luftstoß *m*.
blast furnace Hochofen *m*.
blasting Sprengen *n*.
blasting cap Sprengkapsel *f*.
blasting cartridge Sprengpatrone *f*,
Bohrpatrone *f*.
blasting charge Sprengladung *f*;
Bohrladung *f (borehole)*; Schnell-
ladung *f (emergency)*.
blasting-charge box Ladungskasten
m.
blasting-charge can Ladungsbüchse
f.
blasting-charge container Ladungsgefäß *n*.
blasting fuze Zeitzündschnur *f*, Zeitschnur *f (Engr)*.
blasting machine Glühzündapparat
m (Engr).

blasting oil Sprengöl *n (nitroglycerin)*.
blasting pit Sprenggrube *f (Engr)*.
blasting powder Sprengpulver *n
(black powder)*.
bleach Bleichmittel *n*.
bleaching powder Chlorkalk *m*.
bleed bluten; entlüften *(recoil
mechanism)*.
blend anpassen *(Cam)*.
blimp unstarres Kleinluftschiff.
blind *v* blind machen, blenden.
blind *adj* blind.
blind flying *See* **instrument flying**.
blinker Blinklampe *f. See also*
signal lamp.
blinker light Blinkfeuer *n*, Taktfeuer *n*.
blinker signal Blinkzeichen *n*.
blister Torpedowulst *m (Nav)*; MG.-
Warze *f (Ap)*; Blase *f (Med)*.
blister agent ätzender Kampfstoff
(CWS).
blister gas Hautgift *n*, ätzender
Kampfstoff *(CWS)*.
block Sperre *f (Ft)*; Block *m*,
Klotz *m (Engr)*; Kettenglied *n
(Tk, Trac)*; Haltezeichen *n (RR
block signal)*; Bremsklotz *m
(wheel)*; Sprengkörper *m (explosive)*.
blockade Blockade *f*, Sperre *f*.
block and tackle Flaschenzug *m*.
"blockbuster" schwere Sprengbombe.
blockhouse Blockhaus *n (Ft)*.
blocking Sperrung *f (by means of
obstacles)*.
block warden Blockwart *m (Civ
Defense)*.
blood Blut *n*.
blood donor Blutspender *m*.
blood group *See* **blood type**.
blood plasma Blutplasma *n*.
blood-poisoning Blutvergiftung *f*.
blood type Blutgruppe *f*.
blouse *See* **service coat**.
blowback Rückschlag *m (Ord)*.
blowback-operated weapon Gasdrucklader *m*.
blower Gebläse *n (Ap engine)*.
blown primer Zündhütchenausfall
m.
blowtorch Lötlampe *f*.
blow up sprengen *(blast)*; aufblasen
(inflate).
bludgeon Knüppel *m*.
blue blau.

blueprint Blaupause *f.*
bluff Felsenklippe *f*, Klippe *f (Top).*
board *n* Brett *n (wood);* Ausschuß *m (committee).*
board *v* einsteigen *(a vehicle);* beköstigen, verköstigen *(to supply meals);* in Kost sein *(to receive meals).*
board of officers Ehrenrat *m;* Offizierausschuß *m.*
boardwalk Bretterbahn *f.*
boat Boot *n,* Kahn *m.*
boat crew Fahrtrupp *m (Engr).*
boat ferry Kahnfähre *f (Engr).*
boat hook Bootshaken *m.*
boatswain Bootsmann *m (Nav).*
boat-tail Verjüngung nach hinten *(Am).*
bobbing target Klappscheibe *f*, Verschwindscheibe *f (practice firing).*
body Körper *m;* Walze *f (Am);* Zünderkörper *m,* Zündergehäuse *n (fuze);* Zünderteller *m (powdertrain time fuze);* Aufbau *m (MT);* Fernrohrkörper *m (binocular);* Geschoßhülle *f (projectile);* Gasmaskenkörper *m (gas mask).*
body armor Panzerweste *f (Avn).*
bodyguard Leibgarde *f*, Leibwache *f.*
Bofors gun Bofors-Maschinenkanone *f.*
bog Sumpf *m,* Moor *n,* Morast *m.*
bog down versacken.
bogie Rollenwagen *m (Tk);* Rollbock *m (Arty).*
bogie trailer Rollbock *m (Arty).*
bogie wheel Laufrad *n,* Laufrolle *f (Tk).*
boil *v* kochen.
boiler Kessel *m.*
bolo philippinisches Hackmesser.
bolt Verschluß *m,* Kammer *f (R, pistol);* Verschlußzylinder *m (Small Arms);* Bolzen *m (Mech).*
bolt assembly Schloß *n (MG, R).*
bolt base Schloßfuß *m (MG).*
bolt catch Kammerfang *m (MG).*
bolt-catch piece Kammerfangstück *n (pistol).*
bolt handle Kammerstengel *m (R);* Kammergriff *m,* Schloßhebel *m (MG).*
bolt housing Schloßgehäuse *n (MG).*
bolt knob Kammerknopf *m (R).*
bolt lock Rasthebel *m (MG).*
bolt lug Kammerwarze *f (R).*

bolt mechanism Zylinderverschluß *m,* Schloß *n (R).*
bolt sleeve Schlößchen *n (R).*
bolt slide Kammerbahn *f (R).*
bolt support Schloßhalter *m (MG).*
bolt thread Bolzengewinde *(MT).*
bomb *n* Bombe *f*, Fliegerbombe *f.*
bomb *v* bombardieren, bomben.
bombard bombardieren, bomben.
bombardier Bombenschütze *m.*
bombardier's compartment Bombenschützenstand *m (Ap).*
bombardment Bombardierung *f*, Kanonade *f (Arty);* Bombenangriff *m (Avn).*
bombardment airplane Bomber *m,* Bombenflugzeug *n,* Kampfflugzeug *n,* Kampfmaschine *f.*
bombardment aviation Kampffliegerei *f;* Bombenflieger *mpl,* Kampfflieger *mpl.*
bombardment formation Kampffliegerverband *m (Avn).*
bombardment group Kampfgruppe *f*, Kampffliegergruppe *f (Avn).*
bombardment school Kampfschule *f (Avn).*
bombardment squadron Kampfstaffel *f*, Kampffliegerstaffel *f (Avn).*
bombardment wing Kampfgeschwader *n,* Luftkampfgeschwader *n (Avn).*
bomb bay Bombenkammer *f*, Bombenmagazin *n (Ap).*
bomb-bay doors Bombenklappe *f (Ap).*
bomb case Bombenhülle *f.*
bomb control Bombenabzughebel *m (Ap).*
bomb control mechanism Bombenabwurfvorrichtung *f*, Bombenauslösungsvorrichtung *f (Ap).*
bomb crater Bombenloch *n.*
bomb disposal officer Bombenräumoffizier *m.*
bomb disposal unit Bombenräumtrupp *m,* Sprengkommando *n.*
bomber Bomber *m,* Bombenflugzeug *n,* Kampfflugzeug *n.*
bomber command Kampffliegerkommando *n (USA).*
bomber-fighter *See* fighter-bomber.
bomber formation Kampfverband *m (Avn).*
bomber pilot Kampfflieger *m.*
bomber squadron Kampfstaffel *f.*

bomber wing   Kampfgeschwader *n*, Bombengeschwader *n*.

bomb fuze   Bombenzünder *m*.

bomb hit   Bombeneinschlag *m*, Bombentreffer *m*.

bomb hoist   Bombeneinhängevorrichtung *f*.

bomb hole   Bombenloch *n*.

bombing   Bomben *n*, Bombenwurf *m*, Bombardierung *f*.

bombing altitude   Angriffshöhe *f*, Abwurfhöhe *f*.

bombing approach   Anflug *m*.

bombing attack   Bombenangriff *m*.

bombing formation   Kampfverband *m* (*Avn*).

bombing raid   Bombenangriff *m*.

bomb load   Bombenlast *f*.

bomb nose   Bombenkopf *m*.

bombproof   bombensicher, bombenfest.

bombproof shelter   bombensichere Deckung.

bomb rack   Schacht *m*, Bombenschacht *m*, Abwurfschacht *m* (*Ap*).

bomb rack control   Bombenabzughebel *m* (*Ap*).

bomb release   Wurf *m*, Abwurf *m*, Bombenwurf *m*, Bombenauslösung *f*.

bomb release altitude   Abwurfhöhe *f*.

bomb release controls   Bombenabwurfgerät *n*.

bomb release handle   Bombenhebel *m*.

bomb release line   Auslöselinie *f*.

bomb release mechanism   Bombenabwurfvorrichtung *f*, Bombenauslösungsvorrichtung *f*.

bomb release point   Auslösepunkt *m*.

bomb-resistant   bombensicher, bombenfest.

"Bombs away!"   "Wurf!"

bomb shackle   Tragvorrichtung *f* (*Ap*).

bomb sight   Zielgerät *n*, Abwurfzielgerät *n*, Bombenzielgerät *n*, Bombenzielvorrichtung *f*, Bombenzielapparat *m*, Bombenvisier *n*, Bombenrichtgerät *n*.

bomb target area   Bombenwurfplatz *m*.

bomb trailer   Bomben-Zubringewagen *m*.

bomb train   Bombenreihe *f*.

bomb trajectory   Fallbahn *f*, Wurfbahn *f*, Wurfparabel *f*, Bombenflugbahn *f*, Bombenfallkurve *f*, Bombenabwurfkurve *f*.

bone   Knochen *m*; Gräte *f* (*of fish*).

bonus   Handgeld *n*.

booby trap   Sprengfalle *f*, Schreckladung *f*, Schreckmine *f*.

boom   Ladebaum *m* (*of a crane*); schwimmende Balkensperre (*water obstacle*).

boom defense vessel   Sperrwachboot *n*.

boost   aufladen, verstärken.

booster   Schlagladung *f* (*fuze*).

booster charge   Beiladung *f*, Anfeuerungssatz *m* (*Am*).

boot   Stiefel *m* (*Clo*); Tasche *f*, Schuh *m* (*holster*).

border   Grenze *f*.

border area   Grenzgebiet *n*.

border incident   Grenzzwischenfall *m*.

bore   *n* Rohrseele *f*, Seele *f* (*Ord*); Rohrinneres *n* (*G*); Laufinneres *n* (*Small Arms*); Bohrung *f* (*Mech*).

bore   *v* bohren.

bore brush   Reinigungsbürste *f* (*Ord*).

bore gage   Meßpatrone *f* (*Small Arms*); Kaliberzylinder *m*, Kaliberring *m*.

borehole   Minenrohr *n*, Bohrloch *n*.

borehole blasting charge   Bohrladung *f*.

bore-safe and detonator-safe fuze   rohrsicherer Zünder mit Sprengkapselsicherung (*Am*).

bore-safe fuze   rohrsicherer Zünder.

bore sight   Ziellinienprüfer *m*, Justiergerät *n* (*Ord*).

bore-sight adjustment   Justieren *n* (*G*).

boric acid   Borsäure *f*.

borrow pit   Erdgrube *f*.

bottleneck   Flaschenhals *m* (*figuratively and literally*); Engpaß *m* (*Top*).

bottom chord   Untergurt *m* (*truss*).

bottom gun carriage   Unterlafette *f*.

boulder   Felsblock *m*, großer Stein.

"bouncing baby"   See **bounding mine**.

bound   Sprung *m* (*jump*).

boundary   Grenze *f*, Abschnittsgrenze *f*, Nahtstelle *f* (*between units*), Trennungslinie *f*.

boundary layer   Grenzschicht *f* (*fluid mechanics*).

boundary light   Umrandungsfeuer *n*, Randfeuer *n* (*Adrm*).

bounding mine   S-Mine *f*, Schrapnellmine *f*.

bounds Einzelsprünge *mpl (method of advancing).*
by bounds sprungweise.
bourrelet Zentrierwulst *m;* Führungswulst *m (rear).*
bow Bug *m (Ap, Nav, Tk).*
bow compartment Vorderkaffe *f (Pon).*
bowden control cable Bowdenzug *m.*
bow gun Buggeschütz *n,* Bugfeuergeschütz *n (Tk).*
bow gunner Bugschütze *m (Ap, Tk).*
bow-on Stirnansicht *f.*
bow-on silhouette Stirnschattenriß *m (practice target).*
bow wave Kopfwelle *f (Ballistics).*
box Kasten *m,* Schachtel *f.*
box barrage Feuerabriegelung *f.*
box car gedeckter Güterwagen *(RR).*
box girder Kastenträger *m.*
box in Feuerabriegelung schießen.
box level Dosenlibelle *f.*
box magazine Kastenmagazin *n.*
box-trail gun carriage Kastenlafette *f.*
brace *n* Strebe *f (structures);* Bohrwinde *f (a tool).*
brace *v* abspreizen, absteifen.
,**braced** verspannt.
bracing Auskreuzung *f,* Verspannung *f,* Verstrebung *f.*
bracket *n* Gabelung *f,* Eingabelung *f (Arty).*
bracket *v* gabeln, eingabeln *(Arty).*
bracket adjustment Gabelbilden *n.*
bracket fire Gabelschießen *n.*
bracketing Gabelbildung *f,* Eingabeln *n.*
bracketing correction Gabelschießen *n.*
bracketing elevation Erhöhung zum Gabelbilden.
bracketing method Gabelbilden *n.*
bracketing salvo gabelbildende Salve.
bracket seat Schildlager *n (G).*
braid Borte *f,* Tresse *f (Clo).*
brake *n* Bremse *f (MT, Ord).*
brake *v* abbremsen.
brake arm Bremsarm *m (gun-carriage wheel brake).*
brake band Bremsband *n (MT).*
brake bushing Bremsbuchse *f (recoil mechanism).*
brake cable Zugriemen *m.*
brake cylinder Bremszylinder *m (MT).*
brake drum Bremstrommel *f,* Bremsscheibe *f.*

brake equalization Bremsausgleich *m (MT).*
brake fluid Bremsflüssigkeit *f.*
brake horsepower Bremsleistung *f,* Nutzleistung *f.*
brake lever Bremshebel *m (G, MT).*
brake lining Bremsbelag *m.*
brake pedal Fußbremshebel *m,* Bremsfußhebel *m,* Bremstritt *m,* Bremspedal *n (MT).*
brake release spring Bremsfeder *f (MT).*
brake rod Bremsgestänge *n (MT).*
brakeshoe Bremsklaue *f (gun-carriage wheel);* Bremsbacke *f,* Bremsklotz *m.*
braking effect Bremswirkung *f.*
branch Waffengattung *f (of the Army);* Ast *m,* Zweig *m (of a tree);* Filiale *f,* Zweigstelle *f (of a bank, business);* Nebenstelle *f (of a post office);* Abteilung *f (Adm).*
branch depot Zweigpark *m,* Zweiglager *n.*
branch of the service Dienstzweig *m,* Waffengattung *f,* Truppengattung *f.*
brand Marke *f,* Sorte *f (of commercial product).*
brass Messing *n.*
brassard Armbinde *f.*
brass knuckles Schlagring *m.*
breach *n* Bresche *f,* Sturmlücke *f,* Einbruchstelle *f.*
breach *v* einbrechen *(a line);* eine Bresche schießen *(a wall, etc.).*
breaching charge Sprengladung *f.*
breaching line Trennschnitt *m (demolitions).*
breaching point Sprengstelle *f (demolitions).*
breach of discipline Disziplinarvergehen *n,* Übertretung *f,* Vergehen *n,* Verfehlung *f.*
bread Brot *n.*
break *n* Bruch *m;* Trennung *f (Rad procedure).*
break *v* brechen; degradieren, herabsetzen *(demote).*
breakage Bruch *m.*
break camp das Lager abbrechen.
breakdown Zusammenbruch *m (collapse);* Panne *f (of vehicle);* Betriebsstörung *f (Tp, Com, etc.);* Gliederung *f (analysis).*
break down eine Panne erleiden *(MT);* zusammenbrechen *(physical*

collapse); zerlegen, zergliedern *(analyze, decompose)*.

break in einfahren *(a vehicle)*; einarbeiten *(Pers)*; zureiten, abrichten *(a horse)*.

break-in procedure Dazwischensprechen *n (Rad)*.

break loose losbrechen.

break off combat das Gefecht abbrechen.

break ranks wegtreten.

break-through Durchbruch *m (Tac)*.

break up abschlagen, abweisen *(an a t t a c k)*; auseinandertreiben *(a crowd)*; zerschlagen, zersplittern *(into pieces)*; aufklären *(of clouds, weather)*.

breakwater Wellenbrecher *m*.

breast harness Sielengeschirr *n*.

breastplate Brustblatt *n (harness)*.

breastplate harness Vorderzeug *n*.

breast strap Halskoppel *f (harness)*.

breastwork Brustwehr *f*.

breather Entlüftungsstutzen *m (Mtr)*.

breech Bodenstück *n (G)*.

breechblock Verschlußblock *m (screw-type breech)*; Verschlußkeil *m (wedge-type breech)*; Verschlußstück *n*, Kartuschestück *n*, Ladeklappe *f*, Stoßboden *m (Ord)*.

breechblock carrier Verschlußträger *m (G)*.

breechblock wedge Verschlußkeil *m (G)*.

breech bore gage Kaliberzylinder *m*, Kaliberring *m*.

breech cover Verschlußüberzug *m (G)*.

breeches Reithosen *fpl*.

breeching Umgang *m*, Hinterzeug *n (harness)*.

breechlock Verschluß *m*, Geschützverschluß *m (Ord)*.

breech mechanism Verschluß *m*, Verschlußsystem *n*, Geschützverschluß *m*, Ladevorrichtung *f (Ord)*.

breech piece Laufmundstück *n (R)*.

breech recess Patroneneinlage *f (R)*; Keilloch *n (G)*.

breech ring Verschlußring *m*, Verschraubungsstück *n (G)*.

breech wedge Verschlußkeil *m*.

Bren gun Bren-Maschinengewehr *n*.

brevet rank Rang eines charakterisierten oder ernannten Offiziers.

brevity code Funkverkehrsabkürzungen *fpl (Rad)*.

bribe *v* bestechen; schmieren *(slang)*.

bribery Bestechung *f*.

brickyard Ziegelei *f*.

bridge *n* Brücke *f*; Floßbrücke *f (floating)*; Schnellbrücke *f (hasty)*.

bridge *v* eine Brücke schlagen, eine Brücke bauen.

bridge bay Brückenstrecke *f*.

bridge capacity Verkehrslast *f*.

bridge center line Brückenachse *f*, Brückenlinie *f*.

bridge commander Brückenkommandant *m*.

bridge construction Brückenschlag *m*, Brückenbau *m*.

bridge-construction party Brückentrupp *m*.

bridge diagram Brückenskizze *f*.

bridge equipage *See* **bridge equipment.**

bridge equipment Brückengerät *n*, Kriegsbrückengerät *n*, Brückenbaugerät *n*, Übergangsgerät *n*.

bridge foundation Brückenunterbau *m*.

bridgehead Brückenkopf *m*, Brückenkopfstellung *f (Tac)*.

bridgehead line Brückenkopflinie *f*.

bridge railing Brückengeländer *n*.

bridge roadway Brückenbahn *f*.

bridge site Brückenstelle *f*.

bridge span Brückenstützweite *f*.

bridge structure Brückenbau *m*.

bridge superstructure Brückenüberbau *m*.

bridge traffic control post Ablaufposten *m*.

bridge train Brückenkolonne *f (Engr)*.

bridge trestle Brückenbock *m*.

bridle Zaumzeug *n (harness)*.

brief *v* den Flug besprechen *(Avn)*.

briefing Flugbesprechung *f*, Einsatzbesprechung *f*; Befehlsausgabe *f (issuance of orders)*.

brigade Brigade *f*.

brigade commander Brigadeführer *m*, Brigadekommandeur *m*.

brigade headquarters Brigadekommando *n*.

brigadier general Generalmajor *m*; Generalmajor der Flieger *(Luftwaffe)*; Generalarzt *m (Med)*; Generalveterinär *m (Vet)*.

bright light   Fernlicht *n (on auto headlight).*

bring down   abschießen *(an Ap).*

brisance   Brisanz *f.*

broadcast *n*   Rundfunk *m.*

broadcast *v*   rundfunken.

broadcasting   Rundfunk *m.*

broadcasting station   Rundfunksender *m.*

broadside   Breitseite *f (Nav).*

broken   wolkig, fast bedeckt *(Met).*

broken outlines   zerlegte Formen *(Cam).*

broken stone   Steinschlag *m.*

bromacetone   Bromazeton *n,* B-Stoff *m (CWS).*

brombenzylcyanide   Brombenzylzyanid *n,* T-Stoff *m (CWS).*

bronchitis   Luftröhrenkatarrh *m,* Bronchialkatarrh *m.*

bronze   Bronze *f.*

brow band   Stirnriemen *m* (harness).

Browning automatic rifle   Browning-Selbstladegewehr *n.*

Browning machine gun   Browning-Maschinengewehr *n.*

brush   Bürste *f,* Pinsel *m;* Anstrichpinsel *m (paint);* Gebüsch *n (undergrowth);* Strauch *m (brushwood);* Scharmützel *n (skirmish).*

brush hurdle   Hurde *f.*

brush road   Strauchdamm *m.*

brushwood   Dickicht *n (thicket);* Strauch *m (broken branches, bushes, etc.).*

brushwork   Flechtwerk *n,* Strauchwerk *n,* Strauchpackung *f.*

brushwork revetment   Spreutlage *f.*

bucket   Kübel *m,* Eimer *m.*

buckle *n*   Koppelschloß *n.*

buckle *v*   knicken.

buckling   Knicken *n (march column).*

"buddy"   "Kumpel" *m.*

budget   Etat *m.*

budget item   Etatposten *m.*

buffer   Auffangvorrichtung des Rückstoßes, Puffer *m (Ord).*

buffer spring   Rücklauffeder *f (MG).*

buffing   Polieren *n.*

buggy whip antenna   Stabantenne *f.*

bugle   Horn *n,* Trompete *f.*

bugle call   Trompetensignal *n,* Hornsignal *n.*

bugler   Hornist *m,* Trompeter *m.*

building   Gebäude *n.*

built-up area   bebautes Gelände.

built-up barrel   Ringrohr *n,* Mantelringrohr *n (G).*

bulb   Glühbirne *f,* Birne *f (Elec);* Ballen *m (horse).*

bulk container   Packgefäß *n.*

bulkhead   Spant *m,* Rumpfspant *m,* Schott *n (Ap).*

bulk reduction point   Eisenbahntankstelle *f (RR).*

bulldozer   Planier-Raupenschlepper *m,* mechanischer Pflugbagger.

bullet   Geschoß *n,* Kugel *f.*

bullet drop   Geschoßfall *m (Ballistics).*

bulletin   Ankündigung *f,* Bekanntmachung *f (notice);* Nachrichtenblatt *n (publication).*

bulletin board   Anschlagtafel *f.*

bulletproof   kugelsicher, kugelfest, schußfest, schußsicher.

bulletproof glass   schußsicheres Glas, beschußsicheres Glas, Panzerglas *n.*

bullet-resisting inner tube   schußsicherer Schlauch *(MT).*

bullet tube   Geschoßkanal *m (grenade launcher).*

bullet wound   Schußwunde *f,* Schußverletzung *f.*

bull's eye   Spiegel *m,* Zentrum *n,* Zielschwarze *n,* "Das Schwarze."

bump   Windstoß *m (Avn);* Höcker *m,* Rast *f (road).*

bumper   Stoßfänger *m* Stoßstange *f (MT).*

buna tire   Bunareifen *m (MT).*

bungee   mechanische Hilfsvorrichtung *(Ap).*

bunk   Koje *f.*

bunker   Bunker *m.*

bunting   Fahnentuch *n,* Flaggentuch *n;* Flaggenschmuck *m.*

buoy   Boje *f,* Tonne *f.*

buoyancy   Auftrieb *m,* Hubkraft *f (Avn);* Schwimmkraft *f (Nav).*

bureau   Amt *n,* Bureau *n,* Büro *n.*

burial   Begräbnis *n,* Beerdigung *f,* Bestattung *f.*

burial detail   Bestattungskommando *n.*

burlap   Sackleinen *n.*

burn *n*   Brandwunde *f.*

burn *v*   brennen, verbrennen.

burning rate   Brenngeschwindigkeit *f (cord fuze).*

burning time   Leuchtdauer *f (Sig).*

burst *n*   Stoß *m,* Feuerstoß *m (MG).*

burst *v*   bersten, zerspringen, platzen.

burst center mittlerer Sprengpunkt.
burst effect Zerknallstoß *m*, Sprengwirkung *f (Am)*.
burster Sprengladung *f (Am)*.
burster course Zerschellerschicht *f (Ft)*.
burster tube Kammerhülsenrohr *n*, Sprengladungsröhre *f (Am)*.
bursting charge Sprengladung *f*, Sprengstoffgehalt *m*, Sprengsatz *m (Am)*.
burst interval Aufschlagweite *f (Gunnery)*.
burst of fire Feuerstoß *m (MG)*.
burst wave Verdichtungswelle *f (Sound Ranging)*.
bury begraben, beerdigen; vergraben, verbergen *(to hide)*.
bus Kraftomnibus *m*.
bush fighting Buschgefecht *n*, Waldgefecht *n*.
bushing Buchsring *m (G)*; Futterstück *n (breechblock)*; Lagerschale *f*, Buchse *f*, Futter *n (Tech)*.
busy besetzt *(Tp)*.
busy signal Besetztzeichen *n*, Besetztschauzeichen *n (Tp)*.

butcher Fleischer *m*, Metzger *m*, Schlächter *m*.
butchery platoon Schlächtereizug *m (QMC)*.
butt Kolben *m (MG, R)*; Kugelfang *m (target range)*.
butt assembly Bodenstück *n (MG)*.
butter Butter *f*.
buttock Gesäßbacke *f*.
button Knopf *m*.
butt plate Kolbenkappe *f (R)*.
butt strap Lasche *f (Engr)*.
butt stroke Kolbenhieb *m*.
butt swivel Klammer *f (R)*.
butt-swivel plate Klammerfuß *m (R)*.
buzzer Wecker *m*, Summer *m (Tp)*.
buzzer button Summerknopf *m (Tp)*.
buzzer set Summerzusatz *m (Tp)*.
buzzer signal Summeranruf *m (Tp)*.
bypass *n* Überstromkanal *m (Mtr)*; Ausweichstelle *f (road)*.
by-pass *v* aussparen *(Tac)*.
"By the left flank, march!" "Links, um!"
"By the right flank, march!" "Rechts, um!"

C

cab Fahrerhaus *n (of truck)*.
cabane Spannturm *m*, Rahmenspannturm *m (Ap)*.
cabbage Kraut *n*.
cabin Kabine *f (Ap, Nav)*; Hütte *f (hut)*.
cabinet Truhe *f*, Gehäuse *n (Rad)*.
cable Seil *n*, Tau *n (Nav, etc.)*; Kabel *n (Elec, Tp)*; Drahtzug *m (flexible steel, Ap)*; Drahtseil *n (wire)*. See also **wire**.
cable armor Bewehrung *f*.
cable block Drahtseilhindernis *n (obstacle)*.
cable brake Seilbremse *f*.
cable drum Seilrolle *f*, Seiltrommel *f*.
cable ferry Seilfähre *f*.
cablegram Kabeldepesche *f*.
cable knife Kabelmesser *n*.
cable lead-in point Kabelaufführungspunkt *m (Elec, Tp)*.
cable line Kabelleitung *f (Tp)*.

cable ship Kabelschiff *n*.
cable sleeve Kabelverbinder *m (Tp)*.
cable splice Kabelverbindung *f (Tp)*.
cable-testing instrument Kabelmeßgerät *n (Tp)*.
cable trench Kabelgraben *m (Tp)*.
cable wax Kabelwachs *n (Engr, Tp)*.
cable winch Seilwinde *f*.
cadence Gleichschritt *m*, Zeitmaß *n (Marching)*.
cadet Kadett *m*; Fahnenjunker *m*, Fahnenjunker-Gefreiter *m (junior cadet)*; Fahnenjunker-Unteroffizier *m (cadet Sgt)*.
cadre Cadre *m*, Kader *m*, Stammtruppe *f*.
cadreman Soldat einer Stammannschaft.
cadre personnel Stammannschaft *f*.
caduceus Äskulapstab *m (insigne)*.
caisson Hinterwagen *m*, Munitionswagen *m (Arty)*; Senkkasten *m (Engr)*.

caisson section leader Wagenzug-führer *m (Arty)*.
calcium bleach Chlorkalk *m*.
calcium chloride Chlorkalk *m*.
calculate rechnen, berechnen, aus-rechnen.
calculation Berechnung *f*.
calculator Rechenmaschine *f*, Rechen-gerät *n*.
calculus Infinitesimalrechnung *f*.
calf Wade *f (of leg)*.
caliber Rohrweite *f*, Kaliber *n*, Waf-fenkaliber *n (Ord)*.
calibrate eichen.
calibrated geeicht.
calibration Höhenrichtverbesserung nach Einschießgeschütz *(Gunnery)*; Eichung *f (Tech)*; Funkbeschickung *f (Rad compass)*.
calibration adjustment Frequenz-korrektur *f (Rad)*.
calibration correction Ausschalten der Grundstufe *(Gunnery)*.
calibration firing Vergleichsschießen *n (Arty)*.
calipers Greifzirkel *m*.
calk dichten.
call *n* Ruf *m*, Zeichen *n*, Signal *n*, Anruf *m*, Gesprächsverbindung *f (Sig C)*; Ferngespräch *n*, Gespräch *n*, Spruch *m (Tp)*.
call *v* rufen; anrufen *(Tp)*.
called station Gegenstelle *f (Rad, Tp)*.
calling key Flackertaste *f (Tp)*.
call letters Buchstaben des Rufzei-chens *(Rad)*.
call sign Rufzeichen *n (Rad)*.
call signal Rufzeichen *n (Rad, Tp)*; Anrufzeichen *n (Tp)*.
call the roll Namen aufrufen.
call the shot das Abkommen melden.
call to quarters Locken *n*.
call to the colors *See* **induction**.
call-up Anruf *m (Rad)*.
call up aufrufen, anrufen.
calm *adj* still, ruhig, windstill *(Met)*.
cam Daumen *m*, Nocken *m (Tech)*; Drucknase *f (trigger)*; Lenkschrau-be *f (steering column, MT)*.
cam and lever steering system Schraubenganglenkung *f*, Spindel-lenkung *f (MT)*.
camber Radsturz *m (MT)*; Wölbung *f*, Krümmung *f*.
camera Kammer *f*.
camera gun Lichtbild-MG. *n (Avn)*.

cameraman Photograph *m*.
camera spotting Artillerie-Bildbeob-achtung *f*.
camouflage *n* Tarnung *f*, Tarnen *n*.
camouflage *v* tarnen.
camouflage discipline Tarndisziplin *f*.
camouflage jacket Tarnjacke *f*.
camouflage material Tarnmittel *n*.
camouflage net Maske *f*, Flieger-maske *f*, Tarnnetz *n*.
camouflage paint Tarnungsfarbe *f*, Tarnanstrich *m*.
camouflage troops Tarnungstruppe *f*.
camouflet Quetschladung *f*, Quetsch-mine *f*.
camp *n* Lager *n*, Lagerplatz *m*, La-gerort *m*, Truppenlager *n*; Gefange-nenlager *n (PW)*.
camp *v* das Lager aufschlagen.
campaign Feldzug *m*.
campaign medal Kriegsdenkmünze *f*, Erinnerungsmedaille *f*.
camp hospital *See* **station hospital**.
camp kitchen Lagerküche *f*.
cam plate Kurvenscheibe *f (Ord)*.
camp site Lagerstelle *f*.
camshaft Nockenwelle *f*, Steuerwelle *f*, Daumenwelle *f*.
can Büchse *f*, Blechbüchse *f*, Dose *f*.
canal Kanal *m*.
canard airplane Ente *f*, Entenflug-zeug *n*.
cancel ausstreichen, durchstreichen *(cross out)*; aufheben, absagen, an-nullieren *(annul)*; widerrufen *(re-voke)*.
cancellation Streichung *f (crossing out)*; Aufhebung *f*, Annullierung *f (annulment)*.
candle Kerze *f*.
canister Kartätsche *f (separate-load-ing Am)*; Filterbüchse *f (gas mask)*.
canister filter Büchsenfilter *m (gas mask)*.
canned food Büchsenkonserven *fpl*.
canned meat Fleischkonserve *f*, Büchsenfleisch *n*.
canned ration Büchsenkonserven *fpl*.
cannelure Rille *f (Am)*.
cannibalization Wiederinstandset-zung unter Verwendung von Teilen beschädigten Kriegsgeräts *(Ord)*.
cannon Kanone *f*.
cannonade Bombardierung *f*, Kano-nade *f*.

cannoneer Schütze *m*, Kanonier *m*.
cannon salute Kanonensalut *m*.
cannon transport wagon Rohrwagen *m*.
canopy Baldachin *m (Ap)*; Stoffbahn *f (Prcht)*.
cant *n* schiefer Radstand, Verkantung *f (Arty)*.
cant *v* verkanten *(G, R)*.
canteen Feldflasche *f (water container)*; Kantine *f*, Kamaradschaftsheim *n (place)*.
canteen cover Feldflaschenhülle *f*.
canteen cup Trinkbecher *m*, Becher *m*.
cantilever freitragend.
cantilever beam Kragträger *m*.
cantilever bridge Kragträgerbrücke *f*, Auslegerbrücke *f*.
cantilever wing freitragender Flügel.
cantle Hinterzwiesel *m (saddle)*.
cantonment Barackenlager *n*.
cantonment area Unterkunftsraum *m*.
cantonment building Militärbaracke *f*, Baracke *f*.
canvas Segeltuch *n*.
cap Haube *f*, Kappe *f*, Kopf *m (Am)*; Mütze *f (Clo)*; Geschoßkappe *f (projectile)*; Sprengkapsel *f (blasting)*.
capacitance Kapazität *f (Elec)*.
capacitor Kondensator *m (Rad)*.
capacity Leistung *f*, Leistungsfähigkeit *f (performance)*; Vermögen *n (capability)*; Fähigkeit *f (ability)*; Eigenschaft *f (function)*; Verkehrslast *f (Bdg)*; Fassungsvermögen *n (volume)*.
cap crimper Würgezange *f*.
cape Umhang *m (cloak)*; Kap *n (point of land)*.
cap hole Zündkanal *m (blasting cartridge)*.
capillary tube Haarröhre *f*.
capital Haupstadt *f (of a country)*; großer Buchstabe *(letter)*.
capital offense Kapitalverbrechen *n*.
capital ship Großkampfschiff *n*.
capitulate sich ergeben, kapitulieren.
capitulation Übergabe *f*, Kapitulation *f*.
capsize kentern, umkippen.
capstan Gangspill *m*, Ankerwinde *f (Nav)*; Erdwinde *f (Engr)*.
captain Hauptmann *m (plural:*

Hauptleute)*; Rittmeister *m (Cav, H Arty)*; Stabsarzt *m (Med)*; Stabsveterinär *m (Vet)*; Kapitän zur See *(Nav)*.
captive balloon Fesselballon *m*.
capture *n* Einnahme *f (of a locality)*; Gefangennahme *f (of a person)*.
capture *v* fangen, gefangennehmen *(a person)*; erbeuten *(matériel)*; aufbringen *(a ship)*; einnehmen *(a locality)*.
captured gun Beutegeschütz *n*.
captured matériel erbeutetes Kriegsgerät.
captured officer kriegsgefangener Offizier.
car Wagen *m (MT, RR)*.
carbine Karabiner *m*.
carbine scabbard carrier Karabinertragevorrichtung *f*.
carbolic acid Karbolsäure *f*.
carbon Kohle *f*, Kohlenstoff *m*; Ölkohle *f (Mtr)*.
carbon block Kohleklotz *m (microphone)*.
carbon brush Kohle *f*, Kohlebürste *f (Elec)*.
carbon copy Durchschlag *m (typed)*; Durchschrift *f (written)*.
carbon-copy pad Durchschreibeblock *m*.
carbon dioxide Kohlensäure *f*.
carbon electrode Kohlenelektrode *f*.
carbon filler Kohlenstoffträger *m (in liquid-oxygen blasting charges)*.
carbon lightning arrester Kohleblitzableiter *m*.
carbon microphone Kohlenmikrophon *n*.
carbon monoxide Kohlenoxyd *n*.
carbon paper Kohlepapier *n*.
carbon residue Verbrennungsrückstand *m (Mtr)*.
carbon rod Kohle *f*, Kohlestab *m (Elec)*.
carbon tetrachloride Tetrachlorkohlenstoff *m*.
carbonylchloride Chlorkohlenoxyd *n*, Phosgen *n (CWS)*.
carbon-zinc battery Kohle-Zinksammler *m*.
carbon-zinc cell Kohle-Zink-Element *n (Elec)*.
carburetion Vergaseranordnung *f*, Gemischbildung im Vergaser *(Mtr)*.
carburetor Vergaser *m*.

carburetor engine Vergasermotor *m*.
carcass Kadaver *m*, Leiche *f*.
card Karte *f*, Schein *m*, Zettel *m*.
cardboard Pappe *f*, Pappdeckel *m*, Karton *m*.
card file Kartei *f*.
cardinal point Himmelsrichtung *f*.
care Pflege *f* (*of wounded, equipment, etc.*); Verwundetenbetreuung *f* (*of casualties*); Fürsorge *f* (*welfare*); Vorsicht *f* (*caution*).
cargo Last *f*, Ladung *f* (*load*); Fracht *f* (*freight*); Schiffsladung *f* (*Nav*).
cargo carrier Lastkraftwagen *m*, Transportwagen *m* (*MT*).
cargo-carrying glider Lastensegler *m*, Lastensegelflugzeug *n*.
cargo parachute Lastfallschirm *m*.
cargo tonnage Ladefähigkeit *f* (*capacity*); Ladegewicht *n* (*weight*).
cargo-transport plane Frachtflugzeug *n*.
cargo truck Lastkraftwagen *m*.
carload Wagenladung *f*.
carpenter Zimmermann *m*.
carriage Lafette *f*, Lafettierung *f* (*G*).
carrier Beförderungsmittel *n*, Fahrzeug *n* (*vehicle*); Träger *m* (*Pers*); Flugzeugträger *m* (*Nav*); Tragbeutel *m*, Büchse *f*, Tasche *f* (*container*).
carrier current Trägerstrom *m* (*Tp*).
carrier pigeon Brieftaube *f*, Heeresbrieftaube *f*.
carrier wave Trägerwelle *f* (*Rad*).
carry tragen; halten (*AA SL*).
carrying capacity Tragfähigkeit *f*.
carrying pad Tragepolster *n* (*MG*).
carrying strap Tragband *n* (*gas mask*).
carry light führender Scheinwerfer (*AAA*).
carry out ausführen, durchführen.
cartel ship Austauschschiff *n*.
cartographer Kartenzeichner *m*, Tabellenzeichner *m*.
cartographical sketching Anfertigung von Grundrißskizzen.
cartridge Patrone *f* (*Am*); Kartusche *f* (*semifixed and fixed Am*); **scharfe Patrone** (*ball*); Anlaßpatrone *f* (*for cartridge starter*).
cartridge bag Kartuschbeutel *m*.
cartridge belt Patronengurt *m* (*MG*).

cartridge case Hülse *f*, Patronenhülse *f*, Geschoßhülse *f* (*Am*); Kartusche *f*, Kartuschhülse *f* (*semifixed and fixed Am*).
cartridge chamber Patronenlager *n* (*R*).
cartridge clip Patronenstreifen *m*, Ladestreifen *m* (*Am*).
cartridge feed Patronenzuführung *f* (*Small Arms*).
cartridge starter Anlaßpistole *f* (*Mtr*).
cartridge-type ground signal Leuchtpatrone *f*.
cartwheel Wagenrad *n*.
case Gehäuse *n*, Hülse *f*, Büchse *f* (*Tech*); Kiste *f*, Kasten *m* (*box*); Futteral *n*, Tasche *f*; Kartusche *f* (*semifixed and fixed Am*); Zündschraubengehäuse *n* (*threaded percussion primer*) (*Am*); Fall *m* (*instance*); Schurholzrahmen *m* (*gallery case*); Patronenhülse *f* (*cartridge*); Bombenhülle *f* (*bomb*).
casein glue Kaseinleim *m*.
casemate Kasematte *f* (*Ft, Nav*).
casemate gun mount Kasemattenlafette *f*.
case I pointing direktes Richten (*Gunnery*).
case II pointing Richten mit direkter Seitenrichtung und indirekter Höhenrichtung (*Gunnery*).
case III pointing indirektes Richten (*Gunnery*).
case IV pointing Richten mit vorgeschobener Beobachtungsstelle (*Gunnery*).
cash Bargeld *n*.
cashier *v* aus dem Heere ausstoßen.
casing Deckplatte *f* (*MG telescopic sight*); Laufdecke *f*, Decke *f*, Mantel *m* (*tire*); Gehäuse *n*, Hülle *f*, Hülse *f*, Schalung *f*.
castellated nut Kronenmutter *f*.
caster Nachlauf *m*, Vorlauf *m* (*MT*); Schwenkrolle *f* (*roller*).
casting Guß *m*, Gießen *n* (*action*); Abguß *m* (*thing cast*).
cast iron Gußeisen *n*.
cast-metal case Gußgehäuse *n*.
cast-steel Gußstahl *m*.
casuals zur Verwendung stehendes Militärpersonal.
casualty Verlust *m*, Ausfall *m*.
casualty agent Kampfstoff *m* (*CWS*).

casualty day tägliche Verlustrate.
casualty list Verlustliste *f*.
casualty report Verlustmeldung *f*.
catalog Katalog *m*.
catapult *n* Katapult *m*, Startkatapult *m*, Schleuder *f*, Flugzeugschleuder *f* (*Avn*).
catapult *v* katapultieren (*an Ap*).
catapult airplane Katapultflugzeug *n*.
catapult take-off Schleuderstart *m* (*Avn*).
catch *n* Falle *f* (*MG*); Kammerfang *m* (*MG bolt catch*); Sperrnase *f* (*fuze*); Sperrklinke *f* (*pawl*).
catch *v* fangen, einfangen, auffangen; ergreifen (*seize*); sich zuziehen, anstecken (*a disease*).
catch pivot Fallenachse *f* (*MG*).
caterpillar band Radgürtel *m* (*G*).
caterpillar drive Raupenantrieb *m*, Gleiskettenantrieb *m* (*MT*).
caterpillar prime mover Gleiskettenschlepper *m*, Gleiskettenzugmaschine *f*.
caterpillar track Raupe *f*, Raupenkette *f*, Gleiskette *f* (*MT, Tk*).
caterpillar tractor Gleiskettenschlepper *m*, Gleiskettenzugmaschine *f*, Raupenschlepper *m*.
cathode Kathode *f*.
cathode-ray tube Kathodenstrahlröhre *f*, Elektronenstrahlröhre *f*, Braunsche Röhre.
cattle Vieh *n*.
catwalk Lattenrost *m*, Holzrost *m*.
cause *v* verursachen, veranlassen, bewirken.
causeway Straßendamm *m*.
caustic *n* Ätzmittel *n*.
caustic soda kaustisches Natron, Ätznatron *n*.
caution Vorsicht *f*, Achtung *f*.
cavalry Kavallerie *f*, Reiterei *f* (*H Cav*); motorisierte Kavallerie (*Mecz*).
cavalry brigade Reiterbrigade *f*, Kavalleriebrigade *f*.
cavalry corps Kavalleriekorps *n*.
cavalry division Kavalleriedivision *f*.
cavalryman Kavallerist *m*, Reiter *m*.
cavalry patrol Reiterspähtrupp *m*.
cavalry pioneer Kavalleriepionier *m*.
cavalry reconnaissance detachment Reiteraufklärungsabteilung *f*.
cavalry regiment Reiterregiment *n*, Kavallerieregiment *n*.

Cavalry School Kavallerieschule *f*, Reitschule *f*.
cavalry troop Reiterschwadron *f*.
cave Höhle *f*.
cave in einstürzen.
cave shelter minierter Unterstand (*Ft*).
cavesson Reithalfter *f* (*harness*).
cavity Loch *n*, Vertiefung *f*, Höhle *f*.
cease aufhören, einstellen.
"Cease firing!" "Feuerpause!"
ceiling Wolkenhöhe *f* (*Met*); Gipfelhöhe *f* (*Ap*); Decke *f* (*of a room*).
ceiling light Wolkenscheinwerfer *m* (*Met*).
ceiling ventilator Deckenventilator *m* (*MT*).
celestial navigation astronomische Navigation.
celestial sphere Himmelskugel *f* (*Navigation, Surv*).
cell Zelle *f*, Flügelzelle *f* (*Ap*); Gaszelle *f* (*Airship*); Element *n* (*Elec*).
cell container Elementbecher *m* (*Elec*).
cellophane Zellophan *n*.
cellophane cover Zellophanüberzug *m* (*CWS*).
cellular-type radiator Elementekühler *m* (*MT*).
cellule Zelle *f*, Flügelzelle *f* (*Ap*); Gaszelle *f* (*Airship*).
celluloid Zelluloid *n*.
celluloid templet Zelluloidtafel *f*.
cellulose Zellulose *f*.
cellulose acetate Zellon *n*.
cellulose fiber Zellwolle *f*.
cement Mörtel *m*, Zement *m*.
cemetery Friedhof *m*.
censor Zensor *m*.
censorship Zensur *f*.
center Mitte *f*, Mittelpunkt *m*, Zentrum *n*.
center balk Mittelbalken *m* (*Bdg*).
center line Brückenlinie *f* (*Bdg*).
center of burst mittlerer Sprengpunkt.
center of dispersion *See* center of impact.
center of impact mittlerer Treffpunkt.
center of lift Auftriebsmittelpunkt *m* (*Aerodynamics*).
center of resistance Widerstandszentrum *n* (*Tac*).
center of the front Frontmitte *f* (*Tac*).

center point of target Zielpunkt *m*.
center punch Körner *m*.
centigrade Celsius.
central Vermittlung *f*, Vermittlungsstelle *f (Tp)*.
central control zentrale Feuerleitung *(Arty)*.
Central European time mitteleuropäische Zeit *(15° E standard meridian)*.
central station Zentrale *f (sound ranging)*.
central tube Kammerhülse *f (shrapnel)*.
centrifugal action Fliehkraftantrieb *m (fuze)*.
centrifugal arming device Fliehbacke *f (fuze)*.
centrifugal bolt Fliehbolzen *m (fuze)*.
centrifugal casting Schleuderguß *m (foundry)*.
centrifugal compressor Turbokompressor *m*, Kreiselkompressor *m*.
centrifugal force Fliehkraft *f*, Zentrifugalkraft *f*.
centrifugal fuze Fliehkraftzünder *m*.
centrifugal governor Fliehkraftregler *m (Mtr)*.
centrifugal pump Kreiselpumpe *f*, Zentrifugalpumpe *f*, Schleuderpumpe *f*.
centripetal force Zentripetalkraft *f*.
ceremonial detachment Ehrenwache *f*.
ceremony Zeremoniell *n*, Feierlichkeit *f*, besondere Veranstaltung; Trauerfeier *f (Mil funeral)*.
certificate Bescheinigung *f*, Zeugnis *n*, Schein *m*.
certificate of discharge Entlassungsschein *m*.
certificate of identification Personalausweis *m*.
certificate of rejection Ausmusterungsschein *m*.
certificate of service Dienstbescheinigung *f*.
certified beglaubigt *(documents)*.
certify bescheinigen, bezeugen, beglaubigen.
cessation Einstellung *f*.
cetane rating Cetenzahl *f (Diesel fuel)*.
chain Kette *f*; Gleitschutzkette *f (skid)*; Meßkette *f (Surv)*.
chaining Messen mit Meßkette *(Surv)*.

chain link Kettenglied *n*.
chain of command Befehlsweg *m*, Befehlsverhältnisse *npl*.
chain of evacuation Verwundetenabschublinie *f*.
challenge Anruf *m*, Einspruch *m*, Herausforderung *f*.
chamber Kartuschraum *m (G)*; Patronenlager *n (R)*; Kammer *f*, Raum *m*.
change *v* ändern, sich ändern, umändern; verändern *(to alter)*; wechseln *(money)*; tauschen *(to exchange)*; sich umziehen *(clothes)*; umsteigen *(trains)*.
change lever Umschalthebel *m (automatic R)*.
change of course Kurswechsel *m (Avn)*.
change of height Höhenänderung *f (AA predictor)*.
change of personnel Personalveränderung *f*.
change of position Stellungswechsel *m (Tac)*.
change of station Platzwechsel *m*.
change-over switch Umschalter *m (Elec)*.
change step den Schritt wechseln, den Tritt wechseln.
channel Dienstweg *m (Adm)*; Frequenzbereich *m (Rad)*; Verbindungsweg *m (Com)*.
through channels auf dem Dienstweg.
channel marker Bake *f (Nav)*.
channel of communication Verbindungsweg *m (Tp, Rad)*.
chapel Kapelle *f*.
chaplain Wehrmachtgeistlicher *m*, Feldgeistlicher *m*.
character Buchstabe *m*, Schriftzeichen *n (letter)*; Charakter *m (of a person)*.
characteristic curve Röhrenkennlinie *f (Rad tube)*.
characteristic impedance Wellenwiderstand *m (Elec, Rad)*.
charcoal Holzkohle *f*.
charcoal layer Kohleschicht *f (gas mask)*.
charge *n* Ladung *f (Am, blasting, Elec)*; Attacke *f*, Angriff *m (Cav)*; Betrauung *f (trust)*; Anklage *f (accusation)*; Gebühr *f (rate)*.
charge *v* anstürmen *(Inf)*; attackieren *(Cav)*; laden *(Am, Elec)*; ver-

langen, anfordern *(money)*; beschuldigen *(accuse)*.
charge-placing pole Sprengstange *f.*
charging unit Lademaschinensatz *m,* Aggregat *n (Elec).*
charging voltage Ladespannung *f (battery charger).*
chart *n* Plan *m,* Tabelle *f,* Übersicht *f;* Karte *f (map).*
chartroom Feuerleitstelle *f (Arty);* Kartenraum *m (Nav).*
chase *n* langes Feld *(G).*
chassis Fahrwerk *n,* Fahrgestell *n (MT);* Apparatur *f (Rad).*
chassis clearance Bauchfreiheit *f (MT).*
chassis frame Fahrwerkrahmen *m (MT).*
chassis panel Montageplatte *f (Rad).*
chauffeur Kraftfahrer *m (MT).*
check *n* Scheck *m (banking);* Kontrolle *f (supervision);* Zeichen *n (mark).*
check *v* hemmen, verhindern *(to hinder);* prüfen, nachprüfen, überprüfen *(to test, to verify);* überwachen, kontrollieren *(to supervise).*
check list Kontrolliste *f.*
check point Anhaltspunkt *m,* Bezugspunkt *m.*
check valve Reglerventil *n.*
cheek Backe *f,* Wange *f.*
cheekbone Jochleiste *f (horse).*
cheek strap Backenstück *n (harness).*
cheese Käse *m.*
chemical agent Kampfstoff *m.*
chemical-agent detector kit Gasanzeiger *m.*
chemical barrier Kampfstoffsperre *f,* Kampfstoffriegel *m (CWS).*
chemical battalion Werferabteilung *f (Ger).*
chemical bomb Kampfstoffbombe *f,* Fliegergasbombe *f (Avn).*
chemical candle Giftrauchkerze *f,* Giftnebelkerze *f (CWS).*
chemical cylinder Gasflasche *f,* Gasbehälter *m;* Nebelabblasgerät *n (smoke).*
chemical decontamination *See* **decontamination.**
chemical decontamination company Entgiftungskompanie *f.*
chemical defense Gasschutz *m.*
chemical defense school Heeresgasschutzschule *f.*

chemical fumes Kampfstoffschwaden *mpl (CWS).*
chemical hand grenade Gashandgranate *f.*
chemical land mine chemische Erdmine, Gas-Erdmine *f.*
chemical layer Mundschicht *f (gas mask).*
chemical mine chemische Erdmine, Gas-Erdmine *f.*
chemical mortar Gashandwerfer *m,* Gasmörser *m.*
chemical munitions Gasmunition *f,* chemische Kampfmittel.
chemical officer Gasoffizier *m.*
chemical projectile Gasgeschoß *n.*
chemical projector Werfer *m,* Nebelwerfer *m,* Gaswerfer *m (CWS).*
chemical-projector fire Gaswerfen *n.*
chemical regiment Nebelwerferregiment *n,* Werferregiment *n (Ger).*
chemical security Gasschutz *m.*
chemical shell Gasgranate *f;* Gasbrisanzgranate *f (HE).*
chemical-shell fire Kampfstoffbeschuß *m (CWS);* Gelbkreuzbeschuß *m (vesicant filler, CWS).*
chemical spray apparatus Kampfstoffzerstäuber *m;* Luftstromgerät *n,* Zerstäubungsgerät *n (Ap).*
chemical spraying Versprühen von Kampfstoffen *(CWS).*
chemical tank Nebelgerät *n (for air Cml spraying).*
chemical troops chemische Truppen, Gastruppen *fpl,* Nebeltruppen *fpl.*
chemical warfare chemischer Krieg; Gaskampf *m,* Gaskrieg *m.*
chemical warfare agent chemischer Kampfstoff.
Chemical Warfare Board Gastechnischer Forschungsausschuß *(USA).*
chemical warfare depot Gasschutzpark *m.*
chemical warfare material Gaskampfmittel *npl,* Gaskampfgerät *n.*
chemical warfare officer Gasoffizier *m.*
Chemical Warfare School Gaskriegsschule *f (USA).*
Chemical Warfare Service chemischer Kriegsdienst *(USA).*
chemist Chemiker *m.*
chess Brückenbelag *m (Bdg).*
chest Brust *f (anatomy);* Kiste *f,* Kasten *m (box).*

chest pack parachute Brustfallschirm *m.*
cheval-de-frise spanischer Reiter *(Ft).*
chevron Uniformwinkel *m.*
chewing gum Kaugummi *m.*
chicken wire Maschendraht *m.*
chief Chef *m.*
chief engineer Leitender Ingenieur, Chefingenieur *m,* Oberingenieur *m.*
chief nurse Oberschwester *f.*
chief of ammunition Munitionsunteroffizier *m (Arty).*
Chief of Chaplains Feldbischof *m.*
Chief of Chemical Warfare Service Chef des chemischen Kriegsdienstes *(USA).*
chief of civil affairs section Chef der Zivilverwaltung *(at army Hq).*
Chief of Coast Artillery Chef der Küstenartillerie *(USA).*
chief of corps supply services Korpsnachschubführer *m (Ger).*
chief of division supply services Divisionsnachschubführer *m (Ger).*
Chief of Engineers Inspekteur der Pioniere.
Chief of Naval Operations Chef des Admiralstabs *(USA).*
Chief of Ordnance Chef des Heeres-Waffenamtes.
chief of staff Stabschef *m,* Generalstabschef *m.*
Chief of Staff Chef des Generalstabes.
chief of supply services Nachschubführer *m.*
Chief of the Air Staff Chef des Führungsstabes der **L u f t w a f f e** *(USA).*
Chief of the Veterinary Service Chefveterinär *m.*
chief of transportation Chef des Transportwesens *(Tac, RR).*
chief petty officer Portepeeunteroffizier *m (Nav).*
Chief Signal Officer Inspekteur der Nachrichtentruppen.
Chief Surgeon Armeearzt *m.*
chief transportation officer bevollmächtigter Transportoffizier.
chilled casting Kokillenguß *m.*
chimney Schornstein *m.*
chin Kinn *n.*
chinaware Porzellan *n.*
chin groove Kinnkettengrube *f (horse).*

chin strap Sturmriemen *m,* Kinnriemen *m (headgear);* Kinnstößel *m (harness).*
chin support Kinnstütze *f (gas mask).*
chisel Meißel *m.*
chloracetophenone Chlorazetophenon *n (CWS).*
chloracetophenone solution Chlorazetophenon - Chlorpikrin - Lösung *f,* Tränenstoff *m (CWS).*
chloramine-T Chloramin *n (CWS).*
chlorate explosive Chlorat-Sprengmittel *n.*
chloride of lime Chlorkalk *m.*
chlorination Chlorbeimischung *f,* Chlorzusetzung *f.*
chlorine Chlor *n,* Chlorgas *n (CWS).*
chlorpicrin Chlorpikrin *n (CWS).*
chlorsulfonic acid Chlorsulfonsäure *f (CWS).*
chock Bremsklotz *m.*
chocolate Schokolade *f.*
choke *n* Starterklappe *f (Mtr);* Würgebohrung *f (barrel) (Ord).*
choke *v* ersticken *(suffocate);* erwürgen *(strangle).*
choke coil Drosselspule *f (Elec).*
choke valve Luftklappenventil *n (carburetor).*
cholera Cholera *f.*
chord Gurt *m (truss);* Sehne *f (Geometry).*
Christie tank Christie-Panzerkraftwagen *m.*
chromium Chrom *n.*
chromium-plated verchromt.
chronograph Chronograph *m,* Registrier-Chronograph *m.*
chronology of battle Gefechtszeitangabe *f.*
chronometer Chronometer *n.*
chuck Futter *n (of lathe, etc.).*
church Kirche *f.*
cigarette Zigarette *f.*
cigarette lighter Feuerzeug *n.*
cincha Untergurt *m (saddle).*
cipher *n* Schlüssel *m,* Chiffre *f.*
cipher *v* schlüsseln, chiffrieren, ziffern.
cipher device Chiffriermaschine *f,* Schlüsselmaschine *f.*
cipher disk Verschlüsselungsscheibe *f.*
cipher key Geheimwort *n,* Schlüsselwort *n.*

cipher text Geheimtext *m*, Schlüsseltext *m*.

circle *n* Kreis *m*.

circle *v* Runde(n) fliegen *(Avn)*.

circle of rupture Wirkungskreis *m* *(blasting)*.

circling target kreisendes Ziel *(AAA)*.

circuit Stromkreis *m*, Leitungsnetz *n*, Schaltung *f* *(Elec)*.

circuit arrangement Leitergebilde *n* *(Elec)*.

circuit breaker Stromunterbrecher *m*, Spannungssicherung *f* *(Elec)*.

circuit diagram Schaltplan *m*, Schaltungsschema *n*; Leitungsskizze *f*, Schaltskizze *f* *(Tp)*.

circuit tester Leitungsprüfer *m* *(Elec)*.

circular *n* Rundschreiben *n*, Umlauf *m*.

circular course Kreisflug *m* *(Avn)*.

circular track Kranz *m*, Drehkranz *m* *(MG mount)*.

circular track mount Lafettenkranz *m* *(Ap, Tk)*.

circulation Umlauf *m* *(of money, fluids)*; Kreislauf *m* *(of blood)*; Auflage *f* *(of a newspaper)*; Verbreitung *f* *(of news)*.

circulation map Wegekarte *f*.

circumference Umkreis *m*.

circumstance Sachlage *f*, Zustand *m*.

circumstantial evidence Indizienbeweis *m*.

cirrocumulus Zirrokumulus *m*.

cirrostratus Zirrostratus *m*.

cirrus cloud Cirruswolke *f*, Zirruswolke *f*, Federwolke *f*.

citation Auszeichnung *f*, ehrenvolle Erwähnung.

citizen Staatsbürger *m*, Bürger *m*.

citizenship Staatsangehörigkeit *f*.

city Stadt *f*.

civil staatlich, Staats- *(pertaining to government)*; höflich, anständig *(polite)*.

civil affairs section Zivilverwaltung *f* *(Mil Govt)*.

civil airway Luftverkehrslinie *f*.

civil aviation Zivilluftfahrt *f*.

civil communication lines Postleitungen *fpl*.

civil court Zivilgericht *n*.

civilian *n* Zivilist *m*, Zivilperson *f*.

civilian clothes Zivil *n*, Zivilkleidung *f*, bürgerliche Kleidung.

civilian defense ziviler Luftschutz.

civilian internee Zivilinternierter *m*.

civilian population Zivilbevölkerung *f*.

civil offense Zivilvergehen *n*, nichtmilitärisches Vergehen.

civil service Staatsdienst *m*.

civil war Bürgerkrieg *m*.

claim *n* Anspruch *m*, Anrecht *n*.

clamp *n* Klammer *f* *(Tech)*; Klemmzange *f* *(blasting-cap fuze)*.

clamping collar Schelle *f* *(Mort)*.

clamping lever Klemmhebel *m*, Begrenzungshebel *m* *(MG)*.

clamping mechanism Festklemmvorrichtung *f* *(MG tripod)*.

clamping plate Klemmplatte *f* *(G barrel guide)*.

clamping ring Klemmring *m* *(grenade launcher)*.

clamping screw Klemmschraube *f* *(aiming circle)*.

clarity of sound Klangreinheit *f* *(Rad)*.

clash Zusammenstoß *m* *(Tac)*.

clasp Spange *f* *(decoration)*.

class Klasse *f*; Jahrgang *m* *(age class)*.

classification Einteilung *f*, Gliederung *f*.

classification of artillery fire Feuerformen der Artillerie.

classification of chemical agents Kampfstoffgruppen *fpl*.

classification of equipment Stoffgliederung *f*.

classification of machine-gun fire Feuerformen des Maschinengewehrs.

classification track Richtungsgleis *n*, Abstellgleis *n* *(RR)*.

classified military information geheime Gegenstände.

class of equipment Gerätklasse *f*.

claw hatchet Klauenbeil *n*.

clay pit Lehmgrube *f*.

clean *v* reinigen, säubern, putzen.

cleaning and preserving material Reinigungsgerät *n*.

cleaning brush Reinigungsbürste *f* *(G)*.

cleaning patch Reinigungsdocht *m* *(R)*.

cleaning rag Reinigungslappen *m*, Putzlappen *m*.

cleaning rod Stock *m*, Gewehrstock *m* *(R)*; Wischstock *m* *(G)*.

clean-up party Säuberungstrupp *m*.

clean out säubern *(Tac)*.

clear *v* räumen, säubern.

clear *adj.* wolkenlos *(Met)*; **frei** *(of obstructions)*.

in clear im Klartext *(Com)*.

clearance Spielraum *m (Mech)*; Sicherheitsmaß *n (Gunnery)*; Entlastung *f (of responsibility)*; Freigabe *f (permit)*; Bauchfreiheit *f (chassis)*.

clearance of masks Überschießen von Deckungen *(Gunnery)*.

clearance of the enemy Feindfreiheit *f*.

clearance space Geschoßanlage *f (R)*.

cleared for action gefechtsklar *(Nav)*.

cleared zone Rollfeld *n (Adrm)*.

clear ice glasartige Vereisung.

clearing Waldblöße *f*, Waldlichtung *f (forest or wood)*.

clearing signal Schlußzeichen *n (Tp)*.

clearing station Hauptverbandplatz *m (Med)*.

clearing unit Krankenträgertrupp *m (Med)*.

clear up säubern *(Tac)*.

cleat Greifer *m (MT)*.

clergyman Geistlicher *m*, Pfarrer *m*; Pastor *m (Protestant)*; Priester *m (Catholic)*; Rabbiner *m (Jewish)*.

clerical aptitude test Schreibereignungsprüfung *f*.

clerk Schreiber *m*, Schriftführer *m*, Gefechtsschreiber *m*.

clevis Schäkel *m*.

click *n* Rast *f (Mech)*.

cliff Klippe *f*, Kliff *n*.

climate Klima *n*.

climatic klimatisch.

climb *n* Steigflug *m*, Steigen *n (Avn)*.

climb *v* steigen, besteigen, klettern.

climb-and-dive indicator Statoskop *n (Ap)*.

climbers Steigeisen *npl (for Tp lineman)*.

climbing ability Steigvermögen *n (Ap)*.

climbing iron Klettereisen *n*, Klettersporn *m*.

climbing take-off Kavalierstart *m (Avn)*.

climbing turn gezogene Kurve *(Avn)*.

clincher rim Wulstfelge *f (MT)*.

clinical record Krankenblatt *n*.

clinometer Gefällemesser *m*, Neigungsmesser *m (Arty, Surv)*; Geländewinkelmesser *m (for angle of site, Arty)*; Richtbogen *m (G)*.

clip *n* Patronenrahmen *m*, Ladestreifen *m (R, AA gun)*; Klammer *f (paper clip)*.

clip-fed rifle Mehrlader *m*.

clip loading machine Ladestreifenfüller *m*.

clock Uhr *f (timepiece)*; Borduhr *f (Ap)*; Melderose *f (AWS)*.

clock method Melderoseverfahren *n (Gunnery, AWS)*.

clockwise im Sinne des Uhrzeigers, im Uhrzeigersinn, rechtsgängig, rechtslaufend.

clockwork action Uhrwerkantrieb *m (fuze)*.

clockwork fuze Uhrwerkzünder *m*.

close *v* schließen, zuschließen, zumachen *(a door, etc.)*; abschließen *(an account)*; beenden *(conclude)*.

close billets Ortsbiwak *n*.

close column aufgeschlossene Marschfolge.

close combat Nahkampf *m*.

close-combat range Nahkampfweite *f*.

close-combat weapon Nahkampfwaffe *f*.

closed airdrome Flugplatz außer Betrieb.

close defense Nahabwehr *f*, Nahverteidigung *f*.

closed traverse geschlossener Zug, Polygonzug *m (Surv)*.

closed weather ungünstiges Fliegerwetter *(Avn)*.

close-in security Nahsicherung *f*.

close order geschlossene Ordnung.

close-order drill Exerzieren in der geschlossenen Ordnung.

close range Nahkampfweite *f*; nächste Entfernung *(up to 100 meters)*; nahe Entfernung *(up to 400 meters)*.

close-range fighting Nahkampf *m*.

close-range weapon Nahkampfwaffe *f*.

close reconnaissance Nahaufklärung *f*.

close-reconnaissance airplane Nahaufklärungsflugzeug *n*, Nahaufklärer *m*, Naherkunder *m*.

close support Nahunterstützung *f (Tac)*.

close terrain bewachsenes Gelände.

closing cap Zünderkappe *f*, Verschlußschraube *f (fuze)*.

closing spring cylinder Kraftspeicher *m (AA gun)*.

cloth filter Tucheinsatz *m (MT)*.

cloth garnish bunte Lappen *(Cam)*.

clothing Bekleidung *f*.

clothing account Bekleidungsnachweis *m*.

clothing allowance verabfolgte Kleidungsstücke.

clothing slip Bekleidungsschein *m*.

cloud Wolke *f*.

cloud attack Blasangriff *m (CWS)*.

cloud bank Wolkenfeld *n*.

cloud cover Wolkendecke *f*.

cloud formation Wolkenform *f*.

cloud gas attack Blasangriff *m*.

cloud particle Stäubchen *n (CWS)*.

cloud soaring Wolkensegeln *n (glider)*.

clove hitch Mastwurf *m*.

club Knüppel *m (weapon)*.

cluster Sternbündel *n (Sig)*; Bündel *n (Bombing)*.

cluster adapter Bombenbündelträger *m*.

clutch Kupplung *f (MT)*.

  throw in the clutch einkuppeln.

  throw out the clutch auskuppeln.

clutch cone Kupplungskegel *m*.

clutch housing Kupplungsgehäuse *n*.

clutch lever Kupplungshebel *m*.

clutch pedal Kupplungsfußhebel *m*, Kupplungspedal *n*, Kupplungstritt *m*.

clutch plate Kupplungsscheibe *f*.

clutch shaft Kupplungswelle *f*.

clutch spring Kupplungsfeder *f*.

CN Chlorazetophenon *n (CWS)*.

CNB Tränengasstoff *m*.

CN candle Universalkerze CN *f (CWS, USA)*.

CN capsule Reizwürfel *m (CWS)*.

CN generator Riechtopf *m (CWS)*.

CNS Chlorazetophenon-Chlorpikrin-Lösung *f (CWS)*.

CN solution Tränengasstoff *m*.

coal Kohle *f*.

coarse file Grobfeile *f*.

coarse setting Grobeinstellung *f*.

coarse sight Vollkorn *n*, volles Korn *(R)*.

coast Küste *f*.

coastal area Küstengebiet *n*.

Coast Artillery Corps Küstenartilleriekorps *n (USA)*.

coastal force Küstenverband *m*.

coastal reconnaissance airplane Küstenaufklärer *m*.

coastal squadron Küstenstaffel *f (Avn)*.

coastal waters Küstengewässer *npl*.

coastal zone Küstenvorfeld *n*.

coast artillery Küstenartillerie *f*.

coast artillery district Küstenartilleriebezirk *m (USA)*.

Coast Artillery School Küstenartillerieschule *f (USA)*.

coast battery Küstenbatterie *f (CA)*.

coast defense Küstenverteidigung *f*, Küstenwehr *f*, Küstenwacht *f*.

Coast Guard Küstenwache *f*, Küstenwachkorps *n (USA)*.

coast guard station Küstenstation *f*.

coast reconnaissance Küstenaufklärung *f*.

coat Jacke *f*, Rock *m (of a suit)*; Mantel *m*, Überzieher *m (overcoat)*; Schicht *f (of paint, grease, etc.)*. See also **service coat**.

coaxial gleichachsig, mit gemeinschaftlicher Achse, Doppel-.

coaxial counterrotating propellers Doppelpropeller *m (Ap)*.

cobalt Kobalt *m*.

cock *v* spannen *(Small Arms)*.

cocking bolt Spannriegel *m (breechblock)*.

cocking cam Spannstollen *m (breechblock)*.

cocking lever Spannhebel *m (G, MG)*.

cocking piece Schlagbolzenmutter *f (R)*.

cocking slide Spannschieber *m (MG)*.

cockpit Kabine *f*, Kanzel *f*, Führerraum *m*, Führersitz *m*, Führerstand *m (Ap)*.

code Schlüssel *m*, Geheimschrift *f*.

code book Schlüsselheft *n*.

code call Deckanruf *m (Tp)*.

code chart Signaltafel *f*.

code group Funkabkürzung *f*, Kurzsignal *n*, Schlüsselgruppe *f*.

code name Deckname *m*.

code panel Signaltuch *n*, Signalstreifen *m*, Tuchzeichen *n (Avn)*.

code section Schlüsseltrupp *m*.

code sign Deckzeichen *n*.

code word Deckwort *n.*

coding Verschlüsselung *f,* Schlüsseln *n.*

coefficient Beiwert *m.*

coefficient of form Formwert *m* (*Ballistics*).

coffee Kaffee *m.*

coffin Sarg *m.*

coil Spule *f* (*Elec, Rad*).

coil spring Schraubenfeder *f* (*MT*).

coil unit Spulensatz *m* (*Rad*).

coincidence range finder Halbbildentfernungsmesser *m,* Schnittbildentfernungsmesser *m,* Koinzidenzentfernungsmesser *m.*

cold Erkältung *f,* Schnupfen *m* (*Med*).

cold chisel Kaltmeißel *m.*

cold front Kaltluftfront *f,* Einbruchsfront *f* (*Met*).

cold-resistant kältebeständig.

cold working Kaltrecken *n* (*Ord*).

collapsible boat Faltboot *n.*

collar Kragen *m* (*Clo*).

collar patch Patte *f,* Kragenpatte *f,* Kragenspiegel *m.*

collation of information Nachrichtenbearbeitung *f.*

collecting depot Sammelplatz *m* (*Salvage*).

collecting point Krankensammelpunkt *m* (*Med*).

collecting station Verwundetensammelstelle *f* (*Med*); Leichtverwundetensammelplatz *m* (*for walking wounded*).

collecting unit Bergekommando *n,* Sammelkommando *n* (*Salvage*).

collective call sign Sammelrufzeichen *n* (*Rad*).

collective fire vereinigtes Feuer, zusammengefaßtes Feuer.

collective protection Sammelschutz *m* (*CWS*).

collector ring Kollektor *m,* Schleifring *m* (*Elec*).

collimate berichtigen (*Surv*); justieren (*G*).

collimating mark Kollimationslinie *f.*

collimating sight Richtglas *n.*

collimation Kollimation *f* (*G*); Berichtigung *f* (*Surv*).

collimator Kollimator *m,* Spaltrohr *n.*

collision Zusammenstoß *m.*

collision course Zielanflugkurs *m* (*Avn*).

colonel Oberst *m;* Oberst der Flieger (*AAF*); Oberstarzt *m* (*Med*); Oberstveterinär *m* (*Vet*).

color Farbe *f.*

color bearer Fahnenträger *m.*

color blind farbenblind.

colored cloth bunte Lappen (*Cam*).

color guard Fahnenkompanie *f,* Fahnentrupp *m,* Fahnenwache *f.*

colorless farblos.

colors Fahne *f.*

color salute Senken der Fahne.

color sentinel Fahnenposten *m,* Fahnenwache *f.*

color vision Farbentüchtigkeit *f.*

column Kolonne *f* (*Tac*); Reihe *f* (*Inf drill, Cav*); Pfeiler *m,* Säule *f* (*Engr*).

column commander Kolonnenchef *m* (*MT*).

"Column half left, march!" "Halblinks schwenkt, marsch!"

"Column half right, march!" "Halbrechts schwenkt, marsch!"

"Column left, march!" "Links schwenkt, marsch!" (*followed by* "Augen gerade, aus!").

column of companies Kompaniekolonne *f.*

column of files Kolonne zu Einem.

column of fours Kolonne zu Vieren.

column of groups Gruppenkolonne *f.*

column of platoons Zugkolonne *f.*

column of refugees Flüchtlingskolonne *f.*

column of threes Marschordnung *f* (*Inf drill*); Kolonne zu Dreien (*march Clm*). See also "Fall in!"

column of troopers Reihe *f,* Reiterreihe *f* (*Cav*).

column of twos Doppelreihe *f* (*Inf drill*); Kolonne zu Zweien (*march Clm*). See also "Fall in!"

"Column right, march!" "Rechts schwenkt, marsch!" (*followed by* "Augen gerade, aus!").

column traffic Kolonnenverkehr *m.*

comb Kamm *m.*

combat Kampf *m,* Kampfhandlung *f,* Gefecht *n;* Luftkampf *m* (*Avn*).

combat activity Kampftätigkeit *f,* Gefechtstätigkeit *f.*

combat airplane Kriegsflugzeug *n,* Frontflugzeug *n.*

combat air reconnaissance Gefechtsluftaufklärung *f.*

combatant Frontkämpfer *m*, Frontsoldat *m*.
combat area Kampfraum *m*.
combat at defiles Gefecht um Engen.
combat aviation Kampf- und Jagdflieger *mpl*.
combat car Kampfwagen *m*, Kampffahrzeug *n*, Panzerwagen *m*.
combat command Kampfgruppe *f*
(Armd Comd).
combat conditions Kampfbedingun-
gen *fpl*.
combat crew fliegendes Personal
(Ap).
combat exercise Kampfübung *f*.
combat echelon Kampfstaffel *f*.
combat element Kampftruppe *f*,
kämpfende Truppe, Frontverband *m*.
combat engineer regiment Sturm-
pionier-Regiment *n*.
combat engineers Sturmpioniere *mpl*.
combat firing Gefechtsschießen *n*.
combat formation Gefechtsform *f*,
Gefechtsformation *f*.
combat from fortified positions Stellungskampf *m*.
combat frontage Gefechtsbreite *f*.
combat in snow Gefecht bei tiefem
Schnee.
combat intelligence Ergebnisse der
Gefechtsaufklärung.
combat in towns Ortskampf *m*.
combat in woods Waldgefecht *n*.
combat liaison Gefechtsanschluß *m*.
combat message Gefechtsmeldung *f*;
Kampfnachricht *f (Rad)*.
combat mission Gefechtsauftrag *m*,
Kampfauftrag *m (Tac)*; Feindflug
m (Avn).
combat operation Kampfhandlung *f*
(Tac).
combat order Gefechtsbefehl *m*, Operationsbefehl *m (Tac)*.
combat outpost Gefechtsvorposten *m*.
combat patrol Gefechtsspähtrupp *m*,
Stoßtrupp *m*.
combat performance Kampfleistung *f*.
combat practice Gefechtsexerzieren
n, Gefechtsausbildung *f*, Gefechtsübung *f*, Gefechtsdrill *m*.
combat practice firing gefechtsmäßiges Schießen; Gefechtsschießen *n*
(advanced); Schulgefechtsschießen
n (elementary).
combat preparation Bereitstellung *f*
(Tac).

combat reconnaissance Gefechtsaufklärung *f*.
combat report Gefechtsbericht *m*.
combat sector Gefechtsstreifen *m*,
Gefechtsabschnitt *m*, Kampfabschnitt *m*.
combat situation Gefechtslage *f*.
combat station Gefechtsstand *m*
(Ap).
combat team Kampfgruppe *f*,
Kampfgemeinschaft *f*.
combat train Gefechtstroß *m*.
combat-train echelon Gefechtsstaffel *f*.
combat troops Kampftruppen *fpl*,
Gefechtstruppen *fpl*, Frontverbände
mpl.
combat unit Kampfeinheit *f*,
Gefechtseinheit *f*, Gefechtsgruppe *f*,
Kampfgruppe *f*.
combat unit loading gefechtsmäßiges
Verladen.
combat vehicle Kampffahrzeug *n*,
Gefechtsfahrzeug *n*.
combat zone Gefechtsgebiet *n*.
combination Vereinigung *f*, Zusam-
menschluß *m (group)*; Verbindung *f*
(of group, Cmls, etc.); Kombination
f (Math).
combination fuze Dreifachzünder *m*
(superquick, delay and time); Mehrfachzünder *m*, Doppelzünder *m*.
combination tool Mehrfachwerk-
zeug *n*.
combination wheel-track car Räder-
Raupen-Wagen *m*.
combination wheel-track drive Räder-
Gleiskettenantrieb *m (MT)*.
combination wheel-track vehicle
Hilfskettenfahrzeug *n*, Räder-Raupen-Fahrzeug *n (MT)*.
combine *v* kombinieren, (sich) vereinigen, zusammensetzen, verbinden
(forces, etc.); kombinieren *(Math)*.
combined arms Verband *m*, Kampfverband *m*, gemischter Verband,
verbundene Waffen *(Tac)*.
combined-arms armored force Panzerverband *m*.
combined-arms force gemischter
Verband.
combined-arms unit Verband aller
Waffen, gemischter Verband, Truppenverband *m*.
combined force Kampfgruppe *f*.
combined observation Artilleriebeob-

achtung mit seitlicher Beobachtungsstelle.
combined operations Operationen der
verbundenen Waffen.
combustible composition Anfeuerung
f (Sig cartridge).
combustion Verbrennung *f*.
combustion chamber Verbrennungsraum *m (Mtr)*; Laderaum *m
(G)*.
"come in" signal Einflugzeichen *n
(Inst landing)*.
coming flight Anflug *m*.
command Befehl *m*, Kommando *n
(order) (Tac)*; Führung *f (leadership)*; Kommandobehörde *f (agency)*; Befehlsgewalt *f (authority)*.
command airplane Führerma-
schine *f*.
Command and General Staff School
Führer- und Führergehilfen-Schule
f (USA).
commandant Kommandeur *m (Mil
school)*.
command car Befehlswagen *m*, Kommandowagen *m*.
command channel Befehlsweg *m*.
commandeer requirieren, beitreiben.
command element Stab *m*, Führungsstab *m*, Truppenführer *mpl*.
commander Truppenführer *m*, Befehlshaber *m*; Kommandeur *m (battalion and higher units)*; Kommandant *m (Ap, Tk)*; Fregattenkapitän
m (Nav).
commander-in-chief Oberbefehlshaber *m*, Oberkommandierender *m*.
Commander-in-Chief Oberster Befehlshaber.
**Commander-in-Chief of the Armed
Forces** Oberster Befehlshaber der
Wehrmacht.
commander of a unit Einheitsführer *m*.
commander of communications zone
Kommandant des rückwärtigen Ar-
meegebiets.
commander of the guard Wachvorgesetzter *m*, Wachhabender *m*.
commander of troops Truppenbefehlshaber *m*.
commander's armored truck Panzerbefehlswagen *m (Armd Comd)*.
commander's car Befehlswagen *m*.
commanding officer Führer *m*, Vorgesetzter *m*, Befehlshaber *m*, Truppenführer *m*.

commander's tank Kommandeurpanzer *m*.
command group Führerstab *m*, Befehlsgruppe *f*.
command headquarters Dienststelle *f*.
commanding general Oberbefehlshaber *m*, Kommandierender General.
commanding ground beherrschendes
Gelände *(Tac)*.
commanding height beherrschende
Höhe *(Top)*.
commanding position Höhenstellung *f*.
command liaison Zusammenwirken
mit benachbarten Kommandostellen.
command net Befehlsnetz *n*.
Commando Stoßtrupp *m*, Commando
n (British).
command of execution Operationsbefehl *m (Tac)*; Ausführungskommando *n (drill)*.
command pilot Flugzeugführer mit
über 10 Dienstjahren.
command post Gefechtsstand *m*, Befehlsstelle *f*, Kommandostelle *f*.
command-post exercise Rahmenübung *f (staff training)*.
command-post flag Kommandoflagge
f (battalion or higher unit).
command-post shelter Befehlsstand *m*.
command set Funkanlage für Verkehr von Bord zu Bord, Kommandogerät *n (Ap, Rad)*.
command tank Befehlspanzer *m*,
Kommandopanzer *m*.
command telephone central Führungsvermittlung *f*.
command truck Befehlswagen *m*,
Kommandowagen *m (MT)*.
"Commence firing!" "Feuer frei!"
commencement of firing Feueröffnung *f*.
commencement of hostilities Ausbruch der Feindseligkeiten.
commendation Anerkennungsschreiben *n*.
comment *n* Erklärung *f*, Deutung *f*,
Auslegung *f (interpretation)*; Be-
merkung *f (remark)*; Anmerkung *f
(note)*.
comment *v* Erklärungen geben *(interpret)*; Bemerkungen machen *(remark)*; mit Anmerkungen versehen
(annotate).
commentary Stellungnahme *f (Tac)*.

commercial handelsüblich *(vehicles, etc.);* kaufmännisch, kommerziell.

commercial airplane Verkehrsflugzeug *n.*

commercial aviation Zivilluftfahrt *f,* Verkehrsfliegerei *f.*

commercial loading Verladen mit bestmöglicher Raumausnutzung.

commercial motor truck handelsüblicher Lastkraftwagen.

commercial vehicle Nutzfahrzeug *n.*

commissary Verpflegungsamt *n.*

commissary officer Verpflegungsoffizier *m.*

commission *n* Patent *n,* Offizierspatent *n (written order);* Offiziersrang *m (rank and authority).*

commission *v* das Patent verleihen *(as an officer);* in Dienst stellen *(a vessel).*

commissioned officer patentierter Offizier, Offizier *m.*

commit einsetzen, ansetzen *(Tac);* begehen *(a crime).*

commitment Einsatz *m (Tac).*

commitment of armored units Panzereinsatz *m.*

commitment of major forces Großeinsatz *m,* Masseneinsatz *m (Tac).*

commitment order Einsatzbefehl *m.*

commodore Konteradmiral *m (Nav).*

common battery Zentralbatterie *f (Tp).*

common battery system Zentralbatteriesystem *n (Tp).*

communicable disease ansteckende Krankheit.

communicating file Anschlußmann *m,* Verbindungsleute *mpl.*

communicating trench *See* **communication trench.**

communication Mitteilung *f,* Nachricht *f;* Verbindung *f.*

communication battalion Nachrichtenabteilung *f.*

communication chief Nachrichtenunteroffizier *m.*

communication detail Nachrichtentrupp *m.*

communication facilities Nachrichtenanlagen *fpl.*

communication lines Verbindungslinien *fpl.*

communication net Nachrichtennetz *n.*

communication officer Nachrichtenoffizier *m.*

communication platoon Nachrichtenzug *m.*

communication repair truck Nachrichtenwerkstattkraftwagen *m.*

communication route Verbindungsstraße *f.*

communications Nachrichtenmittel *npl,* Nachrichtenverbindung *f,* Nachrichtenwege *mpl.*

communication section Nachrichtenstaffel *f.*

communication station Fernmeldeanlage *f (Rad, Tg, Tp).*

communications zone rückwärtiges Armeegebiet, rückwärtiges Gebiet, Etappe *f.*

communications zone depot rückwärtiges Nachschublager.

communication transmission Nachrichtenübermittlung *f.*

communication trench Verbindungsgraben *m.*

communication truck Nachrichtenwagen *m.*

communication unit Truppennachrichtenverband *m.*

communiqué Kriegsbericht *m;* Heeresbericht *m (official, Army).*

community Gemeinde *f (religious, territorial);* Gemeinschaft *f (social, political).*

commutation of quarters Wohnungsgeldzuschuß *m.*

commutation of rations Verpflegungszuschuß *m.*

commutation value Vergütungswert *m.*

commutator Kollektor *m (Elec).*

compact *adj* dicht, fest, kompakt; kurz, gedrängt *(figurative).*

company Kompanie *f.*

company aid man Sanitätsunteroffizier *m,* Sanitäter *m.*

company area Kompanierevier *n,* Kompaniebezirk *m.*

company boundary Kompaniegrenze *f.*

company clerk Kompanieschreiber *m.*

company commander Kompaniechef *m,* Kompanieführer *m.*

company command post Kompaniegefechtsstand *m.*

company fund Kompaniegelder *npl.*

company grade Kompanieoffiziersrang *m.*

"Company, halt!" "Abteilung, halt!"

company headquarters Kompanieführung f.
company headquarters personnel Kompanietrupp m.
company litter bearer Kompaniekrankenträger m.
company order Kompaniebefehl m.
company orderly room Schreibstube f.
company street Lagerstraße f.
company transport Kompaniefahrzeuge npl.
company wedge formation Kompaniekeil m.
compartment Kabine f (Ap).
compartment of terrain Geländeabschnitt m.
compass Bussole f, Kompaß m (magnetic); Zirkel m (drawing).
compass azimuth Kompaßkurswinkel m.
compass azimuth ring Bussolenring m.
compass bearing Kompaßpeilung f, Kompaßzahl f.
compass bowl Kompaßkessel m (Ap).
compass card Kompaßrose f, Scheibenrose f.
compass case Bussolengehäuse n.
compass compensation Kompaßausgleichung f.
compass course Kompaßkurs m (Avn).
compass declination Mißweisung, Kompaßmißweisung f, Deklination f.
compass error Deviation f, Kompaßablenkung f.
compass heading Kompaßkurs m.
compass north magnetische Nordrichtung, Kompaßnord m.
compass rose Kompaßrose f.
compass traverse Bussolenzug m (Arty, Surv).
compel zwingen, nötigen.
compensate ausschalten (for error, etc.) (Gunnery).
compensating jet Ausgleichdüse f.
compensation Entschädigung f (reimbursement); Ersatz m (damages); Vergütung f (award).
compensator Ausgleicher m, Kompensator m (Ord, Mech).
compilation Sammlung f, Kompilation f.
complaint Beschwerde f, Klage f, Klageschrift f (Law).

complement Bemannung f, Besatzung f, Stärke f.
complete adj vollzählig, vollständig; vollkommen (perfect); ganz (whole); vollendet (finished).
complete cleaning Hauptreinigung f (R).
complete order Gesamtbefehl m (Tac).
complete round vollständiger Schuß, kompletter Schuß (Am).
completion Erledigung f.
component n Bestandteil m, Einzelteil m, Komponente f.
component adj einen Teil ausmachend, Teil-.
composite connection Doppelbetriebsschaltung f (Tp).
composite construction Gemischtbauweise f.
compound n Einzäunung f (PW); Verbindung f (Cml).
compound-wound motor Verbundmaschine f.
compressed air Druckluft f, Preßluft f.
compressed-air cleaner Blaspistole f (MT).
compressed-air cylinder Preßluftzylinder m.
compressed-air equilibrator Luftausgleicher m (G).
compressed-air flask Preßluftflasche f.
compressed-air starter Preßluftanlasser m (Mtr).
compressed-air tank Luftbehälter m.
compression Verdichtung f, Verdichten n (Mtr).
compression-and-rebound range Verschränkbarkeit der Achsen (of spring suspension) (MT).
compression chamber Kompressionsraum m (Mtr).
compression chord Druckgurt m (Bdg).
compression cylinder Verdrängungszylinder m (counterrecoil mechanism).
compression ratio Verdichtungsverhältnis n (Mtr).
compression stroke Verdichtungshub m (Mtr).
compressor Drucklufterzeuger m.
compulsory zwingend, verbindlich, Zwangs-, Pflicht-.
computation Berechnung f.

compute berechnen; schätzen *(estimate)*.

computed charge Planladung *f (Engr)*.

computer Dreieckrechner *m (circular slide rule, Air Navigation)*; Rechner *m (Pers)*; Rechengerät *n*, Rechenmaschine *f (Inst)*.

computing instrument Rechengerät *n*.

computing slide rule Auswertelineal *n (flash ranging)*.

computing station Auswertestelle *f (sound ranging)*.

concave hohl, ausgehöhlt, konkav.

concave slope hohle Böschung, konkave Böschung, konkave Geländeneigung *(Top)*.

conceal tarnen *(Cam)*; verbergen *(an object or person)*; verhehlen, verheimlichen *(a fact)*.

concealed verdeckt, verschleiert.

concealed machine gun Schweige-MG. *n*.

concealed position verdeckte Stellung.

concealment Deckung *f*, Verdeckung *f*, Verschleierung *f (Tac)*.

concentrate *v* massieren.

concentrated attack geballter Angriff, massierter Angriff.

concentrated charge geballte Ladung *(Engr)*.

concentrated fire zusammengefaßtes Feuer.

concentration Zusammenballung *f*, Zusammenfassung *f*, Ansammlung *f (Tac)*; Dichte *f*, Gehalt *m*, Kampfstoffgehalt *m*, Anreicherung *f*, Luftanreicherung *f (CWS)*; Feuerschlag *m*, Feuerüberfall *m (Arty)*.

concentration area Aufmarschgebiet *n (Tac)*.

concentration camp Konzentrationslager *n*.

concentration fire See concentrated fire.

concentration march Aufmarsch *m*.

concentration of fire Feuervereinigung *f (Arty)*.

concentration of troops Truppenansammlung *f*.

concentration ring Korbring *m (Bln)*.

concentric konzentrisch.

concertina Drahtrolle *f*; Stacheldrahtrolle *f*, S.-Rolle *f (barbed wire)*; Klaviersaitendrahtrolle *f*, K.-Rolle *f (plain wire)*.

conclusion Folge *f*, Folgerung *f*, Schluß *m (deduction, inference)*; Beschluß *m*, Entscheidung *f (decision)*; Abschluß *m (of a treaty)*.

concrete Beton *m (Engr)*.

concrete bridge Betonbrücke *f*.

concrete bunker Betonbunker *m*.

concrete dugout Betonunterstand *m*.

concrete emplacement Bunker *m*, Bunkerstand *m*.

concrete mixer Betonmischmaschine *f*.

concrete obstacle Betonsperre *f*.

concrete paving block Zementfliese *f*.

concrete pillbox Betonbunker *m*.

concrete shelter Bunker *m*, Betonunterstand *m*.

concrete turret Betonturm *m (Ft)*.

concur übereinstimmen.

concurrent gleichzeitig *(at same time)*; übereinstimmend *(corresponding)*; zustimmend *(Law)*.

concussion Luftstoß *m*; Erschütterung *f*.

concussion of the brain Gehirnerschütterung *f*.

concussion plunger Zündbolzen *m (power-train time fuze) (Am)*.

condemn verurteilen *(to sentence)*; tadeln, mißbilligen *(disapprove)*; beschlagnahmen *(Law)*.

condenser Kondensator *m (Rad)*.

condenser microphone Kondensatormikrophon *n*.

condenser plates Belegungen *fpl (Rad)*.

condition Zustand *m*, Beschaffenheit *f (state)*; Bedingung *f (stipulation)*.

condom Vorbeugungsmittel *n*, Schutzmittel *n*, Selbstschutzmittel *n*.

conduct *n* Benehmen *n*, Betragen *n (behavior)*; Führung *f*, Leitung *f (direction, management)*.

conductivity Leitfähigkeit *f (Elec)*.

conduct of battle Kampfführung *f*.

conduction capacitance Leitungskapazität *f (Elec)*.

conduct of field operations Truppenführung *f*.

conduct of fire Feuerregelung *f*.

conductor Leiter *m (Elec)*; Schaffner *m (RR)*.

conduit Schacht *m*, Durchlaß *m*.

cone Kegel *m*; Garbe *f (Ballistics)*; Lautsprechertrichter *m (Rad)*.

cone clutch Kegelkupplung *f*, Konuskupplung *f (MT)*.

cone of dispersion Garbe *f*, Feuergarbe *f*, Schußgarbe *f*, Streukegel *m*.
cone of fire *See* cone of dispersion.
cone of light Lichtkegel *m*.
cone speaker Trichterlautsprecher *m* (*Rad*).
conference Besprechung *f*, Führerbesprechung *f*.
conference call Sammelgespräch *n* (*Tp*).
confidence Zuversicht *f* (*reasonable certainty*); Vertrauen *n* (*trust*).
confidential vertraulich, geheim.
confidential document Kommandosache *f*.
configuration of terrain Geländegestaltung *f*, Bodengestaltung *f*.
confine begrenzen, einschränken (*restrict*); einsperren, einschließen (*imprison*).
confinement Arrest *m*, Arreststrafe *f*, Haft *f*, Beschränkung *f*.
confirm bestätigen.
confirmatory order Befehlsbestätigung *f*.
confiscation Beschlagnahme *f*.
confuse verwirren, aus der Fassung bringen, bestürzt machen (*bewilder*); verwirren, durcheinanderbringen (*create disorder*).
confusion Verwirrung *f*, Unordnung *f*, Durcheinander *n* (*disorder*); Verlegenheit *f* (*embarrassment, perplexity*).
congestion Verkehrsstockung *f* (*traffic*); Anhäufung *f*, Überfüllung *f*.
Congressional Medal of Honor Ehrenmedaille *f* (*USA*).
conical peak Kegel *m* (*Top*).
conical roller bearing Kegelrollenlager *n*.
conic projection Kegelprojektion *f*.
connect vermitteln (*Tp*); verbinden, anschließen (*Tech*).
connecting cord Verbindungsschnur *f* (*Tp*).
connecting elements Verbindungsorgane *npl* (*march column*).
connecting file Anschlußmann *m*, Verbindungsleute *mpl*.
connecting group Verbindungstrupp *m*.
connecting jack Vermittlungsklinke *f* (*Tp*).
connecting piece Anschlußstück *n* (*gas mask*).

connecting plug Anschlußstecker *m* (*Elec*).
connecting point Anschlußpunkt *m* (*in axes of Sig Com*) (*Tp*).
connecting rod Kurbelstange *f*, Pleuelstange *f*.
connecting sleeve Kabelverbinder *m* (*Tp*).
connecting thread Anschlußgewinde *n* (*Mech*).
connecting trench Verbindungsgraben *m*.
connecting wire Drahtverbindung *f*, Anschlußschnur *f* (*Elec*).
connection Vermittlung *f*, Gesprächsverbindung *f* (*Tp*); Schaltung *f* (*Elec*).
connector Kettenkurbel *f* (*MG*); Triebzahn *m* (*caterpillar track*).
conquer erobern (*territory or locality*); besiegen (*the enemy*).
conquest Eroberung *f*.
conscientious objector Kriegsdienstverweigerer *m*.
conscript *v* ausheben.
conscription Aushebung *f*.
consent *v* genehmigen (*approve*); beistimmen, einwilligen (*agree to*).
consider bedenken, erwägen (*ponder*); in Betracht ziehen, berücksichtigen (*take into account*); schätzen, halten für, ansehen für (*to regard*).
consideration Betrachtung *f*, Erwägung *f*; Bedeutung *f*, Wichtigkeit *f* (*importance*); Rücksicht *f* (*thoughtfulness*).
consolidate vereinigen, zusammenbringen; ausbauen (*a position*).
consolidation of position Einrichten einer Stellung.
conspiracy Verschwörung *f*.
conspire sich verschwören.
constant *n* Konstante *f* (*Math*).
constant *adj* beständig, unverändert, unveränderlich (*unchangeable*); fortwährend (*continuous*); konstant, gleichbleibend (*Math*).
constant-mesh transmission Aphongetriebe *n* (*MT*).
constellation Sternbild *n*, Konstellation *f*.
constitute aufstellen (*a unit*).
construct (er)bauen (*build*); errichten (*erect*); konstruieren, entwerfen (*geometry*).

construction Jau *m*, Ausbau *m*, Bauausführung *f*, Fertigung *f*.
construction battalion Baubataillon *n*.
construction company Baukompanie *f* (*Mil*).
construction detail Bautrupp *m*.
construction float Einbaufähre *f*.
construction troops Bautruppen *fpl*.
construction zone Baubezirk *m*.
contact Berührung *f*, Fühlung *f*, Verbindung *f*, Anschluß *m* (*Tac*); Kontaktstück *n* (*Elec*).
"**Contact!**" "Ein!", "Zündung eingestellt!" (*Avn*).
contact fire Stoßzündung *f*, Berührungszündung *f* (*Nav*).
contact flight Sichtnavigation *f* (*Air Navigation*).
contact light Landebahnfeuer *n* (*Adrm*).
contact mine Kontaktmine *f*, Stoßmine *f*, Stoßkappenmine *f* (*Nav*).
contact mission Fühlunghalten *n* (*Avn*).
contact party Werkstatt-Trupp *m*.
contact patrol Verbindungspatrouille *f* (*Tac*); Infanterieflug *m* (*Avn*).
contact piece Druckstück *n* (*R trigger*); Kontaktstück *n* (*Elec*).
contact point Schließstelle *f* (*Elec*).
contact print Abzug *m* (*Photo*).
contact surface Auflagefläche *f*.
contact with the enemy Feindberührung *f*.
contagious disease ansteckende Krankheit.
contain fesseln, festhalten, binden, hinhalten (*Tac*).
container Topf *m* (*hand grenade*); Behälter *m* (*gasoline tank, etc.*); Blechkanister *m* (*metal container for gasoline, water, etc.*); Faß *n*, Tonne *f*, (*barrel or drum*).
containing attack Fesselungsvorstoß *m*.
contaminate vergiften (*CWS*).
contaminated area Gassperre *f*, Kampfstoffsperre *f*, vergiftetes Gelände (*CWS*).
contamination Vergiftung *f* (*CWS*).
contempt Verachtung *f*; Mißachtung *f* (*of court*).
contest *v* streitig machen.
contiguous Nachbar-.
contingent *n* Kontingent *n* (*quota of troops, etc.*).
contingent *adj* abhängig, bedingt.

continuance Aussetzung *f*, Aufschub *m* (*Law*).
continuous fire Dauerfeuer *n* (*MG, AAA*).
continuous interference Dauerstörung *f* (*Rad*).
continuous note Dauerton *m* (*Rad*).
continuous radio alert Funkdauerbereitschaft *f*.
contour *n* Höhenlinie *f*, Höhenschichtlinie *f* (*Top*).
contour interval senkrechter Abstand der Schichtlinien (*Top*).
contour line Höhenlinie *f*, Höhenschichtlinie *f*, Schichtlinie *f* (*Top*).
contour map Höhenlinienkarte *f*.
contraband of war Bannware *f*, Konterbande *f*, Kriegskonterbande *f*.
contract *n* Vertrag *m*.
contract *v* einen Vertrag abschließen (*business*); anstecken (*a disease*); (sich) zusammenziehen, einschrumpfen, eingehen (*shrink*).
contracting powers Vertragsstaaten *mpl* (*treaties, etc.*).
contracting officer zu Vertragsabschlüssen bevollmächtigter Offizier.
contracting parties vertragschließende Teile (*Law*).
contractor Vertragsschließende(r) *m*, Kontrahent *m*; Bauunternehmer *m* (*builder*); Lieferant *m* (*supplier*).
contract surgeon Vertragsarzt *m*.
contradiction Widerspruch *m*.
contrast Gegensatz *m*, Kontrast *m*.
control *n* Kontrolle *f*, Oberaufsicht *f*, Leitung *f*; Kontroll-; Leit-.
control *v* beaufsichtigen, überwachen, kontrollieren; nachprüfen (*check up*); (be)herrschen (*govern*); sich beherrschen (*restrain oneself*).
control airport Flughafen mit Flugsicherungsanlagen.
control aneroid barometrische Reglerdose (*Ap engine*).
control board Schalttafel *f* (*Elec*).
control box Kupplungskasten *m* (*AA director*).
control buoy Minenmarkierboje *f* (*Nav*).
control cabin Führerraum *m*, Führerkanzel *f*, Führerstand *f* (*Ap*).
control cable Bowdenzug *m* (*in flexible steel conduit*).
control car Führergondel *f* (*airship*).

control center Luftschutzwarnzentrale f (AWS).

control column Steuersäule f (Ap).

control device Bedienungseinrichtung f.

control flag Winkflagge f, Winkerflagge f.

control grid Steuergitter n (Rad tube).

control grip Drehgriff m (Mtcl).

controllable kontrollierbar (capable of supervision); steuerbar (Tech); verstellbar (Ap propeller).

controllable-pitch propeller Verstellschraube f, Verstell-Luftschraube f, Dreiblattverstellschraube f (three-blade) (Ap).

controlled mine Grundmine f, Beobachtungsmine f (Nav).

controlled mosaic Bildplan m (aerial Photo).

controlled tower Sprungturm m, Fallschirm-Absprungturm m (Prcht Tng).

controller Bediener m (AA searchlight).

controlling Steuern n.

control officer Marschführer m (march column).

control of the air Luftherrschaft f.

control panel Schalttafel f (Elec).

control point Orientierungspunkt m, Festpunkt m (Surv); Verkehrsposten m, Marschkontrollstelle f (traffic); Auskunftstelle f, Meldestelle f (Sig C).

control rod Verstellwelle f (Ap).

controls Flugzeugsteuerung f, Steuerung f, Steuerorgane npl (Ap).

control servo Hilfsvorrichtung f, Servomotor m, Trimmklappe f (Ap).

control shaft Steuerwelle f (Ap).

control station Scheinwerferrichtungsweiser m (AA SL); Leitfunkstelle f, Hauptfunkstelle f (Rad).

control-station traffic Leitverkehr m (Rad).

control stick Knüppel m, Steuerknüppel m (Ap).

control surface Steuerfläche f (Ap).

control system Steuerung f (Ap).

control tower Abfertigungsgebäude n, Aufsichtsturm m, Befehlsgebäude n, Befehlsstelle f (Adrm).

control wheel Steuerrad n (Ap).

control zone Flugplatzzone f (Adrm).

contusion Quetschung f, Quetschwunde f (Med).

convalescence Genesung f, Konvaleszenz f.

convalescent n Rekonvaleszent m.

convalescent camp Genesungsanstalt f, Genesungsheim n.

convalescent hospital Leichtkrankenkriegslazarett n.

convection Strahlung f, Konvektion f.

conventional sign Kartenzeichen n, Kartensignatur f, Signatur f (Top).

converge zusammenlaufen, konvergieren.

convergence Zusammenlaufen n, Zusammenstrahlen n.

convergent zusammenlaufend, konvergierend.

converging attack konzentrischer Angriff (Tac).

converging fire konzentrisches Feuer (Arty).

conversion Umrechnung f (Math).

conversion table Umrechnungstabelle f, Umrechnungstafel f.

convert v umrechnen (Math); umändern, umwandeln (change); bekehren (to a party, religion).

converter Umformer m (Elec); Chiffriermaschine f, Schlüsselmaschine f (cipher device).

converter unit Umformersatz m (Elec).

convertible umrechenbar (Math); vertauschbar, umwechselbar, umwandelbar.

convex konvex, gewölbt.

convex slope gewölbte Böschung (Top).

convoy Begleitzug m, Geleitzug m.

convoy commander Kraftfahrzeugkolonnenführer m (MT).

convoy guard Geleitschutz m (Nav).

cook n Feldkochunteroffizier m (NCO).

cooking pit Kochloch n.

cool v kühlen, abkühlen.

cool adj kühl, frisch; ruhig (calm).

coolant Kühlmittel n (Mtr).

cooling fin Kühlrippe f, Lamelle f (Mtr).

cooling liquid Kühlflüssigkeit f (Mtr).

cooling system Kühlung *f*, Kühlanlage *f (Mtr)*.
cooperate mitwirken, zusammenarbeiten; beitragen *(contribute to)*; unterstützen *(support)*.
cooperation Mitwirkung *f*, Zusammenarbeit *f*; Unterstützung *f (support)*.
cooperative *adj* mitwirkend; behilflich.
coordinate *n* Koordinate *f*.
coordinate *v* beiordnen, koordinieren, zum Zusammenwirken bringen.
coordinate cards Koordinatenschieber *mpl (Surv)*.
coordinated attack planmäßiger Angriff, einheitlich angesetzter Angriff *(Tac)*.
coordinate map grid Gitternetz *n*.
coordinate scale Planzeiger *m (Arty, Surv)*.
coordinate system Koordinatensystem *n*.
coordination Zusammenwirken *n*.
co-pilot zweiter Flugzeugführer.
copper Kupfer *n*.
copper cup kupfernes Hütchen *(cartridge)*.
copper shell Kupferkapsel *f (detonator cap)*.
copper wire Kupferdraht *m*.
copy *n* Abschrift *f*, Kopie *f*; Durchschlag *m (carbon copy)*; Exemplar *n*, Abdruck *m (of a book)*; Manuskript *n (for printer)*; Nummer *f (of a newspaper)*; Nachahmung *f (imitation)*.
cord Seil *n*, Strick *m (rope)*; Schnur *f (twine)*; Klafter *f (of wood)*.
cord fuze Leitfeuer *n (Engr)*.
cord-fuze detonation Leitfeuerzündung *f (Engr)*.
cord-fuze detonator Leitfeuerzündmittel *n (Engr)*.
cordite Kordit *n (explosive)*.
cord lashing Schnürbund *m (Engr)*.
cordon Gürtel *m (Tac)*.
cord powder Stäbchenpulver *n (Am)*.
corduroy road Knüppelweg *m*, Knüppeldamm *m*, Schwellenbahn *f*.
core of bullet Geschoßkern *m*.
cork Kork *m (substance)*; Kork(en) *m*, Pfropfen *m*, Stöpsel *m (stopper)*.
corkscrew Korkenzieher *m*.
coronet Hufkrone *f (of hoof)*.
corporal Obergefreiter *m*.

corporal of the guard Aufführender *m*.
corps Korps *n*.
corps area Korpsbezirk *m*.
corps artillery Korpsartillerie *f*.
corps artillery commander Artilleriekommandeur *m*.
corps cavalry regiment Korps-Kavallerieregiment *n*.
corps combat order Korpsbefehl *m*.
corps communication battalion Korpsnachrichtenabteilung *f*.
corpse Leiche *f*.
corps engineer Kommandeur der Pioniere.
corps headquarters Generalkommando *n*, Korpskommando *n*.
Corps of Chaplains Wehrmachtseelsorgedienst *m*.
Corps of Engineers Pionierkorps *n*, Pioniertruppe *f*.
corps quartermaster Kommandeur der Korpsnachschubtruppen *(USA)*.
corps supply column Korpsnachschubkolonne *f*.
corps troops Korpstruppen *fpl*.
corrected azimuth berichtigte Teilringeinstellung *(Gunnery)*.
corrected deflection berichtigte Seitenrichtung *(Gunnery)*.
corrected elevation Aufsatzerhöhung *f (Gunnery)*.
corrected range Aufsatzentfernung *f (Gunnery)*.
correction Berichtigung *f*, Verbesserung *f (Gunnery)*; Irrung *f (Rad procedure)*.
correction angle Verbesserungswinkel *m (Gunnery)*.
correction factor Verbesserungswert *m (Ballistics)*.
corrector Brennlängenschieber *m (fuze)*.
corrector pointer Schlüsselschieber *m (hand fuze setter)*.
correlation Wechselbeziehung *f*, Korrelation *f*.
correspondence Schriftverkehr *m*.
correspondence course Fernkurs *m*.
correspondent Kriegsberichter *m (in Ger propaganda Co)*; Berichter *m*, Berichterstatter *m*, Korrespondent *m*.
corresponding range Überschießgrenze *f*.
corridor Geländestreifen *m*.

corroboration Bekräftigung *f*, Bestätigung *f*.

corrugated paper Wellpappe *f*.

cosecant Kosekante *f*.

cosine Kosinus *m*.

cost *n* Preis *m*, Kosten *pl*.

cot Feldbett *n*, Pritsche *f*.

cotangent Kotangens *m* *(function)*; Kotangente *f* *(line)*.

cotter pin Splint *m*.

cotton Baumwolle *f*; Watte *f* *(Med)*.

cotton linters Baumwollabfall *m*.

cotton waste Putzwolle *f* *(for cleaning)*.

counsel Anwalt *m*, Rechtsbeistand *m* *(Law)*; Rat *m* *(advice)*.

count *n* Graf *m* *(title)*; Zahl *f* *(number)*.

count *v* zählen *(enumerate)*; rechnen *(compute)*.

counteract zuwiderhandeln, entgegenwirken; verhindern *(prevent)*; vereiteln *(nullify)*.

counterapproach trench Gegenlaufgraben *m*.

counterattack Gegenangriff *m* *(Tac)*.

counterbalance Massenausgleich *m* *(Ap)*; Gegengewicht *n* *(Mech)*.

counterbattery fire Artilleriebekämpfung *f*.

counterclockwise im Gegensinn zum Uhrzeiger, im Gegenzeigersinn, linksgängig, linkslaufend.

counterespionage Spionageabwehr *f*, Gegenspionage *f*.

counterfire Erwiderungsfeuer *n*, Gegenfeuer *n*, Feuerkampf *m*.

counterintelligence Abwehrdienst *m*.

countermand Gegenbefehl geben.

countermarch Gegenmarsch *m*.

countermeasure Gegenmaßnahme *f*.

countermine Gegenmine *f*, Gegenstollen *m*.

counteroffensive Gegenoffensive *f*.

counterorder Gegenbefehl *m*.

counterpoise Gegengewicht *n* *(Rad, Mech)*; Beschwerungsstück *n*, Beschwerungsrohr *n* *(G)*.

counterpreparation Gegenvorbereitungsfeuer *n*.

counterpropaganda Gegenpropaganda *f*.

counterrecoil Vorlauf *m*, Vorlaufbewegung *f*.

counterrecoil mechanism Vorholeeinrichtung *f*, Vorholer *m* *(G)*.

counterrecoil piston rod Vorlaufhemmstange *f* *(G)*.

counterreconnaissance Gegenaufklärung *f*.

counterreconnaissance screen Gegenaufklärungsstreifen *m*.

counterrotating propellers gegenläufige Luftschrauben *(Ap)*.

countershaft Vorgelegewelle *f* *(MT)*.

countersign Erkennungswort *n*, Gegenlosung *f*.

counterslope Gegenböschung *f*, Gegenhang *m*.

counterthrust Gegenstoß *m* *(Tac)*.

counterweight Beschwerungsstück *n*, Beschwerungsrohr *n* *(G)*; Massenausgleich *m* *(Ap)*; Gegengewicht *n* *(Mech)*.

"Count off!" "Abzählen!"

country Land *n*; Gelände *n* *(terrain)*; Gegend *f* *(region)*.

country of origin Heimatstaat *m*.

couple *v* aufprotzen *(Arty)*.

coupling Kopplung *f* *(Mech, Rad)*; Kupplung *f* *(Mech)*; Anschluß *m* *(Ord)*.

courier Kurier *m*.

courier mail Kurierpost *f*.

course Kurs *m* *(Nav, Avn)*; Flugweg *m*, Flugrichtung *f* *(Avn)*; Lehrgang *m* *(instruction)*.

course determination Flugwegbestimmung *f* *(Air Navigation)*.

course light Streckenfeuer *n*, Flugstreckenfeuer *n*.

course of target Zielweg *m* *(AA gunnery)*.

court Gericht *n*. See also **military court**.

courtesy Höflichkeit *f*, höfliche Formen. See also **military courtesy**.

court-martial Kriegsgericht *n*.

court-martial proceedings Kriegsgerichtsverfahren *n*.

court plaster Leukoplast *n*.

cover *n* Schutz *m*; Decke *f*; Deckel *m*; Überzug *m*; Deckung *f*, Eindeckung *f* *(Ft)*; Aufnahme *f* *(for withdrawal in delaying action, Tac)*; Hülsenbrücke *f* *(R receiver)*.

cover *v* durch Feuer decken, decken, schützen.

coverage Bedeckung *f* *(Met)*; Feuerschutz *m*, Feuerunterstützung *f* *(Tac)*; Geländeausschnitt *m* *(aerial Photo)*.

covering Tarndecke *f (Cam);* Außenhaut *f,* Bespannung *f (Ap);* Verschalung *f.*
covering fire Feuerschutz *m.*
covering force Deckungstruppe *f;* Aufnahme *f (reserve force covering withdrawal from action).*
covering party Deckungstrupp *m.*
covering position vorgeschobene Stellung *(in defense);* Aufnahmestellung *f (covering withdrawal from action).*
"**Cover off!**" "Vordermann!"; "Auf Vordermann gehen!" *(behind file leaders when in platoon front).*
cover off auf Vordermann gehen, auf Vordermann stehen, Vordermann nehmen.
cover plate Abdeckplatte *f (G).*
cover-plate latch Deckelriegel *m (MG).*
cover-plate lock Deckelsperre *f (MG).*
cover position gedeckte Stellung.
cover trench Deckungsgraben *m.*
cowardice Feigheit *f.*
cowl flaps Luftabflußklappen *fpl (Ap).*
cowling Haube *f,* Verkleidung *f (Ap).*
crab Luvwinkel *m (Avn).*
crabbing windschiefer Flug *(Avn).*
crack *n* Riß *m,* Sprung *m,* Spalt *m (split);* Krach *m,* Knall *m (sound).*
crack *v* zerspalten, zersprengen, zerbrechen.
crack-up Bruch *m (Avn).*
cradle Wiege *f,* Rohrwiege *f (G);* Gewehrträger *m (on MG sleigh mount or tripod).*
cradle frame Wiegenträger *m (G).*
cradle guide rails Wiegengleitbahn *f (G).*
cradle lock Wiegenzurrung *f (G).*
craft Wasserfahrzeug *n (stream crossing).*
crane Kran *m (Engr).*
crank *n* Kurbel *f.*
crank *v* andrehen, ankurbeln, anwerfen.
crank arm Kurbelarm *m (crank shaft).*
crankcase Kurbelgehäuse *n (Mtr).*
crank handle Andrehkurbel *f (MT).*
crank mechanism Kurbeltrieb *m (Mech).*
crankpin Kurbelzapfen *m (Mtr).*

crankshaft Kurbelwelle *f (Mtr).*
crankshaft assembly Kurbeltriebwerk *n (Mtr).*
crankshaft throw Kröpfung der Kurbelwelle *(Mtr).*
crank starter Handanlasser *m (Mtr).*
crankwheel Kurbelrad *n (G).*
crankwheel operation exercise Kurbelübung *f (gun laying).*
crash *n* Bruch *m (Avn).*
crash boat Fliegerrettungsboot *n.*
crash helmet Schutzmütze *f (Armd Comd);* Sturzhelm *m.*
crash landing Bruchlandung *f (Avn).*
crash padding Schutzpolsterung *f.*
crater Trichter *m,* Sprengtrichter *m.*
crater charge Trichterladung *f (Engr).*
crawl *v* robben *(on land);* kraulen *(swimming).*
crawl forward sich vorrobben.
crawl trench Kriechgraben *m.*
credit *n* Kredit *m,* Guthaben *n (financial);* Anerkennung *f (acknowledgment).*
creep kriechen.
creeping barrage Feuerwalze *f.*
cremation Einäscherung *f.*
creosote Kreosot *n.*
cresol soap solution Kresolseifenlösung *f,* Kresolwasser *n.*
crest Kamm *m,* Kammlinie *f (Top);* Gewehrauflage *f,* Brustwehrkrone *f (trench);* Krone *f.*
crew Besatzung *f,* Mannschaft *f (Ap, Tk);* Bedienung *f (G, SL).*
crib Stapel *m (Bdg).*
crime Verbrechen *n.*
criminal Verbrecher *m.*
crimp Würgung *f (Am).*
crimper Würgezange *f.*
critical item Sparstoff *m.*
critical point Gefahrpunkt *m,* kritischer Punkt *(Tac);* Wechselpunkt *m (Top).*
critical speed kritische Geschwindigkeit; Durchsackgeschwindigkeit *f (Avn);* kritische Drehzahl *(Mech).*
critical zone Planfeuerwürfel *m (AA firing).*
critique Schlußbesprechung *f.*
cross *n* Kreuz *n;* Zapfenkreuz *n (universal joint) (MT).*
cross *v* überqueren *(a river, etc.);* überschreiten *(a bridge, road, etc.).*

crossbar Traverse *f (split-trail carriage)*; Querverbindung *f (log sled)*.
crossbelt Schulterriemen *m (Clo)*.
cross bracing Auskreuzung *f (Ap)*; Querverstrebung *f (Bdg)*.
cross-country querfeldein; geländegängig; Überland-, Gelände-.
cross-country driving Geländefahren *n*.
cross-country flight Überlandflug *m*.
cross-country mobility Geländegängigkeit *f*.
cross-country vehicle Geländefahrzeug *n (MT)*.
crosscut saw Hirnsäge *f*, Quersäge *f*.
cross-examination Kreuzverhör *n*.
cross-examine einem Kreuzverhör unterwerfen.
cross fire *n* Kreuzfeuer *n*.
cross-fire *v* Feuer kreuzen *(firing)*.
cross hairs Fadenkreuz *n (Optics)*.
cross hole screw Kreuzlochschraube *f*.
crossing Übergang *m*.
crossing of ditches Grabendurchfahrt *f (MT)*.
crossing of rivers Überwinden von Flüssen.
crossing point Übersetzstelle *f*.
crossing station Übergangsbahnhof *m*, Kreuzungsbahnhof *m (RR)*.
crossing target querfahrendes Ziel.
cross level *n* Querlibelle *f*, Verkantungslibelle *f (Optics, Surv, Arty)*; Radstandlibelle *f (G)*.
cross-level *v* die Libelle einspielen.
cross-level drive Verkantungstrieb *m (Optics, Ord)*.
cross leveling Libelleneinstellung *f (firing)*.
cross-leveling mechanism Radstandtrieb *m (G sight)*.
cross lines Kreuzleinen *fpl (of harness)*.
crosspiece Ducht *f (boat)*.
cross pipe fitting Kreuzmuffe *f*.
crossroads Wegekreuzung *f*, Straßenkreuzung *f*.
cross section Profil *n*, Querschnitt *m*.
cross wind seitlicher Schiebewind *(Avn)*.
cross-wind landing Landung mit Seitenwind.
cross-wind takeoff Start mit Seitenwind.
cross wires Fadenkreuz *n (Optics)*.
crouching fox hole Hockloch *n*.

croup Kruppe *f (horse)*.
crowbar Brechstange *f*, Hebebaum *m*.
crown of roadbed Bahnkrone *f (RR)*.
crownpiece Kopfstück *n (harness)*.
crucible steel Tiegelgußstahl *m*.
crude oil Rohöl *n*.
cruise *v* fahren *(vehicle or ship)*; kreuzen *(ship)*; fliegen *(Ap)*.
cruiser Kreuzer *m*.
cruising power rating Reisedauerleistung *f*.
cruising radius Fahrbereich *m (MT, Tk)*.
cruising speed Reisegeschwindigkeit *f (Ap)*; Marschgeschwindigkeit *f (MT)*.
crush (zer)quetschen, zerdrücken, zermalmen.
cryptanalysis Entzifferung *f*, Geheimschriftanalyse *f*.
cryptogram Kryptogramm *n*.
cryptograph *See* cryptogram.
cryptography Geheimschrift *f*.
crystal Kristall *m*.
crystal control Quarzsteuerung *f (Rad)*.
crystal-controlled transmitter quarzgesteuerter Sender *(Rad)*.
crystal detector Kristalldetektor *m (Rad)*.
cube *n* Würfel *m*, Kubus *m*; Kubikzahl *f*, dritte Potenz *(Math)*.
cubed zur dritten Potenz erhoben.
cubic centimeter Kubikzentimeter *n*.
cultivated fields bebaute Felder.
culvert Durchlaß *m*.
cumulus cloud Haufenwolke *f*, Kumuluswolke *f*.
cup Trinkbecher *m (drinking)*; Schmierbüchse *f (grease)*; Hütchen *n (cartridge)*.
cup anemometer Schalenkreuzwindmesser *m (Met)*.
cupola Kuppel *f*, Beobachtungskuppel *f*, Turmkuppel *f*, Beobachtungstürmchen *n*, Turmaufsatz *m (Tk)*.
cupola mount Kuppellafette *f (Ap)*.
curb bit Kandare *f (harness)*.
curb chain Kinnkette *f (harness)*.
curbing Rödelung *f (Bdg)*.
curb lashing Rödeln *n (Bdg)*.
curb rail Rödelbalken *m (Bdg)*.
curb rein Kandarenzügel *m (harness)*.
cure *v* heilen.
curfew Ausgehverbot *n (Mil Govt)*.

currency Währung *f;* Geld *n (money).*
current *n* Strom *m,* Strömung *f.*
current capacity Stromaufnahme *f (Rad).*
current consumer Stromverbraucher *m (Elec).*
current flow Stromfluß *m (Elec).*
current generator unit Stromaggregat *n (Elec).*
current intensity Stromstärke *f (Elec.)*
current-measuring instrument Strommeßgerät *n (Elec).*
current supplies laufender Nachschub.
current supply Stromzufuhr *f,* Stromvorrat *m (Elec).*
current surge Stromstoß *m (Elec).*
currycomb Striegel *m.*
curtain door Gasschutzvorhang *m.*
curtain of antiaircraft fire Flaksperre *f,* Sperrfeuerwand *f.*
curtain of fire Feuerwand *f,* Feuervorhang *m.*
curvature Krümmung *f,* Biegung *f.*
curve *n* Straßenbiegung *f (road);* Krümmung *f,* Kurve *f,* Bogen *m.*
curved-chord truss Parabel-Fachwerkträger *m (Engr).*
curved spur track Gleiskurve *f,* Klaue *f (RR gun).*
curve of the trajectory Gestalt der Flugbahn.
curvilinear flight Kurvenflug *m.*
cushion tire Pneumassivreifen *m,* Hochelastikreifen *m (MT).*
custodian Urkundenbewahrer *m (of documents).*
custody Haft *f,* Gewahrsam *m;* Aufsicht *f,* Hut *f,* Verwahrung *f (care);* Schutz *m (protection).*
custom Gebrauch *m.*
custom house Zollhaus *n.*
customs of the service Truppenbrauch *m.*
customs of war Kriegsbrauch *m,* Kriegsgebrauch *m.*
cut *n* Durchstich *m,* Einschnitt *m (Engr, RR);* Schnitt *m (injury or wound);* Hieb *m (slash).*

cut *v* schneiden, abschneiden *(wire, etc.);* hauen, abhauen *(trees, etc.).*
cut a fuze Zünder einstellen.
cut-and-cover shelter Unterschlupf *m.*
cut film Schnittfilm *m.*
cut off trennen *(Elec, Tp).*
cut-off frequency Grenzfrequenz *f (Rad).*
cutout Auspuffklappe *f (Mtr).*
cutter *See* cutting pliers.
cutting pliers Zwickzange *f (Engr).*
cw tonlos *(marking on Rad set).*
cw transmission Telegraphiesendung *f (Rad).*
cyanogen bromide Bromzyan *n,* Ce-Stoff *m (CWS).*
cyanogen chloride Chlorzyan *n,* Cyanogenchlorid *n (CWS).*
cycle Periode *f,* Hertz *n (Elec);* Kreisprozeß *m (Mtr);* Kreislauf *m.*
cyclic change mechanism Vorrichtung zur Verlangsamung der Schußfolge *(automatic R).*
cyclic rate Schußfolge *f.*
cyclic rate mechanism *See* cyclic change mechanism.
cyclogiro Radflügelflugzeug *n (Avn).*
cyclone Zyklon *m,* Tief *n (low);* Orkan *m,* Taifun *m (tropical);* Wirbelsturm *m,* Tornado *m,* Trombe *f (tornado).*
cylinder Zylinder *m.*
cylinder block Motorblock *m,* Zylinderblock *m (Mtr).*
cylinder grinding Zylinderschleifen *n (Mtr).*
cylinder head Zylinderkopf *m (Mtr).*
cylinder liner Zylinderlaufbüchse *f (Mtr).*
cylinder wall Zylinderwand *f (Mtr).*
cylindrical zylindrisch, walzenförmig.
cylindrical cam Lenkschraube *f (steering column, MT).*
cylindrical grid Zylinderelektrode *f (Rad tube).*
cylindrical mount Walzenblende *f (Tk gun).*

D

dagger Dolch *m.*
daily automatic supply Tagesversorgung *f.*

daily ration Tagesverpflegung *f.*
daily ration strength return Stärkenachweis für die Tagesverpflegung.

daily sick report Krankenmeldung f.
daily stock record Bestandsnachweisung f.
daily strength report Iststärkenachweisung f.
daily telegram tägliche Stärke- und
Bedarfsmeldung.
daily train tägliche Nachschubkolonne (MT).
dam Damm m, Stauanlage f; Talsperre f (across a valley); Buhne f
(diversion).
damage n Beschädigung f, Schaden m.
damage v beschädigen.
damage control Schadenbekämpfung f.
damming Anstauung f (Engr).
damped oscillations gedämpfte
Schwingungen (Rad).
damped waves gedämpfte Wellen
(Rad).
damping Dämpfung f (Elec, Rad).
damping device Dämpfungsvorrich-
tung f.
danger Gefahr f.
danger area Schußbereich m.
danger flag Warnflagge f.
danger of icing Vereisungsgefahr f
(Avn).
danger of interception Abhörgefahr
f (Tp).
dangerous gefährlich.
danger signal Warnsignal n.
danger space Visierbereich m (MG
firing).
darkness Dunkelheit f, Finsternis f.
darkroom Dunkelkammer f.
dash n Strich m (Tg).
dashboard Instrumentenbrett n.
data Grundlagen fpl, Unterlagen fpl,
Angaben fpl, Daten npl.
data board Schreibbrett n (Arty).
data card Merkzettel m.
data computer Kommandogerät n.
data receiver Empfänger m (data
transmission system).
data transmission system Übertragungsgerät n (AAA).
data transmitter Geber m (data
transmission system).
date Datum n.
datum Unterlage f, Angabe f,
Datum n.
datum level Bezugsebene f (Surv).
datum line Bezugslinie f (Surv).

datum plane Bezugsebene f, Bezugsfläche f (Surv).
datum point Bezugspunkt m (Surv).
davit Davit m, Schwenkdavit m
(Nav).
daybook Kriegstagebuch n.
daybreak Tagesanbruch m.
daylight attack Tagesangriff m,
Tagesvorstoß m.
day march Tagmarsch m.
day of fire Munition für einen Tag.
day of supply Tagesverbrauch m,
Vorratsbestand für einen Tag.
day's destination Tagesziel n.
day's march Tagesmarsch m.
day's objective Tagesziel n.
dazzle-painted bunt bemalt (Cam).
dazzle painting Buntfarbenanstrich
m (Cam).
DB boat Hilfsfahrzeug zum Legen
von Grundminen (Nav).
d-c generator Gleichstromerzeuger m.
dead tot.
dead abatis schwere Baumsperre.
dead area toter Schußraum.
dead center Totpunkt m (Mtr).
dead-end road Sackgasse f; Holzweg
m (in a forest).
dead-end station Kopfbahnhof m
(RR).
dead-end street Sackgasse f.
dead file erledigte Akten.
deadline Termin m.
deadman eingebetteter waagerecht
liegender Verankerungspfahl
(Engr).
dead reckoning Koppeln n (Avn).
dead reckoning navigation Koppelnavigation f (Avn).
dead reckoning position Koppelort
m (Air Navigation).
dead space toter Schußraum, toter
Trichter, gedeckter Raum, toter
Winkel (Gunnery).
dead-stick landing Landung mit
abgestelltem Motor (Avn).
dead time Kommando- und Ladeverzugszeit f (Gunnery).
death Tod m.
death sentence Todesurteil n.
debarkation Ausbooten n, Ausbootung f.
debarkation officer Landungsoffi-
zier m.
debouch aus einer Enge heraustreten
(from a defile); aus dem Waldgelände heraustreten (from a wood).

debris Trümmer *pl.*
debt Schuld *f.*
deceive täuschen, vortäuschen.
deception Täuschung *f.*
deceptive irreführend, Täuschungs-, Schein-.
deceptive smoke screen Scheinverneblung *f.*
decibel Phon *n*, Dezibel *n.*
decipher entschlüsseln, entziffern, dechiffrieren.
decision Entschluß *m (Tac).*
decisive ausschlaggebend, entscheidend.
decisive action Entscheidungsgefecht *n (Tac).*
decisive battle Entscheidungskampf *m (Tac).*
deck Deck *n (Tk, Nav);* Oberseite *f.*
declaration of war Kriegserklärung *f.*
declinate Ortsmißweisung bestimmen *(compass).*
declination Mißweisung *f*, Kompaßmißweisung *f (compass).*
declination constant Mißweisung *f*, Ortsmißweisung *f.*
declinator Richtkreis-Bussole *f*, Bussole *f (aiming circle).*
decode entschlüsseln.
decontaminate entgiften *(CWS).*
decontaminating agent Entgiftungsmittel *n*, Entgiftungsstoff *m.*
decontaminating apparatus Entgiftungsgerät *n;* Zerstäubergerät *n (spray).*
decontaminating-powder s p r a y e r Pulverzerstäuber *m (CWS).*
decontaminating sprayer Flüssigkeitszerstäuber für Entgiftung.
decontamination Entgiftung *f.*
decontamination agent Entgiftungsstoff *m (CWS).*
decontamination battalion Entgiftungsabteilung *f.*
decontamination cart fahrbare Entgiftungstrommel.
decontamination drum Entgiftungstrommel *f.*
decontamination point Entgiftungsplatz *m (CWS).*
decontamination service Entgiftungsdienst *m.*
decontamination squad Entgiftungstrupp *m.*
decontamination troops Entgiftungstruppen *fpl.*

decopper entkupfern.
decoppering agent Entkupferungsmittel *n.*
decoration Auszeichnung *f*, Ehrenzeichen *n.*
decoy *n* Lockmittel *n*, Falle *f.*
decoy *v* heranlocken.
decryptograph entziffern, entschlüsseln, dechiffrieren.
deduct abziehen, subtrahieren.
deep-sea diver Torpedotaucher *m.*
deep thrust tiefer Vorstoß *(Tac).*
defeat *n* Niederlage *f.*
defeat *v* schlagen, besiegen.
defecate den Darm entleeren; scheißen *(vulgar).*
defect Fehler *m;* Materialfehler *m (structural);* Konstruktionsfehler *m (design);* Sehfehler *m (vision).*
defective fehlerhaft.
defense Verteidigung *f*, Abwehr *f (as distinguished from* Schutz, *protection, Tac).*
defense area Verteidigungsraum *m.*
Defense Command Landesverteidigungsbezirk *m (USA).*
defense in depth nach Tiefe gegliederte Verteidigung.
defense plan Verteidigungsplan *m.*
defense system Wehrorganisation *f (total armed defense system of a country);* Landesverteidigungsorganisation *f (home defense);* Befestigungsanlagen *fpl (Ft).*
defensive *n* Defensive *f*, Verteidigung *f (Tac).*
defensive *adj* defensiv, in der Verteidigung.
defensive area Verteidigungsraum *m.*
defensive arm Abwehrwaffe *f.*
defensive battle Abwehrschlacht *f.*
defensive coastal area Küstenverteidigungsabschnitt *m.*
defensive combat Abwehrkampf *m*, Abwehrgefecht *n (Tac).*
defensive fire Abwehrfeuer *n*, Notfeuer *n (Arty, MG).*
defensive front Abwehrfront *f.*
defensive installations Verteidigungsanlagen *fpl.*
defensive line Verteidigungslinie *f.*
defensively abwehrweise.
defensive measure Abwehrmaßnahme *f.*
defensive-offensive offensive Verteidigung.

defensive operations Verteidigungsoperationen *fpl.*

defensive position Verteidigungsstellung *f.*

defensive preparation Abwehrvorbereitung *f.*

defensive sector Verteidigungsabschnitt *m.*

defensive weapon Abwehrwaffe *f.*

defensive zone Abwehrzone *f,* Verteidigungszone *f.*

defer zurückstellen.

deferment Zurückstellung *f.*

defilade Geländeschutz *m.*

defiladed area gedeckter Raum.

defile Enge *f,* Engpaß *m (Tac).*

defile between lakes Seenenge *f.*

definition Linsenschärfe *f (of a lens);* Definition *f,* Begriffsbestimmung *f (of a word).*

deflagration Verbrennung *f,* Deflagration *f (powder).*

deflection Seitenabweichung *f (Gunnery);* Ablenkung *f;* Strahlungsablenkung *f (of Rad waves);* Durchbiegung *f (of a beam or girder).*

deflection angle Seitenwinkel *m (Gunnery).*

deflection board Seitenrichtschieber *m (CA).*

deflection change Seitenänderung *f (Gunnery).*

deflection correction Seitenänderung *f,* Seitenverbesserung *f (Gunnery).*

deflection difference Feuervereinigungswinkel *m (Btry firing).*

deflection dispersion Breitenstreuung *f (Ballistics).*

deflection reading Festlegezahl *f (Gunnery).*

deflection scale Seitenrichtteilung *f.*

deflector box Hülsenkasten *m (AA gun).*

degassing Entgasung *f,* Entgasen *n.*

de-gaussing Entmagnetisierung *f (Nav).*

degreasing Entfettung *f (MT).*

degree Grad *m (of circle, temperature);* Stufe *f (stage or step);* Grad *m,* Maß *n (extent).*

dehydrated meat Dörrfleisch *n.*

dehydrated vegetables Dörrgemüse *n.*

de-icer Enteiser *m,* Enteisungsgerät *n,* Vereisungsschutzgerät *n (Ap).*

de-icing system Enteisungsanlage *f.*

delay *v* hinhalten *(Tac).*

delay *n* Verzögerung *f,* Verzug *m;* Aufschub *m.*

delayed-action bomb Bombe mit Verzugszeit.

delayed-action fuze Aufschlagzünder mit Verzögerung, Verzögerungszünder *m.*

delayed-action mine Verzögerungsmine *f (Engr).*

delayed jump Absprung mit verzögerter Öffnung *(Prcht).*

delay fuze Aufschlagzünder mit Verzögerung, Verzögerungszünder *m.*

delaying action hinhaltendes Gefecht *(Tac).*

delaying position Widerstandsstellung im hinhaltenden Gefecht, Aufnahmestellung *f (Tac).*

delaying unit Widerstandsgruppe *f (Tac).*

delay pellet Verzögerungssatz *m.*

delay powder train Verzögerungssatz *m (fuze).*

delegation of authority Übertragung einer Amtsgewalt.

deliberate field fortification planmäßige Feldbefestigung.

deliver liefern, abliefern.

delivery Auslieferung *f.*

delivery container Abwurfkiste *f (airborne operations).*

delivery roadway Ladestraße *f (RR freight station).*

delivery unit Fallschirmlast *f,* Versorgungsbehälter *m (airborne supply).*

delouse entlausen.

delousing Entlausung *f.*

delousing station Entlausungsstation *f.*

delta connection Dreieckschaltung *f (Elec).*

demarcation Abgrenzung *f.*

demilitarize militärisch räumen, entmilitarisieren.

demobilization Demobilmachung *f.*

demobilize demobilmachen.

demolish sprengen *(blow up);* niederreißen, abreißen, abbrechen *(tear down);* zerstören, vernichten *(to ruin).*

demolition Sprengung *f,* Zerstörung *f,* Demolierung *f.*

demolition block Sprengbüchse *f (Engr).*

demolition bomb Sprengbombe *f.*

demolition chamber Minenkammer *f (Bdg, mine)*; Sprengstelle *f (Bdg)*.

demolition detail Sprengtrupp *m*.

demolition equipment Sprenggerät *n*, Zündgerät *n (Engr)*.

demolition installation Minenanlage *f*.

demolition mission Sprengauftrag *m*.

demolition order Sprengbefehl *m*, Sprengauftrag *m*.

demolition party Sprengkommando *n*.

demolition plan Sprengplan *m (Engr)*.

demolition service Sprengdienst *m*.

demolition squad Sprengtrupp *m*.

demonstration Täuschungsmanöver *n*, Scheingefecht *n*, Scheinangriff *m (Tac)*; Vorführung *f*.

demonstration chart Unterrichtstafel *f (Tng)*.

demonstration flight Schauflug *m (Avn)*.

demonstration material Anschauungsmittel *npl (Tng aids)*.

demoralize demoralisieren, entmutigen.

demotion Degradation *f*, Dienstgradherabsetzung *f*.

denim Drillich *m*, Drilch *m*.

densimeter Dichtemesser *m*, Dichtigkeitsmesser *m*.

density Dichte *f*.

density of fire Feuerdichte *f*.

density of fragments Splitterdichte *f (Arty)*.

density of gas coverage Belegungsstärke *f (CWS)*.

density of loading Ladedichte *f (Am)*.

Dental Corps zahnärztliches Korps *(USA)*.

dental officer Sanitätsoffizier *(Z) m*.

dental surgeon Kriegszahnarzt *m*.

dental technician Zahntechniker *m*.

dental treatment Zahnbehandlung *f*.

dentist Zahnarzt *m*.

depart abrücken, abmarschieren, aufbrechen.

departing flight Abflug *m (AA)*.

department Abteilung *f (branch, section)*; Verwaltungsbereich *m (sphere)*; Behörde *f (Adm)*; Ministerium *n (of government)*.

departure Abfahrt *f*, Ausrücken *n*, Abrücken *n*.

departure point Aufbruchsort *m*.

departure time Aufbruchszeit *f*.

dependency benefits Familienunterhalt *m*.

dependent Unterhaltsberechtigter *m*.

deploy entwickeln, ausschwärmen.

deployed riflemen Schützen in Entwicklung.

deployment Entwicklung *f (Tac)*.

deployment for action Gefechtsentwicklung *f (Tac)*.

deport verschicken, verbannen, deportieren; abschieben *(aliens)*.

depot Lager *n*, Park *m (Mil)*; Bahnhof *m (RR station)*; Zweiglager *n (branch depot)*.

depot quartermaster Lagermeister *m (Ger: civilian official)*.

depress senken *(G)*.

depression Mulde *f (Top)*; Tief *n (Met)*.

depression angle Senkungswinkel *m (G)*.

depression position finder Azimutentfernungsmesser *m*.

depth Tiefe *f (Tac)*.

in depth tiefgegliedert, treffenweise.

depth bomb Wasserbombe *f*, Unterwasserbombe *f*.

depth of penetration Eindringtiefe *f*, Eindringungstiefe *f (Tac)*.

depth of profile Profiltiefe *f (Ap wing)*.

depth of wing profile Flügeltiefe *f (Ap)*.

deputy Stellvertreter *m*.

Deputy Chief of Staff Stellvertretender Chef des Generalstabes.

descending air current Abwind *m (Met)*.

descending branch of trajectory absteigender Ast *(Ballistics)*.

description Beschreibung *f*, Schilderung *f*, Darstellung *f*.

desert *n* Wüste *f*.

desert *v* desertieren, fahnenflüchtig werden, Fahnenflucht begehen.

desert area Wüstenzone *f*.

deserter Fahnenflüchtiger *m*, Deserteur *m*; Überläufer *m (to the enemy)*.

desertion Fahnenflucht *f*, Desertion *f*.

desiccated cell Füllelement *n (Elec)*.

design *n* Ausführung *f (Mech).*
designated **target** Punktziel *n (Arty).*
designation **of objective** Zielsetzung *f.*
designer Konstrukteur *m (Mech).*
design **load** Normalbelastung *f (Mech).*
desired **frequency** Nutzfrequenz *f (Rad).*
desk Schreibtisch *m.*
destination Ziel *n.*
destroy zerstören, vernichten.
destroyer Zerstörer *m,* Torpedobootzerstörer *m (Nav).*
destroyer **escort** Korvette *f (Nav).*
destruction Vernichtung *f,* Zerstörung *f.*
destruction **fire** Niederkämpfen *n (Arty).*
detach abkommandieren, ausscheiden, absondern.
detached **duty** *See* detached service.
detached **post** Vorpostenverband *m.*
detached **service** Kommando *n.*
on **detached service** abkommandiert.
detached **unit** Kommando *n.*
detachment Trupp *m,* Abteilung *f.*
detachment **commander** Truppführer *m.*
detail *n* Trupp *m,* Kommando *n,* Abteilung *f (Pers);* Dienst *m (duty).*
detail *v* kommandieren.
detailed **report** Tatbericht *m,* Tatsachenbericht *m.*
"Detail, **halt!**" "Abteilung, halt!" *(given on right foot).*
detain aufhalten *(to delay);* abhalten, verhindern (withhold); in Haft behalten, festhalten *(under arrest).*
detaining **authority** nehmestaatliche Behörde *(PW).*
detaining **power** Nehmestaat *m (PW).*
detect auffangen *(Rad);* entdecken *(discover);* aufdecken *(an action);* ertappen *(to catch).*
detector Audion *n,* Detektor *m (Rad).*
detector **crayon** Gasspürkreide *f (CWS).*
detector **kit** Spürgerät *n,* Gasanzeiger *m (CWS).*
detector **paint** Gasspürfarbe *f (CWS).*
detent Rast *f (Mech).*

detention Haft *f (arrest);* Einbehaltung *f (of pay, etc.).*
detention **of pay** Besoldungseinbehaltung *f.*
detention **room** Haftlokal *n.*
detention **ward** Arrestraum im Lazarett.
deteriorating **supplies** begrenzt lagerungsfähige Vorräte.
determinate **error** regelmäßiger Fehler, systematischer Fehler.
determination **of altitude** Höhenbestimmung *f (Avn).*
determination **of course** Flugwegbestimmung *f (Air Navigation).*
determination **of direction** Richtungsbestimmung *f (Avn, Rad).*
determination **of fix** Kreuzpeilung *f (Air Navigation).*
determination **of position** Ortsbestimmung *f (Avn).*
determine **a fix** anschneiden *(Air Navigation).*
detonate detonieren, sprengen, zünden *(Engr.)*
detonating **agent** Zündmittel *n (Engr).*
detonating **charge** Aufladung *f (blasting cap).*
detonating **cord** Knallzündschnur *f.*
detonating **explosive** Brisanzsprengstoff *m.*
detonating **fuze** Sprengzünder *m.*
detonating **net** Knallennetz *n.*
detonating **slab** Zerschellerschicht *f (Ft).*
detonation Klopfen *n (Mtr);* Zünden *n,* Zündung *f (blasting);* Detonation *f.*
detonation **wave** Verdichtungswelle *f (Ballistics).*
detonator Sprengkapsel *f (Am).*
detonator-safe **fuze** Zünder mit Sprengkapselsicherung *(Am).*
detour *n* Umweg *m.*
detour *v* umgehen.
detraining **of troops** Truppenausladung *f.*
detraining **point** Ausladebahnhof *m.*
detrucking **area** Ausladegebiet *n.*
detrucking **point** Ausladeplatz *m,* Ausladestelle *f.*
devastate verwüsten, verheeren.
devastation Verwüstung *f,* Verheerung *f.*
develop entfalten *(Tac);* entwickeln *(Photo).*

developed armament probable error Treffwahrscheinlichkeit der Waffe.

development Entfaltung *f (Tac)*.

development from march column Entfaltung aus dem Marsch *(Tac)*.

development order Befehl zur Entfaltung *(Tac)*.

deviate abweichen, abkommen.

deviation Geschoßabweichung *f (Gunnery)*; Fehlweisung *f (Rad)*; Versetzung *f (Avn)*; Kompaßlenkung *f*, Deviation *f*.

deviation curve Funkbeschickungskurve *f*, Peilberichtigungskurve *f (Rad)*.

device Vorrichtung *f (Mech, Engr)*; Abzeichen *n (insigne)*.

dew Tau *m*.

dew point Taupunkt *m*.

diagonal *n* Schräglinie *f*.

diagonal *adj* schräg, querlaufend.

diagonal strut Strebe *f (Ap)*.

diagram Plan *m*, Schema *n*, Figur *f*; Abbildung *f (illustration)*.

dial *n* Zifferblatt *n (on Inst)*; Nummernscheibe *f*, Wählerscheibe *f(Tp)*; Gangrolle *f (pivoted dial of speedometer)*.

dial *v* einstellen, wählen *(Tp)*.

dial box Nummernscheibenkästchen *n (field Tp)*.

dial hum Amtszeichen *n*, Freizeichen *n*, Summton *m (Tp)*.

dialing central Wählamt *n (Tp)*.

dial plate Skalenscheibe *f (Rad)*.

dial system Wählerbetrieb *m (Tp)*.

diameter Durchmesser *m*.

diameter of projectile Geschoßdurchmesser *m (Ballistics)*.

diamond formation Rautenformation *f*.

diaphragm Schallblech *n (Tp)*; Membran *f -(microphone)*; Stoßboden *m*, Stoßscheibe *f (shrapnel)*; Blende *f (Photo)*.

diaphragm gas mask Membranmaske *f*.

diaphragm pump Membranpumpe *f (Mtr)*.

diarrhea Durchfall *m*, Diarrhöe *f*.

diary Tagebuch *n*.

diatomite layer Diatomitschicht *f (gas filter, CWS)*.

dichloramine-T Dichloramin *n (CWS)*.

die *n* Gewindebacken *fpl (for cut-*

ting threads); Stanze *f*, Gesenke *n (for stamping or punching)*.

stock and die Schneidkluppe *f*.

die *v* sterben.

die down ausschwingen *(Elec oscillations)*.

dielectric Dielektrikum *n (Rad)*.

Diesel-electric drive dieselelektrischer Antrieb.

Diesel engine Dieselmotor *m*, Dieselmaschine *f*, Schwerölmotor *m*.

Diesel fuel Dieselkraftstoff *m*, Gasöl *n*, Schweröl *n*, Schwerkraftstoff *m*.

Diesel motor *See* **Diesel engine.**

Diesel tractor Dieselschlepper *m*

Diesel truck Diesel-Lastwagen *m (MT)*.

dietitian Diätschwester *f*.

difference Unterschied *m;* Differenz *f (Math)*.

difference chart graphische Schußtafel.

difference in altitude Höhenunterschied *m*.

differential Differential *n (MT)*.

differential calculus Differentialrechnung *f*.

differential case Hinterachsengehäuse *n (MT)*.

differential effects Werte zum Ausschalten der Witterungseinflüsse *(Gunnery)*.

differential gear Ausgleichgetriebe *n (MT)*.

differential lock Ausgleichsperre *f (MT)*.

difficult terrain schwieriges Gelände.

difficulty Schwierigkeit *f;* Verlegenheit *f (trouble)*; Geländeschwierigkeit *f (of terrain)*.

diffuser plate Ladeleitrad *n (Ap engine)*.

dig *v* graben; ausgraben *(excavate)*.

dig in schanzen, einschanzen, sich eingraben.

diglycolnitrate flaked powder Diglykolnitrat-Blättchenpulver *n*.

dihedral V-Form *f*, V-Stellung *f*, Schränkung *f (Ap)*.

dihedral angle V-Formwinkel *m (Ap)*.

dike Deich *m*.

dim *v* abblenden *(a light)*.

dimension Ausmaß *n*.

dimethylsulfate D-Stoff *m (CWS)*.

dim headlights v abblenden (MT).
dim light n Abblendelicht n (headlight, MT).
dim-out n Halbverdunkelung f (Air Defense).
dim out v abblenden (Air Defense).
diode Diode f (Rad).
diode tube Zweielektrodenröhre f, Zweipolröhre f (Rad).
diopter hair Diopterfaden m (Optics).
diopter slit Diopterschlitz m (Optics).
dip n Inklinationswinkel m (compass); Kimmtiefe f (Avn).
dip v dippen, senken.
diphenylaminechlorarsine Adamsit m, Diphenylaminchlorarsin n (CWS).
diphenylchlorarsine Diphenylchlorarsin n, Chlorarsinkampfstoff m (CWS).
diphenylcyanarsine Cyan-Chlorarsinkampfstoff m (CWS).
diphosgene Chlorameisensäurechlormethylester m, Perchlorameisensäuremethylester m, Perstoff m, K-Stoff m (CWS).
dipole antenna Dipolantenne f.
direct-climbing target Flugziel im Steigflug (AA gunnery).
direct current Gleichstrom m.
direct-current ammeter Gleichstrommeßgerät n.
direct-current generator Gleichstromerzeuger m.
direct-current meter Gleichstrommeßgerät n.
direct-current motor Gleichstromelektromotor m.
directed net Nachrichtennetz mit Leitfunkstelle (Rad).
direct fire direktes Feuer.
direct-fire range Visierschußweite f.
direct-fire shot Visierschuß m.
direct-fire sight Notvisier n, Flakvisier n.
direct hit Volltreffer m; Artillerievolltreffer m (Arty).
directing gun Grundgeschütz n.
directing point Nullpunkt m (CA).
directing staff Leitungsstab m (maneuvers).
direction Seite f, Seitenrichtung f, Richtung f (Gunnery).
directional antenna Richtantenne f (Rad).
directional effect Richtwirkung f (Rad).

directional gyro Kurskreisel m.
directional loop antenna Peilrahmen m (Rad).
directional position Antennenstellung f (of antenna).
directional receiving antenna Richtempfangsantenne f (Rad).
directional stability Richtungsstabilität f, Kursstabilität f (Ap).
directional traverse Fluchtlinie f (Surv).
direction board Richtungsanzeiger m (AAA).
direction dispersion Breitenstreuung f (Ballistics).
direction finder Peilfunkempfänger m, Richtempfänger m, Peilempfänger m, Bordpeiler m, Funkpeiler m (Air Navigation).
direction-finder equipment Peilgerät n (Rad, Avn).
direction-finder signal Peilzeichen n (Avn).
direction-finder station Richtempfangsanlage f, Peilanlage f, Peilstelle f (Air Navigation); Bodenpeilstelle f (surface).
direction finding Peilen n, Peilung f (Avn); Funkpeilung f (Rad).
direction-finding equipment Richtgerät n (Rad).
direction-finding set Richtempfänger m, Peilempfänger m (Rad).
direction of air flow Anströmrichtung f, Anblasrichtung f (in a wind tunnel, Avn).
direction of approach Anflugrichtung f (Avn).
direction of attack Angriffsrichtung f.
direction of flight Flugrichtung f (Avn).
direction of the target Zielrichtung f.
directive Weisung f, Anweisung f, Verfügung f.
direct laying direktes Richten (Gunnery).
director Leitender m, oberster Schiedsrichter m (maneuvers); Kommandogerät n (Arty); Zentralrichtgerät n (AAA).
director headquarters Übungsleitung f (maneuvers).
director's aide Leitungsgehilfe m (maneuvers).

direct plate voltage Anodengleichspannung f (Rad).

direct pointing direktes Richten (Gunnery).

direct pressure Nachdrängen n (in pursuit, Tac).

direct pressure detachment Verfolgungsabteilung f (in pursuit, Tac).

direct-reading compass Nahkompaß m.

directrix Nullstrahl des Schußfeldes (Gunnery).

direct-sighting telescope Zielfernrohr n.

direct support unmittelbare Unterstützung (Arty, Tac); taktische Unterstützung (Avn, Tac).

direct vision slit Panzerscharte f (Tk).

direct vision slot Sehschlitz m (Tk).

dirigible Lenkluftschiff n.

dirt Schmutz m, Dreck m; Erde f (earth).

dirt road unbefestigte Straße, ungepflasterte Straße.

disability Kriegsbeschädigung f (war injury); Dienstunfähigkeit f (unfitness for service).

disability pension Versehrtengeld n.

disabled kriegsbeschädigt (injured in war); dienstunfähig, untauglich (unfit for service).

disadvantage Nachteil m.

disappearing armored turret Panzer-Verschwindeturm m (Ft).

disappearing carriage Verschwindlafette f (G).

disappearing target Verschwindscheibe f.

disappearing turret Verschwindeturm m (Ft).

disapproval Mißbilligung f.

disapprove mißbilligen, tadeln; verwerfen, zurückweisen (reject).

disarm entschärfen, unscharf machen (Am); entwaffnen, abrüsten.

disarmament Abrüstung f.

disassemble auseinandernehmen, zerlegen.

disband entlassen, auflösen.

disbursement Auszahlung f.

disbursing agent Zahlmeister m (Ger: civilian official).

disbursing officer Oberfeldzahlmeister m (Ger: civilian official).

discharge n Entlassung f (from service); Entladung f (Am, Elec, etc.).

discharge v entlassen, verabschieden (dismiss); abfeuern, losschießen (shoot); entladen (a gun, Elec); abladen, ausladen (supplies); löschen (ship's cargo).

discharge certificate Entlassungsschein m, Entlassungspapier n.

discharge surge Entladungsstoß m (Elec).

discharge without honor Dienstentlassung f.

disciplinary action Disziplinarverfahren n.

disciplinary barracks Militärgefängnis n, Wehrmachtgefängnis n, militärische Strafanstalt.

disciplinary exercises charakterschulendes Exerzieren.

discipline n Disziplin f, Manneszucht f; Zucht f.

disconnect ausschalten, trennen.

disconnect drop Schlußklappe f (Tp switchboard).

disconnect from binding post abklemmen (Elec).

discrepancy Fehlbestand m (in supplies, etc.); Widerspruch m (contradiction); Unregelmäßigkeit f (irregularity); Vorschriftswidrigkeit f (infraction of regulations).

discretion Ermessen n.

disease Krankheit f.

disembark ausschiffen.

disembarkation Ausschiffung f.

disengage from the enemy sich vom Feinde loslösen.

disengagement Absetzen n, Absetzbewegung f, Loslösung f (Tac).

disengage the clutch auskuppeln (MT).

dishonorable discharge Wehrunwürdigkeitserklärung f.

disinfect entseuchen (Med).

disinfectant Desinfektionsmittel n.

disinfecting agent Entseuchungsmittel n.

disinfecting chamber Desinfektionskammer f, Entseuchungsschrank m (Med).

disinfection Entseuchen n.

disinfestor Entlausungsgerät n, Entlausungsapparat m.

disintegrate auflösen, zerteilen, zerfallen, zerlegen.

disintegrating belt Zerfallgurt *m (MG)*.

disk Scheibe *f*, Lamelle *f (Mech)*; Schallplatte *f (phonograph)*.

disk spider Radkörper *m (wheel)*.

dismantle abbauen, ausbauen; abbrücken *(a bridge)*.

dismantling Abbau *m*.

dismiss abtreten lassen, wegtreten lassen.

dismissal Dienstentlassung *f*.

"**Dismissed!**" "Weggetreten!" *(to a formation)*; "Abtreten!", "Treten Sie ab!" *(formal style, to an individual)*; "Sie können gehen" *(informal, to an individual)*.

dismount absitzen; ausbauen *(Ord)*.

dismounted abgesessen, zu Fuß *(Pers)*.

dismounted defilade mannshohe Deckung.

dismounted drill Exerzieren zu Fuß.

dismounting Absitzen *n (Pers)*.

disobedience Ungehorsam *m*.

disobey nicht gehorchen, den Gehorsam verweigern *(a superior)*; verletzen, nicht befolgen, mißachten *(orders)*.

disorder Unordnung *f*, Verwirrung *f (confusion)*; Aufruhr *m (rioting)*; Störung *f (Med)*.

disorganized in Unordnung gebracht, in Verwirrung gebracht; zerrüttet *(ruined)*; aufgelöst *(disbanded, dispersed)*.

dispatch *n* Meldung *f*, Mitteilung *f*, Nachricht *f*.

dispatch *v* aussenden, entsenden, schicken.

dispatch case Meldetasche *f*.

dispensary Krankenrevier *n*.

dispensary case Revierkranker *m*.

dispersal Zerlegung *f (Tac)*.

dispersal area Abstellplatz *m (Adrm)*.

dispersal landing field Ausweichflugplatz *m*.

dispersed formation in depth Fliegermarschtiefe *f (AA security)*.

dispersed formation in width Fliegermarschbreite *f (AA security)*.

dispersion Auseinanderziehen *n (Tac)*; Streuung *f (Ballistics)*.

dispersion diagram prozentmäßiges Streuungsbild.

dispersion error Streuung *f*.

dispersion ladder prozentmäßiges Streuungsbild.

dispersion pattern Bodentreffbild *n (Ballistics)*.

dispersion zone Streuungsfläche *f (Ballistics)*.

displaced versetzt.

displacement Verschiebung *f (troops, etc.)*; Verdrängung *f*; Seitenabstand *m (Arty)*; Hubraum *m (piston)*.

displacement volume Hubvolumen *n*, Hubraum *m (Mtr)*.

display board Anschlagbrett *n*, schwarzes Brett.

disposition Aufstellung *f (Tac)*; Verfügung *f (availability)*.

disposition in depth treffenweise Aufstellung *(Tac)*.

disposition in width flügelweise Aufstellung *(Tac)*.

disposition of outposts Vorpostenaufstellung *f*.

disposition of troops Truppeneinteilung *f (Tac)*.

disrespect unehrerbietiges Verhalten.

disrupt unterbrechen, sprengen *(enemy communications, etc.)*.

dissemination of information Verbreitung von Nachrichten.

distance Abstand *m (Tac, close order drill)*; Tiefenabstand *m (Tac)*; Entfernung *f*.

distance between march units Marschabstand *m*.

distant control Fernsteuerung *f*.

distant reconnaissance Fernaufklärung *f*.

Distinguished Flying Cross Fliegerverdienstkreuz *n (USA)*.

distinguished marksman Scharfschütze *m*.

Distinguished Service Cross Kriegsverdienstkreuz *n (USA)*.

Distinguished Service Medal Verdienstmedaille *f (USA)*.

distortion Verzerrung *f (Rad)*.

distress landing Notlandung *f*.

distress signal Notsignal *n*.

distribute verteilen; ausgeben *(issue)*.

distributed fire Breitenfeuer *n (R, MG)*.

distributing point Ausgabestelle *f*, Verteilungsstelle *f*.

distribution Verteilung *f*, Gliederung *f*, Aufstellung *f*.

distribution box Verteiler *m*, Verteilerkasten *m* *(data transmission system)* *(Elec, Nav)*.

distribution box boat Hilfsfahrzeug zum Legen von Grundminen *(Nav)*.

distribution in depth Tiefengliederung *f*.

distribution in width Breitengliederung *f*.

distribution of artillery for attack Artillerieaufmarsch *m*.

distribution of forces Kräfteverteilung *f* *(Tac)*.

distribution of rations Portionenausgabe *f*.

distributor Verteiler *m*, Zündverteiler *m* *(Mtr)*.

distributor arm Verteilerlaufstück *n*, Verteilerfinger *m* *(Mtr)*.

distributor cock Brandhahn *m* *(Ap fire extinguisher)*.

distributor head Batteriezündverteilerkopf *m* *(Mtr)*.

distributor plate Verteilerscheibe *f* *(Mtr)*.

distributor rotor Verteilerlaufstück *n* *(Mtr)*.

district Bezirk *m*, Distrikt *m*.

district warning center Luftschutzwarnstelle *f* *(Civ defense)*.

disturbance Störung *f*; Aufregung *f*, Unruhe *f* *(confusion)*; Aufruhr *f* *(rioting)*.

ditch Graben *m*; Entwässerungsgraben *m* *(drainage)*; Straßengraben *m* *(road)*; Panzergraben *m* *(AT)*.

ditching Notwassern *n*, Notwasserung *f* *(Avn)*.

ditch profile Grabenprofil *n* *(Engr)*.

dive *n* Sturzflug *m* *(Avn)*.

dive *v* stürzen, einen Sturzflug machen *(Avn)*.

dive-bomb *v* sturzbomben *(Avn)*.

dive bomber Sturzkampfflugzeug *n*, Stuka *n*.

dive bomber pilot Sturzkampfflieger *m*, Stukaflieger *m*.

dive bomber wing Sturzkampfgeschwader *n* *(Avn)*.

dive bombing Sturzbomben *n*.

dive-bombing attack Sturzangriff *m*, Stukaangriff *m*.

dive-bombing sight Sturzvisier *n* *(Avn)*.

diver Schiffstaucher *m*, Taucher *m* *(Nav)*. See also **deep-sea diver**.

diverge auseinandergehen.

divergence difference Feuerverteilungswinkel *m* *(Btry firing)*.

diversion Ablenkung *f* *(of enemy forces)*; Ablenkungsangriff *m* *(feint attack)*.

diversion dam Buhne *f* *(Engr)*.

divert ablenken; ableiten *(a stream, etc)*.

dive siren Sturzsirene *f* *(dive bomber)*.

divide *v* teilen, absondern, trennen.

dividers Stechzirkel *m*.

diving angle Sturzwinkel *m* *(Avn)*.

diving apparatus Tauchgerät *n* *(Nav)*.

diving brake Stukabremse *f*, Sturzflugbremse *f* *(Ap)*.

diving qualities Sturzflugeigenschaften *fpl* *(Ap)*.

diving speed Sturzgeschwindigkeit *f* *(Ap)*.

division Division *f* *(Mil)*.

division antitank battalion Divisionspanzerabwehrabteilung *f*.

division artillery Divisionsartillerie *f*.

division artillery commander Artillerieführer *m*; Artilleriekommandeur *m* *(when GHQ artillery is attached)*.

division commander Divisionskommandeur *m*.

division command post Divisionsgefechtsstand *m*.

division engineer Pionierführer bei der Division.

division headquarters Divisionsstab *m*.

division order Divisionsbefehl *m*.

division signal battalion Divisionsnachrichtenabteilung *f*.

division supply column Divisionsnachschubkolonne *f*.

division surgeon Divisionsarzt *m*, Divisionschefarzt *m*.

division surgical hospital Divisionsfeldlazarett *n*.

division trains Troß der Division.

division trunk line Divisionsstammleitung *f*.

DM Adamsit *m* *(CWS)*.

DM irritant gas candle Giftnebelkerze DM *f* *(USA)*.

dock *n* Dock *n*.

dock installations Dockanlagen *fpl*.

dockyard Werft *f.*
doctor Arzt *m.*
document Akt *m,* Akte *f (plural:*
Akten); Urkunde *f (permanent record).*
documentary data schriftliche Unterlagen.
documentary evidence Urkundenbeweis *m;* urkundliches Beweistück
(document).
dog Hund *m;* Mitnehmer *m (lathe);*
Klaue *f (clutch);* Sanitätshund *m*
(first-aid).
dog clutch Klauenkupplung *f (MT).*
dog clutch member Schaltklaue *f*
(constant-mesh transmission, MT).
dogfight Kurvenkampf *m (Avn).*
dog handler Hundeführer *m.*
dog-handler party Hundeführerrotte
f (for messenger dogs).
"dog tag" Erkennungsmarke *f.*
dome light Deckenlicht *n (MT).*
door Tür *f;* Luke *f (Ap, Tk).*
dope Klebelack *m,* Spannlack *m (for
Ap fabric);* Betriebsstoffzusatzmittel
n (for Avn gasoline).
dose Portion *f (Med).*
dot Punkt *m (Tg).*
dots and dashes Punkte und Striche.
double action revolver Revolver mit
Wiederspannabzug.
double anchor hitch doppelter Ankerstich *(cow hitch, Engr).*
double-apron entanglement Drahtzaun *m,* Stacheldrahtzaun *m,* Flandernzaun *m (Ft).*
double banking Benutzung beider
Fahrbahnen in gleicher Richtung.
double-barreled machine gun Zwillingsmaschinengewehr *n.*
double base powder nitroglyzerinhaltiges Nitrozellulosepulver *(Am).*
double-bay biplane Zweistieler *m.*
double envelopment Doppelumfassung *f,* Zangengriff *m (Tac).*
double file Doppelreihe *f.*
double rank Linie zu 2 Gliedern.
double-ring snaffle bit Doppelringtrensengebiß *n (harness).*
double-row radial engine Doppelsternmotor *m,* Zweisternmotor *m.*
double sentry Doppelposten *m.*
double slide Doppelschieber *m*
(plotting protractor).
double tent Doppelzelt *n.*
double time Laufschritt *m,* Sturmschritt *m (march).*

"Double time, march!" "Im Laufschritt, Marsch! Marsch!"
double-tracked zweigleisig *(RR).*
doubletree Ortscheit *n (limber).*
double V-type engine Fächermotor *m.*
doubtful fraglich *(Arty Obsn).*
dough Teig *m.*
doughboy Landser *m.*
down *v* zum Absturz bringen,
herunterholen, abschießen *(an Ap).*
downdraft Fallbö *f (Met).*
downdraft carburetor Fallstromvergaser *m (Mtr).*
downhill abwärts, bergab.
downstream unterstrom *(place);*
stromabwärts *(action).*
downstream anchor Windanker *m*
(Pon Bdg).
downstream anchor cable Windankertau *n,* Windankerleine *f (Pon
Bdg).*
downwind *adv* leewärts, windabwärts.
draft Aushebung *f (conscription);*
Pferdezug *m,* Zugkraft *f (horse);*
Tiefgang *m (Nav).*
draftee Ausgehobener *m.*
draft efficiency Zugleistung *f*
(horse).
drafting equipment Zeichengerät *n;*
Reißzeug *n (set).*
draftsman Konstruktionszeichner *m.*
drag Widerstand *m,* Luftwiderstand
m (Avn).
"dragon's teeth" Höckerhindernisse
npl (AT obstacle).
drag washer Zugöse *f (wheel).*
drain *n* Ölablaß *m (Mtr).*
drain *v* abwässern *(water).*
drainage Abwässern *n (Ft).*
drainage ditch Entwässerungsgraben *m.*
drainage pit Sickerschacht *m (Ft).*
drain plug Leerschraube *f.*
drape *n* Tarnnetz *n (Cam).*
draw *v* ziehen *(pull);* zeichnen
(sketch).
drawbar Zugstange *f (MT);* Protzarm *m (limber).*
drawing board Reißbrett *n,* Zeichenbrett *n.*
drawbridge Klappbrücke *f.*
drawing instrument Zeichengerät *n;*
Reißzeug *n (a set).*
drawing paper Zeichenpapier *n.*
drawknife Schalmesser *n.*
dredge *n* Bagger *m (Engr).*

dress *v* ausrichten *(close order drill)*; Toppflaggen setzen *(Nav)*; verbinden *(a wound)*; sich anziehen *(put on Clo)*.

dressing Verband *m (Med)*.

dressing bag Verbandtasche *f (Med)*.

dressing equipment Verbandmittel *npl (Med)*.

dressing station Verbandplatz *m*, Truppenverbandplatz *m (Med)*.

"Dress left, dress!" "Nach links, Richt Euch!"

dress parade Ehrenparade *f*.

"Dress right, dress!" "Richt Euch!"

dress uniform Ausgehanzug *m*; Paradeanzug *m (for ceremonies)*; Gesellschaftsanzug *m (for social occasions)*.

drift *n* Durchschlag *m (pin)*; Versetzung *f*, Abdrift *f (Avn, Nav)*; Drallabweichung *f*, Seitenabweichung *f (Ballistics)*.

drift angle Luvwinkel *m*, Abtriftwinkel *m (Avn)*.

drift correction Seitenverschiebung *f (Gunnery)*.

drift meter Abdriftvisier *n*, Abdriftmesser *m (Ap)*.

drift sand Triebsand *m*.

driftwood Treibholz *n*.

drill *n* Exerzieren *n*, Ausbildung *f*; Bohrer *m (Mech)*.

drill *v* exerzieren *(practice)*; bohren *(Mech)*.

drill ammunition Exerziermunition *f*.

drill bomb Exerzierbombe *f*.

drill formation Exerzierordnung *f*, Exerzierform *f*.

drill ground Exerzierplatz *m*.

drill regulations Exerzierordnung *f*, Exerziervorschrift *f*.

drinking cup Trinkbecher *m*.

drinking water Trinkwasser *n*.

drive *n* Antrieb *m (Mech)*.

drive *v* fahren *(a vehicle)*; einschlagen *(a nail)*.

drive gear Antriebszahnrad *n (gearshift transmission, MT)*.

driver Fahrer *m*, Kraftfahrer *m (MT)*; Fahrer *m (Tk)*.

driver's cab Fahrerhaus *n (Trk)*.

driver's permit Führerschein *m*, Wehrmachtführerschein *m (MT)*.

drive shaft Antriebswelle *f*.

drive wheel Antriebsrad *n (MT)*.

driving axle Treibachse *f*, Antriebsachse *f (MT)*.

driving chain Zahnkette *f (MT)*.

driving range Fahrbereich *m (MT)*.

driving sprocket Triebrad *n (Tk)*.

drizzle *n* Nieseln *n*, Sprühregen *m (Met)*.

droop *n* Wölbung *f*, Durchhängen *n*, Verbiegen *n (Mech)*.

drop *n* Klappe *f*, Fallklappe *f*, Weckerfallklappe *f (Tp)*; Fall *m (action)*; Fallhöhe *f (distance)*; Tropfen *m (of water, etc.)*.

drop *v* absacken *(Avn)*; fallen lassen *(an object)*; fallen, abnehmen *(temperature, etc.)*.

drop-base rim Tiefbettfelge *f (MT)*.

drop-block type breechblock Fallblockverschluß *m (G)*.

drop cover Klappblende *f (Ft)*.

drophammer Rammbär *m (of piledriver)*; Fallhammer *m (Tech)*.

droplet Tröpfchen *n (CWS, Met)*.

drop message Abwurfmeldung *f*.

drop-message bag Meldeabwurfhülle *f*.

dropping angle Bombenabwurfwinkel *m (bombing)*.

dropping ground Meldeabwurfstelle *f*.

drop point Abwurfstelle *f (airborne supply)*.

drop tank Abwurfbehälter *m (Ap)*.

drop-type switchboard Klappenschrank *m*.

drug *n* Arznei *f*, Droge *f*; Rauschgift *n (narcotic)*.

drum *n* Trommel *f (Am, music, etc.)*; Ölfaß *n (container)*.

drum feed Trommelmagazinzuführung *f (MG)*.

drum fire Trommelfeuer *n*.

drum index Trommelzeiger *m (sight mount, panoramic sight)*.

drum magazine Trommelmagazin *n (MG)*.

drum major Bataillonshornist *m*, Tambourmajor *m*.

drummer Trommler *m*.

drum-type smoke container Nebeltrommel *f (CWS)*.

drunk betrunken; besoffen *(slang)*.

dry-bulb thermometer trockenes Thermometer *(Met)*.

dry cell Trockenelement *n (Elec)*.

dry cell rectifier Trockengleichrichter *(Rad)*.
dry dock Trockendock *n.*
dry-sump lubrication Trockensumpfschmierung *f (Mtr)*.
dual controls Doppelsteuerung *f.*
dual-purpose gun Einheitsgeschütz *n.*
dual tires Doppelbereifung *f (MT)*.
dubbin Lederfett *n.*
duckboard Lattenrost *m,* Holzrost *m;* Bretterbahn *f (trench);* Spurtafel *f (Bdg)*.
dud Blindgänger *m,* Bodenkrepierer *m (Arty)*.
duffle bag Bekleidungssack *m.*
dugout Unterschlupf *m (Ft)*.
dumdum bullet Dumdum-Geschoß *n.*
dummy Puppe *f,* Zielpuppe *f,* Strohpuppe *f (bayonet Tng);* Attrappe *f (of a Tk, vehicle, etc.)*.
dummy airfield Scheinplatz *m.*
dummy airport Scheinflughafen *m.*
dummy ammunition Exerziermunition *f (drill);* Verpackungsgeschosse *npl (for vehicle-loading practice)*.
dummy cartridge Exerzierpatrone *f (MG, R)*.
dummy installation Scheinanlage *f (Cam, Ft)*.
dummy mine Scheinmine *f.*
dummy obstacle Scheinsperre *f (Ft)*.
dummy position Scheinanlage *f,* Scheinstellung *f.*
dummy projectile Exerziergeschoß *n.*
dummy site Scheinstellung *f.*
dummy trench Scheingraben *m (Ft)*.
dummy works Scheinanlagen *fpl.*
dump *n* Lager *n,* Sammelstelle *f.*
dump *v* Ballast abwerfen *(Avn)*.

dump car Kipplore *f (field RR)*.
dumping mechanism Kippvorrichtung *f (dump Trk)*.
dump truck Kippwagen *m.*
dunnage Unterlegbohlen *fpl.*
dunnite Dunnit *n (Am)*.
duplex operation Gegensprechen *n (Rad)*.
duplicate *n* Duplikat *n,* Kopie *f.*
duplicate *v* eine Kopie machen, vervielfältigen.
duplicate *adj* zweit-, zweifach-, doppelt.
in duplicate in zweifacher Ausführung.
duralumin Duralumin *n (Ap)*.
duration Dauer *f.*
dust Staub *m.*
dust filtering Entstaubung *f (MT)*.
dust particle Stäubchen *n (CWS)*.
dust respirator Staubschutzmaske *f.*
duty Dienst *m (service);* Pflicht *f (obligation);* Steuer *f (tax)*.
on duty im Dienst, diensttuend.
duty officer Offizier vom Dienst.
duty roster Diensteinteilung *f,* Dienstplan *m,* Kommandierrolle *f.*
duty station Dienststelle *f,* Posten, *m.*
duty with troops Truppendienst *m,* Dienst bei der Truppe.
dynamic speaker elektrodynamischer Lautsprecher *(Rad)*.
dynamite Dynamit *n.*
dynamo Dynamomaschine *f,* Stromerzeuger *m.*
dynamotor Einankerumformer *m (Elec, Rad)*.
dysentery Ruhr *f,* Dysenterie *f.*

E

eagle Adler *m.*
ear Ohr *n;* Öse *f (Mech)*.
ear cup Hörmuschel *f (sound locator)*.
eardrum Trommelfell *n.*
earpiece Hörmuschel *f (Rad, Tp)*.
ear-plug Ohrenverschlußwatte *f,* Ohrenwatte *f (cotton)*.
earth Erde *f.*
earth-bleach mixture Chlorkalk-Sand-Gemisch *n (CWS)*.

earth inductor compass Erdinduktionskompaß *m.*
earthwork Erdwerk *n,* Schanze *f (Ft)*.
east Osten *m,* Ost *m.*
easterlies Ostwinde *mpl (Met)*.
Eastern European time osteuropäische Zeit (30° E standard meridian).
E-boat Schnellboot *n,* Motorschnellboot *n,* Motortorpedoboot *n (Ger)*.

ebonite Hartgummi *m-n.*
eccentric sleeve Exzenterhülse *f (aiming circle).*
echelon Staffel *f (Tac).*
echelonment Staffelung *f.*
echo depth sounder Behmlot *n,* Echolot *n (Nav).*
economic warfare Wirtschaftskrieg *m.*
economy of force Kraftersparnis *f,* Kräftebemessung *f.*
economy of manpower Kräfteersparnis *f.*
E. C. powder Nitrozellulosepulver *n.*
ecrasite Ekrasit *n (explosive).*
E.C. smokeless powder *See* E.C. powder.
ED Äthyldichlorarsin *n,* Äthylarsindichlorid *n (CWS).*
edge Schneide *f (of a bayonet, etc.);* Kante *f,* Rand *m (Mech, Top).*
edge of land Führungskante *f (G barrel).*
edge of slope Böschungskante *f (Top).*
edge of woods Waldrand *m.*
edible eßbar.
Edison storage battery Edisonsammler *m.*
eduction tube Auslaßrohr *n (Cml cylinder).*
effective wirksam, tatsächlich.
effective beaten zone bestrichener Raum der Kerngarbe *(MG).*
effective fire Wirkungsfeuer *n,* Wirkungsschießen *n (Gunnery).*
effective output Nutzleistung *f (Mech).*
effective part of cone Kerngarbe *f (Ballistics);* MG.-Kerngarbe *f (MG fire).*
effective pattern *See* effective beaten zone.
effective pitch Fortschritt *m,* Fortschrittsteigung *f,* wirksame Steigung *(propeller).*
effective range wirksame Schußweite, Wirkungsbereich *m (Ord).*
effective resistance Nutzwiderstand *m (Elec).*
effective strength Iststärke *f,* Iststand *m.*
effective wind Durchschnittswind *m (Ballistics).*
effect of fire Feuerwirkung, *f,* Schußwirkung *f (Arty).*
effect of projectile Geschoßwirkung *f.*

effect of ricochet burst Splitterwirkung des Abprallers.
effect of shell burst Splitterwirkung der Granate.
efficiency Wirkungsgrad *m (Tech);* Leistungsfähigkeit *f (of performance);* Wirtschaftlichkeit *f (economy).*
egg Ei *n (plural:* Eier).
eight-man tent Achterzelt *n.*
eight-speed transmission Achtganggetriebe *n (MT).*
eighty-five percent zone bestrichener Raum der Kerngarbe *(MG).*
ejector Auswerfer *m (Ord).*
ejector mechanism Auswerfervorrichtung *f (Ord).*
elastic *n* Gummiband *n.*
elastic *adj* spannkräftig, federnd, elastisch.
elasticity Spannkraft *f,* Federkraft *f,* Elastizität *f.*
elasticity correction Ausschalten der Temperatureinflüsse *(Gunnery).*
elasticity effect Temperatureinflüsse *mpl (Ballistics).*
elbow Ellbogen *m.*
elbow pipe Krümmer *m.*
elbow rest Armauflage *f (trench).*
elbow telescope Winkelfernrohr *n.*
electric elektrisch.
electrical detonation elektrische Zündung *(Engr).*
electrical engineer Elektrotechniker *m.*
electrically-charged obstacle Starkstromsperre *f,* elektrisches Hindernis *(Ft).*
electric circuit Stromkreis *m.*
electric detonator Glühzündstück *n.*
electrician Elektromechaniker *m.*
electrician's knife Kabelmesser *n.*
electric igniter Glühzünder *m (blasting cap);* Glühzündstück *n (Engr).*
electric meter Elektrizitätszähler *m.*
electric motor Elektromotor *m.*
electric primer elektrische Zündschraube *(G).*
electric wiring Leitungsmaterial *n (equipment);* Leitungsnetz *n (installed).*
electrified obstacle Starkstromsperre *f.*
electrode Elektrode *f (in a spark plug, the grounded electrode; the insulated electrode is called* Zündstift).

electromagnet Elektromagnet *m.*
electromagnetism Elektromagnetismus *m.*
electron Elektron *n.*
electron bomb Elektronbrandbombe *f.*
electron-ray tube magisches Auge *(Rad).*
electrostatic induction Influenz *f (Elec).*
element Element *n (Elec);* Einheit *f,* Truppenteil *n (Tac).*
elementary marksmanship training Schießvorschule *f.*
elephant halbtonnenförmiges Wellblech *(Ft, USA).*
elephant steel shelter Wellblech-Hütte *f (USA).*
elevate nach der Höhe richten, heben *(G).*
elevating and traversing mechanism Richtmaschine *f (G).*
elevating arc Zahnbogen *m (G).*
elevating arm Richthebel *m (MG).*
elevating-arm shaft Richthebelwelle *f (MG).*
elevating-gear housing Richtgehäuse *n (MG).*
elevating-gear lever Höhenhebel *m (MG).*
elevating handwheel Handrad zur Höhenrichtung, Höhenrichtrad *n (G).*
elevating knob Triebscheibe zur Höhenrichtung *(Optics, Ord).*
elevating link Richtgelenk *n (MG).*
elevating mechanism Höhenrichttrieb *m,* Höhenrichtwerk *n,* Höhenrichtmaschine *f (G, MG);* Schraubenspindelrichtmaschine *f (elevating-screw type) (G).*
elevating rack Zahnbogen *m (G).*
elevating sector Höhengradbogen *m (G).*
elevating shaft Höhenrichtwelle *f (G).*
elevating stop Höhenbegrenzer *m (MG).*
elevating worm Kippschnecke *f (aiming circle, BC telescope);* Höhentrieb *m (sighting mechanism).*
elevation Erhöhung *f (Ballistics, G, MG);* Rohrerhöhung *f (G);* Höhe *f,* Richthöhe *f (Gunnery);* Höhe *f,* Bodenerhebung *f (Top);* Höhenrichtfeld *n (total movement in elevation) (G).*

elevation above sea level Höhe über dem Meeresspiegel.
elevation angle Visierwinkel *m,* Aufsatzwinkel *m,* Erhöhungswinkel *m.*
elevation circle Teilkreis des Höhenrichttriebs *(G).*
elevation controller Höhenrichtmann *m (AAA).*
elevation difference Höhenunterschied *m.*
elevation graduations Aufsatzeinteilung *f (sight mount).*
elevation indicator Höhenempfänger *m (AA gun).*
elevation level Höhenlibelle *f (MG sight).*
elevation mechanism Höhenrichttrieb *m,* Höhenrichtwerk *n (G, MG);* Aufsatztrieb *m (G).*
elevation micrometer Teilscheibe *f (panoramic telescope).*
elevation plotting board Höhenmeßplan *m (Gunnery).*
elevation quadrant Winkelmesser *m,* Libellenquadrant *m.*
elevation scale Erhöhungsskala *f,* Höhenteilung *f (G, MG).*
elevation screw Höhenrichtschraube *f (prismatic sight).*
elevation setter Höhenrichtkanonier *m.*
elevation setting Erhöhungseinstellung *f (Gunnery).*
elevation table Schußtafel zum Bestimmen der Erhöhung.
elevation tracking telescope Höhenrichtfernrohr *n (height finder).*
elevator Höhenruder *n,* Höhensteuer *n (Ap);* Aufzug *m (for personnel and freight);* Fahrstuhl *m (for personnel only).*
elevator assembly Höhenleitwerk *n (Ap).*
elevator control Höhensteuerung *f (Ap).*
elevator control lever Steuerhebel *m,* Höhenruderhebel *m (Ap).*
eliminate ausschalten *(errors, etc.);* ausscheiden *(impurities);* ausmerzen *(eradicate);* ausstoßen *(expel);* streichen *(cross out);* eliminieren *(Math).*
elite troops Kerntruppen *fpl.*
embankment Bahndamm *m (RR);* Dammkörper *m (dam).*
embargo Embargo *n,* Handelssperre

f (on commerce); Transportsperre
f, Transportverbot *n (on truck, RR
and ship movements).*
embark einschiffen *(Pers);* verladen *(equipment, etc.).*
embarkation Einschiffen *n*, Einschiffung *f (Pers);* Verladung *f
(equipment, etc.).*
embassy Botschaft *f.*
emblem Wahrzeichen *n,* Sinnbild *n,*
Emblem *n;* Abzeichen *n (insigne).*
embrasure Schießscharte *f (Ft).*
emergency Not *f,* Notfall *m,* Ernstfall *m.*
emergency antenna Behelfsantenne *f.*
emergency blasting charge Schnell-
ladung *f (Engr).*
emergency brake Notbremse *f,*
Handbremse *f.*
emergency bridge Behelfsbrücke *f.*
emergency call Notruf *m (Tp).*
emergency ceiling Gipfelhöhe mit
einem stehenden Motor *(Ap).*
emergency construction material Behelfsmaterial *n (Engr).*
emergency flotation gear Schwimmwerk für Landflugzeuge *(Avn).*
emergency gas protection Behelfsgasschutz *m.*
emergency illumination Notbeleuchtung *f.*
emergency landing Notlandung *f
(on land),* Notwasserung *f (on
water).*
make an emergency landing notlanden.
emergency landing field Notlandehafen *m,* Notlandungsplatz *m,* Notlandeplatz *m.*
emergency landing flare Notlande-
fackel *f (Avn).*
emergency line Notleitung *f (Tp).*
emergency medical tag Begleitzettel
m.
emergency pneumatic boat Behelfsfloßsack *m.*
emergency ration eiserne Portion.
emergency release Blindabwurf *m
(bombing).*
emergency release handle Notzug
m (Ap).
emergency salvo release Notwurf *m,*
Notabwurf *m (bombing).*
emery cloth Schmirgelleinwand *f.*
emery paper Schmirgelpapier *n.*
emery wheel Schmirgelscheibe *f,*
Schmirgelrad *n.*

emigrant Emigrant *m,* Auswanderer
m.
empennage Leitwerk *n (Ap).*
empire Reich *n;* Kaiserreich *n
(country ruled by an emperor).*
emplace in Feuerstellung bringen.
emplacement Stellung *f (Tac);* Nest
n (Ft); Feuerstellung *f (Mort, AT
gun, etc.).*
emplacing Instellungbringen *n
(Arty).*
employment Einsatz *m,* Verwendung
f (Tac).
employment of armored units Pan-
zerverwendung *f.*
employment of chemical agents
Kampfstoffverwendung *f.*
employment of major forces Masseneinsatz *m (Tac).*
employment of prisoners of war
Kriegsgefangeneneinsatz *m.*
employment reconnaissance Einsatz-
Aufklärung *f.*
empower ermächtigen, bevollmächtigen.
empties Leergut *n (Am);* Leermaterial *n (RR).*
empty weight Leergewicht *n.*
encampment Feldlager *n.*
encipher chiffrieren, verschlüsseln,
ziffern.
encipherment Verschlüsselung *f,*
Chiffrierung *f.*
encircle einkesseln *(Tac).*
encircled area Kessel *m (Tac).*
encirclement Einkreisung *f,* Einkesselung *f,* Umklammerung *f
(Tac).*
encircling maneuver Einkreisungsmanöver *n;* überholende Verfolgung
(in pursuit).
enclosure Einzäunung *f,* Umzäunung *f.*
encode schlüsseln. verschlüsseln.
encoding Schlüsseln *n (Rad, Tg).*
encoding and decoding chart Schlüsselunterlage *f.*
encoding section Schlüsseltrupp *m.*
encounter *n* Treffen *n,* Begegnung *f,*
Zusammenstoß *m.*
encrypt *See* **encipher.**
endanger gefährden, in Gefahr
bringen.
end cap Mantelkopf *m (MG jacket).*
end dam Stoßbohle *f (Bdg).*
end plate Endscheibe *f (Ap wing).*
end ramp Kopframpe *f (RR).*

end station Meßstand *m (Gunnery)*.
endurance Flugdauer *f*, Flugzeit *f (Avn)*; Ausdauer *f (Pers)*.
enemy Feind *m*.
enemy action Feindeinwirkung *f (Tac)*.
enemy activity Feindtätigkeit *f*.
enemy alien feindlicher Ausländer.
enemy fire Feindfeuer *n*, Feindbeschuß *m*.
enemy forces Feindkräfte *fpl*, Feindstreitkräfte *fpl*.
enemy movement Feindbewegung *f*.
enemy observation Feindsicht *f*, Feindeinsicht *f*.
enemy pressure Feinddruck *m*.
enemy resistance Feindwiderstand *m*.
enemy terrain Feindgelände *n*.
enemy territory Feindesland *n*.
enemy zone Feindraum *m*.
energy Energie *f*, Kraft *f*.
Enfield rifle Enfield-Gewehr *n*.
enfilade *v* der Länge nach beschießen.
enfilade fire Seitenfeuer *n*, flankierendes Feuer, bestreichendes Feuer, Längsbestreichung *f*, Längsfeuer *n*.
engage in ein Gefecht verwickeln *(Tac)*; einkuppeln *(the clutch) (MT)*.
engagement Gefecht *n*, Gefechtshandlung *f*, Kampfhandlung *f (Tac)*.
engaging of successive targets Zielwechsel *m*.
engine Motor *m*, Maschine *f (MT)*; Lokomotive *f (RR)*.
engine brake Motorbremse *f (MT)*.
engine compartment Motorenraum *m (Tk)*.
engine cowling Motorhaube *f*, Motorverkleidung *f*, Haubenverkleidung *f (Ap)*.
engineer Pionier *m (Army)*; Ingenieur *m (Nav) (also civilian official in Ger Army)*.
Engineer Amphibian Command Pionier-Landungstruppen *fpl (USA)*.
engineer assault platoon Pioniersturmzug *m*.
engineer combat equipment Pionier-Kampfmittel *npl*.
engineer commander Pionierführer *m*.
Engineer Corps Pionierkorps *n*, Pioniertruppe *f*.
engineer depot Pionierpark *m*.

engineer dump Pionierzwischenpark *m*.
engineer equipment Pioniergerät *n*.
engineer explosives Pioniersprengmittel *npl*.
engineer headquarters Pionierstab *m*.
engineer officer Pionieroffizier *m*.
engineer reconnaissance Pionieraufklärung *f*.
Engineer School Pionierschule *f*.
engineer soldier Pionier *m*.
engineer's scale Reduktionsmaßstab *m*.
engineer tool Pionierwerkzeug *n*.
engineer troops Pioniere *mpl*, Pioniertruppen *fpl*.
engineer vehicle Pionierfahrzeug *n*.
engine failure Motorpanne *f*.
engine house Lokomotivschuppen *m (RR)*.
engine preheater Vorwärmer *m*.
engine repair Motoren-Instandsetzung *f*.
engine rpm Motordrehzahl *f*.
engine torque Motordrehmoment *n*.
engine trouble Motorstörung *f*.
engine yard Lokomotivbahnhof *m (RR)*.
enlarge vergrößern.
enlargement Vergrößerung *f*.
enlarging projector Vergrößerungsapparat *m*.
enlist sich freiwillig melden.
enlisted cadre Rahmenheer *n*, Stammtruppen *fpl*.
enlisted man Soldat *m*, Mann *m*; Fliegersoldat *m (Luftwaffe)*.
enlisted men *See* **enlisted personnel.**
enlisted personnel Unteroffiziere und Mannschaften.
enlisted specialists Unteroffiziere und Mannschaften der Sonderlaufbahnen.
enlistment Eintreten als Freiwilliger.
enroll sich freiwillig melden.
en route unterwegs.
ensign Leutnant zur See *(Nav)*; Kriegsflagge *f (flag)*.
entanglement Verhau *m*, Drahtverhau *m*.
entertainment Unterhaltung *f*.
entrain verladen *(RR)*.
entraining officer Verladeoffizier *m (RR)*.
entraining of troops Truppeneinladung *f*.

entraining point Verladeplatz *m* (*RR*).
entraining table Fahrtliste *f*, Verladeplan *m* (*RR*).
entrance Eingang *m*, Eintritt *m*, Zutritt *m*.
entrance hatch Einsteigluke *f* (*Tk*).
entrench schanzen, einschanzen, sich eingraben.
entrenching tools Schanzzeug *n*.
entrenchment Nest *n*, Verschanzung *f* (*Ft*).
entruck verladen (*MT*).
entrucking point Verladeplatz *m* (*MT*).
entrucking table Verladeplan *m* (*MT*).
envelop umfassen (*Tac*).
envelope Ballonhülle *f* (*Bln*); Glasgefäß *n* (*Rad tube*); Umschlag *m* (*for a letter*).
enveloping attack umfassender Angriff.
envelopment Umfassung *f*, Umklammerung *f* (*Tac*).
epaulet Epaulette *f*.
epi Gleiskurve *f*, Klaue *f* (*for RR gun*).
epidemic *n* Seuche *f*, Epidemie *f*.
episcope Episkop *n*.
equal area projection flächentreue Projektion (*mapping*).
equal section charge aus zwei gleichen Teilladungen bestehende Treibladung (*Am*).
equation Gleichung *f* (*Math*).
equator Äquator *m*.
equilibrator Ausgleicher *m* (*G*).
equilibrator anchor Ausgleicherarm *m* (*G*).
equip ausstatten.
equipage Ausrüstungsstücke *npl*.
equipment Gerät *n*, Ausrüstung *f*.
equipment car Gerätewagen *m*.
equipment on hand Istbestand *m*.
equipment truck Gerätekraftwagen *m*.
equipment wagon Gerätewagen *m*.
equivalent circuit Ersatzschaltschema *n* (*Elec*).
eraser Radiergummi *m*.
erect *v* errichten, bauen.
erect *adj* aufrecht.
erect truss Hängewerk *n* (*Bdg*).
erosion Abnutzung *f*, Ausbrennung *f* (*Ord*).

erosion of the bore Rohrabnutzung *f*, Ausbrennung *f* (*Ord*).
error Fehler *m*.
escape *n* Entweichen *n* (*Tac*); Flucht *f*.
escape *v* entlaufen, entweichen.
escape hatch Bodenluke *f* (*Ap, Tk*); Falltür *f* (*Ap*).
escarpment Böschung *f*.
escort *n* Geleit *n*, Geleitmannschaft *f*, Bedeckung *f*, Bedeckungsmannschaft *f*; Begleitschutz *m* (*Avn*).
escort airplane Sicherungsflugzeug *n*.
escort of honor Ehrengeleit *n*.
escort party Begleitkommando *n*.
escort vessel Begleitschiff *n*, Geleitschiff *n*.
escutcheon Abzeichen *f*, Hoheitsabzeichen *n*.
espionage Spionage *f*, Ausspähung *f*.
esprit de corps Korpsgeist *m*.
essential items wehrwichtige Güter.
establishment Heereseinrichtung *f*, Heeresanstalt *f* (*organization or institution*).
establishment of communication Verbindungsaufnahme *f*.
establishment of contact Fühlungnahme *f* (*Tac*).
establishment of liaison Verbindungsaufnahme *f*.
estimate *n* Schätzung *f*, Beurteilung *f*.
estimate *v* schätzen, beurteilen.
estimate of terrain Geländebeurteilung *f*.
estimate of the situation Beurteilung der Lage, Lagebeurteilung *f* (*Tac*).
estimation Schätzung *f* (*Gunnery*).
ether Äther *m*.
ethyldichlorarsine Äthydichlorarsin *n*, Äthylarsindichlorid *n* (*CWS*).
ethyliodoacetate Jodessigester *m* (*CWS*).
evacuate abbefördern (*PW, wounded, etc.*); abtransportieren, abschieben (*supplies, equipment, etc.*).
evacuating officer Abschuboffizier *m*.
evacuation Abschub *m*, Abtransport *m*, Abbeförderung *f*.
evacuation hospital Kriegslazarett *n*.
evacuation hospital battalion Kriegslazarettabteilung *f*.
evacuation of prisoners Gefangenenabschub *m*.

evacuation of the sick Krankenabtransport *m*.

evacuation of wounded Abschub von Verwundeten, Verwundetenabschub *m*, Verwundetenabtransport *m*.

evacue(e) Evakuierter *m*, Abgeschobener *m*.

evade ausweichen.

evading movement Ausweichbewegung *f*.

evaluation Auswertung *f*, Beurteilung *f*.

evaluation of information Nachrichtenbeurteilung *f*.

evaluation of terrain Geländebeurteilung *f*.

evidence Beweismaterial *n* (*Law*).

evolution Formveränderung *f* (*Tac*).

examine prüfen, untersuchen; vernehmen, verhören, ausfragen (*question*).

excavator Baggerwerk *n*, Bagger *m* (*Engr*).

excess stock Mehrbestand *m*.

exchange *n* Austausch *m*, Tausch *m*; Amt *n*, Telephonamt *n* (*Tp*); Wechsel *m* (*currency*); Wechselkurs *m* (*rate*); Marketenderei *f* (*PX*).

exchange of prisoners Gefangenenaustausch *m*.

exchange ship Austauschschiff *n*.

excitation current Erregerstrom *m* (*Elec*).

excitation winding Erregerwicklung *f* (*Elec*).

excite erregen (*Elec*).

exciter Erreger *m* (*Rad*).

excrement Kot *m*, Stuhl *m*.

excused from duty vom Dienst entschuldigt.

execute durchführen, ausführen, vollstrecken (*carry out*); hinrichten (*put to death*).

execution Durchführung *f*, Ausführung *f* (*carrying out*); Hinrichtung *f* (*putting to death*).

executive Batterieoffizier *m* (*firing Btry*).

executive officer Adjutant *m*.

executive order Notverordnung *f*.

exempt *adj* befreit, verschont, frei; zurückgestellt (*deferred*).

exercise *n* Übung *f* (*drill*, *Tng maneuver*); Leibesübung *f* (*physical*).

exhaust *n* Auspuff *m* (*Mtr*).

exhaust *v* erschöpfen (*tire out*, *use up*); aufbrauchen (*use up*).

exhaust duct Auspuffleitung *f*, Auspuffkanal *m* (*Mtr*).

exhaust gases Abgase *npl*.

exhaust manifold Auspuffkrümmer *m*.

exhaust port Auslaßventilkammer *f*.

exhaust stroke Auspuffhub *m*, Auspufftakt *m*.

exhaust turbine Abgasturbine *f* (*Ap*).

exhaust valve Auslaßventil *n*.

exile *n* Verbannung *f*, Exil *n*; Verbannte(r) *m* (*person*).

exile *v* verbannen.

exonerate freisprechen, entlasten.

expedient Behelf *m*, Aushilfe *f* (*aid*); List *f* (*clever act*).

expeditionary force Expeditionsarmee *f*.

expendable verbrauchbar, verzehrbar.

expendable supplies Mittel *npl*, Verbrauchsstoffe *mpl*, Verbrauchsgüter *npl*.

expenditure of ammunition Munitionsverbrauch *m*.

experiment *n* Versuch *m*, Experiment *n*.

experiment *v* Versuche anstellen, experimentieren.

experimental airplane Versuchsflugzeug *n*.

expert *n* Fachmann *m*, Sachverständiger *m*.

expert *adj* ausgezeichnet (*excellent*); qualifiziert (*qualified*).

expiration Ablauf *m*, Beendigung *f* (*termination*); Verfall *m* (*lapse*).

explode bersten, krepieren, explodieren.

exploder Glühzündapparat *m* (*Engr*).

exploit *n* Heldentat *f*.

exploit *v* ausnutzen (*Tac*).

exploitation Ausnutzung *f* (*Tac*).

explosion Explosion *f*.

explosive Sprengstoff *m* (*generic term*); Sprengmittel *n* (*in prepared form*).

explosive block ' Sprengkörper *m*; Sprengbüchse *f* (*in container*).

explosive bomb Sprengbombe *f*.

explosive bullet Sprenggeschoß *n* (*projectile*); Sprengpatrone *f* (*cartridge*).

explosive charge Sprengladung *f* (*Engr.*)

explosive D Ammoniumpikrat *n*.

explosive filler Sprengstoffüllung *f (Am)*.

explosive force Sprengkraft *f (Am)*.

explosive rivet Sprengniete *f*.

explosive train Zündsatz *m*.

exposed offen, ungeschützt, unangelehnt *(Tac)*.

exposed flank unangelehnte Flanke, ungeschützte Flanke.

exposed position offene Stellung *(Tac)*.

exposed wing offener Flügel *(Tac)*.

exposure Aussetzung *f (to danger, cold, disease)*; Belichtung *f (Photo)*; Enthüllung *f (revelation)*.

exposure time Belichtungszeit *f (Photo)*.

express highway Autobahn *f*.

extend auseinanderziehen *(Tac)*; ausfahren *(Ap landing gear)*.

extendable mount Klapplafette *f (Ap MG)*.

extended formation geöffnete Flugordnung *(Avn)*.

extended order geöffnete Ordnung *(Tac)*; geöffnete Linie *(in width)*.

extension arm Klapparm *m (AA sight)*.

extension in depth Tiefenausdehnung *f (Tac)*.

extension in width Breitenausdehnung *f (Tac)*.

extensive smoke screen Großvernebelung *f*.

exterior balk Ortbalken *m (floating Bdg)*.

exterior ballistic factors Witterungseinflüsse *mpl*.

exterior ballistics äußere Ballistik, äußere Schießlehre.

exterior guard Außenwache *f*.

exterior stringer Ortbalken *m (fixed Bdg)*.

exterminate ausrotten, vertilgen, vernichten.

external contracting brake Außenbackenbremse *f (MT)*.

external suspension Außenaufhängung *f (of bombs)*.

extinguish löschen.

extinguisher Feuerlöscher *m*.

extinguisher fluid Löschflüssigkeit *f*.

extract *v* ausziehen.

extraction of root Radizierung *f (Math)*.

extractor Auszieher *m (Ord)*.

extract order Einzelbefehl *m*.

extra duty Strafdienst *m*.

extreme range Höchstschußweite *f (Ord)*.

eye Auge *n*.

eyeguard Augenmuschel *f*.

eyepiece Einblick *m*, Okular *n (Optics)*; Augenfenster *n (gas mask)*.

eyepiece frame Augenring *m (gas mask)*.

eyepiece lens Einblicklinse *f*.

eyepiece mount Einblickstutzen *m*.

eyepiece tube Einblickrohr *n*.

eyesight Sehkraft *f*, Sehvermögen *n*, Sehschärfe *f*.

"Eyes, left!" "Die Augen, links!"

"Eyes, right!" "Augen, rechts!"

F

fabric Stoff *m*.

fabric covering Bespannung *f (Ap)*.

face *n* Gesicht *n*.

face form Maskenspanner *m (to prevent gas-mask distortion)*.

facepiece Maskenkörper *m (gas mask)*.

facing Wendung *f (drill)*.

facing distance Wendungsabstand *m*.

facsimile equipment Bildtelegraphie-Gerät *n (Tg)*; Bildfunkgerät *n (Rad)*.

fact Tatsache *f*.

factor Faktor *m*, Koeffizient *m*; Wert *m (value)*.

factor of safety Sicherheitskoeffizient *m (Mech)*.

factory Fabrik *f*.

fade schwinden, abnehmen *(Rad)*.

fading Fading *n*, Schwund *m (Rad)*.

fading effect Schwundwirkung *f (Rad)*.

fail mißlingen, scheitern, fehlschlagen, versagen.

failure Mißerfolg *m*, Mißlingen *n*; Betriebsstörung *f (Elec, Tp)*; Panne *f (Mtr);* Unterlassung *f,* Versäumnis *n (neglect).*

Fairey gun mount Fairey-Sonderlafette *f (Ap).*

fairing Verkleidung *f,* Profilierung *f (Ap).*

fake gas "Scheingas" *n,* "Schwindelgas" *n (CWS).*

fall *n* Herbst *m (season);* Fall *m (drop).*

fall *v* fallen; sinken *(of prices, temperature, etc.).*

fall back ausweichen, sich absetzen, sich zurückziehen, zurückgehen.

fall in antreten.

"**Fall in!**" "Antreten!" *(not at attention);* "Angetreten!" *(at attention);* "In Marschordnung, angetreten!" *(in column of threes);* "In Doppelreihe, angetreten!" *(in column of twos);* "In Linie, angetreten!" *(in three ranks);* "In Linie zu zwei Gliedern, angetreten!" *(in two ranks);* "In Linie zu einem Glied, angetreten!" *(in one rank);* "In Reihe, angetreten!" *(in single file).*

fall off sich seitlich abrutschen lassen, sich über den Flügel abrutschen lassen *(Avn).*

fall out wegtreten *(drill).*

"**Fall out!**" "Weggetreten!" *(dismissed);* "Heraustreten!" *(to men in barracks).*

false attack Scheinangriff *m.*

false ogive Zünderdeckel *m (Am).*

family allowance Familienunterhalt *m.*

famine Hungersnot *f,* Nahrungsmangel *m.*

fan *n* Windflügel *m (MT).*

fan-marker beacon Kreisfunkfeuer *n (Rad).*

fanning out seitliches Einschwenken *(Tac).*

fan out seitlich einschwenken *(Tac).*

fan-type engine Fächermotor *m.*

far fern, weit, entfernt.

farad Farad *n (Elec).*

fare Fahrpreis *m (RR, etc.).*

fascine Faschine *f,* Reisigbündel *n.*

fascine revetment Strauchwerkbekleidung *f,* Strauchbündelbekleidung *f;* Senkfaschine *f (sunken).*

fascine road Strauchdamm *m,* Faschinenbahn *f;* Faschinendamm *m (raised).*

fasten verbinden *(tie);* leimen

(glue); verkitten, ankleben *(with adhesives);* anstecken *(hitch).*

fathom Faden *m (Nav).*

fathometer Behmlot *n,* Echolot *n (Nav).*

fatigue Arbeitsdienst *m (duty);* Müdigkeit *f,* Ermüdung *f (exhaustion).*

fatigue detail Arbeitskommando *n.*

fatigue duty Arbeitsdienst *m (Mil).*

fatigue strength Dauerfestigkeit *f (Engr).*

fatigue uniform Arbeitsanzug *m,* Drillichanzug *m.*

feathered position Segelstellung *f (propeller).*

feces Kot *m,* Stuhl *m.*

feed *n* Speisung *f (Elec, MT);* Futter *n (for horses).*

feed *v* abfüttern *(horses, etc.);* zu essen geben *(Pers).*

feedback Rückkopplung *f (Rad).*

feed bag Freßbeutel *m.*

feed belt Patronengurt *m,* Gurt *m (MG).*

feed box Zuführungsgehäuse *n (AA gun).*

feeder current Speisestrom *m (Elec).*

feed funnel Patronenschacht *m (Ap MG).*

feeding Verpflegung *f (Pers);* Füttern *n (horses, etc.);* Zuführung *f (Am).*

feeding device Ladevorrichtung *f (Small Arms);* Mehrladevorrichtung *f (magazine) (R).*

feed mechanism Zuführer *m (Ord).*

feint *n* Täuschungsmanöver *n,* Scheinangriff *m,* Scheingefecht *n (Tac).*

feint *v* vortäuschen.

felloe Felge *f.*

felt Filz *m.*

felt boot Filzstiefel *m.*

felt hat Filzhut *m.*

fence Zaun *m.*

fender Abweiser *m (G);* Kotflügel *m (MT).*

ferro-concrete *See* **reinforced concrete.**

ferrule Beschlag *m.*

ferry *n* Fähre *f,* Übersetzfähre *f.*

ferry *v* überführen *(Avn).*

ferryboat Fähre *f.*

ferry cable Fährseil *n (Engr).*

Ferry Command Abholkommando *n,*

Überführungskommando *n*, Lieferkommando *n (USA)*.
ferry embarkation point Fährstelle *f*.
ferry for vehicles Wagenfähre *f*.
ferrying flight Überführungsflug *m*.
ferrying operations Fährbetrieb *m*.
ferrying point Übersetzstelle *f*.
ferrying service Lieferdienst *m (Avn)*.
ferrying site Fährstelle *f*.
fetlock Köte *f (horse)*.
fever Fieber *n*.
fiber Faser *f*.
field Feld *n*.
field airdrome Feldflugplatz *m*, Feldflughafen *m*.
field army Feldarmee *f*.
Field Artillery Artillerie *f*.
field artillery intelligence Nachrichtensammeln über den Gegner *(Arty)*.
Field Artillery School Artillerieschule *f*.
field artillery survey Vermessung von Feuerstellungen *(Arty)*.
field artillery trainer Zimmerschießgerät *n*.
field bag Brotbeutel *m*.
field bakery Feldbäckerei *f*.
field cap Feldmütze *f*.
field cell Feldelement *n (Tp)*.
field development Verbesserung auf Grund von Kampferfahrungen.
field duty Dienst bei der Truppe, Felddienst *m*.
field emplacement Feuerstellung *f*.
field equipment Feldgerät *n*.
field exercise Geländeübung *f*, Felddienstübung *f*.
field firing Gefechtsschießen *n (R)*.
field firing range Gefechtsschießstand *m (R)*.
field forces Feldheer *n*.
field fortification Feldbefestigung *f*, befestigte Feldstellung.
fieldglass Glas *n*, Fernglas *n*, Doppelglas *n*.
field grade Stabsoffiziersrang *m*.
field gun Feldkanone *f*, Feldgeschütz *n*.
field hospital Hauptverbandplatz *m*.
field jacket Windjacke *f (Clo)*.
field kit Wäsche, Putz- und Nähzeug.
field kitchen Feldküche *f*.
field laboratory Feldlaboratorium *n*,

chemische und hygienische Untersuchungsstelle *(Med)*.
field magazine Munitionslager in Geschütznähe, Munitionsnische *f*.
field magnet Feldmagnet *m*.
field maneuvers Truppenübungen *fpl*.
field manual Druckvorschrift *f*.
Field Marshal Feldmarschall *m*, Generalfeldmarschall *m (Ger)*.
field medical record Krankenblatt *n*.
field mess Feldverpflegung *f*.
field message book Meldeblock *m*.
field officer Stabsoffizier *m*.
field of fire Schußfeld *n*, Wirkungsbereich *m*.
field of view Blickfeld *n*, Sehfeld *n*, Gesichtsfeld *n (Optics)*.
field order Sattelbefehl *m*.
field pack Tornister *m*.
field piece Feldkanone *f*, Feldgeschütz *n (G)*.
field position Feldstellung *f*.
field radio *See* **field radio set**.
field radio section Kleinfunktrupp *m*.
field radio set Feldfunksprechgerät *n*.
field radio truck Kleinfunkkraftwagen *m*.
field railroad Feldbahn *f*.
field range Feldkochherd *m (field kitchen)*.
field ration Feldportion *f*, Feldration *f*.
field safe Kriegskasse *f*.
Field Service Regulations Felddienstordnung *f*, Druckvorschriften für Führung und Gefecht der verbundenen Waffen.
field shop Feldwerkstatt *f*.
field strip *v* Waffengruppen auseinandernehmen.
field target Gefechtsscheibe *f*.
field target firing Gefechtsschießen *n (R)*.
field telegraph tragbarer Telegraph.
field telephone Feldfernsprecher *m*.
field telephone line Feldlinie *f*, Feldkabelleitung *f*; Felddauerlinie *f (permanent)*.
field-telephone operator Feldfernsprecher *m*.
field testing box Feldprüfschrank *m (Tp)*.
field testing set Feldmeßkästchen *n*.
field training Geländeausbildung *f*.
field trunk cable Feldfernkabel *n (Tp)*.

field uniform Feldanzug *m*.
field wagon Feldwagen *m*.
field well Feldbrunnen *m*.
field wire Feldkabel *n (Tp)*.
field-wire laying Feldkabelbau *m (Tp)*.
field-wire line Feldkabelleitung *f (Tp)*.
field-wire strand Feldkabelader *f (Tp)*.
fifth column Fünfte Kolonne.
fifth-wheel steering Drehschemellenkung *f*.
fifty percent zone Streifen der 50 %igen oder mittleren Streuung.
fight *v* kämpfen, fechten.
fighter *See* fighter airplane.
fighter airdrome Jägerplatz *m*.
fighter airplane Jäger *m*, Jagdflugzeug *n;* Zerstörer *m (long range)*.
fighter aviation Jagdflieger *mpl*.
fighter-bomber Jagdbomber *m*, Jabo *m*.
fighter command Kommando der Jagdflieger *(USA)*.
fighter defense Jagdabwehr *f (Avn)*.
fighter escort Jägerschutz *m*, Jagdschutz *m*, Begleitschutz *m (Avn)*.
fighter formation Jagdverband *m (Avn)*.
fighter group Jagdgruppe *f (Avn)*.
fighter pilot Jagdflieger *m (Avn)*.
fighter school Jagdfliegerschule *f (Avn)*.
fighter screen Jagdsperre *f (Avn)*.
fighter squadron Jagdstaffel *f (Avn)*.
fighter wing Jagdgeschwader *n (Avn)*.
fighting compartment Kampfabteil *m (Tk)*.
fighting control Flugführung und Feuerleitung *(bombardment formation)*.
fighting power Kampfkraft *f*.
fighting qualities Kampfwert *m (of a unit)*.
fighting spirit Kampfgeist *m*.
filament Glühfaden *m (Elec)*.
filament battery Heizsammler *m*, Heizbatterie *f (Rad)*.
filament circuit Heizkreis *m (Rad)*.
filament current Heizstrom *m (Rad)*.
file Reihe *f (formation);* Feile *f (Tech);* Kartothek *f (card file)*.
   in file treffenweise, in Reihe.
file closer Schließender *m*.

file leader Anführer *m*.
filing cabinet Aktenschrank *m*.
filing card Karteikarte *f*.
fill *n* Damm *m*, Aufschüttung *f (Engr, Top)*.
fill *v* füllen.
filler Füllung *f;* Sprengstoffüllung *f (explosive)*.
filler cap Füllschraube *f (MG)*.
filler charge Sprengfüllung *f (Am)*.
filler cover Verschlußkappe *f (MG)*.
filling Füllung *f (Am, CWS)*.
filling plug Füllzapfen *m*.
filling station Tankstelle *f (MT)*.
film Film *m*.
film-pack adapter Filmkassette *f (Photo)*.
film strip Filmstreifen *m*.
filter *n* Filter *m;* Weiche *f (Rad);* Sieb *n (Mtr, Rad);* Kraftstoffreiniger *m (Mtr)*.
filter *v* filtern, filtrieren.
filter area von einem Flugwachkommando überwachtes Gebiet *(AWS)*.
filter board Kartentisch des Flugmeldedienstes.
filter center Flugwachkommando *n (AWS)*.
filter circuit Sperrkreis *m (Rad)*.
filter container Filtergehäuse *n (gas mask)*.
filter element Filtereinsatz *m*, Atemeinsatz *m (gas mask)*.
filter-element container Einsatztopf *m (gas mask)*.
filter funnel Siebtrichter *m (MT)*.
filtering Sammeln, Auswerten und Weitergeben der eingehenden Flugmeldungen *(AWS)*.
filter officer leitender Offizier beim Flugwachkommando.
filter replacement Filterwechsel *m (gas mask)*.
fin Flügel *m (Mort shell, R grenade, bomb);* Stabilisierungsflügel *m*, Steuerflügel *m (bomb);* Flosse *f*, Seitenflosse *f (Ap);* Kühlrippe *f (cooling fin of engine);* Steuerfläche *f (stabilizing fin of Mort shell)*.
final amplifier Hauptsender *m*, Leistungsstufe *f (of a Rad transmitter)*.
final assembly Bereitstellung *f (Tac);* Fertigmontage *f*, Endmontage *f (Tech)*.
final assembly area Bereitstellungsraum *m*.

final objective Endziel *n.*
final protective line letzte Widerstandslinie *(Tac).*
final stage of amplification Leistungsstufe *f (Rad transmitter)*
finance *n* Kassenwesen *n.*
Finance Department Kassenabteilung *f.*
finance officer Offizier der Kassenabteilung.
finder telescope Sucherfernrohr *n (height finder).*
findings Untersuchungsergebnis *n,* Beschluß *m (Law).*
fine *n* Geldstrafe *f (Law).*
fine grain Feinkorn *n (Photo).*
fine setting Feineinstellung *f (optical Inst).*
fine sight Feinkorn *n (R aiming).*
fine tuning Feineinstellung *f (Rad).*
finger Fin;;;r *m.*
fingernail Nagel *m,* Fingernagel *m.*
fingerprint *n* Fingerabdruck *m.*
fingerprint *v* Fingerabdrücke machen, daktyloskopieren.
fin shaft Flügelschaft *f (Mort shell).*
fin surface Rippenfläche *f (air-cooled engine).*
fire *n* Schießen *n,* Feuer *n,* Beschuß *m.*
fire *v* schießen, feuern, abfeuern; abdrücken *(press the trigger).*
"Fire!" "Feuer frei!" *(R);* "Feuer!" *(Arty).*
fire adjustment Einschießen *n,* Einrichten *n,* Richt- oder Zündereinstellung beim Einschießen.
fire against personnel Schießen gegen lebende Ziele *(Gunnery).*
fire and maneuver *See* **fire and movement.**
fire and movement Feuer und Bewegung *(Tac).*
firearm Feuerwaffe *f,* Schußwaffe *f.*
fire barrage Sperrfeuer *n.*
fire bay Feuerstellung *f (trench).*
firebreak Schneise *f,* Waldschneise *f.*
fire by a battalion Abteilungsschießen *n (Arty).*
fire by command for range Schießen mit Entfernungskommandos.
fire by piece at command geschützweises Feuer *(Arty).*
fire call Feuersignal *n.*
fire command Feuerbefehl *m.*
fire control Feuerregelung *f (Arty).*

fire-control aid Schießbehelf *m (Gunnery).*
fire-control car Gerätewagen *m (RR).*
fire-control code Zeichen für die Feuerleitung *(Arty).*
fire-control equipment Feuerleitgerät *n (Arty).*
fire-control grid Gitterschießplan *m (Gunnery).*
fire-control instruments Beobachtungs- und Vermessungsgerät *n (Arty).*
fire-control map Schießplan *m,* Feuerleitungsplan *m (Gunnery).*
fire-control net Feuerleitungsnetz *n (Arty).*
firecracker Knallkörper *m,* Kanonenschlag *m (simulated fire).*
fire crest Brustwehrkrone *f (trench);* Gewehrauflage *f (Ft).*
fire curtain Feuervorhang *m,* Feuerwand *f,* Feuerschutz *m.*
fire department Feuerwehr *f.*
fire detector selbsttätiger Feuermelder *(Tk).*
fire direction Feuerleitung *f.*
fire-direction center Feuerleitungsstelle *f,* Leitstand *m (Arty).*
fire-direction net Feuerleitungsnetz *n (Arty).*
fire director Kommandogerät *n,* Flakkommandogerät *n (AAA).*
fire-director data Kommandowerte *mpl (AAA).*
fire discipline Feuerzucht *f (Arty).*
fire distribution Feuerverteilung *f (Arty, MG).*
fire duel Feuergefecht *n,* Feuerkampf *m.*
fire effect Feuerwirkung *f.*
fire engine Feuerspritze *f.*
fire extinguisher Feuerlöscher *m.*
fire fight Feuergefecht *n,* Feuerkampf *m.*
fire for destruction Zerstörungsfeuer *n,* Vernichtungsfeuer *n (Arty).*
fire for effect Wirkungsschießen *n (Gunnery).*
fire lane Schußschneise *f.*
fire marshal Brandmeister *m.*
fire mission Schießauftrag *m,* Feuerauftrag *m (Arty).*
fire order Feuerbefehl *m.*
fire plan Feuerplan *m (Tac);* Feuerlöschordnung *f (firefighting).*
fire position Feuerstellung *f.*

firepower Feuerkraft *f.*

fire preparation Feuervorbereitung *f (Tac).*

fire prevention Brandschutz *m.*

fireproof feuerfest, feuersicher.

fire raft Brander *m.*

fire sector Beobachtungs- und Wirkungsstreifen *m*, Zielraum *m*, Zielabschnitt *m (Small Arms).*

fire step Schützenauftritt *m (Ft).*

fire superiority Feuerüberlegenheit *f.*

fire support Feuerunterstützung *f.*

fire trench Schützengraben *m (Ft).*

fire unit Feuereinheit *f (Arty).*

firewall Brandschott *n*, Brandspant *m (Ap).*

firing Schießen *n*, Feuern *n*, Abfeuern *n;* Zünden *n*, Zündung *f (a blasting charge);* Erdzielbeschuß *m (at ground targets);* Flugzielbeschuß *m (at aerial targets).*

firing angle Richtungswinkel *m.*

firing azimuth Seitenrichtung *f.*

firing base Lafettenstütze *f.*

firing battery Gefechtsbatterie *f.*

firing bay Feuerstellung *f (trench).*

firing chart Batterieplan *m*, Planpause *f (Arty).*

firing circuit Abfeuerungsverbindung *f (Tk MG or G).*

firing command Feuerkommando *n (Arty).*

firing correction Schußverbesserung *f (Gunnery).*

firing data Schießgrundlagen *fpl*, Schußwerte *mpl*, Schußelemente *npl (Gunnery).*

firing device Zündvorrichtung *f (mines).*

firing elevation Rohrerhöhung *f.*

firing interval Zeitabstand *m*, Pause *f.*

firing jack Geschützwinde *f.*

firing lever Abzugsstück *n*, Abfeuerungshebel *m*, Abzugshebel *m (G).*

firing line Feuerlinie *f;* Feuerkette *f (Pers).*

firing mechanism Abzugsvorrichtung *f*, Abfeuerungsvorrichtung *f.*

firing order Zündfolge *f (of engine cylinders).*

firing party für die Ehrensalven bestimmte Abteilung *(at graveside service).*

firing pin Nadel *f*, Zündnadel *f (fuze);* Schlagbolzen *m (Ord).*

firing-pin spring Schlagbolzenfeder *f (pistol, fuze).*

firing-pin support Nadelstück *n (fuze).*

firing-pin trip Spannfalle *f (breechblock).*

firing-port shutter Schartenblende *f.*

firing position Feuerstellung *f (place);* Anschlagsart *f (standing, kneeling, etc.).*

in firing position feuerbereit, in Feuerstellung.

firing practice Schießübung *f.*

firing procedure Schießverfahren *n.*

firing range Schußweite *f (distance);* Schießstand *m (place).*

firing regulations Schießvorschrift *f.*

firing spur Stichgleis *n (RR Arty).*

firing squad Erschießungskommando *n (at an execution).*

firing stand Schießgestell *n (MG).*

firing step *See* fire step.

firing table Schußtafel *f;* Artillerierechenschieber *m (graphical).*

firing-table elevation schußtafelmäßige Erhöhung *(Gunnery).*

firing-table range schußtafelmäßige Schußweite *(Gunnery).*

firing technique Schießtechnik *f.*

firing wire Zünderdraht *m*, Sprengkabel *n (blasting).*

first aid erste Hilfe, erster Wundverband.

first-aid dog Sanitätshund *m.*

first-aid kit Verbandzeug *n.*

first-aid packet Verbandpäckchen *n.*

first-aid pouch Notverbandtasche *f.*

first-aid supplies Verbandzeug *n.*

first lieutenant Oberleutnant *m;* Oberleutnant der Flieger *(Luftwaffe);* Oberarzt *m (Med);* Oberveterinär *m (Vet).*

first name Rufname *m.*

first officer Erster Offizier *(Nav).*

first sergeant Hauptfeldwebel *m;* Hauptwachtmeister *m (Arty, Cav).*

first sergeant's call Versammlung der Hauptfeldwebel zur Befehlsausgabe.

fiscal year Haushaltsjahr *n.*

fish *n* Fisch *m.*

fish net Fischnetz *n (Cam).*

fishtail Abbremsen des Flugzeuges bei der Landung durch dauerndes Bewegen des Seitenruders *(Avn).*

fishtail wind ständig wechselnder Wind.

fist Faust *f.*
fit *v* passen; montieren *(assemble).*
fit for duty dienstfähig.
fitting Verpassung *f,* Verpassen *n*
(of uniforms, etc.); Zubehörteil *m,*
Armatur *f,* Paßstück *n (Tech).*
fix *n* Koppelort *m (Air Navigation).*
fix *v* fesseln *(Tac).*
"Fix bayonets!" "Seitengewehr,
pflanzt auf!"
fixed ortsfest, ständig *(Arty, Ft).*
fixed ammunition Einheitsmunition
f, Patronenmunition *f.*
fixed antenna Festantenne *f.*
fixed antiaircraft artillery ortsfeste
Flak.
fixed bayonet aufgepflanztes Seitengewehr.
fixed bridge Brücke mit festen Stützen.
fixed emplacement fest eingebaute
Geschützstellung, ortsfeste Geschützstellung.
fixed fire Punktfeuer *n (MG).*
fixed gun starre Kanone *(Ap).*
fixed gun mount starre Lafette.
fixed hospital feste Krankenunterkunft.
fixed liner festes Seelenrohr *(G).*
fixed machine gun starres Maschinengewehr.
fixed objective festes Ziel.
fixed obstacle fest eingebautes Hindernis.
fixed-pitch propeller Luftschraube
mit gleichbleibender Steigung.
fixed pivot Drehpunkt *m;* Flügelmann am Drehpunkt *(drill).*
fixed round ein Schuß Patronenmunition.
fixed seacoast artillery ortsfeste
Küstenartillerie.
fixed target festes Ziel.
flag Flagge *f,* Fahne *f.*
flagman Winker *m.*
flag officer Flaggoffizier *m (Nav).*
flag of protection Lazarettflagge *f.*
flag of truce Parlamentärflagge *f,*
weiße Flagge.
  bearer of a flag of truce Unterhändler *m,* Parlamentär *m.*
flagpole Fahnenschaft *m,* Fahnenstange *f;* Fahnenmast *m (fixed).*
flag semaphore Nachrichtenübermittlung durch Winkflaggen.
flagship Flaggschiff *n.*
flag signal Flaggensignal *n.*

flag target Schleppziel *n,* Schleppscheibe *f,* Luftsack *m (AAA).*
flake powder Blättchenpulver *n,*
Plattenpulver *n (Am).*
flaksuit Panzerweste *f (Avn).*
flame Flamme *f.*
flame dampener exhaust stack Flammenverzehrer *m (Ap).*
flame-thrower Flammenwerfer *m;*
Nahwerfer *m (short-range);* Weitwerfer *m (long-range).*
flame-throwing tank Flammenwerferpanzerwagen *m (Ger).*
flange Flansch *m.*
flank *n* Flanke *f,* Breitseite *f (Tac);*
Führungsfläche *f (G tube);* Weiche
f, Flanke *f (of horse).*
flank *v* flankieren, umgehen.
flank attack Flankenangriff *m.*
flank guard Seitendeckung *f (Tac).*
flanking fire Flankenfeuer *n,* flankierendes Feuer.
flanking march Flankenmarsch *m.*
flank man Flügelmann *m (drill).*
flank observation Beobachtung von
seitlicher Beobachtungsstelle *(Arty).*
flank patrol Spähtrupp zur Flankensicherung.
flank protection Flankenschutz *m.*
flank protective fire Artilleriefeuer
zur Flankensicherung.
flank security Flankensicherung *f,*
Seitendeckung *f (Tac).*
flank spotting Beobachtung von seitlicher Beobachtungsstelle *(Arty).*
flap Klappe *f (Ap, Clo);* Tornisterklappe *f (pack).*
flare Fackel *f,* Leuchtkugel *f (Sig).*
flareback Vorbeischlagen der Pulvergase *(G).*
flare composition Leuchtsatz *m.*
flare path Leuchtpfad *m (Avn).*
flash Mündungsfeuer *n,* Aufblitzen *n*
(G); Zündstrahl *m (Am);* Blitzstrahl *m (lightning).*
flash defilade Sichtdeckung *f (Arty).*
flash fuze elektrischer Glühzünder
(CWS).
flash hider Feuerdämpfer *m,* Flammendämpfer *m,* Mündungsfeuerdämpfer *m (Ord).*
flash hole Zündkanal *m (fuze).*
flashing light Blinkfeuer *n (Avn).*
flashlight Taschenlampe *f.*
flashlight battery Taschenlampen-
batterie *f.*
flash message dringende Meldung.

flash point Zündpunkt *m (fuels)*.

flash ranging Lichtmessen *n*.

flash-ranging adjustment Einschießen der eigenen Artillerie durch die Lichtmeßbatterie *(Arty)*.

flash-ranging battery Lichtmeßbatterie *f*.

flash-ranging location *See* **flash ranging**.

flash-ranging section Lichtmeßtrupp *m (Arty)*.

flash-ranging station Lichtmeßstelle *f*, Meßstelle *f*.

flash-ranging system Lichtmeßsystem *n*.

flash reconnaissance Gefechtsaufklärung durch Lichtmeßbatterie oder vom Flugzeug aus.

flash-reducing wad Kartuschvorlage *f (Am)*.

flash signal Blinkzeichen *n*.

flash tube Kammerhülse *f (shrapnel)*.

flash-tube charge Kammerhülsenladung *f (shrapnel)*.

flat-base rim Flachbettfelge *f (MT)*.

flat butt strap Flachlasche *f*.

flatcar Plattformwagen *m (RR)*.

flat coil spring Bandfeder *f (fuze)*.

flat feet Plattfüße *mpl*.

flat fire *See* **flat-trajectory fire**.

flat-jawed pliers Flachzange *f*.

flatness of trajectory Rasanz der Flugbahn.

flat spin Flachtrudeln *n*, Tellertrudeln *n (Avn)*.

flatten out abfangen *(Avn)*.

flat-top Maske *f*, Tarndecke *f (Cam)*. *See also* **aircraft carrier**.

flat trajectory gestreckte Flugbahn, gestreckte Geschoßbahn *(Ballistics)*.

flat-trajectory fire Flachfeuer *n*.

flat-trajectory gun Flachfeuergeschütz *n*, Flachbahngeschütz *n*.

flat-trajectory weapon Flachbahnwaffe *f*, Flachfeuerwaffe *f*.

fleet Flotte *f (Nav)*.

fleeting target Augenblicksziel *n*.

flexible schwenkbar *(Ap MG)*; biegsam *(Tech)*.

flexible axle Schwingachse *f (MT)*.

flexible ball mount Kugelblende *f (Tk gun)*.

flexible disk Hardyscheibe *f (MT)*.

flexible-disk joint Trockengelenk *n (MT)*.

flexible drive shaft Gelenkwelle *f*.

flexible gun bewegliches Geschütz.

flexible machine gun bewegliches Maschinengewehr.

flexible shaft Schwinge *f (follow-the-pointer mechanism)*; biegsame Welle *(Tech)*.

flexible steel cable Drahtzug *m (Ap)*.

flexure Durchbiegen *n (Mech)*.

flick Erfassung des Zieles, kurzdauerndes Halten eines erfaßten Zieles *(AA searchlight)*.

flier Flieger *m*.

flight Kette *f (Avn unit)*; Flug *m*.

flight commander Kettenführer *m (Avn)*.

flight control Flugzeugsteuerung *f (Ap)*; Bewegungskontrolle *f (by operations office)*.

flight deck Flugdeck *n*, Landedeck *n (aircraft carrier)*.

flight diagram Auftragskarte *f (aerial Photo)*.

flight echelon fliegendes Personal.

flight engineer Bordwart *m*, Bordmechaniker *m*, Bordmonteur *m (Avn)*.

flight formation Flugform *f*.

flight indicator Neigungsmesser *m*, Gyrorektor *m (Ap)*.

flight instructor Fluglehrer *m*.

flight line Fluglinie *f*, Flugstrecke *f*.

flight log Flugbuch *n*, Flugtagebuch *n*.

flight maneuver Flugfigur *f*.

flight map Fliegerkarte *f*.

flight officer Feldwebelleutnant der Flieger *(USA)*.

flight pay Luftdienstzulage *f*, Fliegerzulage *f*.

flight performance Flugleistung *f*.

flight personnel fliegendes Personal.

flight position Flugrichtung *f*, Fluglage *f*.

flight ration Bordverpflegung *f*.

flight report Flugmeldung *f*.

flight route Flugstrecke *f*.

flight surgeon Sanitätsoffizier bei fliegenden Verbänden, Fliegerarzt *m*.

flinching Mucken *n (Small Arms firing)*.

float Schwimmer *m (Ap, carburetor, gage, etc.)*; Floß *n (Engr)*; Fußplatte *f*, Fußteller *m (AA gun)*; Schwanzblech *n (G trail)*.

float chamber Schwimmergehäuse *n (carburetor)*.

float column Tellersäule *f (AA gun outrigger).*
float gear Schwimmwerk *n*, Schwimmerwerk *n*, Schwimmergestell *n (seaplane).*
floating bridge Brücke mit schwimmenden Stützen, Floßbrücke *f.*
floating dock Schwimmdock *n.*
floating mine Treibmine *f.*
float needle Schwimmernadel *f (carburetor).*
floatplane Schwimmerflugzeug *n.*
float plate Ansteckblech *n (G trail spade);* Fußplatte *f*, Fußteller *m (AA gun).*
floats Schwimmwerk *n (Ap).*
flock Reiterrudel *n (Cav).*
flood *n* Überflutung *f*, Überschwemmung *f.*
flood *v* überfluten, überschwemmen; anstauen *(dam up).*
flooded area Anstauung *f (Engr).*
flooding Anstauung *f*, Überflutung *f (Engr).*
floodlight Flutlicht *n.*
floor Boden *m*, Fußboden *m (buildings);* Fahrbahn *f*, Brückenbahn *f (Bdg);* Stock *m (story).*
floor beam Fahrbahnträger *m (Bdg).*
floor board Bodenbrett *n (MT).*
floor plate Bodenstück *n (MG).*
floor-plate lock Bodenstücksperre *f (MG).*
flotation gear Schwimmwerk *n (Ap).*
flotation stability Schwimmstabilität *f (seaplane).*
flour Mehl *n.*
fluid drive Flüssigkeitsgetriebe *n (MT).*
fluid equalizer Flüssigkeitsausgleicher *m (recoil mechanism).*
fluke Ankerflunken *m (of an anchor).*
fluorescent tube Leuchtröhre *f.*
flush riveting Versenknietung *f.*
flutter *n* Rüttelerscheinungen *fpl (Ap).*
fly *v* fliegen.
fly a sortie Einsatz fliegen *(Avn).*
flying boat Flugboot *n;* Fernaufklärungsflugboot *n (long-range reconnaissance).*
flying bridge *See* **flying ferry.**
flying cadet Fähnrich der Flieger *(USA).*
flying distance Flugweite *f.*

flying ferry Gierfähre mit nur an einem Ufer verankertem Fährseil *(Engr).*
flying field Flugplatz *m.*
Flying Fortress Fliegende Festung.
flying in formation Verbandsflug *m (Avn).*
flying officer Fliegeroffizier *m.*
flying pay Fliegerzulage *f*, Luftdienstzulage *f.*
flying school Fliegerschule *f.*
flying suit Fliegerschutzanzug *m;* Pelzkombination *f (fur-lined coverall).*
flying time Flugzeit *f (Avn).*
fly on instruments blindfliegen.
flyweight Fliehgewicht *n (engine governor).*
flywheel Schwungrad *n*, Schwungmasse *f*, Schwungscheibe *f (Mtr).*
FM Titantetrachlorid *n (CWS).*
FM grenade Nebelhandgranate mit Titantetrachlorid-Füllung *(CWS).*
FM smoke Titantetrachlorid-Nebel *m (CWS).*
focal center Flugmeldekommando *n (AWS).*
focal distance Brennweite *f (Optics).*
focal length *See* **focal distance.**
focal plane Brennebene *f (Optics).*
focus *n* Brennpunkt *m (Optics).*
focusing scale Sehschärfeneinteilung *f (Optics).*
fog Nebel *m.*
fog area Nebelgebiet *n (Met).*
folding wings beiklappbare Tragflügel, Schwenkflügel *mpl*, Klappflügel *mpl (Ap).*
follower Zubringer *m (Small Arms).*
follower spring Zubringerfeder *f (Small Arms).*
follower-spring stud Federkopf *m (self-loading pistol).*
follow-the-pointer drive Folgezeigerantrieb *m (AAA).*
follow-the-pointer indicator Folgezeiger *m.*
follow-the-pointer sight mechanism Zeigerzieleinrichtung *f (G).*
follow-the-pointer system Folgezeigereinrichtung *f.*
follow up *v* nachdrängen *(Tac);* anfragen nach *(inquire).*
food Lebensmittel *npl*, Nahrungsmittel *npl (any means of nutrition);* Essen *n*, Kost *f*, Verpflegung *f*

(meals in general); Eßwaren *fpl* *(food products).*

food ration card Lebensmittelkarte *f.*

foot Fuß *m.*

footbridge Steg *m,* Beselersteg *m;* Schnellsteg *m (hasty);* Floßsacksteg *m (of pneumatic boats);* Uferschnellsteg *m (single span).*

foot-firing mechanism Abzugsvorrichtung mit Fußhebel *(AA gun).*

footgear Schuhzeug *n.*

footpath Fußweg *m.*

foot plate Fußplatte *f,* Fußteller *m (AA gun).*

footrest Fußstütze *f (AA gun).*

foot shifter Fußschaltung *f (MT).*

footsore fußkrank.

foot starter Fußschalter *m (MT).*

foot switch Fußschalter *m (Elec).*

foot troops Fußtruppen *fpl.*

forage *n* Futter *n.*

forage *v* furagieren, verpflegen, Futter und Nahrungsmittel beschaffen.

forage ration Futterration *f.*

foragers Reiter in geöffneter Linie *(Cav).*

force *n* Kraft *f (power);* Kräfte *f pl (Pers);* Kampfeinheit *f (unit);* Kräftegruppe *f (group);* Verband *m (formation).*

in force mit starken Kräften, mit Einsatz aller Kräfte *(Tac).*

force *v* erkämpfen, erzwingen, überwinden *(Tac).*

forced-circulation cooling Pumpenkühlung *f,* Wasserpumpenkühlung *f (Mtr).*

forced crossing Überschreiten des Flusses unter Kampf *(Tac).*

forced landing Notlandung *f (Avn);* Truppenlandung unter Feuer *(Tac).*

make a forced landing notlanden *(Avn).*

forced march Dauermarsch *m,* Gewaltmarsch *m.*

forcing cone Übergangskegel *m (G).*

ford *n* Furt *f.*

ford *v* durchwaten.

fordable durchwatbar.

fording ability Watfähigkeit *f (MT).*

fore-and-aft inclinometer Längsneigungsmesser *m (Ap).*

forearm Schaft *m (automatic R);* Vorarm *m (horse).*

forecast *See* **weather forecast.**

forefinger Zeigefinger *m.*

foreground Vorfeld *n (Tac).*

forehead Stirn *f.*

forehead strap Stirnband *n (gas mask).*

foreign ausländisch, fremd, auswärtig.

foreign country Ausland *n,* fremdes Land.

foreigner Ausländer *m,* Fremde(r) *m.*

foreign port Auslandshafen *m,* ausländischer Hafen.

foreign service Dienst außerhalb der Landesgrenze.

forequarters Vorhand *f (horse).*

foresight Vorsicht *f (Surv).*

forest Wald *m.*

forestalling Unterbindung *f (Tac).*

forest clearing Waldblöße *f,* Waldlichtung *f.*

forest road Waldweg *m;* Waldschneise *f,* Schneise *f (along a firebreak).*

forfeiture Verlust des Wehrsoldes.

forfeiture of pay Verwirkung des Wehrsoldes.

forge *n* Schmiede *f.*

forged iron Schmiedeeisen *n.*

fork Verlegung des mittleren Treffpunktes um die Hälfte des Treffbildes *(Gunnery);* Wegegabel *f (road);* Gabel *f (utensil).*

form Schalung *f (concrete construction);* Vordruck *m,* Formular *n (printed form);* Gestalt *f (shape).*

formation Form *f,* Formation *f,* Gliederung *f (drill, Tac);* Verband *m (Avn);* Flugform *f (flight formation).*

formation flying Verband(s)flug *m,* Fliegen im Verbande.

formation in depth Tiefengliederung *f (Tac).*

formation in width Breitengliederung *f (Tac).*

formation of airplanes Fliegerformation *f,* Fliegerverband *m.*

formation of bombardment airplanes Kampfverband *m.*

formation of dive bombers Sturzkampfverband *m,* Stukaverband *m.*

formation of eddies Wirbelbildung *f (Ballistics).*

formation of pursuit airplanes Jagdverband *m (Avn).*

formation of reconnaissance airplanes Aufklärungsverband *m.*

formation of torpedo bombers Torpedoflugzeugverband m.

formation release Verbandswurf m, Verbandsabwurf m (Bombing).

formula Formel f.

formulation of decisions Entschlußfassung f.

fort Werk n, Festung f.

fortification Befestigung f.

fortified defense system Befestigungsanlage f.

fortified line Stützpunktlinie f.

fortified locality Stützpunkt m (Tac).

fortified position befestigte Stellung.

fortress Festung f.

fortress artillery Festungsartillerie f.

fortunes of war Wechselfälle des Gefechts (Tac).

forward v befördern (supplies, etc.); nachsenden (a letter).

forward area Kampfgebiet n, Kampfraum m.

forward echelon I. Staffel (Hq).

forward gunner's compartment Bugkanzel f (Ap).

forwarding point Weiterleitungsstelle f.

"Forward, march!" "Im Gleichschritt, Marsch!"

forward observation post vorgeschobene Beobachtungsstelle (Tac).

forward observer vorgeschobener Beobachter (Arty).

forward PW camp Frontstalag n.

forward slope Vorderhang m (Top).

forward slope position Vorderhangstellung f (Tac).

forward speed Vorwärtsgang m (MT).

forward velocity Vorwärtsgeschwindigkeit f (Bombing).

fougasse Flattermine f, Fugasse f.

fouling Rückstände im Laufinnern (Ord).

fouling shot erster Schuß zum Entölen des Laufinnern.

foundation Bettung f (G emplacement); Unterbau m (Engr).

foundry Gießerei f.

fountain pen Füllfeder f.

four-cycle engine Viertaktmotor m.

four-man tent Viererzelt n.

fourragère Fangschnur f; Schützenschnur f (marksmanship).

four-way pipe joint Kreuzmuffe f.

four-wheel vehicle Zweiachser m.

foxhole Schützenloch n; Hockloch n (crouching); Schützenloch für stehenden Anschlag (standing).

fraction Bruch m (Math).

fractional charge Teilladung f (Am).

fracture Knochenbruch m (Med).

fracture of the skull Schädelbruch m.

fragment Bruchstück n, Splitter m, Sprengstück n.

fragmentary order Einzelbefehl m, besondere Anordnung (Tac).

fragmentation Splitterwirkung f (Am).

fragmentation bomb Splitterbombe f.

fragmentation effect Splitterwirkung f.

fragmentation hand grenade Eierhandgranate f (egg-shaped).

fragmentation shell Splittergranate f.

frame n Rahmen m; Fahrwerkrahmen m (MT); Protzgestell n (limber); Tragegestell n (pack saddle).

frame rib Trageschiene f (pack saddle).

frame-type gun carriage Rahmenlafette f.

frangible grenade Brandflasche f.

fraudulent enlistment freiwilliges Eintreten mit falschen Angaben oder Verschweigen wichtiger Tatbestände.

fraudulent induction Diensteintritt mit falschen Angaben oder Verschweigen wichtiger Tatbestände.

free air thermometer AußenluftThermometer n (Ap).

free balloon Freiballon m.

freeboard Freibord m.

freedom Freiheit f.

free-space radiation Raumstrahlung f (Rad).

free travel toter Gang (clutch pedal).

freewheeling Freilauf m (MT).

freeze frieren; erfrieren (to death); sich festfressen (piston, etc.).

freeze in position regungslos erstarren.

freight Fracht f.

freight car Güterwagen m (RR).

freighter Frachter m, Frachtdampfer m (Nav).

freight station Güterbahnhof m (RR).

freight train   Güterzug *m (RR)*.

frequency   Schwingungszahl *f*, Frequenz *f (Elec, Rad)*.

frequency band   Frequenzband *n*.

frequency-control element   Steuersender *m*, Steuerstufe *f (Rad transmitter)*.

frequency designation   Frequenzangabe *f (Rad)*.

frequency meter   Wellenmesser *m*, Frequenzmesser *m (Elec, Rad)*.

frequency modulation   Frequenzmodulation *f (Rad)*.

frequency selection   Grobeinstellung *f (Rad)*.

frequency spectrum   Wellenspektrum *n (Rad)*.

friction   Reibung *f*.

frictional resistance   Reibungswiderstand *m*.

friction igniter   Abreißzünder *m*, Zündschnuranzünder *m*.

friction primer   Reibzündschraube *f*.

friction surface   Laufffläche *f (Mech)*.

friction tape   Isolierstreifen *m*, Isolierband *n*.

friendly troops   eigene Truppen.

frog   Strahl *m (hoof)*; Weichenstück *n (RR switch)*.

front   Front *f (Met, Mil)*; Bug *m*, Stirnseite *f (Tk)*.

frontage   Ausdehnung *f*, Breite *f*, Gefechtsbreite *f (Tac)*.

frontage in attack   Angriffsbreite *f*.

frontal area   Stirnfläche *f (Mech)*.

frontal attack   frontaler Angriff, Frontalangriff *m*, Stirnangriff *m*.

frontal fire   Frontalfeuer *n*.

frontal security   Sicherung nach vorne *(Tac)*.

frontal soaring   Frontensegeln *n*, Gewitterflug *m (glider)*.

front arch   Vorderzwiesel *m (packsaddle frame)*.

front armor   Bugpanzer *m (Tk)*.

front axle   Vorderachse *f (MT)*.

front-axle drive   Vorderachsantrieb *m (MT)*.

front cinch   Bauchgurt *m (pack saddle)*.

front gunner   Bugschütze *m (Tk)*.

frontier   Grenze *f*.

frontier area   Grenzgebiet *n*.

frontier district   Grenzbezirk *m*.

frontier force   Grenzschutz *m (Tac)*.

frontier guard   Grenzwache *f*, Grenzwacht *f*.

frontier protection   Grenzschutz *m (Tac)*.

frontier station   Grenzbahnhof *m (RR)*.

front line   Frontlinie *f*, vorderste Kampflinie *(Tac)*.

front outrigger   Vorderholm *m (AA gun mount)*.

front ring sight   Kreiskorn *n (MG)*.

front ring sight base   Kreiskornfuß *m (MG)*.

front ring sight frame   Kreiskornrahmen *m (MG)*.

front ring sight support   Kreiskornhalter *m (MG)*.

front roller   Kletterwalze *f*, Abfangwalze *f (MT)*.

front sector   Frontabschnitt *m*.

front sight   Korn *n (Small Arms)*; Nebenstachel *m (AT gun)*.

front-sight base   Kornfuß *m (R)*.

front-sight cover   Kornschoner *m (R)*.

front-sight holder   Kornhalter *m (R)*.

front-sight stud   Kornwarze *f (R)*.

front-wheel drive   Frontantrieb *m*, Vorderradantrieb *m (MT)*.

frost   Reif *m*, Rauhreif *m (Met)*.

frostbite   Frostbeule *f*.

frosted glass   Milchglas *n*.

frozen   gefroren *(of water, etc., frostbitten)*; erfroren *(frozen to death or point of serious danger)*.

fruit   Frucht *f*; Obst *n (collective)*.

FS solution   Nebelsäure *f (CWS)*.

fuel   Brennstoff *m*, Kraftstoff *m*, Treibstoff *m*, Betriebsstoff *m (Mtr)*. *See also* **gasoline**.

fuel-air mixture   Kraftstoff-Luftgemisch *n (Mtr)*.

fuel cake   Brennstoff *m (DM irritant gas candle)*.

fuel consumption   Brennstoffverbrauch *m*, Kraftstoffverbrauch *m (MT)*.

fuel distributing point   Kraftstoffausgabestelle *f*.

fuel dump   Brennstofflager *n*, Treibstofflager *n*, Kraftstofflager *n*.

fuel economy   Kraftstoffersparnis *f (MT)*.

fuel feed   Kraftstoffzufluß *m*, Kraftstofförderung *f*.

fuel filter   Kraftstoffilter *m*, Kraftstoffreiniger *m*.

fuel gage   Benzinstandmesser *m*,

Kraftstoffmeßuhr *f*, Kraftstoffstand-anzeige *f*.
fuel injector Einspritzdüse *f*.
fuel jet Kraftstoffdüse *f*.
fuel level gage Kraftstoffvorrats-messer *m (Ap)*.
fuel line Kraftstoffleitung *f (MT)*.
fuel mixture Brenngemisch *n*, Kraft-stoffgemisch *n*.
fuel oil Heizöl *n*.
fuel pressure gage Kraftstoffdruck-messer *m (Ap)*.
fuel pump Kraftstofförderpumpe *f*, Kraftstoffpumpe *f*.
fuel shut-off valve Kraftstoffabstell-hahn *m.*
fuel supply Brennstoffvorrat *m*, Kraftstoffnachschub *m*, Betriebs-stoffversorgung *f*, Kraftstoffversor-gung *f*.
fuel-supply column Betriebsstoff-kolonne *f*.
fuel-supply dump Treibstofflager *n*.
fuel-supply truck Betriebsstoff-Last-kraftwagen *m*.
fuel system Kraftstoffanlage *f (Mtr)*.
fuel tank Kraftstofftank *m*, Kraft-stoffbehälter *m*, Treibstoffbehälter *m (MT, Ap)*.
fuel tender Tankprahm *m (Nav)*.
fuel train Kraftstoffzug *m (RR)*.
fulcrum Drehpunkt *m*.
full-automatic fire Dauerfeuer *n (MG, R)*.
full cock Spannrast *f (Small Arms)*.
full dress uniform Paradeanzug *m*.
full pack Marschgepäck *n*.
full sight Vollkorn *n (R aiming)*.
full-track vehicle Vollkettenfahrzeug *n*.
fulminate of mercury Knallquecksil-ber *n*.
fumigate (aus)räuchern, desin-fizieren.
functioning Arbeitsspiel *n (Mech)*.

funeral Trauerfeier *f.*
funeral escort Begleitkommando *n*, Trauergefolge *n*.
funnel Trichter *m*.
fur-lined pelzgefüttert.
fur-lined flying suit Pelzkombination *f*.
furlough Urlaub *m*.
furlough allowance *See* **furlough ra-tion allowance.**
furlough ration allowance Verpfle-gungsgebührnisse bei Urlaub.
furrow Furche *f*, Bodenfalte *f (Top)*.
fuse Sicherung *f*, Schmelzsicherung *f*, Grobsicherung *f (Elec)*. *See also* **fuze.**
fuselage Rumpf *m*, Flugzeugrumpf *m (Ap)*.
fuselage assembly Rumpfmontage *f (Ap)*.
fuselage framework Rumpfgerüst *n (Ap)*.
fuselage skin Rumpfhaut *f (Ap)*.
future position Treffpunkt *m*, Vor-haltepunkt *m (AA gunnery)*.
fuze Zünder *m (Am)*; Zeitzünd-schnur *f (blasting)*. See also **fuse.**
fuze body Zündergehäuse *n*.
fuze composition Zündsatz *m*.
fuze cord Abreißschnur *f (hand grenade)*.
fuze-cord button Abreißknopf *m (hand grenade)*.
fuze-indicator Folgezeigerempfänger *m (follow-the-pointer-type fuze set-ter)*.
fuze-lighter Zündschnuranzünder *m*.
fuze-range Zünderlaufzeit *f*.
fuze-setter Zünderstellschlüssel *m (manual)*; Zünderstellmaschine *f (automatic)*.
fuze-setter support Zünderstellsitz *m (AA gun)*.
fuze setting Zündereinstellung *f*, Zünderstellung *f (Gunnery)*.

G

gabion Schanzkorb *m (Ft)*.
gag Knebel *m*.
gage Spurweite *f (RR)*; Lehre *f (Tech)*.
gain *n* Gewinn *m*.
gain *v* gewinnen.

gait Gangart *f (of horse)*.
gait of march Marschgeschwindig-keit *f (H Cav)*.
gale Sturmwind *m*, stürmischer Wind.
gallery Minengang *m*, Minenstollen

m (mining); Schießhalle *f*, gedeckte Bahn *(shooting)*.

gallery case Schurholzrahmen *m (Engr)*.

gallery of departure Ausgangsstollen *m*, Hauptstollen *m (mine warfare)*.

gallery practice ammunition Zielmunition *f*.

galley Kombüse *f (Nav)*.

galling Reibung *f*.

gallon Gallone *f (3.785 liters)*.

gallon capacity Tragfähigkeit *f (tank Trk)*.

galvanize verzinken.

galvanized verzinkt.

galvanometer Leitungsprüfer *m*, Galvanometer *n*.

galvanoscope Galvanoskop *n*.

gangplank Laufbrücke *f*.

gangrene Brand *m*, Wundbrand *m*.

gap Lücke *f;* Gasse *f (in mine field);* Sturmgasse *f (through obstacles);* Schußfeldlücke *f (in field of fire)*.

garbage Müll *n*.

garbage can Mülleimer *m*.

garlands bunte Lappen *(Cam)*.

garnishing Einflechten bunter Lappenstreifen in ein Tarnnetz *(Cam)*.

garrison Standort *m (place);* Besatzung *f (Pers)*.

garrison belt Leibriemen *m (Clo)*.

garrison cap Feldmütze *f*.

garrison gin behelfsmäßiges Hebezeug aus Dreibock und Winde.

garrison prisoner Garnisonhäftling *m*.

garrison ration Verpflegungsgebührnisse *fpl*, Beköstigungsgeld *n*.

gas *n* Kampfgas *n (CWS)*.

gas *v* vergasen, begasen, mit Kampfstoff vergiften *(CWS)*.

gas alarm Alarm *m*, Gasalarm *m (CWS)*.

gas-alarm signal Gasalarmzeichen *n*.

gas-alarm siren Gasalarmsirene *f*.

gas alert Gasbereitschaft *f*.

gas alert line Gasbereitschaftslinie *f (CWS)*.

gas ammunition Gasmunition *f*.

gas attack Gasangriff *m*.

gas bag Ballonhülle *f (Bln)*.

gas barrier Gassperre *f (CWS)*.

gas bomb Gasbombe *f*.

gas candle Giftnebelkerze *f*, Giftrauchkerze *f (CWS)*.

gas casualty Gasvergifteter *m (plural:* Gasverluste *mpl)*.

gas chamber Gasraum *m (CWS, Bln)*.

gas chamber test Gasraumprobe *f*, Gasraumprüfung *f*.

gas check Gasabdichtung *f*, Liderung *f (breechblock)*.

gas-check pad Kissen *n*, Liderungspolster *n (breechblock)*.

gas-check seat Liderungsplatte *f (breechblock)*.

gas cloud Gaswolke *f*, Giftnebelwolke *f*.

gas concentration Kampfstoffgehalt *m*, Luftanreicherung *f (CWS)*.

gas coverage Kampfstoffbelegung *f (CWS)*.

gas curtain Gasschutzvorhang *m (Ft)*.

gas cylinder Blasflasche *f*, Gasflasche *f (CWS)*.

gas-cylinder attack Blasangriff *m (CWS)*.

gas-cylinder method Blasverfahren *n (CWS)*.

gas-cylinder nozzle Gasdüse *f (CWS)*.

gas-cylinder plug Hülse *f (MG)*.

gas defense Gasabwehr *f*.

gas-defense equipment Gasabwehrmittel *n*.

gas-defense instruction Gasausbildung *f*.

gas-defense regulations Gasschutzvorschrift *f*.

gas-defense weapon Gasabwehrwaffe *f*.

gas detection Gasspüren *n*, Abspüren *n (CWS)*.

gas-detection apparatus Gasspürgerät *n*.

gas-detection equipment Gasspürmittel *npl*, Spürmittel *npl*.

gas-detection paper Spürpapier *n (CWS)*.

gas-detection service Gaserkennungsdienst *m*.

gas detector Gasanzeiger *m*.

gas-detector powder Spürpulver *n (CWS)*.

gas discipline Gasdisziplin *f*, Gaszucht *f*.

gas filter Gasfilter *n (gas mask)*.

gas fumes Gasschwaden *mpl (CWS)*.

gas gangrene Gasbrand *m*.

gas goggles Gasbrille *f (CWS)*.

gas hand grenade Gashandgranate *f.*
gas-identification set Riechprobenkasten *m (CWS).*
gas-impervious gasdicht, gassicher.
gasket Dichtung *f.*
gaskin Unterschenkel *m (horse).*
gas line Gasleitung *f.*
gas main Hauptgasleitung *f.*
gas mask Gasmaske *f,* Maske *f;*
Sondergasmaske *f (special).*
gas-mask accessories Gasmaskenzubehör *n.*
gas-mask carrier Gasmaskentragbüchse *f,* Tragbüchse *f (metal type).*
gas-mask testing apparatus Gasmaskenprüfgerät *n.*
gas noncommissioned officer Gasschutzunteroffizier *m.*
gas officer Gasoffizier *m.*
gas oil Gasöl *n.*
gasoline Kraftstoff *m,* Betriebsstoff
m, Benzin *n,* Brennstoff *m,* Treibstoff *m;* Waschbenzin *n (for cleaning). See also fuel.*
gasoline-air mixture Kraftstoff-
Luftgemisch *n.*
gasoline consumption Brennstoffverbrauch *m,* Kraftstoffverbrauch *m.*
gasoline container Benzinkanister *m*
(Ap, MT).
gasoline distributing point Kraftstoffausgabestelle *f.*
gasoline filling station Tankstelle *f*
(MT).
gasoline filter Kraftstoffilter *m,*
Kraftstoffreiniger *m.*
gasoline-oil mixture Kraftstoffölmischung *f.*
gasoline pressure gage Benzinmanometer *n (Mtr).*
gasoline pump Benzinpumpe *f,*
Kraftstofförderpumpe *f (Mtr).*
gasoline supply Kraftstoffversor-
gung *f,* Kraftstoffnachschub *m,*
Kraftstoffvorrat *m.*
gasoline supply depot Betriebsstoff-
lager *n.*
gasoline supply section Kraftstoffstaffel *f (Tk Bn).*
gasoline supply truck Betriebsstoff-
Lastkraftwagen *m.*
gasoline tank Benzinbehälter *m,*
Benzintank *m,* Kraftstoffbehälter *m.*
gas-operated durch Gasdruck
betätigt *(Ord).*
gas-operated machine gun Gasdrucklader *m.*

gas pipe Gasleitung *f.*
gas pliers Rohrzange *f.*
gas pot Tränenstoffkerze *f (CWS).*
gas pressure Gasdruck *m (Ballistics,*
Ord).
gas projectile Gasgeschoß *n.*
gasproof gassicher.
gas proofing Abdichtung gegen
Kampfgas *(CWS).*
gasproof shelter gassicherer Unterstand, gasgeschützter Unterstand.
gas-protection boots Gasstiefel *mpl.*
gas-protection cloak Gasumhang *m.*
gas-protection equipment Gasschutzgerät *n.*
gas-protection glove Gashandschuh
m.
gas-protection service Gasabwehrdienst *m.*
gas-protection suit Gasanzug *m.*
gas reconnaissance Gasaufklärung *f.*
gas release Abblasen *n (CWS).*
gas-release method Gasabblaseverfahren *n (CWS).*
gas rifle grenade Gasgewehrgranate
f.
gassed-area marker Gasspürfähnchen *n.*
gas sentry Gasspürer *m.*
gas shell Gasgranate *f.*
gas-shell fire Gasschießen *n,* Vergiftungsschießen *n (Arty).*
gassing Begasung *f (CWS).*
gas situation map Kampfstoff-
Lagenkarte *f (CWS).*
gas-spraying apparatus Aus- und
Abgießgerät *n (Ap, CWS).*
gas tank Gasbehälter *m.*
gas trap Gasschleuse *f (CWS).*
gas tube Gasentladungsröhre *f*
(Rad).
gas valve Ballonventil *n (Bln).*
gas-valve operating line Ventilleine
f (Bln).
gas warfare Gaskrieg *m*
gas warning Gaswarnung *f.*
gate Tor *n (large);* Tür *f (small).*
gate-type gear shift Kulissenschaltung *f.*
gauge *See* gage.
gauze Gaze *f.*
gear Zahnrad *n (toothed wheel);*
Gang *m (gear ratio);* Zeug *n*
(equipment).
in gear eingerückt, eingeschaltet.
out of gear außer Eingriff.
gear pump Zahnradpumpe *f (Mtr).*

gear ratio Übersetzungsverhältnis
n, Übersetzung *f*.

gear shaft Spindel *f (elevating
mechanism) (G)*.

gearshift Gangschaltung *f*, Schaltung *f*.

gearshift collar Schaltmuffe *f (MT)*.

gearshift lever Schalthebel *m (MT)*.

gearshift-lever housing Schaltdom *m (MT)*.

gearshift transmission Schaltgetriebe *n (MT)*.

gear transmission Zahnradgetriebe *n (MT)*.

gear wheel Zahnrad *n*.

general *n* General *m;* Generaloberst *m (full general)*.

general *adj* allgemein.

general air defense Gesamtheit aller Luftschutzmaßnahmen.

general call sign Sammelrufzeichen *n (Rad)*.

general counterpreparation Masseneinsatz der Artillerie zum Gegenvorbereitungsfeuer.

general court-martial Oberkriegsgericht *n*.

general depot Heeresfeldzeugdienststelle *f*.

General Headquarters Oberkommando des Heeres. *See also* **GHQ**.

general hospital Heereslazarett *n*, Reservelazarett *n*.

general message Sammelmeldung *f (Rad)*.

general military service allgemeiner Wehrdienst.

general officer General *m*.

General of the Armies Generalfeldmarschall *m*.

general orders allgemeingültige Anordnungen *(Adm)*; allgemeine Postenanweisungen *(guard orders)*.

general outpost Vorposten *m*.

general-purpose airplane Mehrzweckflugzeug *n*.

general-purpose bomb Sprengbombe *f (Avn)*.

general-purpose gun Mehrzweckgeschütz *n*.

general-purpose vehicle Mehrzweckfahrzeug *n (MT)*.

general service allgemeiner Wehrdienst.

generalship Feldherrnkunst *f*.

general staff Generalstab *m*.

General Staff Corps Generalstabskorps *n*.

general staff officer Generalstabsoffizier *m*.

general staff with troops Truppengeneralstab *m*.

general support Unterstützung durch angewiesene Artillerie *(Arty, Tac)*.

generate erzeugen.

generating unit Maschinensatz *m*, Stromaggregat *n;* Kraftquellenwagen *m (mobile);* Tretsatz *m (pedal-operated);* Kleinmaschinensatz *m (portable)*.

generation Erzeugung *f*, Entwicklung *f (Tech);* Generation *f (age group)*.

generator Stromerzeuger *m*, Dynamomaschine *f*, Generator *m (Elec);* Lichtmaschine *f (for lighting);* Zündlichtmaschine *f (MT);* Induktor *m (Tp)*.

generator-starter Lichtanlasser *m (MT)*.

Geneva Convention Genfer Abkommen.

Geneva Cross Genfer Rotes Kreuz.

gentle slope flache Böschung *(Top)*.

geodetic survey Landesaufnahme *f*.

geographic code Schlüssel für Ortsnamen *(Sig C)*.

geographic coordinates geographische Koordinaten.

geographic index number Kartenblattnummer *f*.

geographic map geographische Karte.

geographic north geographisch Nord.

geometrical pitch geometrische Schraubensteigung *(Ap propeller)*.

geometric projection perspektivische Projektion.

geophone Erdhörer *m*.

germ Bazille *f*, Keim *m*.

German Cross Deutsches Kreuz *(decoration)*.

getaway man Gefechtsmelder *m*.

GHQ air force dem Heer unterstellte Fliegerverbände.

GHQ artillery Heeresartillerie *f*.

GHQ cavalry Heereskavallerie *f*.

GHQ medical battalion Heeressanitätsabteilung *f*.

GHQ motor vehicle park Heereskraftfahrpark *m*.

GHQ pool *See* **GHQ troops.**

GHQ reserve Heeresreserven *fpl.*

GHQ reserve tank groups Panzerverbände der Heerestruppen.

GHQ signal communication section Heeresnachrichtenverband *m.*

GHQ supply column Heeresnachschubkolonne *f.*

GHQ troops Heerestruppen *fpl.*

giant tire Riesenluftreifen *m (MT).*

gimbal kardanische Aufhängung *(compass).*

girder Balken *m,* Träger *m,* Unterzug *m.*

girth Sattelgurt *m (of saddle).*

gisement Meridiankonvergenz *f (Surv).*

give ground weichen, zurückweichen.

give way ausweichen.

gland Düse *f (MG);* Stopfbüchse *f (Mech);* Durchführung *f,* Stopfbuchsdeckel *m (Bln);* Drüse *f (Med).*

glare Blendung *f.*

glass Glas *n.*

glass scale Glasmaßstab *m (Optics).*

glaze glasartige Vereisung *(Avn).*

glide *n* Gleitflug *m (Avn).*

glide *v* gleiten, segeln.

glide bombing Angriff aus dem Gleitflug.

glide landing Landung in flachem Gleitflug.

glider Segelflugzeug *n,* Segler *m,* Gleiter *m,* Gleitflugzeug *n;* Motorsegler *m (powered).*

glider bomb Gleitbombe *f (Avn).*

glider flight Luftlandekette *f.*

glider pilot Segelflieger *m.*

glider squadron Luftlandestaffel *f.*

gliding Gleitflug *m,* Gleiten *n (Ap);* Segelflug *m,* Segeln *n (glider).*

gliding ability Gleitfähigkeit *f.*

gliding angle Gleitwinkel *m,* Gleitflugwinkel *m.*

gliding turn Kurve im Gleitflug *(Avn).*

glove Handschuh *m.*

glow plug Glühkerze *f (Diesel engine).*

glue Leim *m,* Fischleim *m.*

glycerin Glyzerin *n.*

gnomonic projection gnomonischer Kartenentwurf, gnomonische Projektion, zentrale Projektion.

goggles Schutzbrille *f.*

going flight Abflug *m.*

gondola Gondel *f (Avn).*

gondola car offener Güterwagen, Bordwandwagen *m (RR).*

goniometer Winkelmesser *m,* Goniometer *n (Surv).*

goniometry Winkelmessung *f,* Goniometrie *f (Surv).*

gonorrhea Tripper *m.*

gooseberry Drahtigel *m (obstacle).*

goose step Exerziermarsch *m,* Stechschritt *m.*

gorge Schlucht *f (Top).*

governing device Regelvorrichtung *f (Mtr).*

government Regierung *f (of a state);* Verwaltung *f (administration);* Militärverwaltung *f (Mil Govt).*

government property Staatsbesitz *m.*

governor Drehzahlregler *m,* Motorregler *m,* Regler *m (Mtr).*

governor arms Reglergabel *f (Mtr).*

governor drive Reglerantrieb *m (Mtr).*

governor housing Drehzahlregler-Gehäuse *n,* Reglergehäuse *n (Mtr).*

governor spring Reglerfeder *f (Mtr).*

grade Dienstgrad *m;* Munitionsart *f (Am);* Steigung *f (Top).*

grade chevron Dienstgradabzeichen *n.*

grade crossing Planübergang *m.*

gradient Steigung *f,* Böschungswinkel *m,* Hangwinkel *m (Top);* Gefälle *n,* Gradient *m (Met).*

graduate *n* Mensur *f,* Meßbecher *m,* Meßglas *n (container);* Absolvent *m (from a school).*

graduate *v* abstufen, einteilen *(into degrees);* absolvieren *(from a school).*

graduated disk Teilscheibe *f (plotting protractor).*

graduated oil dispenser Ölmeßbecher *m (MT).*

graduation Eichstrich *m,* Gradeinteilung *f,* Strich *m.*

grand strategy Gesamtkriegführung *f:*

grand tactics Massentaktik *f.*

granular form Körnerform *f (powder).*

granulation Granulation *f,* Granulieren *n,* Gestalt und Dichte der Pulverkörner *(Am).*

granule Körnchen *n.*

graph Kurvenblatt *n.*

graphical firing table   Artillerie-rechenschieber *m*.

graphite Graphit *m*.

graphite grease Graphitfett *n*.

graphite lubricant Graphitschmier-mittel *n*.

grapnel Ankersucher *m*, Dragge *f*, Suchanker *m*.

grapple den Suchanker über den Grund schleppen *(Engr, Nav)*.

grassland Wiese und Weide.

gratuity Zulage *f*.

gratuity upon death Sterbegeld *n*.

graupel shower Graupelschauer *m* *(Met)*.

gravel pit Kiesgrube *f*.

gravel road Kiesstraße *f*, Schotter-straße *f*.

grave marker Grabkreuz *n*, Grab-tafel *f*.

graveside service Ehrenbezeigungen bei Beerdigung *(Mil funeral)*.

Graves Registration Service Kriegs-gräberfürsorge *f*.

gravitation Erdschwere *f (Physics)*.

gravity *See* **gravitation.**

gravity-system water cooling Ther-mosyphonkühlung *f (Mtr)*.

gravity tank Fallbenzintank *m* *(MT)*.

graze *n* Auftreffpunkt eines Ge-schosses oder Abprallers bei Flach-feuer *(Gunnery)*.

graze *v* bestreichen.

graze burst Zerspringen des Ge-schosses im Augenblick des Auf-schlags beim Schießen mit Zeit-zünder.

grazing fire bestreichendes Feuer, Strichfeuer *n (MG)*.

grease *n* Fett *n*.

grease *v* einfetten.

grease coating Fettüberzug *m*.

grease cup Schmierbüchse *f*.

grease gun Luftdruck-Fettpresse *f*, Fettpresse *f (Mech)*.

great circle Großkreis *m*.

great-circle chart Karte nach dem gnomonischen Kartenentwurf.

great-circle course Kurs auf dem größten Kreis.

green grün.

Greenwich hour angle Greenwicher Stundenwinkel.

Greenwich Time Greenwicher Zeit.

grenade Handgranate *f (hand)*; Gewehrgranate *f (R)*.

grenade court Handgranatenwurf-stand *m*.

grenade launcher Schießbecher *m*.

grid Gitter *n (map, Rad)*.

grid azimuth Richtungswinkel *m* *(Surv)*.

grid base-line direction Gitterrich-tung *f (Gunnery)*.

grid capacitor Gitterkondensator *m* *(Rad)*.

grid circuit Gitterkreis *m (Rad)*.

grid condenser Gitterkondensator *m* *(Rad)*.

grid control Steuerwirkung des Gitters *(Rad)*.

grid coordinates Koordinaten des Gitters *(Surv)*.

grid declination Meridiankonvergenz *f (Surv)*.

gridded map Gitternetzkarte *f*.

grid-leak detector Audion *n (Rad)*.

grid line Gitterlinie *f*, Gitternetz-linie *f*.

grid north Gitter-Nord *m (Surv)*.

grid rectifier Gittergleichrichter *m* *(Rad)*.

grid resistance Gitterwiderstand *m* *(Rad)*.

grid resistor Gitterdrossel *f (Rad)*.

grid sheet Kartenblatt mit Gitter.

grid square Quadrat *n*, Planquadrat *n (map)*.

grid system Gitternetz *n*.

grid voltage Gitterspannung *f* *(Rad)*.

grinding Schleifen *n (Tech)*; Hacken *n (meat, etc.)*.

grinding machine Schleifmaschine *f* *(Tech)*; Fleischhackmaschine *f* *(meat grinder)*.

grip *n* Griff *m*, Griffstück *n*, Hand-griff *m*; Griffigkeit *f (of tires)*; Handstütze *f (pistol)*; Knüppelgriff *m (of control stick, Ap)*.

grip safety Sicherungshebel *m (pis-tol)*.

groin Leistengegend *f*.

grommet Kausche *f*.

groove Nut(e) *m(f)*; Zug *m* *(rifling)*.

grooved piston ring Ölschlitzring *m* *(Mtr)*.

gross tonnage Bruttotonnengehalt *m* *(Nav)*.

gross weight Fluggewicht *n*, Ge-samtgewicht *n (Ap)*.

ground *n* Boden *m*, Erde *f*, Gelände

n, Grund *m (Top);* Erdleitung *f*, Erdschluß *m*, Erdung *f*, Erde *f*, Erder *m (Elec)*.

ground *v* am Boden festhalten *(Avn);* erden *(Elec)*.

ground adjustment target Erdeinschießziel *n (Gunnery)*.

ground alert Bereitschaft zum unverzüglichen Start *(Avn)*.

ground cable Fesselkabel *n*, Fesselseil *n*, Verankerungstau *n (Bln)*.

ground cloth Unterlegeplane *f (Bln)*.

ground commander Befehlshaber von Erdtruppen.

ground crew fliegertechnisches Personal, Bodenbedienung *f*, Bodenpersonal *n (Avn);* Landemannschaft *f (Bln)*.

ground decontamination Geländeentgiftung *f (CWS)*.

grounded geerdet *(Elec);* gestrandet *(ship)*.

grounded electrode Elektrode *f (spark plug)*.

ground elevation Bodenerhebung *f (Top)*.

ground fog Bodennebel *m (Met)*.

ground forces Erdtruppen *fpl*, Erdwaffen *fpl*.

ground form Geländegestaltung *f (Top)*.

ground gear Landevorrichtung *f (Bln)*.

ground-glass plate Mattscheibe *f*.

grounding Erdung *f (Elec)*.

grounding rod Erdstecker *m (Elec, Tp)*.

ground installations Bodenanlagen *fpl*.

ground lead Erdleitung *f*, Erdzuleitung *f (Elec)*.

ground leak Erdschluß *m*, Ableitung *f (Elec)*.

ground level Erdgleiche *f (Ft)*.

ground loop Überschlag auf dem Boden *(Avn)*.

ground mechanic Wart *m (Avn)*.

ground mine Grundmine *f (Nav)*.

ground observation Erdbeobachtung *f (Arty)*.

ground observer Luftspäher *m*, Luftwache *f (AWS)*.

ground panel Auslegezeichen *n*, Tuchzeichen *n (Sig C)*.

ground personnel Bodenpersonal *n*, Bodenorganisation *f (Avn)*.

ground pipe Erdleitungsrohr *n (Elec)*.

ground platform Geschützbettung *f*, Bettung *f (RR gun)*.

ground position signal Ortungsleuchtzeichen *n (ground-air Com)*.

ground pressure spezifischer Bodendruck *(per unit area, MT)*.

ground projector Signalwerfer *m*.

ground radiation Bodenstrahlung *f (Rad)*.

ground radio service Bodenfunkdienst *m (Avn)*.

ground radio station Bodenstelle *f (Avn)*.

ground readiness Flugbereitschaft *f*, Startbereitschaft *f (Avn)*.

ground reconnaissance Erdaufklärung *f*, Geländeerkundung *f (Tac)*.

ground reference points Bodenpunkte *mpl (Surv)*.

ground-return circuit Einfachleitung *f*, Erdrückleitung *f (Tp)*.

ground-return telephone circuit Erdtelegraphieverbindung *f*.

ground-return telephone circuit Erdfernsprechverbindung *f*.

ground school Fliegerschule für technische Ausbildung *(Avn)*.

ground signal Leuchtkugel *f*, Leuchtzeichen *n*, Handleuchtzeichen *n*.

ground signal cartridge Leuchtpatrone *f*, Meldepatrone *f*.

ground signal projector Signalwerfer *m*.

ground sill Grundschwell *f (Bdg)*.

ground speed Zielgeschwindigkeit über Grund, Horizontalgeschwindigkeit des Zieles *(AA Gunnery);* Grundgeschwindigkeit *f (Avn)*.

ground strafing Maschinengewehrangriff gegen Erdziele *(Avn)*.

ground target Bodenziel *n*.

ground troops Landtruppen *fpl*.

ground visibility Bodensicht *f (Avn)*.

ground wave Bodenwelle *f (Rad)*.

ground-wave reception zone Bodenwellenempfangszone *f (Rad)*.

ground wire Erdleitungsdraht *m (Elec)*.

group Gruppe *f (Avn);* Waffengruppe *f (Ord, Small Arms);* Gruppe *f (Tac) (generally in compounds, i.e., Artilleriegruppe, Flakgruppe, etc.)*.

group column of squadron V's Gruppenwinkel *m (Avn)*.

group column of squadron wedges Gruppenkolonne aus geschlossenen Winkeln *(Avn)*.

group commander Gruppenkommandeur *m (Avn)*.

group command post Gruppengefechtsstand *m (Avn)*.

group firing zusammengefaßtes Feuer mehrerer Schützen.

group formation Gruppenflugform *f (Avn)*.

groupment Gruppe *f*.

group of armies Heeresgruppe *f*.

group of squadron javelins Gruppenkolonne *f (Avn)*.

group of squadron javelins echeloned left Gruppenkolonne links *(Avn)*.

group wedge Gruppenkeil *m (Avn)*.

grouser Greifer *m (MT)*.

grub hoe Minenkratze *f (Engr)*.

guard *n* Wache *f*, Posten *m;* Streife *f (patrol);* Parierstange *f (bayonet guard);* Abzugsbügel *m (trigger guard)*.

on guard auf Wache *(guard duty);* auf der Hut *(alert)*.

guard *v* bewachen, Wachdienst ausüben.

guard detail Wachmannschaft *f*, Wache *f*.

guard duty Feldwachdienst *m*, "Wacheschieben" *n*.

guard fence Schutzzaun *m*.

guardhouse Arrestlokal *n*, Wachgebäude *n*.

guarding mission Auftrag zur dauernden Überwachung des feindlichen Funkverkehrs *(Rad, Sig C)*.

guard mount Aufziehen der Wache; Vergatterung *f (bugle call)*.

guard of honor Ehrenwache *f*, Ehrenposten *m*.

guard rail Rödelbalken *m (Bdg);* Radlenker *m (RR)*.

guardroom Wachstube *f*.

guerrilla Partisane *m*, Freischärler *m*, Guerillakämpfer *m*.

guerrilla warfare Kleinkrieg *m*, kleiner Krieg, Guerilakrieg *m*.

guide *n* ortskundiger Führer, Einweiser *m (Tac);* Führer *m*, Anführer *m (file);* Flügelmann *m (line);* Anhalt *m (guiding principle)*.

party of guides Einweisungskommando *n*.

guide lining Klauenfutter *n (G)*.

guide rail Führungsschiene *f*, Gleitschiene *f (G cradle)*.

guide ring Klauenring *m (G)*.

guide roller Führungsrolle *f (Tk)*.

guide slide Gleitschiene *f (G cradle)*.

guidon Standarte *f (Arty, Cav, Armd Comd);* Fahne *f (inf);* Standartenträger *m*, Fahnenträger *m (Pers)*.

guilty schuldig.

gull wing Knickflügel *m (Ap)*.

gully Schlenke *f*.

gun Geschütz *n*, Kanone *f (G);* Gewehr *n (R);* Maschinengewehr *n (MG)*.

gun arm Entfernungslineal *n (plotting board)*.

gun barrel Geschützrohr *n*, Kanonenrohr *n*.

gun battery Geschützbatterie *f*.

gunboat Kanonenboot *n*.

gun book Rohrbuch *n*.

gun car Geschützwagen *m (RR)*.

gun carriage Lafette *f*. See also gun mount.

gun-carriage axle Lafettenachse *f*.

gun-carriage bed Lafettentisch *m*.

gun-carriage side plate Lafettenwand *f*.

gun commander Geschützführer *m*.

guncotton Schießbaumwolle *f*, Schießwolle *f*.

guncotton powder Schießwollpulver *n*.

gun cover Geschützplane *f*.

gun cradle Wiege *f*.

gun crew Bedienungsmannschaft *f*, Geschützbedienung *f*.

gun difference Entfernungsunterschied zwischen Richtkreis-Ziel und Feuerstellung-Ziel.

gun displacement Staffelung *f (within a battery);* Stellungswechsel *m (change of position)*.

gun emplacement Geschützstellung *f*, Geschützstand *m*.

gunfire Geschützfeuer *n*.

gun grease Waffenfett *n*.

gun group Geschützteile *npl*, Waffengruppe *f*.

gun hoist Ladekran *m*, Geschoßkran *m*, Batteriekran *m*.

gun junction box Kupplungskasten *m (AA director)*.

gun loader Ladekanonier *m*.

gun motor carriage Selbstfahrlafette
f.
gun mount Lafette *f;* Bordlafette *f*
*(on Ap or ship). See also terms
under* **gun carriage.**
gun-mount outrigger Lafettenholm
m.
gunner   Kanonier *m (in a general
sense, FA);* Richtkanonier. *m (gunner, FA);* Richtschütze *m (gunner,
MG, AT or Tk G);* Panzerschütze *m
(Tk);* Bordschütze *m,* Fliegerschütze
m (Avn); Granatwerfer *m (Mort
squad).*
gunner's quadrant Winkelmesser *m,*
Libellenquadrant *m.*
gunner's seat Richtsitz *m (G).*
gunner's station   Schützenstand *m,*
Gefechtsstand *m (Ap).*
gunnery Schießwesen *n.*
gunnery instructor Schießlehrer *m.*
gun park Geschützpark *m.*
gun platform Feuerplattform *f.*
gun platform excavation Bettungsloch *n (RR gun).*
gun pointer   Richtschütze *m,* Richtkanonier *m.*
gun pointer's platform Plattform *f
(RR gun).*
gun pointer's shield Schutzschild *m
(G).*
gun pointing data Schießgrundlagen
fpl, Schußelemente *npl,* Schußwerte
mpl (Gunnery).
gun position   Geschützstellung *f
(Arty);* Schützenstand *m,* Gefechtsstand *m (Ap).*
gunpowder Schießpulver *n,* Schwarzpulver *n.*
gun rack   Gewehrmieke *f,* Gewehrmücke *f,* Gewehrstütze *f.*
gun rail   Lafettenschiene *f (MG
mount).*
gun section Geschützstaffel *f (Btry).*

gun shelter Schartenblende *f,* Schartenschild *m,* Klappblende *f (Ft).*
gun shield   Schutzschild *m (G);*
Blende *f (Tk).*
gun shot Kanonenschuß *m,* Schuß *m.*
gun slide Gleitschuh *m (G);* Schieber *m.*
gun sling Gewehrriemen *m,* Riemen
m (R).
gun sling hook Schnalle *f (R).*
gun sling keeper Riemenschieber *m
(R).*
gun squad Geschützbedienung *f,* Bedienung *f,* Geschützmannschaft *f,*
Bedienungsmannschaft *f.*
gun-target line Linie Geschütz-Ziel.
gunwale Dollbord *n (rowboat);* Pontonoberkante *f (Pon).*
gun wave Schallwelle des Mündungsknalls *(Sound Ranging).*
gun-wheel brake Schießbremse *f.*
gusset Eckplatte *f (Engr).*
gust Windstoß *m,* Bö *f (Met).*
guy line   Ankerseil *n,* Haltetau *n,*
Verankerungskabel *n (Engr).*
guy pin Zeltpflock *m (tent).*
guy rope Zeltleine *f (tent).*
gyro compass Kreiselkompaß *m.*
gyro control   Kreiselabfeuergerät *n
(Tk).*
gyro flight indicator Gyrorektor *m.*
gyro horizon indicator Horizont *m,*
künstlicher Horizont *(Ap Inst).*
gyro instrument Kreiselgerät *n.*
gyropilot Selbststeuergerät *n (Ap).*
gyroplane   Tragschrauber *m,* Autogiro *m.*
gyroscope Kreisel *m.*
gyroscopic turn indicator   Kreiselwendezeiger *m,* Kreiselsteuerzeiger
m (Ap).
gyro-stabilizer   Kreiselabfeuergerät
n (Tk).

H

hachures Bergstriche *mpl,* Schraffen *fpl (map).*
hacksaw Metallsäge *f.*
Hague Convention Haager Abkommen.
hail *n.* Hagel *m (Met).*
hailstorm Hagelschlag *m.*

hair Haar *n.*
hairpin curve Spitzkehre *f.*
hair trigger   Stecher *m (Small
Arms).*
half cock Ruhrast *f (Small Arms).*
half left halblinks.
half-loop wingover Fächerturn *m.*

half-mast halbmast, halbstocks.
half right halbrechts.
half roll halbe Rolle *(Avn)*.
half-squad Abmarsch *m (Cav)*.
half-staff halbstocks.
half step halber Schritt *(drill)*.
half-track carrier Zugkraftwagen *m (also used as prime mover)*.
half-track drive Halbkettenantrieb *m (MT)*.
half-track motorcycle Kettenkrad *n*.
half-track motor truck Halbketten-Lastkraftwagen *m*.
half-track motor vehicle Halbketten-kraftfahrzeug *n*.
half-track vehicle Halbkettenfahr-zeug *n*, Zwitterfahrzeug *n*.
halt *n* Halt *m*, Marschhalt *m*, Marschpause *f*; Beobachtungshalt *m (for Obsn)*.
halt *v* halten, anhalten.
"Halt!" "Halt!" *(to an individual)*; "Abteilung, halt!" *(to detail, squad, etc.)*.
halt area Halteplatz *m (Tac)*.
halter Halfter *f (for horse)*.
halter chain Halfterkinnkette *f*.
halter headstall Stallhalfter *f*.
halter tie Halfterriemen *m*.
halt order Befehl zum Halten.
"Halt! who is there?" "Halt, wer da!"
halving Bildteilung im Schnittbild-Entfernungsmesser *(coincidence range finder)*.
halving adjustment Ausschalten der Schnittbildversetzung *(coincidence range finder)*.
halving line Schnittlinie *f (coincidence range finder)*.
ham Schinken *m*.
hammer Hahn *m*, Hammer *m*, Schlagstück *n (Small Arms)*.
hammer gun Hahngewehr *n*.
hammerless gun hahnloses Gewehr, Hammerleßgewehr *n*.
hammock Hängematte *f*.
hand Hand *f*.
hand arm Handwaffe *f*.
handbook Handbuch *n*.
hand brake Handbremse *f*.
hand camera Handkammer *f*.
handcart Handwagen *m*.
hand crank Handkurbel *f (MT)*.
hand-crank generator Kurbeldynamo *m*, Handdrehmaschine *f (Elec)*; Kurbelinduktor *m (Tp)*.

handcuff Handfessel *f*.
hand drill Handbohrmaschine *f*, Brustbohrer *m*.
hand extinguisher Handfeuerlöscher *m*.
hand grenade Handgranate *f*.
hand-grenade bag Standsack *m*.
hand-grenade range Handgranaten-wurfweite *f*.
hand guard Handschutz *m (R)*.
hand hole Handloch *n (G wheel)*.
handle *n* Griff *m*, Handgriff *m*, Stiel *m*.
handle bar Lenkstange *f (Mtcl)*.
hand level Freihandnivellierinstru-ment *n (Surv)*.
handling line Haltetau *n*, Transport-tau *n (Bln)*.
hand-operated handtätig.
hand-operated ventilator Handlüfter *m*.
hand reel tragbare Kabeltrommel *(Tp)*.
hand salute Gruß *m*.
handset Handapparat *m (Tp, Rad (Tp)*.
handset switch Lauthörknopf *m (Tp)*.
handspike Richtbaum *m (G trail)*.
hand sprinkler Handstreutrommel *f (CWS)*.
hand starter Handanlasser *m (Mtr)*.
hand-to-hand fighting Kampf von Mann gegen Mann, Handgemenge *n*.
hand weapon Handwaffe *f*, blanke Waffe.
handwheel Handrad *n*.
hang einhaken *(hook on)*; aufhän-gen *(a picture, etc.)*; hängen *(a criminal)*.
hangar Flugzeughalle *f*, Halle *f*.
hanger bar Auflager *n (harness)*.
hangfire Nachbrenner *m (Am)*.
hang fire nachbrennen *(Am)*.
hangwire Entsicherungsdraht *m*.
harass stören, beunruhigen *(Tac)*.
harassing Beunruhigung *f*, Störung *f*.
harassing agent Ermüdungskampf-stoff *m*, Reizstoff *m (CWS)*.
harassing concentration Erträglich-keitsgrenze *f (CWS)*.
harassing fire Beunruhigungsfeuer *n*, Ermüdungsschießen *n*, Störungs-feuer *n*; Lähmungsschießen *n (with Cml shell)*.

harassing tactics Störungsangriffe *mpl*, Ermattungstaktik *f.*
harbor *n* Hafen *m.*
harbor *v* Schutz gewähren, beherbergen.
harbor area Hafengebiet *n.*
harbor defense Hafenschutz *m.*
harbor defense craft Hafenschutzboot *n (Nav).*
harbor-defense ordnance depot Sperramt *n.*
hard labor Strafarbeit *f.*
hard solder Schlaglot *n.*
harmonic frequency Oberschwingungsfrequenz *f (Rad).*
harmonization Ineinklangbringen *n;* Anschießen *n (Ord).*
harness *n* Bandgestell *n (gas mask);* Geschirr *n (horse);* Gurtwerk *n (Prcht).*
harne s *v* aufschirren.
hash Haschee *n.*
hasty flüchtig, schnell, behelfsmäßig, Behelfs-.
hasty ammunition shelter Munitionsnische *f (Ft).*
hasty bridge Behelfsbrücke *f,* Schnellbrücke *f.*
hasty field fortification flüchtige Feldbefestigung.
hasty footbridge Schnellsteg *m.*
hasty intrenchment flüchtige Feldbefestigung.
hasty landing stage Behelfslandbrücke *f (Engr).*
hasty meteorological message Barbarabehelfsmeldung *f (Arty).*
hasty obstacle Schnellsperre *f.*
hasty profile Höhenumrißskizze *f (Top).*
hasty single-span footbridge Uferschnellsteg *m.*
hasty trestle bridge Bockschnellsteg *m.*
hat Hut *m;* Mütze *f (cap).*
hatch Luke *f,* Einstiegluke *f,* Einsteigklappe *f (Ap);* Einsteigluke *f (Tk).*
hatch cover Lukendeckel *m (Tk).*
hatchet Handbeil *n.*
hatching Schummerung *f (map).*
hat cord Mützenkordel *f.*
haul *v* ziehen, schleppen.
haversack Tornister *m.*
haversack-type radio set Tornister-Funkgerät *n.*

haversack-type receiver Tornisterempfänger *m (Rad).*
hawser Trosse *f,* Kabeltau *n.*
haystack Heuschober *m.*
haze Dunst *m (Met).*
hazy diesig, dunstig.
HC mixture *See* **HC smoke mixture**
HC smoke mixture Zinknebel *m,* amerikanische Bergermischung *(CWS).*
head Kopf *m (anatomy);* Geschoßspitze *f (shell);* Zünderkappe *f (point-detonating fuze);* Patronenboden *m (cartridge);* Reibfläche *f (Small Arms Am);* Kopfstück *n (MG);* Geschoßkopf *m (projectile);* Kolonnenspitze *f,* Spitze *f (of a column);* Haupt *n (chief, especially in compounds).*
head and chest set Brustfernsprecher *m (Tp).*
head harness Kopfbänderung *f (gas mask).*
heading Steuerkurs *m (Air Navigation);* Überschrift *f (on messages, etc.).*
headlight Scheinwerfer *m.*
head nurse Oberschwester *f.*
headphone Hörer *m,* Kopfhörer *m,* Kopffernhörer *m (Tp, Rad).*
headquarters Stab *m,* Kommando *n,* Hauptquartier *n,* Stabsquartier *n,* Kommandostelle *f,* Kommandobehörde *f;* Gefechtsstand *m (Avn).*
headquarters and service company Stabs- und Betriebskompanie *f (USA).*
headquarters battery Stabsbatterie *f (Arty).*
headquarters clerk Stabsschreiber *m.*
headquarters company Stabskompanie *f.*
headquarters detachment Stabstrupp *m.*
headquarters net Nachrichtennetz der Kommandostellen *(Rad).*
headquarters platoon Stabszug *m.*
headquarters section Stabsgruppe *f.*
headquarters squadron Stabsstaffel *f (Avn).*
headquarters troop Kommando- und Stabsschwadron *f (Cav).*
head resistance Stirnwiderstand *m.*
headset Kopfhörer *mpl.*
head space Verschlußabstand *m (Ord).*

headstall Hauptgestell *n*, Kopfgestell *n* (*harness*).

head-strap cushion Kopfplatte *f* (*gas mask*).

head straps Kopfbänder *npl* (*gas mask*).

headway Zeitabstand *m* (*time interval*, *MT*, *RR*).

head wind Gegenwind *m*.

heal heilen.

health Gesundheit *f*.

heart Herz *n*.

heat *n* Wärme *f*, Hitze *f*.

heat *v* erwärmen, erhitzen; heizen (*a room, etc.*).

heater Ofen *m*.

heat of condensation Kondensationswärme *f* (*Met*).

heat of vaporization Verdampfungswärme *f* (*Met*).

heat-resistant hitzebeständig.

heat shrinking Aufschrumpfen *n* (*Ord*).

heatstroke Hitzschlag *m*.

heat-treated steel Vergütungsstahl *m*.

heavier-than-air aircraft Luftfahrzeuge schwerer als Luft.

heavily armored schwergepanzert.

Heaviside layer Heavisideschicht *f* (*Rad*).

heavy schwerst- (*Ord*).

heavy antitank gun s.Pak *f*.

heavy artillery schwerste Artillerie.

heavy-case bomb Panzerbombe *f*.

heavy cruiser schwerer Kreuzer (*Nav*).

heavy machine gun überschweres Maschinengewehr, s.S.MG. *n*.

heavy machine-gun section MG.-Staffel *f* (*Cav*).

heavy machine-gun squad s.M.G.-Bedienung *f*.

heavy ponton battalion schweres Pontonier-Bataillon.

heavy tank schwerer Panzerkampfwagen.

heavy weapons schwere Infanteriewaffen.

heavy weapons company Maschinengewehrkompanie *f* (*Inf*); schwere Kompanie (*Mtz R Regt*).

hedge Hecke *f*.

hedgehog Igel *m* (*AT obstacle*).

hedge-hopping Heckenspringen *n*, Tiefflug *m* (*Avn*).

heel *n* Ballen *m* (*harness*); Ferse *f* (*anatomy*); Absatz *m* (*of shoe*).

heel *v* krängen (*Avn, Nav*).

heeling error Krängungsfehler *m* (*Avn, Nav*).

height Anhöhe *f*, Höhe *f* (*Top*).

height finder Höhenmesser *m*, Höhenentfernungsmesser *m*, Entfernungsmeßgerät *n* (*AAA*).

height of burst Sprenghöhe *f* (*Gunnery*).

height of mask Deckungshöhe *f* (*Ballistics*).

height of muzzle Feuerhöhe *f* (*Arty*).

height-of-range setter Höhenrichtkanonier *m*.

height of rise Steighöhe *f* (*ground Sig*).

height of site Höhe über Normalnull (*CA*).

height of target Zielhöhe *f* (*Gunnery*).

helical spring Schraubenfeder *f*, Spiralfeder *f* (*MT*).

helical wire Drahtspirale *f*.

helicopter Schraubenflugzeug *n*, Hubschrauber *m*.

heliograph Spiegeltelegraph *m* (*Sig C*).

heliotrope *See* **heliograph**.

helium Helium *n*.

helmet Helm *m*; Stahlhelm *m* (*steel*); Fliegerhaube *f*, Kopfhaube *f* (*Avn*); F.T.-Haube *f* (*with built-in headset and throat-type microphone*); Tropenhelm *m* (*sun helmet*); Sturzhelm *m* (*crash helmet*).

helmet cover Helmbezug *m*, Helmüberzug *m*; Tarnkappe *f* (*Cam*).

hemorrhage Blutung *f*.

hernia Bruch *m*, Leistenbruch *m*.

heterodyne frequency Überlagerungsfrequenz *f*.

heterodyne frequency meter Schwebungsfrequenzmesser *m*.

hexachlorethane Hexachloräthan *n* (*CWS*).

hexagonal-head screw Sechskantschraube *f* (*MT*).

H-hour X-Uhr.

high-altitude bombing Höhenbombenwurf *m*.

high-altitude flight Höhenflug *m*.

high-altitude mixture control Höhenmischregelung *f* (*Ap*).

high-angle fire Steilfeuer *n*, Feuer in der oberen Winkelgruppe.

high-angle gun Steilfeuergeschütz *n*.

high-angle weapon Steilfeuerwaffe *f*.

high-burst adjustment target Lufteinschießziel *n* (*Arty*).

high-burst auxiliary target Luftvergleichsziel *n* (*Arty*).

high-burst ranging Einschießen mit hohen Sprengpunkten (*Gunnery*).

high command obere Kommandobehörde (*agency*); Oberbefehl *m* (*function*); Oberkommando *n* (*agency and function*).

High Command of the Air Forces Oberkommando der Luftwaffe (*Ger*).

High Command of the Armed Forces Oberkommando d e r Wehrmacht (*Ger*).

High Command of the Army Oberkommando des Heeres (*Ger*).

High Command of the Navy Oberkommando der Kriegsmarine (*Ger*).

higher echelon obere Führung (*collective*); übergeordneter Truppenteil (*unit*); übergeordnetes Kommando (*command*).

high explosive hochbrisanter Sprengstoff.

high-explosive chemical shell Gasbrisanzgranate *f*.

high-explosive rifle grenade Gewehr-Sprenggranate *f*.

high-explosive shell Brisanzgranate *f*, Sprenggranate *f* (*Am*); Sprenggranaten-Patrone *f* (*fixed Am*).

high-explosive shrapnel Brisanzschrapnell *n*.

high frequency Hochfrequenz *f*.

high-frequency interference Hochfrequenzstörungen *fpl* (*Rad*).

high-frequency oscillator tube Überlagerröhre *f*.

high-octane gasoline Benzin mit hoher Oktanzahl.

high-power radio station Großfunkstelle *f*.

high-pressure area Hochdruckgebiet *n* (*Met*).

high-pressure lubrication Hochdruckschmierung *f*.

high-pressure tire Hochdruckreifen *m* (*MT*).

high-priority material Sparstoff *m*.

high reference point Hochpunkt *m* (*Surv*).

high-tension line Hochspannungsleitung *f* (*Elec*).

high-tension obstacle Starkstromsperre *f*.

high-tension wire Hochspannungsleitung *f* (*Elec*).

high terrain Höhengelände *n* (*Top*).

high tide Hochwasser *n*.

high voltage Hochspannung *f* (*Elec*).

high-voltage line Hochspannungsleitung *f*.

high-voltage obstacle Starkstromsperre *f*.

high-voltage power lines Starkstromnetz *n* (*Elec*).

high-voltage warning device Berührungswarngerät *n*.

highway Landstraße *f*; Autobahn *f*.

high wind steifer Wind.

high-wing monoplane Hochdecker *m*.

high wire entanglement Flandernzaun *m*, Drahtzaun *m* (*Engr*).

hill Hügel *m* (*Top*).

hilltop Gipfel des Hügels, Bergspitze *f*.

hindquarters Hinterhand *f* (*horse*).

hinge Scharnier *n*.

hinged-arch bridge Gelenkbogenbrücke *f*.

hip Hüfte *f*.

hip strap Schweberiemen *m* (*harness*).

hit Treffer *m*, Einschuß *m*; Granattreffer *m* (*shell fire*); Bombentreffer *m* (*bombing*); Torpedotreffer *m* (*torpedo*); Flaktreffer *m* (*AA fire*).

hit-and-run raid Zerstörangriff *m* (*Avn*).

hitch *n* Stich *m* (*rope*).

hitch *v* anstecken (*attach*); einhaken (*hook up*); festmachen (*tie*); anschirren (*harness*).

hock Sprunggelenk *n* (*horse*).

hoe Kratze *f* (*Engr*).

hoist *n* Kran *m*, Munitionsaufzug *m*.

hoist *v* heißen, hissen (*a flag*); in die Höhe ziehen, heben (*lift*).

hold *n* Laderaum *m* (*Nav*); Griff *m* (*grip*).

hold *v* halten, standhalten (*Tac*).

holdfast Verankerung *f* (*Engr*).

holding attack Fesselungsvorstoß *m*, Nebenangriff *m*.

holding garrison Verteidigungstruppen *fpl*.

holding plate Griffplatte *f* (*G sight*).

hold off abfangen, ausschweben *(Avn)*.

hold right or left das Korn klemmen *(R aiming)*.

hole Loch *n*, Mulde *f (Top)*; Öffnung *f (opening)*; Lücke *f (gap)*.

holster Halftertasche *f*.

home Heim *n*, Heimat *f*; Haus *n*, Wohnung *f (dwelling)*.

home base Heimatflughafen *m*, Heimathorst *m (Avn)*.

home defense Landesverteidigung *f*.

home-defense system Landesverteidigungsorganisation *f*.

home field Einsatzhafen *m (Avn)*.

home front innere Front.

home parole Entlassung auf Ehrenwort.

home port Heimatshafen *m*.

home station Standort *m*.

homing Zielflug *m (Air Navigation)*; Rückflug *m (Avn)*.

homing instinct Ortsgedächtnis *n*.

homing pigeon Brieftaube *f*.

honor Ehre *f*.

honorable discharge ehrenvoller Abschied.

honorary rank Ehrenrang *m*.

honor guard Ehrenwache *f*.

hood Motorhaube *f (MT)*; Zünderhülse *f (fuze)*; Schutzhülle *f*, Überzug *m*, Kapuze *f*.

hoof Huf *m*.

hoof coronet Hufkrone *f (horse)*.

hook Haken *m*.

hook switch Gabelumschalter *m*, Hakenumschalter *m (Tp)*.

hoop Schellband *n*, Verstärkungsring *m (G)*; Hülse *f (Mort)*; Eisenreifen *m (wooden barrel or cask)*.

horizon Kimm *f*, Horizont *m*.

horizontal horizontal, waagerecht.

horizontal angle Seitenwinkel *m (Surv)*.

horizontal base Langbasis *f*, Basis *f (Arty Surv)*.

horizontal base method Zielaufnahme mit Langbasisanlage, Langbasisverfahren *n*.

horizontal bombing Waagerechtbombenwurf *m*.

horizontal clock system Windrichtungsangabe nach Melderose *(Gunnery)*.

horizontal fire Flachfeuer *n*, Feuer in der unteren Winkelgruppe *(Gunnery)*.

horizontal-fire table Tafel für das Schießen in der Mündungswaagerechten *(Gunnery)*.

horizontal flight Horizontalflug *m*, Geradeausflug *m*, Waagerechtflug *m (Avn)*.

horizontal plane Horizontalebene *f*, Kartenebene *f (Gunnery)*.

horizontal projection Projektion auf die Horizontalebene.

horizontal range Kartenentfernung *f (Gunnery)*.

horizontal range to future position Kartenentfernung zum Treffpunkt *(AAA)*.

horizontal range to midpoint Kartenentfernung zum Wechselpunkt *(AAA)*.

horizontal range to present position Kartenentfernung zum Abschußpunkt *(at instant of firing, AAA)*.

horizontal shot group Bodentreffbild *n (Ballistics)*.

horizontal target waagerechte Treffläche *(Ballistics)*.

horn Lautsprechertrichter *m (Rad)*; Trichter *m (AA sound locator)*.

horn collector Trichter *m (AA sound locator)*.

horn-type speaker Trichterlautsprecher *m (Rad)*.

horse Pferd *n*.

horse ambulance Pferdetransportwagen *m*.

horse artillery berittene Artillerie, reitende Artillerie.

horse blanket Pferdedecke *f*.

horse cavalry Kavallerie *f*.

horse-drawn pferdebespannt, bespannt.

horse-drawn artillery bespannte Artillerie.

horse-drawn generating unit Kraftquellenwagen *m*.

horse-drawn vehicle Pferdefahrzeug *n*.

horsehide Pferdehaut *f*.

horseholder Pferdehalter *m (Cav, Arty)*.

horsepower Pferdestärke *f (Mech)*.

horseshoe Hufeisen *n*.

horseshoe magnet Hufeisenmagnet *m*.

horseshoer Beschlagschmied *m*.

hose Schlauch *m*; Atemschlauch *m (gas mask, oxygen breathing apparatus)*.

hose coupling Schlauchbinder *m* (*MT*).

hospital Krankenhaus *n*, Lazarett *n*.

hospital boat Lazarettschiff *n*.

hospitalization Lazarettaufnahme *f*, Lazarettbehandlung *f*, Hospitalisierung *f*.

hospital ship Lazarettschiff *n;* Leichtkrankenschiff *n* (*for sitting wounded*).

hospital train Lazarettzug *m;* Leichtkrankenzug *m* (*for sitting wounded*).

hospital transport Lazarettschiff *n*.

hospital treatment Lazarettbehandlung *f*.

hostage Geisel *m-f*.

hostile feindlich. *See also* enemy.

hostile forces Feindstreitkräfte *fpl*.

hostile territory Feindesland *n*.

hostilities Feindseligkeiten *fpl*.

hot cathode Glühkathode *f* (*Rad*).

hot-wire-bridge head Glühköpfchen *n* (*electric igniting device*) (*Engr*).

hour Stunde *f*.

hour angle Stundenwinkel *m*.

hour of operation Betriebsstunde *f* (*Mech*).

house Haus *n*.

house warden Hauswart *m* (*Civ. Defense*).

housewife Nähzeug *n* (*personal equipment*).

housing Gehäuse *n* (*Mech*).

howitzer Haubitze *f* (*105 mm and 150 mm*); Mörser *m* (*210 mm and larger*).

howitzer barrel Mörserrohr *n*.

howitzer carriage Haubitzlafette *f*.

HS vapor detector kit Senfgas-Spürgerät *n* (*CWS*).

hub Nabe *f*.

hub cap Radkappe *f* (*Arty, MT*).

hub flange Nabenscheibe *f* (*G wheel*); Nabenflansch *m* (*MT*).

hull Kasten *m*, Panzerkasten *m*, Panzerkörper *m*, Wanne *f* (*Tk*);

Rumpf *m*, Boot *n* (*flying boat*); Schiffsrumpf *m* (*Nav*).

humidity Feuchtigkeitsgehalt *m*, Feuchtigkeit *f* (*Met*).

hump Ablaufberg *m* (*RR*).

hung striker Schlagbolzen-Versager *m* (*fuze*).

hunt *v* schwingen, wandern (*Mech*).

hurdle *n* Hürde *f*, Verhau *m*, Hindernis *n*.

hurricane Orkan *m*, Taifun *m*.

hut Hütte *f*.

hydraulic brake Öldruckbremse *f* (*MT*).

hydraulic shock absorber Flüssigkeits-Stoßdämpfer *m* (*MT*).

hydrochloric acid Salzsäure *f*.

hydrocyanic acid Hydrozyansäure *f*, Blausäure *f*, Zyanwasserstoff *m*, Zyanwasserstoffsäure *f* (*CWS*).

hydrogen Wasserstoff *m*.

hydrogen peroxide Wasserstoffsuperoxyd *n*.

hydrogen sulfide Schwefelwasserstoff *m*.

hydrographic map Seekarte *f* (*Nav*).

hydrometer Aräometer *n*, Säuremesser *m*.

hydrophone Unterwasserhorchgerät *n* (*Nav*).

hydrostatic bomb fuze hydrostatische Zündvorrichtung, S e e z ü n d e r *m* (*antisubmarine bombs and depth charges*).

hygiene Hygiene *f*, Gesundheitspflege *f* (*care*); Gesundheitslehre *f* (*science*).

hygrograph Feuchtigkeitsschreiber *m*.

hygrometer Feuchtigkeitsmesser *m*.

hygroscopic hygroskopisch, wassergierig.

hypothetical target angenommenes Ziel (*Gunnery*).

hypsometry Höhenmessung *f* (*Surv*).

hysteresis Hysterese *f*, Nachhinken *n* (*Inst, Mech*).

I

ice Eis *n*.

ice apron Eisbrecher *m* (*Bdg*).

ice creepers Steigeisen *npl*.

ice eliminating Enteisung *f:* Warm-

luftenteisung *f* (*thermo method*) (*Avn*).

ice-eliminating system Enteisungsanlage *f* (*Ap*).

ice formation Eisansatz m (Avn).
ice spade Eissporn m (trail spade) (G).
icing Vereisung f (Avn).
icw tönend (marking on Rad set).
identification Identifikation f, Identifizierung f, Erkennen n.
identification card Ausweiskarte f.
identification helmet band Helmband n (maneuvers).
identification light Kennlicht n, Kennscheinwerfer m (Ap).
identification mark Erkennungszeichen n, Kennzeichen n.
identification panel Erkennungstuch n.
identification papers Personalausweis m, Ausweispapier n.
identification signal Kennung f (Avn).
identification tag Erkennungsmarke f.
identify identifizieren (a person, thing); erkennen (a Cml agent); sich ausweisen (identify oneself).
idle v leerlaufen (Mtr).
idler Leitrad n (Tk).
idler adjuster rod Spannschloß n (Tk).
idler jet Leerlaufdüse f (Mtr).
idler wheel Leitrad n (Tk).
idler wheel shaft Leitradachse f (Tk).
idling speed Leerlauf m (Mtr).
igloo Schneehütte f.
igloo magazine Munitionsbunker m.
ignite zünden (a charge, etc.); anzünden, in Brand setzen (set on fire); sich entzünden, Feuer fangen (begin to burn).
igniter Beiladung f (Am); Zünder m (land mine); Glühzündstück n (Elec igniter).
igniter train Zündsatz m (pyrotechnic Sig).
igniting Zünden n (Mtr).
igniting charge Beiladung f (Am); Zündladung f.
igniting flash Zündstrahl m (Am).
igniting fuze Brennzünder m (hand grenade).
igniting mixture Zündmasse f.
igniting powder Beiladung f (Am).
ignition Zünden n, Zündung f (Mtr).
ignition cartridge Zündpatrone f (Am).
ignition charge Zündladung f (Am).

ignition coil Zündspule f (Mtr).
ignition current Zündstrom m (Mtr).
ignition key Zündschlüssel m (MT).
ignition quality Zündwilligkeit f (Diesel fuel).
ignition spark Zündfunke m (Mtr).
ignition switch Zündschalter m (Ap, MT).
ignition system Zündanlage f, Zündvorrichtung f (Mtr).
ill krank.
illegal illegal, ungesetzlich, gesetzwidrig.
illegible unleserlich, unlesbar.
illiterate n Analphabet m.
illiterate adj des Schreibens und Lesens unkundig.
illuminant charge Leuchtsatz m.
illuminating shell Leuchtgranate f.
illuminating window Beleuchtungsfenster n (panoramic sight).
illumination Anleuchten n, Beleuchtung f.
illustrate veranschaulichen.
illustration Abbildung f (visual); Erläuterung f (explanation); Beispiel n (example).
illustrative material Anschauungsmittel npl (training aids).
immediate verzögerungsfrei (Ord); augenblicklich, unverzüglich.
immediate action Beseitigen von Hemmungen.
immediate action letter Vordruck für dringende Meldungen.
immediate objective erstes Angriffsziel.
Immelmann turn hochgezogene Kehrkurve, Immelmann-Turn m (Avn).
immobilize festhalten, lähmen, niederhalten (Tac).
immune geschützt, immun.
immunization Immunisierung f.
impact Aufschlag m, Auftreffen n, Einschlag m, Geschoßeinschlag m.
impact area Aufschlaggelände n.
impacted snow Schneestauung f (MT).
impact fuze Aufschlagzünder m (Am).
impedance Scheinwiderstand m, Impedanz f (Elec).
impedimenta Gepäck n.
impel treiben, antreiben.
impeller Ladelaufrad n (Ap engine); Laufrad n (of pump, etc.).

impermeability Wasserdichtigkeit *f (to water);* Gasdichtigkeit *f (to gas);* Dichtigkeit *f,* Undurchdringlichkeit *f.*

impermeable wasserdicht *(to water);* gasdicht *(to gas);* undurchdringlich *(impenetrable).*

impermeable protective clothing Gasschutzkleidung *f.*

impetigo Eiterflechte *f,* Blasengrind *m,* Impetigo *f.*

impregnate imprägnieren.

impregnite Imprägniermittel *n.*

impress zum Dienst pressen.

imprison ins Gefängnis stecken.

improper uniform unvorschriftsmäßige Uniform.

improve ausbauen *(Ft);* ausbessern, bessern *(a road, etc.).*

improved road unterhaltener Fahrweg.

improvised mount Hilfslafette *f (MG).*

improvised road behelfsmäßige Fahrbahn *(Engr).*

impulse generator mechanism Flugzeug-M.G.-Steuerung *f,* Synchronisator *m (Ap).*

inaccessible unerreichbar *(of a place);* nicht zu sprechen *(said of a busy person)*

inaccurate ungenau *(not precise);* fehlerhaft *(erroneous).*

inactivate aus dem aktiven Dienst entlassen.

inactive inaktiv, nicht aktiv.

Inactive Reserve Inaktive Offiziere.

inadequate unzulänglich, unangemessen.

inboard stabilizing float Stützflosse *f,* Flossenstummel *m (seaplane).*

incandescent cathode tube Glühkathodenröhre *f (Rad).*

incandescent lamp Glühlampe *f.*

incapable unfähig, ungeeignet; untauglich *(unfit).*

incendiary *adj* brandwirkend, Brand-.

incendiary agent Brandstoff *m,* Brandmittel *n.*

incendiary ammunition Brandmunition *f.*

incendiary bomb Brandbombe *f;* Stabbrandbombe *f (stick-type).*

incendiary bottle Brandflasche *f,* Molotowcocktail *m.*

incendiary bullet Phosphorgeschoß *n,* Brandgeschoß *n.*

incendiary cluster Brandbombenbündel *n (bombing).*

incendiary composition Brandmasse *f (Am).*

incendiary grenade Brandgranate *f,* Brand-Handgranate *f.*

incendiary projectile Brandgeschoß *n.*

incendiary shell Brandgranate *f.*

inch Zoll *m (2.54 cm).*

incineration Abbrennen *n (CWS).*

incinerator Kehrichtofen *m.*

incision Einschnitt *m,* Schnitt *m.*

incite aufhetzen.

inclination Neigung *f,* Steigung *f.*

incline *n* Ablaufberg *m (RR);* Steigung *f,* Hang *m (Top).*

inclined sights verkantetes Visier *(Small Arms).*

inclinometer Neigungsmesser *m.*

inclosure Beilage *f.*

income tax Einkommensteuer *f.*

incoming-call signal light Anrufschauzeichen *n (Tp).*

incoming track Einfahrgleis *n (RR).*

increase *n* Zunahme *f (addition);* Gewinn *m (gain);* Steigerung *f (intensification);* Vermehrung *f,* Erhöhung *f (in numbers);* Wachsen *n,* Anwachsen *n (growing).*

increase in range Vorverlegung des Feuers *(Arty).*

increase of efficiency Leistungssteigerung *f (Mtr).*

increasing twist wachsender Drall, zunehmender Drall *(Ord).*

increment Teilladung *f (separate-loading Am).*

increment section *See* **increment**.

indecision Unentschlossenheit *f.*

indelible pencil Tintenstift *m,* Kopierstift *m.*

indemnity Schadenersatz *m.*

independent unabhängig, selbständig.

independent suspension Einzelaufhängung *f (of wheels, MT).*

independent units selbständige Verbände *(Tac).*

index Marke *f,* Stellmarke *f (optical Inst).*

index error Ablesefehler *m.*

index line Ablesemarke *f.*

index map Übersichtsbild *n (aerial Photo).*

index mark Ablesemarke *f (optical Inst).*

index plate Markenplatte *f (on aiming circle or telescopic sight).*

index ring Markenring *m (MG telescopic sight).*

Indian file Gänsemarsch *m.*

indicated air speed Eigengeschwindigkeit *f,* Relativgeschwindigkeit *f,* Geschwindigkeit zur Luft *(Avn).*

indicated horsepower indizierte Leistung.

indicator Anzeiger *m,* Zeiger *m;* Empfänger *m (fuze setter, follow-the-pointer mechanism on AA gun);* Folgezeiger *m,* Gegenzeiger *m (follow-the-pointer mechanism on data transmission system).*

indicator-regulator Empfänger *m (data transmission system) (AA gun).*

indicator slide Anzeigerschiene *f (MG).*

indirect fire indirektes Feuer, indirektes Schießen *(Gunnery).*

indirect laying indirektes Richten *(Gunnery).*

indirect pointing *See* indirect laying.

indirect support operative Unterstützung *(Avn, Tac).*

indispensable unabkömmlich, unentbehrlich.

individual *n* der Einzelne.

individual *adj* Einzel-, persönlich.

individual air raid precautions Selbstschutz *m (Civ defense).*

individual attack Einzelangriff *m.*

individual clothing slip Uniformbezugschein *m.*

individual equipment Einzelausrüstung *f.*

individual pay record Soldbuch *n.*

individual protection Einzelschutz *m.*

individual release Einzel(ab)wurf *m (bombing).*

individual suspension Einzelabfederung *f (of wheels, MT).*

indoctrination Unterweisung *f.*

indoor antenna Zimmerantenne *f.*

indoors in geschlossenen Räumen.

induced detonation Zündübertragung *f (blasting).*

induced-detonation charge Folgeladung *f (Engr).*

induced drag induzierter Widerstand *(Avn).*

induct einberufen.

inductance Belastung *f (Rad).*

induction Einberufung *f (Mil);* Induktion *f (Elec).*

induction coil Sprechspule *f (Tp).*

induction order Gestellungsbefehl *m.*

induction station Einberufungsort *m.*

industrial gewerblich, industriell.

industrial installations Industrieanlagen *fpl.*

industry Industrie *f.*

inefficient untüchtig, unfähig.

inert träge, unentzündbar, neutral.

inertia Beharrungsvermögen *n,* Trägheit *f (Ballistics, Mech).*

inertia pellet Schlagbolzen *m (fuze).*

inertia starter Schwungkraftanlasser *m (Mtr).*

inertia striker pellet Schlagbolzen *m (fuze).*

inert material Gaskampf- und Schutzgerät *n (CWS).*

inexcusable unverzeihlich, unentschuldbar.

infantry Infanterie *f.*

infantry-accompanying gun Infanteriebegleitgeschütz *n.*

infantry assault Infanteriesturm *m.*

infantry battalion Infanteriebataillon *n.*

infantry commander Infanteriekommandeur *m.*

infantry company Grenadierkompanie *f,* Infanteriekompanie *f.*

infantry division Infanteriedivision *f;* Jägerdivision *f (Ger light Mtz Inf Div).*

infantry equipment park Infanteriepark *m.*

infantry howitzer Infanteriegeschütz *n.*

infantryman Grenadier *m,* Infanterist *m;* Landser *m (Slang).*

infantry mil Einheit der 6283-Teilung des Vollkreises *(Gunnery).*

infantry pack Tornister *m,* Rückengepäck *n.*

infantry pioneer Infanteriepionier *m.*

infantry point Infanteriespitze *f (march column).*

infantry rear point Infanterienachspitze *f (march column).*

infantry regiment Grenadierregiment *n,* Infanterieregiment *n.*

Infantry School Infanterieschule *f.*

infantry weapon Infanteriewaffe *f.*

infection Ansteckung *f,* Infektion *f.*

inferior niedriger, unter *(lower)*; unterlegen, schwächer *(in numbers)*; untergeordnet, unterstellt *(in rank)*; minderwertig *(in quality)*.

inferiority Unterlegenheit *f (Tac)*.

infiltrate einsickern *(Tac)*.

infiltration Einsickern *n*, Eindringen *n (Tac)*.

infirmary Krankenstube *f*, Krankenrevier *n*.

infirmary case Revierkranker *m (Med)*.

inflammable feuergefährlich, entzündbar.

inflate aufblasen.

inflow Vorstrom *m*, Saugluft *f (Avn)*.

influenza Grippe *f*.

in force mit starken Kräften, mit Einsatz aller Kräfte *(Tac)*.

inform benachrichtigen, in Kenntnis setzen, mitteilen, informieren.

information Auskunft *f;* Auskunftstelle *f (place)*; Nachricht *f (intelligence)*.

information center Flugmeldekommando *n (AWS, Z of I)*; Flugmeldezentrale *f (AWS, T of Opns)*.

information of objectives Zielunterlagen *fpl (bombing)*.

"Information please" "Bitte Auskunft" *(Tp)*.

initial *n* Initiale *f*, Anfangsbuchstabe *m*.

initial *adj* anfänglich, Anfangs-.

initial charge Anfangsladung *f (Engr)*.

initial data Eingangswerte *mpl (AAA)*.

initial fire order Einschieß-Kommando *n*.

initial issue erste Ausstattung.

initial phase Auftakt *m (of an operation)*.

initial point Anfangspunkt *m*, Ausgangspunkt *m;* Bereitstellung *f (Tac)*.

initial position Ausgangsstellung *f*, Anfangsstellung *f (Tac)*.

initial return Iststärkenachweis *m*.

initial twist Anfangsdrall *m (Ord)*.

initial velocity Anfangsgeschwindigkeit *f*, Mündungsgeschwindigkeit *f (Ballistics)*.

initiate anfangen, beginnen *(begin)*; einführen *(introduce)*; einweihen *(initiate into)*.

initiate an action das Gefecht einleiten *(Tac)*.

initiate an assault zum Sturm antreten.

initiative Initiative *f (Tac)*; Einsatzbereitschaft *f (quality)*.

take the initiative die Initiative ergreifen *(Tac)*.

initiator Initialzünder *m (Am)*.

injection nozzle Einspritzdüse *f*, Zerstäuberdüse *f (Diesel engine)*.

injection pump Einspritzpumpe *f*.

injury Verletzung *f*, Verwundung *f*.

ink Tinte *f*.

in kind in Natur.

inland waterway Binnenwasserstraße *f*.

inlet Einlaß *m;* Bucht *f (creek)*.

inlet valve Einatemventil *n (gas mask, oxygen breathing apparatus)*; Einlaßventil *n (Tech)*.

in-line engine Reihenmotor *m*.

in-line upright engine Reihenstandmotor *m*.

inner cap Innenhütchen *n (blasting cap)*.

inner harbor Innenhafen *m*.

inner sleeve Innenschieber *m (sleeve-valve engine)*.

inner tube Luftschlauch *m*, Schlauch *m;* schußsicherer Schlauch *(bullet-resisting)*.

innocent unschuldig, schuldlos.

inoculate impfen.

inoculation Impfung *f*, Schutzimpfung *f*.

inquire fragen, nachfragen, sich erkundigen.

inquire as to party desired abfragen *(Tp)*.

inquire one's way sich nach dem Wege erkundigen.

inquiry Frage *f*, Nachfrage *f*, Erkundigung *f*.

insensitive to shock stoßsicher *(explosives)*.

inshore patrol Küstenpatrouille *f*.

insignia Abzeichen *n;* Rangabzeichen *n (rank)*; Hoheitsabzeichen *n (national)*; Erkennungszeichen *n (for identification of Ap, Tk, etc.)*.

inspect untersuchen, prüfen, besichtigen.

inspection Inspizierung *f*, Inspektion *f*, Inaugenscheinnahme *f*, Besichtigung *f*.

inspection hole Schauloch *n (Mtr)*.

inspection-mark plate Stempel-platte *f (R)*.
inspector Inspekteur *m*.
inspectorate Inspektion *f (Ger)*.
inspector general Heeresinspekteur *m (USA)*.
Inspector General's Department Generalinspektion *f (USA)*.
installation Anlage *f*, Einrichtung *f*.
instant Moment *m*, Augenblick *m*.
instantaneous current Momentstrom *m (Elec)*.
instantaneous fuze Schnellzünder *m*, Augenblickszünder *m*, Aufschlag-zünder ohne Verzögerung.
instruct unterrichten *(teach)*; an-weisen *(direct)*.
instruction Unterricht *m (teaching)*; Weisung *f (directive)*; Anhalts-punkt *m (in orders, etc., generally in plural)*.
instructional aid Ausbildungsbehelf *m*.
instruction firing Belehrungs-schießen *n*.
instructor Ausbilder *m*, Lehrer *m*.
instructor's license Fahrlehrerschein *m (MT)*.
instrument Gerät *n*, Instrument *n*.
instrumental error Instrument-Feh-ler *m*.
instrument board Armaturenbrett *n*.
instrument case Apparattornister *m (portable Rad)*.
instrument flying Blindflug *m*.
instrument-flying equipment Blind-fluggerät *n*, Blindfluginstrumen-tierung *f*.
instrument landing Blindlandung *f*; A.N.-Verfahren *n (A.N. method of beam bracketing) (Avn)*.
instrument-landing equipment Blind-landungsgerät *n (Avn)*.
instrument-landing receiver Blind-landungsempfänger *m (Rad)*.
instrument light Schaltbrettlaterne *f*, Gerätelicht *n*.
instrument panel Armaturenbrett *n*, Gerätebrett *n*, Instrumentenbrett *n (Ap, MT)*.
insubordination Gehorsamsverwei-gerung *f*.
insulate isolieren.
insulated electrode Zündstift *m (spark plug)*.
insulating material Isolierstoff *m*.

insulating tape Isolierband *n*, Iso-lierstreifen *m (Elec)*.
insulation Isolierschutz *m (Elec)*; Dichtung *f (sealing)*.
insulator Isolator *m*; Isolierstoff *m (insulating substance) (Elec)*.
insurance Versicherung *f*.
intake duct Ansaugleitung *f*, Saug-leitung *f (Mtr)*.
intake line Einlaßkanal *m (Mtr)*.
intake manifold Saugrohr *n (Mtr)*.
intake pipe Ansaugrohr *n (Mtr)*.
intake stroke Ansaughub *m*, Saug-hub *m*, Ansaugetakt *m (Mtr)*.
intake valve Einlaßventil *n*, Saug-ventil *n (Mtr)*.
intake-valve chamber Einlaßventil-kammer *f (Mtr)*.
integral calculus Integralrechnung *f*.
intelligence Nachricht *f (informa-tion)*; Nachrichtenwesen *n (organ-ization)*; Nachrichtenbeschaffung *f (gathering of information)*; Nach-richtendienst *m (service)*.
intelligence map vom Nachrichten-dienst vorbereitete Lagenkarte.
intelligence net Netz des Nachrich-tendienstes.
intelligence officer Nachrichten-offizier *m*.
intelligence section Nachrichtenab-teilung *f*.
intelligence service Nachrichten-dienst *m*.
intelligence situation map vom Nach-richtendienst vorbereitete Lagen-karte.
intensity Intensität *f*, Stärke *f*, Hef-tigkeit *f*.
intensity of light Lichtstärke *f*.
intent Absicht *f*, Vorhaben *n*.
interaircraft communication Ver-ständigung von Bord zu Bord *(Avn)*.
intercept ablauschen *(Rad)*; abfan-gen *(Tac)*.
intercept apparatus Lauschgerät *n (Tg, Tp)*.
intercept board Kontrollkarte *f (AWS)*.
interception Abhören *n (Tp)*; Ab-fangen *n (Tac)*.
interceptor airplane Jäger *m*, Jagd-flugzeug *n*, Zerstörer *m*.
interceptor group Jagdgruppe *f (Avn)*.
intercept post Lauschstelle *f (Tg, Tp)*.

intercept receiver Lauschempfänger *m (Tg, Tp)*.

intercept service Horchdienst *m*, Lauschdienst *m (Rad,˙ Tp)*.

intercept station Mithörstelle *f*, Abhörstelle *f*, Lauschstelle *f (Rad, Tp)*; Funkhorchstelle *f (Rad)*.

interchangeable austauschbar, wechselbar.

interchangeability Austauschbarkeit *f*.

intercommunication Querverbindung *f (intervehicular)*; Eigenverständigung *f (intravehicular)*.

intercommunication channel Funkquerverbindung *f (Rad)*.

intercommunication line Querverbindung *f (Tp)*.

intercommunication system Bordsprechanlage *f*, Bordverständigungsanlage *f (Ap, Tk)*.

intercommunication telephone Bordsprechgerät *n*, Bordgerät *n (Ap, Tk)*.

intercooler Ladeluftkühler *m (Ap supercharger)*.

interdict abriegeln, sperren, ausschließen.

interdiction fire Behinderungsschießen *n*, Feuerriegel *m*.

interfere stören *(Rad)*.

interference Störung *f;* Störgeräusch *n (Rad)*.

interference elimination Entstörung *f (Rad)*.

interior Innenraum *m*.

interior ballistic factors besondere Einflüsse.

interior ballistics innere Ballistik, innere Schießlehre.

interior bracing Innenauskreuzung *f*, Innenverspannung *f (Ap)*.

interior guard Innenwache *f*.

interior guard duty Standortwachdienst *m*.

intermediate circuit Zwischenkreis *m (Rad)*.

intermediate depot rückwärtiges Zweiglager.

intermediate frequency Zwischenfrequenz *f (Rad)*.

intermediate landing field Zwischenlandungsplatz *m*.

intermediate objective Angriffszwischenziel *n*, Zwischenziel *n*.

intermediate position Übergangsstellung *f*, Zwischenstellung *f*.

intermediate range Zwischenentfernung *f (Gunnery)*.

intermediate scale map Karte im Maßstab 1 : 200,000 bis 1 : 500,000.

intermediate section mittlerer Abschnitt des rückwärtigen Gebietes.

intermediate station Zwischenbahnhof *m (RR)*.

intermittent fire stoßweises Feuer.

intermittent light Wechselfeuer *n*.

intern internieren.

internal-combustion engine Brennermotor *m*, Verbrennungsmotor *m*, Verbrennungskraftmaschine *f*.

internal expanding brake Innenbackenbremse *f*.

internal resistance innerer Widerstand *(Elec)*.

international code internationales Signalbuch *(Nav)*. See also **International Morse Code**.

international law Völkerrecht *n*, internationales Recht.

International Morse Code internationales Morsealphabet.

International Red Cross Internationales Rotes Kreuz.

internee Internierter *m*.

internet traffic Querverkehr *m (Rad)*.

internment camp Interniertenlager *n*.

internment camp commander Lagerkommandant *m*.

interphone Bordtelephon *n*, Bordsprechanlage *f*, Eigenverständigung *f (Ap, Tk)*; Hausleitung *f*, Haustelephon *n (in a building)*.

interphone communication Bordverständigung *f*.

interphone equipment Verständigungsgerät *n (Ap)*.

interplane strut Flügelstiel *m*.

interpolating scale Transversalmaßstab *m (Surv)*.

interpolation Interpolieren *n*.

interpret auswerten *(evaluate)*; beurteilen *(estimate, judge)*; verdolmetschen *(translate)*; auslegen, erklären, deuten *(explain)*.

interpretation Auswertung *f*, Verwertung *f*.

interpretation of aerial photographs Luftbildauswertung *f*.

interpretation of photographs Bildauswertung *f*.

interpreter Dolmetscher *m*.

interpupillary distance Augenabstand *m (Optics)*.
interpupillary-distance scale Teilscheibe *f (binocular)*.
interrogate ausfragen, vernehmen, verhören.
interrogation Befragung *f*, Ausfragen *n*, Verhör *n*, Vernehmung *f*.
interrogation officer Vernehmungsoffizier *m (PW)*.
interrogation of prisoners Gefangenenverhör *n*, Gefangenenvernehmung *f*.
interrupt unterbrechen.
interrupted fire stoßweises Feuer.
interrupted-screw-type breechblock Schraubenverschluß *m (G)*.
interrupter Sicherungsklappe *f*, Sicherungsflügel *m*, Sicherungsvorrichtung *f (Am)*; Unterbrecher *m (Elec)*.
interruption Unterbrechung *f*.
intersect anschneiden.
intersection Kreuzung *f*, Straßenkreuzung *f*, Wegekreuzung *f (road)*; Anschneiden *n (Surv)*.
interstation communication Bordverständigung *f (Ap)*.
interurban line Fernleitung *f (Tp)*.
interval Zwischenraum *m (close order drill)*; Pause *f*, Zwischenzeit *f*, Zeitabstand *m (time)*.
intervehicular communication Querverbindung *f*.
intervehicular distance Marschabstand zwischen den einzelnen Fahrzeugen.
interview Unterredung *f*, Interview *n*.
intolerable concentration Schädlichkeitsgrenze *f (CWS)*.
intoxication Trunkenheit *f*, Rausch *m*.
intravehicular communication Eigenverständigung *f*, Bordverständigung *f*.
intrench schanzen, einschanzen, (sich) eingraben.
intrenching tool kleines Schanzzeug.
intrenchment Verschanzung *f*.
intruder Klebeflugzeug *n (Ap)*.
intruding Kleben *n (Avn)*.
intruding airplane Klebeflugzeug *n*.
intrusion Kleben *n (Avn)*.
inundated area Anstauung *f (map)*.
inundation Überflutung *f*, Über-

schwemmung *f (flooding)*; Anstauung *f (by damming)*.
invade einmarschieren, einbrechen, invahieren.
invasion Invasion *f*.
inventory Bestand *m*, Inventar *n*, Bestandsnachweisung *f*.
inverse ratio umgekehrtes Verhältnis.
inverse value Kehrwert *m*.
inverted flight Rückenflug *m*.
inverted-image range finder Invertentfernungsmesser *m*, Kehrbildentfernungsmesser *m*.
inverted truss Sprengwerk *n (Engr)*.
inverted valve Hängeventil *n (Mtr)*.
inverted wedge formation Breitkeil *m (Tac)*.
investigate untersuchen.
investigating officer Untersuchungsoffizier *m*.
investigation Untersuchung *f*.
involuntary unfreiwillig.
involuntary absence without leave unverschuldete Abwesenheit.
iodine Jod *n*; Jodtinktur *f (tincture of iodine)*.
iron Eisen *n*.
iron core Eisenkern *m (Elec)*.
Iron Cross Eisernes Kreuz *(decoration)*.
iron ration eiserne Portion *(for Pers)*; eiserne Ration *(for horses)*.
iron reinforcement Bewehrung *f*, Eiseneinlage *f (in ferro-concrete)*.
iron roller Eisenwalze *f (mine clearing)*.
irregular unregelmäßig; unvorschriftsmäßig *(contrary to regulations)*.
irregularity Verstoß *m (Law)*; Unregelmäßigkeit *f*.
irreplaceable unabkömmlich, unentbehrlich.
irritant *n* Reizstoff *m (CWS)*.
irritant agent reizender Kampfstoff *(CWS)*.
irritant candle Reizkerze *f (CWS)*.
irritant capsule Reizwürfel *m (CWS)*.
irritant gas Giftnebel *m (CWS)*.
irritant-gas candle Giftrauchkerze *f*, Giftnebelkerze *f (CWS)*.
irritant-gas generator Riechtopf *m (CWS)*.
irritant smoke Giftrauch *m (CWS)*.

irritant training agent   Übungsreizstoff *m (CWS)*.
irritating concentration   Reizkonzentration *f*.
island   Insel *f*.
island of resistance   Widerstandsnest *n (Tac)*.
isobar   Isobare *f (Met)*.
isolate   isolieren; abtrennen *(separate)*; abschneiden *(cut off)*; absondern *(Med)*.
isolated internment   Einzelhaft *f*.
isolation   Abtrennen *n*, Abschneiden *n*, Isolierung *f (Tac)*; Absonderung *f (Med)*.

isolation quarters   Absonderungsabteilung *f (Med)*.
issuance of order(s)   Befehlsausgabe *f*, Befehlserteilung *f*.
issue *n*   Verausgabung *f*, Verteilen *n*, Ausgabe *f*.
issue *v*   verausgaben.
Italian method   Rückwärtseinschneiden *n (Surv)*.
item   Stück *n*, Gegenstand *m*, Artikel *m*.
item of equipment   Ausrüstungsstück *n*, Gerätstück *n*.

J

jack   Wagenheber *m (MT)*; Klinke *f (Tp)*; Buchse *f*, Steckdose *f (Elec, Rad)*.
jacket   Mantel *m (Tech)*; Jacke *f (Clo)*; Hülsenmantel *m (of cartridge case)*; Geschoßmantel *m (of bullet)*; Rohrmantel *m (of G)*; Wassermantel *m*, Kühlmantel *m (Mtr, MG)*.
jacket base   Mantelboden *m (MG)*.
jacket cradle   Jackenwiege *f (G)*.
jacket end cap   Mantelkopf *m (MG)*.
jack float   Fußteller *m (AA gun)*.
jackknife   Klappmesser *n*.
jack shaft   Seitenwelle *f (MT)*.
jail *n*   Gefängnis *n*.
jam *n*   Hemmung *f (stoppage, Ord)*; Verkehrsstockung *f (traffic)*.
jam *v*   hemmen *(Ord)*; verklemmen *(Mech)*; stören *(Rad)*.
jamming station   Störstelle *f (Rad)*.
javelin   Kolonne *f (Avn)*.
jaw   Kiefer *m (man)*; Ganasche *f (horse)*.
"jeep"   "Kübel" *m*, Kübelsitzer *m*, Kübelwagen *m*, Kübelsitzwagen *m*.
jeopardy   Gefahr *f*.
jet   Strahl *m (of a liquid)*; Düse *f (Inst)*.
jet-propulsion engine   Rückstoßmotor *m (Ap)*.
jettison   abwerfen *(Avn)*; über Bord werfen *(Nav)*.
jetty   Mole *f*, Hafendamm *m*.
jiu-jitsu   Jiu-Jitsu *n*.

jockey box   Gerätekasten *m*.
joint *n*   Gelenk *n*, Verbindung *f*.
joint operations   Operationen der verbundenen Waffen.
joint piece   Gelenkstück *n (MG tripod)*.
joint plan   Operationsplan für Zusammenwirken von Armee und Flotte.
journal   Zapfen *m*; Wellenzapfen *m (shaft)*; Lagerzapfen *m (crankshaft)*; Tagebuch *n*, Kriegstagebuch *n (diary)*.
judge   Richter *m*.
judge advocate   Kriegsgerichtsrat *m*.
Judge Advocate General   Chef des Heeresjustizwesens *(USA)*.
judo   Judo *n*.
jugular groove   D r o s s e l r i n n e *f (horse)*.
jump   Abgangsfehlerwinkel *m (Gunnery)*; Absprung *m*, Sprung *m (Prcht)*.
jump area   Abdriftplatz *m (Prcht troops)*.
jumpmaster   Absetzer *m (Prcht troops)*.
jump-off   Antreten zum Sturm *(Tac)*.
jump off   zum Sturm vorgehen *(Tac)*.
jump-off line   Ausgangslinie *f*.
jump-off point   Absprungpunkt *m (Prcht)*.

jump-off position Ausgangsstellung *f (Tac)*.
junction Anschlußbahnhof *m*, Trennungsbahnhof *m (RR)*; Straßenspinne *f*, Straßenknotenpunkt *m (road)*.
junction box Kupplungskasten *m (AA director)*; Verteilerkasten *m (data transmission system)*.
junction line Abzweigung *f*, Zweiglinie *f (RR)*.

jungle Dschungel *f*, Urwald *m*.
jungle warfare Dschungelkrieg *m*, Urwaldkriegführung *f*, Urwaldkrieg *m*.
junior officers Hauptleute und Leutnants.
junior umpire Unterschiedsrichter *m (maneuvers)*.
jurisdiction Gerichtsbereich *m*, Gerichtsbarkeit *f*.

K

K Wert zur Verbesserung der Kartenentfernung auf Grund der erschossenen B.W.E. *(FA)*.
katabatic wind Fallwind *m (Met)*.
keel Kiel *m*.
keel fin Kielflosse *f (flying-boat hull or seaplane float)*.
keeper Schieber *m*, Schlaufe *f*, Schluppe *f*, Schlupfe *f (for straps, etc.)*.
kerosene Petroleum *n*.
key Schlüssel *m (to a lock, code, etc.)*; Taste *f*, Morsetaste *f (Rad, Tg)*; Zündschlüssel *m (ignition)*; Keil *m (Mech)*.
keyer Tastgerät *n (Rad)*.
keying Tasten *n*.
key point Schlüsselpunkt *m (Tac)*.
key position Schlüsselstellung *f (Tac)*.
keyway Keilnut *f*, Nut(e) *m(f)*.
khaki Khakituch *n*, Khaki *n*.
kick Rückstoß *m (Ord)*; Fußtritt *m (with the foot)*.
kick starter Kickstarter *m (Mtcl)*.
kill töten; erschießen *(by shooting)*; erschlagen *(by blows)*; erstechen *(by stabbing)*; abschlachten, niedermetzeln, niedermachen *(massacre, slaughter)*; umbringen, ermorden *(murder)*; sich umbringen, Selbstmord begehen *(commit suicide)*.
killed in action im Felde gefallen, vor dem Feind gefallen.
killing concentration tödliche Menge *(CWS)*.
kilocycle Kilohertz *n*.
kind *n* Art *f*, Sorte *f*.
in kind in Natur, Natural-.
kinetic energy kinetische Energie.
kingpin Achszapfen *m*.
kingpost Hängesäule *f*.

kit Tasche *f*.
kitchen Küche *f*, Feldküche *f*.
kitchen car Eisenbahnküchenwagen *m (RR)*.
kitchen police Küchendienst *m*.
kitchen truck Küchenlastwagen *m*.
kite Drache(n) *m*.
kite balloon Drachenballon *m*.
knapsack Rucksack *m*, Tornister *m*.
knee Knie *n*; Zungenstuhl *m (RR switch)*.
kneeling position Anschlag kniend, kniender Anschlag *(in firing)*.
kneeling trench Schützenloch für knienden Schützen, Hockloch *n (Ft)*.
knee pad Kniepausche *f (harness)*.
knife Messer *n*.
knife rest spanischer Reiter *(Engr)*.
knife switch Messerschalter *m (Elec)*.
knife-switch prong Kontaktmesser *n (Elec)*.
knob Knopf *m*, Knagge *f (Tech)*; Triebscheibe *f*, Handrädchen *n (optical Inst, Ord)*; Griff *m (door)*; Kuppe *f (Top)*; Kammerknopf *m (R bolt)*; Abstimmkondensatorgriff *m (tuning knob, Rad)*.
knoll Kupe *f*.
knot Knoten *m (of rope, wood; unit of speed)*.
knots and ties Bunde und Knoten *(Engr, Tp)*.
knuckle Knöchel *m*, Gelenk *n*.
knuckle lug Auflaufstück *n (G)*.
knurl kordieren, rändeln.
knurled nut Kordelmutter *f*.
knurling Kordierung *f*, Kordelung *f (Mech)*.
KP Küchendienst *m*.
K-transfer Erschießen der B.W.E. bei Planschießen *(FA)*.

L

labor camp Arbeitslager *n*.
lace Schnürsenkel *m (of shoe or boot)*.
lace boot Schnürstiefel *m*.
lacerated wound Rißwunde *f*.
lack Mangel *m*.
lacquer Lack *m*.
lacrimator Augenreizstoff *m*, Reizkörper *m*.
lacrimator gas Tränengas *n (CWS)*.
ladder Leiter *f (Engr)*; Reihe *f (Gunnery)*.
ladder fire Reihenfeuer *n*, Reiheschießen *n (Gunnery)*.
lake See *m*.
lamb Schöpsenfleisch *n*, Hammelfleisch *n (meat)*.
Lambert projection Lamberts flächentreue Azimutalprojektion *(Mapping)*.
lamp Lampe *f*; Laterne *f (lantern)*.
lamp case Lampengehäuse *n (Sig lamp)*.
lamp signal Blinkzeichen *n*, Blinksignal *n*, Lichtsignal *n*.
lamp socket Lampenfassung *f (Elec)*.
lance Fahnenstange *f (flagpole)*.
lance pole Baustange *f (Tp)*.
land *n* Land *n*; Feld *n (rifling)*.
land *v* landen *(on land)*; wassern *(on water, Avn)*.
land-based aircraft von Land operierende Luftstreitkräfte.
landing Landung *f*.
landing area Landeplatz *m*, Landungsplatz *m (Avn)*; Abdriftplatz *m (Prcht troops)*.
landing attack Landungsangriff *m*.
landing boat Landungsboot *n*.
landing craft Landungsfahrzeug *n*.
landing deck Flugdeck *n*, Landedeck *n (aircraft carrier)*.
landing-direction light Landelicht *n (Avn)*.
landing field Landeplatz *m (Avn)*; Flugplatzfeld *n*, Rollfeld *n (Adrm)*.
landing flap Landeklappe *f (Ap)*.
landing flare Bordlandefackel *f (Avn)*.
landing gear Fahrwerk *n*, Fahrgestell *n (Ap)*.
landing-gear axle Fahrwerkachse *f (Ap)*.

landing-gear frame Fahrgestell *n (Ap)*.
landing-gear strut Fahrwerkstrebe *f (Ap)*.
landing light Landefeuer *n*, Landelicht *n (Ap)*.
landing operation Landungsunternehmung *f*.
landing party Landungstrupp *m*.
landing ramp Landungsklappe *f*, Klappe *f*, Landesteg *m (landing craft)*; Ablaufbahn *f (for seaplanes)*.
landing run Ausrollen *n (Avn)*.
landing runway Landebahn *f (Avn)*.
landing ski Gleitkufe *f (Ap)*.
landing ski assembly Schneekufengestell *n (Ap)*.
landing smoke signal Landungsrauchzeichen *n (Avn)*.
landing speed Landegeschwindigkeit *f (Ap)*.
landing stage Landbrücke *f (Engr)*.
landing strip Landebahn *f (Adrm)*; Stahlstraße *f (steel)*.
landing T Landekreuz *n (Avn)*.
landing wheel Laufrad *n (Ap)*.
landing zone Landezone *f (Adrm)*.
landmark Geländepunkt *m (Surv)*; Bake *f (Nav)*.
land mine Landmine *f (Engr)*.
lands Felder *npl (Ord)*.
lands and grooves Felder und Züge *(Ord)*.
landscape sketch Ansichtsskizze *f*.
landscape target Geländescheibe *f (Tng)*.
land vehicle Landfahrzeug *n*.
land warfare Landkrieg *m*.
L-antenna L-Antenne *f*.
lantern Laterne *f*.
lanyard Abzugsschnur *f (Ord)*; Pistolengurt *m (pistol)*.
lanyard handle Abzugsgriff *m (G)*.
lapse rate vertikaler Temperaturgradient *(Met)*.
large-caliber machine gun überschweres Maschinengewehr *(Cal .50)*.
large-caliber projectile großkalibriges Geschoß.
large-scale attack Großangriff *m*.
large-scale map Karte im Maßstab 1:20,000 oder größer *(Surv)*.

large unit   strategische Einheit *(USA: Div and up; Ger: corps and up)*.

lashing Bund *n (Engr, Tp)*.

lateral axis Querachse *f (Ap)*.

lateral communication Querverbindung *f*, Seitenverbindung *f (Sig C)*.

lateral conduct of fire Einschießen mit Beobachtung von seitlicher Beobachtungsstelle *(Gunnery)*.

lateral correction Verbesserung für Seite *(Gunnery)*.

lateral deflection angle Seitenwinkelvorhalt in der Horizontalebene *(AA Gunnery)*.

lateral error Seitenfehler *m (Gunnery)*.

lateral fire *See* lateral conduct of fire.

lateral jump Seitenabgangsfehler *m*, Seitenabweichung *f (Gunnery)*.

lateral lead Seitenvorhalt *m (Gunnery)*; Seitenwinkelvorhalt der Seitenvorhaltebene *(AA Gunnery)*.

lateral march Seitenbewegung *f (Tac)*.

lateral road Querverbindungsstraße *f*.

lateral stability Querstabilität *f (Ap)*.

lateral sway Seitenschwankung *f (Bdg)*.

lateral tilt Schrägstellung *f.*

lath Latte *f*.

lathe Drehbank *f*.

lathe operator Dreher *m*.

latitude geographische Breite, Breitenkreis *m*, Breitengrad *m*.

latrine Latrine *f*.

launch *n* Verkehrsboot *n (Nav)*.

launch *v* ansetzen *(an attack)*; vom Stapel lassen *(a ship)*.

launcher Werfer *m*.

launching device Startvorrichtung *f (Avn)*.

launching nose Brückenspitze *f (Bdg)*.

laundry Wäsche *f;* schmutzige Wäsche *(soiled clothes)*; Wäscherei *f (place)*.

law Recht *n (jurisprudence)*; Gesetz *n (statute, scientific formulation)*; Kriegsrecht *n (Mil law)*.

law member Beisitzer *m*.

Laws and Customs of War on Land Gesetze und Gebräuche des Landkrieges *(Hague convention, 1907)*.

laws of war Kriegsrecht *n*.

lay richten *(Gunnery)*; stellen, setzen *(place)*.

layer Schicht *f*, Lage *f (stratum)*.

layer's seat Richtsitz *m (G)*.

laying Richten *n (Gunnery)*.

laying by survey Planrichten *n (Gunnery)*.

laying for direction Nehmen der Seitenrichtung *(Gunnery)*.

laying for elevation Nehmen der Höhenrichtung *(Gunnery)*.

laying mechanism Richtgerät *n*, Richtmaschine *f*, Richtmittel *n (G)*.

lazy strap Strangträger *m*, Tauträger *m*, Stranglaufe *f (harness)*.

lead *n* Blei *n (metal)*.

lead *n* Vorhalt *m (firing)*.

take a lead vorhalten.

amount of lead Vorhaltsmaß *n*, Vorhaltswert *m*.

lead *v* fuhren; vorhalten *(Gunnery)*.

lead azide Bleiazid *n*.

lead chart Planfeuertafel *f (AA firing)*.

lead computer Auswanderungsmesser *m (AA gun)*; Vorhalteeinrichtung *f (AT gun, AA gun)*.

lead curve Vorhaltekurve *f*.

leader Leiter *m*, Führer *m*.

leadership Führerschaft *f*, Führung *f*.

lead graduations Vorhaltemaße *npl (firing at moving targets)*.

lead horse Vorderpferd *n*.

lead-in Einführungsdraht *m*, Zuführungsdraht *m (Rad)*.

lead-in cord Zuleitungskabel *n (Sig lamp)*.

leading airplane Führerflugzeug *n*.

leading car Spitzenwagen *m (MT)*.

leading edge Flügelvorderkante *f*, Flügeleintrittskante *f*, Leitkante *f*, Flügelnase *f (Ap)*.

leading element Spitzengruppe *f (Tac)*.

leading fire Vorhaltefeuer *n*.

leading flight Führungskette *f (Avn)*.

leading tank Spitzenpanzer *m*.

lead-in point Kabelaufführungspunkt *m (Tp)*.

lead jacket Bleimantel *m (Am)*.

lead mark Zielmarke *f (telescopic sight)*.

lead-plate storage battery Bleisammler *m*.

lead rein Führerzügel *m (harness).*
lead seal Bleiplombe *f.*
lead sheath Bleimantel *m (Armd cable).*
lead spatter Bleispritzer *m.*
lead team Vorderpferde *npl.*
lead track Ausziehgleis *n (RR).*
leadup strap Rückenriemen *m (harness).*
lead wire Zünderdraht *m (blasting);* Zuführungsdraht *m (Rad);* Bleidraht *m (wire made of metallic lead).*
leaf Lamelle *f (Tech);* Blatt *n (of a spring);* Klappe *f (of a sight);* Visierklappe *f (of rear sight).*
leaflet Flugblatt *n (propaganda).*
leaf sight Klappvisier *n.*
leaf spring Blattfeder *f (MT).*
leak *n* Leck *n (ship);* Spalte *f,* Loch *n (container).*
to spring a leak leck werden.
leak *v* leck sein *(ship);* undicht sein *(gas container);* rinnen *(liquid container).*
leakage Undichtigkeit *f (of a container);* Ableitung *f,* Stromverlust *m,* Streuung *f (Elec).*
leakproof dicht, wasserdicht.
lean-to tent Halbzelt *n.*
leather Leder *n.*
leather bag Ledertasche *f.*
leather leggins Beinleder *npl.*
leave *n* Urlaub *m*
on leave beurlaubt, auf Urlaub.
leave area Ruhequartier *n.*
lecture Vortrag *m.*
led horse Handpferd *n.*
leeward leewärts, windabwärts.
leeway Abdrift *f (Avn).*
left-about Kehrtwendung links *(drill).*
left bank Linkskurve *f (Avn).*
left dress sich nach links ausrichten *(drill).*
left face Linkswendung *f.*
"Left, face!" **"Links, um!"**
left-handed thread Linksgewinde *n.*
left-handed twist Linksdrall *m (rifling).*
leg Bein *n (limb);* Strecke *f (distance);* Schenkel *m (diagrams, Inst).*
legal legal, gesetzlich, gesetzmäßig; rechtsgültig, rechtskräftig *(valid).*
legal status Rechtsstellung *f,* rechtliche Stellung.
legation Gesandtschaft *f.*

legend Zeichenerklärung *f (key to map signs).*
leggins Gamaschen *fpl;* Beinleder *npl (leather);* Wickelgamaschen *fpl (wrapped).*
lemon Zitrone *f.*
length Länge *f.*
length of barrel Rohrlänge *f (G).*
length of rifling Drallänge *f (Ord).*
lens Linse *f.*
lensatic compass Marschkompaß *m.*
lethal chemical agent tödlicher chemischer Kampfstoff.
lethal concentration tödliche Menge *(CWS).*
letter Brief *m,* Schreiben *n (written message);* Buchstabe *m (of the alphabet).*
letter of instruction Weisung *f.*
letter of transmittal Begleitschreiben *n.*
letter order schriftlicher Befehl.
levee Schutzdamm *m.*
levée en masse allgemeines Aufgebot.
level *n* Libelle *f (Inst);* Setzwaage *f (builder's);* Nivellierinstrument *n (Surv).*
level *adj* eben, flach.
level crossing Planübergang *m.*
level flight Horizontalflug *m,* Geradeausflug *m,* Waagerechtflug *m,* Normalfluglage *f (Avn).*
level flight bombardment Waagerechtbombenwurf *m.*
level housing Libellengehäuse *n (panoramic telescope).*
leveling Einspielen der Libellen *(Gunnery).*
leveling device Horizontierungsvorrichtung *f (AA gun mount).*
leveling jack Horizontierung *f (AA gun outrigger).*
leveling-jack handle Horizontiergriff *m (AA gun outrigger).*
leveling mechanism Einkipptrieb *m (Mort).*
level off abfangen *(Avn).*
level party Nivellier-Meßtrupp *m (Surv).*
level point Fallpunkt *m (Ballistics).*
level-point range waagerechte Schußweite *(Gunnery).*
level setting Libelleneinstellung *f.*
lever Hebel *m.*
lewisite Lewisit *n,* Chlorvinyldichlorarsin *n (CWS).*

liaison   Anschluß *m*, Verbindung *f*, Verbindungsdienst *m* *(Tac)*.

liaison agent   Verbindungsmann *m*.

liaison airplane   Kurierflugzeug *n*, Verbindungsflugzeug *n*.

liaison communication   Nachrichten querverbindung *f*.

liaison detachment   Verbindungstrupp *m*.

liaison net   Verbindungsnetz *n* *(Rad)*

liaison officer   Verbindungsoffizier *m*.

liaison party   Verbindungstrupp *m*.

liaison pilot   Verbindungsflieger *m*.

liberate   befreien, freilassen.

librarian   Bücherwart *m*, Bibliothekar *m*.

library   Bibliothek *f*, Bücherei *f*.

license   Fahrerschein *m*, Führerschein *f* *(driver's)*.

lieutenant   Leutnant *m*; Kapitänleutnant *m* *(Nav)*. See also second lieutenant, first lieutenant, lieutenant junior grade.

lieutenant colonel   Oberstleutnant *m*; Oberstleutnant der Flieger *(Luftwaffe)*; Oberfeldarzt *m* *(Med)*; Oberfeldveterinär *m* *(Vet)*.

lieutenant commander   Korvettenkapitän *m* *(Nav)*.

lieutenant general   General der Infanterie *(Inf)*; General der Artillerie *(Arty)*; General der Kavallerie *(Cav)*; General der Flieger *(Luftwaffe)*; General der Panzertruppen *(Armd Comd)*; General der Flakartillerie *(AAA)*; General der Nachrichtentruppen *(Sig C)*; etc.

lieutenant junior grade   Oberleutnant zur See *(Nav)*.

life belt   Rettungsring *m*.

lifeboat   Rettungsfahrzeug *n*.

lifebuoy   Rettungsboje *f*.

lifeguards   Rettungsleute *mpl*.

life insurance   Lebensversicherung *f*.

life line   Rettungsleine *f* *(for rescue work in river operations)*

life preserver   Rettungsring *m*.

life-saving equipment   Rettungsgerät *n*.

life-saving service   Rettungsdienst *m*.

life vest   Schwimmweste *f*.

lift *n*   Auftrieb *m* *(Avn)*.

lift *v*   heben.

lift fire   das Feuer vorverlegen *(Arty)*.

lifting capacity   Tragfähigkeit *f* *(Ap)*.

light *n*   Licht *n*.

light *v*   beleuchten, erleuchten *(illuminate)*; anzünden *(ignite)*; befeuern *(with beacon lights)*.

light artillery   leichte Artillerie.

light buoy   Leuchtboje *f*, Leuchttonne *f*.

light elephant steel shelter   leichte Wellblech-Hütte *(USA)*.

lighter   Prahm *m* *(Engr, Nav)*.

lighter-than-air aircraft   Luftfahrzeuge leichter als Luft.

light fuel   Leichtöl *n* *(as distinguished from Diesel fuel)*.

lighthouse   Leuchtturm *m*.

light infantry weapons   leichte Infanteriewaffen.

light machine gun   leichtes Maschinengewehr.

light machine-gun squad   leichtes MG.-Halbzug *m*.

lightning   Blitz *m*; Wetterleuchten *n* *(distant lighting)* *(Met)*.

lightning arrester   Blitzschutzsicherung *f*.

light shelter   leichter Unterstand.

lightship   Leuchtschiff *n*, Feuerschiff *n*.

light signal   Leuchtzeichen *n*; Leuchtpatrone *f*.

"lights out!"   "Lichter aus!"

light switch   Lichtschalter *m* *(Elec)*.

light tank   Klein-Panzerkampfwagen *m*, leichter Panzerkampfwagen.

lignite   Braunkohle *f*.

limber *n*   Protze *f* *(Arty)*.

limber *v*   aufprotzen *(Arty)*.

limber ammunition chest   Protzkasten *m* *(Arty)*.

limber drawbar   Protzarm *m* *(Arty)*.

limber frame   Protzgestell *n* *(Arty)*.

limber position   Protzenstellung *f* *(Arty)*.

limber wheel   Protzenrad *n* *(Arty)*.

lime   Kalk *m*.

lime solution   Kalkmilch *f* *(CWS)*.

limit *n*   Grenze *f*.

limit *v*   begrenzen, beschränken.

limited-area smoke screen   Kleinvernebelung *f*

limited attack   Angriff mit begrenztem Ziel *(Tac)*.

limited objective   begrenztes Ziel.

limited radio alert   Funkbereitschaft für begrenzte Zeit.

limited radio silence   Funkbeschränkung *f*.

limited service Wehrdienst für bedingt Taugliche.

line Linie *f (formations, etc.)*; Leitung *f (Tg, Tp)*; Leine *f*, Seil *n*, Tau *n (rope)*.

in line flügelweise, in Linie.

lineal promotion Aufrücken in eine höhere Rang- und Gehaltsklasse nach dem Dienstalter.

linear measurement Längenmessung *f*.

linear speed method lineares System *(AA Gunnery)*.

linear target Breitenziel *n (Gunnery)*.

linear travel of target Auswanderungsstrecke *f*; Vorauswanderungsstrecke *f (during dead time)*, Hauptauswanderungsstrecke *f (during time of flight of projectile, AA Gunnery)*.

line construction Leitungsbau *m (Tp)*.

line-construction unit Leitungsbaueinheit *f (Tp)*.

line formation Linienform *f*, Linienaufstellung *f*.

line jack Anchlußklinke *f (Tp)*.

line maintenance Feldinstandsetzung *f*.

lineman Fernsprecher *m (Tp)*.

line of aim Visierlinie zum Richtpunkt *(Gunnery)*.

line of anchors Ankerlinie *f (Bdg)*.

line of battalions Regiment in Linie.

line of battle Kampflinie *f*, Gefechtslinie *f*.

line of bearing Peillinie *f (Air Navigation)*.

line of breach Trennschnitt *m (demolitions)*.

line of collimation Kollimationslinie *f*.

line of communication Zufuhrstraße *f*, Nachschubstraße *f*.

line of companies Bataillon in Linie.

line of defense Verteidigungslinie *f*.

line of departure Ausgangslinie *f (Tac)*; Abgangsrichtung *f (Ballistics)*.

line of duty Dienst *m*, Pflichterfüllung *f*.

line of elevation verlängerte Seelenachse, Seelenachse am Ende des Einrichtens *(Gunnery)*.

line of fall Tangente an die Flugbahn im Fallpunkt *(Ballistics)*.

line officer Frontoffizier *m*, Truppenoffizier *m*.

line of fire Schußlinie *f*, Schußbahn *f*.

line-offset method Kreisbogen-Absteckung von einer Sehne aus *(Surv)*.

line of future position Schußlinie *f (AA Gunnery)*.

line of impact Tangente an die Flugbahn im Aufschlagpunkt *(Ballistics)*.

line of interception Auffanglinie *f (Avn)*.

line of intersection Anschneidelinie *f*.

line of march Marschlinie *f*, Marschstrecke *f*; Marschordnung *f (formation)*; Marschrichtung *f (direction)*.

line of masses Massierung *f (Tac)*.

line of observation Sehlinie *f*.

line of operations Operationslinie *f*.

line of outguards Vorpostenkette *f (Tac)*.

line of platoons Kompanie in Linie.

line of position Visierlinie *f (Ballistics)*; Standlinie *f (Navigation)*.

line of present position Visierlinie *f (AA Gunnery)*.

line of resistance Widerstandslinie *f*.

line of retirement Rückzugslinie *f (Tac)*.

line of retreat Rückzugslinie *f*, Rückzugsstraße *f*, Rückmarschstraße *f (Tac)*.

line of security Sicherungslinie *f*.

line of sight Visierlinie *f (Gunnery)*; Sehlinie *f (Surv)*.

line of site Schußlinie *f (Gunnery)*; Visierlinie *f (Ballistics)*; Standlinie *f (Navigation)*.

line of skirmishers Feuerkette *f*, Schützenlinie *f*.

line of squads Zug in Linie zu einem Glied.

line of supply Zufuhrstraße *f*, Nachschubstraße *f*.

line of the Army Truppe *f*.

line of wedges Keillinie *f (Tac)*.

line of withdrawal Rückzugslinie *f (Tac)*.

liner Kernrohr *n*, Seelenrohr *n (G)*.

line route map Linienkarte *f (Tp)*.

lines of advance Operationslinien *fpl (Tac)*.

lines of communication Verkehrslinien *fpl (Tac)*.

lines of force Kraftlinien *fpl (Elec)*.

line squall Linienbö *f (Met)*.
line-up stud Markenstück *n (on top gun carriage)*.
line wire Leitungsmittel *n (Tp)*.
link Tasche *f (cartridge belt)*; Kettenglied *n (chain)*.
link belt Metallgliedergurt *m*, Stahlgurt *m (MG)*.
linking station Zwischenstelle *f*.
link-loading machine Gurtfüller *m*.
Link trainer Linktrainer *m (Avn)*.
linseed oil Leinöl *n*.
lip Lippe *f*.
liquid Flüssigkeit *f*.
liquid air flüssige Luft.
liquid-cooled flüssigkeitsgekühlt.
liquid-cooled engine flüssigkeitsgekühlter Motor, Motor mit Flüssigkeitskühlung.
liquid fire Flammenstrahl *m (flame thrower)*.
liquid oxygen flüssige Luft, Sprengluft *f*.
liquid vesicant detector paint Gasspürfarbe *f*.
liquor Schnaps *m (brandy, gin, etc.)*.
list Liste *f (of items)*; Schlagseite *f (of a ship)*.
listener Horchposten *m*.
listen in ablauschen, abhören, mithören *(Rad, Tp)*.
listening post Horchposten *m*, Horchstelle *f*.
Lister bag Listerscher Wasserreinigungssack.
list of balances Bestandliste *f*.
lithographic ink Lithographentinte *f*.
litter Krankentrage *m*, Trage *f (Med)*.
litter bearer Krankenträger *m (Med)*.
litter carrier Räderbahre *f (Med)*.
little dipper Kleiner Bär.
live *adj* scharf *(Am)*; geladen *(Elec)*.
live abatis Baumverhau *m*.
live ammunition scharfe Munition.
Livens projector Livens-Handwerfer *m (CWS)*.
live shell scharfgeladene Granate.
livestock Viehbestand *m*.
live wire geladener Draht.
load *n* Ladung *f (Ord)*; Ladung *f*, Last *f*, Traglast *f (Ap, MT)*; Beanspruchung *f (Mech)*.
load *v* laden; einladen *(a truck, etc.)*.
"**Load!**" "Laden!"

"**Load and lock!**" "Laden und sichern!"
load capacity Ladefähigkeit *f*.
load coefficient Belastungsfaktor *m*.
loader Ladekanonier *m (Arty)*; Ladeschütze *m (Tk)*.
loader's seat Ladesitz *m (G)*.
loading Verladung *f (supplies, etc.)*; Munitionieren *n (Ap weapons)*.
loading action Ladevorgang *m (semi- or full-automatic weapons)*.
loading barrow Munitionskarren *m*.
loading belt Patronengurt *m*.
loading coil Pupinspule *f (Tp)*.
loading crane Batteriekran *m (Arty)*.
loading device Ladevorrichtung *f*.
loading lag Ladeverzug *m*, Ladeverzugszeit *f (Gunnery)*.
loading officer Verladeoffizier *m*, Verladungsoffizier *m (Transportation)*.
loading operations Ladetätigkeit *f (service of the piece)*.
loading party Aufladekommando *n*.
loading platform Laderampe *f*, Verladerampe *f*.
loading point Verladestelle *f*, Verladeplatz *m*.
loading port Verladehafen *m (Nav)*.
loading ramp Rampe *f*.
loading recess Ladeloch *n (G)*.
loading siding Ladegleis *n (RR)*.
loading station Verladebahnhof *m (RR)*.
loading table Verladeplan *m*.
loading time Ladezeit *f*, Verladezeit *f*.
loading tray Lademulde *f*, Ladeschale *f*, Ladetisch *m (G)*.
load line Tiefladelinie *f (Nav)*.
load test Belastungsprobe *f*.
load unit Ladeeinheit *f*.
lobe parachute Stufenfallschirm *m*.
local örtlich, Orts-.
local air defense örtliche Luftabwehr.
local battery Ortsbatterie *f (Tp)*.
local-battery operation Ortsbatterie-Betrieb *m (Tp)*.
local-battery system Ortsbatterie-System *n (Tp)*.
local circuit Querverbindung *f (Tp)*.
local circuit line Nebenanschlußleitung *f (Tp)*.
local counterattack Gegenstoß *m*, örtlicher Gegenangriff.

local engagement lokales Gefecht, örtliches Gefecht, Teilkampf *m.*

local flight Rundflug *m (Avn).*

locality Ort *m,* Punkt *m.*

localizer beam Leitstrahl *m (Inst landing).*

localizer-beam method Leitstrahlverfahren *n (Inst landing).*

local mobilization Teilmobilmachung *f.*

local net Ortsnetz *n (Tp).*

local observation Nahbeobachtung *f.*

local protection örtliche Sicherung.

local reception Ortsempfang *m (Rad).*

local reconnaissance Nahaufklärung *f.*

local security Nahsicherung *f,* örtliche Sicherung.

local smoke screening Kleinvernebelung *f.*

local station Nebenanschluß *m,* Nebenstelle *f (Tp);* Ortssender *m (Rad).*

local support Stoßreserve *f (in assault, Tac).*

locate auffinden *(find);* orten *(establish position);* bestimmen, feststellen *(a point on a map, a shell burst, etc.).*

locate a target das Ziel auffinden.

locator card Wehrstammblatt *n,* Wehrstammkarte *f.*

lock *n* Schloß *n (on door, etc.);* Schleuse *f (of a canal).*

lock *v* absperren, zusperren, schließen, zuschließen *(a door, etc.);* sichern *(Ord).*

locked position Zurrstellung *f (Ord).*

lock frame Verschlußschlitten *m (Ord).*

lock handle Zurrgriff *m (G cradle).*

locking bolt Sperrstück *n (pistol);* Sperriegel *m (MG stock).*

locking device Festhaltevorrichtung *f (MG).*

locking lever Sperrhebel *m;* Bremshebel *m (panoramic telescope).*

locking mechanism Zurrung *f (G, Tk, MG).*

locking pin Schlüsselbolzen *m (limber).*

locking spring Sperrfeder *f (MG).*

locking washer Stoßscheibe *f (wheel bearing, MT).*

locking wheel Sperrad *n (G cradle).*

lockjaw Wundstarrkrampf *m (Med).*

lock lever Zurrhebel *m.*

lock nut Gegenmutter *f,* Sicherungsmutter *f.*

lock rod Zurrstange *f.*

lock-spar support Bocksprengwerk *n (Bdg).*

lock support Zurrlager *n (cradle lock).*

lockwasher Federring *m,* Stahlfederring *m (Mech).*

locomotive Lokomotive *f.*

loft Brieftaubenschlag *m,* Brieftaubenstelle *f (Sig C).*

lofting Formgebung *f (Ap).*

log Baumstamm *m (tree trunk);* Klotz *m (wood);* Log *n (Nav). See also* log book.

logarithm Logarithmus *m.*

logarithmic range scale Rechenschieber zur Entfernungsermittlung *(Arty).*

log book Bordbuch *n (Ap);* Tagebuch *n.*

log crib Balkenstapel *m (Bdg).*

logistics Transport- und Nachschubplanung *f.*

log runner Baumstammkufe *f (log sled).*

loins Lenden *fpl (horse).*

long lang.

long-barreled gun Langrohrkanone *f,* Langrohrgeschütz *n.*

long-base method Langbasisverfahren *n (Gunnery).*

long dash Dauerstrich *m (Tg).*

long-delay fuze Aufschlagzünder mit erhöhter Verzögerung.

long-distance circuit Fernleitung *f (Tp).*

long-distance reception Fernempfang *m (Rad).*

long-distance telephone call Ferngespräch *n,* Durchgangsfernspruch *m.*

longeron Hauptträger *m,* Rumpfholm *m,* Rumpflängsleiste *f (Ap).*

longevity pay Besoldungszulage nach dem Dienstalter.

longhorn Trichter-Richtungshörer *m (AAA).*

longitude geographische Länge, Längenkreis *m,* Längengrad *m.*

longitudinal axis Längsachse *f,* Rumpflängsachse *f (Ap).*

longitudinal cross bracing Tiefenverspannung *f,* Tiefenkreuzverspannung *f (Ap).*

longitudinal deviation Längenabweichung *f (Gunnery)*.

longitudinal level Längslibelle *f (sighting mechanism)*.

longitudinal outrigger Längsträger *m (AA gun)*.

longitudinal stability Längsstabilität *f (Ap)*.

long lunge Ausfall *m (bayonet thrust)*.

long range weite Entfernung *(beyond 800 meters)*.

long-range artillery Fernkampfartillerie *f*.

long-range battery Fernkampfbatterie *f (Arty)*.

long-range bomber Fernbomber *m*, Fernkampfbomber *m*, Langstreckenbomber *m*, Fernkampfflugzeug *n*.

long-range fighter Langstreckenjäger *m*, Zerstörer *m*, Zerstörerflugzeug *n (Avn)*.

long-range fighter wing Zerstörergeschwader *n (Avn)*.

long-range gun Fernkampfgeschütz *n*.

ong-range seaplane Langstrecken-Seeflugzeug *n*.

longshoreman Hafenarbeiter *m*.

long thrust Ausfall *m (bayonet thrust)*.

long-wave direction finder Langwellenpeiler *m (Rad)*.

long waves Langwellen *fpl (Rad)*.

lookout Späher *m*.

lookout hole Sehöffnung *f (Ft, Tk)*.

lookout hole cover Sehklappe *f (Tk)*.

lookout post Hochstand *m*.

lookout slit Sehschlitz *m (Tk)*.

loop Looping *m*, Schleife *f*, Überschlag *m (Avn)*.

oop antenna Rahmenantenne *f;* Peilrahmen *m (directional);* Drehrahmenantenne *f (rotating)*.

loophole Schießscharte *f (Ft)*.

loop maneuver Schleifenflug *m (Avn)*.

loop-tip terminal Kabelschuh *m (Elec)*.

loose contact Wackelkontakt *m (Elec)*.

loose round Patrone mit locker sitzendem Geschoß *(Am)*.

loot *n* Beute *f*.

looting Plünderung *f*.

loss Verlust *m*.

loss of altitude Höhenverlust *m (Avn)*.

loss of velocity Geschwindigkeitsverlust *m (Ballistics)*.

loss replacements Auffülltruppen *fpl*.

lost motion toter Gang *(Mech)*.

lot Lieferung *f (shipment)*.

lot number laufende Nummer der Lieferung.

loud speaker Lautsprecher *m (Rad)*.

louse Laus *f (plural:* Läuse*)*.

louver Kühlerklappe *f*, Luftschlitz *m*.

low-altitude flight Tiefflug *m (Avn)*.

low-angle fire Flachfeuer *n*, Feuer in der unteren Winkelgruppe *(Gunnery)*.

low entanglement niedriger Drahtzaun, n i e d r i g e r Flandernzaun *(Engr)*.

lower *v* herunterlassen *(let down);* ausfahren *(landing gear, etc., Avn)*.

lower band Unterring *m (R)*.

lower chord Untergurt *m (truss)*.

lower gun carriage Unterlafette *f*.

lower shield Unterschild *m (G)*.

lower shield bracket Unterschildträger *m (G)*.

low explosive nichtbrisanter Sprengstoff.

low-flying attack *See* **low-level attack**.

low frequency Niederfrequenz *f (Rad)*.

low-frequency interference Niederfrequenzstörungen *fpl (Rad)*.

low gear Anfahrtsgang *m (MT, Tk)*.

low-level approach Tiefanflug *m (Avn)*.

low-level attack Tiefangriff *m*, Tieffliegerangriff *m*, Tiefflugangriff *m (Avn)*.

low-level bombing attack Bombentiefangriff *m (Avn)*.

low-level flight Tiefflug *m (Avn)*.

low-order burst Fehlzerspringer *m (Am)*.

low position liegender Anschlag *(MG)*.

low-pressure area Tiefdruckgebiet *n*, Tief *n (Met)*.

low-pressure chamber Unterdruckkammer *f*.

low-pressure tire Niederdruckreifen *m (MT)*.

low voltage Niederspannung *f*.

low-wing monoplane Tiefdecker *m*.

low wire entanglement niedriger Drahtzaun, niedriger Flandernzaun *(Engr)*.

loyal loyal, treu, pflichttreu.

lubber line Steuerstrich *m (aircraft compass)*.

lubricant Schmiermittel *n*, Gleitmittel *n*.

lubricate schmieren; einfetten *(grease)*; einölen *(oil)*.

lubricating oil Schmieröl *n*.

lubricating spray Sprühpistole *f (MT)*.

lubricating system Schmierstoffanlage *f (Mtr)*.

lubrication Schmierung *f*.

lubrication point Schmierstelle *f*.

lubrication pump Schmierölpumpe *f (Mtr)*.

lug Vorstecker *m (fuze)*; Dübel *m (G)*; Warze *f*, Kammerwarze *f (R)*;

Aufhängeöse *f (suspension lug of bomb)*.

lull Gefechtspause *f (in combat)*.

lumber Bauholz *n*.

luminous compass Leuchtkompaß *m*.

luminous dial Leuchtblatt *n*, Leuchtzifferblatt *n (Inst)*.

luminous paint Leuchtfarbe *f*, Fluoreszenzfarbe *f*.

lunette Zugöse *f*, Protzöse *f (limber, trailer)*.

lung Lunge *f*.

lunge *n* Stoß *m*, Vorstoß *m*.

lunge *v* ausholen.

lung irritant Lungengift *n*, Lungenreizstoff *m*, erstickender Kampfstoff.

lusterless paint Mattanstrich *m*.

lye kaustisches Natron, Ätznatron *n*.

lysol Lysol *n*.

Lyster bag Listerscher Wasserreinigungssack.

M

macadam Makadam *m-n*.

machete Hackmesser *n*.

machine Maschine *f*.

machine gun Maschinengewehr *n*.

machine-gun *v* mit Maschinengewehrfeuer belegen, unter Maschinengewehrfeuer nehmen.

machine-gun ammunition Maschinengewehrmunition *f*.

machine-gun ammunition belt MG.-Gurt *m*.

machine-gun barrel MG.-Lauf *m*.

machine-gun bolt MG.-Schloß *n*.

machine-gun camera Lichtbildmaschinengewehr *n*.

machine-gun carrier Gewehrträger *m (Pers)*; MG.-Träger *m (vehicle)*.

machine-gun cart MG.-Wagen *m*.

machine-gun company Maschinengewehrkompanie *f*, MG.-Kompanie *f*.

machine-gun crew MG.-Bedienung *f*.

machine-gun detail Maschinengewehr-Bedienung *f*, Maschinengewehr-Bemannung *f*.

machine-gun emplacement Maschinengewehrstand *m*, MG.-Stand *m*.

machine-gun fire Maschinengewehrfeuer *n*, MG.-Feuer *n*.

machine-gunner Maschinengewehrschütze *m*, MG.-Schütze *m*, MG.-Mann *m*.

machine-gun nest MG.-Nest *m*.

machine-gun platoon MG.-Zug *m*.

machine-gun sight MG.-Richtaufsatz *m*.

machine-gun squad Maschinengewehr-Halbzug *m*, MG.-Halbzug *m*.

machine-gun station MG.-Stand *m (Ap)*.

machine-gun telescopic sight MG.-Zielfernrohr *n*.

machine-gun tripod MG.-Dreifuß *m*.

machinery Maschinerie *f*, Maschinen *fpl*; Mechanismus *m (mechanism)*; Maschinenteile *mpl (parts)*.

machine shop Werkstatt *f*.

machine tool Werkzeugmaschine *f*.

machinist Maschinist *m (Nav)*.

macrometer Makrometer *n*, Spiegelentfernungsmesser *m*.

"Mae West" Schwimmweste *f*.

magazine Magazin *n*, Munitionslager *n (Ord)*; Kasten *m (R)*.

magazine belt Patronengurt *m*.

magazine catch Magazinhalter *m (pistol)*.

magazine charge Schlagladung *f* (*fuze*).

magazine-fed rifle Mehrlader *m.*

magazine feeding device Mehrladevorrichtung *f* (*R*).

magazine fire Schnellfeuer *n*, Magazinfeuer *n.*

magazine floor plate Kastenboden *m* (*R*).

magazine holder Magazinhalter *m* (*MG*).

magazine housing Magazingehäuse *n* (*pistol*).

magazine pocket Patronentasche *f.*

magazine rack Magazinlager *n* (*Ord*).

magazine release Magazinhaltehebel *m* (*automatic weapons*).

magazine weapon Mehrlader *m.*

magnesium Magnesium *n.*

magnesium bomb Magnesiumbombe *f.*

magnesium powder Magnesiumpulver *n.*

magnesium thermit Magnesiumthermit *n* (*incendiary bomb*).

magnet Magnet *m.*

magnetic magnetisch.

magnetic azimuth mißweisender Kurswinkel (*Navigation*).

magnetic azimuth reading Nadelzahl *f.*

magnetic compass Magnetkompaß *m.*

magnetic course mißweisender Kurs (*Air Navigation*).

magnetic declination Mißweisung *f*, Ortsmißweisung *f*, Nadelabweichung *f*, Deviation *f.*

magnetic field Magnetfeld *n*, magnetisches Feld (*Elec*).

magnetic heading mißweisender Kurs (*Air Navigation*).

magnetic mine Magnetmine *f.*

magnetic north Magnetisch-Nord *m.*

magnetic tachometer Wirbelstromtachometer *n.*

magnetic variation Mißweisung *f*, Deklination *f.*

magneto Magnetzündapparat *m*, Magnetapparat *m*, Zündmagnet *m.*

magneto ignition Magnetzündung *f.*

magnification Vergrößerung *f.*

magnify vergrößern.

magnitude Größe *f.*

magnitude of oscillations Schwingungsgröße *f* (*Rad*).

Magnus effect Magnus-Effekt *m* (*Ballistics*).

mail Post *f.*

mail call Postaufruf *m.*

mail clerk Postmeister *m.*

mail orderly *See* **mail clerk.**

main attack Hauptangriff *m.*

main body Gros *n* (*march column*) (*Tac*); Hauptmasse *f* (*Tac*).

main bore gezogener Teil (*G tube*).

main charge Hauptladung *f* (*blasting cap*).

main clutch Hauptkupplung *f* (*MT, Tk*).

main column Hauptkolonne *f.*

main deck Hauptdeck *n*, Batteriedeck *n* (*Nav*).

main effort Hauptangriff *m* (*Tac*).

main girder Hauptträger *m* (*Bdg*).

main guard Hauptwache *f.*

main ignition lead Hauptzündung *f* (*Blasting*).

main jet Hauptdüse *f* (*Mtr*).

main line of resistance Hauptkampflinie *f.*

main mooring line Haupt-Ankertau *n*, Haupt-Fesseltau *n* (*Bln*).

main reduction gear Hauptvorgelege *n* (*Tk*).

main shaft Getriebehauptwelle *f* (*transmission*) (*MT*).

main spring Schlagbolzenfeder *f* (*R*); Schließfeder *f* (*pistol*).

main-station intersection method Hauptschnittverfahren *n* (*Flash Ranging*).

main supply road Hauptzufuhrstraße *f*, Hauptnachschubstraße *f.*

maintain instandhalten (*vehicles, etc.*); unterhalten (*roads*); behaupten, aufrechterhalten (*an opinion, position*).

maintenance Instandhaltung *f*, Instandsetzung *f*, Unterhaltung *f*, Wartung *f.*

maintenance and repair Unterhaltung und Instandsetzung.

maintenance area Feldwerkstattsbereich *m.*

maintenance company Werkstattkompanie, *f.*

maintenance crew Instandsetzungsmannschaft *f.*

maintenance detachment Instandsetzungsabteilung *f.*

maintenance man Wart *m* (*Avn*); Störungssucher *m* (*Tp*).

maintenance officer Instandsetzungs-offizer *m.*

maintenance of supply Vorratshaltung *f.*

maintenance park Werkstattplatz *m.*

maintenance party Instandsetzungstrupp *m,* Werkstatt-Trupp *m.*

maintenance personnel Bodenpersonal *n (Avn).*

maintenance plan Instandsetzungsplan *m.*

maintenance platoon Abschleppzug *m (MT);* Werkstattzug *m (Tk Bn).*

maintenance section Gefechtstroß *m (Btry);* Instandsetzungshalbzug *m.*

maintenance service Instandsetzungsdienst *m,* Störungsdienst *m.*

maintenance truck Instandsetzungskraftwagen *m.*

maintenance vehicle Instandsetzungsfahrzeug *n,* Instandsetzungswagen *m.*

main transmission gear Hauptgetriebe *n (MT).*

main trench Hauptgraben *m (Ft).*

major Major *m;* Oberstabsarzt *m (Med);* Oberstabsveterinär *m (Vet).*

major attack Großangriff *m.*

major general Generalleutnant *m;* Generalleutnant der Flieger *(Luftwaffe);* Generalstabsarzt *m (Med);* Generalstabsveterinär *m (Vet).*

major operation Operation in großem Maßstabe *(Tac);* schwere Operation *(Med).*

major repair größere Reparatur.

make machen; verfertigen, herstellen *(manufacture).*

make-and-break device Schaltvorrichtung *f.*

make an emergency landing notlanden *(Avn).*

make contact Verbindung aufnehmen *(with friendly troops);* Fühlung aufnehmen *(with friendly or enemy troops).*

make fast festmachen.

make port in einen Hafen einlaufen *(Nav).*

maker Hersteller *m,* Verfertiger *m (manufacturer).*

make tight dichten *(seal);* zuziehen *(tighten).*

make up montieren, zusammensetzen *(assemble).*

make-up track Aufstellgleis *n,* Ordnungsgleis *n (RR).*

make-up yard Aufstellbahnhof *m (RR).*

malaria Malaria *f,* Sumpffieber *n.*

malfunction Fehlleistung *f.*

malingerer Simulant *m.*

malingering Vortäuschung von Krankheiten, Simulieren *n.*

malleable hämmerbar, schmiedbar.

malleable alloy Knetlegierung *f.*

mallet Fäustel *n,* Handfäustel *n (Engr).*

manage verwalten, führen, leiten *(direct);* auskommen *(get along).*

manager Verwalter *m,* Leiter *m.*

mandatory zwingend, obligatorisch.

maneuver Manöver *n (Tac);* Truppenübung *f (Tng).*

maneuverability Manövrierfähigkeit *f (Tac);* Wendigkeit *f (Ap).*

maneuvering force vordere Angriffstruppen *(Tac).*

maneuvering spider Halteleinenbund *m (Bln).*

maneuvering target kurvendes Ziel *(AAA);* bewegliche Scheibe *(Tng).*

maneuvering valve Manövrierventil *n (Bln).*

manganese Mangan *n.*

manganese dioxide Braunstein *m.*

manhandle mit der Hand bewegen, mit den Händen bewegen.

manhole Kabelbrunnen *m (Tp);* Mannloch *n,* Einsteigöffnung *f.*

manifold Auspuffkrümmer *m (exhaust) (Mtr).*

manifold pressure Ladedruck *m.*

manifold pressure control Ladedruckregler *m (Ap engine).*

manifold pressure gage Ladedruckmesser *m (Ap).*

manipulation Handhabung *f;* Zielwechsel *m,* Zielverlegung *f (Gunnery).*

manning detail Geschützbedienung *f (CA).*

manning table Bemannungsliste *f.*

manometer Manometer *n.*

manta Gepäckdecke *f.*

manual *n* Handbuch *n,* Vorschrift *f.*

manual *adj* handtätig, Hand-.

manual fuze setter Zünderstellschlüssel *m.*

manually-operated handtätig.

manufacture *n* Fertigung *f.*

manufacture *v* verfertigen, herstellen, fabrizieren.

map *n* Karte *f.*

map 341 marking disk

map *v* kartieren.
map code *See* map coordinate code.
map compilation Kartenvervollständigung *f*.
map coordinate code Kartenschlüssel *m*.
map correction Kartenverbesserung *f*.
map course Kartenkurs *m (Navigation)*.
map data Kartenunterlagen *fpl (for making maps)*; Kartenwerte *mpl (as read from maps)*.
map exercise Planspiel *n*, Planübung *f (Tng)*.
map fire Punktfeuer *n*, Planschießen *n*, Schießen mit Karte *(Gunnery)*.
map maneuver Planübung *f (Tng)*.
map measurer Kartenentferungsmesser *m*.
mapping Kartierung *f*.
mapping camera Reihenbildner *m (aerial Photo)*.
mapping photography Reihenbildaufnahme *f (aerial Photo)*.
mapping unit Kartenabteilung *f*.
map problem Planübung *f (Tng)*.
map projection Kartenentwurf *m*, Kartenprojektion *f*.
map protractor Kartenwinkelmesser *m*, Meßdreieck *n*.
map-protractor set Plansektor *m (Arty, Surv)*.
map range Kartenentfernung *f (Gunnery)*.
map reading Kartenlesen *n*.
map reconnaissance Kartenerkundung *f*, Kartenaufklärung *f*.
map scale Kartenmaßstab *m*.
map section Kartenausschnitt *m*.
map sheet Kartenblatt *n*.
map square Gradabteilung *f*, Gradfeld *n*.
map substitute Ersatzkarte *f*.
marauder Plünderer *m*, Marodeur *m*.
march *n* Marsch *m*.
march *v* marschieren.
march collecting post Marsch-Krankensammelstelle *f*.
march column Marschkolonne *f*.
march destination Marschziel *n*.
march discipline Marschdisziplin *f*, Marschzucht *f*.
march formation Marschform *f*; Marschordnung *f (close order)*; Marschgliederung *f (organization of*

march units); Marschfolge *f (sequence of units)*.
march graph Marsch-Diagramm *n*, Marschtafel *f*.
march group Marschgruppe *f*.
march halt Marschhalt *m*, Marschpause *f*.
marching ability Marschfähigkeit *f*.
marching speed Marschgeschwindigkeit *f*, Marschtempo *n*.
march in review Parademarsch *m*, Vorbeimarsch *m*.
march maintenance nach Bedarf durchgeführte Instandsetzung.
march movement Marschbewegung *f (Tac)*.
march objective Marschziel *n*.
march order Marschbefehl *m*.
"March order!" "Marschordnung!" *(Arty)*.
march outpost Marschvorposten *m*.
march performance Marschleistung *f*.
march plan Marschplan *m*.
march readiness Marschbereitschaft *f*.
march rest Marschrast *f*.
march route Marschstraße *f*, Marschstrecke *f*.
march schedule Marschübersicht *f*.
march table Marschtafel *f*.
march unit Marschgruppe *f*, Marschverband *m*.
Marconi antenna Einpolluftleiter *m (Rad)*.
marginal data Randnoten *fpl*, Randbemerkungen *fpl*.
margin of safety Sicherungszuschlag *m (Firing)*.
margin of the sheaf of fire Anschlußteil der Garbe *(Ballistics)*.
marine Seesoldat *m (USA)*.
marine cable Flußkabel *n (river)*; Seekabel *n*, Tiefseekabel *n (ocean)*.
Marine Corps Seesoldatenkorps *n (USA)*.
mark Marke *f*, Kennzeichen *n*.
marker Anzeiger *m (Inst)*; Wegeposten *m (traffic control)*.
marker beacon signal Kennung *f (Rad)*.
marker light Abstandslicht *n (MT)*.
marking Abzeichen *n*, Erkennungszeichen *n*, Kennzeichen *n (Ap, Tk)*; Hoheitsabzeichen *n (national insignia) (Ap, Tk)*.
marking disk Zielkelle *f*, Ziellöffel *m*.

marking gage Strichmaß *n* *(Woodworking)*.

marking out Einfluchten *n* *(Surv)*.

marking panel Fliegertuch *n*.

mark number Kennummer *f*.

marksman Scharfschütze *m*.

marksmanship Schießfertigkeit *f*, Zielsicherheit *f*.

marksmanship fourragère Schützenschnur *f*.

marksmanship training Schießausbildung *f*.

mark time auf der Stelle treten.

marsh Morast *m*, Sumpf *m*.

martial law Standrecht *n*.

martingale Vorderzeug *n* *(harness)*.

mask *n* Deckung *f*, Geländebedeckung *f* *(Gunnery)*; Maske *f* *(Cam)*; Atemmaske *f* *(oxygen equipment)*; Gasmaske *f* *(gas)*.

mask *v* verschleiern, verbergen, verdecken.

mask-clearance table Tafel zum Überschießen von Deckungen *(Gunnery)*.

masked area gedeckter Raum.

masked battery gedeckte Batterie.

mason Maurer *m*.

mass *n* Masse *f*, Massierung *f*, Truppenzusammenziehung *f* *(Tac)*.

mass *v* massieren, zusammenziehen, zusammenbringen *(Tac)*.

mass athletics Massenturnen *n*.

mass attack massierter Angriff.

massed fire Feuerschlag *m* *(Arty)*.

mass effect Massenwirkung *f* *(Tac)*.

massive attack Massenangriff *m*, massierter Angriff *(Tac)*.

mass of maneuver vordere Angriffstruppen *(Tac)*.

mass production Großfertigung *f*, Massenfertigung *f*, Großserienfabrikation *f*.

mast Mast *m*.

master Meister *m*, Kapitän *m*, Kommandant *m* *(Nav)*.

master compass Mutterkompaß *m* *(Avn)*.

master cylinder Druckzylinder *m* *(hydraulic brake)*.

master oscillator Steuerstufe *f*, Schwingungserzeugerstufe *f*.

master oscillator tube Steuerröhre *f*.

master sergeant Oberfeldwebel *m*; Oberwachtmeister *m* *(Arty, Cav)*; Stabsfeldwebel *m* *(Rgtl Sgt Maj)*.

master watch Hauptuhr *f*, Mutteruhr *f* *(timepiece)*.

mastery of the air Luftherrschaft *f*.

match *n* Streichholz *n*, Zündholz *n*.

mate Maat *m* *(Nav)*.

material Material *n*, Werkstoff *m*, Stoff *m*.

material damage Sachschaden *m*.

matériel Gerät *n*, Kriegsmaterial *n*.

Matériel Command Technisches Amt *(AAF)*.

matrix Mischung von Schwarzpulver und Kollophonium *(shrapnel)*.

mattock Tonhacke *f*.

mattock hoe Lettenhaue *f* *(Engr)*.

maul Handramme *f* *(Engr)*.

maximum elevation größte Rohrerhöhung *(Gunnery)*.

maximum gas pressure Höchstgasdruck *m* *(Ballistics, Ord)*.

maximum intensity Maximaleffekt *m* *(sound locator)*.

maximum intensity method Höchstwertverfahren *n* *(sound locator)*.

maximum load Belastung *f*, Höchstlast *f* *(Engr)*.

maximum number Höchstzahl *f*.

maximum ordinate Gipfelhöhe *f* *(Ballistics)*.

maximum power Höchstleistung *f*.

maximum punishment Höchststrafe *f*.

maximum range Flugbereich *m*, Reichweite *f* *(Ap)*; Höchstschußweite *f* *(Firing)*.

maximum speed Größtgeschwindigkeit *f*, Höchstgeschwindigkeit *f*.

maximum thermometer Maximumthermometer *n*.

M-day Mobilmachungstag *m*, X-Tag *m*.

meadow Weide *f*, Wiese *f*.

meal ticket Eßmarke *f*.

mean *adj* mittel, mittler, mittelmäßig; durchschnittlich *(average)*.

mean chord mittlere (Flügel-)Tiefe *(Ap wing)*.

mean deviation mittlere Streuung *(Gunnery)*.

mean error mittlerer Fehler, durchschnittlicher Fehler.

mean height of burst mittlere Sprenghöhe *(Ballistics)*.

mean point of impact mittlerer Treffpunkt *(Ballistics)*.

mean range mittlere Länge *(Gunnery)*.

mean sea level Normalnullpunkt *m*, Normalnull *f*.

means of communication Nachrichtenmittel *n*, Verbindungsmittel *n*.

means of fire control Schießhilfsmittel *npl (Arty)*.

means of identification Erkennungszeichen *n*.

means of supply movement Nachschubmittel *n*.

means of traction Zugmittel *n*.

means of transportation Beförderungsmittel *n*, Transportmittel *n*.

means of wire communication Drahtnachrichtenmittel *n*.

mean solar time mittlere Sonnenzeit.

mean trajectory mittlere Flugbahn.

measure *n* Maß *n (of quantity, etc.)*; Maßnahme *f (step or enactment)*.

measure *v* messen.

measurement Maß *n (measure)*; Messung *f*.

measuring apparatus Meßgerät *n (Inst or equipment)*.

measuring circuit Meßleitung *f (Sound Ranging, Flash Ranging)*.

measuring knob Meßknopf *m*, Meßwalze *f (range finder)*.

measuring line Eichstrich *m (Inst)*.

measuring mark Meßmarke *f (range finder)*.

meat Fleisch *n*.

meat can Kessel *m (mess kit)*.

meat grinder Fleischhackmaschine *f*.

meat inspection Fleischbeschau *f*.

meat loaf Hackbraten *m*.

mechanic Mechaniker *m*, Maschinenschlosser *m*.

mechanical aptitude test technische Eignungsprüfung.

mechanical filter Schwebstoffilter *m*, Schutzsieb *n (gas mask)*.

mechanical fuze mechanischer Zünder.

mechanical pick-up unit Schalldose *f (phonograph)*.

mechanical pilot automatischer Pilot, automatische Kurssteuerung, Selbststeuergerät *n (Ap)*.

mechanical time fuze mechanischer Zeitzünder *(Am)*.

mechanical training technische Ausbildung.

mechanism Vorrichtung *f*.

mechanization Motorisierung *f (Mil)*.

mechanized motorisiert, mechanisiert.

mechanized attack Panzerangriff *m*.

mechanized battalion Schnelle Abteilung.

mechanized cavalry motorisierte Kavallerie.

mechanized gun Geschütz auf Selbstfahrlafette, Sturmgeschütz *n*.

mechanized troops Schnelle Truppen.

mechanized unit motorisierter Verband, moto-mechanisierter Verband.

medal Medaille *f*, Orden *m*, Auszeichnung *f*.

Medal of Honor Ehrenmedaille *f (USA)*.

medical attendance ärztliche Behandlung.

medical battalion Sanitätsabteilung *f*.

medical company Sanitätskompanie *f*.

Medical Corps Sanitätskorps *n*.

medical corps personnel Sanitätspersonal *n*.

medical corps unit Sanitätstruppe *f*.

Medical Department Amt für Gesundheitsdienst *(USA)*.

medical depot Sanitätspark *m*.

medical detachment Sanitätstruppe *f*.

medical equipment Sanitätsausrüstung *f*, Sanitätsgerät *n*.

medical examination ärztliche Untersuchung.

medical examiner Truppenarzt *m*.

medical field manual Kriegssanitätsordnung *f*.

medical inspector Sanitätsinspekteur *m*.

medical installation Sanitätseinrichtung *f*.

medical isolation Kranken-Absonderung *f*, Kranken-Isolierung *f*.

medical laboratory medizinisches Laboratorium.

medical officer Sanitätsoffizier *m*, Truppenarzt *m*.

medical service Sanitätsdienst *m*, Sanitätswesen *n*, Gesundheitsdienst *m*.

medical supply depot Sanitätsmaterialpark *m*.

medical train Sanitätstroß *m*.

medical treatment ärztliche Behandlung.

medical troops Sanitätstruppen *fpl*, Sanitätspersonal *n*.

medical unit Sanitätstruppe *f*.

medicine Medizin *f (science, drug)*; Arznei *f (drug)*.

medium schwer *(Ord)*; mittler, Mittel-.

medium artillery schwere Artillerie.

medium range mittlere Entfernung *(up to 800 meters)*.

medium-scale map Karte im Maßstab 1:50,000 bis 1:125,000.

medium sight gestrichenes Korn *(R aiming)*.

medium tank mittlerer Panzerkampfwagen.

medium tractor mittelschwerer Schlepper *(MT)*.

meet begegnen, treffen.

meeting engagement Begegnungsgefecht *n*.

meeting point Treffpunkt *m (Tac)*.

megaphone Sprachrohr *n*, Megaphon *n*.

member Mitglied *n (of an organization)*; Angehöriger *m (of a unit)*; Glied *n (of the body)*.

memorandum Merkblatt *n*, Mitteilung *f*, Denkschrift *f*.

meningitis Gehirnhautentzündung *f*.

méplat abgeflachter Teil *(Small Arms Am)*.

Mercator chart Mercatorkarte *f*.

Mercator projection Mercatorprojektion *f*.

merchantman Handelsschiff *n*.

Merchant Marine Handelsmarine *f*.

mercury Quecksilber *n*.

mercury fulminate Knallquecksilber *n*.

meridian Meridian *m*.

meridian altitude Breitenhöhe *f (Celestial Navigation)*.

mesh road Drahtstraße *f (Engr)*.

mess Kantine *f*, Kasino *n*, Speiseraum *m*.

message Meldung *f*, Nachricht *f*, Botschaft *f*, Mitteilung *f*.

message blank Meldeblatt *n*, Meldekarte *f*.

message book Meldeblock *m*.

message center Meldesammelstelle *f*, Nachrichtenstelle *f*, Nachrichtenzentrale *f*.

message channel Meldeweg *m*.

message container Meldebüchse *f*, Abwurfpatrone *f (Avn, Sig C)*.

message dropping Meldeabwurf *m (Avn, Sig C)*.

message dropping ground Abwurfstelle *f*, Meldeabwurfstelle *f (Avn, Sig C)*.

message form Vordruck für dringende Meldungen.

message pad Meldeblock *m*.

message pick-up Aufhaken *n (Avn)*.

message relay service Meldedienst *m*.

message transmission service Meldedienst *m*.

mess attendant zum Küchendienst kommandierter Soldat.

mess council Kasinovorstand *m*.

messenger Melder *m*; Meldegänger *m*, Läufer *m (on foot)*; Meldereiter *m (on horse)*; Meldefahrer *m (on vehicle)*; Kradmelder *m (on Mtcl)*.

messenger dog Meldehund *m*.

messenger-dog detail Meldehundtrupp *m*.

messenger-dog handler Meldehundführer *m*.

messenger pigeon Brieftaube *f*, Heeresbrieftaube *f*.

messenger team Meldehundegespann *n*.

messenger vehicle Meldefahrzeug *n*.

mess gear *See* mess kit.

messing Verpflegung *f*.

mess kit Kochgeschirr *n*, Eßgeschirr und -Besteck.

mess-kit cover Kochgeschirrhülle *f*.

mess officer Verpflegungsoffizier *m*.

mess orderly *See* mess attendant.

mess sergeant Küchenunteroffizier *m*, Verpflegungsunteroffizier *m*.

metal Metall *n*.

metal cabinet Metallgehäuse *n (Rad)*.

metal container Blechbehälter *m*, Blechgefäß *n*, Blechkanister *m*.

metal drum Blechtrommel *f*; Trommel *f (for belt Am)*.

metal fittings Beschlag *m (R)*.

metal fouling Metallrückstände im Rohr *(G)*.

metallic circuit Doppelleitung *f (Tp)*.

metallic-link ammunition belt Metallgliedergurt *m*, Stahlgurt *m (MG)*.

metallic telephone circuit Fernsprechdoppelleitung *f*.

metal mesh road Drahtstraße *f (Engr)*.

metalsmith Flugzeugmetaller *m (Nav, Avn)*.

metal tube Stahlröhre *f (Rad)*.

meteorograph Meteorograph *m (Avn, Met)*.

meteorological Wetter-. *See also* metro.

meteorological disturbance Wetterstörung *f.*

meteorological measurement Wettermessung *f.*

meteorological message Wetterfunkmeldung *f*, Wetterfunkspruch *m* *(Rad);* Barbarameldung *f (Arty).*

meteorological service Truppenwetterdienst *m (T of Opns).*

meteorological station Wetterwarte *f.*

meteorologist Meteorologe *m.*

meteorology Wetterkunde *f.*

method Methode *f*, Verfahren *n*, Weise *f*, Art *f.*

method of attack Angriffsart *f.*

method of combat Kampfmethode *f.*

method of execution Art der Durchführung *(Tac).*

method of fire Feuerart *f*, Schießverfahren *n (Arty).*

method of movement Bewegungsart *f.*

method of radio communication Funkverkehrsform *f.*

method of survey Vermessungsart *f (Engr).*

method of warfare Kampfmethode *f.*

methyldichlorarsine Methyldichlorarsin *n (CWS).*

metro Wetter-, Witterungs-, Barbara-. *See also* meteorological.

metro correction Verbesserung für Witterungseinflüsse *(Arty).*

metro data Witterungseinflüsse *mpl. (Gunnery).*

metro message Barbarameldung *f*, Wettermeldung *f (Arty).*

metro platoon Wetterzug *m (Arty).*

mica Glimmer *m.*

microbarograph Mikrobarograph *m.*

microfilm Mikrofilm *m.*

micrometer Teilring *m (optical Inst);* Skalenring *m (angle-of-site Inst);* Mikrometerschraube *f (calipers).*

micrometer calipers Mikrometerschraube *f.*

micrometer drum Trommel *f (panoramic sight).*

micrometer head Triebscheibe *f (optical, Ord).*

micrometer index Stellmarke *f (optical Inst).*

micrometer knob Rändel *m*, Teil-

trommel *f (panoramic telescope, BC telescope).*

micrometer scale Skalenring *m*, Teiltrommel *f (telescopic sight).*

microphone Mikrophon *n.*

middle Mitte *f.*

midpoint Mittelpunkt *m (center);* Wechselpunkt *m (AAA).*

midrange *See* medium range.

midshipman Seekadett *m.*

midwing monoplane Mitteldecker *m.*

mil Teilstrich *m*, Strich *m (Gunnery). See also* Neugrad.

mildew Meltau *m.*

mild steel Weicheisen *n.*

mile Landmeile *f (statute mile of 1.609 km);* Seemeile *f (nautical mile of 1.853 km).*

mileage Kilometerzahl *f. See also* mileage allowance.

mileage allowance Reisekostenvergütung *f.*

mileage indicator Kilometerzähler *m.*

mileage table Reiseverordnung *f.*

milestone Meilenstein *m.*

mil formula Teilstrich-Formel *f (Arty).*

mil graduation Stricheinteilung *f*, Teilstricheinteilung *f;* Richtkreiseinteilung *f (on aiming circle).*

military *n* Militär *n.*

military *adj* militärisch, Wehr-, Heeres-, Kriegs-.

military academy Militärakademie *f.*

military age wehrpflichtiges Alter.

military area Militärbezirk *m (any area under military control);* Wehrersatzbezirk *m (recruiting area, subdivision of a Wehrkreis).*

military attaché Militärattaché *m.*

military authorities Militärbehörde *f.*

military aviation Militärluftfahrt *f.*

military bearing soldatische Haltung.

military bridge Kriegsbrücke *f.*

military bridge equipment Kriegsbrückengerät *n.*

military cemetery Militärfriedhof *m.*

military censorship Militärzensur *f.*

military channel Dienstweg *m.*

military chart Generalstabskarte *f.*

military commission Militärausschuß *m*, Militärkommission *f.*

military correspondence militärischer Schriftverkehr.

military court Militärgericht *n*, Wehrmachtgericht *n.*

military courtesy militärische Formen.

military crest Böschungskante *f* *(Top).*

military custom Truppengebrauch *m.*

military discipline militärische Disziplin, Manneszucht *f.*

military district Militärbezirk *m;* Wehrbezirk *m (subdivision of a* Wehrersatzbezirk).

military district headquarters Feldkommandantur *f (Com Z).*

military education Wehrerziehung *f*, Wehrertüchtigung *f.*

military equipment Heergerät *n*, Kriegsmaterial *n.*

military establishment Wehrmacht-Einrichtung *f.*

military funeral Militärbegräbnis *n;* Trauerfeier *f (service);* Trauerparade *f (procession).*

military geography Wehrgeographie *f.*

military geology Wehrgeologie *f.*

military government Militärverwaltung *f.*

military governor Militärbefehlshaber *m.*

military grid Gitternetz *n.*

military hospital Heereslazarett *n.*

military hygiene Wehrmachtgesundheitsdienst *m*, Gesundheitswesen *n.*

military information wehrwichtige Nachrichten.

military intelligence militärisches Nachrichtenwesen.

Military Intelligence Division Amt für den Militärischen Nachrichtendienst im Generalstab des Heeres *(USA).*

Military Intelligence Service Nachrichtendienst *m (USA).*

military internee Internierter *m.*

military jurisdiction Militärgerichtsbarkeit *f.*

military justice Kriegsgerichtsrechtsprechung *f.*

military law Kriegsrecht *n*, Wehrrecht *n;* Wehrstrafrecht *n (penal code).*

military map Generalstabskarte *f.*

military mining Minenkrieg *m*, Minenkampf *m.*

military mission militärischer Auftrag; Militärmission *f.*

military necessity Kriegsräson *f.*

military objective militärisches Ziel.

military occupation militärische Besetzung.

military offense Wehrvergehen *n*, militärisches Vergehen, militärisches Verbrechen.

military order Heeresbefehl *m.*

military passport Passierschein *m.*

military penal code Wehrmacht-Strafgesetzbuch *n*, Militärstrafgesetzbuch *n (Ger).*

military police Feldgendarmerie *f.*

military policeman Feldgendarm *m.*

military police regulations Feldgendarmerievorschrift *f.*

military police service Ordnungsdienst *m.*

military policy Wehrpolitik *f.*

military post Wehrmacht-Standort *m.*

military prison Arrestanstalt *f.*

military prisoner Arrestant *m*, Militärgefangener *m*, Militärhäftling *m.*

military railroad Militäreisenbahn *f*, Feldeisenbahn *f.*

military railway engineer Feldeisenbahner *m.*

military rank militärischer Rang.

military rating Kurzleistung *f (of an Ap engine).*

military requirements Belange der Truppe, Kriegserfordernisse *npl.*

military reservation Wehrmachtgelände *n.*

military school Heeresbildungsanstalt *f*, Waffenschule *f.*

military science Kriegswissenschaft *f*, Wehrwissenschaft *f.*

military service Wehrdienst *m.*

military sketch Geländeskizze *f.*

military specialist Wehrmachts-Sachverständiger *m*, Angehöriger einer Sonderlaufbahn.

military subdistrict Militärverwaltungsbezirk *m.*

military symbol Kartenzeichen *n*, taktisches Zeichen.

military train Militärzug *m (RR).*

military training Wehrausbildung *f*, Wehrertüchtigung *f.*

military tribunal Militärgericht *n*, Wehrmachtgericht *n.*

military usage Truppengebrauch *m.*

militia Miliz *f.*

milk Milch *f.*

mill Mühle *f.*

milliammeter Milliamperemeter *n.*

milling Fräsen *n (Tech)*.
milling machine Fräsmaschine *f*, Fräswerk *n*.
mil relation Teilstrich-Formel *f (Arty)*.
mine *n* Mine *f (Mil, Nav)*; Bergwerk *n (coal, iron, etc.)*.
mine *v* Minen legen, verminen *(laying mines)*; minieren, unterminieren *(Mil tunneling)*; abbauen *(coal, iron, etc.)*.
mine barrier Minensperre *f*.
mine buoy Minenboje *f*, Minentonne *f*.
mine case Minengefäß *n*.
mine chamber Sprengkammer *f (Blasting)*.
mine clearance Minenräumung *f*.
mine-clearance roller Minenräumwalze *f*.
mine-clearance tank Minenräumpanzer *m*.
mine crater Minentrichter *m*.
mine defense Minensperre *f*.
mine detector Minensuchgerät *n*.
mine dragging Minenschleppen *n (Nav)*.
mine field Minenfeld *n*.
mine gallery Minengang *m (Engr)*.
mine group Minenabteilung *f (harbor defense)*.
mine-infested area minenverseuchtes Gebiet *(Nav)*.
mine layer Minenfahrzeug *n*, Minenleger *m*, Minendampfer *m (Nav)*.
mine-laying airplane Minenflugzeug *n*, Minenflieger *m*.
mine-laying tank Minenlegerpanzerkampfwagen *m*.
mine-locating detail Minensuchtrupp *m*.
mine planter *See* mine layer.
mine planting flotilla Minenlegerflottille *f (Nav)*.
mine-probing rod Minensuchstab *m*.
mine road block Straßensperre mit Minen.
miner's spoon Raumlöffel *m (Engr)*.
miner's tramcar Minenhund *m (Engr)*.
mine shaft Minenschacht *m (Engr)*.
mine-surveying set Markscheidegerät *n (Engr)*.
mine sweeper Minenräumer *m*, Minenräumboot *n*, Minensucher *m*, Minensuchboot *n (Nav)*.
mine sweeping Minenräumung *f*.

mine tunnel Minenstollen *m (Engr)*.
mine ventilation Bewetterung *f (Engr)*.
mine yawl Minenlegermotorboot *n (Nav)*.
miniature kleine Ordensschnalle *f (decoration)*.
miniature range Kleinschießplatz *m*.
minimum Minimum *n*, Kleinste *n*.
minimum altitude attack Tiefangriff *m*, Tieffliegerangriff *m*, Tiefflugangriff *m (Avn)*.
minimum-altitude flight Tiefflug *m (Avn)*.
minimum elevation kleinste Rohrerhöhung *(Gunnery)*.
minimum horizontal range Kartenentfernung zum Wechselpunkt *(AA Gunnery)*.
minimum number Mindestzahl *f*.
minimum range kürzeste Schußentfernung *(Firing)*.
minimum thermometer Minimumthermometer *n*.
mining effect Minenwirkung *f (Am)*.
mining gallery Minengang *m*.
mining system Minenanlage *f*.
mining tools Miniergerät *n (Engr)*.
minor casualty Leichtverwundeter *m*.
mirror Spiegel *m*.
mirror diameter Spiegeldurchmesser *m (searchlight)*.
mirror sight Spiegelvisier *n*.
misalignment of wheels schiefer Radstand, Verkantung *f (MT)*.
misappropriation unrechtmäßige Aneignung.
misbehavior before the enemy militärisches Verbrechen vor dem Feinde, militärisches Vergehen vor dem Feinde.
miscalculate falsch rechnen, sich verrechnen.
misfeed Zufuhrhemmung *f*.
misfire Versager *m*.
miss *n* Fehlgänger *m*, Fehlschuß *m*.
miss *v* verfehlen.
missile Geschoß *n*.
missing in action vermißt.
mission Auftrag *m*, Aufgabe *f*; Gefechtsaufgabe *f*; Einsatz *m (Avn)*.
"Mission accomplished!" "Auftrag erledigt!"
mist Nebel *m*.
mistake grober Fehler.
mister Herr *m*.

mitigation of sentence Urteilsmilderung *f.*

mitten Fausthandschuh *m.*

mixed force Truppenverband *m,* gemischter Verband.

mixed medical commission gemischte ärztliche Kommission.

mixed train gemischter Zug *(RR).*

mixture Gemisch *n;* Lösung *f (solution).*

mixture control Düsenkorrektor *m (Inst);* Gemischregelung *f (process).*

moat Festungsgraben *m,* Wallgraben *m.*

mobile fahrbar, fahrend, beweglich, schnell, motorisiert.

mobile antiaircraft artillery Kraftwagenflak *f.*

mobile artillery fahrende Artillerie, bewegliche Artillerie.

mobile generating unit fahrbarer Stromerzeuger, Kraftquellenwagen *m.*

mobile hospital Feldlazarett *n.*

mobile machine shop fahrbare Werkstatt, Werkstattkraftwagen *m.*

mobile reserve bewegliche Reserve *(Tac).*

mobile reserves beweglich gehaltene Vorräte *(supplies).*

mobile seacoast artillery bewegliche Küstenartillerie.

mobile surgical unit motorisiertes Bereitschaftslazarett.

mobile troops Schnelle Truppen.

mobile warfare Bewegungskrieg *m.*

mobility Wendigkeit *f (MT, Tk).*

mobilization Mobilmachung *f.*

mobilization camp Mobilmachungslager *n.*

mobilization center Mobilmachungslager *n.*

mobilization day Mobilmachungstag *m,* X-Tag *m.*

mobilization plan Mobilmachungsplan *m.*

mobilization point Mobilmachungslager *n.*

Mobilization Regulations Mobilmachungsbestimmungen *fpl.*

mobilize mobilisieren, mobilmachen, aufbieten.

mock combat Scheingefecht *n.*

mock-up Nachbildung *f.*

model Baumuster *n,* Modell *n,* Muster *n,* Typ *m (Ap, MT).*

model designation Typenbezeichnung *f.*

model number Typennummer *f,* Modellnummer *f.*

modulated wave modulierte Welle, gemodelte Welle.

moisture Feuchtigkeit *f.*

moisture content Feuchtigkeitsgehalt *m (Met).*

"Molotov breadbasket" Schüttkasten *m (Avn).*

"Molotov cocktail" Brandflasche *f.*

moment of force Kraftmoment *n.*

moment of inertia Trägheitsmoment *n.*

momentum Bewegungsgröße *f,* Impuls *m.*

monitor *v* überwachen *(Com).*

monitoring station Überwachungsstelle *f (Com).*

monkey wrench Schraubenschlüssel *m.*

monobloc gun barrel Vollrohr *n.*

monocoque construction Schalenbauweise *f (Ap).*

monocular *adj* einäugig, monokular *(optical Inst).*

monoplane Eindecker *m.*

monsoon Monsun *m.*

monument Denkmal *n.*

moon Mond *m.*

moor *v* ankern, verankern, festmachen, vertäuen.

moored mine Ankermine *f.*

mooring band Verankerungsgurt *m (Bln).*

mooring cable Fesselkabel *n,* Fesselseil *n,* Verankerungstau *n (Bln).*

mooring line *See* **mooring cable.**

mooring mast Ankermast *m,* Verankerungsmast *m,* Vertäumast *m.*

mooring tower Ankerturm *m,* Verankerungsturm *m.*

mop Mop *m.*

mopping-up detachment Säuberungstrupp *m.*

mopping-up operation Säuberungsunternehmen *n.*

mop up säubern *(Tac).*

morale Moral *f,* Stimmung *f.*

Morale Branch Truppenbetreuung *f.*

moral effect seelische Wirkung *(Tac).*

morning Morgen *m;* Vormittag *m (forenoon).*

morning report Iststärkenachweisung *f.*

morning-report strength Iststärke *f.*
morphine Morphin *n*, Morphium *n.*
Morse code Morsealphabet *n.*
Morse code character Morsezeichen *n.*
mortar Granatwerfer *m (Ord);* Mörtel *m (building material).*
mortar ammunition Granatwerfermunition *f.*
mortar cart Gasmörser-Karen *m (CWS).*
mortar emplacement Granatwerferstand *m.*
mortar equipment Granatwerfergerät *n.*
mortar fire Granatwerferfeuer *n*, Granatwerferbeschuß *m.*
mortar gunner Werferschütze *m.*
mortar pit Granatwerfernest *n.*
mortar platoon Granatwerferzug *m.*
mortar projectile Granatwerfergeschoß *n.*
mortar section Granatwerfer-Gruppe *f.*
mortar shell Wurfgranate *f.*
mortar-shell fuze Wurfgranatzünder *m.*
mortar smoke shell Nebelwurfgranate *f.*
mortar squad Granatwerfertrupp *m.*
mosaic Reihenbild *n (Photo).*
mosaic assembly Zusammensetzen von Reihenbildern *(Photo).*
mosquito Moskito *m*, Mücke *f.*
mosquito bar See **mosquito net.**
mosquito fleet Schnellboot-Flottille *f (Nav).*
mosquito net Moskitonetz *n.*
motor Motor *m*, Maschine *f.*
motor ambulance Krankenkraftwagen *m.*
motor ambulance train Krankenkraftwagenzug *m.*
motor carriage Selbstfahrlafette *f (G).*
motor column Kraftfahrzeugkolonne *f.*
motor convoy Kraftfahrzeugkolonne *f*, Kraftwagenkolonne *f.*
motorcycle Kraftrad *n*, Krad *n.*
motorcycle infantry Kradschützen *mpl.*
motorcycle messenger Kradmelder *m.*
motorcycle point Kradspitze *f (Adv Gd).*
motorcycle rifle company Krad-

schützenkompanie *f.*
motorcycle rifleman Kradschütze *m.*
motorcycle scout Kradspäher *m*, Kraftradspäher *m.*
motorcycle troop Kradschützenschwadron *f*, Kraftradschützenschwadron *f.*
motorcycle troops Kradschützen *mpl.*
motorcyclist Kradfahrer *m*, Kraftradfahrer *m.*
motor dispatch service Kraftfahr-Verbindungsdienst *m.*
motor ferry Motorfähre *f.*
motor fuel Kraftstoff *m*, Treibstoff *m*, Betriebsstoff *m.*
motorization Motorisierung *f.*
motorize motorisieren.
motorized motorisiert, verlastet.
motorized artillery Kraftzugartillerie *f*, motorisierte Artillerie.
motorized division leichte Division, schnelle Division, motorisierte Division.
motorized gun Kraftzuggeschütz *n.*
motorized infantry motorisierte Infanterie.
motorized infantry division Panzergrenadierdivision *f.*
motorized march Kraftwagenmarsch *m.*
motorized riflemen motorisierte Schützen.
motorized troops verlastete Truppen, schnelle Truppen.
motorized unit motorisierter Verband.
motor messenger Meldefahrer *m.*
motor officer Kraftfahrtransportoffizier *m (USA).*
motor oil Motorenöl *n.*
motor park Kraftwagenpark *m.*
motor pool Kraftfahrpark *m.*
motor torpedo boat Schnellboot *n*, Motorschnellboot *n*, Motortorpedoboot *n*, Torpedoschnellboot *n.*
motor transport Kraftwagentransport *m.*
motor transport equipment Kraftfahrgerät *n.*
motor transport officer See **motor officer.**
Motor Transport Service Kraftfahrwesen *n.*
motor truck Lastkraftwagen *m.*
motor vehicle Kraftfahrzeug *n.*
motor-vehicle column Kraftfahrkolonne *f.*

motor-vehicle concentration Kraftfahrzeugansammlung *f.*

motor-vehicle maintenance unit Kraftfahrzeuginstandsetzungseinheit *f.*

motor-vehicle park Kraftfahrzeugpark *m,* Kraftwagenpark *m.*

motor-vehicle repair shop Kraftwagenwerkstatt *f.*

mount *n* Träger *m (Mech);* Lafette *f (Ord);* Reitpferd *n (horse). See also* gun mount.

mount *v* aufsteigen, besteigen; aufziehen *(Photo).*

mountain Berg *m.*

mountain artillery Gebirgsartillerie *f.*

mountain battery Gebirgsbatterie *f.*

mountain cannon Gebirgskanone *f.*

mountain cap Bergmütze *f (Clo).*

mountain combat Gefecht im Gebirge, Gebirgskampf *m.*

mountain corps Gebirgskorps *n.*

mountain gun Gebirgsgeschütz *n.*

mountain infantryman Gebirgsjäger *m,* Jäger *m.*

mountain pack company Gebirgsträgerkompanie *f.*

mountain pass Gebirgspaß *m.*

mountain range Gebirge *n.*

mountain supply column Gebirgsfahrkolonne *f (H-Dr).*

mountain troops Gebirgstruppen *fpl.*

mountain warfare Gebirgskrieg *m.*

mounted aufgesessen *(on horse or vehicle);* beritten *(on horse);* verlastet *(porté).*

mounted combat Gefecht zu Pferde.

mounted defilade Sichtdeckung für Reiter *(Cav).*

mounted drill Ausbildung zu Pferd *(Cav).*

mounted infantry berittene Infanterie.

mounted maneuver Reitmanöver *n.*

mounted messenger Meldereiter *m (on horse);* Meldefahrer *m (on vehicle).*

mounted officer berittener Offizier, Offizier zu Pferde.

mounted platoon Reiterzug *m (Inf Regt).*

mounted reconnaissance berittene Aufklärung, Aufklärung zu Pferd *(Cav).*

mounted rifle half squad Schützenabmarsch *m (Cav).*

mounted section Gruppe zu Pferde *(Cav).*

mount guard *v* Wache beziehen.

mouth Mund *m (Pers);* Maul *n (animal);* Mündung *f (river, G muzzle);* Stellbecher *m (of fuze setter).*

mouthpiece Atemmundstück *n (oxygen breathing apparatus);* Einsprache *f (Tp);* Mundstück *n (harness).*

movement Bewegung *f,* Fortbewegung *f;* Verlegung *f (from one point to another);* Transport *m (of troops, etc.).*

movement at an angle Schrägfahrt *f (ground target).*

movement by air Lufttransport *m.*

movement by rail Eisenbahntransport *m.*

movement by road Marschbewegungen *fpl;* Kraftfahrzeugtransport *m.*

movement by water Seetransport *m.*

movement order Transportbefehl *m,* Verlegungsbefehl *m.*

moving coil Drehspule *f (Elec).*

moving-coil instrument Drehspulinstrument *n.*

moving picture Film *m.*

moving pivot Drehpunkt *m (drill).*

moving screen Verschleierungsabteilung *f.*

moving target bewegliches Ziel, fahrendes Ziel.

"moving up" Ausrücken *n.*

mud Schlamm *m.*

mud capping Verdämmen *n (blasting).*

mudguard Schutzblech *n,* Kotflügel *m.*

muffler Auspufftopf *m,* Schalldämpfer *m (Mtr).*

mule Maultier *n,* Maulesel *m.*

mule train Maultierkolonne *f.*

multi-axle drive Mehrachsantrieb *m.*

multi-axle vehicle Mehrachser *m.*

multielement tube Verbundröhre *f.*

multiplace mehrsitzig.

multiplace fighter Jagdmehrsitzer *m.*

multiplane Mehrdecker *m (Ap).*

multiple Vielfache *n (Math).*

multiple antiaircraft weapon mehrläufige Fla-Waffe.

multiple-belt entanglement Flächendrahthindernis *n.*

multiple connection Vielfachschaltung *f*, zusammengesetzte Vermittlung *(Tp)*.

multiple disk clutch   Lamellenkupplung *f*, Mehrscheibenkupplung *f*.

multiple-engine mehrmotorig.

multiple-grid tube Mehrgitterröhre *f*.

multiple-gun mount Mehrlauflafette *f*.

multiple-hole nozzle Mehrlochdüse *f (Mtr)*.

multiple-lens camera Mehrfach-Reihenbildkammer *f (aerial Photo)*.

multiplex operation Mehrfachbetrieb *m (Tp)*.

multiplex telephony Mehrfachsprechen *n*.

multiplex utilization Mehrfachausnutzung *f (Tp)*.

multipurpose gun Mehrzweckgeschütz *n*.

multiseater mehrsitzig.

multiseater airplane Mehrsitzer *m*.

multisection charge aus Teilladungen bestehende Triebladung *(Am)*.

municipal police Schutzpolizei *f*.

munitions Munition *f*, Kriegsgerät *n*, Kampfmittel *npl*.

munitions officer Munitionsoffizier *m*.

munitions storage shed Munitionsschuppen *m*.

muscle Muskel *m*.

musette bag Brotbeutel *m*.

mushroom head of obturator Liderungskopf *m*, Pilz *m (G)*.

mustache Schnurrbart *m*.

mustard Senf *m*, Mostrich *m*.

mustard gas   Senfgas *n*, Lost *n*, Yperit *n (CWS)*.

mustard gas shell Senfgas-Granate *f (CWS)*.

mustardization Vergasung mit Senfgas *(CWS)*.

muster Appell *m*, Musterung *f*.

muster roll Stammrolle *f*.

mutilate verstümmeln.

mutiny Meuterei *f*.

mutton Hammelfleisch *n*.

mutual fire support   gegenseitige Feuerunterstützung.

mutual support gegenseitige Unterstützung.

muzzle Mündung *f (Ord)*.

muzzle bell Mundlochfries *m (G)*.

muzzle blast Stoß der Mündungsgase *(G)*.

muzzle-blast smoke Mündungsrauch *m*.

muzzle brake Mündungsbremse *f (G)*.

muzzle cover Mündungsschoner *m*.

muzzle energy Mündungsarbeit *f*, Mündungswucht *f*, Mündungsenergie *f*.

muzzle flash Mündungsfeuer *n*.

muzzle gas pressure Mündungsgasdruck *m*.

muzzle-loader Vorderlader *m*.

muzzle sight Korn *n (Ord)*.

muzzle swell Mundlochfries *m (G)*.

muzzle velocity Anfangsgeschwindigkeit *f*, Mündungsgeschwindigkeit *f*.

muzzle wave Schallwelle des Mündungsknalls *(Sound Ranging)*.

N

N.A.C.A. cowling   NACA-Haube *f (Ap)*.

nacelle Gondel *f (Ap)*.

nadir point Fußpunkt *m*.

nail Nagel *m*.

name plate Typenschild *n*.

narrow eng, schmal.

narrow gage Schmalspur *f (RR)*.

narrow-gage railroad Schmalspurbahn *f*, Kleinbahn *f*.

national anthem Nationalhymne *f*.

National Defense Act Wehrgesetz *n*.

national emblem Hoheitszeichen *n*.

national ensign Reichskriegsflagge *f (Ger Nav)*; Nationalflagge *f (other countries) (Nav)*.

national flag Reichsflagge *f*, Nationalflagge *f*.

National Guard   Nationalgarde *f (USA)*.

national insignia Hoheitsabzeichen *n*, Hoheitszeichen *n*.

nationality Nationalität *f*, Staatsangehörigkeit *f*.

national salute Flaggensalut *m*.

natural obstacle Geländehindernis *n*.

natural oscillation Eigenschwingung *f (Rad)*.

natural rubber Naturkautschuk *m*, Naturgummi *m*.

nausea Brechreiz *m*.

nautical mile Seemeile *f (1.853 km)*.

naval Marine-, See-. *See also* **navy**.

Naval Academy Marineakademie *f*.

naval aircraft pilot Seeflieger *m*.

Naval Air Forces Marineluftwaffe *f (USA)*.

naval airplane Seeflieger *m*, Seeflugzeug *n*.

naval antiaircraft artillery Marineflak *f*.

naval attaché Marineattaché *m*.

naval aviation Marineflugwesen *n*, Seeluftstreitkräfte *fpl*, Seeflieger *mpl*, Marineflieger *mpl*.

naval aviator Marineflieger *m*.

naval base Flottenstützpunkt *m*, Marinestation *f*.

naval district Marinebezirk *m (USA)*.

naval forces Seestreitkräfte *fpl*.

naval patrol airplane Seeaufklärer *m*.

naval pilot Marineflieger *m*.

Naval Reserve Marinereserve *f (USA)*.

naval unit Marineeinheit *f*, Flotteneinheit *f*.

navigate orten.

navigation Navigation *f (Avn, Nav)*.

navigational chart Navigationskarte *f*.

navigation guide Bake *f (Nav)*.

navigation head Schiffsausladestelle *f*, Endhafen *m*.

navigation instrument Navigationsinstrument *n (Avn)*.

navigator Orter *m (Avn)*.

navigator's compass Kurszeiger *m*, Orterkompaß *m*, Peilkompaß *m (Ap)*.

navy Kriegsmarine *f*, Marine *f*.

navy airplane Seeflugzeug *n*, Seeflieger *m*.

Navy Department Marineamt *n (USA)*.

navy patrol airplane Seeaufklärer *m*.

navy yard Marinewerft *f*, Kriegswerft *f*.

NCO Unteroffizier *m*.

NCO training course Unterführerkurs *m*.

near nahe.

near horse Sattelpferd *n*.

near miss Fehltreffer *m*, Nebsttreffer *m*.

neck Hals *m;* Hülsenhals *m (cartridge)*.

neckband Halsbinde *f (Clo)*.

neck groove Halskerbe *f (horse)*.

neck halter Halshalfter *f (harness)*.

neck-halter tie Halshalfterriemen *m (harness)*.

neck strap Nackenband *n (gas mask)*; Nackenriemen *m*, Halsriemen *m (harness)*; Tragriemen *m (pack saddle)*.

necktie Binder *m (Clo)*.

needle Nadel *f*.

needle bearing Nadellager *n (MT)*.

needle dam Nadelwehr *n (Engr)*.

negative stagger Rückwärtsstaffelung *f*, Staffelung nach hinten *(Ap wings)*.

neglect of duty Pflichtverletzung *f*, Pflichtversäumnis *f*.

negligence Fahrlässigkeit *f*, Nachlässigkeit *f*, Vernachlässigung *f*.

negotiate verhandeln.

negotiations for surrender Übergabeverhandlungen *fpl*.

negotiator Unterhändler *m*.

neon lamp Glimmlampe *f*.

nephoscope Wolkenspiegel *m (Met)*.

nest Nest *n (Ft)*.

nest of resistance Widerstandsnest *n*, Verteidigungsnest *n*.

nest of riflemen Schützennest *n*.

net Netz *n (Rad, Eng, Cam)*.

net barrier Netzsperre *f (coast defense)*.

net control station Funküberwachungsstelle *f*, Hauptfunkstelle *f*, Leitfunkstelle *f (Rad)*.

net diagram Funkskizze *f (Rad)*.

netting Tarnungsgeflecht *n (Cam)*.

net weight Nettogewicht *n*.

network Stromnetz *n (Elec)*.

neutral *adj* neutral.

neutral *n* Leerlauf *m (Mtr)*.

neutrality Neutralität *f*.

neutralization Niederkämpfung *f*, Lahmlegung *f (Tac)*; Neutralisierung *f*, Neutralisation *f (CWS)*.

neutralization fire Niederhaltungsschießen *n*, Niederhalten *n (Arty)*.

neutralize neutralisieren; lähmen, lahmlegen *(an attack)*; niederhalten, niederkämpfen *(fire)*.

neutral position Nullstellung *f* (*Mech*).

neutral power neutrale Macht.

neutral troops neutrale Truppen (*Tng*).

news broadcast Nachrichtenübertragung *f*.

newspaper Zeitung *f; Frontzeitung· f* (*T of Opns*).

newsreel Wochenschau *f*.

news service Nachrichtendienst *m* (*Rad*).

next of kin die nächsten Angehörigen.

NH powder nichthygroskopisches Pulver.

niche Munitionsnische *f*, Fuchsloch *n* (*Ft*).

nickel Nickel *m-n*.

nickel-alkaline cell Nickelsammler *m*.

night attack Nachtangriff *m*.

night beacon lighting Nachtbefeuerung *f* (*Avn*).

night bomber Nachtbomber *m*.

night bombing flare Leuchtbombe *f*.

night combat Nachtgefecht *n*.

night fighter Nachtjäger *m* (*Avn*).

night fighting Nachtjagd *f*, Nachtluftkampf *m* (*Avn*).

night firing Nachtschießen *n*.

night flying chart Nachtflug-Karte *f* (*Avn*).

night glasses Nachtglas *n*.

night march Nachtmarsch *m*.

night operation Nachtunternehmung *f*.

night raid Nachtangriff *m* (*Avn*).

night reconnaissance Nachtaufklärung *f*.

ninety-degree turn Flügelspitzenkurve *f* (*Avn*).

nippers Beißzange *f*.

nipple Nippel *f* (*Tech*).

nitrate explosive Sprengsalpeter *m*.

nitration Nitrierung *f* (*Am*).

nitric acid Salpetersäure *f*.

nitrocellulose Nitrozellulose *f*.

nitrocellulose powder Nitrozellulosepulver *n*.

nitrocotton Schießwolle *f*, Schießbaumwolle *f*.

nitrogen Stickstoff *m*.

nitrogen mustard gas Stickstofflost *n* (*CWS*).

nitroglycerin Sprengöl *n*, Nitroglyzerin *n*.

nitroglycerin powder Nitroglyzerinpulver *n*, Sprengölpulver *n*.

noise Geräusch *n*, Lärm *m*; Gefechtslärm *m* (*of battle*); Motorengeräusch *n* (*of engines*).

no man's land Niemandsland *n*.

nomenclature Benennung *f*.

nonbattle injury Wehrdienstbeschädigung *f*.

noncombatant Nichtkämpfer *m*, Nichtkombattant *m*.

noncommissioned officer Unteroffizier *m*.

noncorrosive nichtätzend.

nondelay fuze Schnellzünder *m*, Augenblickszünder *m*, Aufschlagzünder ohne Verzögerung.

nondeteriorating supplies lagerungsfähige Vorräte.

noneffective *n* Dienstunfähiger *m*.

nonexpendable nicht verbrauchbar.

nonexpendable supplies Gerät *n*.

nonhygroscopic powder nichthygroskopisches Pulver.

nonlethal agent nicht tödlich wirkender Kampfstoff, Reizstoff *m* (*CWS*).

nonmilitary objectives nichtmilitärische Ziele.

nonpersistent chemical agent flüchtiger Kampfstoff.

nonpersistent c h e m i c a l munitions Luftkampfstoffmunition *f*.

nonrecoverable unbrauchbar, nicht instandsetzbar.

non-rigid airship unstarres Luftschiff.

nonskid chain Gleitschutzkette *f* (*MT*).

nonskid device Gleitschutzmittel *n* (*MT*).

nonskid tread Gleitschutz *m* (*MT*).

nonstop flight Ohnehaltflug *m* (*Avn*).

nonsystematic error zufälliger Fehler.

nontoxic agent nicht giftig wirkender Kampfstoff, Reizstoff *m* (*CWS*).

nontransportable nicht transportfähig.

normal barrage Sperrfeuer *n* (*Arty*).

normal height of burst richtige Sprenghöhe, normale Sprenghöhe (*Gunnery*).

normal impact senkrechtes Auftreffen (*Ballistics*).

normal landing Dreipunktlandung *f* (*Avn*).

normal position Normalstellung *f* (*Mech*).

normal rating Dauerleistung *f* (*Mtr*).

normal sitting position sitzender Anschlag (*MG*).

north Norden *m* (*point of compass*); Nordrichtung *f* (*direction*).

North Star Polarstern *m*.

nose Bug *m*, Rumpfbug *m*, Rumpfspitze *f*, Rumpfnase *f* (*Ap fuselage*); Nase *f* (*anatomy*).

noseband Nasenriemen *m* (*harness*).

nosebleed Nasenbluten *n*.

nose clamp Nasenklammer *f* (*gas mask*).

nose compartment vordere Kanzel, Bugkanzel *f* (*Ap*).

nose dive Kopfsturz *m* (*Avn*).

nose fuze Kopfzünder *m* (*bomb*).

nose gun Bug-Maschinengewehr *n*.

nose gunner Bugschütze *m* (*Ap, Tk*).

nose-gun station Bugstand *m* (*Ap*).

noseheavy kopflastig, vorderlastig (*Ap*).

nose irritant Nasenrachenreizstoff *m* (*sternutator*) (*CWS*).

nose-over Kopfstand *m* (*Avn*).

nose section of shell Kopfteil *n* (*Am*).

nose spray vorderer Sprengkegel (*air burst*).

nose turret vordere Kanzel, Bugkanzel *f* (*Ap*).

nostrils Nüstern *fpl* (*horse*).

notarized beglaubigt (*documents*).

notice of induction Einberufungskarte *f*.

notify benachrichtigen.

notify next of kin die nächsten Angehörigen verständigen, die nächsten Verwandten verständigen.

nozzle Düse *f*, Spritzdüse *f*.

nuisance raid Störungsflug *m*, Störflug *m*, Störeinsatz *m* (*Avn*).

nuisance raider Störflugzeug *n*, Störflieger *m* (*Ap*).

number Nummer *f*, Zahl *f*, Ziffer *f*.

number of personnel Kopfstärke *f* (*of a unit*).

number of prisoners Gefangenenziffer *f*.

numerical value Zahlenwert *m*.

nurse Krankenschwester *f*.

nurse balloon Ballonamme *f* (*for supplying gas*).

Nurse Corps *See* **Army Nurse Corps.**

nut Schraubenmutter *f*, Mutter *f* (*Mech*).

O

Oak Leaf Cluster Eichenlaub *n* (*decoration*).

oakum Werg *n*.

oar Ruder *n*.

oath of enlistment Diensteid *m*, Fahneneid *m*.

obedience Gehorsam *m*.

objective Ziel *n*, Kampfziel *n*; Angriffsziel *n* (*of an attack*); Zweck *m* (*purpose*).

objective lens Ausblick *m*.

objective-lens socket Ausblickstutzen *m*.

objective plane Zielfläche *f* (*Gunnery*).

objective point Treffpunkt *m*, Aufschlagpunkt *m* (*point of impact*); Zielpunkt *m* (*Tac*).

objective-prism housing Ausblickprismengehäuse *n* (*BC telescope*).

obligation Pflicht *f*.

oblique schräg, schief.

oblique fire Schrägfeuer *n*.

oblique photograph Schrägaufnahme *f* (*aerial Photo*).

obscure situation ungeklärte Lage (*Tac*).

observation Beobachtung *f*, Nahaufklärung *f*; Glasbeobachtung *f* (*with field glass or telescope*).

observation airplane Naherkunder *m*, Nahaufklärungsflugzeug *n*.

observation area Beobachtungsbereich *m* (*Arty*).

observation aviation Nahaufklärungsflieger *mpl*.

observation balloon Beobachtungsballon *m*.

observation battalion Beobachtungsabteilung *f* (*Arty*).

observation battery Beobachtungsbatterie *f* (*Arty*).

observation camp Beobachtungslager *n*, Beobachtungsstation *f*.

observation car Beobachtungswagen *m (MT)*; Aussichtswagen *m (RR)*.

observation group Nahaufklärungsgruppe *f (Avn)*.

observation mine Beobachtungsmine *f*, Grundmine *f (Nav)*.

observation mission Aufklärungsaufgabe *f*, Aufklärungsauftrag *m*.

o' servation of fire Feuerbeobachtung *f*, Schußbeobachtung *f (Arty)*.

observation of the enemy Feindbeobachtung *f*.

observation point Beobachtungspunkt *m*.

observation post Beobachtungstelle *f (Arty)*; Flugwache *f (AWS)*; Beobachtungsstand *m (station or position)*; Baumbeobachtungsstand *m (in a tree)*.

observation post system Beobachtungsnetz *n (Arty)*.

observation post—target line Linie Beobachtungsstelle-Ziel *(Gunnery)*.

observation slit Sehschlitz *m*.

observation squadron Nahaufklärerstaffel *f (Avn)*.

observation station Beobachtungsstelle *f (Arty)*; Flugwache *f (AWS)*.

observation tower Aussichtsturm *m*.

observatory Warte *f*, Sternwarte *f*.

observe beobachten.

observed fire beobachtetes Feuer, beobachtetes Schießen.

observed-fire chart Zieltafel für beobachtetes Schießen.

observer Beobachter *m*; Orter *m (navigator-observer, Avn)*; Luftspäher *m (AWS)*.

observer's basket Beobachtungskorb *m (Bln)*.

observer telescope Beobachterfernrohr *n*.

obsolete veraltet.

obstacle Hindernis *n*, Sperre *f*.

obstacle construction Hindernisbau *m*.

obstacle-construction equipment Sperrmittel *n*.

obstacle construction squad Hindernistrupp *m*.

obstacle course Hindernisstrecke *f*, Hindernisbahn *f*.

obstacle demolition party Hindernissprengtrupp *m (Engr)*.

obstacle field Sperrfeld *n*.

obstacle light Hindernisfeuer *n (Avn)*.

obstacle line Sperrlinie *f*.

obstruction Hindernis *n*, Sperre *f (obstacle)*; Hemmung *f*, Sperrung *f (Mech)*.

obstruction light Hindernisfeuer *n (Avn)*.

obturation Lidern *n*.

obturator Liderung *f (G)*.

obtuse angle stumpfer Winkel.

occluded front Okklusion *f (Met)*.

occlusion Okklusion *f (Met)*.

occulter Blende *f (SL)*.

occupation Besetzung *f*, Okkupation *f*; Einnahme *f (capture or conquest)*; Inbesitznahme *f (taking possession)*.

occupation of position Instellunggehen *n (Tac)*.

occupation troops Besatzungstruppen *fpl*.

occupied area Stellung *f (Tac)*; besetztes Gebiet *(territory)*.

occupied territory besetztes Gebiet.

occupy besetzen, einnehmen *(a locality)*.

ocean Ozean *m*, Meer *n*, See *f*.

ocean-going tug Hochseeschlepper *m*.

octane number Oktanzahl *f*.

octane rating Oktanwert *m*.

octant Oktant *m*, Libellensextant *m (Air Navigation)*.

odometer Kilometerzähler *m (MT)*.

odor Geruch *m*.

odor-detection training agent Übungsriechstoff *m (CWS)*.

odorless geruchlos.

off aus *(a switch, etc.)*.

off-carrier position Ausladeplatz *m*.

off-course correction Kursverbesserung *f (Air Navigation)*.

off duty wachfrei, dienstfrei.

offense Übertretung *f*, Vergehen *n*, Verfehlung *f*.

offensive Offensive *f*, Angriff *m*.

offensive action Angriffsaktion *f*, Angriffshandlung *f (Tac)*.

offensive combat Angriffsgefecht *n*.

offensive defense aktive Abwehr, offensive Verteidigung.

offensive mission Angriffsaufgabe *f*.

offensive operations Angriffsoperationen *fpl*.

offensively angriffsweise *(Tac)*.

off-field landing Außenlandung *f* (*Avn*).
off horse Handpferd *n*.
office Amt *n* (*function and place*); Bureau *n* (*place*).
Office of Civilian Defense Luftschutzamt *n* (*USA*).
officer Offizier *m*.
officer candidate Offiziersanwärter *m*.
Officer Candidate School Kriegsschule *f*.
officer of the day Offizier vom Tagesdienst.
officer of the guard Offizier vom Ortsdienst.
officer of the line Truppenoffizier *m*.
officer on duty Offizier vom Dienst.
officer prisoner kriegsgefangener Offizier.
officers' mess Offizierskasino *n*, Kasino *n*; Offizierheim *n* (*mess and quarters*).
officers' quarters Offizierheim *n* (*quarters and mess*).
Officers' Reserve Corps Reserveoffizierkorps *n* (*USA*).
officer training course Führerkurs *m*.
office supplies Büromaterial *n*.
official *n* Beamter *m*.
official *adj* amtlich, dienstlich.
official correspondence amtlicher Schriftverkehr.
official envelope amtlicher Briefumschlag.
official papers Aktenmaterial *n*.
off limits verbotenes Lokal.
being off limits Besuch eines verbotenen Lokals.
offset Höhenunterschied *m* (*Surv*).
offshore side Strombord *m* (*Pon*).
ogive Bogenspitze *f* (*Am*).
ogive of shell Geschoßspitze *f*.
ohmmeter Ohmmeter *n*, Widerstandsmesser *m*.
oil *n* Öl *n*.
oil *v* ölen, einölen.
oil bomb Ölbombe *f*.
oilcan Ölbüchse *f*.
oilcloth Wachstuch *n*.
oil container Ölkanister *m* (*Ap, MT*).
oil cooler Ölkühler *m*, Schmierstoffkühler *m* (*Mtr*).
oil drain Ölablaß *m* (*Mtr*).
oiler Öltropfer *m* (*R cleaning*).
oil-filler plug Einfüllstutzen *m* (*recoil mechanism*); Öleinfüll-Verschraubung *f* (*Mtr*).

oil film Ölfilm *m*, Schmierölschicht *f*.
oil gage Öldruckmesser *m* (*pressure*); Öldstandanzeiger *m* (*level*); Ölthermometer *n* (*temperature*).
oil level Ölstand *m* (*Mtr*).
oil level gage Schmierstoffvorratsmesser *m* (*Ap*).
oil level plug Ölstandschraube *f* (*Mtr*).
oil overflow Ölüberlauf *m* (*Mtr*).
oil overflow outlet Öl-Überlaufbohrung *f* (*Mtr*).
oil pan Ölwanne *f* (*Mtr*).
oil pressure gage Schmierstoffdruckmesser *m*, Ölmanometer *n* (*Ap, Mtr*).
oil pump Ölpumpe *f*.
oil refinery Ölraffinerie *f*.
oil-resistant ölbeständig.
oilskin Wachstaffet *m*.
oil-storage depot Öllager *n*.
oil tank Ölbehälter *m*, Schmierstoffbehälter *m*, Öltank *m* (*Ap, Mtr*).
oil temperature gage Ölthermometer *n* (*Mtr*).
oiltight öldicht.
oil well Ölbohrloch *n*.
ointment Salbe *f*.
old guard alte Wache.
oleo strut Ölfederstrebe *f* (*Ap*).
olive drab olivgrün.
omnidirectional antenna Antenne mit Rundwirkung.
omnidirectional beacon Kreisfunkfeuer *n* (*Rad*).
on ein (*a switch, etc.*).
on-course zone Anflugsektor *m* (*Inst landing*).
on duty diensttuend, im Dienst.
one-man shelter tent Einerzelt *n*.
one-way Morse-code transmission einseitiges Tasten (*Rad, Tg*).
one-way (radio) telephone transmission einseitiges Sprechen.
one-way radio traffic einseitiger Funkverkehr.
one-way street Einbahnstraße *f*.
one-way telegraphy einseitige Telegraphie.
one-way traffic Einbahnverkehr *m* (*MT*).
on guard auf Wache (*guard duty*); auf der Hut (*alert, watchful*).
onion Zwiebel *f*.
on leave beurlaubt, auf Urlaub.
"On the double!" "Marsch! Marsch!"
open city offene Stadt.
open column zerlegte Marschkolonne.

open culvert Querrinne *f (road).*
open fire Feuer eröffnen.
open flank offene Flanke, nicht geschützte Flanke *(Tac).*
open formation geöffnete Marschordnung.
opening Durchlaß *m,* Öffnung *f.*
opening of fire Feuereröffnung *f (Arty).*
open position offene Stellung, nicht geschützte Stellung *(Tac).*
open tail Gitterschwanz *m (Ap).*
open traverse Streckenzug *m (Surv).*
operating building Operationsbaracke *f (surgical unit).*
operating current Betriebsstrom *m (Elec).*
operating device Bedienungseinrichtung *f.*
operating directions Bedienungsanweisung *f.*
operating handle Öffnerhebel *m (G).*
operating instructions Bedienungsvorschrift *f.*
operating lever Öffnerhebel *m (G).*
operating maintenance nach Bedarf durchgeführte Instandsetzung.
operating panel Bedienungsplatte *f (Rad).*
operating range Fahrbereich *m (MT, Tk).*
operating switch Bedienungsschalter *m (Elec);* Betriebsschalter *m (Tp).*
operation Unternehmung *f,* Operation *f,* Gefechtshandlung *f .(Tac);* Betrieb *m (Rad, Tp, Mech);* Operation *f (Med).*
operational operativ *(Tac).*
operational line Operationslinie *f.*
operations Operationen *fpl (Tac).*
Operations Division Operationsabteilung *f (USA) (corresponds roughly to the department of Oberquartiermeister I in the German General Staff).*
operations map Operationskarte *f.*
operations order Operationsbefehl *m.*
operations plan Operationsplan *m.*
operator Fernsprecher *m (Tp).*
operator's answering jack Abfrageklinke *f (Tp).*
operator's permit Führerschein *m (MT);* Wehrmachtsführerschein *m (Mil).*
operator's telephone Abfrageapparat *m.*
opiate schmerzstillendes Mittel.

opponent Gegner *m.*
oppose Widerstand leisten.
opposed-piston engine Gegenkolbenmotor *m,* Boxermotor *m.*
opposing sides Parteien *fpl (Tng).*
opposition Widerstand *m.*
optical sight optisches Zielgerät *(Ord).*
optician Optiker *m.*
oral message mündliche Mitteilung, mündliche Meldung.
oral order mündlicher Befehl.
order *n* Befehl *m;* Sonderverfügungen *fpl (special orders);* besondere Anordnungen *fpl (administrative details in combat orders, fragmentary orders in this sense).*
order *v* befehlen *(command);* verordnen, anordnen, bestimmen *(prescribe);* bestellen *(goods, meals).*
"Order, arms!" "Gewehr, ab!"
orderly Ordnonnanz *f.*
orderly officer Ordonnanzoffizier *m.*
orderly room Schreibstube *f.*
order of battle Kriegsgliederung *f.*
order of march Marschfolge *f.*
order of the day Tagesbefehl *m.*
Order of the Purple Heart Purpurherz *n (USA).*
orders conference Flugbesprechung *f,* Einsatzbesprechung *f (Avn).*
ordinary telephone call gewöhnliches Ferngespräch.
ordinate Ordinate *f,* Achse *f.*
ordinate of the trajectory Flughöhe *f (Ballistics).*
ordnance Waffen und Gerät.
ordnance battalion Feldzeugbataillon *n.*
ordnance collecting point Gerätesammelstelle *f.*
Ordnance Department Waffenamt *n.*
ordnance depot Arsenal *n,* Feldzeuglager *n.*
ordnance matériel Waffen und Gerät.
ordnance officer Waffenoffizier *m,* Geräteoffizier *m.*
ordnance park Geschützpark *m.*
Ordnance School Heereswaffenmeister- und Heeresfeuerwerkerschule *(USA).*
ordnance service Geräte-, Waffenund Munitionsabteilung *f (USA).*
ordnance stores Lagerbestände der Feldzeuginspektion.
organic Stamm-.

organization Organisation *f*, Gliederung *f*, Einrichtung *f*.

organizational equipment Kriegsausrüstung einer Einheit.

Organization and Training Division Organisations- und Ausbildungsamt im Generalstab des Heeres *(USA)*.

organization chart Gliederungsübersicht *f*.

organization commander Kommandeur eines Truppenteils.

organization of march Marschgliederung *f*.

organization of the ground Geländeverstärkung *f (Tac)*.

organized position befestigte Feldstellung.

Organized Reserves Organisierte Reserve *(USA)*.

organized resistance organisierter Widerstand, planmäßiger Widerstand.

organized tactical locality Stützpunkt *m*.

orient *v* sich zurechtfinden, sich orientieren *(get one's bearings)*; ausrichten, einstellen *(an Inst)*; eine Karte in die Nordrichtung einstellen *(a map)*.

orientation Orientierung *f*, Ausrichtung *f*; Einrichten *n (of a map)*.

orientation by map Geländeorientierung *f (Surv)*.

orientation card Flugmelderose *f*, Melderose *f (AWS)*.

orientation course Schulungskursus *m*.

orientation point Richtungspunkt *m*, Orientierungspunkt *m (Surv)*.

orienting line Richtungslinie *f*, Orientierungslinie *f (Gunnery) (Surv)*.

orienting point *See* orientation point.

origin Ursprung *m*, Ausgangspunkt *m*.

original model Urbaumuster *n (Ap, Tk, etc.)*.

original position Ausgangslage *f (Mech)*.

origin of the trajectory Mündung *f (Ballistics)*.

orographic orographisch *(Met)*.

orthochromatic farbtonrichtig, orthochromatisch.

orthographic projection orthographische Projektion.

oscillate pendeln, schwingen.

oscillating circuit Schwingungskreis *m (Rad)*.

oscillation Schwingung *f (Elec, Rad)*; Nadelschwankungen *fpl (oscillations of compass needle)*.

oscillator Schwingungserzeuger *m (Rad)*.

oscillator-amplifier Hörsaalsummer *m (code practice)*.

oscillator-amplifier transmitter zweistufiger Sender *(Rad)*.

oscillogram Knallbild *n*, Oszillogramm *n (sound ranging)*.

oscillograph Schallaufnahmegerät *n*, Schallmeßaufnahmegerät *n (sound ranging)*.

oscilloscope Oszilloskop *n (Elec, Rad)*.

osnaburg Sackleinen *n*.

Otto engine Ottomotor *m (Mtr)*.

outboard motor Aubomotor *m*, Außenbordmotor *m*.

outbreak Aufruhr *f (riot)*; Ausbruch *m (of an epidemic, hostilities)*.

outcome of battle Ausgang des Kampfes, Schlachtentscheidung *f (Tac)*.

outdoors im Freien.

outer cover Ballonhülle *f (Bln)*.

outer harbor äußerer Hafen, außenhafen *m*.

outer sleeve Außenschieber *m (sleeve-type engine)*.

outer steam tube Sperrohr *n (MG)*.

outfit *n* Ausrüstung *f (equipment, etc.)*; Mannschaft *f (crew)*; Truppenteil *m (unit)*.

outflank flankieren, überflügeln, umgehen.

outflanking maneuver Überflügelung *f*.

outgoing track Ausfahrgleis *n (RR)*.

outguard Feldwache *f*, Feldposten *m*.

outlet Steckdose *f (Elec)*; Auslaß *m*, Auslauf *m*, Durchlaß *m (for liquids, etc.)*.

outlet valve Ausatemventil *n (gas mask)*.

outline *n* Umriß *m*; Entwurf *m (sketch)*.

outlying picket Außenwache *f*.

outnumber an Zahl übertreffen, zahlenmäßig überlegen sein.

out of action außer Gefecht (gesetzt).

"Out of action!" "Abblenden!" *(AA searchlight).*

out of alignment dejustiert *(boresight adjustment).*

out of gear außer Eingriff *(MT).*

out of order außer Betrieb.

out of range außer Schußweite.

out of sight außer Sicht.

outpost Vorposten *m.*

outpost area Vorpostengelände *n,* Vorfeld *n,* Vorgelände *n (Tac).*

outpost duty Vorpostendienst *m.*

outpost engagement Vorpostengefecht *n.*

outpost line vorderste Sicherungslinie.

outpost line of resistance Widerstandslinie der Vorposten *(Tac).*

outpost observer Vorwarner *m (sound ranging).*

outpost position Vorpostenstellung *f.*

outpost reserve Vorpostenreserve *f.*

outpost-sector boundary Vorpostenabschnittsgrenze *f.*

outpost station Vorwarnerstelle *f (sound ranging).*

outpost system Vorpostendienst *m.*

output Leistung *f (Mech).*

output transformer Ausgangstransformator *m (Rad).*

output voltage Ausgangsspannung *f.*

outrank einen höheren Rang bekleiden, den Vorrang haben.

outrigger Ausleger *m (for water craft);* Holm *m (AA gun; plural:* Holme *or* Lafettenkreuz).

outrigger lock Holmzurrung *f (G).*

outrigger-type gun mount Kreuzlafette *f.*

outside antenna Außenantenne *f.*

outworks Außenbefestigungen *fpl,* Außenwerke *npl (Ft).*

oven Ofen *m,* Backofen *m.*

over *n* Weitschuß *m (Gunnery).*

over-all length Länge über alles.

overboard über Bord.

overcast bedeckt *(Met).*

overcoat Mantel *m,* Übermantel *m.*

overcome überwinden, überwältigen, übermannen.

overdrive Schnellgang *m (MT).*

overdrive transmission Schnellganggetriebe *n,* Schonganggetriebe *n (MT).*

overended shot Bodentreffer *m.*

overexposure Überbelichtung *f (Photo).*

overfall dam Überfallwehr *n.*

overflow *n* Überlauf *m.*

overflow pipe Überlaufrohr *n.*

overflow water Überschußwasser *n (dam).*

overhang *n* Überhang *m (MT).*

overhaul *v* überholen.

overhead antenna Luftdraht *m.*

overhead construction Hochbau *m (Tp line).*

overhead firing Überschießen eigener Truppen *(Gunnery).*

overhead firing table Überschießtafel *f (MG tripod).*

overhead line Freileitung *f (Tp).*

overhead line construction Hochbau von Leitungen *(Tp).*

overhead wire Luftkabel *n (Tp).*

overlap *n* Überdeckung *f (aerial Photo).*

overlay Planpause *f.*

overload überlasten.

overloading Übersteuerung *f (Elec, Rad);* Überbeanspruchung *f (Mech).*

overpass Bahnüberführung *f,* Überführung *f (RR).*

overprint *n* Aufdruck *m.*

overseas cap Feldmütze *f.*

overseas expedition Übersee-Expedition *f.*

overseas operation Übersee-Unternehmung *f.*

overshoes Überschuhe *mpl.*

overshoot über etwas hinausschießen.

oversize tire Riesenluftreifen *m.*

overtake überholen, einholen.

overwhelm niederkämpfen.

oxyacetylene cutting Schneidbrennen *n.*

oxyacetylene torch Azetylensauerstoffbrenner *m.*

oxyacetylene welding Sauerstoffazetylenschweißung *f.*

oxygen Sauerstoff *m.*

oxygen apparatus Atemgerät *n,* Höhenatmer *m,* Sauerstoffgerät *n (Avn).*

oxygen breathing apparatus Sauerstoffschutzgerät *n,* Isoliergerät *n,* Selbstretter *m.*

oxygen cylinder Sauerstofflasche *f.*

oxygen mask Atemmaske *f (Avn).*

P

pace *n* Schritt *m.*
pace off abschreiten.
pack *n* Tornister *m*, Rückengepäck
n; Traglast *f* *(Animal Transportation)*; Fallschirmsack *m* *(Prcht).*
pack *v*   dichten, abdichten *(seal)*;
packen *(a trunk, etc.).*
package Bündel *n*, Paket *n.*
pack animal Tragtier *n.*
pack-animal train Tragtierkolonne *f.*
pack artillery Gebirgsartillerie *f.*
pack assembly   Fallschirmsack *m*
(Prcht).
pack frame Tragegestell *n.*
pack horse Tragpferd *n.*
pack howitzer Gebirgskanone *f.*
packing   Packung *f*, Dichtung *f*
(Mech).
pack reel Rückentrage für Feldkabel.
pack rest Ausleger *m* *(harness).*
pack rope Packstrick *m* *(harness).*
pack saddle   Packsattel *m*, Trag-
sattel *m.*
pack strap Packriemen *m* *(harness).*
pack train Tragtierkolonne *f.*
pack transportation   Tragtierbeförderung *f.*
pad   Block *m*, Schreibeblock *m*
(writing); Kissen *n*, Polster *n* *(Clo,
harness, etc.).*
padded unterpolstert.
paddle *n* Stechruder *n.*
padlock Vorhängeschloß *n.*
pail Eimer *m*, Kübel *m.*
paint *n* Farbe *f*, Anstrich *m.*
paint *v* anstreichen.
paint brush   Pinsel *m*, Anstrichpinsel *m.*
palm Handfläche *f.*
pan Pfanne *f.*
pancake *v* absacken, durchsacken
(Avn).
pancake landing "Bumslandung" *f.*
panel Signaltuch *n*, Tuchzeichen *n*
(Sig C); Hüllenbahn *f* *(Bln)*; Stoffbahn *f* *(Prcht).*
panel code   Schlüssel für Tuchzeichen.
panel signal   Sichtzeichen *n*, Tuchzeichen *n.*
panoramic camera Panoramakammer
f *(Avn).*

panoramic photograph Rundbild *n.*
panoramic sight Rundblickfernrohr
n.
panoramic sketch Ansichtsskizze *f.*
panoramic telescope Rundblickfernrohr *n.*
pantograph   Storchschnabel *m*,
Pantograph *n.*
paper Papier *n.*
paper-strip method Papierstreifenverfahren *n* *(aerial Photo).*
paper work Schreibarbeit *f.*
parabola Parabel *f.*
parabolic parabelförmig, parabelähn-
lich.
parabolic mirror Parabolspiegel *m.*
parachute Fallschirm *m*, Schirm *m.*
parachute battalion   Fallschirmjägerbataillon *n.*
parachute canopy Schirm *m.*
parachute equipment   Fallschirmgerät *n.*
parachute flare   Fallschirmleuchtkugel *f*, Fallschirmrakete *f* *(ground
Sig)*; Leuchtfallschirm *m*, Fallschirmleuchtbombe *f* *(Ap Sig).*
parachute harness Fallschirmgurt *m*,
Gurtwerk *n.*
parachute jump Fallschirmabsprung
m.
parachute jump suit   Sprungkombination *f.*
parachute lobe Zusatzfallschirm *m.*
parachute pack Fallschirmsack *m.*
parachute regiment   Fallschirm-
jägerregiment *n.*
parachute rigger Fallschirmwart *m.*
parachute skirt Ringfallschirm *m.*
parachute tower Fallschirmturm *m*,
Fallschirmabsprungturm *m.*
parachute troops   Fallschirmjäger
mpl, Fallschirmtruppen *fpl.*
parachutist Fallschirmjäger *m*, Fallschirmschütze *m*, Fallschirmspringer
m.
parade Parade *f.*
parade ground Paradeplatz *m*, Exerzierplatz *m.*
parados Rückendeckung *f*, Rückenwehr *f* *(Ft).*
parallax Parallaxe *f.*
parallax offset mechanism   Verbesserungsgerät *n* *(sound locator).*

parallel *adj* gleichlaufend, parallel; e n t s p r e c h e n d *(corresponding)*; gleich, ähnlich *(similar)*.

parallel-chord truss Parallel-Fachwerkträger *m (Engr)*.

parallel connection Nebeneinanderschaltung *f*, Parallelschaltung *f (Elec)*.

parallel line Gleichlaufende *f*.

parallel of latitude Breitenkreis *m*.

parallelogram linkage system Visiergestänge *n*, Parallelogrammgestänge *n (AA sight)*.

paralyze lähmen *(Tac)*.

parapet Brustwehr *f (trench)*; Wehr *f (G emplacement)*.

parasite drag schädlicher Widerstand *(Avn)*.

parasol monoplane Schirmeindecker *m*.

parasol-type antenna Gitterantenne *f*.

paratrooper *See* **parachutist.**

paratroops *See* **parachute troops.**

paravane Minenabweiser *m*, Räumotter *f*, Otter *f*.

parent unit Stammtruppenteil *m*, Stammeinheit *f*.

park *n* Park *m*.

park *v* parken, abstellen.

parka Anorak *m*, Schneehemd *n (Clo)*.

parking area Abstellplatz *m (Adrm, MT)*.

parking light Parklicht *n (MT)*.

parking place Abstellplatz *m*.

parlementaire Unterhändler *m*.

parley Unterredung *f*, Verhandlung *f*, Unterhandlung *f*.

parole *n* Ehrenwort *n*.

parry *n* Abwehr *f*, Fangstoß *m*.

parry *v* parieren.

part *n* Teil *m (portion)*; Zubehörteil *m (Tech)*.

participation Beteiligung *f*, Teilnahme *f*.

partisan warfare kleiner Krieg.

party Kommando *n (Tac)*; Teilnehmer *m (Tp)*.

party of guides Einweisungskommando *n*.

pass Erlaubnisschein *m*, Urlaubsschein *m (leave)*; Paß *m (Top)*; Vorbeiflug *m (Avn)*.

passable gangbar; fahrbar *(for vehicles)*.

passage Durchlaß *m*, Durchgang *m*; Gasse *f (through a mine field, etc.)*.

passenger Fahrgast *m*, Passagier *m*; Fluggast *m (Avn)*.

passenger capacity Tragfähigkeit *f (MT)*.

passenger car Personenkraftwagen *m (MT)*.

passenger ferry Personenfähre *f*.

passenger seat Fluggastsitz *m (Ap)*.

passenger station Personenbahnhof *m (RR)*.

passenger vehicle Personenkraftfahrzeug *n (MT)*.

passing Überholung *f (MT)*.

passing flight Vorbeiflug *m*.

pass in review *n* Vorbeimarsch *m*, Parademarsch *m*.

pass in review *v* vorbeimarschieren, defilieren.

passive air defense Luftschutz *m*.

passport Paß *m*.

password Kennwort *n*, Parole *f*, Losung *f*, Kampfruf *m*, Verständigungsmittel *n*.

paste Klebstoff *m*, Klebemittel *n*; Kleister *m (starch)*; Fischleim *m (fish glue)*; Kitt *m (putty)*.

pastern Fessel *f (horse)*.

pastern joint Fesselgelenk *n (horse)*.

patching cord Vermittlungsschnur *f (Tp)*.

path Pfad *m*, Weg *m*; Bahn *f (of a projectile)*; Fußweg *m (footpath)*; Saumpfad *m (for pack animals)*; Schleichweg *m (hidden trail)*; Fahrweg *m (for carts)*; Holzweg *m (dead-end loggers' road)*.

path-of-flight pointer Gegnerpfeil *m*, Flugrichtungspfeil *m (reflector sight)*.

patient *n* Patient *m*, Kranker *m*.

patrol *n* Spähtrupp *m*; Patrouillenflug *m (Avn)*.

patrol *v* abstreifen *(a road, area, etc.)*.

patrol activity Aufklärertätigkeit *f*, Spähtrupptätigkeit *f*, Patrouillentätigkeit *f*.

patrol boat Wachboot *n*.

patrol bomber Seeaufklärer *m*.

patrol leader Spähtruppführer *m*.

patrolling Patrouillenflug *m (Avn)*.

patrol message Spähtruppmeldung *f*.

patrol vessel Bewachungsfahrzeug *n*, Wachschiff *n (Nav)*.

pattern Streuungsbild *n*, Treffbild *n (Gunnery)*; Modell *n (foundry)*.

pattern bombing Abstandwerfen *n*.

paulin Decke *f*, Plane *f*.
paved road gepflasterte Straße, Straße mit fester Decke.
pawl Sperrklinke *f (Mech)*.
pay *n* Sold *m*, Besoldung *f;* Lagergeld *n (PW)*.
pay grade Wehrsoldgruppe *f*.
pay load Nutzlast *f*.
payment Zahlung *f*, Bezahlung *f;* Besoldung *f (wages)*.
pay out auslegen *(a rope, etc.)*.
pay roll Soldliste *f*.
PD *See* **phenyldichlorarsine.**
peace Friede *m*.
peace negotations Friedensverhandlungen *fpl*.
peace organization Friedensorganisation *f (of Armed Forces)*.
peace strength Friedensstärke *f (of Armed Forces)*.
peace training Friedensausbildung *f*.
peak Gipfel *m*, Spitze *f (pointed)*, Kuppe *f (rounded)*.
peak value Scheitelwert *m*, Höchstwert *m (Elec)*.
pedal Fußhebel *m (Ord, MT)*.
pedal-operated generating unit Tretsatz *m (Elec)*.
pedal-operated generator Tretmotor *m*.
pedestal Auflager *n (Bdg)*; Sockel *m (G)*.
pedestal mount Sockellafette *f (G)*.
pedometer Schrittmesser *m*.
"peep" "Kübel" *m*.
peephole Panzerscharte *f*, Sehöffnung *f (Ft, Tk)*.
peephole protector Sehklappe *f (Tk)*.
peep sight Diopterloch *n*.
peep slit Sehschlitz *m (Tk)*.
pelorus Peilaufsatz *m (Avn)*.
pen Feder *f*.
penalty Strafe *f*.
penalty envelope frankierter Dienstumschlag.
pencil Bleistift *m*.
pencil sharpener Bleistiftspitzer *m*, Bleistiftspitzmaschine *f*.
penetrate eindringen, durchdringen, durchstoßen *(Tac)*; durchbrechen, durchschlagen *(armor, etc.)*; einfliegen *(Avn)*.
penetrating power Durchschlagskraft *f (Am)*.
penetration Einbruch *m (Tac)*; Durchschlagskraft *f (Am)*.

penetration and mining effect Durchschlags- und Minenwirkung *f (Am)*.
penetration by assault Durchstoß *m*.
penetration in depth Tiefenstoß *m (Tac)*.
peninsula Halbinsel *f*.
penis Penis *m*, Glied *n*, männliches Glied.
penitentiary Zuchthaus *n*.
pennant Stander *m*, Wimpel *m*.
pension Ruhegehalt *n*.
pepper Pfeffer *m*.
per cent Prozent, vom Hundert.
percentage Prozentsatz *m*.
percussion Aufschlag *m*.
percussion cap Zündhütchen *n (Am)*.
percussion charge Schlagladung *f*.
percussion composition Zündsatz *m*.
percussion fuze Aufschlagzünder *m (Am)*.
percussion plunger Zündbolzen *m (powder-train time fuze, Am)*.
percussion primer Zündhütchen *n (fuze)*.
per diem allowance Tagegeld *n*.
perforated powder Röhrenpulver *n (Am)*.
performance Leistung *f;* Nutzleistung *f (Mech)*; Schußleistung *f (Ord)*; Zugleistung *f (Trac)*; Aufführung *f (theater)*.
performance-type glider Leistungssegelflugzeug *n (Avn)*.
perimeter Umkreis *m*, Umfang *m*.
perimeter positions Randstellungen *fpl (Tac)*.
period Periode *f (Elec)*.
periople Trachte *f (hoof)*.
periphery Umkreis *m*.
periscope Periskop *n*, Sehrohr *n;* Winkelspiegel *m*, Optik *f (Tk)*.
permanent ortsfest, fest eingebaut, dauernd, ständig.
permanent emplacement ortsfeste Geschützstellung.
permanent ferrying operations Dauerfährbetrieb *m*.
permanent field-telephone line Felddauerlinie *f*.
permanent fortification ständige Befestigung, Befestigungswerk *n*, Werk *n*.
permanent line Dauerleitung *f*, Dauerlinie *f (Tp)*.
permanent magnet Dauermagnet *m*.
permanent rank Dienstgrad mit Patent.

permanent way Oberbau *m (RR)*.
permission Erlaubnis *f*, Bewilligung *f*; Einwilligung *f (consent)*.
permit *n* Fahrausweis *m (traveling)*; Passierschein *m (pass)*; Urlaubsschein *m (leave pass)*.
permit *v* erlauben, gestatten, zulassen; dürfen *(to be allowed)*.
perpendicular *n* Senkrechte *f*, Lotrechte *f*.
perpendicular *adj* senkrecht, lotrecht.
persistency Seßhaftigkeit *f*, Wirkungsdauer *f (CWS)*.
persistent chemical warfare agent seßhafter Kampfstoff, Geländekampfstoff *m*.
personal effects persönliche Sachen, persönliche Gegenstände.
personal salute persönlicher Salut.
personal staff persönliche Adjutanten.
personnel Personal *n*, Leute *pl*; Mannschaften *fpl (enlisted Pers below the rank of Cpl)*.
personnel carrier Mannschaftstransportwagen *m*, Mannschaftswagen *m*, Personenkraftwagen *m*, Personenkraftfahrzeug *n (MT)*.
personnel consultant Heerespsychologe *m*.
Personnel Division Heerespersonalamt *n*, Personalamt *n*.
personnel error Beobachtungsfehler *m*.
personnel roster Stammrolle *f*.
personnel section Personalabteilung *f*.
perspective projection perspektivische Projektion.
perspective spatial model Raumbildmodell *n (aerial Photo)*.
petition *n* Gesuch *n*, Bittschrift *f*.
petroleum Erdöl *n*.
petty officer Maat *m (Nav)*.
phantom circuit Doppelsprechschaltung *f*, Viererleitung *f (Tp)*.
phantom connection Viererschaltung *f (Tp)*.
phantoming Doppelsprechen *n (Tp)*.
pharmacist Apotheker *m*.
phase Abschnitt *m (Tac)*; Phase *f (Elec)*; Ausbildungsstufe *f (Tng)*; Entwicklungsstufe *f (of development)*.
initial phase Auftakt *m (Tac)*.
in phases abschnittsweise *(Tac)*.

phase difference Phasendifferenz *f*, Phasenunterschied *m*.
phase line Angriffszwischenziel *n (Tac)*.
phenol Karbolsäure *f*.
phenyldichlorarsine Phenyldichlorarsin *n*, Pfiffikus *n (CWS)*.
phonetic alphabet Buchstabiertafel *f (Com)*.
phonograph Grammophon *n*, Sprechmaschine *f*.
phonograph pick-up unit Schallplatten-Abtastdose *f*.
phonograph record Schallplatte *f*.
phosgene Chlorkohlenoxyd *n*, Phosgen *n (CWS)*.
phosphorus Phosphor *m*.
phosphorus bomb Phosphorbombe *f*, Phosphorfliegerbombe *f*.
phosphorus grenade Phosphorhandgranate *f*.
photo-charting Luftbildherstellung *f (aerial Photo)*.
photo-electric cell Photozelle *f*.
photoflash bomb Blitzlichtbombe *f*.
photogrammetry Bildmeßwesen *n*, Photogrammetrie *f*.
photograph *n* Lichtbild *n*.
photograph *v* lichtbilden, photographieren; eine Aufnahme machen *(take a snapshot)*.
photographer Photograph *m*, Lichtbildner *m*.
photographic interpretation Luftbildauswertung *f*.
photographic map Luftbildkarte *f*.
photographic mapping photographische Kartenaufnahme.
photographic officer Bildoffizier *m*.
photographic overlay Lichtbildpause *f*.
photographic reconnaissance Bildaufklärung *f*, Bilderkundung *f*.
photographic strip Luftbildreihe *f*, Filmstreifen *m*.
photography Photographie *f*, Lichtbildwesen *n*.
photomap Luftbildplan *m*.
photostat *n* Photokopie *f*.
photostat *v* photokopieren.
photo-survey Geländeaufnahme *f*.
phototopography Meßbildverfahren *n*, Lichtbildmessung *f*, Erdmessung *f*, Phototopographie *f*.
physical condition Gesundheitszustand *m*.

physical examination ärztliche Untersuchung.

physical fitness Tauglichkeit *f.*

physical inspection Gesundheitsappell *m.*

pibal Wetterbericht vom Pilotballon *(Met).*

pibal equipment Pilotballonaufstieggerät *n (Met).*

pickaxe Beilpicke *f,* Spitzhacke *f.*

picked troops Kerntruppen *fpl.*

picket Pfahl *m,* Pikettpfahl *m (stake).*

picket line Furagierleine *f,* Halfterstrick *m.*

pick mattock Klapphacke *f.*

pick-up Schallplatten-Abtastdose *f (phonograph)*

pick-up arm Tonarm *m (phonograph).*

pick-up assembly Aufnahmegerät *n (Ap).*

pick-up hook Aufnahmehaken *m (Ap).*

pick-up unit Abtastdose *f (phonograph).*

picric acid Pikrinsäure *f.*

picture Bild *n.*

picture point Bildpunkt *m (aerial Photo).*

piece Artilleriegeschütz *n,* Feldgeschütz *n (Arty);* Gewehr *n (R);* Stück *n (fragment).*

piece of equipment Ausrüstungsstück *n,* Gerätstück *n,* Ausrüstungsgegenstand *m.*

pier Pfeiler *m (Bdg);* Pier *m,* Ladeplatz *m,* Anlegestelle *f;* Löschplatz *m (for unloading cargo).*

pierce durchbrechen, durchlöchern, durchstoßen.

pigeon Taube *f.*

pigeoneer Brieftaubenpfleger *m;* Brieftaubenmeister *m (with rank of Tech Sgt).*

pigeon loft Brieftaubenschlag *m,* Brieftaubenstelle *f.*

Pigeon Service Brieftaubendienst *m.*

pike Fahnenstange *f (flagpole).*

pile *n* Pfahl *m (Engr);* Brückenpfeiler m *(Bdg);* Haufen *m (irregular heap);* Stapel *m (regular heap).*

pile bent Pfahljoch *n (Bdg).*

pile-bent bridge Pfahljochbrücke *f.*

pile driver Ramme *f;* Zugramme *f (drophammer type).*

pile-driver drophammer Rammbär *m (Engr).*

pile-driver frame Rammgerüst *n (Engr).*

pile-driver raft Rammfähre *f (Engr).*

pile-driver staging Rammbühne *f (Engr).*

pile-post obstacle Pfahlsperre *f (AT).*

pillage *n* Beute *f,* Plünderung *f.*

pillar Pfeiler *m (Engr).*

pill box betoniertes Maschinengewehrnest, Bunker *m (Ft).*

pill-box demolition party Schartensprengtrupp *m (Engr).*

pillow Kissen *n.*

pilot *n* Flieger *m,* Flugzeugführer *m (Avn);* Lotse *m (Nav).*

pilotage Bodennavigation *f,* Sichtnavigation *f,* Erdortung *f,* optische Peilung *(Air Navigation).*

pilot balloon Pilotballon *m (Met).*

pilot chart Fliegerkarte *f (Avn).*

pilot light Kontrollampe *f (Ap, MT).*

pilot parachute Hilfsschirm *m.*

pilot's certificate Fliegerzeugnis *n.*

pilot's cockpit Führersitz *m,* Führerstand *m,* Führerkanzel *f (Ap).*

pilot's compartment Führerraum *m (Ap).*

pilot's rating Fliegerzeugnis *n.*

pilot trainee Flugschüler *m.*

pilot training Fliegerschulung *f (Avn).*

pin Stecknadel *f (plain pin);* Sicherheitsnadel *f (safety pin);* Stift *m,* Bolzen *m (Tech);* Pflock *m (stake).*

pincer attack Zangenangriff *m (Tac).*

pincer movement Zangenbewegung *f (Tac).*

pincers Kneifzange *f.*

pinch-bar Brechstange *f .*

pinion Ritzel *m (Mech).*

pinion and sector steering system Zahnstangenlenkung *f (MT).*

pinion shaft Ritzelwelle *f (Mech).*

pinning Fesselung *f (Tac).*

pin nozzle Zapfendüse *f (Mtr).*

pinpointing Herstellung von Einzelbildern *(aerial Photo).*

pinpoint photograph einzelnes Senkrechtbild *(aerial Photo).*

pintle Zughaken *m.*

pintle drawbar Zugstange *f.*

pintle nozzle Zapfendüse *f (Mtr)*.

pioneer Pionier *m*.

pioneer and demolition platoon Pionierzug *m*.

pioneer tools Pionierwerkzeug *n*.

pioneer work Pionierarbeit *f*.

pipe *n* Rohr *n*, Leitung *f*; Schlauch *m (hose)*; Pfeife *f (smoking)*.

pipe cable Röhrenkabel *n (Elec, Tp)*.

pipe wrench Rohrzange *f*.

pistol Pistole *f*.

pistol ammunition Pistolenmunition *f*.

pistol belt Pistolengurt *m*.

pistol cartridge Pistolenpatrone *f*.

pistol course Pistolenausbildungskurs *m*.

pistol grip Handstütze *f*.

pistol holster Pistolentasche *f*.

pistol port Pistolenöffnung *f (Tk)*.

pistol sharpshooter Pistolenscharfschütze *m*.

piston Kolben *m (Mech)*.

piston displacement Hubraum *m*, Hubvolumen *n (Mtr)*.

piston pin Kolbenbolzen *m (Mtr)*.

piston ring Kolbenring *m*.

piston rod Kolbenstange *f*, Pleuelstange *f*.

piston stroke Kolbenhub *m*.

pit Grube *f*.

pitch *n* Gewindegang *m*, Steigung *f (Mech)*; Propellersteigung *f (propeller)*; Pech *n (tar-like substance)*; Tonhöhe *f (sound)*.

pitch-control mechanism Luftschraubenverstellgerät *n (propeller)*.

pitch indicator Längsneigungsmesser *m (Ap)*.

pith helmet Tropenhelm *m*.

pitot tube Pitotrohr *n*, Staudruckfahrtmesser *m*.

pivot *n* Drehzapfen *m (Mech)*; Schwenkungspunkt *m (Tac)*.

pivot *v* einschwenken *(Tac, drill)*.

pivot inclination Achs(zapfen)sturz *m (MT)*.

pivot man Flügelmann am Drehpunkt *(drill)*.

pivot pin Lagerzapfen *m (trail spade)*; Drehbolzen *m (Tech)*.

pivot-type mount Pivotlafette *f (MG)*.

place *n* Punkt *m (Tac)*; Ort *m (locality)*.

place mark Bodenpunkt *m*, Pfahl *m (Surv)*.

plain text Klartext *m*.

plain-wire concertina Klaviersaitendrahtrolle *f*, K.-Rolle *f*.

plan *n* Plan *m*; Zeichnung *f (Tech)*.

plan *v* planen, beabsichtigen.

plane *n* Ebene *f (surface)*; Hobel *m (carpentry)*; Flugzeug *n (Ap)*. See also airplane.

plane of departure Schußebene *f (Gunnery)*.

plane of fire Schußebene *f (Gunnery)*.

plane of position Schußebene *f (at instant of firing) (AA Gunnery)*.

plane of present position Visierebene *f (AA Gunnery)*.

plane of propeller rotation Luftschraubenebene *f (Ap)*.

plane table Kartenunterlage *f*, Meßtisch *m*, Planunterlage *f (Arty, Surv)*.

plane table sheet Meßtischblatt *n*.

planetary gear Planetengetriebe *n*, Umlaufgetriebe *n (MT)*.

planimeter Planimeter *n (Surv)*.

planimetry Planimetrie *f*.

plank Bohle *f*.

plank crib Bretterstapel *m (Bdg)*.

plank floor Brettertafel *f (Bdg)*.

plank flooring Bretterteppich *m (rope Bdg)*.

planking Brückenbelag *m*, Belag *m (Bdg)*.

plank road Bohlenbahn *f*.

plank scaffolding Aufrüstung *f (Pon, Engr)*.

plank trestle Bretterbock *m*.

plan of attack Angriffsplan *m*.

plan of campaign Feldzugsplan *m*, Operationsplan *m*.

plan of fire Feuerplan *m (Tac)*.

plan of operations Operationsplan *m (Tac)*.

plan of telephone communication Betriebsunterlagen *fpl*.

plastic Preßstoff *m*; Kunststoff *m (synthetic)*.

plastic-pad obturator plastische Liderung *(G)*.

plate Lamelle *f*, Platte *f*, Tafel *f (Tech)*; Anode *f (Elec)*; Teller *m (dish)*.

plateau Hochebene *f*, Plateau *n*.

plate battery Anodenbatterie *f (Rad)*.

plate circuit Anodenkreis *m (Rad)*.
plate clutch Scheibenkupplung *f (MT)*.
plate dissipation Anodenverlustleistung *f (Rad)*.
platform Plattform *f*, Bettung *f (Arty)*; Bahnsteig *m (RR)*.
platform underpass Bahnsteigunterführung *f (RR)*.
platoon Zug *m*.
platoon boundary Zuggrenze *f*.
"Platoon, halt!" "Abteilung, halt!"
platoon headquarters detail Zugtrupp *m*.
platoon leader Zugführer *m*.
play *n* Spiel *n (Mech)*.
plead guilty sich schuldig erklären.
plead not guilty sich nicht schuldig erklären.
plexiglas Plexiglas *n*.
pliers Zange *f*.
plot *v* abstecken *(a course on a map)*; abgreifen *(transfer distance with dividers)*; zeichnen *(draw)*; Eintragungen machen *(enter data on a map)*; sich verschwören *(conspire)*.
plotter Rechner *m (Pers)*.
plotting Planzeichnen *n*, Festlegen von Zielpunkten *(Surv)*.
plotting board Flächenmeßplan *m (flash ranging)*.
plotting instrument Zeichengerät *n*.
plotting protractor Meßdreieck *n (Arty)*.
plotting scale Reduktionsmaßstab *m*, Lineal *n (FA)*.
plug *n* Stecker *m (Elec)*; Stöpsel *m*, Anschlußstecker *m (Tp)*; Innenhütchen *n (detonator cap)*; Pfropfen *m (stopper)*.
plug gage Innengrenzlehre *f*.
plug in stöpseln, einstöpseln *(Rad, Tp)*.
plug prong Steckerstift *m (Elec)*.
plumb bob Lot *n*, Senkblei *n*.
plumber Klempner *m*, Installateur *m*.
plumb line Lotschnur *f*.
plunder *v* plündern, ausplündern.
plundering Plünderung *f*.
plunge *n* Absturz *m*.
plunger Zündbolzen *m (powder-train time fuze, Am)*; Reglergestänge *n (engine governor)*.
plunging fire Senkfeuer *n*, Steilfeuer *n (Arty)*.

plus *n* Plus *n*, Mehr *n;* Pluszeichen *n (plus sign)*.
plywood Sperrholz *n*.
pneumatic boat F l o ß s a c k *m*, Schlauchboot *n*.
pneumatic-boat ferry Schlauchbootfähre *f*.
pneumatic-boat footbridge Floßsacksteg *m*.
pneumatic equilibrator Luftausgleicher *m (G)*.
pneumatic float Floßsack *m*.
pneumatic hammer Drucklufthammer *m*, Preßlufthammer *m*.
pneumatic pile driver Druckluftramme *f (Engr)*.
pneumatic ponton Floßsack *m*.
pneumatic raft Floßsack *m*, Schlauchboot *n*.
pneumatic-raft footbridge Floßsacksteg *m*.
pneumatic recuperator Luftvorholer *m (G)*.
pneumatic riveter Druckluft-Niethammer *m*, Preßluft-Niethammer *m*.
pneumatic tire Luftreifen *m*.
pneumonia Lungenentzündung *f*.
pocket *n* Kessel *m (Tac)*; Tasche *f (Clo)*.
pocket *v* einkesseln *(Tac)*.
pocket battleship Panzerschiff *n*, Westentaschenschlachtschiff *n*.
pocket knife Taschenmesser *n*.
pocket of resistance Widerstandskessel *m*.
point *n* Punkt *m (Tac)*; Spitze *f (Adv Gd)*; Himmelsrichtung *f (of the compass)*.
point *v* richten *(a gun)*; zeigen, deuten, weisen *(indicate)*.
point-blank range Kernschußweite *f*.
"point" car Spitzenwagen *m (MT)*.
point designation Punktbestimmung *f*.
point-designation grid Artilleriepunkttafel *f*.
point-detonating fuze Kopfzünder *m*.
pointed-post reticle Zielstachel *m (telescopic sight)*.
pointer Gegenzeiger *m*, Folgezeiger *m (follow-the-pointer mechanism in data transmission system)*.
point fire Punktschießen *n*, Punktfeuer *n*.
pointing Richten *n*, Richtung *f (Gunnery)*.
point location Punktbestimmung *f*.

point of aim Haltepunkt *m (Arty, R)*; Abkommpunkt *m (R)*.
point of air burst Luftsprengpunkt *m (Ballistics)*.
point of burst Sprengpunkt *m (Gunnery)*.
point of contact Berührungspunkt *m*.
point of departure Ausgangsstellung *f (in attack)*; Ausgangsort *m (Air Navigation, Trans)*.
point of fall Fallpunkt *m (Ballistics)*.
point of hock Hacke *f (horse)*.
point of impact Aufschlagpunkt *m*, Auftreffpunkt *m*, Treffpunkt *m (Ballistics)*.
point of intersection Schnittpunkt *m (in plotting, etc.)*.
point of main effort Schwerpunkt *m (Tac)*.
point of origin Ausgangspunkt *m (Arty, Surv)*.
point of penetration Einbruchstelle *f*.
point of rupture Sprengstelle *f (Demolitions)*; Bruchgrenze *f (Mech)*.
point target Einzelziel *n (bombing)*; Punktziel *n (Gunnery)*.
poison *n* Gift *n*.
poisoned vergiftet.
polar air arktische Kaltluft *(Met)*.
polar coordinate Polarkoordinate *f*.
Polaris Polarstern *m*, Nordstern *m*.
pole Stange *f*, Mast *m*; Deichsel *f (limber)*; Pol *m (Elec)*.
pole changer Polwechsler *m (Tp)*.
pole charge Sprengstange mit geballter Ladung *(Engr)*.
pole-location diagram Stangenbild *n (Tp)*.
pole piece Polschuh *m (magnet)*.
pole pin Deichselbolzen *m (limber)*.
pole prop Deichselstütze *f (limber)*.
pole reversal Umpolung *f (Elec)*.
police *n* Polizei *f*; Feldgendarmerie *f (MP)*.
police *v* überwachen, in Ordnung halten.
policeman Polizist *m*, Schutzmann *m*; Gendarm *m (rural)*; Feldgendarm *m (MP)*.
polish *v* putzen, wichsen *(leather, etc.)*; polieren *(Tech)*; putzen *(equipment)*.
polyconic projection polykonische Projektion.
pommel Vorderzwiesel *m (saddle)*.
pommel-pad strap Vorsteckriemen *m*.
poncho Poncho *m*.

pond Teich *m*.
ponton Ponton *m (Bdg)*. *See also* pontoon.
ponton balk Scherbalken *m (Engr)*.
ponton bay Pontonstrecke *f (Pon Bdg)*.
ponton bridge Pontonbrücke *f*.
ponton carrier Pontonwagen *m (MT)*.
pontoneer Pontonier *m*.
ponton ferry Pontonfähre *f*.
ponton train Brückenkolonne *f*.
pontoon Schwimmer *m (Ap float)*. *See also* ponton.
pool *n* gemeinsame Reserve an Truppen und Gerät *(Tac)*.
pool *v* vereinigen, zusammenlegen *(Tac)*.
poppet valve Plattenventil *n*, Tellerventil *n (Mtr)*.
population Bevölkerung *f*; Einwohnerschaft *f (of a town)*.
pork Schweinefleisch *n*.
port Hafen *m (harbor)*; Scharte *f*, Blende *f (Tk)*; Öffnung *f (Mech)*.
portable bridge Kolonnenbrücke *f*.
portable generator tragbarer Stromerzeuger.
portable obstacle bewegliches Hindernis.
portable-radio section Tornisterfunktrupp *m*.
portable radio set Tornister-Funkgerät *n (haversack type)*.
portable receiver Tornisterempfänger *m (Rad, haversack type)*.
portable signal-lamp case Blinktornister *m*.
portable switchboard Klappenschrank *m*, Schaltkästchen *n*, Vermittlungskästchen *n (Tp)*.
porté verlastet.
porté artillery verlastete Artillerie.
port engine Backbordmotor *m*.
porter Gepäckträger *m*, Träger *m (RR)*.
porthole Bullauge *n*.
port installation Hafenanlage *f*.
port of debarkation Ausschiffungshafen *m*.
port of embarkation Einschiffungshafen *m*.
port of entry Einfuhrhafen *m*.
port officer Hafenoffizier *m*.
port side Backbord *m (Nav)*.
position Stellung *f (Tac)*; Standort *m (location)*.

position and aiming drill Ausbildung in den Anschlagsarten.

position defilade verdeckte Feuerstellung *(Tac)*.

position determination Ortsbestimmung *f (Air Navigation)*.

position finder station Peilfunkstelle *f*.

position finding Ortung *f*, Ortsbestimmung *f*.

positioning device for leads Vorhalteeinstellung *f (sight mechanism)*.

position in readiness Bereitstellung *f*.

position light Positionslicht *n (Avn)*.

position of departure Ausgangsstellung *f (Tac)*.

position of target Meßpunkt *m (at instant of range determination)*, Abschußpunkt *m (at instant of firing)*, Treffpunkt *m (at instant of impact)*, Gegnerpunkt *m*, Sprengpunkt *m (at instant of burst)*, Wechselpunkt *m (at midpoint) (AA Gunnery)*.

position of the gun Geschütznullpunkt *m*, Geschützort *m (on firing charts and diagrams)*.

position of the piece Geschützstand *m (Arty)*.

position report Standortmeldung *f (Air Navigation)*.

position warfare Stellungskrieg *m*, Stellungskampf *m*.

positive stagger Vorwärtsstaffelung *f*, Staffelung nach vorne *(Ap wings)*.

post *n* Pfahl *m (Engr)*; Standort *m (station)*.

post *v* aufstellen *(a guard, etc.)*; anschlagen *(a notice, etc.)*.

postage Porto *n*.

postal censor's office Postprüfungsstelle *f*, Postüberwachungsstelle *f*.

post commander Standortältester *m*.

post exchange Marketenderei *f*, Truppenmarketenderei *f*.

poster Plakat *n*, Anschlagzettel *m*.

post hospital Standortlazarett *n*.

posting Aussetzen *n (of guards)*.

postmaster Postmeister *m*.

post obstacle Pfahlsperre *f*.

post office Postamt *n*, Post *f*.

postpone aufschieben, verschieben.

potable trinkbar.

potassium cartridge Kalipatrone *f (oxygen breathing apparatus)*.

potassium permanganate Kaliumpermanganat *n*.

potato Kartoffel *f*.

"potato-masher" hand grenade Stielhandgranate *f*.

pothole Schlagloch *n (road)*.

potentiometer Potentiometer *n*.

pouch Beutel *m*, Tasche *f*.

pouch kit Sanitätstasche *f*.

powder Pulver *n (Am)*.

powder bag Kartuschbeutel *m*.

powder chamber Pulverraum *m*, Ladungsraum *m*, Pulverkammer *f*.

powder charge Pulverladung *f (Am)*.

powder fouling Pulverrückstände *mpl (G)*.

powder grain Pulverkorn *n (Am)*.

powder magazine Pulverhaus *n*.

powder pellet Pulversatz *m (fuze)*; Satzring *m (time fuze)*.

powder thermometer Pulverthermometer *n (Am)*.

powder train Pulversatz *m (fuze)*, Zündsatz *m (blasting)*.

powder-train fuze See **powder-train time fuze.**

powder-train ignition Pulverbrennzündung *f (fuze)*.

powder-train time fuze Brennzünder *m*.

power Energie *f*, Kraft *f (Mech)*; Macht *f*, Staat *m (country)*; Potenz *f (Math)*; Gewalt *f (authority)*.

power amplifier Leistungsstufe *f (Rad)*.

power amplifier tube Leistungsröhre *f*.

power control Leistungsregler *m (Rad)*.

powered glider Motorgleiter *m*, Motorsegler *m*.

powerful mächtig, gewaltig; einflußreich *(influential)*.

power house Kraftwerk *n*.

power lead-in Anzapfleitung *f (Rad)*.

power line Starkstromleitung *f*, Hochspannungsleitung *f (Elec)*.

power loading Leistungsbelastung *f (Ap)*.

power loss Energieverlust *m (Elec, Rad)*.

power pack Speiseteil *m (Rad)*.

power plant Triebwerk *n*, Triebwerksanlage *f (Ap, MT)*; Maschinensatz *m (generating unit)*; Kraftwerk *n (power house)*.

power saw Kraftsäge *f*, Motorsäge *f (Engr)*.

power shovel Bagger *m*, Löffelbagger *m (Engr)*.

power source Kraftquelle *f*, Stromquelle *f*.

power station Kraftwerk *n*, Elektrizitätswerk *n*.

power stroke Arbeitshub *m*, Arbeitstakt *m (Mtr)*.

power supply Energievorrat *m (Mech)*; Speisung *f (Rad)*.

power traction Kraftzug *m (MT)*.

power train Kraftübertragung *f*, Kraftübertragungsteile *mpl (MT)*.

power transformer Netztransformator *m (Rad)*.

power transmission Kraftübertragung *f*.

power transmission line Hochspannungsleitung *f (Elec)*.

power transmission unit Kraftübertragungsteil *m (MT)*.

power unit Maschinensatz *m*.

practice *n* Übung *f (Tng)*; Verfahren *n (procedure)*; Praxis *f (as distinguished from theory)*.

practice *v* üben.

practice alert Luftschutzübung *f (Civ defense)*.

practice ammunition Übungsmunition *f*.

practice bomb Exerzierbombe *f*.

practice-bombing panel Bombenteppich *m*.

practice charge Übungsladung *f (Am)*.

practice firing Schulschießen *n*, Übungsschießen *n*.

practice flight Übungsflug *m*.

practice grenade Übungshandgranate *f*.

practice mine Übungsmine *f*.

practice range Schießstand *m*.

practice shell Übungsgranate *f (Am)*.

practice sight Richtübungsgerät *n (G, MG)*.

prearranged fire vorbereitetes Feuer *(Arty)*.

precedence Vorrang *m*.

precipitation Niederschläge *mpl*.

precipitation area Regengebiet *n (rain)*, Schneefallgebiet, *n (snowfall)*.

precise genau, zielgenau, präzis.

precision Genauigkeit *f*, Präzision *f*.

precision adjustment Feineinstellung *f (Rad)*.

precision adjustment fire genaues Einschießen *(Arty)*.

precision bombing Zielwurf *m*, gezielter Bombenwurf.

precision fire Präzisionsschießen *n*.

precombustion chamber Vorkammer *f (Diesel engine)*.

predict voraussagen, vorhersagen *(forecast)*; den Vorhalt errechnen *(calculate the lead, Gunnery)*.

predicted position of target Vorhaltepunkt *m (Gunnery)*.

predicting interval Vorhaltestrecke *f (AA Gunnery)*.

prediction Voraussage *f*, Vorhersage *f (forecast)*; Errechnung des Vorhalts *(Gunnery)*.

predictor Zielrechenmaschine *f (AA)*.

preflight training theoretische Ausbildung.

preheater Vorwärmer *m*.

preignition Frühzündung *f (Mtr)*.

preliminary action einleitendes Gefecht *(Tac)*.

preliminary mission Vorausaufgabe *f (Tac)*.

preliminary signal Vorsignal *n*.

premature air burst Frühzerspringer *m (Arty)*.

premature ignition Vorzündung *f*.

premium Treugeld *n*.

preparation Vorbereitung *f*; Vorbereitungsfeuer *n (Arty)*.

preparation of fire Vorbereitung des Schießens.

preparatory command Ankündigungskommando *n*.

preparatory marksmanship training Schießvorschule *f*.

preparedness Bereitschaft *f*.

prescribe vorschreiben; verschreiben, verordnen *(Med)*.

prescribed vorgeschrieben; vorschriftsmäßig *(according to regulations)*.

prescribed load vorgesehene Menge, vorgeschriebene Last.

preselector Vorwähler *m (Tp)*.

"Present, arms!" "Achtung! Präsentiert das, Gewehr!"

present position of target Meßpunkt *m (at instant of range determination)*, Abschußpunkt *m (at instant of firing, AA Gunnery)*.

preserved meat Dauerfleisch *n*.

press *v* drücken, pressen.

press report Pressemeldung *f (Rad)*.

pressure Druck *m*.

pressure-board mine Druckbrettmine *f*, Brettstückmine *f*.

pressure cabin Druckkabine *f (Ap)*.

pressure change Betrag der Druckänderung *(Met)*.

pressure equalizer Druckausgleicher *m*.

pressure firing device Druckzünder *m (land mine)*.

pressure gage Gasdruckmeßgerät *n*, Meßei *n (Arty)*.

pressure gradient barometrisches Gefälle, Luftdruckgradient *m (Met)*.

pressure igniter Druckzünder *m*.

pressure line Druckleitung *f (Hydraulics)*.

pressure lubrication Druckschmierung *f*, Druckumlaufschmierung *f (Mtr)*.

pressure plate Druckplatte *f (clutch)*.

pressure plug Druckstempel *m (Arty)*.

pressure point Druckstelle *f*.

pressure regulator Druckregler *m*.

pressure surface Druckseite *f (Ap wing)*.

pressure test Gasdruckprüfung *f (Ord)*.

prevailing wind vorherrschende Winde.

prevent hindern, verhindern *(hinder or stop)*; vorbeugen *(by measures taken in advance)*.

preventive maintenance Pflege *f*.

primacord Knallzündschnur *f (Engr)*.

primacord net Knallnetz *n*.

primary circuit Primärkreis *m (Rad)*.

primary current Primärstrom *m*, Erststrom *m*.

primary target Hauptziel *n*.

primary trainer Schulflugzeug *n*.

primary traverse station trigonometrischer Punkt.

primary weapon Hauptwaffe *f*.

primary winding Primärwicklung *f (Elec)*.

prime mover Kraftzugmaschine *f*, Zugmaschine *f*; Zugkraftwagen *m (Trk)*; Kraftschlepper *m (Trac)*.

primer Zündhütchen *n (SA Am)*; Zündmittel *n (Am)*; Zündsatz *m (Am, blasting)*; Zündladung *f (primer charge)*; Zündschraube *f (threaded primer) (Am)*.

primer charge Zündladung *f*.

primer cup Zündhütchenhülse *f (Am)*.

primer vent Zündkanal *m (cartridge)*.

priming charge Eingangszündung *f*, Zündladung *f (Engr)*.

priming composition Zündsatz *m*.

priming flash Zündstrahl *m (Am)*.

principal course of approach Anfluggrundlinie *f (Inst landing)*.

principal lateral deflection angle Gesamtvorhaltewinkel *m (AA gunnery)*.

principal vertical deflection angle Reglerwinkel *m (AA gunnery)*.

principle Grundsatz *m* Prinzip *n*.

principles of war Grundprinzipien des Krieges.

print *n* Abzug *m*, Lichtpause *f (Photo)*.

print *v* drucken; kopieren, abziehen *(Photo)*.

printed form Vordruck *m*.

priority Vorrang *m (precedence)*; Vorfahrtsrecht *n (Trans)*.

priority list Dringlichkeitsliste *f*.

priority message dringende Meldung.

prismatic compass Marschkompaß *m*.

prison Gefängnis *n*; Arrestanstalt *f (Mil)*; Zuchthaus *n (penitentiary)*.

prisoner Gefangener *m*.

prisoner guard detachment Gefangenenbewachungskommando *n (MP)*.

prisoner of war Kriegsgefangener *m*.

prisoner of war camp Gefangenenlager *n*.

prisoner-of-war collection point Kriegsgefangenensammelstelle *f*.

private Grenadier *m (Inf)*; Jäger *m (in Gebirgsjäger or Jäger unit)*; Panzergrenadier *m (Armd Inf Regt)*; Reiter *m (Cav)*; Kanonier *m (Arty)*; Pionier *m (Engr)*; Fahrer *m (H-Dr Trans)*; Kraftfahrer *m (MT)*; Funker *m (radioman)*; Sanitätssoldat *m (Med)*; Schütze *m (rifleman)*.

private first class Obergrenadier *m (Inf)*; Oberjäger *m (in Gebirgsjäger or Jäger unit)*; Panzer-Obergrenadier *m (Armd Inf Regt)*; Oberreiter *m (Cav)*; Oberkanonier *m (Arty)*; Oberpionier *m (Engr)*; Oberfahrer *m (H-Dr Trans)*; Oberkraftfahrer *m (MT)*; Oberfunker *m (radioman)*; Oberschütze *m (rifleman)*; Sanitätsobersoldat *m (Med)*.

prize Prise *f*, Beute *f*.

probability factor Wahrscheinlichkeitsfaktor *m (Ballistics)*.

probability of hit Treffwahrscheinlichkeit *f (Gunnery);* Treffaussicht *f (bombing).*

probable error wahrscheinlicher Fehler.

probing rod Minensuchstab *m (for land mines).*

problem Aufgabe *f (Tng);* Problem *n.*

procedure Verfahren *n.*

procedure sign Funkabkürzung *f.*

procedure signal *See* procedure sign.

proceed weitergehen, weiterfahren; fortfahren *(continue).*

process *v* bearbeiten, fertigstellen.

proclamation Proklamation *f,* Verkündigung *f,* Bekanntmachung *f (public notice);* Verordnung *f (decree).*

procure anschaffen, beschaffen, verschaffen, besorgen.

procurement Anschaffung *f,* Beschaffung *f,* Besorgung *f.*

produce *v* erzeugen, hervorbringen; herstellen *(manufacture).*

product Erzeugnis *n,* Produkt *n.*

production Erzeugung *f,* Herstellung *f,* Fertigung *f,* Produktion *f.*

profile Profil *n,* Umriß *m.*

profile map Höhenumrißkarte *f.*

profile thickness Profildicke *f (Ap wing).*

profit *n* Gewinn *m.*

progress *n* Fortschritt *m.*

progress of action Gefechtsverlauf *m (Tac).*

progress of an attack Angriffsverlauf *m.*

prohibit verbieten.

prohibited zone Luftsperrgebiet *n (Avn).*

projectile Geschoß *n.*

projection Entwurf *m,* Projektion *f.*

projector Abschußrohr *n,* Werfer *m,* Wurfgerät *n (CWS, Sig);* Filmvorführapparat *m,* Filmprojektor *m (movies);* Bildwerfer *m (stills).*

projector signal Granatsignal *n.*

prolonge Abschlepptau *n,* Handhabungstau *n (Arty).*

promote befördern.

promotion Beförderung *f.*

promotion list Beförderungsliste *f.*

prone position Anschlag liegend *(firing).*

prone shelter Schützenmulde *f.*

prong Streckerstift *m (of a plug),* Kontaktstift *m (of a jack) (Elec).*

proof Beweis *m;* Probebild *n (Photo);* Probeabzug *m,* Probedruck *m (printing).*

prop Stütze *f,* Knagge *f (Engr).*

propaganda Propaganda *f.*

propeliant Treibmittel *n (Am).*

propellent treibend, antreibend.

propellent gases Treibgase *npl (Ballistics).*

propellent primer Zündhütchen *n (Am).*

propeller Luftschraube *f,* Propeller *m (Ap).*

propeller blade Luftschraubenblatt *n,* Luftschraubenflügel *m (Ap).*

propeller boss Luftschraubennabenstück *n (Ap).*

propeller-disk area Propellerkreis *m,* Luftschraubenkreis *m (Ap).*

propeller drive Schraubenantrieb *m (amphibian vehicle).*

propeller hub Propellernabe *f (Ap).*

propeller pitch indicator Luftschraubensteigungsmesser *m.*

propeller post Schraubensteven *m (Nav).*

propeller rpm Luftschraubendrehzahl *f.*

propeller shaft Gelenkwelle *f,* Zwischenwelle *f (MT).*

propeller spinner Luftschraubenhaube *f (Ap).*

propeller thrust Schraubenzug *m (Ap).*

propelling charge Treibladung *f,* Geschützladung *f (Am).*

propelling-charge chamber Patronenraum *m (Mort shell).*

propelling-charge increment Teilladung *f (Am).*

propelling equipment Fahrgerät *n (Engr).*

property Eigentum *n,* Besitz *m.*

property book Bestandsliste *f,* Waffen- und Gerätenachweis *m.*

property officer Geräteoffizier *m.*

prophylactic Sanierungsmittel *n.*

prophylactic station Sanitätsstelle für Schutzbehandlung gegen Geschlechtskrankheiten.

prophylaxis Prophylaxe *f,* Vorbeugung *f.*

propulsion Fortbewegung *f;* Antrieb *m (drive).*

prosig Funkabkürzung *f.*

prosine Funkabkürzung *f.*
protect beschützen, schützen.
protected shelter Unterstand *m (Ft).*
protecting power Schutzmacht *f (PW).*
protection Schutz *m.*
protective awning Gasplane *f (CWS).*
protective clothing Körperschutzmittel *n,* Gasbekleidung *f (CWS).*
protective fire Feuerschutz *m,* Notfeuer *n (Arty, MG).*
protective mat Gasschutzdecke *f (CWS).*
protective ointment Schutzsalbe *f (CWS).*
protective wire Drahthindernis *n.*
protectorate Schutzgebiet *n,* Protektorat *n.*
protectoscope Winkelspiegel *m,* Schutzglas *n,* Schutzscheibe *f (Tk).*
prototype Urbaumuster *n (Ap, Tk, etc.).*
protractor Strahlenzieher *m,* Sektor *m,* Winkelmeßgerät *n,* Winkelmesser *m;* Zelluloidtafel *f (transparent template).*
prove beweisen; sich erweisen, sich bestätigen *(one's ability, etc.);* prüfen, erproben *(test).*
provide versehen, versorgen *(to supply);* besorgen, beschaffen *(to get).*
proving ground Waffenprüfungsplatz *m.*
provisional map Ersatzkarte *f.*
provisional organization Spezialverband *m.*
provisions Proviant *m,* Lebensmittel *npl,* Nahrungsmittel *npl,* Verpflegung *f.*
provost court Feldgericht *n.*
provost marshal Stabsoffizier bei der Feldgendarmerie *(USA).*
prussic acid Hydrozyansäure *f,* Blausäure *f,* Zyanwasserstoff *m,* Zyanwasserstoffsäure *f (CWS).*
psychrometer Psychrometer *n.*
PT boat Schnellboot *n.*
public-address system Kraftverstärker-Anlage *f (Elec).*
public relations officer Presseoffizier *m.*
pull *v* abziehen *(trigger);* ziehen, schleppen.
pulley Riemenscheibe *f,* Rolle *f.*
pull firing device Ziehzünder *m (land mine).*
pull igniter Zugzünder *m (mine).*
pull out durchziehen *(dive bombing).*

pull-pressure igniter Zugdruckzünder *m (mine).*
pull up abheben *(Avn).*
pulmotor Pulmotor *m,* Sauerstoff-Wiederbeleber *m.*
pulsating direct current welliger Gleichstrom.
pulse Puls *m,* Pulsschlag *m.*
pump *n* Pumpe *f.*
punch Durchschläger *m (tool);* Faustschlag *m,* heftiger Stoß, Schlag *m (blow).*
puncture *v* stechen, zerstechen, durchlöchern *(pierce);* platzen *(said of a tire).*
punish strafen, bestrafen.
punishment Strafe *f,* Bestrafung *f.*
punishment book Strafbuch *n.*
punt ferry Kahnfähre *f (Engr).*
punting Staken *n (with punt pole).*
pup tent Einerzelt *n.*
purification unit Trinkwasserbereiterwagen *m (vehicle).*
Purple Heart Purpurherz *n (USA).*
purpose Zweck *m;* Absicht *f (intention);* Ziel *n (aim).*
pursue verfolgen, nachsetzen.
pursuit Verfolgung *f (Tac).*
pursuit airplane Jäger *m,* Jagdflugzeug *n.*
pursuit group Jagdgruppe *f (Avn).*
pursuit squadron Jagdstaffel *f (Avn).*
pursuit troops Verfolgungstruppen *fpl.*
pursuit wing Jagdgeschwader *n (Avn).*
push *v* schieben *(shove);* drücken *(press);* drängen *(crowd);* stoßen *(thrust).*
pushbutton Druckknopf *m.*
pusher airplane Flugzeug mit Druckschraube, Druckschrauber *m.*
pusher propeller Druckschraube *f (Ap).*
push-pull amplifier Gegentakt-Verstärker *m (Rad).*
push rod Stoßstange *f (Mtr).*
puttees Gamaschen *fpl.*
putty Kitt *m.*
pylon Wendeturm *m (Adrm).*
pyrocellulose Nitrozellulose *f.*
pyrocellulose powder Schießwollpulver *n.*
pyrocotton Schießbaumwolle *f,* Schießwolle *f.*
pyro powder Nitrozellulosepulver *m.*

pyro smokeless powder rauchloses Nitrozellulosepulver *n.*
pyrotechnic code Leuchtzeichenschlüssel *m.*
pyrotechnic composition Leuchtsatz *m (illuminant)*; Rauchsatz *m (smoke)*.

pyrotechnic device Leuchtmittel *n.*
pyrotechnic pistol Leuchtpistole *f.*
pyrotechnic projector Leuchtraketengestell *n*, Leuchtgranatwerfer *m.*
pyrotechnics Leuchtmunition *f.*
pyroxylin Kollodiumwolle *f (Am)*.

Q

Q signal Q-Gruppe *f (Com)*.
quadrant Quadrant *m;* Libellenquadrant *m (with spirit level, G)*; Viertelkreis *m (of a circle)*; Winkelmesser *m (G)*.
quadrant angle Erhebungswinkel *m.*
quadrant angle of departure Abgangswinkel *m (Ballistics)*.
quadrant angle of elevation Erhöhungswinkel *m (Arty)*.
quadrant elevation Gesamterhöhung *f*, Erhöhung *f (Arty)*.
quadrant plate Quadrantenfläche *f*, Winkelmesserebene *f (G)*.
quadrant scale Gradbogen *m (G)*.
quadrant sight Quadrantenvisier *n (leaf-type) (R, MG)*; Visiereinrichtung *f (G)*.
qualification Qualifikation *f*, Fähigkeit *f.*
qualification as a lawful belligerent Charakter einer kriegführenden Macht.
qualification card Qualifikationsbericht *m.*
qualification course Preisübung *f.*
qualification in arms Qualifizierung auf Grund erfolgreich beendeter Ausbildung.
qualified qualifiziert, geeignet, befähigt *(fitted)*; berechtigt *(entitled)*.
qualify qualifizieren.
quality Eigenschaft *f (characteristic)*; Qualität *f*, Beschaffenheit *f*, Güte *f (degree of excellence)*.
quantity Größe *f (Math)*; Menge *f (amount)*.
quarantine *n* Quarantäne *f (Med)*.
quarantine *v* isolieren, in Quarantäne stellen.
quarry Steinbruch *m.*
quarter Viertel *n (fourth)*; Stadtviertel *n (of a city)*; Gnade *f*, Pardon *m (mercy)*.

quartering Unterbringung *f.*
quartering area Unterbringungsgebiet *n*, Unterkunftsbezirk *m.*
quartering officer Quartiermacher *m.*
quartering party Quartiermacherkommando *n.*
Quartermaster Quartiermeister *m (USA)*.
Quartermaster Corps Quartiermeisterkorps *n (USA)*.
quartermaster depot Quartiermeisterlager *n (USA)*.
Quartermaster General Generalquartiermeister *m (USA)*.
quartermaster unit Quartiermeistereinheit *f (USA)*.
quarters Unterbringung *f*, Unterkunft *f.*
quarters allowance Quartiervergütung *f.*
quarters and subsistence allowance Quartier- und Verpflegungszuschuß *m.*
quarters in kind freie Unterkunft.
quartz crystal Quarzkristall *m (Rad)*.
quay Kai *m.*
quenching frequency Pendelfrequenz *f (Rad)*.
question *n* Frage *f.*
question *v* ausfragen, befragen, verhören, vernehmen; bezweifeln *(doubt)*.
questioning Vernehmung *f.*
questioning of prisoners Gefangenenverhör *n*, Gefangenenvernehmung *f.*
questionnaire Fragebogen *m.*
quick schnell, rasch.
quick-detachable rim Maderfelge *f (MT)*.
quick fire Schnellfeuer gegen bewegliche Ziele.
quick fuze Augenblickszünder *m (Arty)*.

quicklime ungelöschter Kalk.
quickmatch Zündschnur *f (Prcht flare)*.
quick time Gleichschritt *m.*
"**Quick time, march!**" "Im Gleichschritt!" *(being in march in double time)*.

quiet *n* Ruhe *f*, Stille *f.*
quiet *adj* ruhig, still.
quinine Chinin *n.*
quit verlassen *(leave)*; aufhören *(stop)*.
quota Quote *f.*
quotient Quotient *m.*

R

race *n* Laufring *m (ball bearing)*.
racer Drehring *m (AA gun)*.
rack Zahnstange *f*, Zahnbogen *m (Mech, Ord)*; Gewehrstütze *f (R)*; Bombenschacht *m (Ap)*; Lagergerüst *n (for storage of supplies)*.
rack stick Schnürleiste *f (for cord lashing, Bdg)*.
radar Funkmeßgerät *n.*
radar station Funkmeßturm *m.*
radial engine Sternmotor *m.*
radian Radian *m*, Bogeneinheit *f.*
radiation Ausstrahlung *f*, Strahlung *f (Rad)*.
radiator Kühler *m (Mtr)*; Heizkörper *m (for heating)*.
radiator cap Kühler-Einfüllverschluß *m (MT)*.
radiator guard Kühlerschutzhaube *f (MT)*.
radio *n* Funk *m*; Funkgerät *n (set)*.
by radio auf dem Funkwege, auf dem Funkspruchwege.
radio *v* funken, senden.
radio address Rundfunkrede *f.*
radio alert Funkbereitschaft *f.*
radio antenna truck Funkmastkraftwagen *m.*
radio beacon Funkbake *f*, Funkfeuer *n.*
radio beam Funkstrahl *m*, Leitstrahl *m*, Ansteuerungsfunkfeuer *n.*
radio-bearing signal Peilzeichen *n.*
radio broadcasting station Rundfunkstation *f*, Rundfunksender *m.*
radio-broadcast reception Rundfunkempfang *m.*
radio call signal Funkrufzeichen *n.*
radio car Funkkraftwagen *m.*
radio case Funkkiste *f.*
radio chest *See* **radio case.**
radio command Funkbefehl *m.*

radio command tank Funkpanzerkampfwagen *m.*
radio command truck Funkkraftwagen *m.*
radio communication Funkverbindung *f*, Funkverkehr *m.*
radio communications Funknachrichten *fpl.*
radio compass Bordpeiler *m*, Peilfunkempfänger *m*, Richtempfänger *m*, Peilempfänger *m (Air Navigation)*.
radio compass calibration Funkbeschickung *f (Air Navigation)*.
radio deception Funktäuschung *f.*
radio detector *See* **radar.**
radio direction finder Funkpeiler *m.*
radio direction finder station Bodenpeilfunkstelle *f*, Peilfunkstelle *f*, Peilstelle *f (Avn)*.
radio direction finding Funkpeilung *f.*
radio direction-finding truck Peilkraftwagen *m.*
radio discipline Funkzucht *f.*
radio engineer Funktechniker *m.*
radio engineering Funktechnik *f.*
radio equipment Funkgerät *n*, F.T.-Gerät *n*; F.T.-Anlage *f (Ap, Tk)*.
radio-equipment truck Funkgerätekraftwagen *m.*
radio exercise Funkübung *f.*
radio facility chart Fliegerkarte mit für die Funknavigation notwendigen Angaben *(Avn)*.
radio fix Schnittpunkt zweier Peilstrahlen, Standort *m (Air Navigation)*.
radio frequency Hochfrequenz *f.*
radio-frequency amplifier Hochfrequenzverstärker *m.*
radio-frequency choke Hochfrequenzdrossel *f.*

radio-frequency stage Hochfrequenzstufe *f (Rad)*.
radio-frequency transformer Hochfrequenztransformator *m*.
radio goniometer Funkpeilanlage *f*.
radiogram Funktelegramm *n*.
radio intelligence Funkaufklärung *f*.
radio intercept Funkhorchen *n*.
radio intercept station Funkhorchstelle *f*.
radio jamming Funkstörung *f*.
radio landing beam Leitstrahl des Landefunkfeuers *(Avn)*.
radio log Funkbetriebsbuch *n*.
radioman Funker *m*.
radio marker beacon Navigationsfunkfeuer *n (Air Navigation)*.
radio mast Funkmast *m*.
radio message Funkmeldung *f*, Funkspruch *m*.
radio meteorograph Radiosonde *f*.
radio monitoring Funküberwachung *f*.
radio motor vehicle Funkkraftfahrzeug *n*.
radio navigation Funknavigation *f (Avn)*.
radio net Funknetz *n*.
radio noise suppressor Störungsschutz *m*, Störschutz *m*, Störsperre *f*.
radio officer Funknachrichtenoffizier *m*.
radio operations Funkbetrieb *m*.
radio operator Funker *m*; Bordfunker *m (Avn)*; Funkunteroffizier *m (Sgt)*; Funkgefreiter *m (Cpl)*.
radio operator's station Stand des Funkers *(Ap)*.
radio order Funkbefehl *m*.
radiophoto transmission Bildfunk *m*.
radio position finding Feststellen des Standortes eines feindlichen Senders durch Funkpeilung *(Rad)*.
radio procedure Funkbetriebsverfahren *n*.
radio range Funknavigationsanlage *f*.
radio range beacon Richtfunkfeuer *f*.
radio range station Bodenstelle für Funknavigation, Richtfunkstelle *f*.
radio receiver Funkempfänger *m*.
radio reception Funkempfang *m*.
radio repairman Funkgerätmechaniker *m*.
radio section Funktrupp *m*.
radio set Funkgerät *n*.
radio shield Entstörkappe *f (Mtr)*.
radio signal Funksignal *n*.

radio silence Funkstille *f*, Funkverbot *n*.
radiosonde Radiosonde *f (Met)*.
radio station Funkstelle *f*.
radio technician Funkwart *m*.
radio technology Funktechnik *f*.
radiotelegraph communication funkentelegraphische Verbindung.
radiotelegraph set F.T.-Gerät *n (Ap)*.
radiotelegraphy Funkentelegraphie *f*.
radiotelephone Funksprechgerät *n*.
radiotelephone communication Funksprechen *n*.
radiotelephony Funkentelephonie *f*.
radio tower Funkturm *m*.
radio traffic Funkverkehr *m*.
radio transmission Funksendung *f;* Funktasten *n (keying)*.
radio transmitter Funksender *m*, Sendegerät *n*.
radio truck Funkkraftwagen *m*, Funkwagen *m*.
radio tube Elektronenröhre *f*.
radio voice transmission Funksprechen *n*.
radio wave Funkwelle *f*.
radio wave deflection Strahlungsablenkung *f*.
radio weather station Funkwetterwarte *f*.
radius Halbmesser *m*, Radius *m*.
radius of action Aktionsradius *m*, Wirkungsbereich *m (Ap)*.
radius of rupture Wirkungshalbmesser *m (blasting)*.
radius of visibility Sichtweite *f*.
raft Floß *n*.
raid *n* Streifzug *m*, Überfall *m*, Stoßtruppunternehmung *f (Tac)*; Razzia *f (police)*; Luftangriff *m*, Angriffsflug *m*, Feindflug *m (Avn)*.
raiding party Streifabteilung *f*, Streifkommando *n*.
rail Schiene *f (RR, etc.)*; Holm *m (spar)*; Stange *f (pole)*; Runge *f (rack bar or pole, MT)*.
by rail mit der Eisenbahn.
railhead Eisenbahnendpunkt *m*, Ausladebahnhof *m*, Ausladespitze *f*.
railhead distribution Verteilung der Nachschubgüter vom Ausladebahnhof aus.
railhead reserve area Nachschubsammelgebiet *n*.
railing Geländer *n (Bdg)*.
railing support Geländerstütze *f*.

railroad Eisenbahn *f. See also* **railway.**

railroad antiaircraft artillery Eisenbahnflak *f.*

railroad artillery *See* **railway artillery.**

railroad car Eisenbahnwagen *m.*

railroad crossing Bahnübergang *m;* Überführung *f (overpass);* Unterführung *f (underpass);* Planübergang *m (level).*

railroad depot Bahnhof *m.*

railroad embankment Bahndamm *m.*

railroad engineer troops Eisenbahnpioniere *mpl.*

railroad gun Eisenbahngeschütz *n.*

railroad installation Bahnanlage *f,* Eisenbahnanlage *f.*

railroad junction Eisenbahnknotenpunkt *m.*

railroad line Eisenbahnlinie *f,* Bahnverbindung *f.*

railroad station Bahnhof *m.*

railroad station traffic officer Bahnhofsoffizier *m.*

railroad supply line Eisenbahnnachschublinie *f.*

railroad track Eisenbahngleis *n.*

railroad traffic Zugverkehr *m.*

railroad train Eisenbahnzug *m,* Zug *m.*

railroad transportation Eisenbahnbeförderung *f,* Bahntransport *m.*

r a i l r o a d transportation timetable Eisenbahntransportfolge *f.*

railroad yard Gleisanlage *f.*

railway Eisenbahn *f. See also* **railroad.**

railway artillery Eisenbahnartillerie *f.*

railway artillery battery Eisenbahnbatterie *f.*

railway engineer regiment Eisenbahn-Pionierregiment *n.*

railway gun Eisenbahngeschütz *n.*

railway gun car Geschützwagen *m (RR).*

railway howitzer Eisenbahnhaubitze *f.*

railway mortar Eisenbahnmörser *m.*

railway operating company Betriebskompanie *f.*

rain *n* Regen *m.*

raincoat Regenmantel *m.*

rain gage Regenmesser *m (Met).*

raise *v* heben *(lift);* erhöhen *(increase);* potenzieren *(to a power) (Math).*

rake *n* Rechen *m.* Harke *f.*

rake *v* beschießen, bestreichen *(firing).*

rally *v* sammeln, vereinigen, wiederversammeln *(Tac).*

rallying point Sammelplatz *m (Tac).*

ram *v* ansetzen *(G);* rammen *(Nav).*

rammer Ansetzer *m (G);* Stößel *m (fuze).*

ramp Rampe *f.*

ramp carrier Rampenwagen *m (Bdg train).*

ramp equipment Rampengerät *n (Bdg).*

range Entfernung *f,* Schußweite *f (distance);* Schießplatz *m,* Schießstand *m (place);* Flugbereich *m (Avn);* Wurfweite *f (bombing);* Reichweite *f (of a Rad set);* Bodenstelle für Funknavigation *(Rad range station).*

range adjustment Einschießen nach der Länge *(firing).*

range angle Vorhaltewinkel *m (bombing).*

range butt Kugelfang *m.*

range car Schießwagen *m (on target range).*

range card Punktplan *m (Gunnery).*

range conversion table Kommandotafel *f (Gunnery).*

range correction Längenverbesserung *f,* Verbesserung für Länge *(Gunnery).*

range-deflection fan Zielspinne *f (Gunnery).*

range determination Entfernungsermittlung *f.*

range deviation Höhenabweichung *f,* Längenabweichung *f (Gunnery).*

range difference Entfernungsunterschied *m.*

range dispersion Längenstreuung *f,* Tiefenstreuung *f (on horizontal target);* Höhenstreuung *f (on vertical target).*

range drum Trommel *f,* Übertrommel *f (sight mount).*

range estimation Entfernungsschätzen *n.*

range finder Entfernungsgerät *n,* Entfernungsmeßgerät *n,* Entfernungsmesser *m,* Fernmesser *m,* Fernmeßgerät *n.*

range-finder operator Entfernungsmeßmann *m,* Entfernungsmesser *m.*

range finding Entfernungsmessen *n.*

range indicator Entfernungsmarke *f* (*practice firing*).

range knob Entfernungstrommel *f* (*G*).

range plate Strichplatte *f* (*MG mount*).

range pole Fluchtstab *m* (*Surv*).

range practice Schießübung *f*.

range quadrant Winkelmesser *m*, Libellenquadrant *m* (*G*).

Ranger Soldat der Landungstruppen (*USA*).

range ruler Entfernungslineal *n* (*Arty*).

range scale Entfernungsteilung *f*.

range sensing Festlegen der Längenabweichung (*Arty Obsn*).

range setting Entfernungseinstellung *f* (*Gunnery*).

range spotting Festlegen der Längenabweichung (*Arty Obsn*).

range table Schußtafel für Erhöhung.

range to target Zielentfernung *f* (*Gunnery*).

ranging fire Einschießen nach der Länge (*CA*).

ranging station Meßstelle *f* (*sound ranging, flash ranging*).

rank *n* Glied *n* (*in formation*); Rang *m* (*status*).

ranking *adj* rangältest.

ranks Unteroffiziere und Mannschaften (*Pers*).

rape *n* Notzucht *f*, Vergewaltigung *f*.

rapid fire Schnellfeuer *n*.

rapid-fire breechblock Schnelladeverschluß *m* (*G*).

rapid-fire cannon Schnellfeuerkanone *f*.

rapid-fire gun Schnellfeuergeschütz *n*.

rasp Raspel *f*.

rat Ratte *f*.

ratchet Knarre *f* (*wheel and pawl*); Klinke *f* (*pawl*).

ratchet wheel Sperrad *n*.

rate Satz *m*, Rate *f*; Geschwindigkeit *f* (*speed*); Gebühr *f* (*charge*); Preis *m* (*price*); Tarif *m* (*classified rate*); Honorar *n* (*fee*).

rated horsepower Nennleistung *f*.

rate of angular movement Winkelgeschwindigkeit *f* (*Ord*).

rate of burning Brenngeschwindigkeit *f* (*time blasting fuze*).

rate of climb Steigleistung *f*, Steigzeit *f* (*Avn*).

rate-of-climb indicator Statoskop *n*.

rate of drop Sinkgeschwindigkeit *f* (*Avn*).

rate of fall Fallgeschwindigkeit *f*, Sinkgeschwindigkeit *f*.

rate of fire Feuergeschwindigkeit *f* (*MG*).

rate of fuel consumption Kraftstoffverbrauchssatz *m* (*MT*).

rate of march Marschgeschwindigkeit *f*, Marschtempo *n*.

rate of pay Höhe des Wehrsoldes (*Mil*).

rating Dienstgrad *m* (*Nav*).

ration *n* Portion *f*, Portionssatz *m*, Verpflegungssatz *m*, Verpflegungsportion *f*.

ration *v* rationieren.

ration allowances Verpflegungsgebührnisse *fpl*.

ration and savings account Verpflegungsabrechnung *f*.

ration articles Verpflegungsgegenstände *mpl*.

ration card Kleiderkarte *f* (*Clo*); Lebensmittelkarte *f* (*food*).

ration distributing point Verpflegungsausgabestelle *f*.

ration requirements Verpflegungsbedarf *m*.

ration return Verpflegungsbezugsschein *m*.

rations Verpflegungsmittel *npl*, Verpflegung *f*.

rations and quarters Verpflegung und Unterkunft.

ration savings Geldwert der Verpflegungsersparnisse.

rations delivery unit Verpflegungsbombe *f* (*airborne Opns*).

rations in kind Verpflegung in Natur, Naturalverpflegung *f*.

ration stockage Verpflegungsbestände *mpl*.

ration strength Verpflegungsstärke *f*.

ration supplies Verpflegungsmittel *npl*, Lebensmittel *npl*.

ration supply depot Verpflegungslager *n*.

ration train Verpflegungstroß *m*; Verpflegungszug *m* (*RR*).

ravine Schlenke *f*.

ray Strahl *m*.

rayon Kunstseide *f*.

razor Rasiermesser *n* (*barber's*); Rasierapparat *m* (*safety*).

razor blade Rasierklinge *f*.

reaction Reaktion *f*, Rückstoß *m*.

reaction pressure Rückdruck *m* (*rocket*).

read lesen, ablesen.

readability Lautstärke *f (Rad, Tp)*; Lesbarkeit *f*, Verständlichkeit *f*.

readiness Bereitschaft *f*.

readiness for action Gefechtsbereitschaft *f*.

ready bereit, fertig.

"**Ready!**" "Fertig!" *(Arty)*.

ready-fixed fuze Fertigzünder *m*.

ready-fixed percussion fuze Fertigaufschlagzünder *m (Am)*.

ready for take-off startklar *(Avn)*.

"**Ready, front!**" "Augen gerade, aus!"

ready to fire schußfertig.

reamer Reibahle *f*.

rear *n* Rücken *m (Tac);* Heck *n (Tk)*.

to the rear nach hinten.

rear *adj* rückwärtig.

rear admiral Vizeadmiral *m (Nav)*.

rear area rückwärtiges Gebiet.

rear armor plate Heckpanzer *m (Tk)*.

rear attack Rückenangriff *m (Tac)*.

rear-axle drive Hinterachsantrieb *m (MT)*.

rear bourrelet Führungswulst *m (Am)*.

rear cinch Gurtstrippe *f (pack saddle)*.

rear communications rückwärtige Verbindungen.

rear cover Rückendeckung *f (Tac)*.

rear covering force Rückendeckung *f (Tac)*.

rear drive Heckantrieb *m (MT)*.

rear driver Rückwärtsfahrer *m (of a vehicle with double-end control)*.

rear echelon II. Staffel *(Hq)*.

rear echelon train Kolonnenstaffel *f*.

rear guard Nachhut *f*.

rear-guard action Nachhutgefecht *n*.

rear guard reserve Haupttrupp *m (in rear guard of large unit)*.

rear guard support Nachtrupp *m (in rear guard of large unit);* Haupttrupp *m (in rear guard of smaller unit)*.

rear gunner Heckschütze *m (Avn)*.

rear installations rückwärtige Einrichtungen.

rear outrigger Hinterholm *m (AA gun)*.

rear party Nachspitzenkompanie *f (in rear guard of large unit);*

Nachtrupp *m (in rear guard of smaller unit)*.

rear point Nachspitze *f (Tac)*.

rear position rückwärtige Stellung *(Tac)*.

rear rider Beifahrer *m (Mtcl)*.

rear ring sight Kreiskimme *f (MG)*.

rear services rückwärtige Dienste.

rear sight Visier *n (Ord)*.

rear-sight base Visierfuß *m (MG, R)*.

rear-sight leaf Visierklappe *f (MG, R)*.

rear-sight pin Visierhaltestift *m*, Visierstift *m (MG, R)*.

rear-sight spring Visierfeder *f (MG, R)*.

rear toggle joint Hintergelenk *n (pistol)*.

rear-view mirror Rückblickspiegel *m*.

rearward rückwärtig.

rearward position rückwärtige Stellung *(Tac)*.

rear-wheel drive Hinterradantrieb *m (MT)*.

rear zone rückwärtiges Gebiet.

recapping Profilieren *n*, Reifenerneuerung *f (MT)*.

recapture wiedereinnehmen *(a locality);* wiedergefangennehmen *(a prisoner)*.

receding flight Abflug *m (AA)*.

receding leg Abflugstrecke *f*, Wegflugstrecke *f (AA target)*.

receding target gehendes Ziel.

receipt *n* Empfangsschein *m*, Einnahmeschein *m*.

receiver Empfänger *m (data transmission system) (Rad);* Hülse *f (pistol) (R);* Griffstück *n (pistol);* Kasten *m (MG);* Fernhörer *m*, Hörer *m (Rad Tp, Tp)*.

receiver chassis Empfangsapparatur *f*, Empfängerchassis *n (Rad)*.

receiver circuit Empfangsschaltung *f (Rad)*.

receiver cover Hülsenbrücke *f (R)*.

receiver floor plate Kastenboden *m (MG)*.

receiver top Kastendeckel *m (MG)*.

receiving antenna Empfangsantenne *f*.

receiving frequency Empfangsfrequenz *f (Rad)*.

receiving set Empfangsgerät *n*, Empfänger *m (Rad)*.

receptacle Steckdose *f (Elec)*.

reception Aufnahme *f*, Empfang *m;* Funkempfang *m (Rad).*
reception center Rekrutendepot *n.*
reception zone Empfangszone *f (Rad).*
recess Keilloch *n (G breech).*
reciprocal laying Gleichlaufverfahren *n (Btry).*
reciprocating motion Vor- und Rückgang *m.*

reclaim wieder nutzbar machen, instandsetzen, verwerten.
reclaimed rubber regenerierter Altgummi.
reclamation Wiederinstandsetzung *f (of equipment).*
recocking shaft Spannwelle *f (breechblock).*
recognition Erkennen *n (identification);* Anerkennung *f (acknowledgment).*
recognition signal Erkennungszeichen *n.*
recoil Rücklauf *m*, Rückstoß *m.*
recoil booster Rückstoßverstärker *m (MG).*
recoil brake Rohrbremse *f*, Rücklaufbremse *f (G).*
recoil connection Kupplung *f (pistol).*
recoil cylinder Bremszylinder *m (G).*
recoil lug Hülsenzapfen *m (R).*
recoil marker Rücklaufmesser *m (G).*
recoil mechanism Bremsvorrichtung *f*, Rücklaufeinrichtung *f (G).*
recoil oil Bremsflüssigkeit *f (G).*
recoil-operated mit Rückstoß betätigt.
recoil-operated weapon Rückstoßlader *m.*
recoil piston Bremskolben *m (G).*
recoil spring Rücklauffeder *f.*
recoil-spring lever Kupplungshebel *m (pistol).*
recoil-spring lever bar Kupplungsstange *f (pistol).*
reconnaissance Aufklärung *f*, Erkundung *f (Tac).*
reconnaissance airplane Aufklärer *m*, Aufklärerflugzeug *n*, Aufklärungsflugzeug *n;* Nahaufklärer *m*, Naherkunder *m (close reconnaissance).*
reconnaissance area Aufklärungsgebiet *n*, Aufklärungsraum *m.*
reconnaissance aviation Aufklärungsflieger *mpl.*
reconnaissance boat Floßsack zur Erkundung der Übersetzstellen.

reconnaissance car Spähwagen *m;* Panzerspähwagen *m (Armd).*
reconnaissance company Aufklärungskompanie *f.*
reconnaissance depth Aufklärungstiefe *f.*
reconnaissance detachment Aufklärungstrupp *m;* Reiteraufklärungsabteilung *f (Cav).*
reconnaissance element Erkundungsorgan *n.*
reconnaissance exercise Aufklärungsübung *f.*
reconnaissance flare Fallschirmleuchtbombe *f (Avn).*
reconnaissance flight Aufklärungsflug *m (Avn).*
reconnaissance float airplane Aufklärungsseeflugzeug *n.*
reconnaissance in force gewaltsame Erkundung.
reconnaissance information Aufklärungsmaterial *n.*
reconnaissance mission Aufklärungsflug *m (Avn).*
reconnaissance of position Geländeerkundung *f.*
reconnaissance of route Wegeerkundung *f (Tac).*
reconnaissance party See reconnaissance patrol.
reconnaissance patrol Aufklärungsspähtrupp *m*, Spähtrupp *m.*
reconnaissance platoon Aufklärungszug *m.*
reconnaissance sector Aufklärungsstreifen *m.*
reconnaissance squadron Aufklärungsstaffel *f (Avn).*
reconnaissance troop Aufklärungsschwadron *f (Cav).*
reconnaissance vehicle Erkundungsfahrzeug *n.*
reconnoiter aufklären.
reconstruction Wiederherstellung *f.*
record *n* Aufzeichnung *f*, Niederschrift *f (notation); Akt m*, Urkunde *f (document);* Rekord *m*, Höchstleistung *f*, Bestleistung *f (feat);* Schallplatte *f (phonograph).*
record *v* aufzeichnen, aufschreiben *(write);* aufnehmen *(sound, etc.).*
recorder Aufschreiber *m (Arty).*
recording target Treffbild *n (practice firing).*
recording theodolite Kinotheodolit *m (practice firing).*

record of transactions Bewegungsbuch *n* *(QMC)*.

record service practice Schulschießen *n (Arty)*.

recoupment Entschädigung *f*, Vergütung *f*.

recoverable wiederverwendbar, instandsetzbar.

recoverable item wiederinstandsetzbarer Gegenstand.

recovery Bergen *n*, Bergung *f (of matériel, etc.)*; Genesung *f (from sickness)*; Erholung *f (from fatigue)*.

recovery equipment Bergegerät *n*.

recovery party Sammelkommando *n*.

recovery service Bergedienst *m*.

recreation Unterhaltung *f*, Zeitvertreib *m*.

recruit *n* Rekrut *m*.

recruit *v* rekrutieren.

recruit depot Rekrutendepot *n*.

recruit drill Rekrutenexerzieren *n*.

recruiting center Ersatzdienststelle *f*.

recruiting office Annahmestelle *f*.

rectangle Rechteck *n*.

rectangular coordinates rechtwinklige Koordinaten.

rectification Gleichrichtung *f (Rad)*; Entzerrung *f (aerial Photo)*.

rectifier Gleichrichter *m (Rad)*.

rectifier tube Gleichrichterröhre *f*.

recuperator Vorholer *m*, Luftvorholer *m (pneumatic) (Ord.)*.

recuperator cylinder Luftbehälter des Vorholers *(G)*.

recuperator mechanism Vorholeinrichtung *f (Ord)*.

red rot.

Red Cross Rotes Kreuz.

redesigning Umkonstruktion *f*.

redline ausstreichen.

reduce degradieren, herabsetzen *(in rank)*; bezwingen, niederkämpfen *(Tac)*; abschwächen *(Photo)*; reduzieren *(chemistry)*; beseitigen *(a stoppage) (Ord)*.

reduced charge verminderte Ladung *(Am)*.

reduction Untersetzung *f (Mech)*.

reduction coefficient Verbesserungswert zum Ausschalten des Stellungsunterschiedes *(Gunnery)*.

reduction gear Untersetzungsgetriebe *n*, Reduziergetriebe *n (MT)*.

reel Aufspuler *m (Tp)*.

reel cart Handwagen mit Kabeltrommel, Verlegswagen *m (Sig C)*.

reenlist kapitulieren, sich zu einer längeren Dienstzeit verpflichten, freiwillig weiterdienen.

reenlistment Kapitulation *f*, Verpflichtung zu einer längeren Dienstzeit.

reentrant einspringender Winkel *(Ft)*.

refer festlegen, Teilringzahlen zum Festlegepunkt ermitteln *(Gunnery)*.

reference Hinweis *m (in books, etc.)*; Erwähnung *f (mention)*; Empfehlung *f (recommendation)*; Bezug *m (relation)*.

reference line Bezugslinie *f*, Null-Linie *f (Surv)*.

reference number Kennummer *f*, Kennziffer *f;* Windziffer *f (wind reference number) (Ballistics)*.

reference piece Geschütz, auf das die Grundstufe bezogen wird.

reference point Hilfsziel *n*, Zwischenziel *n (R fire)*; Festlegepunkt *m (Gunnery)*; Festpunkt *m (Surv)*.

reference-point reading Grundzahl *f (Gunnery)*.

referring point Festlegepunkt *m*, Nahfestlegepunkt *m (close at hand) (Gunnery)*.

reflecting projector Episkop *n*.

reflecting sight See **reflector sight.**

reflector Rückstrahler *m*.

reflector sight Reflexvisier *n*.

refresher instruction Wiederholungsunterricht *m*.

refrigerator Kühlschrank *m*.

refrigerator car Kühlwagen *m*.

refrigerator truck Kühlwagen *m*, Sonderlastkraftwagen mit Kühleinrichtung.

refuel nachtanken, auftanken.

refueling station Tankstelle *f (MT)*.

refugee Flüchtling *m*.

refugee evacuation center Flüchtlingssammelstelle *f*.

regeneration Rückkopplung *f (Rad)*; Regeneration *f (of rubber, etc.)*.

regiment Regiment *n*.

regimental adjutant Regimentsadjutant *m*.

regimental commander Regimentskommandeur *m*.

regimental command post Regimentsgefechtsstand *m*.

regimental communication officer Regimentsnachrichtenoffizier *m.*
regimental communication platoon Regimentsnachrichtenzug *m.*
regimental defense area Regimentsabschnitt *m.*
regimental headquarters Regimentsstab *m.*
regimental sector Regimentsabschnitt *m.*
regimental sergeant major Stabsfeldwebel *m;* Stabswachtmeister *m (Arty, Cav).*
regimental staff Regimentsstab *m.*
regimental surgeon Regimentsarzt *m.*
regimental train Regimentstroß *m.*
region Gebiet *n*, Raum *m*, Region *f;* Gegend *f (vicinity).*
regional charts Fliegerkartenblätter *npl (USA).*
register *v* auf ein Ziel einschießen *(Gunnery);* aufgeben *(baggage, etc.);* sich einschreiben *(enroll);* sich melden *(with the authorities).*
registration Einschießen auf ein bestimmtes Ziel *(Gunnery);* Musterung *f (for the draft).*
registration and airworthiness certificate Zulassung *f (Avn).*
registration certificate Zulassung *f (MT).*
registration district Musterungsbezirk *m (for the draft).*
registration target Einschießziel *n*, Hilfsziel *n.*
regrouping Umgruppierung *f.*
regular regelmäßig.
Regular Army Reguläre Armee *(USA);* langdienendes Berufsheer.
regulate regeln, regulieren; verstellen, einstellen *(adjust).*
regulating nut Einstellmutter *f.*
regulating point Umleitungsstelle *f (MT).*
regulating station Verteilerbahnhof *m (RR).*
regulation Regelung *f;* Verstellung *f (Mech);* Dienstvorschrift *f (service regulation).*
regulation of fire Feuerregelung *f (Arty).*
regulation of traffic Regelung des Verkehrs, Verkehrsregelung *f.*
regulator Regelstange *f (G recoil brake).*
rein Zügel *m (harness).*

reinforce verstärken, nähren *(Tac).*
reinforced concertina roll Drahtwalze *f.*
reinforced concrete Eisenbeton *m.*
reinforcements Verstärkungen *fpl.*
reinforcing strap Belag *m (harness).*
related arm Schwesterwaffe *f.*
relative humidity relative Feuchtigkeit *(Met).*
relative rank entsprechender Rang.
relaxation oscillation Kippschwingung *f (Rad).*
relay Schütz *m*, Relais *n (Elec).*
re-lay neu einrichten, wieder richten *(Gunnery).*
relay coil Relaisspule *f (Elec).*
relay message weitergegebene Meldung.
relay messengers Stafetten *fpl.*
relay point *See* **relay station.**
relay station Zwischenstelle *f (Sig C);* Umschlagstelle *(Trans).*
release *n* Abwurf *m*, Auslösung *f (of bombs, etc.);* Freilassung *f (of a prisoner);* Presseaussendung *f (news);* Verzicht *m (Law).*
release button Auslöseknopf *m.*
release hook Sicherungshaken *m (glider).*
release mechanism Auslöseeinrichtung *f*, Abwurfvorrichtung *f*, Abwurfgerät *n (bombing);* Abdrückvorrichtung *f (G);* Abfeuerungseinrichtung *t (Mort).*
release of smoke Nebelabblasen *n (CWS).*
release on parole Freilassung auf Ehrenwort.
release point Auslösepunkt *m (bombing).*
reliable verläßlich, zuverlässig.
reliability Verläßlichkeit *f*, Zuverlässigkeit *f.*
reliability of operation Betriebssicherheit *f (Mech).*
relief Ablösung *f (taking over);* Entlastung *f (of enemy pressure);* Entsatz *m*, Entsetzung *f (of a besieged garrison);* Relief *n (Top);* Abspannung *f (of tension or strain).*
relief map Reliefkarte *f.*
relief valve Entlastungsventil *n.*
relieve ablösen *(take over);* entheben *(of a command, etc.);* entsetzen *(a besieged garrison);* entlasten *(of enemy pressure);* abspannen *(of tension or strain).*

relieve oneself austreten.

religion Religion *f.*

remain bleiben.

remaining velocity Änderungsgeschwindigkeit *f (Ballistics).*

remission of sentence Ermäßigung der Strafe.

remote control Fernsteuerung *f,* Fernantrieb *m,* Fernlenkung *f.*

remote control system Fernrichtanlage *f (AA).*

remote control unit Fernbesprechgerät *n (Rad).*

remote-reading compass Fernkompaß *m (Ap).*

remote-reading c o m p a s s assembly Fernkompaßanlage *f (Ap).*

remount *n* Ersatzpferd *n.*

remount *v* remontieren.

remount area Zuchtgebiet für Truppenpferde und Maultiere.

remount depot Remonteamt *n,* Pferdepark *m.*

Remount Division Remonteinspektion *f.*

remount purchasing board Remonteaufkaufskommission *f,* Remontekommission *f.*

remount service Remontewesen *n.*

removable liner Futterrohr *n,* auswechselbares Seelenrohr *(G).*

removal of obstacles Beseitigung von Sperren.

remove abnehmen, ausbauen *(Mech).*

rendezvous Treffpunkt *m,* Versammlung *f,* Rendezvous *n.*

rendezvous point Versammlungsplatz *m.*

rental allowance Wohnungsgeldzuschuß *m.*

reorganization Reorganisation *f,* Umbildung *f.*

reorganize reorganisieren, umbilden.

repair *n* Instandsetzung *f,* Wiederherstellung *f.*

repair *v* instandsetzen, wiederherstellen, ausbessern.

repair and maintenance Instandsetzung und Unterhaltung.

repair hangar Werfthalle *f (Adrm).*

repair shop Instandsetzungswerkstätte *f.*

repair shop company Werkstattkompanie *f (Inf);* Panzerwerkstattkompanie *f (Armd Comd).*

repair shop truck Werkstattkraftwagen *m (MT).*

repatriation Heimbeförderung *f,* Heimsendung *f,* Repatriierung *f.*

repeat wiederholen; "Bitte wiederholen" *(Rad procedure).*

repeater compass Tochterkompaß *m (Ap).*

repeating coil Übertrager *m;* Ringübertrager *m (ring-through type),* *(Tg, Tp).*

repeating coil unit Übertragerkästchen *n (Tp).*

repeating theodolite Repetitions-Theodolit *m (Surv).*

repel abschlagen, abweisen *(Tac).*

replace ersetzen.

replacement *n* Ersatz *m,* Ersatzmann *m.*

replacement *adj* Ersatz-.

replacement center Ergänzungsstelle *f.*

replacement part Ersatzteil *m.*

replacements Ersatzmannschaften *fpl,* Ersatztruppen *fpl.*

replacement unit Ersatzeinheit *f.*

report *n* Bericht *m,* Meldung *f;* Knall *m (explosive sound);* Mündungsknall *m (produced by gun or muzzle wave),* Geschoßknall *m (produced by shell wave) (Sound Ranging).*

report *v* sich melden *(present oneself);* melden, berichten *(a message, etc.);* melden *(a person).*

report for duty sich zum Dienst melden.

report of approaching target. Einflugsmeldung *f (AWS).*

report of survey Ergebnis der Waffen- und Gerätuntersuchungen *(Ord).*

report sick sich krank melden.

reprimand Verweis *m.*

reprisal Vergeltung *f,* Vergeltungsmaßnahme *f.*

repulse *v* See **repel.**

request *n* Gesuch *n,* Antrag *m.*

request *v* bitten, erbitten, ansuchen, einen Antrag stellen.

request for deferment Zurückstellungsantrag *m.*

request for transfer Gesuch um Versetzung, Antrag auf Versetzung.

require erfordern, bedürfen.

requirements Bedarf *m (Ord);* Erfordernisse *npl.*

requisition *n* Anforderung *f,* Bestellung *f.*

requisition *v* anfordern *(Adm)*; beitreiben *(from civilians)*.
requisitioning Beitreibung *f*.
requisition number Anforderungszeichen *n*, Bestellnummer *f*.
requisition receipt Beitreibungsschein *m* *(for goods requisitioned from civilians)*.
requisition ticket Bestellschein *m*.
re-route umleiten.
rescind aufheben, für ungültig erklären.
rescue *n* Bergung *f*, Rettung *f*.
rescue personnel Rettungsleute *mpl*.
rescue service Rettungsdienst *m*.
rescue squad Rettungsmannschaft *f*; Rettungstrupp *m* *(CWS)*.
rescue vehicle Abschleppfahrzeug *n*.
rescue vessel Bergungsschiff *n*.
resection Rückwärtseinschneiden *n*, Rückwärtseinschnitt *m* *(Surv)*.
reserve Reserve *f* *(Tac)*; Haupttrupp *m* *(Adv or rear Gd of march column)*.
reserve officer Reserveoffizier *m*.
Reserve Officers' Training Corps Reserveoffiziere-Ausbildungskorps *n* *(USA)*.
reserve unit Reserveteil *m*, Ersatzteil *m*.
reservist Reservist *m* *(USA)*.
reservoir Stausee *m*, Reservoir *n*, Wasserreservoir *n* *(water supply)*; Behälter *m* *(container)*.
residence ständiger Wohnsitz.
resident Einwohner *m*.
residential quarter Wohnviertel *n*.
resistance Widerstand *m* *(Elec, Tac)*; Gegenwehr *f* *(Tac)*; Beständigkeit *f* *(of materials)*.
resistance to aging Alterungsbeständigkeit *f*.
resistance to corrosion Korrosionsbeständigkeit *f*.
resistance to heat Wärmebeständigkeit *f*.
resonance Resonanz *f*, Mitklingen *n* *(Rad)*.
resonant circuit Resonanzkreis *m* *(Rad)*.
respirator Staubmaske *f*, Staubschutzgerät *n*, Respirator *m*.
respirator bag Atemsack *m* *(oxygen breathing apparatus)*.
responsible verantwortlich.

responsibility Verantwortlichkeit *f*, Verantwortung *f*.
rest *n* Rast *f*, Marschrast *f* *(march column)*; Rest *m* *(remainder)*; Stütze *f* *(prop)*.
"Rest!" "Rührt Euch!"
rest group Rastgruppe *f* *(march rest)*.
resting command ruhende Truppe.
restitution Entzerrung *f* *(aerial Photo)*.
restricted nur für den Dienstgebrauch *(manuals, etc.)*.
restricted area Sperrgebiet *n*.
restriction Strafmaßnahme *f*, Verbot *n*.
result *n* Ergebnis *n*, Resultat *n*.
retainer Federteller *m* *(valve spring)* *(Mtr)*.
retaining catch Sperrklinke *f* *(breechlock)*.
retaining ring Sprengring *m* *(gas mask)*.
retaliate vergelten.
retaliation Vergeltung *f*.
retaliation attack Vergeltungsangriff *m*.
retaliation fire Erwiderungsfeuer *n*, Gegenfeuer *n*.
retard aufhalten *(stop)*; verlangsamen *(slow up)*; verzögern *(delay)*.
retardation Geschwindigkeitsänderung *f*, negative Beschleunigung *(Ballistics)*.
retarded ignition Spätzündung *f*.
retard spring Sperrfeder *f* *(fuze)*.
reticle Strichplatte *f* *(Optics)*.
reticle image Leuchtkreuz *n* *(reflector sight)*.
reticule See reticle.
retire den Rückzug antreten, sich zurückziehen.
retired im Ruhestand, außer Dienst.
retirement Rückmarsch *m*, Rückzug *m*, planmäßiger Rückzug *m* *(Tac)*; Ruhestand *m* *(from active service)*.
retirement route Rückzugslinie *f*, Rückzugsstraße *f* *(Tac)*.
retractable einziehbar.
retractable landing gear Einziehfahrgestell *n*, Einziehfahrwerk *n*, einziehbares Fahrgestell *(Ap)*.
retreading Reifenerneuerung *f*, Runderneuerung *f* *(MT)*.
retreat *n* Rückzug *m* *(Tac)*; Abend-Flaggenparade *f* *(service call)*.

retreat v zurückgehen, zurückweichen, sich zurückziehen.
retriever boat Rettungsboot n, Bergungsboot n.
retroactive rückwirkend.
retrograde Rück-, rückläufig.
retrograde march Rückmarsch m.
retrograde movement Rückmarschbewegung f.
return n Rückkehr f; Bericht m (report).
return flight Rückflug m (Avn).
return line Rückleitung f.
reveille Wecken n.
revenge n Rache f.
reverse n Rückschlag m (repulse); Niederlage f (defeat); Unglück n (misfortune); Rückseite f (opposite side); Rückwärtsgang m (MT).
reverse v umkehren.
reverse idler gear shaft Rücklaufwelle f (MT).
reverse movement Rückwärtsfahrt f (MT).
reverse slope Hinterhang m (Top).
reverse-slope position Hinterhangstellung f.
reverse speed Rückwärtsgang m(MT).
reversing gear Wendegetriebe n.
revet bekleiden, verkleiden.
revetment Bekleidung f (Ft).
review n Besichtigung f, Parade f.
revised neubearbeitet (manuals, etc.).
revision neubearbeitete Auflage (of a manual, etc.).
revolution Umdrehung f (Mech); Revolution f (political).
revolutions per minute Umdrehungen per Minute; Motorendrehzahl f, Drehzahl f.
revolve sich umdrehen.
revolver Revolver m (Small Arms).
revolver belt Revolvergurt m.
revolving armored turret Panzerdrehturm m (Ft).
revolving beacon light See revolving searchlight.
revolving searchlight Drehlichtscheinwerfer m (Avn).
revolving tank turret Panzerdrehturm m (Tk).
revolving turret Drehturm m, Drehkuppel f (Ap, Ft, Tk).
Reynolds number Reynoldszahl f (Aerodynamics).
r-f See radio frequency.
rheostat Schieberwiderstand m.

rhumb line Schieflaufende f, Loxodrome f (navigation).
rib Rippe f.
ribbed guide Führungsleiste f (breechblock).
ribbon Band n, Ordensband n.
ribbon microphone Bandmikrophon n.
ricochet n Abpraller m, Prallschuß m, Prellschuß n.
ricochet v abprallen.
ricochet fire Abprallerschießen n.
ride n Fahrt f (on vehicle); Ritt m (on animal).
ride v fahren (on vehicle); reiten (on animal).
ridge Kamm m, Rücken m, Höhenrippe f (Top).
ridge line Kammlinie f, Rückenlinie f (Top).
ridge soaring Hangsegeln n (glider).
riding boots Reitstiefel mpl.
riding horse Reitpferd n.
rifle Gewehr n (R); Rohr n (G).
rifle accessories Gewehrzubehör n.
rifle ammunition Gewehrmunition f.
rifle battalion Grenadierbataillon n, Schützenbataillon n.
rifle bullet Gewehrgeschoß n.
rifle butt Gewehrkolben m.
rifle company Grenadierkompanie f, Schützenkompanie f.
rifled gezogen (Ord).
rifle fire Gewehrfeuer n, Schützenfeuer n.
rifle grease Waffenfett n.
rifle grenade Gewehrgranate f.
rifle inspection Gewehrappell m.
rifleman Schütze m, Gewehrschütze m, Gewehrträger m; Grenadier m, Füsilier m (Inf rifleman).
rifle pit Schützenloch n, Schützenmulde f.
rifle platoon Zug m (Inf, Cav); Schützenzug m (Inf); Reiterzug m (H Cav).
rifle rack Gewehrstütze f, Gewehrmieke f, Gewehrmücke f.
rifle range Schießstand m, Gewehrschießstand m.
rifle regiment Grenadierregiment n, Schützenregiment n.
rifle scabbard Gewehrtragevorrichtung f (Cav).
rifle shot Gewehrschuß m.
rifle sling Gewehrriemen m.
rifle squad Gruppe f (Inf).
rifle stock Gewehrschaft m.

rifle unit Schützenverband *m*.
rifling Drall *m (Ord)*.
rifling grooves Drallzüge *mpl (Ord)*.
rigging band Ballongurt *m (Bln)*.
right recht, richtig; rechts *(to the right)*.
right angle rechter Winkel.
right bank Rechtskurve *f (Avn)*; rechtes Ufer *(of a stream)*.
"Right, face!" "Rechts, Um!"
right-hand thread Rechtsgewinde *n (MT)*.
right-hand twist Rechtsdrall *m (rifling)*.
right of way Vorfahrt *f*, Vorfahrtsrecht *n*, Vorfahrtserlaubnis *f*.
right-of-way regulations Vorfahrtregelung *f*.
"Right shoulder, arms!" "Das Gewehr, über!"
rigid airship starres Luftschiff.
rim Felge *f (MT)*; Hülsenrand *m (of cartridge case)*.
rim band Wulstband *n (MT)*.
rime ice Reif *m*.
ring *v* anläuten, rufen *(Tp)*.
ring and bead sight mechanisches Visier *(Ap)*.
ring cowling Ringverkleidung *f (Ap)*.
ring cradle Jackenwiege *f (G)*.
ringer Wecker *m (Tp)*.
ringing current Rufstrom *m (Tp)*.
ring off abrufen *(Tp)*.
ring sight Kreisvisier *n (Ord)*.
ingworm Ringelflechte *f*, Ringflechte *f*.
riot Aufruhr *m*.
rip *n* Riß *m*.
rip *v* reißen, aufreißen, abreißen, zerreißen.
rip cord Abreißschnur *f*, Reißleine *f (Bln, Prcht)*.
rip panel Reißbahn *f (Bln)*.
ripsaw Schrotsäge *f*.
rise *n* Bodenerhebung *f*, Anhöhe *f (Top)*.
river Fluß *m*, Strom *m*.
river bed Flußbett *n*.
river craft Stromfahrzeug *n*.
river crossing Flußübergang *m*.
river-crossing equipment Übersetzmittel *npl*, Werkzeug für Behelfsbrückenbau.
river reconnaissance Flußerkundung *f*.
river-width measuring instrument Flußbreitenmesser *m*.

rivet *n* Niete *f*.
rivet *v* nieten, vernieten.
riveted seam Niet *m*.
riveter Niethammer *m (tool)*.
riveting Nietung *f*; Sprengnietung *f (with explosive rivets)*.
road Straße *f*, Weg *m*.
roadbed Bahnkörper *m*, Bettung *f (RR)*.
road bend Wegebiegung *f*.
road block Straßensperre *f*, Wegsperre *f*.
roadbound straßengängig.
road capacity Kapazität *f*, Aufnahmefähigkeit einer Straße.
road center Straßenknotenpunkt *m (junction)*.
road clearance Bodenfreiheit *f (MT)*.
road conditions Straßenverhältnisse *npl*, Wegeverhältnisse *npl*.
road construction Straßenbau *m*, Wegebau *m*.
road curve Wegebiegung *f*.
road discipline Straßenzucht *f*, Straßendisziplin *f*.
road ditch Straßengraben *m*.
road fork Straßengabel *f*.
road grader and tamper Bodenverdichter *m (Engr)*.
road hole Schlagloch *n (MT)*.
road intersection Wegekreuzung *f*.
road jam Marschstockung *f*.
road junction Straßenspinne *f*, Spinne *f*, Straßenknotenpunkt *m*.
road metal Schotter *m*.
road net Straßennetz *n*, Wegenetz *n*.
road reconnaissance Wegeerkundung *f*.
road roller Straßenwalze *f*, Chausseewalze *f*.
road rule Verkehrsregel *f*.
road screen Straßentarnung *f (Cam)*.
road sign Richtungsschild *n*.
road space Marschlänge *f*, Marschtiefe *f (march column)*.
road surface Straßendecke *f*.
road traction Bodenhaftung *f (MT)*.
roadway Fahrbahn *f*; Brückenbahn *f (Bdg)*.
roadway girder Fahrbahnträger *m (Bdg)*.
rock *n* Fels *m (geology)*; Felsblock *m (boulder)*; Stein *m (stone)*.
rock-blasting explosive Gesteinsprengmittel *n*.
rocker arm Kipphebel *m (Mtr)*.
rocket Rakete *f*.

rocket-assisted take-off Raketenstart *m (Avn)*.

rocket bomb Raketenbombe *f (Avn)*.

rocketeer *See* rocket gunner.

rocket gunner Raketenschütze *m*.

rocket launcher Raketenwurfmaschine *f;* Panzer-Raketenbüchse *f (AT)*.

rocket mortar Werfer *m*, Nebelwerfer *m*.

rocket projector Raketenwurfmaschine *f*.

rocket propulsion Raketenantrieb *m*.

rod Stab *m*.

rod antenna Stabantenne *f (Rad)*.

roll *n* Trommelwirbel *m*, Wirbel *m (drum);* Rolle *f (Avn);* Stammrolle *f (list);* Schlingern *n (Nav, Avn)*.

roll *v* rollen; anrollen *(along runway on take-off run)*.

roll back aufrollen *(Tac)*.

roll by vorbeirollen.

roll call Appell *m*.

roller Rolle *f*, Walze *f*.

roller bearing Rollenlager *n*.

roller bumper Abfangwalze *f*, Kletterwalze *f (MT)*.

roll film Rollfilm *m*.

roll-film camera Filmkammer *f*.

rolling barrage Feuerwalze *f*.

rolling kitchen Feldküche *f*, Fahrküche *f*.

rolling mill Walzwerk *n*.

rolling stock rollendes Material *(RR)*.

roll up aufrollen *(Tac)*.

roof Dach *n*.

roof antenna Dachantenne *f*.

roofing paper Dachpappe *f*.

room Zimmer *n (in a house);* Raum *m (space)*.

root Wurzel *f*.

rope Seil *n*, Strick *m*, Schnur *f*, Leine *f*, Tau *n*.

rope ferry Seilfähre *f*, Zugfähre *f*.

rope ladder Strickleiter *f*.

rope lashing Schnürbund *n*, Leinenbund *n (Engr)*.

roster Kommandierrolle *f*.

rotary engine Umlaufmotor *m (Ap)*.

rotary snowplow Schneefräsmaschine *f*.

rotary sweeper Aufrauhbürste *f (road construction)*.

rotate umlaufen, rotieren, sich drehen.

rotating band Führungsring *m*, Führungsband *n (Am)*.

rotating beacon Drehlichtsignal *n*.

rotating crank Drehkurbel *f*.

rotation Drehbewegung *f (Ballistics)*.

rotations per minute Umdrehungszahl *f*.

rotor Anker *m (Elec)*.

rotor airplane Drehflügelflugzeug *n*.

rotor-type valve Drehschieber *m (Mech)*.

rough ground unebenes Gelände.

round *n* Patrone *f (fixed Am);* Schuß *m (Am);* vollständiger Schuß *(complete round)*.

round *adj* rund.

roundhouse Lokomotivschuppen *m (RR)*.

round timber Rundholz *n*.

rout *n* wilde Flucht, regellose Flucht.

route *n* Route *f*, Strecke *f*, Weg *m*, Straße *f*.

route *v* leiten, regeln.

route column Marschkolonne *f (MT)*.

route formation gelöste Flugordnung *(Avn)*.

route march Marschieren ohne Tritt.

route of advance Vormarschstraße *f*.

route of approach Anmarschstraße *f*, Anmarschweg *m*, Annäherungsweg *m*.

route of march Marschweg *m*.

route reconnaissance Straßenaufklärung *f*.

route step Marschieren ohne Tritt.

"Route step, march!" "Ohne Tritt, Marsch!"

routine message gewöhnliche Meldung.

routine order Dienstbefehl *m*.

routine radio message Betriebsfunkspruch *m*.

roving gun Arbeitsgeschütz *n (Arty)*.

rowboat Ruderboot *n*.

rpm Umdr./Min.; U/Min. *(Umdrehungen per Minute)*.

rub reiben.

rubber Gummi *m-n*, Kautschuk *m;* Radiergummi *m (eraser)*.

rubber band Gummiband *n*.

rubber block Gummipolster *n (caterpillar track)*.

rubber cable Gummikabel *n (Tp)*.

rubber coating Gummierung *f*.

rubberized material Gummistoff *m*.

rubber-tired wheel Gummirad *n*.

rubber track Gummigleiskette *f (Tk)*.

rubber truncheon Gummiknüppel *m*.

rubble Steinschlag *m.*
rucksack Rucksack *m.*
rudder Seitenruder *n (Ap);* Steuerruder *n (Nav).*
rudder assembly Seitenleitwerk *n (Ap).*
rudder lobe Steuersack *m (Bln).*
ruffles gedämpfter Trommelwirbel.
rule Regel *f,* Vorschrift *f,* Ordnung *f.*
Rules of Land Warfare Landkriegsordnung *f.*
rules of war Kriegsrecht *n.*
rumor Gerücht *n.*
run *n* Lauf *m,* Gang *m (Mech);* waagerechter Anflug *(Avn).*
run *v* rennen, laufen; fahren, rollen *(vehicles);* laufen *(Mech);* führen *(drive, manage).*
run aground auflaufen, auffahren, auf den Grund laufen.

runner Fußmelder *m,* Läufer *m,* Meldeläufer *m (messenger);* Kufe *f (sled).*
runner surface Lauffläche *f (sled).*
running board Trittbrett *n (MT).*
running fight laufendes Gefecht.
running gear Fahrwerk *n,* Laufwerk *n,* Räderwerk *n (MT, Tk).*
running light Seitenlicht *n,* Positionslicht *n (Ap).*
runway Laufbahn *f,* Startbahn *f,* Landebahn *f,* Ablaufbahn *f (Adrm).*
runway localizer beacon Landefunkfeuer *n (Rad).*
rupture Bruch *m,* Riß *m.*
rural police Gendarmerie *f.*
ruse Kriegslist *f (Tac).*
rush *v* erstürmen, vorprellen *(Tac).*
by rushes sprungweise.
rust Rost *m.*
rusty rostig, verrostet.
rut Fahrrinne *f,* Spur *f.*

S

saber Säbel *m.*
sabotage Sabotage *f.*
saboteur Saboteur *m.*
saddle Sattel *m (harness) (Top);* Bergjoch *n (Top).*
saddlebag Packtasche *f.*
saddle blanket Woilach *m.*
saddle cover Satteltracht *f,* Tracht *f (for pack saddle).*
saddle covering Sattelbekleidung *f.*
saddle pad Trachtenkissen *n,* Sattelkissen *n.*
saddler Sattler *m.*
saddletree Sattelbaum *m (harness).*
safe gesichert, sicher.
put at safe sichern *(a pistol, etc.).*
safe altitude Sicherheitshöhe *f (Avn).*
safe-conduct Passierschein *m.*
safeguard Schutzschein *m (document);* Schutzwache *f (guard).*
safety Sicherung *f (Small Arms).*
safety angle Erhöhung einschließich der Sicherheitsteilstriche *(overhead firing).*
safety area Sicherheitszone *f (Arty).*
safety belt Anschnallgurt *m (Avn).*

safety cap Sicherungskappe *f (hand grenade).*
safety catch Sperrklinke *f (Mech).*
safety device Sicherungsvorrichtung *f;* Sicherungskappe *f (fuze).*
safety factor Sicherheitskoeffizient *m.*
safety fuze Leitfeuer *n,* Zeitzündschnur *f (Engr).*
safety glass Sicherheitsglas *n.*
safety lever Sicherungshebel *m (pistol).*
safety limit Grenze des Sicherheitsbereiches *(practice firing).*
safety lock Sicherung *f (fuze).*
safety measure Sicherheitsmaßnahme *f.*
safety officer Sicherheitsoffizier *m.*
safety of operation Betriebssicherheit *f (Mech).*
safety pin Sicherungsvorstecker *m,* Vorstecker *m (bombs, mines, etc.);* Sicherungsstift *m (fuze);* Sicherheitsnadel *f (Clo).*
safety pointing observer Sicherheitsunteroffizier *m (practice firing).*
safety regulations Sicherheitsbestimmungen *fpl.*

safety spark gap Sicherheitsfunkenstrecke *f* (*magneto ignition*).
safety wire Sicherheitsdraht *m* (*Ord*).
safety zone gedeckter Raum (*firing*).
sag Durchhang *m*.
sailor Matrose *m*, Seemann *m*.
sailplane Segelflugzeug *n*, Segelflieger *m* (*Avn*).
sales article Marketenderware *f* (*at PX*).
salient Frontvorsprung *m*, Vorsprung *m*, Kniestellung *f*, Knie *n*, Ausbuchtung *f* (*Tac*); ausspringender Winkel (*Ft*).
sally Ausfall *m* (*Tac*).
salt Salz *n*.
saltpeter Salpeter *m*.
salt tablet Kochsalztablette *f*.
salt-water resistant seewasserbeständig.
salute *n* Ehrenbezeugung *f*; Gruß *m* (*hand salute*); Salut *m* (*G*).
salute *v* Ehrenbezeugung erweisen, grüßen.
saluting distance Grußweite *f*.
saluting gun Salutgeschütz *n*.
salvage *n* Bergung *f*, Bergen *n*.
salvage *v* sammeln, bergen.
salvage collecting Sammeltätigkeit *f*.
salvage collecting service Bergedienst *m*.
salvage dump Gerätsammelstelle *f*; Beutestelle *f* (*for enemy matériel*).
salvage service Sammelwesen *n*.
salvage vessel Bergungsschiff *n*.
salvo Lage *f* (*pieces fire in succession*); Salve *f* (*pieces fire simultaneously*).
salvo fire Lagenfeuer *n*.
salvo release Massenabwurf *m*, Schüttwurf *m* (*bombing*).
Sam Browne belt Leibgurt mit Schulterriemen.
sandbag Sandsack *m* (*Ft*).
sandpaper Sandpapier *n*.
sand pit Sandgrube *f*.
sand table Sandkasten *m* (*Tng*).
sand-table exercise Sandkastenspiel *n* (*Tng*).
sand-table instruction Sandkastenunterricht *m* (*Tng*).
sanitary sanitär, gesundheitlich, Gesundheits-.
Sanitary Corps Gesundheitsdienst *m*.
sanitary inspector Sanitätsinspekteur *m*.

sanitary survey Erkundung der hygienischen Verhältnisse eines Gebietes.
sap Sappe *f* (*Ft*).
sap end *See* saphead.
saphead Sappenkopf *m*, Grabenkopf *m* (*Ft*).
saturation Sättigung *f* (*Met*).
sausage Wurst *f*.
saw Säge *f*.
sawhorse ramp obstacle Rampensperre *f* (*Engr*).
sawmill Sägewerk *n*.
scabbard Scheide *f* (*saber, bayonet*); Futteral *n* (*saber*); Tragevorrichtung *f* (*R*).
scaffold Baugerüst *n*, Gerüst *n*.
scale Skala *f*, Einteilung *f*; Maßstab *m* (*proportion*); Lineal *n* (*ruler*).
according to scale maßstabgerecht.
scale disk Skalenscheibe *f* (*Rad*.)
scalp Kopfhaut *f*.
scar Narbe *f*.
scarp Böschung *f* (*Top*).
scatter bomb Streubrandbombe *f*.
scattered heiter (*Met*).
scattering of fire Zersplitterung des Feuers (*Arty*).
schedule Zeittafel *f*.
scheduled maintenance regelmäßig durchgeführte Instandsetzung.
schedule fire vorbereitetes Feuer (*Arty*).
scheme Plan *m*.
scheme of maneuver Gefechtsplan *m*, Operationsplan *m*.
school Schule *f*.
scoop Schöpfeimer *m* (*excavator*).
scorched earth tactics Brand- und Asche-Taktik *f*.
score *n* Trefferergebnis *n* (*firing or bombing*).
score *v* Treffer erzielen, Treffer verzeichnen (*to score hits*).
score book Schießbuch *n*.
scotch tape Klebestreifen *m*.
scour Auskolkung *f*, Kolk *m*, Furche *f* (*in river bed*).
scout *n* Späher *m*, Erkunder *m*.
scout *v* spähen, erkunden, aufklären (*Tac*); aufklären (*Nav, Avn*).
scout bomber Seeaufklärer *m*.
scout car Spähwagen *m*; leichter Panzerspähwagen (*Armd*).
scout car platoon Aufklärungszug *m*.
scouting party Spähtrupp *m*.

scouting raid Erkundungsvorstoß m, Spähtruppvorstoß m.
scout vehicle Erkundungsfahrzeug n.
scraper Kratze f (Engr).
scrap metal Altmetall n.
screen n Schleier m, Aufklärungsschleier m, Sicherungsschleier m (Tac); Maske f (Cam); Drahtnetz n (wire); Sieb n (sifter).
screen v verschleiern (Tac).
screen grid Schirmgitter n (Rad).
screen-grid tube Schirmgitterröhre f (Rad).
screening Tarnung f, Verschleierung f (Cam); Vernebelung f (smoke).
screening agent Nebelstoff m (CWS).
screening force Verschleierungsabteilung f (Tac).
screening smoke künstlicher Nebel (CWS).
screw Schraube f.
screwdriver Schraubenzieher m.
screw pitch gage Gewindeschablone f.
scriber Reißnadel f.
scud roll Böenkragen m (Met).
sculling Wriggeln n.
sea See f, Meer n.
seacoast Küste f, Meeresküste f.
seacoast gun Küstengeschütz n.
seal n Siegel n, Stempel m.
seal v dichten (Mech); siegeln, versiegeln (documents, etc.).
sealed orders versiegelte Anordnung, versiegelter Befehl.
sea level Meeresspiegel m, Meereshöhe f.
sealing band Dichtlinie f (gas mask).
sealing frame Dichtrahmen m (gas mask).
sealing pitch Pech n.
seaman Matrose m (apprentice seaman).
seaman first class Matrosenobergefreiter m; Matrosenhauptgefreiter m (highest rated, with 4½ years seniority).
seaman second class Matrosengefreiter m.
sea mile See nautical mile.
seaplane Seeflugzeug n, Wasserflugzeug n, Seeflieger m.
seaplane base Seefliegerhorst m.
seaplane tender Flugzeugmutterschiff n, Flugzeugtender m.
sear Abzugsstollen m (R); Abzugsstange f (pistol); Spannstück n (G).

search v suchen, absuchen, durchsuchen.
searching and traversing fire Breitenfeuer mit Tiefenfeuer (MG).
searching fire Tiefenfeuer n (MG).
searching sector Beobachtungsraum m, Luftraumausschnitt m (AAA).
searchlight Scheinwerfer m.
searchlight battalion Scheinwerferabteilung f (AAA).
searchlight battery Scheinwerferbatterie f.
searchlight station Scheinwerferstellung f (AAA).
search patrol method Luftabwehr durch Jagdpatrouillen (Avn).
sea rescue airplane Seenotflugzeug n.
sear nose Abzugsstollen m (R).
sear spring Abzugsfeder f (R).
seat Sitz m; Sattelsitz m (saddle).
seating of projectile Geschoßführung f (Ballistics).
seat pack parachute Sitzfallschirm m.
seat strap Sitzriemen m (saddle).
seat-type parachute Sitzfallschirm m.
secant Schnittlinie f.
second Sekunde f (time); an zweiter Stelle, zweit (in order).
secondary air Nebenluft f (Mtr).
secondary attack Nebenangriff m.
secondary circuit Nebenstromkreis m, Sekundärkreis m (Rad).
secondary current Sekundärstrom m (Rad).
secondary effort Nebenangriff m (Tac).
secondary objective Ausweichsziel n (bombing).
secondary operations Nebenoperationen fpl (Tac).
second-in-command stellvertretender Führer.
second lieutenant Leutnant m; Panzerleutnant m (Armd Comd); Leutnant der Flieger (Luftwaffe); Assistenzarzt m (Med); Veterinär m (Vet).
secrecy Geheimhaltung f, Verschwiegenheit f.
secret n Geheimnis n.
secret adj geheim.
secretary Sekretär m, Sekretärin f.
Secretary of War Kriegsminister m (USA).
secret code Geheimschlüssel m.
secret text verschlüsselter Text, geschlüsselter Text, Geheimtext m.

section Staffel *f* *(Arty, Cav)*; Halbzug *m*, MG-Halbzug *m* *(of MG platoon)*; Gruppe *f* *(Cav)*; Granatwerfergruppe *f* *(Mort section)*; Abteilung *f* *(Adm department)*; Schnitt *m* *(cut or sectional view)*; Brückenglied *n* *(Bdg)*; Zelle *f* *(Ap)*.

sectional antenna mast Steckmast *m* *(Rad)*.

sectional liner geteiltes Seelenrohr *(G)*.

section leader Gruppenführer *m* *(Cav)*; Staffelführer *m* *(Cav MG section)*; Halbzugführer *m* *(MG section)*.

section personnel Staffeltrupp *m* *(Cav MG section)*.

section security officer Offizier vom Ortsdienst.

sector Abschnitt *m*, Streifen *m*, Raum *m* *(Tac)*.

sector boundary Abschnittsgrenze *f*.

sector of fire Beobachtungs- und Wirkungsstreifen *m*, Zielraum *m*, Zielabschnitt *m* *(Small Arms)*.

sector reserve Abschnittsreserve *f*.

security Sicherung *f* *(Tac)*.

security detachment Sicherung *f*.

security measure Sicherungsmaßnahme *f*.

security mission Sicherungsauftrag *m* *(Tac)*.

security on the march Marschsicherung *f*.

security patrol(s) Sicherer *mpl* *(Tac)*.

sedative *n* beruhigendes Mittel.

sedition Aufruhr *f*, Aufstand *m*; Meuterei *f* *(mutiny)*.

segregate absondern.

seize sich festfressen *(piston)* *(Mtr)*.

seizure Festnahme *f* *(arrest)*; Einnahme *f* *(of a locality)*; Beschlagnahme *f* *(confiscation)*.

selectee Ausgehobener *m*.

Selective Service Act Wehrpflichtgesetz *n* *(USA)*.

selectivity Trennschärfe *f* *(Rad)*.

selector Wähler *m* *(swtichboard mechanism)*.

selector disk Wahlscheibe *f* *(switchboard mechanism)*.

selector switch Umschalter *m* *(Elec)*; Auslesenknopf *m* *(aircraft armament control)*.

self-destroying fuze Zerlegerzünder *m* *(AA Am)*.

self-exciting selbsterregend *(Rad)*.

self-government Selbstverwaltung *f* *(PW)*.

self-induction Selbstinduktion *f (Elec)*.

self-induction coil Selbstinduktionsspule *f* *(Elec)*.

self-loading pistol Selbstladepistole *f*.

self-loading rifle Selbstladegewehr *n*, Selbstlader *m*.

self-loading weapon Selbstladewaffe *f*.

self-locking differential gear selbstsperrendes Ausgleichgetriebe *(MT)*.

self-mutilation Selbstverstümmelung *f*.

self-propelled auf Selbstfahrlafette.

self-propelled gun Geschütz auf Selbstfahrlafette.

self-propelled mount Selbstfahrlafette *f*.

self-propulsion Selbstantrieb *m*.

self-sealing selbstdichtend.

self-seal tank geschützer Behälter.

semaphore flag Winkflagge *f*.

semiautomatic Selbstlade-, halbautomatisch.

semiautomatic fire Einzelfeuer *n*.

semiautomatic rifle Selbtladegewehr *n*.

semiautomatic weapon Selbstladewaffe *f*.

semicantilever halbfreitragend.

semifixed cartridge Hülsenkartusche *f*.

semiflat-base rim Halbflachbettfelge *f*, Halbflachfelge *f* *(MT)*.

semihigh-wing monoplane Schulterdecker *m*.

semi-motorized teilmotorisiert.

semiparabolic truss Halbparabel-Fachwerkträger *m* *(Bdg)*.

semirigid airship halbstarres Luftschiff.

semi-smokeless rauchschwach.

semitrailer Sattelschlepper *m* *(MT)*.

send schicken, senden; aufgeben *(a telegram, etc.)*; funken, senden *(Rad)*; tasten *(key Rad)*.

sending key Taste *f* *(Tg)*; Drucktaster *m* *(Sig lamp)*.

senior Rangältester *m*; Dienstältester *m*.

seniority Dienstalter *n*; Rangdienstalter *n* *(age-in-grade)*.

senior officer Rangältester *m*.

senior pilot Flugzeugführer mit über fünf Dienstjahren.

sense *n* Sinn *m*.

sense *v* die Abweichung der Schüsse vom Ziel beobachten *(Gunnery)*.

sense of direction Ortsgedächtnis *n*.

sensing Schußbeobachtung *f (Arty)*; Seitenbestimmung *f (Rad Direction Finding)*.

sensing antenna Hilfsantenne *f (Rad direction finder)*.

sensitive empfindlich; stoßempfindlich *(to shock)*; lichtempfindlich *(to light)*.

sensitive altimeter Feinhöhenmesser *m (Ap)*.

sentence of confinement Freiheitsstrafe *f*.

sentence of confinement to a penitentiary Zuchthausstrafe *f*.

sentence of confinement to a prison Gefängnisstrafe *f*.

sentry Posten *m*, Wachposten *m*.

sentry box Schilderhaus *n*.

separate-loading ammunition getrennte Munition, Kartuschmunition *f*.

separator Scheider *m (storage battery)*.

sequence of events Verlauf *m (Tac)*.

sergeant Unteroffizier *m*.

sergeant major *See* regimental sergeant major.

sergeant of the guard dienstältester Unteroffizier der Wache *(interior guard)*.

serial number laufende Nummer.

series circuit Kreisleitung *f (Elec)*.

series connection Hauptschlußschaltung *f*, Hintereinanderschaltung *f*, Reihenschaltung *f (Elec)*.

series motor Hauptschlußmotor *m (Elec)*.

series-parallel connection Gruppenschaltung *f (Elec)*.

serious casualty Schwerverwundeter *m*.

serum Serum *n*.

service *n* Dienst *m*; Wartung *f (maintenance)*.

service *v* warten *(Ap, MT)*.

service cap Schirmmütze *f*.

service ceiling Dienstgipfelhöhe *f*, Volltraghöhe *f (Avn)*.

service coat Feldbluse *f*.

service color Waffenfarbe *f*.

Service Command Wehrkreis *m*.

service commander Wehrkreisbefehlshaber *m*, kommandierender General eines Wehrkreises.

service company Nachschub- und Instandhaltungskompanie *f (USA)*.

service gas mask Dienstmaske *f*.

service manual Dienstvorschrift *f*.

service of the piece Geschützbedienung *f*, Bedienung *f*.

service of the piece drill Geschützexerzieren *n*.

service personnel Bodenpersonal *n (Avn)*.

service pilot Transportflieger *m*.

service practice Ausbildungsschießen *n (Arty)*.

service record Wehrstammbuch *n*.

service regulation Dienstvorschrift *f*.

Services of Supply *See* Army Service Forces.

service status Wehrdienstverhältnis *n*.

service stripe Ärmelborte für je drei Dienstjahre *(USA)*.

service troop Nachschub- und Instandhaltungsschwadron eines Kavallerieregiments *(USA)*.

service uniform Dienstanzug *m*.

service with troops Truppendienst *m*, Dienst bei der Truppe.

servicing Wartung *f*.

servo action Servowirkung *f (servo brake) (MT)*.

servo control Hilfsvorrichtung *f*, Servomotor *m*, Trimmklappe *f (Ap)*.

servo tab Trimmklappe *f (Ap)*.

sesquiplane Anderthalbdecker *m*, Eineinhalbdecker *m (Ap)*.

set *v* einstellen, verstellen *(adjust)*; setzen, stellen *(place)*.

setback Rückstoß *m (Tech)*; Rückschlag *m (Tac)*.

set-forward point Vorhaltepunkt *m (Gunnery)*.

setscrew Klemmschraube *f*, Grenzschraube *f*.

setting Einstellung *f (adjusting)*; Ablesung *f (reading)*.

setting-up exercise Freiübung *f*.

sextant Sextant *m*.

shackle Schäkel *m (chain)*; Federlasche *f (vehicle spring)*; Tragvorrichtung *f (Ap bomb rack)*.

shadow Schatten *m*.

shadow effect Schattenwirkung *f (Cam)*.

shaft Welle *f (Mech)*; Schacht *m (mining)*; Deichsel *f (wagon)*.

shallow seicht *(water)*; flach *(container)*.

shallow trench Kriechgraben *m*.

sham battle Scheingefecht *n*.

shank Ankerrute *f (of an anchor)*.

shape Form *f*, Gestalt *f*.

sharp scharf *(blade)*; spitz *(point)*.
sharpen schärfen; schleifen *(grind)*; wetzen, abziehen *(hone)*; spitzen, zuspitzen *(a point)*.
sharpness Schärfe *f*.
sharpness of resonance Abstimmschärfe *f (Rad)*.
sharpshooter Scharfschütze *m*.
sharp turn kurze Kehrtwendung, Turn *m (Avn)*.
shatter splittern, zersplittern.
shatterproof glass splittersicheres Glas, Sicherheitsglas *n*.
shaving cream Rasiercreme *f*.
shaving soap Rasierseife *f*.
sheaf Garbe *f (Ballistics)*.
sheaf of fire Feuergarbe *f*, Geschoßgarbe *f*, Schußgarbe *f*.
shear *n* Abscheren *n*, Abscherung *f*.
shear lashing Kreuzbund *m (for diagonal timbers)*.
shears Schere *f (Inst)*.
shear strength Scherfestigkeit *f*.
shear stress Scherspannung *f*.
shear wire Scherdraht *m (fuze)*.
shed Schuppen *m*.
sheet Bogen *m*, Blatt *n*, *(paper)*; Bettuch *n*, Leintuch *n (bed)*; Blech *n (metal)*; Schicht *f (coating or layer)*; Kartenblatt *n (map)*.
sheet metal Blech *n*.
sheet-metal case Eisenblechgehäuse *n*, Blechgehäuse *n (Rad)*.
sheet steel Stahlblech *n*.
shell *n* Granate *f (Am)*; Zünderhalter *m (blasting cap)*; Hülse *f (casing)*.
shell *v* mit Artillerie beschießen, unter Artilleriefeuer nehmen, mit Artilleriefeuer belegen.
shellac Schellack *m*.
shell case Granathülse *f (Am)*.
shell cavity Geschoßhöhlung *f (Am)*.
shell crater Granattrichter *m*.
shell filler Granatfüllung *f (Am)*.
shell fragment Sprengstück *n*.
shell hoist Munitionsaufzug *m*.
shell hole Granatloch *n*.
shellproof bombensicher *(heavy)*; schußsicher *(light)*.
shellproof cover bombensichere Deckung *(heavy)*, schußsichere Deckung *(light) (Ft)*.
shellshock *See* battle fatigue.
shell splinter Granatsplitter *m*.
shell wave Kopfwelle *f (Ballistics)*.

shelter Deckung *f (cover)*; Unterstand *m*, Schutzraum *m (Ft)*; Unterkunft *f (billets)*; Luftschutzraum *m (air raid)*.
shelter area Unterkunftsbezirk *m*, Unterkunftsraum *m*.
shelter half Zeltbahn *f*.
sheltering Unterbringung *f*.
shelter tent Zelt *n*.
shield Schild *m*, Brustschild *m*, Schutzschild *m (G)*.
shielding Abschirmung *f (Rad)*.
shield support Schildstütze *f (G)*.
shift *n* Schicht *f (of workmen)*; Feuerverlegen *n (of fire)*.
shift *v* schalten *(MT)*; verlegen, verschieben, versetzen *(move)*.
shifter fork Schaltgabel *f (MT)*.
shift rail Schaltstange *f (MT)*.
shim Lamelle *f (Mech)*; Futterholz *n (Engr)*.
shimmying Flattern *n (MT)*.
shin Schienbein *n*.
shine *v* leuchten, glänzen *(glisten)*; putzen *(to polish)*.
ship Schiff *n*.
ship-based antiaircraft artillery Schiffsflak *f*.
shipboard airplane Bordflugzeug *n*.
shipboard antiaircraft artillery Bordflak *f (Nav)*.
shipboard reconnaissance airplane Bordaufklärer *m*.
shipbuilding Schiffbau *m*.
shipbuilding yard Schiffswerft *f*, Schiffbauwerft *f*.
ship concentration Schiffsansammlung *f*.
shipment Lieferung *f*, Sendung *f*, Versand *m*.
shipment-safe fuze transportsicherer Zünder *(Am)*.
shipping Schiffahrt *f*, Schiffswesen *n (Nav)*.
shipping ticket Lieferschein *m*.
shipwreck Schiffbruch *m*.
shipyard Werft *f*, Schiffswerft *f*.
shipyard installation Werftanlage *f*.
shirt Hemd *n*.
shoals Untiefen *fpl*.
shock Stoß *m*; Schock *m (Med)*; Schlag *m (Elec)*.
shock absorber Stoßdämpfer *m (MT)*.
shock-absorbing strut Federbein *n (Ap)*.
shock power Stoßkraft *f*.
shock strut Flugzeugbein *n (Ap)*.

shock troops Stoßtruppen *fpl.*
shoe Schuh *m (Clo, Tech);* Decke *f (tire);* Kettenglied *n (Trac);* Backe *f,* Klotz *m (brake);* Hufeisen *n (of horse).*
shoe brake Backenbremse *f (MT).*
shoeing Hufbeschlag *m (horse).*
shoelace Schnürsenkel *m.*
shoot schießen, feuern.
shoot down abschießen.
shooting gallery Schießhalle *f,* gedeckte Bahn.
shop Werkstatt *f (Tech);* Laden *m (store).*
shop foreman Werkmeister *m.*
shore Ufer *n (bank);* Küste *f (coast);* Strand *m (beach);* Land *n (land).*
shore anchor line Landankertau *n.*
shore battery Küstenbatterie *f (Arty).*
shore sill Uferbalken *m (Bdg).*
shoreward ponton Landfahrzeug *n.*
shoreward side Landbord *m.*
short *n* Kurzschuß *m (Gunnery);* Kurzschluß *m (Elec).*
short *adj* kurz.
shortage Fehlbestand *m.*
short circuit Kurzschluß *m (Elec).*
short range nächste Entfernung *(up to 100 meters);* nahe Entfernung *(up to 400 meters).*
shorts kurze Unterhose *(Clo).*
short wave Kurzwelle *f (Rad).*
short-wave switch Wellenstufenschalter *m (Rad).*
short-wave transmitter Kurzwellensender *m.*
shot *n* Schuß *m (discharge of fire-arms);* Schrot *m (for shotgun);* Vollgeschoß *n (solid projectile).*
shot group Zieldreieck *n (marksmanship Tng);* Einschlagsgruppe *f (Arty).*
shotgun Flinte *f,* Schrotgewehr *n.*
shotgun shell Schrotpatrone *f.*
shot pattern *See* shot group.
shoulder *n* Schulter *f;* Sommerweg *m (of road).*
shoulder *v* schultern *(rifle, etc.).*
shoulder arms das Gewehr übernehmen.
shoulder blade Schulterblatt *n.*
shoulder loop Schulterstück *n (officers),* Schulterklappe *f (enlisted men, Ger).*
shoulder piece Schulterstück *n (MG).*

shoulder stock Schulterstütze *f (MG).*
shoulder strap Schultergurt *m (gas mask carrier). See also* shoulder loop.
shovel Schaufel *f,* Schippe *f (hand);* Bagger *m,* Löffelbagger *m (power);* Spaten *m (spade).*
shower Regenschauer *m,* Regenguß *m (Met).*
shower bath Duschanlage *f.*
shower-bath truck Badewagen *m.*
shrapnel Schrapnell *n (Am).*
shrapnel ball Schrapnellkugel *f (Am).*
shroud line Fangleine *f (Prcht).*
shrubbery screen Strauchmaske *f (Cam).*
shunt Nebenschluß *m (Elec).*
shunt motor Nebenschlußmotor *m (Elec).*
shut-off valve Abstellhahn *m.*
shutter Weckerfallklappe *f (Tp);* Blende *f (Tk, searchlight, camera).*
shutter cover Blendabdeckung *f (Tk).*
shutter lever Blendenhebel *m (searchlight).*
shuttle traffic Pendelverkehr *m.*
sick krank.
sick bay Schiffslazarett *n (Nav).*
sick call Krankenappell *m.*
go on sick call sich krank melden.
sick leave Krankenurlaub *m.*
sick report book Krankenmeldebuch *n,* Krankenbuch *n.*
side Seite *f.*
sidecar Beiwagen *m,* Seitenwagen *m.*
sidecar motorcycle Beiwagenkrad *n,* Beiwagenmaschine *f.*
sidecar rider Beifahrer *m (Mtcl).*
side door Seitenklappe *f (Tk).*
sidelap seitliche Überdeckung *(aerial Photo).*
side-loading ramp Seitenrampe *f.*
side of receiver Kastenwand *f (MG).*
side outrigger Seitenholm *m (AA gun).*
side plate Lafettenwand *f (G carriage).*
siderail Rödelbalken *m (Bdg).*
siderail clamp Rödelzange *f (Bdg).*
side slip seitliches Abrutschen *(Avn).*
side spillway Umlauf *m (dam).*
side spray seitlicher Sprengkegel *(air burst).*
side street Nebenstraße *f,* Seitenstraße *f.*

sidetone circuit Mithöreinrichtung *f* (*Rad, Tp*).

side view Seitenansicht *f*.

side view flight Vorbeiflug *m* (*AA*).

sidewise-striking projectile Bauchtreffer *m*.

siding Ausweichgleis *n*, Ausweichstelle *f*, Nebengleis *n*, Überholungsgleis *f* (*for passing*) (*RR*).

siege Belagerung *f*.

siege warfare Festungskrieg *m*.

Siegfried Line *See* **West Wall.**

sight *n* Visier *n*, Zielgerät *n* (*Ord*); Gesichtssinn *m* (*sense*).

sight *v* visieren, anvisieren; zielen, anzielen (*aim*); anrichten (*point*); erblicken (*see*).

sight adjustment rod Aufsatzstange *f* (*G*).

sight assembly Visiereinrichtung *f*.

sight base Visierfuß *m*.

sight bracket Visierträger *m*, Aufsatzträger *m* (*Ord*).

sight defilade Sichtdeckung *f*.

sight equipment Richtgerät *n* (*G*).

sight extension Verlängerungsstück *n* (*G sight*).

sight in anschießen.

sighting device Visiereinrichtung *f*.

sighting disk Ziellöffel *m*.

sighting level Nivellierlibelle *f* (*plane table*).

sighting mechanism Zieleinrichtung *f*, Visiereinrichtung *f*, Visiervorrichtung *f*, Zielgerät *n* (*Ord*).

sighting shot Anschuß *m*.

sighting-triangle aiming exercise Dreieckzielen *n* (*Gunnery*).

sight leaf Visierklappe *f* (*Small Arms*).

sight mount Aufsatz *m*, Richtaufsatz *m*.

sight-mount bracket Richtaufsatzträger *m*.

sight-mount housing Aufsatzgehäuse *n* (*G*).

sight notch Kimme *f* (*MG, R*).

sight peephole Fenster *n* (*AA sight*).

sight-port cover Visierklappe *f* (*G shield*).

sight shield Visierschild *m* (*G*).

sight slide Visierschieber *m* (*MG, R*).

sight support Aufsatzträger *m* (*G*).

sign Zeichen *n* (*symbol, signal*); Schild *n*, Richtungsschild *n* (*road*).

signal *n* Signal *n*, Zeichen *n*.

signal ammunition Erkennungsmunition *f*.

signal battalion Nachrichtenabteilung *f*.

signal book Signalbuch *n* (*Nav*).

signal cartridge Signalpatrone *f*, Leuchtpatrone *f*.

signal center Nachrichtenzentrale *f*.

signal communication Nachrichtenverbindung *f*. *See also* **communication.**

signal communications Nachrichtenwesen *n*.

signal communication traffic Nachrichtenverkehr *f*.

signal company Nachrichtenkompanie *f*.

Signal Corps Nachrichtentruppen *fpl*.

Signal Corps School Nachrichtenschule *f* (*USA*).

signal depot Nachrichtenpark *m*.

signal equipment Nachrichtengerät *n*.

signal flag Signalflagge *f* (*Nav*); Winkflagge *f* (*semaphore*).

signaling current Rufstrom *m* (*Tp*).

signaling panel Tuchzeichen *n* (*air-ground Com*).

signal intelligence Nachrichtenaufklärung *f*.

signal lamp Blinkgerät *n*, Blinklampe *f*.

signal-lamp apparatus Blinkgerät *n*.

signal-lamp communication Blinkverbindung *f*.

signal-lamp message Blinkspruch *m*.

signal-lamp spotting squad Blinksuchtrupp *m*.

signal-lamp squad Blinktrupp *m*.

signal-lamp station Blinkstelle *f*.

signal-lamp transmission Blinken *n*; Tasten *n* (*keying*).

signal motor vehicle Nachrichtenkraftfahrzeug *n*.

signal officer Nachrichtenoffizier *m*, Nachrichtenführer *m*.

signal operation instructions dem Operationsbefehl beigefügte besondere Anordnung des Nachrichtenführers.

signal order Befehl für den Nachrichteneinsatz.

signal personnel Nachrichtenleute *mpl*.

signal pistol Leuchtpistole *f*; Kampfpistole *f* (*for Sig and/or incendiary cartridges*).

signal pistol ammunition Leuchtpistolenmunition f.
signal projector Signalwerfer m.
signal rocket Leuchtrakete f, Signalrakete f.
signal strength Lautstärke f (Rad).
signal supplies Nachrichtengerät n.
signal-supply dump Nachrichtengerätpark m.
signal troops Nachrichtentruppen fpl.
signal vehicle Nachrichtenfahrzeug n.
signal wagon Nachrichtenwagen m.
signature Unterschrift f (written name); Kartenzeichen n (maps).
sign post Richtposten m (road).
silence Schweigen n, Stille f, Ruhe f.
silencer Knalldämpfer m (R, pistol, etc.).
silent alarm stiller Alarm.
"silent soldier" S-Mine f, Schützenmine f.
silhouette Schattenriß m.
silhouette target Kampfwagenscheibe f (Tk).
silk Seide f.
sill Schwelle f, Fußlatte f (Bdg).
silt Triebsand m.
silver Silber n.
Silver Star Silberstern m (decoration, USA).
simple einfach.
simple anchor hitch einfacher Ankerstich (with bowline).
simplex coil Ringübertrager m (Tg, Tp).
simplexed connection Simultanschaltung f (Tg, Tp).
simplexed telegraphy Unterlagerungstelegraphie f.
simulate vortäuschen (Tac).
simulated agent Übungsreizstoff m (CWS).
simulated fire Geschützzielfeuer n (representing an enemy gun target); Gewehrzielfeuer n (representing an enemy R or MG target).
simulated mine Scheinmine f.
simultaneous gleichzeitig.
simultaneous two-way radio traffic Funkdoppelverkehr m.
sine Sinus m (Math).
single einzeln (one); allein (alone); ledig (unmarried).
single-barreled einläufig.
single connection einfache Vermittlung (Tp).

single-cylinder engine Einzylindermotor m.
single-engine einmotorig.
single file Reihe f.
single-fuselage airplane Einrumpfflugzeug n.
single-grid tube Eingitterröhre f (Rad).
single-intersection method Einzelschnittverfahren n (Flash Ranging).
single-line charge gestreckte Ladung, Reihenladung f (Engr).
single loader Einzellader m.
single-place fighter Jagdeinsitzer m.
single-plate clutch Einscheibenkupplung f (MT).
single rank Linie zu 1 Glied (Inf).
single release Einzel(ab)wurf m (Bombing).
single-seater einsitzig.
single-seater airplane Einsitzer m.
single-seater fighter Jagdeinsitzer m (Avn).
single shot Einzelschuß m.
single-shot fire Einzelfeuer n (MG).
single-shot weapon Einzellader m.
single-slot wing einschlitziger Schlitzflügel (Ap).
single-span stringer bridge Uferbrücke f.
single-station spotting Einfachanschnitt m.
singletree attachment hook Zughaken m (limber).
sinking Versenkung f (Nav).
siren Sirene f, Heulsignal n.
site Stelle f, Platz m, Ort m. See also angle of site.
site scale See angle of site scale.
sitting position Anschlag sitzend (firing).
situation Lage f, Zustand m.
situation map Lagenkarte f (Tac).
six-engine sechsmotorig.
six-wheel motor vehicle Sechsradkraftfahrzeug n.
six-wheel vehicle Dreiachser m.
size Grösse f; Nummer f (of shoes, gloves).
skeet range Wurftaubenschießstand m, Tontaubenschießstand m.
skeet shooting Taubenschießen n, Tontaubenschießen n.
sketch Skizze f.
ski n Ski m, Schi m.
ski v Ski laufen.
ski battalion Schibataillon n.

skid *n* Kufe *f (sled runner)*.
skid chain Gleitschutzkette *f*, Schneekette *f (MT)*.
skidding Schleudern *n (MT)*.
skid mark Bremsspur *f (MT)*.
skill Geschicklichkeit *f*.
skilled ausgebildet *(Mil)*.
skin Haut *f*, Außenhaut *f*, Bespannung *f (Ap)*.
skin decontamination agent Hautentgiftungsmittel *n*.
skin effect Hautwirkung *f (Rad)*.
skip zone tote Zone *(Rad)*.
skirmish Scharmützel *n*, Plänkelei *f*.
skirmisher's trench Schützenmulde *f*.
skirmishing Plänkeln *n*.
skirt Seitenblatt *n*, Satteltasche *f (saddle)*.
skirting Laufwerkpanzerung *f (Tk)*.
ski troops Skitruppen *fpl*.
skull Schädel *m*.
sky Himmel *m*; Luftraum *m (Avn)*.
sky wave Raumwelle *f (Rad)*.
sky-wave effect Raumwellenwirkung *f (Rad)*.
slack schlaff, locker.
slant plane Seitenvorhaltebene *f (AA gunnery)*.
slant range Schrägentfernung *f (AA Gunnery)*.
slant range to future position Treffpunktentfernung *f (AA Gunnery)*.
slant range to midpoint Wechselpunktentfernung *f (AA Gunnery)*.
slant range to present position Meßentfernung *f (instant of range determination)*, Abschußentfernung *f (instant of firing) (AA Gunnery)*.
slash *n* Streich *m*, Hieb *m (bayonet)*.
slashing weapon Hiebwaffe *f*.
slat Hilfsflügel *m*, Vorflügel *m*, Zusatzflügel *m (Ap wing)*.
sled Schlitten *m*.
sledge hammer Vorschlaghammer *m*.
sled runner Kufe *f*.
sleeping bag Schlafsack *m*.
sleet Frostgraupeln *fpl*, Eisregen *m*.
sleeve Ärmel *m (Clo)*; Schieber *m (sleeve-type engine)*; Kabelverbinder *m (cable connector)*; Muffe *f (pipe connector)*.
sleeve cuff Ärmelaufschlag *m (Clo)*.
sleeve insignia Ärmelabzeichen *n*.
sleeve target Luftsack *m (AAA target practice)*.
sleeve-type engine Schiebermotor *m*, ventilloser Motor.

sleigh Rohrschlitten *m (G)*.
sleigh mount Schlitten *m (MG)*.
slew schwenken *(gun laying)*.
slide Gleitbahn *f (G cradle)*.
slide bearing Gleitlager *n (Mech)*.
slide buckle Schiebeschnalle *f*.
slide fastener Reißverschluß *m*.
slide mechanism Gleitvorrichtung *f (MG)*.
slide plate Gleitwand *f (MG)*.
slide rule Rechenschieber *m*.
sliding bolt Gleitriegel *m (breechblock)*.
sliding lever Gleithebel *m (breechblock)*.
sliding-lever breechblock Gleithebelverschluß *m*.
sliding roof Schiebedach *n (Ap)*.
sliding surface Lauffläche *f (sled)*.
sliding-type breechblock Schubkurbelverschluß *m*, Leitwellverschluß *m (G)*.
sling Gewehrriemen *m (R)*.
"Sling arms!" "Gewehr umhängen!"
sling lashing Schleuderbund *m (Engr)*.
sling psychrometer Schleuderpsychrometer *n (Met)*.
sling swivel Riemenbügel *m (R)*.
slip Abrutschen *n*, Slip *m (Ap)*; Schlupf *m (propeller)*.
slipstream Luftschraubenstrahl *m*, Propellerwind *m*, Nachstrom *m (Avn)*.
slip tank Abwurfbehälter *m (Ap)*.
slit Schlitz *m*.
slit trench Deckungsgraben *m*, Splittergraben *m*, Fliegerschutzgraben *m*.
slogan Schlagwort *n*.
slope *n* Böschung *f*, Abdachung *f*, Geländeneigung *f*, Neigung *f*, Hang *m*, Abhang *m*, Steigung *f (Top)*.
slope *v* abfallen *(Top)*.
slope of fall Tangens des Fallwinkels *(Ballistics)*.
slope position Hangstellung *f (Ft)*.
sloping terrain abfallendes Gelände.
slot Nut(e) *m(f) (Tech)*; Schlitz *m (Ap wing)*; Sehschlitz *m (directvision slot, Tk)*.
slotted aileron Schlitzquerruder *n (Ap)*.
slotted wing Schlitzflügel *m*, Spaltflügel *m (Ap)*.
slow langsam.
slow match Lunte *f (fuze lighter)*.
slow roll gesteuerte Rolle *(Avn)*.
sluice Schleuse *f*.

slurry Losantinbrei *m* *(calcium hypochlorite, CWS)*.

small klein.

small arms Handfeuerwaffen *fpl (Ord)*.

small-bore barrel Kleinkaliberlauf *m (R)*.

small-bore practice Kleinkaliberschießen *n*.

small-bore target range Kleinschießplatz *m (R)*.

small of the stock Kolbenhals *m (R)*.

smallpox Pocken *fpl*, Blattern *fpl*.

smash zerschmettern.

smoke Rauch *m;* Nebel *m (CWS)*.

smoke agent Nebelstoff *m*, Nebelmittel *n (CWS)*.

smoke and flash defilade Sichtdeckung *f (Arty)*.

smoke apparatus Nebelgerät *n (CWS)*.

smoke battalion Werferabteilung *f*.

smoke blanket Nebeldecke *f (CWS)*.

smoke bomb Nebelbombe *f (Avn)*.

smoke candle Schwelkerze *f*, Nebelkerze *f*, Rauchkerze *f (CWS)*.

smoke cartridge Nebelpatrone *f*.

smoke charge Rauchladung *f (Am)*.

smoke cloud Nebelwolke *f*, Rauchwolke *f (CWS)*.

smoke composition Rauchsatz *m*.

smoke container Nebelkasten *m (case)*, Nebeltrommel *f (drum) (CWS)*.

smoke-container firing device Nebelzündmittel *n (CWS)*.

smoke coverage Nebelausdehnung *f (CWS)*.

smoke curtain Nebelwand *f (CWS)*.

smoke effect Raucherscheinung *f (Flash Ranging)*.

smoke equipment Nebelgerät *n (CWS)*.

smoke-filled chemical cylinder Nebelabblasgerät *n (CWS)*.

smoke filler Rauchkörper *m (Am)*.

smoke generator Rauchentwickler *m;* Rauchofen *m (Adrm)*.

smoke grenade Nebelhandgranate *f*.

smokeless rauchschwach, rauchlos.

smokeless powder rauchschwaches Pulver.

smoke party Nebeltrupp *m (Engr)*.

smoke pellet Rauchsatz *m (Am)*.

smoke pot Nebeltopf *m (CWS)*.

smoke-producing unit Nebelabteilung *f (CWS) (Pers)*.

smoke projectile Nebelgeschoß *n*.

smoke-puff charge Kanonenschlag mit Raucherscheinung, Rauchkörper *m (simulated fire)*.

smoke screen Nebelschleier *m;* Nebelwand *f*, Rauchwand *f*, Rauchvorhang *m (vertical);* Nebeldecke *f (horizontal)*.

smoke-screened area Nebelzone *f (CWS)*.

smoke screening Vernebelung *f*, Blenden *n;* Feindvernebelung *f (against enemy Obsn)*.

smoke-screening fire Blendungsschießen *n (Arty)*.

smoke-screening tank Nebelpanzerkampfwagen *m*.

smoke shell Nebelgranate *f*, Rauchgranate *f (Arty);* Nebelwurfgranate *f (Mort)*.

smoke-shell firing Nebelschießen *n (Arty)*.

smoke-shell mortar Nebelwerfer *m*.

smoke signal cartridge Rauchpatrone *f*.

smoke tank Nebelgerät *n (for air Cml spraying)*.

smooth glatt; eben *(even);* flach *(flat)*.

smooth-bore *adj* glatt *(Ord)*.

snaffle Trense *f (harness)*.

snaffle bit Trensengebiß *n (harness)*.

snaffle rein Trensenzügel *m (harness)*.

snap fastener Druckknopf *m*.

snap gage Außengrenzlehre *f*.

sneak raider Störflieger *m (Avn)*.

sneeze gas Niesgas *n (CWS)*.

sniffing test Riechprobe *f (CWS)*.

sniff set Riechprobenkasten *m (CWS)*.

sniper Heckenschütze *m*, Scharfschütze *m;* Baumschütze *m (in a tree)*.

sniping Schießen aus dem Hinterhalt.

sniping post Scharfschützennest *n*.

snow Schnee *m*.

snow chain Schneekette *f (MT)*.

snow flurries Schneetreiben *n (Met)*.

snow-pellet shower Graupelschauer *m (Met)*.

snow pit Schneeloch *n*.

snowplow Schneepflug *m*.

snowshoe Schneereifen *m*, Schneeschuh *m*.

soakage pit Müllgrube *f (for refuse)*.

soaking pit Vergütungsanlage *f* *(Ord)*.

soap Seife *f*.

soaring Segeln *n (glider)*.

socket Hülse *f (G carriage)*; Kugelpfanne *f (Mort)*; Lampenfassung *f*, Fassung *f (Elec)*; Buchse *f*, Stutzen *m*, Zapfenlager *n (Tech)*.

socket connection Sockelschaltung *f (Rad tube)*.

socket wrench Steckschlüssel *m*, Aufsteckschlüssel *m*.

sodium Natrium *n*.

sodium chloride tablet Natriumchloridtablette *f*.

sodium hydroxide kaustisches Natron, Ätznatron *n*.

sodium hypochlorite Chlornatron *n*, Natriumhypochlorit *n*.

sodium sulfide Schwefelnatrium *n*, Natriumsulfid *n*.

sodium sulfite schwefligsaures Natrium, Natriumsulfit *n*.

"softening up" Sturmreifmachung *f*.

soil Erde *f*, Boden *m*, Grund *m*.

solar plexus Sonnengeflecht *n*, Solarplexus *m*.

solder *n* Lötzinn *n*, Lötmetall *n*.

solder *v* löten.

soldering iron Lötkolben *m*.

soldier Soldat *m*.

soldierly qualities Soldatentum *n*.

sole Sohle *f*.

solenoid Magnetspule *f*, Solenoid *n (Elec)*.

solid tire Vollgummireifen *m*, Vollreifen *m*.

solitary confinement Einzelhaft *f*.

solo flight Alleinflug *m*.

solo motorcycle Einzelkrad *n*, Solokrad *n*.

solution Lösung *f*.

solvent Lösungsmittel *n*.

sonic altimeter Echolot *n*, Behmlot *n*, Relativhöhenmesser *m (Ap)*.

sort *v* sortieren, aussondern.

sortie Ausfall *m (Tac)*; Einsatz *m*, Feindflug *m (Avn)*.

sound Ton *m*, Schall *m*, Laut *m*; Geräusch *n (noise)*; Knall *m* (report).

sound and flash ranging Lichtschallmessen *n*.

sound communication Verbindung durch Schallzeichen.

sound-communication device Schallmittel *n*.

sound effect Knallerscheinung *f (Sound Ranging)*.

sounding lotbare Wassertiefe *(depth of water)*.

sounding lead Lot *n*, Peillot *n*, Senkblei *n (Nav)*.

sound intensity Lautstärke *f*.

sound lag Schallverzug *m (AA Gunnery)*.

sound-lag correction Ausschalten des Schallverzugs.

sound location akustische Ortung, Schallortung *f (AAA)*.

sound locator Richtungshörer *m*, Horchgerät *n (AAA)*.

soundproof schalldicht.

sound ranging Schallmessung *f (Arty)*.

sound-ranging altimeter Echolot *n (Avn)*.

sound-ranging microphone Schallmikrophon *n (Arty)*.

sound-ranging net Schallmeßsystem *n (Arty)*.

sound-ranging section Schallmeßtrupp *m*, Meßtrupp *m (Arty)*.

sound-ranging station Schallmeßstelle *f (Arty)*.

sound-recording apparatus Schallaufnahmegerät *n* (Sound Ranging).

sound reproduction Tonwiedergabe *f (Elec)*.

sound signaling *See* **sound communication.**

sound track Knallbild *n (Sound Ranging)*.

sound travel time Stoppzeit *f (Sound Ranging)*.

sound truck Tonwagen *m (film unit)*.

sound wave Schallwelle *f*.

soup Suppe *f*.

source Quelle *f*.

south Süden *m*.

sovereignty of the air Lufthoheit *f*.

soya-bean flour Bratlingspulver *n*.

space Raum *m;* Abstand *m (distance)*; Zwischenraum *m (interval)*.

space charge Raumladung *f (Rad tube)*.

spaced armor Hohlraumpanzerung *f*, Schottpanzerung *f (Tk)*.

spade Sporn *m (G)*; Spaten *m (tool)*.

spade arm Spornarm *m (G)*.

spade plate Spornblech *n (G)*.

spadework Schanzarbeiten *fpl (field Ft)*.

span Spannweite *f (Ap, Bdg);* Brückenstützweite *f,* Stützweite *f (span between supports);* Brückenbogen *m (arch);* Strecke *f (bay).*

spar Holm *m (Ap, Bdg);* Stange *f (pole);* Rundholz *n (round timber);* Stiel *m (compression member);* Strebe *f (tension member).*

spar bracing Verstrebung *f (Bdg).*

spare *adj* Ersatz-, Vorrats-.

spare *v* ersparen *(save);* schonen *(keep intact);* aufheben, aufbewahren *(keep for future use).*

spare barrel Vorratslauf *m (MG).*

spare part Ersatzteil *m,* Vorratsteil *m.*

spare parts truck Werkstattgerätkraftwagen *m (MT).*

spark Funke *m.*

spark adjustment Zündverstellung *f (Mtr).*

spark control Zündhebel *m (lever);* Zündverstellung *f (action or function).*

spark discharge Funkentladung *f.*

spark gap Funkenstrecke *f.*

spark plug Zündkerze *f.*

spark-plug cable Zündkabel *n.*

spark-plug point Elektrode *f.*

spar trestle Stangenbock *m (Bdg).*

speaker Lautsprecher *m (Rad).*

speaker cabinet Lautsprechertruhe *f (Rad).*

spearhead Stoßkeil *m (Tac).*

special *adj* besonder, Sonder-.

special agreement Sonderabkommen *n (Law).*

special announcement Sondermeldung *f (Rad).*

special court-martial Sonderkriegsgericht *n.*

special gas mask Sondergasmaske *f.*

specialist Fachmann *m,* Fachverständiger *m;* Sonderführer *m (uniformed specialist in Ger Armed Forces with nominal rank up to Bn commander but no actual Mil rank).*

special message Sondermeldung *f (Rad).*

special mission Sonderauftrag *m.*

special-missions staff officer Ordonnanzoffizier *m.*

special operations Gefechte unter besonderen Verhältnissen *(Tac).*

special orders Sonderverfügungen *fpl,* Tagesbefehl *m (Adm);* besondere Postenanweisung *(guard duty).*

special-purpose airplane Sonderflugzeug *n.*

special-purpose motor truck Sonderlastkraftwagen *m.*

special-purpose vehicle Sonderfahrzeug *n.*

special radio message Sonderfunkspruch *m.*

special service practice Belehrungs- und Versuchsschießen *n (Arty).*

special services besondere Dienstzweige.

special telephone call Sondergespräch *n.*

specifications Angaben *fpl,* Beschreibung *f.*

specific gravity spezifisches Gewicht, Einheitsgewicht *n.*

speed Geschwindigkeit *f;* Gang *m (gear shifting).*

speedboat Schnellboot *n.*

speed increase Geschwindigkeitssteigerung *f.*

speed of current Stromgeschwindigkeit *f.*

speed of target Zielgeschwindigkeit *f.*

speedometer Geschwindigkeitsmesser *m;* Tachograph *m (with odometer).*

spike Sporn *m (MG tripod);* Spiker *m,* Stift *m (long nail).*

spillway Überfall *m (dam).*

spillway crest Überfallkrone *f (dam).*

spillway weir Überfallwehr *n,* Sturzwehr *n.*

spin Trudeln *n (Ap);* Geschoßdrall *m,* Geschoßdrehung *f (of projectile).*

go into a spin abtrudeln.

spinal column Wirbelsäule *f.*

spindle Schwingschenkel *m (steering-knuckle) (MT).*

spine Wirbel *m.*

spinner Luftschraubenhaube *f,* Propellerhaube *f,* Haube *f (Ap propeller).*

spiral Kurvengleitflug *m (Avn).*

spiral dive Sturzspirale *f;* Korkenzieher *m (Avn).*

spiral spring Spiralfeder *f,* Wickelfeder *f.*

spiral-spring equilibrator Spiralfederausgleicher *m (AA gun).*

spiral wire Drahtspirale *f.*

splash Spritzer *m.*

splash lubrication Spritzumlaufschmierung *f (Mtr).*

splice *n*   Splissung *f*, Spleißung *f*; Kabelverbindung *f* (*Tp wire*).

splice *v*   spleißen, splissen.

spline shaft   Keilwelle *f* (*MT*).

splint   Armschiene *f*, Schiene *f* (*Med*).

splinter   Splitter *m*; Bombensplitter *m* (*bomb*); Granatsplitter *m* (*shell*); Sprengstück *n* (*fragment*).

splinterproof   splittersicher.

splinterproof cover   splittersichere Deckung.

splinterproof shelter   splittersicherer Unterstand *m*.

split-field range finder   Schnittbildentfernungsmesser *m*, Halbbildentfernungsmesser *m*.

split flap   Spreizklappe *f* (*Ap*).

split ring   Spaltring *m* (*breechblock*).

split trail   Spreizlafettenholme *mpl*, Spreizlafettenschwanz *m* (*G*).

split-trail gun carriage   Spreizlafette *f*.

spoil   Bodenaushub *m* (*Ft*); Miniergut *n* (*Mining*).

spoke   Speiche *f* (*wheel*).

sponge   Schwamm *m*.

sponson   Panzerkastenoberteil *m* (*Tk*); Stabilisierungsschwimmer *m* (*Ap*).

spoon   Löffel *m*.

spot *v*   orten (*locate*); sichten (*see*); entdecken (*discover*).

spot landing   Ziellandung *f* (*Avn*).

spotlight   Sucher *m* (*MT*).

spotter   Artilleriebeobachter *m*.

spotting   Schußbeobachtung *f* (*Arty*).

spot welding   Punktschweißung *f*.

sprain   Verstauchung *f* (*Med*).

spray *n*   Sprengkegel *m* (*air burst*); Zerstäuber *m* (*Inst*).

spray attack   Giftregenangriff *m* (*CWS*).

spray effect   Splitterwirkung *f* (*Gunnery*).

spray gun   Druckzerstäuber *m* (*CWS*).

spraying   Versprühen *n* (*CWS*).

spray nozzle   Spritzdüse *f* (*carburetor*); Spritzschlauch *m* (*hose*).

spray-nozzle tube   Tauchrohr *n* (*carburetor*).

spray painting unit   Farb-Spritzanlage *f*.

spray-type decontaminating apparatus   Zerstäubergerät *n* (*CWS*).

spread *v*   auf Streulicht gehen (*searchlight beam*); ausstreuen, ausbreiten.

spread-out formation   auseinandergezogene Formation (*Avn*).

spread the trails   die Holme spreizen (*split-trail gun carriage*).

spring   Quelle *f* (*water*); Feder *f* (*Tech*); Frühling *m* (*season*).

spring action   Federantrieb *m* (*clockwork fuze*).

spring bolt   Federbolzen *m* (*MT*).

spring bracket   Federhand *f* (*MT*).

spring clip   Federbund *m* (*split-trail G carriage*).

spring counterrecoil mechanism   Federvorholer *m*.

spring equilibrator   Federausgleicher *m* (*G*).

spring hanger   Federbock *m* (*MT*).

spring mechanism   Federeinrichtung *f* (*MG*).

spring recuperator   Federvorholer *m* (*G*).

spring shackle   Federlasche *f* (*MT*).

spring suspension   Federaufhängung *f* (*MT*); Federgehänge *n* (*G carriage*).

spring system   Abfederung *f*, Federung *f* (*MT*).

sprinkling can   Tropfkanne *f*.

sprocket   Triebrad *n* (*driving sprocket*) (*Tk*).

spur   Sporn *m* (*Cav*).

spur gear   Stirnrad *n*.

spur track   Eisenbahnklaue *f*.

spy *n*   Spion *m*, Kundschafter *m*.

spy *v*   auskundschaften, ausspähen.

squad   Gruppe *f* (*Inf*); Trupp *m* (*detail, team*); Kommando *n* (*party*).

squad column   Schützenreihe *f*.

"Squad, halt!"   "Abteilung, halt!"

squad leader   Gruppenführer *m*.

squadron   Staffel *f* (*Avn*); Geschwader *n* (*Nav*). Note: No Ger equivalent in Cav.

squadron commander   Staffelführer *m*, Staffelkapitän *m* (*Avn*).

squadron commander's flight   Führungskette *f* (*Avn*).

squadron formation   Staffelform *f*, Staffelverband *m* (*Avn*).

squadron javelin formation   Staffelkolonne *f* (*Avn*).

squadron V formation   Staffelwinkel *m* (*Avn*).

squad room   Mannschaftsstube *f*.

squall   Bö *f*, Windstoß *m*.

squall line   Bölinie *f*.

square *n* Viereck *n*, Quadrat *n;* Platz *m (in city or town).*

square *adj* viereckig, quadratisch; rechtwinklig *(having right angles).*

square centimeter Quadratzentimeter *m.*

squared quadratisch; quadriert, (zum) Quadrat, hoch zwei *(raised to second power).*

square division viergliedrige Division.

square lashing Bockschnürbund *m (Bdg).*

square root Quadratwurzel *f.*

square-wedge breechblock Flachkeilverschluß *m (G).*

squeeze abkrümmen, durchkrümmen *(trigger);* drängen *(Tac).*

squirrel-cage motor Kurzschlußankermotor *m.*

stability Stabilität *f.*

stabilizer Höhenflosse *f (Ap);* Kreiselabfeuergerät *n (Tk).*

stabilizer lobe Stabilisierungswulst *m (Bln).*

stabilizing fin Steuerflügel *m (bomb);* Flügelblech *n (Am);* Steuerfläche *f (Mort shell).*

stabilizing surface Dämpfungsfläche *f,* Stabilisierungsfläche *f (Ap).*

stable *n* Stall *m.*

stable *adj* stabil, fest, dauerhaft, haltbar, stark; beständig *(durable).*

"Stack, arms!" "Setzt die, Gewehre! Zusammen!"

stadia rod Meßlatte *f,* Meßstab *m (Surv).*

staff Stab *m.*

staff administrative order Stabsbefehl *m.*

staff car Befehlswagen *m.*

staff officer Stabsoffizier *m.*

staff order Stabsbefehl *m.*

staff sergeant Unterfeldwebel *m;* Unterwachtmeister *m (Arty, Cav).*

stage Stufe *f (Rad, etc.);* Landbrücke *f (landing stage).*

stagger Staffelung *f (Ap wings).*

stagger distance Stufung *f (formation flying).*

staggered gegeneinander verschoben, gegeneinander versetzt.

staggered biplane gestaffelter Doppeldecker *m.*

stagger formation zerlegter Verband. gestaffelter Verband *(Tac).*

staggering Stufung *f (formation flying).*

stagger wire Gegenseil *n (biplane).*

stake *n* Absteckpfahl *m (Surv);* Stock *m,* Pfahl *m,* Pflock *m.*

stake mine Stockmine *f (Ger concrete antipersonnel mine).*

stake off abstecken *(Engr, Surv).*

stall *n* Überziehen *n (Ap).*

stall *v* abwürgen *(Mtr).*

stalled bewegungsunfähig *(MT).*

stalling Überziehen *n (Avn).*

stalling flight Langsamflug *m (Ap).*

stalling speed Durchsackgeschwindigkeit *(Avn).*

stamp Stempel *m;* Briefmarke *f (postage).*

stamp pad Stempelkissen *n.*

standard *n* Standarte *f (flag);* Norm *f (Tech).*

standard *adj* Einheits-, Normal-, Regel-, genormt, vorschriftsmäßig, regelrecht.

standard fuze Einheitszünder *m (Am).*

standard gage Normalspur *f,* Regelspur *f,* Vollbahn *f (RR).*

standard-gage railroad Vollspurbahn *f.*

standardization Normung *f,* Vereinheitlichung *f.*

standardize normen, vereinheitlichen.

standard maximum load Regellast *f (Bdg).*

standard muzzle velocity schußtafelmäßige Anfangsgeschwindigkeit.

standard nomenclature einheitliche Benennung.

standard operating procedure vorschriftsmäßiges Verfahren.

standard part Normteil *m (MT).*

standard time Zonenzeit *f,* Einheitszeit *f.*

stand-by Alarmbereitschaft *f.*

stand-by message Erwa-Meldung *f (preliminary to metro message) (Arty).*

stand-by operation Horchempfang *m (Rad).*

standing army stehendes Heer.

standing barrage Notfeuer *n,* Sperrfeuer *n,* Feuerriegel *m (Arty).*

standing foxhole Schützenloch für stehenden Anschlag.

standing order Dauerbefehl *m.*

standing position Anschlag stehend *(firing).*

staple *n* Krampe *f (Tech)*.

stapler Hefter *m*.

star Stern *m; Leuchtstern m (Sig)*.

starboard Steuerbord *m*.

starboard engine Steuerbordmotor *m (Ap)*.

star cluster Sternbündel *n (Sig)*.

star gage Seelenmesser *m (G)*.

star shell Leuchtgeschoß *n*, Leuchtgranate *f (Am)*; Granatsignal *n (Sig)*.

start aufbrechen *(set out)*; starten *(Ap take-off)*; anlassen, anwerfen *(an engine)*; abrücken, abmarschieren *(start a march)*.

starter Anlasser *m*, Starter *m (MT)*.

starter battery Starterbatterie *f (MT)*.

starter button Anlaßdruckknopf *m*, Anlaßknopf *m (MT)*.

starter-generator Dynastart *m (MT)*.

starter motor Anlaßmotor *m*.

starter pinion Antriebsritzel *m (on armature shaft of starter)*.

starter switch Anlaßschalter *m (Mtr)*.

starting Anlassen *n*, Ingangsetzen *n (MT)*.

starting equipment Anlaßvorrichtung *f (Mtr)*.

starting point Aufbruchsort *m*.

starting time Aufbruchszeit *f*.

state Staat *m (country)*; Zustand *m (condition)*.

state of emergency Ausnahmezustand *m*.

state of siege Belagerungszustand *m*.

state of war Kriegszustand *m*.

static Störgeräusch *n*, Gewitterstörung *f (Rad)*.

static eliminator Funkentstörer *m (Rad)*.

static line Aufziehleine *f*, Reißleine *f (Prcht)*.

station Bahnhof *m*, Station *f (RR)*; Standort *m (post or garrison)*; Stand *m (position in Ap or vehicle)*; Funkstelle *f (Rad)*.

stationary fest, ortsfest, stehend.

stationary generating unit ortsfester Stromerzeuger.

stationary gun mount ortsfeste Lafette *(G)*.

stationary patrol stehender Spähtrupp.

stationary target stehendes Ziel.

station capacity Bahnhofleistung *f (number of trains loaded or unloaded per day)*.

stationery Briefpapier *n*.

station hospital Standortlazarett *n*.

station list Kommandostellenverzeichnis *n*.

station log Betriebsbuch *n (Rad)*.

station surgeon Standortarzt *m*.

statistics Statistik *f*.

stator Stator *m (Elec)*.

statoscope Variometer *n*.

status Wehrdienstverhältnis *n (service status)*; Rechtsstellung *f*, rechtliche Stellung *(Law)*.

statute Statut *n*, Satzung *f*, Grundgesetz *n*, Gesetz *n*.

statute mile Landmeile *f (1.609 km)*.

statute of limitations Verjährungsgesetz *n*.

stave Daube *f (of a barrel)*.

steadiness Standsicherheit *f (of a mobile G mount, vehicle, etc.)*.

steady fest *(firm)*; anhaltend *(continuous)*; gleichmäßig *(even)*.

steal stehlen.

steam Dampf *m*.

steamboat Dampfschiff *n*.

steam engine Dampfmaschine *f*.

steam roller Dampfwalze *f (Engr)*.

steam tube Dampfrohr *n (MG)*.

steel Stahl *m*.

steel alloy Stahllegierung *f*.

steel and concrete fortification Panzerwerk *n*.

steel-beam obstacle Sperre aus Stahlträgern.

steel bridge Stahlbrücke *f*.

steel bushing Stahlfutter *n (breechblock wedge)*.

steel-core bullet Stahlkerngeschoß *n*.

steel cylinder Stahlflasche *f (container)*.

steel flask *See* **steel cylinder**.

steel helmet Stahlhelm *m*.

steel measuring tape Stahlmeßband *n*.

steel mill Stahlwerk *n*.

steel plank Stahlschwelle *f (Engr)*.

steel plate Stahlplatte *f*.

steel-rail obstacle Sperre aus Schienen.

steel tetrahedron Stahligel *m (AT obstacle)*.

steel tie Stahlschwelle *f (RR)*.

steel treadway Stahlspurbahn *f*.

steel wire armor Stahldrahtbeklöppelung *f (armored cable).*

steep abschüssig, schroff, steil *(Top).*

steep-banked turn Steilkurve *f (Avn).*

steep-bank flight Messerflug *m (Avn).*

steep climb Hochziehen *n (Ap).*

steep grade Steilhang *m (Top).*

steep hill Steigung *f (Top).*

steep slope Steilhang *m (Top).*

steering Steuern *n,* Lenken *n.*

steering arm Lenkstock *m,* Lenkstockhebel *m (MT);* Lenker *m (of a G wheel).*

steering brake Lenkbremse *f (Tk).*

steering column Lenksäule *f,* Steuersäule *f (MT).*

steering-column cam Lenkschraube *f (MT).*

steering gear Lenkung *f,* Lenkgetriebe *n (MT).*

steering-gear connecting rod Lenkschubstange *f (MT).*

steering-gear housing Lenkgehäuse *n (MT).*

steering-knuckle arm Spurstangenhebel *m (MT).*

steering-knuckle gear-rod arm Lenkhebel *m (MT).*

steering-knuckle pivot Achszapfen *m (MT).*

steering-knuckle type steering Achsschenkellenkung *f (MT).*

steering lever Lenkhebel *m,* Lenkknüppel *m (Tk, Trac).*

steering mechanism Lenkeinrichtung *f,* Lenkgetriebe *n (Tk, Trac).*

steering play toter Gang *(MT).*

steering shock suspension Lenkstoßfang *m (MT).*

steering system Lenkung *f,* Steuerung *f (MT).*

steering wheel Steuer *n,* Steuerrad *n,* Lenkrad *n (MT).*

steering worm Lenkschnecke *f (MT).*

steering-worm sector Lenksegment *n (MT).*

stem Vordersteven *m (Nav);* Aufziehachse *f,* Aufziehwelle *f (of a timepiece).*

stencil *n* Matrize *f (typing);* Schablone *f (Tech).*

stencil *v* schablonieren, aufschablonieren.

stenographer Stenograph *m,* Stenographin *f.*

step Stufe *f;* Schritt *m,* Tritt *m (pace);* Stufe *f (Ap float or pontoon).*

stepped-up (-down) formation Stufenformation *f (Avn).*

stereogram Raummeßbild *n (Photo survey).*

stereo-pair *See* stereoscopic pair.

stereo-photogrammetry Raumbildmessung *f.*

stereo range finder *See* stereoscopic range finder.

stereoscope Stereoskop *n.*

stereoscopic complements stereoskopische Meßbildpaare *(Photo survey).*

stereoscopic height finder *See* stereoscopic range finder.

stereoscopic image Raumbild *n.*

stereoscopic pair Raumbildpaar *n.*

stereoscopic range finder Raumbildentfernungsmesser *m.*

sterilization Entwesung *f (of clothing, etc.).*

sterilization truck Sterilisationswagen *m (Med).*

sterilize entkeimen, sterilisieren *(Med).*

stern Heck *n.*

stern compartment Hinterkaffe *f (Pon).*

sternpost Hintersteven *m,* Rudersteven *m.*

sternutator Nasenrachenreizstoff *m,* Blaukreuz *n (CWS).*

stevedore Stauer *m,* Lader *m,* Auslader *m,* Hafenarbeiter *m.*

stick Stock *m* Knüppel *m.*

stick control Knüppelsteuerung *f (Ap).*

stick hand grenade Stielhandgranate *f.*

stick-type incendiary bomb Stabbrandbombe *f.*

sticky klebrig.

stiff steif, starr.

stifle joint Knie *n (horse).*

still projector Bildwerfer *m (Photo).*

Stillson wrench Rohrzange *f.*

stimulant Anregungsmittel *n.*

stirrup Steigbügel *m.*

stirrup pump Luftschutzbrandspritze *f (Civ defense).*

stirrup strap Steigriemen *m.*

stock Schaft *m (R);* Griffschale *f (pistol);* Schulterstütze *f (MG);* Bestand *m,* Lagerbestand *m,* Vorrat *m (of supplies, equipment, etc.);* Schneidkluppe *f,* Kluppe *f (die* *holder);* Ankerbalken *m (of an anchor).*

stockade Einzäunung *f (PW).*

stock and die Schneidkluppe mit Schneidbacken.

stock book Bestandsbuch *n (QM).*

stocking Strumpf *m (Clo).*

stock inventory Bestandsnachweisung *f.*

stock preservative Schaftpflegemittel *n (R).*

stock rail Backenschiene *f (RR).*

Stokes mortar Stokes-Gasmörser *m.*

stop Aufenthaltspunkt *m,* Haltepunkt *m,* Haltestelle *f (RR, MT);* Anschlag *m (Ord).*

stop and taillight Stopp- und Schlußlicht *n (MT).*

stop light Bremslicht *n (MT).*

stoppage Hemmung *f,* Ladehemmung *f (Ord).*

stopping distance Bremsweg *m (MT).*

stopwatch Stoppuhr *f.*

storage Lagern *n,* Lagerung *f,* Aufbewahrung *f.*

storage battery Sammlerbatterie *f,* Sammler *m,* Kraftspeicher *m.*

storage-battery cell Plattensatz *m,* Plattensatz *m (Elec).*

storage-battery truck Sammlerkraftwagen *m (Rad).*

storage dam Staudamm *m.*

storage depot Magazin *n.*

storage rack Lagergerüst *n.*

storage shed Lagerschuppen *m.*

storeroom Lagerraum *m,* Speicher *m.*

storm *n* Sturm *m,* Unwetter *m.*

storm *v* stürmen, erstürmen *(Tac).*

storm trooper SA-Mann *m,* Sturmabteilungsmann *m.*

stove Ofen *m.*

stow unterbringen, verstauen.

stowage chart Beladeplan *m (for vehicle).*

stowage position Unterbringung *f (equipment in vehicle).*

strafe unter Feuer nehmen, mit Maschinengewehrfeuer belegen *(Avn).*

strafing attack Maschinengewehrangriff *m (Avn).*

straggler Versprengter *m,* Nachzügler *m.*

straggler collecting point *See* straggler post.

straggler post Versprengtensammelstelle *f.*

straight gerade.

straight ahead geradeaus.

straightedge Lineal *n.*

straight flight Geradeausflug *m (Avn).*

straight-side rim Geradseitfelge *f (MT).*

strain Dehnung *f (Mech);* Beanspruchung *f,* Belastung *f,* Anstrengung *f.*

strand Kabelader *f (Tp wire);* Strang *m (rope).*

strangle erwürgen, erdrosseln.

strap Gurt *m,* Gürtel *m,* Riemen *m.*

stratagem Kriegslist *f,* List *f (Tac).*

strategic strategisch, operativ.

strategic advance guard Vorausabteilung *f.*

strategic air reconnaissance operative Luftaufklärung.

strategic concentration Aufmarsch *m.*

strategic reconnaissance operative Aufklärung.

strategic withdrawal strategischer Rückzug.

strategist Stratege *m.*

strategy Kriegskunst *f,* Feldherrnkunst *f,* Strategie *f.*

strategy of attrition Ermattungsstrategie *f,* Zermürbungsstrategie *f.*

stratocumulus cloud Stratokumulus *m.*

stratosphere Stratosphäre *f (Avn, Met).*

stratum Lage *f (Met).*

stratus cloud Stratus-Wolke *f,* Schichtwolke *f.*

straw Stroh *n.*

stream Bach *m,* Strom *m,* Wasserlauf *m.*

stream crossing Übergang *m,* Übersetzen über Wasserläufe, Bachübergang *m.*

stream-crossing ability Watfähigkeit *f (MT).*

stream-crossing equipment Übergangsmittel *npl,* Übersetzmittel *npl.*

stream-crossing point Übersetzstelle *f.*

stream-crossing troops Übergangstruppe *f.*

streamlined stromlinienförmig.

streamline shape Stromform *f,* Stromlinienform *f.*

streamward wasserwärts.

street Straße *f,* Gasse *f.*

street fighting Straßenkampf *m.*

strength Stärke *f,* Kopfstärke *f (of a unit);* Kraft *f (of an individual).*

strength of barrel Rohrfestigkeit *f (Ord).*

strength of cover   Deckungsstärke *f (Ft)*.

strength of materials   Festigkeitslehre *f*.

strength report   Stärkenachweisung *f*; Iststärkenachweisung *f (daily strength report)*.

stress *n*   Spannung *f*, Belastung *f*.

stress analysis   statische Berechnung, Festigkeitsnachweis *m*.

stress-strain diagram   Spannungs-Dehnungs-Diagramm *n*.

stretch   Strecke *f (distance)*; Ausdehnung *f (expansion)*; Verspannung *f*, Spannung *f (tension)*.

stretcher   Feldtrage *f*, Krankentrage *f*, Trage *f (Med)*.

stride   Doppelschritt *m (2 paces)*.

strike   Aufschlag *m*, Einschlag *m*, Treffer *m (firing)*; Streik *m (labor)*.

strike a flag   die Flagge streichen *(in token of surrender)*; die Flagge niederholen *(at retreat, etc.)*.

strike a tent   das Zelt abbrechen.

strike camp   das Lager abbrechen.

striker   Schlagbolzenspitze *f (G, R)*.

striking force   Frontverband *m (Avn)*.

striking power   Schlagkraft *f (Tac)*.

striking velocity   Auftreffgeschwindigkeit *f*, Aufschlaggeschwindigkeit *f (of a projectile)*.

string   hochgestufte Reihe *(formation flying)*; Schnur *f*, Bindfaden *m (cord)*.

stringer   Längsträger *m*, Streckbalken *m*, Tragbalken *m; Holm *m (spar)*; Gleisbalken *m (rail support) (Bdg)*.

strip *n*   Streifen *m*, Band *n*.

strip *v*   auseinandernehmen, zerlegen *(Ord)*; Waffengruppen auseinandernehmen *(field strip)*; ausschalen *(concrete forms)*.

strip map   Flugstreckenkarte *f (Avn)*; Marschskizze *f*, Wegskizze *f (MT)*.

strip mosaic   Bildreihe *f*.

strip powder   Stäbchenpulver *n (Am)*.

stroke   Hub *m*, Takt *m (Mtr)*.

strong   stark, kräftig.

strong point   Stützpunkt *m*.

structural defect   Materialfehler *m (of material)*; Baufehler *m (of construction)*.

structural dimensions   Baumaß *n*.

structural-steel obstacle   Sperre aus Stahlträgern.

structural unit   Bauglied *n*.

structural weight   Rüstgewicht *n (plus equipment, Ap)*.

structure   Gebäude *n (building)*; Zusammensetzung *f (composition)*; Bau *m (type of construction)*; Gliederung *f (organization)*; Gestaltung *f (configuration)*.

strut   Stiel *m (compression member)*; Strebe *f (tension member)*.

strut-braced construction   Sprengwerk *n (Engr)*.

stub wing   Ansatzflügel *m (Ap)*.

stuck   bewegungsunfähig *(MT)*.

to get stuck   stecken bleiben *(MT)*.

stud   Seitengewehrhalter *m (R)*.

stuffing box   Stopfbuchse *f*.

stump   Baumstumpf *m*, Stumpf *m*.

stunt flying   Kunstflug *m*.

stunt-flying maneuver   Kunstflugfigur *f*.

styptic *n*   blutstillendes Mittel.

subarea   Teilgebiet *n*, Unterabschnitt *m*.

subcaliber ammunition   Kleinkalibermunition *f*, Zielmunition *f*.

subcaliber barrel   *See* subcaliber tube.

subcaliber firing   Abkommschießen *n*.

subcaliber target practice   Kleinkaliberschießen *n (Arty)*.

subcaliber target range   Kleinschießplatz *m (Arty)*.

subcaliber tube   Einstecklauf *m*, Einlegerohr *n*, Abkommrohr *n*, Kleinkaliberlauf *m (G)*.

subchaser   *See* submarine chaser.

subdepot   Zweiglager *n*, Zweigdepot *n*, Nebendepot *n*.

subdue   bezwingen *(the enemy)*; unterwerfen *(to subject)*; unterdrücken *(to suppress)*.

sub-grade   Bahnplanum *n (RR)*; Unterbau *m (road)*.

submachine gun   Maschinenpistole *f*.

submarine   Unterseeboot *n*, U-Boot *n*.

submarine chaser   U-Bootjäger *m*.

submarine commander   Unterseebootkommandant *m*.

submarine construction yard   U-Boot-Werft *f*.

submarine mine   Seemine *f*.

submarine mine field   Seeminensperre *f*, Minensperre *f*, Minenfeld *n (Nav)*.

submarine mine planter   Minenfahrzeug *n*, Minenleger *m*, Minendampfer *m*.

submarine mining   Minenlegen *n*.

submarine net U-Bootnetz *n*.
submarine pen U-Boot-Bunker *m*.
submarine tender U-Boot-Mutter-schiff *n*.
submarine warfare U-Bootkrieg *m*.
subordinate unterstellt.
sub-port Nebenhafen *m*.
subsector Unterabschnitt *m*.
subsector reserve Unterabschnitts-Reserve *f (Tac)*.
subsistence Quartier und Verpfle-gung.
subsistence allowance Quartier- und Verpflegungsvergütung *f*.
subsistence stores Verpflegungsgegen-stände *mpl*.
subsoil water Grundwasser *n (Engr)*.
substitute Ersatz *m (thing)*; Stell-vertreter *m (Pers)*.
sub-stratosphere airplane Höhenflug-zeug *n*, Substratosphärenflugzeug *n*.
substructure Unterbau *m*.
subtract abziehen.
succeed Erfolg haben, gelingen *(make good)*; folgen, nachfolgen *(follow, replace)*.
success Erfolg *m*.
suction Sog *m*, Ansaugung *f*, An-saugen *n*.
suction line Saugleitung *f (MT)*.
suction stroke Saughub *m*, Ansauge-takt *m (Mtr)*.
suction surface Saugseite *f (Ap wing)*.
suffocate ersticken.
sugar Zucker *m*.
sulfur Schwefel *m*.
sulfuric acid Schwefelsäure *f*.
sulfur trioxide Schwefeltrioxyd *n (CWS)*.
sulfur trioxide-chlorsulfonic acid so-lution Nebelsäure *f (CWS)*.
sulphur *See* sulfur.
summary court-martial Standgericht *n (in USA for noncapital offenses)*.
summit Gipfel *m*.
summit of trajectory Gipfelpunkt *m (Ballistics)*.
sump Sickerschacht *m (Ft)*; Schmier-stoffbehälter *m (Mtr)*.
sun Sonne *f*.
sun-blindness Blendung durch Son-nenlicht.
sunburn Sonnenbrand *m*.
sun helmet Tropenhelm *m*.
sunken road Hohlweg *m*.
sunrise Sonnenaufgang *m*.
sunset Sonnenuntergang *m*.

sunshade Sonnenblende *f*.
sunstroke Sonnenstich *m*.
supercharge vorverdichten *(Mtr)*.
supercharged engine Auflademotor *m*, Gebläsemotor *m*, Kompressormo-tor *m (Avn)*.
supercharger Gebläse *n*, Kompressor *m*, Lader *m*, Vorverdichter *m*; Bo-denlader *m (with low blower ratio)*; Höhenlader *m (with high blower ratio)*.
supercontrol tube Regelröhre *f (Rad)*.
superelevation Aufsatzwinkel *m (AA gunnery)*.
superheterodyne receiver Überlage-rungsempfänger *m*, Zwischenfre-quenzempfänger *m (Rad)*.
superior *n* Vorgesetzter *m*.
superior *adj* überlegen *(in strength, etc.)*; vorgesetzt *(in command, etc.)*; höher *(higher)*.
superiority Überlegenheit *f*, Über-macht *f*.
superior officer Vorgesetzter *m*.
superior provost court Oberfeldge-richt *n (USA)*.
superior strength Übermacht *f (Tac)*.
supernumerary überzählig, über-planmäßig.
superposed circuit Kunstschaltung *f (Tp)*.
superquick fuze empfindlicher Zünder, empfindlicher Aufschlagzünder *(Am)*.
superregenerative receiver Pendelfre-quenzempfänger *m*.
supersaturation Übersättigung *f (Met)*.
supersede ersetzen.
supersensitive fuze hochempfindlicher Aufschlagzünder *(AA Am)*.
superstructure Überbau *m*.
stranded wire Litze *f (Elec)*.
supervise beaufsichtigen, überwachen.
supplementary ergänzend, nachträg-lich, Ergänzungs-.
supplies Nachschubgüter *npl*, Ver-sorgungsgüter *npl*.
supply Nachschub *m*, Versorgung *f*, Heeresversorgung *f*.
supply *v* versorgen, beliefern, liefern.
supply *adj* Nachschub-, Versorgungs-.
supply area Nachschubgebiet *n*, Ver-sorgungsgebiet *n*, Versorgungsbe-zirk *m*.
supply balloon *See* nurse balloon.
supply base Nachschubstützpunkt *m*.
supply boat Nachschubboot *n*.

supply by air Luftversorgung *f*.
supply column Nachschubkolonne *f*.
supply convoy Nachschubgeleit *n* *(Nav)*.
supply delivery unit Versorgungsbombe *f* *(airborne Opns)*.
supply depot Nachschublager *n*, Lager *n*.
Supply Division Heeresnachschubamt im Generalstab des Heeres *(USA)*.
supply dump Nachschublager *n*, Materiallager *n*.
supply line Nachschublinie *f*.
supply party Nachschubtrupp *m*.
supply point Nachschublager *n* *(depot)*; Nachschubumschlagstelle *f*, *(rail or truck head)*; Nachschubausgabestelle *f* *(distributing point)*.
supply port Versorgungshafen *m*.
supply road Nachschubweg *m*.
supply route Nachschubstraße *f*.
supply sergeant Kammerunteroffizier *m*.
supply service Nachschubdienst *m*, Versorgungsdienst *m*.
supply shortage Nachschubmangel *m*.
supply tank Nachschubpanzerkampfwagen *m* *(vehicle)*.
supply traffic Nachschubverkehr *f*.
supply train Nachschubzug *m* *(RR)*; Fahrkolonne *f* *(H-Dr)*; Kraftfahrkolonne *f* *(MT)*; Gefechtstroß *m* *(combat)*; Verpflegungstroß *m* *(rations)*.
supply vehicle Nachschubfahrzeug *n*, Versorgungsfahrzeug *n*.
support Rückhalt *m*, Unterstützung *f* *(Tac)*; Aufnahmen *fpl* *(in delaying maneuver)*; Stütze *f*, Lager *n*, Träger *m* *(Tech)*.
support *v* unterstützen, Rückhalt geben, schützen *(by fire)*, decken *(Tac)*.
support aviation Schlachtflieger *mpl*.
supported flank angelehnter Flügel.
support force Frontverband *m* *(Avn)*.
supporting artillery Unterstützungsartillerie *f*.
supporting fire Unterstützungsfeuer *n*.
support party Deckungstrupp *m*.
suppressor grid Bremsgitter *n*, Schutzgitter *n* *(Rad tube)*.
supreme command Oberbefehl *m*.
surcingle Deckengurt *m*, Obergurt *m*, *(harness)*.
surface Oberfläche *f* *(outside or top)*; Fläche *f* *(area)*; Boden *m* *(ground)*.

surface area Flächeninhalt *m* *(Surv)*.
surface construction Tiefbau *m* *(Tp line)*.
surface direction-finder station Bodenpeilstelle *f* *(Avn)*.
surface forces Überwasserstreitkräfte *fpl* *(Nav)*.
surface line Bodenleitung *f* *(Tp)*.
surface wind Bodenwind *m*.
surge Stromstoß *m* *(Elec)*.
surge chamber Druckraum *m* *(hydraulics)*.
surgeon Sanitätsoffizier *m* *(Mil)*; Chirurg *m*.
Surgeon General Heeres-Sanitätsinspekteur *m*.
surgery Chirurgie *f*.
surgical hospital Feldlazarett *n*, Armeefeldlazarett *n*.
surname Familienname *m*, Zuname *m*.
surplus stock Mehrbestand *m*.
surprise Überraschung *f* *(Tac)*.
surprise attack Überraschungsangriff *m*, Überfall *m* *(Tac)*.
surprise fire Feuerüberfall *m* *(Arty, MG)*.
surprise raid Handstreich *m*.
surrender *n* Kapitulation *f*, Übergabe *f*, Waffenstreckung *f*.
surrender *v* sich ergeben, kapitulieren.
surveillance Überwachung *f* *(Obsn)*; Untersuchung *f* *(Am and CWS supplies)*.
surveillance of fire Feuerbeobachtung *f* *(Arty)*.
survey *n* Vermessung *f*, Vermessung durch Anhängen *(by controlled traverse)* *(Arty, Engr)*.
survey *v* vermessen *(measure)*; besichtigen *(inspect)*.
surveying Vermessung *f*, Einmessen *n* *(Arty, Engr)*.
survey map sheet Meßtischblatt *n*.
surveyor's chain Meßkette *f* *(Surv)*.
surveyor's level Nivellierinstrument *n* *(Engr)*.
surveyor's tape Meßband *n*.
suspend zeitweilig vom Dienst entheben *(from duty)*; hängen *(hang)*; einhängen *(a bomb)*.
suspended camouflage net hängende Fliegermaske *(AA defense)*.
"suspend firing!" "Stopfen!"
suspension zeitweilige Dienstenthebung *(from duty)*; Aufhängung *f* *(of bombs)*; Federung *f* *(MT)*;

Laufwerk *n (Tk)*; Pause *f (of activity)*.
suspension bridge Hängebrücke *f*.
suspension frame Trapez *n (Bln)*.
suspension line Hängeleine *f (Prcht)*.
suspension lug Aufhängeöse *f (bomb)*.
suspension of arms örtliche vorübergehende Waffenruhe.
suspension of fire Feuerpause *f*.
suspension of traffic Verkehrsunterbrechung *f*.
suspensions Laufwerk *n (Tk)*.
suspensions and tracks Fahrwerk *n (Tk)*.
suspension spring Tragfeder *f (split-trail carriage)*.
sustained fire Dauerfeuer *n*.
swamp Sumpf *m*.
swamp atmosphere Sumpfklima *n*.
swamp sector Sumpfstreifen *m*.
swastika Hakenkreuz *n*.
sway brace Verschwertung *f (Engr)*.
swear in vereidigen.
sweat *n* Schweiß *m*.
sweat *v* schwitzen.
sweater Schlupfjacke *f (Clo)*.
sweep *v* absuchen *(searching for mines)*; räumen *(clearing of mines)*; bestreichen *(Gunnery)*; fegen.
sweepback Pfeilform *f (Ap wing)*.
sweeping fire Breitenfeuer *n (MG)*.
swerve pendeln.
swim schwimmen.
swimmer Schwimmer *m*; Freischwimmer *m (qualified swimmer)*.
swing team Mittelpferde *npl*.
switch Schalter *m (Elec)*; Weiche *f (RR)*.
switchboard Klappenschrank *m*, Schalttafel *f*, Schalttisch *m*, Vermittlungseinrichtung *f (Tp)*.
switchboard drop Anrufklappe *f (Tp)*.
switchboard operator Fernsprecher *m*.
switch box Schaltkasten *m (Elec, MT)*; Schaltkästchen *n (sound ranging apparatus)*.

switching Verschieben *n (RR)*.
switching central Vermittlungsstelle *f*, Vermittlung *f*, Fernsprechvermittlung *f (Tp)*.
switching off Ausschaltung *f (Elec)*.
switching on Einschaltung *f (Elec)*.
switch knob Schaltgriff *m (Elec)*.
switch lamp Weichenlaterne *f (RR)*.
switch lever Weichenhebel *m (RR)*.
switch point Herzstück *n (RR switch)*.
switch position Wechselstellung *f (Tac)*.
switch stand Weichenbock *m (RR)*.
switch tower Stellwerk *n (RR)*.
swivel Riemenbügel *m (R)*.
swivel gun Pivotgeschütz *n*, Sockelgeschütz *n*.
sword Degen *m*.
sword knot Faustriemen *m*; Portepee *n (worn by Ger officers and higher NCO's)*.
symbol Zeichen *n*.
sympathetic detonation übertragene Zündung.
synchro-mesh transmission Synchrongetriebe *n (MT)*.
synchronism Gleichlauf *m*.
synchronization Synchronisierung *f*, Steuerung *f*, Zusammenwirken *n*; Maschinengewehrsteuerung *f (Ap MGs)*.
synchronize synchronisieren; gleichstellen *(watches)*.
synchronized machine gun synchronisiertes Maschinengewehr, gesteuertes Maschinengewehr *(Ap)*.
synchroscope Synchronoskop *n (Ap)*.
synthetic *n* Kunststoff *m*.
synthetic material Ersatz *m*, Ersatzstoff *m*.
synthetic rubber künstlicher Gummi, synthetischer Gummi.
syphilis Syphilis *f*.
systematic error regelmäßiger Fehler, systematischer Fehler.

T

table Tafel *f (list)*; Tisch *m (furniture)*.
table of basic allowances Ausrüstungsnachweisung *f*.

table of coordinates Koordinatenverzeichnis *n (Surv)*.
table of equipment Ausrüstungsnachweisung *f*.

table 409 tank battle

table of maximum punishment Verzeichnis der Höchststrafe.

table of organization Stärkenachweisung *f;* Friedensstärkenachweisung *f (peacetime);* Kriegsstärkenachweisung *f (wartime).*

tachometer Drehzahlmesser *m,* Umdrehungszähler *m,* Stichzähler *m.*

tack *n* Stiftzwecke *f (carpet, etc.);* Reißnagel *m (thumbtack).*

tackle *n* Flaschenzug *m.*

tactical taktisch.

tactical airplane Kriegsflugzeug *n.*

tactical employment taktische Verwendung, taktischer Einsatz.

tactical exercise taktische Übung.

tactical fire classification taktische Feuerbegriffe *(Arty).*

tactical grouping taktische Gruppengliederung, Kräfteverteilung *f,* Gefechtsgliederung *f.*

tactical maneuver taktisches Manöver.

tactical march Kriegsmarsch *m.*

tactical obstacle taktisches Hindernis.

tactical offensive taktischer Angriff.

tactical operation Gefechtshandlung *f,* Kampfhandlung *f.*

tactical operations staff Gefechtsstab *m.*

tactical plan taktischer Plan.

tactical protection Gasabwehrmaßnahmen *fpl (CWS).*

tactical reconnaissance taktische Aufklärung.

tactical retreat planmäßiger Rückzug.

tactical ride Geländebesprechung *f (maneuvers).*

tactical situation Kampflage *f,* Kampfverhältnisse *npl,* taktische Lage.

tactical smoke künstlicher Nebel.

tactical symbol taktisches Zeichen.

tactical training Gefechtsausbildung *f.*

tactical unit Kampfeinheit *f,* taktischer Verband.

tactical walk Geländebesprechung *f (maneuvers).*

tactician Taktiker *m.*

tactics Taktik *f,* Gefechtslehre *f.*

tactics and technique Waffenführung *f,* Waffentechnik *f.*

tag Anhänger *m,* Anhängezettel *m (tie-on type),* Klebezettel *m (stick-on type).*

tail Heck *n,* Rumpfende *n,* Schwanz *m (Ap);* Bodenschwanz *m (bomb);* Schweif *m (horse).*

tail assembly Leitwerk *n (Ap).*

tail fin Seitenflosse *f (Ap).*

tail gun Heckwaffe *f (Ap).*

tail gunner Heckschütze *m (Avn).*

tail gun position Heckstand *m (Ap).*

tailheavy schwanzlastig *(Ap).*

tail landing Schwanzlandung *f (Avn).*

taillight Rücklicht *n,* Schlußlicht *n (MT).*

tail skid Sporn *m,* Schwanzsporn *m,* Spornschuh *m (Ap).*

tail spin Trudeln *n.*

tail surface Dämpfungsflosse *f (Ap).*

tail turret Heckkanzel *f (Ap).*

tail turret gun Heckmaschinengewehr *n,* Heckwaffe *f.*

tail unit Leitwerk *n (Ap).*

tail wheel Radsporn *m,* Spornrad *n (Ap).*

tail wind Rückenwind *m.*

"Take, Arms!" "Gewehr in die, Hand!"

take bearings anpeilen, peilen *(Air Navigation) (Rad).*

take-off Abflug *m,* Start *m (Avn).*

take off starten *(Avn).*

take-off distance Startlänge *f,* Anlaufstrecke *f (Avn).*

take-off point Start *m,* Startstelle *f (Adrm).*

take-off rating Abflugleistung *f.*

take-off run Anlauf *m (Avn).*

take-off speed Abfluggeschwindigkeit *f (Avn).*

take-off zone Startzone *f (Adrm).*

take up the slack Druckpunkt nehmen *(Small Arms).*

talking range Sprechverständigung *f (Tp).*

tamping Verdämmen *n (blasting).*

tampion See tompion.

tandem airplane Tandemflugzeug *n.*

tangent Berührungslinie *f,* Tangente *f (geometry);* Tangens *m (trigonometrical function).*

tangent sight Kurvenvisier *n (MG).*

tank Kampfwagen *m,* Panzerkampfwagen *m,* Panzerwagen *m,* Panzer *m,* Tank *m (Tk);* Behälter *m (container).*

tank ammunition Panzermunition *f.*

tank armament Bordwaffen *fpl.*

tank barrier Panzersperre *f,* Panzerkampfwagenhindernis *n.*

tank battle Panzerkampf *m,* Panzerschlacht *f.*

tank car Eisenbahnkesselwagen *m*, Tankwagen *m* (*RR*).

tank commander Panzerführer *m*, Panzerkommandant *m*.

tank crew Panzerbesatzung *f*.

tank cupola Panzerkuppel *f*.

tank destroyer Pakgeschütz auf Selbstfahrlafette (*USA*).

tank destroyer gun Panzerjägergeschütz *n*.

Tank Destroyer School Panzerjägerschule *f* (*USA*).

tank ditch Panzerwagengraben *m*.

tank driver Panzerfahrer *m*.

tank engagement Panzerkampf *m*.

tank engine Panzermotor *m*.

tanker Tanker *m*, Tankschiff *n*, Tankdampfer *m* (*Nav*).

tank factory Kampfwagenwerk *n*.

tank gun Kampfwagenkanone *f*, Kampfwagengeschütz *n*, Panzerkanone *f*.

tank gunner Panzerschütze *m*.

tank hull Panzerkasten *m*, Panzerwanne *f*; Panzeraufbau *m* (*hull and turret*).

tank landing craft Fährprahm *m*, F-Boot *n*.

tank mine Panzermine *f*.

tank obstacle Panzerkampfwagenhindernis *n*.

tank radio operator Panzerfunker *m*.

tank shutter Panzerblende *f*.

tank silhouette Pz.Kw.-Nachbildung *f*, Kampfwagennachbildung *f* (*practice firing*).

tank-silhouette aiming target Panzerrichttafel *f*.

tank-silhouette target Kampfwagenscheibe *f*.

tank track Panzerkette *f*.

tank trap Panzerwagenfalle *f*, Panzerfalle *f*, Panzerfahrzeugfalle *f*, Tankfalle *f*.

tank truck Tankwagen *m*, Brennstofftankwagen *m*, Kesselwagen *m*, Kraftstoff-Kesselkraftwagen *m* (*MT*).

tank turret Panzerturm *m*.

tank warfare Panzerkriegführung *f*.

tank warning Panzerwarnung *f*.

T-antenna T-Antenne *f* (*Rad*).

tap *n* Anzapfung *f* (*Elec*); Gewindebohrer *m* (*Tech*).

tap *v* anzapfen (*a wire, etc.*) (*Elec*); ein (Innen) Gewinde schneiden (*Tech*).

tape *n* Aufnahmestreifen *m* (*tele-*

type); Klebestreifen *m* (*adhesive tape*); Trassierband *n* (*tracing tape*).

taper Verjüngung *f* (*Mech*).

tapered bore Würgebohrung *f* (*barrel*) (*Ord*).

tappet rod Stößel *m*, Stoßstange *f*; Abwälzstößel *m* (*eccentric-cam type*); Gleitstößel *m* (*sliding-cam type*).

taps Zapfenstreich *m*.

tar Teer *m*.

target Ziel *n* (*combat*); Scheibe *f* (*Tng*).

target area Zielgelände *n*, Zielraumfläche *f*, Zielkreis *m*, Bombenwurfraum *m* (*Arty*); Zielgebiet *n*, Zielplatz *m* (*bombing*).

target butt Kugelfang *m*.

target course Zielweg *m* (*AA*).

target designation Zielansprache *f*.

target-designation grid Zielgeviertafel *f* (*Arty Surv*).

target frame Scheibenrahmen *m*.

target image Zielbild *n* (*telescopic sight*).

target length Zielbreite *f* (*moving targets*).

target location Zielfeststellung *f* (*Gunnery*).

target moving at an angle schrägfahrendes Ziel (*ground target*).

target moving parallel to front querfahrendes Ziel (*ground target*).

target of opportunity Gelegenheitsziel *n*.

target practice Schulschießen *n*, Übungsschießen *n*.

target range Schießplatz *m*, Schulschießstand *m*, Schulgefechtschießstand *m*.

target reconnaissance Zielerkundung *f*, Zielaufklärung *f*.

target sector Zielteil *m*.

target ship Zielschiff *n*.

target sled Zielschlitten *m*.

tarpaulin Decke *f*, Plane *f*.

task Auftrag *m*, Aufgabe *f*.

task air force Fliegerverband *m*.

task force Armeegruppe *f* (*usually an army plus miscellaneous units*); Kampfgruppe *f* (*smaller*).

tassel Quast *m*.

taste Geschmack *m*.

tattoo Signal "Lichter .aus!"

taxi *v* rollen (*Avn*).

taxiway neutrale Zone, Rollbahn *f*, Rollstraße *f* (*Adrm*).

team Mannschaft *f (Pers);* Gespann *n,* Bespannung *f (horses, etc.).*
team of horses Gespann *n.*
tear gas Tranengas *n* Tranenstoff *m,* Reizkorper *m (CWS)*
tear-gas candle Tranengaskerze *f (CWS)*
tear-gas pot Tränenstoffkerze *f (CWS)*
technical adviser Fachberater *m.*
technical designer Konstrukteur *m.*
technical inspection Waffen- und Geratuntersuchung *f.*
Technical Manual Bedienungsanleitung *f.* Merkblatt zur Bedienung, Gebrauchsanleitung *f.*
technical sergeant Feldwebel *m;* Wachtmeister *m (Arty, Cav);* Feuerwerker *m (Ord),* Funkmeister *m (Rad);* Schirrmeister *m (maintenance);* Brieftaubenmeister *m (pigeoneer);* Festungspionierfeldwebel *m (Ft Engr).*
technical services technische Dienstzweige.
technician Techniker *m.*
telegram Telegramm *n.*
telegraph Telegraph *m,* Fernschreiber *m.*
telegraph key Morsetaste *f.*
telegraph line Telegraphenleitung *f.*
telegraph pole Telegraphenstange *f.*
telegraph printer Schnelltelegraph *m,* Ferndrucker *m,* Fernschreiber *m.*
telegraphy Telegraphie *f.*
telephone Fernsprecher *m,* Telephon *n.*
by telephone fernmündlich.
telephone call Ferngespräch *n,* Gespräch *n,* Spruch *m.*
telephone central Fernsprechvermittlung *f,* Vermittlung *f,* Vermittlungsstelle *f.*
telephone circuit Sprechverbindung *f.*
telephone communication Sprechverbindung *f.*
telephone - communications company Fernsprechkompanie *f.*
telephone connection Sprechverbindung *f*
telephone-construction company Fernsprechbaukompanie *f.*
telephone-construction detail Fernsprechbautrupp *m.*
telephone construction truck Fernsprechbauwagen *m.*
telephone equipment Fernsprechgerät *n.*

telephone line Fernsprechleitung *f.*
telephone motor truck Fernsprechkraftwagen *m.*
telephone motor vehicle Fernsprechkraftfahrzeug *n.*
telephone operations truck Fernsprechbetriebskraftwagen *m.*
telephone operations vehicle Fernsprechfahrzeug *n.*
telephone operator Fernsprecher *m.*
telephone pole Leitungsmast *m.*
telephone receiver Hörer *m.*
telephone relay Fernsprechrelais *n.*
telephone section Fernsprechtrupp *m.*
telephone station Fernsprechstelle *f,* Sprechstelle *f.*
telephone traffic Fernsprechverkehr *m,* Sprechverkehr *m.*
telephone transcription Fernspruch *m.*
telephoto Fernbild *n,* Fernrohraufnahme *f.*
telescope Fernrohr *n.*
telescope center section Fernrohrhals *m.*
telescope head Fernrohrkopf *m.*
telescope holder Zielfernrohrträger *m (AT gun, R).*
telescope housing Fernrohrhülse *f.*
telescope mount Aufsatz *m,* Richtaufsatz *m (Ord).*
telescope seat Fernrohrlager *n.*
telescope support Fernrohrsteg *m.*
telescope tube Fernrohrkörper *m;* Fernrohrarm *m (BC telescope).*
telescopic sight Zielfernrohr *n,* Richtfernrohr *n,* Fernrohraufsatz *m,* Optik *f.*
with telescopic sight fernrohrbesetzt.
telescopic sight mount Zielfernrohrträger *m.*
teletype Schnelltelegraph *m,* Ferndrucker *m,* Fernschreiber *m.*
teletype circuit Fernschreibleitung *f.*
teletype net Fernschreibnetz *n.*
teletype operator Fernschreiber *m.*
teletype truck Fernschreibwagen *m.*
teletypewriter Schnelltelegraph *m,* Ferndrucker *m,* Fernschreiber *m.*
television Fernsehen *n.*
temperature Temperatur *f.*
temperature difference Wärmeunterschied *m (Met).*
temperature gage Temperaturmesser *m (Mtr).*
temperature gradient Temperaturgradient *m (Met).*

temperature variation Temperaturschwankung *f.*
tempered steel gehärteter Stahl.
template *See* templet.
temple Schläfe *f (anatomy).*
temple strap Schläfenband *n (gas
mask).*
templet Schablone *f (Tech).;* Zellu-
loidplatte mit Einteilung *(Surv).*
temporary grade zeitweiliger Rang.
tenacious zäh.
tender Anhänger *m (RR);* Mutterschiff *n,* Tender *m (Nav).*
tendon Sehne *f.*
tensile strength Zugfestigkeit *f.*
tensile stress Zugspannung *f.*
tension Spannung *f.*
tension chord Zuggurt *m (truss).*
tension line Stromleine *f (Bdg).*
tension member Strebe *f.*
tension wire Spanndraht *m.*
tent Zelt *n.*
tent camp Zeltlager *n.*
tent equipment Zeltausrüstung *f.*
tent pin Zeltpflock *m,* Hering *m.*
tent pitching Zeltbau *m.*
tent pole Zeltstock *m.*
terminal Kabelschuh *m (Elec);* Endbahnhof *m (RR).*
terminal binding post Polklemme *f.*
terminal plate Endplatte *f (Elec).*
terminal repeater Endverstärker *m
(Tp).*
terminal station Endbahnhof *m
(RR).*
terminal twist Enddrall *m (Ord).*
terminal velocity Endgeschwindigkeit
f (Ballistics).
terminal velocity dive Sturzflug mit
Endgeschwindigkeit *(Avn).*
terminology of orders Befehlssprache
f.
terrain Gelände *n.*
terrain appreciation Geländebeurteilung *f (Tac).*
terrain area Gelänéeraum *m.*
terrain compartment Geländeabschnitt *m.*
terrain conditions Geländeverhältnisse *npl.*
terrain contamination Geländevergiftung *f.*
terrain corridor Geländestreifen *m.*
terrain exercise Rahmenübung *f.*
terrain feature Geländegegenstand
m, auffallender Geländepunkt.

terrain intelligence Geländeerkundung *f.*
terrain obstacle Geländehindernis *n.*
terrain photo-survey Geländeaufnahme *f.*
terrain problem Geländeaufgabe *f
(maneuvers).*
terrain representation Geländedarstellung *f (Surv).*
terrain sector Geländeabschnitt *m.*
terrain surveying Geländevermessung *f.*
terrestrial fire Flachfeuer *n,* Feuer
in der unteren Winkelgruppe *(Gunnery).*
terrestrial observation Erdbeobachtung *f (Arty).*
territory Gebiet *n.*
test Prüfung *f,* Versuch *m,* Probe *f.*
test airplane Versuchsflugzeug *n.*
test button Prüfknopf *m (field
Tp).*
test cartridge Meßkartusche *f (Am).*
test firing Probeschießen *n,* Versuchsschießen *n (Ord).*
test flight Probeflug *m,* Einfliegen *n.*
testicle Hoden *m.*
testing apparatus Prüfgerät *n.*
testing block Prüfstand *m (Avn,
(MT).*
testing stand Prüfgestell *n,* Prüfstand *m.*
test key Prüftaste *f (field Tp).*
test pilot Einflieger *m.*
test run Probelauf *m,* Versuchslauf
m (Mtr).
test station Untersuchungsstelle *f
(Tp).*
tetanus Wundstarrkrampf *m (Med).*
tetraethyl lead Bleitetraäthyl *n.*
tetrahedron Igel *m (AT).*
tetryl Tetryl *n.*
text Wortlaut *m,* Text *m.*
text in clear Klartext *m (Sig C).*
theater commander kommandierender General eines Operationsgebiets.
theater of operations Operationsgebiet *n,* Kriegsgebiet *n.*
theater of war Kriegsschauplatz *m.*
theater reserve Hauptreserve des
Operationsgebiets.
theodolite Theodolit *m (Surv).*
theoretical deflection shift schußtafelmäßige Seitenverschiebung.
theoretical range schußtafelmäßige
Schußweite *(Gunnery).*

theoretical time of flight schußtafel-mäßige Flugzeit *(Ballistics)*.
theory Lehre *f*, Theorie *f*.
theory of antiaircraft fire Flak-schießlehre *f*.
theory of flight Fluglehre *f*.
theory of gunnery Schießlehre *f*; Flakschießlehre *f (AA)*.
theory of tactics Gefechtslehre *f*.
thermal soaring Thermiksegeln *n (glider)*.
thermite Thermit *n*.
thermite bomb Thermitbombe *f*.
thermite charge Thermitladung *f (incendiary bomb)*.
thermite grenade Thermithandgra-nate *f*.
thermocouple meter Thermokreuz-instrument *n*.
thermograph Thermograph *m*.
thermo ice elimination Warmluftent-eisung *f (Avn)*.
thermometer Thermometer *n*.
thermos bottle Thermosflasche *f*.
thermostat Thermostat *m*.
thick dick, dicht.
thickness gage Fühlerlehre *f*.
thickness of armor Panzerstärke *f (Tk)*.
thigh Schenkel *m*, Oberschenkel *m*.
thimble Kausche *f (rigging, etc.)*.
thirsty durstig.
Thompson submachine gun Maschi-nenpistole Modell Thompson.
thread Gewinde *n (Tech)*; Faden *m (sewing)*.
threaded anvil Amboßschraube *f (Am)*.
threaded breech hoop Spannschraube *f (G)*.
threaded closing cap Verschluß-schraube *f (fuze)*.
threaded percussion primer Schlag-zündschraube *f (fuze)*.
threaded plug Verschraubung *f*.
threaded sleeve Muffe *f (for pipe connections)*.
threat Drohung *f*, Bedrohung *f*.
three-axle vehicle Dreiachser *m*.
three-bank upright engine Drei-reihenstandmotor *m*, W-Motor *m*.
three-blade controllable propeller Dreiblattverstellschraube *f (Ap)*.
three-blade propeller Dreiflügel-schraube *f (Ap)*.
three-engine dreimotorig.

three-phase alternating current Dreh-strom *m*.
three-point landing Dreipunktlan-dung *f (Avn)*.
three-point resection Einschneiden nach drei Punkten *(Surv)*.
three-seater dreisitzig.
three-speed transmission Dreigang-getriebe *n (MT)*.
three-way selector cock Dreiwege-hahn *m*.
throat Kehle *f*, Rachen *m*, Schlund *m*.
throatlatch Kehlriemen *m (harness)*.
throat-type microphone Kehlkopf-microphon *n (Avn)*.
throttle *n* Drossel *f (Mtr)*.
throttle *v* abdrosseln *(Mtr)*.
throttle grip Drosselgriff *m*.
throttle lever Drosselhebel *m*, Gas-hebel *m*, Regulierhebel *m*.
throttle shaft Drosselklappenwelle *f*.
throttle unit Drosselorgan *n*.
throttle valve Drosselklappe *f*.
throttling Drosselung *f*.
through channels auf dem Dienstweg.
through station Durchgangsbahnhof *m (RR)*.
through track Durchlaufgleis *n (RR)*.
throw *n* Wurf *m*.
throw *v* werfen.
throwing pit Wurfgrube *f*.
throwing range Wurfweite *f*.
throw in the clutch einkuppeln *(MT)*.
throwout Schaltstück *n (sight-mount housing)*.
throwout lever Ausschaltehebel *m (aiming circle)*; Schalthebel *m (pa-noramic telescope)*.
throw out the clutch auskuppeln *(MT)*.
thrust Schraubendruck *m*, Schrau-benzug *m (propeller)*; Stich *m*, Stoß *m (with a weapon)*; Vorstoß *m (Tac)*.
thrusting weapon Stichwaffe *f*, Stoß-waffe *f*.
thrust line Stoßlinie *f (Tac)*.
thumb Daumen *m*.
thumb jump Daumensprung *m (range estimation)*.
thumb nut Drücker *m (sight)*.
thumbscrew Flügelschraube *f*.
thumbtack Heftzwecke *f*, Reißnagel *m*.
thumb width Daumenbreite *f (range estimation)*.
thunder Donner *m*.
thunderstorm Gewitter *n*.

ticket Karte *f*, Schein *m*, Zettel *m*.
ticket office Fahrkartenausgabestelle *f* *(office)*; Fahrkartenschalter *m* *(window) (RR)*.
tide Gezeiten *fpl*.
tide station Gezeitenvermessungsstation *f*, Gezeitendienst *m (CA)*.
tide table Gezeitentafel *f*.
tie *n* Schwelle *f (RR)*; Bund *m (lashing)*; Schlips *m (Clo)*.
tie *v* binden, knüpfen; abbinden *(Tp)*; anstechen *(Engr)*.
tie plate Schienenunterlagplatte *f (RR)*.
tie rod Lenkstange *f*, Spurstange *f (MT)*; Kuppelstange *f (split-trail carriage)*.
tighten zusammenziehen, verspannen.
tightening Verspannung *f*.
tilt *n* Schrägstellung *f*, Verkantung *f*.
tilt *v* verkanten, kippen.
timber raft Balkenfloß *n (Bdg)*.
timber road Balkenbahn *f (Engr)*.
timber road-block Balkensperre *f (Engr)*.
time Zeit *f*.
time announcement Uhrzeitangabe *f*.
time blasting fuze Zeitzündschnur *f (Engr)*.
time bomb Zeitbombe *f*, Bombe mit Verzugszeit.
time-delay relay Verzögerungsschütz *m (Elec, Rad)*.
time difference Zeitunterschied *m*, Stoppzeit *f (sound ranging)*.
time-difference method Zeitunterschiedverfahren *n (sound ranging)*.
time distance Marschzeit *f*.
time fire Brennzünderschuß *m (firing)*.
time fuze Zeitzünder *m (Am)*; Zeitzündschnur *f (blasting fuze)*; Brennzünder *m (hand grenade, powder-train fuze)*.
time heading Zeitgruppe *f (on Rad messages)*.
time interval Zeitabstand *m*, Zeitunterschied *m (AA gunnery)*; Stoppzeit *f (flash ranging)*.
time interval recorder Stoppuhr *f*.
time lag Stoppzeit *f (flash ranging)*.
time length Vorbeimarschdauer *f*.
time of attack Angriffsbeginn *m (Tac)*.
time of departure Abfahrzeit *f*.
time of fall Fallzeit *f*, Bombenfallzeit *f (bombing)*.

time of flight Flugzeit *f;* Flugzeitsekunden *fpl (in seconds)*.
time-of-flight curve Flugzeitkurve *f (Ballistics)*.
time of functioning Zünderlaufzeit *f (fuze)*.
time of starting Abfahrzeit *f*.
time shell Granate mit Zeitzünder.
time signal Zeitzeichen *n*.
timetable Fahrplan *m (RR)*; Zeiteinteilung *f (Tac)*; Zeittafel *f*.
time train ring Satzstück *n (time fuze)*.
timing Zündeinstellung *f*, Zündpunktverstellung *f (ignition)*.
timing gear Steuerrad *n (Mtr)*.
timing system Steuerung *f (Mtr)*.
tin Zinn *n*.
tincture of iodine Jodtinktur *f*.
tin-plated verzinnt.
tinsmith Blechschmied *m*.
tip *n* Spitze *f (point)*; Trinkgeld *n (gratuity)*; Flügelende *n (wing)*.
tip *v* kippen *(tilt)*; umkippen *(turn over)*.
tipping gradient Kippneigung *f (MT)*.
tire *n* Reifen *m*, Radreifen *m;* Luftreifen *m (pneumatic)*; Vollgummireifen *m*, Vollreifen *m (solid)*.
tire *v* ermüden, ermatten.
tire casing Laufdecke *f (MT)*.
tire flap Felgenband *n*, Schlauchschoner *m (MT)*.
tire pressure gage Reifen-Luftdruckprüfer *m*.
tire tool Reifenheber *m*, Montierhebel *m*.
titanium tetrachloride Titantetrachlorid *n (CWS)*.
TNT Sprengmunition 02 *f*, Füllpulver 02 *n (abbr. Fp. 02)*.
tobacco Tabak *m*.
toe Zehe *f*.
toe-in Einschlag *m*, Vorspur *f (MT)*.
toggle joint Kniegelenk *n (pistol)*.
toggle switch Kippschalter *m (Elec)*.
tolerance Toleranz *f*, gestattete Abweichung *f (Tech)*.
tollgate Zollschranke *f*.
toll station Überweisungsamt *n (Tp)*.
"tommy gun" Maschinenpistole *f*.
tompion Mündungskappe *f*, Mündungspfropfen *m*, Mundpfropfen *m*, Mittelpfropfen *m (G)*.
ton Tonne *f (metric ton of 1,000 kg)*.
ton capacity Tragfähigkeit *f (MT)*.
tone Ton *m;* Tönung *f (Photo)*.

tongs Zange *f.*
tongue Zunge *f.*
tonnage Schiffsraum *m,* Tonnengehalt *m (Nav).*
tonneau light Deckenlicht *n (MT).*
tool Werkzeug *n.*
tool bag Werkzeugtasche *f.*
tool box Werkzeugkasten *m.*
tool kit *See* tool bag.
tool steel Werkzeugstahl *m.*
tooth Zahn *m.*
toothache Zahnschmerzen *mpl.*
toothbrush Zahnbürste *f.*
toothpaste Zahnpaste *f.*
tooth powder Zahnpulver *n.*
top carriage Oberlafette *f (G).*
top chord Obergurt *m (truss).*
topographical crest Böschungskrone *f.*
topographical feature Geländeform *f.*
topographical map topographische Karte.
topographical point graphischer Punkt.
topographic survey Erdvermessung *f.*
topographic troops Karten- und Vermessungstruppen *fpl.*
topography Topographie *f.*
top sergeant Spieß *m.*
torch Fackel *f.*
torpedo *n* Torpedo *n.*
torpedo *v* torpedieren.
torpedo boat Schnellboot *n.*
torpedo bomber Torpedoflugzeug *n,* Torpedoflieger *m.*
torpedo-bomber pilot Torpedoflieger *m.*
torpedo-carrying flying boat Flugtorpedoboot *n.*
torpedo defense net Torpedoschutznetz *n.*
torpedoman Torpedo-Waffenleitvormann *m (Nav).*
torpedo plane Torpedoflugzeug *n.*
torpedo release Torpedoabwurf *m,* Torpedowurf *m (Avn).*
torpedo tube Torpedoausstoßrohr *n,* Torpedorohr *n.*
torque Drehmoment *n (Mech, Mtr).*
torque tube Verstellwelle *f (Ap).*
torsional vibration Drehschwingung *f (Mtr).*
torsional vibration damper Schwingungsdämpfer *m (Mtr).*
total elevation Gesamtrohrerhöhung *f (G).*
total loss Totalausfall *m.*
total mileage odometer Gesamtkilometerzähler *m (speedometer).*

total movement in elevation Höhenrichtfeld *n (Ord).*
total movement in traverse Schwenkbereich *m,* Seitenrichtbereich *m,* Seitenrichtfeld *n (G, MG).*
total traverse Gesamtseitenrichtung *f (G).*
total war totaler Krieg.
touch signal Berührungszeichen *n (Tk).*
tough zäh *(tenacious);* schwierig *(difficult).*
tourniquet Aderpresse *f.*
tow *v* schleppen.
towed boat Schleppkahn *m.*
towed-sleeve target Schleppziel *n,* Schleppscheibe *f,* Luftsack *m (AAA).*
towel Handtuch *n.*
tower Turm *m.*
towing Abschleppen *n.*
towing equipment Abschleppgerät *n.*
towline Startseil *n (glider).*
town Stadt *f,* Ortschaft *f.*
town headquarters Stadtkommandantur *f,* Ortskommandantur *f (Mil Govt).*
tow rope Schlepptau *n.*
tow target Schleppscheibe *f,* gezogenes Ziel.
toxic giftig.
toxic agent Giftstoff *m (CWS).*
toxic smoke Giftnebel *m (CWS).*
toxic-smoke candle Giftrauchkerze *f (CWS).*
trace *n* Leuchtspur *f (of tracer projectile);* Geschirrtau *n (harness).*
trace *v* durchpausen *(a map, etc.).*
tracer Leuchtspurgeschoß *n (projectile);* Leuchtspursatz *m (composition).*
tracer ammunition Leuchtspurmunition *f,* Leuchtmunition *f.*
tracer bullet Leuchtspurgeschoß *n.*
tracer shell Leuchtspurgranate *f (Am).*
tracer thread Kennfaden *m (field wire).*
tracing paper Pauspapier *n.*
tracing tape Trassierband *n (CWS, Engr).*
track *n* Geleise *n (RR);* Schiene *f (a rail);* tatsächlich abgeflogener Kurs *(Avn);* Kette *f (Tk);* Spurweite *f (MT);* Rollbahn *f (road).*
track *v* festhalten *(a target).*
track block Kettenglied *n (Tk, Trac).*

track-connecting fixture Kettenspanner *m (Tk, Trac)*.
tracked landing vehicle Kettenschwimmwagen *m*.
tracking dog Spürhund *m*.
track-laying vehicle Gleiskettenfahrzeug *n*, Kettenfahrzeug *n*, Raupenfahrzeug *n*.
track pin Kettenbolzen *m (Tk, Trac)*.
tracks and suspensions Fahrwerk *n (Tk)*.
track shield Kettenabdeckung *f (Tk)*.
track shoe Kettenglied *n (Tk, Trac)*.
track-supporting roller Stützrolle *f (Tk)*.
traction Bodenhaftung *f*, Griffigkeit *f (ground grip)*; Zugkraft *f (tractional power)*.
traction aid Gleitschutzmittel *n (MT)*.
traction device Greifervorrichtung *f (MT)*.
tractional resistance Fahrwiderstand *m (MT)*.
traction band Geländekette *f (MT)*.
tractor Kraftschlepper *m*, Schlepper *m*, Trecker *m;* Planier-Raupenschlepper *m (with angledozer)*.
tractor airplane Zugschrauber *m*.
tractor-drawn artillery Artillerie mit Kraftzug.
tractor propeller Zugschraube *f (Ap)*.
trade test Berufsprüfung *f*.
trade wind Passatwind *m*.
traffic Verkehr *m*, Betrieb *m*.
traffic area Verkehrskreis *m*.
traffic block Verkehrsstoppung *f*.
traffic center Verkehrspunkt *m*.
traffic control Verkehrsregelung *f*.
traffic-control clearance Einfluggenehmigung *f (Avn)*.
traffic control officer Straßenkommandant *m*.
traffic control post Verkehrsposten *m (road)*; Ablaufposten *m (Bdg)*.
traffic diagram Leitungsskizze *f (Tp)*.
traffic element Verkehrsteilnehmer *m*.
traffic installations Verkehrsanlagen *fpl*.
traffic officer Bahnhofsoffizier *m (RR)*.
traffic patrol Verkehrsstreife *f*.
traffic regulation Verkehrsregel *f*, Verkehrsbestimmung *f;* Vorfahrtregelung *f (right-of-way procedure)*.
traffic sign Verkehrsschild *n*.
traffic supervision Verkehrsüberwachung *f*.

traffic symbol Verkehrszeichen *n*.
trail Lafettenschwanz *m (G)*; Holm *m (of split-trail)*; Hinterstütze *f (MG tripod)*; Rücktrift *f (bomb trajectory)*; Pfad *m*, Spur *f*, Piste *f (path)*.
trail angle Rücktriftwinkel *m (bomb trajectory)*.
trail assembly Lafettierung *f (G)*.
trail box Lafettenkasten *m (G)*.
trail bridge *See* **trail ferry**.
trailer Anhänger *m (MT)*.
trailer load Anhängelast *f (MT)*.
trailer mount Lafettenfahrzeug *n (Arty)*.
trail ferry Gierfähre *f (Engr)*.
trail-ferrying Gieren *n (Engr)*.
trail float Schwanzblech *n (G)*.
trail handspike Richtbaum *m (G)*.
trailing edge Hinterkante *f*, Schleppkante *f (Ap)*.
trailing-wire antenna Hängeantenne *f*, Schleppantenne *f (Ap)*.
trail officer Schließender *m (MT column)*.
trail rope Schlepptau *n (Bln)*.
trail spade Erdsporn *m*, Lafettensporn *m*, Sporn *m (G)*.
train Troß *m*, Kolonne *f (supply vehicles, etc.)*; Zug *m (RR)*.
train bombing Reihenabwurf *m*.
train commander Transportführer *m*, Zugkommandant *m (RR)*.
trainee Rekrut *m*, Schüler *m*.
trainer Schulflugzeug *n (Ap)*.
train guard Zugwache *f*, Zugbewachung *f*.
training Ausbildung *f*.
training agent Gasschutzübungsmittel *n (CWS)*.
training airplane Schulflugzeug *n*, Übungsflugzeug *n*.
training aviation Schulflugwesen *n*, Lehrflugwesen *n*.
training center Ausbildungsstelle *m*.
training film Lehrfilm *m*.
training grenade Übungshandgranate *f*.
training installations Übungsanlagen *fpl*.
training instrument Ausbildungsgerät *n*.
training loss Ausbildungsausfall *m*.
training manual Ausbildungsvorschrift *f*.
training mask Übungsmaske *f (CWS)*.

training munitions Übungsmunition *f*, Übungskriegsgerät *n*.

training of instructors Ausbildung von Ausbildern.

training of replacements Ersatzreserveausbildung *f*.

training order Ausbildungsanweisungen *fpl*.

training outlines Ausbildungsrichtlinien *fpl*.

training program Ausbildungsprogramm *n*.

training projectile Übungsgeschoß *n*.

training regulations Ausbildungsrichtlinien *fpl*.

training schedule Ausbildungsplan *m*.

training unit Übungseinheit *f*, Übungsverband *m*.

train of empties Leermaterial *n* (*RR*).

train of oscillations Schwingungszug *m* (*Elec, Rad*).

train release Reihenabwurf *m*, Reihenwurf *m* (*Bombing*).

train schedule Fahrplan *m* (*RR*).

train transportation officer Transportführer *m*.

train vehicle Troßfahrzeug *n*, Versorgungsfahrzeug *n* (*march column*).

traitor Verräter *m*.

trajectory Flugbahn *f* (*Ballistics*).

trajectory chart graphische Schußtafel *f*.

trajectory diagram Flugbahnaufriß *m*, Flugbahngrundriß *m*, Flugbahnbild *n* (*Ballistics*).

tramway Förderbahn *f*.

transceiver Senderempfänger *m* (*Rad*).

transconductance Steilheit *f* (*Rad*).

transcript Abschrift *f*; Fernspruch *m* (*Tp*).

transfer *n* Versetzung *f* (*Pers*); Verlegung *f* (*installation, fire, etc.*).

transfer *v* versetzen (*Pers*); verlegen (*installation, fire, etc.*).

transfer case Gruppengetriebe *n*, Zusatzgetriebe *n*.

transferred versetzt.

transformer Übertrager *m*, Umformer *m*, Transformator *m* (*Elec*).

transformer voltage Umformerspannung *f*.

transient target Augenblicksziel *n*.

transit Universalinstrument *n* (*Surv*).

transition Übergang *m*.

translate übersetzen; verdolmetschen (*interpret*).

translating lever Mitnehmer *m* (*sighting mechanism*).

translator Übersetzer *m*; Dolmetscher *m* (*interpreter*).

transloading point Umschlagstelle *f*.

transmission Wechselgetriebe *n*, Getriebe *n* (*MT*); Übermittlung *f*, Durchgabe *f* (*of messages, etc.*); Senden *n*, Tasten *n* (*keying*) (*Rad*).

transmission brake Getriebebremse *f*.

transmission case Getriebegehäuse *n*.

transmission grease Getriebefett *n*.

transmission in clear Klartextfunken *n* (*Rad*).

transmission main shaft Getriebehauptwelle *f* (*MT*).

transmission oil Getriebeöl *n* (*MT*).

transmission shaft Getriebewelle *f* (*MT*).

transmit funken, senden, geben (*Rad, Tg*); befördern, durchgeben (*Sig C*).

transmitter Sendegerät *n*, Funksender *m* (*Rad*); Geber *m* (*AA director*).

transmitter antenna Sendeantenne *f* (*Rad*).

transmitter tube Senderöhre *f* (*Rad*).

transom Querträger *m*, Unterzug *m* (*Bdg*).

transparent durchsichtig.

transparent reflector Reflexglas *n* (*reflector sight*).

transport Beförderung *f*, Transport *m* (*transportation*); Transporter *m* (*Ap, Nav*); Transportschiff *n*, Truppentransportschiff *n* (*Nav*); Transportflugzeug *n* (*Ap*). See also **motor transport.**

transportation Beförderungsmittel *n*, Transportmittel *n* (*means*); Beförderung *f*, Versand *m*, Verschickung *f*, Transport *m*; Eisenbahnbeförderung *f* (*RR*); Wassertransport *m* (*by water*); Kraftfahrtransport *m* (*MT*).

transportation company Transportkompanie *f*.

Transportation Corps Heerestransportkorps *n* (*USA*).

transportation headquarters Transportkommandantur *f* (*RR*).

transportation officer Transportführer *m*, Transportoffizier *m* (*RR*).

transportation of freight Frachtenbeförderung *f*.

transportation of the wounded Verwundetentransport m.

transportation of troops Truppenbeförderung f.

transportation order Transportbefehl m; Fahrbefehl m (MT).

transportation request Transportantrag m.

Transportation Service See **Transportation Corps.**

transportation system Transportwesen n.

transport aviation Transportluftfahrt f, Transportflugwesen n.

transport command Transportgeschwader n (Avn).

transport commander Transportkommandant m.

transport force Transportgeschwader n (Avn).

transport officer See **transportation officer.**

transposition cipher Kastenschlüssel m (Sig C).

transshipment Umladung f.

transshipment port Umschlagshafen m.

transverse beam Querträger m (Bdg).

transverse shutter Querschnittblende f (Sig lamp).

transverse support Querträger m (Bdg).

trap n Falle f; Hinterhalt m (ambush).

trap v einkesseln (Tac).

trapezoid truss Trapez-Fachwerkträger m (Engr).

trap mine Schreckmine f, Schreckladung f, Sprengfalle f.

travel allowance Reisegeld n (money); Fahrkostenentschädigung f, Reisekostenvergütung f, Reisevergütung f (reimbursement).

traveling capacity Fahrleistung f (MT, Tk).

traveling distance Fahrbereich m (MT, Tk).

traveling position Fahrstellung f (Ord).

travel of target Vorauswanderungsstrecke f (during dead time) (AA gunnery).

travel order Marschbefehl m (official order); Fahrausweis m (traveling permit).

travel pay See **travel allowance.**

travel ration Reiseverpflegung f.

traverse Querdeckung f, Querwall m, Schulterwehr f (Ft); Streckenzug m (Surv).

traverse v schwenken (G); durchqueren (cross).

traverse method Streckenzugverfahren n.

traverse stop Seitenbegrenzer m, Begrenzungsstift m (G, MG).

traversing and searching fire Breiten- und Tiefenfeuer n (MG).

traversing arc Führungsstück n (MG).

traversing drive Seitenrichttrieb m (G, Mort).

traversing fire Breitenfeuer n (MG).

traversing handwheel Handrad zur Seitenrichtung, Seitenrichtrad n (G).

traversing lever Seitenhebel m.

traversing mechanism Seitenrichtmaschine f, Seitenrichtwerk n (G).

traversing rack Zahnkranz m (AA gun, Tk turret).

traversing screw Seitenrichtschraube f (G).

traversing slide Führungshülse f (MG).

traversing stop See **traverse stop.**

tread Tritt m (foot); Schützenauftritt m (firing step); Lauffläche f, Profil n (tire); Spurweite f (lateral distance between wheels) (MT).

treadway Spurtafel f.

treadway bridge Spurtafelbrücke f (duckboard); Kradschützensteg m (floating).

treason Landesverrat m, Kriegsverrat m.

treatment Behandlung f.

treaty Vertrag m.

tree Baum m.

tree stump Baumstumpf m.

tree-top height Baumhöhe f.

tree trunk Baumstamm m.

trellis mast Gittermast m.

trench Graben m, Schützengraben m.

trench board Holzrost m.

trench bottom Grabensohle f (Ft).

trench excavator Grabenbagger m.

trench mortar Granatwerfer m, Handwerfer m. See also **mortar.**

trench mouth Mundschleimhautentzündung f; Stomatitis f (Vincent's infection).

trench periscope Beobachtungsrohr

n, Schützengrabenspiegel *m,* Deckungsspiegel *m.*
trench profile Grabenprofil *n (Ft).*
trench pump Grabenpumpe *f (Ft).*
trench shelter Deckungsgraben *m,* Splittergraben *m.*
trench system Grabensystem *n.*
trench timber Schurzholz *n (Ft).*
trench warfare Grabenkrieg *m.*
trestle Bock *m,* Joch *n (Bdg).*
trestle bridge Bockbrücke *f;* Bockschnellsteg *m (hasty Bdg).*
trestle carrier Bockwagen *m (MT).*
trestle leg Bockbein *n (Bdg).*
trestle setting Bocksetzen *n (Bdg).*
trial *n* Probe *f (test);* Versuch *m (experiment);* Prozeß *m (law).*
trial *adj* versuchsweise, Versuchs-.
trial balloon Pilotballon *m.*
trial fire Einschießen *n (Gunnery).*
trial run Versuchslauf *m (Mtr).*
triangle Dreieck *n.*
triangle exercise Dreieckzielen *n (R practice).*
triangle of error Fehlerdreieck *n (Surv).*
triangle of velocities Geschwindigkeitsdreieck *n (Avn).*
triangular dreieckig, dreigegliedert, dreigliedrig.
triangular division dreigliedrige Division.
triangular road junction Wegedreieck *n.*
triangular timber obstacle Dreieckbalkensperre *f.*
triangulation Triangulation *f,* Dreiecksaufnahme *f (Surv).*
triangulation point trigonometrischer Punkt *(Surv).*
trick List *f.*
tricycle landing gear Dreiradfahrgestell *n,* Bugradfahrgestell *n (Ap).*
trigger Abzug *m (R);* Dauerabzug *m (for full-automatic fire) (MG).*
trigger bar Abzugsschiene *f (AA gun).*
trigger cam Drucknase *f (R).*
trigger frequency Kippschwingung *f (Rad).*
trigger guard Abzugsbügel *m (R).*
trigger-guard screw Kreuzschraube *f (R).*
trigger lever Abzugshebel *m (MG).*
trigger mechanism Abzugsvorrichtung *f (R).*

trigger piece Abzugsstück *n (on G breech mechanism).*
trigger pin Abzugsstift *m (R);* Hahnbolzen *m (MG).*
trigger pull Abzugsgewicht *n (Small Arms).*
trigger sear Abzugsstollen *m (R).*
trigger-sear fork Abzugsgabel *f (R).*
trigger squeeze Abkrümmen *n,* Durchkrümmen *n (R).*
trigonometric function Kreisfunktion *f.*
trigonometry Trigonometrie *f.*
trimming Lastigkeitsregelung *f (Ap).*
trim tab Trimmklappe *f,* Trimmruder *n,* Ausgleichfläche *f (Ap).*
trinitrophenol Pikrinsäure *f,* Trinitrophenol *n.*
trinitrotoluol Trinitrotuoluol *n.* Tolit *n,* Tolita *n,* Trilit *n,* Trotyl *n,* Tutol *n; * Sprengmunition 02, Fp. 02 *(Ger).*
triode grid-leak detector Audion *n.*
triode tube Dreielektrodenröhre *f,* Dreipolröhre *f,* Triode *f (Rad).*
trip *n* Reise *f (journey);* Spannfalle *f (of firing pin, G);* Auslösung *f (Mech).*
trip *v* stolpern *(stumble);* auslösen *(release).*
triplane Dreidecker *m.*
triple mixture Dreiergemisch *n (gasoline 50%, benzol 40%, alcohol 10%).*
triple rank Linie zu 3 Gliedern.
triplicate eine dritte Kopie.
in triplicate in dreifacher Ausführung.
trip mileage odometer Tageskilometerzähler *m (speedometer).*
tripod Dreibein *n,* Dreifuß *m.*
tripod cable support Dreibock *m (Engr).*
tripod extension piece Dreifußaufsatzstück *n,* Lafettenaufsatzstück *n (MG).*
tripod mast Dreibeinmast *m (Nav).*
tripod mount Dreibeinlafette *f.*
trip wire Stolperdraht *m;* Drahtschlinge *f (snare).*
trip-wire entanglement Stolperdrahthindernis *n.*
trip-wire mine Stolperdrahtmine *f.*
troop Schwadron *f (Cav).*
troop carrier Truppentransporter *m (Ap).*
troop-carrying glider Lastensegler *m,* Lastensegelflugzeug *n.*

troop commander Schwadronschef *m*, Schwadronführer *m (Cav)*.

troop concentration Truppenmasse *f*.

trooper Reiter *m*.

troop headquarters detail Schwadronstrupp *m (Cav)*.

troop movement Truppenbewegung *f*.

troops Truppe *f (collective)*; Truppen *fpl (plural)*.

troop school Truppensonderlehrgang *m*.

troopship Truppentransporter *m*, Truppentransportschiff *n*.

troops of occupation Besatzungstruppen *fpl*.

troop train Truppentransportzug *m*.

troop training camp Truppenübungslager *n*.

troop training grounds Truppenübungsplatz *m*.

troop transport Truppentransporter *m (Ap, Nav)*. See also **troopship**.

troop unit Truppeneinheit *f (usually has uniform type of weapons, as distinguished from Truppenverband, combined-arms unit)*; Truppenteil *m*.

tropical tropisch, Tropen-.

tropical air tropische Warmluft *(Met)*.

troposphere Troposphäre *f (Avn, Met)*.

trouble shooter Störungssucher *m (Tp)*.

trouble truck Abschleppwagen *m*.

trough Trog *m*, Wanne *f*.

trousers Hosen *fpl*.

truce Waffenruhe *f*, örtlicher Waffenstillstand.

truck Lastkraftwagen *m (MT)*; Drehgestell *n (RR car)*.

truck driver Lastkraftfahrer *m*, Kraftfahrer *m*.

truckhead Ausladespitze *f*, Umschlagstelle einer Kraftwagenkolonne *(MT)*.

truck-tractor Lastwagenschlepper *m*.

truck trailer Lastanhänger *m (MT)*.

true azimuth rechtweisende Kompaßzahl *f*, rechtweisender Kurswinkel *m*.

true copy beglaubigte Abschrift.

true course rechtweisender Kurs *(Air Navigation)*.

true declination Ortsmißweisung *f*.

true heading rechtweisender Windkurs *(Air Navigation)*.

true north Geographisch-Nord *m (Surv)*.

trumpet Trompete *f (bugle)*; Lautsprechertrichter *m (Rad)*.

trunk Rumpf *m (anatomy)*; Koffer *m (travel)*.

trunk cable Fernkabel *n (Tp)*.

trunk circuit Hauptleitung *f*, Hauptkabel *n*, Stammleitung *f (Sig)*.

trunk line Stammleitung *f (Tp)*.

trunk-line construction Stammleitungsbau *m (Tp)*.

trunk station Hauptanschluß *m*, Hauptstelle *f (Tp)*.

trunnion Tragzapfen *m*, Zapfen *m*; Lagerzapfen *m (aiming circle)*; Schildzapfen *m (G)*.

trunnion bearing Pivotlager *n*, Schildzapfenlager *n (G)*.

trunnion cap Schildzapfenlagerdeckel *m (G)*.

trunnion socket Schildzapfenpfanne *f (G)*.

truss Fachwerkträger *m (Bdg)*.

truss bridge Fachwerkbrücke *f*.

try square Anschlagwinkel *m*.

tube Rohr *n*, Röhre *f*, Schlauch *m*; Kernrohr *n*, Seelenrohr *n (G)*; Elektrodenröhre *f (Rad)*; Luftschlauch *m (inner tube) (MT)*.

tube base Röhrensockel *m (Rad)*.

tube length Seelenlänge *f (Ord)*.

tube-testing apparatus Röhrenprüfgerät *n (Rad)*.

tubular chassis frame Rohrrahmen *m (MT)*.

tubular handle Griffrohr *n (trail spade)*.

tubular mast Röhrenmast *m (Nav)*.

tubular mount Röhrenlafette *f (MG)*.

tubular spirit level Röhrenlibelle *f*.

tubular trail Röhrenlafette *f (G)*.

tug *n* Schlepper *m (Nav)*.

tugboat Schlepper *m*; Hafenschlepper *m (harbor)*; Hochseeschlepper *m (ocean-going)*.

tumble sich überschlagen *(projectile)*.

tune abstimmen *(Rad)*.

tune in einstellen *(Rad)*.

tungsten Wolfram *n*.

tuning coil Abstimmspule *f (Rad)*.

tuning condenser Abstimmkondensator *m (Rad)*.

tuning control Frequenzeinstellung *f (Rad)*.

tuning knob Abstimmkondensatorgriff *m (Rad)*.

tuning out Sperren *n (Rad).*
tuning scale Abstimmskala *f (Rad).*
tunnel Stollen *m,* Tunnel *m (Engr).*
turbine Turbine *f.*
turbo supercharger Zwischengebläse *n (Ap engine).*
turbulence Böigkeit *f (Met).*
turbulence chamber Wirbelkammer *f (Diesel engine).*
turn *n* Kehrkurve *f,* Kurve *f,* Kehrtwendung *f,* Wendung *f (Avn);* Krümmung *f,* Biegung *f (road).*
turn *v* drehen, wenden; schwenken *(to wheel right or left);* umgehen *(to flank).*
turn and bank indicator *See* **bank and turn indicator.**
turnback Verbindungsriemen *m (harness).*
turnbuckle Spannschloß *n.*
turn indicator Wendezeiger *m (Ap).*
turning combat Kurvenkampf *m (Avn).*
turning movement Umgehung *f (Tac).*
turntable Drehscheibe *f (RR);* Drehkranz *m (seaplane catapult).*
turntable gun carriage Drehscheibenlafette *f.*
turret Kanzel *f (Ap);* Turm *m (Tk, Ft, Nav).*
turret basket Kampfabteil *m (Tk).*
turret gun Turmgeschütz *n.*
turret gun mount Turmlafette *f (Tk).*
turret hatch Turmluk *n,* Turmluke *f,* Dachluke *f,* Turmklappe *f (Tk).*
turret hatch cover Turmlukendeckel *m (Tk).*
turret locking clamp Turmzurrung *f (Ap, Tk).*
turret mount Turmlafette *f.*
turret traversing mechanism Turmschwenkwerk *n (Ap, Tk).*
twenty-five percent rectangle 25%ige Trefferfläche *(Ballistics).*
twin barrels Zwillingsläufe *mpl (MG).*
twin-engine zweimotorig.
twin-float seaplane Zweischwimmer-Seeflugzeug *n..*
twin machine gun MG.-Zwilling *m.*
twin mount Zwillingslafette *f (Ord).*
twin rudders Doppelseitensteuer *n (Ap).*
twin-screw elevating mechanism Doppelschraubenrichtmaschine *f (G).*

twin tail Gabelschwanz *m (Ap).*
twist Drall *m,* Windung *f (Ord).*
twist drill Spiralbohrer *m.*
twist effect of slipstream Drallwirkung *f (Avn).*
two-axle vehicle Zweiachser *m.*
two-barreled mount Doppellafette *f (Ord).*
two-blade propeller Zweiflügel-Luftschraube *f (Ap).*
two-conductor firing wire Doppelsprengkabel *n (Demolitions).*
two-cycle engine Zweitaktmotor *m.*
two-man shelter tent Zweierzelt *n.*
two-place airplane Zweisitzer *m.*
two-point landing Radlandung *f (Avn).*
two-point resection Zweipunktverfahren *n (Surv).*
two-ship element Rotte *f,* Zweierverband *m (Avn).*
two-stage zweistufig.
two-stage supercharger Stufenlader *m (Ap).*
two-stage transmitter zweistufiger Sender *(Rad).*
two-station net Funklinie *f (Rad).*
two-station spotting Doppelanschnitt *m.*
two-stranded zweiadrig *(Elec).*
two-way break-in communication Gegensprechen *n (Rad).*
two-way communication Doppelverkehr *m (Rad, Tp).*
two-way radiophone communication Funkwechselsprechen *n.*
two-way radio traffic Funkwechselverkehr *m (alternate);* Funkdoppelverkehr *m (simultaneous).*
two-way telegraphy wechselseitige Telegraphie.
two-way telephone circuit gegenseitige Sprechverbindung.
two-way traffic Doppelverkehr *m (simultaneous),* Wechselverkehr *m (alternate) (Rad).*
type Art *f,* Baumuster *n,* Muster *n,* Typ *m.*
typewrite maschineschreiben, tippen.
typewriter Schreibmaschine *f.*
typhoid fever Typhus *m,* Unterleibstyphus *m.*
typhus Fleckfieber *n,* Flecktyphus *m.*
typist Maschinenschreiber *m,* Maschinenschreiberin *f.*

U

U-boat U-Boot *n*, Unterseeboot *n*.
U-frame U-Rahmen *m* (*tubular chassis*) (*MT*).
uhf *See* ultrahigh frequency.
ultimatum Ultimatum *n*.
ultrahigh frequency Ultrakurzwelle *f*.
ultrahigh frequency receiver Ultrakurzwellenempfänger *m*.
ultrahigh frequency transmitter Ultrakurzwellensender *m*.
umbrella antenna Schirmantenne *f*.
umpire *n* Schiedsrichter *m*; Stabsschiedsrichter *m* (*at Hq*).
unanchored contact mine Treibmine *f*.
unarmed unbewaffnet, waffenlos; unscharf (*fuze, etc.*).
unauthorized eigenmächtig, ohne Erlaubnis, unvorschriftsmäßig.
uncase entrollen (*flag*).
uncock entspannen (*Ord*).
unconditional surrender bedingungslose Unterwerfung, bedingungslose Übergabe.
unconscious ohnmächtig, bewußtlos (*a physical state*); unbewußt (*unaware*).
uncontrolled mosaic Bildskizze *f* (*aerial Photo*).
uncouple abprotzen (*Arty*).
uncover die Kopfbedeckung abnehmen (*remove hat, etc.*); entblößen (*Tac*).
undamped oscillations ungedämpfte Schwingungen (*Rad*).
undamped waves ungedämpfte Wellen (*Rad*).
under arms unter Waffen, bewaffnet.
underbrush Unterholz *n*, Gestrüpp *n*, Gesträuch *n*.
underdrive Geländegang *m* (*MT*).
underground cable Erdkabel *n*, unterirdisches Fernkabel (*Tg, Tp*).
underground movement illegale Bewegung (*political*).
underground water Grundwasser *n*.
undermine unterminieren.
underpass Bahnunterführung *f* (*RR*).
undershirt Unterhemd *m*.
underwater ranging battery Unterwassermeßbatterie *f* (*CA*).
underwear Unterwäsche *f*.
undesired frequency Störfrequenz *f*, fremde Wellen (*Rad*).

unescorted ohne Begleitung, ohne Geleit, ohne Deckung, ohne Schutz.
unescorted by fighters ohne Jägerschutz (*Avn*).
unevacuable nicht evakuierbar.
unevenness of ground Bodenunebenheit *f*.
unexploded bomb nicht explodierte Bombe.
unfavorable ungünstig, unvorteilhaft.
unfavorable weather ungünstige Wetterlage.
unfit untauglich, ungeeignet.
"Unfix, bayonets!" "Seitengewehr, an Ort!"
unfurl entrollen (*flag*).
unharness ausschirren.
uniform *n* Uniform *f*, Anzug *m* (*Clo*).
uniform *adj* einheitlich, gleichförmig, vorschriftsmäßig.
uniform allowance Einkleidungsbeihilfe *f* (*for Clo*).
uniform slope stetige Böschung (*Top*).
uniform twist gleichbleibender Drall, gleichförmiger Drall (*Ord*).
unilateral einseitig.
unimproved road Fahrweg, nicht jederzeit brauchbar.
Union Jack Lotsenflagge *f* (*Nav*).
unit Einheit *f*, Verband *m*, Truppenteil *m* (*Tac*).
unit assemblage Geräteeinheit *f* (*of equipment, etc.*).
unit commander Kommandeur eines Truppenteils.
United States Army Das Berufsheer der Vereinigten Staaten einschließlich der Nationalgarde und der organisierten Reserven. *Compare* Army of the United States.
United States Coast Guard Küstenwachkorps der Vereinigten Staaten.
United States Marine Corps Marinekorps der Vereinigten Staaten.
United States Navy Kriegsmarine der Vereinigten Staaten.
United States of America Die Vereinigten Staaten von Amerika.
unit engineer Pionierführer *m*.
unit fund Kasse eines Truppenteils.
unit of equipment Gerätsatz *m*.
unit of fire Munition für einen Tag.

unit of measurement Maßeinheit *f*.
universal joint Kreuzgelenk *n*.
universal-joint housing Gelenkgehäuse *n (MT)*.
unlimber abprotzen *(Arty)*.
unlimbered feuerbereit, abgeprotzt *(Arty)*.
unload entladen, abladen, ausladen; löschen *(a ship)*; entladen *(a gun, etc.)*.
unloading party Abladekommando *n*.
unloading unit Ausladeeinheit *f*.
unmask enthüllen, verraten *(position of a gun by opening fire)*; freigeben *(field of fire for friendly troops)*.
unmilitary unsoldatisch, unmilitärisch.
unobserved fire Schießen ohne Beobachtung *(Gunnery)*.
unqualified nicht qualifiziert, ungeeignet.
unsaddle absatteln.
unserviceable unbrauchbar, unbenutzbar.
"Unsling arms!" "Gewehr abnehmen!"
unsynchronized fire nicht synchronisiertes Feuer *(Ap gun)*.
updraft carburetor Aufstromvergaser *m (Mtr)*.
uphill bergauf, aufwärts.
upper band Oberring *m (R)*.
upper-band spring Oberringfeder *f (R)*.

upper prism micrometer head Triebschraube *f (panoramic sight)*.
upper shield Oberschild *m (G)*.
upright engine Standmotor *m*.
upside-down flight Rückenflug *m*.
upstream oberstrom *(Engr)*.
upstream anchor Stromanker *m (Bdg)*.
up-sun approach Sturzflug aus der Sonne.
upwind *adv* windwärts.
urgent dringend; KR *(in Rad procedure spoken Konrad Richard in accordance with German phonetic alphabet)*.
urgent call dringendes Gespräch, Ausnahmegespräch *n (Tp)*.
urgent message dringende Meldung.
urgent radio message dringender Funkspruch.
urgent signal Dringlichkeitszeichen *n (Sig Com)*.
urgent telephone call dringendes Ferngespräch.
urinate urinieren, Harn lassen, Wasser lassen.
urine Harn *m*, Urin *m*.
usable rate of fire praktische Feuergeschwindigkeit *(Ord)*.
useful load Nutzlast *f (vehicles)*; Zuladung *f (Ap)*.
utilization of terrain Geländeausnutzung *f*.

V

vacancy freie Planstelle, Fehlstelle *f (Adm)*.
vaccinate impfen.
vaccination Impfung *f*, Schutzimpfung *f*.
vaccination certificate Impfschein *m*.
vacuum Leere *f*, Luftleere *f*, Vakuum *n*; Luftsog *m (resulting from explosion)*.
vacuum pump Vakuumpumpe *f*.
vacuum tank Unterdruckförderer *m (MT)*.
vaccum tube Vakuumröhre *f*.
vacuum-tube amplifier Röhrenverstärker *m (Rad)*.
vacuum-tube oscillator Röhrensummer *m (Rad)*.

vacuum-tube voltmeter Röhrenspannungsmesser *m*.
valley Tal *n*.
valley dam Talsperre *f*.
valve Ventil *n*.
valve arrangement Ventilanordnung *f (Mtr)*.
valve ball Ventilkegel *m (MT)*.
valve chamber Ventilkammer *f (Mtr)*.
valve cord Ventilleine *f (Bln)*.
valve guide Ventilschaftführung *f (Mtr)*.
valve head Ventilteller *m (Mtr)*.
valve lifter Ventilstößel *m*, Stößel *m*, Rollenstößel *m (roller type) (Mtr)*.
valve seat Ventilsitz *m (Mtr)*.

valve spring Ventilfeder *f (Mtr)*.
valve stem Ventilschaft *m (Mtr)*.
valve-timing system Ventilsteuerung *f (Mtr)*.
van *See* vanguard.
van Flügel *m (Cml shell, bomb)*; Flügelkolben *m (pump)*; Wetterfahne *f (weather vane)*.
vapor Dampf *m*, Dunst *m*.
vapor detector kit Gasanzeiger *m (CWS)*.
vapor particle Tröpfchen *n (CWS)*.
vapor trail Kondensstreifen *m (Avn)*.
variable condenser Drehkondensator *m*.
variable μ tube Regelröhre *f (Rad)*.
variation Ortsmißweisung *f (Air Navigation)*.
variometer Variometer *n (Ap, Elec)*.
varnish Firnis *m*, Lack *m*.
veal Kalbfleisch *n*.
vector Vektor *m*.
veer wenden, umschwingen, nach der Seite abgelenkt werden.
vegetable(s) Gemüse *n;* Dörrgemüse *n (dehydrated)*.
vegetation Bodenbewachsung *f (Top)*.
vehicle Fahrzeug *n*.
vehicle assembly area Ablaufplatz *m*.
vehicle-borne verlastet.
vehicle park Kraftfahrpark *m*.
vehicle resistance Rollwiderstand *m (MT)*.
vehicular station in ein Fahrzeug eingebautes Funkgerät *(Rad)*.
velocity Geschwindigkeit *f*.
velocity error abweichende Anfangsgeschwindigkeit *(Ballistics)*.
velocity of fall Fallgeschwindigkeit *f (Bombing, Ballistics)*.
velocity of light Lichtgeschwindigkeit *f*.
velocity of sound Schallgeschwindigkeit *f*.
veneer Furnier *n*.
venereal disease Geschlechtskrankheit *f*.
V-engine Gabelmotor *m*, V-Motor *m*.
vent Düse *f (rocket);* Öffnung *f*, Austritt *m*, Loch *n*.
vent hole Zündkanal *m (obturator)*.
ventilation Lüftung *f*, Belüftung *f;* Bewetterung *f (mines)*.
ventilation system Belüftungsanlage *f;* Wetterführung *f (mines)*.
ventilator Lüfter *m;* Aufbaulüfter *m (Tk hull)*.

ventral gun mount Bodenlafette *f (Ap)*.
ventral turret Bodenkanzel *f*, Wanne *f (Ap)*.
verbal order mündlicher Befehl.
verdict Urteil *n*, Entscheidung *f;* Urteilsspruch *m (Law)*.
verification Prüfung *f*, Nachprüfung *f*.
verification fire Prüfungsschießen *n*.
verify prüfen, nachprüfen; "Bitte prüfen" *(Rad procedure)*.
vernier Nonius *m*.
vernier dial Feineinstellung *f (Rad)*.
vertical senkrecht, lotrecht.
vertical aerial photograph Senkrechtbild *n*, Senkrechtluftbild *n* Senkrechtaufnahme *f*, Senkrechtluftaufnahme *f*.
vertical axis Hochachse *f (Ap)*.
vertical axle displacement Kletterfähigkeit *f (MT)*.
vertical deviation Höhenabweichung *f (Gunnery)*.
vertical dive Kopfsturz *m (Avn)*.
vertical frame Spant *m (Ap)*.
vertical height Flughöhe *f (Ballistics)*.
vertical interval senkrechter Abstand, Höhenabstand *m*, Höhenunterschied *m*.
vertical jump Abgangsfehlerwinkel *m (Ballistics)*.
vertical lead Höhenwinkelvorhalt *m (AA Gunnery)*.
vertical photograph Senkrechtaufnahme *f*, Senkrechtbild *n (aerial Photo)*.
vertical plane Senkrechtebene *f*.
vertical projection Projektion auf die Senkrechtebene.
vertical ring Spant *m (Ap)*.
vertical shot group Scheibentreffbild *n (Ballistics)*.
vertical speed Senkrechtgeschwindigkeit *f (Avn)*.
vertical spotting Beobachtung der Längenabweichung *(Gunnery)*.
vertical stabilizer Seitenflosse *f (Ap)*.
vertical target senkrechte Treffläche *(Ballistics)*.
vertical tracking telescope Höhenrichtfernrohr *n (height finder)*.
vertical visual angle Höhenwinkel *m (AA Gunnery)*.
Very light Leuchtkugel *f*.
Very light signal Leuchtsignal *n*.

Very pistol Leuchtpistole *f*.
Very signal cartridge Leuchtpatrone *f*.
Very signal light Leuchtkugel *f*.
vesicant *n* ätzender Kampfstoff, Hautgift *n*, blasenziehender Kampfstoff, Gelbkreuz *n* (*CWS*).
vesicant *adj* blasenziehend (*CWS*).
vessel Wasserfahrzeug *n* (*Nav*).
veteran Veteran *m*, ehemaliger Kriegsteilnehmer, ehemaliger Frontsoldat.
Veterans Administration Fürsorgeverwaltung für Kriegsteilnehmer (*USA*).
veterinarian Tierarzt *m*, Veterinär *m*.
veterinary aid man Veterinärgehilfe *m*.
veterinary aid station Pferdeverbandplatz *m*.
veterinary ambulance Pferdetransportwagen *m*.
veterinary blood-testing laboratory Tierblutuntersuchungsstelle *f*.
veterinary clearing station Pferdelazarett *n*.
veterinary collecting point Pferdekrankensammelpunkt *m*.
veterinary collecting station Pferdekrankensammelstelle *f*, Pferdekrankensammelplatz *m*.
veterinary company Veterinärkompanie *f*.
Veterinary Corps Veterinärkorps *n* (*USA*).
veterinary depot Veterinärpark *m*.
veterinary dispensary Pferdeverbandplatz *m*.
veterinary equipment Veterinärgerät *n*.
veterinary general hospital Heimat-Pferdelazarett *n* (*Z of I*).
veterinary hospital Pferdelazarett *n*, Krankenstall *m*; Heerespferdelazarett *n* (*GHQ*).
veterinary motor ambulance Pferdekrankenkraftwagen *m*.
veterinary officer Veterinäroffizier *m*.
veterinary personnel Veterinärpersonal *n*.
veterinary service Veterinärdienst *m*.
veterinary station hospital Standort-Pferdelazarett *n*.
V-formation Winkel *m*, Winkelform *f* (*Avn*).

viaduct Viadukt *m*, Überführung *f*.
vibration Schwingung *f* (*Mech*).
vibrator Wechselrichter *m*, Zerhacker *m* (*Rad*).
vice-admiral Admiral *m* (*Nav*).
victim Opfer *n*.
victor Sieger *m*.
victorious siegreich.
victory Sieg *m*.
Victory Medal Interalliierte Siegesmedaille (*USA, World War I*).
Victory ribbon Band der Interalliierten Siegesmedaille (*USA, World War I*).
view Blick *m*, Anblick *m*, Aussicht *f*; Ansicht *f* (*opinion*).
view finder Sucher *m*.
viewing slit Augenschlitz *m* (*telescopic sight*).
vigilance Wachsamkeit *f*.
village Dorf *n*, Ortschaft *f*.
vineyard Weingarten *m*.
violent heftig.
viscometer Dichtigkeitsmesser *m*.
vise Schraubstock *m* (*Tech*).
visible horizon sichtbarer Horizont, Kimm *m*.
visibility Sicht *f*, Sichtigkeit *f*, Sichtbarkeit *f*; Fernsicht *f* (*distant*); Sichtverhältnisse *npl* (*conditions*).
vision Sehkraft *f*, Sehvermögen *n*, Sehschärfe *f*.
vision slit Sehschlitz *m* (*Tk*).
visiting correspondent Sonderberichterstatter *m*.
visit of courtesy Höflichkeitsbesuch *m*.
visor Schirm *m* (*Clo*).
visual communication Zeichenverbindung *f*.
visual indicator Sichtanzeigegerät *n* (*Ap Inst*).
visual reconnaissance Augenaufklärung *f* (*Avn*).
visual signal Sichtzeichen *n*.
voice frequency band Sprachfrequenzband *n* (*Rad, Tp*).
voice radio Sprechfunk *m*; Telefon *n* (*as marked on Rad set*).
voice-radio communication Funksprechen *n*.
voice transmission Sprachübertragung *f*, Sprechen *n* (*Rad, Tp*); Funksprechübermittlung *f*, Funksprechen *n* (*Rad*).

volatile chemical warfare agent Luftkampfstoff m.
volatility Flüchtigkeit f (CWS).
volley Gruppe f (Arty); Salve f Small Arms); Ehrensalve f (at burials).
volley fire Gruppenfeuer n, Gruppenschießen n (Arty).
volt Volt n.
voltage Spannung f (Elec).
voltage across terminals Klemmenspannung f (Elec).
voltage divider Spannungsteiler m (Rad).
voltage drop Spannungsabfall m.
voltage regulator Spannungsregler m.
voltage variation Spannungsschwankung f.
voltmeter Spannungsmesser m, Voltmeter n.
volt-milliammeter Volt-Milliamperemeter n.

volume Lautstärke f (Rad); Rauminhalt m (content).
volume control Lautstärkenregler m (Rad).
volume of fire Feuerstärke f.
volume of reception Empfangslautstärke f (Rad).
volumetric mengenmäßig.
volumetric capacity Fassungsvermögen n.
volunteer n Freiwilliger m.
volunteer adj freiwillig.
volunteer v sich freiwillig melden.
volute spring Kegelfeder f.
voucher Beleg m.
V-turn Straßenknie n, Wegeknie n (road).
V-type belt Keilriemen m (Mtr).
V-type engine V-Motor m.
vulcanize vulkanisieren.
vulnerable verwundbar, verletzlich.

W

wad Pfropfen m.
wade waten.
wagon Wagen m.
waist Gürtellinie f.
waist gun Seiten-MG. n (Ap).
wait v warten.
waiver Erlaß m, Verzichtleistung f, Verzicht m.
wake Kielwasser n (of a ship).
walkie-talkie Feldfunksprecher m, tragbares Kleinfunksprechgerät.
walking wounded marschfähige Verwundete.
wall Wall m (Ft); Mauer f (masonry); Wand f (interior); Trachte f (hoof).
wallet Brieftasche f.
war Krieg m.
war chest Kriegskasse f.
war chevron Kriegsteilnehmerabzeichen für Überseedienst (USA).
war college Kriegsakademie f.
war correspondent Kriegsberichter m.
ward n Krankenstube f, Krankenabteilung f (Med).
ward attendant Krankenwärter (Med).
War Department Kriegsministerium n, Kriegsdepartement n (USA).

War Department General Staff Generalstab des Heeres.
war diary Kriegstagebuch n
ward master Krankenstubenaufseher m, Abteilungsaufseher m (Med).
ward officer leitender Arzt (Med).
war economy Wehrwirtschaft f.
war effort Kriegseinsatz m.
warehouse Lagerhaus n, Warenlager n.
warfare Krieg m, Kriegführung f.
war footing Kriegsfuß m.
war game Kriegsspiel n (map maneuvers).
war gas Kampfgas n (CWS).
warhead Gefechtskopf m (of torpedo).
warm front Aufgleitfront f, Warmluftfront f (Met).
warming-up shot Anwärmeschuß m.
warning Warnung f.
warning district Luftwarnbezirk m.
warning order Vorbefehl m (Tac).
warning signal Ankündigungssignal n.
war of attrition Abnutzungskrieg m.
war of movement Bewegungskrieg m (Tac).

war of position Stellungskrieg *m.*
warp *n* Beiende *n (on a rope).*
war photographer Bildberichter *m.*
war plant Rüstungswerk *n.*
warrant *n* Beförderungsurkunde *f.*
warrant officer Feldwebelleutnant *m (USA).*
war reserves Materialreserven *fpl.*
war service chevron *See* war chevron.
warship Kriegsschiff *n.*
war strength Kriegsstärke *f.*
war traitor Kriegsverräter *m.*
war treason Kriegsverrat *m.*
washer Abdichtungsring *m,* Dichtungsscheibe *f,* Unterlegscheibe *f,* Dichtungsring *m.*
washing soda Natriumkarbonat *n.*
waste *n* Abfall *m,* Altmaterial *n.*
waste of ammunition Munitionsvergeudung *f.*
watch *n* Wache *f (Nav);* Uhr *f (timepiece).*
watchtower Warte *f,* Wachtturm *m.*
watchword Kennwort *n,* Losungswort *n.*
water Wasser *n.*
water bag *See* water-sterilizing bag.
water chest Wasserbehälter *m.*
water circulation Wasserumlauf *m (Mtr).*
water-cooled wassergekühlt, mit Wasserkühlung.
water distributing point Wasserverteilungsstelle *f.*
watering Tränken *n (an animal).*
watering bridle Wassertrense *f (harness).*
water jacket Kühlmantel *m,* Wassermantel *m,* Kühlwassermantel *m.*
water level Wasserstand *m;* Wasserwaage *f (Instr).*
water-level gage Pegel *m (for rivers, lakes, etc.).*
waterline Wasserlinie *f.*
water obstacle Wassersperre *f.*
water pipe Wasserleitung *f.*
waterproof wasserdicht.
waterproof paper Guttaperchapapier *n (Engr).*
water pump Wasserpumpe *f.*
water-repellent wasserabstoßend.
water-sterilizing bag Wasserreinigungssack *m.*
water supply point Wasserversorgungsstelle *f.*
water temperature gage Fernthermometer *n (MT).*

watertight wasserdicht.
water tower Wasserturm *m.*
waterway Wasserstraße *f.*
waterworks Wasserwerk *n.*
watt Watt *n.*
wave *n* Welle *f (Rad, Tac, etc.).*
wave length Wellenlänge *f (Rad).*
wavemeter Wellenmesser *m (Rad).*
wave of tanks Treffen *n.*
wave propagation Wellenausbreitung *f (Rad).*
wave range Wellenbereich *m (Rad).*
wax Wachs *n.*
weapon Waffe *f.*
weapon carrier Waffenfahrzeug *n.*
weapons decontaminating agent Waffenentgiftungsmittel *n.*
weapons duel Feuerkampf *m.*
weapons platoon Maschinengewehr- und Granatwerferzug der Schützenkompanie *(USA).*
weapons troop Schwere Schwadron *(Cav).*
wear *n* Abnutzung *f.*
wear down zermürben *(Tac).*
wear-resistant abriebbeständig.
weather Wetter *n,* Witterung *f. See also* meteorological, metro-.
weather code Wetterschlüssel *m.*
weather conditions Wetterlage *f,* Wetterverhältnisse *npl.*
weather factors Witterungseinflüsse *mpl (Gunnery).*
weather factors and time difference Witterungseinflüsse und Zeitunterschied *(Sound Ranging).*
weather forecast Wettervoraussage *f,* Wettervorhersage *f.*
weather instruments Wetterdienstgeräte *npl.*
weather map Wetterkarte *f.*
weather message Wetterfunkmeldung *f,* Wetterfunkspruch *m (Rad).*
weather observation Wetterbeobachtung *f.*
weather reconnaissance Wettererkundung *f (Avn).*
weather region Wetterbezirk *m.*
weather report Wettermeldung *f.*
weather service Wetterdienst *m.*
weather side Luv *f (stream-crossing Opns).*
weather station Wetterstelle *f,* Wetterwarte *f.*
web Gurt *m,* Gewebe *n.*
web belt Stoffgurt *m.*

web girth Schnurrensattelgurt *m (saddle)*.

wedge Keil *m;* Knagge *f (Engr)*.

wedge formation Keil *m (Tac)*.

wedge-type breechblock Keilverschluß *m;* Rundkeilverschluß *m (cylindrical)*.

weighing anchor Ankerlichten *n.*

weigh off Ballast abwerfen *(Bln)*.

weight Gewicht *n.*

weight of projectile Geschoßgewicht *n (Ballistics)*.

weight per horsepower Leistungsgewicht *n.*

weir Wehr *n,* Stauwehr *n (Engr)*.

weld *n* Schweißung *f,* Schweißnaht *f,* Schweißstelle *f.*

weld *v* schweißen.

welder Schweißer *m.*

welding rod Schweißelektrode *f.*

welding torch Schweißbrenner *m.*

well Brunnen *m,* Quelle *f.*

Western European time westeuropäische Zeit *(zero meridian time)*.

Western Front Westfront *f.*

West Wall Westwall *m.*

wet naß.

wet-bulb thermometer feuchtes Thermometer *(Met)*.

wharf Ladeplatz *m.*

Wheatstone bridge Meßbrücke *f (Elec)*.

wheel *n* Rad *n.*

wheel *v* schwenken *(Tac)*.

wheelbarrow Schubkarren *m.*

wheelbase Radstand *m (MT)*.

wheel block Bremsklotz *m.*

wheel brake Fahrbremse *f (G carriage)*.

wheel chocks Schießklötze *mpl (Mtz Arty)*.

wheel control Radsteuerung *f (Ap)*.

wheeled litter carrier Krankentragenfahrgerät *n (Med)*.

wheeled tractor Radschlepper *m,* Radzugmaschine *f.*

wheeled vehicle Räderfahrzeug *n.*

wheel harness Hintersielengeschirr *n.*

wheel load Raddruck *m (MT)*.

wheel spindle Achsschwingschenkel *m,* Schwingschenkel *m (G);* Achsschenkel *m (MT)*.

wheel team Stangenpferde *npl.*

wheel-track car Räder-Raupen-Wagen *m.*

wheel-track drive Räder-Gleiskettenantrieb *m (MT)*.

wheel-track vehicle Hilfskettenfahrzeug *n,* Räder-Raupen-Fahrzeug *n (MT)*.

whetstone Wetzstein *m.*

whipstall "Männchen" *n (Avn)*.

whisper *v* flüstern.

whistle *n* Pfeife *f (Inst);* Pfiff *m (sound)*.

whistle signal Pfeifensignal *n,* Pfeifsignal *n.*

white weiß.

white dress uniform Sommeruniform *f.*

white line Furche *f (hoof)*.

white phosphorus weißer Phosphor.

wick Docht *m.*

wide-angle photograph Weitwinkelaufnahme *f.*

wide gage Breitspur *f (RR)*.

width Breite *f.*

in width flügelweise.

wigwag Winkzeichen mit einer einzigen Flagge oder Licht geben.

winch Spill *n,* Winde *f;* Windewagen *m (Trk)*.

wind Wind *m.*

windage Einfluß des Querwinds, Ausschaltung des Querwindeinflusses.

wind arrow Windpfeil *m (Met)*.

wind brace Windverband *m (Bdg)*.

windbreak Windschutz *m.*

wind-component indicator Wetterspinne *f (Gunnery)*.

wind cone Luftsack *m,* Windsack *m,* Windkegel *m.*

wind correction Ausschalten des Windes *(Gunnery);* Ausschalten der Windabtrift, Einrechnung des Luvwinkels, Einrechnung des Vorhaltewinkels *(Air Navigation)*.

wind corrector and time scale Wezu-Gerät *n (Sound Ranging)*.

wind deflection Ablenkung durch den Wind *(Gunnery)*.

wind direction Windrichtung *f.*

wind-direction indicator Windrichtungsanzeiger *m (Avn);* Windpfeil *m (Met)*.

wind drift Windabtrift *f.*

winded abgejagt *(worn out)*.

wind factors Windverhältnisse *npl,* Windkomponenten *fpl (Ballistics)*.

wind gage Windmesser *m,* Anemometer *n.*

wind indicator Windanzeiger *m.*

winding Wicklung *f (Elec, Rad)*.

winding stem Aufziehachse *f (on blasting machine)*.
windmill Windmühle *f*.
window Fenster *n*.
wind pressure Winddruck *m*.
wind reference number Windziffer *f (Gunnery)*.
windshield Windschutzscheibe *f*.
windshield wiper Scheibenwischer *m*.
wind sock Windsack *m*, Luftsack *m*.
wind tee T-förmiger Windanzeiger.
wind test Windmessung *f (Met)*.
wind tunnel Windkanal *m (Avn)*.
wind vane Windfahne *f (Met)*.
wind velocity Windstärke *f (Met)*.
windward wirdwärts, windseitig.
wine Wein *m*.
wing Flügel *m (Ap, Tac)*; Tragflügel *m*, Tragfläche *f (Ap)*; Geschwader *n (Avn unit)*.
wing area Flügelinhalt *m (Ap)*.
wing assembly Tragwerk *n (Ap)*.
wing attack Flügelangriff *m (Tac)*.
wing bracing Flügelverspannung *f*.
wing center section Flügel-Mittelstück *n (Ap)*.
wing chord Flügelsehne *f*, Profilsehne *f (Ap)*.
wing column formation Geschwaderkolonne *f (Avn)*.
wing commander Geschwaderkommodore *m*, Kommodore *m (Avn)*.
wing cross section Flügelschnitt *m (Ap)*.
wing dihedral V-Form der Tragflügel *(Ap)*.
wing flap Landeklappe *f (Ap)*.
wing float Stützschwimmer *m (flying boat)*.
wing gun Flugzeug-Flügelkanone *f (G)*; in Tragfläche eingebautes Maschinengewehr *(MG, Ap)*.
wingheavy flügellastig *(Ap)*.
wing loading Flächenbelastung *f (Ap)*.
wing-mounted gun Flugzeug-Flügelkanone *f (G)*; in Tragfläche eingebautes Maschinengewehr *(MG, Ap)*.
wing net Geschwaderfunknetz *n (Avn)*.
wing nut Flügelmutter *f*.
wing over *v* über den Flügel abkippen *(Avn)*.
wing profile Flügelprofil *n (Ap)*.
wing rail Flügelschiene *f (RR)*.
wing rib Flügelrippe *f*.
wing root Flügelwurzel *f (Ap)*.

"wings" Flugzeugführer-Abzeichen *n (insigne)*.
wing setting Flügelanordnung *f*.
wing signal Flügelsignal *n*.
wing skin Flügelhaut *f*.
wing span Spannweite *f (Ap)*.
wing spar Flügelholm *m*.
wing strut Flügelstrebe *f*.
wing strut system Flügelverstrebung *f*.
wing tip Flügelende *n*, Tragflügelende *n (Ap)*.
wing-tip flare Flügelleuchtpatrone *f*, Landefackel *f (Ap)*.
wing wedge formation Geschwaderkeil *m (Avn)*.
winter cap Kopfschützer *m*.
winter equipment Winterausrüstung *f*.
winter warfare Winterkrieg *m*.
wire *n* Draht *m*, Kabel *n*.
wire brace Spanndraht *m*.
wire cable Drahtseil *n*.
wire-cable lashing Drahtbund *m (Engr)*.
wire circuit Drahtverbindung *f (Tg, Tp)*.
wire communication Drahtverbindung *f*.
wire cutters Drahtschere *f*.
wire-cutting party Hindernissprengtrupp *m (Engr)*.
wire entanglement Drahthindernis *n*; Drahtverhau *m (with abatis)*.
wire head Meldekopf *m (Sig Com)*.
wire-laying team Feldfernkabeltrupp *m (Tp)*.
wire lead-in point Kabelaufführungspunkt *m (Elec, Tp)*.
wire line Drahtleitung *f*, Kabelleitung *f (Tp)*.
wire loop Drahtschleife *f (Elec)*.
wire mesh Maschendraht *m*.
wire mesh mat Drahtmatte *f (Engr)*.
wire mesh road Drahtstraße *f (Engr)*.
wire net Drahtnetz *n*; Fernsprechnetz *n (Tp)*; Telegraphennetz *n (Tg)*.
wire netting Drahtnetz *n*, Maschendraht *m*.
wire patrol Störungssuchtrupp *m (field Tp)*.
wire pike Drahtgabel *f (Tp)*.
wire roll Drahtrolle *f*.
wire-roll entanglement Drahtrolle *f*.
wire snare Drahtschlinge *f*.
wire splice Kabelverbindung *f (Tp)*.
wire system Drahtnachrichtennetz *n*.

wire telegraphy Drahttelegraphie *f.*
wire telephony Drahttelephonie *f.*
wire-testing instrument Kabelmeßgerät *n (Tp).*
wire trench Kabelgraben *m (Tp).*
wire turn Drahtschleife *f (Elec).*
wire-wound gun barrel Drahtrohr *n.*
wiring diagram Leitungsplan *m,* Installationsplan *m.*
wiring system Leitungssystem *n (Elec);* Bordnetz *n (Ap).*
withdraw abziehen, ausweichen, absetzen, sich absetzen *(Tac).*
withdrawal Abzug *m,* Entweichen *n,* Absetzbewegung *f,* Rückzug *m (Tac).*
withdrawal from action Abbrechen des Gefechts.
withdrawal route Rückweg *m,* Rückzugstraße *f,* Rückzugslinie *f (Tac).*
withers Widerrist *m (horse).*
witness *n* Zeuge *m.*
woman auxiliary Stabshelferin *f.*
wood Holz *n.*
wood alcohol Holzgeist *m.*
wooded area Waldgelände *n.*
wooden baffle Holzgehäuse *n (Rad).*
wooden grating Holzrost *m.*
wooden railing Holzgeländer *n.*
wood-gas engine Holzgasmotor *m.*
wood-gas generator Holzgasanlage *f,* Gasgenerator *m (MT).*
wood-gas generator trailer Generatoranhänger *m (MT).*
woodland Waldgelände *n.*
wood revetment Holzverkleidung *f.*
woods Wald *m.*
wood separator Holzzwischenlage *f (storage battery).*
wool Wolle *f.*
woolen cap Kopfschützer *m.*
wording Wortlaut *m.*
work Arbeit *f (labor);* Werk *n (Ft).*
working blouse Arbeitsbluse *f,* Drillichrock *m.*
work order Werkstattauftrag *m.*
works Arbeiten *fpl,* Befestigungsarbeiten *fpl (Ft).*

workshop Werkstatt *f;* Werft *f (Adrm).*
work uniform Arbeitsanzug *m,* Drillichanzug *m.*
worm Schnecke *f (Mech).*
worm and sector steering system Schneckenlenkung *f,* Segmentlenkung *f,* Zahnkranzlenkung *f (MT).*
worm drive Schneckenantrieb *m,* Schneckentrieb *m (MT, Mech).*
worm gear Schneckenrad *n (MG).*
worm-gear housing Schneckengehäuse *n (panoramic telescope).*
worm-gear rear-axle drive Schnecken-Hinterachsantrieb *m (MT).*
worm shaft Schneckenwelle *f (Mech).*
worn abgenutzt; abgetragen *(Clo).*
wound *n* Wunde *f.*
wound *v* verwunden.
wound chevron Verwundetenabzeichen in Form eines Uniformwinkels *(USA).*
woven wire Maschendraht *m.*
woven-wire fence Maschendrahtzaun *m.*
wrapped leggins Wickelgamaschen *fpl.*
wrapping Pakethülle *f.*
wrap puttees Wickelgamaschen *fpl.*
wreck *v* zertrümmern, zerstören; Schiffbruch erleiden *(be shipwrecked).*
wrecker *See* wrecking truck.
wrecker platoon Abschleppzug *m (MT).*
wrecking truck Abschleppkraftwagen *m.*
wrecking unit Abschleppkommando *n.*
wrench *n* Schraubenschlüssel *m.*
wrist Handgelenk *n.*
wrist pin *See* piston pin.
wrist watch Armbanduhr *f.*
write schreiben.
writing paper Briefpapier *n.*
written evidence Beweismaterial *n.*
written order schriftlicher Befehl.
wrought iron Schmiedeeisen *n.*

X

X-coordinate Abszisse *f (Math);* Rechtswert *m (on coordinate scale).*

X-line waagerechte Gitterlinie *(map grid).*

X-ray *n* Röntgenaufnahme *f*, Röntgenphoto *n*.

X-ray *v* eine Röntgenaufnahme machen.

X-ray equipment Röntgeneinrichtung *f*.

X-rays Röntgenstrahlen *mpl*.

xylyl bromide Xylylbromid *n*, T-Stoff *m (CWS)*.

Y

yacht Jacht *f*.

yard Hof *m (courtyard)*; Rangierbahnhof *m (RR)*; Yard *n (0.914 m)*.

Y-azimuth Richtungswinkel *m*.

yaw *v* gieren *(Avn, Nav.)*

yawing Seitwärtsbewegung *f (Ap)*.

yawl Jolle *f (Nav)*.

yawmeter Gierungsmesser *m (Ap)*.

Y-connection Sternschaltung *f (Elec)*.

Y-coordinate Ordinate *f (Math)*; Hochwert *m (on coordinate scale in map reading)*.

yellow gelb.

yellow fever Gelbfieber *n*, gelbes Fieber.

yeoman Schreiber *m (Nav)*.

Y-gun Y-förmiger Wasserbombenwerfer *(Nav)*.

Y-line senkrechte Gitterlinie *(map grid)*.

Z

Zenith Zenit *m*, Scheitelpunkt *m*; Gipfel *m (summit)*.

zero *n* Null *f*.

zero *v* auf Null stellen *(a scale, etc.)*; Normalvisier stellen *(a gun sight)*.

zero beat Schwebungsnull *f*, Schwebungslücke *f (Rad)*.

zero hour X-Uhr *f*, Nullzeit *f*.

zero point Nullpunkt *m (Arty, Surv)*.

zigzag *v* zickzack fliegen *(Avn)*; Zickzackkurs fahren *(Nav)*.

zigzagging target kurvendes Ziel *(AAA)*.

zinc Zink *n*.

zinc container Zinkbecher *m (dry cell)*.

zipper Reißverschluß *m*.

zone *n* Zone *f*, Gebiet *n*, Fläche *f*, Bereich *m*, Streifen *m*, Raum *m*.

zone fire Flächenschießen *n*, Flächenfeuer *n*, Streuschießen *n (Gunnery)*.

zone map Kartenblatt *n*.

zone of action Gefechtsabschnitt *m*, Gefechtsstreifen *m (Tac)*; Angriffsabschnitt *m (in attack)*; Aktionsbereich *m (Ap, Tk, etc.)*.

zone of advance Vormarschstreifen *m*.

zone of defense Verteidigungszone *f*, Abwehrzone *f*.

zone of dispersion Streuungsbereich *m (Ballistics)*.

zone of fire Feuerbereich *m*, Feuerzone *f*.

zone of operations Operationsraum *m*, Operationsgebiet *n*.

zone of resistance Widerstandszone *f*; Tiefenzone *f (organized in depth)*.

zone of security Sicherungszone *f*.

zone of the interior Heimatgebiet *n*.

zoom Hochziehen *n (Ap)*.

APPENDIX I
NUMBERS

Cardinal Numbers (Grundzahlen)		Ordinal Numbers (Ordnungszahlen)
Ein(s) (One)	1... (First)	Der, Die, Das, Erste
Zwei	2	Zweite
Drei	3	Dritte
Vier	4	Vierte
Fünf	5	Fünfte
Sechs	6	Sechste
Sieben	7	Sieb(en)te
Acht	8	Achte
Neun	9	Neunte
Zehn	10	Zehnte
Elf	11	Elfte
Zwölf	12	Zwölfte
Dreizehn	13	Dreizehnte
Vierzehn	14	Vierzehnte
Fünfzehn	15	Fünfzehnte
Sechzehn	16	Sechzehnte
Siebzehn	17	Siebzehnte
Achtzehn	18	Achtzehnte
Neunzehn	19	Neunzehnte
Zwanzig	20	Zwanzigste
Einundzwanzig	21	Einundzwanzigste
Dreißig	30	Dreißigste
Vierzig	40	Vierzigste
Fünfzig	50	Fünfzigste
Sechzig	60	Sechzigste
Siebzig	70	Siebzigste
Achtzig	80	Achtzigste
Neunzig	90	Neunzigste
Hundert; Einhundert	100	(Ein)hundertste
Hundertundeins	101	Hundertunderste
Tausend; Eintausend	1,000	(Ein)tausendste
Tausendundeins	1,001	Tausendunderste
Hunderttausend	100,000	(Ein)hunderttausendste
Hunderttausendundeins	100,001	Hunderttausendunderste
Eine Million	1,000,000	(Ein)million(s)te

APPENDIX II

WEIGHTS AND MEASURES

Weight

German — U.S.

1 Gramm	= 0.035 ounce	
1 Pfund	= 1.102 pounds	
	(= 500 Gramm)	
1 Kilogramm	= 2.205 pounds	
	(= 1,000 Gramm)	
1 Zentner	= 110.25 pounds	
	(= 100 Pfund)	
	(= 50 Kilogramm)	
1 Doppelzentner	= 220.50 pounds	
	(= 100 Kilogramm)	
1 Tonne (metric)	= 1.102 tons (short)	
	(= 1,000 Kilogramm)	

U. S. — German

1 ounce	= 28.35 Gramm
	= 0.014 Pfund
1 pound	= 453.6 Gramm
	= 0.454 Kilogramm
	= 0.908 Pfund
1 ton (short)	= 0.907 Tonnen (metric)
	= 907.2 Kilogramm

Length

1 Kilometer	(= 1,000	Meter)	
	= 0.621	mile	
	= 1,094	yards	
	= 3,281	feet	
1 Meter	(= 100	Zentimeter)	
	= 1.09	yards	
	= 3.28	feet	
1 Zentimeter	(= 10	Millimeter)	
	= 0.393	inch	
1 Millimeter	= 0.039	inch	

1 mile = 1.609 Kilometer	
= 1,609 Meter	
1 yard = 0.914 Meter	
= 91.44 Zentimeter	
1 foot = 0.305 Meter	
= 30.48 Zentimeter	
1 inch = 2.54 Zentimeter	
= 25.4 Millimeter	

Area

1 Quadratmeter	= 1.196	square yards
	= 10.76	square feet
1 Quadratzenti-meter	= 0.155	square inch
1 Quadratmilli-meter	= 0.00155	square inch
1 Hektar	(= 100	Ar)
	(= 10,000	Quadratmeter)
	= 2.471	acres

1 square inch	= 6.452 Quadratzentimeter
	= 645.2 Quadratmillimeter
1 square foot	= 0.093 Quadratmeter
1 square yard	= 0.836 Quadratmeter
1 acre	= 0.405 Hektar

Volume

1 Kubikzenti-meter	= 0.061	cubic inch
1 Kubikmeter	= 35.31	cubic feet
	= 1.308	cubic yards
1 Liter	(= 1	Kubikdezimeter)
	= 0.264	gallons
	= 1.057	quarts (liquid)
1 Hektoliter	(= 100	Liter)
	= 26.42	gallons

1 gallon	= 3.785 Liter
1 liquid quart	= 0.946 Liter
1 cubic inch	= 16.39 Kubikzentimeter
1 cubic foot	= 0.0283 Kubikmeter
1 cubic yard	= 0.764 Kubikmeter
1 fluid ounce	= 29.58 Kubikzentimeter

Temperature Conversion

Centigrade (or Celsius) into
Fahrenheit

Multiply by 9/5 and add 32

Fahrenheit into Centigrade

Subtract 32 and multiply by 5/9

Convenient Approximate Conversions

Kilometers into miles:	Multiply by 6/10
Meters into yards:	Add 10%
Meters into feet:	Multiply by 3 and add 10%.
Centimeters into inches:	Multiply by 4/10
Kilograms into pounds:	Multiply by 2 and add 10%
Liters into gallons:	Divide by 4 and add 5%

APPENDIX III
GERMAN MILITARY ABBREVIATIONS

For an exhaustive list of German military abbreviations see Special Series No. 12, MIS 461, 12 Apr 1943. The following list contains only such abbreviations as are not listed in the work mentioned. Abbreviations used as independent words will be found in the body of the dictionary; e.g. *Stuka, Gestapo, Krad,* etc.

A

A.	Ausgabestelle	distribution point
A.B.St.	Artillerie-Beobachtungsstelle	artillery observation post
Abst.Tr.	Abstecktrupp	layout party, staking-out party
Abw.	Abwehr	defense; counterintelligence, security
A.D.	Abwehrdienst	counterintelligence service, security service
A.F.	Artillerieführer	division artillery commander
A.G.	Aufklärungsgruppe	air forces reconnaissance unit
Ah.	Anhänger	trailer
a.m.(d.) F.b.	augenblicklich mit der Führung beauftragt	in temporary command
A.M.L.	Armee-Munitionslager	army ammunition depot
A.O.	Abwehroffizier	counterintelligence officer, security officer
Ao.	Ago	name of an aircraft manufacturing company
A.Pi.Fü.	Armee-Pionierführer	army engineer commander
AR.	Arado	name of an aircraft manufacturing company
A.St.	Abwehrstelle	counterintelligence center, security control center
atü	Atmosphärenüberdruck	pressure difference expressed in atmospheres
Ausb.Abt.	Ausbildungs-Abteilung	training section (*section of Army General Staff*)
a.v.	arbeitsverwendungsfähig	fit for labor duty only
a.v. Heimat	arbeitsverwendungsfähig in der Heimat	fit for labor duty in zone of interior only
A.Z.o.V.	Aufschlagzünder ohne Verzögerung	nondelay fuze

B

Baon.	Bataillon	battalion
B.B.	Backbord	port (*side*)
Bb.	Beobachtung	observation
Bef.Wg.	(Panzer-) Befehlswagen	(armored) command car
Bgb.	Bergbau	mining
B-Gruppe	Buchstabengruppe	group of letters (*code section*)

B.K.	Blendkörper	frangible-glass smoke grenade
Bl.P.	Blättchenpulver	flake powder (*Am*)
B.M.	Bordmechaniker	flight engineer
Br.Kol.	Brückenkolonne	bridge column; bridge train
B.R.T.	Bruttoregistertonne	gross registered ton (2.8316 *cu m*)
Beschr.	Beschreibung	description
B.St.	Beobachtungsstelle	observation post
B.St.	Bereitschaftsstellung	line of support; position of readiness
Bü.	Bücker	designation of airplanes built by Bücker Company
B.Z.A.	Bombenzielapparat	bomb sight
B.Z.G.	Bombenzielgerät	bomb sight

C

C.d.Z.	Chef der Zivilverwaltung	Chief of Civil Affairs Section
C.G.S.	Chef des Generalstabs des Heeres	Chief of General Staff of the Army
Ch.d.ST.	Chef der Schnellen Truppen	Chief of Mobile Troops
Ch.d.St.F.H.	Chef des Generalstabs des Feldheeres	Chief of General Staff of the Field Army
Ch.HRü.u.BdE.	Chef des Heeresrüstung und Befehlshaber des Ersatzheeres	Chief of Army Equipment and Commander of the Replacement Training Army

D

D.	Disziplinar-	disciplinary
D.A.W.	Dienstanweisung	service regulations
D.B.	Daimler-Benz	name of an engine factory
Deut.	Deutpatrone	indicator cartridge
DIN	Deutsche Industrie-Norm	German industrial standard
Div.K.St.	Divisions-Kartenstelle	divisional map center
D.L.	Doppellafette	two-barreled mount
Do.	Dornier	designation of airplanes built by Dornier Company
D.P.	Doppelposten	double sentry
Drh.L.	Drehlafette	pivot mount
D.V.	Divisionsverfügung, Divisionsverordnung	divisional order
D.V. '	Durchgangsvermittlung	long-distance telephone exchange
DWM	Deutsche Waffen- und Munitionsfabriken	name of German armament company
D.Z.	Druckzünder	pressure igniter

E

E.A.Z.	empfindlicher Aufschlagzünder	superquick impact fuze
Ei.V.	Eigenverständigung	interphone, intravehicular communication

E.K.W.	Eisenbahnkesselwagen	railway tank car
E.L.	einfache Lafette	single-barreled mount
Em	Entfernungsmeßgerät	range finder
E.M. 4m	Entfernungsmesser mit 4m-Basis	range finder with 4-meter base
Ents.Kp.	Entseuchungskompanie	disinfection company
Erwa	Erwartung	standing by (*for metro message*)
E.S.	Erkennungssignal	recognition signal
Ex	Exerziermunition	drill ammunition

F

F.	Fallschirm-	parachute
F.	Fern-	long-range, long-distance
F.	Flugzeug	airplane
Fb.K.Kw.	Flugbetriebstoff-Kesselkraftwagen	aviation-gasoline tank truck
Fda.	Feldartillerie	field artillery
F.d.L.	Führer der Luft	air liaison officer with Navy
Fdw.	Feldwebel	technical sergeant
Feba.	Feldbahn	light narrow-gage railway
Feldbr.	Feldbrunnen	field well
F.F.	Festungsflak	fortress antiaircraft artillery
F.G.	Fallschirmjäger-Gewehr	parachutist's rifle
Fi.	Fieseler	designation of liaison airplanes built by the company of that name
Fkm.	Funkmeister	radio technical sergeant
F.Kol.	Fahrkolonne	horse-drawn column
Flb.M.	Flußbreitenmesser	river-width measuring instrument
Fldw.	Feldwebel	technical sergeant
F. Leucht.	Fallschirmleuchtpatrone	parachute-flare signal cartridge
Fl.P.	Festlegepunkt	reference point (*Gunnery*)
FMG	Flakmeßgerät	plane spotter and range finder (*AAA*)
F.M.G.	Fernmeßgerät	range finder
F.P.	Festpunkt	reference point (*Surv*)
Fp.02	Füllpulver 02	filler powder 02 (=*TNT*)
F.S.	Fallschirm	parachute
F.S.	Fernschreiber	teletype
F.S.	Fernschreiben	teletype message
Fsp.Betr.Zg.	Fernsprech-Betriebszug	telephone operating platoon
F.St.	Funkstelle	radio station
F.St.N.	Friedensstärkenachweisung	table of organization (*peacetime*).
F.S.Tr.	Fallschirmtruppen	parachute troops
Fu.M.G.	Funkmeßgerät	radar
Funkm.	Funkmeister	radio technical sergeant
Fu.St(e).	Funkstelle	radio station
Fu.Tr.	Funktrupp	radio section

Fvt. *or*	Feuerverteilung	fire distribution
Fvtg. *or*		
Fvtl.	Focke-Wulf	designation of airplanes built
Fw.		by the company of that name

G

g.	geländegängig	having cross-country mobility *(MT)*
G.	Gruppenführer	squad leader
G.A.St.	Geräteausgabestelle	equipment distributing point
Geb.	Gebäude	building
Geb.I.G.	Gebirgsinfanteriegeschütz	mountain infantry howitzer
geh.Kdos.	geheime Kommandosache	secret military document
Gen.	Genesenden-, Genesenen-, Genesungs-	convalescent; reconditioning *adj*, rehabilitation *adj*
Gen St.d.H.	Generalstab des Heeres	Army General Staff
gep.	gepanzert	armored
G.G.	Gewehrgeschoß	rifle bullet
G.G.	Gewehrgranate	rifle grenade
g.Kdos.	geheime Kommandosache	secret military document
G.N.Abt.	Gebirgs-Nachrichtenabteilung	mountain signal battalion
G.O.	Gasoffizier	gas officer
G.O.	Generaloberst	general *(full general)*
Go.	Gotha	designation of airplanes built by the *Gothaer Waggonfabrik*
Gr.	Grenz-	frontier *adj*
Gr.	Grenzwacht	frontier guard
Gr.B.	Granatbüchse	antitank grenade rifle
Gr.F.88 *or* **Grf.88**	Granatfüllung 88	shell filler 88 (= *picric acid*)
Gr.H.Qu.	Gruppen-Hauptquartier	army group headquarters
G.R.L.	Grundrichtungslinie	base line *(Gunnery)*
G.R.P.	Grundrichtungspunkt	base point *(Gunnery)*
G.U.	Gasschutzunteroffizier	gas noncommissioned officer
G.V.	Goerz-Visier	bomb sight manufactured by Goerz Company
g.v.F.	garnisonsverwendungsfähig (Feld)	fit for garrison duty in the field
g.v.H.	garnisonsverwendungsfähig (Heimat)	fit for garrison duty in zone of interior
G.V.O.	Gräber-Verwaltungsoffizier	graves registration officer
Gw.	Grenzwache	frontier guard

H

H.	Heimat-	home *adj*, Zone of Interior
H.	Horch-	listening *adj*; intercept *adj* *(Rad)*; sound locating *adj* *(AAA)*.
Ha.	Hamburg	designation of airplanes built by Blohm & Voß Company, Hamburg

H.A.	Heeres-Atmer	service oxygen breathing apparatus
Haft-H.	Haft-Hohlladung	magnetic antitank hollow charge
H.B.L.	Heeresbetriebsstofflager	Army gasoline-supply depot
He.	Heinkel	designation of airplanes built by company of that name
Hf.	Heeresfahrzeug	Army vehicle
H.Fu.	Heeres-Funkstelle	Army radio station
H.Gr.	Haubitzgranate	howitzer shell
H.K.	höheres Kommando	higher command, higher echelon
Hkf.	Halbkettenfahrzeug	half-track vehicle
H.M.L.	Heeresmunitionslager	Army ammunition depot
Höh.Arko.	Höherer Artilleriekommandeur	special staff artillery officer
Höh.Pi.Offz.	Höherer Pionier-Offizier	special staff engineer officer
Hpt.	Hauptmann	captain
Hpt.V.Pl.	Hauptverbandplatz	clearing station (*Med*)
Hptwm.	Hauptwachtmeister	first sergeant (*Arty, Cav*)
Hs.	Henschel	designation of airplanes built by company of that name
H.S.S. *or* H.S.S.G.	Heeres-Sauerstoffschutzgerät	service oxygen breathing apparatus
H.SS Pf.	Höherer SS- und Polizeiführer	Senior SS and Police Commander
H.Tr.	Heerestruppen	GHQ troops
H.V.A.	Heeresverwaltungsamt	Army Administration Office
H.V.B.	Hauptverbandplatz	clearing station (*Med*)
H.V.L.	Heeresverpflegungslager	Army ration depot
H.W.	Hauptwachtmeister	first sergeant (*Arty, Cav*)
H.Wa.A.	Heereswaffenamt	Army Ordnance Office
H.W.L.	Hauptwiderstandslinie	main line of resistance (*in delaying action*)

I

I	Ingenieur	engineer
I.d.A.	Inspekteur der Artillerie	Inspector of Artillery
I.d.O.	Inspekteur der Ordnungspolizei	Inspector of Uniformed Police
I.d.Sipo u.d.SD	Inspekteur der Sicherheitspolizei und des Sicherheitsdienstes	Inspector of Security Police and Security Service
I.E.B.	Infanterie-Ersatzbataillon	infantry replacement training battalion
I.E.R.	Infanterie-Ersatzregiment	infantry replacement training regiment
I.G.K.	Infanteriegeschütz-Kompanie	infantry howitzer company
Igr.	Infanteriegranate	infantry howitzer shell
i.L.	in Ladestreifen	loaded in clips (*Am*)
I.L.R.	Infanterie-Lehrregiment	infantry demonstration regiment

Inf.G.K.	Infanteriegeschütz-Kompanie	infantry howitzer company
I.K.	Infanteriekolonne	infantry supply column
I-Staffel	Instandsetzungsstaffel	repair and maintenance section

J

J.	*See* I.	used especially in typewritten documents for capital I; *e.g.*, J.R. for I.R
(J)	Jugoslawien	Jugoslavia (*marking on equipment*)
J.G.	Jagdgeschwader	fighter wing
Ju.	Junkers	designation of airplanes built by company of that name
JuMo	Junkers-Motor	Junkers aircraft engine

K

K	Kraftfahrwesen	motor transport
K.	Kraftrad	motorcycle
K.	Kriegs-	war *adj*
K.	Kriegsgefangenen-	prisoner of war *adj*
K.A.N.	Kriegsausrüstungsnachweisung	table of basic allowances (*wartime*)
Kdr.N.	Kommandeur der Nachrichtentruppen	Chief of Signal Troops
Kdr.Pi.	Kommandeur der Pioniere	Chief of Engineers
K.Em.	Kehrbildentfernungsmesser	inverted-image range finder
K.G.	Kampfgeschwader	bombardment wing
K.Gr.	Kanonengranate	shell for a gun
kHz	Kilohertz	kilocycles per second
K.K.	Kleinkaliber	small caliber, subcaliber, small bore
Kl.	Klemm	designation of airplanes built by company of that name
Kl.	Klartext, Klarschrift	text in clear
KOB.	Kriegsoffizier-Bewerber	applicant for wartime commission
KR		urgent (*Rad procedure; spoken* "Konrad-Richard" *in accordance with Ger phonetic alphabet*).
Krd.	Krad-	motorcycle *adj*, **motorcyclist**
Kr.Gl.	Kriegsgliederung	order of battle
Kr.S.St.	Krankensammelstelle	collecting station (*Med*)
K.S.B.	Kradschützen-Bataillon	motorcycle battalion
K.St.N.	Kriegsstärke-Nachweisung	table of organization (*wartime*)
k.v.	kriegsverwendungsfähig	fit for active service

KVK	Kriegsverdienstkreuz	War Service Cross (*decoration*)
KW	Kampfwagen	tank
Kw.K.	Kampfwagenkanone	tank gun

L

L.	Ladestreifen	ammunition clip
L.	Länge	length
l.	lang	long
L.	Lauf	length of barrel in calibers, *e.g.* L/60
L.	Lehr-	instruction, demonstration
l.	leicht	light *adj*
L.	Lieferung	delivery, lot, shipment
le.I.K(ol).	leichte Infanteriekolonne	light infantry supply column (*H-Dr*)
le.V.	leichtverwundet, Leichtverwundeter	slightly wounded, minor casualty
lfd.Nr.	laufende Nummer	serial number
L.G.	Leichtgeschütz	light gun for airborne operations
L.I.	leitender Ingenieur	chief engineer (*Civ engaged for Mil construction*)
l.I.G.	leichtes Infanteriegeschütz	light infantry howitzer
l.I.K.	leichte Infanteriekolonne	light infantry supply column (*H-Dr*)
L.L.	Luftlande-	airborne
Lm.	Leichtmetall-	light alloy *adj*
L.M.	Luftmine	aerial mine
L.N.R.	Luftnachrichten-Regiment	air forces signal regiment
Ls.	Landesschützeneinheit	regional defense force
L.S.	Lastensegler, Lastensegelflugzeug	cargo transport glider
l.S.	leichtes Spitzgeschoß	pointed light-weight bullet
L.S.	Leuchtspur-	tracer, *adj*
L.S.R.	Luftschutzraum	air raid shelter
L.u.S.Mun.	Leucht- und Signalmunition	signal pistol ammunition

M

M.	Marine	navy, naval
Ma.	Munitionsanstalt	ammunition depot
M.A.A.	Marineartillerieabteilung	naval coast artillery battalion
Ma.N.	magnetisch Nord	magnetic north
Me.	Messerschmitt	designation of airplanes built by company of that name
Mebu	Maschinengewehr-Eisenbetonunterstand	machine-gun reinforced concrete pillbox
m.Fm.W.	mittlerer Flammenwerfer	medium-weight flame thrower
M.G.M.D.	MG.-Meßdreieck	machine-gun plotting protractor
M.G.Rkr.	MG-Richtkreis	machine-gun aiming circle

M.G.Z.	Maschinengewehr-Zielein-richtung	machine-gun sighting mechanism
M.G.Z.F.	Maschinengewehr-Zielfern-rohr	machine-gun telescopic sight
Mineis.	Eisenbahn-Ministerium	Ministry of Railways
M.K.	Marschkolonne	march column
m.K.	mit Kappe	with cap (*Am*)
m.K.	mit Kern	with core (*Am*)
M.K.A.	Marine-Küstenartillerie	naval coast artillery
M.Kpf.	Meldekopf	advance message center, wire head
M.Kw.	Munitionskraftwagen	ammunition truck
M.S.Ger.	Minensuchgerät	mine detector
M.S.St.	Meldesammelstelle	message center

N

N.	Nachmittag	afternoon
N.	Nacht-	night, *adj*
N.A.	Nachrichtenabteilung	signal battalion
N.A.	Nachrichten-Aufklärung	signal intelligence
Nb.Hgr.	Nebelhandgranate	smoke hand grenade
Nb.K.	Nebelkerze	smoke candle
Neb.Ma.	Neben-Munitionsanstalt	branch ammunition depot
N.F.	Niederfrequenz	audio frequency (*Rad*)
Ngl.Bl.P.	Nitroglyzerin-Blättchen-pulver	nitroglycerin flake powder
N.H.	Nachrichtenhelferin	woman signal auxiliary
Nkdo.	Nachkommando	rear detachment
N.L.	Nebenlager	branch camp (*PW*)
N.N.	Normalnull	mean sea level
N.R.	Nachrichtenregiment	signal regiment
Nz.Gew.Bl.P.	Nitrozellulose-Gewehr-Blättchenpulver	nitrocellulose flake powder for rifle ammunition
N.Z., N.Zg.	Nachrichtenzug	signal platoon
Nz.Stb.P.	Nitrocellulose-Staub-Pulver	finely granulated nitro-cellulose powder

O

O.	Oberst	colonel
(ö)	österreichisch	Austrian (*marking on equipment*)
O.	Ordonnanzoffizier	special-missions staff officer
O.	Orts-	garrison *adj*, local
O.B.	Ortsbatterie	local battery (*Tp*)
Ob. (Bfh.)	Oberbefehlshaber	commanding officer
Obfdw.	Oberfeldwebel	master sergeant
OD	Ordnungsdienst	military police service
Offz. (E)	Ergänzungsoffizier	retired officer recalled to active duty
Offz. (W)	Offizier des Waffenwesens; in short: Waffenoffizier	ordnance officer
O.F.K.	Oberfeldkommandantur	military government area Hq

Ofu.	Oberfunker	radio operator with grade of pfc
OQu	Oberquartiermeister	*See entry in body of dictionary*
o.W.	obere Winkelgruppe	angles above 45° *(Gunnery)*

P

p	polnisch	Polish *(imprint on ammunition labels, etc.)*
P.	Posten	sentry
P.	Punkt	point
Patrh.	Patronenhülse	cartridge case
Patr.s.S.i.L.	Patronen, schwere Spitz-, in Ladestreifen	heavy pointed cartridges in clips
Patr.s.S.o.L.	Patronen, schwere Spitz-, ohne Ladestreifen	heavy pointed cartridges without clips
Peilge	Peilgerät	radio compass, direction finder *(Ap)*
P.m.K.	Phosphorgeschoß mit Stahlkern	phosphorus bullet with steel core
P.V.	Planübergang	grade crossing
Pwg.	Panzerwagen	tank
Pz.	panzerbrechend	armor-piercing
Pz.Abt. (F)	Panzerabteilung (Flammenwerfer)	armored flame-thrower battalion
Pz.Dv.	Panzer-Division	armored division
Pz.E.Kol.	Panzerersatzteilkolonne	tank spare-parts column
Pzgr.Patr.	Panzergranate-Patrone	armor-piercing shell *(fixed Am)*
Pz.Kpf.Wg.	Panzerkampfwagen	tank
PzKw 5	Panzerkampfwagen 5	"Panther" tank
PzKw 6	Panzerkampfwagen 6	"Tiger" tank
Pz.Spr.Gr.	Panzersprenggranate	armor-piercing HE shell
Pz.Sp.Tr.	Panzerspähtrupp	armored reconnaissance-car section or patrol

R

R	Radfahrabteilung	bicycle battalion
R.	Richtkreis	aiming circle *(Gunnery)*
(r)	russisch	Russian *(marking on equipment)*
r.A.	rückwärtiges Armeegebiet	rear area of an army *(Com Z)*
Rdf.	Rheindorf	name of a German arsenal
R.Em.	Raumbildentfernungsmesser	stereoscopic range finder
Revi	Reflexvisier	reflector sight
Rh	Rheinmetall	name of a German arms company
r.H.	rückwärtiges Heeresgebiet	rear area of group of armies *(Com Z)*
R.I (II)	Richtkreisunteroffizier I (II)	NCO number 1 (2) in charge of aiming circle

443

Ri.	Richt-	pertaining to aiming, sighting, etc.
Rkr.U.	Richtkreisunteroffizier	NCO in charge of aiming circle
R.O.B.	Reserveoffizier-Bewerber	reserve officer applicant
Rs.	Reizstoff	tear gas, lacrimator (*CWS*)
R.Sp.Tr.	Reiterspähtrupp	mounted reconnaissance patrol
RZ	Rückenfallschirm mit Zwangsauslösung	static-line back-pack parachute

S

S.	Seelenlänge	tube length, barrel length (*Ord*)
S	sicher	"safe" (*Ord*)
sbst.	selbständig	autonomous, independent
Sch.	Schütze	rifleman, private
Sch.F.	Scheinwerferführer	searchlight NCO
schn.Tr.	schnelle Truppen	mobile troops
Schtz.Kp.	Schützenkompanie	rifle company
Schü.Mine	Schützenmine	antipersonnel mine
S.D.	Sicherheitsdienst	SS Security Service
S.F.St.	Scherenfernrohrstand	emplacement of battery commander's telescope
Si.	Siebel	designation of airplanes built by firm of Siebel
S.K.	Sanitätskompanie	medical company
S.K.D.	Selve-Kornbegel-Dornheim	name of a German small-arms ammunition factory
S.L.	Sockellafette	pedestal mount (G)
S-M(ine)	Schützenmine	antipersonnel mine
S.m.E.	Spitzgeschoß mit Eisenkern	pointed bullet with iron core
S.m.K.(H)	Spitzgeschoß mit Stahlkern (hart)	pointed bullet with hardened-steel core
S.Mun.	Spitzmunition	ordinary pointed ball ammunition
Spl.	Splitter	splinter, fragment
Spl.Gr.	Splittergranate	fragmentation shell
Sprgr.Patr.	Sprenggranate-Patrone	high-explosive shell (*fixed Am*)
Spr.W.	Sprengweite	horizontal distance between point of air burst and theoretical point of impact
ss.	schwerst	heavy (*classification of Arty*)
S.Sold.	Sanitätssoldat	private in medical corps
St.	Standort	garrison, post or station
St.	Stelle	place; office; agency; point
St.Ält.	Standortältester	garrison commander
Stb.	Stab	staff Hq
Stb.P.	Staub-Pulver	finely granulated powder (*Am*)
St.Hgr.	Stielhandgranate	stick hand grenade

St.K.G.	Sturzkampfgeschwader	dive-bomber wing
Sto.Mi.	Stockmine	antipersonnel picket-type mine
Stu.G.	Sturmgeschütz	self-propelled assault gun
St.K.	Sturmkanone	self-propelled assault gun
S.Werf.Rgt.	schweres Werferregiment	heavy smoke regiment

T

(t)	tschechisch	Czechoslovakian (*marking on equipment*)
T.	Teich	pond
Tb.	Taube	pigeon
tdu.	tropendienstunfähig	unfit for service in tropics
T.E.	Tageseinflüsse	weather factors (*Gunnery*)
T.E.	Tornisterempfänger	pack-type portable receiver
T.E.K.	Truppenentgiftungskompanie	personnel decontamination company
Tf.	Telefonist	telephone operator
Tp.	Transport	transport
T.P.	trigonometrischer Punkt	triangulation point

U

U.	Urschrift	original (*document*)
Ug/M	Umdrehungen je Minute	revolutions per minute
U.K.	unabkömmlich	indispensable, irreplaceable
U.K.W.	Ultrakurzwelle	ultrashort wave (*Rad*)
UKWE	Ultrakurzwellenempfänger	very-high-frequency receiver (*Rad*)
U.L.	Unterlafette	bottom carriage (*G*)
Umdr/M	Umdrehungen je Minute	revolutions per minute
u.W.	untere Winkelgruppe	angles up to 45° (*Gunnery*)
U.Z.	Uhrzünder	clockwork fuze

V

V.	Vermessung	survey
V.A.	Verpflegungsausgabestelle	rations distributing point
V.A.	Vorausabteilung	advance detachment
Verf.O.K.H.	Verfügung des Oberkommandos des Heeres	Army Regulation
V.O.	Verbindungsoffizier	liaison officer
V.O.	Vernehmungsoffizier	interrogation officer
V.O.	Verpflegungsoffizier	mess officer
Vo	V·Null (*i.e.* Velocitas-Null)	muzzle velocity
V.P.	Vorposten	outpost

W

(W)	(Offizier) des Waffenwesens	ordnance officer
Wa.	Wachregiment	guard regiment (*T of Opns*)
W.A.B.	Waffenabwurfbehälter	parachute weapons container
Wa.Btln.	Wachbataillon	guard battalion
Wewa	Wetterwarte	weather station
Wezu	Witterungseinflüsse und Zeitunterschied	weather factors and time difference (*SR*)
W.G.O.	Wehrmacht-Gräberoffizier	armed forces graves registration officer
Wgr.	Wurfgranate	mortar shell
Wgr.Nb.	Wurfgranate (Nebel)	mortar smoke shell
Wgr.Z.	Wurfgranatzünder	mortar-shell fuze
W.H.	Wehrmacht—Heer	marking on Army vehicles
W.Ka.	Waffenkarren	weapons cart
Wkv.	Winkerverbindung	flag signaling communication
W.L.	Wehrmacht—Luftwaffe	marking on Air Forces vehicles
W.M.	Wehrmacht—Marine	marking on Navy vehicles
Wn.	Wiener Neustadt	designation of airplanes built by *Wiener Neustädter Flugzeugwerke*
W.St.G.B.	Wehrmacht-Strafgesetzbuch	military penal code

Z

(Z)	Sanitätsoffizier des zahnärztlichen Dienstes	dental officer
Z.	Zünder	fuze
Z.G.	Zerstörergeschwader	twin-engine fighter wing
Zgpf.	Zugpferd	draft horse
z.u.	zeitlich untauglich	temporarily unfit
Zugpf.	Zugpferd	draft horse
Z.u.Z.Z.	Zug- und Zerschneidezünder	pull-and-cut igniter
Z.Z.	Zugzünder	pull igniter